COPINGER AND SKONE JAMES
ON
COPYRIGHT

AUSTRALIA
The Law Book Company Ltd.
Sydney : Melbourne : Brisbane

CANADA AND U.S.A.
The Carswell Company Ltd.
Agincourt, Ontario

INDIA
N. M. Tripathi Private Ltd.
Bombay

ISRAEL
Steimatzky's Agency Ltd.
Jerusalem : Tel Aviv : Haifa

MALAYSIA : SINGAPORE : BRUNEI
Malayan Law Journal Pte Ltd.
Singapore

NEW ZEALAND
Sweet & Maxwell (N.Z.) Ltd.
Wellington

PAKISTAN
Pakistan Law House
Karachi

COPINGER and SKONE JAMES
ON
COPYRIGHT

INCLUDING

INTERNATIONAL COPYRIGHT

WITH THE STATUTES AND ORDERS RELATING THERETO

AND

FORMS AND PRECEDENTS

ELEVENTH EDITION

BY

E. P. SKONE JAMES, M.A.
Barrister-at-Law of the Middle Temple

LONDON
SWEET & MAXWELL
1971

First edition	By W. A. Copinger	... ...	1870
Second „	„ „	... ...	1881
Third „	„ „	... ...	1893
Fourth „	„ J. M. Easton	... ...	1904
Fifth „	„ „	... ...	1915
Sixth „	„ F. E. Skone James	... ...	1927
Seventh „	„ „	... ...	1936
Eighth „	„ „	... ...	1948
Ninth „	„ F. E. & E. P. Skone James	...	1958
Tenth „	„ „	... ...	1965
Eleventh „	„ E. P. Skone James	... ...	1971
Second Impression	„	... ...	1977

Published by
Sweet & Maxwell Limited of
11 New Fetter Lane, London
and printed in Great Britain
by Redwood Burn Limited
Trowbridge & Esher

SBN 421 14050 X

PREFACE

THIS being the first occasion on which I have been solely responsible for a new edition of this book I have taken the opportunity of giving careful consideration to the question whether any changes were needed, particularly in the general format. There has, in the past, been both criticism and praise of the format, but I have decided that since major changes in format might cause, not only confusion, but also, possibly, frustration, to regular users of the book, it would be best to retain the existing format, at least for this edition.

However, as on previous occasions, the book has been revised throughout to bring it up to date, taking note of recent cases, statutes and so on and, where necessary, it has been rewritten. In this regard I would particularly like to thank John Mummery, who has rewritten the section dealing with Breach of Confidence and revised the sections dealing with Passing Off, Breach of Statutory Duty and Malicious Falsehood. Also Richard Bramwell, who has rewritten the Income Tax section of the chapter on Income Tax, Estate Duty and Stamp Duty, and revised the rest of that chapter. I am much indebted to Peter Kleiner, who has not only researched the overseas case law and revised the Tables and Index, but also pointed out a number of places where the text could be clarified. As far as I know he is the only person, apart from the Editor, who has read the book from cover to cover! Finally, my thanks are due to proof readers and others who have, in their various ways, assisted me in the preparation of this edition.

In the domestic field, apart from a number of interesting decisions on various aspects of the law, the main development since the last edition has been the enactment of the Design Copyright Act, 1968. This Act radically changes the relationship between artistic copyright, under the Copyright Act, and design copyright, under the Designs Act. This Act will, no doubt, prove to be a fruitful source of litigation since, though having only two sections, it contains no transitional provisions. The Copyright (Amendment) Act, 1971, has added a new section to the Copyright Act, 1956, enabling applications to be made to the Performing Right Tribunal to renew its orders under section 27.

The major developments, however, have been in the international field. There have been further Orders extending the Copyright Act, 1956, to various parts of the Commonwealth, and other Orders amending the 1964 Order which applies that Act to foreign countries. But by far the most important development has been the Stockholm revision of the Berne Convention in 1967. This introduced the controversial Protocol Regarding Developing Countries which has resulted, not only in the position that, to date, none of the major developed countries, including this country, has ratified or acceded to the substantive provisions of the Stockholm revision, but also in proposals to hold revision conferences in mid-1971 for the purpose of revising the Berne Convention and also the Universal Copyright Convention.

It seems probable, therefore, that within the near future, and certainly within the life of this edition, there will be considerable changes, both in the international field and, as a consequence thereof, in the domestic field also.

E. P. SKONE JAMES.

5, NEW SQUARE,
LINCOLN'S INN.
June 1971

CONTENTS

PART III

Copyright in Special Circumstances

PART IV

Arrangements between Authors and Publishers, etc.

PART V

International Copyright and the Protection of Works Originating Outside the United Kingdom

PART VI

Copyright Laws of Commonwealth and Foreign Countries

PART VII

Forms and Precedents

APPENDICES

TABLE OF STATUTES

TABLE OF RULES OF THE SUPREME COURT

TABLE OF STATUTORY INSTRUMENTS

S.R. & O.

TABLE OF CASES

Part I

INTRODUCTORY AND HISTORICAL

Chapter 1

NATURE OF COPYRIGHT

1 **Distinction between copyright and other similar rights.** Copyright law is, in essence, concerned with the negative right of preventing the copying of physical material existing in the field of literature and the arts. Its object is to protect the writer and artist from the unlawful reproduction of his material. It is concerned only with the copying of physical material and not with the reproduction of ideas [1] and it does not give a monopoly to any particular form of words or design. It is thus to be distinguished from the rights conferred by patent, trade mark and design legislation, which give to the registered proprietor an exclusive right to the registered material, even as against a person who has reproduced such material innocently and from an independent source. If it could be shown that two precisely similar works were in fact produced wholly independently of one another, the author of the work that was published first would have no right to restrain the publication by the other author of that author's independent and original work.[2] A patentee, on the other hand, has the right to prevent another from using his invention if it in fact infringes the former's patent, notwithstanding that the latter's invention was the subject of independent investigation on his part. As was said by Diplock L.J. in the case of *Francis Day & Hunter, Ltd.* v. *Bron* [3]: "the copyright work must be the source from which the infringing work was derived."

2 **Copyright not in ideas but in the material that has embodied the ideas.** "The claim is not to ideas, but to the order of words, and this order has a marked identity and a permanent endurance. . . . The order of each man's words is as singular as his countenance, and although, if two authors composed originally with the same order of words, each would have a property therein, still the probability of such an occurrence is less than that there should be two countenances that could not be discriminated. The permanent endurance of words is obvious by comparing the works of ancient authors with other works of their day; the vigour of their words is unabated; the other works have mostly perished. It is true that property in the order of words is a mental abstraction, but so also are many other kinds of property;

[1] See *Donoghue* v. *Allied Newspapers Ltd.* [1938] Ch. 106 at 109 and 110.

[2] *Per* Sargant J., *Corelli* v. *Gray* (1913) 29 T.L.R. 570; *per* Warrington J., *Rees* v. *Melville* [1911–16] Macg.Cop.Cas. 96, 168; *Hollinrake* v. *Truswell* [1894] 3 Ch. 420; *Libraco, Ltd.* v. *Shaw Walker, Ltd.* (1913) 30 T.L.R. 22. There is no copyright in the "plot" of a play: *Rees* v. *Robbins, The Times,* July 4, 1914.

[3] [1963] Ch. 587.

for instance, the property in a stream of water, which is not in any of the atoms of the water, but only in the flow of the stream. The right to the stream is not the less a right of property, either because it generally belongs to the riparian proprietor, or because the remedy for a violation of the right is by action on the case, instead of detinue or trover." [4]

3 **Copyright rightfully called property.** Nothing can with greater propriety be called a man's property than the fruit of his brains. The property in any article or substance accruing to him by reason of his own mechanical labour is never denied him: the labour of his mind is no less arduous and consequently no less worthy of the protection of the law.

4 **Whether copyright protection should be unlimited in time?** Since copyright law does not create a monopoly, it has often been argued that the protection which the law of copyright affords, namely, that of preventing unlawful reproduction, should extend without limit of time. Unlimited protection indeed always has been and still is, with some qualification, given to unpublished literary works [5] and it was at one time contended that this right which subsisted at common law was not taken away by Copyright Acts which gave statutory protection to published works. This question came before the House of Lords in the famous case of *Donaldson* v. *Beckett.*[6] The judges were directed to attend, and the following questions, amongst others, were put to them by the House of Lords:

1st. Whether, at common law, an author of any book or literary composition had the sole right of first printing and publishing the same for sale, and might bring an action against any person who printed, published and sold the same without his consent?

2nd. If the author had such right originally, did the law take it away upon his printing and publishing such book or literary composition? And might any person afterwards reprint and sell, for his own benefit, such book or literary composition, against the will of the author?

3rd. Whether the author of any literary composition, and his assigns, had the sole right of printing and publishing the same in perpetuity by the common law?

5 **Copyright at common law merged in statutory copyright.** The first question was decided in the affirmative by ten judges, against one in favour of the negative: the second was decided in the negative by eight to three: and the third in the affirmative by seven to four. It

[4] *Per* Erle J. in *Jefferys* (*C.*) v. *Boosey* (*T.*) (1855) 4 H.L.C. 815.
[5] Copyright Act, 1956, s. 2 (3).
[6] (1774) 4 Burr. 2408.

was, however, held by the majority of the judges that the common law right which an author had to copyright in his works became merged in the statutory right conferred by the Copyright Act then in force (8 Anne, c. 19), upon publication.

Although, from time to time, there have been cases in which the contrary has been strenuously argued [7] this case must be taken to have finally decided that publication put an end to the common law perpetual right, and that after publication an author had to base his claim for protection upon his statutory right, if any. But, prior to the Copyright Act, 1911, a common law copyright in unpublished works was constantly admitted.[8] The Act of 1911 abolished copyright at common law and in the Act of 1956 it is provided that no copyright or right in the nature of copyright shall subsist otherwise than by virtue of that Act or some other enactment in that behalf.[9] Nevertheless the unlimited term has been maintained in relation to literary works which are unpublished.[10]

6 **Development of law of copyright.** The law of copyright was first concerned only with preventing the unlawful reproduction of copies of books. It has developed in two directions: first, by extending the subject-matter of protection by including dramatic, musical and artistic works and later gramophone records, and, by the Act of 1956, films, broadcast and television performances and published editions, and, secondly, by extending the classes of acts which constitute infringement.

7 **Definitions of copyright.** The expression "copyright" has developed its meaning in a corresponding manner. Before the Act of 1911 it seems that the expression "copyright" was confined to the right of multiplying copies and did not include the performing right in dramatic or musical works,[11] and it is a matter of some doubt whether the expression "copyright" was before that date used only in relation to the right to restrain publication of published works or so as to include also the right of an author to restrain publication of his unpublished works.[12]

Since the Act of 1911, the expression "copyright" has in this country come to be used as meaning all the rights conferred by the Act of 1911 upon authors, composers and artists in respect of their

7 *Jefferys (C.)* v. *Boosey (T.)* (1855) 4 H.L.C. 815; *Read* v. *Conquest* (1861) 9 C.B.(N.S.) 755.

8 *Albert (Prince)* v. *Strange* (1849) 1 M. & G. 25; *Caird* v. *Sime* (1887) 12 App.Cas. 326; *Exchange Telegraph Co., Ltd.* v. *Gregory & Co.* [1896] 1 Q.B. 147; *Exchange Telegraph Co., Ltd.* v. *Central News, Ltd.* [1897] 2 Ch. 48; *Philip* v. *Pennell* [1907] 2 Ch. 577; *Mansell* v. *Valley Printing Co.* [1908] 2 Ch. 441.

9 Copyright Act, 1956, s. 46 (5).

10 s. 2 (3).

11 See Pollock C.B., *Chappell* v. *Purday* (1845) 14 M. & W. 303.

12 *Re Dickens* [1935] Ch. 267.

literary, dramatic, musical and artistic works. But, as has been seen, copyright does not essentially mean a right to do something, but a right to restrict the doing of acts by others,[13] and, when copyright is referred to as "an exclusive right" the emphasis is on the word "exclusive." The Act of 1956 accordingly defines "copyright" as meaning the exclusive right to do and to authorise other persons to do the acts restricted under that Act by the copyright in a work of that description.[14] The Act then proceeds, in the various sections dealing with the various classes of works, to state what are the acts restricted by the copyright in those works.[15]

[The next paragraph is 21]

[13] See § 1, *ante*.
[14] Copyright Act, 1956, s. 1 (1).
[15] *e.g.*, ss. 2 (5), 3 (5).

CHAPTER 2

HISTORICAL REVIEW OF COPYRIGHT LAW

21 **Early control of printing.** It was only after the introduction of printing that any serious question as to the copyright in literary works could be expected to arise. An early statute of Richard III [1] encouraged the printing of books, and permitted their importation, but this statute was repealed fifty years later on protectionist grounds, it being alleged in the preamble of the repealing statute [2] that such a " marvellous number of printed books " were imported into the realm to the prejudice of the " King's natural subjects," who " have given themselves so diligently to learn and exercise the said craft of printing, that at this day there be within this realm a great number cunning and expert in the said science or craft of printing, as able to exercise the said craft in all points as any stranger in any other realm or country." A similar plea is urged on behalf of the bookbinders, who, " having no other faculty wherewith to get their living, be destitute of work and likely to be undone, except some reformation herein be had." [3]

As the number of printers increased in England, the King assumed a prerogative of granting printing privileges, and the earliest copyright protection took the form of printers' licences, and became a source of considerable profit to the King and his favourites.

22 **Original charter of the Stationers' Company.** In the year 1556 the original charter of the Stationers' Company was granted by Philip and Mary. It was the declared object of the Crown at that time to prevent the propagation of the reformed religion, and it seems to have been thought that this could most effectually be brought about by imposing the severest restrictions on the press. About this period there are several decrees and ordinances of the Star Chamber regulating the manner of printing, the number of presses throughout the kingdom, and prohibiting all printing against the force and meaning of any of the statutes or laws of the realm. Until the year 1640 the Crown, through the instrumentality of the Star Chamber, exercised this restrictive jurisdiction without limit, enforcing, by the summary powers of search, confiscation and imprisonment, its decrees, without the least obstruction from Westminster Hall or the Parliament in any instance.

1 1 Ric. 3, c. 9 (1483).
2 25 Hen. 8, c. 15.
3 We recognise in this statute the prototype of the American " manufacturing clause."

23 **Decrees of Star Chamber.** In 1556, by a decree of the Star Chamber, it was forbidden, amongst other things, to print contrary to any ordinance, prohibition, or commandment in any of the statutes or laws of the realm, or any injunction, letters patent, or ordinances set forth, or to be set forth, by the Queen's grant, commission or authority.

By another decree, dated June 23, 1585, every book was required to be licensed, and all persons were prohibited from printing "any book, work, or copy against the form or meaning of any restraint contained in any statute or laws of this realm, or in any injunction made by Her Majesty, or her Privy Council; or against the true intent and meaning of any letters patent, commissions, or prohibitions under the great seal, or contrary to any allowed ordinance set down for the good government of the Stationers' Company."

In 1623, a proclamation was issued to enforce this decree; reciting that it had been evaded, amongst other ways "by printing beyond sea such allowed books, works, or writings, as have been imprinted within the realm, by such to whom the sole printing thereof by letters patent or lawful ordinance or authority doth appertain."

In 1637, the Star Chamber again decreed that "no person is to print or import (if printed abroad) any book or copy which the Company of Stationers, or any person, hath or shall, by any letters patent, order or entrance in their register book, or otherwise, have the right, privilege, authority, or allowance, solely to print." [4]

24 **First Licensing Act.** In 1640, however, the Star Chamber was abolished; the King's authority was set at naught; all the regulations of the press, and restraints previously imposed upon unlicensed printers by proclamations, decrees of the Star Chamber and charter powers given to the Stationers' Company, were deemed and certainly were illegal. The licentiousness of libels induced Parliament to make an ordinance which prohibited printing, unless the book was first licensed. The ordinance prohibited printing without the consent of the owner, or importing (if printed abroad), upon pain of forfeiting the same to the *owner or owners of the copies* of the said books, etc. The provision necessarily presupposed the property to exist; it would have been nugatory if there had been no admitted owner. An owner could not at that time have existed otherwise than by common law. In 1649 the Long Parliament made another ordinance; and in 1662 was passed the Licensing Act (13 & 14 Car. 2, c. 33), which interdicted the printing of any book unless first licensed and entered in the register of the Stationers' Company. It ordered that no person should presume to print "any heretical, seditious, schismatical, or offensive books or pamphlets, wherein any doctrine or opinion shall be asserted or maintained which is contrary to the Christian faith, or the doctrine or

[4] 4 Burr. 2312.

discipline of the Church of England, or which shall, or may, tend to be to the scandal of religion or the church, or the government or governors of the church, state, or common wealth, or of any corporation or particular person or persons whatever." It further prohibited the publication of unlicensed books, prescribed regulations as to printing and empowered the King's messengers, and the master and wardens of the Stationers' Company, to seize books suspected of containing matters hostile to the Church or Government. It was necessary to print in the beginning of every licensed book the certificate of the licenser to the effect that the books contained nothing "contrary to the Christian faith, or the doctrine or discipline of the Church of England, or against the state and government of this realm, or contrary to good life or good manners, or otherwise, as the nature and subject of the work shall require." To prevent fraudulent changes in a book after it had been licensed, a copy was required to be deposited with the licenser when application was made for a licence.

25 The Act further prohibited any person from printing or importing, without the consent of the owner, any book which any person had the sole right to print by virtue of letters patent, or "by force or virtue of any entry or entries thereof duly made or to be made, in the register book of the said Company of Stationers, or in the register book of either of the universities." The penalty of piracy was forfeiture of the books and six shillings and eightpence for each copy; half to go to the King, and half to the owner.

The sole property of the owner is here acknowledged in express terms as a common law right; and the legislature which passed that Act could never have entertained the most distant idea "that the productions of the brain were not a subject-matter of property." To support an action on this statute, ownership had to be proved or the plaintiff could not have recovered, because the action was to be brought by the owner who was to have a moiety of the penalty. The various provisions of this Act effectually prevented piracies, without actions at law or Bills in equity. But cases arose of disputed property. Some of them were between different patentees of the Crown; in some the point was whether the property belonged "to the author, from his invention and labour, or the King, from the subject-matter."

26 The ordinance of 1643 prohibited the printing or importing of any book that had been lawfully licensed and entered in the register of the Stationers' Company, "for any particular member thereof, without the licence and consent of the owner." The penalty prescribed was forfeiture of the book to the owner, "and such further punishment as shall be thought fit." This clause was repeated in the ordinances of 1647, 1649, and 1652.

It has been questioned whether these clauses were applicable to any other than members of the Stationers' Company—in fact, whether they were more than by-laws for the regulation of the members *inter se*, but it is doubtful whether any such restriction can be put upon their scope.

27 The Licensing Act of Car. 2 was continued by several Acts of Parliament, but expired May, 1679; soon after which there is a case in Lilly's *Entries of Hilary Term*, 31 Car. 2, B.R.[5] In this case an action was brought for printing 4,000 copies of the *Pilgrim's Progress*, of which the plaintiff was the true proprietor, whereby he lost the profit and benefit of his copy. There is no account, however, of the case having been proceeded with.

28 **Ordinances of the Stationers' Company.** In 1681, all legislative protection having ceased, the Stationers' Company adopted an ordinance, or by-law, which recited that several members of the company had *great part of their estates in copies*, that by ancient usage of the company, when any book or copy was duly entered in their register to any member, such person had always been reputed and taken to be the proprietor of such book or copy, and ought to have the sole printing thereof. The ordinance further recited that this privilege and interest had of late been often violated and abused; and it then provided a penalty against such violation by any member or members of the company, where the copy had been duly entered in their register. The true view of this ordinance would seem to be, that the members of the Stationers' Company, finding their estates in copies, which belonged to them by the common law, no longer under the protection of the Licensing Act (the repeal of which had incidentally withdrawn the protection that had always been inserted in it, though it had necessarily no connection with the system of licensing), undertook to provide for the failure of legislation, as far as they could, by an ordinance applicable, of course, to their own members only. The ordinance is not to be cited as any other proof of what the common law right was, than that it shows, in connection with other historical proof, what it was then supposed to be. It was much the same as if an association of persons were to agree that any one of their number should pay a penalty for violating the acknowledged rights of property of any other person in the association, provided such rights were duly entered in their common records. It would not be an attempt to create the right, but it would justly be regarded as acknowledgment of the existence of such a right.[6]

In another by-law, passed in 1694,[7] it was stated that copies were constantly bargained and sold amongst the members of the company as their property, and devised to their children and others for legacies

5 *Ponder* v. *Bradyl*, Lilly's *Entries*, 67; see Carter, 89; 4 Burr. 2317; Skinner, 234; 1 Mod. 257.

6 *Curtis on Copyright*, p. 38.

7 In this year expired finally the Licensing Act of 13 & 14 Car. 2, which had been revived by 1 Jac. 2, c. 7, and continued by 4 W. & M. c. 24.

and to their widows for maintenance; and it was ordained that if any member should, without the consent of the member by whom the entry was made, print or sell the same, he should forfeit for every copy twelve-pence.

29 **New legislation sought.** For many years successively, attempts were made to obtain a new Licensing Act. Such a Bill once passed the Upper House, but the attempt miscarried upon constitutional objections to a licence. Proprietors of copyright had so long been protected by summary measures that they regarded an action at law as an inadequate remedy. A Bill in equity was never even thought of: no hope of its success appears at the time to have been entertained.

In one of the petitions presented to the House in support of applications to Parliament in 1709, for a Bill to protect copyright, the last clause or paragraph was as follows: " The liberty now set on foot of breaking through this ancient and reasonable usage is no way to be effectually restrained but by an Act of Parliament. For by common law, a bookseller can recover no more costs than he can prove damage, but it is impossible for him to prove the tenth, nay, perhaps, the hundredth part of the damage he suffers; because a thousand counterfeit copies may be dispersed into as many hands all over the kingdom, and he not be able to prove the sale of them. Besides, the defendant is always a pauper, and so the plaintiff must lose his costs of suit. (No man of substance has been known to offend in this particular, nor will any ever appear in it.) Therefore, the only remedy by the common law is to confine a beggar to the rules of the King's Bench or Fleet, and there he will continue the evil practice with impunity. We therefore pray that confiscation of counterfeit copies be one of the penalties to be inflicted on offenders." [8]

30 **First Copyright Act, 8 Anne, c. 19.** In response to these applications, in the year 1709 the first Copyright Act (8 Anne, c. 19), was passed. This Act gave authors of books then printed the sole right and liberty of printing them for a term of twenty-one years from April 10, 1710, and of books not then printed the sole right of printing for fourteen years, with a proviso that after the expiration of the said term of fourteen years the sole right of printing or disposing of copies should return to the authors thereof, if they were then living, for another term of fourteen years. The titles to books had to be registered in the register book of the Stationers' Company and nine copies had to be delivered to certain libraries.

This statute, passed with a view to giving a greater protection to copyright, had the unexpected result of curtailing it; for in the case of *Donaldson* v. *Beckett* [9] the House of Lords finally decided that the

[8] 4 Burr. 2318.

[9] (1774) 4 Burr. 2408; *Beckford* v. *Hood* (1798) 7 T.R. 620; *Jefferys (C.)* v. *Boosey (T.)* (1855) 4 H.L.C. 815.

effect of the statute was to extinguish the common law copyright in published works, though leaving the common law copyright in unpublished works unaffected.

The universities, alarmed at the consequence of this decision, applied for and obtained an Act of Parliament [10] establishing in perpetuity their right to all the copies given or bequeathed to them or which might thereafter be given to or acquired by them theretofore.

31 **Copyright Act, 1814.** The period for which copyright was capable of existing was somewhat varied by 54 Geo. 3, c. 156, s. 4, which enacted that instead of enduring for fourteen years, and contingently for fourteen more, authors should have the sole liberty of printing and reprinting their works for the term of twenty-eight years, to commence from the day of the first publication of the same; and, further, if the author should be living at the expiration of that period, for the residue of his natural life.

32 **Copyright Act, 1842.** All these Acts were repealed by the Copyright Act, 1842.[11] To Mr. Serjeant Talfourd was due the honour of obtaining this piece of legislative justice. From 1837 to 1842, in spite of the opposition of Macaulay, he used his best endeavours and expended his most eloquent strains to accomplish its passing. In contending for an extension of the period during which protection was afforded to literary works, he bursts forth: "There is something peculiarly unjust in bounding the term of an author's property by his natural life, if he should survive so short a period as twenty-eight years. It denies to age and experience the probable reward it permits to youth—to youth, sufficiently full of hope and joys to slight its promises. It gives a bounty to haste, and informs the laborious student, who would wear away his strength to complete some work which 'the world will not willingly let die,' that the more of his life he devotes to its perfection, the more limited shall be his interests in its fruits. It stops the progress of remuneration at the moment it is most needed; and when the benignity of nature would extract from her last calamity a means of support and comfort to the survivors—at the moment when his name is invested with the solemn interest of the grave—when his eccentricities or frailties excite a smile or a shrug no longer—when the last seal is set upon his earthly course, and his works assume their place among the classics of his country—your law declares that his works shall become your property, and you requite him by seizing the patrimony of his children."

The Act of 1842 extended the period of copyright to the life of the author and seven years after his death, or a term of forty-two years, whichever should be the longer, and in spite of its defects, both in

[10] 15 Geo. 3, c. 53.
[11] 5 & 6 Vict. c. 45.

substance and in draftsmanship, it remained the governing statute as to literary copyright until it was repealed by the Copyright Act, 1911.[12]

33 **Engraving copyright.** In the realm of artistic copyright, engravings were the first subjects to receive legislative protection. In 1734 the Engraving Copyright Act (8 Geo. 2, c. 13) was passed, conferring copyright upon these for a term of fourteen years.

No provision was made in this Act for the protection of any work of which the engraver was not also the designer; and this has been accounted for by the fact that Hogarth, by whose influence the Act was introduced, was invariably the designer as well as the engraver of his celebrated works.

The Engraving Copyright Act of 1766 (c. 38) was passed to remedy this oversight, and extended protection to any person making an engraving from the original work of another. It also enlarged the period of protection to twenty-eight years. A further Act of 1777 [13] enlarged the remedies for piracy; an Act of 1836 [14] extended the provisions of the Engravings Acts to Ireland; and an Act of 1852 [15] to prints taken by lithography or other mechanical process.

34 **Sculpture copyright.** Works of sculpture were the next in order to be protected by the Sculpture Copyright Act, 1814,[16] the term of protection being fourteen years, with a further reversionary term of fourteen years to the author if then living.

35 **Musical and dramatic performing rights.** Musical and dramatic compositions were held to be " books " within the meaning of the Copyright Acts relating to literary works [17]; but the performing right was not statutorily protected until the year 1833, when the Dramatic Copyright Act, commonly known as Bulwer Lytton's Act,[18] conferred an exclusive right of public performance for twenty-eight years, with a reversionary period to the author for the residue of his life, provided the work was printed and published; if the work was not printed or published the term of protection was uncertain.

Bulwer Lytton's Act only referred to dramatic pieces, but section 20 of the Literary Copyright Act, 1842,[19] dealt with the performing rights both in musical and dramatic pieces, and extended protection to the performing rights in both classes of works for a like period to that provided for the duration of copyright in books, namely, a period of

12 1 & 2 Geo. 5, c. 46.
13 17 Geo. 3, c. 57.
14 6 & 7 Will. 4, c. 59.
15 15 & 16 Vict. c. 12, s. 14.
16 54 Geo. 3, c. 56.
17 *Bach* v. *Longman* (1777) 2 Cowp. 623; *Storace* v. *Longman* (1809) 2 Camp. 26, note.
18 3 & 4 Will. 4, c. 15.
19 5 & 6 Vict. c. 45. Lectures were protected by the 5 & 6 Will. 4, c. 65.

forty-two years, or the life of the author and seven years after, whichever should be the longer.

Certain abuses arose with respect to the performing rights in musical works. In particular, a man named Wall gained considerable notoriety by purchasing performing rights and enforcing payment of penalties—which penalties were fixed at 40s. a performance by Bulwer Lytton's Act—from innocent infringers.

36 This led to the passing of the Copyright (Musical Compositions) Acts of 1882 and 1888,[20] which required that notice of reservation of rights of public performance of any musical composition should be printed on every published copy thereof and left the question of payment of costs and amount of penalties to the discretion of the court.

37 Owing to the injury caused to proprietors of the copyright in musical compositions by the practice of selling pirated copies of songs and music through the medium of street hawkers, and the difficulty of ascertaining any substantial person to proceed against for infringement, the Musical (Summary Proceedings) Act, 1902, and the Musical Copyright Act, 1906,[21] were passed providing summary methods of procedure against infringers of musical copyright. Both these last-mentioned Acts remained unrepealed by the Act of 1911, but have been repealed by the Copyright Act, 1956.

38 **Paintings, drawings and photographs.** The last class of works to receive statutory protection were paintings, drawings and photographs, which were, for the first time, protected by the Fine Arts Copyright Act, 1862.[22] This Act purported to protect paintings, drawings and photographs for the term of the life of the author and seven years after his death, but the wording of the Act was such as to produce the somewhat remarkable result that, unless the work was executed upon commission, so as to vest the copyright initially in the person commissioning the work, the copyright was lost altogether upon the first sale of the work unless, on that occasion, there was some written instrument signed by the artist dealing with the copyright, either by way of express assignment to the purchaser, or by way of express retention by the artist.[23] It should be observed that this requirement probably also applied to works of foreign origin, the copyright wherein in this country was secured by Convention or Order in Council, though it seems unlikely that foreign artists would have been aware of this peculiar provision of English law on a first sale to a dealer in their own country.

[20] 45 & 46 Vict. c. 40; 51 and 52 Vict. c. 17.
[21] 2 Edw. 7, c. 15; 6 Edw. 7, c. 36.
[22] 25 & 26 Vict. c. 68.
[23] Copinger (4th ed.), pp. 366, 367.

39 **Royal Commission of 1875.** Having regard to the number of Acts in force dealing with different branches of the law of copyright, a consolidating statute was urgently required. In 1875 a Royal Commission was appointed to inquire into the working of the Copyright Acts, and the Commissioners presented their Report in 1878. In this Report they stated[24]: "The first observation which a study of the existing law suggests is that its form, as distinguished from its substance, seems to us bad. The law is wholly destitute of any sort of arrangement, incomplete, often obscure, and, even when it is intelligible upon long study, it is in many parts so ill-expressed that no one who does not give such study to it can expect to understand it. The common law principles, which lie at the root of the law, have never been settled. The well-known cases of *Millar* v. *Taylor, Donaldson* v. *Beckett*, and *Jefferys* v. *Boosey* ended in a difference of opinion amongst many of the most eminent judges who have ever sat upon the Bench. The fourteen Acts of Parliament which deal with the subject were passed at different times between 1735 and 1875.[25] They are drawn in different styles, and some are drawn so as to be hardly intelligible. Obscurity of style, however, is only one of the defects of these Acts. Their arrangement is often worse than their style. Of this the Copyright Act of 1842 is a conspicuous instance."

40 **The Berne Convention.** In spite, however, of the recommendations of the Commissioners, no consolidating statute was passed—difficulties with the colonies particularly standing in the way of any settlement which should include any alterations in the existing law. In the year 1885, Great Britain was represented at the Conference of Powers held at Berne, which resulted in the framing of the Berne Convention, to which Great Britain adhered. Previously to doing so the International Copyright Act, 1886,[26] was passed, making the necessary alterations and additions to the International Copyright Act, 1844,[27] to enable Great Britain to give the required protection to foreign authors.

In the year 1908 the considerable modifications of the original Berne Convention, which were carried at the Conference of the Powers held at Berlin, rendered it imperative that Great Britain should amend her copyright laws, if she was to fall into line with the other Powers, and be in a position to give to foreigners the protection required by the Revised Convention.

41 **Committee of 1909.** In 1909 a committee was appointed "to examine the various points in which the revised International Copyright Convention, signed at Berlin on November 13, 1908, is not in accordance with the law of the United Kingdom, including those points

24 paras. 7, 8, 9.
25 Several more were added between 1875 and 1910.
26 49 & 50 Vict. c. 33.
27 7 & 8 Vict. c. 12.

which are expressly left to the internal legislation of each country, and to consider in each case whether that law should be altered so as to enable His Majesty's Government to give effect to the Revised Convention." This committee after hearing evidence, reported to Parliament [28] generally approving the provisions of the Revised Convention, and recommending the passing of a consolidating and amending Act.

42 **Copyright Act, 1911.** In the year 1910 a Bill to give effect to these recommendations was drafted and introduced into the House of Commons, but was dropped for that Session. In 1911, however, another Bill was introduced which, after being modified in several particulars during its passage through Parliament, was at length passed by both Houses, and received the Royal Assent on December 16, 1911.[29] This Act repealed all previous statutes on the subject of literary and artistic copyright, with the exception of the Musical Copyright Acts of 1902 and 1906,[30] and one section of the Fine Arts Copyright Act, 1862. The Act of 1911 came into force on July 1, 1912.

43 **Committee of 1951.** The Berne Convention was further revised at Rome in 1928 and at Brussels in 1948, and, in 1951, a further Committee was appointed " to consider and report whether any, and, if so, what changes are desirable in the law relating to copyright in literary, dramatic, musical and artistic works with particular regard to technical developments and to the revised international convention for the protection of literary and artistic works signed at Brussels in June 1948 and to consider and report on related matters." The Committee also took into consideration the Universal Copyright Convention which was subsequently signed at Geneva in 1952 under the auspices of UNESCO.[31] This Committee, after hearing evidence, reported to Parliament [32] recommending that Her Majesty's Government should accede to the Convention as revised at Brussels in 1948, and proposing a number of changes in the law.

44 **Copyright Act, 1956.** In the year 1955 a Bill to give effect to these recommendations was introduced into the House of Lords and, after a number of modifications introduced in both Houses, received the Royal Assent on November 5, 1956.[33] This Act repealed the Copyright Act of 1911 (except sections 15, 34 and 37) and the Musical Copyright Acts of 1902 and 1906 and the outstanding section of the Fine Arts Copyright Act, 1862. It came into force on June 1, 1957.[34]

[The next paragraph is 51]

28 Report of the Committee on the Law of Copyright, 1909, Cd. 4976.
29 1 & 2 Geo. 5, c. 46.
30 *Ante*, § 37.
31 As a result this Convention is variously referred to as the Universal, Geneva or UNESCO Convention.
32 Report of the Committee on the Law of Copyright, 1952, Cmd. 8662.
33 4 & 5 Eliz. 2, c. 74.
34 S.I. 1957 No. 863.

Part II

THE GENERAL LAW OF COPYRIGHT

CHAPTER 3

UNPUBLISHED WORKS, AND PUBLICATION

1.—UNPUBLISHED WORKS

51 **Protection at common law.** Except in the cases of paintings, drawings and photographs,[1] unpublished works received no statutory protection prior to the commencement of the Act of 1911,[2] but were protected under the common law.[3]

The nature of this common law protection was fully discussed in the case of *Re Dickens*,[4] in which a question at issue was whether the common law right in an unpublished manuscript passed under a bequest, taking effect before the passing of the Act of 1911, of "all my private papers." The Court of Appeal after considering the judgments in the cases of *Millar* v. *Taylor*,[5] *Mansell* v. *Valley Printing Co.*,[6] and *Macmillan & Co.* v. *Dent*,[7] were unanimously of opinion that the right was an incorporeal right existing independently of the property in the manuscript and one which did not pass to a legatee or donee on a bequest or gift of the manuscript itself. The Act of 1911, however, abolished common law copyright,[8] and conferred statutory copyright upon all works as from the date when the same were made.[9]

52 These provisions are substantially repeated in section 46 (5) of the Act of 1956. It is there provided that, "Subject to the preceding provisions of this section, no copyright, or right in the nature of copyright, shall subsist otherwise than by virtue of this Act or of some other enactment in that behalf." The preceding provisions in question are those preserving university copyright,[10] Crown copyright,[11] and the rules of equity relating to breaches of trust or confidence.[12]

53 **Under the Copyright Act, 1956.** The Act of 1956 confers copyright on unpublished works, as to literary, dramatic or musical works

1 *Tuck & Sons* v. *Priester* (1887) 19 Q.B.D. 48; Fine Arts Copyright Act, 1862 (25 & 26 Vict. c. 68), s. 1.
2 July 1, 1912: Copyright Act, 1911, s. 37 (2).
3 *Millar* v. *Taylor* (1769) 4 Burr. 2303; *Donaldson (A.)* v. *Beckett (T.)* (1774) 4 Burr. 2408, *ante*, § 30; *Jefferys (C.)* v. *Boosey (T.)* (1855) 4 H.L.C. 815; *Mayall* v. *Higbey* (1862) 1 H. & C. 148; *Mansell* v. *Valley Printing Co.* [1908] 2 Ch. 441; *Bowden Bros.* v. *Amalgamated Pictorials, Ltd.* [1911] 1 Ch. 386.
4 [1935] Ch. 267.
5 (1769) 4 Burr. 2303.
6 [1908] 2 Ch. 441.
7 [1907] 1 Ch. 107.
8 Copyright Act, 1911, s. 31.
9 s. 1.
10 Copyright Act, 1956, s. 46 (1); Chap. 19.
11 s. 46 (2) (3); Chap. 19.
12 s. 46 (4), *post*, § 88.

by section 2 (1), and as to artistic works by section 3 (2). Copyright is also conferred by section 12 (1) on unpublished sound recordings [13] and by section 13 (1) on unpublished cinematograph films.[14] The word "unpublished" does not occur in these subsections but since in each case there is a following subsection conferring copyright upon the respective work when published, it is clear that these subsections are intended to confer copyright on the works while unpublished.

54 **Proprietor of copyright.** In determining who is the first proprietor of the copyright in an unpublished work the Act draws no distinction between a published and an unpublished work, and for a consideration of this question the reader is referred to the later chapters in this work. Subsection (2) of section 17 of the Act of 1911 provided that where an author's unpublished manuscript is acquired "under a testamentary disposition made by the author," the ownership of the manuscript is prima facie proof of ownership of the copyright. This section applied and still applies to deaths before the commencement of section 38 of the Act of 1956,[15] whether the death of the person making the testamentary disposition occurred before or after the commencement of the Copyright Act, 1911. It had no effect where the court had the disposition before it to construe, and was able to decide, as a matter of construction, that the copyright was not intended to pass with the manuscript.[16] In order to raise this presumption the title to the manuscript must be derived from the "author" and under a testamentary disposition. Apparently, therefore, there would be no similar presumption in the case of a person deriving title under an assign of the author [17] and it was unnecessary to extend the provisions of the subsection to a case where the author died intestate, for in such a case the manuscript and the copyright would clearly devolve upon the deceased's administrator for the benefit of his next-of-kin.[18] Further, the subsection only applied to "manuscripts" and not to works of art.

55 **Presumption arising from bequest of manuscript.** Section 38 of the Act of 1956 has a superficial resemblance to the above-mentioned section of the Act of 1911, but is really quite different in effect. This provides that, where under a bequest, whether specific or general, a person is entitled beneficially or otherwise to the unpublished manuscript of a literary, dramatic or musical work, or to an artistic work, the bequest shall, unless a contrary intention is indicated in the testa-

13 Chap. 17.
14 Chap. 16.
15 Copyright Act, 1956, Sched. 7, Part VI, para. 29.
16 *Re Dickens* [1935] Ch. 267.
17 For example in the case of a receiver of a letter. Under s. 3 of the Literary Copyright Act, 1842, copyright in any book first published after the author's death belonged to the proprietor of the manuscript. This section received a strict construction in *Macmillan & Co.* v. *Dent* [1907] 1 Ch. 107.
18 *Latour* v. *Bland* (1818) 2 Stark. 382.

tor's will or a codicil thereto, be construed as including the copyright in the work in so far as the testator was the owner of the copyright immediately before his death. " Manuscript," by section 48 (1) of the Act, means the original document embodying the work whether written by hand or not. This section therefore provides a rule of construction and not a rule of evidence, as did the Act of 1911. It only applies in the case of an author who died after the commencement of the Act. Section 17 (2) of the Act of 1911 will continue in operation in respect of the copyright of an author who has died before the commencement of section 38 of the Act of 1956.[19] It is to be observed that, in addition to the basic distinction above indicated, section 38 of the Act of 1956 applies to an artistic work and applies whether or not the work has been performed in public prior to the author's death. The words " beneficially or otherwise " presumably indicate that the section is to apply to a bequest to trustees on trust.

56 **Term and assignment of copyright.** Questions relating to the term of copyright in an unpublished work are dealt with in a later chapter, as are also questions of assignment.[20]

57 **Conditions for obtaining copyright.** It is a condition precedent to the subsistence of copyright in an unpublished work that the author was a " qualified person " at the time when the work was made.[21]

58 **Qualified person.** A qualified person is defined as the following classes of persons, namely: A British subject, a British protected person, a citizen of the Republic of Ireland, a person domiciled in the United Kingdom, a person resident in the United Kingdom, a person domiciled or resident in another country to which the relevant provision extends, a body corporate incorporated under the laws of the United Kingdom and a body corporate incorporated under the laws of another country to which the relevant provision extends.

59 Since the British Nationality Act, 1948,[22] every person who under that Act is a citizen of the United Kingdom and Colonies, or who under any enactment for the time being in force in certain specified countries [23] is a citizen of that country, has the status of a " British subject." There is also a class of British subjects without citizenship.[24]

[19] Copyright Act, 1956, Sched. 7, Part VI, para. 29.
[20] See *post*, Chaps. 6 and 8.
[21] Copyright Act, 1956, ss. 2 (1), 3 (2), 12 (1), 13 (1).
[22] British Nationality Act, 1948, (11 & 12 Geo. 6, c. 56), s. 1 (1) as amended.
[23] s. 1 (3) as amended. The countries are Canada, Australia, New Zealand, India, Pakistan, Ceylon, the Republic of Cyprus, Nigeria, Sierra Leone, Ghana, Malaysia, Tanzania, Jamaica, Trinidad and Tobago, Uganda, Kenya, Malawi, Zambia, Malta, the Gambia, Guyana, Singapore, Botswana, Lesotho, Barbados, Swaziland, Mauritius, Tonga and Fiji.
[24] ss. 13 and 16 as amended.

60 A " British protected person " is defined by section 32 (1) of the British Nationality Act, 1948, as a person who is a member of a class of persons declared by Order in Council, made in relation to any protectorate, protected State, mandated territory or trust territory, to be, for the purposes of that Act, British protected persons by virtue of their connection with that protectorate, State or territory.[25]

61 **" Domicile."** Domicile may be obtained either by birth, operation of law (*e.g.*, by marriage), or by choice. Domicile of origin prevails in the absence of a domicile of choice, that is if a domicile of choice has never been acquired or, if once acquired, has been abandoned. Further, a domicile of choice is acquired when a man fixes voluntarily his sole or chief residence in a particular place with an intention of continuing to reside there for an unlimited time.[26] A domicile of choice will be abandoned when, after a departure from a country, a man no longer has an intention to return there and this is so, even if his intention of returning has merely withered away and he has not formed any positive intention never to return to live in the country. The death of the old intention suffices, without the birth of any new intention.[27]

62 **" Residence."** Where there is nothing to show that it is used in a more extensive sense, " residence " denotes the place where an individual eats, drinks and sleeps, or where his family or his servants eat, drink and sleep.[28] It seems clear that " residence " implies something more than a visit, but the degree of permanence is hard to define.[28a] It is submitted that it will be sufficient to show that the author, at the time the work was made, was living at a place within the country in question as his home. The meaning of " residence " has been considered in cases under the Income Tax Acts.[29]

63 **When is a work " made."** In the case of literary, dramatic, musical or artistic works, if the making of the work extended over a period, the test is satisfied if the author was a qualified person for a substantial part of the period of making.[30] In the case of a literary, dramatic or musical work, " making " means reduction to writing or some other

[25] As to position where a territory has ceased to be a protectorate, protected state or trust territory when Order made, see British Nationality (No. 2) Act, 1964 (1964 c. 54), s. 5.

[26] *In the estate of Fuld, decd.* (No. 3) [1968] P. 675.

[27] In *Re Flynn* [1968] 1 W.L.R. 103, where the standard of proof required from those asserting that a change of domicile has taken place is considered; see also *In the estate of Fuld decd., supra.*

[28] *R.* v. *The Overseers of Norwood* (1866) L.R. 2 Q.B. 457.

[28a] See *MacRae* v. *MacRae* [1949] P. 397 and *Stransky* v. *Stransky* [1954] P. 428.

[29] *Lloyd (T.)* v. *S.I.R.* (1883) 11 Sess.Cas. (4th Ser.) 687; *Levene* v. *C.I.R.* [1928] A.C. 217; *C.I.R.* v. *Lysaght* [1928] A.C. 234.

[30] Copyright Act, 1956, ss. 2 (1), 3 (2).

material form.[31] In the case of a sound recording it means the production of the first record embodying the recording.[32] There is no statutory definition of " making " in relation to an artistic work or a cinematograph film but the maker of a cinematograph film is defined as the person by whom the arrangements necessary for the making of the film are undertaken.[33]

64 **Copyright in works in existence before being " made."** While the foregoing provisions make it clear that a work cannot be protected under the Act until it is reduced to a material form since, until it is " made," it cannot be established that the maker was a qualified person, it is not expressly stated that copyright protection does not exist for a work which has not been " made." It is arguable, therefore, that once it is " made," the copyright which is then created relates back to the moment at which the work comes into existence. This may be material in the case of music which is composed and played before being written down, and in the case of a dramatic work performed without having been previously written. If a person who has heard these performances reproduces them after the author has himself recorded them, it seems to remain a question, as it was prior to 1956, whether an infringement has been committed.[34]

Apart from any copyright claim, a claim based upon breach of confidence may arise when a person who has heard a private performance of a new work makes use of the information.[35]

65 **Corporate bodies.** It would not appear that a body corporate can be an author, except in the case of photographs where the " author " is defined as being the person who, at the time when the photograph is taken, is the owner of the material on which it is taken, and such a person could be a body corporate.[35a] It therefore appears that the references to a body corporate in the definition of " qualified person " relate, apart from photographs, solely to sound recordings and cinematograph films, in relation to which the person who has to be a qualified person is the maker and not the author.[36] In the case of a sound recording the maker is the person who owns the first record embodying the recording,[37] and in the case of a cinematograph film it is the person as above stated who made the arrangements.[38]

[31] s. 49 (4).
[32] s. 12 (8).
[33] s. 13 (10).
[34] See *post*, Chap. 9.
[35] See *Gilbert* v. *The Star Newspaper Co., Ltd.* (1894) 11 T.L.R. 4; *post*, § 98.
[35a] Copyright Act, 1956, s. 48 (1); but see s. 3 (3) (*c*).
[36] ss. 1 (5), 12 (1), 13 (1).
[37] Copyright Act, 1956, s. 12 (8).
[38] s. 13 (10).

2.—PUBLICATION

66 **Importance of determining when a work is published.** Under the Act of 1911, the subsistence of copyright in a published work depended solely on the place of first publication and consequently copyright could often be lost or gained by publication. The loss of copyright was particularly the case in relation to works emanating from the United States of America, since by Order in Council copyright was extended to the unpublished works of subjects or residents of the United States, but not to works first published there.[39] Under the Act of 1956 the copyright in published works depends, not only upon the place of first publication but, whatever that place, will be enjoyed if the author was a qualified person at the time when the work was first published or, if he died before publication, was a qualified person immediately before his death.[40] These provisions, however, do not apply to works which were first published before the commencement of the Act of 1956.[41] Consequently, it remains of substantial importance to determine whether or not a work was published. Even in the case of a work published after the commencement of the Act of 1956 it will be observed that a different date is relevant in determining whether or not the author was a qualified person, so that if the work was not first published in the United Kingdom or in another country to which the relevant provisions extend, it will become necessary to ascertain different information about the author than while the work was unpublished. Moreover the term of copyright in certain cases runs from first publication.[42]

67 **What is meant by "publication."** We therefore propose to consider what is meant by "publication" of a work; in other words, the circumstances under which a work ceases to fall within the class of unpublished works and becomes a published work.

Prima facie a literary, dramatic or musical work, or an edition of such a work or an artistic work, is published if, but only if, reproductions of the work have been issued to the public[43] and for the purpose of this provision the reproduction of a substantial part of the work is not a reproduction of the work or edition.[44] A sound recording is published if records embodying the recording or any part thereof are issued to the public.[45] A cinematograph film is published if copies of the film are sold, let on hire, or offered for sale or hire to the public.[46] On the other hand, the performance,

[39] S.R. & O. 1915 No. 130.
[40] Copyright Act, 1956, ss. 2 (2), 3 (3).
[41] Sched. 7, Part I, para. 1.
[42] See Chap. 6, *post*.
[43] s. 49 (2) (*c*).
[44] s. 49 (2).
[45] Copyright Act, 1956, s. 12 (9).
[46] s. 13 (10).

or the issue of records, of a literary, dramatic or musical work, the exhibition of an artistic work, the construction of a work of architecture, and the issue of photographs or engravings of a work of architecture or of a sculpture, are not to constitute publication of the work.[47]

68 **"Reproductions" must be issued.** Inasmuch as publication is to mean the issue of "reproductions" to the public, it follows that a work cannot be orally published,[48] and that there can be no publication of a work of which there only exists a single example. The writer of a literary work may permit his manuscript to be viewed or read by any number of persons without thereby publishing his work. It is even doubtful whether an artist can "publish" his work by issuing a single replica, for the Act speaks of "reproductions." Having regard to the special provision as to works of sculpture, it seems that these can only be published by means of castings from the original work.

69 **What is a reproduction.** Since it was thought necessary to provide specifically that the issue of photographs of works of sculpture should not constitute publication, it appears to have been considered by the legislature that such photographs would have been "reproductions" for the purpose of this provision, and it seems to follow that the legislature contemplated that the issue to the public of authorised photographs of paintings would constitute publication of the paintings. On the other hand, it is arguable that, while a photograph of a painting may be a "reproduction" for the purposes of proceedings for infringement, it is not a "reproduction" in the sense in which that word is used in dealing with the question of publication.[48a] And a similar question may arise with regard to other works. For instance, if A were to translate his manuscript work and publish the translation before the original, would this be a publication of the original? Upon the whole, it is thought that it would not. It is suggested that the proper view of the matter is that where what is published so differs from the original that it is capable of existing as a separate copyright work, it is this separate copyright work which is published and not the original.[48a] This reasoning would apply to a dramatisation of an unpublished novel as well as to a translation. It is thought that the legislature were giving effect to this principle in the specific provision in regard to works of sculpture, but that the existence of a specific provision in that case does not exclude the more general application of the principle to other cases. Thus, it is submitted that the publication of a pianoforte arrangement of an opera, or that of a few of the

[47] s. 49 (2) (*a*).

[48] In this respect the law was altered by the Act of 1911: see *Boucicault* v. *Chatterton* (1877) 5 Ch.D. 267; *Walter* v. *Lane* [1900] A.C. 539; *Caird* v. *Sime* (1887) 12 App.Cas. 326.

[48a] But compare Copyright Act, 1956, s. 13 (5) and (10), where the word "copy" is used in relation both to infringement and publication; see also ss. 7 and 18 (3).

orchestral parts, would not be a publication of the opera itself,[49] and if, say, specimen pages of a literary work were distributed prior to the entire work being published this could not be more than a publication of the specimen pages. These views are confirmed by the fact that in section 2 (5) and (6) of the Act of 1956 the making of an adaptation is treated as distinct from reproduction, and by the provisions of section 49 (2).[49a]

70 **When a work is " issued " to the public.** In order that there shall be a publication of a work, not only must the reproductions be made, but reproductions must be " issued " to the " public." Clearly, issue for the purposes of sale is not essential, although, no doubt, if reproductions are issued for such a purpose, this would amount to publication.[50] A presentation of copies on the part of the author to individuals, or to a limited class, or even the sending of advance copies to the press for review would not, it is thought, be publication, but gratuitous circulation generally would seem to be so.[51] Thus in *Prince Albert* v. *Strange*,[52] it appeared that her late Majesty Queen Victoria and the late Prince Consort had given to their intimate friends lithographic copies of drawings and etchings which they had made for their own amusement. This was held to be a private circulation of copies, and hence not a publication.

71 **Not by public performance.** The performance in public of a dramatic or musical work, and the delivery in public of a lecture, are not publication of the work or lecture.[53] This would have been reasonably clear without any express provision to that effect, for obviously a performance is not an " issue of reproductions," but it is perhaps as well to emphasise the point. The Act of 1911 effected an alteration in the law, it having been held under the old law that a dramatic work was published by being publicly performed.[54]

72 **Nor by public exhibition.** Neither is the exhibition in public of an artistic work, nor the construction of a work of architecture, publication of it.[54a] It was held prior to 1911 that exhibition of a painting in a public gallery, the rules of which forbade the public to copy, was not a publication of the work.[55]

[49] *Boosey* v. *Fairlie* (1877) 7 Ch.D. 301.
[49a] In *Merchant Adventurers Ltd.* v. *M. Grew & Co. Ltd.* [1971] F.S.R. 233, held that drawings for light-fittings were published by the sale to the public of the three dimensional fittings made from the drawings.
[50] *White* v. *Geroch* (1819) 2 B. & Ald. 298.
[51] *Novello* v. *Ludlow* (1852) 12 C.B. 177.
[52] (1849) 1 M. & G. 25.
[53] Copyright Act, 1956, s. 49 (2) (*a*), and see definition of " performance," s. 48 (1).
[54] *Boucicault* v. *Delafield* (1863) 1 H. & M. 597; *Boucicault* v. *Chatterton* (1877) 5 Ch.D. 267; *Falcon* v. *The Famous Players Film Co. Ltd.* [1926] 2 K.B. 474 (C.A.).
[54a] Copyright Act, 1956, s. 49 (2) (*a*).
[55] *Turner* v. *Robinson* (1860) 10 Ir.Ch. 121, 510.

73 **Nor by issue of records.** It was submitted in previous editions of this work that, under the Act of 1911, the issue to the public of records or mechanical contrivances by which a musical work may be performed in public did constitute a publication of the music since such contrivances constituted just as much a fixed and permanent record of the music as publication of a musical score but, as has been seen,[56] it is now clearly provided under the Act of 1956, that the issue of records of a literary, dramatic or musical work is not to constitute publication.

74 **Place of publication.** In cases where the place of publication is material it would appear that it is the place where copies are received by the public, or at least capable of being so received, and not the place where copies are printed or produced.[57]

75 **Unauthorised publication.** A work is not published if its publication is unauthorised. If copyright subsisted in the work, as an unpublished work, then it is unauthorised if done without the licence of the copyright owner. If the work, as an unpublished work, did not enjoy protection, then it is not published if published without the consent of the author or, in the case of a sound recording, cinematograph film, or an edition of a literary, dramatic or musical work, the consent of the maker or publisher as the case may be.[58]

76 **Simultaneous publication.** A literary, dramatic, musical or artistic work is entitled to copyright, if first published in the United Kingdom or a country to which the relevant provision extends, or if the author was a qualified person at the time when the work was first published, or at his death if this occurred before first publication.[59] Unless the makers were qualified persons at the time of making, sound recordings and cinematograph films are entitled to copyright only if the first publication took place in the United Kingdom or in another country to which the provision extends,[60] and copyright subsists in published editions if the first publication thereof took place in the United Kingdom or another country to which the provision extends, or the publisher was a qualified person at the date of first publication.[61] In all these cases, therefore, it is essential to determine what is meant by " first " publication. It is provided by the Act of 1956 that publication in any country shall not be treated as being other than the first publication by reason only of an earlier publication elsewhere if

[56] Copyright Act, 1956, s. 49 (2) (*a*), and *ante*, § 67.
[57] *McFarlane* v. *Hulton* [1899] 1 Ch. 884. As to publication in parts, see *Low* v. *Ward* (1868) L.R. 6 Eq. 415.
[58] Copyright Act, 1956, s. 49 (3).
[59] ss. 2 (2), 3 (3).
[60] ss. 12 (2), 13 (2).
[61] Copyright Act, 1956, s. 15 (1).

the two publications took place within a period of not more than thirty days.[62] What is frequently in copyright law described as "simultaneous" publication therefore means any two or more publications which take place within a period of thirty days. And a copyright owner, seeking to rely upon first publication as establishing copyright in his work, may rely upon any publication that has taken place within this period of thirty days. Under the Act of 1911 the relevant provision provided a period of fourteen days only, and this period still applies in the case of a publication effected before the commencement of the Act of 1956.[63]

It must be borne in mind that works may also enjoy copyright in the United Kingdom by virtue of Orders in Council made under section 32, applying the Act to works first or simultaneously published in foreign countries.[64]

77 **"Colourable" publication.** The Act of 1956 repeats the Act of 1911 in providing that a publication which is merely colourable and not intended to satisfy the reasonable requirements of the public shall be disregarded.[65]

78 The question as to what is a "colourable" publication arose in the case of *Francis, Day & Hunter* v. *Feldman & Co.*[66] There the plaintiffs were the owners of the copyright in a song called "You made me love you (I didn't want to do it)," which was composed by an American author, who assigned his copyright in it to a firm in New York. This firm published the song simultaneously in New York and Canada on May 5, 1913.[67] In April 1913 they sent twelve copies of the song to the plaintiffs with instructions to copyright the song in the United Kingdom on May 5, 1913. On that day the plaintiffs sent one copy to the British Museum and one copy they filed at their London office. They also sent four copies to the agent for receiving copies for the university libraries, and the remaining six copies they exposed for sale on the counter in the retail department of their business premises in London. They did not advertise the song, and there was no immediate demand for it, but subsequently it became a great success, made large sales, and the plaintiffs acquired the copyright for the United Kingdom. It was held that the publication in England on May 5, 1913, was not "colourable only," and that it was sufficient

62 s. 49 (2) (*d*).

63 Copyright Act, 1911, s. 35 (3) and Copyright Act, 1956, Sched. 7, Part VI, para. 33 (1).

64 See *post*, Chap. 25.

65 Copyright Act, 1911, s. 35 (3) and Copyright Act, 1956, s. 49 (2) (*b*).

66 [1914] 2 Ch. 728.

67 Canada was not at that date a part of His Majesty's dominions to which the Act extended.

to show that there was an intention to satisfy the demands of the public if such demand should arise.[67a]

In *Copex Establishment* v. *Flegon*,[68] on an application for interlocutory relief to restrain threatened publication of a book, the question whether copyright subsisted in the book depended solely on whether it had been published here. The plaintiffs' evidence was to the effect that 169 copies of the book in the Russian language had been placed on sale at more than 50 booksellers. On the first occasion of sale the demand did not exceed the supply but, since the publicity given to the case, there had been extra demand which had exceeded the supply, and it was intended to meet the extra demand. The defendant argued that this was not "publication," that it was not intended to satisfy the reasonable requirements of the public and that there had been deliberate undersupplying of the work in Russian to protect the forthcoming publications of the book in volume form and serial form in English. No decision was reached on the issue of "publication" as, during the course of the hearing, the defendant gave an undertaking not to publish the book until the trial of the action.

79 **Subsequent acquisition of copyright for an unprotected work.** Although the Orders made in pursuance of the Brussels Convention and Universal Copyright Convention must make the event more unusual than in the past, circumstances may still occur in which an unpublished work was unprotected in England, but subsequently became protected by publication here.[68a] For instance, apart from international arrangements, a foreign artist does not, by exhibiting his painting in England, become entitled to copyright there. Until he has issued reproductions to the public, any person is at liberty (unless acting in breach of confidence) to photograph, engrave, or otherwise copy, the original work, and to sell those reproductions in England. This, again, being done without the consent of the artist, does not "publish" the work,[69] and, therefore, if the artist subsequently himself issues reproductions to the public he thereby gains copyright in his original. What, then, is the position of the first copyist? Clearly, he cannot be sued for piracy merely because he has in his possession copies of the work, for those copies were lawfully made, and the subsequent acquisition of copyright by the author cannot, prima facie, have a retrospective effect so as to render an act unlawful which was perfectly lawful at the time it was committed. It is equally clear that

[67a] In *Grossmann* v. *Canada Cycle Co.* [1901–04] Macg.Cop.Cas. 36, the posting of copies of a newspaper to subscribers in this country was held not to amount to publication here. Further that even delivery here of such copies would probably not be a sufficient publication as it was not making the paper available to the general public.

[68] *The Times*, August 18, 1967; see § 555, *post*.

[68a] See *Copex Establishment* v. *Flegon, supra*, where the authoress was Mrs. Svetlana Alliluyeva, Stalin's daughter.

[69] Copyright Act, 1956, s. 49 (3).

the copyist cannot make or print any further copies, but it is not so clear whether he can dispose of copies which he has on hand at the date when the artist acquired his copyright. It is, however, submitted that the first copyist does not infringe the copyright of the artist by selling or otherwise disposing of copies lawfully made by him. It is, no doubt, provided by section 5 (3) of the Act of 1956 that copyright shall be deemed to be infringed by a person who (*inter alia*) sells or exposes for sale any article if to his knowledge the making of the article constitutes an infringement of that copyright. In the case supposed, the copies were not " made " in contravention of the provisions of this Act, and it is submitted that it follows that the copies lawfully made may be disposed of without exposing the copyist to an action for infringement of copyright. The case seems to be somewhat analogous to the case of a person who has assigned his copyright, or granted a licence to publish for a term which has expired. It was held, under the old law, that an assignor could dispose of copies manufactured before the date of his assignment,[69a] and that a licensee could do the same with regard to copies manufactured before his licence ran out.[70] In the latter case, Wood V.-C. remarked, " the Copyright Acts were directed against unlawful printing; and when, as in this case, the defendant had acquired the right of lawfully printing the work, he was at liberty to sell at any time what he had so printed." No doubt, the dicta in the case of *Monckton* v. *Pathé Frères Ltd.*,[71] in which it was held that gramophone records lawfully made could not be lawfully sold without payment of royalties, are contrary to the view here expressed, but, whatever may have been the proper construction of section 2 (2) of the Copyright Act, 1911, it seems quite clear that under the Act of 1956 the view here expressed must be correct.

3.—LETTERS AND LECTURES

(a) *Letters*

80 Two classes of works which frequently remain unpublished call for some special observations, namely, letters and lectures.[71a]

A letter is an " original literary work," and therefore entitled to copyright. The fact that the letters are of no literary value is quite immaterial.[72] The writer of a letter is clearly the author and, therefore, the owner of the copyright unless he is under a contract of service or apprenticeship [73] or is a mere clerk or amanuensis.[74] It is clear

69a *Taylor* v. *Pillow* (1869) L.R. 7 Eq. 418.
70 *Howitt* v. *Hall* (1862) 6 L.T. 348.
71 [1914] 1 K.B. 395.
71a See " Copyright in Letters " [1905–10] Macg.Cop.Cas.
72 *Walter* v. *Lane* [1900] A.C. 539; *British Oxygen Co., Ltd.* v. *Liquid Air, Ltd.* [1925] Ch. 383.
73 Copyright Act, 1956, s. 4.
74 *Walter* v. *Lane* [1900] A.C. 539; *Donoghue* v. *Allied Newspapers, Ltd.* [1938] Ch. 106.

that the writer of an ordinary private letter does not, by sending the same to his correspondent, thereby publish the letter, although it would be different if the letter was published in a newspaper with his consent. Generally, therefore, the writer of a letter can restrain any publication of copies of his letter as an infringement of copyright, but circumstances may imply a licence to publish. The case of a letter to a newspaper is an extreme example, in which case, not only does the newspaper obtain the right to publish the letter, but also, by customary implication, the right to alter it, so long as the alterations are not of a nature to affect the credit or literary reputation of the writer.[75] Again, a licence to publish commercial letters will be more readily implied than in the case of private correspondence.[76] Under the old law it was clear that letters might be published if the object of doing so is to vindicate the character of the receiver [77]; but not for the purpose of representing to the public as true that which the receiver has, in legal proceedings upon that very question, admitted to be false.[78] It is doubtful if this doctrine, which receives no support from the Act of 1956, can stand where the action is founded upon infringement of copyright as distinguished from breach of confidence; it could only do so upon the ground of an implied licence or consent, and it seems difficult to imply such a consent under the circumstances of necessity existing.[79]

81 Apart from copyright the publication of letters and even the communication of their contents by the receiver has often been restrained as a breach of trust or confidence.[80]

82 **Rights of the receiver.** The position of the receiver of a letter is that, in the absence of some limitations, imposed either by the subject-matter of the letter or the circumstances under which it is sent, he has an unqualified title to the material upon which it is written,[80a] and he can deal with it as absolute owner, subject only to the proprietary right retained by the author and his representatives to the publication

75 *Springfield* v. *Thame* (1903) 89 L.T. 242, in which case it was held that the alterations were such as to make the editor the "author" of the communication. *Cf. Lee* v. *Gibbings* (1892) 67 L.T. 263; *Hogg* v. *Kirby* (1803) 8 Ves. 215.

76 *Perceval* (*Lord and Lady*) v. *Phipps* (1813) 2 V. & B. 19.

77 *Lytton* (*Earl of*) v. *Devey* (1884) 52 L.T. 121; *Labouchere* v. *Hess* (1898) 77 L.T. 559; *Folsom* v. *Marsh* (1841) 2 Story (Amer.) 100; *Howard* v. *Gunn* (1863) 32 Beav. 462.

78 *Palin* v. *Gathercole* (1844) 1 Col.C.C. 565.

79 *British Oxygen Co., Ltd.* v. *Liquid Air, Ltd.* [1925] Ch. 383.

80 *Pope* v. *Curl* (1741) 2 Atk. 341; *Thompson* (*C.*) v. *Stanhope* (*E.*) (1774) 2 Amb. 737; *Granard* (*Earl*) v. *Dunkin* (1809) 1 Ball & B. 207; *Gee* (*A. P.*) v. *Pritchard* (*W.*) (1818) 2 Swans. 402; *Palin* v. *Gathercole* (1844) 1 Col.C.C. 565; but see *Perceval* (*Lord and Lady*) v. *Phipps* (1813) 2 V. & B. 19; *British Oxygen Co., Ltd.* v. *Liquid Air, Ltd.*, *supra*; see also § 88, *post*.

80a *Thurston* v. *Charles* (1904) 21 T.L.R. 659.

or non-publication of the ideas in their particular verbal expressions.[81] The receiver is under no obligation to preserve the letter for the benefit of the writer: he is at liberty to destroy it, or to sell it for waste paper, or for the value of the autograph signature, or for any other purpose, if he pleases.[82] It is submitted, however, that whilst the signature on a letter would not in itself amount to a literary work,[83] the reproduction of which would amount to an infringement of literary copyright, it might, in certain cases, be protected as an artistic work.

83 **Power of government to publish or withhold letters.** It would appear that governments have a right, upon grounds of public policy, to publish or to withhold all letters addressed to the public offices.[84] This exception in favour of the government is not supposed to make such communications common property, to be published by any person who may see fit, without the sanction of the government, nor to take away the property of the writers or their representatives. " In respect to official letters addressed to government," observed Story J. in *Folsom* v. *Marsh*,[85] " or any of its departments, by public officers, so far as the right of the government extends from principles of public policy to withhold them from publication, or to give them publicity, there may be a just ground of distinction. It may be doubtful whether any public officer is at liberty to publish them, at least in the same age, when secrecy may be required by the public exigencies, without the sanction of the government. On the other hand, from the nature of the public service, or the character of the documents, embracing historical, military, or diplomatic information, it may be right, and even the duty, of the government, to give them publicity, even against the will of the writers. But this is an exception in favour of the government, and stands upon principles allied to, or nearly similar to, the right of private individuals, to whom letters are addressed by their agents, to use them, and publish them, upon fit and justifiable occasions. But assuming the right of the government to publish such official letters and papers, under its own sanction, and for public purposes, I am not prepared to admit that any private persons have a right to publish the same letters and papers without the sanction of the government for their own private profit and advantage. Recently the Duke of Wellington's despatches have, I believe, been published by an able editor, with the consent

[81] *Pope* v. *Curl* (1741) 2 Atk. 341; *Oliver* v. *Oliver* (1861) 11 C.B.(N.S.) 139; *Howard* v. *Gunn* (1863) 32 Beav. 462; *Labouchere* v. *Hess* (1898) 77 L.T. 559; *Macmillan & Co.* v. *Dent* [1907] 1 Ch. 107; *Philip* v. *Pennell* [1907] 2 Ch. 577 and see *post*, § 97.

[82] *Baker* v. *Libbie* (1912) 210 Mass. 599, an American case.

[83] See *post*, § 230 *et seq.*

[84] *Curtis on Copyright* (Amer.) 98.

[85] (1841) 2 Story (Amer.) 100.

of the noble duke and under the sanction of the government. It would be a strange thing to say, that a compilation involving so much expense and so much labour to the editor in collecting and arranging the materials, might be pirated and republished by another bookseller, perhaps to the ruin of the original publisher and editor. Before my mind arrives at such a conclusion, I must have clear and positive lights to guide my judgment, or to bind me in point of authority."

84 **Statutory power to publish old letters.** Under section 7 (6) and (7) of the Copyright Act, 1956, provision is made to enable unpublished manuscripts which are more than a hundred years old and are deposited in a library, museum or institution to be published.[86] This applies to letters so deposited, and will enable collections of correspondence of biographical or historical interest to be published.

(b) *Lectures*

85 The protection afforded to lecturers was, under the law prior to the Copyright Act, 1911, of a very unsatisfactory character, and there was no copyright in an unpublished lecture. The definition of " performance " in section 48 (1) of the Act of 1956, includes the delivery of lectures, addresses, speeches and sermons. Copyright, however, can only subsist in a lecture if it is a literary work, *i.e.*, a work expressed in print or writing,[87] and it would appear, therefore, that there is still no copyright in a mere extempore speech. It is submitted, however, that where a speech is made from notes it might be held that anyone copying the speech was infringing the copyright in the notes.

A lecture is not published by delivery,[88] but it would appear that the issue of reports, or even of copies of notes from which it was made, with the acquiescence of the author, would constitute publication, since such reports would be copies of the literary work in which the copyright subsists. A lecturer would probably be held to license the publication if he delivered his lecture knowing that reporters were present.

86 **Newspaper reports of public lectures.** The provision of section 2 (1) (v) of the Copyright Act of 1911 to the effect that the publication of a report of a lecture in public was not an infringement, unless the report was prohibited by conspicuous notice, is not repeated in the Act of 1956. Presumably, however, section 6 (3) of the Act of 1956, which provides that no fair dealing with a literary work for the purpose of reporting current events in a newspaper, magazine or similar

86 See *post,* Chap. 12.

87 *University of London Press, Ltd.* v. *University Tutorial Press, Ltd.* [1916] 2 Ch. 601. See Copyright Act, 1956, s. 49 (4).

88 See definition of " performance," Copyright Act, 1956, s. 48 (1), as applied to s. 49 (2) (*a*).

periodical, or by means of broadcasting or in a cinematograph film, is to constitute an infringement, would have substantially similar effect. Indeed it is probably less favourable to the lecturer, since it may well be contended that the newspaper would be entitled to publish the contents of a public speech as reporting current events even though the speaker expressly forbade the publication. Furthermore this licence extends to broadcasting and films.

87 Of course, if a speech or lecture is not delivered in public there may be an express or implied obligation on the part of those who hear the speech or lecture not to publish it, in which case publication would—apart altogether from copyright—be restrained by injunction.[89] If, however, pupils are admitted to a lecture given for their instruction, they may go to the extent, if desirous and capable, of taking down the whole by means of shorthand, for the purposes of their own information; but they may not publish.[90]

4. PUBLICATION IN BREACH OF TRUST OR CONFIDENCE

88 **Rule stated.** The Act of 1956, repeating in substance section 31 of the Act of 1911, provides that nothing in the Act shall affect the operation of any rule of equity relating to breaches of trust or confidence.[91] This rule has been stated as follows. There is a broad principle of equity that he who has received information in confidence shall not take unfair advantage of it. He must not make any use of it to the prejudice of him who gave it, without obtaining his consent or, at any rate, without paying him for it.[92] It has for long been clear that the courts can restrain a breach of confidence arising out of a contract or any right to property.[93] For example, under the old law, prior to the Copyright Act, 1911, there were many cases in which publication of an unpublished literary work was restrained upon the ground of breach of confidence, but inasmuch as, under that law, all unpublished works were entitled to common law copyright [94] it is often difficult to know how far the injunctions granted were based on a breach of the common law copyright and how far upon breach of confidence. In recent years, however, a number of cases have estab-

[89] *Nicols* v. *Pitman* (1884) 26 Ch.D. 374; *Caird* v. *Sime* (1887) 12 App.Cas. 326.

[90] Copyright Act, 1956, ss. 6 and 9. In an American case, *Keene (L.)* v. *Kimball (M.)* (1860) 16 Gray (82 Mass.) 545, Hoar J. said: "The student who attends a medical lecture may have a perfect right to remember as much as he can, and afterwards to use the information thus acquired in his own medical practice, or to communicate it to students or classes of his own, without involving the right to commit the lecture to writing, for the purpose of subsequent publication in print or by oral delivery."

[91] Copyright Act, 1956, s. 46 (4). See generally "Restitution of benefits obtained in breach of another's confidence," 86 L.Q.R. 463.

[92] *Seager* v. *Copydex* [1967] 1 W.L.R. 923 at 931.

[93] *Argyll (Duchess)* v. *Argyll (Duke)* [1967] Ch. 302 at 318; *Seager* v. *Copydex* [1967] 1 W.L.R. 923; *Fraser* v. *Evans* [1969] 1 Q.B. 349. *Morison* v. *Moat* (1851) 20 L.J.Ch.(N.S.) 513 at 522; *McNicol* v. *Sportsman's Book Stores* [1928–35] Macg. Cop.Cas. 116.

[94] *Ante*, §§ 51 and 52.

lished that the action for breach of confidence is independent of any right of property or contract or right of law [93] and rests upon an equitable obligation of confidence which may be implied from the circumstances of the case. If, therefore, a defendant is proved to have used confidential information, directly or indirectly obtained from a plaintiff, without his consent, express or implied, he will be guilty of an infringement of the plaintiff's rights.[95] So stated the rule may seem somewhat too wide. It is, therefore, necessary to elaborate upon that rule by expounding, with reference to the decided cases, what is meant by describing information as "confidential," in what circumstances the obligation not to disclose or use such information is implied or imposed, to what extent the courts will enforce such obligation and what remedies are available for that purpose. Particular reference will be made to those cases which concern literary and other copyright works.

89 **Relation between copyright and confidence.** The right to restrain the publication of a work upon the ground that to do so would be a breach of trust or confidence is, it is submitted, a broader right than the proprietary right of copyright. There can be no copyright in ideas or information, and it is no infringement of copyright to adopt or appropriate the ideas of another or to publish information received from another, provided there is no copying of the language in which those ideas have, or that information has, been previously embodied.[96] As Lord Denning remarked in *Fraser* v. *Evans* [97] *à propos* a written report, "copyright does not subsist in the information contained in the report. It exists only in the literary form in which the information is dressed." But if the ideas or information have been acquired by a person under such circumstances that it would be a breach of good faith to publish them and he has no just cause or excuse for doing so, the court will grant an injunction against him.[97] For example, this may be of considerable importance with regard to unpublished manuscripts submitted, and not accepted, for publication or use. In general, it is thought, that in such circumstances an obligation not to use would be implied, and this would extend to a mere plot which would not, in general, be protected under the law of copyright.[98]

90 **Elements of action for breach of confidence.** In order to succeed in an action for breach of confidence, the plaintiff must establish, to

95 *Saltman Engineering Co., Ltd.* v. *Campbell Engineering Co., Ltd.* (1948) 65 R.P.C. 203 at 213 (C.A.); *Nichrotherm Electrical Co., Ltd.* v. *Percy* [1957] R.P.C. 207 (C.A.); *Brian D. Collins (Engineers) Ltd.* v. *Charles Roberts & Co. Ltd.* [1965] R.P.C. 429.

96 *Ante*, § 2; *Hollinrake* v. *Truswell* [1894] 3 Ch. 420; *Walter* v. *Steinkopff* [1892] 3 Ch. 489; *Chiltern* v. *Progress Printing, etc., Co.* [1895] 2 Ch. 29; *Rees* v. *Melville* [1911–16] Macg.Cop.Cas. 96 at 98; but see *Corelli* v. *Gray* (1913) 30 T.L.R. 116.

97 [1969] 1 Q.B. 349 at 361, 362.

98 *Moore* v. *Edwards* [1901–4] Macg.Cop.Cas. 44; *Fraser* v. *Edwards* [1905–10] Macg.Cop.Cas. 10.

the satisfaction of the court, three elements: firstly, that the information which he is seeking to protect is of a confidential nature; secondly, that the information in question was communicated in circumstances importing an obligation of confidence; and, thirdly, that the defendant is about to make, or has made, an unauthorised disclosure or use of that information.[99]

91 **Definition of information.** Unlike copyright, it is not necessary that the information should be embodied in any document, though, as documents are more specific than other kinds of information, it may be easier to identify them and restrain their use and disclosure.[1] The information must, however, be traced to a particular source or be identifiable in reasonably specific terms, and the courts will not protect information which has become so completely merged in the mind of the person informed that it is impossible to say from what precise source or quarter he derived the information which led to the knowledge which he is found to possess.[1] This point is well illustrated in the cases in which employers have sought to restrain former employees from disclosing or using confidential information acquired by them in the course of their employment.[2] It has been held that the granting of an injunction against an ex-employee is not prevented by the fact that the information is carried in his head rather than being embodied in a document. The true test of protectability is whether the information in question can fairly be regarded as a separate part of the employee's stock of knowledge which a man of ordinary honesty and intelligence would recognise to be the property of his old employer and not his own to do as he likes with.[3] Where there are trade secrets which an employee will inevitably carry away in his head, it is not generally the proper course to invoke the general equitable doctrine to prevent breaches of confidence, but to exact from the employee a contract of service restricting, in reasonable terms, the employee's field of activity after he has left his employment.[3]

92 **Requirement of confidentiality.** Having defined or identified the relevant information, the court must then determine whether that information has the requisite quality of confidentiality about it to merit protection. It is difficult to enunciate any general test by which the courts decide whether the information which is sought to be protected is of a confidential nature or not. In some cases, the courts have paid attention to considerations which also arise in cases where they have to determine whether copyright subsists in a particular

[99] *Coco* v. *A. N. Clark (Engineers), Ltd.* [1969] R.P.C. 41.
[1] *Terrapin, Ltd.* v. *Builders' Supply Co. (Hayes), Ltd.* [1967] R.P.C. 375.
[2] *Printers & Finishers, Ltd.* v. *Holloway* [1965] 1 W.L.R. 1; *Coral Index, Ltd.* v. *Regent Index, Ltd.* [1970] R.P.C. 147; *Stevenson, Jordan & Harrison, Ltd.* v. *MacDonald & Evans* [1952] 1 T.L.R. 101; *P. A. Thomas & Co.* v. *Mould* [1968] 2 Q.B. 913.
[3] *Printers & Finishers, Ltd.* v. *Holloway, supra.*

work; for example the amount of time, skill and labour expended on its creation. Thus, it has been said that what makes a document confidential is the fact that the maker of the document has used his brain and has produced a result which can only be produced by somebody who goes through the same process; and a person breaches that confidence when he dispenses with the necessity of going through the process which has been gone through in compiling the document or collecting the information and avails himself of the fruits of the other's efforts, thereby saving himself a great deal of labour and calculation.[4] This consideration has, for example, been emphasised in the various cases in which news agencies have sought to protect the improper acquisition and use of information supplied by them to subscribers. Thus, in the case of *Exchange Telegraph Co., Ltd.* v *Central News Ltd.*[5] Stirling J. said: "By the expenditure of labour and money the plaintiffs had acquired this information, and it was, in their hands, valuable property in this sense—that persons to whom it was not known were willing to pay, and did pay, money to acquire it." On the other hand, as was remarked in a recent case: "Equity ought not to be invoked to protect trivial tittle-tattle, however confidential."[6] There must be brought into existence, by the application of the skill and ingenuity of the human brain, some novel or confidential information.

93 **Private or secret information.** It is submitted, however, that although the expenditure of time, skill and labour on the acquisition of information may often be relevant to determining whether information has a confidential quality, it is not of itself a necessary or sufficient condition of the confidentiality of that information. For example, there are cases where the courts have prevented publication of facts relating to a person's private life[7] on the grounds of breach of confidence. No time, labour or skill has in these cases been spent by the plaintiff on the acquisition of information: the facts themselves are protected from disclosure simply because they are private, because the knowledge of them was acquired by the person seeking to publish them in the course of a confidential relationship and because the publication cannot be justified as being in the public interest. It is therefore submitted that the necessary condition of confidentiality is that the information in question is private or secret. Something which is public property or public knowledge cannot *per se* provide any foundation for proceedings for breach of confidence.[6] Something which has been constructed solely from materials in the public domain

[4] *Saltman Engineering Co., Ltd.* v. *Campbell Engineering Co., Ltd.* (1948) 65 R.P.C. 203 at 215 (C.A.); *Industrial Furnaces, Ltd.* v. *Reaves* [1970] R.P.C. 605 at 617.

[5] [1897] 2 Ch. 48.

[6] *Coco* v. *A. N. Clark (Engineers), Ltd.* [1969] R.P.C. 41 at 48; *Franchi* v. *Franchi* [1967] R.P.C. 149.

[7] See § 96, *post*.

may, however, possess the necessary quality of confidentiality, for something new and confidential may have been created by the effort of the human brain; novelty or confidentiality depend upon the thing or information itself rather than upon the quality of its constituent parts.[6] The principle is, therefore, clear enough when the whole of the information is private.

94 **Mixed information.** Difficulties can arise when the information is in part public and in part private, as, for example, when some of the information is published in the form of a patent specification. "When the information is mixed, being partly public and partly private, then the recipient must take special care to use only the material which is in the public domain. He should go to the public source and get it, or, at any rate, not be in a better position than if he had gone to the public source. He should not get a start over others by using the information which he received in confidence. At any rate, he should not get a start without paying for it."[8] It has been said that this "springboard" principle extends so far as to prevent a person who has received information in confidence from using that information even after it has been published by or with the consent of the person from whom the information was originally acquired. Thus in *Terrapin, Ltd.* v. *Builders' Supply Co. (Hayes), Ltd.* Roxburgh J. said[9]: "As I understand it, the essence of this branch of the law, whatever the origin of it may be, is that a person who has obtained information in confidence is not allowed to use it as a springboard for activities detrimental to the person who made the confidential communication, and springboard it remains even when all the features have been published or can be ascertained by actual inspection by any member of the public." Similarly in the *Saltman* case Lord Greene pointed out[10] that while the recipient of the confidential information could, like any one else, buy the article, measure it and make his own mould, he could not lawfully shorten his labours by resort to the confidential know-how he had learned. On this view the recipient of the confidential information is placed under a special and permanent disability in the field of competition in order to ensure that he does not get an unfair start. On the other hand, it was argued for the defendants in *Peter Pan Manufacturing Corporation* v. *Corsets Silhouette, Ltd.*[11] that these views were inconsistent with the decision of the House of Lords in *Mustad (O.) & Son* v. *Dosen.*[12] The point was not decided as being a future question but, in *Cranleigh Precision*

[8] *Seager* v. *Copydex* [1967] 1 W.L.R. 923 at 931.
[9] [1967] R.P.C. 375 at 391. Approved in *Seager* v. *Copydex, supra*; and see *Ackroyds (London), Ltd.* v. *Islington Plastics, Ltd.* [1962] R.P.C. 97.
[10] (1948) 65 R.P.C. 203 at 215; *Underwater Welders & Repairers, Ltd.* v. *Street* [1967] F.S.R. 194.
[11] [1963] R.P.C. 45.
[12] [1963] R.P.C. 41.

Engineering, Ltd. v. *Bryant* [13] Roskill J. held that there was no conflict.

95 **Examples of confidential information.** Most of the cases in which the courts have laid down the principles on which the courts decide what information should, or should not, be protected concern trade secrets and industrial designs, but the principles contained in these decisions would seem equally applicable in other areas. While, as has been seen, ideas or plots are not protected under copyright law,[14] they may be protected by an action for breach of confidence if they are private or confidential and knowledge of them has been acquired in confidence. Examples of this kind of protection in the general field of copyright law are given below.

96 **Private and personal facts.** A leading case upon the subject is that of *Prince Albert* v. *Strange* [15] in which Prince Albert successfully applied to the court for an injunction restraining the defendants from exhibiting, publishing copies of, and publishing a catalogue of, drawings and etchings made by Queen Victoria and Prince Albert of their children and other subjects of interest to the family for their private use and amusement. Impressions of these drawings and etchings had, by some means, come into the defendants' hands, without the consent of Queen Victoria or Prince Albert, as a result of a breach of confidence committed by an employee of a printer, who had been entrusted with plates for the purpose of printing off impressions for Queen Victoria and Prince Albert. The defendants contended that a man who acquired knowledge of another man's property without his consent was not forbidden from communicating or publishing that knowledge to the world, or from informing or describing to the public what the property was, even though the other man might have kept, or tried to keep, his property secret. It was further argued that as regards portraits there were three distinct and independent rights: first, the property in the physical canvas itself; secondly, the copyright in the portrait painted on the canvas and, thirdly, the knowledge of the existence of the portrait on the canvas. On this basis, it was conceded that a person might be restrained from reproducing the portrait on the canvas, but contended that there was no legal principle which could restrain a person from describing the attributes of the portrait as was sought, for example, to be done in the case of the catalogue. These arguments were rejected by both Knight-Bruce V.-C., in the first instance, and by Lord Cottenham on appeal, and an injunction was granted both on the ground of infringement of the plaintiff's proprietary rights in the copyright of the pictures and upon

[13] [1964] 3 All E.R. 289 at 302.
[14] See § 2, *ante*.
[15] (1849) 1 M. & G. 25.

the ground of breach of confidence. Lord Cottenham said that he was bound to assume that the possession of the impressions of the etchings by the defendants had its foundation in a breach of trust, confidence or contract. It could not be suggested by the defendants that the impressions had been properly obtained from the plaintiff. He said: " But this case by no means depends solely on the question of property, for a breach of trust, confidence or contract would entitle the plaintiff to an injunction . . . the matter or thing of which the party had obtained knowledge, being the exclusive property of the owner, he has a right to the interposition of this court to prevent any use being made of it, that is to say, he is entitled to be protected in the exclusive use and enjoyment of that which is exclusively his."

The same principle was applied in the case of *Argyll* (*Duchess*) v. *Argyll* (*Duke*)[16] in which the plaintiff obtained an injunction to restrain the publication by the defendant of the secrets of the plaintiff relating to her private life, personal affairs and private conduct communicated by her to the defendant during the subsistence of their marriage to each other. Ungoed-Thomas J. held that communications between husband and wife during their marriage were protected against breach of confidence and that even the subsequent adultery of the plaintiff resulting in divorce did not relieve the defendant from the obligation to preserve earlier confidences.

97 **Private letters.** The nature of confidential information was also recognised by Kekewich J. in the case of *Philip* v. *Pennell.*[17] In that case the plaintiffs sought to restrain the defendants from publishing letters written by the artist, Whistler, or the information contained in them, in a biography of Whistler which the defendants proposed to publish. Inasmuch as the letters were in the lawful possession of the defendants, Kekewich J. refused to prohibit them from making use of the information they might derive from a perusal of the letters, although he indicated that he might have arrived at a different conclusion if there had been any circumstances which would have rendered it a breach of confidence on the part of the defendants to make use of that information.

98 **Plots of plays and literary ideas and information.** In the case of *Gilbert* v. *The Star Newspaper Co., Ltd.*[18] Mr. W. S. Gilbert obtained an *ex parte* injunction restraining the publication of the plot of his play, *His Excellency*, then being rehearsed but not yet publicly performed, on the ground that the defendants had obtained the information with the knowledge that it was given to them in breach of

16 [1967] Ch. 302.

17 [1907] 2 Ch. 577; see also *McNicol* v. *Sportsman's Book Stores* [1928–35] Macg. Cop.Cas. 116; *Cooksley* v. *Johnson & Sons* (1906) 25 N.Z.L.R. 834.

18 (1894) 11 T.L.R. 4; *cf. Exchange Telegraph Co., Ltd.* v. *Central News, Ltd.* [1897] 2 Ch. 48.

confidence. Similarly, in *Macklin* v. *Richardson*[19] the defendant was restrained from publishing the text of a play *Love à la Mode* which a short-hand writer, employed by him, had taken down upon its performance at the theatre. In other cases injunctions have been granted to restrain the printing of conveyancing precedents stolen from the plaintiff's chambers,[20] though a pupil might make copies for his own use, as long as he did not publish them[21]; the printing of notes copied by a clerk of a gentleman to whom the plaintiff had lent them[22]; the selling or exhibiting of copies of a photograph without the sitter's consent[23] and the publishing of the text of private lectures on the part of persons attending them.[24] There have also been cases in which the plaintiff has recovered substantial damages against a defendant who has rejected a scenario for a play submitted to him by the plaintiff, but has then gone on to make considerable use of the dramatic ideas, characters and plot contained in the scenario.[25]

99 **News.** In a number of cases the courts have protected information in the form of news which has been collected by news agencies and has been surreptitiously obtained from a subscriber to the agency's news service. But it is difficult to say how far the decisions are based upon infringement of common law copyright, and how far upon the breach of confidence. For example, in *Exchange Telegraph Co., Ltd.* v. *Gregory & Co.*,[26] the plaintiffs, under a contract with the committee of the London Stock Exchange, obtained valuable information as to the prices of stocks and shares from time to time during the day. This information the plaintiffs handed on to their subscribers by means of tape machines, the subscribers expressly agreeing not to sell or communicate to non-subscribers the information which had been supplied to them. The defendants had been at one time subscribers of the plaintiffs, but the latter had recently refused to continue them as such, and they had succeeded in surreptitiously obtaining the information from another subscriber, and posted the information thus received in their offices. The court granted an injunction restraining the defendants from infringing the plaintiffs' copyright and from continuing to induce any subscriber of the plaintiffs to supply them with the information in breach of his contract with the plaintiffs. This case was

19 (1770) 2 Amb. 694.
20 *Webb* v. *Rose* (1732) cited (1766) 4 Burr. 2303 at 2330.
21 *Abernethy* v. *Hutchinson* (1825) 3 L.J.(O.S.) Ch. 209; *Lamb* v. *Evans* [1893] 1 Ch. 218.
22 *Forrester* v. *Waller* (1741) cited (1766) 4 Burr. 2303 at 2331; see also *Turner* v. *Robinson* (1860) 10 Ir.Ch. 121, 510; *Southey* v. *Sherwood* (1817) 2 Mer. 435; *Gee (A. P.)* v. *Pritchard (W.)*. (1818) 2 Sw. 402.
23 *Pollard* v. *Photographic Co.* (1889) 40 Ch.D. 345; *cf. Ellis* v. *Marshall (H.) & Son* (1895) 64 L.J.Q.B. 757; and see § 315, *post.*
24 *Caird* v. *Sime* (1887) 12 App.Cas. 326.
25 *Moore* v. *Edwards* [1901–4] Macg.Cop.Cas. 44; *Fraser* v. *Edwards* [1905–10] Macg.Cop.Cas. 10.
26 [1896] 1 Q.B. 147; and see *Tillett* v. *The Cosmopolitan Press, Ltd.* [1928–35] Macg.Cop.Cas. 331; *cf. Chilton* v. *Progress Printing, etc., Co.* [1895] 2 Ch. 29.

followed in *Exchange Telegraph Co., Ltd.* v. *Central News, Ltd.*,[27] where an injunction was sought to restrain the defendants from improperly copying information as to the results of horse-races at Manchester, collected by the plaintiffs' subscribers, and from communicating the information so copied to the defendants' subscribers. It was sought to distinguish this case from the case of *Exchange Telegraph Co., Ltd.* v. *Gregory & Co., supra*, on the ground that the result of a horse-race is public property, but Stirling J. refused to acknowledge the distinction. "The information," he said, "was not made known to the whole world; it was, no doubt, known to a large number of persons, but a great many more were ignorant of it. By the expenditure of labour and money the plaintiffs had acquired this information, and it was, in their hands, valuable property in this sense —that persons to whom it was not known were willing to pay, and did pay, money to acquire it. . . . I think that it is established as against the syndicate that they published for their own benefit information acquired from or through some subscribers to the plaintiffs, with knowledge or notice on the part of their manager, that it was acquired contrary to the terms imposed on the plaintiffs' subscribers." An injunction was accordingly granted.

100 **Confidential relationships.** However secret and confidential the information may be, there can be no binding obligation of confidence unless the information is communicated or acquired in circumstances importing an obligation of confidence.[28] It is difficult to deduce from the decided cases any precise, comprehensive test for determining whether the circumstances of a particular case import an obligation of confidence. One general test which has been suggested is that a confidential relationship exists if the circumstances are such that any reasonable man, standing in the shoes of the recipient of the information, would have realised that upon reasonable grounds the information was being given to him in confidence.[28] For example, it would be relatively easy for a plaintiff to establish a confidential relationship where information which is of commercial or industrial value is communicated during business negotiations with a view to a joint venture or to the commercial exploitation of the information by one party for, or with the co-operation of, the other party. The plaintiffs in both *Seager* v. *Copydex*[29] and *Coco* v. *A. N. Clark (Engineers), Ltd.*[28] were inventors who alleged that they had disclosed to the defendants details of their invention during the course of negotiations with a view to the defendants using the information in

[27] [1897] 2 Ch. 48; *The Exchange Telegraph Co., Ltd.*, v. *Howard* (1906) 22 T.L.R. 375; *Press Association, Ltd.* v. *Northern and Midland Reporting Agency* [1905–10] Macg.Cop.Cas. 306; *London & Provincial Sporting News Agency, Ltd.* v. *Levy* [1923–28] Macg.Cop.Cas. 340.

[28] *Coco* v. *A. N. Clark (Engineers), Ltd.* [1969] R.P.C. 41.

[29] [1967] 1 W.L.R. 923.

the manufacture of articles under agreements with the plaintiffs. In both cases the court found that those circumstances gave rise to a confidential relationship.

101 **Confidence in contracts.** The initial obligation to keep the information confidential often arises from an express or implied contract under which the information was originally communicated.[30] Such a case involves the determination of the nature and extent of the contract. A common example is when a contract, under which documents, drawings and technical information have been supplied for the purpose of assisting the manufacture of goods, has been terminated. In that case the court can restrain the use of the drawings and information for the purposes of continuing to manufacture the goods.[31]

A similar situation arose in the case of *Saltman Engineering Co., Ltd., & Ors.* v. *Campbell Engineering Co.*[32] where the defendants had been entrusted under a contract with certain engineering designs for the purpose of carrying out an order for the manufacture of a quantity of goods. The defendants thereafter used the designs for purposes outside the contract and it was held that such action was a breach of a confidential relationship which could be restrained by the court. Lord Greene said that if two persons make a contract under which one of them obtains, for the purposes of the contract or in connection with it, some confidential material, the law will imply an obligation to treat that confidential material in a confidential way as one of the implied terms of the contract. He added, however, that the obligation to respect confidence is not limited to cases where the parties are in a contractual relationship.

Another common contractual situation which can import a confidential obligation is the contract of service between employer and employee. A servant may not disclose or use confidential information, knowledge of which he has acquired during his employment,[33] nor make unauthorised copies of documents belonging to his master,[34] for to do so would be a breach of the confidence reposed in him. For example, in the case of *Amber Size Co.* v. *Menzel* [33] the court

30 See *Fraser* v. *Evans* [1969] 1 Q.B. 349 for an example of an express covenant.

31 *Brian D. Collins (Engineers), Ltd.* v. *Charles Roberts & Co., Ltd.* [1965] R.P.C. 429.

32 (1948) 65 R.P.C. 203 (C.A.).

33 *Lamb* v. *Evans* [1893] 1 Ch. 218; *Merryweather* v. *Moore* [1892] 2 Ch. 518; *Robb* v. *Green* [1895] 2 Q.B. 315; *Measures Bros., Ltd.* v. *Measures* [1910] 2 Ch. 248; *Amber Size, etc., Co., Ltd.* v. *Menzel* [1913] 2 Ch. 239; *Reid & Sigrist, Ltd.* v. *Moss & Mechanism, Ltd.* (1932) 49 R.P.C. 461; *Printers & Finishers, Ltd.* v. *Holloway* [1965] 1 W.L.R. 1; *Coral Index, Ltd.* v. *Regent Index, Ltd.* [1970] R.P.C. 147; *British Industrial Plastics, Ltd.* v. *Ferguson* (1941) 58 R.P.C. 1; *Lord Ashburton* v. *Pape* [1913] 2 Ch. 469; *Initial Services, Ltd.* v. *Putterill* [1968] 1 Q.B. 396; *Litholite, Ltd.* v. *Thomas Travis, etc., Ltd.* (1913) 30 R.P.C. 266, 532; *Industrial Furnaces, Ltd.* v. *Reaves* [1970] R.P.C. 605.

34 *Louis* v. *Smellie* [1895] W.N. 115; *Tuck & Sons* v. *Priester* (1887) 19 Q.B.D. 48.

granted an injunction against a dismissed servant of the plaintiff company, restraining him from making use of information as to a secret process of manufacture obtained in the course of his confidential employment with the plaintiffs, although the defendant had not abstracted anything tangible, such as a list of customers, and was not proposing to publish the information he had gained, but simply to use the same for the benefit of a rival firm into whose employment he had subsequently entered. Astbury J. granted an injunction in general terms restraining the defendant from using the whole or any material part of the plaintiffs' secret method or process of manufacture, the knowledge of which was acquired or obtained by him during his employment by the plaintiffs and from disclosing to any other person any information with respect thereto. The case of *Stevenson Jordan & Harrison, Ltd.* v. *MacDonald & Evans* [35] illustrates the limits of the confidential obligations inherent in a contract of employment. The plaintiffs there contended that the defendant, who had written a textbook with regard to the subject-matter of his employment, had in so doing disclosed confidential information. Lord Evershed said that if an employee writes a book which discloses confidential information learnt by him in the course of his employment, the court would restrain the publication. He added, however, that this did not apply to "know-how" learned in the course of his employment. "Know-how" indicates the way in which a skilled man does a job and is an expression of his individual skill and experience. Denning L.J. said that a servant, when he leaves his employment, cannot be restrained from using knowledge he has acquired so long as he does not take away trade secrets or lists of customers. Thus, not all information which is given to a servant in confidence and which it would be a breach of his duty for him to disclose to another person during his employment, is a trade secret which he can be prevented from using for his own advantage or for the benefit of a future employer after the employment is over.[36]

102 **Other examples of confidential relationships.** In *Argyll (Duchess)* v. *Argyll (Duke)* [37] it was held that the obligation of confidence was implied in the relationship of marriage. The confidential nature of the relationship was of its very essence and so obviously and necessarily implicit in it that there was no need for it to be expressed; it was the policy of the law to preserve the close confidence and trust between husband and wife and an injunction would therefore be granted to restrain the publication of communications made between spouses during the subsistence of that relationship.

[35] [1952] 1 T.L.R. 101; *Morris (B. O.), Ltd.* v. *F. Gilman (B. S. T.), Ltd.* (1943) 60 R.P.C. 20; *Canada Bonded Attorney and Legal Dictionary, Ltd.* v. *Leonard-Parmeter, Ltd.* (1918) 42 D.L.R. 342; *Nichrotherm Electrical Co., Ltd.* v. *Percy* [1957] R.P.C. 207.

[36] *Printers & Finishers, Ltd.* v. *Holloway* [1965] R.P.C. 239 at 253; *cf. Industrial Furnaces, Ltd.* v. *Reaves* [1970] R.P.C. 605 at 618.

[37] [1967] Ch. 302.

If a person lends his manuscript to another, there will generally be implied an obligation that the latter shall not publish it.[38] Similarly, where a person sits for his portrait to a photographer, there will usually be implied on the part of the latter an obligation that he will not sell or exhibit copies without the sitter's consent,[39] and an obligation may be implied on the part of persons attending private lectures not to take them down and publish them.[40]

103 **Wrongful use of confidential information.** Once a person has acquired confidential information in the course of a confidential relationship, he is generally under a duty not to disclose or use that information without the consent of the person who imparted that information. He is liable even if he uses the information unconsciously.[41] This is not, however, an absolute duty. It has been said that in some cases the duty is more accurately expressed in a qualified form as a duty not to use the information without paying a reasonable sum for it.[42] This might be the case in the fields of industry and commerce where there are difficulties involved in granting an injunction when a person has added information of his own to the information he has acquired in confidence and the two have become commercially inextricable. In such cases damages are a more appropriate remedy. But in other fields, such as the protection of privacy or the preservation of marital confidences, the duty probably exists in a more stringent form, and an injunction will be a more appropriate remedy, as the object of the plaintiff is to ensure the preservation of secrecy, rather than to obtain compensation for its ultimate exploitation.

104 **Justifiable use.** Although a person is not generally permitted to divulge to the world information which he has received in confidence, there are circumstances in which he has a just cause or excuse for doing so. If the information, which has been acquired in confidence, relates to misconduct of such a nature that it ought in the public interest to be disclosed to one who had a proper interest to receive it, the courts will not restrain its disclosure.[43] For example, in *Initial Services, Ltd.* v. *Putterill*[44] the plaintiffs tried to restrain the defendant, a former employee, from disclosing to a newspaper information to the effect that the plaintiffs had entered into agreements which should have been registered under the Restrictive Trade Practices Act, 1956. It was held that the law would not lend its assistance to anyone

38 *Queensberry (Duke)* v. *Shebbeare* (1761) 2 Eden 329; and see as to letters *ante*, § 80.
39 *Pollard* v. *Photographic Co.* (1889) 40 Ch.D. 345.
40 *Caird* v. *Sime* (1837) 12 App.Cas. 320.
41 *Seager* v. *Copydex* [1967] 1 W.L.R. 923.
42 *Coco* v. *A. N. Clark (Engineers), Ltd.* [1969] R.P.C 41; *Bostitch Inc.* v. *McGarry & Cole, Ltd.* [1964] R.P.C. 173.
43 *Fraser* v. *Evans* [1969] 1 Q.B. 349 at 361.
44 [1968] 1 Q.B. 396.

who was proposing to commit, and to continue to commit, a breach of statutory duty imposed in the public interest. It was also suggested that there may be cases where the misdeed is of such a character that the public interest may demand, or at least excuse, publication to a broader field, even to the press. There is, therefore, no breach of confidence in the disclosure of iniquity and that principle is not confined to cases of fraud, or the contemplated commission of a crime or civil wrong.

105 **Benefit of confidence.** Further, there may be cases in which, although it is established that information has been wrongfully disclosed or used in breach of confidence, yet the plaintiff has no right to relief. Such a case was *Fraser* v. *Evans*[45] where the plaintiff was a public relations consultant who had entered into a contract with the Greek Government, which contained an express term that he would not reveal any information about his work for the Government either during or after his contract. The defendant newspaper proposed to publish an article based on a report the plaintiff had made to the Greek Government in pursuance of the contract. An injunction was refused on the ground that the party complaining must be the person who is entitled to the confidence and to have it respected. In this case no duty of good faith was owed by the Greek Government or the defendants to the plaintiff. There was a duty of confidence owed to the Greek Government, but they were not the plaintiffs in the action. There was thus no duty, express or implied, owed to the plaintiff.

106 **Liability of third parties.** It was once thought that a further limitation on the liability for wrongful use or disclosure of confidential information was that the remedies for such breach probably only lay against persons who had either committed a breach of contract or confidence themselves, or were at least fully aware of all the circumstances. It was doubtful whether the remedies could be pursued against a purchaser for value of the information without notice of the fact that it was acquired in confidence. In *Stevenson, Jordan & Harrison, Ltd.* v. *Macdonald & Evans*[46] the point was raised, but not decided, whether the publisher of a book could be restrained from publication if he had acquired the manuscript for value without notice, but was given notice of a breach of confidence prior to publication. It might be argued that as the liability arises from the breach of an equitable obligation and not from the infringement of a proprietary right, such as copyright where ignorance is generally no defence,[47] a

[45] [1969] 1 Q.B. 349 at 362; *Gartside* v. *Outram* (1858) 26 L.J.Ch. 113 at 114; See also *Butler* v. *Board of Trade* [1970] 3 W.L.R. 822.

[46] [1952] 1 T.L.R. 101; See also *Nichrotherm Electrical Co., Ltd.* v. *Percy* [1957] R.P.C. 207 at 215; *Cranleigh Precision Engineering, Ltd.* v. *Bryant* [1964] 3 All E.R. 289; *Philip* v. *Pennell* [1907] 2 Ch. 577.

[47] *Mansell* v. *Valley Printing Co.* [1908] 2 Ch. 441; see Copyright Act, 1956, ss. 17 (2) and 18 (2).

purchaser for value without notice ought not to be liable to restraint. In several recent cases, however, it has been held that, even if a person comes by the information innocently, nevertheless if he gets to know that it was originally given in confidence, he can be restrained from breaking that confidence.[48]

107 **Damages for breach of confidence.** Where the obligation of confidence also involves an implied contract, damages for past breaches, as well as an injunction to prevent future breaches, can be readily obtained. However, if the act complained of also involves infringement of copyright, the damages are alternative, and not cumulative, under these two heads.[49] But there are circumstances in which a breach of an obligation of confidence may occur, though no contractual relationship exists between the parties, and so there is no common law cause of action. In such a case it had been doubted whether damages as well as an injunction could be obtained.[49] It has now been held that compensation is recoverable and that the proper basis for assessing such compensation is to determine the market value of the confidential information on a sale between a willing seller and a willing buyer.[50] That value depends on a decision by a competent tribunal, such as a patent judge, of the question whether the information involved a true inventive step, or was such as could have been provided by any competent consultant. In the former case compensation would be the capitalised value of the royalty payable on a sale of the invention, while, in the latter case, its value would be the reasonable fee payable to such a consultant. Once the compensation, as assessed, has been paid, the right to exploit the information belongs to the defendant as on an outright purchase under an agreement for sale.[50]

It would appear that an account of profits can be ordered as an alternative to damages.[51]

108 **Delivery up.** In addition to damages and an injunction the court can also make an order for delivery up of material containing confidential information. This may be ordered as an alternative to destruction of such material on oath and is useful where a defendant has shown, by his past conduct, that his oath is not to be relied upon. If the defendant has added material of his own to the information which he has obtained from the plaintiff in breach of confidence he can still be ordered to deliver up the material.[52]

[The next paragraph is 111]

48 *Fraser* v. *Evans* [1969] 1 Q.B. 349; *Argyll (Duchess)* v. *Argyll (Duke)* [1967] Ch. 302; *Printers & Finishers, Ltd.* v. *Holloway* [1965] 1 W.L.R. 1 at 7.

49 *Nichrotherm Electrical Co., Ltd.* v. *Percy* [1957] R.P.C. 207.

50 *Seager* v. *Copydex, Ltd.* (No. 2) [1969] 1 W.L.R. 809.

51 *Peter Pan Manufacturing Corp.* v. *Corsets Silhouette* [1963] R.P.C. 45 at 57 and see *Seager* v. *Copydex, Ltd.* [1967] 1 W.L.R. 923.

52 *Industrial Furnaces, Ltd.* v. *Reaves* [1970] R.P.C. 605 at 627, 628; see § 560, *post.*

CHAPTER 4

ORIGINALITY

1.—WHAT IS "ORIGINAL"

111 **Statutory provisions.** By sections 2 (1) and (2) and 3 (2) and (3) of the Copyright Act, 1956, copyright is to subsist in every original literary, dramatic, musical and artistic work. There is no substantial difference between these provisions and those of the Act of 1911 so far as concerns the word "original," and decisions on the point under the Act of 1911 remain valid.

112 **Of form not ideas.** The question of what is meant by "original" in the law of copyright is one which has given rise to difficulty both before and since the commencement of the Act of 1911. While the mere copyist of a written document does not obtain copyright in his copy,[1] it is clear that neither original thought nor original research is essential, and that the standard of originality required is a low one.[1a] But it is difficult to state any principle upon which the standard is based.

113 Copyright protection is given to literary, dramatic, musical and artistic works and not to ideas, and therefore it is original skill or labour in execution, and not originality of thought which is required.[2] It is for this reason that mathematical tables are protected,[3] if their author has worked them out for himself, even though identical tables have previously been published; although the idea or information embodied in the tables is not novel, the result of the author's labour of compilation is a set of tables upon which the author has done original work. This may be contrasted with the supposititious case of an author who has copied existing tables, but by some device of coloured inks has rendered them of greater practical utility; it is thought that the author, in this latter case, though, in one sense of the word, he has employed greater "originality," will not be protected because his originality has lain in the sphere of ideas and not of composition.

[1] See *per* Lord James in *Walter* v. *Lane* [1900] A.C. 539 at 554; *Barfield* v. *Nicholson* (1824) 2 Sim. & St. 1; *Leslie* v. *Young (J.) & Sons* [1894] A.C. 335.
[1a] See *Jagdish Prasad Gupta* v. *Parmeshwar Prasad Singh* [1966] A.I.R. Patna 33.
[2] See *Kilvington Bros., Ltd.* v. *Goldberg* (1957) 8 D.L.R. (2d) 768, copyright in tombstone, and *Martin* v. *Polyplas Manufacturers, Ltd.* [1969] N.Z.L.R. 1046, copyright in three-dimensional engravings of two-dimensional designs for coins.
[3] *Bailey* v. *Taylor* (1830) 1 Russ. & My. 73; see also *Stevenson (A.)* v. *Crook (H. F.)* [1938] Ex.(Can.) 299.

114 It may also be contrasted with the standard at present required for registered designs under the Registered Designs Act, 1949. The requirement for registration under that Act is of novelty, so that if a design in fact resembles an existing design it may not be registered, even though the designer of the second design has not seen the former one.

115 Similarly it has been held in a Scottish case [4] that the author of a collection of precedents or " styles " constructed by following the directions of a statute was entitled to copyright protection, although any two persons with a knowledge of the subject would be bound to arrive at a similar result. Lord Fullerton observed: " It is said that owing to the particular nature of the styles they cannot be the subject of copyright, because they are drawn up precisely after the form prescribed in the statute, and because any styles relating to the same subjects as those given by the complainer must, if the directions of the statutes and phraseology of conveyancers were used, be expressed in the same manner exactly as those proposed by the complainer. Now it may be quite true that if the statute had supplied certain forms by which the operations intended to be thereby regulated were to be done; if the statute had contained, as such statutes sometimes do, an appendix exhibiting certain schedules of forms which it was only necessary for anyone to copy in order to avail himself of the provisions of the Act, then I hold that the reprinting of such forms in a separate publication would not give him a copyright in these forms. But the case here is different, for the statute only gives very general directions and descriptions of the styles that are to be used. The schedules are very general in their terms, and it is no doubt of great practical importance to suit these general directions to each case falling under the statute as it may arise. The preparing and adjusting of such writings require much care and exertion of mind As to invention, that is a different thing; it does not require the exercise of original or creative genius, but it requires industry and knowledge."

116 **Photographs.** Again, while it may be that there is no copyright in a photograph of an existing photograph,[5] it is thought that, if a person takes a photograph of a scene in nature which is identical with a former photograph of the same scene, he will have copyright in his photograph although the idea of taking the photograph was derived from his having seen the first photograph; and, if two

[4] *Alexander (W.)* v. *Mackenzie (R.)* (1846) 9 Sc.Sess.Cass. (2nd Ser.) 748; see also *Real Estate Institute of N.S.W.* v. *Wood* (1923) 23 S.R.(N.S.W.) 349, *Capital Finance Co. Ltd.* v. *Bowmaker (Commercial), Ltd.* [1964] R.P.C. 463 and *Capital Finance Co., Ltd.* v. *Lombank, Ltd.* [1964] R.P.C. 467.

[5] See § 130, *post*.

persons should make separate pictures to illustrate the same text of a story, although there might be a strong similarity between the two pictures, each would be entitled to a separate copyright.[6]

117 But a different view may be entertained as to the nature of copyright in a photograph. It may be contended that, in order that copyright may subsist, there must be original skill and labour, either in grouping or arranging the subject photographed or, at least, in selecting the exact moment to seize for the photograph of a moving scene. In the case of *Bauman* v. *Fussell*[7] in 1953 the Court of Appeal had to consider whether a photograph of a cock-fight was infringed by a painting admittedly derived from the photograph. The matter came before the Court of Appeal on appeal from the county court, so that the judgments largely turned upon whether any question of law arose, or whether the matter was disposed of by the county court judge as a question of fact, with the result that there was no ground for appeal to the Court of Appeal, but parts of the judgments are very relevant to the point now under consideration.

Somervell L.J. said: " A man takes a photograph of a procession or the laying of a foundation stone. He, of course, has chosen when and from where the photograph should be taken. The relative position of those in the procession, or their taking part in the ceremony, is not, however, his work, or his design, in the same sense in which the relative position of the figures on the ceiling of the Sistine Chapel was the work and design of Michelangelo. The order and arrangement of the procession has been, no doubt, carefully planned and designed by someone else. It is an individual's work that the Act is intended to protect. I do not think that a painter who was minded to make a picture of the procession, in his own style, would be committing a breach of copyright if he used a photograph to enable him to get accurately the relative positions of those taking part. What he would be taking would not be a substantial portion of the plaintiff's work. At the other end of the photographic scale one can imagine a case where the photographer has made an original arrangement of the objects animate and inanimate which he photographs in order to create a harmonious design representing, for example, Spring. Here the design would be his work."

Romer L.J. in a dissenting judgment said: " The photograph is of two birds engaged in the one activity for which they were reared and trained; and I cannot but think that the positions in which the camera caught them are of the essence of the plaintiff's skilful presentation of that activity. It is clear that in certain photographs

[6] See *Blackwell* v. *Harper* (1740) 2 Atk. 92.

[7] This case is only reported in *The Times*, May 19, 1953, and *The Author* (1954) LXIV, No. 363, but the material in the text is taken from a shorthand note of the judgments.

of bird or animal life the attitudes of the subjects are the prime essentials."

118 There is therefore ground for argument that the decision of the court at any rate threw doubt on the subsistence of copyright in a simple snapshot of a still scene in nature. On the other hand, the Act of 1956 in defining artistic work in relation to photographs, uses the expression "irrespective of artistic quality."[8] If quality is to be disregarded in a photograph, it is submitted that all that remains is the necessity that the photograph should not be a copy of an existing photograph, but should be original in the sense that it is a fresh photograph of some object in nature or art. Some support for this view may also be found in the fact that the legislature has given to photographs only a relatively short term of protection, which would seem to suggest that copyright was not being conferred in respect of artistic qualities, but only in respect of something in the nature of an industrial production; and further that the "author" is defined as the person who is the owner of the material on which the photograph is taken.[9]

119 **Examination papers.** The meaning of the word "original" in the Act of 1911, was discussed in a judgment of Petersen J. in the case of *University of London Press, Ltd.* v. *University Tutorial Press, Ltd.*,[10] which has frequently been cited with approval in subsequent cases.[11]

The learned judge, after holding that certain examination papers were "literary works" for the purposes of the Act, went on to consider whether they were "original." He said: "The word 'original' does not in this connection mean that the work must be the expression of original or inventive thought. Copyright Acts are not concerned with the originality of ideas, but with the expression of thought, and in the case of 'literary work' with the expression of thought in print or writing. The originality which is required relates to the expression of the thought. But the Act does not require that the expression must be in an original or novel form, but that the work must not be copied from another work—that it should originate from the author. In the present case it was not suggested that any of the papers were copied. Professor Lodge and Mr. Jackson proved that they had thought out the questions which they set, and that they made notes or memoranda for future questions and drew on these notes for the purposes of the questions which they set. The papers which they prepared originated

8 Copyright Act, 1956, s. 3 (1) (*a*).
9 s. 48 (1).
10 [1916] 2 Ch. 601 at 608; and see *Ascot Jockey Club, Ltd.* v. *Simons* (1968) 64 W.W.R. 411.
11 See *Macmillan & Co., Ltd.* v. *Cooper (K. & J.)* (1923) 40 T.L.R. 186 at 190; *British Broadcasting Co.* v. *Wireless League Gazette Publishing Co.* [1926] Ch. 433 at 440; *Ladbroke (Football), Ltd.* v. *William Hill (Football), Ltd.* [1964] 1 W.L.R. 273 at 277.

from themselves and were, within the meaning of the Act, original. It was said, however, that they drew upon the stock of knowledge common to mathematicians, and that the time spent in producing the questions was small. These cannot be tests for determining whether copyright exists. If an author, for purposes of copyright, must not draw on the stock of knowledge which is common to himself and others who are students of the same branch of learning, only those historians who discovered fresh historical facts could acquire copyright for their works. If time expended is to be the test, the rapidity of an author like Lord Byron in producing a short poem might be an impediment in the way of acquiring copyright, and, the completer his mastery of his subject, the smaller would be the prospect of the author's success in maintaining his claim to copyright. Some of the questions, it was urged, are questions in book work, that is to say, questions set for the purpose of seeing whether the student has read and understood the books prescribed by the syllabus. But the questions set are not copied from the book; they are questions prepared by the examiner for the purpose of testing the student's acquaintance with the book, and in any case it was admitted that the papers involved selection, judgment, and experience. The objection has not, in my opinion, any substance; if it had, it would only apply to some of the questions in the elementary papers, and would have little, if any, bearing on the paper on advanced mathematics. Then it is said that the questions in the elementary papers were of common type; but this only means that somewhat similar questions have been asked by other examiners. I suppose that most elementary books on mathematics may be said to be of common type, but that fact would not give impunity to a predatory infringer. The book and the papers alike originate from the author and are not copied by him from another book or other papers. The objections with which I have dealt do not appear to me to have any substance, and after all, there remains the rough practical test that what is worth copying is prima facie worth protecting."

120 **Compilations.** The question of originality was further considered by the Privy Council in the case of *Macmillan & Co., Ltd.* v. *Cooper (K. & J.)*,[12] in which it was alleged that there was copyright in a selection or abridgment of a non-copyright work.

Lord Atkinson, in delivering the judgment of the court, said: "It will be observed that it is the product of the labour, skill, and capital of one man which must not be appropriated by another, not the elements, the raw material, if we may use the expression, upon which the labour and skill and capital of the first have been expended. To secure copyright for the product it is necessary that labour, skill, and

[12] (1923) 40 T.L.R. 186. And see *Dutt (S. K.)* v. *Law Book Co.* [1954] A.L.J. 125; *Gouindan* v. *Gopalakrishna Kone* (1955) Mad.W.N. 369.

capital should be expended sufficiently to impart to the product some quality or character which the raw material did not possess, and which differentiates the product from the raw material." Lord Atkinson then referred with approval to a decision of the Supreme Court of the United States [13] bearing on the same point, and continued: " It brings out clearly the distinction between the materials upon which one claiming copyright has worked and the product of the application of his skill, judgment, labour, and learning to these materials, which product, though it may be neither novel nor ingenious, is the claimant's original work in that it originates from him, and is not copied."

121 **Measure of independent labour required.** At a later stage in his judgment Lord Atkinson said: " What is the precise amount of the knowledge, labour, judgment or literary skill or taste which the author of any book or other compilation must bestow upon its composition in order to acquire copyright in it within the meaning of the Copyright Act of 1911 cannot be defined in precise terms." [14]

It is here, as was pointed out by Maugham J. in *Cambridge University Press* v. *University Tutorial Press, Ltd.*,[15] that the real difficulty arises. There is no guiding principle as to the quantum of skill or judgment required. But an examination of the decisions on the subject is useful as indicating the degree of labour which the courts have considered requisite in various sets of circumstances.

122 **Law before 1911.** Before referring to particular decisions it is desirable to point out that, before the commencement of the Copyright Act, 1911, there was no general statutory requirement of " originality " for copyright works. Neither the Literary Copyright Act, 1842,[16] nor the Engravings Copyright Act, 1766,[17] use the expression " original," but the Sculpture Copyright Act, 1814,[18] and the Fine Arts Copyright Act, 1862,[19] referred respectively to " original " sculptures and " original " paintings.

123 **Report of a speech.** The absence of the word " original " in the Literary Copyright Act, 1842, was specifically referred to in the judgment of Lord Halsbury L.C. in the case of *Walter* v. *Lane.*[20] The point in that case was whether a reporter was entitled to copyright in his verbatim report of a public speech. The defendant had published

13 *Emerson* v. *Davies*, Storey's U.S.Rep. 768 (1845).

14 This statement was accepted by the House of Lords in *G. A. Cramp & Sons, Ltd.* v. *Frank Smythson, Ltd.* [1944] A.C. 329, as laying down a guiding principle: see also *Ladbroke (Football), Ltd.* v. *William Hill (Football), Ltd.* [1964] 1 W.L.R. 273.

15 (1928) 45 R.P.C. 335.

16 5 & 6 Vict. c. 45.

17 7 Geo. 3, c. 38.

18 54 Geo. 3, c. 56.

19 25 & 26 Vict. c. 68.

20 [1900] A.C. 539.

a book called "Appreciations and Addresses delivered by Lord Rosebery," containing almost exact copies of the reports of Lord Rosebery's speeches appearing in *The Times* newspaper. Lord Rosebery made no claim to copyright in the speeches, and the action was brought by *The Times.* North J. granted an injunction, but, upon appeal, the Court of Appeal reversed his decision, holding that the Copyright Act, 1842, was passed to protect authors, not reporters.[21] On appeal to the House of Lords, the decision of the Court of Appeal was reversed. Lord Halsbury L.C. said: "I observe that the Court of Appeal introduces the words 'original composition' as if those were the words of the statute; and at another part of the judgment it is said that 'the report and the speech reported are, no doubt, different things, but the author or publisher of the report is not the author of the speech reported, which is the only thing which gives any value or interest to the report.' The sentence is a little difficult to construe, but, as I understand it, it means to convey that the thing to which the statute gives protection must be of some value or interest. Again, I am compelled to point out that such words are not to be found in the statute. The producer of this written composition is, to my mind, the person who is the author of the book within the meaning of the statute, and, as I have pointed out, the words 'original composer' are not to be found in the statute at all; and, as I understand, the judgment of the Court of Appeal is entirely based on the thing protected being an original composition in the sense that the person who claims the protection of the statute must not have obtained his words or his ideas from somebody else, but must be himself an original author in the sense in which that word is generally used in respect of literary composition." [22] Later on he says: "Though I think in these compositions there is literary merit and intellectual labour, yet the statute seems to me to require neither, nor originality, either in thought or in language . . . I do not find the word 'original' in the statute, or any word which imports it, as a condition precedent, or makes originality of thought or idea necessary to the right." In the Lord Chancellor's view, copyright "is given by the statute to the first producer of a book, whether that book be wise or foolish, accurate or inaccurate, of literary merit or of no merit whatever." [23] Likewise Davey L.J. did not think "the fact that the subject-matter of the report had been made public property, or that no originality or literary skill was demanded for the composition of the report, have anything to do with the matter, . . . but it is a sound principle that a man shall not avail himself of another's skill, labour, and expense by copying the written product of it." [24]

21 [1899] 2 Ch. 749.
22 [1900] A.C. 546 and 547.
23 *Ibid.* p. 549.
24 *Ibid.* p. 552. *Collis* v. *Cater, etc., Ltd.* (1898) 78 L.T. 613; see also *Jarrold* v. *Houlston* (1857) 3 K. & J. 708.

124 **Copyright in report not speech.** It must be clearly understood that the House of Lords did not decide that the reporter obtained the copyright in Lord Rosebery's speeches, but only in the reports of those speeches. Lord Rosebery did not—and, indeed, could not—claim to prevent the publication of his speeches either in newspaper or pamphlet form.[25] Any other persons present at Lord Rosebery's meetings were at liberty to take his speeches down in shorthand and each of them to obtain copyright in his original report, but no person was entitled to annex the results of *The Times* reporter's labour. The reporter had added something " original," in that he reduced to writing what previously had only been oral, and that added " something " was considered to be worthy of protection.

125 **Effect of addition of word " original " in Acts of 1911 and 1956.** The view was expressed in earlier editions that the insertion of the word " original " in the Act of 1911 did not, having regard to the limited meaning attached thereto in the decisions previously referred to, alter the law. But Cross J. more recently [26] said that, while it was not necessary for him to decide the point, in view of the change in the law brought about by the introduction of the word " original " into the Acts of 1911 and 1956, it was at least arguable that *Walter* v. *Lane* is no longer good law. He also pointed out that counsel for the shorthand writers, in his argument in the Court of Appeal in *Walter* v. *Lane*, expressly conceded that, if Lord Rosebery had written his speech out and had read it or repeated it from memory, the shorthand writers would have had no copyright in their reports of it.[27] His lordship expressed the view that this concession of counsel might well have been justified.

2.—KINDS OF SKILL OR LABOUR

126 **Use of existing subject-matter.** As has been seen [28] where the author has produced his result without reference to any pre-existing subject-matter, it is immaterial that the result is not novel, or that anyone else could have produced the same result, or that the idea or scheme from which the result has been produced is open to the public. But where the author has made use of existing subject-matter more difficulty arises and it has to be determined whether he has done sufficient independent labour to justify copyright protection for his result.[28a]

25 Under the law prior to 1911, it was very difficult to retain any copyright in a speech publicly delivered; see *post,* Chap. 20, and as to present law, see *post,* Chap. 7.

26 *Robertson* v. *Lewis, The Times,* June 1, 1960.

27 [1899] 2 Ch. 749 at p. 766.

28 See *ante,* § 113.

28a *Martin* v. *Polyplas Manufacturers Ltd.* [1969] N.Z.L.R. 1046.

127 **Kinds of use.** The kinds of skill or labour which may be employed to make a copyright work from existing subject-matter may be classified into: change of medium, arrangement, abridgment, and selection.

128 **Change of medium.** The work of the reporter, as in *Walter* v. *Lane*, *supra*, is an example of the first class. Another example is the work of a translator which has always been protected,[29] and it is fairly clear, in the realm of artistic works, that any change of medium will entitle a reproduction of an existing artistic work to independent protection. For example, it was held under the Fine Arts Copyright Act, 1862,[30] that a photograph of an engraving was entitled to protection.[31]

129 Again, an engraver is almost invariably a copyist, but although his work may infringe copyright in the original painting if made without the consent of the owner of the copyright therein, his work may still be original in the sense that he has employed skill and judgment in its production. He produces the resemblance he is desirous of obtaining by means very different from those employed by the painter or draughtsman from whom he copies: means which require great labour and talent.[31a] The engraver produces his effect by the management of light and shade, or, as the term of his art expresses it, the *chiaroscuro*. The due degree of light and shade are produced by different lines and dots; he who is the engraver must decide on the choice of the different lines or dots for himself, and on his choice depends the success of his print.[32]

130 **Mere copy.** It may be argued that, since the copying, even in the same medium, of an artistic work, requires a higher degree of skill and judgment than the mere reproduction of a literary work, the mere copyist of an artistic work should have protection for his copy; and it is indeed a little difficult to distinguish on principle the reproduction by photography of a painting from the reproduction by the same means of an existing photograph. It is thought, however, that where the reproduction is in the same medium as the original, there must be more than an exact reproduction to secure copyright. If the original, in the case of a painting, is used merely as a model to give the idea of the new work or, in the case of a photograph, merely as a basis to be worked up by photographic process to something substantially different, then

29 *Byrne* v. *Statist Co.* [1914] 1 K.B. 622; *Wyatt* v. *Barnard* (1814) 3 V. & B. 77.
30 25 & 26 Vict. c. 68.
31 *Graves' Case* (1869) L.R. 4 Q.B. 715.
31a See *Martin* v. *Polyplas Manufacturers, Ltd.* [1969] N.Z.L.R. 1046, copyright in three-dimensional engravings of two-dimensional designs for coins.
32 *Newton* v. *Cowie* (1827) 4 Bing. 234; *Martin* v. *Wright* (1833) 6 Sim. 297.

the new work may be entitled to protection, but, if the result is simply a slavish copy, it will not, it is thought, be protected.[33]

131 **Compilations.** The labour and skill employed in selecting and arranging existing subject-matter may give copyright protection to the resulting work. This was recognised by the definition of "literary work" in section 35 of the Copyright Act, 1911, which included "compilations," and by section 48 (1) of the Act of 1956 which defines "literary work" as including "any written table or compilation."

Protection has been given to such compilations as an arrangement of broadcasting programmes,[34] school textbooks,[35] a book of receipts,[36] a book of scientific questions and answers,[37] a directory,[38] a trade advertisement,[39] a mining report,[40] a list of registered bills of sale and deeds of arrangement extracted from official sources,[41] a list of foxhounds and hunting dogs,[42] a list of Stock Exchange prices,[43] biographical notes of prominent golfers published in a golf annual,[44] a list of brood mares with their sires and a list of stallions with daughters at the stud,[45] a list of weights and acceptances for horse racing,[46] a list of books,[47] a list of characteristics of racehorses,[48] a manual of classified information for the use of motor car insurers,[49] an alphabetical list of railway stations contained in "Bradshaw's Railway Guide,"[50] chronological fixture lists of football clubs,[51] football coupons,[52] columns of

[33] *Cf. Re Martin (T. J.)* (1884) 10 V.L.R. 196; see *ante*, § 116.

[34] *British Broadcasting Co.* v. *Wireless League Gazette Publishing Co.* [1926] Ch. 433.

[35] *Educational Co. of Ireland, Ltd. (The)* v. *Fallon Bros., Ltd.* [1919] 1 I.R. 62

[36] *Matthewson* v. *Stockdale* (1806) 12 Ves. 270.

[37] *Jarrold* v. *Houlston* (1857) 3 K. & J. 708.

[38] *Kelly* v. *Morris* (1866) L.R. 1 Eq. 697; *Morris* v. *Ashbee* (1868) L.R. 7 Eq. 34; *Morris* v. *Wright* (1870) 5 Ch. 279.

[39] *Maple & Co.* v. *Junior Army and Navy Stores* (1882) 21 Ch.D. 369.

[40] *Kenrick* v. *Danube Collieries, etc., Co., Ltd.* (1891) 39 W.R. 473.

[41] *Trade Auxiliary Co.* v. *Middlesbrough, etc., Association* (1889) 40 Ch.D. 425; *Cate* v. *Devon, etc., Newspaper Co., ibid.* 500.

[42] *Cox* v. *Land and Water Journal Co.* (1869) L.R. 9 Eq. 324.

[43] *Exchange Telegraph Co., Ltd.* v. *Gregory & Co.* [1896] 1 Q.B. 147.

[44] *Nisbet (J.) & Co., Ltd.* v. *The Golf Agency* (1907) 23 T.L.R. 370.

[45] *Weatherby & Sons* v. *International Horse Agency and Exchange, Ltd.* [1910] 2 Ch. 297.

[46] *Winterbottom* v. *Wintle* (1947) 50 W.A.L.R. 58.

[47] *J. Whitaker & Sons, Ltd.* v. *Publishers' Circular, Ltd.* [1946–47] Macg.Cop.Cas. 10.

[48] *Portway Press, Ltd.* v. *Hague* (1957) R.P.C. 426; and see *Canterbury Park Race Course Co., Ltd.* v. *Hopkins* (1932) 49 W.N.(N.S.W.) 27; *Demerara Turf Club* v. *Phang* (1963) 6 W.I.R. 177 and *Ascot Jockey Club Ltd.* v. *Simons* (1968) 64 W.W.R. 411.

[49] *Underwriters Survey Bureau, Ltd.* v. *Amer. Home Fire Ass. Co.* (1939) 4 D.L.R. 89.

[50] *Blacklock (H.) & Co., Ltd.* v. *Arthur Pearson (C.), Ltd.* [1915] 2 Ch. 376; *cf. Leslie* v. *Young (J.) & Sons* [1894] A.C. 335.

[51] *Football League, Ltd.* v. *Littlewoods Pools, Ltd.* [1959] Ch. 637.

[52] *Ladbroke (Football), Ltd.* v. *William Hill (Football), Ltd.* [1964] 1 W.L.R. 273.

birth and death announcements in a newspaper,[53] contract forms,[54] sheets of election results[55] and business literature.[56] But the mere selection of various tables of an ordinary character for insertion in a pocket diary was held not to constitute a copyright work on the ground that the labour of selection was negligible.[57]

132 The case of *Purefoy Engineering Company, Ltd.* v. *Sykes, Boxall & Co., Ltd.*[58] illustrates the nature of the originality required in the preparation of a trade catalogue. The plaintiffs had decided to commence a new business in the manufacture and supply of parts suitable for sale to manufacturers so as to be combined into the various kinds of jigs and fixtures used in different industries. A great deal of time and skill was employed in selecting the most suitable parts and the most suitable range of sizes in each part and the selection so chosen was ultimately embodied in a trade catalogue. The Court of Appeal felt no difficulty in deciding that the catalogue was an original work because the arrangement of the catalogue itself had, in the view of the court, involved a sufficient amount of labour and skill to constitute it as an original compilation. The court, however, decided that the copyright so constituted existed in the catalogue and not in the selection of parts and sizes embodied in the catalogue. Consequently, those parts of the defendants' catalogue which were not proved to have been copied from the plaintiffs' catalogue were held not to constitute an infringement, although they resembled the plaintiffs' catalogue. The fact that the defendants, in preparing that part of the catalogue which was held not to constitute an infringement, had nevertheless made use of the plaintiffs' compilation and selection of parts and sizes, was held not to be an infringement of any material in which copyright could be claimed.

133 It should be observed, however, that the basis of the decision was that, on the facts of the case, what had been copied was a physical collection of parts and not the catalogue made therefrom by the plaintiffs. The decision was distinguished in *Ladbroke (Football), Ltd.* v. *William Hill (Football), Ltd.*[59] where it was held that copyright subsisted in the plaintiffs' compilation of pools, notwithstanding that these

[53] *John Fairfax & Sons Pty., Ltd.* v. *Australian Consolidated Press, Ltd.* [1960] S.R.(N.S.W.) 413.

[54] *Capital Finance Co.* v. *Bowmaker* [1964] R.P.C. 463 and *Capital Finance Co.* v. *Lombank, ibid.* 467; see also *Alexander (W.)* v. *Mackenzie (R.)* (1846) 9 Sc.Sess. Cass. (2nd Ser.) 748; *Real Estate Institute of N.S.W.* v. *Wood* (1923) 23 S.R. (N.S.W.) 349 and § 115, *ante*.

[55] *Press Association, Ltd.* v. *Northern and Midland Reporting Agency* [1905–10] Macg.Cop.Cas. 306.

[56] *Coral Index Ltd.* v. *Regent Index Ltd.* [1970] R.P.C. 147.

[57] *G. A. Cramp & Sons, Ltd.* v. *Frank Smythson, Ltd.* [1944] A.C. 329.

[58] (1955) 72 R.P.C. 89.

[59] [1964] 1 W.L.R. 273: see *Warwick Film Productions, Ltd.* v. *Eisinger* [1969] Ch. 508 and *Industrial Furnaces, Ltd.* v. *Reaves* [1970] R.P.C. 605.

might be considered in a sense to be a collection of parts and that that copyright had been infringed because the defendants had in fact copied the plaintiffs' compilation.

134 **Selections.** Selections of poems or prose compositions may also be protected,[60] and selections of incidents from real life.[61] Also arrangements of private letters. Thus, in the case of *Parry* v. *Moring*,[62] the plaintiff published a book entitled "Letters from Dorothy Osborne to Sir William Temple, 1652–54." These letters were, at the time when the plaintiff issued his book, in a private collection, whilst most of them were undated and in old English spelling. The plaintiff had had these letters copied, translated them into modern English spelling, arranged them in the order of date in which he considered they had been written, and published them with notes. Subsequently the original MSS. were bought by the British Museum authorities, and it was in evidence that they claimed no copyright in these originals. The defendants then published an edition of these same letters, and in their edition the letters were placed in practically the same order as the plaintiff's. The plaintiff moved for an interlocutory injunction restraining the infringement of his copyright,[63] and, on the defendants admitting that they had sent the plaintiff's book to their printers, and had the text of the letters printed direct from this, without having taken the trouble to get the letters copied from the originals in the British Museum, the judge expressed such a strong opinion that this method could not be defended, that the defendants submitted to an injunction and an inquiry as to damages, and to treat the motion as the trial of the action.

135 **Adaptation of old play.** Copyright may be secured in the adaptation of a play which is itself common property. Thus, in *Hatton* v. *Keane*,[64] where it appeared that the defendant had designed a dramatic representation, consisting of one of Shakespeare's plays, with certain alterations in the text, original music, scenic effects, and other accessories, the court did not doubt that the production, as a whole, was a proper subject of copyright, although the play itself was, in its original form, common property.

136 **New arrangement of music.** So in the case of musical compositions, not only an original composition but any substantially new

[60] *Macmillan & Co.* v. *Suresh Chunder Deb* (1890) 17 Indian L.R.(Calcutta) 951.

[61] See *Harman Pictures N.V.* v. *Osborne* [1967] 1 W.L.R. 723, *Poznanski* v. *London Film Production, Ltd.* [1936–45] Macg.Cop.Cas. 107 and *MacGregor* v. *Powell* [1936–45] Macg.Cop.Cas. 233.

[62] *The Times,* April 13 and 14, 1903, before Farwell J.

[63] The plaintiff complained of infringement in respect of (1) Notes; (2) Arrangement; (3) Text; and (4) Title. The defendants admitted infringement in the matter of the text and it became unnecessary to go into the other matters.

[64] (1859) 7 C.B. 268.

arrangement or adaptation of an old piece of music is a proper subject of copyright; and the man who makes the new arrangement or adaptation is the " author " of it and entitled to the copyright. If A makes a pianoforte score of the music of B's opera,[65] or if he writes words and accompaniments to an old non-copyright melody,[66] A is, in either case, properly described as the author of the new composition.

137 **Writing down of traditional air.** In the case of *Roberton* v. *Lewis* [67] in 1960 it was contended that copyright had been acquired in a traditional air by writing it down, at any rate to the extent that anyone who was proved to have made a copy directly or indirectly from the version so written down infringed such copyright. Cross J. held that copying in this sense was not proved, but he also indicated that he was by no means satisfied that such copyright could exist where there was no suggestion of original additions or arrangements by the plaintiff and where the probability was that others had from time to time also made written records of the tune. On the other hand, it may be argued that to write down, from ear, in musical notation, any tune, requires a degree of skill and labour not less than in some of the other instances which have been discussed, and that where direct copying can be clearly proved there is no reason why protection should not be afforded.

138 **The pianoforte score of an opera.** The pianoforte score of an already existing opera, whether arranged by the composer himself or by another person, is the subject of copyright and, as such, is entitled to protection, subject to the rights of the proprietor of the copyright in the original work. The arrangement of the opera score for the pianoforte, involving as it does labour as well as intelligence and skill, constitutes it a new work.[68]

In deciding the point in the case of *Wood* v. *Boosey*, Sir A. Cockburn C.J. said [69]: " It seems impossible to believe that any musician, however great his talent, whether as a composer or an executant, from the mere circumstance of having the opera in its entirety before him, that is to say, with all the score for all the instruments, which neither eye nor mind could take in at the same time, could be able to play the accompaniment while singing the music of the opera at the piano. It requires time, reflection, skill, and mind so to condense the opera score as to compose the pianoforte accompaniment. . . . I cannot, therefore, bring myself to think that the pianoforte arrangement of the music of an opera, which originally consisted

[65] *Wood* v. *Boosey* (1867) L.R. 3 Q.B. 223; (1866) L.R. 2 Q.B. 340.
[66] *Leader* v. *Purday* (1848) 7 C.B. 4; *Austin* v. *Columbia Graphophone Co., Ltd.* [1917–23] Macg.Cop.Cas. 398.
[67] *The Times*, June 1, 1960.
[68] *Wood* v. *Boosey, supra*; *Boosey* v. *Fairlie* (1877) 7 Ch.D. 301.
[69] (1866) L.R. 2 Q.B. 340 at 350.

of vocal music and instrumentation to be executed by some half-hundred instruments, can be said to be anything else than a specific, separate, and distinct work from the opera itself. And it seems to me to hold otherwise would lead to very serious consequences. Operas are very frequently arranged, sometimes by the composer of the opera himself, sometimes by other persons, with the consent or without the consent of the original composer. It may be, if the arrangement be made without the consent of the composer of the opera, such an adaptation would be an infringement of his copyright, which would subject the adapter to an action. It is not necessary to decide that. But it may be that, after the copyright has expired, an arrangement for the pianoforte may be made in the first instance, or some musical composer, thinking that an arrangement that already existed of some well-known and popular opera is not as good as it can be made, might apply his hand to the work and make a new arrangement. Can it be said that such an arrangement, useful as regards the musical world, shall not be the subject of protection under the Copyright Acts? "

139 And on appeal Sir Fitzroy Kelly C.B.,[70] in affirming the decision of the Queen's Bench, clearly pointed out the difference between the pianoforte score and the original score, and the fact that each might be the subject of copyright. " The opera," said he, " is composed and is published in score, and contains in each line of what is called the entire score the music for some one particular instrument, these instruments being some twenty in number. Now let us come to what the arrangement is for the pianoforte. Undoubtedly there are portions of it which are identical, as in the case before the Exchequer, and might subject, as I have already observed, the author of the adaptation to an action if it had been published without the authority of the author of the opera. But what is the pianoforte arrangement? It is an arrangement of the whole of the music of this opera for the pianoforte, a part of which is the ordinary pianoforte accompaniment, the bass and the treble, played with both hands, and which is independent of the melody. There may be, as it appears, the line of music for one voice, or two or three voices, as the case may be; and there are separate and distinct lines for the accompaniment for the pianoforte; and no doubt, here and there throughout this accompaniment, and by going line by line through the score of the original opera, there may be found the same notes; but there are other parts of the accompaniment which are merely the pianoforte accompaniment, the notes forming which are nowhere to be found in the score at all. The accompaniment for the pianoforte is a work of greater or less skill. In some cases, perhaps in many cases—it may be in this for aught I know—the operation of adaptation is little more than mechanical, and what any-one acquainted with the science of music, any composer of experience,

[70] (1867) L.R. 3 Q.B. 223 at 229.

might have been able to do without difficulty; but it may be, and often is, as in the case of the six operas of Mozart, by Mazzinghi, a work—I would hardly use the term of great genius, but a work—of great merit and skill of that eminent composer and pianist, Mazzinghi. If such a work be published as the adaptation to the pianoforte by a composer, other than the composer of the original opera, no doubt it is a piracy of the opera, and the composer may maintain an action against the adapter or the publisher of the adaptation; but, whenever the copyright in the original opera has expired, if after that, and for the first time, another composer composes another adaptation of that opera to the pianoforte, it is a new substantive work, in respect of which he is just as much entitled to the benefit of the copyright in this country as the original composer of the opera; and if anyone had by an adaptation pirated that arrangement, he would be liable to an action for that piracy. I consider that an infallible test to show the difference between the one work and the other—between the original opera and the arrangement of it for the pianoforte. It is perfectly clear, therefore, that in point of fact—for it is rather a matter of fact than anything else—the adaptation to the pianoforte, or the arrangement for the pianoforte, of an opera already published, is itself a new and separate work, and is not one and the same with the original opera." In this same case Bramwell B. said [71]: "It has been said that there is nothing inventive on the part of the person who makes the arrangement. In one sense, there is not—that is to say, he neither invents the tune nor the harmony; but there is invention in another sense, or rather there is composition in the adaptation to the particular instrument. Of that, the adapter is the author, and it is perfectly certain that the man who wanted to arrange this opera for a pianoforte would find it a great deal easier to copy what Brissler had done than to take the score and do it over again."

140 **Abridgments.** Copyright may likewise exist in a genuine and just abridgment, for it is said that an abridgment may with great propriety be called a new book,[72] and therefore is an original literary work. Whether an abridgment is, or is not, a piracy of the original work is more doubtful; but this matter will be more appropriately dealt with in the chapter on "Infringement of Copyright," [73] and there are reasons for holding that the fact that a work is a piracy ought not of itself to disentitle it to copyright.[74]

To constitute a true and equitable abridgment the entire work must be preserved in its precise import and exact meaning, and then the act of abridgment is an exertion of the understanding, employed in

[71] (1867) L.R. 3 Q.B. 223 at 232.
[72] *Per* Lord Hardwicke, *Gyles* v. *Wilcox* (1740) 2 Atk. 141.
[73] Chap. 9, *post*.
[74] *Post*, § 145.

moulding and transfusing a large work into a small compass, thus rendering it less expensive, and more convenient both to the time and use of the reader. Independent labour must be apparent, and the reduction of the size of a work, by copying some of its parts and omitting others, confers no title to authorship; and the result will not be an abridgment entitled to protection. To shorten a work by leaving out the unimportant parts is not to abridge it in a legal sense. To abridge in the legal sense of the word is to preserve the substance, the essence of the work, in language suited to such a purpose—language substantially different from that of the original. To make such an abridgment requires the exercise of the mind; labour, skill and judgment are brought into play, and the result is not merely copying.[75]

141 In the case of *Macmillan & Co., Ltd.* v. *Cooper (K. & J.)* [76] the Privy Council held that the plaintiff had not established any claim to copyright in the text of an edition of North's "Life of Plutarch" by merely cutting down the original for the use of schools and joining together the remainder so as to make a continuous narrative.

142 **Headnotes.** The digest of a law report, usually included in and known as the headnote, is a species of abridgment. "The headnote, or the side or marginal note of a report," said Crowder J. in *Sweet* v. *Benning*,[77] "is a thing upon which much skill and exercise of thought is required, to express in clear and concise language the principles of law to be deduced from the decision to which it is prefixed, or the facts and circumstances which bring the case in hand within the same principle or rule of law or of practice." It may indeed be considered, perhaps, as in itself a species of brief and condensed report, the reporter furnishing in each case two reports, in one of which he gives the facts, the arguments, and the judgment at length; and in the other, an abstract of the decision, conveying the principle upon which it is founded and the pith and substance of the case. But whether thus regarded, or viewed in the manner adopted by Maule J. in the above-cited case, namely, in the nature of an independent deduction from the report, and a succinct statement of the legal principles involved, or of the doctrine of law established by the decision, there is a sufficient exertion of mental power in the formation to render it substantially a subject of copyright.

143 **New editions.** It is thought that the position with regard to new editions of existing works is not quite the same since the commencement of the Copyright Act, 1911, as it was before. Under the Act of

[75] This passage, which appeared in former editions of this work, was cited with approval in *Macmillan & Co., Ltd.* v. *Cooper (K. & J.)* (1923) 40 T.L.R. 186.
[76] (1923) 40 T.L.R. 186.
[77] (1855) 16 C.B. 459. See *D'Almaine* v. *Boosey* (1835) 1 Y. & C.Ex. 288 at 301.

1842, no action could be brought in respect of infringement of copyright in a book, unless the book was duly registered at Stationers' Hall.[78] Consequently, if a new edition were registered, and the date of publication entered as the date of publication of the new edition, it had to be considered whether the new edition, regarded as a whole, was a new book or not. If it were a new book, the registration was correct; if it were only the old book with slight variations, then the registration was invalid.[79]

144 But it would appear that such considerations are not now of importance. The court has not to consider whether a work has been properly registered, but whether there has been any infringement of any original work done by the editor of the new edition. Such original work may consist of additions to, or alterations of, the text which, if they are not merely trivial, will, it is thought, be protected in the same way as any original literary work,[80] whether they form a substantial part of the complete work or not; or they may consist of new arrangement of the existing subject-matter.[81] With regard to the latter, it would seem that the same considerations arise as in the case of alterations of any other existing subject-matter. For instance in the case of *Blacklock (H.) & Co., Ltd.* v. *Arthur Pearson (C.), Ltd.*,[82] it was held that the index to a new edition of Bradshaw was an original book. Joyce J. said: "A book which consists of a specification of the conditions at the present moment of a constantly changing subject-matter is a new work even though some of the particulars given may not have altered from what they were, and were stated to be, at some prior date, perhaps years before."

It follows therefore that where a work not out of copyright is edited by a person different from the original author, there may be two copyrights in the second edition; namely, the copyright in the original text vested in the original author, or his representatives or assigns; and the copyright in the additions and rearrangements of the text vested in the person who makes the new edition.

145 **Copyright in a work which itself infringes copyright.** The question whether copyright can subsist in a work which is a piracy of another copyright work is a difficult one. It is submitted that copyright can subsist in such a work, provided it is not a slavish copy, since, in such a case, there would be no "originality," that is nothing originating from the author of the piracy.[83] But, in the case of a translation of a

78 5 & 6 Vict. c. 45, s. 24.

79 *Thomas* v. *Turner* (1886) 33 Ch.D. 292; *Black (A. & C.), Ltd.* v. *Murray (A.) & Son* (1870) 9 Sc.Sess.Cas. (3rd Ser.) 341.

80 See § 119, *ante*.

81 See § 131, *ante*.

82 [1915] 2 Ch. 376.

83 See *University of London Press, Ltd.* v. *University Tutorial Press, Ltd.* [1916] 2 Ch. 601 at 608, and s. 2 (1) and (2) of the Copyright Act, 1956, for instance, under which all original literary works are entitled to copyright without qualification in respect of plagiarised works.

copyright work into another language, for instance, involving the expenditure of considerable time, skill and labour by the translator, there would seem no reason why such a work, even though unauthorised, should not be entitled to its own copyright.[83] What would be the position if the original copyright owner later gave permission? But if there is such copyright, is it enforceable and, if so, against whom?

146 Until recently the authorities on the subject have not been clear and, even now, the position is not entirely settled. Thus, in the case of *Cary* v. *Faden*,[84] Lord Loughborough, in refusing an injunction to restrain an infringement of the copyright in a road book, appears to have been influenced by the fact that the plaintiffs' work was an infringement of the copyright in an earlier work. But this decision goes only to relief and not to the question of subsistence. However, in *Wood* v. *Boosey*,[85] a case concerned with an arrangement by one Brissler of the score of an opera, Kelly C.B. said,[86] " But although the work of Brissler, if published without the authority of the composer of the original opera or his representatives, would be the piracy of that work, yet it may be a new and substantive work in itself, and be the subject of a copyright at Berlin, probably according to the law of Prussia, certainly in this country under the Copyright Acts in force. . . . The accompaniment for the pianoforte is a work of greater or less skill. In some cases, perhaps in many cases—it may be in this for aught I know—the operation of adaptation is little more than mechanical, and what anyone acquainted with the science of music, any composer of experience, might have been able to do without difficulty; but it may be, and often is, as in the case of the six operas of Mozart's, by Mazzinghi, a work—I would hardly use the term of great genius, but a work—of great merit and skill of that eminent composer and pianist, Mazzinghi. If such a work be published as the adaptation to the pianoforte by a composer other than the composer of the original opera, no doubt it is the piracy of the opera, and the composer may maintain an action against the adapter or the publisher of the adaptation; but whenever the copyright in the original opera has expired, if after that, and for the first time, another composer composes another adaptation of that opera to the pianoforte, it is a new substantive work, in respect of which he is just as much entitled to the benefit of the copyright in this country as the original composer of the opera; and if anyone had, by an adaptation pirated that arrangement, he would be liable to an action for that piracy."

[84] (1799) 5 Ves. 23, and see *Edward Thompson & Co.* v. *American Law Book Co.* [1905–10] Macg.Cop.Cas. 16.

[85] (1866) L.R. 2 Q.B. 340; (1867) L.R. 3 Q.B. 223; and see *Sailendra Nath De* v. *Chayanika Chitra Mandir* (1950) 55 Cal.W.N. 713; *Gouindan* v. *Gopalakrishna Kone* [1955] Mad.W.N. 369 and *Walter* v. *Lane* [1900] A.C. 539 at 558.

[86] (1867) L.R. 3 Q.B. at p. 229, and see *Leader* v. *Purday* (1884) 7 C.B. 4.

It would appear from this decision that copyright will subsist in the piracy, the preparation of which involved the expenditure of time, skill and labour by its originator. On the other hand, it is interesting to note that, in *Gramophone Co. Ltd.* v. *Stephen Cawardine and Co.*,[87] Maugham J., in considering the nature of the protection afforded to gramophone records under section 19 of the Copyright Act, 1911, said,[88] " Using the word ' record ' as sufficient to cover for the purpose of brevity the phrase I have read, it is manifest that the record must be made from a literary, dramatic or musical work and it is clear that in such a work there may well be copyright under section 1 of the Act. It is not difficult to make a record without the leave of the owner of the original copyright, for records are made in private, and I think it is a little surprising that there is nothing in section 19, subsection (1), which says whether the record is assumed to be a record lawfully made. . . . For the purpose of the present case, however, I shall assume that the section gives protection only in respect of records lawfully made, which is the case with the record I am dealing with today."

147 In the recent case of *Warwick Film Productions Ltd.* v. *Eisinger*,[89] the plaintiffs alleged infringement of copyright in two books, one entitled *The Trials of Oscar Wilde* edited by Mr. Montgomery Hyde, and the other entitled *Oscar Wilde: Three Times Tried* written anonymously. Plowman J. held that both books were entitled to copyright, but that the plaintiffs had not established any title to the copyright in *Three Times Tried*. It appeared that part of the Hyde book consisted, in part, of trial scenes taken from *Three Times Tried*, without any proper authority. The defendants argued that, since when Mr. Hyde wrote his book, he had no permission from anyone who had been proved to be the owner of the copyright in *Three Times Tried* to use that book, his accounts of the trials must be regarded as piratical and that no copyright exists in a pirated book or, at any rate, in so much thereof as was pirated. In the alternative the defendants argued that, as a matter of law, copyright can subsist in some parts of a literary work without subsisting in other parts, and that no copyright will be held to subsist in those parts which consist of copied raw material on which no labour and skill have been expended.

Plowman J., however, in dealing with these arguments, referred to the different approach to the problem propounded in the case of *Ladbroke (Football), Ltd.* v. *William Hill Football, Ltd.*,[90] which he said arose " where a literary work includes unoriginal or pirated material." [91] In the *Ladbroke* case the defendants had copied certain

[87] [1934] Ch. 450.
[88] *Ibid.* at p. 457.
[89] [1969] Ch. 508.
[90] [1964] 1 W.L.R. 273; and see *Industrial Furnaces, Ltd.* v. *Reaves* [1970] R.P.C. 605 at 624.
[91] [1969] Ch. at p. 530.

parts of the plaintiffs' coupon and they sought to argue that, for the purpose of deciding whether or not copyright subsisted, the plaintiffs' coupon should be dissected and each part considered separately. The House of Lords, however, decided that the plaintiffs' coupon must be treated as a whole, and that only when it had been decided whether the work as a whole was original and entitled to copyright was it correct to inquire whether the part taken by the defendant was a substantial part. Further, that the reproduction of a part which, by itself, has no originality, will not normally be a substantial part. For that which would not attract copyright, except by reason of its collocation, will, when robbed of that collocation, not be a substantial part of the copyright, and therefore the courts will not hold its reproduction to be an infringement. It is when one is debating whether the part reproduced is substantial that one considers the pirated portion on its own.

Plowman J., in the *Warwick Film* case, said that Mr. Hyde's copying from *Three Times Tried* was of two kinds, namely edited copying and unedited copying. As regards the edited copying, this had been copied by the defendant Eisinger only to a limited extent which, by itself, did not constitute a substantial part of the Hyde book. As to Mr. Hyde's unedited copying, it had no originality and attracted copyright, as part of the whole book, only by reason of its collocation. When robbed of that collocation it did not represent a substantial part and so did not involve an infringement of it. In the result he held that there had been no reproduction of a substantial part of the Hyde book and no infringement of copyright.[91a]

148 There was no question in the *Ladbroke* case of any part of the plaintiffs' work having been pirated by the plaintiffs. However, it would appear from the decisions in that case and in the *Warwick Film* case, first that, where pirated material is joined with original material the whole may be entitled to copyright, secondly, if no work has been done on the pirated material, if copied, it will not be considered a substantial part for the purposes of infringement, but, thirdly, if work has been done on the pirated material it may be considered a substantial part for such purposes.

149 This still leaves uncertain two matters. First, what is the position where an entire work is alleged to be a piracy, rather than just a part of it? Is such a work entitled to copyright? It is submitted that, in the light of the decisions in the *Ladbroke* and *Warwick Film* cases, there will be copyright in such a work if the originator of the work has expended time, skill and labour on the material pirated, such as would be involved in preparing a translation, for instance. But, secondly, even if such a work is entitled to copyright, will the courts grant relief

[91a] See *Industrial Furnaces, Ltd.* v. *Reaves* [1970] R.P.C. 605 at 624.

where a substantial part of it has been copied? Will the courts grant relief in the case of a work which consists in part of pirated material, on which time, skill and labour has been expended and where the part copied, though a substantial part of the whole work, consisted entirely of pirated material? In the circumstances this point did not arise in the *Warwick Film* case, but it is submitted that the courts might well be unwilling to do so, in either case, on the grounds of public policy, and certainly not against the original copyright owner, unless, perhaps, he had later given permission.[92]

[The next paragraph is 151]

[92] See *Glyn* v. *Western Feature Film Co.* [1916] 1 Ch. 261 at 269 and §§ 224 to 229, *post.* See also *Slingsby* v. *Bradford Patent Truck, etc., Co.* [1905] W.N. 122, [1906] W.N. 51; *Cary* v. *Faden* (1799) 5 Ves. 23; *Edward Thompson & Co.* v. *American Law Book Co.* [1905–10] Macg.Cop.Cas. 16 and *Sweet* v. *G. W. Bromley & Co.* [1905–10] Macg.Cop.Cas. 203, and §§ 559, 560, *post.*

CHAPTER 5

THE SUBJECTS OF COPYRIGHT

1.—LITERARY WORKS

151 **Statutory definitions.** By section 2 (1) and (2) of the Copyright Act, 1956, copyright is conferred in respect of " literary " works. This repeats, in substance, section 1 of the Copyright Act, 1911. In that Act, however, " literary work " was defined, by section 35, as including " maps, charts, plans, tables and compilations " whereas, in the Act of 1956, it is defined, by section 48 (1), as including " any [1] written table or compilation," so that maps, charts and plans are no longer protected as literary works but are protected as artistic works under the definition of " drawing." [2] The Act of 1956, by section 48 (1), defines " writing " as including any form of notation, whether by hand or by printing, typewriting or any similar process. Presumably this definition would also be applied to " written," so that a compilation expressed in any form of notation will be protected as a literary work, for example in braille or shorthand.

152 **" Literary work."** In the case of *University of London Press, Ltd.* v. *University Tutorial Press, Ltd.*,[3] Petersen J., in speaking of the meaning of the word " literary " in the Act of 1911, said:

" It may be difficult to define ' literary work ' as used in this Act, but it seems to me plain that it is not confined to ' literary work ' in the sense in which that phrase is applied, for instance, to Meredith's novels and the writings of Robert Louis Stevenson. In speaking of such writings as literary works one thinks of the quality, the style, and the literary finish which they exhibit. Under the Act of 1842, which protected books, many things which had no pretensions to literary style acquired copyright; for example, a list of registered bills of sale, a list of foxhounds and hunting dogs, and trade catalogues; and I see no ground for coming to the conclusion that the present Act was intended to curtail the rights of authors. In my view the words ' literary work ' cover work which is expressed in print or writing, irrespective of the question whether the quality or style is high. The word ' literary ' seems to be used in a sense somewhat similar to the use of the word ' literature ' in political or electioneering literature, and

1 It appears that the addition of the word " any " has not added anything to the definition; *per* Upjohn J. *Football League, Ltd.* v. *Littlewoods Pools, Ltd.* [1959] Ch. 637 at 650.

2 Copyright Act, 1956, ss. 3 (1) (*a*) and 48 (1).

3 [1916] 2 Ch. 601 at 608.

refers to written or printed matter." He therefore decided that examination papers constituted "literary" work within the meaning of the Act of 1911.

153 **Some form of notation essential.** But the work must be expressed in some form of notation. Thus, a speech or lecture, even if recorded on a dictaphone, sound film or other recording device, would not be entitled to copyright protection as a literary work, though the recording itself might be protected as a sound recording under section 12 of the Act of 1956. On the other hand, because some form of notation is sufficient, there seems no reason why items of computer software such as punched cards, punched tapes, magnetic tapes and even magnetic cores should not be protectable as "literary works," apart from the more obviously literary works, such as print outs and so on.[3a] The report of the Banks Committee,[3b] whilst acknowledging that computer programs did not seem to fall easily within any existing industrial property legislation, and stating that at present a favoured proposal for protection appeared to be the use of copyright with a possible extension of the law, recommended that computer programs should not be patentable.

If an author dictates to a stenographer, it is thought that he will acquire copyright in his material as a literary work at the moment it is recorded in the notation of shorthand. This would seem to be on the basis that the person dictating the material is in fact the author of the material, so that he would not have to rely upon section 4 of the Copyright Act, 1956, to become the owner of the copyright therein.[3c] It would, it is thought, be immaterial that the shorthand writer was not an employee, to whom section 4 would apply, but a relative or friend. But, if this is true, it is difficult to exclude the case of a shorthand record of a speech, at any rate where the speaker is well aware that his speech is being recorded. As has been pointed out, the authority of *Walter* v. *Lane* on this kind of question as a decision affecting the law under the Act of 1956 is of some uncertainty.[4] At any rate it is important to keep in mind that there may be separate copyrights in separate ownership in an original speech, lecture, or court judgment and in records thereof whether they be mechanical or shorthand.

[3a] See Copyright Act, 1956, ss. 2, 48 (1) (definition of "writing") and 49 (4) and definition of "notation" in *Shorter Oxford English Dictionary.* See also *Badger Co. Incorporated's Application* [1970] R.P.C. 36, *Gevers' Application* [1970] R.P.C. 91. "Legal Protection of Software" by Leslie Melville (1969) 119 New L.J. 1169 and "Software Protection. The legal protection of computer programs" Report of Proceedings at a Conference in November 1969 arranged by the British Computer Society.

[3b] The British Patent System, 1970 Cmnd. 4407, Chap. 17.

[3c] See *Donoghue* v. *Allied Newspapers, Ltd.* [1938] Ch. 106.

[4] *Ante*, § 125.

154 **"Writing" is sufficient though it has no meaning in language.** But so long as something in "writing" exists, it is sufficient and it is not necessary that what is written should express a meaning in language. Thus, there may be copyright in a list of meaningless words used as a telegraph code,[5] or in a catalogue of type,[6] or in a system of shorthand.[7]

155 Again, so long as there is a sufficient amount of skill and labour in constructing or selecting the material, no particular skill in the literary form is needed. Thus, copyright has been conferred in respect of newspaper telegrams,[8] in the rules of a game,[9] in the rules and coupon for a football competition [10] and in tallies for bridge parties.[10a]

156 **But some skill and labour of arrangement of words required.** Thus there is no copyright in a title of a book or magazine. [11] And it has been held, on the ground of triviality, that there is no copyright in the advertisement slogan, "youthful appearances are social necessities, not luxuries," [12] nor in the stringing together for advertisement purposes of a number of commonplace sentences.[13]

157 It must also be borne in mind that copyright protection is not given to ideas or information, however novel or valuable, unless reduced into some form which can be characterised as literary work.

The court declined, under the old law, to grant copyright in respect of a cardboard pattern sleeve containing upon it scales, figures, and descriptive words for adapting it to sleeves of any dimensions [14]; a list of sporting selections [15]; a scoring sheet used for cricket [16]; or an album for holding photographs [17]; and, under the later law, in respect of a card containing spaces and certain directions for

5 *Anderson (D. P.) & Co., Ltd.* v. *The Lieber Code Co.* [1917] 2 K.B. 469; *Ager* v. *P. & O. Steam Navigation Co.* (1884) 26 Ch.D. 637; *Ager* v. *Collingridge* (1886) 2 T.L.R. 291.

6 *Masson, Seeley & Co., Ltd.* v. *Embosotype Manufacturing Co.* (1924) 41 R.P.C. 160.

7 *Pitman* v. *Hine* (1884) 1 T.L.R. 39.

8 *Walter* v. *Steinkopf* [1892] 3 Ch. 489; *Exchange Telegraph Co., Ltd.* v. *Central News, Ltd.* [1897] 2 Ch. 48.

9 *Caley (A. J.) & Son, Ltd.* v. *Garnett (G.) & Sons, Ltd.* [1936–45] Macg.Cop.Cas. 99.

10 *Ladbroke (Football), Ltd.* v. *William Hill (Football), Ltd.* [1964] 1 W.L.R. 273.

10a *Stevenson (A.)* v. *Crook (H. F.)* [1938] Ex.(Can.) 299.

11 See § 230, *post.*

12 *Sinanide* v. *La Maison Kosmeo* (1928) 139 L.T. 365 (C.A.).

13 *Kirk* v. *Fleming (J. & R.), Ltd.* [1928–35] Macg.Cop.Cas. 44.

14 *Hollinrake* v. *Truswell* [1894] 3 Ch. 420; followed *Boosey* v. *Wright* [1900] 1 Ch. 122.

15 *Chilton* v. *Progress Printing, etc., Co.* [1895] 2 Ch. 29; *Fournet* v. *Pearson, Ltd.* (1897) 14 T.L.R. 82; *Smith's Newspapers, Ltd.* v. *The Labor Daily* (1925) 25 S.R.(N.S.W.) 593.

16 *Page* v. *Wisden* (1869) 20 L.T. 435.

17 *Schove* v. *Schmincké* (1886) 33 Ch.D. 546.

filing particulars under the National Health Insurance Act, 1911 [18]; a race card containing the names of competitors in a race in the order in which they were drawn [19]; and a selection of tables for use in a diary.[20]

158 **Tradesmen's catalogues.** It is clear that tradesmen's catalogues can be the subject-matter of copyright.[21] It was at one time thought that the fact that a book was used solely for the purpose of advertising the goods of the author militated against its being held to be the subject of copyright [22]; but this view was overruled.[23] It is, of course, always open to doubt whether the component parts of the catalogue are original or merely taken from a common source,[24] but a catalogue is generally a compilation upon which the compiler has exercised skill and judgment.[25]

159 The nature of the copyright in tradesmen's catalogues has been the subject of discussion in relation to other compilations. It has been argued that, in so far as skill and labour has been employed merely in selecting a desirable aggregate of saleable commodities, this was irrelevant to the creation of a copyright compilation. This argument has been used with regard to the compilation of the Football League fixture list, it being said that the selection of appropriate dates upon which the teams should meet was for the purposes of the League activities and not for the compilation of its fixture list. But Upjohn J.[26] held that copyright subsisted in the list and that part of the skill and labour involved in its preparation was that of working out the appropriate dates of matches. This view has more recently been upheld in the House of Lords in connection with the copyright in a compilation of football pools.[27]

The copyright in catalogues was considered in the case of *Purefoy Engineering Co., Ltd.* v. *Sykes, Boxall & Co., Ltd.*[28] In that

[18] *Libraco, Ltd.* v. *Shaw Walker, Ltd.* (1913) 30 T.L.R. 22.
[19] *Greyhound Racing Association, Ltd.* v. *Shallis* [1923–28] Macg.Cop.Cas. 370; but see *Canterbury Park Race Course Co., Ltd.* v. *Hopkins* (1932) 49 W.N.(N.S.W.) 27, *Odhams Press, Ltd.* v. *London and Provincial Sporting News Agency, etc., Ltd.* [1936] Ch. 357, *Demerara Turf Club* v. *Phang* [1963] 6 W.I.R. 177 and *Ascot Jockey Club, Ltd.* v. *Simons* (1968) 64 W.W.R. 411.
[20] *G. A. Cramp & Sons, Ltd.* v. *Frank Smythson, Ltd.* [1944] A.C. 329.
[21] *Hotten* v. *Arthur* (1863) 1 H. & M. 603; *Grace* v. *Newman* (1875) L.R. 19 Eq. 623; *Maple & Co.* v. *Junior Army and Navy Stores* (1882) 21 Ch.D. 369; *Davis* v. *Benjamin* [1906] 2 Ch. 491.
[22] *Cobbett* v. *Woodward* (1872) L.R. 14 Eq. 407.
[23] *Maple & Co.* v. *Junior Army and Navy Stores, supra.*
[24] *Collis* v. *Cater, etc., Ltd.* (1898) 78 L.T. 613; *Harpers, Ltd.* v. *Barry, Henry & Co., Ltd.* (1892) 20 Sess.Cas. (4th Ser.) 133; *cf. Cooper* v. *Stephens* [1895] 1 Ch. 567; *Marshall (W.) & Co., Ltd.* v. *Bull (A. H.), Ltd.* (1901) 85 L.T. 77.
[25] *Lamb* v. *Evans* [1893] 1 Ch. 218; *Collis* v. *Cater, etc., Ltd.* (1898) 78 L.T. 613; *Kelly* v. *Morris* (1866) L.R. 1 Eq. 697; *Morris* v. *Ashbee* (1868) L.R. 7 Eq. 34.
[26] *Football League, Ltd.* v. *Littlewoods Pools, Ltd.* [1959] Ch. 637; and see *J. & C. Moores* v. *Customs and Excise Commrs.* [1963] 1 W.L.R. 1105; [1964] 1 W.L.R. 817.
[27] *Ladbroke (Football), Ltd.* v. *William Hill (Football), Ltd.* [1964] 1 W.L.R. 273.
[28] (1955) 72 R.P.C. 89.

case, the question of infringement was considered in respect of different parts of a catalogue. The catalogue consisted of certain illustrations of machinery parts, certain diagrammatic engineers' drawings, and a number of tables consisting of a series of figures arranged in columns to indicate the specifications of different sizes of standard parts. The Court of Appeal had no difficulty in deciding that copyright subsisted in the whole of the catalogue and in each part of it, and the real issue between the parties was as to the extent of the infringement.

160 **Illustrations in catalogues.** It will be apparent that the illustrations in a catalogue will be protected as artistic works and not as literary works. This was otherwise under the Copyright Act of 1842, when copyright was conferred in respect of " books " and the protection comprehended the whole contents of the book, and even under the Act of 1911 the whole catalogue might have been regarded as a " compilation." But it is submitted that under the Act of 1956 the definition of " literary work ", by section 48 (1), as " any written table or compilation " makes it clear that, under the present law, illustrations must be protected as artistic works and not as part of the catalogue.

At one time, it was considered that illustrations of articles of manufacture in a catalogue might not be protected because of the exemption from copyright protection of industrial designs, but, as will be seen, this will no longer arise.[29]

2.—DRAMATIC AND MUSICAL WORKS

161 **Performing right.** The next class of works referred to in section 2 (1) and (2) of the Copyright Act, 1956, after literary works, are, as in the case of section 1 of the Act of 1911, " dramatic " and " musical " works. These works naturally fall to be considered together, because, in both cases, the authors probably expect to reap at least some portion of their reward from the public performance of their work. Under the law prior to 1911, performing rights could only be claimed in respect of any " tragedy, comedy, play, opera, farce, or any other dramatic piece or entertainment," [30] or in respect of " any musical composition " [31]; but under the Acts of 1911 and 1956, the right to perform a work in public is included in the copyright of all literary, dramatic and musical works.[32]

162 **Importance of distinction between literary and dramatic and musical works.** The distinction, therefore, between a dramatic work

[29] *Post*, § 197.
[30] Dramatic Copyright Act, 1833 (3 & 4 Will. 4, c. 15), s. 1.
[31] Copyright Act, 1842 (5 & 6 Vict. c. 45), ss. 20, 21.
[32] See now Copyright Act, 1956, s. 2 (5).

or musical work and a literary work is not of the same importance under the present law as under the law prior to 1911, yet it is one that is not wholly immaterial. For instance, it is only in the case of a dramatic work that the conversion of it into a novel or other non-dramatic work is forbidden.[33] Again, short passages may be taken for school books from published literary or dramatic works, but not from musical works,[34] and it is only " musical works " which may be compulsorily reproduced mechanically upon the terms of payment of a royalty.[35]

163 **Statutory definition of " dramatic work."** The definition of dramatic work in the Act of 1956 is slightly different from that in the Act of 1911, and the difference may be of material importance. In the Act of 1911, dramatic work was defined as including " any piece for recitation, choreographic work or entertainment in dumb show, the scenic arrangement or acting form of which is fixed in writing or otherwise." [36] In the Act of 1956, dramatic work is defined as including " a choreographic work or entertainment in dumb show, if reduced to writing in the form in which the work or entertainment is to be presented." [37]

164 " Any piece for recitation " is left out, presumably because its special mention was thought unnecessary. But the change from " is fixed in writing or otherwise " to " if reduced to writing in the form in which the work or entertainment is to be presented " may have significance. It was thought that, under the Act of 1911, a sketch or dramatic performance might acquire copyright protection if filmed or recorded at the moment of performance, but it would seem clear that this is not so under the Act of 1956. There must be some existing writing or notation before a copyright work comes into existence, though it may perhaps still be argued that, by reason of the provision of section 49 (4) of the Act of 1956, that a work is made when " reduced to writing or some other material form," it still admits of argument that a dramatic work which has been recorded on a recording device has a material form entitled to protection. The record itself may, of course, be protected in any event, but this is not the same thing, since the infringement may not be derived from the record, but directly from the performance of the dramatic work.

165 In the circumstances, there seems, therefore, under the present law, to be little difference between a literary and a dramatic work, so far as concerns the kind of material in which copyright subsists. In either

[33] Copyright Act, 1956, s. 2 (5) (6).
[34] s. 6 (6).
[35] s. 8, though associated words may be included in the record.
[36] Copyright Act, 1911, s. 35.
[37] Copyright Act, 1956, s. 48 (1).

case, it would appear to be a necessary condition for the existence of copyright that something should exist in writing or other notation.

The words " the acting form of which is fixed in writing or otherwise " in the Act of 1911 were derived from Article 2 of the Berne Convention, repeated in the Brussels Convention but not in the Stockholm Convention which leaves any requirement of fixation to domestic legislation.

166 **Scenic effects.** The words " scenic arrangement " have been dropped from the definition, and this, again, may be thought to limit its scope and to confine the protection to something which has dramatic action without regard to any elements of background or production.

167 Under the law prior to 1911, possibly, neither a pantomime nor a choreographic work was entitled to protection.[38] In *Tate* v. *Fullbrook*[39] it was stated by the Court of Appeal that a dramatic work was not entitled to be protected against piracy by public performance unless it was capable of being printed and published. " Scenic effects, taken by themselves and apart from the words and incidents of the piece are not," said Farwell L.J., " the subject of copyright,[40] because they cannot be the subject of printing and publication. Nor do I say that scenic effects may not be protected as part and parcel of the drama; scenes do, of course, form part of a drama, and it is the dramatic piece, as a whole, that is protected by the Act. It is essential, however, to such protection that there should be something in the nature of a dramatic entertainment, for a mere spectacle standing alone is no more within the Act than a singer who sings in character costume is within it."[41] The facts of that case were that the plaintiff complained of the piracy of his sketch called " Motoring " by the defendant's sketch called " Astronomy." Both sketches were entertainments in the form of comic dialogue grounded on very slight dramatic action. The defendant used different words, but the plaintiff complained that the defendant copied certain incidents, the " make-up " of the actors from his sketch, and also that he used the same " gag." The court held that the plaintiff could have no copyright in the incidents, the " make-up," or the " gag."[42]

38 *Karno* v. *Pathé Frères, Ltd.* (1909) 100 L.T. 260. In *Lee* v. *Simpson* (1847) 3 C.B. 871, the written introduction to a pantomime was protected, but it is not clear that the protection extended to the pantomime itself.

39 [1908] 1 K.B. 821.

40 This is contrary to the dictum of Brett J. in *Chatterton* v. *Cave* (1876) as reported in 33 L.T. 255.

41 [1908] 1 K.B. at 832.

42 In *Rees* v. *Melville* [1911–16] Macg.Cop.Cas. 96, 168, the court doubted whether there could be copyright in the plot of a play: see *post*, § 485.

168 While this decision, in so far as it was based upon the necessity for the existence of some work capable of being printed and published for dramatic copyright to be claimed, is no doubt overridden by the definitions in the Acts of 1911 and 1956, a similar decision that mere scenic effects could not be protected was given under the Act of 1911.[43] It would appear that both under the Act of 1911 and under the Act of 1956, a work must be a dramatic work, pure and simple, or a choreographic work, or a dumb show. A dramatic work, pure and simple, probably predicates words spoken or sung; choreographic works and dumb shows predicate action. Scenic effects, characters, " get-up," and so forth are not the subjects of protection, apart from either words or defined movements, but as was admitted by the Lords Justices in *Tate* v. *Fullbrook*,[44] once you have dialogue, scenic effects become accessory to the dramatic work, and the whole becomes the subject of copyright in the sense that they are the background of the dramatic action and therefore part of it. If the scenic effects are fitted to a totally different dialogue, complaint apparently cannot be made; but, if the dialogue is not dissimilar, the fact that the scenic effects also correspond with those found in the earlier work may be evidence of plagiarism. It is probable that the use of mere scenic effects, coupled with the use of a name, might give rise to a passing-off action.[45] Furthermore, some scenic effects are capable of protection as artistic works.[46]

169 **" Gag."** " Gag " was held not to be the subject of copyright in *Tate* v. *Fullbrook*[47] upon the grounds that, generally speaking, the author of the " gag " is not the writer of the play, but the actor who speaks the words, and that, even if the writer of the play and the speaker of the " gag " should happen to be the same person, the " gag " is not a permanent part of the play, but is intended to be changed from time to time. There must be some certainty in the subject-matter of copyright.[48] But if such certainty is attained, there seems no reason why the author of the " gag " should not have copyright therein.

170 As regards what is necessary to constitute a " dramatic work," the judges under the old law were somewhat hampered by the

43 *Tate* v. *Thomas* [1921] 1 Ch. 503.
44 [1908] 1 K.B. 821; see *Bishop* v. *Viviana & Co.* [1905–10] Macg.Cop.Cas. 211, where it was held under the law prior to 1911 that there could be no copyright in a dance.
45 See § 230 *et seq., post.*
46 This is possibly the explanation of the decision in *Perkin* v. *Ray Bros.* [1911–16] Macg.Cop.Cas. 288, where copyright was held to subsist in the *mise en scène* of a revue.
47 [1908] 1 K.B. 821.
48 *Tate* v. *Thomas* [1921] 1 Ch. 503.

definition contained in the Dramatic Copyright Act, 1833,[49] which gave to the authors of " any tragedy, comedy, play, opera, farce, or other dramatic piece or entertainment," the sole liberty of performing it. The Literary Copyright Act 1842 [50] further declared that " the words ' dramatic piece ' shall be construed to mean and include every tragedy, comedy, play, opera, farce, or other scenic, musical, or dramatic entertainment." The courts held that the words " other dramatic entertainment " must be construed *ejusdem generis* with the words " tragedy, comedy, play, opera, and farce." It was mainly for this reason that the Lords Justices held, in the case of *Tate* v. *Fullbrook*,[51] above alluded to, that a dramatic work, in order to become entitled to copyright, must be capable of being printed and published.

171 **Definition of " musical work."** There was no definition of musical work in the Act of 1911 and there is none in the Act of 1956. The Musical (Summary Proceedings) Copyright Act, 1902,[52] which has now been repealed, defined a musical work as meaning " any combination of melody and harmony, or either of them, printed, reduced to writing, or otherwise graphically produced or reproduced," thus expressly confining musical works to those which are printed or written.

172 If the question is whether, if A improvises a tune in B's presence, which B carries away in his head and subsequently publishes, A has copyright in the tune, which he can sue B for infringing, probably A has no copyright in his tune, and in any case, the difficulties in the way of proving that B's published work is an infringement of A's improvised tune will be well-nigh insuperable. What the Acts protect is a musical " work " and the expression seems to imply that the tune shall be recorded in some permanent form before it becomes entitled to copyright. This view is confirmed by the provision that, in the case of an entertainment in dumb show or a choreographic work, it must be reduced to writing in the form in which the work or entertainment is to be presented,[53] and also by the requirement that a work is made when first reduced to writing or some other material form.[54]

On the other hand, it seems clear that the words " graphically produced or reproduced " in the Act of 1902, are too narrow in present circumstances. If A, having improvised a tune, has his tune recorded on tape or other record, it seems clear that he at once

49 Dramatic Copyright Act, 1833 (3 & 4 Will. 4, c. 15).
50 Literary Copyright Act, 1842 (5 & 6 Vict. c. 45).
51 [1908] 1 K.B. 821.
52 2 Edw. 7, c. 15, s. 3.
53 Copyright Act, 1956, s. 48 (1) definition of " dramatic work," *cf. Rees* v. *Melville* [1911–16] Macg.Cop.Cas. 96, 168.
54 *Ibid.* s. 49 (4).

enjoys copyright in his musical work under the Act of 1956, and this is confirmed by section 49 (4) to which reference has already been made in relation to dramatic works. But in the case of a musical work, there is not the same difficulty about copyright being created merely by recording on a record, since there is no definition such as occurs in the case of literary and dramatic works involving the existence of writing or other notation.[55] It is submitted that the subject-matter of copyright, in the case of music, is not any graphic or other representation, but the actual tune and that the recording is required, not to create a protectable work, but to afford permanent evidence of the nature of the work. This is of particular importance in relation to much of the modern " pop " type music which is played straight onto tapes without having first been written down.

It seems quite clear that, in these circumstances, A is the author and first owner of the copyright in the tune apart from special circumstances. On the other hand, the sound recording embodied in the record or tape could be a separate subject-matter of copyright vested in the owner of the record.[56]

173 **Musical work also a dramatic work.** Before the Act of 1911 the question arose, in a number of cases, whether a particular work was a dramatic piece as well as a musical work.[57] This question is now of less importance since, under the Acts of 1911 and 1956, the owner of copyright in a dramatic work had and has no separate rights from those enjoyed by the owner of copyright in a musical work. These decisions may, however, have some relevance to the question of what constitutes dramatisation of a non-dramatic work.[58]

174 A distinction, however, which is sometimes overlooked is that, whereas the musical accompaniment of a song enjoys copyright as a musical work, the words themselves generally enjoy copyright as a literary work. As has been seen,[59] there are still cases in which the law regarding musical works differs from that regarding literary works. In such cases it may be contended that the words ought to be assimilated to the music by treating them as a dramatic work, and the cases cited in the last paragraph may be relevant to this contention.

3.—ARTISTIC WORKS

175 **Statutory definitions.** Previously to the Copyright Act, 1911, the copyright in artistic works was the subject of various statutes which

[55] *Ante*, §§ 153 and 163.
[56] *Post*, Chaps. 7 and 17.
[57] *Russell* v. *Smith* (1848) 12 Q.B. 217; *Clark* v. *Bishop* (1872) 25 L.T. 908, *Roberts* v. *Bignell* (1887) 3 T.L.R. 552; *Fuller* v. *The Blackpool Winter Gardens, etc., Co. Ltd.* [1895] 2 Q.B. 429.
[58] See *post*. Chap. 9.
[59] See *ante*, § 162.

dealt separately with engravings, paintings, drawings, photographs, and works of sculpture.[60] Under the Act of 1911 these all fell under one compendious phrase, section 1 conferring copyright upon "every original artistic work."

The Act of 1956 also gives copyright to every original artistic work, which is defined as follows: (a) the following, irrespective of artistic quality, namely, paintings, sculptures, drawings, engravings[61] and photographs; (b) works of architecture, being either buildings or models for buildings; (c) works of artistic craftsmanship, not falling within either of the preceding paragraphs.[62]

"Drawing" includes any diagram, map, chart or plan.[63] "Engraving" includes any etching, lithograph, wood-cut, print or similar work, not being a photograph.[63] "Photograph" means any product of photography or any process akin to photography, other than a part of a cinematograph film.[63] "Sculpture" includes any cast or model made for purposes of sculpture.[63]

176 **Artistic quality.** It will be observed that, in the case of works described under sub-paragraph (a), the words "irrespective of artistic quality" occur. It was generally considered under the Act of 1911 that the word "artistic" was merely used as a generic term to include the different processes of creating works set out in the definition section and that, provided that a work was produced by one of such processes, and that its creation involved some skill or labour on the part of the artist, it was protected. The use of the word "artistic" was thought to be akin to that of the word "literary," which, as already pointed out,[64] was held to refer only to the nature of the material being written or printed matter. In fact, under the Act of 1911, merely commercial designs were protected.[65] This matter is now clarified, as above mentioned.

On the other hand, it will be observed that the words "irrespective of artistic quality" do not apply in the case of the works mentioned in sub-paragraphs (b) and (c). This again follows the interpretation given under the Act of 1911 to works of artistic craftsmanship.

177 Clauson J., in *Burke, etc., Ltd.* v. *Spicers Dress Designs*,[66] in considering whether a lady's dress was capable of enjoying copyright protection as a work of artistic craftsmanship, cited definitions of

60 *Post*, Chap. 20.
61 As to labels, see *Charles Walker & Co., Ltd.* v. *The British Picker Co., Ltd.* [1961] R.P.C. 57, and *Tavener Rutledge, Ltd.* v. *Specters, Ltd.* [1959] R.P.C. 83.
62 Copyright Act, 1956, s. 3 (1).
63 s. 48 (1); as to protection of maps and plans of imaginary things, see *Braithwite Burn and Co.* v. *Trustees of the Port of Madras* (1956) 2 Mad.L.J. 486.
64 *Ante*, § 152.
65 *Waters* v. *Huygen (M. A.) & Co.* [1923–28] Macg.Cop.Cas. 17; *Purefoy Engineering Co., Ltd.* v. *Sykes, Boxall & Co., Ltd.* (1955) 72 R.P.C. 89.
66 [1936] Ch. 400.

"artistic" and "artist" in the *Oxford English Dictionary* as showing that the proper question was whether a designer who designs and makes a frock was thereby cultivating "one of the fine arts in which the object is mainly to gratify the aesthetic emotions by perfection of execution whether in creation or representation." In the particular case the actual decision was that there was no copyright vested in the firm who executed the design because their servants, who made the frock from a third party's design, did not originate any artistic element which might subsist. But Clauson J. was clearly doubtful whether copyright would have subsisted, even if the plaintiff had both designed and made the frock.

In two cases, one in Australia, *Cuisenaire* v. *Reed*,[67] and the other in Canada, *Cuisenaire* v. *South West Imports Ltd.*,[68] it was decided that a set of rods, specially designed for teaching mathematics, was not a work of artistic craftsmanship. There was no craftsmanship in the making of the rods as no skill was involved in cutting or colouring them. Nor were they artistic.

In the Australian case, Pape J. said,[69] "In my opinion, the words 'artistic' and 'craftsmanship' each refer to some quality in the acts performed by the maker or author of the article in which copyright is alleged to subsist in the course of performing the physical operation of making that article as distinct from the earlier cogitation and thought which produced the idea upon which the work was based. The true test, I think, is whether the author, in making the article in which copyright is alleged to subsist, was applying his skill and taste to its production with the main object of creating an article which, even if it be utilitarian, nevertheless will have a substantial appeal to the aesthetic tastes of those who observe it. Put another way, it may be said that the test is whether the author was, in creating the article, cultivating one of the fine arts with the main object of appealing to the aesthetic tastes of those who view it, provided that the expression 'the fine arts' is given the wide meaning of any application of skill and taste to the production of articles which are beautiful in themselves or which have an appeal to aesthetic taste. The emphasis is thus upon the object of the author in creating the work, rather than in the reaction of the viewer to the completed work, for it is commonplace in copyright law that it is immaterial whether the work has any merit: *Walter* v. *Lane*.[70] In stating that the emphasis is on the object of the author, I do not desire to be taken as saying that the sole test of whether the work of a craftsman is a work of artistic craftsmanship is the intention or object of the craftsman at the time he made the work. As a general rule, the court adjudicating on the

[67] [1963] V.R. 719.
[68] [1968] 1 Ex.C.R. 493; 37 Fox's C.P.C. 93; 40 Fox's C.P.C. 81.
[69] [1963] V.R. at p. 730.
[70] [1900] A.C. 539, *per* Lord Halsbury L.C. at p. 549.

matter will apply a purely objective test by an examination of the article itself. When, however, as in this case, such an objective test may be thought to deny that the work is one of artistic craftsmanship, and it is sought to establish the contrary, the object of the creator of the work must, in my view, play a dominant part in the resolution of the question. The best evidence concerning that is the evidence of the creator of the work himself, although, if he were dead, I am inclined to think that evidence from qualified viewers of the work that it had an aesthetic appeal to them may be some evidence from which a court could hold that the creator of the work intended, when he made it, that it should have such an appeal. But evidence that a particular section of the community in viewing the work found that it appealed to their aesthetic emotions cannot be a ground for ascribing copyright to that work if it is clear that its author had no such object in view when he created it." In the Canadian case, Noel J. said,[71] "An artistic work, in my view, must to some degree at least, be a work that is intended to have an appeal to the aesthetic senses not just an incidental appeal, such as here, but as an important or one of the important objects for which the work is brought into being. The plaintiff's rods may have a certain attraction to children, but this, in my view, is a very secondary purpose which, I am afraid, is not a sufficient basis for a finding that the rods are artistic."

It is interesting to note that the Court of Appeal, in *Amp Incorporated* v. *Utilux Pty., Ltd.*,[72] decided that the phrase, features of shape or configuration which "appeal to and are judged solely by the eye," in section 1 (3) of the Registered Designs Act, 1949, did not impose any requirement for the presence of aesthetic or artistic appeal, Megaw L.J. adding that,[73] "Courts of law should not be made arbiters on matters of aesthetic taste."

178 **Drawings not ideas protected.** It must always be remembered that ideas, however original, are not protected under the Copyright Act. Consequently, where a very simple diagram embodies an original idea, it is the diagram and not the idea which is protected. Thus, a plaintiff conceived the idea of printing and publishing cards bearing a representation of a hand holding a pencil in the act of completing a cross within a square, with a view to such cards being used at elections by illiterate voters, and procured an artist to make, under his directions, a drawing of the representation above described. Subsequently the defendants published similar cards with a hand holding a pencil, in the act of completing a cross in a particular square of a voting paper, but the hand in the defendant's cards was in a slightly different position, though the idea was clearly taken from the plaintiff's cards.

71 [1968] 1 Ex.C.R. at p. 514.
72 [1970] R.P.C. 397.
73 *Ibid.* p. 432.

It was held that the defendants had not infringed the plaintiff's copyright. There was no copyright in the idea; the defendants' work was not an exact reproduction of the plaintiff's, and the plaintiff was not entitled to prevent anyone from producing such a simple design as a hand in a square in any form.[74] The case could probably have been put on the ground that there was no evidence of copying the actual drawing although the idea of making and using such a drawing was no doubt copied.

179 **Maps, etc.** Under the law prior to 1911 a map might be protected either as a " book," under the Literary Copyright Act, 1842, or as an engraving, under the Engraving Acts, 1734 and 1766, according to whether the owner of the copyright chose to call his work a " map " or an " engraving." [75] The Act of 1911—somewhat illogically, perhaps—included " maps, charts, and plans " in the definition of " literary works." [76]

Under the Act of 1956, as has been seen, maps, charts and plans are included in the definition of " drawing " and are therefore artistic works,[77] though, if finally produced by an engraving process or by photography, they may also enjoy a separate copyright under these heads, and, while still artistic works, may have two copyrights in different ownership. The only difference in the change from the 1911 Act would appear to be that the term of copyright in such works, whether published or unpublished, will now, unless they are engravings, be fifty years from the death of the author,[78] whereas, as literary works, such works, if unpublished, were entitled, by virtue of section 17 (1) of the Act of 1911, to copyright until publication and then for fifty years thereafter.

4.—INDUSTRIAL DESIGNS

Comparison of Copyright and Design Protection

180 **Industrial designs and artistic copyright.** As has been pointed out,[79] the Copyright Act of 1911 generalised the protection of artistic works to cover any work produced by artistic process in a broad sense and this has been continued by the Act of 1956. Moreover, both Acts make it an infringement of the copyright in an artistic work to

[74] *Kenrick & Co.* v. *Lawrence & Co.* (1890) 25 Q.B.D. 99. *Cf. Nottage* v. *Jackson* (1883) 11 Q.B.D. 627; and *Commercial Signs* v. *General Motors Products of Canada, Ltd.* (1937) 2 D.L.R. 310.

[75] This seems to be the effect of the two somewhat puzzling decisions of *Stannard* v. *Lee* (1871) L.R. 6 Ch. 346, and *Stannard* v. *Harrison* (1871) 19 W.R. 811, both relating to maps of the scene of war in 1870.

[76] Copyright Act, 1911, s. 35 (2).

[77] *Ante*, § 151.

[78] Copyright Act, 1956, s. 3 (4).

[79] *Ante*, § 175.

reproduce the work in any material form.[80] This was held under the Act of 1911 to include the reproduction of a two-dimensional artistic work in a three-dimensional form [81] and this is expressly provided in the definition of " reproduction " in section 48 (1) of the Act of 1956. Consequently, if no limit was placed on the protection so conferred, the manufacture and sale of purely industrial articles might be restrained as an infringement of the copyright in any sketch, catalogue or diagram upon which the article was based,[82] also in the case of lamp-standards, book-ends and other articles derived from a model which could be described as a work of sculpture or of artistic craftsmanship, as an infringement of such work.[83]

As it had generally been considered that it was not within the proper field of artistic copyright to protect purely industrial designs, measures were taken both under the Act of 1911 and the Act of 1956 to limit artistic copyright in this respect and to secure that works of this class should only receive protection under the Designs Acts. Under the latter Acts, protection is only afforded to works in respect of which a design is registered, the term of protection is much shorter, and a stricter view taken of the requirement of originality. On the other hand registration under the Designs Acts gives an exclusive right to make use of the registered design and not merely, as under the Copyright Acts, a right to prevent copying. The method adopted in the two Copyright Acts of limiting artistic copyright in this connection has, however, been entirely different. Under the Act of 1911, works were excluded altogether from artistic copyright, if capable of registration under the Designs Acts and if intended for use as a model or pattern for industrial production.[84]

The Act of 1956 adopted a different principle and excluded from artistic copyright all designs actually used for industrial purposes and in respect of which a design had not been registered under the Designs Acts, but only in so far as so used, so that the copyright protection was retained as against any other form of user. The position was similar if a design was registered under the Designs Acts.[85] Since the copyright protection was therefore not qualified from the creation of the work, but only from the date of use (or registration), it was necessary to amend the Registered Designs Act, 1949, so that prior publication as a purely artistic work should not prevent registration as a design when such use was first contemplated.[86]

[80] Copyright Act, 1911, ss. 1 (2) and 2 (1) and Copyright Act, 1956, s. 3 (5).
[81] *King Features Syndicate* v. *O. & M. Kleeman, Ltd.* [1941] A.C. 417.
[82] Under s. 9 (8) of the Act of 1956, the industrial object must, however, appear to be a reproduction to the eye of a non-expert.
[83] Copyright Act, 1956, s. 48 (1), s. 3 (1) (*a*) and (*c*), and ss. 3 (5) and 9 (8).
[84] Copyright Act, 1911, s. 22 (1).
[85] Copyright Act, 1956, s. 10, before amendment.
[86] s. 44.

181 **Report of Designs Committee, 1962.** A committee was appointed in 1959 by the Board of Trade to consider and report whether any, and if so what, changes were desirable in the law relating to the protection of industrial designs. The committee reported in August 1962.[87] An entirely new proposal was the introduction, in addition to the existing system, of a new form of protection to be known as "Design Copyright." Protection would be obtained, without registration, by the deposit of a copy of the design. It would not, as in the case of present Registered Design law, be necessary to establish absolute novelty of the design but only "originality" in the sense hitherto used in the law of artistic copyright but, on the other hand, infringement would only be established on proof of copying, and not, as under Registered Design law, merely on proof of similarity.

The majority of the committee favoured the continuation of the system introduced by the Act of 1956 under which artistic copyright protection would be cut down where a design is used for industrial purposes with the consent of the copyright owner, but recommended simplification of procedure. A minority, however, would apparently have preferred a return to the system operating under the Act of 1911 with modifications.

182 **Design Copyright Act, 1968.** Notwithstanding such Report, in October 1968 the Design Copyright Act, 1968,[88] was enacted, which radically changed the position of industrial designs under the Act of 1956. Thus, instead of cutting down the artistic copyright in designs actually used for industrial purposes, or in respect of which a design has been registered, to the extent above mentioned, the Act of 1968 has amended the Act of 1956 in such a way that the Act of 1956 now allows full artistic copyright to such designs for a limited time, even if used for industrial purposes and even if a design is registered. However the Act of 1968 does not contain any transitional provisions and, therefore, the scope of its operation is not clear.[89]

Artistic Works Created before June 1, 1957

183 Since provisions of the Act of 1956 equivalent to those of the Act of 1911 apply in respect of artistic works made before the commencement of the Act of 1956,[90] it will be convenient to discuss in detail the effect of the provisions of the Act of 1956 applicable to old works, before proceeding to explain the provisions of the Act of 1956 applicable to new works and thereafter to consider the provisions of the Design Copyright Act of 1968.

87 Cmnd. 1808.
88 1968, c. 68.
89 See § 222, *post*.
90 Copyright Act, 1956, Sched. 7, para. 8.

184 The main provisions as to old works in the Copyright Act, 1956, are contained in the Seventh Schedule, para. 8 and the Eighth Schedule, para. 2, and these substantially reproduce the provisions of section 22 of the Copyright Act, 1911, as interpreted by the court and brought up to date so as to refer to the Registered Designs Act, 1949, instead of to the Patents and Designs Act, 1907.[91]

These provisions are as follows. Under paragraph 8 (2) it is provided that copyright shall not subsist by virtue of the Act of 1956 in any artistic work made before the commencement of section 10 which, at the time when the work was made, constituted a design capable of registration under the Registered Designs Act, 1949, or under the enactments repealed by that Act, and was used, or intended to be used, as a model or pattern to be multiplied by any industrial process. Paragraph 2 of the Eighth Schedule provides that a design shall be deemed to be used as a model or pattern to be multiplied by any industrial process (a) when the design is reproduced or is intended to be reproduced on more than fifty single articles unless all the articles on which the design is reproduced or is intended to be reproduced together form only a single set of articles as defined in subsection (1) of section 44 of the Registered Designs Act, 1949, or (b) when the design is to be applied to (i) printed paper hangings, (ii) carpets, floorcloths or oil-cloths, manufactured or sold in lengths or pieces, (iii) textile piece goods, or textile goods manufactured or sold in lengths or pieces, or (iv) lace, not made by hand. " Set of articles " is defined in section 44 (1) of the Registered Designs Act, 1949, as a number of articles of the same general character ordinarily on sale or intended to be used together, to each of which the same design, or the same design with modifications or variations not sufficient to alter the character or substantially to affect the identity thereof, is applied.

By way of explanation of the foregoing provisions it may be pointed out that a drawing or painting to be reproduced upon hardware is not excluded from the Copyright Act unless more than fifty articles are intended to be manufactured bearing the same design, but a drawing or painting to be reproduced upon textile goods manufactured in lengths or pieces is so excluded, whatever be the quantity manufactured. Again, for example, a dinner-service consisting of seventy-six pieces would be regarded as one article.

185 **Intention at time when work was made.** Section 22 of the Copyright Act, 1911, was as follows: " This Act shall not apply to designs capable of being registered under the Patents and Designs Act, 1907, except designs which, though capable of being so registered, are not used or intended to be used as models or patterns to be multiplied by any industrial process." This section involved an awkward double

[91] 7 Edw. 7, c. 29; see *Usher* v. *Barlow* [1952] Ch. 255.

negative, as was pointed out by Lord Maugham in *King Features Syndicate* v. *O. & M. Kleeman, Ltd.*[92] Furthermore, it involved a doubt as to the time at which the use or intention to use as models or patterns to be multiplied by industrial process was to be established until this doubt was set at rest by the decision of the House of Lords in the same case that the question whether protection was excluded by section 22 had to be decided once and for all at the time when the work was made. As has been seen,[93] both these points are clarified in the new definition; and unless it can be said that at the time when the work was made it was used or intended to be used as a model or pattern to be multiplied by industrial process it will enjoy protection under the Copyright Act, notwithstanding that it is afterwards used for such a purpose.[94] The same case decided that the material intention is that of the artist.[95]

186 **"Capable of registration."** A further point arises which, however, seems still somewhat uncertain. This is whether "capable of registration under the Registered Designs Act, 1949, or under the enactments repealed by that Act" refers only to capacity as a possible subject-matter for registration or includes also capacity on the ground of originality. It was held, under the Act of 1911, that a work which existed before the commencement of that Act, if it had not been registered under the Patents and Designs Act, 1907, was entitled to copyright under the Act of 1911 because, at the commencement of that Act, it was not capable of registration as a design, for lack of novelty.[96] Under the Act of 1907, a design was registrable unless a similar design had been used on an article in the same class or on an article of an analogous character.[97] But section 1 (2) of the Registered Designs Act, 1949, somewhat extends the restriction by providing that a design shall not be registered unless it is new or original, in particular if it is the same as a design which before the date of the application for registration, has been registered or published in the United Kingdom in respect of the same or any other article or differs from such a design only in immaterial details or features which are variants commonly used in the trade. Occasions may occur, therefore, of a design incapable of registration for lack of novelty, but still sufficiently original from the point of view of artistic copyright to be entitled to protection under the Copyright Act. It is arguable, however, that the word "constituted" in paragraph 8 (2) of the Seventh Schedule to the Act of 1956, indicates that the words "capable of

92 [1941] A.C. 417 at 427.
93 *Ante*, § 184.
94 *King Features Syndicate* v. *O. & M. Kleeman, Ltd.* [1941] A.C. 417; *Ware* v. *Anglo-Italian, etc., Agency, Ltd.* (*No.* 1) [1917–23] Macg.Cop.Cas. 346.
95 *King Features Syndicate* v. *O. & M. Kleeman, Ltd.*, *supra*, at p. 427.
96 *Stevenson Blake* v. *Grant, Legros, Ltd.* (1917) 86 L.J.Ch. 93.
97 *Stenor, Ltd.* v. *Whitesides* (*Clitheroe*), *Ltd.* [1948] A.C. 107.

registration" refer only to the nature of the design and not to the actual facts of its prior user or otherwise so that, if it is the kind of design which is capable of registration and use or intention to use is proved, it will lose its copyright protection notwithstanding that it is not sufficiently original to be able, in fact, to obtain protection under the Designs Act.

However this may be, the primary question involved in the expression "capable of registration" is what kind of artistic works are capable of registration.

187 **Definition of a design.** By section 93 of the Patents and Designs Act, 1907, as amended by the Patents and Designs Act, 1919,[98] a "design" was defined as meaning "only the features of shape, configuration, pattern or ornament applied to any article by an industrial process or means, whether manual, mechanical, or chemical, separate or combined, which in the finished article appealed to and are judged solely by the eye; but does not include any mode or principle of construction, or anything which is in substance a mere mechanical device"; and by the same section "article" is defined as meaning "(as respects designs) any article of manufacture and any substance artificial or natural or partly artificial and partly natural."

It will be observed that this definition is directed rather to distinguishing "designs" from "patents" than from "artistic works." Moreover, the "design" defined is not the model or pattern in material form protected by the Copyright Act, but the notional "features" which, when applied to an article, will assume a material form. In view of the wide definition of "article," it is difficult to arrive at any principle for excluding the design of any artistic work from the possibility of being registered.

188 The foregoing definitions are the relevant definitions where the work was made before the Registered Designs Act, 1949, being the definitions in "the enactments repealed by that Act." The Act of 1949 [99] did not substantially alter the definition of "design," but somewhat narrowed the definition of "article," leaving out the reference to substance. But for the purposes of the present discussion the alterations do not appear to have made any real difference.

189 **What designs capable of registration?** It is clear that it cannot have been intended that every artistic work, the design of which is reproduced or is intended to be reproduced in more than fifty articles, was to be excluded from protection under the Copyright Act, since

[98] 9 & 10 Geo. 5, c. 80, s. 19. It was held by Clauson J. in *Pytram, Ltd.* v. *Models, etc., Ltd.* [1930] 1 Ch. 639, that the amending provisions of the Act of 1919 had to be regarded although this Act was not passed at the date of the Act of 1911.

[99] s. 44 (1).

this would affect many engravings and photographs of a purely artistic character. The only guide given is that the section only applies to designs capable of registration under the Designs Act, but, as has been pointed out, this affords little assistance. There seems no reason, upon a literal reading of the Designs Act, why the design for a poster or a Christmas card should not be registered as a design, since features of pattern or ornament are to be applied to paper in such cases just as much as in the case of a design for wallpaper, which has always been regarded as registrable. It is submitted, however, that the fundamental distinction between a " design " and a simple " artistic work " lies in the applicability of the former to another article. That is to say, an artistic work is bought purely and simply for its artistic properties, an article to which a design has been applied is bought, not simply because of the artistic qualities of the design, but because of the utility of the article apart from the design, and that this distinction may be implied from the obvious purpose of the Designs Acts, and from the use of the words " pattern or ornament," which are not properly applicable to such designs as are not merely appurtenances but are the essence of the thing created. For example, the plate from which an engraving is to be printed is intended to be applied to a sheet of paper or other material, but an engraving is not usually purchased for the material on which it is printed. Therefore, engravings are prima facie entitled to protection under the Copyright Act. But if it were intended that this engraving should be applied to, say, a wallpaper, then it would be different; for nobody would be likely to purchase an engraving printed upon a wallpaper, unless it was for the purpose of papering a room. In such a case the engraving would fall under the law as to designs. Applying these principles, it is submitted that a drawing or painting intended to be reproduced upon a Christmas card falls under the Copyright Act.[1] Similarly with regard to an advertisement poster, for the object of a person in designing a poster is not to cover the hoarding upon which it is to be pasted, but to produce a picture which will attract the passer-by. Picture postcards possibly present greater difficulty, for it may be contended that a purchaser of a postcard purchases the same as a means for carrying on a correspondence. It is, nevertheless, submitted that these are entitled to the protection of the Copyright Act, the postcard being subsidiary to the picture upon it.

190 **Rules under the Registered Designs Act, 1949.** These difficulties have, to some extent, been resolved as a result of section 1 (4) of the Registered Designs Act, 1949. Under that section, rules may be made

[1] It was so held under the law prior to 1911, which did not expressly exclude designs from the benefit of the Copyright Acts: *Hildesheimer* v. *Dunn & Co.* (1891) 64 L.T. 452; *Millar & Lang, Ltd.* v. *Polak* [1908] 1 Ch. 433; and see as to football pool coupon, *Re Littlewoods Pools, Ltd.* (1949) 66 R.P.C. 309 and *Ladbroke (Football), Ltd.* v. *William Hill (Football), Ltd.* [1964] 1 W.L.R. 273.

by the Board of Trade providing for excluding from registration thereunder designs for articles which are primarily literary or artistic in character. Rules have, in fact, been made excluding from registration under the Designs Act: (1) works of sculpture other than casts or models used or intended to be used as models or patterns to be multiplied by any industrial process, (2) wall plaques and medals, and (3) printed matter primarily of a literary or artistic character, including bookjackets, calendars, certificates, coupons, dress-making patterns, greetings cards, leaflets, maps, plans, postcards, stamps, trade advertisements, trade forms, and cards, transfers, and the like.[2]

In *Klarmann (H.) Ltd.* v. *Henshaw Linen Supplies*,[3] Roxburgh J. pointed out the difficulty of the definition and that it was wholly uncertain whether the *ejusdem generis* rule applied. He also expressed the view that the test could not be whether the combination of article and words or picture superimposed had a primarily literary or artistic purpose, as this could not apply to a calendar or birth certificate. It is submitted, however, that this, after all, may be the correct test for the reasons suggested in the preceding paragraphs. Using " literary " in the copyright sense, a calendar is primarily literary in that it supplies information by its use of words and figures: this applies also to a birth certificate. The actual decision was that a plastic cover having a picture thereon retains its artistic copyright.

191 **Wall plaques, etc., made before 1949.** The case of *Usher* v. *Barlow*[4] decided that wall plaques, though in existence before 1949, were entitled to artistic copyright after 1949, since, at the date of the issue of the writ, they were not capable of registration, having regard to the rules in question and to the fact that, by virtue of the Interpretation Act, 1889, the Registered Designs Act, 1949, was deemed to be substituted for the Patents and Designs Act, 1907, in section 22 of the Copyright Act, 1911. It seems doubtful, however, if this decision would still apply in the case of an artistic work created before 1949 since, under paragraph 8 (2) of the Seventh Schedule to the Copyright Act, 1956, copyright is not to subsist in a work which, at the time of making, constituted a design capable of registration under enactments repealed by the Registered Designs Act, 1949. Therefore, if the work was made before 1949 and was, at the time of making, capable of registration under the Act of 1907, it is not now entitled to artistic copyright, notwithstanding the existence of the rules. It of course still remains arguable that many of the articles specified in the rules are, in any event, not capable of registration on the grounds set forth above.

[2] Designs Rules, 1949 (S.I. 1949 No. 2368), r. 26.
[3] [1960] R.P.C. 150.
[4] (1952) 69 R.P.C. 27.

192 **Medals.** It has been decided that "medal" in the rules abovementioned was not confined to awards or decorations but applied to anything in the nature of a medal, such as a Coronation medal.[5]

193 **Works of sculpture.** The difficulty in determining what is a registrable design in the case of a two-dimensional work does not apply so forcibly to works of sculpture, since the words in the Designs Act, "features of shape or configuration," seem capable of being applied to designs, which are the essence of the object created.

194 Clauson J. in *Pytram, Ltd.* v. *Models, etc., Ltd.*[6] said: "Now let me take the case, immediately after the Act of 1911 comes into force, of an ordinary piece of sculpture, sculptured by a sculptor according to the usual methods used by sculptors, say a portrait bust, or something of that kind. As I read the Act, the copyright in that article of sculpture is given to the author of it in the first instance, but that copyright is taken away by the first part of section 22, if (as would at all events in many cases, if not all, be the fact) the sculpture comes within the term 'design' as defined in the Act of 1907, and is, accordingly, capable of being registered under that Act, so that, although in the first instance the sculptor is prima facie given copyright under the Act of 1911, the first part of section 22 takes that copyright away, if his artistic work is a design which is capable of being registered under the Patents and Designs Act of 1907; but by the following words in the same section, section 22, the work is replaced in the category of works carrying copyright under the Copyright Act, 1911, if it is a design which is 'not used or intended to be used as a model or pattern to be multiplied by any industrial process'—words which, of course, would apply in the case of what I may call an ordinary piece of artistic sculpture."

195 And in the case of *Con Planck, Ltd.* v. *Kolynos Inc.*[7] cut-out figures of pierrots, to be used for advertisement purposes, were held not to be the subject-matter of copyright protection.

196 **Original sketch of a design.** It will be observed that paragraph 8 of the Seventh Schedule to the Act of 1956, as was the case with section 22 of the Act of 1911, only applies to a case where the artistic work is used or intended to be used as a model or pattern. It might be said that this only strictly covered a model for a piece of sculpture or other three-dimensional article, such as the design for a work of artistic craftsmanship, and did not apply, therefore, to an inventor's sketch of a design to be produced in three dimensions, since the sketch

5 *Reliance (Nameplates), Ltd.* v. *Art Jewels, Ltd.* [1953] 1 W.L.R. 530.
6 [1930] 1 Ch. 639.
7 [1925] 2 K.B. 804

itself is not multiplied. The Board of Trade rules endeavoured to get over the difficulty by indicating that if the design is multiplied the work is to be deemed to be used as a model or pattern, but the rule itself cannot extend the scope of the section. However, in *King Features Syndicate* v. *O. & M. Kleeman, Ltd.*,[8] the House of Lords appear to have assumed that the two-dimensional works there in question would have lost protection under the Copyright Act if they had in fact, been intended to be used for the reproduction of brooches. It is thought that the narrower view would be held to be an unreasonable interpretation of the provisions.

197 **Subsequent reproduction of design.** On the other hand, where the design is subsequently produced in an artistic form, *e.g.*, by a photograph of the industrial object, the subsequent work, though embodying the design, is not excluded from copyright protection.[9]

Artistic Works Created on or after June 1, 1957, and before October 25, 1968

198 **Copyright subsists in all artistic works.** Turning now to works created after the commencement of the Copyright Act, 1956, and before the commencement of the Design Copyright Act, 1968, the basic provisions are to be found in section 10 of the Act of 1956 before its amendment by the Act of 1968.

This section, instead of providing, as did the Copyright Act, 1911, that, in the circumstances stated, the Act should not apply to certain works, provided that certain acts should not constitute an infringement of copyright. Copyright therefore subsisted in all artistic works, irrespective of whether or not they were used or intended to be used as designs, and the effect of the section was to put a limit upon the acts which constituted an infringement of that copyright and not to affect the subsistence of the copyright.

Corresponding Design Registered

199 There were two main sets of circumstances which brought the section into operation. The first concerned the case where an artistic copyright subsisted and a corresponding design was registered under the Registered Designs Act, 1949. "Corresponding design" is defined in section 10 (7) of the Act of 1956 as meaning a design which, when

8 [1941] A.C. 417.

9 *Ware* v. *Anglo-Italian, etc., Agency, Ltd.* (*No.* 2) [1917–23] Macg.Cop.Cas. 371. See also *Masson Seeley & Co., Ltd.* v. *Embosotype Manufacturing Co.* (1924) 41 R.P.C. 160. In the Australian case of *Buzacott & Co., Ltd.* v. *Dutch* (1929) 30 S.R.(N.S.W.) 22, however, it was held that representations in a catalogue of designs for articles are not protected under the Copyright Act if the designs are capable of registration under the Designs Act, but the correctness of this decision must be doubted.

applied to an article, results in a reproduction of that work. "Reproduction" is defined in section 48 (1) of the Act of 1956 as including, in the case of an artistic work, a version produced by converting the work into a three-dimensional form, or, if it is in three dimensions, by converting it into a two-dimensional form. In section 9 (8) of the Act of 1956 it is provided that the making of an object of any description which is in three dimensions shall not be taken to infringe the copyright in an artistic work in two dimensions, if the object would not appear, to persons who are not experts in relation to objects of that description, to be a reproduction of the artistic work. Though this provision does not in terms qualify reproduction, but rather infringement, it does, in effect, amount to a limit upon what is meant by "reproduction," and it is submitted that anything which is not a reproduction in this sense is not a corresponding design because it would have been unnecessary to apply section 10 of the Act of 1956 to a case where, as a result of section 9 (8) of that Act, the industrial article would not infringe copyright in the artistic work. "Design" is not defined in the Copyright Act, but presumably, in this section, has the same meaning as in the Registered Designs Act, 1949, to which attention has already been called.

200 **Corresponding design registered without the knowledge of the copyright owner.** Normally a corresponding design would have been registered by the owner of the copyright in the artistic work. To safeguard the copyright owner, where this was not the case, provision is made in the First Schedule to the Copyright Act, 1956.[10] Thus where copyright subsists in an artistic work and proceedings are brought under the Copyright Act, 1956, and a corresponding design has been registered, but it is proved or admitted that the person registered was not the proprietor thereof for the purposes of the Act of 1949 and was registered without the knowledge of the owner of the copyright in the artistic work, then for the purposes of the copyright proceedings the registration is to be treated as never having been effected: accordingly in relation to that registration section 10 (1) of the Act of 1956 is not to apply and nothing in section 7 of the Act of 1949 is to provide any defence. If, however, the act of infringement alleged was done in pursuance of an assignment or licence from the registered proprietor in good faith in reliance upon the registration, and without notice of any proceedings for cancellation or rectification, then section 10 (1) of the Copyright Act, 1956, would apply. Section 10 (1) has now been deleted by the Design Copyright Act, 1968, which Act also amended the First Schedule to the Copyright Act, 1956, to accord.[11]

[10] See *Ornamin (U.K.), Ltd.* v. *Bacsa, Ltd.* [1964] R.P.C. 293.
[11] See § 221, *post*.

201 **Design " proprietor " and copyright " owner " not necessarily the same.** By section 2 of the Registered Designs Act, 1949, it is provided that the author of a design shall be treated as the proprietor of the design provided that, where the design is executed by the author for another person for good consideration, that other person shall be treated, for the purposes of the Act, as the proprietor; and where a design or the right to apply a design to any article becomes vested, whether by assignment, transmission or operation of law, in any person other than the original proprietor, either alone or jointly with the original proprietor, that other person, or, as the case may be, the original proprietor and that other person, shall be treated for the purposes of the Act as the proprietor of the design or as the proprietor of the design in relation to that article. It follows that the proprietor of the design may not be the same person as the owner of the artistic copyright under the Copyright Act. For example, under section 4 of the Act of 1956, it is only in the case of a photograph, portrait or engraving that the copyright in a commissioned work of art will vest in the person placing an order. However, having regard to the amendment to section 6 of the Registered Designs Act, 1949, mentioned below, it should not normally be possible for the person who was to be proprietor of the design to obtain registration without the consent of the owner of the artistic copyright.

202 **Effect of such registration.** The purport of these provisions therefore seems clear, namely, that they applied whenever a design was registered under the Designs Act with the consent of the owner of the artistic copyright for articles, the reproduction of which would, under the Copyright Act, constitute an infringement of the artistic copyright.

In these circumstances, it was provided that it should not be an infringement of the artistic copyright to do anything during the subsistence of the copyright in the registered design under the Registered Designs Act, 1949, which was within the scope of the copyright in the design, or to do anything after the copyright in the design has come to an end which, if it had been done while the copyright in the design subsisted, would have been within the scope of that copyright as extended to all associated designs and articles.[12]

203 **" Scope of the copyright."** By section 10 (6) of the Act of 1956 the expression " scope of the copyright in a registered design " is defined as referring to the aggregate of the things, which, by virtue of section 7 of the Registered Designs Act, 1949, the registered proprietor of the design has the exclusive right to do. " Scope of the copyright . . . in a registered design as extended to all associated designs and articles "

12 Copyright Act, 1956, s. 10 (1).

is defined by the same subsection as referring to the aggregate of the things which, by virtue of section 7 aforesaid, the registered proprietor would have had the exclusive right to do if, (a) when the design was registered there had at the same time been registered every possible design consisting of that design with modifications or variations not sufficient to alter the character or substantially to affect the identity thereof, and the said proprietor had been registered as the proprietor of every such design, and (b), the design in question, and every other design such as is mentioned in paragraph (a), had been registered in respect of all the articles to which it was capable of being applied.

204 Section 7 of the Registered Designs Act, 1949, gives to the proprietor the exclusive right, in the United Kingdom and the Isle of Man, to make or import for sale or for use for the purposes of any trade or business, or to sell, hire or offer for sale or hire, any article in respect of which the design is registered, being an article to which the registered design or a design not substantially different from the registered design has been applied, and to make anything for enabling any such article to be made as aforesaid, whether in the United Kingdom, or the Isle of Man, or elsewhere.

205 **Extent of artistic copyright during period of registration.** It should be noted, therefore, that during the period of registration artistic copyright continued to protect the owner thereof in respect of any infringement not concerned with the article in respect of which the design was registered and even in respect of such an article against any infringement not concerned with purposes of trade. Moreover the words " as aforesaid " in the last sentence involve making " for sale or use for the purposes of a trade or business," so that the making of kits of parts to be sold to amateurs to enable them to make the article for their private use was not within the section.[1]

206 **Extent of artistic copyright after determination of designs copyright.** After the determination of the designs copyright, the artistic copyright only protected the owner of the artistic copyright in relation to infringements not capable of being protected under the Designs Act by any design registration, either of a design corresponding to the original artistic work, or of a design corresponding to the artistic work with modifications or variations. To some extent, this reintroduced the problem of what was capable of registration under the Designs Act, which has been discussed at length above in relation to section 22 of the Act of 1911.[2] The meaning of " the articles to which it was capable of being applied " in section 10 (6) (*b*) of the Act of 1956, is akin to the question under section 22 of the Act of 1911, of what is

[1] *Dorling* v. *Honnor Marine, Ltd.* [1965] Ch. 1.
[2] *Ante*, § 190; Designs Rules, 1949 (S.I. 1949 No. 2368), r. 26.

meant by designs capable of being registered under the Patents and Designs Act, 1907. However, as has been seen, a good deal of this difficulty has now been removed by section 1 (4) of the Registered Designs Act, 1949, and rules made thereunder.[2]

Artistic Copyright Used for Industrial Purpose and No Design Registered

207 The second set of circumstances envisaged by the original section 10 of the Act of 1956 was where the artistic copyright was used for an industrial purpose and no design was registered.

These circumstances were described in section 10 (2) of the Act of 1956 and arose where (a) a design corresponding to an artistic work in which copyright subsisted was applied industrially by or with the licence of the owner of the copyright in the work and (b) articles produced by so applying the design were sold, let for hire, or offered for sale or hire, and (c) at the time when those articles were sold, let for hire, or offered for sale or hire, the design had not been registered under the Registered Designs Act, 1949. It is to be noted that these three conditions were cumulative. If, therefore, one condition was not satisfied it would seem that section 10 (2) would not have applied. This could have occurred, it is submitted, if, for instance, the industrial application took place in America and the relevant articles were sold in America and this country. That is to say, neither the condition relating to industrial application, nor the condition relating to sale specified where that activity had to take place for the condition to be satisfied. It is submitted that, in the circumstances, both were confined to this country since it would seem surprising if, by reason of industrial application and sale in for instance, America alone, there should be a limitation on the English artistic copyright. Some support for this submission is to be found in the Design Copyright Act, 1968, which, in amending section 10, inserts the words " whether in the United Kingdom or elsewhere " at the end of the condition relating to sale, but makes no similar provision in relation to the condition relating to industrial application.[3]

The meaning of " corresponding design " has already been discussed.[4] Here the expression used in relation thereto was " applied industrially " and thus " design " had its normal meaning of the idea of shape or form involved. By section 10 (5) of the Act of 1956 the Board of Trade is given power to make rules for the purpose of determining the circumstances in which a design is to be taken to be applied industrially.

[3] See Registered Designs Act, 1949, s. 6 (4); *Bissell A.G.'s Design* [1964] R.P.C. 125 and para. 148 of the 1962 Report of the Departmental Committee on Industrial Designs, Cmnd. 1808; see also § 219, *post*.

[4] See § 199, *ante*.

208 **Use for industrial purpose.** Under the rules a design is to be taken to be applied industrially if it is applied by any process to, or is reproduced on or in, more than fifty articles not together constituting a single set, or to goods manufactured in lengths or pieces other than hand-made goods.[5] The word "industrially" therefore merely has the signification of quantity and has no relation to the method of application.

209 **Only designs which infringe.** It is again assumed that, if the design is a design which, by virtue of section 9 (8) of the Act of 1956, would not be an infringement of the artistic work, the provision would not have operated. It would not, for example, have imposed any restriction upon the artistic copyright in a plan or engineer's drawing for an industrial design, if the design would not have appeared to non-experts to be a reproduction of the plan or drawing.

210 **Effect of industrial use.** If the circumstances envisaged as aforesaid occurred then, during the period of fifteen years beginning with the date on which articles to which the design had been so applied were first sold or otherwise dealt with as aforesaid, it was not an infringement of the artistic copyright to do anything which would have been within the scope of the copyright in the design, if the design had been registered in respect of all such articles. After the expiration of the period of fifteen years the copyright owner's artistic copyright was cut down in respect of all designs within the scope of such design as extended to all associated designs and articles.

The effect of the two branches of the section was therefore similar. If a corresponding design was registered, or if it was applied industrially without registration, artistic copyright during fifteen years would not protect against infringements within the scope of the design and, after fifteen years, would not protect against infringements within the scope of the design as extended.

211 **Test of capacity for registration no longer applicable.** It is, however, to be observed that the test "applied industrially" is different in kind from the test "capable of registration" in the Act of 1911. A design might be applied industrially although not capable of registration.

212 **Certain designs excluded.** The Act of 1956 therefore provides some relief to meet such cases. In the first place, by virtue of section 1 (4) of the Registered Designs Act above mentioned, the Board of Trade may exclude from registration certain designs for articles of a primarily literary or artistic character. Accordingly section 10 (4) of

[5] Copyright (Industrial Designs) Rules, 1957 (S.I. 1957 No. 867) (Appendix B, § 1617).

the Copyright Act, 1956, provides that, for the purposes of section 10 (2) and 10 (3), no account is to be taken of articles in respect of which the design in question was excluded by rules made under section 1 (4) of the Registered Designs Act, 1949.[6] It is further provided that, for the purposes of proceedings for infringement of copyright, a design shall be conclusively presumed to have been so excluded if, before the commencement of the proceedings, an application for registration of the design in respect of those articles has been refused and one of the reasons for refusal was such rules, and no appeal from such refusal has been allowed or is pending.

213 **Certain designs not "designs."** But there are also cases where a design is not capable of registration because it is not a "design" within the meaning of section 1 (3) of the Act of 1949, for instance where it constitutes features of shape or configuration dictated solely by function. Nevertheless, it could still have constituted a corresponding design and have been applied industrially for the purposes of section 10 (2) of the Act of 1956. This problem arose in *Dorling* v. *Honnor Marine, Ltd.*[7] where the plaintiffs alleged that the defendants had infringed the plaintiffs' copyright in plans for a boat, by the making of boats, by the making of kits or parts for the construction of boats, and by photographs of the parts. Cross J. and the Court of Appeal took the view that the design of the kits of parts was not registrable as purely functional and the Court of Appeal took the view that the design of the boat itself was functional. Consequently, as no design, at least for the kits of parts, could have been registered, even though section 10 (2) applied, section 10 (3) did not.

214 **Lack of "novelty" in copyright work not necessarily bar to registration.** But this does not meet the difficulty that an artistic work issued to the public would prima facie be incapable of registration for lack of novelty.

It is for this reason that it has been necessary to amend the Registered Designs Act, 1949, since otherwise, the prior publication of the artistic work might prevent registration under that Act but, an article to which a corresponding design is applied having been sold or disposed of, section 10 (2) of the Act of 1956 would have applied to defeat any claim of the owner of the artistic copyright to protection.

Section 44 (1) of the Copyright Act, 1956, accordingly provides for a new subsection to be inserted in section 6 of the Registered Designs Act, 1949, as follows: "Where copyright under the Copyright Act, 1956, subsists in an artistic work, and an application is made by, or with the consent of, the owner of that copyright for the registration of a corresponding design, that design shall not be treated for the

[6] *Ante*, § 190.
[7] [1965] Ch. 1.

purposes of this Act as being other than new or original by reason only of any use previously made of the artistic work, unless—(*a*) the previous use consisted of or included the sale, letting for hire, or offer for sale or hire of articles to which the design in question (or a design differing from it only as mentioned in subsection (2) of section one of this Act) had been applied industrially, other than articles of a description specified in rules made under subsection (4) of section one of this Act, and (*b*) that previous use was made by, or with the consent of, the owner of the copyright in the artistic work." [8]

215 In relation to this provision, reference should be made to section 4 of the Registered Designs Act, 1949, which provides, in effect, that where a design has been registered in respect of any article, it may be subsequently registered in respect of other articles notwithstanding the previous registration, but the term of copyright under the Designs Act for all such articles shall not exceed that in respect of the original registration. There is a further provision of the same section enabling an assignee of the original proprietor to obtain additional registrations under the section.

216 **Summary.** The general effect of the foregoing provisions was as follows. Unless and until an industrial design was either registered or used, full copyright protection was preserved for the artistic work. If the copyright owner of the artistic work decided to embark upon an industrial use for his work, he was at liberty to register under the Designs Act, notwithstanding the previous copyright publication. If he registered in respect of one article, he continued to enjoy copyright protection in respect of use on other articles during the term of designs registration in the article which he had registered and during that period he could have obtained additional designs registrations for other articles, but only for the original period. When the original period expired his copyright protection continued but only in respect of use which was not use for industrial purposes. Now, by reason of the Design Copyright Act, 1968, the position may be different.[9]

217 **Limit on duration of designs copyright.** Section 44 (2) and (3) of the Act of 1956 contain amendments of the Registered Designs Act, 1949, providing that, where a design corresponding to an artistic work has been registered and the period of copyright protection in the artistic work determines, the designs copyright shall also determine and may be cancelled. This only applies where there had been a previous use of the artistic work so that the design would not have been registrable but for the new section above referred to.[10]

[8] See *Bissell A.G.'s Design* [1964] R.P.C. 125.
[9] See § 222, *post*.
[10] *Ante*, § 214.

Artistic Works Created on or After October 25, 1968

218 **Design Copyright Act, 1968.** The relationship between artistic copyright under the Copyright Acts, and designs copyright under the Designs Acts, was radically changed by the Design Copyright Act, 1968,[11] which came into force on October 25, 1968. As has been mentioned,[12] under the Act of 1911, works were excluded altogether from artistic copyright, if capable of registration under the Designs Acts and if intended for use as a model or pattern for industrial production.[13] Under the Act of 1956, however, before amendment by the Act of 1968, full artistic copyright subsisted from the creation of the work, although the protection afforded by that Act was cut down if, either a corresponding design was registered under the Designs Acts, or a corresponding design was applied industrially without a design being so registered.[14]

219 The Act of 1968 adopts a completely new approach and permits full artistic copyright to subsist without restriction for a limited period, whether or not a corresponding design is registered under the Designs Acts, and whether or not a corresponding design is applied industrially without a design being so registered. As a result, subject to the questions of novelty[15] and registrability,[16] it is now possible to have a duality of protection, that is under the Copyright Acts and, if a corresponding design has been registered, also under the Designs Acts.[17] This will be a great advantage to many owners of artistic copyrights in works whose viable exploitation time is of short duration, such as toys.

The manner in which this has been achieved is that the Act of 1968 has amended section 10 of the Act of 1956, which applies to works made after the commencement of the Act of 1956, first of all by deleting subsection (1), which contained the limiting provisions where a corresponding design had been registered under the Designs Acts and, secondly, by amending subsection (2), and substituting a new subsection (3) which, together, contained the limiting provisions where a corresponding design was applied industrially and no design had been so registered.

The amended subsection (2) now reads as follows: " Where copyright subsists in an artistic work, and (*a*) a corresponding design is applied industrially by or with the licence of the owner of the copyright in the work, and (*b*) articles to which the design has been so

[11] 1968 c. 68: see as to the Isle of Man, the Copyright (Isle of Man) Order, 1970 (S.I. 1970 No. 1437).
[12] *Ante*, § 180.
[13] Copyright Act, 1911, s. 22 (1).
[14] Copyright Act, 1956, s. 10.
[15] See Registered Designs Act, 1949, ss. 1 (2) and 6 (4) and (5), and § 214, *ante*.
[16] See Designs Rules, 1949, r. 26; Registered Designs Act, 1949, s. 1 (3), and §§ 190, 212 and 213, *ante*.
[17] See *Merchant Adventurers Ltd.* v. *M. Grew & Co. Ltd.* [1971] F.S.R. 233. But see ss. 8 and 11 of the Registered Designs Act, 1949, and § 217, *ante*.

applied are sold, let for hire, or offered for sale or hire whether in the United Kingdom or elsewhere, [and [18]] the following provisions of this section shall apply." The words "whether in the United Kingdom or elsewhere" have been added to what was the original subsection (2) (*b*), but not to what was the original subsection (2) (*a*) which, again, raises the question, since these conditions are cumulative, as to when the subsection applies. That is to say, if it is necessary to provide expressly that sale anywhere is relevant, presumably industrial application is only relevant if it takes place in the United Kingdom. Therefore it would seem that, if industrial application takes place, say, in America, but sale takes place in this country and America, the subsection will not apply.[19]

220 **Extent of protection where corresponding design applied industrially.** Although the Act of 1968 permits full artistic copyright to subsist without restriction, this is only for a limited term. Thus, the new subsection (3) provides that, after the end of "the relevant period of fifteen years," it will not be an infringement of the copyright in the work to do anything, which, at the time when it was done would, if a corresponding design had been registered under the Registered Designs Act, 1949, immediately before that time, have been within the scope of the copyright in the design as extended to all associated designs and articles. Such new subsection defines "the relevant period of fifteen years" as meaning the period of fifteen years beginning with the date on which articles such as are mentioned in subsection (2) (*b*) were first sold, let for hire or offered for sale or hire, whether in the United Kingdom or elsewhere. Again, no account is to be taken of articles in respect of which the design in question was excluded by rules made under section 1 (4) of the Registered Designs Act, 1949.[20] "Scope of the copyright in a registered design as extended to all associated designs and articles" is defined by subsection (6).[21]

In the result, there is unrestricted artistic copyright for fifteen years from first sale, and so on, of articles to which the design has been applied industrially.[22] After that period the position will be the same as it was under the original subsection (3) at the end of the relevant period of fifteen years there mentioned.[23]

221 **Corresponding design registered without the knowledge of the copyright owner.** As has been mentioned,[24] a corresponding design is

18 Although deleting sub-para. (*c*), the Act of 1968 does not, in fact, delete the word "and" which joined sub-para. (*c*) with sub-para. (*b*).
19 See *Bissell A.G.'s Design* [1964] R.P.C. 125 and para. 148 of the 1962 Report of the Departmental Committee on Industrial Designs, Cmnd. 1808; see also § 207, *ante*.
20 Copyright Act, 1956, s. 10 (3) and (4), and see § 212, *ante*.
21 See §§ 203 and 204, *ante*.
22 See as to possible extension to 25 years, *Copyright*, November 1968, p. 235.
23 See § 210, *ante*.
24 § 200, *ante*.

normally registered by the owner of the copyright in the artistic work and, to safeguard the copyright owner, where this was not the case, provision is made in the First Schedule to the Act of 1956. Reference is made, in paragraphs 2 and 3 of the First Schedule, to section 10 (1) and, in view of the deletion of section 10 (1) by the Act of 1968, that Act also amends the First Schedule accordingly. Thus, now, where copyright subsists in an artistic work, and proceedings are brought under the Act of 1956, and a corresponding design has been registered, but it is proved or admitted that the person registered was not the proprietor thereof for the purposes of the Registered Designs Act, 1949, and was registered without the knowledge of the owner of the copyright in the artistic work, then, for the purposes of the copyright proceedings, the registration is to be treated as never having been effected; accordingly, in relation to that registration, nothing in section 7 of the Act of 1949 is to provide any defence. If, however, the act of infringement alleged was done in pursuance of an assignment or licence from the registered proprietor in good faith in reliance upon the registration, and without notice of any proceedings for cancellation or rectification, then this will be a good defence.

222 **Transitional provisions.** The biggest problem created by the Act of 1968 arises from the fact that such Act has no transitional provisions. In view of the important changes in the law effected by this Act, and the benefit it was no doubt intended to confer on a large section of the public, it is, perhaps, unfortunate that the position has been left uncertain as to how the Act affects works created before it came into force on October 25, 1968.

That is to say, the Act clearly applies to works created after it came into force in respect of which any acts of infringement must take place after that date. But the position is not clear as to works created before that date, either in respect of acts of infringement which occurred before that date, or in respect of acts of infringement which occur after that date. It therefore becomes necessary to examine the position under section 10 of the Act of 1956 before amendment,[24a] and then to consider the effect of such amendment.

As has been mentioned,[25] the Act of 1956, unlike the Act of 1911, permits full artistic copyright to subsist from the creation of the work. However, under section 10 before amendment, this protection was cut down if, either a corresponding design was registered under the Designs Acts, or a corresponding design was applied industrially without a design being so registered. The manner in which section 10 cut down this protection was to provide that, in those circumstances, " it shall not be an infringement of the copyright in the work " to do

[24a] This applies to works made after the commencement of the Act of 1956.
[25] §§ 198 and 218, *ante*.

certain things.[26] The effect of such provisions, it is submitted, was not to destroy part of the artistic copyright but, whilst leaving the whole of such copyright intact, to provide a defence to proceedings for infringement of such copyright in the circumstances mentioned.[26a] Thus, by way of comparison, section 6 (1) of the Act of 1956 provides that " No fair dealing with a literary, dramatic or musical work for purposes of research or private study shall constitute an infringement of the copyright in the work "; section 9 (1) of that Act is similarly worded. Section 7 (1) of that Act provides that " The copyright in an article contained in a periodical publication is not infringed " by certain acts; again, section 8 (1) of that Act provides that " The copyright in a musical work is not infringed " by certain acts. All these provisions are, in effect, defences to what would otherwise be infringements.[27]

This view would appear to be supported by the judgment of Cross J., at first instance, in the case of *Dorling* v. *Honnor Marine Ltd.*,[28] who said,[29] " The general effect of section 10 is clear enough. If the owner of the copyright in an artistic work exploits it industrially, he does not lose his copyright under the 1956 Act, but, whether or not he actually registers the design which corresponds to the artistic work under the Registered Designs Act, 1949, he ceases to be entitled to protection under the 1956 Act in respect of matters which are—or, if he had registered the design, would have been—infringements of the design copyright. When the period of design copyright expires, his copyright protection under the 1956 Act goes on, but only in respect of non-industrial use." The judgments in the Court of Appeal are not so clear, both Harman and Danckwerts L.JJ. saying, in effect, that section 10 was designed to prevent duality of protection.[30] However, Danckwerts L.J. also said,[31] " If the shape of the completed boat ought to have been registered as a design under the Registered Designs Act, 1949, the plaintiff is deprived of his remedies under the Copyright Act, 1956, by virtue of section 10 of that Act."

If this view of the effect of section 10 before amendment is correct, what is the effect of the amendment on works created after the commencement of the Act of 1956 and before the Act of 1968 came into force, bearing in mind that the amended section 10 gives unrestricted artistic copyright for the relevant period of fifteen years, where there has been industrial application, by removing the provisions of section 10 which gave what, it is submitted,

26 Copyright Act, 1956, s. 10 (1) and (3) before amendment.

26a This was the view taken by Whitford J. in *I.M.I. Developments, Ltd.* v. *F. C. Harrison, Ltd.* [1970] R.P.C. 299.

27 See *Hawkes & Son (London) Ltd.* v. *Paramount Film Service Ltd.* [1934] Ch. 593; *Johnstone* v. *Bernard Jones Publications Ltd.* [1938] Ch. 599.

28 [1964] Ch. 560.

29 *Ibid.* 573.

30 [1965] Ch. 1 at 15, 18, 19 and 20.

31 *Ibid.* 21.

was a statutory defence during that period? It is suggested that the position as to such works is that they are now entitled to the full unrestricted artistic copyright for the relevant period of fifteen years. Further, that that being so, proceedings can now be brought for infringements of that copyright which occur after October 25, 1968 (when the 1968 Act came into force) and before the expiry of that period, because no part of the copyright was ever destroyed and the statutory defences are now removed. But, proceedings cannot now be brought in respect of " infringements " which occurred before the Act of 1968 came into force since they were not infringements when they occurred and, it is submitted, they cannot become infringements by reason of the removal of the statutory defences.[32]

A further difficulty, arising from the fact that the Act of 1968 merely amends section 10 of, and the First Schedule to, the Act of 1956, is the effect of paragraph 8 of the Seventh Schedule to the Act of 1956 following such amendment. Thus, paragraph 8 (1) provides that section 10 and the First Schedule to the Act of 1956 are not to apply to artistic works made " before the commencement of that section." Clearly, before the Act of 1968 came into force, this was a reference to the commencement of the original section 10 and First Schedule on June 1, 1957. It is submitted that, notwithstanding that the Act of 1968 merely amends section 10 and the First Schedule, paragraph 8 (1) of the Seventh Schedule does not mean, following such amendment, that the amended section 10 and First Schedule do not apply to works created before the Act of 1968 came into force, particularly in view of paragraph 8 (2) and (3) of the Seventh Schedule and section 50 of the Act of 1956.

5.—PUBLISHED EDITIONS OF EXISTING WORKS

223 **Protection for typographical arrangements.** Evidence was given before the 1952 Copyright Committee that protection was required for typographical arrangements. A publisher who had gone to considerable trouble and expense in setting up in type a new edition of a non-copyright work appeared to have no remedy under the Act of 1911 if another publisher, having purchased a copy of the edition, proceeded to reproduce copies thereof by photographic process. The Copyright Committee therefore recommended that protection should be given in such circumstances.[33]

[32] See *Ex p. Todd* (1887) 19 Q.B.D. 186; *Lauri* v. *Renad* [1892] 3 Ch. 402 and Interpretation Act, 1889, s. 38 (2) (*b*). The effect of the amendment of s. 10 was considered, but not decided upon, by Whitford J. in *I.M.I. Developments Ltd.* v. *F. C. Harrison, Ltd., supra.*

[33] Cmd. 8662, paras. 308 and 310.

By section 15 (1) of the Act of 1956 it is provided that copyright shall subsist in every published edition of any one or more literary, or dramatic, or musical works first published in the United Kingdom or in another country to which the section extends, or the publisher whereof was a qualified person at the date of first publication, provided that the subsection does not apply to an edition which reproduces the typographical arrangement of a previous edition of the same work or works.

The protection given to publishers of works of this class is of a limited character and merely restricts the making, by any photographic or similar process, of a reproduction of the typographical arrangement of the edition.[34] The period of copyright is twenty-five years from the end of the calendar year in which the edition was first published [35] and certain exemptions are envisaged in the case of copying by libraries.[36]

6.—SUBJECT-MATTER NOT PROTECTED ON GROUNDS OF PUBLIC POLICY OR SIMILAR GROUNDS

224 **Libellous, immoral, obscene or irreligious works.** A claim of copyright in a work of libellous, immoral, obscene or irreligious tendency will not be enforced.[37] This has been put upon the ground that in order to establish such a claim the author must, in the first place, show a right to sell; and this he cannot possibly do, he himself not being able to acquire a property therein.[38] It is probably more accurate to say that the ground for refusal by the courts to intervene is that it is against public policy to protect rights of publication and sale of works, where publication and sale would be against the public interest; not that there is no copyright in the work, but that the courts will not enforce such copyright.[39]

It would also appear that if the infringing work is of a nature which the court would not protect, a plaintiff, although his work is

[34] Copyright Act, 1956, s. 15 (3).
[35] s. 15 (2).
[36] ss. 15 (4) and 7 (1) to (5).
[37] *Stockdale* v. *Cnwhyn* (1826) 5 B. & C. 173; *Hime* v. *Dale* (1809) 2 Camp. 27n; *Walcot* v. *Walker* (1802) 7 Ves. 1; *Poplett* v. *Stockdale* (1825) 1 Ry. & M. 337; *Gee (A. P.)* v. *Pritchard (W.)* (1818) 2 Swans. 402; *Southey* v. *Sherwood* (1817) 2 Mer. 435; *Murray* v. *Benbow* (1822) Jac. 474n; *Lawrence* v. *Smith* (1822) Jac. 471; *Fores* v. *Johnes* (1802) 4 Esp. 95; *Gale* v. *Leckie* (1817) 2 Stark.N.P. 107; *Baschet* v. *London Illustrated Standard Co.* [1900] 1 Ch. 73; *Glyn* v. *Western Feature Film Co.* [1916] 1 Ch. 261; *Pasickniak* v. *Dojacek* [1928] 2 T.L.R. 545; but a form for credit betting on football matches has been held not to be against public policy: *Barnard* v. *White & Co.* [1923–28] Macg.Cop.Cas. 218.
[38] *Stockdale* v. *Onwhyn, supra.*
[39] See Copyright Act, 1956, s. 2 (1) and (2), for instance, which gives copyright to all original literary works without qualification in respect of public policy. In *Chaplin* v. *Leslie Frewin (Publishers), Ltd.* [1966] Ch. 71, although both Danckwerts and Winn L.JJ. considered the book in question contained blasphemous passages, the point was not taken as to whether this affected the subsistence of copyright in the book, or the court's willingness to intervene if there was copyright: see § 559, *post.*

unobjectionable, cannot succeed since, in claiming that the work is a copy of his work, he is trying to obtain protection for a work of an objectionable kind, whereas his proper remedy would be to disaffirm the work and claim that it was a libel upon his own work.[40]

225 **Works of an irreligious tendency.** In *Lawrence* v. *Smith*[41] the doctrine was carried very far. Lord Eldon, in dissolving the injunction, said: "Looking at the general tenor of the work, and at many particular parts of it, recollecting that the immortality of the soul is one of the doctrines of the Scripture, considering that the law does not give protection to those who contradict Scripture,[42] and entertaining a doubt, I think a rational doubt, whether this book does not violate the law, I cannot continue the injunction. The plaintiff may bring an action, and when that is decided, he may apply again." From a note by the editor, we learn that in 1822, in *Murray* v. *Benbow*, Mr. Shadwell, on the part of the plaintiff, moved for an injunction to restrain the defendants from publishing a pirated edition of Lord Byron's poem of "Cain." The Lord Chancellor, after reading the work, refused the motion, on the grounds similar to those stated in the above judgment; and in another case, Leach V.-C. dissolved an injunction which had been granted restraining an infringement of the same poet's work, "Don Juan."[43]

Referring to Lord Eldon's decisions in the above cases, Story J. says: "The soundness of the general principle can hardly admit of question. The chief embarrassment and difficulty lie in the application of it to particular cases. If a court of equity, under colour of its general authority, is to enter upon all the moral, theological, metaphysical, and political inquiries, which in the past times have given rise to so many controversies, and in the future may well be supposed to provoke many heated discussions, and if it is to decide dogmatically upon the character and bearing of such discussions, and the rights of authors growing out of them, it is obvious that an absolute power is conferred over the subject of literary property, which may sap the very foundations on which it rests, and retard, if not entirely suppress, the means of arriving at physical as well as at metaphysical truths. Thus, for example, a judge who should happen to believe that the immateriality of the soul, as well as its immortality, was a doctrine clearly revealed in the Scriptures (a point upon which very learned and pious minds have been greatly divided), would deem

40 *Glyn* v. *Western Feature Film Co., supra.*

41 (1822) Jac. 471.

42 "Christianity is part and parcel of the law of the land": Kelly C.B. in *Cowan* v. *Milbourn* (1867) L.R. 2 Ex. 230; but, at the present day, it is generally considered permissible to attack the Christian religion so long as it is not done in an offensive manner. It would probably be held equally objectionable to attack the religious beliefs of any body of persons in an offensive manner.

43 *Murray* v. *Benbow* (1822) Jac. 474n.

any work anti-Christian which should profess to deny that point, and would refuse an injunction to protect it. So, a judge who should be a Trinitarian might most conscientiously decide against granting an injunction in favour of an author enforcing Unitarian views, when another judge, of opposite opinions, might not hesitate to grant it." [44]

226 The very case surmised by Story J., arose in the year 1874 in the Scottish courts. The plea put forward by the defendant was that the pursuer could not claim the protection of the law for the book, as it was blasphemous and heretical, denying tacitly or expressly the divinity of Christ. To this the pursuer replied that, apart from the fact that it was written by a Unitarian, and set forth the Unitarian view of the Saviour's life, a more unobjectionable book did not exist. Mr. Sheriff Buntine, of the Sheriff's Court of Lanarkshire, declared the interdict perpetual, and found the defendant liable in expenses, holding that, though the doctrine that Jesus Christ is the Second Person of the Trinity is statute law, yet the public are entitled to criticise and controvert any part of the statute law, provided they do it in such a way as not to endanger the public peace, safety or morality. The pursuer, the sheriff considered, violated none of the conditions, and was entitled to the protection of the law.

227 **Works of a scandalous nature.** In the case of *Hime* v. *Dale*,[45] referred to in *Clementi* v. *Golding*,[46] counsel called attention to the libellous nature of the publication, and contended that it was of such a description that it could not receive the protection of the law. Lord Ellenborough, however, stated that though if the composition had appeared on the face of it to be a libel so gross as to affect the public morals, he should advise the jury to give no damages, as he knew the Court of Chancery on such an occasion would grant no injunction, yet he thought the particular publication ought not to be considered one of that kind. But in another case [47] where an action was brought for the purpose of recovering compensation in damages for the loss alleged to have been sustained by the publication of a copy of a book which had been first published by the plaintiff; and at the trial, it was proved that the work was a memoir of Harriette Wilson, which professed to be a history of the

[44] 2 Story's Eq.Jur., p. 938.
[45] (1809) 2 Camp. 27n.
[46] (1809) 2 Camp. 25. And see *Goeie Hoop Vitgewers (Eiendoms) BPK* v. *Central News Agency*, 1953 (2) S.A. 843.
[47] *Stockdale* v. *Onwhyn* (1826) 5 B. & C. 173; see *Poplett* v. *Stockdale* (1825) 1 Ry. & M. 337, where it was held that the printer of the work, the subject of the last case, could not maintain an action for his bill against the publisher who employed him. Best C.J. said the defendant was equally guilty with the plaintiff, but that he would not, as Lord Kenyon once said, sit to take an account between two robbers on Hounslow Heath.

amours of a courtesan, that it contained in some parts matter highly indecent, and in others matter of a slanderous nature upon persons named in the book, Abbott C.J. directed a nonsuit, and in refusing a rule nisi for a new trial said: " In order to establish such a claim (*i.e.*, to compensate for infringement of his copyright), he must in the first place show a right to sell, for if he has not that right, he cannot sustain any loss by an injury to the sale. Now I am certain no lawyer can say that the sale of each copy of this work is not an offence against the law. How then can we hold that by the first publication of such a work a right of action can be given against any person who afterwards publishes it? It is said that there is no decision of a court of law against the plaintiff's claim. But upon the plainest principles of the common law, founded as it is, where there are no authorities, upon common sense and justice, this action cannot be maintained. It would be a disgrace to the common law could a doubt be entertained upon the subject, but I think that no doubt can be entertained, and I want no authority for pronouncing such a judicial opinion."

228 **Works intended to deceive the public.** In an action for pirating a work of a devotional character, falsely professing to be a translation from the German, of an author who had a high reputation for writings of this kind, the object being to deceive purchasers, and give the work a value which it would not otherwise have possessed, judgment was given for the defendants. Tindal C.J., in the case referred to,[48] drew a distinction between such a work and books of instruction or amusement which have been published as translations, whilst they have, in fact, been original works, or which have been published under an assumed instead of a true name. Such, for instance was the case of " The Castle of Otranto," professing to be translated from the Italian, and of innumerable works published under assumed names—voyages, travels, biographies, works of fiction or romance, and even works of science and instruction; for, in all these instances the misrepresentation is innocent and harmless. But the facts stated in the pleas in the case under consideration imported a serious design on the part of the plaintiff to impose on the credulity of each purchaser, by fixing on the name of an author who had a real existence, and who possessed a large share of weight and estimation in the opinion of the public. The object of the plaintiff was not merely to conceal the name of the genuine author, and to publish opinions to the world under an innocent disguise, but it was to practise upon some of the best feelings of the public, namely, their religious feelings; and thus to induce them to believe that the work was the original work of the author whom he named, when he knew it not to be so. The transaction, therefore,

[48] *Wright* v. *Tallis* (1845) 1 C.B. 893.

ranged itself under the head of *crimen falsi.* It was a species of obtaining money under false pretences; and as the very act of publishing the work, and the sale of the copies to each individual purchaser, were each liable to the objection above stated, the Chief Justice thought the plaintiff could not be considered as having a valid and subsisting copyright in the work, the sale of which produced such consequences, or that he was capable of maintaining an action in respect of its infringement. Cases in which a copyright has been held not to subsist, where the work is one which is subversive of good order, morality or religion, did not bear, he thought, on the case before him, but they had so far analogy that the rule which denied the existence of copyright in those cases was the rule established for the benefit and protection of the public.

229 In another case [49] the plaintiff published an illustrated catalogue of trucks, trolleys, and barrows made by him. Many of the odd pages were headed "Inventor, patentee, and sole maker," and many of the even pages were headed "Slingsby's Patents." The plaintiff had no English patent for the various articles represented, though he had certain foreign patents. The catalogue also contained pictures of buildings on which the plaintiff's name was written in large letters, although he did not occupy the whole of them. The defendants had admittedly copied the plaintiff's catalogue, but the latter was refused an injunction upon the ground that his statements as to his being patentee, etc., were calculated to deceive the public, and that he was attempting to get trade regardless of the way in which it was obtained.

Where a defendant succeeds in a proceeding on the ground that the work infringed will not be protected owing to its objectionable character he will not recover costs.[50]

7.—TITLES AND SIMILAR SUBJECT-MATTER PROTECTED BY "PASSING-OFF" ACTION

Titles

230 The titles to books, newspapers, and periodicals, though often coming before the courts on the question of copyright therein, are not generally in themselves the proper subjects of this right. It is difficult to say that there is any original literary work in the formation of one or two words into a title. The words or phrase chosen may be original in their application to the subject-matter of the work to which they are applied, and it may require much skill and judgment to produce an apt title. But that skill and judgment is generally employed in

[49] *Slingsby* v. *Bradford Patent Truck, etc., Co.* [1905] W.N. 122; [1906] W.N. 51.
[50] *Glyn* v. *Western Feature Film Co.* [1916] 1 Ch. 261; *Baschet* v. *London Illustrated Standard Co.* [1900] 1 Ch. 73.

choosing and selecting from common words and phrases, and not in stringing together words in a novel form.

In the case of *Weldon* v. *Dicks* [51] the plaintiff was the assignee of the copyright in a novel bearing the title "Trial and Triumph." The defendant had published a novel under the title of "Trial and Triumph" at the price of sixpence. The plaintiff claimed an injunction to restrain the defendant from publishing or selling any book or publication under that title, and the injunction was granted by Malins V.-C., though the defendant was in entire ignorance that the title "Trial and Triumph" had been previously used, and though his work was quite distinct in its plot and subject-matter from the plaintiff's book. This case, in so far as it rested upon infringement of copyright, was virtually overruled in a later case.[52] In that case, *Dicks* v. *Yates,*[53] the defendant had published a novel in the *World,* a sixpenny newspaper, with the title "Splendid Misery," in ignorance that that was the title of a novel which had appeared a few years before in the plaintiff's periodical *Every Week,* published at a penny a number. It was, however, proved that many years before the plaintiff's novel was published, another novel had borne the same title. The Court of Appeal, reversing Bacon V.-C., refused the plaintiff an injunction, Jessel M.R. and Lush L.J. on the ground of lack of originality or likelihood of mistake on the part of the public, and James L.J. on the ground that there had been no infringement. "I do not say," said the Master of the Rolls, "that there could not be copyright in a title, as, for instance, in a whole page of title, or something of that kind, requiring invention. However, it is not necessary to decide that. But assuming that there can be copyright in a title, what does this copyright mean? It means the right of multiplying copies of an original work. If you complain that part of your work has been pirated, you must show that that part is original, and if it is not original, you have no copyright. How can the title 'Splendid Misery' be said to be original, when the very same words, for the very same purpose, were used nearly eighty years ago?" Later on, however, he stated that it appeared to him that no authority binding on that court had been produced to show that there could be copyright in such a title as that, and with this opinion James L.J. expressed his concurrence, Lush L.J. desiring to keep the point open.

231 In the case of *Broemel* v. *Meyer* [54] the plaintiff had written a play which she had entitled "Where there's a Will there's a Way," the plot of which turned upon the fortunes of two lovers, whose happiness

51 (1878) 10 Ch.D. 247.
52 *Per* Lindley L.J. in *Licensed Victuallers' Newspaper Co.* v. *Bingham* (1888) 38 Ch.D. 139.
53 (1881) 18 Ch.D. 76.
54 (1912) 29 T.L.R. 148.

depended upon a will, and the word "will" in the title of the play meant testamentary disposition. The defendant was the author of the play entitled "Where there's a Will——," and in that title the word "will" also meant testamentary disposition. The plaintiff contended that the use of these words as the title of a play with the *double entendre* rendered the title an original one, and claimed copyright in it, but Warrington J. held that she could not appropriate the words of a familiar proverb to herself by giving to them a peculiar meaning, and he refused to grant her the injunction.

In *Francis, Day and Hunter, Ltd.* v. *Twentieth Century Fox Corporation, Ltd.*[55] the Privy Council held that the title of a song was not infringed by its use as the title of a film which did not use any other part of the song. Lord Wright said: "The theme of the film is different from that of the song, and their Lordships see no ground in copyright law to justify the appellants' claim to prevent the use by the respondents of these few obvious words, which are too unsubstantial to constitute an infringement, especially when used in so different a connection."

232 In *Ladbroke (Football), Ltd.* v. *William Hill (Football), Ltd.*[56] Lord Hodson stated that neither *Dicks* v. *Yates*[57] nor *Francis, Day and Hunter, Ltd.* v. *Twentieth Century Fox Corporation, Ltd.*[58] supported the proposition that, as a matter of law, copyright cannot subsist in titles. "No doubt," he said, "they will not as a rule be protected, since alone they would not be regarded as a sufficiently substantial part of the book or other copyright document to justify the preventing of copying by others. In any event, there is good authority for the protection of headings in a proper case in *Lamb* v. *Evans*[59] where the headings in question were elaborate and given in each case in English, French, German and Spanish."

It is submitted, therefore, that a title, unless it is sufficiently lengthy to have had labour in construction as well as in choice expended upon it, will not be protected as an original literary work.

Actions for "Passing Off"

233 But titles of books are, in certain circumstances, protected from imitation by means of a "passing-off" action.

The action for "passing off" lies where the defendant has represented to the public that his goods or business are the goods or

[55] [1940] A.C. 112.
[56] [1964] 1 W.L.R. 273 at 286.
[57] *Supra.*
[58] *Supra.*
[59] [1893] 1 Ch. 218.

business of the plaintiff.[60] A defendant may make himself liable to this action by publishing a work under the same title as the plaintiff's,[61] or by publishing a work where title and "get up" so resemble that of the plaintiff as to deceive the public into the belief that it is the plaintiff's work.[62]

234 The general nature of this action was considered in the case of *Draper* v. *Trist*,[63] where it was pointed out that it was not necessary for a plaintiff to prove actual damage, since the law assumed damage to the plaintiff's right of property in the goodwill of his business where "passing off" occurred. There have, in fact, been a number of cases in which publishers of books or periodicals have obtained protection on this ground for the goodwill in the title.[64]

235 In all such cases the plaintiff must prove first that his publication has been in the market long enough to acquire a public reputation,[65] and, secondly, that the title used by the defendant is calculated to deceive the public.[66] A reputation or goodwill can be built up by substantial sales within a short period of time.[67] It is doubtful whether publication in another country without publication here, could amount to a user of the title in this country sufficient to acquire a reputation in the sense material for a passing-off action.[68] Mere intention to deceive is not sufficient, there must be grounds for apprehending actual deception.[69] But it is not necessary to establish that anyone, as a result of the passing off, is induced to deal with the defendant in the mistaken view that he was dealing with the plaintiff; it

60 See *Spalding (A. G.) & Bros.* v. *A. W. Gamage, Ltd.* (1915) 32 R.P.C. 273 and *Clock (The), Ltd.* v. *The Clock House Hotel, Ltd.* (1936) 53 R.P.C. 269; *Brestian* v. *Try* [1958] R.P.C. 161 at 162, 171. See as to goodwill in fictional characters *Conan Doyle* v. *London Mystery Magazine* (1949) 66 R.P.C. 312; *Chaplin* v. *Amador* (1928) 269 *Pacific Reporter* 544 (U.S.); *Patten* v. *Superior Talking Pictures, Inc.* (1934) 8 Fed.Supp. 196 (U.S.); *Lone Ranger, Inc.* v. *Cox* (1942) 124 Fed.Rep. (2d) 650 (U.S.); *Lone Ranger, Inc.* v. *Currey* (1948) 79 Fed.Supp. 190 (U.S.) and *Shaw Bros. (Hong Kong), Ltd.* v. *Golden Harvest (H.K.), Ltd.*, April 1971, (a Hong Kong decision as yet unreported). And see Bulletin of Copyright Society of U.S.A. (1965) Vol. 12, No. 4, p. 210.

61 *Primrose Press Agency Co. (The)* v. *Knowles (M.)* (1885) 2 T.L.R. 404; *Clement* v. *Maddick* (1859) 1 Giff. 98; *Kelly* v. *Hutton* (1867) 3 Ch.App. 703.

62 *Metzler* v. *Wood* (1878) 8 Ch.D. 606; *Spottiswoode* v. *Clark* (1846) 2 Phil. 154; *Reddaway (F.), etc.* v. *Banham (G.), etc.* [1896] A.C. 199; *Lord Byron* v. *Johnston* (1816) 2 Mer. 29; and see *Tavener Rutledge, Ltd.* v. *Spectres, Ltd.* [1959] R.P.C. 83. A useful exposition of the legal propositions relevant to an action for "passing-off" concerned with "get up" is to be found in a Scottish case, *John Haig and Co., Ltd.* v. *Forth Blending Co., Ltd.* (1953) 70 R.P.C. 259.

63 [1939] 3 All E.R. 513.

64 See § 230, *ante*.

65 *Licensed Victuallers' Newspaper Co.* v. *Bingham* (1888) 38 Ch.D. 139; *Oerth A.G.* v. *Bowman (London), Ltd.* [1957] R.P.C. 388.

66 See *Hall* v. *Barrows* (1863) 4 De G.J. & S. 150; *Chappell* v. *Davidson* (1855) 2 K. & J. 123; *cf. Warwick Tyre Co., Ltd.* v. *New Motor, etc., Co., Ltd.* [1910] 1 Ch. 248.

67 *Stannard* v. *Reay* [1967] R.P.C. 589; see as to abandonment of goodwill *Norman Kark Publications, Ltd.* v. *Odhams Press, Ltd.* [1962] 1 W.L.R. 380 and *Ad-Lib Club, Ltd.* v. *Granville* [1971] F.S.R. 1.

68 See *Alain Bernardin et Compagnie* v. *Pavilion Properties, Ltd.* [1967] R.P.C. 581.

69 *Borthwick* v. *The Evening Post* (1888) 37 Ch.D. 449.

is sufficient to show probability of injury to the plaintiff's goodwill.[70] Evidence of mere postal confusion, however, may not be sufficient to show a likelihood of confusion, being merely embarrassment and inconvenience rather than loss of trade.[71] Where there is a close resemblance in general style and arrangement of the contents of the book itself,[72] particularly in the case of a new publication which is alleged to resemble an old publication,[73] or a claim of certain attributes which are known to belong to the original work,[74] or a sudden change from an unobjectionable title, style of publication, and arrangement of contents to a title, style and arrangement more closely resembling the plaintiff's,[75] an intention to deceive may be established. For example, the publishers of a work entitled "My Life and Loves by Frank Harris" obtained an injunction against another firm of publishers who later published an abridged version of the same book, which had been previously published under the title "Frank Harris: My Life and Adventures," under an identical title to the plaintiff's book. It was held the plaintiffs had acquired a distinctive reputation in the title although it was descriptive; that the defendants' publication under a similar title was calculated to deceive the public into buying copies of the defendants' book in the belief that they were copies of the plaintiffs' book; and that the plaintiffs had not lost their right to bring a passing-off action simply because they had granted rights in the book to some other person.[76] However, the fact that the title chosen consists of common words makes it more difficult for a plaintiff to succeed.[77] Thus the plaintiffs who marketed a series of books called "The Pet Library" failed to restrain the defendants from displaying their books on a stand bearing the legend "Ellson's Pet Library," because in the case of common descriptive words comparatively small

[70] *Illustrated Newspapers, Ltd.* v. *Publicity Services (London), Ltd.* (1938) 55 R.P.C. 172.

[71] *Rubber & Technical Press, Ltd.* v *Maclaren & Sons, Ltd.* [1961] R.P.C. 264; *George Outram and Co., Ltd.* v. *The London Evening Newspapers Company, Ltd.* (1910) 27 T.L.R. 231; *Street* v. *Union Bank of Spain and England* (1885) 30 Ch.D. 156; *Scottish Union and National Insurance Co.* v. *Scottish National Insurance Co., Ltd.* (1909) 26 R.P.C. 105 at 110.

[72] *Mack* v. *Petter* (1872) L.R. 14 Eq. 431; *Corns* v. *Griffiths* [1873] W.N. 93; *Norman Kark Publications, Ltd.* v. *Odhams Press, Ltd.* [1962] 1 W.L.R. 380 at 392. *Masson Seeley & Co., Ltd.* v. *Embosotype Manufacturing Co.* (1924) 41 R.P.C. 160 where the catalogue in question was an infringement of copyright; *cf. Crotch* v. *Arnold* [1905–10] Macg.Cop.Cas. 227 where the titles were identical "Cottage Homes of England") but the subject-matter was totally different, as was the price.

[73] *Rubber & Technical Press, Ltd.* v. *Maclaren & Sons, Ltd.* [1961] R.P.C. 264 at 266.

[74] *Chappell* v. *Sheard* (1855) 2 K. & J. 117.

[75] *Corns* v. *Griffiths, supra; Metzler* v. *Wood* (1878) 8 Ch.D. 606; see *Rubber & Technical Press, Ltd.* v. *Maclaren & Sons, Ltd.* [1961] R.P.C. 264.

[76] *W. H. Allen & Co.* v. *Brown Watson, Ltd.* [1965] R.P.C. 191.

[77] *Ridgeway Co. (The)* v. *The Amalgamated Press, Ltd.* (1911) 28 T.L.R. 149; *Ridgeway Co. (The)* v. *Hutchinson* (1923) 40 R.P.C. 335 at 344; *Pearl Cooper, Ltd.* v. *Richmond Hill Press, Ltd.* [1957] R.P.C. 363; *Technical Productions (London), Ltd.* v. *Contemporary Exhibitions & Whittaker (G.)* [1961] R.P.C. 242; and see *Brittain Publishing Co. (London), Ltd.* v. *Trade and Commercial Press, Ltd. (No.* 2) [1957] R.P.C. 271.

differences are accepted as sufficient to avert confusion. Megarry J. remarked that " the success of a claim to monopolise such words as the ' Pet Library ' would be to fence off from commercial employment many phrases compounded of ordinary English words in general use; and I have nothing to persuade me of the justice of authorising such a literary enclosure." [78]

236 Thus where the title is purely descriptive of the contents no passing off can arise by virtue of the use of the title alone unless such title is shown to be distinctive. On the other hand if the title is a fancy title it will be relatively easy to establish a claim. But the difficult cases are where the titles, though descriptive, have an element of fancy.[79]

237 **Examples where injunctions granted.** " The Wonderful Magazine," " The Wonderful Magazine, New Series, Improved." [80] " Minnie," " Minnie Dale." [81] " Minnie," " Minnie, Dear Minnie." [82] " The John Bull and Britannia," " The True Britannia." [83] " London Journal," " Daily London Journal." [84] " Bell's Life," " Penny Bell's Life." [85] " Church and State," " Church and State." [86] " The Decorators and Painters Magazine," " The Decorator." [87] " My Life and Loves by Frank Harris," " My Life and Loves by Frank Harris." [88]

238 **Examples where injunctions refused.** " Magazine of Fiction," " Monthly Magazine of Fiction." [89] " Post Office Directory of the West Riding of Yorkshire," " The Post Office Bradford Directory." [90] " Punch," " Punch and Judy." [91] " Evening Times," " Evening

[78] *The Pet Library (London) Ltd.* v. *Walter Ellson & Son Ltd.* [1968] F.S.R. 359. See also cases on similar descriptive trade names: *Office Cleaning Services Ltd.* v. *Westminster Window and General Cleaners, Ltd.* (1946) 68 R.P.C. 39; *Associated Booking Corporation* v. *Associated Booking Agency* [1964] R.P.C. 372; *Industrial Furnaces, Ltd.* v. *Reaves* [1970] R.P.C. 605 at 625.

[79] *Mathieson* v. *Sir I. Pitman & Sons, Ltd.* (1930) 47 R.P.C. 541; *International Press, Ltd.* v. *Tunnell* [1938] 1 D.L.R. 393 (Can.); *Houghton* v. *Film Booking Offices, Ltd.* (1931) 48 R.P.C. 329; *Legal & General Assurance Society Ltd.* v. *Daniel* [1968] R.P.C. 253.

[80] *Hogg* v. *Kirby* (1803) 8 Ves. 215. In *Hulton Press, Ltd.* v. *White Eagle Youth Holiday Camp, Ltd.* (1951) 68 R.P.C. 126, an injunction was granted to the proprietors of the " Eagle " magazine to prevent the use of the name " White Eagle Youth Holiday Camp " for a children's holiday camp.

[81] *Chappell* v. *Sheard* (1855) 2 K. & J. 117.

[82] *Chappell* v. *Davidson* (1855) 2 K. & J. 123.

[83] *Prowett* v. *Mortimer* (1856) 4 W.R. 519.

[84] *Ingram* v. *Stiff* (1859) 5 Jur. 947.

[85] *Clement* v. *Maddick* (1859) 1 Giff. 98.

[86] *Primrose Press Agency Co. (The)* v. *Knowles (M.)* (1885) 2 T.L.R. 404.

[87] *Dale Reynolds & Co.* v. *Trade Papers Publishing Co.* [1901–04] Macg.Cop.Cas. 32.

[88] *W. H. Allen & Co.* v. *Brown Watson, Ltd.* [1965] R.P.C. 191.

[89] *Stevens (W.), Ltd.* v. *Cassell & Co., Ltd.*, *The Times*, February 7, 1913.

[90] *Kelly* v. *Byles* (1879) 13 Ch.D. 682.

[91] *Bradbury* v. *Beeton* (1869) 18 W.R. 33.

Times." [92] "Morning Post," "Evening Post." [93] "Everybody's Magazine," "Everybody's Weekly." [94] "Adventure," "Hutchinson's Adventure Story Magazine." [95] "How to Appeal against your Rates in the Metropolis," "How to Appeal against your Rates within the Metropolis." [96] "London Weekly Advertiser" and "National Advertiser," "National Weekly." [97] "Sports Car and Lotus Owner," "Sports Cars Illustrated." [98] "Rubber and Plastics Age," "Rubber and Plastics Weekly." [99] "Courier" incorporating "Today," "Today, The New John Bull." [100] "The Field," "The Field and Kennel." [1] "Mainly About People," "People Talked Of." [2] "The Evening Express," "The North Express." [3] "The Pet Library," "Ellson's Pet Library." [4]

239 **Other instances of passing off.** In addition to the protection afforded to authors in respect of titles, there are other instances of the extension of this "passing off" action to the protection of owners of literary and artistic works. The court has restrained a publisher from advertising a new work in such a way as to be calculated to lead the public to believe that such work was the plaintiff's work.[5] In the case of *Samuelson* v. *Producers' Distributing Co., Ltd.*,[6] the owner of the copyright in a dramatic sketch, of which there existed no film version, was granted an injunction to restrain a producer of a film from representing to the public that the film was a film version of the sketch on the ground that such a representation was an injury to the plaintiff's sole right under the Act of 1911 of producing the

[92] *George Outram and Co., Ltd.* v. *The London Evening Newspapers Co., Ltd.* (1910) 27 T.L.R. 231; the plaintiffs' was a Scottish paper and the defendants' a London paper.

[93] *Borthwick* v. *The Evening Post* (1888) 37 Ch.D. 449.

[94] *Ridgeway Co. (The)* v. *The Amalgamated Press, Ltd.* (1911) 28 T.L.R. 149.

[95] *Ridgeway Co. (The)* v. *Hutchinson* (1923) 40 R.P.C. 335.

[96] *Mathieson* v. *Sir I. Pitman & Sons, Ltd.* (1930) 47 R.P.C. 541.

[97] *Brittain Publishing Co. (London), Ltd.* v. *Trade & Commercial Press, Ltd.* [1957] R.P.C. 271.

[98] *Pearl Cooper, Ltd.* v. *Richmond Hill Press, Ltd.* [1957] R.P.C. 363.

[99] *Rubber & Technical Press, Ltd.* v. *Maclaren & Sons, Ltd.* (1961) R.P.C. 264.

[100] *Norman Kark Publications, Ltd.* v. *Odhams Press, Ltd.* [1962] 1 W.L.R. 380.

[1] *Cox* v. *Sports Publishing Co.* [1901–04] Macg.Cop.Cas. 27.

[2] *C. Arthur Pearson, Ltd.* v. *T. P. O'Connor* [1905–10] Macg.Cop.Cas. 43.

[3] *Dillon* v. *Pearson* [1901–04] Macg.Cop.Cas. 17.

[4] *The Pet Library (London), Ltd.* v. *Walter Ellson & Son, Ltd.* [1968] F.S.R. 359.

[5] *Seeley* v. *Fisher* (1841) 11 Sim. 581; *Dr. Barnardo's Homes: National Incorporated Association* v. *Barnardo Amalgamated Industries, Ltd.* (1949) 66 R.P.C. 103.

[6] [1932] 1 Ch. 201. See also *Cheyney* v. *Rialto Productions, Ltd.* [1936–45] Macg. Cop.Cas. 386. In *Menchen* v. *Elite Sales Agency, Ltd.* (*The Times*, December 18, 1912), both plaintiff and defendant had given the title of "The Miracle" to a cinematograph production, and upon an application for an interlocutory injunction the defendant, at the judge's suggestion, agreed to alter his title. In *Elkin & Co.* v. *Francis, Day and Hunter* [1905–10] Macg.Cop.Cas. 294, the defendants were restrained from publishing the "Blue Bird Valse," as calculated to lead to the belief that it was the music of an opera of that name which was published by the plaintiffs; see also *Flamland* v. *Société Radio-Canada* (1967) 53 C.P.R. 217.

sketch in film form. But in *O'Gorman* v. *Paramount Film Service, Ltd.*,[7] it was held, distinguishing the *Samuelson* case, that the plaintiff, as author of a play called "Irish and Proud of it" produced during the years 1914 to 1934, was not entitled to an injunction in respect of a film of the same title, since there was no evidence at the date of the action that the plaintiff contemplated producing a film version of his play. On the other hand, in the case of *Francis, Day and Hunter Ltd.* v. *Twentieth Century Fox Corporation Ltd.*,[8] the Privy Council decided that no case of passing off was made out where the title of a song was used as the title of a film, on the ground that the thing said to be passed off must resemble the thing for which it is passed off, and the song and the film were incapable of comparison in any reasonable sense. Again in *McCulloch* v. *L. A. May (Produce Distributors), Ltd.*[9] it was held that the broadcaster "Uncle Mac" was not entitled to complain of the sale of Puffed Wheat under the name "Uncle Mac's Puffed Wheat" on the ground that there was no common field of activity in which, however remotely, both the plaintiff and the defendant were engaged. The decision in *McCulloch* v. *L. A. May (Produce Distributors) Ltd.* has, however, been criticised in the High Court of Australia in *Henderson and Another* v. *Radio Corporation Pty., Ltd.*[10] where it was held that it was not necessary, in order to establish passing off, that there should be an actual or potential area in which the activities of the plaintiff and the defendant conflicted. The plaintiffs in that case were well-known professional dancers and the defendants had, without their consent, published, on the sleeve of a gramophone record, a photograph of the plaintiffs dancing so as to represent that the plaintiffs had sponsored or recommended the record. It was held that the defendants had thereby wrongfully appropriated the plaintiffs' professional reputation: "In our view once it is proved that A is falsely representing his goods as the goods of B or his business to be the same as or connected with the business of B, the wrong of passing off has been established and B is entitled to relief." [10a] The essence of the wrong lies in the fact that the plaintiffs had acquired a reputation which placed them in a position to earn a fee for any recommendation which they might be disposed to give and the defendants had for their own commercial advantage appropriated the benefit of that recommendation without payment for the value of it. The authority of the case is somewhat weakened

7 [1937] 2 All E.R. 113.

8 [1940] A.C. 112.

9 [1947] 2 All E.R. 845; *Marathon Oil Co.* v. *Marathon Shipping Co., Ltd.* [1968] R.P.C. 443.

10 [1969] R.P.C. 218. *Cf. Corelli* v. *Wall* [1905–10] Macg.Cop.Cas. 4 and *Palmer* v. *The National Sporting Club Ltd.* [1905–10] Macg.Cop.Cas. 55 where injunctions to restrain the unauthorised publication of a person's likeness were refused; see also *Totalizator Agency Board* v. *Turf News Pty. Ltd.* [1967] V.R. 605. The case of *Corelli* v. *Wall, supra*, was not followed in *Krouse* v. *Chrysler* (1970) 12 D.L.R. (3d) 465 (Can), which concerned a claim for invasion of privacy.

10a *Ibid. per* Evatt J. at 234.

by the finding that the activities of the parties were, in any event, competitive in a broad sense.

240 **"Nom de plume."** Where a common field of activity is established, an author or artist who has acquired a reputation under a *nom de plume* is entitled to protect it by a "passing off" action.[11] In several cases, the point has arisen whether an employee, who has acquired a reputation under a *nom de plume,* is entitled to use it after the employment has been discontinued.[12] The effect of these decisions seems to be that, in the absence of some clear term to the contrary, the name is the name of the individual for whom the reputation has been acquired and that he alone is entitled to use it after the severance of his relationship with the employer.

241 Thus, the general principle of applying the action in "passing off" to personal goodwill of authors and artists is now well established. The limited nature of the protection afforded in this action has been well illustrated in the recent case of *Gordon Fraser Gallery, Ltd.* v. *Tatt* [13] where the court refused to grant an injunction to the plaintiff, who published a distinctive style of greetings card, restraining the defendants from offering for sale cards bearing a distinct resemblance to the plaintiff's. The defendants' cards were not copies of, but were obviously derived from, the plaintiff's cards. The court held that merely imitating the style of an artist was a difficult ground on which to base a claim for passing off. Similarity of artistic style and content, not amounting to breach of copyright, were not sufficiently defined features on which to base an allegation that somebody would be persuaded to buy the defendants' goods in the belief that they were the plaintiff's goods.

As has been seen from the *Henderson* case, *supra,* this area of the law is being expanded by judicial decision to adapt to changing economic and social conditions. For example, it has been recently held [14] that the law of passing off has been expanded to cover aspects of unfair trading which do not give rise to deception or confusion. It is a wrong, actionable at the suit of a person thereby injured, to sell goods under an unlawful trade description.[14a] In this new fangled tort of "unlawful competition" the concepts of confusion and deception are irrelevant. Thus it is actionable for a person

[11] *Marengo* v. *Daily Sketch, etc., Ltd.* [1948] 1 All E.R 406; *Serville* v. *Constance* [1954] 1 W.L.R. 487.

[12] *Maitland-Davidson* v. *The Sphere and Tatler, Ltd.* [1917–23] Macg.Cop.Cas. 128; *Hines* v. *Winnick* [1947] Ch. 708; *Modern Fiction, Ltd.* v. *Fawcett* [1948–49] Macg.Cop.Cas. 22; *Forbes* v. *Kemsley Newspapers, Ltd.* [1951] 2 T.L.R. 656; *Landa* v. *Greenberg* (1908) 24 T.L.R. 441, apparently decided on the ground that the defendants were using the name in a manner calculated to deceive the public.

[13] [1966] R.P.C. 505.

[14] *Bollinger* v. *Costa Brava Wine Co.* [1960] R.P.C. 16, [1961] R.P.C. 116; *Vine Products, Ltd.* v. *Mackenzie & Co., Ltd.* [1969] R.P.C. 1; *John Walker & Sons, Ltd.* v. *Henry Ost & Co., Ltd.* [1970] R.P.C. 489; *Shaw Bros. (Hong Kong), Ltd.* v. *Golden Harvest (H.K.), Ltd.*, April 1971 (Hong Kong).

[14a] See also Trade Descriptions Act, 1968.

to call his alcoholic product "sherry" without further qualification if it does not come from the Jerez district of Spain.[14]

This new tort may cover cases where there has been previously held to be no wrong. Thus it has been held in the past that a representation that an old work of an author was a new work of that author does not give a cause of action,[15] and that a representation that the defendant's work had some quality possessed by the plaintiff's work would not give a cause of action unless the quality was unique.[16]

It will be observed from the foregoing that, although an author probably has no copyright in his title and cannot restrain its use in all cases, he has a valuable right, in that he may be able to prevent its use upon any similar publication, and that this right is akin to that in a trade mark.[17]

Statutory Remedies

242 The Copyright Act, 1956, has created new statutory remedies to deal with matters in the nature of "passing off." These, however, are of somewhat limited character. The Copyright Committee[18] considered Article 6 *bis* of the Brussels Convention which dealt with the protection of what is known as the author's "droit moral" but did not consider that any substantial alteration in the law was necessary.

243 **Affixing non-author's name as author.** These provisions are contained in section 43 of the Act of 1956, and restrict the doing of various acts in the United Kingdom. The primary provision restricts any person, without licence, from inserting or affixing the name of another in or on a work of which that other is not the author, or in or on a reproduction of such a work, in such a way as to imply that the other person is the author of the work.[19] This provision applies to literary, dramatic, musical or artistic works, but not to the other classes of works protected by that Act, *e.g.*, sound recordings and films.[20] "Name" is defined as including initials or a monogram[21] and presumably would include a pseudonym where such pseudonym would be recognised by the public as meaning a particular author or artist. The section further restricts the publication, selling, letting for hire by way of trade, offering or exposing for sale or hire or by way of trade, exhibiting in public a work or reproductions of a work or the distribu-

15 *Harris & Co.* v. *Warren and Philipps* [1917–23] Macg.Cop.Cas. 44.
16 *Cambridge University Press* v. *University Tutorial Press, Ltd.* (1928) 45 R.P.C. 335.
17 *Longman (T. N.)* v. *Tripp (J.)* (1805) 2 Bos. & P. 67; *Ex p. Foss* (1858) 2 De G. & J. 230; *Bradbury* v. *Dickens* (1859) 27 Beav. 53.
18 Cmd. 8662, paras. 219–226.
19 Copyright Act, 1956, s. 43 (2) (*a*). See *Humphreys* v. *Thompson & Co., Ltd.* [1905–10] Macg.Cop.Cas. 148.
20 s. 43 (1).
21 s. 43 (11).

tion of reproductions of a work on which a name is so inserted or affixed if, to the offender's knowledge, the person named is not the author of the work,[22] It will be observed that this is a somewhat narrow form of restriction and only arises where the name is affixed and not where the work or reproductions of the work are otherwise passed off as being those of a particular author. On the other hand they would appear to apply whether or not there is a common field of activity.

244 **Performing in public or broadcasting work of non-author as work of claimant.** In the case of literary, dramatic, musical or artistic works a breach of duty is committed if the work is performed in public or broadcast as being the work of an author if, to the offender's knowledge, that person is not the author of the work.[23]

245 **Publishing, selling or distributing reproductions of artistic work of non-author as work of claimant.** In the case of an artistic work in which copyright subsists, the restrictions of the section are contravened by a person who publishes, or sells, or lets for hire, or by way of trade offers or exposes for sale or hire, or by way of trade exhibits in public a reproduction of the work as being a reproduction made by the author of the work, or distributes reproductions of the work as being reproductions made by the author of the work, if such reproduction or reproductions was or were to his knowledge not made by the author.[24]

All the preceding provisions, other than the last-mentioned provision in regard to artistic works, apply whether or not copyright subsists in the work, and apply after the author's death during a period of twenty years from such death.[25] They further apply where, contrary to the fact, a work is represented as being an adaptation of the work of another person.[26] " Adaptation " is defined in section 2 (6) of the Act of 1956 and refers to dramatisations, translations, cartoon versions and arrangements of music. It is submitted that the provisions of section 49 (1) must apply to the preceding provisions, with the result that, if a substantial part of the work to which the name of the claimant is affixed is not the work of the claimant, the section will apply.

246 **Publication, etc., of artistic works altered after author parted with possession as unaltered work of the author.** In addition to the foregoing matters, which all relate to acts in the nature of passing off,

[22] s. 43 (2) (*b*) and (*c*). See Copyright Act, 1956, Seventh Sched., para. 32.
[23] Copyright Act, 1956, s. 43 (2) (*d*).
[24] s. 43 (6).
[25] s. 43 (5).
[26] s. 43 (3).

the section provides, in the case of artistic works, a remedy akin to that which was contained in section 7 of the Fine Arts Copyright Act, 1862, a section which was left unrepealed by the Act of 1911, but is repealed by the Act of 1956. The wrongful act is committed if an artistic work has been altered after the author has parted with possession of it and there is published, sold, let for hire, or by way of trade offered or exposed for sale or hire, the work as so altered or a reproduction of the work as so altered with a representation that it is the unaltered work or a reproduction of the unaltered work of the author, and the offender knows that it is not the unaltered work or a reproduction of the unaltered work of the author.[27] The offence may be committed whether or not the author retains the copyright and up to twenty years from his death.[28]

Section 7 of the Act of 1862 made it an offence, after the sale of the work, if it had been altered by addition or otherwise, for any person knowingly to sell or publish such work, or any copies thereof, so altered, or any part thereof, as or for the unaltered work of such author.

247 **Decisions under Fine Arts Copyright Act, 1862.** There were certain decisions on the construction of section 7 of that Act and it is thought that they may be to some extent relevant to the present section, section 43 of the Copyright Act, 1956.

In the case of *Carlton Illustrators* v. *Coleman & Co., Ltd.*,[29] the plaintiff was an artist who was the author of a fine line drawing made for the purpose of being used as an advertisement in newspapers and periodicals by the defendants, and the copyright was vested in them. The defendants produced and published, without the consent of the plaintiff, on public hoardings throughout the country, in the form of large coloured posters, a reproduction of the plaintiff's drawing, and, for this purpose, they caused various alterations to be made in the original drawing by someone other than the plaintiff, leaving the plaintiff's signature on such posters. Channell J. held that an offence had been committed under the fourth clause of section 7 of the Act of 1862, although no suggestion of fraud was made. In dealing with the question of what would be an "alteration" of the work within the clause, the learned judge pointed out that there might be some alterations which would not come within the clause. He did not think that an alteration in the artist's signature, for instance would have been within that clause, for that would have been an alteration immaterial with reference to the object for which the clause was passed. "To come within the enactment," he said, "an alteration must be a material alteration, having regard to the object with which

[27] Copyright Act, 1956, s. 43 (4).
[28] s. 43 (5).
[29] [1911] 1 K.B. 771.

the enactment was passed; and that which would be material in that sense would be some alteration which might affect the credit and reputation of the artist. To my mind, that is what is prohibited. I do not think it would be necessary to find in any particular case the alteration had affected the character and reputation of the artist; it is sufficient if the alteration is of such a character that it might affect his character and reputation. Applying that principle, I think that this case is brought within the clause." [30] He then dealt with the question whether a change in the colouring of a picture would be such an "alteration" as to be an offence under the clause, and expressed the opinion that that must depend upon the facts of each case. He thought that if the drawing was coloured originally, the putting of different colours would obviously be an alteration; but that the mere addition of colour to a drawing, which originally had none, would not necessarily be an alteration, although in the majority of cases it probably would be so.[31]

248 The work must be sold as and for the unaltered work of the author. It has been decided that this means that there must be a selling or publishing under circumstances in which, to the knowledge of the seller or publisher, there is made, either expressly or by necessary implication, a representation that the author is the author of the work sold or published in the form in which it is sold and published. The necessary implication does not arise merely from the fact that some persons might know who was the author of the work sold from the style of the work.[32]

249 **Remedy an action for breach of statutory duty not criminal proceedings.** The provisions of section 43 of the Act of 1956 were, as has been seen, in part in replacement of section 7 of the Act of 1862, which contained penalties for breach. The section of the Act of 1956 provides that the restrictions imposed thereby are not to be enforceable by criminal proceedings, but to be actionable at the suit of the person affected or, if he is dead, at the suit of his personal representatives as a breach of statutory duty.[33] Any damages recovered by personal representatives are to devolve as part of the author's estate as if the right of action had subsisted and had been vested in the author immediately before his death.[34] The corresponding provision of the Act of 1862 entitled the author to obtain an injunction to restrain future breaches of the clause [35] and presumably this is equally

30 [1911] 1 K.B. at p. 780.
31 At p. 780.
32 *Preston* v. *Raphael Tuck, etc., Ltd.* [1926] Ch. 667.
33 Copyright Act, 1956, s. 43 (8); see *Wood* v. *Butterworth* [1901–04] Macg.Cop. Cas. 16.
34 s. 43 (9).
35 Fine Arts Copyright Act, 1862 (25 & 26 Vict. c. 68), s. 8.

the case under the present Act. It is further provided that nothing under the section now in question is to derogate from any right of action or other remedy in proceedings instituted otherwise than by virtue of this section, provided that this is not to be construed as requiring any damages recovered by virtue of this section to be disregarded in assessing damages in proceedings instituted otherwise than by virtue of this section and arising out of the same transaction.[36] Presumably, therefore, in a suitable case, a plaintiff could maintain an action for passing off at common law as well as an action under this section, but the damages recoverable would not be cumulative.

250 **Provisions apply to acts done in relation to two persons.** The section further provides that it is to apply with respect to acts done in relation to two or more persons in connection with the same work.[37] This presumably covers misrepresentations as to ownership in the case of joint works or works containing material of more than one author.

8.—ACTIONS FOR " MALICIOUS FALSEHOOD "

251 **Nature of action.** Actions of this type have received many appellations in the course of time, for instance " slander of title," " slander of goods," " injurious falsehood," but the description " malicious falsehood " is used in the Defamation Act, 1952,[38] as a comprehensive definition for such actions.

An action will lie for malicious falsehood where there has been a malicious and false statement, written or oral, made to some third party about, for instance, a person's business or his goods.[39] A material omission from a statement which would create an erroneous impression may itself justify a finding of falsity.[39a] Claims based upon malicious falsehood sometimes arise in the fields of literature or art and, when they do so, are often the reverse of the action for passing-off. If a publisher publishes the work of the unknown author A under the name of the well-known writer B, this could be the subject of a passing-off action at the suit of B. But if the publication is made with the approval of B and without the consent of A, because A has produced a clever book which the publisher thinks will sell better under B's name, the only action open to A is for malicious falsehood. His damage is loss of reputation, but his difficulty is to prove malice unless, as suggested below, an intent to deceive the public is sufficient malice. The editor recalls a case, which was not reported, in which a translator obtained damages against a publisher

[36] Copyright Act, 1956, s. 43 (10).
[37] s. 43 (7).
[38] 15 & 16 Geo. 6 and 1 Eliz. 2, c. 66, s. 3.
[39] *Ratcliffe* v. *Evans* [1892] 2 Q.B. 524 at 527 and 532: And see *Eothen Films, Ltd.* v. *Industrial & Commercial Education—Macmillan, Ltd.* [1966] F.S.R. 356.
[39a] *Pfizer Corporation* v. *D.D.S.A. Pharmaceuticals, Ltd.* [1965] R.P.C. 8 at 14.

in an action so constituted for loss of reputation because the translation was attributed to someone else. The right "to claim authorship" was one of the rights conferred by Article 6 *bis* of the Brussels Convention now Article 6 *bis* of the Stockholm Convention. It is understood that the United Kingdom ratified the Brussels Convention and the previous Rome Convention on the basis that this right exists at common law in England, and this view was expressed by the 1952 Copyright Committee,[40] but it is difficult to see what right to claim authorship exists at common law except in so far as the action now under discussion applies.[41]

252 **Whether necessary to prove damage.** Before the Defamation Act, 1952, it was always necessary for a plaintiff to show, in addition, that his material interests had been damaged, but, if the statement was intended or reasonably likely to produce, and in the ordinary course of things did produce, a general loss of business as distinct from the loss of particular known customers, evidence of such general decline of business was admissible and sufficient to support the action.[42] However, the Act now provides that it is not necessary to allege, or prove, special damage in such actions in certain circumstances. These are where, either the words upon which the action is founded are calculated to cause pecuniary damage to the plaintiff and are published in writing or other permanent form (including the broadcasting of words by means of wireless telegraphy), or where such words are calculated to cause pecuniary damage to the plaintiff in respect of any office, profession, calling, trade or business held or carried on by him at the time of the publication.[43] Damages can only be recovered for actual or probable money loss, and not for injured feelings.[44]

253 **Examples.** Thus a plaintiff succeeded where a statement had been published in a newspaper by the defendant importing that the plaintiff had ceased to carry on his business [45]; also, where the defendants had falsely stated that they were selling the plaintiff's hairdriers at cost price [46]; similarly where the plaintiff was tenant of certain premises for the purposes of his motor tyre business, the defendant being his landlord, and the defendant informed the tyre makers that the plaintiff's tenancy had ceased [47]; and where the plaintiff company's production of a play was falsely described by the defendants as a

40 Cmnd. 8662, paras. 219–226.
41 See § 1131, *post*.
42 *Ratcliffe* v. *Evans, supra,* at pp. 528 and 533.
43 Defamation Act, 1952, s. 3 (1).
44 *Fielding* v. *Variety Incorporated* [1967] 2 Q.B. 841.
45 *Ratcliffe* v. *Evans, supra*; *Plant Location International A.S.B.L.* v. *Yaseen* [1964] R.P.C. 345.
46 *Rima Electric, Ltd.* v. *Rolls Razor, Ltd.* [1964] F.S.R. 138.
47 *Joyce* v. *Motor Surveys, Ltd.* [1948] Ch. 252.

"disastrous flop."[47a] It would also be actionable if a person wrongly alleged that the sale of copies of a work in any form would be an infringement of that person's copyright.[48] However, there is not under the Copyright Act, 1956, as under the Patents Act, 1949, in respect of patents[49] and under the Registered Design Act, 1949, in respect of registered designs,[50] a statutory remedy against any person threatening any other person with proceedings for infringement of copyright.

254 **Meaning of "malice."** The most difficult aspect of this type of action is the question of malice in view of the various interpretations thereof given by the courts on different occasions. Thus, in one case[51] it was said to be "without just cause or excuse." But, in a later case,[52] it was said "'Maliciously,' not in the sense of illegally, but in the sense of being made with some indirect or dishonest motive. Honest belief in an unfounded claim is not malice; but the nature of the unfounded claim may be evidence that there was not an honest belief in it. It may be so unfounded that the particular fact that it is put forward may be evidence that it is not honestly believed." More recently it was said[53] that it meant the wilful and intentional doing of damage without just occasion or excuse. On the other hand, the making of careless statements, believing them to be true, and without any indirect motive, and without any intention of injuring the plaintiff, is not malicious.[54] And statements merely "puffing" a person's goods, that is, saying that they are better than another's, are not actionable, unless, possibly, where it was done intentionally to injure the other and maliciously and falsely.[55]

255 A useful summary of the position was given by Stable J. in the case of *Wilts United Dairies, Ltd.* v. *Thomas Robinson Sons & Co., Ltd.*,[56] a decision after the Defamation Act, 1952. In that case it was alleged that the defendants, knowing what they were doing, purchased

47a *Fielding* v. *Variety Incorporated* [1967] 2 Q.B. 841.

48 *Dicks* v. *Brooks* (1880) 15 Ch.D. 22 at 40. *Cf. Mackay* v. *Edwardes* [1905–10] Macg.Cop.Cas. 69.

49 12, 13 & 14 Geo. 6, c. 87, s. 65.

50 12, 13 & 14 Geo. 6, c. 88, s. 26.

51 *Royal Baking Powder Co. (The)* v. *Wright Crossley & Co.* (1901) 18 R.P.C. 95 at 99.

52 *Greers, Ltd.* v. *Pearman & Corder, Ltd.* (1922) 39 R.P.C. 406 at 417.

53 *Joyce* v. *Motor Surveys, Ltd.* [1948] Ch. 252 at 254; *Plant Location International A.S.B.L.* v. *Yaseen* [1964] R.P.C. 345.

54 *Balden* v. *Shorter* [1933] Ch. 427 at 431; *Mackay* v. *Edwardes* [1905–10] Macg. Cop.Cas. 69; *Ucan Products Ltd.* v. *Hilti (Great Britain), Ltd.* [1968] F.S.R. 248.

55 *White* v. *Mellin* [1895] A.C. 154 at 164 and 165; and see *Hubbuck & Sons, Ltd.* v. *Wilkinson, etc., Ltd.* [1899] 1 Q.B. 86 at 94; *Lyne* v. *Nicholls* (1906) 23 T.L.R. 86 and s. 3 of the Defamation Act, 1952.

56 [1957] R.P.C. 220 at 237; affirmed on appeal [1958] R.P.C. 94, though the question of malicious falsehood was not specifically dealt with by the Court of Appeal. See also *London Ferro-Concrete Co., Ltd. (The)* v. *Justicz* (1951) 68 R.P.C. 261 at 265.

a large quantity of the plaintiffs' "British Maid" tinned condensed milk, which they knew was old stock and stale stock, and put that milk into circulation through various wholesalers and retailers as being the normal standard of "British Maid" milk. The plaintiffs complained that that was an injurious falsehood, or alternatively or additionally that it was a passing-off of milk as being milk of the current production, milk that had, in the course of time, been relegated to a class of old or stale milk. The learned judge held that there had been such passing-off and that there was injurious falsehood, and, after reviewing the decisions on the meaning of "malice" said, "As I understand the law it is this, that if you publish a defamatory statement about a man's goods which is injurious to him, honestly believing that it is true, your object being your own advantage and no detriment to him, you obviously are not liable. If you publish a statement which turns out to be false but which you honestly believe to be true, but you publish that statement, not for the purpose of protecting your own interests and achieving some advantage to yourself, but for the purpose of doing him harm, and it transpires, contrary to your belief, that the statement that you believed to be true has turned out to be false, notwithstanding the bona fides of your belief because the object you had in mind was to injure him and not to advantage yourself, you would be liable for an injurious falsehood.

"The third proposition which I derive from the cases is this, that if you publish an injurious falsehood which you know to be false, albeit that your only object is your own advantage and with no intention or desire to injure the person in relation to whose goods the falsehood is published, then provided that it is clear from the nature of the falsehood that it is intrinsically injurious—I say 'intrinsically,' meaning not deliberately aimed with intent to injure but as being inherent in the statement itself, the defendant is responsible, the malice consisting in the fact that what he published he knew to be false."

256 It is thought that "knew to be false" may be too wide, but that, if the defendant has made a false representation with intent to defraud a third party or the public, the plaintiff can rely upon such false representation so made as evidence of a dishonest motive.

[The next paragraph is 261]

CHAPTER 6

THE TERM OF COPYRIGHT

261 **What is a fair term for copyright?** The proper period of copyright has long been a matter of controversy. Some have contended that the period ought, in the interests of literature, to be a very short one; others urge, in the same interests, that it ought to be perpetual.

Those who argue in favour of a restricted period for copyright speak of it as a monopoly [1]; whilst upholders of copyright in perpetuity speak of the author's right to prevent others multiplying copies of his work as a right of property. In truth, the controversy is not one that can be decided by a mere phrase, but by a consideration of what protection an author can reasonably demand to ensure an adequate return for his labours, it being generally admitted that literature cannot, in these days, be expected to flourish in a country possessing lax, or insufficient, copyright laws.

It is sometimes argued that the existence of the copyright laws militates against cheap literature, but it is exceedingly doubtful whether this argument is sound. Complaint can hardly be made that books are not cheap enough at the present day, and this may be said, not only of books the copyright of which has run out, but of those which are still the subject of copyright. Indeed a publisher may think it worth while to bring out a cheap edition of a work of which he is secure of a monopoly in the market for some considerable period, but could not afford to do so if he ran the risk of other cheap editions of the same work being brought out by other publishers. At the same time, it seems proper that some period should be put to copyright, at least in published works, since it is unreasonable to give to the remote successors of the author, long after his death, a monopoly in what has in fact been made public; moreover, the practical difficulty of tracing title after a long period to a kind of property of which there can be no physical possession renders undue protraction of the period of protection undesirable.

262 **The present period of protection.** At the conference of the Powers held at Berlin in the year 1907 for the purpose of considering what modifications ought to be made in the Berne Convention,[2] it was decided that the minimum period of protection accorded to an author should be during his life and for a period of fifty years after his death. This appears to be a reasonable period, and it was adopted by the

[1] As to how far this is correct, see *ante*, §§ 4 and 5.
[2] See *post*, " International Copyright," Part V, Chap. 24

British Copyright Act, 1911, for all works, with certain minor exceptions.[3] The present law has, moreover, the very considerable advantage over the law prior to 1911, that the date of publication has—save in the excepted cases, which will be dealt with later on—no bearing upon the determination of copyright protection. Under the law prior to 1911, which gave an alternative period of copyright for literary works, either for the life of the author and seven years after his death or a gross period of forty-two years from the date of publication, whichever should be the longer,[4] the works of the same author were liable to fall into the public domain at different times; but since 1911 all the works of the same author will—save in the excepted cases—fall into the public domain at one and the same time, namely, fifty years after his death. Furthermore, proof of the date of death is generally much easier to secure than proof of date of first publication.

263 **Brussels Convention.** The Brussels Convention, while maintaining the standard period of fifty years from the death of the author, proposed, with the object of removing any uncertainty which might otherwise arise through difficulty in determining the precise date of death or other event, that the term of protection should always be deemed to begin on January 1, of the year following the event.[5] The Stockholm Convention follows the Brussels Convention on this matter. This procedure has been adopted in the Act of 1956.

264 **Universal Copyright Convention.** The Universal Copyright Convention of 1951 provided that the Convention States should give to works of Convention nationals, or first published in Convention States, protection for the period given to their own nationals, but in any event a minimum of twenty-five years.[6] As this minimum is less than that required by the Brussels Convention, this country in formulating terms of protection had regard to the latter Convention.

265 **The Act of 1956.** The Copyright Act of 1956 provides, in sections 2 (3) and 3 (4), for a normal period of protection for literary, dramatic, musical and artistic works lasting until the end of the period of fifty years from the end of the calendar year in which the author died.

266 **Special periods.** But the Act of 1956 provides special periods in respect of (1) photographs, (2) sound recordings, (3) cinematograph films, (4) published editions, (5) broadcasts, (6) government publications, (7) joint works, (8) posthumous works, and (9) anonymous and pseudonymous works.

[3] Copyright Act, 1911, s. 3.
[4] *Ante*, § 32.
[5] See *post*, "International Copyright," Part V, Chap 24
[6] *Ibid.*

The first five of these classes of works involve in their creation an element of industrial, as distinct from literary or artistic ability, and it has generally been felt that a shorter term is therefore appropriate. Moreover, their creation is not conveniently referable to any ascertainable author. The term of copyright in works of joint authorship, cinematograph films, sound recordings and broadcasts is dealt with in the separate chapters dealing with these classes of works.[7] The term in published editions has already been referred to in a previous chapter.[8]

267 **Photographs.** The period of protection for photographs under the Copyright Act of 1911 was fifty years from the making of the original negative from which the photograph was directly or indirectly derived.[9] And in substance this period is preserved in the case of photographs taken before the commencement of the Act of 1956, since paragraph 2 of the Seventh Schedule to that Act provides that, in relation to a photograph taken before the commencement of that Act, copyright shall continue to subsist until the end of the period of fifty years from the end of the calendar year in which the photograph was taken. The only difference is that the end of the calendar year is prescribed for the reasons already mentioned and the expression "taking of the photograph" is used, rather than "making of a negative." Possibly the making of the negative referred to actual development and not taking the photograph, but the object of the change would seem to be that modern photography does not necessarily involve the use of a negative at all.

268 The Act of 1956 provides a different period of protection for photographs taken after the commencement of that Act. By section 3 (4) (*b*) of that Act it is provided that the copyright in a photograph shall continue to subsist until the end of the period of fifty years from the end of the calendar year in which the photograph is first published. There is therefore conferred on photographs a perpetual copyright until publication and it is only in the case of published photographs that a limited term is given, namely, fifty years from publication. By section 49 (2) (*a*) and (*c*) of the Act of 1956, publication consists in the issue of reproductions of the work to the public, but the exhibition of an artistic work is not publication. It should be observed that publication does not involve the issue of copies for value and the general nature of publication has been discussed in an earlier chapter.[10]

[7] See *post*, Part III, Chaps. 14, 16, 17 and 18.
[8] *Ante*, § 223.
[9] Copyright Act, 1911, s. 21.
[10] *Ante*, § 66 *et seq.*

269 **Government works.** By section 39 (1) (2) and (3) of the Act of 1956, a copyright in literary, dramatic, musical and artistic works made by or under the direction or control of Her Majesty or a Government Department is vested in the Crown. In the case of literary, dramatic or musical works, the copyright is perpetual until publication and, after publication, continues until fifty years from the end of the calendar year in which the work was first published.

In the case of engravings or photographs, copyright subsists until first publication and then for fifty years from the end of the calendar year of first publication.[11] It will again be observed that exhibition of an artistic work is not publication.[12] In the case of other artistic works, however, copyright expires at the end of fifty years from the making of the work without regard to whether the work is published or not.[13]

In the case of photographs made before the commencement of the Act of 1956, copyright, however, will subsist for fifty years from the making of the work whether published or not.[14] This may involve a change in the term of copyright of such works because, while under section 21 of the Act of 1911 the term of copyright in photographs was fifty years from their making, that in all Government publications, under section 18 of that Act, was fifty years from first publication.

The term of copyright in Government cinematograph films and sound recordings is the same as in other works of this nature which will be dealt with in the chapters on these subjects.[15]

270 **Anonymous and pseudonymous works.** Since the term of copyright is normally fixed by reference to the date of death of the author, the provisions of Article 15 of the Brussels Convention,[15a] which are directed to securing that an author can, if he desires it, preserve his anonymity, create a practical difficulty.[16] It is accordingly provided in paragraph 1 of the Second Schedule to the Copyright Act, 1956, that where the first publication of a literary, dramatic, musical or artistic work, other than a photograph, is anonymous or pseudonymous, the term of copyright, in lieu of being fixed by reference to the date of the death of the author, is to subsist until the end of the period of fifty years from the end of the calendar year in which the work was first published. But it is further provided, in paragraph 2 of the same Schedule, that this shall not apply in the case of a work if, at any time before the end of the period mentioned, it is possible for a person,

[11] Copyright Act, 1956, s. 39 (4), proviso.
[12] s. 49 (2) (*a*).
[13] s. 39 (4).
[14] Sched. VII, para. 30.
[15] See *post*, Part III, Chaps. 16 and 17.
[15a] See Article 15 of the Stockholm Convention.
[16] See *post*, § 1111.

without previous knowledge of the facts, to ascertain the identity of the author by reasonable inquiry. As in most cases it will be in the interest of the author or his representatives to extend the time of copyright, if willing to reveal his identity, it is presumed that the simplest way of complying with this procedure will be for the publisher to disclose the identity of the author if asked. Obviously, if a publisher is willing to disclose this fact, this is a reasonable inquiry, which would comply with the paragraph.

271 **What are anonymous and pseudonymous works?** The last provisions also, in effect, define what is meant by "anonymous or pseudonymous works." They mean any work where no name is given on the work sufficient for a reasonable person to identify the author. Thus, in some cases, a publication under initials or a pseudonym might not constitute a pseudonymous work because it was a matter of common knowledge that these initials or words represented a particular author.

Since there are no relevant transitional provisions, these provisions appear to apply to all works, whether published before or after the commencement of the Copyright Act, 1956.

For provisions in regard to joint works, where the works are anonymous or pseudonymous, reference should be made to a separate chapter.[17]

272 **Posthumous literary, dramatic and musical works.** If a literary, dramatic or musical work in which copyright subsists has not, before the death of the author, been published, performed in public, or broadcast, and no device recording the work has been offered for sale to the public, copyright will subsist until the end of fifty years from the end of the calendar year which includes the earliest occasion on which one of these acts is done.[18] The publication, performance in public, broadcasting, or offering for sale of a recording device of an adaptation of a work will bring this provision into operation,[19] where adaptation means, in the case of a non-dramatic work, a dramatic version thereof, in the case of a dramatic work, a non-dramatic version thereof, in the case of a literary or dramatic work, a translation or a picture-version thereof and, in the case of a musical work, an arrangement or transcription thereof.[20]

273 **Posthumous artistic works**. In the case of an engraving not published before the death of the author, copyright will continue to subsist until the end of a period of fifty years from the end of the calendar year in which the work is first published.[21] But in the case

[17] *Post*, § 699.
[18] Copyright Act, 1956, s. 2 (3).
[19] s. 2 (4).
[20] s. 2 (6).
[21] s. 3 (4) (*a*).

of other artistic works, the copyright therein, whether they are published or unpublished, expires fifty years from the end of the calendar year in which the author died.[22]

274 **Pre-Act posthumous works.** Again, there are no relevant transitional provisions, so that the foregoing provisions appear to apply to works in existence at the commencement of the Act of 1956 as well as to new works. These do not differ substantially from the similar provisions contained in section 17 (1) of the Copyright Act, 1911, save that the issue of records of a work may not have constituted publication of the work under that Act.

275 **Compulsory licences.** The power to grant compulsory licences conferred by section 4 of the Copyright Act, 1911, is not repeated in the Act of 1956. It had never in fact been used and was inconsistent with the Brussels Convention and its repeal was recommended by the 1951 Copyright Committee.

276 **Compulsory right to reproduce on payment of royalties.** The Copyright Act, 1956, has also not repeated the provisions of section 3 of the Copyright Act, 1911, giving power to reproduce for sale, on royalty terms, any work, after the expiration of twenty-five or, in the case of pre-1911 works, thirty years from the date of the death of the author. This provision, again, was inconsistent with the Brussels Convention and its continuance was not recommended by the Copyright Committee. However, it is provided by paragraph 9 (1) of the Seventh Schedule to the Act of 1956 that, where a person has, before the repeal of section 3 of the Act of 1911, given the notice requisite under the said proviso, then, as respects reproductions by that person of that work after the repeal of that section, that proviso shall have effect as if re-enacted in the Act of 1956 as a proviso to subsection (2) of section 1 thereof. Section 1 (2) is the primary provision of the Act of 1956 defining infringement of copyright as the doing, without licence of the copyright owner, of any act restricted by the copyright.

It is therefore still necessary to consider the terms of the proviso to section 3 of the Act of 1911 and the rules made thereunder, which are now deemed to have been made under the Act of 1956.[23]

The proviso to section 3 was as follows:

> "Provided that at any time after the expiration of twenty-five years, or in the case of a work in which copyright subsists at the passing of this Act thirty years, from the death of the author of a published work, copyright in the work shall not be deemed to be infringed by the reproduction of the work for sale if the person

[22] Copyright Act, 1956, s. 3 (4).
[23] Sched. VII, para. 9 (2).

reproducing the work proves that he has given the prescribed notice in writing of his intention to reproduce the work, and that he has paid in the prescribed manner to, or for the benefit of, the owner of the copyright royalties in respect of all copies of the work sold by him calculated at the rate of ten per cent. on the price at which he publishes the work; and, for the purposes of this proviso, the Board of Trade may make regulations prescribing the mode in which notices are to be given, and the particulars to be given in such notices, and the mode, time, and frequency of the payment of royalties, including (if they think fit) regulations requiring payment in advance or otherwise securing the payment of royalties."

277 **Application to posthumous works.** The above proviso applies to posthumous works as if the author had died at the date when his work was first published, performed, or delivered in public.[24]

278 **Conditions of the right to reproduce a work.** In order to be entitled to reproduce a copyright work, a person, other than the owner of the copyright,[25] must prove: (a) that he has given the prescribed notice of his intention to reproduce the work, and (b) that he has paid to, or for the benefit of, the owner of the copyright, royalties in respect of all copies of the work sold by him calculated at the rate of 10 per cent. on the price at which he publishes the work.

279 **Board of Trade Regulations as to notice.** The Board of Trade, in accordance with the power conferred on them by the above-mentioned section, issued regulations prescribing the measures to be taken by those who desired to publish works during the period of their non-exclusive protection.[26] Not less than one month before any copies of the work are delivered to a purchaser notice must have been sent by registered post to the owner of the copyright, or his agent for the receipt of notice, if the name and address of such owner or agent can with reasonable diligence be ascertained.[27] The notice must contain the following particulars: (a) the name and address of the person intending to reproduce the work; (b) the name of the work which it is intended to reproduce, and (if necessary) a description sufficient to identify it; (c) the manner in which it is intended to reproduce the work (*e.g.*, whether by painting, lithography, photography, etc.); (d) the price or prices at which it is intended to publish the work;

24 Copyright Act, 1911, s. 17. As to joint works, see Part III, Chap. 14, *post*.

25 The copyright returns automatically to the representatives of the author, if he was the first owner of the copyright, twenty-five years after his death: Copyright Act, 1911, s. 5 (2), *post*, "Assignment and Transmission of Copyright." Chap. 8: see Copyright Act, 1956, Sched. 7, para. 28 (3).

26 Copyright Royalty System (General) Regulations, 1912 (S.R. & O. 1912 No. 532). See Copinger, *Copyright*, 8th ed., p. 423.

27 reg. 3 (*a*).

(e) the earliest date at which any of the copies will be delivered to a purchaser.[28]

280 **As to payment of royalties.** Payment of the royalties is, in the absence of contrary agreement, to be made by means of adhesive labels to be affixed to the copies of the work. After notice of intention to reproduce the work has been given it is the duty of the owner of the copyright to intimate, by registered post, to the person who has given the notice, some reasonably convenient place within the United Kingdom from which adhesive labels can be obtained, and, upon tender of the price, to supply from such place adhesive labels of the required denominations at a price equal to the amount of royalty represented thereby.[29]

281 **Regulations in event of owner not being known or not delivering labels.** It was held,[30] under the corresponding rules made under section 19 (6) of the Act of 1911, with regard to the royalties payable in respect of mechanical contrivances,[30a] that payment by means of adhesive labels is a perfectly legitimate method of " securing " payment of the royalties to the author. If the owner of the copyright cannot with reasonable diligence be found, notice is to be given to him by advertisement in the *London Gazette*,[31] but the regulations then go on to provide that, in cases where royalties are payable by means of adhesive labels, if at any time labels of the required denomination are not available either because (a) after the expiration of fourteen days from the date of the notice the owner of the copyright has not sent to the person reproducing the work an intimation of some reasonably convenient place within the United Kingdom from which such labels can be obtained; or (b) the owner of the copyright refuses or neglects to supply such labels within fourteen days after demand duly made, then copies of the work may be delivered to purchasers without having labels affixed thereto, and the amount of royalties is to be a debt due from the person reproducing the work to the owner of the copyright, the person reproducing the work keeping an account of all such copies sold by him.[32]

282 **Where mode of payment is agreed.** Where royalties are by agreement payable in any other mode than by means of adhesive labels,

[28] reg. 2.

[29] reg. 4 (*a*). As to size and design of labels, see reg. 4 (*c*). And, as to what is meant by " adhesive," see *Boosey & Co., Ltd.* v. *Goodson Gramophone Record Co., Ltd.* [1930] 1 Ch. 448, § 802, *post*.

[30] *Monckton* v. *Pathé Frères, etc., Ltd.* [1914] 1 K.B. 395.

[30a] Copyright Royalty System (Mechanical Musical Instruments) Regulations 1912 (S.R. & O. 1912 No. 533); see Copinger, *Copyright*, 8th ed., p. 425.

[31] reg. 3 (*b*).

[32] reg. 4 (*b*).

the time and frequency of the payments are to be such as are specified in the agreement.[33]

283 **Only published works may be compulsorily reproduced.** It is only "published" works that were liable to be compulsorily reproduced on payment of royalties. A dramatic or musical work was not published by public performance, nor was an artistic work by public exhibition, nor were works of sculpture and architectural works of art by the issue of photographs and engravings.[34] Dramatic and musical works which had been publicly performed, but not sold in print, could not, therefore, have been reproduced upon the royalty system, nor could a picture, unless copies had been issued to the public.

284 **No right to "perform" a work upon the royalty system.** The mode of reproduction is also limited. The work can only be reproduced "for sale," not for any other purpose which would be an infringement of copyright, for instance, for the purpose of gratuitous distribution. The right is to "reproduce" the work, and this reproduction must result in a saleable article, for the amount of royalty payable is to be determined by the price at which the reproducer publishes his work. Performing rights, therefore, remain exclusive throughout the entire period of protection.

285 **Right to reproduce in another form.** It seems also to be doubtful whether a work can be reproduced under this proviso except in a similar form to the original publication, or whether part only of the work can be reproduced. The proviso in question does not give the right to reproduce "in any material form whatsoever," nor does it give the right to reproduce the work, or any substantial part thereof, as in subsection (2) of section 1. It is probable, therefore, that the making of a translation, or of a novel from a dramatic work, of a dramatic work from a novel, or of a mechanical contrivance, would not be licensed under this proviso.

286 **Or a part of a work.** No doubt prima facie the right to reproduce the whole work should include a right to reproduce a part, but the fact that the copyright proprietor is to be remunerated by payment of 10 per cent. upon the published price of the reproduction rather militates against this construction. This fact also raises difficulties if it should be desired to incorporate the whole of a published work in a larger work. For instance, can a published engraving, the author of which has been dead for over twenty-five years, be taken to illustrate a book, or can a literary work be included in an encyclopedia

[33] reg. 4 (*d*).
[34] Copyright Act, 1911, s. 1 (3).

or other collective work? If so, what is the basis for the ascertainment of the royalty payable to the owner of the copyright? If a picture is inserted in a volume, it cannot fairly be said that the publisher "publishes the work"—that is, the picture—at any price, and yet the section makes the royalty 10 per cent. of that price. But if this argument be overruled, there is absolutely no machinery for determining what is the proper proportion of the price of the volume to be attributed to the picture. It has been suggested that where it is impossible to arrive at any basis for the ascertainment of the royalty, such royalty would have to be calculated at 10 per cent. of the published price of the whole work.[35] Some support seems to be lent to the argument that a work cannot be reproduced compulsorily as part of another work by the Board of Trade Regulations, which require, in the absence of contrary agreement, that the royalty shall be payable by means of adhesive labels "affixed to the copies of the work."[36] The publisher of an encyclopedia might well hesitate before issuing a work dotted here and there with adhesive labels! The section, in a sense, expropriates the property of another, and the burden seems to be upon the reproducer to show that he has a right to do so. But it has been held that, where it is proposed to publish together several works of the same author in reliance upon this section, "work," by virtue of section 1 of the Interpretation Act, 1889, may be read as "works," so that the 10 per cent. can be calculated upon the published price of each copy of the several works published together.[35]

287 **Abandonment of copyright.** It has been said that an author may by his conduct, or by his express desire, abandon his copyright, and give to the public a right to publish his work before the time when his copyright would expire.[37] There is no direct authority on the point,[37a] and it is difficult to say what amount of evidence the court would require as to the fact of a dedication of a copyright to the public.

But it is clear that a proprietor of a copyright does not lose his right of publication by permitting his book to remain out of print and obsolete for any number of years.[38] The copies may have been all sold, but he may exercise the right he has of republication at such periods as he thinks likely to answer his purpose and when he considers he can best find purchasers. It is a matter on which he has a right to exercise his own judgment.

[The next paragraph is 301]

35 *Osbourne* v. *Dent (J. M.) & Sons, Ltd.* [1925] Ch. 369.
36 Copyright Royalty System (General) Regulations, 1912, reg. 4 (*a*), *ante*, § 280.
37 In *Millar* v. *Taylor* (1769) 4 Burr. 2303 at 2346; *Platt* v. *Button* (1813) 19 Ves. 447; *Rundell* v. *Murray* (1821) Jac. 311 at 316.
37a See *Romesh Chowdhry* v. *Kh. Ali Mohamad Nowsheri* [1965] A.I.R. Jammu and Kashmir 101.
38 *Weldon* v. *Dicks* (1878) 10 Ch.D. 247.

CHAPTER 7

THE FIRST OWNER OF THE COPYRIGHT

1.—AUTHORSHIP

301 **Author is first owner.** With exceptions, which will be more fully considered hereafter, under the Copyright Act, 1956, the "author" of a work is to be the first owner of the copyright therein.[1]

302 **Meaning of "author."** As a general rule there will be no difficulty in determining who is the author of the work, notwithstanding that the Act of 1956 contains no definition of "authorship," or of "author" except in the case of photographs.[1a] But cases may arise in which the question is not so easy of solution. It is clear that the person who merely suggests the plot of a novel or a play to the writer, or the subject of a picture to an artist, is not the author of the novel, play or picture.[2] It is equally clear that a mere amanuensis is not an author.[3] As was pointed out by Farwell J. in *Donoghue* v. *Allied Newspapers, Ltd.*,[4] in considering this question it is necessary to see in what it is that copyright exists. There is no copyright in ideas and, consequently, if a person who has an idea for a story, or for a picture, or for a play, communicates it to another,[4a] the production which is the result of the communication of the idea is the copyright of the person who has clothed the idea in form. The copyright in reminiscences, for instance, which are "ghost written" therefore belongs to the "ghost writer" and not to the person who relates the reminiscences to the "ghost writer."[4b] On the other hand, if an author employs a shorthand

[1] s. 4 (1). The exceptions to the rule, besides those dealt with in this chapter, are (1) Government publications, see *post*, Chap. 19; (2) sound recordings, see *post*, Chap. 17; (3) cinematograph films, see *post*, Chap. 16; (4) broadcasts, see *post*, Chap. 18; and (5) published editions, see *ante*, § 223.

[1a] See *post*, § 309.

[2] *Shepherd* v. *Conquest* (1856) 17 C.B. 427; *Tate* v. *Thomas* [1921] 1 Ch. 503.

[3] *Walter* v. *Lane* [1900] A.C. 539. In the curious case of *Cummins* v. *Bond* [1927] 1 Ch. 167, it was held that a spiritualist medium was the owner of the copyright in a script which she believed to be dictated to her by a spirit. It would appear that this was clearly right, since, even admitting the hypothesis that a spirit supplied the ideas, the form of words in which copyright subsists came from the medium's brain; and see *Leah* v. *Two Worlds Publishing Co., Ltd.* [1951] Ch. 393.

[4] [1938] Ch. 106.

[4a] The person who had the idea may be able to prevent its use by the person to whom he communicated it, on the grounds of breach of confidence; see *Gilbert* v. *The Star Newspaper Co. Ltd.* (1894) 11 T.L.R. 4; *Moore* v. *Edwardes* [1901–04] Macg.Cop.Cas. 44 and *Fraser* v. *Edwards* [1905–10] Macg.Cop.Cas. 10 and § 88 *et seq.*, *ante*.

[4b] See *Donoghue* v. *Allied Newspapers, Ltd.*, *supra*, *Housden* v. *Marshall* [1959] 1 W.L.R. 1 and *Chaplin* v. *Leslie Frewin (Publishers), Ltd.* [1966] Ch. 71.

writer to take down a story word for word in shorthand, the author is the owner of the copyright and not the shorthand writer.[5] But between these two extremes there may be gradations. It is submitted, however, that prima facie the author of a literary work is the person who originates the language used, and the author of an artistic work is the person who actually executes the design. If A's manuscript is corrected and improved by B it will probably be a question of the amount and value of the corrections and improvements as to whether the author is A or B, or whether they are joint authors.[6]

303 **" Author " of drawing.** In the case of *Kenrick & Co.* v. *Lawrence & Co.*[7] the plaintiffs were a firm of printers, and J., a member of the firm, conceived the idea of printing and publishing cards, bearing a representation of a hand holding a pencil in the act of completing a cross within a square, with a view to such cards being used at parliamentary and other elections for the guidance and instruction of illiterate voters in the marking of their ballot papers. J., being unable to draw, employed an artist in the service of the firm to make, under his direction, a drawing of the representation above described. The plaintiffs registered the drawing under the Fine Arts Copyright Act, 1862,[8] and in the memorandum stated J. to be the author of the drawing. The court however, held that J. was not the author of the drawing, and, that the registration was consequently void. Wills J. remarked: " I do not see how a gentleman who is incapable of drawing even such a very simple picture as a rough sketch of the human hand, and who did not in fact set pencil to paper in the matter, can be called the author of the drawing. He suggested the subject and made such limited suggestions as to the treatment as the subject admitted of; but it seems to me that in an Act which gives copyright to drawings the author must mean a person who has at least some substantial share in putting the touches on to paper." [9]

304 The case of *Stannard* v. *Harrison,*[10] which, at first sight, appears to be contrary to the case just cited, is distinguishable by reason of the difference in wording of the Engraving Acts [11] under which it was decided and the Fine Arts Copyright Act, 1862, under which *Kenrick & Co.* v. *Lawrence & Co.* was decided.

5 See § 125, *ante*.
6 See *Springfield* v. *Thame* (1903) 89 L.T. 242, where the plaintiff had sent an account of an incident he had witnessed to a newspaper, and the account was so altered by the sub-editor of the paper that the latter was held to be the " author " of the newspaper paragraph.
7 (1890) 25 Q.B.D. 99.
8 25 & 26 Vict. c. 68.
9 The court also held that, in any case, the drawing was not one entitled to the benefit of copyright: see *ante*, § 178.
10 (1871) 19 W.R. 811.
11 8 Geo. 2, c. 13; 7 Geo. 3, c. 38.

The Engraving Acts vested the copyright in the person who " shall invent or design, engrave, etch, or work or from his own work, design, or invention, shall *cause or procure* to be designed, engraved etched, or worked " (*inter alia*) a map or plan; whereas the Fine Arts Copyright Act vested the copyright in a drawing in the " author." *Kenrick & Co.* v. *Lawrence & Co.* is therefore an authority under the Act of 1911, but *Stannard* v. *Harrison* is not. And, although the decision in *Kenrick & Co.* v. *Lawrence & Co.* would have actually been different if it had been decided under the Act of 1911 or the Act of 1956, because of the contract of service existing between the artist and the conceiver of the design,[12] yet it seems to be a distinct authority that the person who has no part in the physical operation of producing an artistic work cannot be its " author."

305 **" Author " of collective work.** The decisions in some other cases are also liable to misconception. Thus, in *Barfield* v. *Nicholson* [13] Sir John Leach said: " I am of opinion that, under the statute (8 Anne, c. 19), the person who forms the plan, and who embarks in the speculation of a work, and who employs various persons to compose different parts of it, adapted to their own peculiar requirements, that he, the person who so forms the plan and scheme of the work, and pays different artists of his own selection, who, upon certain conditions contribute to it, is the author and proprietor of the work, if not within the literal expression, at least within the equitable meaning of the statute of Anne, which, being a remedial law, is to be construed liberally."

In this case, it must be pointed out, the Master of the Rolls was referring to collective or composite works, such as encyclopaedias, where there are distinct copyrights, namely, the copyright in the entire work and the copyright in the various separate contributions. The person who plans a collective work may perhaps be the author of the work as a whole although he makes no actual written contribution to the work, but the case of *Barfield* v. *Nicholson* must not be taken as an authority that he becomes the " author " of the separate contributions.[14] On the other hand, it has been held [15] that in the case of a compilation in the nature of a directory the compiler of the work is the author of the actual entries although these may have in fact been in the first place written down at his request by the persons to whom they refer. To take a single contribution from a collective work is not necessarily an infringement of the collective work.[16]

12 Copyright Act, 1911, s. 5 (1) (*b*); Copyright Act, 1956, s. 4 (4).
13 (1824) 2 Sim. & St. 1.
14 See *post*, Chap. 13.
15 *Black (A. and C.), Ltd.* v. *Claude Stacey, Ltd.* [1929] 1 Ch. 177; *James Nisbet & Co., Ltd.* v. *The Golf Agency* [1905–10] Cacg.Cop.Cas. 79.
16 *Walter* v. *Howe* (1881) 17 Ch.D. 708.

306 **"Author" of musical play.** The cases of *Hatton* v. *Keane*[17] and *Wallerstein* v. *Herbert*[18] are cases in which one person composed music for a play arranged by another. They decide that the composer cannot, in the circumstances, complain of the performance of his music in conjunction with the play, by a person deriving title from the arranger of the play, on the ground that he has consented to its use thereafter with such play; but they do not decide that such composer is not the owner of the copyright in the music.

307 **Of plot.** In the case of *Tate* v. *Thomas*[19] Eve J. decided that a person who contributed suggestions for the plot and arrangement of a musical play of which the plaintiffs were the authors of the music and lyrics, was not a joint author with them, and had no copyright therein. And it has been held that, where persons have provided incidents from their own lives as the basis of articles or stories in which these incidents have been written up by others, the person providing the incidents is not the author of the written matter on the ground that he did not take any part in producing the express matter which is the original literary work, the subject-matter of copyright.[20] On the other hand, in the case of *Samuelson* v. *Producers' Distributing Co., Ltd.*[21] it was held by the Court of Appeal that the writer of an original version of a dramatic sketch was the sole author, notwithstanding that another person had revised and altered it for performance.

308 **Of artistic works.** In the case of artistic works, other than photographs, it is the person whose hands fix the picture upon the canvas, paper, stone, copperplate or wood who is the author. Even in the case of lithographs it is submitted that the author is the person who does the drawing upon the stone. Although it is usual to employ a special lithographic designer to draw the design for the express purpose of having the same lithographed, the latter is not, it is thought, the author of the lithograph.

309 **Of photograph.** The difficulty, under the law prior to 1911, of determining who was the "author" of a photograph,[22] was solved, under the Act of 1911, by providing that the person who was the owner of the original negative at the time when such negative was made was to be deemed the author of the work.[22a]

Under the Act of 1956 it is provided that "author," in relation to

17 (1859) 8 W.R. 7.
18 (1867) 16 L.T. 453; see *Hazlitt* v. *Templeman* (1866) 13 L.T. 593.
19 [1921] 1 Ch. 503.
20 *Donoghue* v. *Allied Newspapers, Ltd.* [1938] Ch. 106; *Evans* v. *E. Hulton & Co., Ltd.* [1923–28] Macg.Cop.Cas. 51; *Housden* v. *Marshall* [1959] 1 W.L.R. 1.
21 (1932) 48 R.P.C. 580.
22 See *Nottage* v. *Jackson* (1883) 11 Q.B.D. 627; *Melville* v. *Mirror of Life Co.* [1895] 2 Ch. 531.
22a Copyright Act, 1911, s. 21.

a photograph, means the person who, at the time when the photograph is taken, is the owner of the material on which it is taken.[23] This is really the same definition, altered in form, because modern photography does not necessarily involve the use of a negative. A "photograph," for copyright purposes, is therefore the material on which the photograph is taken and, if a negative is used, it is the negative and not the positive, the latter being a reproduction of the photograph.

2.—COMMISSIONED WORKS

310 By section 4 (3) of the Copyright Act, 1956, it is provided that, where a person commissions the taking of a photograph or the painting or drawing of a portrait or the making of an engraving, and pays or agrees to pay for it in money or money's worth, and the work is made in pursuance of that commission, the person who so commissioned the work shall be entitled to any copyright subsisting under the Act.[24] This provision is expressed to be "subject to the last preceding subsection," referring to the provision hereafter to be mentioned under which a work made in the course of the author's employment by the proprietor of a newspaper, magazine or similar periodical, vests in such proprietor only for the purpose of publication in a newspaper, magazine or similar periodical, leaving the balance of the copyright in the author. "Engraving" is defined as including any etching, lithograph, woodcut, print, or similar work, not being a photograph,[23] and "photograph" as any product of photography or of any process akin to photography other than a part of a cinematograph film.[23]

311 **Similar provisions in earlier Acts.** The Copyright Act, 1911,[25] contained a somewhat similar provision and that provision continues to operate in the case of a work made in pursuance of a contract made before the commencement of the Act of 1956.[26]

It was provided, by section 5 (1) (*a*) of the Act of 1911, that where, in the case of an engraving, photograph or portrait, the plate or other original was ordered by some other person, and was made for valuable consideration in pursuance of that order, then, in the absence of any agreement to the contrary, the person by whom such plate or other original was ordered should be the first owner of the copyright.

The Copyright Act, 1911,[27] contained very similar definitions of "engravings" and "photographs" to those in the Act of 1956, save that the words "other than a part of a cinematograph film" did not occur in the definition of photograph, since, under the Act of 1911, a

23 Copyright Act, 1956, s. 48 (1).
24 See *Williams* v. *Settle* [1960] 1 W.L.R. 1072.
25 s. 5 (1) (*a*).
26 Copyright Act, 1956, Sched. VII, para. 3.
27 s. 35 (1).

film was protected as a photographic work. It is therefore provided, in the Act of 1956, that the provisions of that Act shall have effect in relation to photographs forming part of a cinematograph film made before the commencement of that Act, as those provisions have effect in relation to photographs not forming part of a cinematograph film.[28]

312 There was a somewhat similar provision in the Fine Arts Copyright Act, 1862,[29] to the effect that, where a painting, drawing or the negative of any photograph should be " made or executed for or on behalf of any person for a good or a valuable consideration," the copyright should belong to " the person for or on whose behalf the same shall be so made or executed." [30] Under this Act it was necessary, if the commissioned author was to retain the copyright in himself, that he should do so in writing.

313 The differences between the Act of 1911 and the Act of 1862 were (1) that under the Act of 1911 writing is not required if the artist desires to retain his copyright; the proviso only says " in the absence of any agreement to the contrary "; (2) that the 1862 Act refers to a work " made " for another, and the Act of 1911 speaks of a plate or original " ordered " by some other person; (3) that the 1862 Act uses the expression " a good or a valuable consideration," whereas the Act of 1911 only has the words " valuable consideration."

The Copyright Act, 1956, though expressed in somewhat different words, seems to have the same meaning, in this relation, as the Act of 1911. It is possible that " money or money's worth " may have a narrower construction than " valuable consideration." [31]

314 **The cases before 1911.** In the case of *Stackemann* v. *Paton*,[32] Farwell J. laid some stress upon the fact that the Fine Arts Copyright Act employed the word " good," in addition to " valuable," consideration, and seemed to suggest that there might be a difference between the two. In that case the plaintiffs were photographers who were in the habit of taking photographs of schools and the pupils attending them. This they did as a speculation. Their practice was to seek permission from the principals to take the photographs, it being clearly understood that no one was to be compelled to purchase copies, although, no doubt, the photographers had reasonable expectations of being able to effect sales amongst the pupils and others. In the particular case that came before the court the plaintiffs had obtained permission from the principal, who had gone to some trouble in

28 Copyright Act, 1956, Sched. VII, para. 16.
29 25 & 26 Vict. c. 68.
30 *Petty* v. *Taylor* [1897] 1 Ch. 465; *Boucas* v. *Cooke* [1903] 2 K.B. 227.
31 But see definitions in the Law of Property Act, 1925 (15 Geo. 5, c. 20), s. 205 (1) (xxi).
32 [1906] 1 Ch. 774.

showing the photographer over the interior of the school buildings, in gathering the pupils and grouping them for the purpose of being photographed. A certain number of copies were sold to pupils and others. The defendants were publishers of a book, the purpose of which was to advertise schools, and the proprietors of the school in question had supplied them with a block made from the plaintiffs' photographs to be used for advertising the school in the defendants' publication.

Farwell J., in these circumstances, held that the copyright in the photographs was vested in the proprietors of the school, and that, therefore, the plaintiffs had no right to complain of their reproduction in the defendants' publication. The ground for this decision was that the school proprietors had given "good" consideration by reason of their permitting the photographer to have access to private buildings.[32a]

315 It is not easy to reconcile this decision with the cases of *Ellis* v. *Marshall (H.) & Son* [33] and *Melville* v. *Mirror of Life Co.*,[34] in both of which it was held that celebrities who were requested by photographers to give sittings, without any charge being made for the taking of the photographs, did not acquire the copyright in the photographs, notwithstanding that they subsequently purchased some copies. The learned judge, in *Stackemann* v. *Paton,* sought to distinguish these cases upon the ground that the only possible consideration given by the celebrities was that they took the trouble to walk up to the photographer's room and to sit in his chair. But, even if quantity of consideration is a matter which ought to be considered at all, the consideration given by the principal who permitted access to his buildings seems, at least, no greater than that given by a celebrity who sacrifices his time to attend a photographer's studio. But whether or not the case of *Stackemann* v. *Paton* was rightly decided under the law prior to 1911, it is submitted that, if similar facts were to recur, the decision would not be the same under the Act of 1956.

316 **Present law.** As was pointed out by MacKinnon J., in *Sasha, Ltd.* v. *Stoenesco*,[35] the question at issue in such cases under the Act of 1911 was whether, in the hypothetical circumstances that the sitter declined to buy any copies of the photograph, the photographer would, in the circumstances of the case, be entitled to sue the sitter for work and labour done in the preparation of the negative. No express agreement about this is normally made in practice, so that it

[32a] See as to the granting of exclusive photographic rights at shows, and so on, *Sports and General Press Agency, Ltd.* v. *"Our Dogs" Publishing Co., Ltd.* [1916] 2 K.B. 880; aff. [1917] 2 K.B. 125.
[33] (1895) 64 L.J.Q.B. 757.
[34] [1895] 2 Ch. 531.
[35] (1929) 45 T.L.R. 350. And see *Hartnett* v. *Pinkett* (1953) 103 L.J. 204.

is a matter of implication from the circumstances. Where the sitter approaches the photographer, without any kind of prior invitation, the implication would be that the sitter would have to pay for the negative if he did not pay for it indirectly by buying copies, and the copyright would belong to the sitter.[36] But, if the sitter is the kind of person whom photographers are normally willing to photograph without payment, the fact that, in the particular instance, the approach was made by the sitter and not the photographer, does not give rise to an implication that the sitter is to pay, and therefore the copyright rests with the photographer.[37]

317 **" Original " of engraving.** In an earlier case it was held that, where the plaintiff submitted to the defendants a sketch, which was intended to be reproduced by lithographic process for advertisement purposes, and where the defendants asked him to submit a second sketch in different colours, the second sketch was the " original " of the lithograph within the meaning of the section, and was ordered for valuable consideration.[38]

318 **Limits of the subsection.** It must not, however, be forgotten that it is only in the case of engravings and photographs *of any subject* that the copyright could, under the proviso to section 5 (1) of the Act of 1911, and can, under section 4 (3) of the Act of 1956, vest in the first instance in the person ordering the engraving or photograph. There is no such provision in either Act in the case of any other artistic work, unless that work falls under the description of a "portrait." Consequently, in the case of drawings, not being portraits, even if commissioned, the copyright remains with the artist, unless expressly assigned. This often produces unexpected severances of copyright in the case of commercial art. The advertiser places an order for an advertisement and, therefore, having commissioned the print, is the owner of the copyright therein. But it is overlooked that the advertisement probably started as a sketch or drawing, unaffected by this subsection, so that there is an outstanding copyright which may cause trouble if the advertiser wishes to repeat the main design in a new advertisement.

[36] *Boucas* v. *Cooke* [1903] 2 K.B. 227.

[37] Of course the copyright in a " snapshot " will be in the owner of the negative, for it will not have been ordered, nor will consideration have been given, and there seems to be no legal ground, unless it be " breach of confidence," upon which a person who has been " snapshotted " can object to publication of the " snapshot "; it must be considered one of the risks of the highway.

[38] *Con Planck, Ltd.* v. *Kolynos, Inc.* [1925] 2 K.B. 804. *Cf. Nicol* v. *Barranger* [1917–23] Macg.Cop.Cas. 219. But a sketch which was never in fact used as an original for an engraving, though intended for that purpose, has been held, in Canada, not to fall within the similar provisions of the Canadian Act: *Toronto Carton Co.* v. *Manchester McGregor, Ltd.* [1935] 2 D.L.R. 94.

319 **What is a "portrait"?** There is no definition of a "portrait" in the Acts of 1911 and 1956. The dictionary definition of the word is "a representation or delineation of a person especially of the face, made from life by drawing, painting, photography, engraving etc." [39] The meaning of the word was much discussed in the case of *Duke of Leeds* v. *Earl Amherst*,[40] in which the question arose, upon the construction of a will, whether a picture of the Duke of Schomberg sitting, clad in armour, upon horseback, a battle scene forming the background of the picture, passed under a bequest of "portraits"; and it was held that it did. Whether a picture is a portrait or not seems to depend upon what is the main purpose of the picture. If the main object is the likeness of a person, it is not the less a portrait because of the presence of subordinate accessories in the picture. It is fairly clear that a "portrait" might include the likeness of more than one individual, but that, on the other hand, the mere fact that real persons happen to be delineated in a picture does not necessarily make that picture a "portrait."

320 In the case of *Leah* v. *Two Worlds Publishing Co., Ltd.*[41] Vaisey J. decided that a picture, painted by a spiritualist medium, of a dead person whom he had not seen, was a "portrait" for the purposes of section 5 of the Copyright Act, 1911. He said that it was a "portrait" because it was intended to represent the deceased person as that person was when living, and that it was nonetheless a "portrait" because the materials that the artist used were entirely subjective. As, however, the father of the dead man only agreed to pay for the portrait after he had seen it, Vaisey J. held that it was not "ordered" within the meaning of the section.

3.—The Work of Employees

321 The Act of 1956 provides for two other special classes of cases in which the author is not the first owner of the copyright. The first is concerned with newspapers, magazines and other periodicals and the second with employees generally.

322 **Works made for publication in a newspaper, magazine or similar periodical.** As to the first class, it is provided, in section 4 (2) of the Act of 1956, that where a literary, dramatic or artistic work is made by the author in the course of the author's employment by the proprietor of a newspaper, magazine or similar periodical under a contract of service or apprenticeship, and is so made for the purpose of

[39] *New English Dictionary.* In a copyright Bill drafted by the Artistic Copyright Society, a "portrait" was defined as follows: "Any work shall be considered a portrait whose principal object is the likeness in any form of art of any specified person."

[40] (1845) 14 L.J.Ch. 73.

[41] [1951] Ch. 393.

publication in a newspaper, magazine or similar periodical, the said proprietor shall be entitled to the copyright in the work in so far as the copyright relates to publication of the work in any newspaper, magazine or similar periodical, or to reproduction of the work for the purpose of its being so published; but in all other respects the author shall be entitled to any copyright subsisting in the work by virtue of that Act. What is meant by " contract of service " is discussed below, but it should be noted that this provision does not apply in the case of musical works.

323 The Copyright Act, 1911, contained a somewhat similar provision limiting the vesting of copyright in the case of employees, namely that, where the work made by the employee was an article or other contribution to a newspaper, magazine or similar periodical, there was to be deemed to be reserved to the author a right to restrain the publication of the work otherwise than as part of a newspaper, magazine or similar periodical.[42] It was doubted whether, under that Act, this provision gave to the employee anything except a bare right to restrain publication by others.[43] However, it seems clear that, under the Act of 1956, the employee, unless there is an express agreement to the contrary, will himself retain the full book copyright and be entitled to publish any article or material in book form. This matter is further discussed in a later chapter.[44]

324 **Works made by employees.** The second class of exception is contained in section 4 (4) of the Act of 1956, which provides that, where a work is made in the course of the author's employment by another person under a contract of service or apprenticeship, that other person shall be entitled to any copyright subsisting in the work by virtue of that Act. This class of exception applies to all works, and thus includes musical works, but only applies where the previous provisions regarding works of employees of newspapers and regarding commissioned photographs, portraits and engravings do not apply.[45] This class of exception is substantially the same as was provided in section 5 (1) (*b*) of the Copyright Act, 1911, and decisions under that Act are no doubt in point in regard to the construction of the provision of the Act of 1956.

325 **What is a " contract of service "?** Whether a person is engaged under a " contract of service " or not is a question of fact and not of law.[46]

42 Copyright Act, 1911, s. 5 (1) (*b*).
43 *Sun Newspapers, Ltd.* v. *Whippie* (1928) 28 S.R.(N.S.W.) 473.
44 *Post*, Chap. 13.
45 Copyright Act, 1956, s. 4 (4).
46 *Smith* v. *General Motor Cab Co., Ltd.* [1911] A.C. 188; *Wilmerson* v. *Lynn, etc., Steamship Co., Ltd.* [1913] 3 K.B. 931; *Doggett* v. *Waterloo Taxi-Cab Co., Ltd.* [1910] 2 K.B. 336.

326 In *Short* v. *J. and W. Henderson, Ltd.*,[47] a case in the House of Lords under the Workmen's Compensation Acts, Lord Thankerton recapitulated, with approval, the four indicia of a contract of service derived by the Lord Justice-Clerk in the Court of Session in *Park* v. *Wilsons and Clyde Coal Co., Ltd.*[48] from the authorities. These were (1) the master's power of selection of his servant; (2) the payment of wages or other remuneration; (3) the master's right to control the method of doing of the work; and (4) the master's right of suspension or dismissal. He went on to say that the principal requirement of a contract of service was the right of the master, in some reasonable sense, to control the method of doing the work, and that this factor of superintendence and control had frequently been treated as critical and decisive of the legal quality of the relationship.[49] In *National Federation of Sub-Postmasters* v. *Minister of Health*[50] Branson J. said that he did not think there was any real dispute as to what "employment under a contract of service" meant. The distinction was not in doubt and depended on the amount of control which the employer exercises over the person whom he employs. Where a man employs another to do work for him under his control, so that he can direct the time when the work shall be done, the means to be adopted to bring about the end, and the method in which the work shall be carried on, then the contract is a contract of service. If, on the other hand, a man employs another to do certain work, but leaves it to that other to decide how that work shall be done, what steps shall be taken to produce the desired effect, then it is a contract for services.

The meaning of the expression "contract of service" was also discussed in the case of *Simmons* v. *Heath Laundry Co.*,[51] another case decided under the Workmen's Compensation Acts,[52] where a similar expression is to be found; and the meaning given to the words in the judgments in that case was applied to this section of the Act of 1911 by Petersen J. in *University of London Press, Ltd.* v. *University Tutorial Press Ltd.*[53] A "contract of service" is not the same thing as a "contract for services." In the case of *Simmons* v. *Heath Laundry Co.*,[51] it was held that the applicant, who attended at a pupil's residence to give her music lessons, was not under a contract of service with her employer. The question really turns upon the degree of control exercised by the employer over the employee. "The greater the amount of direct control exercised over the person rendering the services by the person contracting for them, the stronger the

47 (1946) 39 B.W.C.C. 62; *Ready Mixed Concrete (South East), Ltd.* v. *Minister of Pensions and National Insurance* [1968] 2 Q.B. 497.
48 (1928) Sess.Cas. 121 at 133.
49 See *Gould* v. *Minister of National Insurance* [1951] 1 K.B. 731.
50 (1939) 161 L.T. 337 at 338.
51 [1910] 1 K.B. 543; see also *Sadler* v. *Henlock* (1855) 4 E. & B. 570; *Yewens* v. *Noakes* (1880) 6 Q.B.D. 530.
52 The expression also occurs in other statutes.
53 [1916] 2 Ch. 601.

ground for holding it to be a contract of service; and, similarly, the greater the degree of independence of such control, the greater the probability that the services rendered are of the nature of professional services, and that the contract is not one of service." [54] "In each case the question to be asked is, what was the man employed to do? Was he employed upon the terms that he should, within the scope of his employment, obey his master's orders, or was he employed to exercise his skill and achieve an indicated result in such manner as, in his judgment, was most likely to ensure success? " [55]

327 In the case of *Stevenson Jordan & Harrison, Ltd.* v. *Macdonald & Evans* [56], an accountant, who was employed under a contract of service, during a period of his employment prepared and wrote lectures for delivery to universities and to learned and professional societies dealing with the business in which he was employed. The giving of the lectures was helpful to the company in that it served as an advertisement for the company and, on that account, the company paid to the accountant the expenses he incurred. In that case Sir Raymond Evershed M.R. said [57] that, without attempting the difficult—perhaps impossible—task of definition, he thought that the two expressions clearly indicated the distinction between, for example the case of a man engaged to do some specific work under a considerable measure of control extending not only to the work which he did but to the way in which he did it, on the one hand, and that of a man engaged more in the capacity of an independent contractor,[57a] for example, a man engaged professionally.[57b] In the same case Denning L.J. said [58] that one feature was that, under a contract of service, a man is employed as part of the business, and his work is done as an integral part of the business,[58a] whereas, under a contract for services, his work, although done for the business, is not integrated into it, but is only accessory to it.

It is clear, therefore, that if an author or an artist is employed by a publisher to write a book or draw a picture, he does not necessarily become the servant of the publisher. The person who employs him must have the right under his contract to require the author or artist to produce such a work as the employer desires, and if the work does not meet with his approval, to require the author or artist to alter his work. Subject to these general principles, each case must depend upon its own facts.

54 *Per* Fletcher Moulton L.J., *Simmons* v. *Heath Laundry Co., supra,* at p. 550; and see *Cassidy* v. *Ministry of Health* [1951] 2 K.B. 343 at 352.
55 *Per* Buckley L.J., *Simmons* v. *Heath Laundry Co., supra,* at p. 553.
56 [1952] 1 T.L.R. 101.
57 *Ibid.* at p. 105.
57a See *Ready Mixed Concrete (South East), Ltd.* v. *Minister of Pensions and National Insurance* [1968] 2 Q.B. 497.
57b See *Morren* v. *Swinton and Pendlebury Borough Council* [1965] 1 W.L.R. 576.
58 *Stevenson, Jordan & Harrison, Ltd.* v. *Macdonald & Evans, supra* at p. 111.
58a See *Whittaker* v *Minister of Pensions and National Insurance* [1967] 1 Q.B. 156.

328 Thus, in an Australian case,[59] it was held that a cartoonist who was employed by a newspaper on terms including a provision that he should obey and comply with all orders and directions of his employers, was held to be employed under a contract of service. The expression "contract of service" appears in other statutes and there are a number of cases as to the construction of the words.[60]

329 **Course of employment.** In order that the copyright may vest in an employer it is not sufficient that the work is made by his servant. It must also be made "in the course of his employment." In the case of *Byrne* v. *Statist Co.*,[61] it was held that the copyright in a translation made by a person on the regular staff of a newspaper, but during his spare time, did not vest in his employers, but remained in the translator.

330 In the case of *Stevenson, Jordan & Harrison, Ltd.* v. *Macdonald & Evans*,[62] it was held that the lectures were not prepared in the

[59] *Sun Newspapers, Ltd.* v. *Whippie* (1928) 28 S.R.(N.S.W.) 473.

[60] As examples, the following have been held not to be under a contract of service: clergy and ministers (*Re National Insurance Act, 1911* [1912] 2 Ch. 563; *Re National Insurance Act, 1911* (1912) 107 L.T. 143); doctors, surgeons and anaesthetists employed at a hospital (*Scottish Insurance Commissioners (The)* v. *The Royal Infirmary of Edinburgh*, 1913 S.C. 751; but see *Gold* v. *Essex County Council* [1942] 2 K.B. 293 and *Cassidy* v. *Ministry of Health* [1951] 2 K.B. 343 as to permanent hospital staff); a lecturer employed to explain the merits of an airship to persons attending an exhibition (*Waites* v. *The Franco-British Exhibition Inc.* (1909) 25 T.L.R. 441); a sporting representative of a newspaper (*Re Ashley and Smith, Ltd.* [1917–23] Macg.Cop.Cas. 54); a music-hall artiste (*Gould* v. *Minister of National Insurance* [1951] 1 K.B. 731); a concrete carrier (*Ready Mixed Concrete (South East), Ltd.* v. *Minister of Pensions and National Insurance* [1968] 2 Q.B. 497); a part-time teacher (*Argent* v. *Minister of Social Security* [1968] 1 W.L.R. 1749); compare *Market Investigations, Ltd.* v. *Minister of Social Security* [1969] 2 Q.B. 173 where a part-time interviewer was held to be under a contract of service. On the other hand, a pupil teacher (*Re National Insurance Act, 1911* [1913] 1 Ir.R. 219), and a professional footballer (*Walker* v. *The Crystal Palace Football Club, Ltd.* [1910] 1 K.B. 87), have been held to be engaged under contracts of service; in the last case it was held sufficient that the footballer was bound to follow the general instructions of his employers. In *Amalgamated Engineering Union* v. *Minister of Pensions and National Insurance* [1963] 1 W.L.R. 441 the sick steward of the branch of the trade union of which he was a member was held to be under a contract of service; see also *Unsworth* v. *Pease, etc., Ltd.* [1937] 2 K.B. 504. In *Binding* v. *Great Yarmouth, etc., Commissioners* (1923) 16 B.W.C.C. 28, a salvage contractor was held to be under a contract of service, as was a resident-engineer in *Morren* v. *Swinton and Pendlebury Borough Council* [1965] 1 W.L.R. 576, a trapeze artiste in *Whittaker* v. *Minister of Pensions and National Insurance* [1967] 1 Q.B. 156, and a part-time interviewer in *Market Investigations, Ltd.* v. *Minister of Social Security*, *supra*. In the case of *Re National Insurance Act, 1911* (1913) 108 L.T. 894, the contract of service was admitted, and the only question was as to whether they were manual labourers. In *Re Beeton & Co.* ([1913] 2 Ch. 279), the question was as to whether persons employed regularly to contribute articles to a magazine were "clerks or servants" within the meaning of the Companies (Consolidation) Act, 1908 (8 Edw. 7, c. 69, s. 209); this case is more fully set out in Chap. 13, *post*. See also examples mentioned in *Stevenson, Jordan & Harrison, Ltd.* v. *Macdonald & Evans* [1952] 1 T.L.R. 101.

[61] [1914] 1 K.B. 622.

[62] *Supra*, § 327.

course of the accountant's employment, and that the copyright in the lectures remained with the accountant.

331 **Apprenticeship.** As to apprenticeship, "in legal acceptation an apprentice is a person bound to another for the purpose of learning his trade or calling, the contract being of that nature that the master teaches and the other serves the master with the intention of learning." [63]

332 **Works made before 1957.** The foregoing provisions are not applicable to works made under contract of service if made before the commencement of the Act of 1956, or to works made, whether before or after that date, which were commissioned before that date.[64] In such cases the provisions of the Copyright Act, 1911, to which reference has been made, apply.

333 4.—AGREEMENT TO THE CONTRARY

Both the Copyright Act, 1911, and the Copyright Act, 1956, expressly provide that the exceptions referred to are subject to agreement to the contrary, and such agreement may, it is assumed, be oral or be implied from conduct or circumstances.[65] Under the Act of 1911, however, the reverse case was not possible, that is to say it was not possible, in a case not within the provisions, to agree to an initial vesting of copyright in someone other than the author. If any such agreement were made, the author nevertheless became the first owner of the copyright in law and the person entitled to have the copyright became the owner in equity only and took subject to the rights of a purchaser for value without notice. This still continues to be the case if the agreement was made before the commencement of the Act of 1956.[65a] But, in the case of an agreement signed by or on behalf of a prospective owner of a copyright after the commencement of the Act of 1956, copyright may now vest initially in the assignee as soon as the work is made.[66] In the case of an oral or implied agreement, however, the copyright will still vest in the author, subject to a right in equity of the person with whom the agreement is made to have an assignment in his favour. Where an

[63] *Per* Cockburn C.J., *Clapham* v. *St. Pancras* (1860) 6 Jur.(N.S.) 700; see *Fraser* v. *Minister of National Insurance* (1947) Sess.Cas. 594, *Horan* v. *Hayhoe* [1904] 1 K.B. 288, *Re Marryat* [1948] Ch. 298 and *Dunk* v. *George Waller & Son, Ltd.* [1970] 2 W.L.R. 1241.

[64] Copyright Act, 1956, Sched. VII, para. 3.

[65] See *Massine* v. *De Basil* [1936–45] Macg.Cop.Cas. 223, in which the court implied such an agreement in the case of the author of the choreography of a ballet; see *Christopher Bede Studios, Ltd.* v. *United Portraits, Ltd.* [1958] N.Z.L.R. 250, where agreement to contrary was in writing and for valuable consideration.

[65a] Copyright Act, 1956, Sched. VII, para. 28.

[66] Copyright Act, 1956, s. 37 (1).

author is employed by a publisher to write a book or an article for a capital sum, the law will generally presume that it was the intention of the parties that the copyright shall belong to the publisher.[67]

334 5.—OWNERSHIP BY UNINCORPORATED BODY

The question of the vesting of copyright in an unincorporated body of persons was discussed in a Canadian case.[68] It was held that, in the circumstances of that case, certain of the copyrights in question vested in the members as tenants in common so that any one or more of them could sue for infringement.

[The next paragraph is 341]

[67] *Sweet* v. *Benning* (1855) 16 C.B. 459; *Lawrence, etc., Ltd.* v. *Aflalo* [1904] A.C. 17, considered further in §§ 665–667, *post.*
[68] *Massie & Renwick, Ltd.* v. *Underwriters' Survey Bureau, Ltd.* [1940] S.C.R. 218.

CHAPTER 8

ASSIGNMENT AND TRANSMISSION OF COPYRIGHT

341 **Distinction between title to copyright and to the material object.** Copyright is to be distinguished from the material object which is the subject of the copyright. The assignment of the material object does not necessarily transfer the title to the copyright, any more than the transfer of the copyright necessarily transfers the title to the material object.[1] Probably, no purchaser of a book would suppose that he, by his purchase, acquired the right to multiply copies of it, but it is quite possible that the purchaser of an artistic work, such as a picture, not made to his order,[2] may be surprised to find that his purchase does not include the right to reproduce it by such means as engravings and photographs, nor even the right to prevent the artist or anyone else from making reproductions, unless it amounted to a breach of confidence or trust.[3] It is, nevertheless, the fact that such a purchaser can only obtain the right to reproduction of the work he has purchased by insisting upon a licence, or assignment of copyright.[4] Thus, in *Cooper* v. *Stephens*,[5] the plaintiffs sold certain electro blocks for the purpose of printing certain drawings. The purchasers lent these blocks to the defendants in order that they in turn, might print from them; but Romer J. held that the plaintiffs were entitled to restrain the defendants from doing so, notwithstanding the permission of the purchasers. "The sale of the blocks," said the learned judge, "could not have had the effect of an assignment of copyright." [6] At the same time the courts consider that the retention by the vendor of a picture of the copyright therein, involves an "unnatural dissociation of two kinds of property," and, consequently, they will lean towards construing any document given at the time of the sale as an assignment of copyright.[7] An assignment of copyright must, however, be made in writing.[8]

342 **Death of proprietor of copyright.** Section 36 (1) of the Copyright Act, 1956, provides that, subject to the provisions of that section,

[1] See § 82, *ante*.
[2] As to which see Copyright Act, 1956, s. 4.
[3] *Ante*, § 88 *et seq.*
[4] Copyright Act, 1956, s. 36. An equitable title may, however, arise from an implied agreement, see § 333, *ante*.
[5] [1895] 1 Ch. 567, followed by the C.A. in *Marshall (W.) & Co., Ltd.* v. *Bull (A. H.), Ltd.* (1901) 85 L.T. 77.
[6] At 571.
[7] *London Printing, etc., Alliance, Ltd.* v. *Cox* [1891] 3 Ch. 291 at 304.
[8] Copyright Act, 1956, s. 36 (3).

copyright shall be transmissible by assignment, by testamentary disposition, or by operation of law, as personal or movable property.[9] Therefore, upon the death of the proprietor, it will pass to his personal representatives for the benefit of the person to whom he has bequeathed it, or, if the proprietor has died intestate, for the benefit of his next-of-kin.[10]

343 In the case of *Novello & Co., Ltd.* v. *Hinrichsen Edition, Ltd.*,[11] questions arose whether certain copyrights had been owned by enemies during a period after September 3, 1939. In the course of the discussion of these points, Wynn-Parry J. held that, on the death of a foreign owner of English copyrights, the copyrights in question vested in the President of the Probate, Divorce and Admiralty Division of the High Court or in the Crown, being liable to be divested on an administrator of the estate being appointed in England. It seems to follow from this decision that, at least in the case of an intestacy, title cannot be made to English copyrights except through an administrator appointed by the English court.

Section 38 of the Copyright Act, 1956, supplies a rule of construction to the effect that a bequest of an unpublished manuscript of a literary, dramatic or musical work or an artistic work shall be deemed to comprise the copyright therein.[12]

344 **Bankruptcy of proprietor.** The copyright in a published work will also pass to the trustee in bankruptcy of the proprietor, without any assignment in writing.[13] As regards unpublished literary works, copyright is conferred upon an author as soon as his work is "made," and presumably, therefore, the right in such works also passes to the trustee, though the trustee could not compel the author either to finish his MS., or to see the work through the press.[14]

345 **Execution.** There would appear to be no process whereby copyright can be taken in execution by a judgment creditor of the proprie-

9 It was expressly so provided by the Literary Copyright Act, 1842, s. 25. There was no express provision to that effect in the Act of 1911.

10 *Thompson (C.)* v. *Stanhope (E.)* (1774) 2 Amb. 737; *Burnett* v. *Chetwood* (1817) 2 Mer. 441; *Latour* v. *Bland* (1818) 2 Stark. 382. As to rights to royalties as between tenant for life and remainderman, see *Re Sullivan* [1930] 1 Ch. 84; and as between trustee in bankruptcy and equitable assignee, see *Re Trytel* [1952] W.N. 355.

11 [1951] Ch. 595; see also *Novello & Co., Ltd.* v. *Eulenburg (E.), Ltd.* [1950] 1 All E.R. 44 (C.A.).

12 As to similar provision in the Act of 1911, s. 17 (2), see § 54, *ante*.

13 *Mawman* v. *Tegg* (1826) 2 Russ. 385; *Re Curry (W.), etc. & Co.* (1849) 12 Ir. Eq.R. 382; *Re Grant Richards* [1907] 2 K.B. 33. But not a personal right to publish: *Lucas* v. *Moncrieff* (1905) 21 T.L.R. 683. As to an author's right to royalties upon the bankruptcy of his publisher, see now the Bankruptcy Act, 1914, *post*, § 991.

14 *Gibson* v. *Carruthers* (1842) 8 M. & W. 343.

tor,[15] although, of course, royalties due to the judgment debtor might be attached by garnishee proceedings or other process of execution.

346 **Transfer of title to copyright under the Act of 1956.** The main provisions of the Copyright Act, 1956, dealing with transfer of title, are contained in sections 36 and 37, and the main change introduced by that Act is the provision in section 37 enabling the copyright in a future work to be assigned so as to vest the copyright in the assignee as soon as the work is created. Section 19 contains procedural provisions to enable an exclusive licensee to sue an infringer, and some general provisions relevant to changes in title occur in section 49 (5) (7) and (8).

347 **Assignment.** By section 36 (3) of the Act of 1956 it is provided that no assignment of copyright (whether total or partial) shall have effect unless it is in writing signed by or on behalf of the assignor. It should be borne in mind, having regard to the comparative youth of many composers of "pop" music, for instance, that infants [15a] can own and dispose of copyrights in the same way as adults, but subject to the usual rules as to infants' contracts.[16]

Section 36 (2) describes what is meant in that Act by a "partial assignment." It comprises any, or any combination of any, of the following classes of cases, that is to say: an assignment of one or more, but not all, of the exclusive rights given to the owner of copyright including any not separately designated; an assignment of rights for any one or more, but not all, of the countries in relation to which the owner has the exclusive right; and an assignment for part, but not the whole, of the period for which copyright is to subsist.[16a]

348 **Transfer of prospective copyright.** The Copyright Act, 1956, also, as stated, contains provisions under which an agreement may be made before a work is created which will have the effect of vesting the copyright initially in the person with whom the agreement is made as soon as the work is created.[17]

349 **Not possible under Act of 1911.** The Copyright Act, 1911, provided, in section 5 (2) and (3), that the owner of the copyright might assign the right, either wholly or partially, and either generally or subject to limitations to the United Kingdom or to one of His Majesty's Dominions, and either for the whole term or any part thereof and might grant an interest in the right by licence; and that

[15] *Edwards & Co.* v. *Picard* (1909) 78 L.J.K.B. 1108.
[15a] See Family Law Reform Act, 1969 (1969 c. 46).
[16] *Chaplin* v. *Leslie Frewin (Publishers), Ltd.* [1966] Ch. 71.
[16a] See Copyright Act, 1956, s. 49 (5).
[17] Copyright Act, 1956, s. 37 (1).

under a partial assignment of copyright the assignee should be treated for the purposes of the Act as the owner of the copyright in respect of the rights so assigned. Any assignment had to be in writing signed by the owner of the right or his duly authorised agent.

350 This section had no application to a document purporting to assign the copyright in a non-existent work, since a document could not be signed by the owner of the right, and the author became the first owner of the copyright in such a work. Consequently, although such a document might be enforced as an equitable assignment,[17a] it would not entitle the assignee to sue for infringement without joining the author or legal owner.[18] It was suggested, however, that the section might apply to the assignment of equitable rights in existing works.[18] An assignment of the copyright in all works then or thereafter belonging to the assignor was held to be a valid legal assignment in respect of all works of which the copyright was vested in the assignor at the date of the assignment.[19]

351 In the case of *Macdonald (E.), Ltd.* v. *Eyles* [20], Petersen J. held that publishers who had an option to publish the next three future works of an author upon terms that would have made them owners in equity of the copyrights in the works upon their exercising their option, had a sufficient interest, after the author had written another work, but before they exercised their option, to restrain another publisher, who was aware of all the circumstances, from publishing the new work. In this case the legal owner was a party to the suit, though a defendant, so that the court was in a position to enforce an equitable title without prejudice to the legal owner.

352 **Position uncertain before Act of 1911.** There appears to be authority for thinking that, prior to 1911, there could not be a legal assignment of a work not in existence at the date of the alleged assignment [21]. However in the case of *Ward, Lock & Co., Ltd.* v. *Long* [22], Kekewich J. held the contrary. In that case the plaintiffs offered to an author "£200 for the complete copyright of a story containing not less than 80,000 words," on the lines of a synopsis which had been submitted by the author to the plaintiffs, and this offer was accepted. The story, when written, consisted of only about 70,000 words, and the plaintiffs paid the author the sum of £160, and declined to make any

17a *Leader* v. *Purday* (1848) 7 C.B. 4; *Simms* v. *Marryat* (1851) 17 Q.B. 281; *Tailby (E.)* v. *The Official Receiver* (1888) 13 App.Cas. 523.
18 *Performing Right Society, Ltd.* v. *London Theatre of Varieties, Ltd.* [1924] A.C. 1.
19 *Canadian Performing Right Society* v. *Famous Players Canadian Corporation, Ltd.* (1927) 60 O.L.R. 280 and 614.
20 [1921] 1 Ch. 631.
21 *Colburn* v. *Duncombe* (1838) 9 Sim. 151; *Sweet* v. *Shaw* (1839) 3 Jur. 217.
22 [1906] 2 Ch. 550.

further payment. The author thereupon purported to assign his copyright in the story to the defendants, who published the same in ignorance of the author's contract with the plaintiffs. Kekewich J. granted an injunction against the infringement of the plaintiff's copyright. The decision is far from being satisfactory. The learned judge seems to have hesitated to say that the letters which had passed between the author and the plaintiffs amounted to an assignment, but "an agreement to assign in matters of this kind is quite as good as a direct assignment in words, is enforceable in equity, and as between business men is complete." [23] With all deference to the learned judge, it is submitted that there is a great deal of difference between a legal and an equitable assignment, for the one is enforceable, and the other is not enforceable, against a purchaser for value without notice, and if the assignment to the plaintiffs in that case was an equitable assignment only, it is submitted that it was an entire departure from principle to hold that the same held good against the innocent defendants, who appear to have had a legal assignment. But the learned judge seems to have based his decision, in some respects, upon the wording of sections 2 and 3 of the Literary Copyright Act, 1842,[24] which differs from that contained in the Act of 1911.

353 **Transfer of prospective copyright under the Act of 1956.** The Copyright Act, 1956, as has been stated, creates a new method of assigning rights before they come into existence. After defining "future copyright" as copyright which will or may come into existence in respect of any future work or class of works or other subject-matter or on the coming into operation of any provisions of that Act or in any other future event, and providing that "prospective owner" is to be construed accordingly, that Act provides, in section 37 (1), that where, by an agreement made in relation to any future copyright, and signed by or on behalf of the prospective owner of copyright, the prospective owner purports to assign the future copyright (wholly or partially) to another person then if, on the coming into existence of the copyright, the assignee or a person claiming under him would, apart from this subsection, be entitled as against all other persons to require the copyright to be vested in him (wholly or partially, as the case may be), the copyright shall, on its coming into existence, vest in the assignee or his successor in title accordingly by virtue of this subsection and without further assurance. The expression "entitled as against all other persons" presumably refers to the rules of priority which would have applied apart from that Act, if the prospective owner were claiming in a court of equity specific performance of an agreement to assign the future copyright to him.

Subsection (2) of section 37 of the Act of 1956 deals with the case

[23] [1906] 2 Ch. at 557.
[24] 5 & 6 Vict. c. 45.

where the person who would be entitled to the copyright has died before the copyright comes into existence and provides that the copyright shall then devolve as if it had subsisted immediately before his death and he had then been the owner of the copyright. Presumably, therefore, it will vest in his personal representatives.

354 **Not limited to one agreement.** Section 37 of the Act of 1956 contemplates, not merely a simple agreement between the author and one individual or company, as a result of which the copyright when it comes into existence will vest in such individual or company, but also a chain of assignments before the copyright comes into existence, in which case the copyright, when it comes into existence, will vest in the person or persons who, as a result of such documents, will then be the person or persons entitled thereto.[24a] This result follows from subsection (5) of section 37, which defines " prospective owner " as including a person prospectively entitled to the copyright by virtue of such an agreement as is mentioned in subsection (1) of that section.

These provisions, however, do not apply to documents made before the commencement of the Act of 1956.[25] The general effect on the title to works of transactions effected before 1956 will be more fully considered in a later chapter.[26]

355 **What words will effect an assignment.** The Act of 1956, as in the case of the Act of 1911, does not state that the assignment of copyright shall be in any special form, beyond that it shall be in writing, signed by or on behalf of the assignor,[27] and a purported assignment made orally, would, no doubt, avail to protect the assignee against an action for infringement by the assignor, and might, if the consideration was executed, be treated as an equitable assignment. A mere receipt for the purchase-money may, under some circumstances, amount to an assignment of the copyright.[28] Since no particular form of words is required to constitute an assignment it has frequently been a matter

24a See *Chaplin* v. *Leslie Frewin (Publishers), Ltd.* [1966] Ch. 71.

25 Copyright Act, 1956, Sched. VII, para. 28 (2) (*b*).

26 *Post,* Chap. 20.

27 Under the law prior to 1911 an assignment of the copyright in a literary work was required to be in writing: *Leyland* v. *Stewart* (1876) 4 Ch.D. 419. The assignment of the copyright in an engraving had to be in writing, attested by two witnesses (Engraving Copyright Act, 1734 (8 Geo. 2, c. 13) s. 1); in a work of sculpture by deed, attested by two witnesses (Sculpture Copyright Act, 1814 (54 Geo. 3, c. 56), s. 4); and in a painting, drawing, or photograph in writing, signed by the proprietor of the copyright or his agent (Fine Arts Copyright Act, 1862 (25 & 26 Vict. c. 68), s. 3). It was generally considered that an assignment of literary copyright did not require to be attested, and the Acts of 1911 and 1956 do not appear to require any attestation (*Cumberland* v. *Copeland* (1862) 1 Hurl. & C. 194; but see 8 Jur.(N.S.), Part II, p. 148). As to an assignment by a foreigner, see *Jefferys (C.)* v. *Boosey (T.)* (1855) 4 H.L.C. 815.

28 *Jeffreys (C.)* v. *Kyle (M.)* (1855) 18 Sess.Cas. (2nd Ser.) 906; *Howitt* v. *Hall* (1862) 6 L.T. 348; *Levy* v. *Rutley* (1871) L.R. 6 C.P. 523; *Colburn* v. *Duncombe* (1838) 9 Sim. 151; *Ornamin (U.K.)* v. *Bacsa* [1964] R.P.C. 293.

of difficulty to determine upon the construction of a particular document whether it is an assignment, or a mere permission, or bare licence,[29] but it is necessary to distinguish an assignment from an agreement to assign which gives only equitable rights.[30]

356 In *London Printing, etc., Alliance, Ltd.* v. *Cox*[31] the words on an invoice, " For pastel picture and entire copyright, ' On the Threshold,' £52 10s.," and in *Savory (E. W.), Ltd.* v. *The World of Golf, Ltd.*[32] the words on a receipt, " Received of Messrs. E. W. S., Ltd., the sum of £2 6s. 6d. for five original card designs, inclusive of all copyrights. Subjects: Four Golfing subjects; one Teddy Bear painting," were held to be sufficient assignments in writing of the copyright and, in the latter case, oral evidence was admitted to identify the golfing subjects.

357 In both these cases, however, the property in the pictures themselves passed to the purchasers, and in such cases the courts strive to hold that the copyright is not severed from the picture.[33] In *Lacy* v. *Toole*[34] it was held that an agreement to " let A have " a certain work in discharge of a debt owing to A, was sufficient to pass the copyright in the work to A. The intention of the parties must, however, always be regarded, and therefore, in the case of an agreement with publishers whereby the publishers agreed to pay to an author a royalty of sixpence per copy on every copy of the work sold " in consideration of Mr. W. St. J. (author) giving Mr. W. C. N. (publishers) the sole and exclusive right of printing and publishing the series of ' Music and the Higher Life,' and issuing the same in volume form," it was held that the agreement was a publishing agreement only and not an assignment of copyright.[35]

358 **Assignor may not reproduce the work.** An author who has assigned the copyright in his work may, like any other person, be restrained by the assignee from reproducing the work[36] except to the extent permitted by section 9 (9) of the Act of 1956. However, it may

29 *British Actors Film Co., Ltd.* v. *Glover* [1918] 1 K.B. 299; *Macdonald (E.), Ltd.* v. *Eyles* [1921] 1 Ch. 631; *Barstow* v. *Terry* [1924] 2 Ch. 316; *Re " Clinical Obstetrics "* [1905–10] Macg.Cop.Cas. 176; *Neilson* v. *Horniman* [1905–10] Macg. Cop.Cas. 234; *Booth* v. *Richards* [1905–10] Macg.Cop.Cas. 284; *Chaplin* v. *Leslie Frewin (Publishers), Ltd.* [1966] Ch. 71; *Frisby* v. *British Broadcasting Corporation* [1967] Ch. 932. See *post*, § 998 *et seq.*

30 *Ward, Lock & Co., Ltd.* v. *Long* [1906] 2 Ch. 550; *London Printing, etc., Alliance, Ltd.* v. *Cox* [1891] 3 Ch. 291.

31 [1891] 3 Ch. 291.

32 [1914] 2 Ch. 566.

33 *Ante*, § 341.

34 (1867) 15 L.T. 512.

35 *Re Jude's Musical Compositions* [1907] 1 Ch. 651; *cf. Edwardes* v. *Cotton* (1903) 19 T.L.R. 34.

36 *Rooney* v. *Kelly* (1861) 14 Ir.Com.Law Rep. 158; *Colburn* v. *Simms* (1843) 2 Ha. 543; *Educational Co. of Ireland, Ltd. (The)* v. *Fallon Brothers, Ltd.* [1919] 1 I.R. 62.

be a matter of greater difficulty to prove infringement in such a case, because mere similarity is not, in itself, an infringement, without proof of copying, and, when the works are by the same author, such similarity is natural and does not raise any necessary inference of improper use of former works.[36a] An artist who assigns copyright in a work does not, it is submitted, thereby assign his method of portraying similar subjects.[37]

359 **Derivative works.** Where an author has created a second work by using material in an earlier work, questions may arise as to whether there are separate copyrights capable of being vested by assignment in different persons. In *Metzler & Co. (1920), Ltd.* v. *Curwen (J.) & Sons, Ltd.*[38] it was held that an assignee of the copyright in a second work incorporating matter of a first work could maintain an action for infringement against a person using the first work under a subsequent assignment from the author. This decision, however, appears to have rested upon the construction of the assignment in that case. It is submitted that, if the derivative work is a work involving such skill and labour as to constitute it a new original work, the copyright in the first work and the derivative work respectively are capable of being separately assigned so that neither of the respective assignees should have any right of complaint against the other by reason of any exercise of the respective rights assigned to each.[38a]

360 **Divisibility of copyright.** As has been seen,[39] the Act of 1956 contemplates partial assignments limited as to time, as to locality, and as to means of reproduction.

361 **Time.** Copyright might be assigned for a limited time under the law prior to 1911, and it was determined that, in the absence of a special contract to the contrary, the assignor of a copyright was entitled, after the assignment, to continue selling copies of the work printed by him before the assignment and remaining in his possession.[40]

362 In *Howitt* v. *Hall* [41] it appeared that the defendants, having bought the copyright for four years in a book of which the plaintiff was the author, were still continuing, several years after the end of that term, to sell copies which they had printed during the four years. The

36a But see *Francis Day & Hunter Ltd.* v. *Bron* [1963] Ch. 587 and *Industrial Furnaces, Ltd.* v. *Reaves* [1970] R.P.C. 605 at 624.

37 *Preston* v. *Raphael Tuck, etc., Ltd.* [1926] Ch. 667.

38 [1928–35] Macg.Cop.Cas. 127.

38a But see §§ 145 *et seq.* and 358, *ante.*

39 *Ante,* § 347.

40 *Taylor* v. *Pillow* (1869) L.R. 7 Eq. 418; see *Tuck & Sons* v. *Priester* (1887) 19 Q.B.D. 48; *Tuck* v. *The Continental Printing Co.* (1887) 3 T.L.R. 150, 661, 826; *Troitzsch* v. *Rees* (1887) 3 T.L.R. 773.

41 (1862) 6 L.T. 348.

court, in refusing an injunction to restrain such sales, held that the purchase of the copyright carried the right of printing; and that, while this right reverted to the author at the end of four years, the publishers were entitled to sell, after the expiration of that term, all copies which had been printed in good faith during the term. "The Copyright Acts," said Wood V.-C., "were directed against unlawful printing . . . ; and when, as in this case, the defendant had acquired the right of lawfully printing the work, he was at liberty to sell at any time what he had so printed." [42] This case was not affected by the Acts of 1911 and 1956, since it is only the sale of works which infringe copyright which was prohibited by section 2 (2) of the Act of 1911, now section 5 (3) and (4) of the Act of 1956.

363 **Locality.** Whether, under the law prior to 1911, copyright was divisible as to locality, is not so clear, but the balance of authority was in favour of so holding.[43] But the Act of 1911,[44] since it used the words "either generally or subject to limitations to the United Kingdom or any self-governing Dominion or other part of His Majesty's Dominions to which this Act extends," clearly contemplated divisibility as to locality, but it appeared that the assignment must be in respect of a separate country.[45] This was confirmed by the Act of 1956, s. 36 (2) (*b*), which provides that an assignment of copyright may be limited so as to apply to any one or more, but not all, of the countries in relation to which the owner of the copyright has, by virtue of that Act, an exclusive right. It follows that it is not possible to have a separate assignment of copyright in respect of parts of one country.

364 **Mode of reproduction.** There is yet a third manner in which copyright may be divided, and that is as to the mode of reproduction. The words of the Act of 1911 were very wide, permitting an assignment of the copyright "wholly or partially." Thus, the performing rights, the translation rights, the gramophone rights, the photographic rights, the engraving rights, and so forth, were all capable of separate assignment, and it followed, from subsection (3) of section 5 of the Act of 1911, that the assignee of these separate rights could sue for the infringement of his own particular right without making the assignor a party to his action.

365 **"Serial rights."** While, however, the author could, under the Act of 1911, assign separately any one or more of the rights conferred

42 *Ibid.* at 350. But see *ante*, § 79.
43 *Jefferys (C.)* v. *Boosey (T.)* (1855) 4 H.L.C. 815; *Pitt Pitts* v. *George & Co.* [1896] 2 Ch. 866. As to the meaning of "London Right" in the case of a partial assignment of dramatic rights, *cf. Taylor* v. *Neville* (1878) 47 L.J.Q.B. 254.
44 s. 5 (2).
45 *Holt* v. *Woods* (1896) 17 N.S.W.R. 36; *Pitt Pitts* v. *George & Co.* [1896] 2 Ch. 866.

upon him by that Act, it is submitted that a separate assignment of one of these rights, limited to a particular purpose, was invalid. For example, it is submitted that an assignment of " serial rights " in a work was ineffective. The infringement is committed once and for all when the work is printed and, at that stage, it is impossible to know for certain whether printed sheets will be bound over for a single separate publication or for publication in parts over a period. If a grant of " serial rights " were to vest the legal title in the assignee, it would be impossible to know who was the proper plaintiff in an action for infringement by printing. It is suggested that the only effect of a grant of " serial rights," under the Act of 1911, was to give to the grantee a licence to print so long as the printed matter was published in serial form, but to leave the legal title in the copyright vested in the assignor. The same was true, it is suggested, of any other grant of rights limited, not as to mode of reproduction, but as to mode of use when reproduced.

366 Nevertheless, in the case of *Jonathan Cape, Ltd.* v. *Consolidated Press, Ltd.*[46] a person to whom had been granted the right to print in " volume form " was held entitled to sue in his own name as assignee. This case, however, principally turned upon the construction of the document there in question, and the point here alluded to does not seem to have been argued.

The Act of 1956, in dealing with partial assignments of this character, uses the expression " including any one or more classes of acts not separately designated in this Act as being restricted by the copyright, but falling within any of the classes of acts so designated." [47] Moreover, section 49 (5) of the Act of 1956 provides that, in the case of any copyright to which, " whether in consequence of a partial assignment or otherwise," different persons are entitled in respect of the application of the copyright (a) to the doing of different acts or classes of acts, or (b) to the doing of one or more acts or classes of acts in different countries or at different times, the owner of the copyright, for any purposes of that Act, should be taken to be the person who is entitled to the copyright in respect of an application to the doing of the particular act or class of acts, or, as the case may be, to the doing thereof in the particular country or at the particular time, which is relevant to the purpose in question; and, in relation to any future copyright to which different persons are prospectively entitled, references in that Act to the prospective owner of the copyright should be construed accordingly. While none of these provisions wholly meets the point made above in regard to the Act of 1911, it is thought probable that, at least so far as concerns documents executed after the commencement of the Act of 1956, a court would

[46] [1954] 1 W.L.R. 1313 and see § 1001, *post*.
[47] Copyright Act, 1956, s. 36 (2) (*a*).

recognise the right of the grantee of serial or volume rights to be treated as the owner of copyright in respect thereof and to sue alone. The Act of 1956 itself contemplates cases in which the intention of the maker as to the use of the material at the time of making determines whether or not the making is an infringement.[48]

367 **Separate owners of separate rights.** Section 49 (5) of the Act of 1956 above referred to makes clear that there will be separate and independent owners of copyright in respect of the doing of different acts, or different classes of acts, in different countries and at different times. Each owner can only sue in respect of those acts which he himself is entitled to control. This was so under the old law[49] and was true, even though the infringement of some other part of the copyright might commercially damage the owner of the right under the partial assignment. Thus, in *Dicks* v. *Brooks*[50] it was held that the proprietor of the engraving rights in a picture called "The Huguenot" had no right to bring an action against a defendant who had published a chromo-printed pattern for woolwork copied from the original picture. And the assignee of the performing rights in an opera was held not to be entitled to sue in respect of an infringement of the cinematograph rights.[51]

368 **Assignment of "copyright."** Having regard to the various derivative rights which flow from ownership of copyright, an assignor of copyright should always take care that the assignment is drawn in such a way as not to carry rights in excess of those intended to be assigned. Under section 22 of the Literary Copyright Act, 1842,[52] it was provided that no assignment of any book, consisting of or containing a dramatic piece of musical composition, should, prima facie, be taken to convey to the assignee the performing rights. There were, and are, no similar provisions in the Acts of 1911 and 1956, and an assignment of "copyright" would, no doubt, operate, in the absence of contrary intention, to convey to the assignee all the rights which go to make up copyright.[53]

369 **The twenty-five year period.** There was, under the Act of 1911, a limitation on the power of an author to assign his copyright for the full term of life and fifty years. This limitation, forming the proviso to section 5 (2) of the Act of 1911, provided that, where the author was the first owner of the copyright, no assignment of the copyright

48 See, for example, Copyright Act, 1956, ss. 6 (4) and 8 (1) (*c*).
49 Copyright Act, 1911, s. 5 (3).
50 (1880) 15 Ch.D. 22.
51 *British Actors Film Co., Ltd.* v. *Glover* [1918] 1 K.B. 299.
52 5 & 6 Vict. c. 45.
53 Copyright Act, 1956, s. 1 (1); *Cumberland* v. *Planché* (1834) 1 A. & E. 580; *cf. Ex p. Hutchins & Romer* (1879) 4 Q.B.D. 483.

or grant of any interest therein made by him (otherwise than by will) should be operative to vest in the assignee or grantee any rights with respect to the copyright in the work beyond the expiration of twenty-five years from the death of the author, and the reversionary interest in the copyright expectant on the determination of that period should, on the death of the author, notwithstanding any agreement to the contrary, devolve on his legal personal representatives as part of his estate, and that any agreement entered into by him as to the disposition of such reversionary interest should be null and void; but that nothing in the proviso should be considered as applying to the assignment of the copyright in a collective work, or to a licence to publish a work or part of a work as part of a collective work.

By paragraph 28 (3) of the Seventh Schedule to the Act of 1956, it is provided that this proviso, as re-enacted in the Eighth Schedule to that Act, is to apply to assignments and licences having effect with regard to copyright under that Act by the operation of any document made before the commencement of that Act. This means that unless some further assignment has been made since the commencement of the Act of 1956 (June 1, 1957), any assignments or licences made before the commencement of that Act will only operate until the end of the first twenty-five-year period. Consequently, while the proviso does not affect post-1957 documents, even in regard to pre-1957 copyrights, it will continue for many years to affect titles to pre-1957 copyrights which have been the subject of pre-1957 transactions.

370 **Proviso only applied if the author was the first owner of the copyright.** It is to be noticed that this proviso only applied in a case where the author was the first owner of the copyright. In the case, therefore, of an engraving, photograph, or portrait, where the plate or other original was ordered by some other person and was made for valuable consideration, or in the case of a work made by an author in the employment of some other person under a contract of service or apprenticeship, the proprietor of the copyright was at liberty to assign it for the full term, for in neither of these cases did the copyright vest in the author in the first instance.[54]

371 **Proviso did not apply to collective works.** The proviso in question did not apply " to the *assignment* of the copyright in a collective work or a *licence* to publish a work or part of a work as part of a collective work." [55] The words here employed should be noticed. In a collective work there may be several distinct copyrights —that is, the copyright in the complete work, considered as a whole

54 Copyright Act, 1911, s. 5 (1) (*a*) and (*b*).

55 A " collective work " meant (a) an encyclopedia, dictionary, year-book, or similar work; (b) a newspaper, review, magazine, or similar periodical; and (c) any work written in distinct parts by different authors, or in which works or parts of works of different authors are incorporated (Copyright Act, 1911, s. 35 (1)).

and the various copyrights in the distinct contributions to the work. An "assignment" of the copyright in the complete work could have been made for the full period of protection, and a "licence" to publish a contribution as part of the collective work could also have been granted for the like full period. But an "assignment" of the copyright in the contribution could not have been made for the period commencing twenty-five years after the author's death.[56]

372 **Nor to posthumous works.** Inasmuch as it is only the author himself who was prohibited from assigning the entire copyright, the proviso could not apply to posthumous works, which were entitled to protection until publication and for a period of fifty years thereafter.[57]

373 **Proviso did apply to existing works, but not to existing assignments.** On the other hand, while the proviso applied to works in existence prior to the Act of 1911, it did not apply to assignments made before the date of the passing of that Act (December 16, 1911), or between that date and the date of the commencement of that Act (July 1, 1912), because the rights of an assignee under an assignment made before the commencement of that Act were determined once and for all by the provisions of section 24 of that Act.[58]

374 **Quaere, as to photographs and mechanical instruments.** It is questionable whether the proviso against assignment applied to photographs and mechanical instruments, the copyright in both of which was for a period of fifty years from the date of the making of the negative or plate as the case may be, and vested in the owner of the negative or plate, who was to be "deemed to be the author of the work." [59] The proviso did not form part of the Bill as it was originally laid before the House of Commons, but was drafted and added to the Bill during its passage through Committee of the House. It would almost seem as though the draftsman of the proviso had overlooked the fact that, in the case of some works, the period of copyright protection bore no relation to the lives of their authors, and although the words of the proviso, at first sight, seem wide enough to cover photographs and records, it is submitted that the court ought to endeavour to exclude its application to such works. One reason, no doubt, for fixing the period of twenty-five years from the death of an author as the limit of the assignability of copyright was because, at that date, a work ceased to have exclusive copyright, and any person —including, of course, the assignee of the copyright, who then ceased to have the benefit of his assignment—could have published the

[56] Possibly an assignment for the full term might be construed as a licence.
[57] Copyright Act, 1911, s. 17.
[58] *Coleridge-Taylor* v. *Novello & Co., Ltd.* [1938] Ch. 850.
[59] Copyright Act, 1911, ss. 19 and 21.

work upon a royalty basis.[60] It is, however, doubtful whether a photograph or a record could have been published upon this basis.[61] The assignee of the copyright in a photograph or record, whose author died shortly after the making of the negative or plate, would, therefore, be in an unfair position as compared with an assignee of, say, literary copyright. Another reason for excluding photographs and records from the proviso against assignment is that a corporation may be deemed to be the " author " of either of these works, and, in such a case, the proviso could have no possible application. Again, the proviso refers to the interest of the author after the termination of the period of his assignment as " the reversionary interest in the copyright expectant on the termination of that period." If works as to which the existence of any reversionary period is problematical (for the author of a photograph might live for twenty-five years after the making of the photograph) were intended to be included, it would have been more in accordance with the rules of good draftsmanship to have added, after the words " reversionary interest," the words " if any."

375 **Illusory nature of the benefits enforced by the proviso.** The proviso to section 5 (2) of the Act of 1911 was, of course, inserted in the interest of an author's family, to prevent, if possible, a successful author from making improvident contracts to the detriment of his dependants. In practice the benefits to the author's family or dependants have been found to be somewhat illusory. The proviso rendered null and void any attempt by a living author to dispose of the reversionary interest in his copyright, and declared that this reversionary interest should " on the death of the author," devolve on his legal personal representatives " as part of his estate." This reversionary interest, unassignable during the author's lifetime, therefore became an asset of the author's estate and assignable immediately upon his death. It was consequently liable to be sold by his executors for the payment of his debts, and, even if not required for that purpose, it was frequently the duty of the executors to realise the interest for the purpose of winding up the author's estate.[62] Supposing the author made a specific bequest of his reversionary interest in his copyright, the specific legatee would probably be ready to sell that interest forthwith, rather than wait for a chance of income twenty-five years later. The only possible purchaser, at any rate in the case of a literary work, would, save in exceptional cases, be the author's publisher, and the

[60] Copyright Act, 1911, s. 3, proviso, *ante,* § 276 *et seq.* In the case, however, of works existing prior to the Act of 1911, this right did not arise until after thirty years from the death of the author (Copyright Act, 1911, s. 3). There was thus left a hiatus of five years.

[61] *Ante,* § 283.

[62] For instance, the rule well known to equity lawyers as the rule in *Howe* v. *Lord Dartmouth* ((1802) 7 Ves. 137a) would apply. *Cf. Pickering* v. *Evans* [1921] 2 Ch. 309.

amount which he would be prepared to give for a reversionary interest in a copyright falling into possession twenty-five years later would not be likely to be very large, particularly having regard to the fact that he would, even if he declined to purchase the reversion, be entitled to continue to publish the work, if he thought it worth while to do so, upon payment of a royalty to the owner of the copyright, and that, if he did purchase, he could not acquire an exclusive copyright.[63]

376 **Recommendation of Copyright Committee.** The 1952 Copyright Committee recommended that this proviso should not be continued on the ground that they were recommending the omission of the proviso to section 3 of the Act of 1911, which entitled anyone to publish works on compulsory royalty terms at the end of the twenty-five-year period, and considered that the proviso to section 5 (2) of that Act must also go, since it would seem to have been inserted so as to give the royalty, under section 3 of the Act of 1911, to the personal representatives of the author.[64]

377 **Summary of law affecting transfers of title.** Before proceeding to the question of licences, it may be convenient to summarise the legal effect of documents in the classes already dealt with, namely, complete assignments, partial assignments, and transfers of prospective copyright.

First, in these cases, the transferee can sue for infringement in his own name without adding any other party. Secondly, so far as assignments are concerned, it would appear that the transferee, whether for value or not, acquires a good title as against a later transferee, whether or not the latter had notice of the previous transfer. On the other hand, a transferee of future copyright only acquires title if " apart from this subsection he would be entitled as against all other persons to require the copyright to be vested in him." [65] As already submitted, therefore, it would seem that the title has to be considered on the basis of an applicant for specific performance, and although, prima facie, assignments will take effect in their priority of time, equities which could be raised in proceedings for specific performance are material.

378 A further class of case arises where (a) any of the foregoing transactions are carried out orally,[66] or (b) in the case of an assignment of an existing copyright the document executed is not in terms a transfer of copyright, but only an agreement to transfer. It is submitted that, in any such case, the transferee can sue only if he joins

[63] Copyright Act, 1911, s. 3.
[64] Cmd. 8662, para. 23.
[65] Copyright Act, 1956, s. 37 (1).
[66] *e.g., Cooper* v. *Stephens* [1895] 1 Ch. 567; *Dennison* v. *Ashdown* (1897) 13 T.L.R. 226; *Boucas* v. *Cooke* [1903] 2 K.B. 227, 236; *Drabble (Harold), Ltd.* v. *The Hycolite Manufacturing Co.* (1928) 44 T.L.R. 265.

the legal owner of the right, either as plaintiff or defendant,[67] and that his title is not binding on an assignee without notice.

379 **Licences.** Licences are referred to in various sections of the Act of 1956. By section 1 (2) of that Act it is provided that copyright is infringed by any person who, not being the owner of the copyright and without the licence of the owner thereof, does any of the acts restricted by such copyright. Section 49 (7) of that Act, provides for sub-licences by stating that, where the doing of anything is authorised by the grantee of a licence, or a person deriving title from the grantee, and it is within the terms (including any implied terms) of the licence for him to authorise it, it shall, for the purposes of that Act, be taken to be done with the licence of the grantor and of every other person (if any) upon whom the licence is binding. Section 36 (4) of that Act states on whom licences are binding by providing that a licence granted in respect of any copyright by the person who, in relation to the matters to which the licence relates, is the owner of the copyright, shall be binding upon every successor in title to his interest in the copyright except a purchaser in good faith for valuable consideration and without notice (actual or constructive) [68] of the licence, or a person deriving title from such a purchaser. Section 36 (4) continues that references in that Act, in relation to any copyright, to the doing of anything with, or (as the case may be) without, the licence of the owner of the copyright shall be construed accordingly. By section 37 (3) of that Act, it is provided that subsection (4) of section 36 of that Act shall apply in relation to a licence granted by a prospective owner of any copyright as it applies in relation to a licence granted by the owner of a subsisting copyright, as if any reference in that subsection to the owner's interest in the copyright included a reference to his prospective interest.

380 The licensee of copyright, or of prospective copyright, therefore, to the extent of the licence, can do acts restricted by the copyright as against the owner and anyone claiming through him, except a purchaser for value without notice. Except in connection with exclusive licences, as hereafter mentioned, there is no requirement that a licence shall be in writing, and it can therefore presumably be oral, or implied from conduct. But a licence which amounts merely to a consent does not confer any interest in the right.[68a] As it was put by Tindal C.J. in *Muskett* v. *Hill* [69] " a dispensation or licence properly passes no interest, but only makes an action lawful which, without it, would

67 *Neilson* v. *Horniman* (1909) 26 T.L.R. 188; *cf. Heap* v. *Hartley* (1889) 42 Ch.D. 461; *Woolley* v. *Broad* [1892] 1 Q.B. 806; *Macmillan & Co.* v. *Dent* [1907] 1 Ch. 107; *Marshall (W.) & Co., Ltd.* v. *Bull (A. H.), Ltd.* (1901) 85 L.T. 77.

68 See Law of Property Act, 1925 (15 Geo. 5, c. 20), s. 199.

68a See *Neilson* v. *Horniman* [1905–10] Macg.Cop.Cas. 234.

69 (1840) 5 Bing.N.C. 694.

have been unlawful." Clearly, a licence which is not sole and exclusive cannot pass any interest in the right, since if it did, nothing would remain in the grantor out of which to grant subsequent licences.[70] On the other hand a licence, if coupled with an interest in the right, would seem to be irrevocable.[71]

381 **Right of exclusive licensee to sue under Act of 1911.** Before 1956, the position of an exclusive licensee was somewhat doubtful as it had never been clearly decided whether or not he could sue in his own name. Having regard to the provisions of paragraph 28 of the Seventh Schedule to the Act of 1956, the operation of documents under the provisions of the Act of 1911 is still material where such documents were made before the commencement of the Act of 1956 and it may therefore still be necessary to consider the meaning of the expression " grant of any interest " in section 5 (2) of the Act of 1911. One view of the matter was that these words conferred a legal interest in the right which would give the licensee an indefeasible title and enable him to sue in respect of infringements in his own name. The point was left open in the case of *British Actors Film Co., Ltd.* v. *Glover* [72] and in the more recent case of *Jonathan Cape, Ltd.* v. *Consolidated Press, Ltd.*,[73] and has been much debated since the Act of 1911 was passed.

As an argument against the grantee being able to sue, it is to be noted that, while there was an express provision that the assignee under a partial assignment was to be treated as the owner of such part, there was no similar provision with regard to a grantee by way of licence. It is thought, however, that the legislature inserted the provision with regard to a grantee by way of licence to cover the case of a transfer which was, in substance, a partial assignment, but, in form, was expressed as a licence, and might be difficult to construe as an assignment,[74] and that the real effect of this provision was to make it easier to construe a document as a partial assignment though, in form, expressed as a licence [75] while leaving unaffected the law relating to documents which were of necessity licences only in the narrower sense, because they were not exclusive, or purported to deal with rights which were not susceptible of separate assignment.[76]

70 *Warne* v. *Routledge* (1874) L.R. 18 Eq. 497; *Rundell* v. *Murray* (1821) Jac. 311; *Chaplin* v. *Leslie Frewin (Publishers), Ltd.* [1966] Ch. 71.

71 *Hurst* v. *Picture Theatres, Ltd.* [1915] 1 K.B. 1; *British Actors Film Co., Ltd.* v. *Glover* [1918] 1 K.B. 299; *Hart* v. *Hayman, etc., Ltd.* [1911–16] Macg.Cop.Cas 301; *Willams* v. *Feldman* [1911–16] Macg.Cop.Cas. 98; *Chaplin* v. *Leslie Frewin (Publishers), Ltd.* [1966] Ch. 71. See as to irrevocability of licences not coupled with an interest, *Hounslow London Borough Council* v. *Twickenham Garden Developments, Ltd.* [1971] Ch. 233.

72 [1918] 1 K.B. 299.

73 [1954] 1 W.L.R. 1313.

74 *e.g.*, *Re Jude's Musical Compositions* [1907] 1 Ch. 651; see also *Withers* v. *Nethersole* [1946] 1 All E.R. 711; [1948] 1 All E.R. 400.

75 *Messager* v. *British Broadcasting Co., Ltd.* [1929] A.C. 151.

76 See *ante*, § 363.

382 **And under the Act of 1956.** Section 19 of the Copyright Act, 1956, however, has given an exclusive licensee, as defined in that section, the right to sue in his own name.[77] It should be observed, however, that this is only a right as against persons claiming no title through the copyright owner, and does not put an exclusive licensee in any stronger position than any other licensee as against persons claiming through the legal owner of the copyright. This follows from section 19 (4) of the Act of 1956, which provides that, in any action brought by the exclusive licensee, any defence which would have been available to a defendant in the action if that section had not been enacted and the action had been brought by the owner of the copyright, shall be available to that defendant as against the exclusive licensee. It would appear, therefore, that if the owner of the copyright grants a later licence in breach of his obligations to the exclusive licensee, the later licensee will be protected, since he could rely upon his licence in an action brought by the owner of the copyright. In such a case the remedy of the exclusive licensee would appear to lie in damages only against the owner of the copyright.

383 **Definition of "exclusive licence."** "Exclusive licence" is defined by subsection (9) of section 19 of the Act of 1956 as a licence in writing, signed by or on behalf of an owner or prospective owner of copyright, authorising the licensee, to the exclusion of all other persons, including the grantor of the licence, to exercise a right which, by virtue of the Act, would, apart from the licence, be exercisable exclusively by the owner of the copyright. Section 19 is to take effect, as if, instead of the licence, there had been granted, subject to terms and conditions corresponding as nearly as may be with those subject to which the licence was granted, an assignment of the copyright in respect of its application to the doing, at the places and times authorised by the licence, of the acts so authorised.[78] Having regard to this provision it is possible that a licence to exercise the rights of a class not capable of being the subject of an assignment as, for example, rights in one part of the United Kingdom only, are not capable of being the subject of an exclusive licence for the purposes of this section. It should be observed, however, that this definition of exclusive licence is for the purposes of this section only, and that there is no objection to an oral grant of an exclusive licence which will be effective as between the parties as a matter of contract.

384 **Rights of exclusive licensee.** The main operative part of section 19 is in subsection (2), which provides that the exclusive licensee is to have the same rights of action, and to be entitled to the same remedies

[77] The section does not apply to a licence granted before the commencement of the Act of 1956 (Copyright Act, 1956, Sched. 7, para. 22).
[78] Copyright Act, 1956, s. 19 (9).

for infringement, as if the licence had been an assignment, and such rights and remedies are to be concurrent with the rights and remedies of the owner of the copyright. Furthermore, the exclusive licensee is to have the same rights of action, and to be entitled to the same remedies for conversion, as if the licence had been an assignment, and the owner of the copyright is not to be entitled to these remedies.[79] Nevertheless, these rights are not exercisable against the owner of the copyright. The rights of the exclusive licensee against the owner of the copyright lie in contract only and may, of course, be defeated by a purchaser for value of the copyright without notice.[80]

385 **Where necessary to join owner of copyright as party.** It is further provided that, where an action is brought, either by the owner of the copyright, or by the exclusive licensee, and the action relates to an infringement in respect of which they have concurrent rights of action, the owner or licensee, as the case may be, is not to be entitled, except with the leave of the court, to proceed with the action unless the other party is either joined as a plaintiff in the action or added as a defendant.[81] The importance of this provision is that the exclusive licensee may proceed in the absence of the owner of the copyright with the leave of the court, and this may be a great convenience where the owner of the copyright is dead and no grant has been taken to his estate or he cannot be found. It is further provided that, where the other party is added as a defendant, he is not to be liable for any costs of the action, unless he enters an appearance and takes part in the proceedings.[82] It is further provided that an interlocutory injunction may be granted on the application of either the owner of the copyright or the exclusive licensee.[81]

386 **Special provisions as to damages, and accounts of profits.** It is provided that the exclusive licensee and the owner of the copyright are to have concurrent remedies for damages for infringement,[83] but that the exclusive licensee shall alone be entitled to damages for conversion.[84]

If, however, the owner of the copyright and the exclusive licensee are not both plaintiffs in the action, the court, in assessing damages in respect of infringement, shall, if the plaintiff is the exclusive licensee,

[79] s. 19 (2) (*b*) and (*c*).

[80] s. 36 (4).

[81] Copyright Act, 1956, s. 19 (3); see *Warwick Film Productions, Ltd.* v. *Eisinger* [1963] 1 W.L.R. 756. R.S.C., Order 52, r. 19, which dealt specifically with applications, under s. 19 (3) of the Act of 1956, for leave to proceed with an action without joining the other party as a plaintiff or adding him as a defendant has not been repeated in the revised Rules. However, no doubt the procedure under the old Order 52, r. 19, namely, by summons in the action, will still be the appropriate method of making such an application.

[82] s. 19 (8).

[83] s. 19 (2) (*a*).

[84] s. 19 (2) (*b*).

take into account any liabilities in respect of royalties or otherwise to which the licence is subject, and shall, whether the plaintiff is the owner of the copyright or the exclusive licensee, take into account any pecuniary remedy already awarded to the other party in respect of the infringement or, as the case may require, any right of action exercisable by the other party in respect thereof.[85] If in such action, and whether the owner of the copyright and the exclusive licensee are both parties or not, an account of profits is directed to be taken in respect of the infringement, then, subject to any agreement of which the court is aware determining the application of the profits, the court is to apportion the profits between them as the court may consider just, and to give such directions as the court may consider appropriate for giving effect to that apportionment.[86] Again, in such an action, no judgment or order for payment of damages in respect of an infringement is to be given if a final judgment or order has been given or made awarding an account of profits to the other party in respect of the same infringement, and similarly no judgment or order for an account of profits in respect of infringement is to be given if a final judgment or order has been given or made awarding either damages or an account of profits to the other party in respect of the said infringement.[87]

387 **Whether assignable.** Prima facie, a licence is assignable, but this will not be so if there is any evidence that the licensee was chosen on account of his personal skill or reputation.[88]

388 **Sound films and television.** It has been held in *Pathé Pictures, Ltd.* v. *Bancroft*,[89] that a licence to produce a work " in moving picture films " does not authorise the production of a sound film of the work, but it was stated by Swift J., in the same case, that " cinematograph films " would include sound films, and " cinematograph rights " would include the right to reproduce by means of a sound film.

389 A similar question arose in the Australian case of *Williamson (J. C.) Ltd.* v. *M.-G.-M. Theatres, Ltd.*,[90] and it was decided that a reservation of motion picture rights included sound films, on the ground that, at the date of agreement, the use of sound films commer-

85 s. 19 (5).
86 s. 19 (6).
87 Copyright Act, 1956, s. 19 (7).
88 *Re Jude's Musical Compositions* [1907] 1 Ch. 651; *Stevens* v. *Benning* (1855) 1 K. & J. 168; *Hole* v. *Bradbury* (1879) 12 Ch.D. 886; *Griffith* v. *Tower Publishing Co., Ltd.* [1897] 1 Ch. 21. See *Messager* v. *British Broadcasting Co., Ltd.* [1927] 2 K.B. 543, reversed on other grounds [1929] A.C. 151. See Copyright Act, 1956, s. 49 (7).
89 [1928–35] Macg.Cop.Cas. 403.
90 [1937] V.L.R. 140; (1937) 56 C.L.R. 567.

cially was " threatened," so that the parties must have contracted with this in view. It is thought, however, that in documents executed before the commercial use of sound films was contemplated, " cinematograph " or " moving picture rights " must be taken to be confined to the right to make contrivances for the visual performance of the work, and not to comprise the quite distinct right to make contrivances for the audible performance thereof.

Support for this view is to be found in the decision of Buckley J., in *Hospital for Sick Children* v. *Walt Disney Productions, Inc.*,[91] when he held that the grant, by Sir James Barrie, in an agreement made in 1919, of a licence to produce all his literary and dramatic works, for the term of their respective copyrights, " in cinematograph or moving picture films," was only effective to grant silent film rights and not sound film rights also. The learned judge held that the proper conclusion to reach, in that case, as to the effect of the 1919 agreement depended upon what was then properly to be regarded as being in the contemplation of the parties. No help was to be gained from the use of the words " cinematograph " as well as " moving pictures " for if, at the date such agreement was entered into, the only kind of cinematograph or moving picture films that were known as being commercial propositions, or likely to become commercial propositions, within the period contemplated by the agreement were silent films, it was impossible to conclude that, by using the word " cinematograph," the parties intended to refer to something other than the production of silent films.

However, in a limited appeal from the decision of Buckley J.,[92] Lord Denning M.R. said that the decisions in *L. C. Page & Co.* v. *Fox Film Corporation*[93] and *Williamson (J. C.) Ltd.* v. *M.-G.-M. Theatres, Ltd.*[90] showed that, even before sound films were a commercial proposition, a grant of moving picture film rights was capable of carrying the right to make, not only a silent film, but also a sound film. But the provisions of the 1919 agreement did not comprehend sound films. That agreement was made in 1919 when sound films were very remote. Neither of the parties had them in mind. Harman L.J. considered that, to construe a document rightly, the court must seek, not merely what it thinks to be the intention of the parties; it must seek that intention in the words the parties have used. The words used in the 1919 agreement were wide enough to cover talking films with living actors and, without coming to a concluded opinion, Harman L.J. thought that Buckley J. took too narrow a view,

[91] [1966] 1 W.L.R. 1055; and see *Serra* v. *Famous-Lasky Film Service, Ltd.* (1922) 127 L.T. 109; *Messager* v. *British Broadcasting Co.* [1927] 2 K.B. 543; *Ricordi* v. *Paramount Pictures, Inc.* (1950) 92 Fed.Supp. 537; *Rosenberg and Lesser* v. *Wright* (1934) 20 Copyright Decisions 599; *Murphy* v. *Warner Bros. Theatres* (1940) 112 Fed.Rep. 2d 946; *Macloon* v. *Vitagraph Inc.* (1929) 30 Fed.Rep. 2d 634.

[92] [1968] Ch. 52; § 752, *post.*

[93] (1936) 83 Fed.Rep. 2d 196.

and that the better opinion would accord with the decision in the case of *Williamson* v. *M.-G.-M. Theatres.*[90] Salmon L.J. considered that the words of the 1919 agreement were capable of passing, and would normally pass, the talking picture rights, even though commercial talking pictures were not in existence, and therefore not in the minds of the parties to the contract, at the time it was written. However, he went on to say that, although not dissenting from the judgments of Lord Denning M.R. and Harman L.J. that, although the words of the 1919 agreement themselves were wide enough to cover sound films, taking the agreement as a whole they applied only to silent films, he was not so confident that that view was correct, and he preferred to express no concluded opinion on this question.

A similar question could arise as to whether a licence to broadcast included a right to broadcast by television.

390 **Assignment of copyright not bona fide.** Where the proprietors of the copyright in two pictures assigned the same to the plaintiffs upon the plaintiffs undertaking not to reproduce the same without the assignors' consent, the purpose of the assignment being to enable the plaintiffs to sue for infringement of the copyright in the pictures, it was held that the assignment was not bona fide, and that the plaintiffs could not sue without joining the assignors as co-plaintiffs.[94]

The question as to the rights of an assignee of copyright to make alterations in the work is treated in another place,[95] as are also special provisions in regard to television and broadcasting rights.[96]

[The next paragraph is 401]

94 *Landeker & Brown* v. *Wolff (L.) & Co., Ltd.* (1907) 52 S.J. 45.
95 See Chap. 21, *post,* which see generally upon the subject of assignment.
96 See Chap. 18, *post.*

CHAPTER 9

INFRINGEMENT OF COPYRIGHT

1.—GENERAL AND LITERARY

401 Since copyright now subsists only under and in accordance with the provisions of the Act of 1956,[1] all questions relating to what is, and what is not, an infringement of copyright depend upon the terms of that Act.

Infringements of copyright may be divided into direct infringements, which consist of the unauthorised exercise by persons not being the copyright owner of rights restricted by that Act, and indirect infringements, which consist of unauthorised dealings with works which are themselves direct infringements or unauthorised importations.[2]

2.—DIRECT INFRINGEMENT BY COPYING

402 So far as concerns direct infringements, the Act of 1956 provides, in section 1 (2), that the copyright in a work is infringed by any person who, not being the owner of the copyright, and without the licence of the owner thereof, does, or authorises another person to do, any of those acts in relation to the work which are designated as the acts restricted by the copyright in the work. The Act therefore introduces the new expression " restricted by the copyright " and, throughout the Act, various acts in relation to different classes of works are referred to as being " restricted by the copyright " in such works. In this chapter, the acts restricted by the copyright in respect of literary, dramatic, musical and artistic works are considered and in other chapters [3] there are dealt with the acts restricted by the copyright in cinematograph films, sound recordings and other special classes of works.

403 **Reproduction in a material form.** The acts restricted by the copyright in a literary work are set forth in section 2 (5) of the Act of 1956 and the primary act so restricted is " reproducing the work in any material form." This is the general phrase used as well in connection with literary works as in connection with dramatic, musical and artistic works and many of the general observations in this section of this chapter are applicable to all kinds of works. After dealing with infringement by copying, there will further be considered, in

[1] s. 46.
[2] See *post*, § 471.
[3] See *post*, Chaps. 16 and 17.

this chapter, other acts restricted by the copyright in literary works and also the indirect infringements above referred to.

The doing, within the area within which the Copyright Act, 1956, extends, of any of these acts, by a person other than the copyright owner, and without his licence, is, therefore, an infringement of copyright, unless such exercise falls within one of the statutory exceptions.[4] On the other hand, any dealing with the work of the copyright owner which does not involve an exercise of one of these rights is not a direct infringement. Thus to make use of a book is not a piracy, if copies are not multiplied. To take a familiar instance, it is the custom for many Law Societies to print general conditions relating to the sale of real estate. A and B enter into a contract for sale and incorporate by reference into their agreement " the Conditions of Sale of the X Y Law Society." Assuming these conditions to be the subject of copyright, A and B are not infringing that copyright if they confine themselves to a reference and do not copy the conditions into their agreement. The exercise by an unauthorised person of each of such sole rights constitutes a separate tort.[5]

404 **Licence and consent.** The use of the expression " without the licence of the owner," instead of " without the consent of the owner," which was the phrase used in section 2 (1) of the Act of 1911, has not, it is apprehended, made any change in the law. Such licence or consent may, it is apprehended, be verbal, or implied from conduct, or may result from a formal licence.[6]

405 **Infringement under the Act of 1911.** Many of the cases cited in this chapter in regard to what constitutes infringement of copyright are decisions upon the law as it existed before the commencement of the Act of 1911, or are decisions under that Act. While the Act of 1956 has not, it is thought, made any change in the basic nature of infringement of copyright, it may be well in order, to appreciate the decisions under the Act of 1911, to set out here the primary provisions of the Act of 1911 as to infringement. The Act of 1911 [7] provided that copyright should be deemed to be infringed by any person who, without the consent of the owner of the copyright, did anything the sole right to do which was by that Act conferred on the owner of the copyright. The primary right so conferred was " the sole right to produce or reproduce the work or any substantial part thereof in any material form whatsoever." [8] So far as decisions on the law before 1911 are concerned, it must be kept in mind that the language of the

[4] See §§ 458–470, *post*.
[5] *Ash* v. *Hutchinson & Co. (Publishers), Ltd.* [1936] Ch. 489.
[6] *Drabble (Harold), Ltd.* v. *The Hycolite Manufacturing Co.* (1928) 44 T.L.R. 265, and see § 380, *ante*.
[7] s. 2 (1).
[8] Copyright Act, 1911, s. 1 (2).

earlier statutes giving copyright protection differed substantially from that used in the Acts of 1911 and 1956, and that, prior to the Act of 1911, there were a number of different statutes giving protection in different language to different classes of works.

406 **Form, not idea, protected.** A preliminary observation is that it is essential to have in mind, in approaching any question of infringement, the nature of the thing protected by copyright law. What is protected is not original thought or information, but the original expression of thought or information in some concrete form.[9] Consequently, it is only an infringement if the defendant has made an unlawful use of the form in which the thought or information is expressed. The defendant must, to be liable, have made a substantial use of this form; he is not liable if he has taken from the work the essential idea, however original, and expressed the idea in his own form, or used the idea for his own purposes.[10] Protection of this kind can only be given, if at all, under the patent law, or by invoking the principles applicable to confidential information.[11]

407 **Infringement involves copying.** A further essential matter, and one which—rather strangely—is not anywhere precisely stated in the Act of 1956, is that there can be no infringement unless use has been made, directly or indirectly, of the plaintiff's work.[11a] Two photographs of the same scene or person, for example, may be almost identical, and so may two mathematical tables or two directories, but in every case each may have been made without reference to the other. It is thought that there can be no doubt that, in all such cases, where neither work has been taken from the other, there is no infringement, however great the similarity, and although, in one sense, it may be said that the later work " reproduces " the earlier.[12] It is submitted that it would make no difference to the result that the defendant was proved to have obtained his idea from the earlier work, provided that he took his photograph or prepared his table or his directory independently.[13] Although the word " reproducing " in section 2 (5) of the Act of 1956 may be more ambiguous from this point of view than the words " printing or otherwise multiplying copies " in the Act of 1842, it is submitted that the word " copyright " itself indicates that the right given is confined to copying in some form the work to which copyright protection is afforded and does not extend to an independent production of the original. As Lord

[9] See Chap. 1.

[10] *Hollinrake* v. *Truswell* [1894] 3 Ch. 420; *McCrum* v. *Eisner* (1918) 87 L.J.Ch. 99; *Wilmer* v. *Hutchinson & Co., etc., Ltd.* [1936–45] Macg.Cop.Cas. 13.

[11] *Corelli* v. *Gray* (1913) 29 T.L.R. 570. See § 88 *et seq., ante.*

[11a] See *Francis Day & Hunter, Ltd.* v. *Bron* [1963] Ch. 587 at 611.

[12] *Corelli* v. *Gray, supra.* See § 403, *ante.*

[13] See § 130, *ante.*

Atkinson pointed out in *Macmillan & Co., Ltd.* v. *Cooper (K. & J.)*,[14] the moral basis upon which the protective provisions of the Copyright Act, 1911, rested was the Eighth Commandment: "Thou shalt not steal." This, then, is a second way in which copyright protection differs from that afforded to patents. In the case of the latter, any person who produces the patented invention infringes the patent though he has arrived at his result by independent investigation.

408 It follows from what has been said in the last two paragraphs that in any case of infringement the plaintiff has to establish, not only that the work in respect of which complaint is made in fact so nearly resembles his as to be capable of being an infringement, but also that it has in fact been produced by the use of those features of his work which, by reason of the knowledge, skill and labour employed in their production, constitute it an original copyright work.[15] Such use, however, may consist, not of a direct use of the plaintiff's work, but of the use of some other work derived from the plaintiff's work and being itself either an infringement or a licensed production.[16] The foregoing may be summarised by saying that there is no infringement unless it is established that the defendant has produced a work which both closely resembles the plaintiff's work [16a] and has been produced by a direct or indirect use of those features of the plaintiff's work in which copyright subsists.

409 In *Francis Day & Hunter, Ltd.* v. *Bron* [17] Diplock L.J. said: "The necessity for a causal connection between the copyright work and the infringing work, although well established under the Copyright Act, 1911, either as being implicit in the legal concept of 'copyright' or in the word 'reproduce,' is, I think, more easily deduced from the wording of the current Copyright Act of 1956. Section 1 (1) defines 'copyright' in relation to a work as the exclusive right to do and to authorise other persons to do certain acts 'in relation to that work' and subsection (2) defines 'infringement' as the doing of any of those acts by a person who is not the owner of the copyright or his licensee, the acts, which are defined in section 2, and include 'reproducing the

[14] (1923) 40 T.L.R. 186.

[15] *McCrum* v. *Eisner*, *supra*, at p. 102; *De Manduit* v. *Gaumont, etc., Corp., Ltd.* [1936–45] Macg.Cop.Cas. 292. See *Coral Index, Ltd.* v. *Regent Index, Ltd.* [1970] R.P.C. 147, where reference is made to similarity of language, the order of describing a scheme and the format of the documents, in considering whether a substantial part of business literature had been copied.

[16] *King Features Syndicate* v. *O. & M. Kleeman, Ltd.* [1941] A.C. 417; *Cate* v. *Devon, etc., Newspaper Co.* (1889) 40 Ch.D. 500; *Ex p. Beal* (1868) L.R. 3 Q.B. 387; and see *Hanfstaengl* v. *Empire Palace* [1894] 3 Ch. 109; *Purefoy Engineering Co., Ltd.* v. *Sykes, Boxall & Co., Ltd.* (1954) 71 R.P.C. 227 and *Dorling* v. *Honnor Marine, Ltd.* [1965] Ch. 1.

[16a] As to alleged three-dimensional reproduction of literary work in two dimensions, see *Cuisenaire* v. *Reed* [1963] V.R. 719 and *Cuisenaire* v. *South West Imports, Ltd.* [1968] 1 Ex.C.R. 493.

[17] [1963] Ch. 587.

work in any material form,' if they are to constitute infringement must thus be done ' in relation to the work,' an expression which connotes a causal connection between the copyright work and the act relied upon as an infringement."

410 **Ignorance no excuse.** If, however, the defendant has in fact derived his work, either directly or indirectly, from the plaintiff's, the fact that the defendant was unaware that the work he has used was the plaintiff's, or was the subject of copyright, affords no defence to the action,[18] although, in the latter case only, it may affect the remedy.[19] Copyright being a proprietary right, ignorance is no excuse for infringement.[20] Similarly, it is no defence that the defendant has relied upon a licence or assignment, which he believed to have been granted by the owner of the copyright, if this is not the case.

411 **Infringement actionable without damage.** Nor is it a defence that the infringement has caused the plaintiff no damage. The right of the owner of copyright is not determined or measured by the amount of actual damage to him by reason of the infringement. Copyright is a right of property, and he is entitled to come to the court for the protection of that property, even though he does not show or prove actual damage.[21]

412 **Subconscious copying.** In *Francis Day & Hunter, Ltd.* v. *Bron, supra*, the Court of Appeal discussed the possibility of " subconscious copying," that is to say, whether there could be infringement where the defendant honestly stated that he was unaware that his work was a copy of the plaintiff's, even if the court was satisfied that he must have made subconscious use of it. In a previous case of musical copying subconscious copying was mentioned as a possibility[22] and U.S.A. decisions were cited in which such a claim has succeeded. It was argued for the plaintiffs that the proper test, in all cases, involved four propositions: (1) In order to constitute reproduction within the meaning of the Act there must be (a) a sufficient degree of objective similarity between the two works, and (b) some causal connection. (2) It is quite irrelevant to inquire whether the defendant was or was not consciously aware of such causal connection. (3) Where there is a

[18] In the case of indirect infringements, knowledge is material; see § 475, *post*.

[19] Copyright Act, 1956, ss. 17 (2), 18 (2). See Chap. 10, *post*.

[20] *Mansell* v. *Valley Printing Co.* [1908] 2 Ch. 441; *Lee* v. *Simpson* (1847) 3 C.B. 871; *Wittman* v. *Oppenheim* (1884) 27 Ch.D. 260; *Byrne* v. *Statist Co.* [1914] 1 K.B. 622.

[21] *Per* Parkes J. in *Weatherby & Sons* v. *International Horse Agency and Exchange, Ltd.* [1910] 2 Ch. 297, approved in *Hawkes & Son (London), Ltd.* v. *Paramount Film Service, Ltd.* [1934] Ch. 593.

[22] *Ricordi (G.) & Co., etc., Ltd.* v. *Clayton & Waller, Ltd.* [1928–35] Macg.Cop. Cas. 154; and see *Rees* v. *Melville* [1911–16] Macg.Cop.Cas. 168, *Sinanide* v. *La Maison Kosmeo* (1927) 44 T.L.R. 371 and *Seager* v. *Copydex, Ltd.* [1967] 1 W.L.R. 923 at 931.

substantial degree of objective similarity, this, of itself, will afford prima facie evidence to show that there is a causal connection between the plaintiff's and the defendant's work; at least it is a circumstance from which the inference may be drawn. (4) The fact that the defendant denies that he consciously copied affords some evidence to rebut the inference of causal connection arising from the objective similarity, but is in no way conclusive.[22a] Willmer L.J. thought these propositions represented the right approach to the subject, but felt unable to disturb the finding of fact adverse to the plaintiffs in the court below. Upjohn L.J. declined to express a decided opinion whether " unconscious " copying could ever constitute an infringement. Diplock L.J. felt unable to deal with allegations of subconscious copying without evidence of the nature of the mental process involved.

413 **Substantial part.** It is unusual for an infringement to consist of an exact reproduction of the whole of the plaintiff's work. Consequently, difficult questions arise as to the amount of copying and the degree of resemblance necessary to constitute infringement. First as to the amount of copying. Section 49 (1) of the Act of 1956 provides that the doing of an act in relation to a work or other subject-matter shall be taken to include a reference to the doing of that act in relation to a substantial part thereof, and that any reference to a reproduction, adaptation or copy of a work shall be taken to include a reference to a reproduction, adaptation or copy of a substantial part of the work. The Act of 1911 used the expression " substantial part " in defining the sole right to reproduce, perform and publish in section 1 (2) of that Act, and the same expression was to be implied in connection with the other sole rights, that is, to dramatise, and so on.[23] The expression " substantial " is not and was not, however, defined, and some guidance as to its meaning may be obtained from the pre-1911 decisions.

414 **Old law.** Historically, copyright law was first directed to the prevention of reprints, and extended to prevent the evasion of its provisions by the publication of parts of books, or the publication of imitations. Even under the Act of 1842 there is no general statutory prohibition of the multiplication of parts of books, except in the single instance of " parts of a volume."

At an early date, however, it was established that the copying of a part of the work might be restrained.[24] As Lord Eldon said, in *Wilkins* v. *Aikin* [25]: " There is no doubt that a man cannot, under the pretence of quotation, publish either the whole or part of another's book although he may use, what in all cases is difficult to define, fair

[22a] See as to subconscious copying where defendant author of both works, *Industrial Furnaces, Ltd.* v. *Reaves* [1970] R.P.C. 605 at 623.
[23] *Corelli* v. *Gray* (1913) 30 T.L.R. 116.
[24] *Mawman* v. *Tegg* (1826) 2 Russ. 385.
[25] (1810) 17 Ves. 422.

quotation." And it became established, before the Act of 1911, that any " unfair use " of another's work could be restrained.[26]

415 **Quantity taken only slight test.** It was decided, before the Act of 1911, that the quality of the piracy was frequently more important than the proportion which the borrowed passages bore to the whole work.[27]

If so much was taken that the value of the original was sensibly diminished, or that labours of the original author were substantially, to an injurious extent, appropriated by another, that was sufficient, in point of law, to constitute a piracy *pro tanto*.

416 Lord Cottenham, in the cases of *Bramwell* v. *Halcomb*[28] and *Saunders* v. *Smith*,[29] adverting to this point, said: " When it comes to a question of quantity, it must be very vague. One writer might take all the vital part of another's book, though it might be but a small proportion of the book in quantity. It is not only quantity, but value, that is always looked to. It is useless to refer to any particular cases as to quantity." In short, it was said, we must often, in deciding questions of this sort, look to the nature and objects of the selections made, the quantity and value of the materials used, and the degree in which the use may prejudice the sale, or diminish the profits, direct or indirect, or supersede the objects of the original work. Many mixed ingredients enter into the discussion of such questions. In some cases a considerable portion of the materials of the original work may be fused into another work, so as to be indistinguishable in the mass of the latter, which has other professed and obvious objects, and cannot fairly be treated as a piracy; or they may be inserted as a sort of distinct and mosaic work into the general texture of the second work, and constitute the peculiar excellence thereof, and then it may be a clear piracy. If a person should, under colour of publishing " elegant extracts " of poetry, include all the best pieces at large of a favourite poet, whose volume was secured by copyright, it would be difficult to say why it was not an invasion of that right, since it might constitute the entire value of the volume. In short, it is submitted that the substantiality of the infringement will be considered having regard to all the circumstances.

417 **Present law.** It seems reasonable to assume that the Act of 1911, in using the words " substantial part," was using them with a view to giving effect to the above-mentioned decisions under the law prior to 1911, and that this construction will be followed with regard to the

[26] *Weatherby & Sons* v. *International Horse Agency and Exchange, Ltd.* [1910] 2 Ch. 297.

[27] *Tinsley* v. *Lacey* (1863) 1 H. & M. 747; *Warne & Co.* v. *Seebohm* (1888) 39 Ch.D. 73; *Kelly* v. *Hooper* (1840) 4 Jur. 21; and see *Trade Auxiliary Co.* v. *Middlesbrough, etc., Association* (1889) 40 Ch.D. 425.

[28] (1836) 3 My. & Cr. 737; *Neale* v. *Harmer* (1897) 13 T.L.R. 209.

[29] (1838) 3 My. & Cr. 711; see also *Chatterton* v. *Cave* (1878) 3 App.Cas. 483.

Act of 1956. It was held that "substantial," in this connection, is related to quality, rather than quantity, so that even a few bars of music may be a substantial part if they constitute a recognisable reproduction of an essential part of the melody.[30] As was said by Lord Reid, in *Ladbroke (Football), Ltd.* v. *William Hill (Football), Ltd.*[31]: "And, if he does copy, the question whether he has copied a substantial part depends much more on the quality than on the quantity of what he has taken." Lord Reid, like Lord Pearce,[31a] approved, in this connection, the words of Petersen J. in *University of London Press, Ltd.* v. *University Tutorial Press, Ltd.*,[31b] namely, that "what is worth copying is prima facie worth protecting." It may be doubted, however, if the question whether the alleged infringement is likely to compete with or damage the plaintiff's work would be held to be relevant in determining whether what has been taken is "substantial." [32]

418 **Colourable imitation.** In many cases the alleged infringement does not consist of an exact, or verbatim, copy, of the whole, or any part, of the earlier work, but merely resembles it in a greater or lesser degree. In such a case the first question will be whether there has been copying at all. As was pointed out by Sargant J., in *Corelli* v. *Gray*,[33] similarities between the plaintiff's work and the defendant's may be due to any one of four hypotheses, namely: (1) to mere chance; (2) to both works being taken from a common source; (3) to the plaintiff's work being taken from the defendant's; or (4) to the defendant's work being taken from the plaintiff's. It is only on the fourth hypothesis that there can exist an infringement.

419 **Imitation and reproduction.** But, assuming that the court is satisfied that the fourth hypothesis applies, can there be infringement without exact reproduction? In fact the court has never allowed a defendant to evade the provisions of the statutes by merely altering the form of the words in the original work. But there was not, under the Act of 1911, and there is not, in the Act of 1956, any direct statement that an imitation is to be treated as a reproduction. "Adaptation," in

[30] *Hawkes & Son (London), Ltd.* v. *Paramount Film Service, Ltd.* [1934] Ch. 593; in *Ricordi (G.) & Co., etc., Ltd.* v. *Clayton and Waller, Ltd.* [1928–35] Macg. Cop.Cas. 154, it was indicated that even eight bars of an air might constitute a substantial part of the air; see also *Canadian Performing Right Society* v. *Canadian National Exhibition Association* [1934] 4 D.L.R. 154; *Chappell & Co., Ltd.* v. *Thomson (D. C.) & Co., Ltd.* [1928–35] Macg.Cop.Cas. 467; *Frankenburg* v. *Gibbens* (1952) *The Author*, LXIII, No. 2, at 36; *Fernald* v. *Jay Lewis Productions, Ltd.*, *The Times*, February 6, 1953; *Pitman and Turner* v. *Fletcher and Macdonald* (1953) *The Author*, LXIV, No. 1, at 13.

[31] [1964] 1 W.L.R. 273 at 276; and see *Industrial Furnaces, Ltd.* v. *Reaves* [1970] R.P.C. 605 at 623, 625.

[31a] *Ibid.* at pp. 279 and 293.

[31b] [1916] 2 Ch. 601 at 610.

[32] The question is, however, relevant to the defence of "fair dealing" in the limited class of cases in which this defence is applicable: see § 458 *et seq.*, *post.*

[33] (1913) 29 T.L.R. 570.

section 2 (6) of the Act of 1956, has a special and restricted meaning, but does not limit the generality of the word "reproduction." [34] Section 35 (1) of the Act of 1911, in defining "infringing copy," employed the expression "colourable imitation," but this expression does not appear in the Act of 1956. The question therefore appears to turn solely upon the interpretation of the expression "reproduction," and the definition of that word in section 48 (1) of the Act of 1956 does not assist, as this definition merely includes certain special forms of reproduction. It is apprehended, however, that the word "reproduction" in the Act of 1956 has the same sense as the word "copy" has acquired in copyright law.[35]

420 **Suggested test of "copy."** Various definitions of "copy" have been suggested,[35a] but it is submitted that the true view of the matter is that, where the court is satisfied that a defendant has, in producing the alleged infringement, made a substantial use of those features of the plaintiff's work in which copyright subsists, an infringement will be held to have been committed; if he has made such use, he has exercised unlawfully the sole right which is conferred upon the plaintiff. If this view is correct, it follows that the degree of resemblance between the two works is not in itself the test of infringement, but is only one factor in determining whether an unlawful use of the plaintiff's work has been made. For example, assume two cases in which advertising posters resemble the plaintiff's original and that, in the one case in which the resemblance is less close, it is proved *aliunde* that the defendant's artist had the plaintiff's work in front of him and slavishly imitated certain specific features of the design, but in the other, though the general appearance is closer, the artist is able to establish that, though he made use of the plaintiff's basic idea, his execution was quite independent; it is submitted that the former and not the latter would be an infringement.[35b]

The problem is further illustrated by the cases of infringement of copyright in compilations which are dealt with hereafter.[36] In such cases, if it is proved that the defendant has made substantial use of the skill and labour of the compiler, an infringement is committed, whether or not there is any exact reproduction of language, and, on the other hand, an exact reproduction of language, in the case of works such as dictionaries and tables, will not constitute an infringe-

[34] *Francis Day & Hunter, Ltd.* v. *Bron* [1963] Ch. 587.

[35] See *Daily Calendar Supplying Bureau* v. *United Concern* [1967] A.I.R. Madras 381.

[35a] *King Features Syndicate* v. *O. & M. Kleeman, Ltd.* [1941] A.C. 417; *McCrum* v. *Eisner* (1918) 87 L.J.Ch. 99 at 102; *Hanfstaengl* v. *W. H. Smith & Sons* [1905] Ch. 519 at 524; *West* v. *Francis* (1822) 5 B. & Ald. 737 at 743.

[35b] See *Twentieth Century Fox Film Corp.* v. *Anglo Amalgamated Film Distributors, Ltd.*, *The Times*, January 22, 1965, *post*, § 440; and *Daily Calendar Supplying Bureau* v. *United Concern*, *supra*.

[36] *Post*, § 421 *et seq.*

ment if the defendant has worked independently. In the case of dramatic and musical works [37] the principle is, it is submitted, the same, subject to the qualification that, in this class of works, copyright subsists, not in a particular form of words, but in a particular series of dramatic incidents or of musical notes, and it is an unlawful use of these incidents or series of notes which has to be established.

421 **Copying of compilations.** In the case of compilations, such as dictionaries, gazetteers, grammars, maps, arithmetics, almanacs, encyclopedias and guide-books, new publications dealing with a similar subject-matter must, of necessity, resemble existing publications, and the defence of " common source " is frequently made where the new publication is alleged to constitute an infringement of an earlier one.

This defence may merely consist in pointing out that the defendant's work might have been taken from earlier non-copyright matter, and that its similarity to the plaintiff's does not create any necessary inference that it has been copied from the plaintiff's, rather than from other similar works. In *Harman Pictures N.V.* v. *Osborne*,[37a] where the plaintiffs sought interlocutory relief, the defendants alleged that both works dealt with a common subject, which was a famous event in history, on which there was a wealth of non-copyright literature and information, and that they had simply drawn on this. However, in the absence of any explanation by the defendant as to how or when he worked and as to how long it took him, but only a bare assertion that he did not base his work on the plaintiffs' work, Goff J. made an order in the plaintiffs' favour. Whereas, with strictly original work, any identity of phrase is sufficient evidence of copying, with many compilations it is only from external evidence, or from a minute examination of textual errors, that an infringement can be established.[38]

422 Alternatively, the defence may be that the plaintiff has no copyright in his work, because it is not original, but a mere reproduction of earlier non-copyright matter. This question has been dealt with in detail in an earlier chapter.[39] But it must not be forgotten that, though a plaintiff has no copyright in the words, he may have copyright in the arrangement as a compilation.[39a] In *Football League, Ltd.* v. *Littlewoods Pools, Ltd.*,[40] Upjohn J., in holding that the systematic

[37] *Post*, §§ 480, 488.
[37a] [1967] 1 W.L.R. 723.
[38] *Kelly* v. *Morris* (1866) L.R. 1 Eq. 697; *Pike* v. *Nicholas* (1870) L.R. 5 Ch. 251; *Cox* v. *Land and Water Journal Co.* (1869) L.R. 9 Eq. 324; *Jarrold* v. *Heywood* (1870) 18 W.R. 279; *Cadieux* v. *Beauchimin* [1901–04] Mac.C.C. 4; *Mathieson* v. *Universal Stock Exchange* [1901–04] Mac.C.C. 80.
[39] See §§ 112 *et seq.* and 145 *et seq.*, *ante*.
[39a] See, as to format, *Coral Index, Ltd.* v. *Regent Index, Ltd.* [1970] R.P.C. 147 and *Ladbroke (Football), Ltd.* v. *William Hill (Football), Ltd.* [1964] 1 W.L.R 273.
[40] [1959] Ch. 637.

pirating by the defendants of the relevant part of the plaintiffs' chronological fixtures list, in the same order as the plaintiffs, was an infringement, left open the question whether there would have been an infringement if the order had been "scrambled." However, in *Demerara Turf Club* v. *Phang*,[40a] it was held that the publication in the defendants' coupon of a list of names of all horses in a race, taken from the plaintiffs' programme and coupon, but in a "scrambled" form, was an infringement.

423 **Lawful use of existing publications.** But there is a large class of cases which present a further difficulty. While, as has been pointed out above, there is no monopoly in a copyright work, yet, with strictly original works, any user of the earlier work to produce a similar result is an infringement. Published compilations, however, are intended, not merely to be read, but to be used, and the question arises how far they may be used in the preparation of a subsequent compilation.

It is no doubt true that the publication of certain books of this character implies a licence to reproduce their contents. Thus, clearly, a book of legal precedents is intended to be used by practitioners, unless otherwise stated, and it is submitted that a writer is entitled to use prior compilations on a similar subject in order to ascertain where he must go for his material. It is thought, however, that the limits upon this implied licence from publication are fairly clear; and in no case authorise the use of the copyright material in the first work for the purpose of producing a second work of a similar nature. Thus the author of the precedent book authorises the use of his forms for use in practice, unless otherwise stated, but not in a competing book of precedents. And the compiler of a directory may use a prior directory in the same way as any other member of the public as a guide to what streets he must go to for his information, but he may not copy the information into a competing work. The point is illustrated by the following decisions.

424 **Statistics.** In *Scott* v. *Stanford*,[41] the plaintiff had published statistical returns of all coal imported into London, and the defendant, in giving the universal statistics of the United Kingdom, had copied from the plaintiff's work to the extent of one-third of the whole of the defendant's work, at the same time acknowledging the source from which his information was derived. Wood V.-C. decided that, having regard to the quantity and matter of the information which

40a (1963) 6 W.I.R. 177.

41 (1867) L.R. 3 Eq. 718; *Morris* v. *Ashbee* (1868) L.R. 7 Eq. 34; *Mawman* v. *Tegg* (1826) 2 Russ. 385; *Jarrold* v. *Houlston* (1857) 3 K. & J. 708; *Cox* v. *Land and Water Journal Co.* (1869) L.R. 9 Eq. 324; *Trade Auxiliary Co.* v. *Middlesbrough, etc., Association* (1889) 40 Ch.D. 425; *Cate* v. *Devon, etc., Newspaper Co.* (1889) 40 Ch.D. 500.

had been republished without the exercise of any independent thought and labour, and the prejudice to the plaintiff in having the sale of his work superseded by this republication, the plaintiff was entitled to an injunction. If the defendant, after collecting the information for himself, had checked his results by the plaintiff's tables, that would have been a widely different thing from the wholesale extraction of the vital part of his work. No man is entitled to avail himself of the previous labours of another for the purpose of conveying to the public the same information, even though he append additional information to that already published. This is consonant with the law as laid down in *Kelly* v. *Morris*,[41a] which was in the following terms: "In the case of a dictionary, map, guide-book, or directory, where there are certain common objects of information which must, if described correctly, be described in the same words, a subsequent compiler is bound to set about doing for himself that which the first compiler has done. In the case of a road-book, he must count the milestones for himself, . . . and the only use that he can legitimately make of a previous publication is to verify his own calculations and results when obtained."

425 **Directories.** From these observations it is not to be inferred that in compiling a directory the compiler may not look into the previous directory of another for the purpose of ascertaining where a particular person lives and for the purpose of ascertaining from that book whether or not it is worth his while to call upon that person.[42] They imply no further than that he may not take a passage from the directory, and go and see whether it happens to be accurate and, if it be accurate, bodily copy it into his directory.

426 This latter is precisely what was done in *Morris* v. *Ashbee*.[43] The defendants copied the plaintiff's book, and then sent out canvassers to see if the information so copied was correct. If the canvasser did not find the occupier of the house at home, or could get no answer from him, then the information copied from the plaintiff's book was repeated bodily, as if it were a question for the occupier of the house merely, and not for the compiler of the previous directory. The copying was as direct as in the case of *Kelly* v. *Morris, supra.* Not only were the slips for the purpose of canvassing copied, but the course pursued was that when a slip was presented to the person who was canvassed, and his permission

[41a] (1866) L.R. 1 Eq. 697.

[42] *Morris* v. *Wright* (1870) L.R. 5 Ch. 279; *Scott* v. *Stanford* (1867) L.R. 3 Eq. 718; *Cox* v. *Land and Water Journal Co.* (1869) L.R. 9 Eq. 324; *Pike* v. *Nicholas* (1870) L.R. 5 Ch. 251; *Hogg* v. *Scott* (1874) L.R. 18 Eq. 444; *Lamb* v. *Evans* [1893] 1 Ch. 218; *Kelly's Directories, Ltd.* v. *Gavin* [1902] 1 Ch. 631; *Kemps' Commercial Guides, Ltd.* v. *Fashion Publications, Ltd.* (1955) *The Author*, LXV, No. 4, at 88.

[43] (1868) L.R. 7 Eq. 34.

received for the insertion of the particular entry, the slip was forthwith copied into the book. "Now it is plain," observed Giffard L.J., "that it could not be lawful for the defendants simply to cut the slips, which they have cut from the plaintiff's directory, and insert them in theirs. Can it then be lawful to do so, because in addition to doing this, they sent persons with the slips to ascertain their correctness? I say, clearly not."[44] "In *Pike* v. *Nicholas*[45] we had this: two rival books were published with reference to the same subject-matter, and we thought certainly that the defendant had been guided by the plaintiff's book, more or less, to the authorities which the plaintiff had cited; but it was a perfectly legitimate course for the defendant to refer to the plaintiff's book, and if he did, taking that book as his guide, himself go to the original authorities, and compile his book from the original authorities, he made no unfair or improper use of the plaintiff's book."[46] "The true principle in all these cases," said Hall V.-C. in *Hogg* v. *Scott*,[46a] "is that the defendant is not at liberty to use or avail himself of the labour which the plaintiff has been at for the purpose of producing his work; that is, in fact, merely to take away the result of another man's labour, or, in other words, his property."

427 **Other compilations.** In *Jarrold* v. *Houlston*[47] the publishers of Dr. Brewer's "Guide to Science" obtained an injunction against the publication of "The Reason Why." The works in controversy were written on the same plan, and presented, in the form of question and answer, popular information on a variety of scientific subjects. The earlier book, Dr. Brewer's "Guide to Science," had evidently been used to a considerable extent in the preparation of the later one, although copying was denied. The judge said: "I take the illegitimate use, as opposed to the legitimate use, of another man's works on subject-matters of this description to be this: if, knowing that a person whose work is protected by copyright has, with considerable labour, compiled from various sources a work in itself not original, but which he has digested and arranged, you, being minded to compile a work of a like description, instead of taking the pains of searching into all the common sources, and obtaining your subject-matter from them, avail yourself of the labour of your predecessor, adopt his arrangements, adopt, moreover the very questions he has asked, or adopt them with but a slight degree of colourable variation, and thus save yourself pains and labour by availing yourself of the pains and labour which he has employed, that I take to be an illegitimate use."

44 *Ibid.* at p. 41.
45 (1870) L.R. 5 Ch. 251.
46 *Per* Giffard V.-C., *Morris* v. *Wright* (1870) 22 L.T. 78, at 82.
46a (1874) L.R. 18 Eq. 444.
47 (1857) 3 K. & J. 708.

428 So, in the case of a descriptive catalogue of fruit and trees, the court was of opinion that the later compiler might use the work of his predecessor as a guide or instructor, but might not copy the descriptions from it, even though he verifies and corrects them from specimens of fruit before him. Though he could not be prevented from getting much aid in the way of information, suggestions, and so on from the protected work open before him, he must write his own descriptions from actual specimens, or common sources of information.[48]

429 **How far originality of result relevant.** In certain cases before 1911 it appears to have been suggested that a test of whether or not an infringement had been committed, in respect of works of this character, was whether the efforts of the defendant had been such as to produce " an original work." [49] It is submitted that, if this test means that a compiler may use earlier copyright material to any extent, provided that he adds sufficient labour of his own to produce something original, it is not a true test—at any rate at the present day. In order to judge of infringement one has to ascertain whether or not the defendant has copied the plaintiff's material; the originality of the result may be evidence that he has not copied, but is not a final test.[49a]

430 **Compilations involving selection.** While, as has been seen, the compiler of certain kinds of works may lawfully use prior compilations for the purpose of ascertaining the sources available, the position is not the same in regard to those compilations in which part of the merit lies in selection of apt quotations. Thus, in a case of this character,[50] it was said by Collins M.R.: " Counsel justified annexing another man's quotations on the ground that you may follow an indication given in another book as to the place where you will find authorities; that you have the right to consult them; and that all the defendant Mr. Marshall does, being directed by a reference to a particular quotation, is to go and look to the author and see

[48] *Hogg* v. *Scott* (1874) L.R. 18 Eq. 444; *Cary* v. *Kearsley* (1802) 4 Esp. 167; *Matthewson* v. *Stockdale* (1806) 12 Ves. 270; *Longman (T. N.)* v. *Winchester* (1809) 16 Ves. 269; *Baily* v. *Taylor* (1830), 1 Russ. & My. 73; *Bramwell* v. *Halcomb* (1836) 3 My. & Cr. 737; *Kelly* v. *Hooper* (1840) 4 Jur. 21; *Murray* v. *Bogue* (1853) 1 Drew. 353.

[49] *Spiers* v. *Brown* (1858) 6 W.R. 352; *Reade* v. *Lacy* (1861) 1 J. & H. 524; and, in the case of a catalogue, *Hotten* v. *Arthur* (1863) 1 H. & M. 603; *vide*, *Wilkins* v. *Aikin* (1810) 17 Ves. 422; *Bramwell* v. *Halcomb* (1836) 3 My. & Cr. 737; *Cornish* v. *Upton* (1861) 4 L.T. 862.

[49a] See § 440, *post*.

[50] *Moffatt and Paige, Ltd.* v. *Gill (G.) & Sons, Ltd.* (1902) 86 L.T. 465, at 471; *cf. Macmillan & Co.* v. *Suresh Chunder Deb* (1890) 17 I.L.R. (Calcutta) 951, where an infringement of the " Golden Treasury " was restrained; *Black (A. and C.), Ltd.* v. *Murray (A.) & Son* (1870) 9 Sc.Sess.Cas. (3 Ser.) 341. See also *Harman Pictures N.V.* v. *Osborne* [1967] 1 W.L.R. 723, selection of incidents from real life.

whether the quotation corresponds with the text, and, if so, the text being common property, he is at liberty to annex that quotation. I cannot admit that for a moment. He rather suggested that it was justified by the cases relating to directories, which say that though you cannot, where another man has compiled a directory, simply take his sheets and reprint them as your own, you are entitled, taking the sheets with you to go and see whether the existing facts concur with the description in the sheets, and if you do that, you may publish the result as your own. Certainly; but are you at liberty to apply the same principle to a series of quotations—to take the reference given by one author, although he quotes such and such a passage as illustrating this particular matter—to say: 'I will just go and see if that is correctly copied or not, and if it is correctly copied, I propose to introduce it with any other quotation which illustrates the particular passage, and I propose to adopt that as my own work'? That leaves out the whole merit; the felicity of the quotation; its adaptability to a particular end; its illustration of a particular characteristic. All those things enter into the choice of one quotation as apart from another. That is a process which may involve gifts both of knowledge and intelligence. The aptness of quotation does not depend on the particular page or number of lines in which it is found; and that is all you find if you obey a certain direction to go to a certain place and take it. It does not entitle you to annex the skill and judgment and taste which has dictated the selection. . . . It seems to me that the law is clearly such as to entitle the plaintiff to complain if quotations selected and arranged by him are imitated and adopted by the defendant."

431 In the case of *Cambridge University Press* v. *University Tutorial Press, Ltd.*[51] Maugham J., in dealing with an alleged infringement of copyright in a selection of essays, said: "in the case of an infringement of a selection the court is really dealing with something closely analogous to the copying of a list, a list, of course, involving skill or judgment or some sort of discrimination in the elimination of the things or articles not needed for that sole purpose."

432 **Abridgments.** It is thought that the question whether abridgments, précis, synopses and similar works infringe copyright must now depend upon the answer, in each case, to the question whether the production has involved a substantial use of copyright material, or only of ideas and information. Any work which consists of extracts from the original, either verbatim, or with merely colourable alterations of language, would constitute an infringement. On the other

[51] [1923–28] Macg.Cop.Cas. 349. *Cf. Blackie & Sons, Ltd.* v. *The Lothian Book Publishing Co., etc., Ltd.* (1921) 29 C.L.R. 396; and *Graves* v. *Pocket Publications, Ltd.* (1938) 54 T.L.R. 952 (infringement of a compilation in narrative form by a list setting out a series of figures derived from the narrative).

hand a mere epitome of the plot of a novel, or of the general development of a learned work, would not. Some of the earlier authorities suggest a greater licence to abridgers.

433 Thus in *Dodsley* v. *Kinnersley* [52] it appeared that not one-tenth part of the first volume had been abstracted. The Master of the Rolls, Sir Thomas Clarke, refused the injunction, saying: "I cannot enter into the goodness or badness of the abstract. It may serve the end of an advertisement. In general, it tends to the advantage of an author if the composition be good; if it be not, it cannot be libelled. What I materially rely upon is that it could not tend to prejudice the plaintiffs when they had before published an abstract of the work in the *London Chronicle*. If I were to determine this to be elusory, I must hold every abridgment to be so."

434 In *Hawkesworth* v. *Newbery* [53] Apsley L.C., having spent some hours in consultation with Blackstone J., decided that an abridgment, where the understanding is employed in retrenching unnecessary and uninteresting circumstances which rather deaden the narration, is not an act of plagiarism upon the original work, nor against any property of the author in it, but an allowable and meritorious work. It requires both invention and judgment, and displays frequently a deal of learning. Lord Hardwicke thus stated the rule [54]: "Where books are colourably shortened only, they are undoubtedly within the meaning of the Act of Parliament, and are a mere evasion of the statute, and cannot be called an abridgment. But this must not be carried so far as to restrain persons from making a real and fair abridgment; for abridgments may, with great propriety, be called a new book, because not only the paper and print, but the invention, learning, and judgment of the author is shown in them, and in many cases is extremely useful,[55] though in some instances prejudicial, by mistaking and curtailing the sense of an author." [56]

But an injunction has been granted where the facts and the *terms* in which the facts are related are merely the same in both books.[57]

435 In the case of *Butterworth* v. *Robinson*,[58] a motion was made to restrain the defendant from selling a work entitled "An Abridgment

[52] (1737) 1 Amb. 402; *Gyles* v. *Wilcox* (1740) 2 Atk. 141.
[53] (1776) Lofft. 755; *Butterworth* v. *Robinson* (1801) 5 Ves. 709.
[54] *Gyles* v. *Wilcox* (1740) 2 Atk. 141.
[55] *Hodges* (*J.*) v. *Welsh* (*T.*) (1840) 2 Ir.Eq.Rep. 266.
[56] This paragraph seems to confuse the distinct questions (a) whether an abridgment is an original work entitled itself to copyright, and (b) whether the abridgment is a piracy of the abridged work. There is little doubt that an abridgment is, subject to the rights of the proprietor of the copyright in the original itself, capable of acquiring copyright: see *ante*, § 140.
[57] *Bell* v. *Walker* (1784) 1 Bro.C.C. 450; *Story* v. *Holcombe*, 4 McLean 306 (Amer.) (1847).
[58] (1801) 5 Ves. 709.

of Cases argued and determined in the Courts of Law, etc." until answer or further order. In support of the motion, it was stated that this work was by no means a fair abridgment; that, except in colourably leaving out some parts of the cases, such as the arguments of counsel, it was a mere copy verbatim of several of the reports of cases in the courts of law, and among them of the "Term Reports," of which the plaintiff was proprietor. In support of the motion *Bell* v. *Walker* [59] was cited. The Lord Chancellor said: "I have looked at one or two cases, with which I am pretty well acquainted, and it appears to me an extremely illiberal publication. Take the injunction."

436 In the case of *Sweet* v. *Benning* [60] the defendants were restrained from taking verbatim the head-notes from a series of law reports and arranging them in a different manner. In the course of his judgment Jervis C.J. remarked as follows: "I admit that a digest may be made from a copyright work without piracy upon it, but that is a work in which a man applies his mind to the labour of extracting the principles of the original work, and by his labour really produces a new work. It is not so where he merely reduces extracts or passages of another man's work to an alphabetical order, which is a work a clerk might accomplish, and requires neither learning nor study, but may be little more than a merely mechanical operation of cutting out and classifying under certain letters of the alphabet."

437 In *D'Almaine* v. *Boosey* [61] Lord Lyndhurst, then Lord Chief Baron, observed: "No doubt such a modification may be allowed in some cases, as in that of an abridgment or a digest. Such publications are in their nature original. Their compiler intends to make of them a new use; not that which the author proposed to make. Digests are of great use to practical men, though not so, comparatively speaking, to students. The same may be said of an abridgment, of any study; but it must be a bona fide abridgment, because if it contains many chapters of the original work, or such as made that work most saleable, the maker of the abridgment commits a piracy."

438 In *Dickens* v. *Lee* [62] Knight-Bruce V.-C. is reported to have said that he was not aware that one man had the right to abridge the works of another; on the other hand, he did not mean to say that there might not be an abridgment which might be lawful, which might be protected; but to say that one man had the right to abridge, and so publish in an abridged form, the work of another, without more, was going much beyond his notion of what the law of this country was.

[59] (1784) 1 Bro.C.C. 450.
[60] (1855) 16 C.B. 459.
[61] (1835) 1 Y. & C.Ex. 288.
[62] (1844) 8 Jur. 183.

439 Finally, Lord Hatherley, when Vice-Chancellor, in the case of *Tinsley* v. *Lacy*,[63] spoke very unfavourably in regard to the rights of an abridger; he said he must confess that he did not agree with the reasons for upholding such a work given by some learned judges, *viz.*, that an abridger was a benefactor. He should have himself regarded him rather as a sort of jackal to the public, to point out the beauties of authors.

440 **Burlesques.** Similar considerations seem to arise whether a burlesque can be an infringement. If the burlesque consists of what is, in substance, a new work parodying an existing one, but not making substantial use of its language or incidents, it is submitted there is no infringement.[64] But a work which slavishly used the plot and incidents of another would not be defensible under the cloak of burlesque, and an important test is whether the defendant has bestowed such mental labour upon what he has taken and has subjected it to such revision and alteration as to produce an original work.[65]

This test was applied in *Joy Music, Ltd.* v. *Sunday Pictorial Newspapers (1920), Ltd.*,[65a] where McNair J. decided that a parody was not an infringement of the words of a popular song. However, in *Twentieth Century Fox Film Corporation* v. *Anglo Amalgamated Film Distributors, Ltd.*,[65b] where the defendants' poster advertising the defendants' film was based on the plaintiffs' poster advertising the plaintiffs' film, the only difference being that the defendants showed their own actors on the poster instead of the plaintiffs', the defendants' claim that their poster was not a copy but a parody of the plaintiffs' poster, failed. Plowman J. said that, in spite of the differences between the two posters, on the evidence of his own eyes it seemed that the defendants' poster came so near as to suggest the plaintiffs' poster to every person seeing it. The test as to whether a parody infringed a literary work, laid down in *Joy Music, Ltd.* v. *Sunday Pictorial Newspapers (1920), Ltd.*, *supra*, was a test in relation to literary and not artistic copyright. Even applying the test, it did not displace the view one would form on a visual comparison, namely, that the defendants' poster did reproduce a material part of the plaintiffs' poster.

3.—DIRECT INFRINGEMENT BY OTHER ACTS

441 Having dealt with the general nature of infringement by copying it is now proposed to describe other acts restricted by the copyright

63 (1863) 1 H. & M. 747.

64 *Glyn* v. *Western Feature Film Co.* [1916] 1 Ch. 261; *Francis Day & Hunter* v. *Feldman & Co.* [1914] 2 Ch. 728; *Carlton* v. *Mortimer* [1917–23] Macg.Cop.Cas. 194.

65 *Glyn* v. *Western Feature Film Co.* [1916] 1 Ch. 261 at 268.

65a [1960] 2 Q.B. 60.

65b *The Times*, January 22, 1965.

in a literary work. In the first place, "reproducing" extends not only to actual copying, but to reproduction in "any material form" and includes reproduction in the form of a record or of a cinematograph film, where record means any disc, tape, perforated roll or other device in which sounds are embodied so as to be capable (with or without the aid of some other instrument) of being automatically reproduced therefrom.[66] It is submitted, therefore, that reproduction in the form of computer software, such as punched cards, punched tapes, magnetic tapes and even magnetic cores, apart from more obvious forms of reproduction such as print outs, could be infringements of copyright.[66a] Other acts restricted are publishing the work, performing the work in public, broadcasting the work, and making any adaptation of the work.[67]

442 **Corresponding provisions of the Act of 1911.** The corresponding provisions of the Act of 1911 gave to the owner of the copyright the sole right to perform, or, in the case of a lecture, to deliver the work; in the case of an unpublished work, to publish the work; the right to produce, reproduce, perform or publish any translation of the work; the right to convert a dramatic work into a novel or other non-dramatic work; the right to convert a novel or other non-dramatic work or an artistic work into a dramatic work by way of performance in public or otherwise; and the right to make any record, perforated roll, cinematograph film or other contrivance by means of which the work might be mechanically performed or delivered.[68]

443 **Infringement by publication.** It will be observed that the Act of 1956 does not confine the act of publishing the work to unpublished works. If the definition of "publication," in section 49 (2) of the Act, is also to be regarded as a definition of "publishing" for the purpose of infringement, as seems to be the case from the words in sub-clause (*b*) of that subsection, "except in so far as it may constitute an infringement of copyright," an infringement by publication occurs, subject to sub-clause (*a*) of the subsection, whenever reproductions of the work are issued to the public. There is no reference in sub-clause (*c*) of that subsection to first publication. If this be so, the Act of 1956 may have created a new form of infringement by distribution which, unlike the indirect infringements hereafter described,[69] does not require that the distributor should be proved to have knowledge that the material distributed was infringing material.

66 Copyright Act, 1956, s. 48 (1).

66a See "Legal Protection of Software" by Leslie Melville (1969) 119 New L.J. 1169 and "Software Protection. The Legal Protection of Computer Programs," Report of Proceedings at a Conference in November 1969 arranged by the British Computer Society.

67 Copyright Act, 1956, s. 2 (5).

68 Copyright Act, 1911, s. 1 (2). *Byrne* v. *Statist Co.* [1914] 1 K.B. 622.

69 *Post*, § 471.

444 **By public performance.** Under the Literary Copyright Act, 1842,[70] the author of a literary work had no right to complain of portions of his work being recited or read aloud in public.[71] It was fairly clear that the Act of 1911 had altered the law in this respect and the Act of 1956 includes, in the acts restricted by the copyright in a literary work, performing the work in public and broadcasting the work, and defines performing so as to include delivery in relation to lectures, addresses, speeches and sermons, and generally to include any mode of visual or acoustic presentation, including any such presentation by the operation of wireless-telegraphy apparatus, or by the exhibition of a cinematograph film, or by the use of a record, or by any other means.[72] The definition of broadcasting is somewhat complex and is dealt with hereafter.[73]

445 **By " adaptation."** The expression " adaptation " is new to the Act of 1956, and is used to define the making of a dramatic version of a non-dramatic work, the making of a non-dramatic version of a dramatic work, the making of a translation of the work and the making of a version in which the story or action is conveyed wholly or mainly by means of pictures in a form suitable for reproduction in a book, or in a newspaper, magazine or similar periodical.[74]

446 The acts restricted include the reproducing, publishing, performing or broadcasting of any of the types of adaptation which have been referred to.[75]

447 **By translation.** Copyright may therefore be infringed by reproducing the whole or part in the form of a translation.

If there was any doubt, under the law prior to 1911, as to whether a translation infringed the copyright in the original work,[76] it was set at rest by the Act of 1911, and, by the Act of 1956, the making of a translation is one of the forms of adaptation restricted.

It should be noted that two separate rights may exist where there has been an authorised translation, namely, the right of the author of the original work to restrain publication of any other translation thereof, and the right of the author of the translation to restrain publication of his translation. Anyone wishing to reproduce a

[70] 5 & 6 Vict. c. 45.

[71] *Per* Stirling J., *Hanfstaengl* v. *Empire Palace* [1894] 3 Ch. 109 at 116.

[72] Copyright Act, 1956, s. 48 (1).

[73] *Post*, § 530.

[74] s. 2 (6).

[75] Copyright Act, 1956, s. 2 (5) (*g*).

[76] *Burnett* v. *Chetwood* (1817) 2 Mer. 441; *cf. Cate* v. *Devon, etc., Newspaper Co.* (1889) 40 Ch.D. 500. Under the law then in force, a translation was held not to be a piracy in America (*Stowe* v. *Thomas* (1853) 23 Fed.Cas. 201) and in India (*Macmillan & Co.* v. *K. B. Shamsul Ulama M. Zaka* (1895) 19 I.L.R. (Bombay) 557).

particular translation should therefore obtain a licence from both author and translator or their assigns.

448 **By re-translation.** If A's work is with permission translated by B, and C without permission re-translates from B's translation into the original language, or, presumably, into any other language, C infringes A's and B's copyrights.[77]

449 **By dramatisation of non-dramatic works.** Since 1911 it has not been permissible, as it was under the law prior to 1911, provided the actual words were not copied,[78] to convert a novel, or other non-dramatic work, or an artistic work into a dramatic work.[79] The Act of 1911 effected a considerable extension of the rights of the proprietor of the copyright in a novel, because the result was to give protection, not merely to the form of the words in the novel, but sometimes to the situations contained in it, so that, if it was found that a series of incidents in combination had been taken from a copyright novel, an injunction would be granted, even though there was not a single sentence in the dramatic work which was similar to one used in the novel.[80]

450 This result is probably confirmed under the Act of 1956 since, in defining " adaptation " in relation to conversion into a dramatic work, the expression " whether in its original language or a different language " is employed.[81] On the other hand, it would appear that " language " is now required whereas, under the Act of 1911, a work could be converted into a dramatic work by way of performance in public and presumably, therefore, by a performance in dumb show.[82] However, it is thought that, under the Act of 1956, such a performance would be an infringement of the performing right in the non-dramatic work.

451 **By making a pictorial version.** Infringement by the making of a pictorial version of a work is new. It is probable that the production of such a version was not an infringement under the Act of 1911 if no words were used in connection with the version.

452 **By authorising infringements.** Questions have, from time to time, arisen with regard to the liability of persons for infringements of copyright by other persons with whom they stand in some contractual

[77] *Murray* v. *Bogue* (1853) 1 Drew. 353 at p. 368.
[78] *Read* v. *Conquest* (1861) 9 C.B.(N.S.) 755; *Tinsley* v. *Lacey* (1863) 32 L.J.Ch. 535; *Warne & Co.* v. *Seebohm* (1888) 39 Ch.D. 73.
[79] Copyright Act, 1911, s. 1 (2) (*c*), now Copyright Act, 1956, s. 2 (6) (*a*) (i).
[80] *Corelli* v. *Gray* (1913) 30 T.L.R. 116; and see § 484, *post*.
[81] Copyright Act, 1956, s. 2 (6) (*a*) (i), and see *Harman Pictures N.V.* v. *Osborne* [1967] 1 W.L.R. 723.
[82] Copyright Act, 1911, s. 1 (2) (*c*).

or other relation. These matters have been discussed in relation to the wording of particular statutes. Under the law prior to 1911 it was an infringement to cause a piracy to be printed or represented, and, under the Act of 1911, it was an infringement to authorise an infringing act. This is, in effect, reproduced in the Act of 1956 since, in section 1 (1) of that Act, copyright is defined as the exclusive right to do and "to authorise other persons to do" the various acts restricted by the copyright under the various provisions of the Act.

453 It was held in *Karno* v. *Pathé Frères, Ltd.*,[83] under the law prior to 1911, that a person was only liable for infringements committed by his servants or agents. Thus a man will be liable for any infringement committed by his servant in the course of his employment,[84] but, if the infringer is not the servant of the defendant, he will only be liable if he authorised the particular act complained of,[84a] and it must be a question of fact in each case whether he gave such authority—a question which gave rise to the real difficulty in most of the decided cases.[84b]

454 In *Monaghan* v. *Taylor*,[85] it was decided that a man who employed a singer, and took no pains to ascertain what songs he proposed to sing, and was present at the performance, had caused him to sing the songs, including one which was in fact an infringement. In the case of *Performing Right Society, Ltd.* v. *Ciryl Theatrical Syndicate, Ltd.*,[86] the Court of Appeal held that there was no evidence of authorisation by a managing director who had engaged a band on behalf of a limited company and was himself away at the time of an infringing performance. But, in *Performing Right Society, Ltd.* v. *Bray Urban District Council*,[87] it was held that the defendants, having approved of the performance by a band of certain pieces of music, had "authorised" the performance.

455 Questions of liability by "authorising" have arisen in connection with automatic gramophones installed in shops or bars and operated by customers inserting a coin. In the Canadian case of *Vigneux* v.

83 (1909) 100 L.T. 260.
84 *Performing Right Society, Ltd.* v. *Mitchell and Booker, etc., Ltd.* [1924] 1 K.B. 762; *Canadian Performing Right Society* v. *Canadian National Exhibition Association* [1934] 4 D.L.R. 154.
84a See *Australasian Performing Right Association, Ltd.* v. *Miles* [1962] N.S.W.R. 405.
84b See *Australasian Performing Right Association, Ltd.* v. *Koolman* [1969] N.Z.L.R. 273.
85 (1885) 2 T.L.R. 685. See also *Bolton* v. *London Exhibitions, Ltd.* (1898) 14 T.L.R. 550; *Green* v. *Irish Independent Co., Ltd.* [1899] 1 I.R. 386; *Colburn* v. *Simms* (1843) 2 Ha. 543 at 547.
86 [1924] 1 K.B. 1.
87 [1930] A.C. 377 (P.C.). See *Australasian Performing Right Association, Ltd.* v. *Canterbury-Bankstown Leagues Club, Ltd.* [1964–65] N.S.W.R. 138; and *Australasian Performing Right Association, Ltd.* v. *Koolman, supra.*

Canadian Performing Right Society, Ltd.,[88] it was held that the firm who provided and installed the apparatus for a fixed rent, payable by the owner of the shop, had not authorised the performance; the case, however, turned largely upon the special provisions of the Canadian Act. In the Australian case of *Winstone* v. *Wurlitzer, etc., Ltd.*,[89] the court, after reviewing all the authorities, held that the company providing the machine (who, in this case, divided the takings with the shopowner) were engaged with the shopowner in a joint venture for profit, and both were liable for authorising the playing of infringing music; importance was attached to the fact that the company providing the installation selected the records, presumably with a view to making as much profit as possible.

456 It was doubted, in *Performing Right Society, Ltd.* v. *Ciryl Theatrical Syndicate, Ltd.*, whether the word "authorise," in the Act of 1911, added anything to the law, but it has been held by the Court of Appeal, in the case of *Falcon* v. *The Famous Players Film Co., Ltd.*[90] that the Act of 1911 overruled the decision in *Karno* v. *Pathé Frères, Ltd.*, and that anyone who "sanctions, approves or countenances" an infringement may be liable, although the infringer is not his servant or agent, and, in *Mellor* v. *Australian Broadcasting Commission*,[91] Viscount Maugham expressed the view that a broadcaster who knew that his broadcast would be performed in public at hotels and other public places, and did not attempt to limit the performance to private sets, would be "authorising" a number of public performances.

457 There was some authority for the proposition that the word "authorise," in the Act of 1911, made it an infringement to authorise the commission of an infringement, whether the actual infringing act be done or not.[92] This view, however, has been doubted,[93] and it seems improbable that a mere instruction, which might be revoked before it caused damage, can, of itself, be an actionable wrong, though if the defendant, after request, refused to revoke the authority, a case for an injunction might, it is thought, be made out.

4.—STATUTORY DEFENCES

458 **Fair dealing.** The Copyright Act, 1911, provided certain statutory defences to direct infringements, the most important of which was that any fair dealing with any work for the purposes of private study,

88 [1945] A.C. 108 (P.C.).
89 [1946] V.L.R. 338.
90 [1926] 2 K.B. 474. See also *Fiel* v. *Lemaire* (1939) 4 D.L.R.(Can.) 561.
91 [1940] A.C. 491.
92 *Fenning Film Service, Ltd.* v. *Wolverhampton, etc., Cinemas, Ltd.* [1914] 3 K.B. 1171.
93 *Performing Right Society, Ltd.* v. *Mitchell and Booker, etc., Ltd.* [1924] 1 K.B. 762 at 773.

research, criticism, review or newspaper summary, should not constitute an infringement.[94]

459 The corresponding provisions of the Copyright Act, 1956, are that no fair dealing with a literary, dramatic or musical work for purposes of research or private study shall constitute an infringement,[95] that no fair dealing with a literary, dramatic or musical work shall constitute an infringement if it is for purposes of criticism or review, whether of that work or of another work, and it is accompanied by a sufficient acknowledgment,[96] and that no fair dealing with a literary, dramatic or musical work shall constitute an infringement if it is for the purpose of reporting current events in a newspaper, magazine or similar periodical,[96a] or by means of broadcasting, or in a cinematograph film, and, in the case of a newspaper, magazine or similar periodical, is accompanied by a sufficient acknowledgment.[97] "Sufficient acknowledgment" is defined as meaning an acknowledgment identifying the work in question by its title or other description and, unless the work is anonymous or the author has previously agreed or required that no acknowledgment of his name should be made, also identifying the author.[98]

460 **Pre-1911 decisions on "fair dealing."** As has been seen,[99] the question of what amounted to "fair dealing" frequently arose under the law prior to 1911 in determining whether enough use had been made of the plaintiff's work to constitute an infringement, and, for this purpose, a test of "fair dealing" was whether the alleged infringement competed with the plaintiff's work. In *Bradbury* v. *Hotten* [1] the publication complained of was "The Man of his Time," the object of which was to illustrate the career of Napoleon III by caricatures taken from leading English and foreign illustrated papers. Nine caricatures, with their original headings and references, but much reduced in size, were copied from nine numbers of "Punch," comprised within the period extending from 1849 to 1867. It was declared that the selections had been taken for the sole purpose of

94 Copyright Act, 1911, s. 2 (1) (i).
95 Copyright Act, 1956, s. 6 (1), as to artistic works, see *post*, § 506.
96 s. 6 (2).
96a See *Fraser* v. *Evans* [1969] 1 Q.B. 349.
97 s. 6 (3). In recommending the extension of control over the exporting of documents to certain documents between 100 and 30 years old, a Working Party set up by the Government suggested that the supply by the exporter of a copy of the document concerned for retention in this country should suffice. Since to do so without the permission of the copyright owner would be an infringement, it was also suggested that the Act of 1956 be amended to exempt copying for this purpose; see "Export Control of Documents," H.M. Stationery Office, 1970.
98 Copyright Act, 1956, s. 6 (10).
99 *Ante*, §§ 415 and 416.
1 (1872) L.R. 8 Ex. 1; *cf. Leslie* v. *Young (J.) & Sons* [1894] A.C. 335; *Smith* v. *Chatto* (1874) 31 L.T. 775; *Cambridge University Press* v. *University Tutorial Press, Ltd.* [1923–28] Macg.Cop.Cas. 349.

illustrating the career of Napoleon. While admitting that limited extracts might be taken from copyright works for a fair purpose of this kind, the court found that the defendant had published the caricatures in " Punch " for the same purpose as they were originally published, namely, to excite the amusement of his readers. It was held that the defendant had gone beyond the privilege of fair quotation, and therefore a case of piracy was made out.

In the course of his judgment in this case, Kelly C.B. gave the following illustrations: " A traveller publishes a book of travels about some distant country like China. Amongst other things, he describes some mode of preparing food in use there. Then the compiler of a cookery book republishes the description. No one could say that that was piracy. So again, an author publishes a history illustrated with woodcuts of the heads of kings, and another person, writing another history of some other country, finds occasion to copy one of these woodcuts. That again, would not be a piracy. Yet, on the other hand, the copying of a single picture may, under some circumstances, be an infringement. For example, take the case of a work illustrated by one engraving of the likeness of some distinguished man, where no other likeness is extant. No one could have a right to copy that into a book upon any subject whatever, and a jury would in such a case rightly find that there had been an infringement of the copyright."

461 **Relation of substantiality to fair dealing.** It is submitted that, in the examples given, substantial parts of the author's works were taken, and the only defence under the present law would lie in sections 6 and 9 of the Copyright Act, 1956. It should be pointed out in this connection that, at the present time, the question of whether a substantial part has been taken is quite distinct from whether there has been fair dealing. As said in a case under the Act of 1911,[2] it is only when the court has determined that a substantial part has been taken that any question of fair dealing arises. Though, once this question arises, the degree of substantiality, that is to say, the quantity and value of the matter taken, is an important factor in considering whether or not there has been fair dealing. Further, it is thought that, even under the present law, in considering whether a dealing with a particular work was fair, it would have to be considered whether any competition was likely to exist between the two works. But each case will depend on its own facts, and what may be fair in one case will not necessarily be fair in another case.

In fact the limitation of purposes in regard to which the defence of fair dealing can be set up probably did not alter the law, but it has prevented any attempt to extend the defence to new purposes.

[2] *Johnstone* v. *Bernard Jones Publications, Ltd.* [1938] Ch. 599; and see *Hawkes & Son (London), Ltd.* v. *Paramount Film Services, Ltd., infra.*

462 **Meanings of "research," "private study," "criticism" and "review."** The meanings of the expressions "research," "criticism" and "review" seem to require no further consideration. It was held that the reproduction in a news film of a topical event of the playing of music by a band shown in the film could not be justified as a "newspaper summary," and that these words must be confined to their literal meaning.[3] But, as has been seen, the law is now altered, and fair dealing with a musical work for purposes of reporting current events in a cinematograph film would not now be an infringement.[4] "Private study," it is submitted, only covers the case of a student himself copying out a book for his own use, but not the copying by anyone else on his behalf,[4a] nor the circulation of copies among other students.[5]

However, the Act of 1956 contains elaborate provisions enabling works to be copied by libraries for the use of students, and these are discussed in a later part of this work.[6]

463 **Criticism or review.** The copying of reported cases by the writers of legal textbooks now, no doubt, falls to be considered in the light of this proviso. The matter was left in some doubt under the law prior to 1911,[7] but it is submitted that the proper consideration is whether the case is one of bona fide criticism of cases, or whether, under the guise of criticism, the textbook is really a collection of reports intended to be used as such.

Similar considerations are no doubt involved in the case of reviews [7a] and newspaper summaries.[8] In the case of examination papers it had been held that their publication with a few lines of criticism for the use of students could not be justified under the proviso of the Act of 1911.[9]

Further, it was doubted whether that proviso could ever have applied to unpublished literary works—any premature publication of these for any purpose could hardly be a "fair dealing." [10] Dramatic and musical works may be performed without being published, and the publication of portions of these for the purposes of review or criticism could, no doubt, be justified.

3 *Hawkes & Son (London), Ltd.* v. *Paramount Film Service, Ltd.* [1934] Ch. 593.
4 Copyright Act, 1956, s. 6 (3).
4a See Report of Copyright Committee 1952, Cmd. 8662, para. 43, and Chap. 12, *post*.
5 *University of London Press, Ltd.* v. *University Tutorial Press, Ltd.* [1916] 2 Ch. 601.
6 *Post*, Chap. 12.
7 *Saunders* v. *Smith* (1838) 3 My & Cr. 711; *Butterworth* v. *Kelly* (1888) 4 T.L.R. 430; *Hodges (J.)* v. *Welsh (T.)* (1840) 2 Ir.Eq.R. 266.
7a *Harper & Bros.* v. *Biggs & Sons* [1905–10] Macg.Cop.Cas. 89.
8 *Whittingham (C.)* v. *Wooler (T. J.)* (1818) 2 Swan. 428; *Bell* v. *Whitehead* (1839) 8 L.J.Ch. 141; *Maxwell* v. *Somerton* (1874) 30 L.T. 11; *Weatherby & Sons* v. *International Horse Agency and Exchange, Ltd.* [1910] 2 Ch. 297.
9 See note 5, *ante*, § 462.
10 *British Oxygen Co., Ltd.* v. *Liquid Air, Ltd.* [1925] Ch. 383.

464 **Work reproduced need not be work criticised.** It should be observed that it is now possible to rely upon the defence of criticism or review whether the work reproduced is that criticised or not.[11] Thus, in criticising a work in a foreign language, it is now permissible to quote from an English translation, though there is no criticism of the translation as such. Again, in criticising one work, it is permissible to quote from other comparable works for the purpose of exemplifying the criticism.

465 **Acknowledgments.** It has been stated that, under the Act of 1911, if the work is set out and criticised, that is enough to bring the matter within the words " purposes of criticism," and that it is not essential that the source should be acknowledged or should be attributed to the author.[12]

466 But it is expressly provided in the Act of 1956 that, where exemption is claimed on the grounds of criticism, review or reporting, there must be a sufficient acknowledgment,[13] except in the case of reporting current events in a broadcast or film.. It should be noted that the title of the work must now always be given if exemption is claimed under these provisions, and that it is only the author's name which may be omitted, if he is anonymous, or has agreed or required that no acknowledgment of his name should be made.[14] Presumably, if he has required that his name should not be mentioned and it has nevertheless been mentioned, there will not be a " sufficient acknowledgment " within the meaning of the Act. In the case of very short quotations it may be possible to rely on the defence that they are not a substantial part of the original, so that it is not necessary to rely upon the fair dealing provisions and, if this is so, no acknowledgment would be required.

467 **Judicial proceedings.** A new provision of the Act of 1956 is that the copyright in a literary, dramatic or musical work is not infringed by reproducing it for the purposes of a judicial proceeding, or for the purposes of a report of a judicial proceeding.[15] Where an order has been made under section 10 of the Theatres Act, 1968, a police officer may require the person named in the order to produce a script on which the performance of the offending play was, or will be, based, and may require the person so named to afford him an opportunity of causing a copy thereof to be made. Presumably, if such person is not the owner of the copyright in the script,[16] the making of the

[11] Copyright Act, 1956, s. 6 (2).
[12] *Johnstone* v. *Bernard Jones Publications, Ltd.* [1938] Ch. 599.
[13] Copyright Act, 1956, s. 6 (2) and (3).
[14] s. 6 (10).
[15] Copyright Act, 1956, s. 6 (4).
[16] Theatres Act, 1968, s. 9 (2).

copy will be covered by section 6 (4) of the Act of 1956, as such copy can be used in proceedings under the Act of 1968 as evidence of what was performed.[16a]

468 **Reading or recitation of extracts in public.** The provision that the reading or recitation in public by one person of any reasonable extract from a published literary or dramatic work, if accompanied by a sufficient acknowledgment, is not to constitute an infringement,[17] is substantially the same as the corresponding provision of the Act of 1911,[17a] but the Act of 1956 continues, " provided that this subsection shall not apply to anything done for the purpose of broadcasting." This proviso is new, as the situation was not contemplated in 1911.

469 **Use for educational purposes.** Section 6 (6) of the Act of 1956 states that the copyright, in a published literary or dramatic work, is not infringed by the inclusion of a short passage therefrom in a collection intended for the use of schools if (a) the collection is described in its title, and in any advertisements thereof issued by or on behalf of the publisher, as being so intended, and (b) the work in question was not published for the use of schools, and (c) the collection consists mainly of material in which no copyright subsists, and (d) the inclusion of the passage is accompanied by a sufficient acknowledgment. It is, however, provided that the subsection shall not apply in relation to the copyright in a work if, in addition to the passage in question, two or more other excerpts from works by the author thereof (being works in which copyright subsists at the time when the collection is published) are contained in that collection, or are contained in that collection taken together with every similar collection (if any) published by the same publisher within the period of five years immediately preceding the publication of that collection. This is substantially the same as the corresponding provision of section 2 (1) (iv) of the Act of 1911.

470 It is further provided, in section 41 (1) of the Act of 1956, that, where copyright subsists in a literary, dramatic, musical or artistic work, copyright shall not be taken to be infringed by reason only that the work is reproduced, or an adaptation of the work is made or reproduced (a) in the course of instruction, whether at a school or elsewhere, where the reproduction or adaptation is made by a teacher or pupil otherwise than by the use of a duplicating process, or (b) as part of the questions to be answered in an examination, or in an answer to such a question. The expression " school " is defined by relation to the Education Acts and " duplicating process "

16a Theatres Act, 1968, ss. 9 (1) and 10 (5).
17 Copyright Act, 1956, s. 6 (5).
17a Copyright Act, 1911, s. 2 (1) (vi).

as meaning any process involving the use of an appliance for producing multiple copies.[18] It is further provided that nothing in the preceding subsection shall apply to the publication of a work or adaptation of a work.[19] These provisions are new.

5.—INDIRECT INFRINGEMENTS

471 It is not only the person who reproduces, or publicly performs, in whole, or in part, a copyright work who is liable to an action for infringement: persons who deal with infringing copies may also be exposed to a like action, but, in this case, only if they do so knowingly. Section 5 (3) and (4) of the Copyright Act, 1956, provides that the copyright in a literary, dramatic, musical or artistic work is infringed by any person who, in the United Kingdom, or in any other country to which the section extends, and without the licence of the owner of the copyright in the country in which the act is done,[20] sells, lets for hire, or by way of trade offers or exposes for sale or hire any article; or by way of trade exhibits any article in public; or distributes any article for purposes of trade; or distributes any article for other purposes, but to such an extent as to affect prejudicially the owner of the copyright in question; but in any such case, only if, to his knowledge, the making of the article constituted an infringement of that copyright, or, in the case of an imported article, would have constituted an infringement of that copyright, if the article had been made in the place into which it was imported.[21]

These provisions are substantially unchanged from those in the corresponding section 2 (2) of the Act of 1911.

472 **Selling or exposing for sale infringing works.** To sell a work which has been lawfully made, unless it was made in a foreign country, is not, therefore, an infringement of copyright.[22]

A person who simply attempts to effect a sale does not thereby infringe copyright,[23] unless he " by way of trade offers or exposes for sale or hire " the infringing article. The Act of 1911 did not go so far as the Literary Copyright Act, 1842, which made it an infringement of copyright for anyone knowingly " to have in his possession for sale or hire " an imported book which infringed copyright.[24]

18 Copyright Act, 1956, s. 41 (7).

19 s. 41 (2).

20 s. 49 (6).

21 Either under the Act of 1911 or the Act of 1956 (Copyright Act, 1956, Sched. VII, para. 4).

22 This point seems to have been overlooked in the case of *Monckton* v. *Pathé Frères, etc., Ltd.* [1914] 1 K.B. 395.

23 *Wolff* v. *Wood, The Times,* October 31, 1903; *Britain* v. *Kennedy* (1903) 19 T.L.R. 122.

24 5 & 6 Vict. c. 45, s. 17.

473 **Distribution for trade purposes.** Although it is no defence to anyone who has directly infringed copyright to say that he did so without the intention of making any profit thereby,[25] in order to render liable a person who merely *distributes* an article which, to the knowledge of the distributor, infringes copyright, it must be shown that he has done so " either for the purposes of trade or to such an extent as to affect prejudicially the owner of the copyright." It is not, however, very easy to imagine a case in which gratuitous distribution would not prejudicially affect the owner of the copyright. Likewise, " exhibition " must be " by way of trade."

It would seem that a defendant, who has delivered copies of an infringing article to a purchaser "on sale or return," is not liable if he did not know that the copies were infringing copies at the time he made the delivery, because he cannot demand the return of the articles delivered.[26]

474 **Infringement by importation.** It is also an infringement of the copyright in a literary, dramatic, musical or artistic work, by virtue of section 5 (2) of the Copyright Act, 1956, to import, without the licence of the owner of the copyright in the country into which the article was imported,[27] an article, otherwise than for private and domestic use, if, to the knowledge of the importer, the making of that article constituted an infringement of that copyright, or would have constituted such an infringement if the article had been made in the place into which it was so imported. Under section 17 of the Literary Copyright Act, 1842, it was an offence to import piracies, whether or not the importer had knowledge that the works were piracies.[28] Under the Act of 1911, to render the importer liable to be sued as an infringer of copyright, it had to be proved that he imported for " sale or hire " and also, as in the Act of 1956, that the imported works, to his knowledge, would infringe copyright, if made within the part of His Majesty's Dominions into which the importation took place. The Act of 1956, therefore, makes an important change in the nature of infringement by importation, in that the onus is now on the importer to show that the articles were imported for private and domestic use, whereas, under the Act of 1911, it was for the copyright owner to show that they had been imported for sale or hire.

Further, provision is made, in section 22 of the Act of 1956, to enable the owner of copyright to restrict unlawful importation. This is by giving notice to the Commissioners of Customs and Excise, and this matter is dealt with more fully in a later chapter.[29]

25 *Novello* v. *Ludlow* (1852) 12 C.B. 177.

26 *Schofield & Sims, Ltd.* v. *Gibson (R.) & Sons, Ltd.* [1928–35] Macg.Cop.Cas. 64; but *cf. Savory (E. W.), Ltd.* v. *The World of Golf, Ltd.* [1911–16] Macg.Cop. Cas. 149.

27 Copyright Act, 1956, s. 49 (6).

28 *Cooper* v. *Whittingham* (1880) 15 Ch.D. 501.

29 *Post*, Chap. 11.

475 **Necessity to prove knowledge.** As has been seen, in all cases of indirect infringement, it is necessary to prove knowledge on the part of the defendant that the making of the article in question infringed copyright. This distinguishes indirect infringements from direct infringements, where innocence on the part of the defendant is no defence to the claim, although it may, in a limited class of cases, afford some restriction on the remedy.[30] Having regard, however, to the remedies open to the copyright owner, in respect of dealings with infringing copies where proof of knowledge is not necessary,[31] it is often possible for the copyright owner to take proceedings against people dealing with infringing material without relying upon the indirect infringement sections, though greater protection is given to the innocent party under the Act of 1956 in this respect than under the Act of 1911. A further possible basis for proceeding against distributors, without proof of knowledge, has already been suggested in relation to infringement by " publishing " the work.[32]

476 **Burden of proof.** The burden of proof, as to knowledge, appears to lie upon the plaintiff,[33] and the best method of proving knowledge is by giving notice prior to instituting proceedings.[34] But, where such a notice is given, the defendant must be given a reasonable opportunity of ascertaining whether an infringement is in fact being committed before the issue of the writ.[35] The defendant's ignorance must, however, be of the facts and not of the law,[36] and probably the knowledge of an agent would be imputed to his principal.

477 **Works made abroad.** With regard to works made abroad, however, knowledge is obviously more difficult to establish. It may be impossible to give notice before a work is imported, and the importer may be quite unaware of the circumstances under which a work is made abroad.[37] Another difficulty, in regard to such works, would seem to arise where the work was made in the foreign country, under a licence which does not extend to permitting such works to be made in this country. It is suggested that, in such a case, the work would still be one which would have infringed copyright if made in this country, and that the actual lawfulness of the production, where made, cannot be considered.

30 Copyright Act, 1956, ss. 17 (2) and 18 (2).

31 See *post*, § 479.

32 *Ante*, § 443.

33 *Cf.* Copyright Act, 1956, ss. 5 (5), 17 (2) and 18 (3), where the burden of proof is thrown upon the defendant.

34 *Cooper* v. *Whittingham, supra*; *Merchant Adventurers, Ltd.* v. *M. Grew & Co., Ltd.* [1971] F.S.R. 233 at 243.

35 *Van Dusen* v. *Kritz* [1936] 2 K.B. 176.

36 *Burton* v. *Bevan* [1908] 2 Ch. 240.

37 See *Clarke, Irwin & Co.* v. *C. Cole & Co.* (1960) 22 D.L.R. (2d) 183 as to the effect of a copyright notice on the imported works.

478 Section 5 (2) of the Act of 1956, in dealing with infringement by importation, sets out two separate alternatives, namely, that the making of the article constituted an infringement, or that the making of the article would have constituted an infringement if the article had been made in the place into which it is imported. It seems to follow that it is an infringement to import into a country to which the Act extends, articles made in another such country, if the making in such other country was an infringement, although, in the country into which the importation is made, the making would not have been unlawful. It was doubtful whether this was so under the Act of 1911, because the two alternatives, though employed in section 2 (2) of the Act of 1911, could have been explained on the ground that one was dealing with imported works and the other with works sold or offered for sale, and so on.

479 **Conversion of infringing copies.** A further remedy to prevent any dealing with infringements is provided by section 18, Copyright Act, 1956, whereby all infringing copies are to be deemed to be the property of the owner, and any person dealing with them is liable in an action for conversion. Since the definition of "infringing copy," in section 18 (3), does not, as in the Act of 1911, involve any element of knowledge, this would seem to enable owners of copyright to avoid the necessity of proof of knowledge in actions against persons dealing with infringing copies.

6.—DRAMATIC

480 The kinds of infringement of copyright particularly affecting dramatic works consist of the production of dramatic versions, or films, of non-dramatic material, and the performance and broadcasting of works. The nature of infringement of copyright by performance in public and broadcasting, as it applies to all classes of works, is dealt with in later sections of this chapter, and the law concerning cinematograph films is dealt with in a later chapter of this book.[38] A basic distinction between literary works and dramatic works is that, in the latter, the choice of dramatic incident and the arrangement of situation may constitute, to far greater extent, the real value of the work than in the case of the former class. This section of this chapter is devoted to the question of whether, in the case of a dramatic infringement, either by the dramatisation of a non-dramatic work, or by the infringement of one play by another, a claim can succeed where there is no copying of language, but only of situation or plot.

481 **Provisions of the Act of 1956.** The Act of 1956 provides that, in the case of a non-dramatic work, it is an infringement to make a

[38] *Post*, Chap. 16.

version of the work, whether in its original language or a different language, in which it is converted into a dramatic work.[39] As there is a separate provision about translations,[40] it is assumed that the word "language" here refers to a different expression, in the same tongue, of the plot or story. While this may appear somewhat more restricted than was section 1 (2) (*c*) of the Act of 1911, which made it an infringement to convert a non-dramatic work into a dramatic work by way of performance in public or otherwise, which would seem to have included the performance of the plot in dumb show, yet it does appear to contemplate a complete change of language and thus something more remote from the original than would probably constitute an infringement of copyright in the case of two literary works. Again, in the Act of 1956, infringement by performance includes any mode of visual or acoustic presentation of the work [41] and, although literary works may also be infringed by performance, it is thought that, where the work infringed is dramatic, it can be said to have been visually presented if the incidents of the plot are presented without the use of the same language.

482 **Old law.** There is some doubt whether, under the law prior to 1911, a dramatic work could be infringed unless actual words and phrases were used or colourably imitated. Two leading cases on infringement of dramatic copyright were the cases of *Planché* v. *Braham*,[42] and *Chatterton* v. *Cave*.[43] In the first of these cases the defendant used the words of two or three songs of the plaintiff as the vehicle of some airs in an English version of Weber's opera "Oberon." The rest of the version had been written by another person. There was no question as to appropriation of the music, and Tindal L.C.J. left it to the jury to say whether there had been a representation of a part of the plaintiff's dramatic production. The jury found that there had been, and gave a verdict accordingly for the statutory penalty.

483 The second case was an action against the defendant in respect of his having committed an infringement of the copyright of the plaintiffs, in a drama founded on the novel by Eugène Sue, called "The Wandering Jew." The judge found as follows: "I find in this case that two scenes or points of the drama of the defendant have been taken direct from the drama of which Mr. Lewis was the author and the plaintiffs the assignees. I find that the drama of the defendant is not, except in these respects, a copy from or a colourable imitation of the drama of the plaintiffs. . . . I direct the verdict to be entered for the

[39] Copyright Act, 1956, s. 2 (6) (*a*) (i).
[40] s. 2 (6) (*a*) (iii).
[41] s. 48 (1).
[42] (1838) 4 Bing.N.C. 17.
[43] (1878) 3 App.Cas. 483.

defendant." The plaintiffs appealed to the House of Lords, but the House affirmed the decisions of the courts below, Lord Hatherley saying: "I think, my Lords, regard being had to the whole of the case, to the finding of the Lord Chief Justice that the parts which were so taken were neither substantial nor material parts, and the impossibility of damage being held to have accrued to the plaintiff from such taking, and the concurrence of the other judges before whom the case was brought, this appeal should be dismissed, and dismissed with costs." [44]

In *Scholtz* v. *Amasis, Ltd. & Fenn*,[44a] the Court of Appeal decided that there could be no infringement of the performing right in a comic opera if nothing was taken but parts of the plot and scenic effects. Unless the embodiment of the plot in words had, to a substantial extent, been appropriated, the plaintiff's case must break down.

484 **Present law.** But it was clearly settled that, under the Act of 1911, the copyright in a non-dramatic work could be infringed by a dramatic work though no words are taken. In the case of *Corelli* v. *Gray*,[45] where Miss Corelli, the novelist, complained that her novel, "Temporal Power," had been dramatised by the defendant in a sketch called "The People's King," it was held that there might be an infringement of copyright, although no single sentence in the defendant's play was similar to any sentence used in the plaintiff's novel. The Master of the Rolls based his judgment on his view that section 1 (2) of the Act of 1911, including subsection (*c*) of that section, had created such an enlarged right that it deserved to be termed a new right. And, in *Kelly* v. *Cinema Houses, Ltd.*,[46] Maugham J., in dealing with a question of infringement of copyright in a novel by dramatisation, after saying that it was trite law that there could be no book copyright in ideas, said: "As was pointed out in the Court of Appeal in the case of *Corelli* v. *Gray* [45] a new kind of right has been created by section 1, subsection 2, of the Act of 1911—a statutory monopoly of a special character; and protection is now given to the situations copied from the novel if the performance in public of a play founded on the novel involves the representation of these situations in a dramatic form; but I do not think it follows that mere ideas contained in the novel can be protected. If the plot of a story, whether it be found in a play or in a novel, is taken bodily with or without some minor additions and subtractions for the purposes of a stage play or cinema film, there is no doubt about the case. But if a character only is, so to speak, 'lifted' or one or two single situations, the problem becomes more difficult. Can it be said that in relation to

[44] 3 App.Cas. 483, 492, 493.
[44a] [1905–10] Macg.Cop.Cas. 216; but see *Nethersole* v. *Bell* [1901–04] Macg.Cop. Cas. 64.
[45] (1913) 29 T.L.R. 570; on appeal, 30 T.L.R. 116.
[46] [1928–35] Macg.Cop.Cas. 362; see also *Dagnall* v. *British and Dominions Film Corporation, Ltd.* [1928–35] Macg.Cop.Cas. 391, and *post*, Chap. 16.

performing right, and to that right alone, individual ideas can be protected under the Act? " And later on he continued: " The plaintiff has to show that the combination or series of dramatic events in the infringing work have been taken from the like situation in the plaintiff's work."

485 It was considered that it was equally true, under the Act of 1911, that an existing dramatic work might be infringed by a second dramatisation which reproduced dramatic incidents without using or imitating language. In *Rees* v. *Melville*,[47] a case of alleged infringement of one melodrama by another, Swinfen Eady L.J. said: " In order to constitute an infringement it is not necessary that the words of the dialogue should be the same, the situations and incidents, the mode in which the ideas are worked out and presented may constitute a material portion of the whole play, and the court must have regard to the dramatic value and importance of what, if anything, is taken, even though the portion may in fact be small and the actual language not copied. On the other hand, the fundamental idea of two plays may be the same, but if worked out separately and on independent lines they may be so different as to bear no real resemblance to one another." Again, in *Sutton Vane* v. *Famous Players Film Co., Ltd.*,[48] Scrutton L.J., after referring to the fact that the Act of 1911 defined copyright as the sole right to reproduce the work in any material form, discussed tests of infringement by imitation of incidents, without distinguishing cases in which the alleged infringement of a play was another play or a film.

It is not thought that the alteration in language above referred to between the provisions of the Act of 1956 regarding dramatic infringement and those of the Act of 1911 has altered the effect of the cases which have been cited.[48a]

It would appear, therefore, that although the reproduction of a plot alone is not an infringement of copyright, being a thing in the nature of an idea, which is not the subject of copyright protection, the reproduction of incidents and dramatic situations or points in substantially the order and arrangement of the original will be restrained. Though, where the incidents taken are such as are common to many plays, it may be difficult to show that a defendant has taken anything from the plaintiff's work,[49] for a man who has dressed up an old incident in new words can only have a copyright in the words.

486 **Alteration in method of performance.** Having regard to such developments as broadcasting, sound and television, cases arise of

[47] [1911–16] Macg.Cop.Cas. 96 and 168.
[48] [1928–35] Macg.Cop.Cas. 6.
[48a] See *Harman Pictures N.V.* v. *Osborne* [1967] 1 W.L.R. 723.
[49] *Reichardt* v. *Sapte* [1893] 2 Q.B. 308; *Robl* v. *Palace Theatre* (1911) 28 T.L.R. 69; *Bagge* v. *Miller* [1917–23] Macg.Cop.Cas. 179.

alleged infringements of dramatic works prepared for one medium by performance in a different medium. It is submitted that, in all such cases, if a substantial use is made of a series of dramatic incidents in which copyright subsists, there will be an infringement, whatever medium is employed, since it is in the series of incidents, as well as in their original mode of expression, that the copyright subsists. Thus, in one case,[50] it was held that a story was infringed by conversion into a ballet, though no words were used.

487 **Making of play into a novel.** The right to convert a dramatic work into a novel, or other non-dramatic work, is not infringed by the publication of a mere description of the dramatic action in the work. The alleged infringement must be in the nature of a novel or story.[51] It would appear that the test is whether the work complained of appeals to the dramatic interest of the reader, or is merely informative. It is thought, however, that, as in the opposite case, infringement can take place, without reproduction of actual words, if numerous incidents are reproduced.

7.—MUSICAL

488 The acts restricted by the copyright in a musical work are the same as those restricted by the copyright in a literary or dramatic work, save that, in the case of a musical work, there is a different definition of "adaptation." "Adaptation" in relation to a musical work means an arrangement or transcription of the work.[52]

It was argued, in *Francis Day & Hunter, Ltd.* v. *Bron*,[53] that, in the case of a musical work, unless the alleged infringement was an arrangement or a transcription, it must be an exact reproduction for the plaintiff to succeed. But this view was not accepted by the Court of Appeal; all that the plaintiff had to show was substantial similarity. On the other hand, the Court of Appeal accepted the argument that arrangement and transcription could only be the result of a conscious and deliberate process.

489 **How musical copyrights may be infringed.** Composers of musical works at the present day are chiefly concerned with the exercise of their rights by public performances, cinematograph films, recordings, whether on gramophone records or tapes, and broadcasts, and these matters are dealt with in other parts of this book.[53a] Nevertheless, whether an infringement by one of these means is alleged, or the infringement is by reproduction in graphic form, the primary question

50 *Holland* v. *Vivian Van Damm Productions, Ltd.* [1936–45] Macg.Cop.Cas. 69.
51 *Valcarenghi* v. *The Gramophone Co., Ltd.* [1928–35] Macg.Cop.Cas. 301.
52 Copyright Act, 1956, s. 2 (6) (*b*).
53 [1963] Ch. 587; for a further discussion of this case, see § 412, *ante*.
53a *Post*, Chaps. 9, 16, 17, 18.

is whether the alleged infringer has made use of a substantial part of the skill and labour of the original composer.

Whether this has been done or not, does not depend upon a note for note comparison. As was pointed out by Lord Lyndhurst, in *D'Almaine* v. *Boosey* [54]: "The most unlettered in music can distinguish one song from another, and the mere adaptation of the air, either by changing it to a dance or by transferring it from one instrument to another, does not, even to common apprehensions, alter the original subject. The ear tells you that it is the same. The original air requires the aid of genius for its construction, but a mere mechanic in music can make the adaptation or accompaniment. Substantially, the piracy is when the appropriated music, though adapted to a different purpose from that of the original, may still be recognised by the ear. The adding of variations makes no difference in the principle." [55] In another case [56] evidence was given that a musical work could be clearly and deliberately copied, without taking a single note directly from the original.

490 Difficult cases have arisen where the work alleged to have been infringed consisted of an arrangement of non-copyright tunes,[57] or where the infringing work was produced by using an intervening work. In all such cases the question is one of fact whether the plaintiff's skill and labour has been appropriated, and similar musical errors may be evidence of such appropriation. In dealing with an indirect copy the Court of Appeal judgment, in *Boosey* v. *Fairlie*, was expressed as follows: "There is scarcely any popular opera the score of which is not, within a short time after its first performance, arranged for the piano, and if by reconversion of the pianoforte arrangement into an operatic score, a task which could be executed by any skilled musician, and performance of that score the penalties of infringement could be escaped, the protection given to operatic compositions would be almost nugatory." [58]

8.—ARTISTIC

491 The acts restricted by the copyright in an artistic work are reproducing the work in any material form; publishing the work; and including the work in a television broadcast.[59]

492 **Reproduction.** "Reproduction," in the case of an artistic work, includes a version produced by converting the work into a three-

[54] (1835) 1 Y. & C.Ex. 288; *Francis Day & Hunter, Ltd.* v. *Bron* [1963] Ch. 587.
[55] *Boosey* v. *Fairlie* (1877) 7 Ch.D. 301; on appeal (1879) 4 App.Cas. 711. See also *Leader* v. *Purday* (1848) 7 C.B. 4; *Wood* v. *Boosey* (1867) L.R. 2 Q.B. 340; L.R. 3 Q.B. 223.
[56] *Austin* v. *Columbia Graphophone Co., Ltd.* [1917–23] Macg.Cop.Cas. 398.
[57] *Ante*, §§ 136 and 137.
[58] (1877) 7 Ch.D. at 317.
[59] Copyright Act, 1956, s. 3 (5).

dimensional form, or, if it is in three dimensions, by converting it into a two-dimensional form.[60] But the making of an object of any description which is in three dimensions is not to be taken to infringe the copyright in an artistic work in two dimensions if the object would not appear, to persons who are not experts in relation to objects of that description, to be a reproduction of the artistic work.[61] Danckwerts L.J., in *Dorling* v. *Honnor Marine, Ltd.*,[62] discussed this provision, and appeared to indicate that evidence of " non-experts " should have been obtained, but both he and Cross J. (in the court below) expressed a view on the facts as " non-experts." Whitford J. did the same thing in *I.M.I. Developments, Ltd.* v. *F. C. Harrison, Ltd.*,[62a] the learned judge taking the view that evidence on this point was not always necessary.[62b]

493 **Publishing.** As has already been pointed out in regard to literary works, it would appear that, under the Act of 1956, infringement by publishing a work occurs whenever copies of the work are issued to the public and is not confined, as was the case under the Act of 1911, to the act of first publishing an unpublished work. But the issue of photographs or engravings of a work of architecture, or of a sculpture, is not publication of such work.[63]

494 **Inclusion in television broadcast or cinematographic film.** The third class of acts restricted under the Act of 1956 is probably new, since, under the Act of 1911, unless the work was actually copied for the purpose of the broadcast, the inclusion of an artistic work in a broadcast would not, it is thought, have involved an infringement of any right under that Act. Broadcasting, for the purposes of the Act of 1956, is defined by reference to the Wireless Telegraphy Act, 1949,[64] but the inclusion of the work in a broadcast is not to constitute an infringement if its inclusion therein is only by way of background or is otherwise only incidental to the principal matters broadcast.[65] There is a similar qualification on the right of the artist, if his work is included in a cinematograph film,[65] but in this case the limitation may involve a diminution of his rights as existing under the Act of 1911, because the inclusion of a work in a film involves actual copying.

495 **Old law.** Before proceeding to consider the various decided cases about infringement of artistic copyright, it may be well to point out the differences in language employed in various Copyright Acts.

[60] s. 48 (1).
[61] s. 9 (8).
[62] [1965] Ch. 1.
[62a] [1970] R.P.C. 299.
[62b] See further Graham J. in *Merchant Adventurers, Ltd.* v. *M. Grew & Co., Ltd.* [1971] F.S.R. 233 at p. 242.
[63] s. 49 (2) (*a*).
[64] s. 48 (2).
[65] s. 9 (5).

The Fine Arts Copyright Act, 1862,[66] provided, by section 1, that the copyright in a picture, drawing, or photograph should confer " the sole and exclusive right of copying, engraving, reproducing, and multiplying such painting or drawing, and the design thereof, or such photographs, and the negative thereof, by any means and of any size "; and, by section 6 of the same statute, penalties were imposed upon any person who, without the consent of the proprietor of the copyright, should " repeat, copy, colourably imitate, or otherwise multiply . . . any such work or the design thereof." In the case of engravings, copyright was infringed by any person who " shall copy in the whole, or in part, by varying, adding to, or diminishing from the main design " [67]; and, in the case of works of sculpture, by any person who should make or import " any pirated copy or pirated cast " of the original sculpture.[68]

Under the Copyright Act, 1911, the proprietor of the copyright in an artistic work had the sole right to produce or reproduce his work or any substantial part thereof in any material form whatever,[69] and his copyright was infringed by any person who invaded this right without his consent.[70] There was no reference in this Act to the " design " of the artistic work, except in section 22 (1), which did not deal with infringement.

496 **General principles.** The general principles, which have already been discussed,[71] are equally applicable in cases of infringement of artistic copyright. It has to be determined whether the defendant has used a substantial part of those features of the plaintiff's work, upon the preparation of which skill and labour has been employed. Once it is established that there has been such a use of the plaintiff's work, there will be an infringement, whether or not the defendant has used a different medium, and whether or not the infringing work has been derived directly from the plaintiff's. With regard to truly original artistic works, the question whether the defendant has made such a use of the plaintiff's can generally be answered merely by a comparison of the two works. It is to such cases that the well-known definition of copy, in *West* v. *Francis*,[72] is most readily applicable. In that case Bayley J. said: " A copy is that which comes so near to the original as to give to every person seeing it the idea created by

66 25 & 26 Vict. c. 68.
67 17 Geo. 3, c. 57.
68 Sculpture Copyright Act, 1814 (54 Geo. 3, c. 56), s. 3.
69 Copyright Act, 1911, s. 1 (2).
70 s. 2 (1).
71 § 402 *et seq.*, *ante*.
72 (1822) 5 B. & Ald. 737 at 743; cited with approval in the House of Lords in *King Features Syndicate* v. *O. & M. Kleeman, Ltd.* [1941] A.C. 417. But, as has been pointed out above (see § 420, *ante*), this form of definition is not complete, and does not take into account the necessity of proving actual copying. See *Merchant Adventurers, Ltd.* v. *M. Grew & Co., Ltd.* [1971] F.S.R. 233 at 237.

the original." In *Hanfstaengl* v. *W. H. Smith & Sons*,[73] Kekewich J. preferred the definition "a copy is that which comes so near to the original as to suggest that original to the mind of every person seeing it." Whether or not there has been an infringement must be a matter of degree and, in the case of an artistic work, the degree of resemblance is to be judged by the eye. But in the case of commercial designs, general resemblance is not so good a test, since resemblance may be due to common subject-matter or stock designs, and it is necessary to make a close examination of detail to see whether there has been infringement.[74]

497 **Infringement predicates reproduction.** Subject to section 5 of the Act of 1956, and to the case of inclusion in a television broadcast, the work must be actually reproduced without the consent of the copyright owner in order to constitute an infringement of copyright. The fact that copies lawfully produced are used for purposes other than those permitted by the proprietor of the copyright, does not constitute an infringement of copyright, though it may be a breach of contract. Thus, in a case where the owners of the copyright in an engraving gave a licence to a publisher to use the picture once only as a small wood block in a pamphlet illustrative of certain pictures, the defendants, who had purchased a number of pamphlets, and cut out the woodcut in question, and mounted it on cards, which they sold, were held not to be guilty of infringement of copyright.[75] Similar considerations apply where pictures are cut out and used for table tops, and the like, under glass sheets.

498 **Tests of infringement.** It is equally an infringement of copyright whether the size of the copy has been increased or reduced,[76] and whether the whole or part only of the original has been copied.

Thus, where a man had a drawing of his wife made, having attached to her arm and dress a dress holder, a patented invention of his own, and substituted for his wife's head that of the Princess of Wales, taken from a photograph, the copyright in which belonged to the plaintiff, and from the combination so obtained made and printed cabinet-size photographs for the purpose of advertising his invention, that was held to be an infringement.[77]

[73] [1905] 1 Ch. 519 at 524: see *Twentieth Century Fox Film Corp.* v. *Anglo Amalgamated Film Distributors, Ltd.*, *The Times*, January 22, 1965, *ante*, § 440.

[74] *Kenrick & Co.* v. *Lawrence & Co.* (1890) 25 Q.B.D. 99; *Nicol* v. *Barranger* (*C. A.*) [1917–23] Macg.Cop.Cas 219; *Hanfstaengl* v. *Empire Palace* [1895] A.C. 20.

[75] *Frost and Reed* v. *The Olive Series Publishing Co.* (1908) 24 T.L.R. 649; *cf. Murray* v. *Heath* (1831) 1 B. & Ad. 804.

[76] *Hanfstaengl Art Publishing Co.* (*The*) v. *Holloway* [1893] 2 Q.B. 1; *cf. Gambart* v. *Ball* (1863) 14 C.B.(N.S.) 306; *Cooper* v. *Stephens* [1895] 1 Ch. 567; *Marshall* (*W.*) *& Co., Ltd.* v. *Bull* (*A. H.*), *Ltd.* (1901) 85 L.T. 77.

[77] *London Stereoscopic, etc., Co., Ltd.* (*The*) v. *Kelly* (1888) 5 T.L.R. 169: see *Weldons, Ltd.* v. *United Press, Ltd.* [1905–10] Macg.Cop.Cas. 293, where fashion plates were held to have been infringed, notwithstanding that the dresses and heads had been taken from different figures.

499 In *Brooks* v. *Religious Tract Society*,[78] the plaintiff was the owner of the copyright in a picture and engraving known as " Can't you talk? ", which represented a collie dog seated on his haunches on a stone floor looking down at the upturned face of a child. There was a wall in the background with a door on one side through which a cat was looking; above the dog was a table on which was a tub with a spoon in it. The defendants were the owners of a periodical in which was a wood-cut that almost exactly reproduced the whole of the plaintiff's engraving, with the exception of the child, whose position was replaced by a tortoise and two cats. The wood-cut was given as an illustration of a story entitled " A Strange Visitor." It was held that, as the defendants had taken a substantial portion of the plaintiff's engraving and reproduced it in the wood-cut with slightly different surroundings, this constituted an infringement of the plaintiff's copyright, and that the latter was accordingly entitled to an injunction.

500 In the case of *Bauman* v. *Fussell*,[79] where it was alleged that a painting of two cocks fighting was a copy of a photograph of the same subject, it was admitted that the defendant had made use of the photograph for the purposes of his design. Somervell L.J. referred to a passage in the judgment in *Brooks* v. *Religious Tract Society*, *supra*, namely, " it was not only the dog which was taken, but also the feeling and artistic character of the plaintiff's work." He said that, in the case before him, the feeling and artistic character of the painting were the work of the defendant. He agreed, however, that there might be an infringement, although the feeling and artistic character of the two works were different. He took the view, however, that although the artist had used the plaintiff's work as an inspiration, he had not copied it, but had made a new work of art of his own. Birkett L.J., after pointing out that expert evidence was properly called to point out similarities, coincidences and the like in order to support a contention of copying, but that the expert must stop short of giving his opinion that the work under criticism was in fact a copy, said that a question of infringement or otherwise was a question of fact, and he was therefore not prepared to disturb the finding in the court below. Romer L.J., however, in a dissenting judgment, came to the conclusion that the trial judge had misdirected himself. He pointed out that the inquiry should be rather as to what has been reproduced than what has not, and that, if the proper view was that the defendant had taken the outline or form of the birds, he would be infringing the copyright in the photograph.

501 In another case the plaintiff was the proprietor of the copyright in an oil-painting of considerable size, called " Nature's Mirror," which portrayed the draped figure of a " Psyche " with wings, kneeling on a

78 (1897) 45 W.R. 476.
79 (1954) *The Author*, LXIV, No. 3, 63.

rock, and looking into a pool of water, there being a suitable background to the picture. In the advertisement page of a magazine a number of photographic reproductions of pictures used in well-known advertisements appeared, one such reproduction being a rude copy of the figure in "Nature's Mirror," without the wings, and without the background, the reproduction being about the size of an old halfpenny. This was held to be an infringement of the copyright in the picture.[80]

502 **Indirect copies.** Copyright may be infringed by copying something which is itself a copy of the plaintiff's work. If the original work has been reproduced it is no answer to say that it has been copied from a work which was itself, whether licensed or unlicensed, a copy of the original.[81] This is so, even if the intervening work is of a nature not capable of being an infringement of copyright or enjoying copyright.[81] But in the case of *Purefoy Engineering Co., Ltd.* v. *Sykes, Boxall & Co., Ltd.*,[82] it was contended that a catalogue made from the plaintiffs' machinery parts, as offered for sale by them, infringed the copyright in the plaintiffs' catalogue, although the defendants' catalogue had been compiled without any reference to the plaintiffs' catalogue or any copy thereof. The Master of the Rolls, in rejecting this contention, said: "In our judgment, it is not true to say that the parts made and offered by the plaintiffs 'represented' in physical form the descriptions in the catalogue—at least in any sense relevant to the consideration of copyright in the latter, as a literary work. Rather, the contents of the catalogue described the parts made and offered by the plaintiffs. And the considerable skill and labour devoted by the plaintiffs in making their selection was devoted to the selection of the range of goods in which the plaintiffs were to trade, and not for the purpose of bringing into existence the literary work, namely, the catalogue. No doubt, skill and labour were employed for the latter purpose, but skill and labour of a different order. The selected range of goods existed or was capable of existing for trading purposes independently altogether of the plaintiffs' catalogue or of any catalogue. . . . What we will call the intermediate stage or subject-matter copied by the alleged infringer must in some real and intelligible sense, in our judgment, be a 'copy' or representation of the original work." But in *Dorling* v. *Honnor Marine, Ltd.*,[83] the Court of Appeal had no difficulty in finding "indirect" copying, where the plaintiff's plans had been reproduced in three-dimensional form and the form photographed, with the result that the photograph reproduced a substantial

80 *Hanfstaengl* v. *W. H. Smith & Sons* [1905] 1 Ch. 519.

81 *Hanfstaengl* v. *Empire Palace* [1894] 3 Ch. 109; *King Features Syndicate* v. *O. & M. Kleeman, Ltd.* [1941] A.C. 417.

82 (1954) 71 R.P.C. 227; (1955) 72 R.P.C. 89.

83 [1956] Ch. 1; and see *Merchant Adventurers, Ltd.* v. *M. Grew & Co., Ltd.* [1971] F.S.R. 233.

part of the plaintiff's plan. Where the plaintiff is the owner of the right to reproduce the work in a particular form only, for example, as an engraving, he must show that the work of which he complains was copied from his work, and not from the original.[84]

503 **Reproduction by different process.** The question as to whether the copyright in an artistic work could be infringed by the design being transferred to an article of manufacture, arose in the case of *Dicks* v. *Brooks*.[85] However, the Act of 1956 is not directed to the means of reproduction, but to the result, so that, if a manufactured article in fact reproduces the details which go to make the copyright in the artistic work, it is submitted that the method of reproduction is immaterial.

In this case the defendants were not the proprietors of the copyright in the original picture, "The Huguenot," and it is submitted that the decision goes no further than that a Berlin wool pattern, published by the plaintiffs, was not an infringement of the engraving rights, which were the only rights vested in the defendants. It is not clear that, if the action had been brought against the proprietor of the copyright in the picture, the decision would have been to the same effect. Even if this be not so, it is submitted that, whatever the law may have been prior to the Act of 1911, the copying of a picture upon an article of manufacture was, under that Act, and is, under the Act of 1956, an infringement of copyright, the Acts forbidding the reproduction of a work in "any material form." [86] Little weight would, it is thought, be attached at the present day to the argument that the infringing article is not likely to compete in the market with the original.[87]

504 **Reproduction in a different dimension.** Under the Act of 1956 a work in two dimensions may be infringed by a work in three. Under the law prior to 1911 there was some doubt about this, and it had been held that *tableaux vivants* were not infringements of copyright in pictures.[88] But in *Bradbury, Agnew & Co.* v. *Day*,[89] Coleridge J. held that section 1 (2) of the Act of 1911 had the effect of making "living pictures" possible subjects of infringement of copyright in an artistic work. And in *King Features Syndicate* v. *O. & M. Kleeman, Ltd.*,[90] it was held that certain brooches, plaster dolls, and mechanical toys representing the figure of "Popeye the Sailor," infringed copyrights in certain drawings and cartoons. In this case

84 *Lucas* v. *Cooke* (1880) 13 Ch.D. 872.
85 (1880) 15 Ch.D. 22.
86 Copyright Act, 1956, s. 3 (5) (*a*). Copyright Act, 1911, s. 1 (2).
87 *Weatherby & Sons* v. *International Horse Agency and Exchange, Ltd.* [1910] 2 Ch. 297.
88 *Hanfstaengl* v. *Empire Palace* [1894] 2 Ch. 1.
89 (1916) 32 T.L.R. 349.
90 [1941] A.C. 417; followed in *Walt Disney Productions* v. *H. John Edwards Publishing Co., Pty., Ltd.* (1954) 71 W.N.(N.S.W.) 150.

Simonds J. said that it would be contrary to the plain meaning and spirit of the Act of 1911 if a copy of an artistic work were only an infringement if made in the same dimensions. The change of medium might make proof of infringement more difficult, but this was only a question of degree. The principle applicable in the case of works of two dimensions reproduced in three is now clear,[91] but it is necessary that the thing as reproduced should itself resemble the original to non-experts.[92] The fact that a dress, when worn, might resemble the original, will not make the dress in itself an infringement.[93]

505 **Public exhibition.** The Act of 1956 does not make it an infringement of copyright to exhibit in public an original picture, whether for trade or otherwise,[94] and it is only an infringement of copyright to exhibit unlawful copies when it is done " by way of trade." [95]

506 **Statutory defences.** As in the case of literary, dramatic or musical works, fair dealing with an artistic work is permitted for purposes of research or private study,[96] and, if accompanied by a sufficient acknowledgment, for purposes of criticism or review, whether of the work in question or of another work.[97] The same exemption is also provided in the case of reproduction for the purpose of a judicial proceeding or a report of a judicial proceeding.[98]

507 **Making of a subsequent work by same author.** There are, however, certain additional circumstances in which the reproduction of an artistic work will not constitute an infringement.

It is not an infringement of copyright in an artistic work for the same author to make a subsequent work not repeating or imitating the main design of the earlier work, notwithstanding that part of the earlier work is reproduced in the subsequent work, and is so reproduced by the use of a mould, cast, sketch, plan, model or study made for the purposes of the earlier work.[99]

In *Hansfstaengl* (*F.*) v. *Baines* (*H. R.*) *& Co., Ltd.*[1] Lord Watson expressed the opinion that the " design " of a work " means nothing more than the particular forms and arrangements (whether of lines or colouring) which the copyright author has selected as the vehicle for

[91] Copyright Act, 1956, s. 48 (1). The same has been held in America: *Bracken* v. *Rosenthal* (1907) 151 Fed.R. 136; *cf. King Features Syndicate* v. *Fleischer* [1923–28] Macg.Cop.Cas. 170; and see *Buzacott & Co., Ltd.* v. *Dutch* (1929) 30 S.R. (N.S.W.) 22.

[92] Copyright Act, 1956, s. 9 (8).

[93] *Burke, etc., Ltd.* v. *Spicers Dress Designs* [1936] Ch. 400.

[94] *Cf. Martin* v. *Wright* (1833) 6 Sim. 297; *Turner* v. *Robinson* (1860) 10 Ir.Ch. 121, 510.

[95] Copyright Act, 1956, s. 5 (3).

[96] s. 9 (1).

[97] s. 9 (2).

[98] s. 9 (7).

[99] s. 9 (9).

[1] [1895] A.C. 20, 27; see also *Preston* v. *Raphael Tuck, etc., Ltd.* [1926] Ch. 667.

conveying his idea to those who see his work." If, therefore, a picture is made up of a group of persons or things, each the subject of separate study, the artist will be at liberty to make replicas of the separate studies, but not to group them in such a way as to give the general impression of the completed work for which the studies were originally made. The expression that the artist is to be at liberty to " use " his studies is peculiar, but, probably, it includes the right, not only to " use " them for the purpose of making other artistic works, but also to sell the studies themselves, or make exact copies of them.

508 **Works of sculpture and artistic craftsmanship.** The copyright in a work of sculpture and a work of artistic craftsmanship [2] which is permanently situated in a public place, or in premises open to the public, is not infringed by the making of a painting, drawing, engraving, or photograph of the work, or the inclusion of the work in a cinematograph film or in a television broadcast.[3] The words " in premises open to the public " are new in the Act of 1956, and may have extended the licence conferred by the section to premises to which the public are admitted only on licence or on payment. The permission to include the work in a film or television broadcast is also new. Where, however, the public is only admitted on licence, there would seem to be nothing to prevent the owner of the premises imposing conditions in the licence restricting the copying of the material exhibited.[3a] But such conditions, while binding on the licensee, will not make any photographs taken infringing copies so that, in the hands of an ultimate purchaser, they would be free from any obligation to the owner of the premises.

509 **Works of architecture.** A similar exemption is granted in respect of the making of a painting, drawing, engraving or photograph of a work of architecture, whether in a public place or not, or the inclusion of such work in a cinematograph film or television broadcast.[4] Moreover, the publication of any painting, drawing, engraving, photograph or film permitted under the provisions aforesaid is not to constitute an infringement.[5]

510 **Special rights of artists.** An artist has certain specific rights in respect of his work in addition to his rights to restrain infringements. These rights, of which the principal one is to prevent publication of

[2] Works of sculpture include " casts and models made for purposes of sculpture," Copyright Act, 1956, s. 48 (1); works of artistic craftsmanship are not defined by the Act of 1956, see s. 3 (1) (*c*) of that Act.

[3] Copyright Act, 1956, ss. 9 (3) and 3 (1) (*c*).

[3a] See *Sports and General Press Agency, Ltd.* v. " *Our Dogs* " *Publishing Co., Ltd.* [1916] 2 K.B. 880; [1917] 2 K.B. 125.

[4] s. 9 (4). As to architecture, see also Chap. 15, *post*.

[5] s. 9 (6), or if permitted under the Act of 1911 (Copyright Act, 1956, Sched. VII, para. 7 (1)).

altered copies under his name, are exercisable even though he has parted with the copyright.[6]

9.—PUBLIC PERFORMANCE

511 **Definition of performance.** The Copyright Act, 1956, defines " performance " as including delivery, in relation to lectures, addresses, speeches and sermons, and in general as including any mode of visual or acoustic presentation, including any such presentation by the operation of wireless telegraphy apparatus, or by the exhibition of a cinematograph film, or by the use of a record, or by any other means.[7] The definition of wireless telegraphy apparatus is discussed later in this chapter.[8] " Cinematograph film " means any sequence of visual images recorded on material of any description (whether translucent or not) so as to be capable by the use of that material, either of being shown as a moving picture, or of being recorded on other material (whether translucent or not) by the use of which it can be so shown.[9] " Record " means any disc, tape, perforated roll or other device in which sounds are embodied so as to be capable (with or without the aid of some other instrument) of being automatically reproduced therefrom.[7] This definition, however, is expressly subject to subsection (5) of section 48 of the Act of 1956 which provides that broadcasting, or the causing of a work or other subject-matter to be transmitted to subscribers to a diffusion service, is not to be taken to constitute performance and that, where visual images or sounds are displayed or emitted by any receiving apparatus to which they are conveyed by the transmission of electro-magnetic signals (whether over paths provided by a material substance or not), the operation of any apparatus whereby the signals are transmitted, directly or indirectly, to the receiving apparatus shall not be taken to constitute performance. The method adopted by the Act of 1956 of excluding, from the meaning of " performance," these kinds of acts which would have been treated as performances under the old law, instead of treating all the acts as performances, but making special provision as to certain kinds of performances, seems inconvenient in that it is no longer possible to use the expression " performing right " in a broad sense to include all possible methods of performance. It seems likely that this will lead to difficulties in interpreting documents where it may well be that the parties intend, by the word " performance," to include all performing rights, including the right to broadcast. The acts hereby excluded from performance are dealt with specifically in a later section of this chapter.

6 *Ante,* § 246.
7 Copyright Act, 1956, s. 48 (1).
8 *Post,* § 528.
9 Copyright Act, 1956, s. 13 (10).

512 **"In public."** By the Act of 1956 the performing right, as such, is only conferred in respect of literary, dramatic or musical works,[10] the restricted act being "performing the work in public." But the words "in public" also occur in relation to records, in respect of which it is an infringement to cause the recording to be heard in public [11]; in relation to cinematograph films in respect of which it is an infringement to cause the film, so far as it consists of visual images, to be seen in public, or in so far as it consists of sounds, to be heard in public,[12] and in relation to television broadcasts, in respect of which it is an infringement to cause it, in so far as it consists of visual images, to be seen in public, or in so far as it consists of sounds, to be heard in public, but in this case there is the further qualification that it must be seen or heard by a paying audience.[13]

513 Under the law prior to 1911 the performance, to be an infringement of copyright, had to be represented at a place of dramatic entertainment. But it was held that this condition was fulfilled if the performance was at any place in public, since, to hold otherwise, would deprive an author of his right to the profits of his work.[14] The Act of 1911 did not, in section 1 (2), confine the author's rights to performances at a place of dramatic entertainment, but gave effect to decisions under the law prior to 1911 by giving to such author the sole right of performance in public, and this is followed in the Act of 1956.

514 **Performance in public a question of fact.** Whether a particular performance takes place in public or not is a question of fact.[15] There are, however, certain tests which it is material to consider when considering this question of fact.

In a case under the law prior to 1911,[16] the Master of the Rolls said: "It is not necessary that there should be profit made by the representation." He considered that the place need not be habitually kept for the exhibition of dramatic entertainments. A representation in a nursery by children, or by grown-up persons in a drawing-room, is not an infringement because it is obviously domestic and private. So, too, a "representation for the amusement of friends in an unfurnished house hired for the occasion." The representation in that case is also "domestic and private." There must be present a sufficient part of the public who would also go to a performance licensed by the author as a commercial transaction. "Suppose that a member

10 s. 2 (5) (*c*).
11 s. 12 (5) (*b*).
12 s. 13 (5) (*b*).
13 s. 14 (4) (*c*).
14 *Russell* v. *Smith* (1848) 12 Q.B. 217.
15 *Harms (Inc.), Ltd.* v. *Martans Club, Ltd.* [1927] 1 Ch. 526 (C.A.).
16 *Duck* v. *Bates* (1884) 13 Q.B.D. 843, followed in *Jennings* v. *Stephens* [1936] Ch. 469 (performance at a women's club is in public); *cf. Caird* v. *Sime* (1887) 12 App.Cas. 326; *Glenville* v. *Selig Polyscope Co.* (1911) 27 T.L.R. 554.

for a Parliamentary borough organises dramatic entertainments to which the inhabitants are admitted without payment. Suppose that an amateur company chooses to act some drama for a charitable object, with admission upon payment of money or by tickets issued generally. In each of these instances an infringement of the statute has been committed." Bowen L.J. said, however: "But profit is a very important element; the question of numbers also is very important—these are matters to be taken into consideration."

515 In the case of *Harms* (*Inc.*) *Ltd.*, v. *Martans Club, Ltd.*,[17] it was decided that a performance of music by a dance band at a dance club was a performance in public. The Court of Appeal, after approving the application of the tests above mentioned to a decision of questions arising under the Act of 1911 and, in particular, the dictum of the Master of the Rolls in *Duck* v. *Bates*,[18] where he said, "I agree that what was intended to be protected was the value of the author's invention, that is the key to the construction of the Act," suggested that other relevant questions were whether the performance was for profit, whether the public were freely admitted, the kind of place at which the performance occurred, the number of persons present, and whether the performance was likely to injure the owner of the copyright.

516 In the case of *Jennings* v. *Stephens* [19] it was decided that a dramatic performance, given at a village Women's Institute, was a performance in public though the performers were all members of a neighbouring institute, no one was present except members and no charge was made for admission. It was decided that the true criterion, whether the performance was public or quasi-domestic, was the character of the audience. In view of the fact that any woman in the village could become a member of the institute on payment of a small entrance fee, the audience, in this case, could not be held to have any domestic or quasi-domestic character.

517 In *Ernest Turner, etc., Ltd.* v. *Performing Right Society, Ltd.*,[20] it was decided that performances of music given at a factory to workers during working hours were performances in public. The Master of the

17 [1927] 1 Ch. 526 (C.A.). In the case of *Performing Right Society, Ltd.* v. *Hawthornes Hotel* (*Bournemouth*), *Ltd.* [1933] Ch. 855, it was held that a performance in a hotel lounge was a performance in public; *cf. Brearley* v. *Morley* [1899] 2 Q.B. 121 (a licensing case). In *Performing Right Society, Ltd.* v. *Camelo* [1936] 3 All E.R. 557, it was held to be a public performance to perform music on private premises with the object of its being heard in public; and see *Australian Performing Right Association, Ltd.* v. *Canterbury-Bankstown League Club Ltd.* [1964–65] N.S.W.R. 138.

18 (1884) 13 Q.B.D. 843 at 845.

19 [1936] Ch. 469.

20 [1943] Ch. 167. This case is reported jointly with *Performing Right Society, Ltd.* v. *Gillette Industries, Ltd.*, a case in which the facts were very similar.

Rolls pointed out that, in this class of case, it was important to consider the relationship of the audience to the owner of the copyright rather than its relationship to the performer.

On this view it can be contended that any group of persons, who might be contemplated by the owner of the copyright as a possible source of revenue from public performances, constituted the public for the purposes of determining what amounts to an infringement.

518 **Statutory exceptions.** The Act of 1956 contains certain express limitations upon the scope of public performance. In section 12 (7) of that Act there are limitations upon what constitutes causing a sound recording to be heard in public, which are more fully discussed in a later chapter,[21] since these only affect the copyright in the sound recording, and not the copyright in the recorded music. But section 41 (3) of that Act provides that, for the avoidance of doubt, a performance in the course of the activities of a school, by a person who is a teacher in or a pupil who is in attendance at the school, is not to be a performance in public, if the audience is limited to persons who are teachers in or pupils in attendance at the school, or are otherwise directly connected with the activities of the school, whether the performance is in class or otherwise in the presence of an audience. It does not, therefore, appear necessary that the performance should be on the school premises. But a person is not to be taken to be directly connected with the activities of a school by reason only that he is a parent or guardian of a pupil in attendance at the school,[22] so that performances at which parents or guardians are present, may, notwithstanding the section, constitute public performances. The matter would presumably depend upon whether parents were present merely as an audience, or because of some special relationship to the particular performance. " School " has the same meaning as in the Education Act, 1944.[23]

10.—PERMITTING PUBLIC PERFORMANCE

519 In addition to the general liability of persons for infringements of copyright committed with their authority,[24] which, of course, arises in cases of infringement by public performance as in other infringements, section 5 (5) of the Copyright Act, 1956, provides that " the copyright in a literary, dramatic or musical work is also infringed by any person who permits a place of public entertainment to be used for a performance in public of the work, where the performance constitutes an infringement of the copyright in the work." " Place of public entertainment " is defined as including premises occupied mainly for other

21 *Post*, Chap. 17.
22 Copyright Act, 1956, s. 41 (4).
23 s. 41 (7) (*a*).
24 See § 452.

purposes, but from time to time made available for hire to such persons as may desire to hire them for purposes of public entertainment.[25] It is, however, provided that an infringement will not be committed where the person permitting the place to be used was not aware, and had no reasonable grounds for suspecting, that the performance would be an infringement of copyright, or gave the permission gratuitously, or for a consideration which was only nominal, or (if more than nominal) did not exceed a reasonable estimate of the expenses to be incurred by him in consequence of the use of the place for the performance.[26]

While the form of this provision is a little different from that in section 2 (3) of the Act of 1911, the main question remains the same, namely whether the defendant has permitted the premises to be used for a public performance.

Liability only arises where a person has permitted the place to be used. Permission may be inferred from acts which fall short of being direct and positive, and may be inferred from indifference, but it will not be inferred from a mere general authority to use a theatre for the performance of musical or dramatic works.[27]

520 **Who is liable.** Under the law prior to 1911 a person was liable if he caused a dramatic piece to be represented. It was held that a person who had let for hire a place of entertainment for public performance of songs and music was not, from the mere fact of letting, to be held liable if copyright songs were sung without the consent of the proprietors of the copyright.[28] But in the case of *Marsh* v. *Conquest* [29] the defendant was the owner and manager of the Grecian Theatre, and, for £30, he had let, for one night, to his son, who was the stage manager, the use of the theatre, company, and all persons employed. The son selected and brought out a play, for which representation the court held the defendant liable. The judgment was based on the fact that the defendant had the control and management of the theatre and the company during that performance. "I think," said Erle C.J. "the defendant is responsible for that representation. He was the proprietor of the theatre, and had entire control over the establishment and all belonging to it; and what was done by his son was done by his permission. The case of *Lyon* v. *Knowles* seems to me to recognise that distinction. There the defendant merely let his theatre with the scenery, scene-shifters, bands, lights, etc., to Dillon, who brought his own company to represent pieces of his own selection,

[25] Copyright Act, 1956, s. 5 (6).
[26] s. 5 (5), proviso.
[27] *Performing Right Society, Ltd.* v. *Ciryl Theatrical Syndicate, Ltd.* [1924] 1 K.B. 1.
[28] *Russell* v. *Briant* (1850) 8 C.B. 836; *Lyon* v. *Knowles* (1863) 3 B. & S. 556.
[29] (1864) 17 C.B. 418; and see *Kelly's Directories, Ltd.* v. *Gavin and Lloyds* [1902] 1 Ch. 631.

the plaintiff having no control whatever over any person employed in the representation. Here, however, the piece is performed by the defendant's own *corps dramatique,* his son being one of them; and the performance takes place for the defendant's profit to the extent of £30. I think, therefore, it is impossible to say that the defendant did not cause the piece to be represented."

521 So in the case of *Monaghan* v. *Taylor,*[30] the defendant was the proprietor of a music-hall, and had engaged a singer who, on numerous occasions, sang a song called " We are going to reform some day," the copyright of which was in the plaintiff as assignee. The defendant at the trial, denied that he had directed the song to be sung; he was in the hall when it was being sung, but had never heard the whole of it. The court held that, inasmuch as the singer was hired by the defendant to sing what songs he liked, and no supervision or control was exercised as to copyright, there was evidence of agency and authority to sing the song complained of.

522 But, in *Performing Right Society, Ltd.* v. *Ciryl Theatrical Syndicate Ltd.*,[31] the Court of Appeal, while approving the decision in *Monaghan* v. *Taylor,* distinguished that case from that of an absent person who had merely given a general authority to a band.

523 And, in an Australian case,[32] it has been held that the owners of a hall who, under the terms of their contract of letting, cannot prevent the performance of which complaint is made, do not " permit " the performance.

524 **The user must not be gratuitous.** In order to bring the case within section 2 (3) of the Act of 1911 the defendant must have permitted user " for his private profit," so that a person who gratuitously allowed a place to be used for a public performance was not liable under the subsection. Liability was extended to a corporation who permitted their hall to be used for concerts to lessen the burden on the rates, though it was difficult to see in what sense such profit was private.[33]

The Act of 1956 puts the onus the other way, so that the defen-

[30] (1885) 2 T.L.R. 685.

[31] [1924] 1 K.B. 1.

[32] *Australian Performing Right Association, Ltd.* v. *Adelaide Corporation* (1928) 40 C.L.R. 481; see also *Canadian Performing Right Society* v. *Canadian National Exhibition Association* (1934) 4 D.L.R. 154; but *cf. Australian Performing Right Association, Ltd.* v. *Turner (J.) & Son* (1927) 27 S.R.(N.S.W.) 344.

[33] *Performing Right Society, Ltd.* v. *Bradford Corporation* [1917–23] Macg.Cop.Cas. 309; approved in *Performing Right Society, Ltd.* v. *Bray Urban District Council* [1930] A.C. 377 (P.C.); see also *Canadian Performing Right Society* v. *Canadian National Exhibition Association* (1934) 4 D.L.R. 154, as to meaning of " without profit " in the Canadian Copyright Act, 1931.

dant has to show that the permission was gratuitous, or for a nominal consideration.

525 **"Place of public entertainment."** Under the Act of 1911 the performance had to be at a "theatre or other place of entertainment," and doubt existed whether an infringement, under section 2 (3) of the Act of 1911, was committed, if the place was not one habitually used as a theatre or resort for music, dancing or similar amusement.[34] The definition of "place of public entertainment," in the Act of 1956, seems to settle this difficulty, but to raise another one by the use of the word "hire." Section 2 (3) of the Act of 1911 was treated as creating a remedy available, not only against a person who hired out premises for an entertainment, but also as an additional or alternative remedy against a person who himself provided an entertainment at his own premises.[35] The word "hire," in the definition of place of public entertainment, and the words "gave the permission gratuitously, etc.," rather suggest that section 5 (5) of the Act of 1956 is a remedy available only against a person who makes premises available to someone else to give the performance.

In view of the wider definition in the Act of 1956, references to definitions in earlier Acts are probably not now of great importance. Under the Dramatic Copyright Act, 1838,[36] the performance had to be at a "place of dramatic entertainment," and the question arose, in several cases, as to the meaning of this expression. The cases of *Russell* v. *Smith* [37] and *Wall* v. *Taylor* [38] appear to be authorities to the effect that the very fact that a dramatic entertainment, to which the public are invited, is given in a particular building, makes the building, for the time being, a "place of dramatic entertainment," and that that is sufficient to satisfy the statute. In the latter case, Brett M.R. is reported to have definitely stated "performing a dramatic piece makes the place where it is performed a place of dramatic entertainment." [39] In the later case of *Duck* v. *Bates*,[40] however, the Master of the Rolls qualified this dictum. "In describing the place to which the statute is to apply, the Legislature uses the words, 'any place of dramatic entertainment.' From these words it is obvious to me that there is some place where a dramatic piece may be represented without an infringement of the statute: if it is not a place of dramatic entertainment, no breach is committed: the statute requires that the dramatic representation shall be performed at a place of dramatic entertainment."

34 In *Lyons (J.) & Co., Ltd.* v. *Fox* [1919] 1 K.B. 11, it was held that a restaurant was an "entertainment" for the purposes of another statute.
35 *Sarpy* v. *Holland* [1908] 2 Ch. 198; *Monaghan* v. *Taylor, supra.*
36 3 & 4 Will. 4, c. 15.
37 (1848) 12 Q.B. 217.
38 (1882) 11 Q.B.D. 102.
39 At p. 208.
40 (1884) 13 Q.B.D. 843.

11.—BROADCASTING (SOUND AND TELEVISION) AND DIFFUSION SERVICES

526 **Broadcasting under the Act of 1911.** There was some doubt whether the broadcasting of a work constituted a public performance of the work under the Copyright Act, 1911.[41]

In the case of *Messager* v. *British Broadcasting Co., Ltd.*,[42] McCardie J. did, in the course of his judgment, decide the point and, although his judgment in that case was reversed on other grounds, the part of his judgment dealing with broadcasting was cited with approval by the Court of Appeal in *Performing Right Society, Ltd.* v. *Hammond's Bradford Brewery Co., Ltd.*[43] McCardie J., in the course of his judgment, said: "It was by means of electrical instruments that the defendants, by modulating the waves in the ether, were able to affect, as they intended to affect, a vast number of electrical instruments possessed by members of the public and thereby to render audible to that public the performance given within the walls of the defendants' studio. In my view, however, the defendants, in doing what they did, clearly gave a public performance. Instead of gathering the public into a vast assembly room, they set in motion certain ether waves knowing that millions of instruments in houses and flats were tuned to the waves sent forth, and knowing and intending also that acoustic representation of the opera would thereby be given to an enormous number of listeners."

527 But, in delivering the judgment of the Privy Council in the case of *Mellor* v. *Australian Broadcasting Commission*,[44] Viscount Maugham expressed a somewhat different view. He said: "If there is merely a broadcast from the studio where the piece is performed in private there is obviously no performance in public at all. A broadcast *per se* is not an acoustic representation of the work. If the broadcast is picked up only by listeners in private it might be difficult to establish that there is a public performance; for each performance would be separate, and each would be private; but it is not necessary to express an opinion on this point. It cannot be doubted that a broadcast to all and sundry listeners in such a case as we are dealing with will include hotels and other places of entertainment or refreshment who, if not forbidden, will perform the piece to a number of members of the public." He then went on to say that a broadcaster, who did not attempt to limit the general right of the owners of receiving sets to

41 The point was decided in Australia in *Chappell & Co., Ltd.* v. *Associated Radio Co. of Australia, Ltd.* [1925] V.L.R. 350; see also (in the U.S.A.) *Remick (J. H.) & Co.* v. *American Auto-Accessories Co.* [1923–28] Macg.Cop.Cas. 173.

42 [1927] 2 K.B. 543.

43 [1934] Ch. 121.

44 [1940] A.C. 491.

private performance, would be liable as having "authorised" public performance at hotels or other public places.[45]

This latter point followed on the decision in *Performing Right Society, Ltd.* v. *Hammond's Bradford Brewery Co., Ltd.*[46] that, independently of any performance at the broadcasting studio, a separate performance was given by switching on a receiving set and loud speaker at a hotel. Maugham J. (as he was then) said [47]: "The sounds are produced by an instrument under the direct control of the hotel proprietor, and to my mind they are as much under his control as if his employee were turning a barrel organ or one of those distressing mechanical players that we sometimes used to hear. The fact that there is no power of selection is, I think, irrelevant to the question whether the sound amounts to a performance. The reproduction is, in my opinion, as much a performance as is a reproduction of a musical piece by a gramophone apparatus."

This view was confirmed by the Court of Appeal.

528 **Under the Act of 1956.** The Copyright Act, 1956, as has been seen, defines "performance" as including a presentation by the operation of a wireless telegraphy apparatus, or by the exhibition of a cinematograph film, or by the use of a record, or by any other means. "Wireless telegraphy apparatus" is given the wide meaning of that term in the Wireless Telegraphy Act, 1949,[48] and, in substance, covers any apparatus for the sending, transmission or receiving of sound or visual wireless communications. Apart from the express exceptions to be mentioned below, it is clear that, under the Act of 1956, a performance would be given by any person operating wireless apparatus at any stage and also, in view of the other words of the definition, operating at any stage any kind of cinematograph, gramophone, or electrical equipment directly or indirectly conducive to a representation of copyright material.

529 **"Broadcasting" and "diffusion" not "performance."** But, as has been seen, "broadcasting" and "causing to be transmitted to subscribers to a diffusion service," are not to constitute "performance," [49] and these acts are, as described below, the subject of separate and distinct exclusive rights, having somewhat different qualifications from those applicable to the right of public performance. First however, it is proposed to endeavour to indicate what precisely has been excluded from the right of performance.

[45] As to "authorise" see § 452 *et seq.*, *ante*.
[46] [1934] Ch. 121.
[47] *Ibid.* p. 128.
[48] 12 & 13 Geo. 6, s. 19. See Appendix A, § 1553, *post.*
[49] Copyright Act, 1956, s. 48 (5), *ante*, § 511.

530 **Meaning of "broadcasting."** The Act of 1956 states that references in that Act to broadcasting are references to broadcasting by wireless telegraphy, whether by way of sound broadcasting or television, and that a television broadcast or sound broadcast is to be taken to be made by the body by whom, at the time when, and from the place from which, the visual images or sounds in question, or both, as the case may be, are broadcast.[50] This appears to indicate that the act of broadcasting is the act of initiating the sending of wireless waves resulting in a representation of the work, but the expression "broadcast" itself is not defined. It might have a subjective meaning, that is to say that it only applies where the person sending out the signals contemplated their reception by the public or a class of the public, but it is thought that the meaning is objective, and that signals are broadcast if they are in fact sent out in such a way that anyone having a suitable type of reception apparatus could receive them.

531 **Meaning of "diffusion."** The other excluded act is that of "causing material to be transmitted to subscribers to a diffusion service," and this is defined as distributing broadcast programmes or other programmes (whether provided by the person operating the service or other persons) over wires, or other paths provided by a material substance, to the premises of subscribers to the service.[51] This right therefore applies to transmissions over wires and not to wireless transmissions, but it extends to all performances so transmitted, whether they be live performances or performances by means of films or records, and whether the actual performances are provided by the person operating the service or not. On the other hand, it only applies where there is a transmission to the premises of subscribers to the service, and would therefore not apply to a transmission by the proprietor of a hotel to separate rooms in the hotel.[52] This presumably is one of the reasons for the further general exclusion from performance of the operation of any apparatus whereby signals are transmitted directly or indirectly, whether over wires or not, to a receiving apparatus.[53]

532 **"Broadcasting" may still involve "performance."** It should be observed that what is excluded under the foregoing provisions is only performances so far as they are given by the acts of broadcasting or diffusion, and that the actual performances themselves at the point of origin, whether they be live performances, or by means of films or records, will still be infringements of the basic right to perform in

[50] ss. 14 (10) and 48 (2).
[51] Copyright Act, 1956, s. 48 (3): see *ante*, § 511.
[52] The proviso to the subsection also expressly excludes a service operated as part of amenities provided for residents: see *post*, § 535.
[53] Copyright Act, 1956, s. 48 (5).

public if they are in the presence of the public at the point of origin. So also will performances given at the point of reception.[54]

533 **" Broadcasting " and " diffusion " are separate rights.** So far the acts of broadcasting and diffusion have been considered as exceptions from the definition of public performance. These acts are also separate rights of the copyright owner. Thus, the acts restricted by the copyright in a litererary, dramatic or musical work include broadcasting the work, and causing the work to be transmitted to subscribers to a diffusion service [55]; the acts restricted by the copyright in an artistic work include the inclusion of the work in a television broadcast, and causing a television programme which includes the work to be transmitted to subscribers to a diffusion service [56]; the acts restricted by the copyright in a sound recording include broadcasting the recording, but, in this case, do not include any reference to a diffusion service [57]; in the case of a cinematograph film the acts include broadcasting the film and causing the film to be transmitted to subscribers to a diffusion service.[58]

These types of infringement, so far as they consist of infringement of the copyright in cinematograph films and sound recordings, are considered elsewhere.[58a] So also is the copyright in broadcast programmes themselves.[58b] Here it is proposed to consider further the nature of the broadcast and diffusion rights conferred upon the owners of copyright in literary, musical, dramatic and artistic works.

534 **Where infringement occurs.** As has been seen, " broadcasting," in the Act of 1956, refers to broadcasting by wireless telegraphy, and " wireless telegraphy " has the elaborate definition contained in the Wireless Telegraphy Act, 1949,[59] but the word " broadcasting " is not itself further defined. The definition, in section 14 (10) of the Copyright Act, 1956, however, though directly applicable to the copyright in the programmes themselves, which is the subject of that section, is a definition for the purposes of the Act, and not merely for the purpose of the section. It therefore seems to follow that, for the purposes of proceedings for infringement of the broadcasting right conferred upon the owners of copyright, this definition applies, and establishes that the act of infringement is committed by the body by whom the infringing programme is transmitted, and occurs at the time and from the place when and from which the

[54] *Post*, § 541.
[55] Copyright Act, 1956, s. 2 (5).
[56] s. 3 (5).
[57] s. 12 (5).
[58] s. 13 (5).
[58a] Chaps. 16 and 17, *post*.
[58b] Chap. 18, *post*.
[59] s. 19. See Appendix A, § 1553, *post*.

programme is broadcast. It would seem that the word " broadcast " must refer to the act of transmitting waves at large, so that the place in question is the transmitter, and not the studio or other place where the programme is observed by a television camera or microphone. Under the Act of 1911 it was considered arguable that the act of infringement of the performing right by broadcasting was committed where the programme was received, so that an action might lie in respect of a broadcast from a foreign station intended to be received in this country. This would seem to be unarguable under the Act of 1956, at least where the foreign broadcast itself was lawful by the law of the country where the transmission took place. Although the person immediately responsible for the infringement is the body responsible for the actual transmission, the restricted acts consist, not only of broadcasting, but, by virtue of section 1 (2) of the Copyright Act, 1956, also of authorising another person to broadcast, so that persons responsible for the programme may also be made liable. But it may again be noted that this only applies to persons authorising the act to be done in the United Kingdom, or in any other country to which the Act extends.

535 **Infringement of " diffusion " right.** It has been seen that the act of transmission to subscribers to a diffusion service is defined as transmission in the course of a service of distributing broadcast programmes or other programmes (whether provided by the person operating the service or other persons) over wires or other paths provided by a material substance to the premises of the subscribers to the service.[60] It is provided, however, that no account is to be taken of a service of distributing broadcast or other programmes where the service is only incidental to a business of keeping or letting premises where persons reside or sleep, and is operated as part of the amenities provided exclusively or mainly for residents or inmates therein.[61] The provision of a communal loud-speaker service to rooms in a hotel, or to flats in a block of flats is, therefore, not transmission to subscribers to a diffusion service. It would also appear that the reference in the definition to " subscribers " to the service involves that the person taking the service should pay for it, and it is arguable, therefore, that if a free service of this kind were inaugurated in association, perhaps, with advertising, such a service would not fall within the definition. Whatever activities are excluded in this way from the definition of transmitting material to subscribers to a diffusion service are not thereby, as has been seen, necessarily put back again into the field of public

[60] Copyright Act, 1956, s. 48 (3). See *C.A.P.A.C.* v. *C.T.V. Television Network* (1966) 57 D.L.R. (2d) 5; (1968) 68 D.L.R. (2d) 98.

[61] s. 48 (3), proviso; see *Phonographic Performance, Ltd.* v. *Pontins, Ltd.* [1968] Ch. 290 as to the meaning of the similar provisions of s. 12 (7) (*a*) of the Act of 1956, and § 816, *post*.

performance, because of the general words at the end of section 48 (5) of the Act of 1956 which seem to exclude, from public performance, all transmissions of electro-magnetic signals.

536 The person directly responsible for an infringement by transmission to subscribers to a diffusion service is the person operating the service, which is defined as the person who, in the agreements with subscribers to the service, undertakes to provide them with the service whether he is the person who transmits the programmes or not,[62] and it is further provided that no person, other than the person so operating the service, is to be taken to be causing it to be so transmitted, notwithstanding that he provides any facilities for the transmission of the programmes.[62] This appears to exclude the persons responsible at any stage for the technical transmission, but it is thought that it would not exclude any person who would otherwise be liable for authorising the person operating the service to include therein a particular programme.

537 **Statutory defences.** There are certain general defences open in the case of alleged infringement, either by broadcasting, or diffusion. Fair dealing with a literary, dramatic or musical work for the purpose of reporting current events by means of broadcasting, is not to constitute an infringement.[63] But the reading or recitation in public of extracts from published literary or dramatic works, which is permitted, where done directly, is not permitted where done for the purposes of broadcasting.[64] These provisions apply equally where a literary, dramatic or musical work is caused to be transmitted to subscribers to a diffusion service.[64a] The inclusion in a television broadcast of sculpture and works of artistic craftsmanship permanently situated in a public place, or in premises open to the public, is not an infringement of the copyright therein.[65] This applies also to a work of architecture whether permanently situated in a public place, or in premises open to the public, or not.[66] It is further generally provided that the copyright in an artistic work is not infringed by the inclusion of the work in a television broadcast, if its inclusion therein is only by way of background, or is otherwise only incidental to the principal matters broadcast.[67] These provisions apply equally to artistic works in a television programme caused to be transmitted to subscribers to a diffusion service.[68]

[62] Copyright Act, 1956, s. 48 (3).
[63] s. 6 (3).
[64] s. 6 (5).
[64a] s. 6 (9).
[65] s. 9 (3).
[66] s. 9 (4).
[67] s. 9 (5).
[68] s. 9 (11).

538 **Where " diffusion " is of broadcast by B.B.C. or I.T.A.** Additional protection is given to a person operating a diffusion service where the material is the subject of a broadcast by the British Broadcasting Corporation or the Independent Television Authority. If the broadcast is made by or with the licence of the owner of the copyright in the work broadcast, any person who causes the programme to be transmitted to subscribers to a diffusion service is to be in the like position as if he had been the holder of a licence granted by the owner of the copyright to include the work in any programme caused to be transmitted by him to subscribers to that service by the reception of the broadcast.[69] If, on the other hand, the copyright owner had not authorised the broadcast, no proceedings are to be brought against the person causing the programme to be transmitted to subscribers to a diffusion service, but, in assessing damages in any proceedings against the Corporation or the Authority, there is to be taken into account any further infringement involved as a result of the transmission.[70] The liability of the Corporation or the Authority as the case may be would appear to be unaffected by the fact that they may not have known of the transmission. Section 40 of the Copyright Act, 1956, which contains the above provisions, also contains provisions about cinematograph films and sound recordings which are dealt with in the appropriate chapters of this work.[71]

539 **Where by organisation other than B.B.C. or I.T.A.** It will be observed that the foregoing protection given to persons causing broadcast material to be transmitted to subscribers to a diffusion service only applies to broadcasts by the Corporation or the Authority. Where the material distributed consists of programmes broadcast from a place outside the United Kingdom, by an organisation other than the Corporation and the Authority, special powers are conferred by section 28 of the Copyright Act, 1956, upon the Performing Right Tribunal. The general effect of this section is that, where, under the arrangements for the foreign broadcast, charges are payable to a body entitled under the relevant copyright law to authorise the broadcasting of the work, no fee is to be paid for a licence for the transmission of the work to subscribers to a diffusion service, unless and to the extent that the Tribunal is satisfied that the charges payable by the foreign organisation make no allowance for the transmission of the work to subscribers to diffusion services in the United Kingdom, or do not adequately reflect the extent to which it is likely that the works will be so transmitted. It is to be observed that this section only

[69] s. 40 (3) and (5).
[70] s. 40 (4).
[71] Chaps. 16 and 17, *post*.

operates where the Performing Right Tribunal has jurisdiction to deal with disputes about licences, that is to say where the licences are the subject of a licence scheme, or a licensing body has failed or refused to grant a licence. It would not apply, therefore, where the material broadcast is a play, or other copyright material, not controlled by a licensing body.

540 **Infringement by recording of broadcasts.** The persons concerned with the broadcasting of material may not only infringe authors' rights by the act of broadcasting, but may commit separate infringements if they cause the programmes to be recorded, since reproduction, in the case of a literary, dramatic or musical work, includes reproduction in the form of a record or cinematograph film.[72] It is, however, provided, in section 6 (7) of the Act of 1956, that a person entitled to broadcast a literary, dramatic or musical work under an assignment or licence,[73] shall be entitled to make a reproduction of the work solely for the purpose of broadcasting it, provided that the reproduction is not used for making any further reproduction therefrom, or for any other purpose except that of broadcasting in accordance with the assignment or licence, and that the reproduction is destroyed before the end of a period of twenty-eight days beginning with the day on which it is first used for broadcasting the work in pursuance of the licence, or such extended period as may be agreed. This provision was introduced into the Act of 1956 to give effect to Article 11 *bis* (3) of the Brussels Convention which provided that it shall be a matter for legislation in the countries of the Union to determine the regulations for ephemeral recordings made by a broadcasting body by means of its own facilities and used for its own emissions.

541 **Operation of a receiving set is a separate performance.** While as has been seen, the act of broadcasting, or causing a work to be transmitted to subscribers to a diffusion service, is not to constitute performance, the decision, in *Performing Right Society, Ltd.* v. *Hammond's Bradford Brewery Co., Ltd.*,[74] that the operation of a receiving set is a separate performance, is left unaffected by the Act of 1956. This appears from the definition of performance itself,[75] and also from the provision, in section 48 (5) of the Act of 1956, that, in so far as the display or emission of images or sounds by any receiving apparatus to which they are conveyed by the transmission of electro-magnetic signals, whether over paths pro-

[72] s. 48 (1).
[73] If made or granted after the commencement of the Act of 1956 (Copyright Act, 1956, Sched. VII, para. 5).
[74] [1934] Ch. 121.
[75] Copyright Act, 1956, s. 48 (1).

vided by a material substance or not, constitutes a performance, the same shall be taken to be effected by the operation of the receiving apparatus. It is further expressly provided [76] that, in the case of such apparatus provided by or with the consent of the occupier of the premises where the apparatus is situated, the occupier of those premises is to be taken to be the person giving the performance, whether he is the person operating the apparatus or not. This latter provision applies, both to a receiving apparatus for broadcast transmissions, and to any apparatus for reproducing sound by the use of a record. This would apply, for example, to the occupier of premises where coin-operated record-players were provided.

[The next paragraph is 551]

[76] Copyright Act, 1956, s. 48 (6).

CHAPTER 10

CIVIL REMEDIES FOR INFRINGEMENT OF COPYRIGHT

551 **The remedies open.** The remedies given by the Copyright Act, 1956, for infringement of copyright are of two classes, civil and summary. As to the civil remedies, section 17 (1) of the Copyright Act, 1956, provides as follows:

> " Subject to the provisions of this Act, infringements of copyright shall be actionable at the suit of the owner of the copyright; and in any action for such an infringement all such relief, by way of damages, injunction, accounts or otherwise, shall be available to the plaintiff as is available in any corresponding proceedings in respect of infringements of other proprietary rights."

552 **Who may sue.** The remedies are given to the " owner of the copyright," that is to say, the original owner, or a person deriving title under him by assignment or otherwise.

Under the Act of 1911, in the case of an assignment of an interest in copyright not in existence at the time of the assignment, the assignee had no right to sue in his own name for infringements of copyright.[1] The older cases in which courts of equity had enforced the rights of equitable assignees [2] were cases of interim injunction only,[1] and, unless the legal owner was a party to the proceedings, either as joint plaintiff or defendant,[3] a perpetual injunction could only be granted under very special circumstances.

Under the Act of 1956, however, provision is made for an assignment by a prospective owner of copyright so that, on the coming into existence of the copyright, the assignee, or a person claiming under him, acquires the legal title forthwith and, consequently, is entitled to sue and obtain all remedies open to an owner of copyright.[4]

A mere agent to sell has not such an interest in the work as to entitle him to claim relief.[5] A simple licensee is not the owner of the

1 *Performing Right Society, Ltd.* v. *London Theatre of Varieties, Ltd.* [1924] A.C. 1.

2 *Sweet* v. *Cater* (1841) 11 Sim. 572; *Hodges (J.)* v. *Welsh (T.)* (1840) 2 Ir.Eq.R. 266; *Simms* v. *Marryat* (1851) 17 Q.B. 281; *Hazlitt* v. *Templeman* (1866) 13 L.T. 593; *Grace* v. *Newman* (1875) L.R. 19 Eq. 623; *Bohn* v. *Bogue* (1846) 10 Jur. 420.

3 *Performing Right Society, Ltd.* v. *London Theatre of Varieties, supra*; *Macdonald (E.), Ltd.* v. *Eyles* [1921] 1 Ch. 631; *University of London Press, Ltd.* v. *University Tutorial Press* [1916] 2 Ch. 601; *Photocrom Co., Ltd. (The)* v. *Nelson (H. & W.), Ltd.* [1923–28] Macg.Cop.Cas. 293.

4 Copyright Act, 1956, s. 37 (1).

5 *Nicol* v. *Stockdale* (1818) 3 Swans. 687; *Petty* v. *Taylor* [1897] 1 Ch. 465.

copyright or any part of it, and it was held that the licensee under a "sole licence" could bring an action for infringement in his own name, but had to join the proprietor of the copyright, either as co-plaintiff with himself, or as defendant.[6]

553 **Exclusive licensee.** But section 19 of the Copyright Act, 1956, provides that an exclusive licensee is to have the same rights of action as the owner of the copyright except against the owner of the copyright, but so that a defendant is to have any defence available which he would have had if the action had been brought by the owner of the copyright. The details of these provisions have been discussed elsewhere.[7]

554 **Infringement abroad.** It has been doubted whether the English courts have jurisdiction to entertain an action for infringement of copyright in a foreign country.[8] But it is submitted that, where the defendant is within the jurisdiction and, as in the case of a Berne Convention country, the nature of the wrong is similar under both sets of laws, an action should be maintainable here.[8a] In *Jonathan Cape, Ltd.* v. *Consolidated Press, Ltd.*[9] an action was brought in England in respect of an infringement in Australia and the plaintiff succeeded, but no point seems to have been taken as to jurisdiction. At the time, however, the terms of the Copyright Act, 1911, were in force both in England and Australia.

With regard to an infringement of copyright committed on a British ship on the high seas, the matter is more difficult. The courts have jurisdiction over torts committed on such ships[10] and statutes normally extend thereto.[11] But the provisions of sections 1 (1) and 31 of the Act of 1956 appear to limit that Act to the United Kingdom and territories to which the Act has been specifically applied.

555 **Remedy by injunction.** The first and most usual remedy for infringement of copyright is by means of an injunction, but this remedy is not open to an architect suing for infringement of a work of architecture, if construction of the infringing building has been

6 *Neilson* v. *Horniman* (1909) 26 T.L.R. 188; see, however, § 381, *ante*.

7 § 382, *ante*.

8 "*Morocco Bound*" *Syndicate, Ltd.* v. *Harris* [1895] 1 Ch. 534. It would seem, however, that the decision in this case largely turned upon the impossibility of enforcing an injunction if granted. As to place of infringement where goods are delivered on sale or return, see *Savory (E. W.), Ltd.* v. *The World of Golf, Ltd.* [1914] 2 Ch. 566; *Schofield & Sims, Ltd.* v. *Gibson (R.) & Sons, Ltd.* [1928–35] Macg.Cop.Cas. 64.

8a See *Boys* v. *Chaplin* [1969] 3 W.L.R. 322 and *John Walker & Sons, Ltd.* v. *Henry Ost & Co. Ltd.* [1970] R.P.C. 489 at 509.

9 [1954] 1 W.L.R. 1313.

10 *Lloyd* v. *Guibert* (1865) L.R. 1 Q.B. 115; *Davidson* v. *Hill* [1901] 2 K.B. 606.

11 *Schwartz* v. *The India Rubber etc. Co., Ltd.* [1912] 2 K.B. 299.

actually commenced.[12] An injunction may be either interlocutory—that is, one granted prior to the trial and only until that trial, or further order—or final. An interlocutory injunction is usually granted upon evidence by affidavit only and the plaintiff must show that the case is of some urgency, particularly where the application is for *ex parte* relief.

The principles governing the granting of interlocutory relief have been considered recently in *Donmar Productions Ltd.* v. *Bart* [13] and *Harman Pictures N.V.* v. *Osborne.*[14] In the former case, Ungoed-Thomas J. said [15] that, in an application for an interlocutory injunction, the applicant must establish a probability, or a strong prima facie case, that he is entitled to the right of whose violation he complains and, subject to this being established, the governing consideration is the maintenance of the status quo pending the trial. In deciding whether the matter should be maintained *in statu quo*, regard must be had to the balance of convenience and to the extent to which any damage to the plaintiffs can be cured by payment of damages rather than by the granting of an injunction.[15a] The burden of proof lies on the applicant throughout. In the latter case, Goff J. agreed [16] that a plaintiff had first to establish a strong prima facie case for the existence of the right on which he sued.[17] He must show that he was likely to succeed. However, if he did that, or his right was not disputed, then although he must go on to show a prima facie case of infringement, yet for that purpose, he did not have to show that he is likely to be successful, or more likely to be so than the defendant, but only that he had a case reasonably capable of succeeding. Even then the remedy was still discretionary, and in exercising its discretion, the court will have regard to the balance of convenience, but the governing principle is the preservation of the status quo.

Applications for interlocutory relief are frequently made in copyright actions since damages are rarely an adequate remedy.[18] Further, many such applications seek *quia timet* relief where, for instance, a publication is threatened. Thus, in *Copex Establishment* v. *Flegon* [19] the defendant had threatened to publish the book *Twenty Letters to a Friend* by Mrs. Svetlana Allilueva, Stalin's daughter, and, on an interlocutory application by the plaintiff to restrain such threatened publication, the defendant gave an undertaking not to publish the book until trial of the action.

12 1956 Act, s. 17 (4). 13 [1967] 1 W.L.R. 740; *Spottiswoode* v. *Clark*, 2 Phil. 154.
14 [1967] 1 W.L.R. 723. 15 [1967] 1 W.L.R. at 742.
15a See *Merchant Adventurers, Ltd.* v. *M. Grew & Co. Ltd.* [1971] F.S.R. 233 at 243.
16 [1967] 1 W.L.R. at 738.
17 See Copyright Act, 1956, s. 20 (1), under which title will be presumed unless put in issue; *Universities of Oxford and Cambridge (The)* v. *Richardson* (1802) 6 Ves. 689; *Platt* v. *Button* (1813) 19 Ves. 447.
18 See, for instance, *Coral Index, Ltd.* v. *Regent Index, Ltd.* [1970] R.P.C. 147. See *Merchant Adventurers, Ltd.* case [1971] F.S.R. 233 at 239 as to the right of an equitable owner of copyright to seek interlocutory relief.
19 *The Times*, August 18, 1967; see § 78, *ante*.

In *Fraser* v. *Evans* [20] where the defendants were the editor, publishers and owners of *The Sunday Times,* the plaintiff obtained an injunction *ex parte* to restrain the threatened publication of an article based *inter alia* on a version of a written report, made by the plaintiff to the Greek Government, on the grounds that it would be both in breach of confidence and defamatory. At the subsequent hearing *inter partes* the injunction was continued in modified terms to restrain publication of the report, or extracts from it, or any matter derived solely from it. On appeal by the defendants it was contended for the plaintiff that, in any event, he was entitled to interim relief to restrain a breach of his copyright by the proposed publication. The Court of Appeal allowed the appeal, holding that the court will not grant relief against alleged infringement of copyright in *quia timet* proceedings in respect of a proposed article, the contents of which are unknown at the time of the proceedings; *a fortiori* where the proposed publishers claim that they intend fair dealing with the work within section 6 (3) of the Act of 1956.

556 It is submitted that, in the particular circumstances of this case, this decision was unfortunate, especially since the relevant authorities do not appear to have been cited to the Court of Appeal and it may therefore be that the Court of Appeal came to its decision on copyright as a result of a misunderstanding of the nature of the statutory defences provided by the Act of 1956. The decision also appears to conflict with certain of the general principles laid down in the *Donmar* and *Harman* cases, *supra.*

In the *Fraser* case, Lord Denning M.R. said [21] that the plaintiff was the author of the report and entitled to the copyright in it. He also said that the defendants were not going to print the entire report, but only short extracts from it; that the court had not seen what was going to be published; that the defendants said that what they were going to do would be a "fair dealing" such as is permitted by section 6 (3) of the Act of 1956; and that the court could not say there was going to be an unfair dealing when the defendants said it was to be a fair dealing. That being so, no injunction would be granted to prevent them publishing.

As has been seen,[1] the copyright in a literary work is infringed by copying a substantial part of it without the permission of the copyright owner. However, as has also been seen,[2] the Act of 1956, like the Act of 1911, provides certain statutory defences to what would otherwise be an infringement. That is to say, where an act

20 [1969] 1 Q.B. 349; and see "Unfair Dealing?" *Law Guardian*, Feb. 1969, No. 45, p. 23.
21 [1969] 1 Q.B. 349 at 362.
1 §§ 413–417, *ante*.
2 § 458 *et seq.*, *ante*.

is done which is proved or admitted to be a prima facie infringement, the Act of 1956 provides that, in certain specified circumstances, such act is not, in fact, to constitute an infringement. But such defences are not relevant until a prima facie infringement is proved or admitted.[3] One of such defences is contained in section 6 (3) of the Act of 1956 which provides, *inter alia*, that no fair dealing with a literary work is to constitute an infringement if it is for the purpose of reporting current events in a newspaper and if it is accompanied by a sufficient acknowledgment.

In the *Fraser* case, the defendants admitted they were going to print extracts from the report, but said that would be a fair dealing within section 6 (3). However, they produced no evidence to support this. The defendants therefore appear to have been admitting, not only that they were going to publish some part of the report, but also that it would be a substantial part and therefore a prima facie infringement. That is to say, if it was not a substantial part and therefore a prima facie infringement, it would not have been necessary to rely on section 6 (3).

56a It is understandable that a court may be unwilling to grant *quia timet* relief where there is doubt as to whether what the defendant intends to do will be an infringement, for instance if the defendant denies an intention to publish anything. But the result of the Court of Appeal's decision in the *Fraser* case appears to be that the court will not grant *quia timet* relief, even where the defendant admits that he intends to commit a prima facie infringement, provided the defendant alleges that his action will be covered by one of the statutory defences. And this will be so, even if this allegation is unsupported by any evidence.

Lord Denning also said that, if the defendants were going to print the report in full, it might well be a case for an injunction to restrain infringement. But, as has been mentioned above, an infringement is committed, even if only a part is copied, provided it is a substantial part. On the other hand, though the whole may be copied, and therefore a prima facie infringement committed, the defendant might be protected on the basis that this was, nevertheless, in the particular circumstances, a fair dealing.

Finally, Lord Denning said that the defendants should be allowed to publish the article and, if they were guilty of breach of copyright, that could be determined by an action thereafter and damages awarded against them. But it is submitted the defendants had, in effect, admitted that they were going to infringe by reason of their

[3] See *Hawkes and Son (London), Ltd.* v. *Paramount Film Service, Ltd.* [1934] Ch. 593; *Johnstone* v. *Bernard Jones Publications, Ltd.* [1938] Ch. 599 and § 461, *ante*: see also *E. M. Forster* v. *A. N. Parasuram* [1964] A.I.R. Madras 331.

admitting that they were going to print extracts from the report, though alleging that their action would be covered by section 6 (3).

557 **Delay in taking proceedings.** Delay, unless explained [4] is generally fatal to an application for an interlocutory injunction,[5] though the courts will balance the question of delay against the likelihood of the plaintiff ultimately succeeding in the action,[6] and will take into account whether or not the defendant has been led into expense or lulled into security or misled by the inaction of the plaintiff.[6] But the tendency of modern decisions is not to refuse an injunction at the hearing of the action merely on account of delay in instituting proceedings,[7] subject to the provisions of the Limitation Act, 1939. Under certain circumstances delay might be held to amount to a tacit permission to reproduce the work.[8]

558 **Actual damage need not be proved.** If the plaintiff proves that his copyright has been infringed, the court will grant an injunction without proof of actual damage.[9] But he must show that there is a probability of damage,[10] that the defendant is likely to continue his infringement, and that this is not simply trivial.[11] In *Performing Right Society, Ltd.* v. *Berman*,[12] Lewis J. said,[13] that it seemed to him that the plaintiff must show positively that the defendant is likely to continue his infringement in cases where the prima facie position was that the infringement had occurred once and for all and was finished and done with. If, in addition, the defendant had given a bona fide undertaking not to repeat the infringement, that was an important factor which would influence the court in refusing an injunction. However, he also said that, in the majority of cases, it would be very difficult for a plaintiff, whose rights had been infringed, to prove positively a definite likelihood of a repetition of the infringement. In that case infringement was alleged by the playing by a band of music at a club operated by the defendants. No undertaking had been given not to repeat the infringement and

4 See *Park Court Hotel, Ltd.* v. *Trans-World Hotels, Ltd.* [1970] F.S.R. 89.

5 *Southey* v. *Sherwood* (1817) 2 Mer. 435; *Mawman* v. *Tegg* (1826) 2 Russ. 385, 393; *Lewis* v. *Chapman* (1840) 3 Beav. 133.

6 *Cavendish House (Cheltenham), Ltd.* v. *Cavendish-Woodhouse, Ltd.* [1968] R.P.C. 448; [1970] R.P.C. 234, C.A.; *Effluent Disposal, Ltd.* v. *Midlands Effluent Disposal, Ltd.* [1970] R.P.C. 238.

7 *Hogg* v. *Scott* (1874) L.R. 18 Eq. 444; *Morris* v. *Ashbee* (1868) L.R. 7 Eq. 34: and see *Fullwood* v. *Fullwood* (1878) 9 Ch.D. 176 and *Reliance Rubber Co., Ltd.* v. *Reliance Tyre Co., Ltd.* (1925) 42 R.P.C. 91 as to effect on final judgment of delay in prosecuting the action.

8 *Rundell* v. *Murray* (1821) Jac. 311; *Saunders* v. *Smith* (1838) 3 My. & Cr. 711.

9 *Weatherby & Sons* v. *International Horse Agency and Exchange, Ltd.* [1910] 2 Ch. 297 at 305; *Smith* v. *Johnson* (1863) 33 L.J.Ch. 137.

10 *Borthwick* v. *The Evening Post* (1888) 37 Ch.D. 449 at 462.

11 *Whittingham (C.)* v. *Wooler (T. J.)* (1818) 2 Swans. 428; *Baily* v. *Taylor* (1830) 1 Russ. & My. 73; *Cox* v. *Land and Water Journal Co.* (1869) L.R. 9 Eq. 324.

12 1966 (2) S.A. 355.

13 *Ibid.* p. 357.

the learned judge granted an injunction, notwithstanding that the club had subsequently closed down.

Moreover, an injuction will not be granted to restrain infringements of future numbers of a periodical, although the defendants have systematically copied from numbers already published.[14] Upjohn J., in *Football League, Ltd.* v. *Littlewoods Pools, Ltd.*,[15] declined, on this basis, to grant an injunction in respect of the next season's fixture list. It is submitted, however, that in an appropriate case, in which the subject-matter of the injunction can be clearly defined, an injunction may be granted in respect of infringement of future copyright material on the footing that the circumstances justify *quia timet* relief. An injunction may be refused on grounds of public policy.[16]

559 **Where portion only of the work is piratical.** Where only part of a work has been copied, and the part which has been copied from the plaintiff's work can be separated from that which has not been copied, an injunction will be granted only against the objectionable part or parts.[17] But even where a very large proportion of a work of a piratical nature is unquestionably original, if the parts which have been copied cannot be separated from those which are original without destroying the use and value of the original matter, he who has made an improper use of that which did not belong to him must suffer the consequences of so doing, for an injunction will be issued against the whole.[18]

560 The opinion of Lord Hardwicke [19] appears to have been that an injunction might be granted against the whole, although only a portion was pirated; and in the instance of Milton's " Paradise Lost," with Dr. Newton's notes, there being nothing new in that work except the notes, he granted an injunction against the entire book. There is the record of a case tried before Lord Kenyon,[20] in which he states that the question whether an injunction could be issued against the whole of a book on account of the piratical quality of a part, came before Lord Bathurst; and Lord Bathurst seems to have held it could not, unless the part pirated was such that granting an injunction against such part necessarily destroyed the whole. Lord Kenyon, who possessed great information on this

14 *Cate* v. *Devon, etc., Newspaper Co.* (1889) 40 Ch.D. 500 at 507; *Sweet* v. *G. W. Bromley & Co.* [1905–10] Macg.Cop.Cas. 203; but see *Bradbury Sharp* [1891] W.N. 143.

15 [1959] Ch. 637.

16 *Massie & Renwick, Ltd.* v. *Underwriters' Survey Bureau, Ltd.* [1940] S.C.R. 218; and see §§ 149 and 224, *ante*.

17 *Jarrold* v. *Houlston* (1857) 3 K. & J. 708; *Lamb* v. *Evans* [1892] 3 Ch. 462.

18 See *Trengrouse* v. " *Sol* " *Syndicate* [1901–04] Macg.Cop.Cas. 13.

19 *Millar* v. *Taylor* (1769) 4 Burr. 2303.

20 See *Cary* v. *Longman* (1801) 1 East 358; *Trusler* v. *Murray* (1801) 1 East 363n.

subject, states himself to have been perfectly satisfied with the opinion of Lord Bathurst, as bearing upon the judgment of Lord Hardwicke and the other cases. In the case referred to before Lord Kenyon the declaration at law contained a count for publishing the whole work, and another for publishing a part; and Lord Kenyon's direction to the jury seems to have been to find damages for publishing the part only.

"As to the hard consequences which would follow from granting an injunction," said Lord Eldon, in *Mawman* v. *Tegg*,[21] "when a very large proportion of the work is unquestionably original, I can only say that, if the parts which have been copied cannot be separated from those which are original, without destroying the use and value of the original matter, he who has made an improper use of that which did not belong to him must suffer the consequences of so doing. If a man mixes what belongs to him with what belongs to me, and the mixtures be forbidden by law, he must again separate them, and he must bear all the mischief and loss which the separation may occasion. If an individual chooses in any work to mix my literary matter with his own, he must be restrained from publishing the literary matter which belongs to me; and if the parts of the work cannot be separated, and if by that means the injunction, which restrained the publication of my literary matter, prevents also the publication of his own literary matter, he has only himself to blame."

Where the court, upon the evidence, was led to conclude that, if the parts affected with the character of piracy were taken away, there would be left an imperfect work which could not, to any useful extent, serve the purpose intended by the publication, the injunction to restrain the publication of any parts pirated from the plaintiff's work was granted, without waiting till all the parts pirated could be distinctly marked.[22]

561 **Form of.** The injunction is usually directed to restraining the commission of the act by servants and agents of the defendants as well as by the defendant. Farwell L.J., in referring to this practice, said[23]: "It is true that persons who are not parties to an action, and are therefore not bound by the injunction so as to be committed for a breach of it, may yet be amenable to the jurisdiction of the court if the injunction be negative, *i.e.*, forbids something to be done, but it can only be on the ground of contempt in obstructing the course of justice by aiding and abetting in breach of an injunction of the court; and this is the ground on which 'servants and agents' are rendered

[21] (1826) 2 Russ. 385 at 391. See as to films, *Finn* v. *Pugliese* (1918) 18 S.R. (N.S.W.) 530.
[22] *Lewis* v. *Fullarton* (1839) 2 Beav. 6; *Kelly* v. *Morris* (1866) L.R. 1 Eq. 697.
[23] *Brydges* v. *Brydges* [1909] P. 187 at 191; the present form was approved by the House of Lords in *Marengo* v. *Daily Sketch, etc., Ltd.* (1948) 65 R.P.C. 242.

liable for contempt whether they are mentioned in the order or not. The practice of mentioning them probably arose in order to give them warning." The terms of the injunction must be clear, otherwise the court will not grant it.[24]

562 **Enforcement of injunctions.** Injunctions may be enforced against a defendant who is an individual by committal and sequestration; and against a defendant who is a body corporate, by sequestration; and also by committal and sequestration against its directors and other officers.[25] In less serious cases the court may, instead of these penalties, impose a fine and payment of costs,[26] or merely the payment of costs.[27] Breach of an undertaking to the court is punishable in the same way as breach of an injunction.[27a]

563 **Damages.** The next remedy is damages. Under section 17 (1) of the Copyright Act, 1956, a successful plaintiff will be entitled to recover damages for the infringement of his right. The measure of damage is the depreciation caused by the infringement to the value of the copyright as a chose in action.[28] Thus there will be taken into account any loss which the copyright owner has suffered by reason of the diminution of the sales of his work, or the loss of profit which he might otherwise have made,[29] but there will not be taken into account under this head any benefit which may have accrued to the defendant by the use of his work. The fact that the pirated work may have injured the reputation of and vulgarised the original is also a fact that may be taken into consideration in assessing the amount of damages,[30] and generally the damages may be said to be at large.[31]

24 See *Wilson & Whitworth, Ltd.* v. *Express & Independent Newspapers, Ltd.* [1969] R.P.C. 165.

25 R.S.C., Orders 45, r. 5, 46, r. 5 and 52.

26 R.S.C., Order 52, r. 9; *Phonographic Performance, Ltd.* v. *Amusement Caterers (Peckham), Ltd.* [1964] Ch. 195; *Steiner Products, Ltd.* v. *Willy Steiner, Ltd.* [1966] 1 W.L.R. 986; *Ronson Products, Ltd.* v. *Ronson Furniture, Ltd.* [1966] R.P.C. 497, *Re Mileage Conference Group, etc., Ltd.'s Agreement* [1966] 1 W.L.R. 1137 and *Re W. (B.) (An Infant)* [1969] 2 Ch. 50.

27 *Ronson Products, Ltd.* v. *Ronson Furniture, Ltd., supra.*

27a *Re Mileage Conference Group, etc., Ltd.'s Agreement, supra.*

28 *Per* Lord Wright M.R., *Sutherland Publishing Co., Ltd.* v. *Caxton Publishing Co., Ltd.* [1936] Ch. 323 at 336.

29 *Birn Bros., Ltd.* v. *Keene & Co., Ltd.* [1918] 2 Ch. 281; *Fenning Film Service, Ltd.* v. *Wolverhampton, etc., Cinemas, Ltd.* [1914] 3 K.B. 1171. With regard to damages recoverable by an architect, see Chap. 15, *post*.

30 *Hanfstaengl* v. *W. H. Smith & Sons* [1905] 1 Ch. 519. In *Mansell (V.) & Co., Ltd.* v. *Wesley (H.), Ltd.* [1936–45] Macg.Cop.Cas. 288, it was held that the plaintiff was justified in withdrawing his stock, the design of which had been vulgarised, and adding to his claim for damages the loss so suffered.

31 See as to damages for performing musical works in public, *Performing Right Society, Ltd.* v. *Bradford Corporation* [1917–23] Macg.Cop.Cas. 309; *Performing Right Society, Ltd.* v. *Berman*, 1966 (2) S.A. 355; *Performing Right Society, Ltd.* v. *Thompson* (1917) 34 T.L.R. 351; *Performing Right Society, Ltd.* v. *Ciryl Theatrical Syndicate, Ltd.* [1923] 2 K.B. 146; *Performing Right Society, Ltd.* v. *Mitchell and Booker, etc., Ltd.* [1924] 1 K.B. 762 and *Performing Right Society, Ltd.* v. *Camelo* [1936] 3 All E.R. 557. See also as to the possibility of recovering as damages the costs of employing inquiry agents, *British Motor Trade Association* v. *Salvadori* [1949] Ch. 556.

564 **Additional damages.** The Act of 1956 provides for additional damages in suitable circumstances. Where the court having regard, in addition to all other material considerations, to the flagrancy of the infringement and any benefit shown to have accrued to the defendant by reason of the infringement, is satisfied that effective relief would not otherwise be available to the plaintiff, the court in assessing damages for the infringement shall have power to award such additional damages as the court may consider appropriate in the circumstances.[32] It is thought that damages under this section might be appropriate where a defendant adopts a policy of continual infringement, but an injunction is not an appropriate remedy because the defendant reproduces different material on each occasion. It seems that a claim for such additional damages need not be specially pleaded.[32a]

565 In *Williams* v. *Settle*,[33] the Court of Appeal approved of an order of a county court judge awarding £1,000 damages against a photographer, who sold to the Press photographs taken by him for a client in circumstances in which the copyright vested in the client. Sellers L.J. referred to the flagrancy of the infringement, saying it was in total disregard, not only of the legal rights of the plaintiff regarding copyright, but of his feelings.

566 **Damages for conversion.** There is, however, another section of the Act upon which the plaintiff may base his claim for damages, By section 18 (1) of the Act of 1956, it is provided that " the owner of any copyright shall be entitled to all such rights and remedies, in respect of the conversion or detention by any person of any infringing copy, or of any plate used or intended to be used for making infringing copies, as he would be entitled to if he were the owner of every such copy or plate and had been the owner thereof since the time when it was made." " Infringing copy " is defined, in relation to a literary, dramatic, musical or artistic work, as an article the making of which constituted an infringement of the copyright in the work, or, in the case of an imported article, would have constituted an infringement of that copyright if the article had been made in the place into which it was imported.[34] The article in question may be any kind of reproduction which would constitute an infringement, including a record and, in the case of an artistic work, a version in different dimensions. However, it expressly does not include a reproduction in the form of a cinematograph film of a literary, dramatic, musical or artistic work, or of a published edition.[35] Further,

[32] 1956 Act, s. 17 (3); and see *Rookes* v. *Barnard* [1964] A.C. 1129 at 1225.
[32a] See *Broome* v. *Cassell & Co., Ltd.* [1971] 2 W.L.R. 853 at 868 and Halsbury's *Laws of England*, 3rd ed., Vol. 30, p. 13.
[33] [1960] 1 W.L.R. 1072.
[34] Copyright Act, 1956, s. 18 (3); see also § 474, *ante*; and as to " infringing copy " in relation to works of architecture, see *post*, Chap. 15.
[35] Copyright Act, 1956, s. 18 (3) (*a*).

since the making of an adaptation of a literary, dramatic or musical work is, under the Act of 1956, a separate infringement from the reproduction of the work,[36] it may be arguable that such an adaptation is not an infringing copy. "Infringing copy" is further defined, in relation to a sound recording, as a record embodying the recording; in relation to a cinematograph film, as a copy of the film; in relation to a television broadcast or a sound broadcast, as a copy of a cinematograph film of it, or a record embodying a sound recording of it; and, in relation to a published edition, as a reproduction of it.[34] "Plate" is defined as including any stereotype, stone, block, mould, matrix, transfer, negative or other appliance.[34]

567 **Articles made or imported before the commencement of the Act of 1956.** In the case of articles made or imported before the commencement of the Act of 1956, the foregoing provisions are not to apply, but proceedings may be brought or continued in respect of such articles in accordance with the corresponding provisions of section 7 of the Copyright Act, 1911.[37] By section 7 of the Act of 1911 it was provided that "all infringing copies of any work in which copyright subsists, or of any substantial part thereof, and all plates used or intended to be used for the production of such infringing copies, shall be deemed to be the property of the owner of the copyright, who accordingly may take proceedings for the recovery of the possession thereof or in respect of the conversion thereof."

In the Act of 1911, s. 35 (1), it was provided that "'infringing,' when applied to a copy of a work in which copyright subsists, means any copy, including any colourable imitation, made or imported in contravention of the provisions of this Act." But the importation of a work only contravened the provisions of the Act if the work was imported for sale or hire and if the importer knew that the making of the work would have infringed copyright if the work had been made in the United Kingdom. It was therefore often difficult to establish that imported copies were infringing copies. Under the Act of 1956, however, as has been seen, the definition of "infringing copy" is not related to whether its importation would have constituted an infringement, but only to whether its making would have been an infringement if it had been made in the place of importation. Consequently it will be much easier to show that imported copies are infringing copies. On the other hand, as will be seen, innocence may be a defence in an action for the conversion of infringing copies as was not the case under the Act of 1911.

568 **Damages for detention.** So far as proceedings for detention are concerned it would seem that the section contemplates the common

[36] s. 2 (5).
[37] Sched. 7, para. 21.

law action for detinue,[38] in which a plaintiff claims delivery of chattels or their value. A claim in this form may be necessary where no act of conversion has been committed, or where the plaintiff actually desires delivery to him of the infringing copies. In the latter case it is assumed that the court has a discretion to refuse an order for specific delivery in similar circumstances to those in which an order has been refused in normal cases of detinue,[39] and that the provisions of Order 45 of the Rules of the Supreme Court would apply. On the other hand, Stirling J., in *Boosey* v. *Whight* (*No.* 2),[40] took the view that a plaintiff was entitled, as of right, under the provisions of the similar section of the Act of 1842,[41] to an order for delivery up; but it does not seem to have been argued in that case that damages were an alternative remedy. Apart from the statutory provision, the court has an inherent jurisdiction to order the delivery up of articles which have been created in violation of a plaintiff's rights, but it seems only for destruction.[42] This jurisdiction extends to articles not in themselves infringing copies, if brought into being as the result of use of infringing copies.[43]

Where the defendant has mixed the plaintiff's work with work of his own, then, if it is physically possible to sever one from the other, the order for delivery up will apply only to the infringing material,[44] but where the parts are practically inseparable the order may go to the whole work.[45]

Where the claim in respect of detinue is for damages, it is apprehended that similar considerations arise to those discussed below relating to conversion. A plaintiff may, in the same proceedings, claim in detinue in respect of some copies, and in conversion in respect of others.[46] But since the remedy under section 18 of the Act of 1956 is distinct from that under section 17 of that Act, he must claim both remedies, and an inquiry as to damages for infringement of copyright does not authorise the master to assess the damages on the basis of conversion.[47]

38 This was clear in the similar section of the Act of 1842 (5 & 6 Vict. c. 45), s. 23; and see *J. Whitaker & Sons, Ltd.* v. *Publishers' Circular, Ltd.* [1946–47] Macg. Cop.Cas. 10.

39 *Cf. Whiteley, Ltd.* v. *Hilt* [1918] 2 K.B. 808.

40 (1900) 81 L.T. 265; see also, *per* Lord Wright M.R., in *Sutherland Publishing Co., Ltd.* v. *Caxton Publishing Co., Ltd.* [1936] Ch. 323 at 338.

41 See note 44, *post*.

42 *Hole* v. *Bradbury* (1879) 12 Ch.D. 886.

43 *Chappell & Co., Ltd.* v. *Columbia Graphophone Co.* [1914] 2 Ch. 124.

44 See *Warne & Co.* v. *Seebohm* (1888) 39 Ch.D. 73, where an appropriate form of order is set out.

45 *Stevens* v. *Wildy* (1850) 19 L.J.Ch. 190. See discussion of similar problem in Salmond, *Torts*, 15th ed., pp. 147–150.

46 *Birn Bros., Ltd.* v. *Keene & Co., Ltd.* [1918] 2 Ch. 281.

47 *Caxton Publishing Co., Ltd.* v. *Sutherland Publishing Co., Ltd.* [1939] A.C. 178.

569 **Damages for conversion and infringement cumulative.** A question of difficulty arose whether damages for infringement under section 6 of the Act of 1911, and damages for conversion under section 7 of that Act, were alternative or cumulative, and it has now been finally determined by the House of Lords that they are cumulative. Presumably this decision is equally applicable to the provisions of the Act of 1956. But, though the two sets of damages can be cumulative, they must not overlap. This latter point is explained by Greene L.J.[48] as follows: "As an example of what I mean by overlapping let me take the following case. The owner of a copyright in a book proves that, whereas if it had not been for the infringement he could have sold 1,000 copies, he has only been able to sell 500, the infringer having printed and sold 500 copies. It is obvious that as the possible market for the book is limited to 1,000 copies, if the damages for infringement under section 6 are fixed on the basis that the copyright owner would have sold 1,000 copies but for the infringement, and at the same time the value of the 500 copies sold by the infringer is fixed for the purposes of section 7 at the amount for which they were sold, the result will be that the copyright owner will have recovered damages on the footing that there was an available market for 1,500 copies instead of the real market for 1,000 copies only. If he had sold 1,000 copies there would have been no market for the 500 copies made by the infringer, which would accordingly have had no value. Conversely, if the 500 copies sold by the infringer were worth what they were sold for, this could only be so on the basis that the copyright owner was only going to sell 500. In such a case it appears to me that to award to the copyright owner damages for infringement based on his inability to sell 500 copies and at the same time to award him damages based on the sale price of the 500 copies sold by the infringer would not be permissible." The illustration given was, of course, a simple case, and the principle is more difficult to apply where the defendant's work has been sold at a different price than the plaintiff's, or contains additional subject-matter, or was in a form which vulgarised the plaintiff's work. In such cases the court must presumably estimate on the facts available how far any overlap is involved and make provision accordingly.[49]

570 **Measure of damages for conversion.** The measure of damages for conversion is the value of the article converted at the date of the

[48] In *Sutherland Publishing Co., Ltd.* v. *Caxton Publishing Co., Ltd.* [1936] Ch. 323 at 342; the judgment of the Court of Appeal was affirmed by the House of Lords on this point.

[49] See *per* Lord Wright M.R. in *Sutherland Publishing Co., Ltd.* v. *Caxton Publishing Co., Ltd.* [1936] Ch. 323 at 327.

conversion.[50] The question of how that value is to be assessed was discussed in the same case. Lord Porter[51] said: "I do not accept the view that an article has no value or a diminished value to its owner because he has no machinery for selling it," and "The value is not necessarily the price for which the owner could sell the article. Is a publisher who infringes an author's copyright to make a large profit out of an unexpectedly successful book because he could have bought the copyright cheaply if before the publication he had approached the author and paid his price?" and "It is the value known or unknown, which has to be paid, and that value is not necessarily the price which the owner could have obtained or would have taken. It may have to be ascertained by finding out what price for the infringing matter, in the form in which it is offered, the public or some individual is prepared to pay, or in some other way in the light of after events." Lord Roche said[52]: "It is true enough to say that the value is the value to the owner; but it is wrong to say this if you mean what the owner will make out of the thing in money if it is not taken away from him." Where infringing copies are in fact sold by the defendant, the value is usually assessed by reference to the sale price, but allowing to the defendant all expenses which he proves to have been properly and necessarily incurred by him after the conversion in effecting the sale in so far as these expenses would not have been incurred but for the sale; such expenses might be the cost of binding, and the cost of collection and delivery, and the expense of advertising and selling.

571 **The relevant act for calculating damages.** What is the relevant act of conversion was also discussed. Lord Porter said[53]: "Conversion was defined by Atkin J. as he then was, in *Lancashire & Yorkshire Ry.* v. *MacNicoll.*[54] 'Dealing,' he said, 'with goods in a manner inconsistent with the right of the true owner amounts to a conversion, provided that it is also established that there is also an intention on the part of the defendant in so doing to deny the owner's right or to assert a right which is inconsistent with the owner's right.' Atkin J. goes on to point out that, where the act done is necessarily a denial of the owner's right or an assertion of a right

[50] *Birn Bros., Ltd.* v. *Keene & Co., Ltd., supra*; *Caxton Publishing Co., Ltd.* v. *Sutherland Publishing Co., Ltd.* [1939] A.C. 178 at 192. Normally the value will be ascertained at the date of the first act of conversion and subsequent changes of value will not affect the matter (see Salmond, *Torts*, 15th ed., pp. 757–759). The question whether a subsequent rise in value not due to any act of the defendant can be taken into account (see *Greening* v. *Wilkinson* (1825) 1 C. & P. 625) was expressly reserved in *Sutherland Publishing Co., Ltd.* v. *Caxton Publishing Co., Ltd., supra*; but see now Salmond, *Torts*, 15th ed., pp. 758–759.

[51] *Caxton Publishing Co., Ltd.* v. *Sutherland Publishing Co., Ltd.* [1939] A.C. 178 at 203.

[52] *Ibid.* at p. 192.

[53] *Ibid.* at 201.

[54] (1919) 88 L.J.K.B. 601 at 605.

inconsistent therewith, intention does not matter. Another way of reaching the same conclusion would be to say that conversion consists in an act intentionally done inconsistent with the owner's right though the doer may not know of or intend to challenge the property or possession of the true owner." The decision was that, where the infringement complained of consisted of a work which incorporated the plaintiff's material with non-infringing material, the binding together of the sheets constitutes a conversion. Until that stage was reached, the infringing matter could still have been delivered up to the plaintiff. But, once the infringing material was incorporated with the defendant's own property into a composite article, it was considered that the plaintiff had unequivocally dealt with this material as his own. It would seem that, where the infringing work is wholly the plaintiff's, so that no question of incorporation arises, the position may be different and the first act of conversion may be sale or the delivery of copies to a purchaser.[55] The exact moment at which the act of conversion is committed may be material, either by reason of the fact that time will begin to run from the date for the purposes of the statutory period of limitation,[56] or because variations of value after the date of conversion are not in general to be taken into account.[57]

572 **Where part only infringes.** A difficult question arises where the work produced by the defendant consists in part of infringing matter and in part of innocent matter. It has been decided [58] that, in such a case, the value of the whole work has first to be assessed as though the whole work had been converted.[59] It is then necessary to ascertain the proportion of this sum which is properly attributable to the infringing material; this proportion will represent the damage recoverable. No exact method of calculation is prescribed. Clearly the respective lengths of infringing and non-infringing articles cannot be conclusive, since it is the value, and not the length of the material, which has to be taken into account.[60] The court must, by what has been called *rusticum judicium*, determine, on the materials before it, the value of the plaintiff's part of the composite work at the date of conversion.[61]

55 *Caxton Publishing Co., Ltd.* v. *Sutherland Publishing Co., Ltd.* [1939] A.C. 178: and see *J. Whitaker & Sons, Ltd.* v. *Publishers' Circular, Ltd.* [1946–47] Macg. Cop.Cas. 10.

56 § 593, *post.*

57 § 570, note 50, *ante.*

58 *John Lane, etc., Ltd.* v. *Associated Newspapers, Ltd.* [1936] 1 K.B. 715; *Ash* v. *Dickie* [1936] Ch. 655; *Caxton Publishing Co., Ltd.* v. *Sutherland Publishing Co., Ltd.* [1939] A.C. 178.

59 See § 570, *ante.*

60 See cases in note 58, *supra,* and *Mansell (V.) & Co., Ltd.* v. *Wesley (H.), Ltd.* [1936–45] Macg.Cop.Cas. 288.

61 § 570, note 50, *ante.*

573 **Account of profits.** Another remedy is an account of profits, which is an equitable remedy incidental to the right to an injunction.[62] But a plaintiff cannot obtain both an account of profits and damages either for infringement or conversion, since a claim for an account condones the infringement.[63] The principles upon which such an account is granted were thus stated by Wigram V.-C. in *Colburn* v. *Simms*.[64] "It is true," he said, "that the court does not, by an account, accurately measure the damage sustained by the proprietor of an expensive work from the invasion of his copyright by the publication of a cheaper book. It is impossible to know how many copies of the dearer book are excluded from sale by the interposition of the cheaper one. The court, by the account, as the nearest approximation which it can make to justice, takes from the wrongdoer all the profits he has made by his piracy, and gives them to the party who has been wronged. In doing this the court may often give the injured party more, in fact, than he is entitled to, for *non constat* that a single additional copy of the more expensive book would have been sold, if the injury by the sale of the cheaper book had not been committed. The court of equity, however, does not give anything beyond the account." While an account of profits may be a useful remedy in a simple case, it is very difficult to take where part only of the infringing material infringes the plaintiff's copyright.

A plaintiff is entitled to discovery for the purposes of the account. The defendant must give full particulars, upon oath, of the number of copies printed and sold, and the cost of publication and distribution, verified by the production of all proper vouchers and receipts.[65] An account will be refused if it is clear that there are no profits.[66] In such a case the plaintiff may elect to claim damages and an inquiry as to the same.[67]

574 **The innocent infringer.** Inasmuch as copyright is a proprietary right, it is usually no defence to prove that the defendant acted innocently, though, in the case of the indirect infringements by sale, importation, and so on, it is necessary to prove that the defendant was aware of the infringement.[68]

However, it is provided, in section 17 (2) of the Copyright Act, 1956, that a plaintiff, though entitled to an account of profits and

[62] *Hogg* v. *Kirby* (1803) 8 Ves. 215; *Baily* v. *Taylor* (1830) 1 Russ. & My. 73; *Sheriff* v. *Coates* (1830) 1 R. & M. 159; *Kelly* v. *Hooper* (1840) 4 Jur. 21.

[63] *Caxton Publishing Co., Ltd.* v. *Sutherland Publishing Co., Ltd.* [1939] A.C. 178 at 198; *De Vitre (J. D.)* v. *Betts (W.)* (1873) L.R. 6 H.L. 319.

[64] (1843) 2 Ha. 543, 560; see *Pike* v. *Nicholas* (1870) L.R. 5 Ch. 251.

[65] *Stevens* v. *Brett* (1863) 12 W.R. 572.

[66] *Lee* v. *Alston* (1789) 1 Ves. 78; *Colburn* v. *Simms* (1843) 2 Ha. 543; *Powell* v. *Aiken* (1857) 4 K. & J. 343.

[67] *Mawman* v. *Tegg* (1826) 2 Russ. 385 at 400.

[68] § 475, *ante*.

other relief, is not to be entitled to damages in respect of an infringement, if it is proved or admitted that, at the time of the infringement, the defendant was not aware, and had no reasonable ground for suspecting, that copyright subsisted in the work or other subject-matter to which the action relates. By section 18 (2) of the Act of 1956, it is further provided that a plaintiff is not to be entitled, under that section, to any damages, or to an account of profits, in the circumstances there mentioned. Section 18 of the Act of 1956 is the section which gives a right to a plaintiff in respect of conversion or detention, and it is to damages on this basis that this subsection refers. The circumstances which have to be proved or admitted to enable a defendant to take advantage of this subsection are that the defendant was not aware, and had no reasonable ground for suspecting, that copyright subsisted in the work; or that the defendant believed, and had reasonable grounds for believing, that the articles converted or detained were not infringing copies; or, where what is converted or detained was a plate used or intended to be used for making articles, the defendant believed, and had reasonable grounds for believing, that the articles so made or intended to be made were not, or would not be, infringing copies.

575 **Old law.** The only corresponding provision of the Copyright Act, 1911, was contained in section 8, which provided that, where proceedings were taken in respect of the infringement of the copyright in any work, and the defendant in his defence alleged that he was not aware of the existence of the copyright in the work, the plaintiff was not to be entitled to any remedy other than an injunction or interdict in respect of the infringement if the defendant proved that, at the date of the infringement, he was not aware, and had no reasonable ground for suspecting, that copyright subsisted in the work.[69]

576 This section was discussed in the case of *Byrne* v. *Statist Co.*[70] There the plaintiff was employed by the proprietors of a newspaper to translate and summarise, in his spare time, a speech of the Governor of the State of Bahia, Brazil, reported in a foreign language, for the purpose of publication as an advertisement in their paper. The summarised translation was duly published in this way with the words " translated from the Portuguese language by F. D. Byrne " at the end. The defendants saw this advertisement, obtained permission from the Governor to publish it as an advertisement in their papers, for which they were duly paid, and they reproduced the plaintiff's translation verbatim. In an action for infringement of copyright the

[69] Compare with the similar s. 59 of the Patents Act, 1949 (12, 13 & 14 Geo. 6, c. 87) and s. 9 of the Registered Designs Act, 1949 (12, 13 & 14 Geo. 6, c. 88).
[70] [1914] 1 K.B. 622. See also *Gribble* v. *Manitoba Free Press, Ltd.* [1932] 1 D.L.R. 169.

defendants pleaded section 8 of the Copyright Act, 1911, but without success. In dealing with this plea, Bailhache J. remarked as follows: " The defendants suggested that they had no reasonable ground to suspect that there was any copyright in the advertisement at all; but the advertisement contained upon its face an intimation that it was translated by the plaintiff. The defendants' witnesses admitted that that was an unusual and unprecedented fact, but stated that it was one to which they, as men of experience, attached no importance. In that I think they were wrong, and I find as a fact that there was reasonable ground to suspect that there was copyright in the plaintiff's translation. The position of the defendants in fact was not so much that they did not suspect copyright, as that they supposed the copyright was in the Governor of Bahia, whose instructions for its reproduction they had obtained. This merely amounts to saying that they supposed themselves to have the authority of the owner of the copyright, a very different thing from alleging and proving that they did not suspect that any copyright existed. It is this latter state of mind that section 8 requires to be proved, and section 8 is no protection to a person who, knowing or suspecting that copyright exists, makes a mistake as to the owner of the copyright, and under that mistake obtains authority to publish from a person who is not in fact the owner." The plaintiff was awarded £150 damages. It would appear that this decision is equally applicable to section 17 (2) of the Act of 1956.

Section 17 (2) of the Act of 1956 thus affords no defence in a class of case that not infrequently arises. A photograph is submitted to a newspaper for publication. The proprietors of the newspaper accordingly publish the same and pay for it, upon receiving an assurance that the copyright belongs to the person who submitted the photograph to them, and they only become aware of the fact that they have been misinformed when a claim is made for damages for infringement of copyright. Clearly, the newspaper proprietors cannot urge that they did not suspect that copyright existed, but were only deceived as to the person in whom the copyright was vested, and so they have no defence upon the ground of ignorance under section 17 (2).[70a]

577 **To what cases section 17 (2) might apply.** In what cases, then, can this section apply? What " reasonable ground " can a direct copyist have for not suspecting the work he copies to be the subject of copyright? It is submitted that the proper attitude of mind of a copyist towards a work that he copies is that copyright in the latter subsists unless he has evidence to the contrary. The only grounds for not suspecting that copyright subsists appear to be, either (a) that the

[70a] But see § 578, *post.*

period of copyright protection has run out; or (b) that the work is of such a character that it ought not to be a subject of copyright; or (c) that the work is a foreign work.

If a copyist were to ascertain that the author of the original work was born 130 years ago, or that the work was published 100 years ago but, after due inquiry, he could not discover the date of the author's death, he might, perhaps, have reasonable grounds for thinking the copyright had run out. Or, again, if a work, bearing no author's or publisher's name, is pronounced by experts to be the work of A, who died sixty years ago, whereas it, in fact, is the work of B, who died only forty years ago, this, perhaps, is another case in which this section might be successfully pleaded.[70b] But it is submitted that no person has a right to assume, without inquiry, that a work published anonymously is not the subject of copyright.

If it is hard to imagine a case in which the section will be of any avail to a copyist at first hand, it is still harder to imagine a case in which a person deriving title under the original pirate could plead the section. We have seen that this section does not apply if the defendant publishes a work under a wrong impression as to who is the proprietor of the copyright. Take another case that may arise. A publisher publishes a work of X which, unknown to the publisher, contains large extracts from the work of Y. Y is a living person well known to the publisher. He cannot, it is thought, plead, successfully, that he did not suspect copyright to subsist in Y's work. All he could urge is that he did not suspect that X had copied from Y's work, and that, apparently, would not bring him within this section. Further if the defendant pleads that he did not think the pirated work was of a character which ought to be entitled to copyright protection, upon the court holding the contrary, the defendant may have some difficulty in convincing the court that he had no "reasonable grounds" for anticipating the court's decision.[71] Of course, it might be different if the defendant's belief was based upon a decision of the courts which was subsequently overruled.

Finally, if the work was a foreign work, it might yet be entitled to protection in this country, either because the Act of 1956 had been extended or applied to the works of such countries by Order in Council, or because the work was simultaneously published in this country. It is thought that, while a defendant would not be allowed

[70b] See *J. Whitaker & Sons, Ltd.* v. *Publishers' Circular, Ltd.* [1946–47] Macg.Cop. Cas. 10.

[71] See *Pytram, Ltd.* v. *Models, etc., Ltd.* [1930] 1 Ch. 639, where a mistaken view of the construction of s. 22 of the Act of 1911 was stated by Clauson J. not to afford a defence under s. 8 of that Act; he later held that, in fact, the view was not mistaken so that it was unnecessary to rely upon s. 8 of that Act. See also *Fiel* v. *Lemaire* (1939) 4 D.L.R. 561 (Can.); in *Cramp (G. A.) & Sons, Ltd.* v. *Frank Smythson, Ltd.* [1944] A.C. 329, Lord Macmillan expressly reserved his opinion on the application of s. 8 of the Act of 1911.

to plead ignorance of an Order in Council, he might be able to say that he was unaware of simultaneous publication.

578 **Section 18 (2).** As has been seen, however, the Act of 1956 gives a defendant a greater measure of protection where damages are claimed on the conversion basis. In this case, it is sufficient for him to establish that he believed, and had reasonable grounds for believing, that the copies converted were not infringing copies.[72] This provision was primarily intended, it is thought, to protect the printer, who is generally not in a position to know whether material which he is asked to print is, or is not, an infringement of copyright. Unless what he is given to reproduce is obviously matter obtained from an existing work, it is thought that, under section 18 (2) of the Act of 1956, he will generally be protected, if he is acting on the instructions of a person whose good faith he has no reason to doubt. But it would seem that this provision will also protect a publisher who has acquired a right to reproduce a work, which he believes to be the original material of the author with whom he has made a publishing agreement, or where he believes he has obtained a valid licence from the owner of the copyright.[72a]

579 **Matters of procedure.** The court will not make a declaratory order to the effect that copyright will subsist in documents not yet in existence, but which it is anticipated will be brought into existence. There must be before the court specific documents, the character of which can be established.[73]

580 If reasons of urgency exist, application may be made upon notice of motion in the Chancery Division, or upon summons in the Queen's Bench Division for interlocutory relief and an injunction granted upon the plaintiff's undertaking to pay damages for any loss thereby occasioned if he is unsuccessful in the action. Upon such applications evidence is adduced by affidavit. In cases of extreme urgency an application may be made *ex parte* when the plaintiff can rely on the presumptions in section 20 of the Act of 1956 without fear of rebuttal until the effective hearing of the interlocutory application.

581 Where a joint proprietorship exists, either party may sue; and where a plaintiff has an assignment from some only of several part-owners, he is entitled to sue to prevent a stranger from interfering with his rights,[74] or even a co-owner.[75]

[72] Copyright Act, 1956, s. 18 (2) (*b*).
[72a] See *Smith* v. *Daily News, Ltd.* [1905–10] Macg.Cop.Cas. 302.
[73] *Odhams Press, Ltd.* v. *London and Provincial Sporting News Agency, etc., Ltd.* [1936] Ch. 357.
[74] *Lauri* v. *Renad* [1892] 3 Ch. 402.
[75] *Cecinski* v. *George Routledge & Sons, Ltd.* [1916] 2 K.B. 325.

The Vice-Chancellor, in *Sweet* v. *Maugham*,[76] said "It has always been considered sufficient to allege, generally, that the defendant's work contains several passages which have been pirated from the plaintiff's work. Then, when the injunction has been moved for, the two works have been brought into court, and the counsel have pointed out to the court the passages which they rely upon as showing the piracy." This, however, is not the modern practice. A plaintiff, whether on motion for interlocutory relief, or in an action, is expected to indicate, in an exhibit to an affidavit or in particulars to a statement of claim, by reference to parallel passages or otherwise, the parts he mainly relies upon as constituting an infringement, though he may well reserve the right at the trial to rely upon general similarities as further evidence of piracy. If a plaintiff brings an action to protect a work, being only entitled to copyright in a small part of such work, he ought to tell the defendant in his claim what that part is, otherwise costs unnecessarily incurred must be borne by the plaintiff.[77]

582 In an action for infringement of copyright in a picture it is not necessary to produce the original from which the alleged copy has been made.[78]

583 A plaintiff may confine his claim to copyright to part of an unpublished work and, in that case, will not be required, on discovery, to disclose the remainder.[79]

584 **Presumptions as to copyright and title.** The Copyright Act, 1956, contains a series of presumptions designed to assist a plaintiff [79a] in a copyright action whether on an application for interlocutory relief, or at the trial.

In the first place, if the defendant does not put in issue the subsistence of copyright in the work which is the subject-matter of the action, or the ownership thereof, respectively, then copyright is to be presumed to subsist in the work and the plaintiff is to be presumed to be the owner thereof.[80] These presumptions are absolute if the issues are not raised.[80a]

Where the issue of title is raised, and a name purporting to be that of the author appeared on copies of a literary, dramatic, musical

[76] (1840) 11 Sim. 51; *Hotten* v. *Arthur* (1863) 1 H. & M. 603. As to points arising upon the form of the statement of claim in particular cases, see *Oliver* v. *Dickin* [1936] 2 All E.R. 1004; *Ash* v. *Hutchinson & Co.* (*Publishers*), *Ltd.* [1936] Ch. 489.

[77] *Page* v. *Wisden* (1869) 17 W.R. 483; and generally a defendant can obtain an order for particulars.

[78] *Lucas* v. *Williams & Sons* [1892] 2 Q.B. 113.

[79] *Sitwell* v. *Sun Engraving Co., Ltd.* (1938) 107 L.J.Ch. 68.

[79a] Though in some cases they will assist a defendant; see § 585, *post*.

[80] Copyright Act, 1956, s. 20 (1).

[80a] As to the standard of proof where the presumptions are put in time in interlocutory proceedings, see *Merchant Adventurers, Ltd.* v. *M. Grew & Co., Ltd.* [1971] F.S.R. 233 at 236, 239.

or artistic work as published or, in the case of an artistic work, appeared on the work when it was made, the person whose name so appeared is to be presumed, unless the contrary is proved, to be the author of the work.[81] If, however, the name purports to be that of an "arranger," the only presumption is that the "name" in question did some work of arrangement.[82] It is further to be presumed, unless the contrary is proved, that the work was not made in circumstances, such as on commission or in the course of employment by another person, which would result in the copyright vesting initially in that other person.[81] The name may be either the true name of the author, or a name by which he was commonly known.[81] The effect of this provision is that, where an author's name appears in the circumstances indicated, it will not be necessary for the plaintiff to prove that the person so named as author actually wrote, composed or painted the work, and it will be sufficient for the plaintiff to establish a documentary title commencing from such author. Where the work is alleged to be a work of joint authorship, a similar presumption is made in relation to each person alleged to be one of the authors of the work.[83]

585 Where the foregoing provision does not apply, that is to say, where an author's name does not appear on the work, then, if it is established that the work was first published in the United Kingdom or another country to which the Act extends, and was so published within the period of fifty years ending with the beginning of the calendar year in which the action was brought, and that a name purporting to be that of the publisher appeared on copies of the work as first published, copyright is presumed to subsist in the work, and the person whose name so appeared is presumed to have been the owner of the copyright at the time of publication.[84] This presumption applies unless the contrary is proved.[84] This presumption, which is differently worded, appears to be more definite than the similar one contained in section 6 (3) (*b*) of the Copyright Act, 1911, which did not state that, in the given circumstances, copyright should be presumed to subsist in the work. It was held that the presumption, under that Act, did not assist a publisher in a case in which the publisher also produced earlier works from which the work relied upon was reprinted,[85] and it was doubted whether it even shifted the onus of proof where the issue was whether or not copyright subsisted in the work.[86] It was further held, under that section, that the name of an unincorporated body appearing on a work did not create a

[81] s. 20 (2).
[82] *Per* Cross J. in *Roberton* v. *Lewis, The Times*, June 1, 1960.
[83] Copyright Act, 1956, s. 20 (3).
[84] s. 20 (4).
[85] *Hogg* v. *Toye & Co., Ltd.* [1935] Ch. 497.
[86] *Cramp (G. A.) & Sons, Ltd.* v. *Frank Smythson, Ltd.* [1944] A.C. 329.

presumption that copyright was vested in the members of the body at any particular time.[87]

In *Warwick Film Productions Ltd.* v. *Eisinger*,[87a] on an application for interlocutory relief, the defendants successfully relied on the presumption in section 20 (4) of the Act of 1956. In that case, the plaintiffs claimed that the executor of the alleged author of the anonymous book entitled *Oscar Wilde: Three Times Tried*, had assigned the copyright in that book to them, but the defendants contended, in reliance on this presumption, that the publishers of the book must be presumed to have been the owner of any copyright therein at the time of publication, and that the author's executor would have had no copyright to assign. Plowman J. said that it was common ground (1) that this was an action brought by virtue of " this Part of this Act " with respect to a literary work; (2) that subsection (2) of section 20 did not apply; (3) that the book was first published in the United Kingdom; (4) that it was so published within the period of fifty years ending with the beginning of the calendar year in which the action was brought; and (5) that a name purporting to be that of the publisher appeared on copies of the work as first published.

The learned judge said it therefore followed, unless the contrary was shown, that copyright must be presumed to subsist in the work, and the person named must be presumed to have been the owner of that copyright at the time of publication. It followed from this that the plaintiffs, to succeed, must either accept the benefit of the presumption and trace title through the publishers, or else (as a first step) establish that the person named was not the owner of the copyright at the time of publication. They had not attempted to do the former and, in his judgment, they had not succeeded in doing the latter. In order to establish that the publisher of a book was not the owner of the copyright at the date of publication it was not enough to show that he was not the author. The statutory presumption could not be based on any inherent probability. Moreover, if the publisher was to be presumed to have been the owner of the copyright at the time of publication, it must follow that the author is to be presumed not to have owned the copyright at that time. The onus was on the plaintiffs to prove affirmatively, not that the alleged author was the author, but that the person named did not own the copyright when the book was published, and that they had failed to do.

Plowman J. distinguished the case of *Hogg* v. *Toye & Co. Ltd.*[85] on the grounds that this was a decision on the differently worded, though similar, section 6 (3) of the Act of 1911. He also held that it was not legitimate to speculate on what facts might have existed

[87] *Massie & Renwick, Ltd.* v. *Underwriters' Survey Bureau, Ltd.* [1940] S.C.R. 218.
[87a] [1969] 1 Ch. 508; see §§ 147–149, *ante*.

which would render the statutory presumption true as a matter of fact. The plaintiffs had argued that, if the alleged author had assigned the copyright to the person named then, as a matter of law, the copyright would have automatically reverted to his estate in 1953 or 1954, thus enabling his executor to sell it to the plaintiffs.

586 **Deceased or anonymous authors.** The foregoing presumptions are substantially the same as those in section 6 of the Act of 1911,[88] but the Act of 1956 adds additional presumptions. In the case of a literary, dramatic, musical or artistic work, which was published anonymously, or of which the author is dead, the work is to be presumed to be an original work unless the contrary is proved.[89] Furthermore, in the like cases, if it is alleged by the plaintiff that a publication specified in the allegation was the first publication of the work, and that it took place in a country and on a date so specified, that publication is to be presumed, unless the contrary is proved, to have been the first publication of the work, and to have taken place in that country and on that date.[89] For the purpose of this provision, a publication is to be treated as anonymous, if it is not shown that the work has ever been published under the true name of the author, or under a name by which he was commonly known, or that it is possible for a person, without previous knowledge of the facts, to ascertain the identity of the author by reasonable inquiry.[90] Under similar conditions, the presumptions will arise if the work was published under a pseudonym.[91]

587 **Presumptions regarding sound recordings.** There are further presumptions which can be relied upon in any action brought with respect to the copyright in a sound recording. If records embodying a recording, or part thereof, have been issued to the public bearing a label or other mark comprising any one or more of the following statements—(a) that a person named on the label or mark was the maker of the record; (b) that the record was first published in a year specified on the label or mark; (c) that the record was first published in a country specified on the label or mark—that label or mark shall be sufficient evidence of the facts so stated, except in so far as the contrary is proved.[92]

588 **Form of defence.** The defendant to an action for infringement of copyright must, if he desires to dispute the subsistence of copyright

[88] These will apparently still apply in actions in respect of infringements committed before the commencement of the Act of 1956 (Copyright Act, 1956, Sched. 7, paras. 20 and 21).
[89] Copyright Act, 1956, s. 20 (5) and (6).
[90] s. 20 (6) (*b*).
[91] s. 20 (6) (*a*).
[92] s. 20 (7).

in the work, or the plaintiff's title to such copyright or both, specifically raise the point on his pleading [93]; also any plea of innocence with supporting facts, must be pleaded. But he is not required, as he was under the Literary Copyright Act, 1842,[94] to state in his defence the person he alleges to be the author or the proprietor of the copyright, though, in a proper case, the defendant might be ordered to answer interrogatories on the point.

589 **Infringement of each right a separate tort.** It was held that the various rights conferred upon an author by section 1 (2) of the Copyright Act, 1911, including the right "to authorise any such acts as aforesaid," were separate and distinct rights, and the infringement of each was a distinct and separate tort. Consequently, judgment against the author of an infringing work for having authorised its printing was no bar to an action against the printer, though it was a bar to an action against the publisher for also authorising the printing.[95] Although the Act of 1956 is differently framed, it is thought that in similar circumstances the same result follows, since section 1 (2) of that Act treats the doing and the authorising of restricted acts as separate infringements.

590 **Expert evidence.** Expert evidence may be called to point out coincidences, similarities or identical omissions with a view to establishing copying, but it is not proper for an expert witness to state, as a matter of opinion, that the work was copied from another.[96]

591 **Points as to costs.** A person whose copyright has been infringed is not bound to rest satisfied with the promise of the defendant not to commit any further infringement, but he has a right to have an injunction, and is entitled to the costs of such injunction.[97] It is not sufficient to entitle the defendant to escape being ordered to pay the plaintiff's costs of obtaining an injunction that he has, before issue of the writ, offered the plaintiff all that he was entitled to. But if, having made such an offer prior to action brought, the defendant were later to repeat the offer, enlarging it by including the costs of the action up to date, the costs of persisting in his action from the time of an offer to submit to an order might, perhaps, be cast upon the plaintiff. This, it has been said, is the only way in which, where a wrong has been done, the defendant can escape from the liability of having the infringed rights asserted in court, and a proper order

93 s. 20 (1).

94 5 & 6 Vict. c. 45, s. 16.

95 *Ash* v. *Hutchinson & Co.* (*Publishers*), *Ltd.* [1936] Ch. 489.

96 *Deeks* v. *Wells* [1928–35] Macg.Cop.Cas. 353 (P.C.); *Bauman* v. *Fussell* (1954) *The Author* LXIV, No. 3, 63.

97 *Geary* v. *Norton* (1846) 1 De G. & Sm. 9; *Savory* (*E. W.*), *Ltd.* v. *The World of Golf, Ltd.* [1914] 2 Ch. 566; *Performing Right Society, Ltd.* v. *Ciryl Theatrical Syndicate, Ltd.* [1923] 2 K.B. 146; *Samuelson* v. *Producers' Distributing Co., Ltd.* (1932) 48 R.P.C. 580; *Hall-Brown* v. *Iliffe & Sons, Ltd.* [1928–35] Macg. Cop.Cas. 88.

obtained.[98] Moreover, cases of infringement of copyright should be heard in open court, and, therefore, even if the defendant admits liability, and consents to the requisite order being made in chambers, the plaintiff is entitled to the costs of a motion for judgment in court.[99] It has been held that, where a plaintiff claims damages for infringement, detinue and conversion, the defendant may be given leave, under the old Rules of the Supreme Court to pay into court one sum of money in respect of the whole action. Although the separate claims represent separate causes of action the possibility of overlapping of damages [1] may embarrass the defendant unless he is allowed to pay in a single sum.[2] Under the present Rules, Order 22, r. 1 (1) and (4), leave is not necessary.

592 The question of whether a plaintiff can be deprived of costs for any reason short of misconduct, for instance for failure to give notice before issue of writ, has been discussed. In *Cooper* v. *Whittingham*,[3] Jessel J. thought that where a plaintiff came to enforce a legal right, and there had been no misconduct on his part, the court had no discretion, and could not take away his right to costs; and Chitty J. took the same view in *Upmann* v. *Forester*.[4] But in *Walter* v. *Steinkopff*,[5] North J. said that he could not understand that view—it was in the teeth of the General Orders and Act of Parliament, which say the judge has a discretion which he is to exercise; and, in the case of *American Tobacco Co.* v. *Guest*,[6] Stirling J. was of the same opinion. North J. considered that, in the case in question, the defendants had been hardly dealt with by being pulled up all at once without notice for doing what they had been doing for twelve years past and decided that the defendants should pay all the costs of the action down to a certain day, and also such further costs as would have been properly incurred by the plaintiffs in proceedings upon a motion, unopposed by the defendants, to make the interlocutory order perpetual, leaving all other costs to be borne by the parties who incurred them. But the mere fact that the damages are trifling is not a sufficient reason for depriving the plaintiff of his costs.[7] If the defendant is successful he may, nevertheless, be deprived of his costs if the court thinks that he has conducted his case improperly,

[98] *Per* Neville J. in *Savory (E. W.), Ltd.* v. *The World of Golf, Ltd., supra.* See *Mate & Son* v. *Samuel Stephen, Ltd.* [1928–35] Macg.Cop.Cas. 257; *Oliver* v. *Dickin* [1936] 2 All E.R. 1004.

[99] *Smith (J. T.) and Jones (J. E.), Ltd.* v. *Service, Reeve & Co.* [1914] 2 Ch. 576 but see *Hanfstaengl* v. *Lewis* [1901–04] Macg.Cop.Cas. 68.

[1] See § 569, *ante*.

[2] *Tallent* v. *Coldwell* [1938] Ch. 653; *Robertson* v. *Aberdeen Journals, Ltd.* [1954] 1 W.L.R. 1084.

[3] (1880) 15 Ch.D. 501: and see *Customagic Manufacturing Co., Ltd.* v. *Headquarters & General Supplies, Ltd.* [1968] F.S.R. 150.

[4] (1883) 24 Ch.D. 231.

[5] [1892] 3 Ch. 489.

[6] [1892] 1 Ch. 630.

[7] *Hanfstaengl* v. *W. H. Smith & Sons* [1905] 1 Ch. 519.

or his conduct prior to action has been, in the opinion of the court, unfair.[8] A defendant has been allowed costs, incurred before any statement of claim was delivered, in investigating common sources in order to show that his work was not derived from the plaintiffs, although such material was not required in the court because the plaintiff did not proceed with the action.[9]

593 **Period of limitation.** The Copyright Act, 1911, provided that no action in respect of infringement of copyright was to be commenced after the expiration of three years next after the infringement.[10] And it was held that proceedings in respect of conversion or detinue were proceedings in respect of infringement, so that such proceedings were barred, whenever the act of detinue or conversion occurred, unless commenced within three years of the act of infringement which caused the articles detained or converted to be treated as infringing copies.[11] These provisions continue to apply to acts of infringement committed before the commencement of the Copyright Act, 1956, and to acts of conversion or detention committed before or after the commencement of that Act if the relevant infringement occurred before such commencement.[12] The Copyright Act, 1956, itself provides no special limitation period, so that the six-year period provided in the Limitation Act, 1939,[13] for actions of tort will now operate, both in respect of actions for infringement, and in respect of actions for conversion. Moreover, it would appear that the limitation period in respect of an action for conversion will now run from the date of the conversion, and not from the date of the infringement. On the other hand it is expressly provided, in section 18 (1) of the Copyright Act, 1956, that if, by virtue of section 3 (2) of the Limitation Act, 1939, the title of the owner of the copyright to an infringing copy would, if he had been the owner of such copy, have been extinguished at the end of the period mentioned in that subsection, he is not to be entitled to any rights and remedies under section 18 of the Copyright Act, 1956, in respect of anything done in relation to that copy after the end of the period. The effect of section 3 (2) of the Limitation Act, 1939, is that, where a cause of action for conversion or detention has accrued, and the period of six years has elapsed, and the owner has not recovered possession, the title of the owner of the chattel is extinguished.

[The next paragraph is 601]

8 *Cobbett* v. *Woodward* (1872) L.R. 14 Eq. 407; *Pike* v. *Nicholas* (1870) L.R. 5 Ch. 251; *Kelly's Directories, Ltd.* v. *Gavin* [1901] 1 Ch. 374; *cf. Liverpool, etc., Association, Ltd.* v. *Commercial Press, etc., Ltd.* [1897] 2 Q.B. 1.

9 *Scheff* v. *Columbia Picture Corporation, Ltd.* [1936–45] Macg.Cop.Cas. 254.

10 Copyright Act, 1911, s. 10.

11 *Caxton Publishing Co., Ltd.* v. *Sutherland Publishing Co.* [1939] A.C. 178; *Massie & Renwick, Ltd.* v. *Underwriters' Survey Bureau, Ltd.* [1940] S.C.R. 218.

12 Copyright Act, 1956, Sched. 7, paras. 20 and 21.

13 2 & 3 Geo. 6, c. 21, Appendix A., § 1551, *post*.

CHAPTER 11

SUMMARY REMEDIES

1—SUMMARY PROCEEDINGS FOR INFRINGEMENT OF COPYRIGHT

601 **Old law.** The Copyright Act, 1911, imposed certain summary remedies for infringement of copyright and also maintained unrepealed certain earlier Acts imposing summary remedies in respect of dealings with musical works. These Acts are now repealed [1] and, under the Copyright Act, 1956, the only summary proceedings in respect of infringement are those contained in section 21 thereof.

602 **Section 21 of the Act of 1956.** Under this section, subsection (1), an offence is committed by any person who, at a time when copyright subsists in a work, makes for hire or sale, sells or lets for hire, or by way of trade offers or exposes for sale or hire, or by way of trade exhibits in public, or imports into the United Kingdom, otherwise than for his private and domestic use, any article which he knows to be an infringing copy of the work. An offence is also committed under subsection (2) of this section if any person, for purposes of trade or for other purposes, but to such an extent as to affect prejudicially the owner of the copyright, distributes articles which he knows to be infringing copies of the work. An offence is also committed under subsection (3) of this section by any person who, at a time when copyright subsists in a work, makes, or has in his possession, a plate, knowing that it is to be used for making infringing copies of the work.

603 **The meaning of "infringing copy."** For the purposes of these provisions, "infringing copy" means an article the making of which constituted an infringement of the copyright in the work or, in the case of an imported article, would have constituted an infringement of that copyright if the article had been made in the place into which it was imported.[2] The article must, in the case of a literary, dramatic, musical or artistic work, or a published edition, be a reproduction otherwise than in the form of a cinematograph film; in the case of a sound recording, be a record embodying the recording; in the case of a cinematograph film, be a copy of the film; and in the case of a television broadcast or a sound broadcast be a copy of a cinematograph film of it, or a record embodying a sound recording of it.[2] Reproduction, in the case of a literary, dramatic or musical work,

[1] Copyright Act, 1956, s. 50 (2), and Sched. IX.
[2] s. 18 (3). Including an infringement under the Act of 1911 (Sched. VII, para. 23).

includes a record or other device in which sounds are embodied so as to be capable, with or without the aid of some other instrument, of being automatically reproduced therefrom and, in the case of an artistic work, includes a version produced by converting the work into a three-dimensional form or, if it is in three dimensions, by converting it into a two-dimensional form.[3] But in this connection regard must no doubt be had to section 9 (8) of the Act of 1956, which states that the making of an object of any description in three dimensions is not to be taken to infringe the copyright in an artistic work in two dimensions if the object would not appear to persons who are not experts in relation to objects of that description to be a reproduction of the artistic work. Plate, for the purposes of these provisions, includes any stereotype, stone, block, mould, matrix, transfer, negative or other appliance.[2]

604 **Public performance.** A further offence is committed by any person who causes a literary, dramatic or musical work to be performed in public, knowing that copyright subsists in the work and that the performance constitutes an infringement of the copyright.[4] This appears to be directed against the person responsible for a performance and not against the actual performer. The expression used, " causes to be performed," is similar to the expression " causes to be represented " under the law before 1911 and cases upon that expression may be in point.[5]

605 **Proof.** It should be observed that the presumptions provided by section 20 of the Act of 1956 only apply in an action and do not therefore apply to criminal proceedings in which the copyright must, no doubt, be strictly proved. It will also be observed that knowledge is an essential element of all the offences.

606 **Penalties.** The offences above described are punishable on summary conviction.[6] The offences of making, selling, exhibiting, importing or distributing infringing copies are punishable, on first conviction, with a fine not exceeding £2 for each article and, in any other case, by such a fine or imprisonment for a term not exceeding two months.[7] The fines are not to exceed £50 in respect of articles comprised in the same transactions.[7] The offences of having in possession plates, and of causing a work to be performed, are punishable, in the case of first conviction, by a fine not exceeding £50 and, in any other case, by such a fine or imprisonment for a term not exceeding two months.[8]

[3] Copyright Act, 1956, s. 48 (1).
[4] s. 21 (5).
[5] See *ante*, § 452.
[6] s. 21 (7) and (8).
[7] s. 21 (7).
[8] s. 21 (8).

It is further provided that the court before which a person is charged with any of these offences may, whether he is convicted of the offence or not, order that any article in his possession which appears to the court to be an infringing copy, or to be a plate used or intended to be used for making infringing copies, shall be destroyed or delivered up to the owner of the copyright in question or otherwise dealt with as the court may think fit.[9] An appeal lies to a court of quarter sessions from any order to this effect made by a court of summary jurisdiction.[10]

607 **Conspiracy to infringe copyright.** Apart from the summary remedies aforesaid it may be possible to prosecute infringers for a conspiracy at common law. To create this offence, two or more persons must have conspired together to deprive the proprietor of the copyright of his property, for example, by printing for sale piratical copies of a copyright work.[11]

2.—PERFORMERS' RIGHTS

608 **Dramatic and Musical Performers' Protection Act, 1925.** The 1952 Copyright Committee was invited to make recommendations in favour of creating new rights for the protection of performers of musical and dramatic works. The Committee, however, felt that if a right of this kind was conferred, it would add to the number of licences which were needed when performances by mechanical means were given in public and that the further extension of copyright, or a similar right, in this direction was not justified. It therefore only recommended certain modifications of the existing provisions of the Dramatic and Musical Performers' Protection Act, 1925,[12] which, while not creating any right, gives to performers a summary remedy in the cases therein mentioned.[13] Thus this Act was only modified and not repealed by the Copyright Act, 1956.

609 **Performers' Protection Acts, 1958 and 1963.** However, the Act of 1925, together with the amending provisions of the Act of 1956, were repealed and re-enacted by the Dramatic and Musical Performers' Protection Act, 1958.[14] The Act of 1958 has itself been amended by the Performers' Protection Act, 1963,[15] in order to give effect to the International Convention for the Protection of Performers' Producers of Phonograms and Broadcasting Organisations [16]

[9] s. 21 (9).
[10] s. 21 (10).
[11] *R.* v. *Willetts* (1906) 70 J.P. 127; *R.* v. *Bokenham*, *The Times*, July 22, 1910.
[12] 15 & 16 Geo. 5, c. 46.
[13] Cmd. 8662, para. 172.
[14] 6 & 7 Eliz. 2, c. 44.
[15] c. 53.
[16] Cmnd. 2425, Appendix C, § 1791, *post*: ratified by the United Kingdom on October 30, 1963, and entered into force on May 18, 1964.

entered into at Rome on October 26, 1961. As a result protection extends to the performers of literary and artistic works as well as of dramatic and musical works as from August 31, 1963, when the Act of 1963 came into force. It is clear that the introduction of the word "artistic" into subsection (1) of section 1 of the Act of 1963 resulted from a misapprehension. The Convention uses the expression "literary or artistic works" in the same sense as they were used in the Brussels Convention as including everything in the general field of art, such as drama and music, which are not specifically mentioned. But the Copyright Act, 1956, section 3 (1), uses "artistic" in the narrower sense of drawing, painting and architecture. By failing to appreciate this, and repeating the copyright words "literary, dramatic, musical or artistic works" in subsection (1) of section 1 of the Act of 1963 this statute has created the odd conception of a performer performing a drawing, a painting or a house.

Section 1 of the Act of 1958, as modified by the Act of 1963, gives to actors, singers, musicians, dancers or other persons who act, sing, deliver, declaim, play in or otherwise perform literary, dramatic, musical or artistic works a summary remedy [17] in the case of a person knowingly making a record of the performance of such performers without the consent in writing of such performers. The Act of 1958 applies as respects anything done in relation to a performance notwithstanding that the performance took place out of the United Kingdom, though this will not cause anything done out of the United Kingdom to be treated as an offence.

610 It is also an offence to sell, hire, distribute or perform a record so made; further, if such record is made in a country outside the United Kingdom and the law of that country contains a provision requiring the consent of any person to the making of the record, such record is deemed to have been made contrary to the Act of 1958, if, whether knowingly or not, it was made without such consent and without the consent in writing of the performers.

611 The Act of 1958 also makes it an offence, by section 4 thereof, to possess contrivances for the making of such records, and, by section 5 thereof, gives power to the court to order the destruction of such records and contrivances.

612 The Act of 1958, as modified by the Act of 1963, creates further offences in relation to cinematograph films and broadcasting.[18] "Broadcast" means broadcast by wireless telegraphy within the meaning of the Wireless Telegraphy Act, 1949,[19] whether by way of

[17] No civil action can be brought under this section: *Musical Performers' Protection Association, Ltd.* v. *British International Pictures, Ltd.* (1930) 46 T.L.R. 485: see also *Bollinger* v. *Costa Brava Wine Co., Ltd*: [1960] R.P.C. 16 at 33.

[18] Dramatic and Musical Performers' Protection Act, ss. 2, 3.

[19] 12, 13 & 14 Geo. 6, c. 54.

sound broadcasting or of television.[20] Like the Act of 1925, it also narrows the circumstances in which records of performances may lawfully be made, by substituting the words " made for private and domestic use only " for the words " not made for purposes of trade." [21]

613 The Act of 1963 creates another offence in relation to transmission to subscribers to a diffusion service or over wires or other paths provided by a material substance so as to be seen or heard in public; in relation to this offence, section 48 (3) of the Copyright Act, 1956, is to apply.[22]

614 **Meaning of " knowingly."** It has been held that " knowingly," in the Act of 1925, applies both to the making of the record and to the fact that such making was without the consent in writing of the performer[23]: this, it is submitted, will continue to be so under the Acts of 1958 and 1963.

615 **Meaning of " consent in writing."** The amended Act of 1958, like the amended Act of 1925, provides that the consent in writing is given, if given either by the performers themselves, or by a person who, at the time of giving the consent, represented that he was authorised by the performers to give it on their behalf and the person making the record, film, broadcast or transmission had no reasonable grounds for believing that the person giving the consent was not so authorised.[24] However, if the person giving the consent was not so authorised, he commits an offence under the Act of 1963.[25] It is to be noted that consideration for the giving of this consent is not required. Bearing in mind that the performers of much of the present-day recorded " pop " music, for instance, are infants,[25a] if consideration is given for the consent of an infant performer, regard should be had to the rules governing infants' contracts.[25b]

3.—SEIZURE OF IMPORTED COPIES

616 **Section 22 of the Act of 1956.** Section 22 of the Copyright Act, 1956, gives to the owner of the copyright in any published literary, dramatic or musical work, the right to give notice to the Commissioners of Customs and Excise requesting them to prohibit the import of infringing copies. The notice must specify the period during which the goods are to be treated as prohibited and the period must not

[20] Dramatic and Musical Performers' Protection Act, 1958, s. 8.
[21] ss. 1 and 2.
[22] Performers' Protection Act, 1963, s. 3. The Acts of 1958 and 1963 are set out in Appendix A, §§ 1580 and 1590, *post*.
[23] *Gaumont British Distributors, Ltd.* v. *Henry* [1939] 2 K.B. 711.
[24] Dramatic and Musical Performers' Protection Act, 1958, s. 7.
[25] Performers' Protection Act, 1963, s. 4.
[25a] See Family Law Reform Act, 1969 (1969 c. 46).
[25b] See *Chaplin* v. *Leslie Frewin (Publishers), Ltd.* [1966] Ch. 71.

exceed five years, or, in any event, the period for which the copyright is to subsist.[26] The copies which may be prohibited as a result of such notice are copies made outside the United Kingdom which, if made in the United Kingdom, would have been infringing copies of the work.[27] But though " infringing copy " in general, in the Act of 1956, includes any reproduction otherwise than in the form of a cinematograph film, in this section the only copies to which the notice can apply are printed copies, so that records are clearly excluded.

The restriction on importation is not to apply to the importation of any article by a person for his private and domestic use.[28]

617 **Power of Commissioners to make regulations.** The Commissioners are empowered to make regulations prescribing the form in which notices are to be given and requiring a person giving such a notice, either at the time of giving the notice, or at the time when the goods are imported, or at both those times to furnish the Commissioners with such evidence, and to comply with such other conditions (if any), as may be specified in the regulations.[29] It is further provided that the regulations may provide for the payment of fees or the giving of security to the Commissioners in respect of any liability or expense which they may incur in consequence of the detention and for keeping the Commissioners, whether security is given or not, indemnified against any such liability or expense.[30]

618 **Importance of this remedy.** In view of the fact that, under the Act of 1956, an imported copy of a work, which would have infringed copyright if made in the United Kingdom, is an infringing copy, without the necessity of proving that the importer knew that it would be an infringement,[30a] as was the case under the Act of 1911,[31] this method of restricting importation of infringing material is probably of less importance than it was prior to the commencement of the Act of 1956. On the other hand, it affords a simple method of enabling an English publisher to prevent the flooding of his market with cheap foreign reprints. Such reprints may well have been made under licence from the author for sale abroad, but they can still be restricted under these provisions, if imported, because the licence would not cover manufacture in England.

[The next paragraph is 631]

26 Copyright Act, 1956, s. 22 (1). Notices given under s. 14 of the Act of 1911 were continued in effect for six months after the commencement of the Act of 1956 (Sched. VII, para. 24).

27 s. 22 (2).

28 s. 22 (3).

29 Copyright Act, 1956, s. 22 (4). See the Copyright (Customs) Regulations, 1957, *post*, Appendix B, § 1629.

30 s. 22 (5).

30a s. 18 (2).

31 See § 567, *ante*.

CHAPTER 12

PROVISIONS AS TO LIBRARIES

1.—DEPOSIT OF BOOKS

631 **History of the privilege.** The Copyright Act, 1911, in obedience to Article 4 of the Revised Convention of Berne, which provided that the enjoyment and exercise of the rights conferred by the Convention should not be subject to the performance of any formality, abolished all necessity for registration of copyright, but substantially re-enacted sections 6 to 9 of the Copyright Act, 1842,[1] relating to the deposit of published books at the British Museum and other libraries.[2] A strong protest was made by the publishing trade during the passage of the Act of 1911 through Parliament with a view to getting these provisions, which were alleged to be an undue tax upon the trade, modified in favour of the publishers, but these efforts failed, and, in fact, the old law was slightly extended by the Act of 1911, inasmuch as the National Library of Wales was added to the list of libraries which can, under certain circumstances, demand delivery of a copy of a published book.

Certain representations were made to the 1952 Copyright Committee that the delivery of copies of books to the libraries free of charge was unfair to publishers, but the Committee recommended that the privilege of the libraries of deposit to receive copies of published works should not be discontinued.[3] The Copyright Act, 1956, in fact left unrepealed section 15 of the Copyright Act, 1911, under which this privilege was conferred.[4]

632 **The libraries entitled to the privilege.** Section 15 (1) of the Act of 1911 requires the publisher of every book published[5] in the United Kingdom to deliver, at his own expense, one copy of the book, within one month after publication, to the trustees of the British Museum, who are to give a receipt for the same. But by the Copyright (British Museum) Act, 1915,[6] power was given to the Board of Trade, on application of the trustees of the British Museum, to exempt from the obligations of this section trade publications unless copies

[1] 5 & 6 Vict. c. 45.
[2] Copyright Act, 1911, s. 15.
[3] Cmd. 8662, para. 58.
[4] Copyright Act, 1956, s. 50 (2).
[5] Presumably "publication" now has to be construed by reference to the definition in s. 49 of the Act of 1956; see Sched. VII, para. 44, of that Act and *ante*, § 67 *et seq.*
[6] 5 & 6 Geo. 5, c. 38.

thereof are demanded by the trustees, and this power was exercised, in the cases of certain classes of trade publications, by a regulation of August 9, 1915.[7] By the British Museum Act, 1932,[8] it was provided that works of the classes mentioned in the Schedule (*i.e.*, trade publications, time tables, texts and similar works) need not be supplied to the trustees unless demanded, if such classes were prescribed by regulations made by the trustees, and regulations were made by the trustees on October 12, 1932.[9] It is understood that, although registers of voters are listed in these regulations, these are now regularly demanded. The Act of 1915 was repealed, but regulations made thereunder are to be deemed to have been made under the Act of 1932, which is unaffected by the Copyright Act, 1956. Copies are likewise to be delivered for the benefit of the Bodleian Library, Oxford, the University Library, Cambridge, the Library of the Faculty of Advocates at Edinburgh,[10] the Library of Trinity College, Dublin and, subject to certain restrictions, the National Library of Wales, at any time within a month after a written demand made within twelve months after publication or within one month after publication if demand is made before publication. In the case of an encyclopedia, newspaper, review, magazine, or work published in a series of numbers or parts the written demand may include all numbers or parts of the work which may be subsequently published.[11]

633 **National Library of Wales.** As regards the National Library of Wales, the Board of Trade has power to make regulations specifying classes of books whereof copies need not be delivered to that library. Accordingly the Board has issued regulations whereby copies cannot be demanded of certain classes of books.[12]

634 **Meaning of " book."** For the purposes of section 15 of the Act of 1911, the expression " book " includes every part or division of a book, pamphlet, sheet of letterpress, sheet of music, map, plan, chart or table separately published, but does not include any second or subsequent edition of a book, unless such edition contains additions or alterations either in the letterpress or in the maps, prints, or other engravings belonging thereto.[13]

635 **What copies are to be delivered.** The copy to be delivered to the British Museum must be one of the best copies published,[14] but the

7 S.R. & O. 1915 No. 773, Appendix B, § 1606.
8 22 & 23 Geo. 5, c. 34, Appendix A, § 1549.
9 S.R. & O. 1935 No. 278, Appendix B, § 1608.
10 It is provided by the National Library of Scotland Act, 1925, that the privileges enjoyed by this body shall thereafter be transferred to the National Library of Scotland.
11 Copyright Act, 1911, s. 15 (2).
12 The National Library of Wales (Delivery of Books) Regulations, 1924, as amended in 1956, Appendix B, § 1607; and see Copyright Act, 1911, s. 15 (5).
13 Copyright Act, 1911, s. 15 (7).
14 s. 15 (3).

copy for each of the other libraries is to be one of the copies of which the largest number is printed for sale.[15]

636 **Effect of failure to deliver copies.** Section 15 of the Act of 1911 does not make delivery of the copies a condition of copyright. The only effect of non-compliance with the requirements of the section is to expose the publisher, upon whom, and not upon the author, the duty is imposed of delivering the requisite copies of the work, to a fine, not exceeding £5 and the value of the book, upon summary conviction.[16] That is to say, he is liable to a separate fine for each library in respect of which default is made.

637 **Foreign books published in England.** Section 29 of the Copyright Act, 1911, provided that, where that Act was applied by Order in Council to works first published in a foreign country, the provisions of that Act as to the delivery of copies of books should not apply to works first published in such country except so far as was provided by the Order.[17] This provision is not repeated in the Act of 1956. Moreover, it must be pointed out that section 15 of the Act of 1911 deals with all books published in the United Kingdom, irrespective of whether they are entitled to copyright protection or not, and does not use the expression " first published." It is understood that, while the libraries of deposit do not claim that every book, copies of which are issued to the public in the United Kingdom, falls within the section, they do make this claim where copies are so issued of a book upon which the imprint of a London publisher appears, whether alone or jointly with a foreign publisher, whether or not the work has been first published in another country.[18]

2.—DEPOSIT OF SCRIPTS

638 **Deposit of scripts of new plays.** Quite apart from the Copyright Acts, the Theatres Act, 1968,[19] requires delivery of copies of scripts of plays to the trustees of the British Museum. Thus, the Act of 1968 provides [20] that, with certain limited exceptions,[21] where there is given in Great Britain a public performance of a new play, being a performance based on a script, a copy of the actual script on which that performance was based must be delivered to the trustees of the British Museum free of charge within the period of one month beginning with the date of the performance; the trustees are required to give a written receipt for every script so delivered.

15 s. 15 (4).
16 s. 15 (6).
17 s. 29 (1), proviso (iii).
18 See discussion in Report of 1952 Copyright Committee, Cmd. 8662, paras. 60–65.
19 c. 54.
20 s. 11 (1).
21 s. 11 (4).

639 The Act of 1968 contains definitions of "script," "play," "public performance" and "public performance of a new play." Thus, "script" is defined as the text of the play (whether expressed in words or in musical or other notation) together with any stage or other directions for its performance, whether contained in a single document or not.[22] "Play" is defined as (a) any dramatic piece, whether involving improvisation or not, which is given wholly or in part by one or more persons actually present and performing and in which the whole or a major proportion of what is done by the person or persons performing, whether by way of speech, singing or action, involves the playing of a role, and (b) any ballet given wholly or in part by one or more persons actually present and performing, whether or not it falls within paragraph (a) of this definition.[23] "Public performance" is defined as including any performance in a public place within the meaning of the Public Order Act, 1936,[24] and any performance which the public or any section thereof are permitted to attend, whether on payment or otherwise.[23] Finally "public performance of a new play" is defined as a public performance of a play of which no previous public performance has ever been given in Great Britain, but does not include a public performance of a play which, either is based on a script substantially the same as that on which a previous public performance of a play given there was based, or is based substantially on a text of the play which has been published in the United Kingdom.[25]

640 **Effect of failure to deliver copies.** If the above mentioned requirements as to delivery are not complied with, then any person who presented the relevant performance is liable, on summary conviction, to a fine not exceeding £5.[26] However, it is provided that a person is not to be treated as presenting a performance of a play by reason only of his taking part therein as a performer.[27]

3.—SPECIAL EXCEPTIONS AS RESPECTS LIBRARIES AND ARCHIVES

641 **Position before the Act of 1956.** Evidence was given before the 1952 Copyright Committee that, having regard to technical developments, such as contact photography or micro-photography, facilities were now available for study and research which had not been considered at the passing of the Act of 1911. Demands were frequently made upon public libraries for photo-copies, of articles or parts of periodicals and books in their possession, by students and research workers. It was further pointed out that this problem was not met

22 s. 9 (2).
23 s. 18 (1).
24 1 Edw. 8 & 1 Geo. 6, c. 6.
25 s. 11 (3).
26 s. 11 (2).
27 s. 18 (2).

by the exemption contained in section 2 (1) (i) of the Copyright Act, 1911, in respect of fair dealing with a work for the purposes of private study or research. This provision would, no doubt, protect the student who, himself, copied out passages from a book in a library for his own private use, but would not, it was thought, protect a librarian who produced such copies by photographic means. On the other hand, there were serious practical difficulties in obtaining permission to copy, without undue delay and expense. It was understood that the Royal Society had already taken into consideration this problem, as far as concerns periodical literature of a scientific or technical kind, and made arrangements under which non-profit-making organisations were authorised to deliver a single reproduction of a part of an issue to a person establishing that he required it solely for the purpose of private study or research and gave suitable undertakings. The Committee recommended a more general application of an arrangement of this sort.[28]

642 **Section 7 of the Act of 1956.** The Act of 1956, in section 7, in fact, deals with three classes of cases of copying by libraries, namely, the copying of articles from periodicals, the copying of parts of published works, and the copying of complete works for use by other libraries.

643 **Copying of articles from periodicals.** In the first place, the librarian of a library is entitled to make and supply a copy of an article contained in a periodical publication, subject to regulations to be made by the Board of Trade as in the section provided.[29] " Article " is defined as including an item of any description [30] and, where the article is accompanied by one or more artistic works provided for explaining or illustrating it, such illustrations may also be copied.[31]

The regulations to be made by the Board of Trade are to prescribe the class of library to be entitled to the privilege and, in particular, that they are not established or conducted for profit.[32] They are also to make provision to secure that the copies are supplied only to persons satisfying the librarian, or a person acting on his behalf, that they require them for purposes of research or private study and will not use them for any other purpose; that no person is furnished with two or more copies of the same article; that no copy extends to more than one article in any one publication, and that the persons to whom copies are supplied are required to pay for them a sum not less than the cost attributable to their production, including a contribution to the general expenses of the library.[33]

28 Cmd. 8662, para. 45.
29 Copyright Act, 1956, s. 7 (1).
30 s. 7 (10).
31 s. 7 (9).
32 s. 7 (1) (2).
33 s. 7 (2).

644 **Copying of parts of published works.** Libraries, to be prescribed in the same manner, are also to be entitled to make and supply copies of parts of published literary, dramatic or musical works, which will, again, include any illustrations.[34] Similar safeguards are to be prescribed by regulations to be made by the Board of Trade.[35] Furthermore, this privilege is only to be exercised if the name and address of a person entitled to authorise the making of the copy is not known to the librarian and could not be ascertained by him by reasonable inquiry.[35] It will be observed that, if the name and address of such a person is known, the fact that it may be difficult to communicate with him because of distance, does not entitle the librarian to make use of the privilege. In connection with the copying of parts of published works, the Board of Trade is to make regulations securing that no copy to which the regulations apply extends to more than a reasonable proportion of the work in question.[36]

645 **Copying of complete works for use by other libraries.** The third privilege is similar to the second, save that it only entitles the librarian to copy for purposes of supply to the librarian of another library of the class prescribed by the regulations.[37] This privilege, however, is wider than the second, in that it entitles the librarian to copy the whole of the work in question. If what is copied, in exercise of the third privilege, is an article in a periodical publication, it is not necessary for the librarian to establish that he did not know the identity of the owner of the copyright and could not, by reasonable inquiry, have ascertained it.[38]

646 **Copying typographical arrangements.** A further protection for librarians is contained in section 15 of the Copyright Act, 1956. That section confers copyright on the typographical arrangement of published editions; but it is provided, in subsection (4), that such copyright is not infringed by the making, by or on behalf of a librarian, of a reproduction of the typographical arrangement of the edition, if he is a librarian of a library of a class prescribed by regulations made by the Board of Trade, and the conditions prescribed by those regulations are complied with.

647 **Prescribed libraries.** Under Regulations made by the Board of Trade [39] the classes of library for the purposes of the foregoing provisions are prescribed. These include the libraries to which section 15 of the Copyright Act, 1911, applies, libraries of schools and universities, public libraries, parliamentary libraries and libraries of establishments conducted for various learned purposes.[40] The powers

[34] s. 7 (3) (9).
[35] s. 7 (3).
[36] s. 7 (2) (4).
[37] s. 7 (5).
[38] s. 7 (5), proviso.
[39] Copyright (Libraries) Regulations, 1957 (S.I. 1957 No. 868), Appendix B, § 1618.
[40] Regs. 1, 2 and 3, and First and Second Scheds.

to copy articles or parts of published works are only exercisable by such libraries, if not conducted for profit.[41] The power to copy for purposes of supply to another librarian, is exercisable by and for the benefit of any such libraries as aforesaid, and any library which makes works in its custody available to the public free of charge, and whether the supplying library is established or conducted for profit or not.[42] Moreover, the power extends to the supply of copies to a library of a similar class outside the United Kingdom, though this regulation will not necessarily protect the foreign librarian if the copy should be deemed an infringing copy by his local law. The wider class of libraries aforesaid is prescribed for the purposes of section 15.[43]

648 **Prescribed conditions.** The Regulations also prescribe the relevant conditions for the exercise of the respective powers. In the case of the powers to copy articles or parts of published works the applicant is required to sign a prescribed declaration and undertaking.[44] In the case of the power to copy for purposes of supply to another librarian, a second copy is not to be supplied unless the supplying librarian is satisfied that the former copy has been lost, destroyed or damaged, and any copy supplied is to be paid for with a sum not less than the cost.[45] In the case of copies of typographical arrangements, the Regulations provide that these may be made or supplied only in the circumstances, and upon the conditions, in and upon which a copy of that work or part may, by virtue of the provisions of Part I of the Act, be made or supplied without infringing the copyright in that work under Part I; provided that, in this case, it does not matter that the librarian knows or could obtain the name and address of the person entitled to authorise such copy.[46] This Regulation is somewhat uncertain in its effect since the original work, which is the subject of the typographical arrangement, may well be in the public domain. Presumably the Regulation means that the same conditions must be complied with, apart from the proviso, as would have been necessary under section 7 of the Act if the original work had been the subject of an existing copyright.

649 **Reproduction of unpublished works kept in libraries.** The remainder of section 7 of the Copyright Act, 1956, deals with a different kind of problem, which was also the subject of some discussion by the 1952 Copyright Committee.[47] In an increasing number of cases it is found that unpublished letters and manuscripts of historical or literary interest have been deposited with libraries or other institutions, and it may be in the general public interest that these should be published. In view, however, of the law regarding the

41 Reg. 1.
42 Regs. 2, 5 (*c*).
43 Reg. 3.
44 Reg. 4, Third Sched.
45 Reg. 5.
46 Reg. 7.
47 Cmd. 8662, para. 53.

term of copyright in unpublished works, in accordance with which a literary, dramatic or musical work which has not been published or performed in public at the death of the author, namely, that such copyright is to continue to subsist until the end of the period of fifty years from the end of the calendar year which includes the earliest occasion on which the work is published or performed,[48] copyright in unpublished manuscripts is perpetual. On the other hand, after the expiry of a long period, it is impracticable for anyone desiring to publish the material to ascertain with certainty in whom the copyright is vested. However, it might well be difficult to find a publisher prepared to take the risk of publishing, when a person might come forward able to prove a good title to the copyright.

Section 7 (6) of the Act of 1956 accordingly provides that, where the manuscript or a copy of an unpublished work kept in a library, museum or other institution at which it is open to public inspection, and more than fifty years has elapsed from the end of the calendar year in which the author died, and more than 100 years has elapsed after the end of the making of the work, then the work may be reproduced for purposes of research or private study, or with a view to publication.

650 **Publication thereof.** The point of the licence to reproduce with a view to publication is shown by subsection (7) which deals with a new work incorporating the whole or part of a work to which the provisions of the previous subsection apply. Subsection (6) enables the original unpublished work to be copied with a view to publication, and subsection (7) permits it to be lawfully published if, before the new work incorporating it is published, such notice of intended publication has been given as is prescribed by regulations made by the Board of Trade, and if the identity of the owner of the copyright in the old work was not known to the publisher of the new work. It is contemplated, therefore, that the proposed publication incorporating the manuscript work should be advertised and, if no one comes forward establishing a valid title, then the work may be safely published. It is further provided that any subsequent publication of the new work, either in the same or in an altered form, shall not be treated as an infringement of the copyright in the old work, provided that, if the subsequent publication incorporates a part of the old work which was not included in the new work as originally published, then a fresh notice will have to be given, and it will have to be established that the owner of the old work was not known at the date of the subsequent publication.[49] Although these provisions primarily apply only to literary, dramatic or musical works they may, as in the cases above referred to, also apply in respect of artistic

[48] Copyright Act, 1956, s. 2 (3).
[49] Copyright Act, 1956, s. 7 (7).

works provided for explaining or illustrating the work.[50] Where a work is lawfully published under these provisions it may also lawfully be broadcast, transmitted to subscribers to a diffusion service, performed in public or recorded.[51]

651 The Regulations[52] prescribed by the Board of Trade provide for two notices, one not less than three months and the other not less than two months before the intended date of publication with not less than one month between them. The notices are to be in a daily or Sunday newspaper with a national circulation in the United Kingdom, and the particulars to be given in the notices are set out.

4.—PUBLIC RECORDS

652 **Public records under the Act of 1956.** Section 42 of the Copyright Act, 1956, makes special provision as to public records. This section was originally concerned, by reason of subsection (1) (*a*) thereof, with records belonging to Her Majesty and under the charge and superintendence of the Master of the Rolls by virtue of an Order in Council under section 2 of the Public Record Office Act, 1838, and which were open to public inspection in accordance with rules made under that Act. The records in question were documents such as writs, proceedings, decrees, accounts, papers and documents of a public nature which were, by the Act of 1838, placed in the custody of the Master of the Rolls and directed to be deposited in the Public Record Office to be established under that Act.[53] The Act of 1838 was repealed by the Public Records Act, 1958,[54] s. 13 and Sched. 4, and, by virtue of section 11 and Schedule 3 of the Act of 1958, as respects any reproduction made after the commencement of that Act, the reference in section 42 (1) (*a*) of the Act of 1956 to records of the description there mentioned is to be taken as a reference to public records which are open to public inspection in pursuance of the provisions of the Act of 1958.[55] Section 42 of the Copyright Act, 1956, provides that the copyright in such a work is not infringed by the making or the supplying to any person of any reproduction of the work by or under the direction of any officer appointed under the Act of 1838. Since the Act of 1838 has been repealed by the Act of 1958 it is a little difficult to see how this exception is to apply in future. There are similar provisions in regard to records to which the Public Records Act (Northern Ireland), 1923, applies.[56]

[The next paragraph is 661]

50 s. 7 (9).
51 s. 7 (8).
52 The Copyright (Notice of Publication) Regulations, 1957 (S.I. 1957 No. 865), Appendix B, § 1611.
53 Copyright Act, 1956, s. 42 (2) (*a*).
54 6 & 7 Eliz. 2, c. 51.
55 See Public Records Act, 1958, ss. 5 and 10 and Sched. 1.
56 Copyright Act, 1956, s. 42.

Part III

COPYRIGHT IN SPECIAL CIRCUMSTANCES

CHAPTER 13

NEWSPAPERS, MAGAZINES AND PERIODICALS ENCYCLOPEDIAS AND OTHER COLLECTIVE WORKS

61 **Relevant definitions.** The Copyright Act, 1956, uses the expression " newspaper, magazine or similar periodical " in section 2 (6) (*a*), in defining an adaptation by means of pictures of a literary or dramatic work; in section 4 (2) of that Act dealing with the ownership of copyright in works made under a contract of service; and in section 6 (3) of that Act, in giving an exemption in respect of publication for the purpose of reporting current events. Section 7 of that Act refers to periodical publications in authorising copying of articles by certain libraries. These expressions are not defined in the Act of 1956, but their characteristic is clearly that there should be an element of recurrence in their form of publication. It must be doubted whether a publication, which is not intended to be repeated, would fall within the above expressions although published in a magazine format.

The Act of 1956 does not use the expression " collective work " as did the Act of 1911.

62 A " collective work " was defined by section 35 (1) of the Copyright Act, 1911, as meaning " (a) an encyclopedia, dictionary, year book, or similar work; (b) a newspaper, review, magazine, or similar periodical; and (c) any work written in distinct parts by different authors, or in which works, or parts of works, of different authors are incorporated."

Although the Act of 1911 gave a definition of a " collective work," it did not create copyright therein, and there were only two sections of that Act in which the expression occurred, namely, in section 5 (2), the proviso to which was not to apply to an assignment of the copyright in a collective work or a licence to publish a work, or part of a work, as part of a collective work, and section 24 (1) (*a*) (ii), which gave to the proprietor of a collective work the benefit of the extended term of copyright granted by the Act of 1911 to works which were the subject of copyright at the date of the commencement of that Act.[1] The expression is, nevertheless, a useful one to indicate a class of works which differ in principle from ordinary literary, dramatic or artistic works.

Moreover, the two sections of the Act of 1911 may still have

1 *Post*, Chap. 20.

importance in respect of works already in existence at the commencement of the Act of 1956.[2]

663 **Copyright in collective works.** The works dealt with in this chapter are to be distinguished from works of joint authorship which are works of two or more authors in which the contributions of the authors are not distinct.[3]

In the case of a collective work which is a compilation, there appear to be two distinct types of copyright, namely, (1) a copyright in the collective work, considered as a whole; and (2) separate copyrights in the works of the various contributors to the collective work. The "author" of the collective work as a whole will be the person who edits the work or arranges the various contributions. On the other hand, each contributor is the author of his own contribution.

664 **Ownership of such copyright.** The Copyright Act, 1956, however, contains special provisions as to the ownership of copyright in a literary, dramatic or artistic work made for the purpose of publication in a newspaper, magazine or similar periodical in the course of the author's employment by the proprietor of a newspaper, magazine or similar periodical under a contract of service or apprenticeship. In that event such proprietor is entitled to the copyright in the work, but only in so far as the copyright relates to publication of the work in any newspaper, magazine or similar periodical, or to reproduction of the work for the purpose of its being so published.[4] The author remains entitled to the remainder of the copyright in the work.[4] It is, however, provided that these provisions are to have effect subject, in any particular case, to any agreement excluding the operation thereof.[5] It is not provided that either the contract for the making of the work, or the agreement excluding the operation of the section, shall be in writing and, presumably, these may be implied, either from the terms of a particular contract, or from the circumstances of any particular case. It must also be borne in mind that the Act of 1956 not only provides for express assignments and licences in respect of copyright, but for agreements by the prospective owner of a future copyright which will have the effect of vesting the copyright in accordance with the agreement when the work is made.[6] Such assignments or agreements, however, must be in writing, unless they amount only to a bare licence not vesting any right in the licensee.[6]

665 **Old decisions.** Certain decisions before the commencement of the Copyright Act, 1911, might afford ground for argument that, even

[2] See, for instance, Copyright Act, 1956, Sched. 7, para. 28.
[3] *Post*, Chap. 14.
[4] Copyright Act, 1956, s. 4 (2).
[5] s. 4 (5).
[6] Copyright Act, 1956, ss. 36 and 37.

apart from contract of service, the copyright in articles commissioned for a collective work might belong to the proprietor. These cases decided that the court ought generally to draw the inference that, if an author is employed by the proprietor of an encyclopedia or similar work to contribute articles to that work, and is to be paid for his work, it is the intention of the parties that the copyright shall belong to the employer. The cases to this effect are *Sweet* v. *Benning*,[7] *Lamb* v. *Evans*,[8] and *Lawrence, etc., Ltd.* v. *Aflalo*,[9] all decided under section 18 of the Literary Copyright Act, 1842, the effect of which was to vest in the proprietor of any encyclopedia, review, magazine, periodical work, or work published in a series of books or parts, the copyright in articles contributed to the composite work, if those articles were paid for and were contributed " on the terms that the copyright therein shall belong to such proprietor."

666 It will be sufficient to set out the facts in *Lawrence, etc., Ltd.* v. *Aflalo.* There the respondent Aflalo was employed by the appellants, a firm of publishers, to edit an encyclopedia on sport, and it was a term of the agreement that the former was to be remunerated for his editorial services by a lump sum, for which he was to contribute certain articles without further fee. The respondent Cooke was also employed by the appellants to contribute certain articles to the encyclopedia at so much per thousand words. No express agreement was made as to copyright. The respondents duly contributed their articles, and the encyclopedia was published. Afterwards the appellants published a book called *The Young Sportsman*, containing copies of articles written by the respondents for the encyclopedia, and the respondents sought to restrain them from doing so. Joyce J. held that the circumstances were not such as to warrant the inference that the copyright was to belong to the publishers, and granted an injunction to restrain the publishers from publishing the articles in separate form.[10] Upon appeal this decision was affirmed by Romer L.J. and Stirling L.J., Vaughan Williams L.J. *dissentiente*,[11] but the House of Lords reversed the decisions of both Joyce J. and the Court of Appeal, holding that, upon the facts, the copyright was vested in the proprietors of the encyclopedia.[12] The House of Lords considered that the question in whom the copyright was vested depended on an inference of fact, and not of law, to be drawn by a reasonable man, from the nature of the contract and all the circumstances. From this point of view the House considered it was not reasonable to suppose that the appellants had paid their money for the right to publish the

[7] (1855) 16 C.B. 459.
[8] [1893] 1 Ch. 218.
[9] [1904] A.C. 17; and see *Chantry, etc., Co.* v. *Dey (T. H.)* (1912) 28 T.L.R. 499.
[10] [1902] 1 Ch. 264.
[11] [1903] 1 Ch. 318.
[12] [1904] A.C. 17.

articles in their encyclopedia, at the same time leaving it open to the respondents to publish their articles the next day in separate form. The House considered that the case was covered by the earlier decisions of *Sweet* v. *Benning* and *Lamb* v. *Evans* [13] to the same effect.

667 It is, upon the whole, submitted that the Acts of 1911 and 1956 have altered the inference to be drawn in cases where the facts are similar to those in *Lawrence, etc., Ltd.* v. *Aflalo.* It is clear that the case is overruled so far as it decided that the *legal* right to the copyright vested in the proprietors of the encyclopedia, for the respondents were not under a contract of service with the proprietor,[14] and it is only in such a case, or where there is an agreement in writing that, under the Act of 1956, the copyright could vest in the proprietor in the first instance. But if there is an agreement on the part of the contributor that the copyright in his contribution is to belong to the proprietor, an assignment of the copyright could be compelled, and in the meantime, the proprietor would have an equitable title thereto.[15] But it is submitted that, when the Act of 1956 provides that where an author is in the employment of some other person under a contract of service or apprenticeship, and the work is made in the course of his employment by that person, the legal right to the copyright is, in the absence of agreement to the contrary, to vest in the employer, it ought not to be held that the equitable right to the copyright in a work contributed by a paid contributor, not under a contract of service, vests in the employer, unless there is something more than mere employment and payment from which a contract to that effect can be inferred. Otherwise the contributor to a newspaper, magazine, or similar periodical, not under a contract of service, would be worse off than one who was under a contract of service, for the latter is deemed to have reserved to him the right to restrain the publication of the work otherwise than as part of a newspaper, magazine or similar periodical, whereas no such reservation would, presumably, be implied in favour of the former.

668 **Rights reserved to author.** The reservation, in Act of 1956, to the author, of the copyright in the work, otherwise than for publication in a newspaper, magazine or similar periodical, goes further than the similar provision of the Act of 1911 which merely, in the case of an author under a contract of service, reserved to the author the right to restrain the publication of the work otherwise than as part of a newspaper, magazine or similar periodical.[16] This provision, which remains applicable to works created before the commencement of the

[13] But see *Bishop of Hereford* v. *Griffin* (1848) 16 Sim. 190; *Walter* v. *Howe* (1881) 17 Ch.D. 708, where, however, *Sweet* v. *Benning* was not cited.
[14] See *ante*, § 325 *et seq.*, as to the meaning of "contract of service."
[15] *Ante*, § 353. See *Massine* v. *De Basil* [1936–45] Macg.Cop.Cas. 223.
[16] Copyright Act, 1911, s. 5 (1) (*b*).

Act of 1956,[17] was somewhat obscure in its operation. It is thought that the right reserved was not a limited copyright in the work, as the expression " the right to restrain " is inadequate to describe a limited copyright which would be the sole right to publish in any form other than in a newspaper, etc. On the other hand, there is nothing to limit the right to restrain to a right against the employer; such a limit would render the reservation valueless if the employer assigned. It is thought therefore that what the author obtained by the reservation was an arbitrary statutory right to restrain anyone from publishing the contribution except in a newspaper, but that this right did not allow the author or any licensee from him to publish, since this would be an infringement of the copyright in the contribution which was vested in the employer.[18]

The provision of the Act of 1956, however, clearly confers on the author complete rights of copyright in respect of publication otherwise than in a newspaper, magazine or similar periodical, and there is, in effect, a severance of the copyright just as in the case of a partial assignment. While the operation of section 4 (2) of the Act of 1956 may be excluded by agreement, it does not appear that it can be extended by agreement not amounting to an assignment, so that the employer or person placing the order cannot merely, by oral agreement, acquire more than the newspaper right in the work. If he wants to acquire more than this, it must be done by an agreement in writing under section 37 of the Act of 1956.

669 **Contract of service.** The meaning of a contract of service has been already discussed.[19] Persons on the regular staff of a periodical will, no doubt, usually be under contracts of service if their engagements are practically exclusive, but the mere fact that anyone is employed to supply contributions to a periodical at a fixed salary does not necessarily involve a contract of service. In the case of *Re Beeton & Co., Ltd.*,[20] questions arose as to whether certain contributors to a weekly periodical, belonging to a company which was in process of liquidation, were " clerks or servants " of the company within the meaning of section 209 of the Companies (Consolidation) Act, 1908,[21] so as to be entitled to preferential payment of the arrears of salary due to them. A was a director of the company and was also appointed " dress editress " at a fixed salary per annum. Her duties occupied practically the whole of her time and she did no similar work for a rival paper. B was also employed by the company at a fixed salary per annum to supply " fashion drawings " for the periodical, the company had a first call on her services, and her work occupied most

[17] Copyright Act, 1956, Sched. VII, para. 3.
[18] See *Sun Newspapers, Ltd.* v. *Whippie* (1928) 28 S.R.(N.S.W.) 473.
[19] *Ante*, § 325 *et seq.*
[20] [1913] 2 Ch. 279.
[21] 8 Edw. 7, c. 69.

of her time, but occasionally she did work for other publishers. C was employed at a fixed salary per annum to supply weekly articles and other information for the periodical, but she also wrote for other publishers. The court held that A was a "clerk or servant" of the company, but that B and C were not.

Of course, even though a person be on the regular staff of a paper and under a contract of service, he will retain the copyright in work done by him in his spare time and outside the scope of his employment.[22]

670 **Who can sue for piracy of any particular article?** The proprietor of a collective work can only sue in respect of the infringement of separate articles in so far as he is the owner of the copyright therein by assignment or under the provisions of section 4 of the Act of 1956, or under the provisions of section 19 of the Act of 1956, relating to an exclusive licensee. Of course, in so far as he is the owner of the copyright in the arrangement of the compilation he may sue for any infringement of his arrangement and, in the case of contributions to a directory, although the entries may be written by the persons referred to, the editor has been treated as the author of the complete set of contributions.[23]

671 **Copyright in news.** There can be no doubt that newspapers are "literary works" and, as such, entitled to copyright.[24]

There can be no copyright in news, as such, but only in the literary form given to news.[25] The courts have, nevertheless, in more than one case protected news agencies from having information obtained by them disseminated in breach of faith.[26]

672 In the case of *Walter* v. *Steinkopff*,[27] the proprietors of *The Times* brought an action against the proprietor and the publisher of the *St. James's Gazette* to restrain the defendants from further publishing any copy of a newspaper containing any copy of an article by Mr. Rudyard Kipling, or substantial portions thereof, and also certain other extracts taken from *The Times* and contained in twenty-two separate paragraphs of the *Gazette* of April 13. It was not denied by the defendants that they had copied some two-fifths of the Kipling

22 *Byrne* v. *Statist Co.* [1914] 1 K.B. 622.

23 *Black (A. and C.), Ltd.* v. *Claude Stacey, Ltd.* [1929] 1 Ch. 177.

24 *Cox* v. *Land and Water Journal Co.* (1869) L.R. 9 Eq. 324; *Walter* v. *Steinkopff* [1892] 3 Ch. 489; *Johnson* v. *George Newnes, Ltd.* [1894] 3 Ch. 633; *Walter* v. *Lane* [1900] A.C. 539. As to the right to the title of a newspaper, see *Licensed Victuallers' Newspaper Co.* v. *Bingham* (1888) 38 Ch.D. 139; *Borthwick* v. *The Evening Post* (1888) 37 Ch.D. 449; and *ante*, § 230 *et seq.*

25 *Per* North J., *Walter* v. *Steinkopff* [1892] 3 Ch. 489: and see *Football League, Ltd.* v. *Littlewoods Pools, Ltd.* [1959] Ch. 637 at 651.

26 *Exchange Telegraph Co., Ltd.* v. *Gregory & Co.* [1896] 1 Q.B. 147; *Exchange Telegraph Co., Ltd.* v. *Central News, Ltd.* [1897] 2 Ch. 48; *ante*, § 99.

27 [1892] 3 Ch. 489.

article, and all the extracts from *The Times*, practically verbatim, but it was contended that the consent of the proprietors of *The Times* might be assumed if the four following conditions were observed: (i) that the source of the information was acknowledged; (ii) that the paper copying and the paper copied were not direct rivals or competitors; (iii) that the paper copied from had also copied, thereby implying that it agreed to a free interchange of literary and other matter; (iv) that the editor of the paper copied had given no notice of his objection to matter being copied. It was proved by *The Times* that the copyright in the Rudyard Kipling article, and in some of the twenty-two paragraphs was vested in them. North J., in delivering judgment, said that it was said that there was no copyright in news, but there was or might be in a particular form of language or modes of expression by which information was conveyed, and not the less so because the information might be with respect to the current topics of the day. With regard to the quality of the matter copied, the paragraphs pirated were taken in their entirety for the very purpose for which they were used in *The Times, viz.*, to convey information to the readers of the paper. It was not a case of the selection of a part or quotation, or an extract. The defendants had failed to prove that the first three of the four alleged conditions had been observed, but even if they had, the plea of the existence of such a custom or practice of copying as was set up could no more be supported when challenged than the highwayman's plea of the custom of Hounslow Heath. It had often been relied on, but had always been repudiated by the courts. In the result, therefore, the defendants were entirely wrong.

673 **Letters, etc., sent to newspapers.** It may be mentioned here that letters and other manuscripts sent to the editor of a newspaper, as agent for the proprietor, are the property of the latter, and if the editor, after ceasing to be editor, attempts to use them for his own purposes, he will be restrained on the application of the proprietor, and be compelled to hand over such letters or other manuscripts.[28]

The normal custom in such matters recognises no obligation on the part of the proprietor of a newspaper to insure, or to preserve, any manuscript sent to him uninvited, and if the manuscript be lost or destroyed, the author cannot recover for its value.[29] Of course, if an editor or proprietor undertook to return unaccepted communications the case would be different.

674 The sending of a manuscript to a newspaper or periodical implies a licence to publish and, if the article is published, the publisher will be liable to pay the normal fee. If, however, before publication, there are

[28] *Hogg* v. *Kirby* (1803) 8 Ves. 215: see as to gift of manuscript *Thomas* v. *Times Book Company, Ltd.* [1966] 1 W.L.R. 911 and § 984, *post*.
[29] But see *Stone* v. *Long* [1901–04] Macg.Cop.Cas. 66.

detailed discussions about the form of publication and these never fructify, no licence to publish will be implied.[30]

675 **Alterations in communications made to newspapers.** Difficulties sometimes arise by reason of alterations made in the matter communicated by correspondents and others to newspapers. It is necessary to consider two cases. Where the author has assigned his copyright to the newspaper his only cause of action is for the injury to his reputation [31] or, possibly malicious falsehood.[32] Where, however, he has only granted a licence to publish, it may be a term of the licence, express or implied, that no alteration shall be made. If such term is a condition precedent to the licence, a publication, with alterations, would give rise to an action for infringement of copyright, but, if not, there would merely be a right of action for breach of contract. Apart from special contract, contributors to newspapers will probably be taken to have accepted the ordinary custom that editors may make alterations in unsigned articles, but the court will readily imply a term that no substantial alteration may be made to a signed article without the author's consent.[33] Goff J., in approving this passage and a further passage [34] in the case of *Frisby* v. *British Broadcasting Corporation*,[35] said that a licence may expressly or impliedly require publication in an unaltered form or that no substantial alteration be made, but that, in the absence of such a prohibition, the licensee had a right to make alterations, even substantial ones. He continued that a licence did not, *per se,* require the licensee to do anything. It merely protected him from an action for infringement. Without the licence he could not make any substantial use of the copyright material. If a person did that without a licence, then he was liable whether he had reproduced it verbatim or made alterations, even substantial ones. But if he had a licence, then he could set that up as a defence equally whether he had copied verbatim or made alterations, unless and save in so far as the terms of the licence, expressly or impliedly, required him not to make alterations, but he added, the court would readily imply a term limiting the right to make alterations.

Alterations may be so substantial as to make the editor the author of the work [36] or to raise a question of joint authorship.

676 **Strip cartoon may infringe.** A new right which is conferred in respect of literary and dramatic works by the Act of 1956, affects

[30] *Hall-Brown* v. *Iliffe & Sons, Ltd.* [1928–35] Macg.Cop.Cas. 88.

[31] *Archbold* v. *Sweet* (1832) 5 C. & P. 219; but see *Lee* v. *Gibbings* (1892) 67 L.T. 263; *Humphreys* v. *Thomson & Co., Ltd.* [1905–10] Macg.Cop.Cas. 148; *post,* Chap. 21.

[32] See § 251 *et seq., ante.*

[33] *Joseph* v. *National Magazine Co., Ltd.* [1959] Ch. 14.

[34] § 988, *post.*

[35] [1967] Ch. 932.

[36] *Springfield* v. *Thame* (1903) 89 L.T. 242.

newspapers. Under section 2 (6) (*a*) (iv) of that Act it is provided that a version of a work, in which the story or action is conveyed wholly or mainly by means of pictures in a form suitable for reproduction in a book or in a newspaper, magazine or similar periodical, shall be treated as an adaptation of the work and, consequently, the reproduction or publication of such an adaptation will be an infringement of copyright in the literary or dramatic work adapted.[37] A pictorial representation of the plot of a book or play will, therefore, now constitute an infringement, although no words are employed in the representation.

677 **Statutory defences.** Certain of the exceptions from acts which would otherwise constitute infringements of copyright particularly affect newspapers. Thus it is not an infringement of the copyright in a literary, dramatic or musical work to make a fair reproduction for purposes of criticism or review, whether of the work reproduced or of another work, provided that there is a sufficient acknowledgment.[38] There is a similar exception in the case of artistic works.[39] Again it is not an infringement of copyright in literary, dramatic or musical works to make a fair reproduction for the purpose of reporting current events in a newspaper, magazine or similar periodical, provided that there is a sufficient acknowledgment.[40] Such an acknowledgment must identify the work reproduced by its title or other description, and must identify the author, unless the work is anonymous, or the author has agreed or required that no acknowledgment of his name should be made.[41] The copyright in a literary, dramatic, musical or artistic work is not infringed by reproducing it for the purposes of a report of a judicial proceeding.[42] The Act of 1956 does not, as did the Act of 1911,[43] contain special provisions about reporting lectures or addresses, but it is thought that the foregoing provisions, about fair reproduction for the purpose of conveying news, have substantially the same effect.

Periodicals of a scientific or technical nature may be affected by the provisions of section 7 of the Act of 1956 which give powers to libraries to copy articles from periodicals, with accompanying illustrations, for the use of students, or for the use of other libraries.[44]

678 **Newspapers and damages for conversion.** Newspapers and periodicals with large circulations will be particularly affected by the remedy, given to the copyright owner, to recover damages for conversion of infringing copies. Damages in such cases are assessed by

37 Copyright Act, 1956, s. 2 (5) (*g*).
38 s. 6 (2).
39 s. 9 (2).
40 s. 6 (3).
41 s. 6 (10).
42 ss. 6 (4) and 9 (7).
43 Copyright Act, 1911, ss. 2 (1) (i) and (v) and 20.
44 See § 641 *et seq.*, *ante*.

reference to the value of all infringing material circulated and, if a substantial part of an issue with a large circulation is held to be an infringement, the damages may be considerable. Section 18 (2), of the Act of 1956, provides that a plaintiff shall not be entitled to damages or other pecuniary remedy on the conversion basis, if the defendant proves that he believed and had reasonable grounds for believing that the material did not constitute infringing copies of the work. If, therefore, the editor of a newspaper or periodical takes reasonable steps to ascertain that the material he publishes does not infringe copyright, he should escape liability on this basis, although damages for infringement, as distinct from damages for conversion, will remain recoverable.

679 **Pictures submitted by press photographers.** A common feature of newspaper production is the publication of pictures and photographs illustrating the topics of the day, and various agencies exist for supplying the press with such illustrations. The practice is for these agencies to submit prints of photographs to the newspapers, upon the understanding that these papers shall be at liberty to use such of these prints as they desire, but without any obligation upon the papers to use all or any of the prints. If they publish any of the prints, then an agreed fee is payable for each picture used. The legal effect of this arrangement is that, in the absence of any evidence to the contrary, the agency makes an offer to the papers to permit them to use the pictures submitted for publication in the papers, upon payment of the agreed sum. Like all offers, however, made without consideration, this offer is liable to be revoked by notice, and therefore the proprietors of the papers cannot insist upon a right to publish pictures which have been submitted to them by the agency, after the agency has given notice of the withdrawal of their permission, and this notwithstanding that the papers have used any picture previously to the revocation of the permission and have the necessary blocks for printing the same in their possession.[45]

680 **Advertisements.** While, under the law before 1911, some doubt had been expressed on the point,[46] there can be no question but that advertisements are now entitled to copyright protection, either as literary works, or as artistic works or as a combination of both. The copyright, or copyrights, in each individual advertisement is or are vested in the advertiser or his agent, but the proprietor of the newspaper may have a copyright in the arrangement of classified advertisements as a compilation.[47] The ownership of copyright, or

[45] *Bowden Bros.* v. *Amalgamated Pictorials, Ltd.* [1911] 1 Ch. 386.
[46] *Lamb* v. *Evans* [1892] 3 Ch. 462, on appeal [1893] 1 Ch. 218.
[47] See *John Fairfax & Sons Pty., Ltd.* v. *Australian Consolidated Press, Ltd.* [1960] S.R.(N.S.W.) 413.

copyrights, as between advertiser and agent may present some difficulty, particularly where the material is supplied by the advertiser and arranged by the agent.

681 **Nom de plume.** Although there cannot be any copyright in a *nom de plume,* in a case where the plaintiff had been in the habit of contributing articles to a newspaper under a *nom de plume* which she had invented, the court held that, as against the proprietor of the paper, the plaintiff was entitled to the exclusive right to print, publish, and use her *nom de plume* after her connection with the publication had ceased, upon the ground that the newspaper, by continuing to publish articles under the same *nom de plume,* was likely to deceive the public into the belief that the articles were contributed by the plaintiff.[48] In a more recent case [49] the court came to the same conclusion, although the *nom de plume* had been suggested by the editor of the newspaper. The court treated the matter as a question of the proper implication to be derived from the contractual relationship between the parties, and came to the conclusion that, apart from express provision, it would be reasonable to imply that an author would not allow his identity to be cloaked under a *nom de plume,* unless he was entitled to continue to use it after the severance of his relationship with the paper. In the case of *Crookes* v. *Petter,*[50] a dispute arose between the proprietors and editor of a journal, and the court refused to restrain the proprietors from omitting the editor's name from the title page on the ground that it formed no part of the title.

[The next paragraph is 691]

48 *Landa* v. *Greenberg* (1908) 24 T.L.R. 441; and see generally as to the right to a name or title, *ante,* §§ 230 *et seq.*, 240.

49 *Forbes* v. *Kemsley Newspapers, Ltd.* [1951] 2 T.L.R. 656.

50 (1860) 6 Jur.(N.S.) 1131.

CHAPTER 14

WORKS OF JOINT AUTHORSHIP

691 **Definition.** For the purposes of the Copyright Act, 1956, a work of joint authorship means " a work produced by the collaboration of two or more authors in which the contribution of each author is not separate from the contribution of the other author or authors." [1] All the collaborators must answer the description of " authors," and, therefore, if one person is merely the medium for transmitting to paper or canvas the original work of another, that is not a joint work,[2] and a person who merely suggests the idea without contributing anything to the literary or dramatic form in which copyright subsists is not a joint author,[3] nor is a person who revises and makes minor additions to an existing work.[4]

692 **Rights of co-authors inter se.** Co-authors hold the copyright as tenants in common rather than as joint tenants,[5] and, presumably, in the absence of agreement to the contrary, in equal shares. Upon the death of one co-author, therefore, his interest does not pass to his co-authors, but to his personal representatives as part of his estate. One of several authors cannot, therefore, grant a licence to publish which will be binding upon the others [6]; but, on the other hand, one of the joint authors can sue in respect of an infringement and obtain an injunction and his share of damages [7] without joining the other authors as plaintiffs, and an author can obtain an injunction to restrain a joint author from publishing the joint work without his consent.[8]

693 **Subsistence of copyright in joint works.** If, however, the subsistence of copyright in a work depends upon the author being a qualified person, that is to say, if it is an unpublished work, or a work

1 Copyright Act, 1956, s. 11 (3); and see *Taylor (R. A. R.)* v. *Prior (L.)* (1957) *The Author,* LXVII, No. 3 at 60.
2 *Ante,* § 302.
3 *Tate* v. *Thomas* [1921] 1 Ch. 503; *Evans* v. *Hulton E. & Co., Ltd.* [1924] W.N. 130.
4 *Samuelson* v. *Producers' Distributing Co., Ltd.* (1932) 48 R.P.C. 580.
5 *Lauri* v. *Renad* [1892] 3 Ch. 402. It is true that the authority of this decision is diminished by the fact that Kekewich J. considered that *Powell* v. *Head* (1879) 12 Ch.D. 686, was conclusive on the point, whereas no such point was involved in that decision, for the persons there held to be tenants in common were each assignees of a moiety of the copyright from the author. It is, nevertheless, submitted that it is reasonably clear that the statement in the text is correct. See, however, *Marzials* v. *Gibbons* (1874) L.R. 9 Ch. 518.
6 *Powell* v. *Head, supra.*
7 *Quaere,* whether he could not recover the full amount of damages, subject to a liability to account to his co-authors.
8 *Cescinsky* v. *George Routledge & Sons, Ltd.* [1916] 2 K.B. 325.

first published otherwise than in the United Kingdom or a country to which the Act of 1956 extends, then, if one or more of the authors is, or are, not qualified persons, and another or others is, or are, qualified persons, the work is to be treated as a work in which copyright subsists,[9] but the author or authors who is, or are, qualified persons are to be treated as the sole owner, or sole owners, of the copyright for the purposes of the Act of 1956.[10]

Suppose that A and B jointly produce a work, A being a British subject, and B a foreigner not resident in the United Kingdom, at the time when the work was made, nor entitled to protection under the international provisions of the Act of 1956.[11] In such a case B would not, while the work is unpublished, be entitled to any protection if he were the sole author,[12] and consequently A is to be treated, for the purposes of the Act, as if he were the sole author.

Although A is to be treated as the sole author for ascertaining legal ownership of copyright under the Act of 1956, it does not, of course, follow that B, in the circumstances we are now supposing, has no rights as against A. A is no doubt considered to be the legal owner of the entire copyright, and he—and he alone—could bring an action for infringement, but he may have contractual obligations towards B, and, in the absence of agreement to the contrary, he would probably be regarded as trustee of the copyright for himself and B in equal shares.

But A, apparently, could, while the work remained unpublished, alone grant licences in respect of the work.[13]

694 If, however, the work is first published in the United Kingdom all the authors become legally entitled to the copyright.[14] What, then, is the position, supposing the author who, prior to publication, was considered as the sole author, granted a licence to publish contrary to the wishes of his co-author? It is thought that the publisher is not exposed to an action for infringement at the instance of the latter, but that he can rely upon the licence obtained from the author who, at the time when the licence was given, had the legal right to grant it.

695 **Publication of joint works.** It is provided by section 49 (3) of the Act of 1956 that, in determining, otherwise than in relation to questions of infringement, whether a work has been published, first published, or published in the lifetime of a person, no account is to be taken of any unauthorised publication. If copyright did not subsist in the work, publication is to be taken to have been unauthorised, if

[9] Copyright Act, 1956, Sched. III, para. 1.
[10] Sched. III, para. 4.
[11] s. 32.
[12] See *ante*, § 57.
[13] *Lauri* v. *Renad* [1892] 3 Ch. 402; *Powell* v. *Head* (1879) 12 Ch.D. 686; *Trade Auxiliary Co.* v. *Middlesbrough, etc., Association* (1889) 40 Ch.D. 425.
[14] *Ante*, § 66 *et seq.*

done otherwise than by or with the licence of the author or persons lawfully claiming under him.[15] Here the question of authorship arises without reference to ownership of copyright and it would seem, therefore, that the consent of all authors is required, whether any are or are not qualified persons in accordance with the general provision at the end of the Third Schedule to the Act of 1956 (paragraph 6), that, subject to the provisions of the Schedule, any reference in that Act to the author of a work is to be construed, in relation to a work of joint authorship, as a reference to all the authors of the work.

696 **Husband and wife co-authors.** It was provided by subsection (4) of section 16 of the Act of 1911 that, where a married woman and her husband are joint authors of a work, the interest of the married woman should be her separate property. The Law Reform (Married Women and Tortfeasors) Act, 1935,[16] having, in section 1, provided that a married woman should be capable of acquiring, holding, and disposing of, any property in all respects as if she were a *feme sole*, the Second Schedule of the Act amended section 16 (4) by repealing the word " separate." Section 16 (4) of the Act of 1911 is not repeated in the Act of 1956, presumably being thought unnecessary, as it seems clear that the interest of a married woman in a joint work is her own property, whether or not the other author is her husband.

697 **Term of copyright in joint works.** There was no definite decision as to the term of copyright in a joint work under the law before 1911, but probably a literary work was entitled to protection during the life of the longest liver of the co-authors and for a period of seven years from his death or for a period of forty-two years, whichever period was the longer.[17]

The Act of 1911 provided that, in the case of a work of joint authorship, copyright was to subsist during the life of the author who first died and for a term of fifty years after his death, or during the life of the author who died last, whichever period was the longer.[18]

The Act of 1956 has altered the law again in favour of the longer period and provided that the duration of copyright in a work of joint authorship is to be determined by reference to the date of death of the author who died last [19] but, where the copyright in a work of joint authorship has expired before the commencement of the Act of 1956 in accordance with the provisions of the Act of 1911, the extended term conferred by the Act of 1956 will not apply to the work.[20] It would seem that a joint author may be the person to be considered

[15] Copyright Act, 1956, s. 49 (3).
[16] 25 & 26 Geo. 5, c. 30.
[17] *Nottage* v. *Jackson* (1883) 11 Q.B.D. 627, 637.
[18] Copyright Act, 1911, s. 15 (1).
[19] Copyright Act, 1956, Sched. III, para. 2.
[20] Copyright Act, 1956, Sched. VII, para. 10.

for the purpose of establishing the term of copyright in the work, notwithstanding that he is not a qualified person and therefore not to be considered in relation to the subsistence or ownership of copyright in the work. This was expressly stated in the proviso to section 16 (2) of the Act of 1911 but, although this proviso is not repeated in the Third Schedule to the Act of 1956, there seems no reason to doubt that the expression " author," in paragraph 2 of that Schedule, is used in its normal and natural meaning.

698 **The present period of protection.** Summarising the position, the normal period of copyright in the case of a joint literary, dramatic, musical or artistic work will be a term continuing until the end of a period of fifty years from the end of the calendar year in which the last surviving author dies.[19] In the case, however, of literary, dramatic and musical works and engravings which have not been published, performed in public, offered for sale as records or broadcast during the life of the last surviving author, copyright will subsist for a different period, namely, until the end of the period of fifty years from the end of the calendar year which includes the earliest occasion on which one of these acts is done.[19]

699 **Pseudonymous and anonymous joint works.** Where a joint work other than a photograph is published, and the names of all authors are pseudonyms, and the identity of the authors is not known and cannot be ascertained by reasonable inquiry, copyright will continue to subsist until the end of the period of fifty years from the end of the calendar year in which the work was first published and will then expire.[21] If, however, a joint work is published under a pseudonym or pseudonyms, but one or more of the authors' true names is disclosed, or becomes known, or capable of being ascertained by reasonable inquiry within fifty years of publication of the work, then the authors or author whose name is known, or can be so ascertained are, or is, to be treated as the sole authors, or author, for the purpose of ascertaining the term of copyright in the work by reference to a period from their deaths, or death.[22] There is no similar provision about anonymous works which are in fact works of joint authorship. Presumably, however, if an author admits that his work was a joint work in collaboration with a person whose name is not to be disclosed, the term of copyright would in fact be reckoned by reference to the date of death of the known author since this, alone, would be an ascertainable fact.

700 **Statutory presumptions and joint works.** It is expressly provided, in section 20 (3) of the Act of 1956 that, in the case of a work alleged

[21] Sched. II, paras. 1, 2 and 3.
[22] Sched. III, para. 3.

to be a work of joint authorship, the presumption that a person named as author on published copies is the author and did not make the work in circumstances vesting the work in someone else is to apply in relation to each person alleged to be one of the authors of the work as if references, in the subsection conferring the presumption, to the author, were references to one of the authors. There is no similar provision in relation to the presumptions under subsections (5) and (6) of that section, and, accordingly, paragraph 6 of the Third Schedule to the Act of 1956 presumably applies, so that the word "author," in subsections (5) and (6) of section 20 of that Act, has to be construed as a reference to all the authors of the work.

701 **Application of twenty-five-year period.** It will be remembered that, by section 3 of the Act of 1911, it was provided that, in the case of the work of a single author published in his lifetime, the period of post-mortem copyright should be divided into two periods during the first period of twenty-five years the work being entitled to unrestricted protection, but during the last twenty-five years anybody being at liberty to reproduce the work upon payment of a royalty.[23] Further, it was provided by section 5 (2) of that Act, that this latter modified copyright was to be incapable of assignment by an author, except by will.[24] Section 3 of the Act of 1911 continues to be applicable where a notice to reproduce was given before the commencement of the Act of 1956 [25] and the proviso to section 5 (2) of the Act of 1911 continues to apply to assignments made before the commencement of the Act of 1956.[26] It is still, therefore, material to consider how these provisions apply to joint works. There was no mention of joint authorship in section 3 of the Act of 1911 and, therefore, it seemed open to contend that its proviso did not apply to joint works at all. Section 16 of the Act of 1911, again, did not in so many words refer, as section 17 of that Act did, to this proviso, but it contained a general provision that "references in this Act to the period after the expiration of any specified number of years from the death of the author shall be construed as references to the period after the expiration of the like number of years from the death of the author who dies first or after the death of the author who dies last, whichever period may be the shorter." This provision was not, perhaps, a model of clear draftsmanship, but, in applying it to the proviso to section 3 of the Act of 1911, its effect would appear to be that, the period of absolute copyright ends, either at the expiration of twenty-five years from the death of the author who dies first, or immediately upon the death of the author who dies last, whichever

23 *Ante*, § 276.
24 *Ante*, § 369.
25 Copyright Act, 1956, Sched. VII, para. 9.
26 Sched. VII, para. 28 (3).

date happens to be the later. In this way it secured—as was only fair—that so long as any of the joint authors was still living the copyright was absolute, but that, if the period between the death of the author who died first and the author who died last was more than twenty-five years, the period (if any) during which anybody was at liberty to reproduce the work upon a royalty basis commenced immediately upon the death of the latter author. This view is confirmed by the fact that paragraph 9 of the Seventh Schedule to the Act of 1956, continuing the effect of section 3 of the Act of 1911 where notice has been given, expressly refers to sections 16 and 17 of the Act of 1911.

So far as the revesting under section 5 (2) of the Act of 1911 is concerned, paragraph 28 of the Seventh Schedule to the Act of 1956 provides that a document made before the commencement of the Act of 1956 is to have the same effect in regard to title under the Act of 1956 as it had in regard to title under the Act of 1911 including the operation of section 5 (2). Accordingly it would appear that, where an assignment has been made in respect of a work of joint authorship before 1956, and the copyright is still subsisting at the commencement of the Act of 1956, then the work enjoys an extended term, because it is now ascertained by reference to the author who died last. The benefit of the extended term will pass to the personal representatives of the authors.[27]

702 **Meaning of " author " in relation to joint works under the Act of 1956.** It has been stated that, in general, the word " author," in the Act of 1956, is to be construed as a reference to all the authors of the work.[28] This is, of course, subject to what has already been said in regard to ownership and term of copyright and two other special cases. In the first place, the right to copy unpublished manuscripts deposited in a library or institution is not to be exercised, in the case of a joint work less than fifty years from the end of the calendar year in which the last surviving author died.[29] Again, the permission to include a short passage from a published literary or dramatic work in a collection intended for use of schools is specially modified in connection with a work of joint authorship.[30] Permission does not apply, if, in addition to the passage in question, two or more other excerpts from works by the author thereof are contained in that collection, or are contained in that collection taken together with every similar collection published by the same publisher within a period of five years preceding the publication of the collection.[31] In this proviso the expression " excerpts from works by the author " is to be taken to

[27] Copyright Act, 1956, Sched. VII, para. 28.
[28] Sched. III, para. 6.
[29] Sched. III, para. 2.
[30] Sched. III, para. 5.
[31] s. 6 (6).

include a reference to excerpts from works by the author in collaboration with another person, and, if the passage is from a work of joint authorship, is to be taken to include a reference to excerpts from works by any one or more of the authors of that passage, or by any one or more of those authors in collaboration with any other person.[30]

[The next paragraph is 708]

CHAPTER 15

WORKS OF ARCHITECTURE

708 **History of architects' protection.** Architects, for many years, claimed for their works similar protection to that accorded to works of sculpture. The justice of this claim was recognised in some foreign countries, even prior to the revision of the Berne Convention after the conference of the Powers at Berlin in the year 1908, but, prior to that revision, no party to the Berne Convention was compelled to accord copyright protection to architectural works themselves, as distinguished from architectural plans and sketches. But, under the Revised Convention, works of architecture were included amongst the subjects to which all countries, parties to that Convention, were bound to grant protection.[1]

709 The committee appointed by the British Government, in the year 1909, to consider what alterations in the English law were necessary or advisable in order that England should come into line with the other countries who were parties to the Revised Convention of Berne, only by a majority reported in favour of the inclusion of works of architecture amongst the subjects of copyright. Further opposition to the claims of architects was met during the passage of the Copyright Bill through Parliament. The architects, however, triumphed to this extent, that " architectural works of art " were included amongst the works to be protected under the Copyright Act, 1911, although the remedies for the infringement of the copyright in those works were considerably less drastic than those inserted in the Bill as originally laid before Parliament.

710 The Act of 1911, therefore, not only preserved the right of the architect to copyright in his plans, which had existed under the old law, but created a new right by including " architectural works of art " amongst artistic works capable of enjoying copyright protection. It was unsuccessfully contended in the case of *Meikle* v. *Maufe*[2] that there could not be a separate copyright in a building, as distinct from a copyright in the plans on which the building is based, and in fact there seems no reason to doubt that the Act of 1911 created a new and distinct right.

711 **Present law.** The Act of 1956 has confirmed the position of architects in this respect by including, in the definition of artistic work,

[1] See Chap. 24, *post*.
[2] [1941] 3 All E.R. 144.

"works of architecture, being either buildings or models for buildings." [3]

712 So far as plans and sketches are concerned it was a little curious that, under the Act of 1911, plans were protected as "literary works," and sketches as "artistic works." This resulted from the definition of "literary works" contained in that Act, which included, amongst literary works, "maps, charts, plans, tables, and compilations," whereas an "artistic work" included a "drawing." [4] The Act of 1956, however, while continuing to include "drawings" in the definition of "artistic work," [5] then proceeds to define "drawing" as including any diagram, map, chart or plan.[6] Consequently, under the present law, all an architect's work is included in the definition of "artistic work," whether consisting of sketches, plans, elevations, diagrams or other two-dimensional representations, or whether it consists of actual buildings or models for buildings.

713 **Ownership of property and copyright in plans.** Copyright law does not alter the rule as to the prima facie ownership of an architect's plans, namely, that these generally become the property of the client.[7] But this rule does not mean more than that the sheets of paper, with the plans drawn upon them, belong to the client; it does not imply that the copyright in the plans passes to the client. This would only be so if the architect assigned the copyright in writing,[8] or he were under a contract of service with his client.[9] It should be observed, however, that under the Act of 1956, an architect, by an agreement in writing made before the plan or building is created, can confer on the client the future copyright in the work so that, when the work comes into existence, the client will be the owner of the copyright therein.[10] This provision, while not altering the position as to the ownership of the copyright in plans where no written contract exists, makes it easier, by suitable documents, to create the situation in which the copyright in the plans will vest in the client. Moreover, since the proviso to section 5 (2) of the Copyright Act, 1911, under which an author was not able to assign the last twenty-five years of the copyright term, is not repeated in the Act of 1956, it is now possible for the architect to vest the entire copyright for its full term in the client.

3 Copyright Act, 1956, s. 3 (1) (*b*).
4 Copyright Act, 1911, s. 35 (1).
5 Copyright Act, 1956, s. 3 (1) (*a*); see *Inala Industries Pty., Ltd.* v. *Associated Enterprises Pty., Ltd.* [1960] Q.S.R. 562.
6 Copyright Act, 1956, s. 48 (1).
7 *Gibbon* v. *Pease* [1905] 1 K.B. 810; *Ebdy* v. *M'Gowan* (1870), *Hudson's Building Contracts*, 4th ed., Vol. II, p. 9; see *Inala Industries Pty., Ltd.* v. *Associated Enterprises Pty., Ltd., supra.*
8 Copyright Act, 1956, s. 36.
9 s. 4.
10 s. 37 (1).

714 But unless the client has acquired the copyright in the plans, he may not copy them, nor may he reproduce the building in which copyright subsists as a work of architecture. It was held, under the Act of 1911, that a client for whom an architect had designed an existing building could not reproduce the plans or the building, even for the purpose of making extensions to that building.[11] This appears still to be the law, though it is provided in the Act of 1956 that where copyright subsists in a building as a work of architecture, the copyright is not infringed by any reconstruction of that building.[12] Also that, where a building has been constructed in accordance with architectural drawings or plans in which copyright subsists, and has been so constructed, by or with the licence of the owner of that copyright, any subsequent reconstruction of the building by reference to those drawings or plans is not to constitute an infringement of that copyright.[12] On the other hand, where the architect has parted with the copyright, it is not an infringement of the copyright for the architect to reproduce part of his work in a subsequent work by the use of sketches, plans, models or studies made for the purposes of the earlier work if the architect, in making the subsequent work, does not repeat or imitate the main design of the earlier work.[13] Furthermore, where the property in the completed plans passes to the client, it is doubtful whether the architect does not retain the property in all notes, sketches and other material used by him in preparation of the plans.[14]

715 Where the client has not acquired the copyright in the plans a problem which often arises is over the extent of the implied licence to use the plans where there are no express terms. The problem usually falls into two parts. First, what is the extent of use covered by the licence? For instance, does it extend to application for planning permission alone, or to obtaining planning permission and thereafter for use in constructing the building and so on? Secondly, who is entitled to the benefit of the licence, the original client, or the original client and anyone to whom he sells the site with the benefit of the planning permission, for instance? Clearly each case must depend on its own facts, but it is submitted that the wider the implied licence is alleged to be, the less likely the courts will be to find its existence.[14a]

716 The question of the extent of an implied licence to use an architect's plans has been considered recently in two cases, namely, *Stovin-Bradford* v. *Volpoint Properties, Ltd.*,[14a] and *Blair* v. *Osborne & Tomkins.*[15] In the first case it was held, on the facts, that the

11 *Meikle* v. *Maufe* [1941] 3 All E.R. 144.
12 Copyright Act, 1956, s. 9 (10).
13 s. 9 (9).
14 See *Leicestershire County Council* v. *M. Faraday & Partners, Ltd.* [1941] 2 K.B. 205.
14a *The Times*, July 29, 1970; aff. *The Times*, May 25, 1971.
15 [1971] 2 W.L.R. 503.

defendants had a licence to use the plaintiff's drawings to get planning permission, but were not entitled to use them thereafter without paying the plaintiff a further fee. Graham J. distinguished this case from the Australian case of *Beck* v. *Montana Constructions Pty., Ltd.*,[15a] where the parties contemplated that the plans might be used after the obtaining of planning permission. In the second case the plaintiff had prepared plans for the client for the purpose of obtaining full planning permission to build two houses on a site and had been paid the scale fee under the 1962 R.I.B.A. conditions for that work. The client sold the site with the benefit of the planning permission and the plaintiff's plans were used by another firm in erecting houses on the site. The Court of Appeal held that, in the circumstances of that case, the plaintiff had impliedly licensed the use of the plans for building on the site in substantial accordance with them, and whether by the client, or by the people to whom the plans were transferred.

717 The Court of Appeal in the second case approved the decision in *Beck* v. *Montana Constructions Pty., Ltd., supra.* In that case Jacobs J. held that the engagement for reward of a person to produce material of a nature which is capable of being the subject of copyright implies a permission, or consent, or licence in the person giving the engagement to use the material in the manner and for the purpose in which and for which it was contemplated between the parties that it would be used at the time of the engagement. Applying that principle to the case in question he concluded that the payment for plans included a permission or consent to use those plans for the purpose for which they were brought into existence, namely for the purpose of building a building in substantial accordance with them and for the purpose of preparing any necessary drawings as part of the task of building the building. The learned judge further held that it must inevitably be implied that the site owner, having commissioned the plans and having obtained the right to use them for the purpose of erecting on that site a building in substantial accordance with them, should have the right to transfer them to a new owner of the site.

718 **Works of architecture.** Under the Act of 1911 " architectual works of art " were included amongst " artistic works," and such a work was defined as meaning " any building or structure having an artistic character or design, in respect of such character or design, or any model for such building or structure, provided that the protection given by this Act shall be confined to the artistic character and design, and shall not extend to processes or methods of construction." [16]

15a [1964–65] N.S.W.R. 229; and see *Netupsky* v. *Dominion Bridge Co., Ltd.* (1969) 68 W.W.R. 529.

16 Copyright Act, 1911, s. 35 (1).

The Act of 1956, however, employs a much simpler definition and protects original works of architecture, being either buildings or models for buildings,[16a] "building" being defined as including any structure.[17] It is thought, however, that the simpler definition has not produced any substantial alteration in the law. While drawings and plans are protected "irrespective of artistic quality," these words are omitted in relation to works of architecture. Thus the position under the Act of 1911, under which architectural works were required to have "an artistic character or design" is, in effect, restored.

719 **How infringed.** Copyright is infringed by the production of something which, to the eye, is a copy of the original, and the use of processes or methods of construction would not, it is thought, constitute an infringement. No great significance seems to have been attached, in decisions under the Act of 1911, to the requirement of "artistic character or design," and it is doubted whether this meant more than that there must be something beyond the use of common stock features which would not be sufficient to constitute a copyright work. It was held that the requirement of originality did not imply more than that the work was the personal effort of the architect.[18] Again it was held that there was copyright in the design of certain semi-detached villas on the ground that they exhibited something apart from the common stock of ideas and which struck the eye as uncommon.[19]

But it is naturally more difficult to prove infringement of copyright in a plain building than in one showing marked originality. An architect, who has erected a facade showing six windows and a door, clearly could not complain of another building showing the like number of windows and doors, for each architect may have drawn from common sources. But if his plain building has been servilely copied down to the smallest detail, there seems no good reason for depriving him of the right to complain. Slight differences between buildings of no marked originality will prevent them from being held to be copies of each other, which would not be the case if the buildings were of an original character.

720 **Building or structure.** The design to be protected must be a building, or structure, or a model for the same. No general definition of the word "building" can be given,[20] although it has been said that, prima facie, a "building" means "a block of brick or stone work covered in by a roof." [21] But the words must be construed reasonably, having

16a Copyright Act, 1956, s. 3 (1) (*b*).
17 s. 48 (1).
18 *Chabot* v. *Davies* (1936) 155 L.T. 525.
19 *Blake* v. *Warren* [1928–35] Macg.Cop.Cas. 268.
20 *Per* Byles J., *Stevens* v. *Gourley* (1860) 7 C.B.(N.S.) 99.
21 *Moir* v. *Williams* [1892] 1 Q.B. 264. See also *Waite's Exors.* v. *Commissioners of Inland Revenue* [1914] 3 K.B. 196.

regard to the object of the statute.[22] Upon this principle, it is thought, that the building or structure must be of such a character as is usually erected upon the ground from plans with elevations, but that, if it be of such a character, it will be entitled to protection, not only as a whole, but in every architectural detail. For instance, a chimney-piece might, it is thought, be entitled to copyright. It has been held that a garden, consisting of a layout including steps, walls, ponds and other structures in stone, was capable of protection as "a structure." [23]

721 **First owner of copyright.** The copyright in a work of architecture will vest, in the first instance, in the person who has been the author of the artistic design.[24] It had been suggested, by Farwell J., that, in the case of a building, the author was the builder and not the architect.[25] But, in a more recent case,[26] Uthwatt J. held that the author of the copyright work in a building was the architect, on the ground that copyright protection was limited to the artistic character or design embodied in the building, in the creation of which the builder played no part. And it would seem that the same position arises under the Act of 1956. It will not be usual for an architect to be under a "contract of service or apprenticeship" [27] with the client who employs him to design a building, and the latter must remember that, if his building is copied, it will be the architect, and not himself, who will have the right to complain, unless he has obtained an assignment of the copyright in writing from the architect.[28] So the client will have no right to build other buildings from the plans which, as we have seen, will generally be his property, or even to make an enlargement of his existing building in the same design,[29] whilst the architect, unless he has expressly or impliedly agreed to the contrary,[30] will be at liberty to repeat the building.

Of course there are many cases in which architects are employed by companies or institutions on a full-time salaried basis where, in general, plans or designs created in the course of such employment will vest in the employer.

22 *Per* Lindley L.J. *Lavy* v. *London County Council* [1895] 2 Q.B. 577, 582. *British Transport Docks Board* v. *Williams* [1970] 1 W.L.R. 652. It is submitted, therefore, that cases decided under other Acts, *e.g.*, the London Building Acts, have little or no application. As to the erections that have been held to be "buildings or structures" under the London Building Act, see 3 Halsbury's *Laws of England*, 3rd ed., p. 428. See also *H. E. Dibble, Ltd.* v. *Moore* [1970] 2 Q.B. 181.

23 *Vincent* v. *Universal Housing Co., Ltd.* [1928–35] Macg.Cop.Cas. 275.

24 Copyright Act, 1956, s. 4 (1).

25 *Jackson* v. *Jones* (1934) unreported.

26 *Meikle* v. *Maufe* [1941] 3 All E.R. 144.

27 Copyright Act, 1956, s. 4; see § 321 *et seq., ante.*

28 See § 347, *ante.*

29 *Meikle* v. *Maufe, supra,* and see § 714, *ante,* as to right to reconstruct.

30 Probably an agreement not to repeat the building might be readily implied.

722 **"Publication."** It would seem that an architectual work of art will rarely be a published work. "Publication," for the purposes of the Act of 1956, means "the issue of reproductions of the work to the public," and the issue to the public of "photographs and engravings" of architectural works is not to be deemed publication. It is submitted that, not even the repetition of a building down to the smallest detail, would be a "publication" within the meaning of that Act, for that could hardly be regarded as an issue of reproductions "to the public." [31] Moreover, it is expressly provided that the construction of a work of architecture is not to constitute publication.[32] "Engravings" include etchings, lithographs, woodcuts, prints, and other similar works,[33] but do not include paintings and drawings. It would seem that the only way in which the architect could publish a work of architecture would be by issuing paintings or drawings to the public,[34] but this is a highly unlikely event. What would normally be issued would be an "engraving" of the painting or drawing.

723 **Foreign architects and works.** It consequently follows that, apart from international regulations, a foreign architect does not obtain copyright in buildings erected according to his designs in England, unless he is—as, no doubt, he usually would be—a "qualified person" during a substantial portion of the period during which the work was being made.[35] On the other hand, it follows, from the fact that construction is not publication, that a British architect could claim protection in England in respect of a piracy in England of the features of artistic character or design of a building erected by him in a foreign country.

724 **Term of copyright.** The fact of non-publication of an architect's work does not make any difference to the term of copyright. The period of protection will, in any case, be during the life of the author and fifty years after his death.[36]

725 **Infringement.** Architects are therefore concerned with infringements of their rights in three different forms. These are the copying of plans in the form of other plans,[37] the copying of plans in the form of buildings, and the copying of a building by another building.[38]

31 Copyright Act, 1956, s. 49 (2) (*c*). For the same reason the building will not be a publication of the plans: see note 37, below.
32 s. 49 (2) (*a*).
33 s. 48 (1).
34 Paintings and drawings do not infringe the copyright in the structure (Copyright Act, 1956, s. 9 (4)).
35 1956, ss. 1 (5), 3 (2). It is not very clear, however, whether the making of the work, in the case of an architectural work, consists in the preparation of the plans or the erection of the building. Copyright Act, 1956, s. 49 (4), does not apply to artistic works.
36 Copyright Act, 1956, s. 3.
37 See *Czezowski* v. *George W. Warr & King* (1959) 173 *Estates Gazette* 735, which was also concerned with the question of publication of plans.
38 See *Hay and Hay Construction Co., Ltd.* v. *Sloan* (1958) 12 D.L.R. (2d) 397 and *Hay* v. *Saunders & Saunders* (1959) 17 D.L.R. (2d) 352.

Where plans are alleged to be infringed by other plans or sketches, the question to be decided is similar to that arising in connection with other artistic works.

726 **Infringement of plan by building.** As an example of the second type of infringement, it has been held,[39] that an architect's elevation representing a shop front was infringed, by the erection of an actual shop incorporating the elevation, on the ground that the same was a reproduction of the elevation "in a material form." It is submitted that this decision is confined to cases in which the appearance of the complete building appeals to the eye as being a reproduction of what appears on the architect's plan or elevation, and that it would not be an infringement of the copyright in a plan, such as a ground plan, to erect a building based thereon, if the resulting erection bore no resemblance to the plan unless the resemblance was established by dissection and measurement. This view would seem to follow from the decision in *Burke, etc., Ltd.* v. *Spicers Dress Designs* [40] which was distinguished in the case just referred to. Moreover, it receives statutory confirmation, by virtue of the provisions of section 9 (8) of the Act of 1956, which provides that the making of an object of any description in three dimensions shall not be taken to infringe the copyright in an artistic work in two dimensions, if the object would not appear, to persons who are not experts in relation to objects of that description, to be a reproduction of the artistic work.

727 **Infringement of building by building.** The third form of infringement is confined to copying that in which copyright subsists, namely the features of the building having artistic quality. Moreover, the copyright in a work of architecture has other limitations.

The Act of 1956 provides that the copyright in a work of architecture is not infringed by the making of a painting, drawing, engraving or photograph of the work, or the inclusion of the work in a cinematograph film, or in a television broadcast.[41] Nor is it infringed by the publication of any such painting, drawing, engraving, photograph or cinematograph film.[42] While, therefore, the reproduction of an artistic work, which will constitute an infringement is, in general, defined as including, in the case of a work of three dimensions, the conversion of it into a two-dimensional form,[43] it would not appear that there is any two-dimensional form which could constitute an infringement of the copyright in a work of architecture. The only form of infringement, therefore, is the reproduction of the building, or the reproduction of a substantial part of the building, in another building.

[39] *Chabot* v. *Davies* (1936) 155 L.T. 525.
[40] [1936] Ch. 400.
[41] Copyright Act, 1956, s. 9 (4).
[42] s. 9 (6).
[43] s. 48 (1).

728 **Statutory defences.** In addition to the specific sections which have been mentioned, the defences of fair dealing, open in respect of claims for infringement of other artistic works, are also open in the case of architects' plans and works of architecture. For instance, an artistic work may be reproduced for the purposes of research or private study, for the purposes of criticism or review when accompanied by a sufficient acknowledgment, and for the purposes of a judicial proceeding or a report of a judicial proceeding.[44]

729 **Remedies for infringement.** The Act of 1956 expressly provides that no injunction or other order shall be made in an action for infringement of copyright so as to prevent the completion of a building the construction of which has been begun, or require the demolition of a building which has been constructed.[45] On the other hand, the Act of 1956 does not, as did the Act of 1911, exclude works of architecture from the definition of "infringing copy."[46] It is arguable, therefore, that damages on the conversion basis can now be obtained in respect of an infringing building, though, on the other hand, it may be said that, as a building is not a chattel, it is not a possible subject for conversion or detention.

The copyright owner will, however, in any case, be entitled to damages for infringement.[47] While an estimate of the sum which the architect would have charged for the use of his plans and designs may be a basis of assessing damages in such cases,[48] the profit which the architect would have made, if he had been employed, is not the proper basis.[49]

[The next paragraph is 741]

[44] Copyright Act, 1956, s. 9 (1), (2) and (7).
[45] s. 17 (4).
[46] s. 18 (3).
[47] s. 17 (1).
[48] *Chabot* v. *Davies* (1936) 155 L.T. 525; *Stovin-Bradford* v. *Volpoint Properties, Ltd.*, *The Times*, July 29, 1970; aff. *The Times*, May 25, 1971.
[49] *Meikle* v. *Maufe* [1941] 3 All E.R. 144.

CHAPTER 16

CINEMATOGRAPH FILMS

1.—AS INFRINGEMENTS OF OTHER WORKS

741 THE cinematograph film has to be considered, first from the point of view of its capacity to infringe the rights of owners of other subject-matters of copyright and, secondly, in respect of the acquisition, by the makers of films, of rights in the films themselves.

742 **Old law.** Under the law before 1911 it was not an infringement of copyright to dramatise a novel, provided the expressions employed by the novelist were not copied,[1] and the making of a cinematograph film was, presumably, no infringement of copyright. But whether the exhibition of a film in public could be fairly said to be a public "performance" of a dramatic work was, it is believed, never actually decided.[2]

743 **The Act of 1911.** By subsection (2) (*d*) of section 1 of the Copyright Act, 1911, it was provided that "copyright" should include the sole right, in the case of a literary, dramatic or musical work, to make any cinematograph film or other contrivance by means of which the work may be mechanically performed.

Furthermore, under the Act of 1911, it was an infringement of the copyright in a novel, or other non-dramatic work, or an artistic work, to convert it into a dramatic work by way of performance in public or otherwise,[3] and "dramatic work" was defined as including any cinematograph production where the arrangement or acting form or the combination of incidents represented gave the work an original character.[4]

744 In *Sutton Vane* v. *Famous Players Film Co., Ltd.*,[5] Scrutton L.J., in speaking of the alleged infringement of a play by a silent film,

[1] *Read* v. *Conquest* (1861) 9 C.B.(N.S.) 755.

[2] The point was raised in *Glenville* v. *Selig Polyscope Co.* (1911) 27 T.L.R. 554; see also *Karno* v. *Pathé Frères, Ltd.* (1909) 100 L.T. 260; *Newmark* v. *The National Phonograph Co., Ltd.* (1907) 23 T.L.R. 439. In the case of *London Theatre of Varieties, Ltd.* v. *Evans* (1914) 30 T.L.R. 258, the court held that a music-hall artiste, who performed a sketch with the object of enabling a cinematograph film to be made, thereby broke a covenant "not to permit any colourable imitation, representation or version of his performance to be given."

[3] Copyright Act, 1911, s. 1 (2) (*c*).

[4] Copyright Act, 1911, s. 35 (1).

[5] [1928–35] Macg.Cop.Cas. 6 at 8; see also *Glyn* v. *Western Feature Film Co.* [1916] 1 Ch. 261; *Kelly* v. *Cinema Houses, Ltd.* [1928–35] Macg.Cop.Cas. 362;

said: "A play, as printed, consists of words to be spoken and acting directions as to the presentation of incidents on the stage, without spoken words. A cinematograph film contains very few words, but is mainly a pictorial representation of the play as acted, of the scenes which a deaf spectator would see on the stage, with a few words or descriptions forming some guide of what is seen. The definitive section in the Act (s. 35), in speaking of a film as a 'dramatic work,' treats it as 'a representation of a combination of incidents,' and its 'performance' as the 'visual representation of the dramatic action in the work.' It follows that a film, to infringe a printed or acted play, must either use in its captions a substantial part of the words of the play, or colourable imitations thereof, or must use in its pictures, a substantial part of the dramatic incidents represented, or colourable imitations thereof. The copyright protected is not the idea or motive of the play, but the words and dramatic incidents or action in which the idea is embodied."

745 **The Act of 1956.** The Copyright Act, 1956, deals with the matter rather differently. The acts restricted by the copyright in a literary, dramatic or musical work, and in an artistic work, include reproducing the work in any material form,[6] and reproducing a literary, dramatic or musical work is to be construed as including a reproduction in the form of a cinematograph film.[7] On the other hand, although under the Act of 1956 it is also an infringement in the case of a non-dramatic literary work to make a version of the work in which it is converted into a dramatic work,[8] "dramatic work" is defined as not including a cinematograph film, although a scenario or script for a cinematograph film may be a dramatic work.[7] "Cinematograph film," for the purposes of the Act of 1956, means a sequence of visual images recorded on material of any description (whether translucent or not) so as to be capable, by the use of that material, either of being shown as a moving picture, or of being recorded on the material (whether translucent or not) by the use of which it can be so shown.[9] At the present time films for television purposes often consist of records on tape of electrical impulses (videotape). It has been argued that as these are not "visual images" such a tape is not a "cinematograph film" for the purposes of the Act of 1956. It is submitted, however, that, in such a case, a sequence of visual images is recorded

Dagnall v. *British and Dominions Film Corporation, Ltd.* [1928–35] Macg.Cop. Cas. 391; as to infringement of copyright in dramatic works, see § 480 *et seq.*, *ante.* See also *Bolton* v. *British International Pictures, Ltd.* [1936–45] Macg. Cop.Cas. 20; *Poznanski* v. *London Film Production, Ltd.* [1936–45] Macg.Cop. Cas. 107; *MacGregor* v. *Powell* [1936–45] Macg.Cop.Cas. 233; *De Manduit* v. *Gaumont, etc., Corporation, Ltd.* [1936–45] Macg.Cop.Cas. 292.

6 Copyright Act, 1956, ss. 2 (5) (*a*) and 3 (5) (*a*).

7 s. 48 (1).

8 s. 2 (5) (*f*) and (6) (*a*) (i).

9 Copyright Act, 1956, s. 13 (10).

so as to be capable of being shown as a moving picture, even though the record itself is not a " visual image." A cinematograph film is to be taken to include the sounds embodied in any sound track associated with the film.[10] The expression " sound track associated with a cinematograph film " means any record of sounds which is incorporated in any print, negative, tape or other article on which the film or part of it, in so far as it consists of visual images, is recorded, or which is issued by the maker of the film for use in conjunction with such an article.[11]

746 **What constitutes infringement.** These definitions appear to have been introduced into the Act of 1956 because that Act, for the first time, creates a separate copyright in cinematograph films, as is discussed later in this chapter. But, from the point of view of determining what is to constitute an infringement of literary, dramatic, musical or artistic works by the making of films, the definitions seem to have made the position less clear than it was under the Act of 1911. While, under the Act of 1911, the film was regarded as a production consisting of a combination of incidents,[12] under the Act of 1956, it is a piece of celluloid or other material, and while the Act of 1956, as above stated, makes it an infringement to reproduce a literary, dramatic or musical work in the form of a cinematograph film, it affords no guidance as to the circumstances in which such a reproduction is to be recognised. It seems probable, however, that the line of authorities which have established that there is no infringement of a literary or dramatic work by a film, unless a substantial number of detailed incidents are reproduced, will be followed under the Act of 1956.[13] On the other hand, it could be argued that the Act of 1956 has diminished the protection afforded to authors of literary works, and that such works are not reproduced by a film unless the sound track reproduces, or closely imitates, a substantial part of the language of the literary work.

747 **Must be of a copyright work.** The mere reproduction by cinematography of a scene of actual events—as a film of a cricket-match or a horse-race—cannot infringe any copyright. There appears to be nothing in English law that ordinarily gives anyone a right to object to his being " snapshotted " in a public place, although any " faking " of the photograph might perhaps bring the photographer under the law of libel,[14] and sometimes the taking of a photograph might be restrained by injunction, upon the ground that it was done in breach of confidence.

[10] s. 13 (9).
[11] s. 13 (10), and see as to infringing copy, § 780, *post*.
[12] Copyright Act, 1911, s. 35 (1).
[13] See cases under note, 5, *supra*.
[14] *Ante*, § 316, note 37, *Corelli* v. *Wall* (1906) 22 T.L.R. 532.

The person taking the film may be guilty of trespass if he comes on the plaintiff's land without authority to take the film, but apparently he commits no tort if he takes the film from adjoining land.[15]

748 **Infringement of works by performing films.** The Act of 1956 defines " performance " as including any mode of visual or acoustic presentation, including any such presentation by the exhibition of a cinematograph film.[16] Here again the position does not seem as clear as was the case under the Act of 1911 where " performance " was defined as including any visual representation of any dramatic action in a work,[17] so that it was clear that the performance of a film embodying incidents in a literary work infringed that work. It seems arguable that, under the Act of 1956, the literary work is not presented by the performance of a film unless some part of the actual language of the work is reproduced or imitated on the sound track. The position seems even less clear where a film embodying incidents in a literary work is broadcast. Broadcasting is not in itself a performance [18] and, though " broadcasting " is a separate right reserved to the owner of the literary work,[19] there is no definition of " broadcasting " of the same kind as there is of " performance " so as to include any mode of presentation. Assuming, however, that the copyright in a literary work is infringed by broadcasting or diffusion of a film, or by means of a public exhibition of the film at a television receiver, then the same considerations will apply as have been already discussed in connection with the direct broadcasting and diffusion of literary works.[20]

749 **And by authorising the performance of films.** Under the Act of 1956, as under the Act of 1911, it is an infringement of copyright to authorise the doing of an infringing act,[21] and it had been held that the hiring out of a film to the owner of a cinema theatre on terms requiring advertising posters to be obtained from the hirer amounted to " authorising " the performance of a film in public.[22]

750 **Statutory defences.** Certain of the exemptions from infringement apply specifically to cinematograph films as well as to other means of

[15] See case of broadcasting from adjoining land: *Victoria Park, etc., Co., Ltd.* v. *Taylor* (1937) 37 S.R.(N.S.W.) 322; (1938) 38 S.R.(N.S.W.) 33 and see *Sports and General Press Agency, Ltd.* v. *" Our Dogs " Publishing Co., Ltd.* [1916] 2 K.B. 880; [1917] 2 K.B. 125.

[16] Copyright Act, 1956, s. 48 (1).

[17] Copyright Act, 1911, s. 35 (1).

[18] Copyright Act, 1956, s. 48 (5).

[19] s. 2 (5) (*d*).

[20] *Ante*, § 526 *et seq.*

[21] Copyright Act, 1956, s. 1 (1).

[22] *Falcon* v. *The Famous Players Film Co., Ltd.* [1926] 2 K.B. 474; *Fenning Film Service, Ltd.* v. *Wolverhampton, etc., Cinemas, Ltd.* [1914] 3 K.B. 1171; compare—prior to the Act of 1911—*Glenville* v. *Selig Polyscope Co.* (1911) 27 T.L.R. 554; see also *Karno* v. *Pathé Frères, Ltd.* (1909) 100 L.T. 260. In America the contrary has been held: *Kalem Co.* v. *Harper Bros.* (1911) 222 U.S.R. 55.

reproduction. Fair dealing with a literary, dramatic or musical work, for the purpose of reporting current events in a cinematograph film, is not to constitute an infringement.[23] It had been held that the corresponding section of the Act of 1911 did not apply to cinematograph films.[24] Again, it is not to constitute an infringement of copyright in sculptures or works of artistic craftsmanship permanently situated in a public place or in premises open to the public, to include the work in a cinematograph film.[25] Nor is it an infringement of copyright in a work of architecture to include the work in a cinematograph film.[26] And, in general, the copyright in an artistic work is not infringed by the inclusion of the work in a cinematograph film if its inclusion therein is only by way of background, or is otherwise only incidental to the principal matters represented in the film.[27]

751 **Who can authorise filming of old works?** Questions of some difficulty arose under the Act of 1911 as to the proper person to authorise the making and performance of films, where the original work was in existence before the Act of 1911, and the copyright and performing rights were in separate hands. Since it not infrequently happens that films are based upon old works, these questions may still be of importance since, under paragraph 28 of the Seventh Schedule to the Act of 1956, documents or events which affected the title to copyright in the work under the Act of 1911 are to have the corresponding operation in relation to copyright under the Act of 1956. Again, paragraph 36 of the Seventh Schedule to the Act of 1956 maintains the position subsisting under the Act of 1911 in regard to the separation of the copyright and the performing right in dramatic or musical works.

The problem arose by reason of the provisions of section 24 of the Act of 1911.

The short effect of section 24 (1) of that Act was that the person who, at the date of the commencement of that Act, was entitled to any such right in a work, as was specified in the first column of the First Schedule to that Act, was to be entitled to the substituted right specified in the second column of that Schedule, subject, where there had been an assignment of the right, to the author becoming entitled to the benefit of the extra period of protection allowed by that Act. By virtue of such Schedule the person entitled at the commencement of that Act to copyright in a work " other than dramatic and musical works " became entitled to " copyright as defined by this Act." If, therefore, the author of a literary work had, prior to the commencement of that Act, assigned his copyright to a publisher, it was

[23] Copyright Act, 1956, s. 6 (3).
[24] *Hawkes & Son (London), Ltd.* v. *Paramount Film Service, Ltd.* [1934] Ch. 593.
[25] Copyright Act, 1956, s. 9 (3).
[26] s. 9 (4).
[27] s. 9 (5).

reasonably clear that it was the publisher, and not the author, who had the right to dramatise the work and make and exhibit cinematograph films. Similarly, in the case of a musical or dramatic work, if both copyright and performing right had been assigned, the assignee had all cinematograph rights, for he, too, was given by the First Schedule " copyright as defined by this Act." But what if the author of a dramatic or musical work had assigned his performing rights, but retained his copyright, or vice versa? Here, the effect of the Act of 1911 is not so clear. The First Schedule provided that, in such case, the owner of the copyright was to be entitled to " copyright as defined by this Act, except the sole right to perform the work or any substantial part thereof in public," and that the owner of the performing rights was to be entitled to " the sole right to perform the work in public, but *none of the other rights* comprised in copyright as defined by this Act." " Performance," as we have seen, under the Act of 1911 included any visual representation of the dramatic action in a work " by means of any mechanical instrument." [28]

It appears that the right of *public exhibition* of the work by means of a cinematograph film belongs to the proprietor of the performing right and not to the proprietor of the copyright. But has the former the right to *make,* as distinct from the right to *exhibit,* a cinematograph film? It is submitted that he has not, inasmuch as section 1 (2) (*d*) of the Act of 1911 treats the right to " make " a cinematograph film as a totally distinct right from the right of public performance.[29] If this be so, then the result is to produce a kind of stalemate. The owner of the copyright has the right to " make " the film, but not to " exhibit " it; the owner of the performing rights has the right to " exhibit " the film, but not to " make " it. Practically, therefore, a cinematograph exhibition can only be given by mutual arrangement between the respective owners of the performing rights and the copyright, and this seems to be a perfectly fair result. This difficulty has not been solved by the cases of *Barstow* v. *Terry* [30] and *Falcon* v. *The Famous Players Film Co., Ltd.*[31] since, in the former case, the person who was held, as against the owner of the copyright in the novel from which a play was adapted, to have the right to make a film thereof, was the owner, not only of performing rights, but apparently of the graphic rights in the dramatic version of the novel. In the latter case it was only the performance of the film which was restrained by the owner of the performing right, since the making of the film took place in America and was not attacked.

[28] Copyright Act, 1911, s. 35 (1).
[29] *British Actors Film Co., Ltd.* v. *Glover* [1918] 1 K.B. 299; and see *Thompson* v. *Warner Bros. Pictures, Ltd.* [1929] 2 Ch. 308; *Serra* v. *Famous-Lasky Film Service, Ltd.* (1922) 127 L.T. 109.
[30] [1924] 2 Ch. 316.
[31] [1926] 1 K.B. 393; [1926] 2 K.B. 474 (C.A.).

752 **Construction of assignments of cinematograph rights.** Doubts have arisen as to the construction of assignments of cinematograph rights with regard to whether the right to make sound, as well as silent, films has been included in the assignment. Swift J., in *Pathé Pictures, Ltd.* v. *Bancroft*,[32] expressed the view that the words "cinematograph films," in an assignment or licence, would include sound films. In that case the agreement in question was dated in August, 1927, and there was evidence that sound films had been exhibited in June, 1927, but it was held that a licence to produce a work "in moving picture films" did not entitle the licensee to make a sound film of the work. This question has been considered recently in the case of *Hospital for Sick Children* v. *Walt Disney Productions Inc.*,[32a] where it was held that a grant of moving picture rights was capable of conveying the right to make, not only a silent film, but also a sound film, but that the provisions of the agreement in question did not comprehend sound films, the agreement having been made when sound films were very remote.

2.—As a Separate Subject-Matter of Copyright

753 **The Act of 1911.** Turning now to the protection which is accorded to the film itself, the Act of 1956 has made a complete change in the law. Under the Act of 1911, there was no copyright in a film as such. Regarded as a series of photographs, each photograph was protected as an artistic work.[33] The sound track of the film was protected as a contrivance by means of which sounds might be mechanically reproduced.[34] The production was protected as a dramatic work where the arrangement or acting form, or the combination of incidents represented, gave the work an original character.[35] There was also a separate literary or dramatic copyright in any scenario or script[36] and, of course, as has been seen,[37] the making and exhibition of the film might well involve infringement of the separate copyrights of authors and composers whose separate works were embodied in the film.

754 **The Act of 1956.** The Act of 1956, on the other hand, confers an additional independent copyright in respect of a cinematograph film, but so as not to affect the copyright in any literary, dramatic, musical or artistic work from which it is wholly or partially derived.[38]

32 [1928–35] Macg.Cop.Cas. 403.
32a [1966] 1 W.L.R. 1055; [1968] Ch. 52; § 389, *ante*.
33 *Pathé Pictures, Ltd.* v. *Bancroft* [1928–35] Macg.Cop.Cas. 403; *Barker, etc., Ltd.* v. *Hulton (E.) & Co., Ltd.* (1912) 28 T.L.R. 496; *Nordisk Films Co., Ltd.* v. *Onda* [1917–23] Macg.Cop.Cas. 337.
34 Copyright Act, 1911, s. 1 (2) (*d*).
35 s. 35 (1).
36 *Milligan* v. *The Broadway Cinema Productions, Ltd.* 1923 S.L.T. 35.
37 *Ante*, § § 743 and 744.
38 Copyright Act, 1956, s. 16 (6).

But, when the copyright in the cinematograph film expires, the film may be reproduced thereafter without infringing the copyright in any literary, dramatic, musical or artistic work embodied in the film.[39]

755 **Meaning of "cinematograph film."** A "cinematograph film" is defined as any sequence of visual images recorded on material of any description (whether translucent or not) so as to be capable, by the use of that material, either of being shown as a moving picture, or of being recorded on other material (whether translucent or not) by the use of which it can be so shown,[40] and includes any associated sound track.[41] The work protected, therefore, is the physical thing, rather than any dramatic or artistic matter embodied therein.

756 **Conditions necessary for copyright to subsist in a film.** In order that copyright may subsist in a cinematograph film, either the maker must have been a qualified person for the whole or a substantial part of the period during which the film was made[42] or, if the film has been published, if the first publication of the film took place in the United Kingdom or in another country to which the Act extends.[43] For the purposes of these provisions the maker of the film is the person by whom the arrangements necessary for the making of the film are undertaken[40] and, presumably, "person" may here include a body corporate, since "qualified person" includes, in the case of a body corporate, a body incorporated under the laws of any part of the United Kingdom or of another country to which the provisions of the Act extend.[44] "Publication," in relation to a cinematograph film, has a wider definition than for other classes of works and means the sale, letting on hire, or offer for sale or hire, of copies of the film to the public[40]; "copy" means any print, negative, tape or other article on which the film or part of it is recorded.[40] In the case of other classes of works, reproductions have to be issued to the public in order to constitute publication,[45] and it is thought that merely letting on hire would not constitute an issue. It is not clear, however, whether, in the case of a film, it is sufficient, in order to constitute publication, that copies should be let for hire to exhibitors.

757 **Foreign films** The question may be of importance in connection with foreign films. Hitherto, films have been regarded as unpublished works, so that the ownership of copyright under the Act of 1911

[39] Copyright Act, 1956, s. 13 (7).
[40] s. 13 (10).
[41] s. 13 (9).
[42] s. 13 (1).
[43] s. 13 (2).
[44] s. 1 (5) (*b*). See s. 19 of the Interpretation Act, 1889 (52 & 53 Vict. c. 63) and *Rolloswin Investments, Ltd.* v. *Chromolit, etc., S.A.R.L.* [1970] 1 W.L.R. 912.
[45] s. 49 (2) (*c*).

depended upon residence or nationality.[46] Under the wider form of protection given to works of foreign origin as a result of the Universal Copyright Convention,[47] the matter is no longer of great importance, save in the case of old films. But, since, in general, protection is only given here to works of U.S.A. origin first published in the U.S.A., if publication took place on or after September 27, 1957,[48] the point may still have significance.

758 **Term of copyright in films.** Copyright in a cinematograph film is to subsist until the film is registered under the provisions of the Films Act, 1960, or, if not registrable under that Act, until the film is published and thereafter until the end of the period of fifty years from the end of the calendar year in which it is so registered or published.[49] But in the case of newsreels, such as are mentioned in section 38 (1) (*a*) of the Films Act, 1960, the copyright in the film is not infringed by causing it to be seen or heard in public after the end of the period of fifty years from the end of the calendar year in which the principal events depicted in the film occurred.[50]

759 **Ownership of copyright in films.** The owner of the copyright in a cinematograph film is the maker,[51] that is to say, the person by whom the arrangements necessary for the making of the film are undertaken.[52]

760 **Infringement of copyright in films.** Copyright in a film is infringed by copying the film by means of any print, negative, tape or other article, by causing the film, so far as it consists of visual images, to be seen in public and, so far as it consists of sounds, to be heard in public, by broadcasting the film and by causing the film to be transmitted to subscribers to a diffusion service.[53] But where the sounds embodied in the sound track of a film are also embodied in a record, other than a sound track or a record derived (directly or indirectly) from such a sound track, the copyright in the film is not infringed by any use made of that record.[54] This provision is presumably required because it might otherwise be argued that the copyright in a film (including sounds) could be infringed by performing or broadcasting recorded words or music subsequently incorporated in the film. The copyright in a film is not infringed by making a copy

[46] Copyright Act, 1911, s. 1 (1) (*b*).
[47] *Post*, Chap. 24, and Appendix C, § 1730.
[48] Copyright (International Conventions) Order 1957 (S.I. 1957 No. 1523), Appendix D, § 1862, *post*, and Copyright (International Coventions) Order, 1964 (S.I. 1964 No. 690), Appendix D, § 1874, *post*: and see § 1184, *post*.
[49] Copyright Act, 1956, s. 13 (3) (*a*) and (*b*).
[50] s. 13 (8).
[51] s. 13 (4).
[52] s. 13 (10).
[53] s. 13 (5); as to meaning of copy in relation to a film, see s. 13 (10).
[54] s. 13 (9), proviso.

of it for the purposes of a judicial proceeding, or by causing it to be seen or heard in public for the purposes of such a proceeding.[55]

761 **Where the copyright in a film has expired.** Where the copyright in the film has expired, copyright in any literary, dramatic, musical or artistic work embodied therein is not infringed by the public showing of the film.[56] Presumably, however, it will still be an infringement of any subsisting literary, or other copyright, to make further copies of the film, since this would involve a further infringement by reproduction.

762 **Provisions to prevent overlapping of remedies.** Until the copyright in the film so expires, however, it is additional to and independent of the copyright in any material embodied in the film, and the rights of the owners of such copyrights, except in so far as covered by licences granted to the maker of the film, will continue to operate and be enforceable in respect, for example, of public performances of the film. It is, indeed, provided that all the different copyrights subsisting under the Act of 1956 are to be independent of one another.[57] In order to prevent this operating with undue harshness, special provisions are contained in section 40 of the Act of 1956. While broadcasting and diffusion of a film are not to constitute causing the same to be seen or heard,[58] it may be caused to be seen or heard by the operation of receiving apparatus,[59] whereupon, if this is in public, the occupier of the premises may be liable.[60] Further the owner of the copyright in the film is given separate broadcasting and television rights.[61] Provision is therefore made to meet the case of cinematograph films, which are the subject of a television or sound broadcast, with the result that their public performance might be an infringement both of the broadcast right and of the cinematograph right. Where such a film is broadcast and it is an authorised broadcast, that is to say, if it is made by or with the licence of the owner of the copyright in the film, a person who causes the film to be seen or heard in public by the reception of the broadcast, does not infringe the copyright in the film.[62] If, however, the broadcast was not an authorised broadcast, the owner of the copyright in the film is nevertheless not entitled to take proceedings against a person who causes the film to be seen or heard by the reception of the broadcast, but any damage resulting thereby may be taken into account in assessing damages in any proceedings against the British

[55] Copyright Act, 1956, s. 13 (6).
[56] s. 13 (7).
[57] s. 16 (6) and (7).
[58] s. 48 (5).
[59] s. 48 (5) (*b*).
[60] s. 48 (6).
[61] s. 13 (5).
[62] s. 40 (2) and (4).

Broadcasting Corporation or the Independent Television Authority in respect of the copyright in the film.[62] These provisions, however, only protect a person who performs a film by the reception of a broadcast received, either directly, or by means of a relay or re-broadcast, and do not protect a person who performs a film made from a broadcast. Nor do they protect a person who makes a film from a broadcast. There are provisions restricting the diffusion rights in films similar to those applying to the diffusion of literary, dramatic or musical works.[63]

763 **Films performed by schools.** It is provided, in section 41 of the Act of 1956, that a cinematograph film shall not be treated as having been performed in public, if performed in the course of the activities of a school, by a person who is a teacher in or a pupil in attendance at the school, to an audience limited to persons who are teachers in or pupils in attendance at the school, or are otherwise directly connected with the activities of the school. However, such section provides that a parent or guardian shall not be included in persons directly connected with such activities by reason only that he is a parent or guardian.

764 **Indirect infringement.** In addition to the direct forms of infringement aforesaid, it is made an infringement of copyright in a film to deal with copies, known to constitute infringements, in the same way as it is an infringement of the copyright in literary, dramatic, musical and artistic works to deal with such copies thereof. There are, in fact, similar provisions in regard to importing, selling, exhibiting and distributing such copies.[64] Moreover, the definition of "infringing copy" includes a copy of a cinematograph film,[65] so that the provisions of section 18 of the Act of 1956, in regard to detinue and conversion, apply also to copies of films.

765 **Remedies for infringement.** In general the same remedies are open to the owner of the copyright in a cinematograph film as are open to the owners of other copyright material, and, in addition, the summary remedies available against persons making, selling, importing and distributing infringing copies are equally available against persons so dealing with infringing copies of cinematograph films.[66]

[The next paragraph is 771]

[63] Copyright Act, 1956, s. 40 (3) and (4), and see *ante*, § 526 *et seq.*
[64] s. 16 and Sched. VII, para. 19.
[65] s. 18 (3) (*c*).
[66] s. 21 (4).

CHAPTER 17

RECORDS AND SOUND RECORDINGS

1.—HISTORICAL

771 In the year 1886, the date of the Berne Convention, the only mechanical means generally known for reproducing music were musical boxes and Barbary organs. When, therefore, at the request of the Swiss delegates to the Conference of Powers which preceded that Convention, it was, in the interests of a national Swiss industry, declared, by Article 3 of the Final Protocol, that mechanical reproduction of musical airs should not be an infringement of copyright, musical composers did not feel that they were abandoning rights of any great value to themselves. But when instruments were invented capable of reproducing, not one or two tunes, but any number of tunes, and even the words of songs, by means of perforated rolls, discs and cylinders, and it was found that these evidently supplied a public need and met with a ready market, composers became perturbed. Actions were instituted in many countries with a view to testing whether the manufacture and sale of these contrivances were not an infringement of the composer's copyright.

772 **Boosey v. Whight.** Composers met with varying success in different countries.[1] In England the Court of Appeal, affirming Stirling J., held that the interchangeable parts of a machine for reproducing sounds could not reasonably be taken to be "copies" of sheets of music, and therefore that they did not infringe the composer's copyright under the Copyright Act, 1842.[2] The correctness of this decision was doubted by many, but the case was not taken to the House of Lords, and an attempt, in the year 1909, to convince the court that the law had been altered on this point by the Musical (Summary Proceedings) Act, 1902,[3] met with no success [4]; and a like attempt, in the year 1912, to obtain a decision to the effect that the mechanical

[1] In Italy and Belgium the decisions of the courts appear to have been uniformly in favour of the composers. The French courts were hampered by domestic legislation similar in effect to Clause 3 of the Protocol to the Berne Convention, to which, however, a strict construction was given. Thus the French courts held that the permission to reproduce a "musical air" does not authorise the reproduction of the *words* of a song. The American courts followed the English decisions, and held that mechanical instruments could not reasonably be held to be "copies" of musical works: *White-Smith, etc., Co.* v. *Apollo Co.* (1907) 147 Fed.R. 226. In Germany legislation was introduced expressly dealing with mechanical instruments in the year 1901.

[2] *Boosey* v. *Whight* [1899] 1 Ch. 836; [1900] 1 Ch. 122.

[3] 2 Edw. 7, c. 15.

[4] *Newmark* v. *The National Phonograph Co., Ltd.* (1907) 23 T.L.R. 439.

contrivances infringed a composer's common law copyright met with the same fate.[5]

773 **Opposition to amendment.** Upon the assumption that the case of *Boosey* v. *Whight* correctly expounded the British copyright law, a very large industry in the manufacture of these mechanical devices was built up in this country. In the Revised Convention of Berne, 1908, a clause was inserted requiring that signatories to the Convention should give protection to composers against reproductions of their works by mechanical means.[6] When, therefore, in the year 1910, a Parliamentary Committee was formed to report to the Houses of Parliament how far it was advisable to alter the British law in order to comply with the requirements of the Revised Convention, musical composers met with very powerful opposition from the manufacturing interests. On behalf of the manufacturers it was urged that an industry in which much capital was invested, which gave employment to large numbers, and brought good music into the houses of the poor, ought not to be ruined by any alteration of the law, to all of which arguments it was replied that no industry ought to be permitted to flourish upon the methods of the highwayman. In fairness to the manufacturers, it should be said that they all willingly recognised that some remuneration was due to composers whose works were adapted to mechanical reproduction, their chief fear being that, if composers were allowed unlimited powers, either to permit, or prohibit, the reproduction of their works by these means, the result might be that the largest and wealthiest firms engaged in the industry would be able to obtain a monopoly in the most popular works to the prejudice of their smaller competitors in business. With the object of preventing any such result, they urged that some provisions similar to those which had recently been introduced into the American Copyright Act,[7] giving compulsory powers to acquire licences to reproduce musical works by mechanical means upon payment of a fixed royalty, should be inserted in the English Bill. The manufacturers failed to convince the Copyright Committee, who reported, with some few dissentients, in favour of allowing composers full control over the reproduction of their works by mechanical means. The manufacturers thereupon changed the scene of their efforts to the lobbies of the House of Commons, where they met with better success.

774 **Amendment in Committee.** The Copyright Bill, as originally drawn, gave effect to the views of the majority of the Copyright Committee, and left to composers the full control over mechanical repro-

5 *Monckton* v. *The Gramophone Co., Ltd.* (1912) 106 L.T. 84.
6 Article 13, Revised Convention of Berne.
7 United States Copyright Act, 1909, s. 1 (*e*).

duction of their works, but, in Committee of the House of Commons, a clause—section 19 of the Act of 1911—was inserted, the short effect of which was to compel a musical composer, if he has granted a licence to one person to reproduce his work mechanically, to grant to any other person a licence to reproduce the same work in like manner upon payment of a certain royalty to the composer.

775 **Copyright in records under the Act of 1911.** This system has been found to work satisfactorily over the years since the passing of the Act of 1911, and the 1952 Copyright Committee was faced with acute controversy over a rather different matter. The Act of 1911, besides conferring upon the composer of music the right to prevent its being recorded on gramophone records without his consent, conferred on the manufacturers of gramophone records themselves copyright in the records " in like manner as if such contrivances were musical works." [8] It was originally supposed that this right was to protect manufacturers against copying of their recordings by rival manufacturers. But, in the case of *Gramophone Co., Ltd.* v. *Stephen Cawardine & Co.*[9] decided in the year 1934, it was held that the right conferred upon the manufacturers by the Act of 1911 also included a performing right in the record. As a result of this decision it became necessary for people giving public performances of music by means of gramophone records, not only to obtain licences from the owners of the copyright in the music, but also to obtain licences from the gramophone manufacturers. This right was turned to advantage by the Musicians' Union who were able to secure that licences issued by the gramophone manufacturers should restrict public performances where such performances might lead to the substitution of mechanical appliances for the use of musicians. A good deal of evidence was given before the Committee suggesting that hardship was thus caused to promoters of performances, particularly to small audiences, while, on the other hand, the Musicians' Union defended the practice on the ground that no other way existed of protecting the musicians whose performances gave value to the records employed. The Copyright Committee recommended that the performing right in gramophone records should be maintained, but that certain classes of performances should not be deemed to infringe performing rights in gramophone records.[10]

776 **1961 Convention.** An International Convention for the Protection of Performers, Producers of Phonograms, and Broadcasting Organisations was signed at Rome on October 26, 1961.[11] So far as concerns

[8] Copyright Act, 1911, s. 19 (1).
[9] [1934] Ch. 450.
[10] Cmd. 8662, para. 184.
[11] Cmnd. 2425, Appendix C, § 1791: ratified by the U.K. on October 30, 1963, and entered into force on May 18, 1964.

sound recordings, it requires signatories to grant national treatment to producers of sound recordings who are nationals of a contracting state, or where the sound was recorded in a contracting state, or published in a contracting state. The minimum protection required is from copying of records.

777 **Questions now to be considered.** Questions concerning mechanical contrivances fall, therefore, under three main groups. First of all the protection given to the owners of copyright in literary, dramatic and, particularly, musical works in respect of the making and performance of contrivances reproducing such works. Secondly, the special provisions entitling manufacturers of gramophone records to make records of musical works which have once been recorded on the terms of paying a statutory royalty. And, thirdly, the rights conferred upon the manufacturers of gramophone records in respect of such records.

2.—RECORDING AS AN INFRINGEMENT

778 So far as the first point is concerned, the Act of 1956 includes among the acts restricted by the copyright in a literary, dramatic or musical work, reproducing the work in any material form, making any adaptation of the work, and performing in public the work or any such adaptation.[12] "Adaptation," in the case of a non-dramatic work, means a version in which it is converted into a dramatic work and, in relation to a musical work, means an arrangement or transcription of the work.[13] "Reproduction" in the case of a literary, dramatic or musical work includes a reproduction in the form of a record.[14] And "record" means any disc, tape, perforated roll or other device in which sounds are embodied so as to be capable (with or without the aid of some other instrument) of being automatically reproduced therefrom.[14] The definition continues that references to a "record of a work or other subject-matter" are references to a record (as therein defined) by means of which it can be performed. This set of definitions seems more complex than the provisions of the Act of 1911 which provided that copyright in a literary, dramatic or musical work included the sole right to make any record, perforated roll or other contrivance by means of which the work might be mechanically performed or delivered.[15] But the effect seems to be the same. Thus, the copyright in any literary, dramatic or musical work is infringed by the making of a gramophone record, the sound track of a cinematograph film, a tape recording or any other device embodying sounds capable of being automatically reproduced and so that, when reproduced, the work will be performed. It will also

[12] Copyright Act, 1956, s. 2 (5).
[13] s. 2 (6).
[14] s. 48 (1).
[15] Copyright Act, 1911, s. 1 (2) (*d*).

be an infringement if what is embodied in the device is an adaptation of the work as hereinbefore defined.

779 **Performance by means of a record.** The copyright in a literary, dramatic or musical work is also infringed by performing the work, or any adaptation of the work, in public, broadcasting the work, or any adaptation, and causing the same to be transmitted to subscribers to a diffusion service.[16] A performance includes any presentation of the work by the use of a record, as already defined.[14] The public performance of a musical work by means of records has probably always been an infringement, even before the making of the records was an infringement.[17]

The provisions of the Copyright Act, 1956, in regard to broadcasting and diffusion of live programmes and in regard to performances given by the operation of receiving apparatus, appear to apply equally to programmes consisting of records in so far as concerns the rights in the recorded material.[18]

780 **Importation or sale of records.** The provisions of the Act of 1956 restricting the importation, sale and distribution of infringing material would appear to apply equally to records.[19] These sections refer to dealings with any article the making of which constituted an infringement, and a record would appear to be an article for the purpose of these provisions.[19] The word " article " also appears in the definition of " infringing copy " in section 18 of the Act of 1956, and it would seem to follow that a record may be an infringing copy for the purposes of this section and so involve claims based upon conversion or detention. Interlocutory orders have been made by the court on this footing. It should also be noted that an imported record may be an infringing copy, if its making would have been an infringement if made in England, without the necessity of proving guilty knowledge by the importer. A difficult question, however, arises where the record is made abroad with the consent of the person who owns the copyright in the music, both in the country of origin and in England, but who has granted an exclusive licence to someone else in England. The exclusive licensee appears to be in difficulties by reason of section 19 (4) of the Copyright Act, 1956.

In the definition of " infringing copy," in section 18 of the Act of 1956, it is provided that the reproduction in the form of a cinematograph film shall not be deemed an infringing copy of a literary, dramatic or musical work. Since under section 13 (9) of the Act of

16 Copyright Act, 1956, s. 2 (5).

17 *Newmark* v. *The National Phonograph Co., Ltd.* (1907) 23 T.L.R. 439; *Thompson* v. *Warner Bros. Pictures, Ltd.* [1929] 2 Ch. 308.

18 § 526 *et seq.*, *ante.*

19 See Copyright Act, 1956, s. 5 (2) (3) and (4), and definition of " reproduction " in s. 48 (1).

1956, it is provided that for the purpose of that Act a cinematograph film shall be taken to include the sound embodied in any sound track associated with the film, it would seem to follow that, though such sound track falls within the definition of " record " and is therefore a reproduction, it is not to be regarded as an infringing copy.

781 **Summary remedies apply to records.** The word " article " is also used in section 21 of the Act of 1956, and it would seem, therefore, that the summary remedies thereby imposed for the making, importation or sale of infringing articles also apply to gramophone records. But since in this section, unlike section 5 of the Act of 1956, the offence is only committed if the infringer knows the article to be an " infringing copy," it apparently would not apply in the case of the sound track of a cinematograph film.

782 **Customs control.** The provisions of section 22 of the Act of 1956, empowering copyright owners to restrict the importation of infringing material by notice to the Commissioners of Customs, apply only to printed copies of works and this phrase obviously excludes mechanical contrivances. The Commissioners have taken this view and declined to control the importation of infringing records.

783 **" Passing-off."** On the other hand, it would appear that the provisions of section 43 of the Act of 1956, giving a statutory remedy in the case of " passing-off " by affixing a name to a work of which the person named is not the author, would apply in the case of a gramophone record where a name was so affixed to the label.

784 **Issue of records, not publication of works.** It should be further observed that, in section 49 of the Act of 1956, it is provided that the issue of records of a literary, dramatic or musical work is not to constitute publication of the work.[20] The primary object of this provision is to secure that, where copyright in a work depends upon first publication in a particular country, the issue of records is to be disregarded. But the provision appears to have the incidental effect that the issue of records is not to constitute an infringement of copyright by publication. This is probably immaterial, since, even if the defendant who has issued the records is not the maker, he will probably, in any case, be liable for infringement by selling or importing, or can be made liable for the conversion of infringing copies.

785 **Assignment of mechanical rights.** Copyright may, therefore, be infringed either (a) by making a reproduction in the form of a record

[20] Copyright Act, 1956, s. 49 (2) (*a*).

or (b) by using a record in such a manner as to cause the work to be performed in public. Both these rights belong to the author, and, if there has been an assignment of his rights by the author, it is submitted that he retains all rights which he does not expressly, or by necessary implication, assign. It is thought, therefore, that whereas an assignment of copyright out and out will carry the right of reproduction by mechanical instruments and the right of public performance by means of the like instruments to the assignee, the assignment of the right to print and publish a piece of music, alone, will not carry the right to make a record by which the work can be mechanically reproduced, for this is a distinct right.[21] On the other hand, the right of public performance by mechanical instruments is not, it is submitted, a right distinct from the right of public performance by other means, and would pass to the assignee of the performing rights, unless expressly excepted from the assignment.[22]

786 **Words and music.** If the work that has been unlawfully reproduced by means of a record, or other device, be a musical work consisting of words and music, it may not infrequently arise that the copyright in words and music will be vested in different persons. It is submitted that, in that case, the manufacturer is liable to be sued for infringement by both or either of those persons, and that the permission to reproduce the song upon a mechanical instrument must be obtained from both authors.[23] Even if the author of the words has permitted them to be used by the author of the music for publication as a song, that does not, it is submitted, authorise the latter to reproduce the words upon a record or other like contrivance. The Act of 1956, no doubt, authorises the reproduction of words for the purposes of the compulsory royalty provisions,[24] but this provision of the Act has not, it is thought, the effect of including the words with the music for any other purpose.

3.—COMPULSORY LICENCE TO RECORD

787 The second matter to be dealt with is the special exception entitling manufacturers to make records of musical works which have once been recorded with the consent of the copyright owner on the terms of paying a statutory royalty. These provisions, contained in section 8 of the Act of 1956, substantially reproduce the corresponding provi-

21 See as to assignments made prior to the commencement of the Act of 1911, s. 19 (7) (*c*), of that Act, *post*, § 809.

22 See *Thompson* v. *Warner Bros. Pictures, Ltd.* [1929] 2 Ch. 308.

23 In the case of *Rubens* v. *Pathé Frères, etc., Ltd.* (*The Times*, December 20, 1912), it was held that the composer of the music could sue in respect of a gramophone record made without his consent without joining the author of the words as his co-plaintiff.

24 Copyright Act, 1956, s. 8 (5).

sions of section 19 of the Act of 1911, but with considerable modifications in form and detail.[25]

788 **Licence to make for retail sale only.** Section 8 of the Act of 1956 throughout uses the expression "record," and it will be recalled that "record" is defined so as to include, not only gramophone records, but all mechanical devices for reproducing sounds.[26] On the other hand, the Act of 1956 makes clear, what was left somewhat doubtful under the Act of 1911, that the exception only applies where records are reproduced for the purpose of retail sale. The exception therefore clearly does not apply where music is required to be embodied in the sound track of a cinematograph film, but it would apply if what is to be sold retail is not a gramophone record in the ordinary sense, but is, for example, a tape recording. Moreover, if the music has once been recorded for retail sale on one type of record, it can afterwards be recorded, on the terms of the section, for retail sale, embodied in some other type of recording appliance.[27]

789 **Must have been previously recorded.** The first condition is that records of the work or, as the case may be, of a similar adaptation of the work, have previously been made in, or imported into, the United Kingdom for the purposes of retail sale, and were so made or imported by, or with the licence of, the owner of the copyright in the work,[28] in the United Kingdom.[29] Adaptation of a work is to be taken to be similar to a former adaptation if the two adaptations do not substantially differ in their treatment of the work, either in respect of style, or (apart from any difference in numbers), in respect of the performers required for performing them.[30] It is not altogether clear whether the last requirement refers to the quality of the performers, or to the instruments used, or to both these matters. It is further provided that the exception is not to apply to a record of the whole of a work, or adaptation, unless the previous records were records of the whole of the work, or of a similar adaptation.[31] Similarly, the exception is not to apply to a record of part of a work, or adaptation, unless the previous records were records of, or comprising, that part of the work, or of a similar adaptation.[32] From this, it seems to follow that

25 Records made before the commencement of the Act of 1911 are still protected under the provisions of section 19 of that Act and the regulations made under that section, the Copyright Royalty System (Mechanical Musical Instruments) Regulations 1912 (S.R. & O. 1912 No. 533; Copinger, *Copyright*, 8th ed., p. 425) (Copyright Act, 1956, Sched. VII, para. 6 (2)).

26 Copyright Act, 1956, s. 48 (1).

27 A record which is supplied for a consideration partly of money and partly of coupons or tokens is not reproduced for the purpose of retail sale: *Chappell & Co., Ltd.* v. *Nestlé Co., Ltd.* [1960] A.C. 87 (H.L.).

28 Copyright Act, 1956, s. 8 (1) (*a*).

29 s. 49 (6).

30 s. 8 (6).

31 s. 8 (8), proviso (*a*).

32 s. 8 (8), proviso (*b*).

less, but not more, of a work may be recorded than was previously recorded, but subject to the overriding condition that, by taking parts only of the work, such an adaptation is not produced as would create a different treatment of the work from that constituted by the former authorised recording.

790 **Associated words.** Section 8 of the Act of 1956 further provides that, where a record comprises (with or without other material) a performance of a musical work, or of an adaptation of a musical work, in which words are sung, or are spoken incidentally to or in association with the music, and either no copyright subsists in that work or, if such copyright subsists, the conditions of the section are fulfilled in relation to that copyright, then if (i) the words consist or form part of a literary or dramatic work in which copyright subsists, (ii) such previous records as are referred to in paragraph (*a*) of subsection (1) of the section were made by, or with the licence of, the owner of the copyright in that literary or dramatic work, and (iii) the conditions as to notice and royalty are fulfilled ,the making of the record is not to constitute an infringement of the copyright in the literary or dramatic work.[33] The normal case covered by this provision is clearly the making of a record including associated words, where a similar record incorporating the same words has previously been made for retail sale with the consent of the owner of the copyrights both in the musical and in the literary or dramatic work. In this case, the exception clearly applies. But it seems possible to contend that this provision authorises the recording of the words of a song which have previously been recorded in association with different music from that with which the song was associated in the original record. This arises because it is not clear that "previous records" in sub-paragraph (ii) above means more than a previous record of the words of the song.

It is to be noticed that, except as aforesaid, section 8 of the Act of 1956 only applies to "musical works," and no compulsory rights can be acquired under that Act to reproduce either literary or dramatic works by means of mechanical contrivances.

791 **No licence to copy music.** Although a manufacturer has the right to make records in accordance with the terms of this section, he is not thereby entitled to copy the music in its graphic form in order to enable a performance to be given from which such records may be made.[34]

33 s. 8 (5).

34 *Chappell & Co., Ltd.* v. *Columbia Graphophone Co.* [1914] 2 Ch. 124, 745, where an order was made for delivery up of records made from music unlawfully copied.

792 **Previous recordings: Where made.** It is to be noted that to comply with this section, records must previously have been made in or imported into the United Kingdom. It has been held in Australia, on the construction of the similar provision in the Act of 1911, that the making of contrivances with the consent of the owner of the copyright in any Dominion to which that Act applied, released the work throughout the jurisdiction of that Act, although the owner in a different Dominion had not given any consent.[35] But that decision seems to have arisen from the fact that the Act of 1911 was regarded as a single code applicable throughout Her Majesty's Dominions. The first condition of section 8 of the Act of 1956 is that records have previously been made or imported with the licence of the owner of the copyright in the work and it is provided, in section 49 (6) of that Act, that in such a case the relevant owner of the copyright is the owner in the country into which the record was imported. The fact that that person may also be the owner of copyright in a foreign country under the law of that country and has consented to the making of records in that country would not, it is thought, be a compliance with the condition aforesaid.

793 **Inquiries as to previous recordings.** It is provided by subsection (7) of section 8 that, where a manufacturer requires to know whether previous records were made or imported by or with the licence of the owner of the copyright in the work, the manufacturer may make the prescribed inquiries and, if the owner of the copyright fails to reply to those inquiries within the prescribed period, the previous records are to be taken to have been made or imported, as the case may be, with the licence of the owner of the copyright.

794 **Further conditions.** The manufacturer having satisfied himself that the work he desires to record has been previously recorded as hereinbefore mentioned, there are three further conditions which have to be fulfilled in order that the making of the record shall not constitute an infringement of copyright.[36] The manufacturer must give to the owner of the copyright the prescribed notice of his intention to make the record. The manufacturer must intend to sell the record by retail, or to supply it for the purpose of its being sold by retail by another person, or must intend to use it for making other records which are to be so sold or supplied. Finally, in the case of every record which is sold by retail, the manufacturer must pay to the owner of the copyright, in the prescribed manner and at the prescribed time, a royalty of an amount ascertained in accordance with the provisions of section 8 of the Act of 1956.

[35] *Albert* v. *Hoffnung (S.) & Co., Ltd.* (1922) 22 S.R.(N.S.W.) 75; *Leo. Feist Incorp.* v. *The Gramophone Co., Ltd.* [1928] V.L.R. 420.
[36] Copyright Act, 1956, s. 8 (1) (*b*) (*c*) and (*d*).

795 **To whom notice is to be given.** The notice must, it is thought, in a case where the copyright in the work to be reproduced is vested in more than one person, be given to all such persons; and it is expressly provided in subsection (5) of section 8 of the Act of 1956 that, where it is proposed to reproduce on the record associated words, the notice must also be given to the owner of any literary or dramatic work in the associated words.

796 **Amount of royalty.** The normal standard royalty is to be an amount equal to $6\frac{1}{4}$ per cent. of the ordinary retail selling price of the record calculated in the prescribed manner.[37] But it is provided that, if the amount so calculated includes a fraction of a farthing, that fraction shall be reckoned as one farthing, and if, apart from this proviso, the amount of the royalty would be less than three-farthings, the amount thereof shall be three-farthings.[38] It is further provided that, in the case of a record which comprises (with or without other material, and either in their original form or in the form of adaptations) two or more musical works in which copyright subsists (a) the minimum royalty shall be three-farthings in respect of each of those works, and (b) if the owners of the copyright in the works are different persons, the royalty shall be apportioned among them in such manner as they may agree or as, in default of agreement, may be determined by arbitration.[38]

797 **Royalty where associated words.** On the other hand, although the right to use on a record associated words is also dependent upon the payment of the prescribed royalty, it is provided that, where associated words are used, not more than one royalty is to be paid in respect of a record on that account and, if copyright subsists both in the musical work and in the literary or dramatic work, and the owners are different persons, the royalty is to be apportioned among them (or among them and any other person entitled to a share thereof because there is more than one musical work on the record) as they may agree or as, in default of agreement, may be determined by arbitration.[39]

798 **Mechanical reproduction of works published before commencement of the Act of 1911.** As has already been mentioned,[40] mechanical rights were first conferred on owners of copyright by the Act of 1911, and consequently that Act provided that any work published before July 1, 1912, might be mechanically reproduced upon the prescribed notice, notwithstanding that the owner of the copyright

[37] s. 8 (2).
[38] s. 8 (4): see Decimal Currency Act, 1969, ss. 10 and 11.
[39] s. 8 (5).
[40] *Ante*, § 774.

had never authorised reproduction by records.[41] This position is maintained in the Act of 1956, which provides, in subsection (9) of section 8 of the Act of 1956 that, in relation to musical works published before July 1, 1912, the provisions of section 8 are to apply as if paragraph (*a*) of subsection (1), paragraph (*b*) of subsection (5), subsections (6) and (7), and the proviso to the last preceding subsection were omitted. In relation to records of music this seems clear and means that a manufacturer, in the case of a musical work so published, does not have to prove that records of the work, or of a similar adaptation of the work, have previously been made for the purposes of retail sale by or with the licence of the owner of the copyright in the work, but must comply with the other conditions, namely must manufacture for retail sale, must give the prescribed notice and must pay the prescribed royalty. The reduced royalty payable in respect of musical works so published under the provisions of the Act of 1911 [42] is not maintained. But the effect of this subsection in relation to associated words is not clear. If subsection (5) of section 8 of the Act of 1956 is read without sub-paragraph (*b*) there seems nothing to link the associated words with any previous recording. Presumably, however, what is meant is that, where a musical work was published before July 1, 1912, with associated words, then the work may be recorded with those words, notwithstanding that there has been no previous recording, on giving the prescribed notice and paying the prescribed royalty.

799 **Alteration of statutory rate of royalty.** The Act of 1911 enabled the statutory rate of royalty to be altered after a Board of Trade inquiry and an alteration was in fact made in the year 1928.[43] The Act of 1956 provides [44] that, if at any time after the end of a year from the commencement of the section it appears to the Board of Trade that the ordinary rate of royalty, or the minimum amount thereof in accordance with the provisions of the section, or in accordance with those provisions as last varied by an order made under this provision, has ceased to be equitable, either generally, or in relation to any class of records, the Board may hold a public inquiry. If in consequence of such an inquiry the Board are satisfied of the need to do so, the Board may make an order prescribing such different rate or amount, either generally, or in relation to any one or more classes of records, as the Board may consider just. Such an order has to be laid before Parliament and approved by resolution of each House.

[41] Copyright Act, 1911, s. 19 (7): *Chappell & Co., Ltd.* v. *Columbia Graphophone Co.* [1914] 2 Ch. 124; 745.

[42] Copyright Act, 1911, s. 19 (7) (*b*).

[43] s. 19 (3): Copyright Order Confirmation (Mechanical Instruments, Royalties) Act, 1928 (18 & 19 Geo. 5, c. 52).

[44] Copyright Act, 1956, s. 8 (3).

If an order is made, no further order is to be made less than five years after the date of the last previous order.

800 **Board of Trade regulations.** It is provided, in subsection (11) of section 8 of the Act of 1956, that regulations may be made by the Board of Trade to deal with the notice to be given by the manufacturer, the manner and time of payment of royalties and the nature of the inquiries to be made by a manufacturer to ascertain whether the previous recording was made by or with the consent of the owner of the copyright. So far as concerns the manner and time of payment of royalties, the Board of Trade is authorised to provide that the taking of such steps as may be specified in the regulations (being such steps as the Board consider most convenient for ensuring the receipt of the royalties by the owner of the copyright) shall be treated as constituting payment of the royalties in accordance with that paragraph.[45] This last provision was no doubt inserted in view of doubts raised in the case of *Monckton* v. *Pathé Frères, etc., Ltd.*[46] whether the system of adhesive labels set up by regulations under the Act of 1911 was a method of "securing" payment of royalties within subsection (6) of section 19 of the Act of 1911.

801 **As to notice of intention to make.** Board of Trade Regulations have been made pursuant to this power.[47] They prescribe the particulars to be set forth in the notice to be given by the manufacturer to the owner of the copyright of intention to make records of a work, and that such notice is to be given not less than fifteen days before any record is delivered to a purchaser or supplied for retail sale. If the name and address within the United Kingdom of the owner of the copyright or his agent is known, or can by reasonable inquiry be ascertained, the notice is to be sent to such owner or agent at such address, otherwise notice is to be given in the *London Gazette*.[48] These requirements are substantially the same as those prescribed under section 19 of the Act of 1911,[48a] save that the period of the notice has been increased from ten days to fifteen days and that the manufacturer has now to state the address at which he intends to make the records and sufficient particulars to identify the previous recording upon which he relies for the right to make records.

802 **As to mode of payment of royalty.** The Regulations then prescribe the method of payment of royalties which, as under the Act of 1911,

45 s. 8 (11).

46 [1914] 1 K.B. 395.

47 Copyright Royalty System (Records) Regulations, 1957 (S.I. 1957 No. 866), and Copyright Royalty System (Records) (Amendment) Regulations, 1962 (S.I. 1962 No. 2076), *post*, Appendix B, § 1612.

48 Reg. 1.

48a Copyright Royalty System (Mechanical Musical Instruments) Regulations 1912 (S.R. & O. 1912 No. 533): Copinger, *Copyright*, 8th ed., p. 425.

in default of agreement, is by means of adhesive labels. It was decided, under the Act of 1911, that there was no obligation upon the owner of the copyright to provide labels which will adhere to the type of contrivances manufactured; it was sufficient to provide labels which were, in fact, " adhesive " and it was for the manufacturer to see that they were made to adhere.[49] This would seem to be equally the case under the Act of 1956.

The procedure to be followed [50] is that the owner of the copyright is, within seven days of the date of the notice of intention to make records, to intimate to the manufacturer the place in the United Kingdom where labels can be obtained. The manufacturer is then required to specify the labels required and to tender the proper royalty. If labels are duly supplied, no records are to be supplied unless labels are attached thereto or, if the record is of a type that it is not reasonably practicable to attach an adhesive label thereto, to the container. If the manufacturer takes these steps he is deemed to have paid the royalties payable. If the owner of the copyright fails to intimate where labels can be obtained or to supply labels, the manufacturer may supply records without labels. In that case he is to keep an account, and the amount of the royalties due to the owner of the copyright is to be transferred to a special account and held in trust for the owner of the copyright. The comparable Regulation under the Copyright Act, 1911 provided that, in the like case, the amount of the royalties should be a debt due to the owner of the copyright. The change would appear to have important consequences in the event of the insolvency of the manufacturer, and may also affect a claim by the manufacturer to set up a defence based upon the Limitation Act, 1939.

803 **Where more than one work on one record.** It was held in Australia, under the Act of 1911, that where more than one work is placed on the same record and there has been no arbitration or agreement between the respective owners for apportionment of royalty, the manufacturers can only comply with the royalty provisions of the Act by paying to each the maximum royalty [51] or, if one only is known, by paying the maximum royalty to that one and remaining liable for the same amount to the other as a debt.[52] There does not appear to be anything in section 8 of the Act of 1956, or the Regulations made thereunder, substantially to affect the reasoning which led to these decisions.

804 **As to inquiries about previous recordings.** Finally the Regulations deal with the prescribed inquiries to be made by a manufacturer who

[49] *Boosey & Co., Ltd.* v. *Goodson Gramophone Record Co., Ltd.* [1930] 1 Ch. 448.
[50] Reg. 2.
[51] *Leo. Feist Incorp.* v. *The Gramophone Co., Ltd.* [1928] V.L.R. 420.
[52] *Albert* v. *The Gramophone Co., Ltd.* (1927) 28 S.R.(N.S.W.) 70.

requires to know whether previous records have been made or imported. These closely follow the provisions on this subject under the Act of 1911 and enable the inquiries, if the name of the owner is not known, to be addressed in general terms to the owner of the copyright in the work in question, and to be advertised in the *London Gazette*.[53]

805 **Effect of non-compliance with Regulations.** If there is any breach by the manufacturer of a record of any of the provisions of the Act or the Board of Trade Regulations, the effect will be that the record will be an infringement of the copyright in the work reproduced,[54] and not only will the manufacturer be exposed to an action for infringement, but also any person who sells the record knowing that such provisions have not been complied with.[55] It is to be noticed, however, that all the requirements of the Act and the Regulations have not to be complied with at one and the same time, and, in particular, that payment of the royalties does not become due until a record is sold. The only conditions precedent to the actual "making" of the record appear to be that records have been previously made or imported and that the prescribed notice has been given.[56] The Regulations do not require that any notice need be given of intention to make the record until fifteen days prior to the date when any record is "delivered to a purchaser."[57] But, unlike the Act of 1911, section 8 (1) (*b*) of the Act of 1956 requires the notice to be given before the record is made. On the other hand payment of the royalties is to be made at the time when adhesive labels are supplied by the proprietor of the copyright, and these labels must be procured before a record is sold.[58]

806 A contrivance, therefore, which has been lawfully made may subsequently be deemed to have been unlawfully made if the maker defaults in payment. By virtue of section 18 of the Act of 1956 such a contrivance would then become the property of the owner of the copyright and could be claimed by him from the person in whose hands it then was.

807 **No licence to cover imported records.** Under the Act of 1911 there was some uncertainty whether foreign manufacturers could comply with the provision of section 19 of that Act in respect of imported records. But section 8 (10) of the Act of 1956 expressly provides that nothing in section 8 is to be construed as authorising

53 Reg. 4.
54 *Monckton* v. *Pathé Frères, etc., Ltd.* [1914] 1 K.B. 395.
55 Copyright Act, 1956, s. 5.
56 Copyright Act, 1956, s. 8 (1) (*a*) and (*b*).
57 Reg. 1.
58 Reg. 2.

the importation of records which could not lawfully be imported apart from that section and that, where a question arises whether the making of a record made outside the United Kingdom would have constituted an infringement of copyright if the record had been made in the United Kingdom, that question is to be determined as if section 8 (1) had not been enacted. The importer therefore cannot argue, either for the purposes of section 5 (2), or section 18, that an imported record would not have constituted an infringement if it had been made in the United Kingdom on the ground that, if so made, the requirements of section 8 would have been complied with.

808 **Who is the relevant owner of copyright.** The person whose licence is required for previous recordings, and to whom notice must be given of intention to record, and to whom royalties have to be paid, is described in section 8 of the Act of 1956 as "the owner of the copyright." Where the copyright has been severed by assignment, this no doubt means the owner of that part of the copyright which restricts the reproduction of the work in the form of records. And it is expressly provided, in the Seventh Schedule to the Act of 1956, that references in section 8 of the Act to records previously made by, or with the licence of, the owner of the copyright in a work include references to records previously made by, or with the consent of, the owner of the copyright in that work under the Act of 1911.[59]

809 **In the case of pre-1911 works.** But in the case of musical works published before the commencement of the Act of 1911, that Act provided that, notwithstanding any assignment made before the passing of that Act of the copyright in a musical work, any rights conferred by that Act in respect of the making, or authorising the making, of contrivances by means of which the work might be mechanically performed, should belong to the author or his legal personal representatives and not to the assignee.[60] In view of the provisions of paragraph 28 of the Seventh Schedule to the Act of 1956, it would appear that the foregoing provision of the Act of 1911 remains operative in relation to musical works first published before the commencement of that Act. But it is thought that this provision would not apply to a specific pre-1911 assignment of the mechanical rights to be created by that Act, but was merely directed to negativing the effect of section 24 (1) of that Act and the Schedule thereto upon an assignment in general terms. It has been decided that, notwithstanding this provision, an assignee, before the Act of 1911, of the performing right in the work is entitled to perform the work in public by means of a mechanical contrivance; in other words, this provision does not reserve to the author the sole right to perform the work in

[59] Copyright Act, 1956, Sched. VII, para. 6 (1).
[60] Copyright Act, 1911, s. 19 (7) (*c*).

public by means of any contrivance.[61] It is doubtful whether the provisions of section 19 (7) (*c*) of the Act of 1911 apply to a pre-Act of 1911 assignment of words associated with music.

4.—COPYRIGHT IN SOUND RECORDINGS

810 So far this chapter has dealt with the mechanical rights of owners of the copyright in literary, dramatic or musical works. A quite separate matter is the copyright conferred by the Act of 1956 in respect of the records themselves. This copyright is conferred primarily by section 12 of the Act of 1956 and is conferred in respect of " sound recordings," which are defined as meaning the aggregate of the sounds embodied in and capable of being reproduced by means of a record of any description other than a sound track associated with a cinematograph film.[62] The Act of 1911 conferred copyright on records, perforated rolls and other contrivances " in like manner as if such contrivances were musical works," but for a term of fifty years from the making of the original plate.[63] The Act of 1956 does not make the copyright in sound recordings equivalent to that in musical works, but deals separately with the nature of such copyright.

811 **Conditions for subsistence of copyright.** In order that copyright shall subsist under the Act of 1956 in a sound recording it is necessary, either that the maker should have been a qualified person at the time when the recording was made, or that, if the recording has been published, the first publication should have taken place in the United Kingdom or in another country to which section 12 of that Act extends.[64] For the purposes of this provision the maker of a sound recording is the person who owned the record at the time when the recording was made,[65] and the recording is made at the time when the first record embodying the recording is produced.[65] Having regard to the definitions in the Act of 1956 of " sound recording " and " record," it would seem that, as soon as some kind of device is made from a live performance of a musical work, there is an initial making which will be treated as the making, not only of that device, but of any device reproduced directly or indirectly therefrom. " Publication," in relation to a sound recording, is defined as meaning the issue to the public of records embodying the recording or any part thereof,[66] and it seems, therefore, to follow that a sound recording is published as soon as any record or any other device derived directly or indirectly therefrom is issued to the public, and that such

61 *Thompson* v. *Warner Bros. Pictures, Ltd.* [1929] 2 Ch. 308.
62 Copyright Act, 1956, s. 12 (9).
63 Copyright Act, 1911, s. 19 (1).
64 Copyright Act, 1956, s. 12 (1) and (2).
65 s. 12 (8).
66 s. 12 (9).

publication will cover the whole range of pressings, however derived, which comprise the same sounds. Thus, in the case of published records, the subsistence of copyright does not depend on the place where the music is recorded from a live performance, but on the place where records directly or indirectly derived therefrom are first issued to the public. On the other hand, until records are issued to the public, the subsistence of the copyright in the sound recording will depend upon the place of incorporation of the company making the recording. It is assumed that, in most cases, the maker will be in fact a limited company though, if it is not, then the usual requirements for a qualified person who is an individual, namely, citizenship, domicile, or residence, will apply.[67]

812 **First owner of copyright.** The first owner of the copyright in a sound recording is normally the maker, as above defined, but, where a person commissions the making of a sound recording, and pays or agrees to pay for it in money or money's worth, and the recording is made in pursuance of that commission, that person, in the absence of any agreement to the contrary, is to be entitled to the copyright.[68] The position with regard to commissioned recordings is thus similar to that existing under section 4 of the Act of 1956 with regard to commissioned photographs. It is further stated that these provisions as to commissioned sound recordings are subject to the provisions of Part VI of the Act,[68] presumably referring to assignments of prospective copyrights and to the rights of government departments.

813 **Term of copyright.** The term of copyright in a sound recording is from the making of the sound recording until the end of the period of fifty years from the end of the calendar year in which the recording is first published.[69] This period is different from that conferred by the Act of 1911,[70] and, consequently, special provisions had to be made in respect of sound recordings made before the commencement of the Act of 1956.[70] In the case of such sound recordings the term of copyright is to subsist until the end of the period of fifty years from the end of the calendar year in which the recording was made.

814 **Acts restricted by copyright.** The acts restricted by the copyright in a sound recording are the making of a record embodying the recording, causing the recording to be heard in public, and broadcasting the recording,[71] including, in each case, a substantial part

[67] s. 1 (5) (*a*).
[68] s. 12 (4).
[69] s. 12 (3).
[70] Sched. VII, para. 11.
[71] s. 12 (5); as to " causing," see §§ 520, 541, *ante*.

thereof.[72] Any such acts will constitute an infringement, whether a record embodying the recording is utilised directly or indirectly in doing them.[71] It is therefore an infringement of the copyright in the sound recording to make any kind of device whereby the same sounds may be mechanically recorded, but it would not be an infringement of that copyright to reproduce the recorded material in musical notation or other written form. It is to be noted, however, that causing a recording to be heard in public, and broadcasting a recording, are not restricted acts in respect of sound recordings originating in foreign countries, and protected by virtue of the Order in Council made in pursuance of section 31 of the Act, except in the case of specified countries which give similar protection to United Kingdom sound recordings.[73]

815 **Labelling of records.** The Act of 1956 contains special provisions designed to secure that records shall be labelled with the year of first publication so that it may be known when the copyright expires.[74] It is provided that the copyright in a sound recording is not infringed, by a person who does an act which would otherwise be an infringement, if records embodying that recording, or the part of the recording used, had previously been issued to the public in the United Kingdom and, at the time when those records were so issued, they did not bear a label or other mark indicating the year in which the recording was first published. It is, however, provided that this exemption will not apply if it is shown that the records in question were not issued by or with the licence of the owner of the copyright, or that the owner of the copyright had taken all reasonable steps for securing that records embodying the recording, or the part thereof in question, would not be issued to the public in the United Kingdom without such a label or mark, either on the records themselves, or on their containers. Furthermore, these provisions do not apply to a sound recording made before the commencement of section 12 of the Act of 1956.[75] While obligations are thus imposed on record manufacturers with regard to labelling, such labelling will help to establish the title to the copyright in view of the presumptions established in section 20 (7) of the Act.[76]

816 **Restriction on performing rights.** As already mentioned,[77] representations were made before the 1952 Copyright Committee that the performing right in sound recordings should be restricted. Accord-

72 s. 49 (1).
73 The Copyright (International Conventions) Order, 1964 (S.I. 1964 No. 690), Art. 3. The countries in question are set out in the Third Sched. thereto, *post*, § 1880.
74 Copyright Act, 1956, s. 12 (6).
75 Sched. 7, para. 12.
76 *Ante*, § 587.
77 *Ante*, § 775.

ingly it is provided, in subsection (7) of section 12 of the Copyright Act of 1956, that the copyright in a sound recording is not infringed (a) by its performance at any premises where persons reside or sleep, as part of the amenities provided exclusively or mainly for residents or inmates, or (b) if it is performed as part of the activities of, or for the benefit of, a club, society or other organisation, which is not established or conducted for profit and whose main objects are charitable or are otherwise concerned with the advancement of religion, education or social welfare. It is, however, provided [78] that the exemption of premises where persons reside or sleep shall not apply if a special charge is made for admission to the part of the premises where the recording is to be heard. It is also provided [79] that the exemption shall not apply in the case of an organisation, if a charge is made for admission to the place where the recording is to be heard, and any of the proceeds of the charge are applied otherwise than for the purposes of the organisation. This would appear to involve that no part of the admission charge may be used for administration expenses.

In *Phonographic Performance, Ltd.* v. *Pontins, Ltd.*[80] the plaintiffs sought to restrain the playing of records of musical works over loudspeakers at a holiday camp, but the defendants, by their defence, relied on section 12 (7) (*a*) of the Act of 1956. The camp covered a considerable area of land. There were rows of chalets where visitors and their children slept, and there were other chalets where the staff slept. There were a number of other buildings, in particular, a large central block, called the amenity block, containing a dining room, cafe, television lounges, a sun-lounge, a bar and a shop. There was also a covered swimming pool, a reception block and a number of lavatory blocks. In the open dotted about the camp were tennis courts and a paddling pool for children, and lawns. The visitors could stay for as long as they liked, but the normal period of stay was one week. Day visitors, friends of the campers, were admitted. The recorded music was transmitted through eighteen loudspeakers in the amenity building, two in the reception building, one in the swimming pool and several placed in the open at suitable positions, so that the sounds transmitted from them could reach practically all over the camp.

It was common ground that records were being caused to be heard in public without the plaintiff's licence and, therefore, it was simply a question of whether section 12 (7) (*a*) applied. The proviso could not apply as no special charge was made for admission to any part of the camp where the records could be heard. Cross J.

78 Copyright Act, 1956, s. 12 (7), proviso (i).
79 s. 12 (7), proviso (ii).
80 [1968] Ch. 290.

decided[81] that section 12 (7) (*a*) did apply, namely that, in the circumstances of this particular holiday camp, the records were caused to be heard at premises where persons resided or slept, as part of the amenities provided exclusively or mainly for residents or inmates therein.

It was contended, by the plaintiffs, that one could not take the camp, as a whole as being " premises," but that there were a number of different premises—chalets, amenity hall and so on. But the learned judge said he could not draw any distinction between the camp in question and a seaside hotel; the camp as a whole could properly be regarded as the premises. In considering the connection between " reside or sleep " and " residents or inmates " the learned judge thought that the words " sleep " and " inmates " were probably used in contradistinction to " reside " and " residents " to cover institutions such as prisons and asylums. But, in that case, he had to consider the words " reside " and " residents " and, although " reside " had different meanings in different contexts, in his judgment visitors to the camp were residents residing in the premises for the purposes of section 12 (7) (*a*).

In relation to the expression " as part of the amenities provided " the learned judge said that, although it was true there was more organised entertainment for visitors to the camp than one would find at an ordinary hotel, the music, though there was a good deal of it, was only part of the whole amenities provided by those running the camp. Finally he considered the words " exclusively or mainly for residents or inmates therein." He said that the camp was unlike an ordinary hotel in that members of the public could not enter the camp freely and have a drink or meal. Day visitors were only allowed if they were friends of resident guests. Visiting hours were restricted, an entry fee was charged and tickets had to be purchased for their visitors by the resident guests. The learned judge found great force in the defendants' argument that, in these circumstances, it could fairly be said that the amenities were provided exclusively for the residents but that, even if the amenities were provided in part for the day visitors, the number of day visitors was trifling compared with the total number of residents and the amenities were, therefore, provided mainly for the residents.

817 **Decisions under the Rating, etc., Act 1955.** The words " organisation which is not established or conducted for profit and whose main objects are charitable or are otherwise concerned with the advancement of religion, education or social welfare," also appear in section 8 of the Rating and Valuation (Miscellaneous Provisions)

[81] *Ibid.* at p. 296.

Act, 1955.[82] Whether the objects of an organisation are charitable or not is a question of the general law of charity upon which there is a great mass of authority. Legal charities have to fall into one of four classes, namely, the relief of poverty, the advancement of education, the advancement of religion, and other purposes beneficial to the community: *Income Tax Commissioners* v. *Pemsel.*[83] But, in addition to this, there must be an element of public benefit, so that a trust for the education of employees of a particular company is not a valid legal charity: *Oppenheim* v. *Tobacco Securities Trust Co., Ltd.*[84] The expression " social welfare " in the Rating Act has been the subject of a number of decisions. It has been held that the expression means the well-being (whether in the physical, mental or material sense) of individuals as members of society,[85] and that the words " concerned with the advancement of " involve that the organisation does more than enable individuals to advance their own welfare,[86] and that such advancement must be a direct object of the organisation.[87] But it seems doubtful whether the element of public benefit necessary for a charity need subsist.[88] There have also been decisions upon the words " religion "[89] and " education "[90] in the Rating Act.

It will be noted that, where such an organisation is held to exist, the exception applies whether the record is performed as part of the activities of the organisation, which would presumably mean for the entertainment of those whose education or whose social welfare is being advanced, or if it is performed for the benefit of the organisation, which would include a performance given to outsiders where the proceeds of the performance are applied for the purposes of the organisation.

818 **Broadcasting and diffusion of sound recordings.** It is to be observed that the acts restricted by the copyright in a sound recording do not include, as in the case of other copyright material, causing

82 4 Eliz. 2, c. 9. See also the Miners' Welfare Act, 1952 (15 & 16 Geo. 6 & 1 Eliz. 2, c. 23), s. 16.

83 [1891] A.C. 531.

84 [1951] A.C. 297.

85 *National Deposit Friendly Society (Trustees)* v. *Skegness U.D.C.* [1959] A.C. 293; *Berry* v. *St. Marylebone B.C.* [1958] Ch. 406.

86 *National Deposit Friendly Society (Trustees)* v. *Skegness U.D.C., supra*; *Independent Order of Oddfellows, etc.* v. *Manchester Corporation* [1957] 1 W.L.R. 1059.

87 *General Nursing Council, etc.* v. *St. Marylebone B.C.* [1957] 1 W.L.R. 941; [1958] Ch. 921; but compare *Royal College of Nursing* v. *St. Marylebone B.C.* [1958] 1 W.L.R. 95.

88 *Berry* v. *St. Marylebone B.C., supra*; *National Deposit Friendly Society (Trustees)* v. *Skegness U.D.C., supra*, but compare *Derbyshire Miners' Welfare Committee* v. *Skegness U.D.C.* [1957] 1 W.L.R. 764; [1958] 1 Q.B. 298.

89 *United Grand Lodge, etc.* v. *Holborn B.C.* [1957] 1 W.L.R. 1080; *Berry* v. *St. Marylebone B.C., supra.*

90 *Chartered Insurance Institute* v. *London Corporation* [1957] 1 W.L.R. 867.

it to be transmitted to subscribers to a diffusion service.[91] Furthermore, while it seems to follow from the words " directly or indirectly," in section 12 (5) of the Act of 1956, that an infringement of the right to cause the record to be heard in public would be committed by the operation of a receiving set, whether such set picks up a broadcast performance directly from wireless waves or indirectly by means of diffusion, it is expressly provided, in section 40 (1) of the Act of 1956, that where a sound broadcast or television broadcast is made by the B.B.C. or the I.T.A., and a person, by the reception of that broadcast, causes a sound recording to be heard in public, he does not thereby infringe the copyright in that recording under section 12 of that Act. If, however, the sound broadcast or television broadcast is not made by the Corporation or the Authority, the right in the sound recording may be infringed by a public performance at the receiving end, and, in this case, there is not, as in the case of the rediffusion of foreign broadcasts,[92] any special provision requiring the Performing Right Tribunal to take into account charges made to the foreign broadcast authority for the use of the material.

819 **Sound tracks not " records."** As already stated, the definition of sound recording excludes a sound track associated with a cinematograph film,[93] and this phrase is defined in section 13 (10) of the Act of 1956 as meaning any record of sounds which is incorporated in any print, negative, tape or other article on which the film or part of it, in so far as it consists of visual images, is recorded, or which is issued by the maker of the film for use in conjunction with such an article. Such a sound recording is protected as part of the cinematograph film and not as a sound recording. It is provided, in section 13 (9) of the Act of 1956 that, where the sounds embodied in any sound track are also embodied in a record other than such a sound track, or a record derived (directly or indirectly) from such a sound track, copyright in the film is not infringed by any use made of the record, but this is a limitation upon the copyright in the sound track of films, not upon the copyright in sound recordings existing apart from, though associated with, such sound track. It would appear, therefore, that if the sounds embodied in a sound track are also embodied in some other form of record, then copyright will subsist in such sound recording under section 12 of the Act of 1956. This might happen if a live performance was recorded on a record other than a sound track at the same time as it was recorded on a sound track, or if a record other than the sound track was made from the sound track.

[91] Copyright Act, 1956, s. 12 (5).
[92] Copyright Act, 1956, s. 28.
[93] *Ante*, § 810.

820 **Indirect infringements.** Section 16 of the Act of 1956 creates infringements of the copyright in sound recordings by importation, sale and distribution of articles, the making of which would have constituted an infringement of the copyright in the sound recording, similar to those conferred by section 5 of the Act of 1956, with regard to literary, dramatic, musical or artistic works.[94]

821 **Copyright in records is an additional and independent right.** It is, however, expressly provided, in section 16 (6) of the Act of 1956, that copyright in a sound recording is in no way to affect the copyright in any literary, dramatic, musical or artistic work from which the subject-matter is wholly or partly derived, so that the copyright in the sound recording is to be additional to, and independent of, any copyright subsisting in such material. This had been held to be the case in respect of the corresponding provision of the Act of 1911.[95]

822 **Records "infringing copies."** Section 18 (3) of the Act of 1956 includes, in the definition of "infringing copy," a record embodying a sound recording, so that the provisions of that section in regard to the conversion or detention of infringing copies are applicable to infringing copies of sound recordings.

823 **Statutory presumptions.** While, however, the remedies both for conversion and infringement are the same in the case of infringements of sound recordings as in the case of infringement of other material, it is only the first set of presumptions in section 20 of the Act of 1956 that apply to sound recordings.[96]

824 **Summary proceedings.** The summary proceedings provided by section 21 of the Act of 1956 apply to sound recordings, except subsection (5) which is limited to performances of literary, dramatic or musical works. As already stated in relation to infringements of mechanical rights, the power to stop infringing copies, by notice to the Commissioners of Customs, is only applicable to printed copies and therefore does not include records.[97]

825 **Government sound recordings.** There are special provisions about Government sound recordings which are dealt with in the relevant part of this book.[98]

94 Including articles which would have constituted an infringement under the Act of 1911 (Copyright Act, 1956, Sched. 7, para. 19).

95 *Gramophone Co., Ltd.* v. *Stephen Cawardine & Co.* [1934] Ch. 450; *Chappell & Co., Ltd.* v. *Columbia Graphophone Co.* [1914] 2 Ch. 124 and 745; *Australian Performing Right Association, Ltd.* v. *3 D.B. Broadcasting Co. Pty., Ltd.* [1929] V.L.R. 107.

96 See *ante*, § 587.

97 Copyright Act, 1956, s. 22.

98 See § 882, *post*.

826 **Use of material by schools.** The special exemptions with regard to the use of material by schools apply to sound recordings.[99]

827 **Records made before the commencement of the Act of 1911.** Copyright is not to subsist in a sound recording made before July 1, 1912, unless copyright subsisted therein under section 19 (8) of the Act of 1911.[100] This subsection in fact conferred copyright on contrivances made before the commencement of the Act of 1911 in like manner, and for the like term, as if the Act of 1911 had been in force at the making of the original plate from which the contrivance was directly or indirectly derived. The only qualification was that the making of that contrivance must not have been such as to have infringed the copyright in some other contrivance if the Act of 1911 had then been in force. In general, therefore, copyright would seem still to subsist in sound recordings made within the last fifty years.

[The next paragraph is 841]

[99] Copyright Act, 1956, s. 41 (5).
[100] Sched. 7, para. 13.

Chapter 18

TELEVISION BROADCASTS AND SOUND BROADCASTS

841 **Old law: no copyright in broadcast as such.** Under the Copyright Act 1911 no copyright subsisted in a broacast as such, since it was not a literary, dramatic, musical or artistic work. This is equally the case so far as concerns the works protected under Part 1 of the Copyright Act, 1956. Of course, in so far as a programme which is broadcast consists of a musical or dramatic work or is broadcast from a script, which is a literary work in which copyright subsists, the public performance of the material broadcast would constitute an infringement of copyright in the material, and, if the material is reproduced on a record or device, this will also constitute an infringement of the copyright in the original material. For instance, it has been held, in the case of *Performing Right Society, Ltd.* v. *Hammond's Bradford Brewery Co., Ltd.*,[1] that a person who switches on a receiving set in a public place infringes the author's copyright in music broadcast by giving a fresh public performance at the place where the receiving set is situate.

842 In so far, however, as the material broadcast did not enjoy copyright protection in itself, a performance by a person who received the programme in a public place did not involve an infringement of copyright, nor was it an infringement of copyright to record the performance on a record or other device. This would apply, in particular, to broadcasts of outside programmes such as sporting events, processions, historic occasions and the like. It would also apply where the programme broadcast consisted of unscripted dialogues or discussions, quiz programmes and such material as music-hall sketches or gags, where the value of the performance consists in the visual " business " in which copyright, in the ordinary sense, does not subsist.

843 **Copyright Committee.** Strong representations were made before the 1951 Copyright Committee that a new form of copyright should be conferred in respect of broadcast programmes. It was contended that, unless a right of this sort was conferred, it would be difficult to obtain permission to broadcast, particularly by television, sporting spectacles and outside events because the promoters would require some control over the area and extent of the use of the material. It was also pointed out that, without control, broadcast programmes

[1] [1934] Ch. 121.

were being reproduced on records or other devices and distributed to the public; that some of these reproductions were of an indifferent character and reflected adversely on the programme and those taking part in its preparation and presentation. The Committee recommended that a broadcasting authority should have the right to prevent the copying of its programmes, and should have a performing right in television programmes but not in sound programmes.[2]

844 **Present law.** The provisions of the Copyright Act, 1956, in regard to television and sound broadcasts, are principally contained in section 14 of that Act. Such copyright is conferred in respect of every television broadcast and every sound broadcast, made by the British Broadcasting Corporation or by the Independent Television Authority, from a place in the United Kingdom or in any other country to which section 14 of the Act of 1956 is extended.[3] This right, however, is conferred only in respect of a television broadcast or a sound broadcast made after the commencement of that Act.[4]

845 **Commonwealth and foreign organisations.** Copyright protection may, by Order in Council, be made to apply to television broadcasts and sound broadcasts made from foreign countries by organisations constituted under the laws of such countries.[5] A European Agreement on the Protection of Television Broadcasts was concluded on June 22, 1960,[6] and in pursuance thereof protection was applied by Orders in Council [7] to France, Sweden and Denmark. By the Copyright (International Conventions) Order, 1964,[8] Article 8, protection is given, in respect of sound broadcasts, to the countries named in the Fifth Schedule thereto and, in respect of television broadcasts, to the countries named in the Sixth Schedule thereto. Such protection also

[2] Cmd. 8662, paras. 117, 186 and 192.

[3] Copyright Act, 1956, s. 14 (1). s. 14 has been extended to the Isle of Man (1959, No. 861 and 1970, No. 1437), Sarawak (1959, No. 2215), Gibraltar (1960, No. 847), Fiji (1961, No. 60), Uganda (1961, No. 2462), Zanzibar (1961, No. 2463 and 1962, No. 629), Bermuda (1962, No. 1642), North Borneo (1962, No. 1643), Bahamas (1962, No. 2184), Virgin Islands (1962, No. 2185), Falkland Islands (1963, No. 1037), St. Helena (1963, No. 1038), Seychelles (1963, No. 1039), Kenya (1963, No. 1147), Mauritius (1964, No. 689), Montserrat (1965, No. 1858), St. Lucia (1965, No. 1859), Bechuanaland (1965, No. 2009), Cayman Islands (1965, No. 2010), Grenada (1965, No. 2158), British Guiana (1966, No. 79), British Honduras (1966, No. 685), and Saint Vincent (1967, No. 974).

[4] Copyright Act, 1956, Sched. 7, para. 17.

[5] s. 32

[6] Cmnd. 1163. See text, *post*, Appendix C., § 1757; ratified by the United Kingdom on October 30, 1963, and entered into force on May 18, 1964. A Protocol to such Agreement was concluded on January 22, 1965, and entered into force on March 24, 1965; Cmnd. 2744. It was signed without reservation in respect of ratification by the United Kingdom on February 23, 1965. See text, *post*, Appendix C, § 1772. See also European Agreement concerning Programme Exchanges by means of Television Films concluded on December 15, 1958 (Cmnd. 1509, text, *post*, Appendix C, § 1778) signed by the United Kingdom on December 15, 1958, and entered into force on July 1, 1961.

[7] 1961, No. 993 and 1962, No. 165.

[8] 1964, No. 690, as amended, *post*, §§ 1882 and 1883.

obtains in Gibraltar,[9] and Bermuda.[9a] Further, by an Order in Council made in 1961 [10] (replacing one made in 1959 [11]) protection is given to organisations in countries to which section 14 of the Act of 1956 has been extended.[8]

846 **Definitions.** The expression "television broadcast" is defined as meaning visual images broadcast by way of television together with any sounds broadcast for reception along with those images, and the expression "sound broadcast" is defined as meaning sounds broadcast otherwise than as part of a television broadcast.[12] The copyright, therefore, is conferred in respect of visual images and sounds. Copyright is only conferred if these are broadcast by one of the two bodies mentioned and from such a place as is mentioned. Further, it is provided that a broadcast is to be taken to be made by the body by whom, at the time when, and from the place from which, the visual images or sounds in question, or both, as the case may be, are broadcast.[12]

847 **"Broadcasting."** Broadcasting, for the purposes of the Act of 1956 is defined [13] by reference to the same expression in the Wireless Telegraphy Act, 1949, and means, in substance, the emission of messages by electro-magnetic energy otherwise than over wires. It will be observed that the expression "broadcast" is not defined in such a way as to distinguish it from other forms of wireless communication, but it is assumed that the expression necessarily involves that the messages shall be received, or be capable of being received, by a large public.

848 **Rights transmissible.** The copyright thus created vests initially in the British Broadcasting Corporation or the Independent Television Authority as the case may be, but the provisions of sections 36 and 37 of the Act of 1956 apply equally in this form of copyright, so that the bodies in question may assign or license their rights to, or vest them initially and before the actual broadcast in, some other person.

849 **Restrictions on transmissibility in respect of performing rights in television broadcasts.** In this connection, however, there is an express limitation on the powers of the Corporation and the Authority in so far as concerns the performing right in television broadcasts.[14] This

[9] 1966, Nos. 945 and 1409, 1968, No. 1858, 1970, Nos. 290 and 637.
[9a] 1969, No. 743, 1970, Nos. 290 and 637.
[10] 1961, No. 2460.
[11] 1959, No. 2214.
[12] Copyright Act, 1956, s. 14 (10).
[13] s. 48 (2).
[14] Copyright Act, 1956, s. 37 (4), and Sched. 5, para. 1.

right may not be assigned by these bodies, except to an organisation duly appointed for the purposes of the Fifth Schedule to the Act of 1956, and, where such a right has been assigned to such an organisation, it shall not be assignable by the organisation, except to the Corporation or the Authority, as the case may be, or to another organisation subsequently appointed for the purposes of the said Fifth Schedule.[15]

The general effect of the provisions of the Fifth Schedule to the Act of 1956 is that the Corporation and the Authority may jointly appoint an organisation, or each of them separately may appoint an organisation for the purposes of negotiating or granting licences in respect of the performing right in television broadcasts.[16] The appointment or the termination of the appointment of such an organisation must be advertised, not less than fourteen days before the appointment or termination is to take effect in the *London Gazette*, the *Edinburgh Gazette* and the *Belfast Gazette*, and such advertisement must specify the name and address of the organisation and the date on which the appointment or termination is to take effect, and must state whether the appointment or termination of appointment is made by the Corporation or the Authority, or by both of them.[17] Neither the Corporation or the Authority, nor any such organisation, is to authorise any organisation or person, other than a person in their respective employment under a contract of service, to negotiate or act for them with respect to the granting of licences in respect of the rights aforesaid.[18] These provisions, however, apply only in respect of the performing right in television broadcasts,[19] and the other rights granted by section 14 of the Act of 1956 may, presumably, be subject to assignment or other dealing in the same way as any other copyright under that Act.

850 **Term of copyright.** The term of copyright in a television or sound broadcast is a period until the end of fifty years from the end of the calendar year in which the broadcast is made.[20] If a broadcast is repeated, no copyright is to subsist in the repetition if it is made after the end of the period of fifty years from the end of the calendar year in which the first broadcast was made, and if it is made before the end of that period, any copyright subsisting therein is to expire at the end of the period.[21] This means, in effect that no addition to the term of copyright can be acquired by virtue of a repetition of a broadcast, but, presumably, if a repetition involves any substantial alteration of the material, a new copyright will be acquired

15 Sched. 5, para. 4.
16 Copyright Act, 1956, Sched. 5, para. 1, 2 and 3.
17 Sched. 5, para. 6.
18 Sched. 5, para. 5 (1) and (2).
19 Sched. 5, para. 1.
20 s. 14 (2).
21 s. 14 (3).

in respect of the additional matter. It is further provided that a television broadcast or sound broadcast made before the commencement of section 14 of the Act of 1956 is to be disregarded,[22] so that, if a broadcast so made is repeated after the commencement of the section, copyright will subsist therein as if it were a new broadcast.

851 **Acts restricted.** The copyright conferred by section 14 of the Act of 1956 in respect of broadcasts restricts two classes of acts, namely, the recording of such broadcasts on some recording device, and the performance of such broadcasts.[23] So far as the first class of rights is concerned, it is provided that, in the case of a television broadcast, in so far as it consists of visual images, the making, otherwise than for private purposes, of a cinematograph film of it, or a copy of such film, is a restricted act. In the case of a sound broadcast or of a television broadcast, in so far as it consists of sounds, the making, otherwise than for private purposes, of a sound recording of it, or a record embodying such a recording, is a restricted act. With regard to the second class of restriction, it is provided that, in the case of a television broadcast, causing it, in so far as it consists of visual images, to be seen in public, or, in so far as it consists of sounds, to be heard in public, if it is seen or heard by a paying audience, is a restricted act. But there is no similar restriction in respect of simple sound broadcasts. It is further provided that, in the case either of a television broadcast or of a sound broadcast, rebroadcasting it is a restricted act. Again, it is provided that the restrictions aforesaid in relation to a television broadcast or sound broadcast made by the Corporation or the Authority, shall apply whether the act in question is done by the reception of the broadcast, or by making use of any record, print, negative, tape or other article on which the broadcast in question has been recorded.[24] "Reception of a television broadcast or a sound broadcast" receives an extended definition to cover simultaneous transmissions, other than by way of broadcasting, and retransmissions, in section 48 (4) of the Copyright Act, 1956.

852 **Infringement of television broadcasts consisting of visual images.** So far as concerns television broadcasts consisting of visual images, it is provided that the restrictions imposed are to apply to any sequence of images sufficient to be seen as a moving picture, and that, for the purpose of establishing an infringement of such copyright, it is not necessary to prove that the act in question extended to more than such a sequence of images.[25] It appears, however, to be implied

22 Sched. 7, para. 18.
23 Copyright Act, 1956, s. 14 (4).
24 s. 14 (5).
25 s. 14 (6).

from this provision that the reproduction, or exhibition, of a single picture, or series of separate pictures, which could not be used as a moving picture, would not constitute an infringement.

853 **"Otherwise than for private purposes."** The making of films or records of broadcasts is only an infringement of the broadcasting rights if made otherwise than for private purposes. It is provided that a film or record shall be taken to be made, otherwise than for private purposes, if made for the purposes of sale or letting for hire of any copy of the film or record, broadcasting the film or record, or causing the film or record to be seen or heard in public.[26] It should be observed that the expression here is " in public " and not " by a paying audience" and may, therefore, have a more extensive operation. As will be seen,[27] it may not be an infringement of the broadcasting rights to cause television programmes to be seen by certain clubs or associations, but it may well be an infringement of the recording rights for such associations to record performances for future exhibition to their members.

854 **Causing a television broadcast to be seen in public.** The performing rights in television broadcasts are infringed by causing them to be seen or heard in public by a paying audience.[28] The expression " causing to be seen in public " does not seem to involve any difference in meaning from the more usual phrase " performing in public." A direct act will be done by anyone who operates a television set, or exhibits a film on which a broadcast has been recorded. It will be observed that section 5 (5) of the Act of 1956, dealing with infringements by permitting a place of public entertainment to be used for a performance, does not apply to television broadcasts. But the general provision of section 1 (1) of the Act of 1956, including in " copyright " the right to authorise other persons to do restricted acts, applies equally to television broadcasts, since it is provided, in section 1 (4) of that Act, that the provisions of that section are to apply in relation to any subject-matter of a description to which any provision of Part 2 of that Act relates as they apply in relation to a work. Furthermore, decisions, such as *Marsh* v. *Conquest*[29] on the liability under the law before 1911 for " causing a dramatic piece to be represented," may be in point in regard to the liability of owners or licensees of premises at which television broadcasts are shown in public.

855 **Causing a television broadcast to be seen by a paying audience.** Liability, however, is restricted to performances before a paying

[26] Copyright Act, 1956, s. 14 (7).
[27] § 855, *post.*
[28] Copyright Act, 1956, s. 14 (4) (*c*).
[29] (1864) 17 C.B. 418. See § 520, *ante.*

audience, and it is provided that a television broadcast shall be taken to be seen or heard by a paying audience if it is seen or heard by persons who had been admitted for payment to the place where the broadcast is to be seen or heard, or have been admitted for payment to a place of which that place forms part.[30] It is also to be taken to be seen or heard by a paying audience if the persons have been admitted to the place where the broadcast is to be seen or heard in circumstances where goods or services are supplied there at prices which exceed the prices usually charged at that place, and are partly attributable to the facilities afforded for seeing or hearing the broadcast.[31] It is, perhaps, a little surprising that the condition is that the prices should exceed the prices usually charged at that place, rather than prices usually charged for equivalent services at other places, since it would seem that if enhanced prices are regularly charged because of broadcasting facilities, the place is not within the section. It is further provided that, in deciding whether persons have been admitted for payment to the place where the broadcast is to be seen or heard, no account is to be taken of persons admitted to the place in question as residents or inmates therein, or of persons admitted to that place as members of a club or society, where the payment is only for membership of the club or society, and the provision of facilities for seeing or hearing television broadcasts is only incidental to the main purposes of the club or society.[32] It is to be noted that this is only an exception to the first provision, so that if the residents or members are supplied with goods or services at enhanced prices attributable to the television facilities, performance may nevertheless be within the second provision. These provisions may be compared with those of section 12 (7) of the Act of 1956, which contain exemptions from the infringement of performing rights in records in the case of performances at premises where persons reside or sleep, or as part of the activities of a club or organisation.[33] There is a further provision, in section 41 of the Act of 1956, to the effect that a television broadcast shall not be treated as being heard or seen in public, if performed in the course of the activities of a school, by a person who is a teacher in or pupil in attendance at the school, and if the audience is limited to persons who are teachers in or pupils in attendance at the school or otherwise directly connected with the activities of the school: a parent or guardian is not to be taken as a person directly connected with the activities of a school by reason only that he is a parent or guardian of a pupil in attendance at the school.[34] It would seem, however, that this class of

[30] Copyright Act, 1956, s. 14 (8) (*a*).

[31] Copyright Act, 1956, s. 14 (8) (*b*).

[32] s. 14 (8), proviso.

[33] See *Phonographic Performance, Ltd.* v. *Pontins, Ltd.* [1968] Ch. 290 and § 816, *ante*.

[34] Copyright Act, 1956, s. 41 (3) (4) and (5).

performance would not, in any event, be a performance before a paying audience.

856 **Judicial proceedings.** There is a further provision that the copyright in a television broadcast or sound broadcast is not infringed by anything done in relation to the broadcast for the purposes of a judicial proceeding.[35]

857 **No performance of broadcasts by operation of broadcast relay stations, etc.** The Act of 1956 further provides that the causing of subject-matter to be transmitted to subscribers to a diffusion service shall not be taken to constitute causing visual images or sounds to be seen or heard, nor shall the operation of any apparatus whereby signals are transmitted, directly or indirectly, to a receiving apparatus, whether over paths provided by a material substance or not. But, in so far as the display or emission of the images or sounds causes them to be seen or heard, the same shall be taken to be effected by the operation of the receiving apparatus.[36] While, therefore, the performance or use of material relayed from a broadcast relay station may constitute an infringement of the broadcasting rights, the operation of the relay station itself will not constitute such an infringement. It is further to be observed that, while it is only rights in a television broadcast which are infringed by causing the broadcast to be seen or heard in public, the act of rebroadcasting is an infringement, both of television broadcasts and of sound broadcasts.

858 **Copyright in broadcast does not prejudice copyright in material broadcast.** While, as has been seen, the broadcasting rights exist in all visual images and sounds broadcast, including those which represent musical, dramatic, literary and artistic works in which copyright subsists under Part I of the Act of 1956, the existence of the broadcasting rights do not prejudice the rights of the owner of such copyright. It is expressly provided, in section 16 (6) of the Act of 1956, that copyright subsisting by virtue of Part II of that Act is to be additional to, and independent of, any copyright subsisting by virtue of Part I. It is further provided that the subsistence of copyright under any of the sections of Part II is not to affect the operation of any other of those sections [37]; this refers, in addition to broadcasting rights, to sound recording rights, cinematograph film rights and rights in published editions.

859 **Licences required to perform or record a broadcast.** It follows, therefore, that, in general, a person desiring to perform or record a

[35] s. 14 (9).
[36] Copyright Act, 1956, s. 48 (5), and see § 541, *ante*.
[37] s. 16 (7).

broadcast programme may require to obtain a licence, not only from the broadcasting authority, but also from the owners of musical or other material, films and gramophone records used in the programme.

860 **Statutory limitations on duplication of licensing.** Some limit upon this duplication of licensing is afforded by section 40 of the Act of 1956. In the first place it is provided that, where a sound broadcast or television broadcast is made by the British Broadcasting Corporation or the Independent Television Authority, and a person, by the reception of that broadcast, causes a sound recording to be heard in public, he shall not thereby infringe the copyright (if any) in that recording. This means, in effect, that the owner of the copyright in the sound recording under section 12 of the Act of 1956, by licensing a sound broadcast of his record, impliedly licenses any public performance involved in the operation of a receiving set in public.

861 Section 40 of the Act of 1956 contains more elaborate provisions to cover the case of a person who, by operating a television set or radio set, causes a cinematograph film transmitted by the Corporation or the Authority to be seen or heard in public. In the first place, if the transmission is an authorised broadcast, that is to say, if it is made by or with the licence of the owner of the copyright in the film,[38] the person causing it to be seen or heard shall be in the like position, in any proceedings for infringement, as if he had been the holder of a licence granted by the owner of that copyright to cause the film to be seen or heard in public by the reception of the broadcast.[39] If, on the other hand, the film was not an authorised broadcast, so that its broadcasting involved an infringement of copyright by the Corporation or the Authority, as the case may be, then the owner of the copyright in the film may sue the Corporation or the Authority, but may not sue the person who has performed the film in public by the operation of the receiving set.[40] In such proceedings, however, infringements at the receiving end may be taken into account in assessing damages against the Corporation or the Authority.[41] The substantial effect of these provisions is that the person who indirectly performs in public a gramophone record or a cinematograph film by operating a wireless receiving set, is concerned only to obtain a licence from the Corporation or the Authority in respect of the broadcast itself and a licence from the owner of any musical, dramatic or literary copyright involved, but is not concerned with the sound recording or cinematograph film rights, as the case may be. It is to be observed, however, that this protection is only in relation to performing rights and not recording rights, and, so far as performing rights

[38] Copyright Act, 1956, s. 40 (5).
[39] s. 40 (2), and see definition of "reception" in s. 48 (4).
[40] s. 40 (4) (*a*).
[41] s. 40 (4) (*b*).

are concerned, only applies where the performance is given by receiving the broadcast directly, or from a relay station, or a rebroadcast, and not where it is given by the use of any film, record or other article on which the broadcast has been recorded.

862 **Remedies for infringement of broadcasts.** The remedies for infringement of broadcasting rights are the same as those for the infringement of other copyrights. Since a performance of a broadcast programme is an operation unlikely to be repeated in respect of that programme, it may be doubted whether an injunction will be an effective remedy. It may be, therefore, that this is a class of case in which the new provision contained in section 17 (3) of the Act of 1956, enabling the court to award additional damages where satisfied that effective relief would not otherwise be available to the plaintiff, will constitute a suitable remedy.

863 The definition of "infringing copy," in section 18 (3) of the Act of 1956, includes, in relation to a television broadcast or a sound broadcast, a copy of a cinematograph film of it, or a record embodying a sound recording of it, and consequently the remedies made available by that section, in respect of damages for detinue or conversion, will apply. Furthermore, by section 16 of the Act of 1956 it is made an infringement to import, sell, let for hire, by way of trade offer or expose for sale or hire, by way of trade exhibit or, for purposes of trade or to such an extent as to affect the owner of the copyright, to distribute articles the making of which, to the knowledge of the person doing the act, infringed or would, if done in the United Kingdom, have infringed the broadcasting rights aforesaid.

864 In addition to the civil remedies aforesaid, it is expressly provided, in section 21 (4) of the Act of 1956, that the summary remedies exercisable against persons dealing with infringing copies of copyright material are to apply in relation to copyright subsisting in any subject-matter by virtue of Part II of the Act, thus including sound recordings or films of broadcasts.

[The next paragraph is 871]

CHAPTER 19

CROWN AND UNIVERSITY COPYRIGHT

1.—CROWN COPYRIGHT

871 IT has already been noticed that printing, on its first introduction, was considered in England, as in other countries, to be a matter of State, and that the Crown claimed the right to authorise all species of publication whatsoever.[1] When the Crown lost this prerogative, it still claimed the exclusive right to print certain works. The claim has been made in respect of the Authorised Version of the Bible,[2] the Books of Common Prayer, Acts of Parliament [3] and other government publications, law books,[4] and even almanacks.[5]

872 **Bibles and Prayer Books.** The Queen's Printer and the Universities of Oxford and Cambridge hold patents from the Crown for the printing of Bibles and Prayer Books, and their right to prevent others from printing these works is well established.[6] Various reasons have been given for the existence of this prerogative of the Crown. Some have given it as their opinion that it is founded on the circumstances of the authorised translation of the Bible having been actually paid for by King James, and its having thus become the property of the Crown. But there seems little justification for this view. The better opinion would appear to be that the prerogative is to be referred to another consideration, namely, to the character of the duty imposed upon the chief executive officers of the Government to superintend the publication of the Acts of legislature and Acts of state of that description; and also of those works upon which the established doctrines of our religion are founded, that it is a duty imposed upon the first executive magistrate, carrying with it a corresponding prerogative. That was the opinion of Lord Camden, as expressed in the case of *Donaldson (A.)* v. *Beckett (T.)*,[7] and of Skinner C.B. in *Eyre and Strahan* v. *Carnan*.[8]

1 *Ante*, § 21.

2 *Universities of Oxford and Cambridge (The)* v. *Richardson* (1802) 6 Ves. 689; *Manners* v. *Blair (D. H.)* (1828) 3 Bli. 391; *Re "Red Letter New Testament (Authorised Version) (The)"* (1900) 17 T.L.R. 1.

3 *Basket* v. *University of Cambridge (The)* (1758) 1 W. Blackstone 105.

4 *Roper* v. *Streater* (1685) (cited in *Stationers' Company* v. *Parker*, Skinner 233 at 234); *Millar* v. *Taylor* (1769) 4 Burr. 2303.

5 *Stationers (The Co. of)* v. *Partridge* (1725) 10 Mod. 105; see *Gurney* v. *Longman* (1806) 13 Ves. 493.

6 See cases cited above in note 2.

7 (1774) 4 Burr. 2408.

8 (1781) 6 Bac.Ab. (7th ed.) 509.

873 The authorities on this subject were reviewed in a full and exhaustive manner by the Supreme Court of New South Wales,[9] and the conclusion was reached that the right of the court in connection with such works is a proprietary right entitling the Crown, either to issue patents conferring upon the patentee the exclusive right of printing, or to enforce such right directly against an infringer. It was also considered that the Crown's prerogative rights in this respect could not be lost by non-user.

874 In *Universities of Oxford and Cambridge* v. *Eyre & Spottiswoode, Ltd.*[10] the plaintiffs, as owners of the copyright in a new translation of the New Testament, sued the defendants for infringements of copyright for having printed and published a copy of part of the new translation without licence. The defendants contended that they were entitled to do so as holders of a patent from the Crown giving them the exclusive right to print books including New Testaments. They could not prevent the Universities from publishing the new work because they also enjoyed a patent from the Crown, but the defendants, as Queen's printers, claimed an equal right. Arguments in the case covered the whole ground of the nature and extent of the prerogative and of the patents thereunder, but Plowman J. decided the case in favour of the plaintiffs on the ground that the royal prerogative did not include a right to infringe a modern copyright and could not, therefore, have conferred such a right by patent. The savings of the prerogative, contained in section 18 of the Act of 1911 and section 46 (2) of the Act of 1956, were intended to preserve the Crown rights to prevent the publication of material covered by the prerogative, but not to override the rights of others created by these Acts.

875 In fact prior to this case no attempt has been made to interfere with modern translations of the Bible, and no attempt has ever been made to prevent any person from publishing a translation of one Book, or of a part of the Bible, from the original text, and enjoying a copyright in his production.

876 **Copyright in government publications prior to 1911.** With regard to other works prepared and published by or on behalf of the Government, such as ordnance maps, blue books and so on, there appear to have been no decisions under the law before 1911, but it would seem that the Crown could only have been entitled to copyright therein under the general provisions of the Copyright Act, which primarily gave the copyright to the author.[11]

9 *Att.-Gen. for New South Wales (The)* v. *Butterworth & Co. (Australia), Ltd.* (1938) 38 S.R.(N.S.W.) 195.
10 [1964] Ch. 736.
11 *Ante*, § 301 *et seq.* This is subject to s. 18 of the Literary Copyright Act, 1842, *ante*, § 665.

877 **Provisions of Act of 1911.** The Act of 1911 provided [12] that, without prejudice to any rights or privileges of the Crown, where any work was, whether before or after the commencement of that Act,[13] prepared or published by or under the direction or control of His Majesty or any government department, the copyright in the work was, subject to any agreement with the author, to belong to His Majesty, and in such case was to continue for a period of fifty years from the date of the first publication of the work.

878 **Provisions of Act of 1956.** The Copyright Act, 1956, deals with the matter in a more elaborate manner. In the first place, it is provided, in section 46 (2) thereof, that nothing in that Act is to affect any right or privilege of the Crown subsisting otherwise than by virtue of an enactment, and that nothing in that Act is to affect any right or privilege of the Crown, or of any other person, under any enactment (including any enactment of the Parliament of Northern Ireland), except in so far as that enactment is expressly repealed, amended or modified by that Act. Thus the Act of 1956 preserves any special copyrights of the Crown subsisting in the Bible and Prayer Book.

879 **Crown copyright in works not otherwise protected.** The Act of 1956 then provides that, where an original literary, dramatic, musical or artistic work is made by or under the direction or control of Her Majesty or a government department,[14] copyright is to subsist therein if, apart from this provision, copyright would not subsist therein.[15] In other words, in the case of an unpublished work of which the author is not a qualified person, and which, accordingly, would not otherwise be protected, copyright is conferred if the work was made by or under such direction or control as aforesaid.

880 **Crown copyright generally.** Furthermore, subject to agreement as described below, the copyright in every unpublished work, made by or under such direction or control, in which copyright subsists, either under this section or the general provisions of the Act, is to vest in the Crown.[16] In the case of a published literary, dramatic, musical or artistic work, which is first published in the United Kingdom or in another country to which the Act of 1956 extends, and which is published by or under the direction or control of Her Majesty or a government department, the copyright is to vest in the Crown.[17] Presumably if the work, while unpublished, has obtained copyright and vested in the Crown under the preceding provision while unpublished, it will continue to be protected, and to be so vested, even

[12] Copyright Act, 1911, s. 18.
[13] *i.e.*, July 1, 1912; see Copyright Act, 1911, s. 37.
[14] As defined in Copyright Act, 1956, s. 39 (9).
[15] s. 39 (1) (*a*).
[16] s. 39 (1) (*b*).
[17] Copyright Act, 1956, s. 39 (2).

though first published out of the United Kingdom. But, in any other case, if a work is first published out of the United Kingdom, and any such other country as aforesaid, no special protection is acquired, notwithstanding that the publication may be under the direction of a government department. It will be observed that "direction or control" is a much wider expression than "contract of service," and works which have been commissioned by the Crown, from authors who are not under a contract of service, may well vest in the Crown under this section. It is, however, expressly provided that these provisions are to have effect subject to any agreement made by or on behalf of Her Majesty or a government department with the author of the work whereby it is agreed that the copyright in the work shall vest in the author or in another person designated in the agreement in that behalf.[18] A work published under licence from the Crown is not to be treated as being published under the direction or control of a government department.[19]

881 **Term of Crown copyright.** It is further provided that the copyright in a literary, dramatic, or musical work which vests in the Crown in accordance with either of the preceding provisions shall, in the case of an unpublished work, continue to subsist so long as the work remains unpublished and, in the case of a published work, is to subsist until the end of the period of fifty years from the end of the calendar year in which the work was first published.[20] In the case of an artistic work, which vests in the Crown, as aforesaid, copyright is to continue to subsist until the end of the period of fifty years from the end of the calendar year in which the work was made, except that, in the case of an engraving or a photograph, the copyright is to subsist until the end of the period of fifty years from the end of the calendar year in which the engraving or photograph was first published.[21] It would appear, however, that if, by agreement, the copyright in a work commissioned by the Crown is to vest, not in the Crown, but in the author, then the normal term of copyright, in accordance with section 2 or section 3 of the Act of 1956, will subsist.

882 **Crown copyright in records and films.** The Act of 1956 further provides that, where a sound recording or cinematograph film is made by or under the direction or control of Her Majesty or a government department, then, if apart from section 39 of that Act, copyright would not subsist in the recording or film, copyright is to subsist therein.[22] Furthermore, the copyright in a sound recording or cine-

[18] s. 39 (6).
[19] *British Broadcasting Company* v. *Wireless League Gazette Publishing Co.* [1926] Ch. 433; *Att.-Gen. for New South Wales (The)* v. *Butterworth & Co. (Australia), Ltd.* (1938) 38 S.R.(N.S.W.) 195.
[20] Copyright Act, 1956, s. 39 (3).
[21] s. 39 (4).
[22] Copyright Act, 1956, s. 39 (5) (*a*).

matograph film so made is, in any case, subject to agreement to the contrary, to vest in the Crown, and is to subsist for the same period as is provided in section 12 or section 13, as the case may be, of the Act of 1956.[23]

883 **Crown copyright in photographs, records and films made before the Act of 1956.** In relation to photographs made before the commencement of the Act of 1956, copyright is to subsist for the period of fifty years from the end of the calendar year in which the photograph was made [24] and, in the case of sound recordings made before the commencement of that Act, copyright is to subsist for the period of fifty years from the end of the calendar year in which the recording was made.[25] In the case of cinematograph films made before the commencement of the Act of 1956, copyright will not subsist therein as a cinematograph film, but, in so far as it was an original dramatic work as defined in the Act of 1911, copyright will subsist therein as if it were a dramatic work for the purposes of the Act of 1956.[26] Furthermore, in so far as such a cinematograph film is made up of photographs, these will be protected in the same way as other Crown photographs are protected under the Act of 1956.[27]

884 **Application of other provisions of the Act of 1956 to Crown works.** It is provided, in section 39 (7) of the Act of 1956, that, except for the provisions relating to subsistence or ownership or, in the case of literary, dramatic, musical or artistic works, also to duration of copyright, the provisions of Part I and Part II of that Act are to apply in respect of works made or published by or under the direction or control of Her Majesty or a government department. Thus, the ordinary provisions as regards the nature of infringement of copyright and the acts which will not constitute an infringement apply.[28]

885 **Crown Proceedings Act, 1947.** It is expressly provided that, for the avoidance of doubt, the provisions of section 3 of the Crown Proceedings Act, 1947,[29] relating to infringements of industrial property by servants or agents of the Crown, are to apply to copyright.[30] That section provides that, where any servant or agent of the Crown infringes any copyright and the infringement is committed with the authority of the Crown, then, subject to the provisions of the Act, civil proceedings in respect of the infringement shall lie against the

23 s. 39 (5) (*b*).
24 Sched. 7, para. 30.
25 Sched. 7, para. 31 (1).
26 Sched. 7, para. 31 (2) (*a*) and (*b*).
27 Sched. 7, para. 31 (2) (*c*).
28 See as to photographic copies of birth certificates, etc., for purposes of judicial proceedings or reports thereof (1960) 57 L.S.Gaz. 126.
29 10 & 11 Geo. 6, c. 44.
30 Copyright Act, 1956, s. 39 (8).

Crown, but, save as so expressly provided, no proceedings shall lie against the Crown in respect of the infringement of any copyright. "Agent" is defined in section 38 (2) of that Act as including an independent contractor employed by the Crown.

886 **Treasury Circular of 1958.** Proceedings for protection of Crown copyright will be governed by the procedure indicated in the same Act,[31] but not all Crown copyrights are enforced. The practice with regard to Crown copyrights is indicated in a Treasury Circular dated January 9, 1958,[32] which divides Government publications into the following classes:

(i) Bills and Acts of Parliament, Statutory Rules and Orders and Statutory Instruments.

(ii) Other Parliamentary papers, including reports of Select Committees of both Houses and papers laid before Parliament by statute and by command.

(iii) The official report of the House of Lords and House of Commons debates (*Hansard*).

(iv) Non-Parliamentary publications, comprising all papers of Government Departments not contained in the first three classes.

(v) Charts and Ordnance maps.

Since it is in the public interest that the information contained in publications falling in the first three classes should be diffused as widely as possible, no steps will normally be taken to enforce the rights of the Crown in respect of copyright,[33] but all Crown rights in respect of these are reserved and will be asserted in cases considered by the Controller of H.M. Stationery Office as exceptional, for instance reproduction of any part of any such publication in undesirable contexts, or a substantial part of any such publication, either as a separate document or as a major part of another work, in such a way as to result in a significant loss to public funds. Documents within class (i) (Acts of Parliament, etc.), other than those reproduced by the authority of the Stationery Office, must not purport to be published by authority. Reproductions from *Hansard* in connection with advertising are not permitted. And there is a warning as to privilege. The rights of the Crown with regard to works in classes (iv) and (v) will normally be enforced, and these will bear an indication that Crown copyright is reserved. Accordingly, acknowledgment of source and of the permission of the Controller of

[31] Crown Proceedings Act, 1947, s. 13. The Queen in her personal capacity has the same rights as the subject: *Prince Albert* v. *Strange* (1849) H. & T. 1.

[32] *Post*, Appendix B, § 1675. This supersedes Treasury Minutes of 1887 and 1912 and has itself been amended by a Treasury Circular dated March, 1965. By a Press Notice, dated June 25, 1969, the Controller of H.M. Stationery Office has given notice that, in future, under normal circumstances, no action will be taken to enforce the Crown's rights in patent specifications published in the United Kingdom by H.M. Stationery Office.

[33] See *Bhagga* (*J. N.*) v. *State* [1959] 3 All I.R. 492.

H.M. Stationery Office will be required for publication, and suitable fees imposed,[34] which may be waived or reduced in respect of publications where the commercial aspect is relatively unimportant.

2.—COPYRIGHT OF THE UNIVERSITIES AND COLLEGES

887 Upon the introduction of the art of printing into England by Henry VI a press was set up in Oxford, and an important dominion over the publication of books was, for many years, assumed by Oxford University. The sway was extended to Cambridge University, and increased in power, by Charters and grants conferred upon them by the liberality and bounty of several kings.

888 Immediately after, and in consequence of, the decision of *Donaldson (A.)* v. *Beckett (T.)*,[35] the universities hastened to Parliament, and, in the same year, obtained an Act[36] for enabling the two universities in England, the four universities in Scotland, and the several colleges of Eton, Westminster, and Winchester, to hold in perpetuity their copyright in books given or bequeathed to them for the advancement of useful learning and other purposes of education.

The right was to exist in all such books as had been before 1775, or should thereafter be, given or bequeathed by the authors of the same, or their representatives, to or in trust for those universities, or any college or house of learning within them, or to or in trust for the colleges of Eton, Westminster, and Winchester, or any of them, for the beneficial purpose of education within them or any of them.

The exception in favour of the universities and colleges was to extend only to their own books, so long as they were printed at the college press and for their sole benefit; and any delegation of the right was to work a forfeiture, and the privilege become of no effect.

A power was given, by the Act, to the universities, to sell or dispose of the copyright given or bequeathed to them, but if they should delegate, grant, lease, or sell the copyright of any book, or allow any person to print it, their privilege was to cease to exist. The copyright of any work presented to the universities was required to be registered at Stationers' Hall within two months after any such gift should come to the knowledge of the officers of the universities. Special penalties were imposed for any infringement of copyright.

889 By an Act passed in the forty-first year of Geo. 3, c. 107, a similar copyright was given to Trinity College, Dublin, and, by section 27 of

[34] On October 23, 1913, a person was convicted at the Guildhall of piracy of the four mile Ordnance survey map and ordered to pay a fine of 40s., with fifteen guineas costs, and also to give up or destroy all remaining copies (*R.* v. *Mutch, The Times*, October 24, 1913).

[35] (1774) 4 Burr. 2408, *ante*, § 4.

[36] Copyright Act, 1775, 15 Geo. 3, c. 53.

the Literary Copyright Act, 1842,[37] the rights of the respective universities and colleges above enumerated were saved from the operation of that Act.

890 **Provision of Act of 1956.** It is provided, by section 46 (1) of the Act of 1956, that any rights conferred on universities and colleges by the Copyright Act, 1775, which continue to subsist in accordance with section 33 of the Copyright Act, 1911, notwithstanding the repeal of the said Act of 1775, are to continue to subsist in accordance with the said Act of 1775, notwithstanding any repeal effected by the Act of 1956. It is, however, provided that no proceedings shall be brought under the Copyright Act, 1775, but that the provisions of Part 3 of the Act of 1956 are to apply for the enforcement of those rights as if they were copyright subsisting by virtue of the Act of 1956. But it is further provided that no copyright, or right in the nature of copyright, is to subsist otherwise than by virtue of the Act of 1956, or of some other enactment in that behalf,[38] so that, while all existing perpetual copyrights are preserved, no new perpetual copyright can be created.

[The next paragraph is 901]

[37] 5 & 6 Vict. c. 45.
[38] Copyright Act, 1956, s. 46 (5).

Chapter 20

TRANSITIONAL PROVISIONS

1.—Works in Existence at the Commencement of the Copyright Act, 1956

901 **Repeal of Act of 1911.** It is proposed to deal, in this section of the present chapter, with the general provisions of the Copyright Act, 1956, affecting works in existence at its commencement, and to deal, more particularly, in a subsequent section, with older works which were in existence at the commencement of the Act of 1911. The Act of 1956,[1] as from its commencement on June 1, 1957,[2] repealed the Copyright Act, 1911, except sections 15 and 34 thereof which deal with the supply of copies of works to libraries, and section 37 thereof which deals with the date of commencement of the Act of 1911 in different places. This repeal is subject to the transitional provisions set forth in the Seventh Schedule to the Act of 1956.[1]

Except to the limited extent hereinafter described in regard to the investigation of title to existing works, copyright law in the United Kingdom is now wholly to be found in the Copyright Act, 1956,[3] as amended.

902 **Rights to compulsory licences abolished.** Most of the provisions of the Copyright Act, 1911, reappear in the Copyright Act, 1956, subject to modifications and additions. But the right, conferred by section 4 of the Act of 1911, to apply to the Judicial Committee of the Privy Council for a compulsory licence to publish or perform in public, has been abolished, and the provisions of section 3 of the Act of 1911, under which a compulsory licence for the reproduction of works for sale could be obtained on compulsory royalty terms after the expiration of twenty-five or thirty years from the death of the author, have been abolished, except in so far as notices under that section had been given before the commencement of the Act of 1956.[4]

903 **Transitional provisions under 1911 and 1956 Acts compared.** The Copyright Act, 1956, provides an entirely different system for dealing with the transition of rights under the old law to rights under the new. Under the Copyright Act, 1911, any person entitled to copyright under the previous law at the commencement of that Act thereupon obtained copyright, as defined by the Act of 1911, subject

[1] Copyright Act, 1956, s. 50.
[2] Copyright Act, 1956 (Commencement) Order, 1957 (S.I. 1957 No. 863).
[3] Copyright Act, 1956, s. 46 (5).
[4] Sched. 7, para. 9.

to certain modifications in respect of rights forming part of the copyright under the Act of 1911 which had not existed before the commencement of that Act.[5] The Copyright Act, 1956, on the other hand, is to be treated as having always applied to existing works, subject to any modifications in the Seventh Schedule.[6] Paragraph 45 (1) of that Schedule states that the provisions of the Act of 1956 are to apply, in relation to things existing at the commencement of the Act, as they apply in relation to things coming into existence thereafter.

904 **Subsistence of copyright in unpublished works.** The distinction may be explained by reference to a simple case. Section 2 (1) of the Act of 1956 states that copyright shall subsist in every original literary, dramatic or musical work which is unpublished and of which the author was a qualified person at the time when the work was made. Having regard to paragraph 45 of the Seventh Schedule above referred to, it is clear that the test of being a qualified person applies, even though the work was made before the commencement of the Act of 1956, and therefore the conditions for subsistence of copyright under the previous law are irrelevant. While section 1 (1) (*b*) of the Copyright Act, 1911, is expressed in somewhat similar form, this Act contained no provision equivalent to paragraph 45 of the Seventh Schedule to the Act of 1956, and it is clear, from the form of section 24 of the Act of 1911 and the First Schedule to that Act, that copyright only subsisted under the Act of 1911 in works in existence when that Act commenced, if it subsisted immediately before such commencement under the then existing law. This, apparently, had the effect that a foreign author, who was not resident in any place to which the Act of 1911 extended at the time of the making of his work, and had made it before the commencement of that Act, was better off than if he had made it after that date. If he made his work after the commencement of that Act, he would be entitled to no protection until he published his work. But there seemed to be no ground for thinking that a foreigner was not entitled under the law before 1911 to common law copyright in England for his unpublished works and, therefore, it appeared that section 24 (1) of the Act of 1911 gave to him the copyright until first publication. Again, under the law before 1911, a person acquired performing rights by first performance in public in the United Kingdom and, therefore, performing rights under the Act of 1911 were vested in him by section 24 of that Act. But, under the Act of 1911 itself, public performance did not amount to publication,[7] so that first public performance in the United Kingdom would not constitute a ground for obtaining copyright there.

[5] Copyright Act, 1911, s. 24.
[6] Copyright Act, 1956, s. 50 (2).
[7] Copyright Act, 1911, s. 1 (3).

905 **And in published works.** A somewhat similar point arises with regard to published works. Section 35 (3) of the Act of 1911 provided that a work should be deemed to be first published in a place to which the Act extended, notwithstanding that it had been published simultaneously in some other place, and a work should be deemed to be published simultaneously in two places, if the time between the publication in one place and the publication in the other place did not exceed fourteen days. Under section 49 (2) (*d*) of the Act of 1956 it is provided that a publication shall not be treated as being other than a first publication, by reason only of an earlier publication elsewhere, if the two publications took place within a period of not more than thirty days. While it is true that, in dealing with existing works, the words " fourteen days " are to be substituted for " thirty days," [7a] it is clear that it is the provision of the 1956 Act, and not the provision of the 1911 Act, which applies, even in respect of works published before the commencement of the Act of 1956.

906 **Term of copyright.** Similarly with regard to the term of copyright. In the case of works existing at the commencement of the Act of 1911 it is necessary to ascertain whether the term of copyright therein under the pre-existing law had expired before the commencement of the Act of 1911.[8] But the term of copyright provided by the Act of 1956 applies to existing works, as well as to new works, although, in the case of photographs, there is a modification,[9] and, in the case of joint works, the 1911 term is applied to determine whether copyright exists at the commencement of the Act of 1956.[10]

907 **Distinction summarised.** The substance of the matter, therefore, is this. Whereas, in the case of works existing before the commencement of the Act of 1911, it was necessary, and remains necessary,[11] to interpret the law as it stood before the commencement of that Act to see whether there was a subsisting copyright at the commencement of that Act, under the Act of 1956 all questions of subsistence and term depend upon the provisions of the Act of 1956 itself.

908 **Detailed provisions of Seventh Schedule.** Since, therefore, the modifications introduced by the Seventh Schedule to the Act of 1956 are, for the most part, in effect, modifications of the substantive sections of that Act in their application to existing works, it has been most convenient to deal with these provisions, in detail, in the respective chapters of this book dealing with the several subjects. It is sufficient to summarise the more important here.

7a Copyright Act, 1956, Sched. 7, para. 33.
8 Sched. 7, para. 35.
9 Sched. 7, para. 2.
10 Sched. 7, para. 10.
11 See § 928, *post*.

909 **Subsistence of copyright.** The subsistence of copyright in works first published before the commencement of the Act of 1956 depends upon the place of first publication only, and such works do not enjoy the alternative basis of protection conferred by the Act of 1956 in respect of published works of which the author was a qualified person.[12]

910 **Term of copyright in photographs.** The term of copyright in a photograph taken before the commencement of the Act of 1956 is the period of fifty years from the end of the calendar year in which the photograph was taken, and not of the calendar year in which the photograph was published.[13]

911 **Ownership of copyright.** The ownership of the copyright in works created by employees, or on commission, depends upon the provisions of the Act of 1911 set forth in the Eighth Schedule to the Act of 1956, and not upon the provisions of the Act of 1956 itself.[14]

912 **Artistic works and industrial designs.** In the case of artistic works made before the commencement of the Act of 1956, the industrial design provisions based upon those of the Act of 1911, and set forth in paragraph 8 of the Seventh Schedule, and paragraph 2 of the Eighth Schedule, to the Act of 1956, and not the provisions of the Act of 1956 itself, apply.

913 **Joint works.** There is no copyright under the Act of 1956 in a work of joint authorship, the copyright wherein has expired under the provisions of the Act of 1911 set forth in paragraph 4 of the Eighth Schedule to the Act of 1956.[15]

914 **Sound recordings.** There are modifications in the copyright in sound recordings made before the commencement of the Act of 1956.[16]

915 **Films.** There is no copyright in cinematograph films made before the commencement of the Act of 1956,[17] and provision is made preserving the dramatic and artistic copyright in such films corresponding to the rights so subsisting by virtue of the Copyright Act, 1911.[18]

12 Copyright Act, 1956, Sched. 7, para. 1. The various paragraphs of the Seventh Schedule use the phrase " commencement of these provisions " which is defined as meaning coming into operation in the United Kingdom (Sched. 7, para. 46 (2)). See, however, para. 5 of Sched. 4 to the Copyright (International Conventions) Order, 1957, and Art. 2 of the Copyright (International Conventions) Order, 1964, *post*, Appendix D, §§ 1870 and 1875.

13 Copyright Act, 1956, Sched. 7, para. 2.

14 Sched. 7, para. 3.

15 Copyright Act, 1956, Sched. 7, para. 10.

16 Sched. 7, paras. 11, 12 and 13.

17 Sched. 7, para. 14.

18 Sched. 7, paras. 15 and 16.

916 **Television and sound broadcasts.** There is no copyright in television broadcasts and sound broadcasts made before the commencement of the Act of 1956.[19]

917 **Crown copyright.** There are certain modifications in Crown copyright so subsisting.[20]

918 **Existing proceedings.** The repeal of the Act of 1911 will not affect or prejudice existing causes of action, and proceedings in respect of existing infringements may, therefore, be commenced or continued without regard to the commencement of the Act of 1956.[21]

919 **Provisions not strictly transitional.** While, therefore, the provisions of the Act of 1956, in regard to existing works, do not constitute strictly transitional provisions, in the sense of transforming existing rights under one code into new rights under another, it will be convenient to deal in this chapter, at somewhat greater length, with the title to the copyright in works existing before the commencement of the Act of 1956.

920 **Title to existing works.** In the first place, it is provided that any document or event which was made or occurred before the commencement of the Act of 1956, and had any operation affecting the title to copyright in the work under the Act of 1911, or would have had such an operation if the Act of 1911 had continued in force, is to have the corresponding operation in relation to the copyright in the work under the Act of 1956.[22] " Operation affecting the title " is defined as meaning any operation affecting the ownership of copyright, or creating, transferring or terminating an interest, right or licence in respect of copyright.[23] It is further provided that, if the operation of any document was or would have been limited to a period specified in the document, it is not to have any operation in relation to the copyright under the Act of 1956 except in so far as that period extends beyond the commencement of the Act of 1956.[22]

921 **The reversionary twenty-five-year period.** One of the matters affecting title under the Act of 1911 was the proviso in section 5 (2) of that Act which had the effect that no assignment by an author should be operative to vest in the assignee rights beyond the expiration of twenty-five years from the death of the author. It is expressly provided [24] that the effect of this proviso shall apply to assignments operating with reference to copyright under the Act of

19 Sched. 7, para. 17.
20 Sched. 7, paras. 30 and 31.
21 Sched. 7, paras. 20, 21, 22, 23 and 24.
22 Sched. 7, para. 28 (1).
23 Copyright Act, 1956, Sched. 7, para. 28 (5).
24 Sched. 7, para. 28 (3).

1956 by virtue of the foregoing provisions. In other words, a pre-1957 assignment for the full term by an author of copyright under the Act of 1911, takes effect as an assignment of copyright under the Act of 1956, but, nevertheless, only for the period limited by the proviso. But, as the proviso does not apply to assignments made after the commencement of the Act of 1956, the author can, if he has made no pre-1957 assignment, assign for the full term after the commencement of the Act of 1956. Further, if he has only assigned, by a pre-1957 assignment, for no more than his life and twenty-five years, he can assign the residue of the term by an assignment after the commencement of the Act of 1956.

922 **Provisions as to title summarised.** The general effect of these provisions would seem to be that one should first construe any assignment or licence effected before the commencement of the Act of 1956 to ascertain what would have been its effect if the Act of 1911 had continued in force. Having reached this conclusion, it will follow that the title to copyright, conferred by the Act of 1956, will vest as it would have vested if the Act of 1911 had continued. This method of tracing title would produce a difficulty, of course, if there were any case in which the first owner of the copyright under the Act of 1956 could be a different person from the first owner under the Act of 1911. But, in view of what has been said about the provisions of the Seventh Schedule in regard to the works of employees and commissioned works, it does not appear that this difficulty can arise.

923 **Construction of documents made before the commencement of the Act of 1956.** As a guide to construction it is expressly provided that expressions used in a document made before the commencement of that Act are to be construed in accordance with their effect immediately before such commencement, notwithstanding that a different meaning is assigned to them for the purposes of that Act.[25] On the other hand, any enactment, or other document, referring to copyright, or to works in which copyright subsists, is to be construed as referring, or as including a reference, to copyright under the Act of 1956, or to works or any subject-matter in which copyright subsists under that Act.[26] It would seem, therefore, that an assignment made before the commencement of the Act of 1956, which, in terms, purports to assign copyright subsisting by virtue of the Act of 1911, will be construed as passing the copyright conferred under the Act of 1956. On the other hand, it would appear that, if the expression "sound recordings" were used in an assignment or licence made before the commencement of the Act of 1956, this might be construed

[25] Copyright Act, 1956, Sched. 7, para. 28 (2) (*a*).
[26] Sched. 7, para. 44 (*b*).

as including the sound track of a film, notwithstanding the definition of "sound recording" in section 12 (9) of the Act of 1956. It is expressly provided that section 37 (1) of the Act of 1956 shall not apply for the purpose of the operation of documents made before the commencement of the Act of 1956.[27] This is the section under which assignments of future copyright are permitted.

2.—WORKS IN EXISTENCE AT THE COMMENCEMENT OF THE COPYRIGHT ACT, 1911

General Provisions

924 The provisions of the Seventh Schedule to the Copyright Act, 1956, already discussed, apply, in general, to all works in existence at the commencement of the Act of 1956, including works which were in existence at the commencement of the Act of 1911. But, in relation to these latter works, there are modifications in relation to the subsistence of copyright in such works and the title to such copyright.

925 **Subsistence of copyright under the Act of 1956.** The Act of 1956 provides, with regard to works made before the commencement of the Act of 1911, that the provisions of sections 2 and 3 of the Act of 1956, stating the conditions under which copyright under the Act of 1956 shall subsist in works, shall not apply, unless a substituted right, by virtue of section 24 of the Act of 1911, was conferred in respect of such work in place of a right subsisting immediately before the commencement of the Act of 1911 and continued to subsist immediately before the commencement of the Act of 1956.[28] In order, therefore, that copyright shall subsist in a work in existence before the commencement of the Act of 1911, it has to be shown (a) that the work is a work in which copyright can subsist under the Act of 1956 (section 2 (1) or (2) in the case of literary, dramatic or musical works, or section 3 (2) or (3) in the case of artistic works), subject, in each case, to the qualifications introduced in paragraph 1 of the Seventh Schedule to the Act of 1956, (b) that copyright under the Act of 1911 was substituted for pre-1911 copyright by virtue of section 24 of the Act of 1911, and (c) that such substituted right continued to subsist at the commencement of the Act of 1956.

926 **Section 24 of the Act of 1911.** Section 24 of the Copyright Act, 1911, provided that, where any person was, immediately before the commencement of that Act, entitled to copyright, including Common Law copyright in unpublished works, he should, as from the commencement of the Act, be entitled to copyright as defined by the Act of 1911. The Court of Appeal expressed the view that the prima facie construction of the Act of 1911 was that section 24,

[27] Sched. 7, para. 28 (2) (*b*).
[28] Copyright Act, 1956, Sched. 7, para. 35.

subject to section 19 (7) and (8) dealing with mechanical rights, was alone to be looked at in regard to pre-1911 works, not only in questions regarding the subsistence of copyright, but also in questions of title between author and assignee.[29] In order to ascertain, therefore, whether any person was entitled to copyright under the Act of 1911 in a work in existence at its commencement, it is necessary to determine whether, under the law as it existed before the commencement of the Act of 1911, there was a subsisting copyright at the commencement of that Act, and whether the person in question was the owner of that copyright. Once, however, copyright was conferred upon an existing work in this manner, it was provided that the copyright should subsist for the term for which it would have subsisted if the Act of 1911 had been in force at the date when the work was made, and the work had been one entitled to copyright under the Act of 1911.[30]

927 Section 24 of the Act of 1911 further provided that, where a person, immediately before the commencement of that Act, was entitled to "copyright but not performing right" in a musical or dramatic work, there should vest in him copyright as defined by the Act of 1911, except the sole right to perform the work or any substantial part thereof in public.[31] On the other hand, if the person was entitled, at the commencement of that Act, to "performing right but not copyright" in a musical or dramatic work, there should vest in him the sole right to perform the work in public, but none of the other rights comprised in copyright as defined by the Act of 1911.[31] It has been held that the right to perform, so conferred, included the right to perform by means of a mechanical contrivance.[32] To deal with these cases, it is provided in the Act of 1956 that, where the right conferred by the Act of 1911 did not include the sole right to perform the work in public, then the acts restricted by the copyright under the Act of 1956 are to be treated as not including (a) performing the work or an adaptation thereof in public, (b) broadcasting the work or an adaptation thereof, and (c) causing the work or an adaptation thereof to be transmitted to subscribers to a diffusion service.[33] Alternatively, if the right conferred by the Act of 1911 consisted only of the sole right to perform the work in public, the restricted acts are to consist only of the acts above mentioned.[34]

928 **Title to copyright under the Act of 1956 in pre-1911 works.** The question of the title to copyright, under the Act of 1956, in respect of pre-1911 works, is one of some complication. The first

29 *Coleridge-Taylor* v. *Novello & Co., Ltd.* [1938] Ch. 850.
30 Copyright Act, 1911, s. 24 (1).
31 First Sched., Copyright Act, 1911.
32 *Thompson* v. *Warner Bros., Pictures, Ltd.* [1929] 2 Ch. 308.
33 Copyright Act, 1956, Sched. 7, para. 36 (1) and (3).
34 Sched. 7, para. 36 (2) and (3).

owner of copyright under the various Copyright Acts in force before the commencement of the Act of 1911 was not necessarily the same person as would have been the first owner if the Act of 1956 had been in force when the work was made. For example, the Literary Copyright Act, 1842, did not contain provisions for vesting in an employer work done by an employee under a contract of service, though it did contain somewhat involved provisions for vesting copyright in articles contributed to periodicals in the proprietor of the periodical.[35] Again, the Fine Arts Copyright Act, 1862, contained provisions for the vesting of copyright in commissioned works different from those contained in the Acts of 1911 and 1956.[36] So far as the Act of 1911 was concerned, it was clear that the provisions of that Act with regard to first ownership did not apply in respect of works created before its commencement because, under section 24 thereof, copyright under the Act of 1911 vested in the person who was the owner of the pre-1911 copyright at the commencement of the Act of 1911 and, therefore, this person's title depended solely upon the previous Copyright Acts. On the other hand, the Act of 1956, at first sight, would seem to apply its first ownership provisions to works created at any time, since paragraph 3 (2) of the Seventh Schedule applies the first ownership provisions there mentioned, which are in fact the first ownership provisions of section 5 of the Act of 1911, to any work made before the commencement of the Act of 1956. It might be contended, therefore, that, after the commencement of the Act of 1956, in cases in which the first owner, if the provisions of section 5 of the Act of 1911 had applied, would be a different person from the first owner under the pre-1911 statutes, a change of title is effected. It is thought, however, that this effect, which cannot have been intended, is avoided by paragraph 28 of the Seventh Schedule. This provides that any "event" which occurred before the commencement of the Act of 1956, and had any operation affecting the title to copyright under the Act of 1911, shall have the corresponding operation in relation to copyright under the Act of 1956. An operation affecting title is defined as including an operation affecting the ownership of copyright.[37] It would seem, therefore, that, if a work was created before 1911 in circumstances which, under the law then in force, vested the copyright in A as first owner, this would be an "event." This event undoubtedly had an operation affecting ownership under the Act of 1911 because section 24 of that Act vested the copyright, under that Act, in the person who was the owner of the pre-1911 copyright at the commencement of that Act. Accordingly it is suggested that the operation of this "event" overrides the provisions of paragraph 3 (2) of the Seventh Schedule where the effect of those provisions would be to

[35] See *post*, § 949.
[36] See *post*, § 963.
[37] Copyright Act, 1956, Sched. 7, para. 28 (5).

make someone other than A the first owner of the copyright under the 1956 Act.

929 **Contributions to periodicals.** Moreover, one difference between the provisions of the Acts of 1911 and 1956 on the one hand, and the previous law on the other, in regard to first ownership of copyright, is expressly dealt with in the Seventh Schedule to the Act of 1956.[38] Section 18 of the Literary Copyright Act, 1842, while providing for the vesting of the copyright in articles contributed to a periodical in the proprietor thereof, also provided that the author of such an article was to be at liberty, after a lapse of twenty-eight years from the date of publication, to publish his articles in a separate form.[39] The Act of 1911 accordingly provided that, in the case of an essay, article, or portion forming part of and first published in a review, magazine, or other periodical or work of a like nature, the right conferred by section 24 of the Act of 1911 should be subject to any right of publishing the essay, article, or portion in a separate form to which the author was entitled at the commencement of the Act of 1911, or would, if that Act had not been passed, have become entitled under section 18 of the Copyright Act, 1842.[40] This right is maintained by paragraph 37 of the Seventh Schedule to the Act of 1956 where immediately before the commencement of section 2 of the Act of 1956, a right of publishing the work in a separate form subsisted by virtue of the above-mentioned provision of the Act of 1911.

930 **Devolution of title before commencement of Act of 1911.** With regard to the devolution of title to works created before 1911, during the period between their creation and the commencement of the Act of 1911, it would appear that paragraph 28 of the Seventh Schedule to the Act of 1956 will apply for the same reason as has been indicated above in relation to first ownership. The Act of 1911, by section 24, recognised title subsisting at its commencement in accordance with the old law of devolution, and therefore any document or event affecting such devolution during the period in question will have had operation in relation to the 1911 copyright according to its effect by the law in force at the time when the document was made or the event occurred. Therefore, so far as concerns devolution of 1956 copyright, such document or event will have corresponding operation, notwithstanding that a different effect might have ensued if the Act of 1956 had been in force at the time when the same was made or occurred.

931 **Effect of para. 28 (2), Seventh Schedule to the Act of 1956.** A doubt, however, arises, with respect to sub-clause (2) of paragraph

[38] Sched. 7, para. 37.
[39] See *post*, § 949.
[40] Copyright Act, 1911, footnote to Sched. 1.

28 of the Seventh Schedule to the Act of 1956, which provides that expressions used in a document shall be construed in accordance with their effect immediately before the commencement of the Act of 1956, notwithstanding that a different meaning is assigned to them for the purposes of that Act. At first sight, this might appear to mean that a document, executed in 1900, should be construed as if it had been executed immediately prior to 1 June 1957. For example, it is thought that an assignment of "copyright" in a musical or dramatic work, made before 1911, might well not pass performing rights, whereas such an assignment, executed after 1911, would do so. It would seem, however, that the proper construction of this sub-clause is that a document executed before 1911 is to be construed, now, as it would have been construed during the operation of the Act of 1911, that is to say, having regard to the law in force at the time when it was executed.

932 **Effect of events occurring before 1911.** Similarly, it is thought that any event which, before 1911, had the effect of terminating the copyright under the then existing law, such as failure to print with the necessary copyright notice under the Copyright (Musical Compositions) Act, 1882, or failure to grant or reserve copyright on the sale of an artistic work under the Fine Arts Copyright Act, 1862, will still have the same effect with regard to copyright under the Act of 1956.

Special Provisions Affecting Pre-1911 Assignments and Licences

933 The term of copyright under the Copyright Act, 1911, was, in general, longer than that subsisting under the pre-existing law.[41] The Act of 1911, accordingly, contained provisions under which assignments or licences subsisting at the commencement of that Act should determine when the old period of copyright ran out, and the 1911 copyright thereafter revested in the author or his personal representatives.[42] On the other hand, the assignee or licensee was given certain options to be exercised when the old term of copyright expired.[42] The Act of 1956 seeks, in a series of somewhat complicated provisions, to maintain the respective rights of interested parties, so that it is necessary, first, to examine the nature of the provisions in this respect of section 24 of the Act of 1911, and then to inquire how far these have been affected by the Act of 1956.

934 **The revesting proviso.** Proviso (*a*) to section 24 (1) of the Act of 1911 was as follows:

"if the author of any work in which any such right as is

[41] See *post*, § 947.
[42] Copyright Act, 1911, s. 24.

specified in the first column of the First Schedule to this Act subsists at the commencement of this Act has, before that date, assigned the right or granted any interest therein for the whole term of the right, then at the date when, but for the passing of this Act, the right would have expired the substituted right conferred by this section shall, in the absence of express agreement, pass to the author of the work, and any interest therein created before the commencement of this Act and then subsisting shall determine; . . ."

935 **Partial assignment.** The above provision only applied to the case of an assignment or grant of an interest covering the whole term of copyright. If the author had parted with his copyright for a period less than the whole original term, he would have a reversionary interest which would automatically confer upon him, by virtue of the earlier provisions of the section, the substituted right, which would become exercisable by him upon the falling in of his reversion. If, however, the author had granted a licence to one person for a portion of the old term, and then to another for the residue of that term, it is conceived that he would have granted an "interest" in his copyright "for the whole term" within the meaning of the proviso.

936 **Assignment by a person other than the author.** It is, however, important to observe that the proviso only applied to a case where the assignment or licence has been made or granted by "the author" of the work. If, in any case, the copyright vested in the first instance in any person other than the author,[43] then an assignment or licence by such person prima facie passed to the assignee or licensee the benefit of the extended term conferred by the Act of 1911.

937 **Rights of assignee notwithstanding revesting.** Although the benefit of any extended term of copyright conferred by the Act of 1911 prima facie vested in the original author of the work, and not in his assignee or licensee, it would have been unfair to deprive the assignee or licensee of the right to reap any advantage from the market which he had created. It often happens that the publisher, to whom the copyright belonged during the period of its existence, still retains an advantage over his trade competitors after the period of copyright protection has ceased. The Act of 1911 recognised this by providing [42] that the person who, immediately before the date when the copyright would have expired under the repealed statutes, was the owner of any right or interest in the copyright, is to be entitled at his option either:

[43] For example, in the case of collective works (*ante*, § 665 *et seq.*), or works of art executed upon commission (*ante*, § 310 *et seq.*). In the case of collective works, the right of the author to publish his article separately after 28 years (Copyright Act, 1842 (5 & 6 Vict. c. 45)) was expressly reserved by the note to Sched. 1 to the Act of 1911.

"(i) on giving such notice as hereinafter mentioned, to an assignment of the right or the grant of a similar interest therein for the remainder of the term of the right for such consideration as, failing agreement, may be determined by arbitration; or

(ii) without any such assignment or grant, to continue to reproduce or perform the work in like manner as theretofore subject to the payment, if demanded by the author within three years after the date at which the right would have so expired, of such royalties to the author as, failing agreement, may be determined by arbitration, or, where the work is incorporated in a collective work and the owner of the right or interest is the proprietor of that collective work, without any such payment."

The notice referred to had to be given not more than one year, nor less than six months, before the date at which the right would have so expired, and to be sent by registered post to the "author," [44] or, if he could not with reasonable diligence be found, advertised in the *London Gazette* and in two London newspapers.[45]

938 **First option.** It is submitted that the true construction of the first option given was that a person, who had obtained an assignment of the old term of copyright, was entitled to an assignment of the right, but not to the grant of a licence, and, vice versa, that a person who had obtained a licence for the whole of the old term was entitled to a "similar" licence for the residue of the new term, but not to an assignment of the right.

939 **Second option.** If the assignee elected to adopt the second option given him by the proviso, he was not required to give any notice to the proprietor of the copyright, who forfeited any right to royalties if he failed to demand them within three years after the date when the old copyright would have expired. It has been held, by the Court of Appeal,[46] that the effect of the second option was to give to the former assignee a non-exclusive licence to continue to exercise the same rights as he had proviously enjoyed exclusively.

940 **Sale of stock on hand.** The point arises as to whether, if the assignee elects to take neither of the options conferred upon him by proviso (*a*), he is at liberty to sell any stock remaining on hand without any payment to the author or his personal representatives. It

[44] This expression includes his personal representatives; Copyright Act, 1911, s. 24 (2).

[45] The giving of this notice presumably bound the person giving it to purchase the right or interest. It is not clear how the assignment or grant, as the case may be, was to be obtained if the author or his personal representatives could not be found. The person giving the notice, however, would obtain an equitable title.

[46] *Loew's Inc.* v. *Littler* [1958] Ch. 650

would seem that he can, since it is thought that there are no provisions under which a sale of copies, lawfully made, constitutes an infringement.

941 **Collective works.** It was provided by proviso (*a*) (ii) to section 24 (1) of the Act of 1911, that where a work, the copyright in which was assigned before the commencement of that Act was incorporated in a collective work, and the owner of the assigned right or interest was the proprietor of that collective work, such proprietor was to be entitled, during the extended term of copyright, to continue to reproduce the work without any payment to the author or his personal representatives. He could, however, only reproduce " in like manner as theretofore," so that he could not reproduce, without payment, an article contributed to the collective work, except as part of that collective work. Under section 18 of the Literary Copyright Act, 1842,[47] it often happened that the copyright of an article contributed to a collective work vested, *ab initio,* in the proprietor of the work.[48] In that case there would have been no assignment by " the author," and therefore proviso (*a*), to section 24 (1), had no application. The extended term of copyright would belong to the proprietor of the collective work, subject to the concurrent right of the author, if the collective work was of a periodical nature—not otherwise—to publish his article in " separate form " when twenty-eight years had elapsed since the original publication.[49] If however, either because the author expressly reserved the copyright in his article, or for any other reason, the copyright did not originally vest in the proprietor of the collective work, but became the property of the author, then, notwithstanding any subsequent assignment or grant of a licence to publish during the whole period of the old copyright made or given by him, the benefit of the extended term would belong to the author or his personal representatives, but the proprietor of the collective work would have the right, as against the author or his representatives, to continue to publish the article " in like manner as theretofore " without payment.

942 **Provisions of the Act of 1956.** As from the commencement of the Act of 1956, two classes of cases have to be considered, namely (a) cases in which the pre-1911 copyright has already expired, and, (b) cases in which the pre-1911 copyright has not yet expired. It may be pointed out that, while the period of forty-two years from first publication must have already expired in the case of works published before 1911, the alternative period of seven years from the death of the author may well subsist in a substantial number of cases.

47 *Ante*, § 665 *et seq.*
48 *Lawrence, etc., Ltd.* v. *Aflalo* [1904] A.C. 17.
49 See note to Sched. 1 to the Act of 1911

943 **Where the pre-1911 copyright term has expired.** Dealing first with cases in which the pre-1911 copyright term has already expired before the commencement of the Act of 1956, it is provided in paragraph 38 (2) of the Seventh Schedule to that Act that, if before its commencement, any event occurred or notice was given which in accordance with paragraph (*a*) of the proviso to subsection (1) of section 24 of the Act of 1911 had any operation affecting the ownership of the right conferred by the Act of 1911 in relation to the work, or creating, transferring or terminating an interest, right or licence in respect of that right, that event or notice is to have the corresponding operation in relation to the copyright in the work under the Act of 1956. Under this provision, therefore, where the copyright under the 1911 Act has revested in the author or his personal representatives under the proviso, the copyright under the 1956 Act will revest also, and the operation of any notice given under the first option is also preserved. It is further provided that any right which, at a time after the commencement of the Act of 1956 would, by virtue of paragraph (*a*) of the said proviso to section 24 of the Act of 1911, have been exercisable in relation to the work or to the right conferred by the Act of 1911 if the Act of 1956 had not been passed, shall be exercisable in relation to the work, or to the copyright therein under the Act of 1956, as the case may be.[50] This would appear to preserve the right conferred upon the assignee under the second option.

944 **Where the pre-1911 copyright term has not expired.** As to the case in which the old term does not expire until after the commencement of the Act of 1956, it is provided that if, in accordance with paragraph (*a*) of the said proviso, the right conferred by the Act of 1911 would have reverted to the author or his personal representatives on the date referred to in that paragraph, and the said date falls after the commencement of the Act of 1956, then on that date (a) the copyright in the work under the Act of 1956 is to revert to the author or his personal representatives as the case may be and, (b) any interest of any other person in that copyright which subsists on that date, by virtue of any document made before the commencement of the Act of 1911, is thereupon to determine.[51] It will be observed that this provision does not deal with the options given to the prior assignee. It is thought, however, that the provision above-mentioned, under which any right which after the commencement of the Act of 1956 would have been exercisable if the Act of 1956 had not been passed, is to be exercisable in relation to the copyright under the Act of 1956, is wide enough, not only to include the second option in respect of works which have reverted before the commencement of

[50] Copyright Act, 1956, Sched. 7, para. 38 (3).
[51] Sched. 7, para. 38 (4).

the Act of 1956, but also the rights conferred by both options, upon the original assignee, where the pre-1911 term expires after the commencement of the Act of 1956.

3.—SURVEY OF THE LAW OF COPYRIGHT IMMEDIATELY PRIOR TO THE ACT OF 1911

945 As has already been pointed out,[52] questions affecting the subsistence, title and ownership of copyright under the Act of 1956 in works created before the commencement of the Act of 1911 still depend upon the provisions of the statutes and law as existing before the commencement of the Act of 1911. It is not possible to deal fully here with these provisions, but a general outline may be of assistance.

946 **Literary copyright.** First, as to literary copyright. The governing statute was the Literary Copyright Act, 1842.[53] This related to "books," which expression included every volume, part, or division of a volume, pamphlet, letterpress sheets, music sheets, maps, charts, and plans,[54] and the copyright extended throughout the British dominions. A work, to be entitled to protection, need not have been original,[55] although a mere copy was not protected.[56]

947 **Term of copyright.** The term of copyright was the life of the author and seven years, or forty-two years from publication, whichever period was the longer, and, in the case of posthumous works, was forty-two years from publication.[57] Copies of books were required to be delivered at the British Museum and certain libraries, and other institutions, but the failure to make delivery did not imperil the copyright.[58]

948 **Registration.** The Act also made provisions for registration at Stationers' Hall.[59] This, however, was not compulsory, but had to be effected before any action could be brought against infringers.[60] Nevertheless, once registration was effected, actions might be brought for infringements made prior to the date of registration.[61]

949 **To whom the copyright belonged.** The copyright—except in the case of a contribution to a collective work—vested in the author,[62]

52 *Ante*, § 928.
53 5 & 6 Vict. c. 45.
54 Literary Copyright Act, 1842, s. 2.
55 *Walter* v. *Lane* [1900] A.C. 539.
56 *Per* Lord James [1900] A.C. at p. 554.
57 s. 3.
58 ss. 6, 7, 8; *cf.* s. 15 of Copyright Act, 1911, *ante*, § 636.
59 ss. 11–14.
60 s. 24.
61 *Warne* v. *Lawrence* (1886) 54 L.T. 371; *Goubard* v. *Wallace* [1877] W.N. 130.
62 There have been cases in which it has been held that an employer who has had a share in designing, or has solely designed, a work executed by another, is the "author": *Barfield* v. *Nicholson* (1824) 2 Sim. & St. 1; *Hatton* v. *Keane* (1859) 8 W.R. 7; *Nisbet (J.) & Co., Ltd.* v. *The Golf Agency* (1907) 23 T.L.R. 370.

provided he first published his work on British soil.[63] A foreigner was clearly entitled to protection if he was resident within the dominions at the date of first publication, and probably he became so entitled, even if he were resident in a foreign country at that date.[64] With regard to collective works, the Literary Copyright Act of 1842 contained a very ill-drafted and puzzling section,[65] under which the copyright in articles contributed to such a work vested in the proprietor of the work in certain cases. The proprietor had, however, to prove (i) that he employed the writer to compose the articles; (ii) that the articles were composed on the terms that the copyright should belong to the proprietor [66]; and (iii) that the articles were paid for by him.[67] In the case, however, of *periodicals,* the author was at liberty, after a lapse of twenty-eight years from the date of publication, to publish his articles in a " separate form," and, during the term of twenty-eight years, the proprietor could not publish the articles separately or singly without the author's consent. The general opinion [68] was that the section now being dealt with only applied to works of the character of encyclopedias, magazines, and periodicals.

950 **Posthumous works.** In the case of a posthumous work, the copyright vested in the proprietor of the author's manuscript from which the book was first published.[69]

951 **Assignment.** Every assignment of copyright was required to be in writing,[70] and, if the work had been previously registered at Stationers' Hall, it might be assigned by entry in the register.[71]

952 **Lectures.** The only statute conferring protection upon lecturers was the Lecturers Copyright Act, 1835.[72] The protection was only against printing and publishing, and no protection was given without two days' previous notice to two magistrates living within five miles of the place of delivery, or to lectures delivered in any university or public school or college, or any public foundation, or by any individual in virtue of or according to any gift, endowment, or foundation. The period of protection was twenty-eight years.[73]

63 *Routledge* v. *Low* (1868) L.R. 3 H.L. 100.
64 *Routledge* v. *Low, supra.*
65 s. 18.
66 There was a prima facie presumption that this was so: *Lawrence, etc., Ltd.* v. *Aflalo* [1904] A.C. 17. See § 666, *ante.*
67 Actual payment was necessary: *Richardson* v. *Gilbert* (1851) 1 Sim.(N.S.) 336.
68 Kekewich J., however, in the case of *Ward, Lock & Co., Ltd.* v. *Long* [1906] 2 Ch. 550, expressed the opinion that the section extended to books generally.
69 s. 3; *Macmillan & Co.* v. *Dent* [1907] 1 Ch. 107.
70 *Leyland* v. *Stewart* (1876) 4 Ch.D. 419.
71 s. 13.
72 5 & 6 Will. 4, c. 65. This statute relates to *published* lectures. Unpublished lectures were frequently protected from publication upon the ground of breach of confidence: *Caird* v. *Sime* (1887) 12 App.Cas. 326; and see §§ 85 and 88 *et seq.*, *ante.*
73 s. 4.

953 **Musical and dramatic works.** As regards musical and dramatic works,[74] the musical scores and books of words were protected as literary works under the Literary Copyright Act, 1842. The statutes relating to the performing rights were the Dramatic Copyright Act, 1833, commonly known as "Bulwer Lytton's Act," which only originally applied to dramatic works—and sections 20 and 21 of the Literary Copyright Act, 1842, which applied to both musical and dramatic compositions. The effect of these provisions, as regards the performing rights in a musical or dramatic piece, were: (a) if the work had been published as a book, the author was entitled to protection during his life and for seven years after his death or forty-two years from the date of the first public representation or performance of the work; (b) if the work had not been published as a book, but was in manuscript only, the term of performing right was doubtful, for the Dramatic Copyright Act, 1833, did not prescribe any term in such a case, and it is not clear that the Literary Copyright Act, 1842, altered this. Possibly, therefore, the right was perpetual, but, more probably, the term was the same as in the case where the work was printed and published. If the dramatic work was first represented in a foreign country (such country not being one within the International Copyright Acts), it lost any right to protection in this country.[75]

954 **Reservation of performing rights.** In the case of the performing rights in a musical piece, it was required by the Copyright (Musical Compositions) Act, 1882,[76] that these should be expressly stated to be reserved on the title page of every published copy of the work. Failure to print such notice involved the loss of the performing rights,[77] but notice in a foreign language was sufficient.[78]

955 **Registration.** Registration was not necessary to protect performing rights.[79]

956 **Assignment.** The assignment of the copyright in a dramatic or musical piece did not convey the performing rights unless an entry to that effect was made in the register.[80]

957 **Infringement.** It was no infringement of the copyright in a novel to dramatise the same,[81] provided that the dramatic version was not

74 Performing rights were not recognised under the old law except in the case of dramatic or musical works. Probably no action would lie for reciting or singing the words of a song, unless the song was dramatic.

75 *Boucicault* v. *Delafield* (1863) 1 H. & M. 597; *Boucicault* v. *Chatterton* (1877) 5 Ch.D. 267.

76 45 & 46 Vict. c. 40.

77 *Fuller* v. *The Blackpool Winter Gardens, etc. Co., Ltd.* [1895] 2 Q.B. 429.

78 *Sarpy* v. *Holland* [1908] 2 Ch. 198.

79 *Clark* v. *Bishop* (1872) 25 L.T. 908.

80 Literary Copyright Act, 1842 (5 & 6 Vict. c. 45), s. 22.

81 *Read* v. *Conquest* (1861) 9 C.B.(N.S.) 755.

printed or copied.[82] Again, mechanical instruments were not infringements of musical copyright.[83]

958 **Artistic copyright.** Turning, next, to artistic copyright, the old law distinguished between three classes of artistic works, to which different statutes applied, namely: (1) engravings, prints, and lithographs; (2) works of sculpture; (3) paintings, drawings and photographs.

959 **Engravings, prints and lithographs.** As regards engravings and prints, the main statutes in force were the Engraving Copyright Acts of 1734 and 1766,[84] and the Prints Copyright Act, 1777.[85] Prints taken by lithograph, or any other mechanical process for multiplying prints, were brought under the earlier Acts relating to engravings by section 14 of the International Copyright Act, 1852.[86]

960 **Terms and conditions of copyright.** The period of protection was twenty-eight years from the date of publication. No registration was necessary, but the copyright was lost, unless the name of the proprietor of the copyright and the date of the first publication, were engraved on each plate, and printed on each print.[87] It was, however, held that, where engravings formed part of a book, and the copyright in the book and the engravings was vested in the same person, the pictures were protected as part of the book,[88] but not if the copyrights were separated.[89] Maps were protected sometimes under the Literary Copyright Act, and sometimes under the Engraving Copyright Acts,[90] and the latter Acts extended to designs transferred to articles of manufacture.[91]

The Engraving Copyright Acts made no express provisions as to assignment of the copyright, and it was generally considered advisable to assign in writing in the presence of two witnesses.[92]

961 **Sculptures.** Works of sculpture were protected under the Sculpture Copyright Act, 1814.[93] The term of copyright was fourteen years

82 *Warne & Co.* v. *Seebohm* (1888) 39 Ch.D. 73.

83 *Boosey* v. *Whight* [1900] 1 Ch. 122; *Mabe* v. *Connor* [1909] 1 K.B. 515.

84 8 Geo. 2, c. 13; 7 Geo. 3, c. 38.

85 17 Geo. 3, c. 57. The Acts were extended to Ireland by the Copyright Act, 1836, 6 & 7 Will. 4, c. 59.

86 15 & 16 Vict. c. 12.

87 *Newton* v. *Cowie* (1827) 4 Bing. 234; *Rock* v. *Lazarus* (1872) L.R. 15 Eq. 104.

88 *Bogue* v. *Houlston* (1852) 5 De G. & Sm. 267; *Maple & Co.* v. *Junior Army and Navy Stores* (1882) 21 Ch.D. 369; *Davis* v. *Benjamin* [1906] 2 Ch. 491.

89 *Petty* v. *Taylor* [1897] 1 Ch. 465.

90 *Stannard* v. *Lee* (1871) L.R. 6 Ch. 346; *Stannard* v. *Harrison* (1871) 19 W.R. 811.

91 *Dicks* v. *Brooks* (1880) 15 Ch.D. 22.

92 *Jefferys (C.)* v. *Boosey (T.)* (1855) 4 H.L.C. 815, 994, 995.

93 54 Geo. 3, c. 56.

from first publication, and a further fourteen years if the first proprietor was then living and had not divested himself of the copyright. His name had to be put on the work, together with the date of publication,[94] but registration was not required. All assignments had to be by deed, signed by the proprietor in the presence of and attested by two witnesses.[95]

962 **Paintings, drawings and photographs.** By the Fine Arts Copyright Act, 1862,[96] a British subject, or any person resident in the British Dominions, the author of a painting, drawing or photograph made in the British Dominions or elsewhere, and his assigns, was granted copyright during his life and for seven years after his death. Copyright under this Act attached upon the creation of the work, not upon publication,[97] but registration was necessary to obtain the full benefit of the Act.[98] No action would lie in respect of the making of copies of a published work prior to registration, but if any of such copies were sold after the date of registration, damages could be obtained.[99] If the work were unpublished, alongside the statutory copyright was a common law copyright,[1] the term of which, however, would run out with the statutory copyright.

963 **In whom copyright vested.** The first owner of the copyright was the author, except in a case where the work was executed upon commission, in which case the copyright vested, without any agreement, in the party for whom the work was executed. A curious proviso to section 1 of the Act, however, had the effect of causing the work to fall into the public domain, unless the author took the precaution, upon the occasion of his first selling his painting, drawing or negative, as the case might be, of reserving the copyright to himself, by writing under the hand of the vendee or assignee of the work, or of granting the same in writing to such vendee or assignee.[2] The authorship of a photograph was not always an easy matter to determine. Generally speaking, the author was the person who superintended the arrangement of the picture and placed the object in position,[3] but the proprietor of the photographic business was held to be the author

94 *Britain* v. *Hanks Bros. & Co.* (1902) 86 L.T. 765.
95 s. 4.
96 25 & 26 Vict. c. 68.
97 *Tuck & Sons* v. *Priester* (1887) 19 Q.B.D. 48.
98 s. 4.
99 *Tuck & Sons* v. *Priester, supra*; *cf. Savory (E. W.), Ltd.* v. *The World of Golf, Ltd.* [1914] 2 Ch. 566.
1 *Mansell* v. *Valley Printing Co.* [1908] 1 Ch. 567; *Bowden Bros.* v. *Amalgamated Pictorials, Ltd.* [1911] 1 Ch. 386.
2 It is perhaps strange that there never appears to have been any actual decision to this effect, but this was the generally accepted construction of the proviso: see Copinger (4th ed.), p. 366.
3 *Nottage* v. *Jackson* (1883) 11 Q.B.D. 627.

in some cases.[4] The sitter obtained the copyright if he gave valuable consideration.[5]

Copyright in a painting, drawing or photograph could be assigned by any note or memorandum in writing.[6]

964 Protection under the Fine Arts Copyright Act, 1862, did not extend beyond the United Kingdom, and no action for infringement could have been brought in any other part of the British Dominions.[7]

965 **Architecture.** Works of architecture (except architects' plans, which were protected as artistic works), choreographic works, pantomimes, and musical and other records were not entitled to any copyright under the old law.

966 **Summary.** The law of copyright as it stood at the commencement of the Act of 1911 may therefore be conveniently summarised as follows:

1. Unpublished works were protected at common law, and any work[8] unpublished on July 1, 1912, was, therefore, protected under the Act of 1911.

967 2. Literary works, including the literary rights in musical and dramatic works, were protected during the life of the author and for a period of seven years after his death, or during a gross period of forty-two years from publication, whichever was the longer period. Any such work published after July 1, 1870, or any work the author of which died on or after July 1, 1905, was, therefore, protected under the Act, of 1911, notwithstanding that there had been no registration of the copyright.[9]

968 3. Speeches and lectures delivered in public and without restrictions lost all right to protection, unless certain onerous formalities were complied with.[10] But a *report* of a speech might be entitled to copyright.[11]

969 4. Performing rights were only recognised in the case of dramatic or musical works. The term of copyright, if these works were published in manuscript, was for the life of the author and seven years after his death, or for a gross period of forty-two years from the date

4 *Melville* v. *Mirror of Life Co.* [1895] 2 Ch. 531.
5 *Pollard* v. *Photographic Co.* (1881) 40 Ch.D. 345; *Boucas* v. *Cooke* [1903] 2 K.B. 227; *Stackemann* v. *Paton* [1906] 1 Ch. 774.
6 Fine Arts Copyright Act, 1862, s. 3.
7 *Graves (Henry) & Co., Ltd.* v. *Gorrie* [1903] A.C. 496.
8 But as to paintings, drawings and photographs, see § 972.
9 *Savory (E. W.), Ltd.* v. *The World of Golf, Ltd.* [1914] 2 Ch. 566.
10 *Ante,* § 952.
11 *Walter* v. *Lane* [1900] A.C. 539.

of the first public performance of the work. If the work had not been published in manuscript, the term of the performing rights was uncertain.[12] In the case of musical works—not of dramatic works—it was essential to the preservation of performing rights that a notice of reservation of those rights should be printed on the title page of every publication of a work published after 1882. No musical work, therefore, published after 1882, but before July 1, 1912, which omitted to print such notice of reservation obtained any performing rights under the Act of 1911.

970 5. Engravings were protected for a period of twenty-eight years from the date of first publication, provided the name of the author and the date of first publication was printed on each copy. In order, therefore, to be entitled to protection under the Act of 1911, engravings must have been published since June 30, 1884, and have had the name of the author and date of first publication printed on every copy.[13]

971 6. Sculptures were protected for fourteen years after first publication, and for a further fourteen years if the sculptor was still living at the expiration of the first period and had not assigned his copyright, but the name of the sculptor and date of first publication had to be put upon the work.[14] The following works of sculpture, therefore, received no protection under the Act of 1911, *viz.*: (a) all works published before July 1, 1884; (b) all works published between June 30, 1884, and July 1, 1898, unless the author were living fourteen years after first publication and had not assigned his copyright; and (c) all works published before July 1, 1912, which did not bear the name of the sculptor and date of first publication.

972 7. The law with regard to paintings, drawings, and photographs was peculiar.[15] The statutory term was during the life of the author and for seven years after his death, and this statutory copyright commenced from the date of the making of the work, whether the same was published or unpublished; and although, if the work were unpublished, a common law copyright existed alongside the statutory copyright, probably the common law copyright ran out at the same time as the statutory copyright. Further, except in the case of works executed on commission, copyright was liable to be destroyed if the author did not, upon the occasion of the first sale of his work, reserve the copyright to himself in writing. It consequently follows that no painting, drawing or photograph made before July 1, 1912, was

[12] *Ante*, § 953.
[13] *Ante*, § 959.
[14] *Ante*, § 961.
[15] *Ante*, § 962.

entitled to protection under the Act of 1911, (a) if the author died before July 1, 1905, or (b) if the author failed to reserve the copyright in his work on the occasion of the first sale of his work and the work was not executed on commission. No action could be brought in respect of any infringement committed prior to the date when the copyright was registered, but the copyright itself was not imperilled by failure to register. Therefore, the owner of the copyright can sue in respect of any infringement committed after,[16] but not before,[17] July 1, 1912, notwithstanding that the copyright was not registered under the Act of 1862.

973 8. Works of architecture (except architects' plans, which were protected as artistic works), choreographic works, pantomimes, and mechanical contrivances for reproducing sounds [18] were not entitled to any protection before the Act of 1911, and, with the exception of mechanical contrivances,[19] none of these works, if made or published before July 1, 1912, was entitled to protection under the Act of 1911.

[The next paragraph is 981]

16 *Savory (E. W.), Ltd.* v. *The World of Golf, Ltd.* [1914] 2 Ch. 566.
17 *Evans* v. *Morris* [1913] W.N. 58.
18 *Quaere* as to cinematograph films, see *ante*, § 742.
19 *Ante*, § 827.

Part IV

ARRANGEMENTS BETWEEN AUTHORS AND PUBLISHERS, REVENUE PROVISIONS AND PERFORMING RIGHT TRIBUNAL

CHAPTER 21

PUBLISHING AGREEMENTS

981 **No formalities required.** Contracts between authors and publishers are not, as in some countries, regulated by any special law, but their validity, construction, and enforcement depend upon the ordinary rules of law governing contracts relating to dealings with personal property. In practice, such arrangements vary, through many gradations of formality, from an oral or implied licence to publish a single article, to a full-length publishing agreement. It is the informal agreement, leaving many essential terms to implication, that most often renders difficult the determination of the respective rights of the parties.

982 **Necessity of writing.** An assignment of copyright or an exclusive licence must be in writing [1]; but an oral or implied consent to publish will afford a good defence to an action for infringement.[2]

983 **Implication from dispatch of manuscript.** The simplest form of contract is where a manuscript is sent to a publisher without anything being said about terms. It seems probable that, in the case of an article sent to the editor or publishers of a newspaper or journal, the sending of the manuscript would by custom, or necessary implication, be treated as an offer of a licence to publish in consideration of payment of the usual terms for such a publication, and that such offer can at once be accepted by the editor or publisher without further communication.[3]

984 On the other hand, in the case of a larger work, it would seem that the sending of the manuscript is merely an offer to enter into negotiations and does not constitute an offer capable of immediate acceptance so as to form a binding contract. What, short of actual publication, amounts to an acceptance of an author's manuscript will depend upon the circumstances of the case, but if the publisher retain the article and has it put into type and a proof sent for revision to the writer, the latter may generally treat this as an acceptance of his manuscript and sue the publisher for the price, though the article is never, in fact, published.[4] Whether the manuscript itself becomes

1 Copyright Act, 1956, ss. 36 (3) and 19 (9).
2 See § 404, *ante*.
3 See *Hall-Brown* v. *Iliffe & Sons, Ltd.* [1928–35] Macg.Cop.Cas. 88, where, on the special facts, it was held that there was no licence.
4 *Macdonald* v. *National Review*, Westminster County Court, May 16, 1893; *Pall Mall Gazette*, May 17, 1893.

the property of the publisher must depend, it is submitted, on the nature of the work and the circumstances surrounding the submission of the manuscript to the publisher, including the terms of any contract between the publisher and the author.[5]

985 **Forms of agreement in common use.** Agreements between authors and publishers fall roughly into four classes: outright sales of copyright in consideration of a single payment; licences for a period on royalty terms; profit-sharing agreements; and publication on commission, no rights in the work being vested in the publisher.

986 **Agreements for sale of copyright outright.** It will be remembered that, in the case of literary copyright, the Copyright Act, 1956,[6] provides that the copyright shall vest, in the first instance, in the author, and not in the publisher, unless the relationship of master and servant subsists between the author and publisher.[7] This, however, is not necessarily so in the case of engravings, photographs or portraits, for section 4 (3) of that Act provides that, where such works have been commissioned, the person who has given the commission shall be the first owner of the copyright.[8] If, therefore, the terms of the arrangement between the author and publisher be that the copyright in a literary work is to belong to the publisher upon payment to the author of a fixed sum, an assignment in writing of the copyright by the author to the publisher should be made, even though the work has been written to the order of the publisher[9]; but, in the case of an engraving, photograph or portrait made to the order of the publisher, no such assignment will be necessary.

However, it should be observed that, under the Act of 1956,[10] an assignment in writing of the copyright in a work not yet created will operate to vest the copyright in the work in the assignee as soon as the work comes into existence and without further assurance. This will have a very important effect, since it overcomes the difficulty, which has hitherto existed, that a purported assignment of the copyright in a non-existent work gave the assignee equitable rights only, so that such assignee could not, without further assurance, bring proceedings for infringement without joining the assignor. On the other hand, it should be observed that the section only operates if, on the coming into existence of the copyright, the

5 See § 673, *ante*, and *Hogg* v. *Kirby* (1803) 8 Ves. 215; *Stone* v. *Long* [1901–04] Macg.Cop.Cas. 66; *Thomas* v. *Times Book Co., Ltd.* [1966] 1 W.L.R. 911, see also *Copyright*, No. 5, May 1966, p. 144.

6 Copyright Act, 1956, s. 4 (1), *ante*, § 301.

7 s. 4 (4), *ante*, § 324 *et seq.*

8 *Ante*, § 310.

9 As to what would amount to an assignment, see *ante*, § 355. If no assignment has been executed, however, the publisher may have equitable rights; see *ante*, §§ 350 and 351.

10 Copyright Act, 1956, s. 37.

assignee would, apart from the section, be entitled as against all other persons to require the copyright to be vested in him. Consequently, if the author has made an agreement with one publisher to assign the copyright in the next book written by him to that publisher, and subsequently, when about to write a particular book, he agrees to assign the copyright in that book to a second publisher, the copyright will, it appears, vest in the first publisher and not in the second publisher. Both agreements will operate as agreements only until the work is in fact created, so that their priority would seem to depend merely upon the dates of the respective agreements and be unaffected by any question of notice.

987 **Distinction between assignment and licence.** In the case of more formal agreements the most important point to determine is whether any copyright is to be vested in the publisher, or whether a licence only is intended. In the former case the publisher will enjoy the full legal title to the copyright and will alone be entitled to enforce the right against third parties. In the case of a licence which, in a publishing agreement, will normally be an exclusive licence, certain new provisions are introduced by section 19 of the Act of 1956. An exclusive licensee may sue for infringements of copyright, but must joint the assignor as a party to the action, except where an interlocutory injunction is sought. However, it is provided [11] that any defence which would have been available to a defendant in the action, if the action had been brought by the owner of the copyright, shall be available to that defendant as against the exclusive licensee. It does not appear, therefore, that this section has substantially altered the existing law, since an exclusive licensee remains liable to have the value of his licence prejudiced by a later assignment of copyright by the author to an assignee taking without notice of the licence.[12] Other important distinctions between the rights of the parties, according to whether an assignment or licence has been executed, arise with regard to the publisher's right to alter the work, with regard to the liability of an assign of the publisher to royalties payable to the author, with regard to the position which arises on the publisher's bankruptcy, and with regard to the assignability of the benefit of the agreement by the publisher.

988 **Right to alter.** If a publisher be the absolute owner of the copyright, he is entitled, without the consent of the author, to publish successive editions of the work with additions and corrections; and, in bringing out new editions, may make such omissions and other changes in the original as will not injure the reputation of the

[11] Copyright Act, 1956, s. 19 (4).
[12] s. 36 (4).

author.[13] Whereas, in the case of a licence, the licence may expressly, or by implication, only extend to publication in unaltered form, so that the publisher, if he publishes in an altered form, may commit an infringement.[14] This passage, and another passage [15] were approved by Goff J. in *Frisby* v. *British Broadcasting Corporation* [16] who held that, in the absence of a prohibition against publication in an altered form, the licensee had a right to make alterations, even substantial ones; but the court would readily imply a term limiting the right to make alterations.

However, even after assignment, such revision, when done by another, cannot lawfully be represented as having been made by the author of the original, if the public are induced to believe that it is the work of the author, and the author is damaged or deprived of sales thereby.[17] And the publication under an author's name of a work not his own and without his consent in circumstances that would injure his character or reputation may constitute actionable defamation.[18] Furthermore, publication of works of art in an altered form may be actionable under section 43 (4) of the Copyright Act, 1956.

989 **Right to royalties.** The position of an author who assigns his copyright and stipulates for payment on royalty terms may be a difficult one. If the publisher assigns the copyright to a third party, the author cannot sue the third party for his royalties because no privity of contract exists between them,[19] and the original publisher may become insolvent. The rights of an author who had assigned his copyright on royalty terms and then sought to sue a purchaser from the assignee for royalties, were fully considered in the case of *Barker* v. *Stickney* [20] by the Court of Appeal. The claim was put on three grounds, namely, for a vendor's lien, for a charge on the copyright assigned, and on the basis of a covenant the burden of which ran with the copyright. The court held that, so far as a claim based

13 See *Lee* v. *Gibbings* (1892) 67 L.T. 263, where the court declined to interfere in a case in which a purchaser of a stock of books rebound them in a mutilated form.

14 See *Joseph* v. *National Magazine Co., Ltd.* [1959] Ch. 14.

15 § 675, *ante*.

16 [1967] Ch. 932; and see *Cox* v. *Cox* (1853) 11 Hare 118; *Crookes* v. *Petter* (1860) 6 Jur.(N.S.) 1131; *Booth* v. *Edward Lloyd, Ltd.* (1909) 26 T.C.R. 549; *Gilbert* v. *Workman* [1905–10] Macg.Cop.Cas. 235.

17 *Ridge* v. *The English Illustrated Magazine, Ltd.* [1911–16] Macg.Cop.Cas. 91; *Springfield* v. *Thame* (1903) 89 L.T. 242; see *ante*, § 243, and see Copyright Act, 1956, s. 43 (2).

18 *Ridge* v. *The English Illustrated Magazine, Ltd., supra*; See *Lee* v. *Gibbings, supra*; *Mosely* v. *Stanley Paul & Co.* [1917–23] Macg.Cop.Cas. 341; *Glyn* v. *Western Feature Film Co.* [1916] 1 Ch. 261; *Archbold* v. *Sweet* (1832) 1 Moo & Rob. 162; *Humphreys* v. *Thomson & Co., Ltd.* [1905–10] Macg.Cop.Cas. 148.

19 *Bagot Pneumatic Tyre Co.* v. *Clipper Pneumatic Tyre Co.* [1902] 1 Ch. 146 and see *Beswick* v. *Beswick* [1968] A.C. 58.

20 [1919] 1 K.B. 121.

on lien was concerned, this failed since the vendor had accepted the purchaser's covenant to pay royalties in satisfaction of his claim for the price, and, therefore, was not an unpaid vendor. A charge could only arise if it was clearly and expressly created by the document and this was not the case. So far as the burden running with the copyright, Scrutton L.J. said: " but as to personal property it was found that the general rule of Knight-Bruce L.J. (in *De Mattos* v. *Gibson* [21]) was quite impracticable and *Taddy & Co.* v. *Sterious & Co.* [22]; *McCruther* v. *Pitcher* [23]; and *Dunlop Pneumatic Tyre Co. Ltd.* v. *Selfridge & Co. Ltd.*[24] had settled the law that the purchaser of a chattel is not bound by mere notice of stipulations made by his vendor unless he was himself a party to the contract in which the stipulations were made. I see nothing to distinguish a chose in action such as copyright from chattels or land, and I think it is clear that a person acquiring a chose in action is not bound by mere notice of a personal covenant by his predecessor in title." Whether this last point should be reconsidered in the light of the decision in *Lord Strathcona Steamship Co., Ltd.* v. *Dominion Coal Co., Ltd.*[25] where the principle of *De Mattos* v. *Gibson* [26] was applied in the case of a ship, remains undecided.[27] It seems fairly clear, however, that as the law now stands, an author who has entered into a publishing agreement in which the copyright is assigned to the publisher on royalty terms, has no right of action for the royalties against an assign of the publisher. Authors, therefore, should keep the copyright themselves and assign no more than a right to publish conditional upon royalties being paid and only assignable if they are provided for.[28]

990 **Bankruptcy of publisher.** A further example of the difference between a licence and an assignment is afforded by a consideration of the effect, in the two cases, of the bankruptcy of the publisher. In the case of *Re Grant Richards*,[29] it was held that, where an author had assigned his copyright in consideration of the payment of royalties, and, upon the bankrupty of the publisher, his trustee continued the publisher's business for some time, the author had no right to claim payment of the royalties in full, but could only prove

21 (1859) 4 De G. & J. 276.
22 [1904] 1 Ch. 354.
23 [1904] 2 Ch. 306.
24 [1915] A.C. 847.
25 [1926] A.C. 108.
26 *Supra*.
27 In *Port Line, Ltd.* v. *Ben Line Steamers, Ltd.* [1958] 2 Q.B. 146, Diplock J. decided that the *Strathcona* case was wrongly decided but even if it was rightly decided, the defendants did not come within its principles.
28 *Barker* v. *Stickney* [1919] 1 K.B. 121 at 133, 134; see *Farmer* v. *Grant Richards* [1901–04] Macg.Cop.Cas. 78 as to an author's right to royalties on remainder sales.
29 [1907] 2 K.B. 33.

in the bankruptcy for damages. On the other hand, in a case where there was an agreement by the publisher to pay a share of profits to the author, and the copyright still remained vested in him, it was held that the agreement was terminated by the bankruptcy of the publisher, whose trustee in bankruptcy was restrained from reprinting or republishing the book, even on the terms of continuing to pay the author his share of profits, but without prejudice to the right of the trustee to dispose of stock.[30]

991 The undoubted hardship caused to authors by the decision in the case of *Re Grant Richards*[31] was removed by section 60 of the Bankruptcy Act, 1914,[32] whereby it is provided as follows:

> " Where the property of a bankrupt comprises the copyright in any work or any interest in such copyright, and he is liable to pay to the author of the work royalties or a share of the profits in respect thereof, the trustee shall not be entitled to sell, or authorise the sale of, any copies of the work, or to perform or authorise the performance of the work, except on the terms of paying to the author such sums by way of royalty or share of the profits as would have been payable by the bankrupt, nor shall he, without the consent of the author or of the court, be entitled to assign the right or transfer the interest or to grant any interest in the right by licence, except upon terms which will secure to the author payments by way of royalty or share of the profits at a rate not less than that which the bankrupt was liable to pay."

992 This section only, in terms, applies to a case where the bankrupt is liable to pay royalties or a share of profits " to the author." However, it seems probable that the courts would not give a stringent construction to the section, but would hold that it applies equally to a case where the royalties or share of profits is payable to the personal representatives, or to an assign, of the author. It is further to be noticed that the section deprives the trustee in bankruptcy, not only of the right to continue to manufacture copies of an author's work without payment of royalties or share of profits, but also of the right to dispose of stock on hand without making like payment. It has been held[33] that the section was applicable in a case in which a publisher having a mere licence had, with the consent of the author, granted a right to publish to a second publisher on royalty terms, part of which royalty was payable to the author by the first publisher.

30 *Lucas* v. *Moncrieff* (1905) 21 T.L.R. 683.
31 [1907] 2 K.B. 33.
32 4 & 5 Geo. 5, c. 59. S. 102 of the Bankruptcy (Scotland) Act, 1913 (3 & 4 Geo. 5, c. 20), is to the same effect.
33 *Henham* v. *Alston Rivers, Ltd.* [1911–16] Macg.Cop.Cas. 330.

The judge made a declaration that, notwithstanding the insolvency of the first publisher, the author's share of the royalty from the second publisher was payable to him in full, presumably on the ground that the representative of the first publisher could only, having regard to the section, continue to authorise the second publisher to publish on the terms that the author's share of the royalties was paid to him in full. If it is assumed, from the decision in this case, that the section does apply to a mere licence to publish, it might be argued that the section authorises the court to order the assignment of the benefit of a licence which would not otherwise be assignable. It is thought, however, that the section would not be held to have this effect, but only to authorise the court to direct an assignment where the publisher himself could have assigned before bankruptcy.

993 But it has been held that the above-mentioned section does not apply in the case of the winding up of a company [34] and, consequently, if the publisher is a company and is wound up, the liquidator may, unless the publishing agreement otherwise provides, dispose of the copyright in the work and leave the author to prove in the liquidation. Consequently the danger of assigning copyright on royalty terms still remains where the publisher is a limited company.

994 **Assignability.** Again, the distinction between a licence and an assignment is important in connection with the question of the assignability by the publisher of the benefit of a publishing agreement. Where the publisher takes an assignment of copyright, he has a right which he can transfer at will and, in default of an express agreement not to assign, he cannot be deprived of that right. Further, even if there is such an express agreement, it would seem to be ineffective as against a subsequent assignee without notice. Moreover, the mere fact that the publisher is to pay royalties or a share of profits to the author will not give rise to any implication of an agreement not to assign.[35] On the other hand, a licence can expressly be made personal and terminable upon any purported assignment of its benefit and, even without such express provision, will, in general, be read as containing an implied provision to this effect.

995 In such cases the question whether the benefit of a publishing agreement is assignable by the publisher turns upon whether the agreement ought to be regarded as of a personal nature or not. Contracts of a personal character are not assignable,[36] and wherever the author is to be remunerated either by a share of profits or by

[34] *Re Health Promotion, Ltd.* [1932] 1 Ch. 65.
[35] *Simms* v. *Marryat* (1851) 17 Q.B. 281.
[36] See *Booth* v. *Richards* [1905–10] Macg.Cop.Cas. 284.

royalties, prima facie the contract is of a personal nature. Thus, where there was an agreement in writing between an author and certain publishers that they should print, reprint and publish his book, upon the condition that the author should prepare it all before a certain day, and should correct it for the press, and that the publishers should direct the mode of printing, and pay all the expenses and take all risk of publishing, and out of the produce should first repay such expenses, and then divide the profits between themselves and the author equally; and that if all copies should be sold and a new edition should be required, the author should prepare the same, and the publisher should print and publish it on the same conditions; and that, if all the copies of any edition should not be sold in five years from the date of publication, the publishers might sell the remaining copies by auction or otherwise, in order to close the account; it was held to be a personal contract with the author, and not an assignment of the copyright; and, consequently, the benefit thereof could not be assigned by the publishers.[37]

"The principal question then is," said Wood V.-C. in *Stevens* v. *Benning*,[38] "whether this agreement is a personal engagement or not. It would be difficult for me to say that, in a contract of this kind, the author is utterly indifferent into whose hands his interests under such an engagement are to be entrusted. It is not merely a question of his literary interests, but certain publishers undertaking to incur the expenses of bringing out the work, and fixing the price; the author is to have a share of the profits; and they are to decide in what shape the book is to come out, and at what price it is to be sold, and are to account with him. I must say, that, in my opinion, these are peculiarly personal considerations; and that this contract bears the impress of being a personal contract in all these respects. It could not be a matter of indifference to Mr. Forsyth that the assignees in bankruptcy of Mr. Benning should be at liberty to transfer the future right of fixing the price of this and subsequent editions, and the right to call upon him to fulfil his duty of preparing a new edition, and the risk which might be incurred in conducting it, and the other benefits and obligations of the agreement, to anyone they might think proper; possibly to someone not even carrying on the trade of a bookseller, as might happen in the case of an absolute sale to the best bidder. Regarding the agreement as a contract for the purchase of a limited right, according to the view of the Vice-Chancellor of England in *Sweet* v. *Cater*,[39] it is still impossible that it should be indifferent to Mr. Forsyth that it should pass from a respectable firm in London to booksellers residing in a remote part

37 *Stevens* v. *Benning* (1855) 1 K. & J. 168; affirmed 6 D.M. & G. 223; *Reade* v. *Bentley* (1858) 3 K. & J. 271; *Hole* v. *Bradbury* (1879) 12 Ch.D. 886.

38 (1855) 1 K. & J. 168 at 174.

39 (1841) 11 Sim. 572; *Lucas* v. *Moncrieff* (1905) 21 T.L.R. 683.

of the country, or to other persons unable to fulfil the engagements entered into with him. The contract, therefore, is one which involves personal consideration; and framed as it is, I must regard it as a special kind of agency, under which the agents were bound to sell, and to take the risk of there being no profits upon themselves."

996 **If the publishers are a limited company.** The same principles have been held to apply in a case where the publishers were a limited company, and the proposed assignment was to be made by a receiver and manager of the company appointed in a debenture-holder's action. The court declined to accede to the view that a distinction ought to be drawn between a limited company and an individual publisher, and considered that an author might repose confidence in a company, notwithstanding that the constitution of the company might alter and its officers might be changed at any time.[40]

997 **If the publishers are to pay a fixed sum.** If, on the other hand, the publisher is under an obligation to pay to the author a definite sum of money for the privilege of publishing his works, it seems probable that the publisher would have the right, in the absence of express provision, to assign the benefit of the agreement, though the literary interests of the author might possibly be affected to some extent, yet the change of publishers could not, at least directly, cause him any pecuniary injury.

998 **How to distinguish assignment and licence as a matter of construction.** It will have been seen, from the foregoing, that it is of high importance to distinguish between an assignment and a licence. But it is often not easy to make this distinction, as a matter of construction of the words used in agreements between authors and publishers. Thus, in the case of *Sweet* v. *Cater*,[41] the agreement, after reciting that the author had prepared a tenth edition of his work, which the publisher was desirous of *purchasing*, and that it had been agreed that a certain printer should print a given number of copies, and the publisher should pay to the author *for the said tenth edition* a certain sum, went on to direct that the work should be in a given number of volumes, and should *be sold* to the public for a given price. It was objected that the plaintiff, the publisher, was not, under this agreement, the *proprietor of the copyright* within the meaning of the statute 54 Geo. 3, c. 156, s. 4, but a mere licensee to sell a given number of copies. The court overruled the

[40] *Griffith* v. *Tower Publishing Co., Ltd.* [1897] 1 Ch. 21. McCardie J. in *Messager* v. *British Broadcasting Co., Ltd.* [1927] 2 K.B. 543, held that a licence to a theatrical producer terminated with the death of the producer. The decision was overruled in the House of Lords [1929] A.C. 151, on the ground that the document was an assignment and not a licence.

[41] (1841) 11 Sim. 572 and see § 355 *et seq., ante*.

objection, holding that the copyright was equitably vested in the purchaser until the whole edition referred to in the contract was sold, on the ground that the contract was obligatory on both parties, that the plaintiff was bound to sell, and, therefore, the author was bound to abstain from doing anything which would interfere with the sale. The court, moreover, were of opinion that the equitable right to the copyright endured until the number of copies fixed by the terms of the agreement had been exhausted.

999 **Presumption against assignment.** But wherever there are continuous obligations on the part of the publisher—for instance, the payment of royalties to the author—the tendency of the courts is to construe the agreement as conferring upon the publisher a conditional licence to publish, rather than as giving him an equitable title to the copyright. Thus, in *Re Jude's Musical Compositions*,[42] the plaintiff was the proprietor of the copyright in a series of musical compositions called " Music and the Higher Life." In the year 1900 the defendant company, through their managing director, agreed, in consideration of the plaintiff giving to the company " the sole and exclusive right of printing and publishing " this series in volume form, first, to bear the whole cost of printing and issuing the volume, secondly, to pay the plaintiff 6d. on every copy sold, and thirdly, to supply the plaintiff with such copies as he should require at 1s. 6d. per copy, such copies not to be liable to the royalty of 6d. It was held by the Court of Appeal, affirming Kekewich J.,[43] that this was a mere publishing agreement and not an assignment of copyright. The Court of Appeal based their decision largely upon the fact that the defendants were only to be at liberty to publish the musical compositions in " volume form," but Kekewich J. appears to have thought that the fact that the defendants were to be under continuing obligations to the plaintiff was evidence of an intention not to assign the copyright. This view was supported by the case of *Stevens* v. *Benning*,[44] where Page Wood V.-C. remarked as follows: " Then it is argued, that the sole power of printing, reprinting and publishing is, in fact, the copyright. And no doubt if an author, in consideration of a sum of money paid to him, agrees that certain persons shall have the sole power of printing, reprinting and publishing a certain work for all time, that would be a parting with the copyright; but, if the agreement is that the publishers, performing certain conditions on their part, should, so long as they do perform such conditions,

42 [1907] 1 Ch. 651.
43 [1906] 2 Ch. 595.
44 (1855) 1 K. & J. 168, aff. 6 D.M. & G. 223; *cf. Hales* v. *Fisher Unwin (T.), Ltd.* [1923–28] Macg.Cop.Cas. 31. It should be noted that, even in the case of a licence, there may be an implied term, enforceable by injunction, restraining the author from making any other publication until all copies are sold: *Reade* v. *Bentley* (1858) 3 K. & J. 271. See *post*, § 1011.

have the right of printing and publishing the book, that is a very different agreement." But where the agreement indicates that the publishers are to sue in respect of infringements of copyright of the work published it is an indication that an assignment of copyright is intended.[45]

1000 The distinction between an assignment and a licence was further considered by the House of Lords in the case of *Messager* v. *British Broadcasting Co., Ltd.*[46] in connection with an agreement regarding dramatic rights. In that case clause 1 of the agreement provided: "The licensors hereby grant to the licensee the sole and exclusive right of representing or performing the play in the United Kingdom." This was held to be in plain terms an assignment of the performing right the effect of which was not curtailed merely because of the use of the words "licensors" and "licensee" or because payment was to be made on a royalty basis. In arriving at this decision weight was given to the fact that the document contained a provision that in certain events the rights should "revert to and become again the absolute property of the licensors." In *Chaplin* v. *Leslie Frewin (Publishers), Ltd.*[47] the Court of Appeal held that the words "the publishers shall during the legal term of the copyright have the exclusive right of producing, publishing and selling the said work," constituted an assignment. Danckwerts L.J. said[48] that the use of the word "assigns" in other clauses and the absence of an express provision for reverter did not affect the matter. It would, he thought, be reasonable to imply a reverter where necessary. He also said that, even if the words "grant" or "assign" were not used, the intention to assign might appear from the context.

1001 Again, in *Barstow* v. *Terry*[49] a provision that, on certain conditions, "the entire rights for the United Kingdom, etc., in the play become theirs inalienably and they shall present it when and where they will within the countries aforesaid paying fees on the following scale," was held an assignment of the entire performing rights in the play, and in *Jonathan Cape, Ltd.* v. *Consolidated Press, Ltd.*[50] an agreement whereby the author granted to publishers, their successors and assigns the exclusive right to print and publish an original work or any part or abridgment thereof, in volume form, during the legal

45 *Macdonald (E.) Ltd.* v. *Eyles* [1921] 1 Ch. 631.
46 [1929] A.C. 151; see also *Canadian Performing Right Society* v. *Famous Players Canadian Corp., Ltd.* (1927) 60 Ont.L.R. 280, 614; [1929] A.C. 456.
47 [1966] Ch. 71; compare *Frisby* v. *British Broadcasting Corporation* [1967] Ch. 932 where the agreement was held to be a licence: see also *Re "Clinical Obstetrics"* [1905–10] Macg.Cop.Cas. 176; *Neilson* v. *Horniman* [1905–10] Macg.Cop.Cas. 234 and *Booth* v. *Richards* [1905–10] Macg.Cop.Cas. 284.
48 [1966] Ch. at 94.
49 [1924] 2 Ch. 316.
50 [1954] 1 W.L.R. 1313.

term of unrestricted copyright in the English language, throughout the British Commonwealth, on royalty terms, was held to be an assignment of part of the copyright in the work to the publishers. It was also held in this case that it was an infringement of that part of the copyright consisting of the right to publish in volume form to publish substantially the whole of the work in a single issue of a magazine, and that it was immaterial that it was not published in the form of an object with thick cardboard sides and back and merely had a paper cover.[51]

It seems to follow, from these decisions, that the only safe course to adopt, where a licence only is intended, is to say expressly " by way of licence only " or to use words to that effect.

1002 **Outright sale.** It now remains to summarise the four classes of agreements in common use. Where copyright is sold for a single payment, the matter is relatively simple because the rights of the parties are concluded at once.

If an author is employed to write for a fixed payment, the employer is not entitled to complain because the result is unsatisfactory; he has agreed to accept the product of the skill and taste of the author.[52]

After an author has parted with the copyright in a book he is not at liberty to reproduce substantially the same matter in another work. Even in the absence of any special agreement, the second publication would be an infringement of the copyright in the first.[53]

1003 **Royalty agreement.** The necessity in the case of a royalty agreement, from the point of view of the author, of securing that a licence only is granted has already been discussed.[54]

If the royalty payable to the author is a certain proportion of the price of the work, the agreement should fix a minimum price at which the work is to be sold,[55] which may be a " long " price, enabling a discount to be allowed to the general public, or a " net " price, allowing no such discount. The royalty payable to the author will, generally, be calculated upon the retail price at which copies of the work are supplied to the " trade." [56]

[51] The meaning of the expressions " volume form " and " serial form " were considered in this case: see *Heinemann* v. *Smart Set Publishing Co.* [1905–10] Macg.Cop.Cas. 221 as to the meaning of " serial rights " and " magazine rights."

[52] *Ellis* v. *British Filmcraft Productions, Ltd.* [1928–35] Macg.Cop.Cas. 51.

[53] *Colburn* v. *Simms* (1843) 2 Hare 543.

[54] § 989, *ante*.

[55] As to price maintenance agreements and fixing of minimum prices by suppliers, see §§ 1030–1033, *post*.

[56] If the book is published in different bindings this must be taken into consideration in the agreement. Royalties are not usually paid on press or other free copies.

1004 **Profit-sharing agreement.** An agreement between author and publisher to the effect that the former shall contribute the manuscript, and the latter shall, in the first place, defray the cost of the bringing out of the work, and repay himself out of the proceeds of the sale, and that the net profits shall be divided, generally creates a profit-sharing agreement in the nature of a partnership in the sale of the work, though not in the copyright. It is probable, however, that the author would not be liable for paper and printing supplied where the entire risk is taken by the publisher, and no credit is given to the author.[57]

1005 **But is a joint adventure terminable by notice?** The true relationship between author and publisher under a profit-sharing agreement was the subject of discussion in the case of *Reade* v. *Bentley*.[58]

It was contended by the plaintiff, author, that the case was one of simple agency; that by the effect of the agreement the defendant, publisher, became a mere agent of the plaintiff. "But," observed the Vice-Chancellor,[59] "it is clear that he became more than that. A mere agent may be paid, as the defendant was to be paid, by a share of the profits; but a mere agent never embarks in the risk of the undertaking; and here the defendant took upon himself the whole expense and risk of bringing out the work. Clearly, therefore, the case is something more than one of simple agency." He held, accordingly, that the enterprise was in the nature of a "joint adventure" which the author was at liberty to terminate by reasonable notice.

After considering and distinguishing the cases of *Sweet* v. *Cater* [60] and *Stevens* v. *Benning*,[61] the Vice-Chancellor remarked as follows [59]:

"On the other hand, it was contended for the defendant that if the effect of the agreement was not an assignment of the copyright (which it is now clearly decided that it could not be), it resulted in a joint adventure, in which the defendant was to have a licence to publish the work; and that, from the nature of the case, and by the terms of the agreement, that licence was irrevocable. In *Stevens* v. *Benning* [61] I considered the agreement must be regarded as creating, to a certain extent, a joint adventure, and Knight-Bruce L.J. adopted the same view. He says, it must be observed, that such interest, if any, in the copyright of the author's work as the other parties to the agreement acquired under it, they acquired, not exclusively of the author, 'but by the way of joint adventure with him, or of partnership with him, in respect and for the objects of which he undertook the fulfilment by himself personally

57 See *Gardiner* v. *Childs* (1837) 8 C. & P. 345.
58 (1858) 4 K. & J. 656.
59 *Ibid.* p. 662.
60 (1841) 11 Sim. 572.
61 (1855) 6 D.M. & G. 223.

of certain duties to them, and they undertook the fulfilment by themselves personally of certain duties to him.' [62] Community of risk does not appear to me to be by our law, any more than it was by the civil law, essential to constitute a partnership; one partner being at liberty to contract with another that he will take all the losses of the concern upon himself. Turner L.J. looked upon the agreement in *Stevens* v. *Benning* [61] in the double light of a licence and a partnership, speaking, however, less decidedly as to its being a partnership. He says: 'Next, if there was a partnership, then, if the agreement does not affect the copyright, the partnership was not in the copyright, but in the copies printed under the licence contained in the agreement' [63]—viewing it, therefore, as a licence for the publication of the work, and then a joint adventure between the author and the publisher in the copies so to be published. If that were the effect of the agreement in the present case, the question would still remain, whether the licence be irrevocable."

1006 "[The plaintiff] does not attempt to interfere with the publication of an edition which the defendant had commenced, and incurred expense in preparing for publication, before he exercised the option of determining the agreement. His claim is limited to editions about which no such expense had been incurred by the defendant; and his argument is, that, unless he has a right to determine the agreement as to all such editions, the consequence will be, that, during the whole of the defendant's life, he may be under an obligation to the defendant, while the defendant will be under no reciprocal obligation to him. It is true that, according to *Stevens* v. *Benning* [61] a licence like the present would, I apprehend, be restricted to the defendant personally, and would not extend to his executors, or to any future partner or assignee; but if the defendant's construction be correct, it follows that, so long as he lives and is willing to continue publishing fresh editions of the work, so long, according to the doctrine in *Sweet* v. *Cater*, [60] the plaintiff will be precluded from asserting a right to publish any competing edition. The defendant could compel the plaintiff to abstain from publishing a single copy of the work, so long as he expressed his readiness to continue publishing. But the plaintiff has no reciprocal power. He could never compel the defendant to publish more than a single edition of the work. His powers are limited to what the contract gives him; and according to the contract, when the defendant has published a single edition the contract on his part is fulfilled. That is a position of considerable hardship for an author, and one which ought to be clearly shown, upon the face of a contract, to have been contemplated by the parties

[62] 6 D.M. & G. at p. 229.
[63] 6 D.M. & G. at p. 231.

who entered into it. . . . In the present case, no new expense has been incurred by the defendant, either in printing, advertising, or otherwise, as regards 'Peg Woffington,' since the publication of the second edition, and, as regards 'Christie Johnstone,' since the publication of the fourth edition; and that being, as I have already intimated, the true test in construing the agreement, it appears to me that, when those editions were published, the period had arrived at which the parties intended a division of profits to take place and at which the plaintiff became entitled to terminate his agreement with the defendant. This is the only conclusion at which I can arrive, after a very careful consideration of the contracts. But it is much to be regretted that contracts should be framed with such uncertainty, when it would have been so easy to make them certain." [64]

1007 **Profit-sharing involves fiduciary relationship.** A profit-sharing agreement between an author and a publisher establishes a fiduciary relationship between the parties, and the author is entitled to an account from the publisher.[65] For this purpose the publisher must produce all books and documents necessary for the proper vouching of the accounts; he is not entitled to charge the author at a higher rate for the expenses of printing, paper, etc., than he himself actually pays, and must give the author the benefit of all trade commissions and discounts.[66] Where the author may terminate the contract at the end of each edition the damages recoverable by an author against a publisher are limited to the profits which he would have received from one reasonable edition.[67]

1008 **Works published on commission.** Where an author is prepared to run the entire risk of the publication of a work, he usually employs a publisher to publish and sell the work on his behalf at a fixed commission.[68] In this case the publisher is simply agent for the author, and the entire liability for the expenses of printing and publishing the work falls upon the latter; but he receives the gross proceeds of sales, less the publisher's commission. It is, however, a well-known practice of publishers, in accounting for sales, to reckon "thirteen copies as twelve" or "twenty-five copies as twenty-four," and it should be made clear in the agreement whether this practice is intended to apply as between the parties. It should further be made clear whether the particular publisher is to have

64 4 K. & J. 664 to 669. *Cf. Holland* v. *Methuen & Co., Ltd.* [1928–35] Macg.Cop. Cas. 247, where in a case of a royalty agreement and not a profit-sharing agreement, it was held that there was no right to determine.

65 *Barry* v. *Stevens* (1862) 31 Beav. 258.

66 See an opinion of counsel obtained in the year 1893, by the Society of Authors.

67 *Abrahams* v. *Reiach, Ltd.* [1922] 1 K.B. 477.

68 See *Colles* v. *Maugham* [1905–10] Macg.Cop.Cas. 267 as to literary agent entitlement to commission.

the exclusive right of publication, or whether the author is to be at liberty to make similar contracts with other publishers.[67]

1009 **Points in drafting publishing agreements.** Every well-drafted agreement between an author and a publisher should clearly state what are the precise rights which the publisher is to acquire. As we have seen,[69] copyright is divisible as to time, place and classes of acts. Is the agreement to include all translations, abridgments, selections, dramatisations, film rights, television rights, and so on, or are these to be reserved to the author? Is the publisher to have foreign rights as well as local rights? In the case of musical and dramatic works, is the publisher to have the performing rights and the right to authorise reproduction by records or other mechanical instruments? Has the Performing Right Society Limited any rights? Does the author retain film rights? In the case of music a distinction may be made between use of the music as background or incidental music for a film and use as an essential part of a dramatico-musical work. In the case of novels intended to be published in "serial form" in magazines, is the right of publication in "volume form" included, or is the author to be left free to arrange for "volume form" publication independently? The serial publisher may require the right to serialise before any "volume form" publication, but in such case some time limit should be required. In the case of pictures, is the publisher to have the right of reproduction by all processes, or only by photography, engraving, lithography, or what other process, and is the original to become the property of the publisher or to be returnable within any, and what, time to the artist? In whom is the secondary copyright in the negative or plate to be vested? All these are points which should be made clear upon the face of the agreement. If, again, the publisher is to have the right to publish only a single edition of a work, the number of copies of which the edition is to consist should be declared, for otherwise a publisher might, if so disposed, print 20,000 as one edition.[70]

1010 **Construction of the word "edition."** The meaning of the word "edition," and the construction to be placed upon it, were fully discussed in *Reade* v. *Bentley*.[71] It was argued that where a work has once been stereotyped, the term "edition" was no longer applicable; and that when a work is published in what are called "thousands," 20,000 or 30,000 being circulated, each thousand

69 *Ante*, § 360 *et seq.*

70 *Per* Wood V.-C. in *Reade* v. *Bentley* (1858) 4 K. & J. 656 at 667; *Sweet* v. *Cater* (1841) 11 Sim. 572; *Stevens* v. *Benning* (1855) 1 K. & J. 168; *Benning* v. *Dove* (1831) 5 C. & P. 427.

71 (1858) 4 K. & J. 656.

could not properly be called an "edition." Wood V.-C., however, thought that not merely in point of etymology, but having regard to what actually takes place in the publication of any work, an "edition" of a work was the putting of it forth before the public, and if this were done in batches at successive periods, each successive batch was a new edition; and the question whether the individual copies had been printed by means of movable type or by stereotype did not seem to him to be material. If movable type were used, the type having been broken up, the new edition was prepared by setting up the type afresh, printing afresh, advertising afresh, and repeating all the other necessary steps to obtain a new circulation of the work. In that case the contemplated break between the two editions was more complete, because, until the type was again set up, nothing further could be done. It made no substantial difference as regards the meaning of the term "edition," whether the new "thousand" had been printed by a resetting of movable type, or by stereotype, or whether they had been printed at the same time with the former thousand or subsequently. A new "edition" is published whenever, having in his storehouse a certain number of copies, the publisher issues a fresh batch of them to the public. This, according to the practice of the trade, is done, as is well known, periodically. And if, after printing 20,000 copies, a publisher should think it expedient, for the purpose of keeping up the price of the work, to issue them in batches of a thousand at a time, keeping the rest under lock and key, each successive issue would be a new "edition" in every sense of the word.[72]

1011 **Agreements as to number of copies.** Where the agreement is for the exclusive publication of a specified number of copies, that number only can be printed and sold, and, until their sale, the author cannot revoke the authority given to the publishers, or himself publish the work.[73]

An agreement that the publishers shall publish a second edition, if demanded by the public, and print as many copies as they can sell, gives them the right, when such demand arises, to publish and sell as many copies as can properly be considered to belong to that edition, and to prevent the author, or any other person, from publishing until such copies shall be sold.[74]

72 *Per* Wood V.-C., in *Reade* v. *Bentley* (1858) 4 K. & J. 656 at 666, 667. See *Blackwood* (*R.*) v. *Brewster* (*D.*) (1860) 23 Sess.Cas. (2nd Ser.) 142. In this case it was held that an editor, under an agreement that he should prepare every new edition of a work, and should receive a certain sum for his services, is not entitled to superintend, or to claim payment for, the reprinting of a part of the work to replace copies destroyed by fire. The copies reprinted under such circumstances do not form a new edition but go to replace the part of the edition destroyed.

73 *Reade* v. *Bentley* (1858) 3 K. & J. 271; (1858) 4 K. & J. 656.

74 *Pulte* v. *Derby* (1852) 20 Fed.Cas. 51.

If the agreement is silent as to the number of copies to be published, the publisher must publish such a number as is reasonable in all the circumstances.[75]

1012 **Agreements as to style of publication.** The publisher is bound to observe the terms of the contract between himself and the author as to the manner and style of the publication, and the price at which it shall be issued to the public, but if the price at which the work is to be sold be not fixed by the agreement, or otherwise arranged by the author and publisher, the latter is the proper person to determine the same. At the same time, he would not be permitted to fix upon a style, or sell at a price, which would be clearly injurious, either to the literary reputation, or the pecuniary interests of the author, without his consent. The writer of a signed article is entitled to complain of alteration in the text made without his consent.[76]

1013 **Implications of the number of editions.** When neither the time during which the publication is to last, nor the number of editions or copies to be published, is specified, the publisher is not bound to publish more than the first edition; and the author, by giving proper notice, may end the contract and prevent the publication of any further editions.[77] But the publisher is at liberty to continue publishing successive editions on the terms of the contract until the receipt of such notice; and the author is not entitled to restrain the publication or sale of any edition on which the publisher has incurred expenses before receiving notice to end the agreement.[78]

1014 **Warranty on sale of copyright.** Where the executor and son of the deceased author, in reply to an offer from a publishing house relating to one of his father's works, replied that he would be happy to treat with them "respecting the copyright" in it; and, in another letter, said he had accepted their offer "for the exclusive right of publishing it," and gave a receipt for the money paid "for permission to publish the work so long as the copyright may endure; that right to be exclusively their own for ten years from this date," it was held that this amounted to an express warranty of title, and an equitable assignment of the copyright having, unknown to the executor, been previously made to another publisher, the executor was held liable to an action for breach of the warranty.[79]

[75] *Abrahams* v. *Reiach, Ltd.* [1922] 1 K.B. 477.
[76] *Joseph* v. *National Magazine Co., Ltd.* [1959] Ch. 14.
[77] *Reade* v. *Bentley* (1858) 3 K. & J. 271; 4 K. & J. 656; *Warne* v. *Routledge* (1874) L.R. 18 Eq. 497. In this last case it was held that no agreement could be implied on the part of the author not to bring out a second edition until all the first edition was sold. See, however, *Holland* v. *Methuen & Co., Ltd.* [1928–35] Macg.Cop.Cas. 247.
[78] *Reade* v. *Bentley, supra.*
[79] *Simms* v. *Marryat* (1851) 17 Q.B. 281.

1015 **Assignment comprising world rights.** In *Campbell Connelly & Co., Ltd.* v. *Noble* [80] Wilberforce J. had to consider the U.S.A. law of renewal copyright. He was required to construe a purely English contract assigning the full copyright for all countries for the period of copyright as far as it was assignable by law, together with all rights therein which the author then had or might thereafter become entitled to. Notwithstanding U.S.A. authorities to the effect that U.S.A. renewal copyright did not pass unless expressly mentioned the learned judge held that the assignee under the English contract had become entitled to the renewal right. The American decisions were decisions as to the construction and effect of American contracts. He was entitled to look at U.S.A. law to ascertain the nature of the renewal right, but not to enable him to construe the assignment.

1016 **Failure to supply work.** If an author agrees in writing to supply a bookseller or publisher with a manuscript of a work to be printed by the latter, an action for damages can be maintained for refusing to furnish the same,[81] and the publisher can recover as damages any outlay made in reliance on the contract and the estimated loss of profit,[82] provided the work be not one which, if published, would be libellous,[83] or would subject the author to punishment.[84]

1017 **Payment for part of work finished.** Where a work called the "Elements of Mechanical Philosophy" was published in parts, the agreement between the author and publisher being that each part should be paid for when issued, and after the publication of a complete part the progress of the work was interrupted by the death of the author, it was held that the representatives of the deceased author were entitled to payment of the stipulated price of the published part.[85]

1018 **Screen credit.** Where a licence is granted to use a work as part of a film, there is an implied term that credit for the work will not be given to some other person in presenting and advertising the film.[86]

1019 **Specific performance.** A court of equity will not decree specific performance of an agreement to write a book. It has no power to go so far, and were it capable of making such an order, there would be no means of enforcing it.[87]

80 [1963] 1 W.L.R. 252.
81 *Gale* v. *Leckie* (1817) 2 Stark.N.P. 107. The Court of Chancery, however, could not compel him to write.
82 *Clarke* v. *Price* (1819) Wils.C.R. 157.
83 *Lyne* v. *Sampson, Low, The Times*, February 17, 1873.
84 *Gale* v. *Leckie, supra.*
85 *Constable (A.) & Co.* v. *Robison's Trustees* (1808) 14 Fac.Dec. 166.
86 *Miller* v. *Cecil Film, Ltd.* (1937) 53 T.L.R. 544.
87 *Clarke* v. *Price* (1819) Wils.C.R. 157: see *Page One Records, Ltd.* v. *Britton* [1968] 1 W.L.R. 157. But specific performance of an agreement to assign a copyright may be decreed: *Thombleson* v. *Black* (1837) 1 Jur. 198.

On the other hand, whereas, while a publishing agreement remains completely unperformed, it may be impracticable for the court to decree specific performance by the publisher of his agreement to publish, yet, in a case where the order could be enforced without practical difficulty, such a decree may be made. Thus, in the case of *Barrow* v. *Chappell & Co., Ltd.*[88] where the plaintiff claimed specific performance of an oral contract made with the defendant company that the defendant company should publish in a certain journal a musical work composed by the plaintiff, Danckwerts J. felt able to make an order for specific performance against the publishers on the basis that the plaintiff had fully performed everything required on his part, and damages for failure to publish would be difficult to assess and not an adequate remedy. In *Joseph* v. *National Magazine Co., Ltd.*[89] Harman J. distinguished the former case. He said the court could not order specific performance of an agreement to publish where the exact terms of the subject-matter to be published had never been agreed.

1020 **Damages for failure to publish by agreed date.** In the *Barrow* case *supra*, the judge made an order for payment by the publishers of damages in respect of delay in publication, having found as a fact that the contract was a contract to publish in November 1949, or within a reasonable time thereafter, and that this contract had been broken.[90] In another case [91] the Court of Appeal awarded to an author damages against a publisher for failure to publish by an agreed date. The damages were based upon an estimate of what the plaintiff would have got if the defendants had carried out their bargain and the court left open the question whether, in an appropriate case, the plaintiff might also have recovered some damages for loss of publicity. In *Joseph* v. *National Magazine Co., Ltd.*,[89] damages were assessed on the loss to the plaintiff as an expert in jade of the enhancement of his reputation which would have resulted from the publication.

1021 **Purchaser of copyright not bound to publish.** It may be well to mention here that it is apprehended that where the copyright in a work is sold outright, and there is no express agreement to publish the same, the proprietor may decline to publish, notwithstanding that the author may fail by reason of this to acquire additional

[88] (1951) *The Author*, LXII, No. 2, at 38.

[89] [1959] Ch. 14: and see *Tolnay* v. *Criterion Film Productions, Ltd.* [1936] 2 All E.R. 1625, damages awarded for deprivation of screen credit.

[90] See *White* v. *Constable & Co.* [1901–04] Macg.Cop.Cas. 2; and see *Planché* v. *Colburn* (1831) 8 Bing. 14 as to an author's right to claim *quantum meruit* for work done when publication abandoned.

[91] *Goffin* v. *Staples & Staples, Ltd.* [1946–47] Macg.Cop.Cas. 1; *Abrahams* v. *Herbert Reiach, Ltd.* [1922] 1 K.B. 477.

reputation.[92] The author should have made the publication by the purchaser part of the agreement, had he considered this material to his interests. But where there is an agreement to publish, without stating any date of publication, an undertaking to publish within a reasonable time will be implied.[93]

1022 **Restrictions undertaken by authors.** In *Morris* v. *Colman*,[94] where Colman had contracted with the proprietors of the Haymarket Theatre not to write dramatic pieces for any other theatre, the Lord Chancellor maintained that such a contract was not unreasonable upon either construction, whether it was that Mr. Colman should not write for any other theatre without the licence of the proprietors of the Haymarket Theatre, or whether it gave to those proprietors merely a right of pre-emption. " If," said he, " Mr. Garrick was now living, would it be unreasonable that he should contract with Mr. Colman to perform only at the Haymarket Theatre, and Mr. Colman with him to write for the Theatre alone? Why should they not thus engage for the talents of each other? . . . I cannot therefore see anything unreasonable in this; on the contrary, it is a contract which all parties may consider as affording the most eligible, if not the only, means of making this Theatre profitable to them all, as proprietors, authors, or in any other character which they are by the contract to hold." And in *Macdonald* (*E.*), *Ltd.* v. *Eyles,*[95] an authoress who had agreed that a publisher should have an option to acquire the copyright in her next three books was restrained from publishing them with another publisher; and the second publisher, who had purchased the copyright in her next work with knowledge of the agreement, was also restrained.

However in *Brooke* v. *Chitty*,[96] where the defendant had undertaken not to write or edit any work upon the criminal law, except a work of which the plaintiff had purchased the copyright, and an advertisement of an edition of Burn's " Justice of the Peace," by the defendant, had appeared, Lord Brougham refused to grant an injunction, observing that the defendant was at liberty to write in his closet what he pleased, and that the court would not interfere until there was a violation of the alleged undertaking by actual printing and publication.

So, when an author sells the copyright of a work published under his own name, and covenants with the purchaser not to publish any other work to prejudice the sale of it, it seems that another publisher, who has no notice of this covenant, may be restrained from publishing

92 See *Nichols* v. *The Amalgamated Press* [1905–10] Macg.Cop.Cas. 166.
93 *Crane* v. *C. Arthur Pearson, Ltd.* [1936–45] Macg.Cop.Cas. 125.
94 (1812) 18 Ves. 437.
95 [1921] 1 Ch. 631 ; but any time-limit in such an option will be construed strictly: *Martin Hopkinson, Ltd.* v. *Muspratt* [1928–35] Macg.Cop.Cas. 334.
96 (1847) 2 Coop.C.C. 216; *cf. Brook* v. *Wentworth* (1795) 3 Anst. 881.

a work subsequently purchased by him from the same author, and published under his name, on the same subject, but under a different title, and though there be no piracy of the first book.[97]

1023 The authority of these decisions may now require to be reconsidered in the light of the *Petrofina (Gt. Britain), Ltd.* v. *Martin*[98] and *Esso Petroleum Co. Ltd.* v. *Harper's Garage (Stourport), Ltd.*[99] cases.

1024 **Undertaking to work personal.** If an author undertakes to compose a work and dies before completing it, his executors or administrators are discharged from the contract, for the undertaking was merely personal in its nature, and, by the intervention of the contractor's death, has become impossible to be performed.[1] And if an author becomes bankrupt his trustee has no power to compel him to complete the work.[2]

1025 **Author at liberty to publish a continuation of his work.** But where no such covenant had been entered into, and the publisher had agreed with an author for an edition of a history to be written by the latter, in four volumes, and had obtained subscriptions for all that could fall within his edition, the court held that the author was at liberty to publish a continuation of the history which embraced part of the period and also much of the matter contained in the last of the four volumes.[3]

1026 **Agreement to employ author on similar terms.** An author and publisher entered into an agreement under which the author was to edit the whole of the plays of Shakespeare (to be called the *Temple Shakespeare*), and was to write an introduction, notes, and glossary for each play. The publisher was to pay the author a royalty, and the copyright was vested in the publisher. One of the clauses of the agreement was that, in the event of a cheaper or other form of edition of any of the plays being thought advisable by the publisher, it should form the subject of an agreement with the author on similar *pro rata* terms to those embodied in that agreement. Subsequently, the publisher produced a *Temple Shakespeare* for schools, with notes,

[97] *Barfield* v. *Nicholson* (1824) 2 Sim. & St. 1; but see *Sweet* v. *Archbold* (1833) 10 Bing. 133.
[98] [1966] Ch. 146.
[99] [1968] A.C. 269.
[1] *Marshall* v. *Broadhurst* (1831) 1 Tyrwh. 348 at 350; *Cooke* v. *Colcraft* (1773) 2 W. Blackstone 856.
[2] *Gibson* v. *Carruthers* (1842) 8 M. & W. 343.
[3] *Blackie, etc., & Co.* v. *Aikman (J.)* (1827) 5 Sess.Cas. 719. As to the respective rights of a writer and publisher of a periodical to continue to publish the periodical in the old name after termination of their agreement, see *Ingram* v. *Stiff* (1859) 5 Jur. 947; *Clowes* v. *Hogg* [1870] W.N. 268; *Constable (A.) & Co.* v. *Brewster* (1825) 3 Sess.Cas. 215.

introduction, and glossary written by a person other than the author. The court held this to be breach of the publishing agreement and, on the author bringing his action, whilst refusing an injunction restraining the publication of the school edition, ordered a reference to chambers to assess the damages the plaintiff had suffered.[4]

1027 **Rights of owners of chattels which are copyright works.** A few observations may, perhaps, not be out of place here as to the rights of the owner of a material object, which is the subject of copyright, to deal with that object in any way he pleases. We have already pointed out that the transfer of the material object does not, even in the case of a picture, prima facie operate to transfer the copyright.[5] On the other hand the right of selling the material object is not part of the copyright conferred upon an author by the Copyright Act, 1956. Copyright is infringed by reproduction of a work, not by sale of it. It is true that a person who sells a work, which to his knowledge infringes copyright, is, by section 5 of the Act of 1956, exposed to an action for infringement of copyright, but no person can, it is thought, be sued on that ground for selling a work which has been lawfully made, save only in the case of a work lawfully made in another country, but improperly imported into this country.[6] Prima facie, therefore, any owner of a work which is the subject of copyright may sell it to any person, and at any price that he pleases, but may not make copies of it, or authorise the making of copies of it, unless he owns the copyright in it, or is given permission by the copyright owner.

1028 **Stock in hand.** It consequently follows that, if a publisher is given a right to publish a copyright work for a limited period, which has expired, he is entitled to sell stock which he has on hand, provided he has not manufactured in excess of the numbers permitted by his contract. Thus, in the case of *Howitt* v. *Hall*,[7] the defendants paid to the plaintiff, the author of a work entitled " A Boy's Adventures in Australia," the sum of £250, " being the purchase-money, as agreed, for the copyright and sole right of sale for four years " of that work. At the expiration of the term of four years the defendants still had a number of unsold copies of the work in stock, and these the court held he was entitled to dispose of as he pleased. Wood V.-C. in giving judgment said[8]: " The Copyright Acts were directed against unlawful printing; and when, as in this case, the defendant had acquired the right of lawfully printing the work, he was at liberty to sell at any time what he had so printed. The words ' sole

4 *Gollancz* v. *Dent* (1903) 88 L.T. 358.

5 *Ante*, § 341.

6 Copyright Act, 1956, s. 5. But see *Monckton* v. *Pathé Frères, etc., Ltd.* [1914] 1 K.B. 395.

7 (1862) 6 L.T. 348.

8 *Ibid.* p. 350.

right of sale' might or might not have been superfluous, but after four years the right to print the work reverted to the author, who had taken care to secure himself in this respect. It had been suggested that the effect might be to destroy the copyright in the author altogether, as the publisher who had purchased the copyright for a limited period only might during that period print off copies enough to last for all time. Probably a nice question might have arisen as to the number of copies of which an edition might consist, but a publisher was not likely to incur the useless expense of printing copies enough to exhaust the demand for all time, and have them lying on his hands unprofitably. But the answer was palpable, that, if the author wished to guard against such a contingency he might easily secure himself by stipulating what number of copies was to be printed. Should, however, a case of fraud be established against a publisher under such a state of circumstances, the court could deal with it. But no case of fraud was alleged in the present case. What the defendants had done appeared to him to have been done perfectly bona fide, and they were entitled under the contract to do what they had done. The motion for the injunction must therefore be refused." [9]

1029 **Stock made prior to an assignment.** On the same principles, it has been held that the assignor of the copyright in a work is equally at liberty to sell any copies of the work manufactured prior to the date of the assignment,[10] and, prior to the last Bankruptcy Act, the trustee in bankruptcy of a publisher, whose publishing agreement was terminated by the bankruptcy, could also have disposed of stock.[11]

1030 **Price maintenance agreements before new legislation.** Questions regarding price maintenance agreements in regard to the selling price of books have been raised from time to time, and, until quite recent legislation, the position seems to have been as follows. The Copyright Act, 1956,[12] does not include amongst the monopolies conferred upon the copyright owner the exclusive right of selling the work, and, therefore, the patent cases in which it has been held that the purchaser of a patented article is bound by any restrictions imposed by the owner of the patent with regard to user of the patented article, provided there is knowledge of the contract between his immediate vendor and the pat· nt owner at the time of the purchase,[13] have no

[9] In consequence it is usual in publishing agreements, which are liable to determination, to provide that, upon such determination, the author is to be at liberty to purchase stock undisposed of, at cost price.

[10] *Taylor* v. *Pillow* (1869) L.R. 7 Eq. 418.

[11] *Lucas* v. *Moncrieff* (1905) 21 T.L.R. 683; *Re Curry (W.), etc., Co.* (1849) 12 Ir.Eq.R. 382; but see now s. 60 of the Bankruptcy Act, 1914, *ante*, § 991.

[12] See § 1027, *ante*.

[13] See *National Phonograph, etc., Ltd.* v. *Menck* [1911] A.C. 336, and the cases there cited. In America it has been held that, notwithstanding that, under the American Act, the copyright owner is given the exclusive right of vending the work, a sale in breach of a notice not to sell at less than a stated price is not an infringement of copyright: *Bobbs-Merrill Co.* v. *Straus* (1908) 210 U.S.R. 339.

application to copyright works. The owner of a copyright work was not bound by any restrictions in regard to the use or sale of the work, unless he had contracted to observe such restrictions. If a copyright owner sells to a purchaser upon the footing that the work shall not be sold at less than a certain price, and the purchaser does so, he is liable, not for infringement of copyright, but for breach of contract.[14] Such contract, however, does not, under the ordinary law, run with the work, so that a sub-purchaser is not liable to the copyright owner for selling under the stipulated price, even though he had full knowledge of the contract between his immediate vendor and the copyright owner, unless such sub-purchaser has himself contracted to observe the stipulations as to price, because of lack of privity of contract.[15] Sometimes, as affording some additional protection to the copyright owner, an agreement was entered into by the purchaser, not only that he would not himself sell under a certain stipulated price, but that he would, on the occasion of any sub-sale, procure that the sub-purchaser should enter into a similar agreement. Such an agreement was not in restraint of trade, so that an action would lie if the purchaser failed to obtain any such agreement from the sub-purchaser.[16] But if the sub-purchaser did enter into such a contract, there would generally be no privity of contract between the copyright owner and the sub-purchaser, so that the former would have no direct right of action against the sub-purchaser for breach of his contract.[17]

1031 **New legislation.** This position was altered by the Restrictive Trade Practices Act, 1956,[18] which allows an individual supplier to enforce conditions as to minimum prices against any dealer, including one not a party to the original sale, who acquired the goods with notice of the conditions, despite the lack of privity of contract.[19] Moreover, such conditions may be enforced by an injunction restraining the defendant from reselling in breach of any such condition goods thereafter to be sold by the plaintiff, whether of the same description as the goods proved to have been resold in breach of the condition, or of any other description.[20] This seems to provide for a much wider form of injunction than would normally be granted

14 *Benning* v. *Dove* (1831) 5 C. & P. 427.
15 *Taddy & Co.* v. *Sterious & Co.* [1904] 1 Ch. 354; *McGruther* v. *Pitcher* [1904] 2 Ch. 306; *Dunlop Pneumatic Tyre Co., Ltd.* v. *Selfridge & Co., Ltd.* [1915] A.C. 847; *Barker* v. *Stickney* [1919] 1 K.B. 121; *cf. Lord Strathcona Steamship Co., Ltd.* v. *Dominion Coal Co., Ltd.* [1926] A.C. 108, but see *Port Line, Ltd.* v. *Ben Line Steamers, Ltd.* [1958] 2 Q.B. 146.
16 *Elliman Sons & Co.* v. *Carrington & Son, Ltd.* [1901] 2 Ch. 275. As to agreements between manufacturers to keep up prices, see *Urmston* v. *Whitelegg Bros.* (1890) 63 L.T. 455.
17 *Dunlop Pneumatic Tyre Co., Ltd.* v. *Selfridge & Co., Ltd., supra.*
18 4 & 5 Eliz. 2, c. 68; and see Restrictive Trade Practices Act, 1968 (1968 c. 66).
19 s. 25 (1).
20 s. 25 (4).

by a court, which will usually limit the injunction to any repetition of the precise acts of which complaint has been made and proved.

1032 The Restrictive Trade Practices Act, 1956,[18] prohibits any collective agreement between suppliers as to the prices and conditions on which they will supply goods which is declared by the Restrictive Practices Court to be contrary to the public interest.[21] The court has declared a number of agreements not to be contrary to the public interest, including the Net Book Agreement, under which most British publishers impose a common set of conditions as to minimum prices when selling books to retailers.[22] The Act absolutely prohibits agreements for the collective enforcement of conditions as to resale prices.[23]

1033 The Resale Prices Act, 1964,[24] prohibited the fixing of minimum resale prices by suppliers[25] except in relation to classes of goods exempted by the court.[26] Books are included among the classes of goods which have been so exempted.[27]

[The next paragraph is 1034]

21 s. 20 (3).
22 *Re Net Book Agreement 1957* [1962] 1 W.L.R. 1347.
23 4 & 5 Eliz. 2, c. 68, s. 24.
24 c. 58.
25 s. 1 (1).
26 s. 5.
27 See *Re Net Book Reference*, *The Times*, March 2, 1968 and *Board of Trade Journal*, May 10, 1968.

CHAPTER 22

INCOME TAX, ESTATE DUTY AND STAMP DUTY

1.—INCOME TAX

034 **Introduction.** How the fruits of authorship are taxed depends upon the manner in which a number of factors are combined. At the outset it may be helpful to summarise the most important of these factors:

(i) the nature of the receipt (whether a royalty or a lump sum);

(ii) the identity of the recipient (whether the author, or a third party);

(iii) the status of the recipient (whether or not resident or ordinarily resident in the United Kingdom);

(iv) the date of the receipt (whether before or after the author ceases to practise his profession);

(v) the location of the profession (whether or not practised in the United Kingdom).

It is convenient to treat the identity of the recipient as the primary classification and to consider the other factors as each of the two classes of recipient are dealt with. In what follows, references to a person being " taxable " or to " taxation " are references to income tax and surtax unless otherwise stated.

035 **Sums received by an author.** An author who is resident in the United Kingdom and who is carrying on his profession here is taxable upon any royalties he receives whether or not they are received in the United Kingdom.[1] He is similarly taxable upon any lump sums received on the grant of a licence to use a copyright or the total or partial assignment of a copyright.[2]

036 The fact that a person produces copyright by an isolated piece of writing rather than in the course of a profession does not mean, of itself that any profit escapes tax.[3] Where, for example, an individual collaborates with a journalist to produce a series of articles, the individual is taxable upon sums received from the transaction unless

[1] Under Case II of Schedule D, Income and Corporation Taxes Act (I.C.T.A.), 1970 (1970 c. 10), s. 109 (2).

[2] *Glasson* v. *Rougier* [1944] 1 All E.R. 535; 26 T.C. 86; *Howson* v. *Monsell* [1950] 2 All E.R. 1239; 31 T.C. 529.

[3] But the appropriate case of Schedule D would be VI rather than II: I.C.T.A., 1970, s. 109 (2).

the individual is being paid mainly for publication rights, any services that he renders being incidental.[4]

1037 **(i) Post-cessation receipts.** As a matter of general revenue law an author is not taxable on:

(a) lump sums received on the sale of a book *after* the discontinuance of his profession [5] or

(b) royalties received after the discontinuance of his profession from a royalty contract made *before* the discontinuance of his profession.[6]

The view is widely held that the special " post-cessation receipt " provisions [7] subject all such receipts to tax, but it is considered that on their true construction these provisions do not have this result. These provisions are considered below.[8]

On any view, however, one [9] of the post-cessation receipt provisions does catch lump sums and royalties that were payable before the discontinuance but which are not paid until afterwards.

As will have been inferred from their exclusion from (b) above, royalties payable under a royalty contract formed *after* the discontinuance of an author's profession are taxable on general principles.[10]

1038 **(ii) Capital gains.** On the footing that the post-cessation receipt provisions do not charge to income tax a lump sum received on the sale of copyright after the discontinuance of the author's profession, the sale will result in a charge to capital gains tax on the difference between the consideration received for the copyright and the allowable expenditure incurred in its creation. Normally, however, expenditure on the creation of the copyright will have been allowed in an income tax computation, in which case it will not be allowable expenditure for the purposes of capital gains tax.[11]

1039 A person who is resident or ordinarily resident in the United Kingdom is chargeable to capital gains tax on the disposal of copyright wherever it is situate,[12] but an individual who, whilst being

[4] Compare *Hobbs* v. *Hussey* [1942] 1 K.B. 491 with *Housden* v. *Marshall* (1958) 38 T.C. 233.

[5] *Withers* v. *Nethersole* [1948] 1 All E.R. 400; 28 T.C. 501, a case of the partial assignment of a copyright. The same principle applies to a lump sum received for a licence, provided that the grant of the licence substantially diminishes the capital value of the copyright: see *Haig's Trustees* v. *I.R.C.*, 1939 S.C. 676; 22 T.C. 725; *Beare* v. *Carter* [1940] 2 K.B. 187.

[6] *Stainer's Executors* v. *Purchase* [1952] A.C. 280; 32 T.C. 367; *Carson* v. *Cheyney's Executor* [1959] A.C. 412; 38 T.C. 240.

[7] I.C.T.A., 1970, ss. 143, 144.

[8] § 1052 *et seq.*

[9] I.C.T.A., 1970, s. 144 (1).

[10] Under Case III of Schedule D: *ibid.* s. 109 (2).

[11] Finance Act, 1965 (1965, c. 25), Sched. 6, para. 5 (1).

[12] Finance Act, 1965, s. 20 (1).

resident or ordinarily resident [13] in the United Kingdom is not domiciled here, is taxable only on a remittance basis [14] in respect of gains arising on the disposal of copyright situate abroad.[15]

1040 Capital gains tax is considered in other contexts elsewhere in this chapter.[16]

1041 **(iii) Gifts.** Where a trader disposes of an item of trading stock otherwise than in the course of his trade (for example by giving an item away otherwise than to further the interests of the trade), he is treated for tax purposes as if he had earned, as a trading receipt, an amount equal to the market value of the item at the time of the disposal.[17] It has been held,[18] however, that this rule does not apply to persons carrying on a profession and accordingly an author who gives away his copyright is not treated as if he had received as income an amount equal to the market value of the copyright at the date of the gift. However, such a transaction results in a charge to capital gains tax upon the author on the difference between the market value of the copyright at the date of the gift and any allowable expenditure incurred in creating the copyright.[19] If, as will normally be the case, the expenditure has already been allowed in an income tax computation, it will not be allowable expenditure for the purposes of capital gains tax.[20]

1042 If an author gives away future copyright (that is, for instance, copyright not yet in existence [21]) so that when the copyright does come into existence it automatically vests in the donee,[22] it is considered that for the purposes of capital gains tax the author disposes of the copyright at the date when it comes into existence, notwithstanding that it may never have vested in him.[23]

1043 The donee of copyright is treated for capital gains tax purposes as having acquired it for market value,[24] but if the copyright has less

13 "Resident" and "ordinarily resident" have the same meanings for the purposes of capital gains tax as they have for income tax: *ibid.* s. 43 (1) see § 1047, *post.*

14 *Ibid.* s. 20 (7), and see *ibid.* s. 45 (6) for the definition of remittance for these purposes.

15 Copyrights and copyright licences are situate in the United Kingdom if they, or any right derived from them, are exercisable in the United Kingdom; *ibid.* s. 43 (3 (*h*).

16 See §§ 1041, 1042, 1043 and 1050, *post.*

17 *Sharkey* v. *Wernher* [1956] A.C. 58; 36 T.C. 275.

18 *Mason* v. *Innes* [1967] Ch. 1079.

19 Finance Act, 1965, s. 22 (4) (*a*).

20 *Ibid.* Sched. 6, para. 5 (1).

21 See s. 37 (5) of the Copyright Act, 1956.

22 Copyright Act, 1956, s. 37.

23 *Contra Wheatcroft on Capital Gains Taxes*, para. 6–35: "The word disposal must, it is suggested, involve there being some proprietary or beneficial right in the disposer at the time [of the disposal]." Some support for the view expressed in Wheatcroft is to be derived from the Finance Act, 1965, s. 22 (1) (*c*), which seems to contemplate that the person making the disposal will at least own the property that is the subject-matter of disposal.

24 Finance Act, 1965, s. 22 (4) (*a*).

than fifty years to run the donee's acquisition cost will be written down over his period of ownership.[25]

1044 **(iv) The foreign element.** If an author is not resident in the United Kingdom, but is carrying on his profession of author here, receipts from his United Kingdom writings are prima facie liable to United Kingdom taxation [26] and will probably also be prima facie liable to taxation in the country where he is resident. Provided that the country of his residence has a double-tax treaty with the United Kingdom, the author will normally be exempted from United Kingdom taxation by the treaty. But notwithstanding any such exemption, a person paying a royalty to a person who is normally resident abroad is obliged to deduct tax at standard rate from the payment and account to the Revenue for the tax.[27] It is then up to the non-resident to claim the tax so deducted from the Revenue. Where any royalty payment is made through the hands of an agent resident in the United Kingdom, and the agent is entitled as against the author to deduct commission from the payment, the sum from which he must deduct tax at standard rate is the residue of the royalty payment after the deduction of the commission.[28] If the amount of the commission is not ascertained at the time of the payment, tax is deductible from the gross amount of the payment, but when the amount of the commission becomes ascertained, the agent may reclaim from the Revenue an amount equal to tax at standard rate on the commission.[29]

1045 An author who is resident in the United Kingdom, but who is practising his profession wholly abroad, is liable to tax only on the receipts that he enjoys in the United Kingdom as cash, either by bringing the receipts in as cash, or by reconverting them in the United Kingdom to cash from any form in which they had been converted abroad (the "remittance basis" of taxation).[30] Moreover, on any view of the post-cessation receipt provisions, a resident author who carries on his profession wholly abroad is not liable to tax on sums remitted to the United Kingdom in a year after that in which he ceases to practise his profession, even though they arose before the cessation.[31]

25 *Ibid.* Sched. 6, para. 10.

26 I.C.T.A., 1970, s. 108.

27 *Ibid.* s. 391 (1); unless the royalties are from exported copies of a work: *ibid.* and unless the Revenue has agreed that tax need not be deducted. It has been held that a lump sum is a royalty for the purposes of this provision: *I.R.C.* v. *Longmans Green*, 17 T.C. 272.

28 *Ibid.* s. 391 (2).

29 *Ibid.*, proviso.

30 Under Case V of Schedule D: *ibid.* ss. 109 (2), 122 (2) (*b*), (3) (*b*).

31 Because they apply only to professions taxable under Case II of Schedule D: *ibid.* ss. 143 and 144.

1046 Royalties arising in any year in which an author is not resident and in which he does not practise his profession in the United Kingdom, are taxable if remitted in a subsequent year in which he is resident, provided that he is still carrying on his profession abroad.[32]

1047 **(v) "Residence."** The term "residence" does not admit of a single definition for tax purposes and generally the question of whether a person is resident or not is determined by reference to such factors as the regularity, purpose and duration of his visits to the United Kingdom and, the existence of a home in the United Kingdom. A comprehensive survey of the meaning of residence is beyond the scope of this chapter, but attention is drawn to the following points:

(i) any person who is present in the United Kingdom in any financial year for periods exceeding six months is resident in that year [33];

(ii) any person conducting a profession in the United Kingdom who maintains a home here in any year is resident for any such year in which he visits the United Kingdom [34];

(iii) it is the Revenue's view that a person who visits the United Kingdom for periods averaging at least three months per year becomes resident after four years of such visits, unless his arrangements indicated from the start that regular visits of such duration were to be made, in which case he would be resident from the first year [35];

(iv) If a British subject who has hitherto been resident leaves the United Kingdom for some temporary purpose only, he does not thereby cease to be resident,[36] but it appears to be Revenue practice to treat anyone who is absent from the United Kingdom for the whole of any financial year as being non-resident for that year.

1048 **(vi) Top-slicing relief: lump sum on sale of copyright after ten years or more.** If more than ten years after the first publication of a work the copyright is assigned in whole or in part, or licensed [37] by the author [38] and the duration of the assignment or licence is not less than two years, any lump sum [39] receivable for such an

[32] *Elmhirst* v. *I.R.C.*, 21 T.C. 381.
[33] *Ibid.* s. 51 (1) (income tax); Finance Act, 1965, s. 43 (2) (capital gains tax).
[34] *Loewenstein* v. *De Salis*, 10 T.C. 424.
[35] See Revenue leaflet "Visitors from other Countries: Liability to United Kingdom Income Tax," reprinted in the *British Tax Encyclopedia* at para. 6–146. See also *I.R.C.* v. *Lysaght* [1928] A.C. 234; 13 T.C. 511.
[36] *Ibid.* s. 49.
[37] Both ss. 389 and 390 of the I.C.T.A., 1970, use the expression "grants any interests in the copyright by licence." A similar provision is to be found in s. 5 (2) of the Copyright Act, 1911, which is not repeated by the Copyright Act, 1956, and which has never been satisfactorily construed: see § 381, *ante*.
[38] Including a joint author: *ibid.* s. 390 (11).
[39] Including an advance on account of royalties that is not returnable: *ibid.*

assignment or licence is taxable as if it were receivable over more than one year. If the duration of the assignment or licence exceeds six years, the sum is treated as if it were receivable in six equal instalments at yearly intervals, the first of which becoming due in the year in which the sum actually becomes receivable.[40] If the duration is less than six years, the sum is similarly spread over a period corresponding to the actual duration.[41] If the author dies during the period over which the sum is to be spread, subject to an election that can be made by his personal representatives, any instalments which are notionally outstanding at the death are treated as having become receivable on the date when the last instalment before the death became receivable.[42] The election that the personal representatives may make is that the tax payable on the instalments notionally outstanding at the date of death is not to exceed the tax that would have been payable on *all* the instalments had they been spread over the period from the date of the assignment or licence to the date of death.[43] A corresponding rule (which is subject to a corresponding election to be made by the author) applies where instalments are notionally outstanding at the retirement of the author.[44]

A claim for the relief at present under consideration cannot be made in respect of a payment if a prior claim for relief has been made under the provision considered below.[45]

1049 **(vii) Top slicing: other circumstances.** If no prior claim has been made for the relief considered above,[46] where an author grants a licence[47] to use, or totally or partially assigns, a copyright that has taken him more than twelve months to create, his taxability for certain sums receivable by reason of the grant or assignment is computed as if the sums had become receivable over a period of more than one year.[48] The sums to which this relief applies are:

(a) lump sums, including an advance on account of royalties which is not returnable, at any time after the first publication of the work, and

(b) royalties receivable within two years of the first publication of the work.[49]

If the author spent between one and two years in producing the copyright, half the receipt is taxed as income of the year in which

40 *Ibid.* s. 390 (1) and (2).
41 *Ibid.* s. 390 (1) and (3).
42 *Ibid.* s. 390 (4).
43 *Ibid.* s. 390 (5).
44 *Ibid.* s. 390 (6).
45 *Ibid.* s. 390 (9).
46 *Ibid.* s. 389 (6).
47 See note 37, *ante*.
48 *Ibid.* s. 389 (1).
49 *Ibid.* s. 389 (4).

it became receivable and half as income of the preceding year.[50] If the time exceeded two years, one-third of the receipt is taxed as income of the year in which it became receivable, one-third as the income of the preceding year and the final third as the income of the year before that.[51]

1050 **Sums received by third parties and personal representatives.** How royalties, and lump sums derived from copyright should be taxed in the hands of third parties and personal representatives is a matter of some complexity. The position depends upon how two groups of special provisions modify what may be termed the general principles of revenue law. The provisions in question are the "post-cessation"[52] receipt provisions and the "alienation of income derived from personal activities"[53] provisions. As a matter of general revenue law, unless he is a dealer in copyright,[54] a third party or a personal representative is taxable only upon royalties derived from a royalty contract made either by himself or another third party at any time, or by the author after his retirement. Accordingly, as a matter of general revenue law, royalties paid under a contract made by the author in the course of his profession and later assigned to a third party,[55] or which later vest in personal representatives, and lump sums received by a third party or a personal representative from the sale by him of copyrights,[56] escape the charge to income tax. In the case of a sale of copyright, however, unless the receipt is chargeable to income tax under the provisions considered below, the sale will bring about a charge to capital gains tax on the difference between the amount by which the lump sum exceeds the acquisition cost of the third party of the copyright. If he acquired the copyright otherwise than by way of the bargain made at arm's length, the acquisition cost is treated as having been the market value of the copyright at the date of the acquisition.[57] Personal representatives are always treated as having acquired assets from the deceased for market value.[58]

1051 Dealing first with the "alienation of income, etc." provisions, if either of the receipts referred to above as not being chargeable to income tax in the hands of a third party, comes into his hands by reason of a transaction, the main object or one of the main objects of

50 *Ibid.* s. 389 (2).
51 *Ibid.* s. 389 (3).
52 *Ibid.* ss. 143 and 144.
53 *Ibid.* ss. 487 and 489.
54 *Cf. Shiner* v. *Lindblom* (1960) 39 T.C. 367.
55 *Hume* v. *Asquith* [1969] 2 Ch. 58.
56 *Withers* v. *Nethersole* [1948] 1 All E.R. 400; *Haig's Trustees* v. *I.R.C.* (1939) 22 T.C. 725.
57 Finance Act, 1965, s. 22 (4) (*a*).
58 *Ibid.* s. 24 (1). Accordingly, personal representatives are chargeable only on increases in value after that date.

which was the avoidance or reduction of liability to income tax, the *author* is chargeable to income tax on the receipt,[59] although he is entitled to recover the tax from the third party.[60]

1052 Turning to the "post-cessation receipt" provisions, it is widely accepted that they charge to tax lump sums derived from copyright sold *after* the discontinuance of the author's profession and royalties payable under a royalty contract made *before* that discontinuance, in either case, by whomsoever they are received. The provisions are expressed to apply to ". . . sums arising from the carrying on of the trade, profession or vocation during any period before the discontinuance (not being sums otherwise chargeable to tax)."[61]

1053 It is considered that neither of the foregoing receipts arise "during any period before the discontinuance" and accordingly are not within the provisions. "During any period," etc. cannot modify "carrying on" because it is not possible to carry on a profession *otherwise* than before its discontinuance. It may have been thought that the provisions have a wider meaning than that which is here contended for because there is excluded from their ambit: "a lump sum paid to the personal representatives of the author of a literary . . . work as consideration for the assignment *by them,* wholly or partially, of the copyright in the work."[62]

1054 Whatever may be the true construction of these provisions, as they apply only to sums received after a profession has been discontinued, *so long as the author continues to practise his profession,* they are not apt to catch royalties received by a third party under a royalty contract that has been assigned to him by the author or lump sums received, by a third party, on the sale of a copyright.

2.—ESTATE DUTY

1055 On the death of an author estate duty will be payable on the value of any copyrights vested in him at his death and, in so far as he has assigned his copyrights on royalty terms, on the value of his interest passing on his death under any publishing agreements. The basis of valuation of the property passing for the purposes of estate duty is that established in section 7 (5) of the Finance Act, 1894,[63] namely, the price which in the opinion of the Commissioners the property would fetch if sold in the open market at the date of the author's death. In the case of published works a valuation by a publisher or literary agent would usually be accepted. In

59 I.C.T.A., 1970, ss. 487 (1) and (2), 489 (13).
60 *Ibid.* s. 489 (8).
61 *Ibid.* ss. 143 (2), 144 (1).
62 *Ibid.* ss. 143 (3) (*b*), 144 (1) (*b*).
63 57 & 58 Vict. c. 30.

the case of unpublished material it is apprehended that little value could be placed upon the property unless active steps for its exploitation were already in existence at the date of death.

1056 **Gifts or settlements of copyrights.** It is not uncommon for authors to make gifts or settlements of their copyrights. In order that estate duty should not be payable in respect of such property on the death of the author it is necessary that he should survive seven years after the gift or settlement and that no benefit should be reserved to him. Until the Finance Act, 1957,[64] duty on gifts was payable on the value of the property given as at the death of the donor, and consequently if the copyright had been exploited in the meantime and was of little value at the date of death the amount of duty would be equally reduced. The Finance Act, 1957, however, contains complicated provisions designed to secure that duty should not be escaped by the reduction in value of the property between the date of gift and the date of death.

1057 **Author dying domiciled out of the U.K.** If an author dies domiciled out of the United Kingdom, duty on his death is payable only in respect of his copyright situate in the United Kingdom. As in respect of any particular work separate copyrights subsist in different parts of the world under the laws of different countries, it is apprehended that copyright in a particular work only subsists in the United Kingdom in so far as it is protected by the Copyright Act, 1956, and that the copyright in the work which is protected in other countries by other laws is situate in those countries and not in the United Kingdom.

3.—STAMP DUTY

1058 Assignments of copyright, as of other property, are liable to stamp duty as a conveyance or transfer assessed *ad valorem* upon the value of the consideration. If the consideration is a royalty of uncertain amount a duty of 50p is imposed, but, if there is a minimum royalty, the *ad valorem* duty is payable upon the amount of such minimum. It is apprehended that a grant of an exclusive licence is also treated for purposes of stamp duty as a transfer of property incurring an *ad valorem* stamp on the same basis. On the other hand, a non-exclusive licence is treated as a mere agreement. In the case of a gift of copyright the stamp should be adjudicated under section 74 of the Finance Act, 1910.[65] An agreement for the sale of any interest in copyright will be liable to *ad valorem* stamp duty under section 59 of the Stamp Act, 1891.[66]

[The next paragraph is 1061]

64 5 & 6 Eliz. 2, c. 49.
65 10 Edw. 7, c. 8; *R.* v. *C.I.R., ex p. Evill* (1951) 67 T.L.R. 857.
66 54 & 55 Vict. c. 39.

CHAPTER 23

PERFORMING RIGHT TRIBUNAL

1061 **Organisations controlling the exercise of performing rights.** In most countries over the last thirty years a development in the field of copyright protection has been the creation of organisations to control the exercise of copyright and in particular of performing rights. Such organisations either acquire copyrights from their members or act as agents on behalf of their members to enforce copyrights. They issue licences to persons owning places of public entertainment or desirous of giving public entertainments, and they appoint inspectors to see that unauthorised performances of works controlled by them do not take place. In the last resort they enforce the rights of their members by legal action. From the point of view of composers of music and owners of musical copyright the system has great advantages, in that no individual composer or copyright owner can, in practice, secure adequate protection for his work, or deal with the very large number of persons and bodies desirous of exploiting such works. On the other hand, the system has considerable advantages, from the point of view of the public and those giving entertainments, in that licences can be obtained from a single organisation, whereas without such a system, it would be necessary to obtain individual licences from a large number of owners of copyright, and the delay and inconvenience, and the risk of performing music without having obtained a licence from the person entitled to give one, would greatly add to the difficulty and expense of performing music in public on any substantial scale.

1062 But the existence of such organisations has given rise to complaints of the abuse of monopoly rights, since virtually all popular music is now controlled by such societies. Moreover, the creation of additional rights, such as the performing right in gramophone records, and, more recently, the creation of sound broadcasting and television rights, has created the possibility that there could be a number of different organisations and that a licence will be required from each for a particular public performance.

1063 **Necessity for public control.** It has therefore come to be felt, in a number of countries, that some measure of public control over the activities of such organisations is necessary in the public interest. In Canada, for example, the system of requiring the tariffs of fees charged by collecting organisations to be approved by a Copyright

Appeal Board was in force for a number of years. Any society which carries on in Canada the business of acquiring copyrights of dramatico-musical or musical works or of performing rights therein and deals with the issue of licences for the performance in Canada of such works, is required annually to file a statement of its proposed fees for the next year, and the Copyright Appeal Board considers objections to the proposed fees, makes such alterations to the statements as it think fit, and transmits the statements, altered or revised or unchanged, to the Minister certified as the approved statements. The Minister publishes them in the *Canada Gazette* and the statements of fees, so certified as approved, are then binding for the ensuing year. This system appears to have worked with satisfaction in Canada.

1064 **Copyright Committee, 1952.** At the Brussels Copyright Conference, the United Kingdom delegation, in accepting the provisions of Article 11 of the proposed Convention, declared that H.M. Government remained free to enact such legislation as they might consider necessary in the public interest to prevent or deal with any abuse of the monopoly rights conferred upon owners of copyright by the law of the United Kingdom.[1] In view of this declaration it was open to the 1952 Copyright Committee, notwithstanding that they were recommending adherence to the Brussels Convention, to make proposals for the compulsory adjustment of tariffs charged by such copyright organisations. One method suggested was that of compulsory arbitration, but this did not seem wholly satisfactory, in that it was necessary to envisage, not only disputes between a collecting organisation and an organisation of performers, but also cases where individual persons were aggrieved, and, moreover, what was really required was some method of arriving at tariffs which would be binding, not only between the parties to the reference, but in respect of any other persons desiring to exercise similar rights. The Committee therefore proposed that a standing tribunal should be established to decide disputes between collecting organisations and would-be users of controlled works.[2] This proposal has been accepted by the legislature and is embodied in sections 23 to 30 (inclusive) of the Copyright Act, 1956.

1065 **Performing Right Tribunal.** Section 23 enacts that there shall be established a tribunal, to be called the Performing Right Tribunal, for the purposes of exercising the jurisdiction conferred by the provisions of the Act. The Tribunal is to consist of a chairman appointed by the Lord Chancellor, who is to be a barrister, advocate or solicitor of not less than seven years' standing, or a person who has held

[1] See *post*, Appendix C, §§ 1696, 1706.
[2] Cmd. 8662, para. 210.

judicial office, and of not less than two, nor more than four, other members appointed by the Board of Trade.

1066 **Rights with which tribunal is concerned.** The tribunal is to be concerned with three types of rights only.[3] First, the right to perform in public, to broadcast or to diffuse, a literary, dramatic, or musical work or an adaptation thereof. Secondly, the right to cause a sound recording to be heard in public or to be broadcast. Thirdly, the right to cause a television broadcast to be seen or heard in public. The rights, therefore, cover, in effect, the whole of the performing and broadcasting rights conferred by the Act of 1956, other than the right to include an artistic work in a television broadcast, the right to cause a film to be seen in public or heard in public or to be broadcast, and the right to re-broadcast a television broadcast or a sound broadcast.

1067 **Functions of tribunal.** The tribunal has two principal functions. The first is to confirm or vary licence schemes put into operation by organisations under which licences are to be granted to the public in stated classes of cases. The second is to deal with applications by individuals who are aggrieved, either because an organisation operating a licence scheme refuses to grant him a licence in accordance therewith, or because he claims that there is no applicable licence scheme and the organisation refuses to grant him a licence. These two functions appear to be quite distinct, the one being concerned with general tariffs and the other with individual complaints.

1068 **" Licensing bodies."** It must be observed, however, that the tribunal has no jurisdiction except in cases where rights are controlled by organisations described in the Act as " licensing bodies." " Licensing body " is defined in section 24 (3) of the Act of 1956 and, in relation to performing rights in literary, dramatic or musical works or sound recordings, means a society or other organisation which has as its main object, or one of its main objects, the negotiation or granting of licences, either as owner or prospective owner of copyright or as agent for the owners or prospective owners thereof. In relation to rights in television broadcasts, it means the British Broadcasting Corporation or the Independent Television Authority, or any organisation appointed by them or either of them in accordance with the provisions of the Fifth Schedule to the Act of 1956. The definition, however, is limited, in the case of performing rights in literary, dramatic or musical works in that, in the case of such rights, it is not to apply to an organisation by reason that its objects include the negotiation or granting of individual licences, each relating to a

[3] Copyright Act, 1956, s. 24 (1) and (2).

single work or the works of a single author, if they do not include the negotiation or granting of general licences, each extending to the works of several authors. It would appear, therefore, that, for example, a publisher of dramatic works, whose practice is to grant individual licences in respect of particular plays, would not be a licensing body for the purposes of the Act of 1956.

On the other hand, this limitation on the definition does not apply in the case of sound recordings, and it is expressly provided that in relation thereto " licensing body " means any owner or prospective owner of copyright in sound recordings.[4]

1069 **" Licence scheme."** As pointed out, the first function of the tribunal is to deal with licence schemes. " Licence scheme " is defined [5] as a scheme made by one or more licensing bodies, setting out the classes of cases in which they, or the persons on whose behalf they act, are willing to grant licences of any description, and the charges (if any) and terms and conditions, subject to which licences would be granted in those classes of cases. The word " scheme " is to include anything in the nature of a scheme, whether described therein as a scheme, or as a tariff, or by any other name. The jurisdiction of the tribunal arises where a licence scheme is in operation and a dispute arises with respect to the scheme between the licensing body operating the scheme and an organisation claiming to be representative of persons requiring licences in cases of a class to which the scheme applies, or any person claiming that he requires a licence in a case of a class to which the scheme applies.[6]

1070 **Who may refer the scheme?** In such a case, either the organisation, or the person in question, may refer the scheme to the tribunal in so far as it relates to cases of that class. It should be observed, however, that, if the licence scheme contains terms and conditions other than terms and conditions relating to the amount of a charge for a licence which have the effect that a particular case or class of cases is not covered by the licence scheme, that case or class of cases is not within the scheme, and therefore is not subject to revision by the tribunal.[7] Such a case, however, might be the subject of an application by an individual under section 27 (3) of the Act of 1956. Again the tribunal may refuse to entertain the application on the ground that the organisation referring the case is not reasonably representative of the class of persons which it claims to represent.[8]

[4] Copyright Act, 1956, s. 24 (3) (*b*).

[5] s. 24 (4). It includes a scheme made before the commencement of the Act (Sched. VII, para. 25).

[6] s. 25 (1).

[7] ss. 24 (5) and 27 (1).

[8] s. 25 (4).

1071 **Order confirming or varying the scheme.** Where a licence scheme is referred as aforesaid, the tribunal is empowered to make such order, either confirming or varying the scheme, in so far as it relates to cases of the class to which the reference relates, as the tribunal may determine to be reasonable in the circumstances, and so that such order may be either for an indefinite period or for such period as the tribunal may determine.[9]

1072 **Effect of order.** The effect of an order of the tribunal with respect to a licence scheme is that, if, during the continuance of the order, a person has complied with the terms and conditions, which, in accordance with the licence scheme as confirmed or varied by the order, would be applicable to a licence granted in accordance with the scheme, and has paid any charges payable in respect of such licence or, if the amount payable could not be ascertained, has given an undertaking to pay such charges, then, for the purpose of defending proceedings for infringement, he is to be in the same position as if he had been the holder of a licence under the scheme.[10] The exact effect of these provisions would have to be considered in the light of the precise form of any scheme as varied or confirmed by the tribunal. It would seem, however, that once a licence scheme has been confirmed or varied by the tribunal, as covering a particular class of case, it will not be necessary for an actual licence to be issued to a person desiring to pursue activities covered by that class, since it will be sufficient if he complies with the terms and conditions of a licence scheme and pays fees as required thereby. A person complying with a licence scheme as aforesaid is also protected from enforcement of copyright by summary proceedings.[11]

1073 **Effect of order on the scheme.** Once a licence scheme has been referred to the tribunal, and an order made in respect of some class of case covered by the scheme, the scheme will remain in force in respect of that class of case for the period directed by the order, notwithstanding anything contained in the licence scheme to the contrary.[12] In order to preserve the position after reference and before an order is made, it is provided that, once a licence scheme has been referred to the tribunal, it is to remain in operation until the tribunal has made an order in pursuance to the reference, unless the reference has been withdrawn or has been discharged on the ground that the organisation referring the matter has not satisfied the tribunal that it is reasonably representative.[12]

[9] Copyright Act, 1956, s. 25 (5) and (6).
[10] s. 29 (1) and (2).
[11] s. 29 (7).
[12] s. 25 (7).

1074 **Second reference.** However, where the tribunal has made an order with respect to a licence scheme, the scheme may be again referred to the tribunal in relation to cases of the class to which the order applies.[13] On the second reference, application may be made, not only by such an organisation or person as may initiate a first reference, but also by the licensing body operating the scheme.[14] In order, however, to avoid constant references with regard to the same class of case, it is provided that a licence scheme shall not, except with the special leave of the tribunal, be referred again to the tribunal within twelve months of the date on which the order was made, if the order was made for an indefinite period or a period exceeding fifteen months, or, in the case of an order made for a less period, before the beginning of the period of three months ending with the date of expiry of the order.[15] On a further reference, as aforesaid, the tribunal may make a further order as in the case of an initial reference, and the other provisions relating to an initial reference, including provisions for a further reference, will apply.[16]

1075 Where an order of the tribunal, on an initial reference, relates to some classes of case under a licence scheme only, or where the order has been made for a fixed period and expires, the provisions in regard to an initial reference and not those in regard to a re-reference apply.[17]

1076 **Individual application: (i) Where licence scheme.** As has been said, the other function of the tribunal is to deal with individual applications. The first class of case is where a licence scheme applies, but it is alleged that the licensing body operating the scheme had refused or failed to grant to the applicant a licence in accordance with the provisions of the scheme, or to procure the grant to him of such a licence.[18] The licensing body is to be treated as having failed to grant or procure the grant of a licence, if it fails to grant it or to procure the grant of it within a reasonable time after being requested to do so.[19] However, if the licence scheme contains terms or conditions, other than terms or conditions relating to the amount of a charge for a licence which exclude from the licence scheme the class of case in respect of which the applicant has asked for a licence, this form of application, which relates only to the person who claims in a case covered by a licence scheme, is not open.[20] On an application for

13 Copyright Act, 1956, s. 26 (1).
14 s. 26 (1) (*a*).
15 s. 26 (2).
16 s. 26 (4) (5) and (6).
17 s. 26 (7).
18 s. 27 (2). This section does not apply where the refusal or failure occurred before the commencement of the Act (Sched. 7, para. 26).
19 s. 27 (6).
20 ss. 24 (5) and 27 (1).

a licence under a licence scheme, the tribunal, if satisfied that the claim of the applicant is well founded, is to make an order declaring that, in respect of the matters specified in the order, the applicant is entitled to a licence on such terms and conditions, and subject to the payment of such charges (if any), as the tribunal may determine to be applicable in accordance with the licence scheme.[21]

1077 **Effect of order.** Where such an order has been made, and the applicant has complied with the terms and conditions specified in the order and, in a case where the order requires the payment of charges, has paid those charges to the licensing body in accordance with the order, or, if the order so provides, has given to the licensing body an undertaking to pay the charges when ascertained, the applicant is to be in the like position, in any proceedings for infringement of copyright, as if he had, at all material times, been the holder of a licence granted by the owner of the copyright on the terms and conditions specified in the order.[22] It should be observed that, where a licence scheme has been confirmed by the tribunal under section 25 of the Copyright Act, 1956, an application under section 27, for a licence in accordance with the scheme, would appear to be unnecessary, since, as already pointed out, where a scheme has been confirmed, it is not an infringement to do anything covered by the scheme after complying with the terms and conditions thereof and paying fees due thereunder if it would not be an infringement for a person to do so if he were the holder of a licence granted in accordance with the scheme. It is, however, perhaps worth pointing out that there seems to be a distinction between section 29 (1) of the Act of 1956, which deals with the effect of an order on the reference of a scheme, and section 29 (3) of that Act, which deals with an order on an application, namely, that, in the first case, the applicant is to be in the same position as if he had been the holder of a licence, while, in the second case, he is to be in the same position as if he had been the holder of a licence granted by the owner of the copyright. This seems to produce a distinction where, owing to some error, it is found that the licensing body does not, in fact, control the copyright in a work thought to be covered by a licence scheme.

1078 **(ii) Where no licence scheme.** The second form of application, under section 27 of the Act of 1956, is probably the more important one. This is where the applicant requires a licence, in a case not covered by a licence scheme, and claims that a licensing body has refused or failed to grant a licence, or to procure the grant thereof, and that it is unreasonable, in the circumstances, that the licence

[21] Copyright Act, 1956, s. 27 (5).
[22] s. 29 (3).

should not be granted, or that the charges, terms or conditions, subject to which a licensing body proposes that the licence should be granted, are unreasonable.[23] If the tribunal decides that the licensing body has acted unreasonably in either of these respects, the tribunal is to declare the applicant entitled to a licence on such terms and conditions, and subject to the payment of such charges (if any), as the tribunal may determine to be reasonable in the circumstances.[24] If such an order is made, section 29 (3) of the Act will again apply. Unlike schemes which may be referred back to the tribunal where an order has been made (§1074, *ante*), the Act of 1956 did not provide for the review by the tribunal of orders made under section 27. However, a new section, 27A, has been added to the 1956 Act [25] to enable orders made under section 27 to be reviewed by the tribunal.

079 **Special provisions as to: (i) licences relating to television broadcasts.** The Act of 1956 contains certain special provisions about certain types of licences. It is provided that, in the exercise of its jurisdiction in respect of licences relating to television broadcasts, the tribunal is to have regard to any conditions proposed by the promoters of any entertainment, or other event, which is to be comprised in the broadcast, and not to hold a refusal or failure to grant a licence to be unreasonable, if it could not have been granted consistently with those conditions, provided that such conditions do not purport to regulate the charges to be imposed for the grant of licences, or the payments to be made to the promoters in consideration of the grant of facilities for broadcasting.[26] It is apprehended that the object of this provision is to entitle promoters of entertainments, or other events, to impose conditions respecting the area in which broadcasts may be made, or the type of place of entertainment where they may be shown. Such promoters may well only be willing to permit an event to be televised subject to conditions of this sort and, unless the tribunal were to respect such conditions, the result might well be to lead to total prohibition of television of events of this class. Such prohibition could, of course, in practice, be secured in many cases by refusing to give facilities for the presence of television cameras.

080 **(ii) Licences relating to sound recordings or television broadcasts required for purposes of certain organisations.** Again it is provided that, in the case of references or applications relating to licences in respect of sound recordings or television broadcasts required for the purposes of certain organisations, the tribunal may give special reduction of charges, or exemption of charges, for such organisation.[27] The

23 Copyright Act, 1956, s. 27 (3).
24 s. 27 (5).
25 By the Copyright (Amendment) Act, 1971, see §§ 1457A, and 1459, *post*.
26 Copyright Act, 1956, s. 29 (4).
27 s. 29 (5).

organisations in question are the organisations mentioned in section 12 (7) (*b*) of the Act of 1956, namely, a club, society or other organisation which is not established or conducted for profit and whose main objects are charitable or are otherwise concerned with the advancement of religion, education or social welfare. As has been seen,[28] this definition has also been used in another Act in relation to which there have been a number of decisions. It should be appreciated that, under section 12 (7) of the Act of 1956, a licence will not be required for the performance of a sound recording as part of the activities or for the benefit of such an organisation unless a charge is made for admission to the place where the recording is to be heard, and any of the proceeds of the charge are applied otherwise than for the purposes of the organisation. It seems, therefore, a little surprising that the Act of 1956, having given a total exemption in the case of such organisations in the conditions mentioned, should then give the tribunal the right to exempt the organisations from the payment of a licence fee where they do not comply with the requisite conditions. In the case of television broadcasts, however, there is no express exemption in section 14 of the Act of 1956 in respect of performances for the benefit of such organisations, the exemption in subsection (8) of such section being of a different nature, namely, where performances are made to members of a club or society, and the provision of facilities for seeing or hearing television broadcasts is only incidental to the main purpose of the club or society. It should be observed, however, that this provision with regard to television broadcasts is only a provision in regard to charges, so that it would not affect the power to refuse a licence in compliance with a condition imposed by promoters of the entertainment and not concerned with fees.

1081 **(iii) Licences relating to the diffusion of foreign broadcasts.** There are further special provisions with regard to licences for the diffusion of foreign broadcasts. Section 40 (3) of the Act of 1956 makes it unnecessary to obtain a licence to diffuse a broadcast made by the B.B.C. or the I.T.A. where the broadcast itself has been authorised by the copyright owner. But, in the case of the diffusion of a foreign broadcast, such diffusion would prima facie, by section 2 (5) (*e*) of the Act of 1956, be an infringement of the right conferred upon the owner of the copyright in any music concerned. It is accordingly provided, in section 28 of the Act of 1956, that, in the case of a reference or application relating to licences for the diffusion in the United Kingdom of programmes broadcast from a place outside the United Kingdom, the tribunal may exempt such licences from charges, if satisfied that charges are payable by the organisation broadcasting the programme to a body entitled under the relevant

[28] *Ante*, § 817.

copyright law to authorise such broadcasting. If, however, the tribunal is satisfied that such charges make no allowance for the diffusion in the United Kingdom, or do not adequately reflect the extent of such diffusion, then the tribunal is to secure that the charges are on a scale requisite for making good any deficiency in the charges payable by or on behalf of the organisation broadcasting the work.

1082 **Procedure in proceedings before the tribunal.** The Lord Chancellor has made certain rules regulating the procedure to be followed in respect of proceedings before the Performing Right Tribunal.[29] The Fourth Schedule to the Act of 1956 provided the necessary powers to make rules, and made provision as to the appointment and resignation of members of the tribunal and other procedural matters.

1083 **Commencement.** Proceedings, whether the reference of a licence scheme under section 25, or further reference under section 26 of the Act of 1956, or an application under section 27, or an application for the review of an order under section 27A of that Act, are to be commenced by notice in the prescribed forms to be served [30] on the secretary of the tribunal.[31] The originator, that is, the organisation, licensing body or person who has referred a scheme to the tribunal under section 25 or section 26 of the Act of 1956, or who has applied to the tribunal under section 27 or section 27A of that Act,[32] must, at the same time, serve on the secretary of the tribunal, a statement in writing setting out the case he intends to make together with a list of the documents relevant to the reference or application, which are, or have been, in his possession.[31] The secretary of the tribunal, as soon as may be practicable, must serve copies of the originator's notice, statement of case and list of documents, in the case of a reference under section 25 or an application under section 27, on the licensing body named in the notice, or, in the case of a further reference under section 26, on every party other than the originator to the reference including an intervener whose application is pending,[32] on which the tribunal made the latest previous order with respect to the licence scheme,[31] or in the case of an application under section 27A on every party to the application other than the originator, including an intervener whose application is pending.

Any such notice will then be advertised [33] and any organisation or person may apply to be made a party by serving a notice on the

29 The Reforming Right Tribunal Rules, 1965 (S.I. 1965 No. 1506), as amended by the Performing Right Tribunal (Amendment) Rules 1971 (S.I. 1971 No. 636), *post*, Appendix B, § 1633 *et seq.*, which revoked the Performing Right Tribunal Rules, 1957 (S.I. 1957 No. 924), as amended by the Performing Right Tribunal (Amendment) Rules, 1959 (S.I. 1959 No. 1170), and the Performing Right Tribunal (Amendment) Rules, 1960 (S.I. 1960 No. 2428).

30 *Ibid.* r. 26: r. 25 and Sched. 2 prescribe the fees payable.

31 *Ibid.* r. 3: see r. 4 as to applications for special leave under s. 26 (2) and s. 27A (2). References and applications may be withdrawn: r. 17.

32 *Ibid.* r. 2.

33 *Ibid.* r. 5.

secretary in the prescribed form within the time limited by the advertisement.[34] On being served with such notice the secretary must, as soon as practicable, serve copies of the notice on every other party to the proceedings, including an intervener whose application is pending,[32] and serve on the intervener, that is, the organisation or person who has applied to be made a party,[32] copies of the originator's statement of case and list of documents and any other notice of intervention which has been served upon him.[34]

A licensing body [34a] on whom there has been served a copy of the originator's statement of case must, within forty-two days of such service, serve on the secretary of the tribunal a written answer to the originator's statement, together with a list of the documents relevant to the reference or application which are or have been in its possession; and the secretary of the tribunal must, as soon as practicable, serve copies of such answer and list of documents on every other party,[35] including an intervener whose application is pending.[32] Every intervener must, within twenty-one days of the expiration of the time limited by the advertisement, serve upon the secretary of the tribunal a statement in writing setting out the case he intends to make, together with a list of the documents relevant to the reference or application which are or have been in its possession; and the secretary of the tribunal must, as soon as practicable, serve copies of every intervener's statement of case and list of documents on every other party,[36] including an intervener whose application is pending.[32]

Any party, including an intervener whose application is pending,[32] may, at any time, amend his statement of case or answer by serving on the secretary of the tribunal the amended statement or answer. On being served with an amended statement of case or answer, the secretary of the tribunal must, as soon as practicable, serve copies thereof on every other party, including an intervener whose application is pending.[32] However, no amended statement of case or answer can be served after such date as the chairman of the tribunal shall direct, when giving directions as to the further conduct of the proceedings, without the leave of the tribunal or the chairman.[37]

1084 **Objections to credentials.** The next step is to determine objections to the originator's credentials, that is, the validity of the originator's claim to be representative of the class of persons which it claims to represent.[32] Such objections may be raised by a licensing body or by an organisation or person on whom notice of a reference under section 25 or section 26 of the Act of 1956 has been served, or by an intervener, or by the tribunal, the proceedings being stayed meanwhile.[38] The originator, any objector and any other party, including

[34] *Ibid.* r. 7 and see r. 27.
[34a] Or other party.
[35] *Ibid.* r. 9.
[36] *Ibid.* r. 10.
[37] *Ibid.* r. 11.
[38] *Ibid.* r. 6.

an intervener whose application is pending,[32] may be heard or make written representations, and the objections will be considered at an oral hearing, unless the chairman of the tribunal otherwise directs.[38] If, after considering the objections, the tribunal is not satisfied of the originator's credentials, it is to direct that no further proceedings are to be taken by any party in connection with the reference, except as to any order for costs made by the tribunal.[38] If, on the other hand, the tribunal is satisfied of the originator's credentials, it will direct that the reference shall proceed.[38] Various forms are prescribed for raising and dealing with such objections.[38]

Objections may also be made to an intervener's credentials, that is, the possession by the intervener of a sufficient interest in the matter in dispute.[32] Objections may be made by any party, including an intervener whose application is pending,[32] or by the tribunal.[39] Unless the chairman of the tribunal makes any direction, when giving directions as to the future conduct of the proceedings, an objection to an intervener's credentials is not to operate as a stay of the proceedings, and will be considered by the tribunal at the same time as the reference or application in question.[39] Again, forms are prescribed for raising such objections.[39]

1085 **Directions.** As soon as may be practicable after every party, including an intervener whose application is pending,[32] has delivered his statement of case or answer, or the time limited by the rules for doing so has expired, the chairman of the tribunal is to appoint a date and place for the attendance of the parties for the purposes of his giving directions as to the further conduct of the proceedings.[40] Provision is made for the attendance of the other parties, including such an intervener, at the hearing. At the hearing, the chairman is to give directions as to the date and place of the oral hearing if any, the procedure to be followed in regard to the submission and exchange of written arguments if there is not to be an oral hearing, the date after which no amended statement of case or answer is to be delivered without leave, the preparation and delivery by the originator of an agreed schedule setting out the issues to be determined and the contentions in relation thereto, the admission of facts and documents, the discovery and inspection of documents, the giving of evidence on affidavit and the consideration by the tribunal of any objection made to an intervener's credentials.[40] Further directions may be given at a later date.[40] Failure to comply with a direction may result in the party concerned being debarred from taking any further part in the proceedings without leave of the tribunal.[41]

39 *Ibid.* r. 8.
40 *Ibid.* r. 12. Consolidation of proceedings can be ordered: see rr. 13 and 14.
41 *Ibid.* r. 29.

1086 **The hearing.** The hearing is to be in public,[42] and the tribunal may regulate its procedure.[43] Every party to a reference or application, which includes an intervener whose application is pending,[32] which is considered at an oral hearing before the tribunal, is entitled to attend the hearing and to address the tribunal and to call evidence.[42] Evidence is to be given orally or, if agreed, or the tribunal or the chairman of the tribunal so orders, by affidavit, but the tribunal may, at any stage of the proceedings, require the personal attendance of any deponent for examination and cross-examination.[42] Any party may authorise some other person to act for him in the proceedings, and may be represented at any hearing by counsel or solicitor, or by any other person allowed by the tribunal or the chairman to appear on his behalf or, except in the case of a corporation or unincorporated body, in person.[44] The tribunal is to give its decision in writing, including a statement of the tribunal's reasons and, where on a reference, the tribunal has varied the scheme, a copy of the scheme as so varied is to be annexed to the decision.[45] Unless the operation of the order is suspended, the secretary of the tribunal is to send every party a copy of the tribunal's decision and is to make a copy available for public inspection at the office of the tribunal.[45] Short particulars of the decision may be advertised.[45] The costs of and incidental to any proceedings are in the discretion of the tribunal, which may direct that any party against whom an order for costs is made shall pay to any other party a lump sum by way of costs, or such proportion of the costs as may be just, and, in the last case, may assess the sum to be paid, or may direct that it be assessed by the chairman, or taxed, including taxation by a taxing officer.[46]

1087 **Reference by the tribunal to the court of questions of law.** The Act of 1956 provides that any question of law arising in the course of the proceedings may, at the request of any party, be referred by the tribunal to the court for decision, whether before or after the tribunal has given its decision in the proceedings,[47] and that, if the tribunal refuses any such request, the party by whom the request was made may apply to the court for an order directing the tribunal to refer the question to the court.[48] If the court decides that the question was erroneously determined by the tribunal, the tribunal is to reconsider the matter in conformity with the decision of the court.[49] A request

[42] *Ibid.* r. 15.
[43] *Ibid.* r. 30, and see r. 22.
[44] *Ibid.* r. 16.
[45] *Ibid.* r. 18; decisions of the tribunal are referred to in *Current Law*, published by Sweet & Maxwell, Ltd.
[46] *Ibid.* r. 24; and see Copyright Act, 1956, Sched. IV, para. 5.
[47] Copyright Act, 1956, s. 30 (1), and see R.S.C., Ord. 56, rr. 7, 8, 9, 10 and 11 and Ord. 93, rr. 10 and 14.
[48] s. 30 (2) and see, in respect of proceedings in Northern Ireland, s. 7 of and First Schedule to the Northern Ireland Act, 1962 (10 & 11 Eliz. 2, c. 30).
[49] s. 30 (4).

to refer a question of law to the court is to be made by notice in writing to the secretary of the tribunal at any time before or within fourteen days after the tribunal has given its decision in the proceedings, or may be made at the hearing.[50] Any reference of questions by the tribunal to the court is to be by way of stating a case for the opinion of the court.[51] Where the tribunal refers a question of law to the court after giving its decision, it may, if it thinks fit, suspend the operation of any order made in the proceedings.[52] Where a question of law has been referred to the court, the tribunal is not to make any further order on the reference or application in connection with which the question arose until the court has given its decision thereon.[52]

088 **References to the tribunal.** Since the commencement of the Act of 1956, a number of schemes have been referred to the tribunal and, after hearings, the tribunal has approved them with or without variation. In 1965 the Isle of Man Broadcasting Company Limited applied to the tribunal, under section 27 (3) of the Act of 1956, claiming to require a licence from Phonographic Performance Limited to broadcast recorded music and, in 1967 the British Broadcasting Corporation applied to the tribunal, under the same subsection, claiming to require a licence from the Performing Right Society Limited to broadcast music. In each case the tribunal made an order declaring that the respective applicants were entitled to a licence on the terms and conditions and subject to the charges determined by the tribunal.

[The next paragraph is 1091]

50 The Performing Right Tribunal Rules, 1965 (S.I. 1965 No. 1506), r. 19, as amended by the Performing Right Tribunal (Amendment) Rules, 1971 (S.I. 1971 No. 636).
51 Copyright Act, 1956, s. 30 (5).
52 The Performing Right Tribunal Rules, 1965, r. 20. See as to suspension by the court R.S.C., Ord. 93, r. 14. As to the effect of suspension, see the Performing Right Tribunal Rules, 1965, r. 21.

Part V

INTERNATIONAL COPYRIGHT AND THE PROTECTION OF WORKS ORIGINATING OUTSIDE THE UNITED KINGDOM

CHAPTER 24

INTERNATIONAL COPYRIGHT

1.—SCOPE OF INTERNATIONAL COPYRIGHT

1091 **Scope of international copyright.** International copyright is concerned with treaties or conventions between nations requiring their signatories to respect, in their own countries, the copyright of nationals of other signatories. There is no general principle of international law requiring such protection [1] and, before the making of international agreements regarding the matter, a book written by a foreigner and published abroad could obtain no protection in this country.[2]

In some countries such conventions or treaties are regarded by the courts as part of the law of the land but, in the United Kingdom, this is not the case. The courts, except in very limited circumstances,[3] are not concerned to interpret treaties or conventions, but only Acts of Parliament and Orders in Council made for the purpose of giving effect thereto.

It becomes necessary, therefore, in considering copyright from the international aspect, to deal first with the general body of conventions and treaties regulating the copyright relations between different countries, and, secondly,[3] with the protection actually afforded to foreign works by the law of this country.

1092 **Early treaties.** Prior to 1886, international copyright was regulated by treaties between a number of European nations. In England the Crown was authorised by the International Copyright Act, 1844,[4] and various amending Acts,[5] by Order in Council, to direct that foreign works should be entitled to copyright in the United Kingdom, and pursuant to these Acts a large number of Orders in Council were promulgated to give effect to these treaties. The general purport of these treaties was to give the authors of works first published in one of the federated States the same privileges in the other States as would have been enjoyed if the work had been first published there.

1 Curtis, *Copyright*, p. 22; "*Morocco Bound" Syndicate, Ltd.* v. *Harris* [1895] 1 Ch. 534.

2 *Guichard* v. *Mori* (1831) 9 L.J.Ch. 227. The question of how far under the Acts of Anne and of 1842 an alien could obtain copyright at all in England (apart from the International Copyright Acts) was discussed in *Jefferys (C.)* v. *Boosey (T.)* (1855) 4 H.L.C. 815, and *Routledge* v. *Low* (1868) L.R. 3 H.L. 100.

3 *Post*, § 1161.

4 7 & 8 Vict. c. 12.

5 15 & 16 Vict. c. 12; 25 & 26 Vict. c. 68; 38 & 39 Vict. c. 12.

2.—THE BERNE CONVENTION AND ITS REVISIONS

1093 A complicated state of circumstances arose, for the rights of an author in foreign countries varied according to the particular treaty or Order in Council, and in 1885 an attempt was made by several of the great Powers meeting in Conference to secure uniformity throughout their dominions. Great Britain was a party to this Conference, which resulted in the framing of a Convention, known as the Berne Convention, whereby the contracting States were "constituted into a Union for the protection of the rights of authors over their literary and artistic works."[6] To enable Great Britain to give effect to this Convention by Orders in Council the International Copyright Act, 1886,[7] was passed.

1094 **Additional Act of Paris, 1896.** In the year 1896 another Conference of the Powers was held in Paris to consider certain modifications of the original Convention which experience had shown to be necessary or expedient. This Conference resulted in what was called the "Additional Act of Paris, 1896." This was adopted by Great Britain on March 7, 1898, but Great Britain was then unable to accept an "Interpretative Clause" that was agreed to by the other Powers.

1095 **The Revised Berne Convention of Berlin, 1908.** In the year 1908 a further Conference of the Powers was held in Berlin, the object of which was "to secure, if possible, a general agreement to such a revision of the Berne Convention and the Additional Act of Paris as would enable the contracting States to sign a single new instrument containing stipulations of a more complete and simple character, with a view not only to afford a more effectual protection to the author, but also to remove the more salient difficulties which had been encountered in the working of the existing arrangements."[8] The result of the Conference was the Revised Berne or Berlin Convention, 1908, which replaced the original Convention of 1887, and the Additional Act of Paris, 1896, except that States who were signatories of the original Convention and the Additional Act of Paris could still elect to be bound by the provisions of these Conventions in preference to those of the Revised Convention.[9] An additional Protocol was agreed to on March 20, 1914.

1096 **Rome and Brussels Conventions.** The Berne Convention was revised at Rome in 1928 and again at Brussels in 1948. The latter

[6] Berne Convention, 1887, Art. 1. Great Britain adhered to this Convention on November 28, 1887.

[7] 49 & 50 Vict. c. 33.

[8] Report of British Commissioners, Blue Book, 1909, Miscellaneous (No. 2) Cd. 4467, p. 5.

[9] Revised Convention, Art. 27.

revision involved alterations which could only be given effect in the United Kingdom by new legislation and one of the reasons for the passing of the Copyright Act, 1956, was to enable the United Kingdom to ratify the Brussels Convention.[10]

1097 **Stockholm Convention.** The Berne Convention was again revised at Stockholm in 1967.[11] This introduced the controversial Protocol Regarding Developing Countries [12] designed to meet the wishes of certain developing countries who considered the extent of protection provided by the Berne Convention too great in the light of the particular domestic circumstances of such countries. The Protocol therefore provides that any such country which ratifies or accedes to the Convention may make reservations in respect of certain matters which would have the effect of giving less protection in that country than is afforded in other countries of the Berne Union.

1098 The adoption of the Protocol, despite opposition, has led to a serious situation in the international copyright field. Thus, although Article 21 of the Stockholm Convention makes the Protocol an integral part of the Convention, Article 28 provides that any country ratifying or acceding to the Convention may declare that its ratification or accession is not to apply to the substantive provisions of the Convention and the Protocol. As a result three years after the Stockholm revision none of the major developed countries has ratified or acceded to the substantive provisions thereof and this country, for instance, has acceded only to the administrative provisions and final clauses thereof, Articles 22 to 38. The present position of this country is, therefore, the same as that which obtained before the Stockholm revision except to the extent that Articles 22 to 38 of the Stockholm revision are now in force between this country and those other Union countries which have validly ratified or acceded to such Articles: Article 32.

1099 This situation is particularly unfortunate since it had been hoped that one of the results of the Stockholm revision would have been that the United States of America would eventually join the Berne Union after revising its domestic law. However, such hopes have faded as a result of what transpired at Stockholm.[13] Serious attempts have, therefore, been made following Stockholm to try and resolve

[10] See text, *post*, Appendix C, § 1681.

[11] Cmnd. 4412. See text, *post*, Appendix C, § 1681, and "Analysis of the Protocol Regarding Developing Countries" by Dorothy M. Schrader, *Bulletin of the Copyright Society of the U.S.A.*, February 1970, Vol. 17, No. 3, p. 160.

[12] See *Protocol Regarding the Developing Countries* by R. F. Whale.

[13] See "A New Horizon for International Copyright" by Barbara A. Ringer, *Bulletin of the Copyright Society of the U.S.A.*, December 1969, Vol. 17, No. 2, p. 81.

this situation, including proposals to revise the Universal Copyright Convention and to further revise the Berne Convention. At the moment of writing recommendations have been made for the holding of revision Conferences in mid-1971 for the purpose of revising both the Conventions, for which purpose draft texts have been prepared.[14] Depending on what may result at such revision Conferences, more countries, including this country, may adhere to the substantive provisions of the Stockholm Convention which, at the moment of writing, are not yet in force. Because of some of the alterations in the Stockholm Convention, there will have to be amendments of the Copyright Act, 1956, before this country can adhere to such provisions: Article 36. However, on the basis that this country will adhere to the substantive provisions of the Stockholm Convention in the foreseeable future, this part of this chapter is concerned mainly with an examination of such provisions.[15]

1100 **Principles underlying the Convention.** Two systems are possible for an international copyright convention. The theoretically most satisfactory system would be a complete copyright code to be applied in each country of the Union both for nationals and subjects of other countries of the Union. A less satisfactory system is one which merely requires each member state to give to the nationals of other member states the same protection as it gives to its own members with the result that the measure of protection will vary from state to state. The system in fact adopted in the Berne Convention represented a compromise of the two systems and the revisions of the Convention alluded to above have tended to extend the principle of the common code. In fact the Stockholm Convention embodies a reasonably complete code but, as will be seen, specifically reserves to members the right to deal with certain matters by their own legislation.

1101 **Eligibility for protection.** Articles 4, 5 and 6 of the Berlin, Rome and Brussels Conventions contained the fundamental dual principle of mutual protection and code protection. Articles 4, 5 and 6 (1) of the Brussels Convention have been redrafted and rearranged to form Articles 3, 4 and 5 of the Stockholm Convention.

Article 3 contains the general criteria for eligibility for protection and provides as follows:

"(1) The protection of this Convention shall apply to:

(*a*) Authors who are nationals of one of the countries of the Union, for their works, whether published or not;

[14] See *Copyright*, October 1970, pp. 209 and 223.

[15] For an examination of the equivalent provisions of the Brussels Convention, see Chap. 24 of the 10th ed. of this work.

(*b*) Authors who are not nationals of one of the countries of the Union, for their works first published in one of those countries, or simultaneously in a country outside the Union and in a country of the Union.

(2) Authors who are not nationals of one of the countries of the Union but who have their habitual residence in one of them shall, for the purposes of this Convention, be assimilated to nationals of that country."

This Article is broader in scope than the Brussels Convention since works of nationals of Union countries are to be protected, even if first publication takes place in a non-Union country. The previous position was that first publication in a non-Union country would have meant loss of protection: Article 4 of Brussels. Further, protection is to be afforded to nationals of non-Union countries habitually resident in a Union country.[16] It is to be noted that the Stockholm Convention provides, in a similar way to the Brussels Convention, that it is open to any country of the Union to restrict protection of works whose authors are nationals of a non-Union country which does not give reciprocal rights and are not habitually resident in a country of the Union: Article 6.

The Stockholm Convention (Article 4) contains new and special criteria of eligibility for protection in respect of cinematographic works and works of architecture, which latter will necessitate amendment of the Copyright Act, 1956. This Article provides:

" The protection of this Convention shall apply, even if the conditions of Article 3 are not fulfilled, to:

(*a*) Authors of cinematographic works the maker of which has his headquarters or habitual residence in one of the countries of the Union;

(*b*) Authors of works of architecture erected in a country of the Union or of other artistic works incorporated in a building or other structure located in a country of the Union."

102 **What is " publication "?** As has been seen, under Article 3 of the Stockholm Convention protection, in the case of authors who are not nationals of one of the countries of the Union, depends upon first publication of the work in a Union country, or simultaneously in a non-Union country and in a Union country. Article 3 (3) provides that the expression " published works " is to mean works published with the consent of their authors, whatever may be the means of manufacture of the copies, provided that the availability of such copies has been such as to satisfy the reasonable requirements of the public, having regard to the nature of the work. The performance of a dramatic, dramatico-musical, cinematographic or

16 See Copyright Act, 1956, s. 1 (5).

musical work, the public recitation of a literary work, the communication by wire or the broadcasting of literary or artistic works, the exhibition of a work of art and the construction of a work of architecture is not to constitute publication.

This definition has been changed in certain respects from that in Article 4 (4) of the Brussels Convention. Thus the present definition is to apply generally whereas, under Article 4 (4) the definition was only to apply for the purposes of Articles 4, 5 and 6 of the Brussels Convention. Again, whereas previously it had been understood that there could be no publication unless it was authorised, the new definition expressly limits publication to works published with the consent of the authors.[17] Finally, the language used is now more suitable to cover various kinds of works, in that publication depends, to some extent, on the nature of the work. The concept of publication in the Stockholm Convention is, therefore, similar to that adopted by the Copyright Act, 1956,[18] and all that is required to constitute publication in a particular country is that copies should be made available for sale in that country, with the consent of the copyright owner, sufficient to satisfy the reasonable requirements of the public there, having regard to the nature of the work.

1103 It will have been noted that the performance of a dramatic or musical work, the exhibition of a work of art and the construction of a work of architecture do not constitute publication. How then can such works be published? In the case of a dramatic work and a musical work, by printing and publishing the text or score. In the case of a work of art, such as a picture, presumably by publishing sketches, photographs and so on of the work. The Copyright Act, 1956, however, provides [19] not only that the construction of a work of architecture is not to constitute publication thereof, but also that the issue of photographs or engravings of a work of architecture or of a sculpture is not to constitute publication of the work. That Act also provides [17] that the issue of records of a literary, dramatic or musical work is not to constitute publication of the work. It is possible that, in this respect, the Act differs from the provisions of the Stockholm Convention which, as stated above, includes, in publication, the availability of copies " whatever may be the means of manufacture of the copies," which might be thought to comprehend copies in the form of recordings.

1104 **Simultaneous publication.** The alternative to first publication in a Union country, to entitle authors who are nationals of non-Union

[17] See Copyright Act, 1956, s. 49 (3).
[18] s. 49 (2) and see ss. 12 (9) and 13 (10).
[19] s. 49 (2) (*a*).

countries to the protection of the Stockholm Convention, is simultaneous publication in a non-Union country and in a Union country: Article 3. Prior to the Brussels Convention the only provision dealing with "simultaneous publication" was Article 4 in connection with country of origin. As there was no definition of this term, "simultaneous" prima facie appeared to involve publication on the same day. However, Article 4 (3) of the Brussels Convention added a definition which is substantially repeated in Article 3 (4) of the Stockholm Convention. That is that a work is to be considered as having been published simultaneously in several countries if it has been published in two or more countries within thirty days of its first publication.[20]

1105 **Extent of protection.** The extent of protection is dealt with in Article 5 of the Stockholm Convention which provides as follows:

"(1) Authors shall enjoy, in respect of works for which they are protected under this Convention, in countries of the Union other than the country of origin, the rights which their respective laws do now or may hereafter grant to their nationals, as well as the rights specially granted by this Convention.

. . . . .

(3) Protection in the country of origin is governed by domestic law. However, when the author is not a national of the country of origin of the work for which he is protected under this convention, he shall enjoy in that country the same rights as national authors."

A distinction is made between the extent of protection in the country of origin and in other countries of the Union, since protection in the country of origin is governed by the domestic law but, in countries other than the country of origin, the author is given, not only the rights which are given under their domestic laws, but also the rights granted by the Convention. In theory, therefore, an author can be worse off in the country of origin than in other countries of the Union.

1106 **Country of origin.** It will be noted that, under Article 5, authors are protected in countries other than the country of origin. Also that a distinction is made as to the type of protection afforded in the country of origin and in other countries. Country of origin is defined in Article 5 (4) as follows:

"The country of origin shall be considered to be:

(*a*) in the case of works first published in a country of the the Union, that country; in the case of works published simultaneously in several countries of the Union which grant different

[20] See Copyright Act, 1956, s. 49 (2) (*d*).

terms of protection, the country whose legislation grants the shortest term of protection;

(*b*) in the case of works published simultaneously in a country outside the Union and in a country of the Union, the latter country;

(*c*) in the case of unpublished works or of works first published in a country outside the Union, without simultaneous publication in a country of the Union, the country of the Union of which the author is a national, provided that:

(i) when these are cinematographic works the maker of which has his headquarters or his habitual residence in a country of the Union, the country of origin shall be that country, and

(ii) when these are works of architecture erected in a country of the Union or other artistic works incorporated in a building or other structure located in a country of the Union, the country of origin shall be that country."

1107 **Rights of nationals of a Union country.** The result of the above Articles is that nationals of a Union country are to be accorded protection in every Union country for (a) unpublished works, (b) works published in the Union country in which protection is sought, (c) works published in another Union country, and (d) works published in a non-Union country. This last is a change from the Brussels Convention under which, subject to simultaneous publication, protection was lost if a work was first published in a non-Union country: Article 4 (1) of Brussels. Thus, a British subject can claim in, say, France, national treatment of his unpublished works and for his published works wherever published.

It has been mentioned above that nationals of non-Union countries, but habitually resident in one of them, are to be assimilated to nationals of that country: Article 3 (2) of Stockholm. Also that cinematographic works and works of architecture may be protected in certain circumstances irrespective of the nationality of their authors.

1108 **Rights of nationals of a non-Union country.** Nationals of a non-Union country, other than those habitually resident in a Union country, are to be accorded protection for their works first published in a Union country, or simultaneously published in a non-Union country and in a Union country. No protection is, therefore, given to unpublished works of nationals of non-Union countries unless they are habitually resident in a Union country.[21] This means that an American author habitually resident in, say, France is protected in France under the Convention for his unpublished works, which would not be the case if he was habitually resident in

[21] See ss. 1 (5), 2 (1) and 3 (2) of the Copyright Act, 1956. As to the meaning of "publication," see § 1102, *supra*.

America. However, it has been mentioned above that cinematographic works and works of architecture may be protected, in certain circumstances, irrespective of the nationality of their authors.

1109 **No formalities.** It was provided by Article 2 of the original Berne Convention that enjoyment of the rights conferred by the Convention should be " subject to the accomplishment of the conditions and formalities prescribed by the law of the country of origin of the work," and in order to make it clear that the formalities of the country in which protection was sought need not be complied with the Interpretative Declaration of Paris provided that the copyright should depend upon these conditions and formalities " solely." It followed from these provisions that it was always necessary, where a foreigner sought protection in a country other than that in which he first published his work, to inquire as to what formalities were prescribed by the country of origin of the work, and, moreover, the question was raised whether if a work was totally unprotected in its country of origin it could claim any protection in other Unionist countries. Obviously, such a question might involve inquiries into difficult points of foreign law upon which the local tribunal might find it hard to pronounce a correct decision.[22] The Berlin Convention, however, marked a considerable advance in principle by providing, in Article 4,[23] that " the enjoyment and exercise of " copyright in the various countries " shall not be subject to the performance of any formality," and that " such enjoyment and such exercise are independent of the existence of protection in the country of origin of the work "—that is to say, there are not to be any formalities precedent to obtaining copyright, for instance, reservation of copyright, nor any formalities precedent to the bringing of an action for infringement, such as the registration which was necessary, under the repealed English legislation, prior to the commencement of proceedings to enforce copyright in a literary work. " Consequently "—as the paragraph proceeded—" apart from the express stipulations of the present Convention, the extent of protection, as well as the means of redress secured to the author to safeguard his rights, shall be governed exclusively by the laws of the country where protection is claimed."

22 For instance, the point was raised in the German courts as to whether Oscar Wilde's work, *Salome*, would have been debarred from copyright in England upon the ground that the work was blasphemous. In England it was provided by s. 2 (3) of the International Copyright Act, 1886 (now repealed), that " the International Copyright Acts and an Order made thereunder shall not confer on any person *any greater right* or longer term of copyright in any work than that enjoyed in the foreign country in which such work was first published." As to the difficulties that arose upon the words " any greater right," see *Hanfstaengl* v. *Empire Palace* [1894] 3 Ch. 109; and as to compliance with the conditions of the country of origin, *Sarpy* v. *Holland* [1908] 2 Ch. 198.

23 Equivalent provisions are contained in the Rome, Brussels and Stockholm Conventions.

However, it is to be noted that this paragraph, now Article 5 (2) of Stockholm, only applies to the rights conferred in Article 5 (1) of Stockholm, that is to say, to the rights enjoyed in countries other than the country of origin of the work. The equivalent Article 4 (2) of the Brussels Convention only applied to the rights in Article 4 (1) of that Convention which was concerned with the rights of nationals of a Union country. Article 5 (1) of the Stockholm Convention, however, applies both to the rights of nationals of non-Union countries as well as to the rights of nationals of Union countries.

1110 **The term of protection.** By Article 2, paragraph 2, of the original Convention it was provided that copyright " must not exceed, in the other countries, the duration of the protection granted in the said country of origin." At the meeting of the representatives of the Powers at Berlin in 1908, an effort was made to induce the Powers to agree to a uniform term of protection as a condition of membership of the Union. This effort did not, however, entirely succeed, and Article 7 (revised in the Brussels Convention) of the Berlin Convention was agreed to as a compromise.

1111 Article 7 was again revised in the Stockholm Convention and contains some new provisions. The basic term of protection is still to be the life of the author and fifty years after his death: Article 7 (1). However, unlike the Brussels Convention, minimum terms of protection have now been laid down for cinematographic works, photographic works and works of applied art. Thus, in the case of cinematographic works the countries of the Union may provide that the term of protection is to expire fifty years after the work has been made available to the public with the consent of the author,[24] or, failing such an event within fifty years from the making of such a work, fifty years after the making: Article 7 (2). This will require amendment of the Copyright Act, 1956.[25] In the case of photographic works and works of applied art in so far as they are protected as artistic works, it is to be a matter for legislation in the countries of the Union to determine the term of protection thereof. However, this term is to last at least until the end of a period of twenty-five years from the making of such a work: Article 7 (4). In the case of anonymous or pseudonymous works where the identity of the author remains undisclosed, the period is fifty years after the work has been lawfully made available to the public: Article 7 (3). Article 7 (4) of the Brussels Convention referred to fifty years from the date of publication.[24] However, the Stockholm Convention now provides that countries of the Union are not required to protect

[24] See § 1102, *supra*, and Copyright Act, 1956, Sched. 2.
[25] See s. 13 (3) of the Copyright Act, 1956.

anonymous or pseudonymous works in respect of which it is reasonable to presume that their author has been dead for fifty years.

Article 7 (5) of the Stockholm Convention provides that the term of protection subsequent to the death of the author and the terms provided by paragraphs (2) (cinematographic works), (3) (anonymous and pseudonymous works), and (4) (photographic works and works of applied art) are to run from the date of death or of the event referred to in those paragraphs, but such terms are to be deemed to begin on January 1st of the year following the death or such event.

1112 The Brussels Convention omitted the provisions of Article 7 (2) of the Rome Convention which entitled countries of the Union to provide a shorter period of protection than those laid down in Article 7, and this necessitated the abolition in the Copyright Act, 1956, of the proviso to section 3 of the Copyright Act, 1911, allowing works to be published under a compulsory licence at the expiration of twenty-five years from the death of the author. On the other hand, a new provision of the Stockholm Convention permits those countries of the Union bound by the Rome Act of the Convention which grant in their domestic legislation shorter terms of protection than those in Article 7, to maintain such terms when ratifying or acceding to the Stockholm Act: Article 7 (7).

1113 The Stockholm Convention further provides that the countries of the Union may grant a term of protection in excess of those provided by Article 7: Article 7 (6). Again, the Stockholm Convention provides that in any case the term is to be governed by the legislation of the country where protection is claimed but, unless the legislation of that country otherwise provides, the term is not to exceed the term fixed in the country of origin of the work: Article 7 (8).

1114 It will be noticed that the Stockholm Convention does not, in respect of the basic term of protection, draw any distinction between published and unpublished works as does the Copyright Act, 1956.

1115 The Rome Convention added, for the first time, provisions with regard to the minimum term of copyright in works of joint authorship, namely one expiring with the death of the author who dies last. However, the Brussels Convention dropped this provision and, instead, provided that, in the case of a work of joint authorship, the term of protection was to be calculated from the date of the death of the last surviving author: Article 7 *bis*. As a result, the maximum term of fifty years from the death of the last surviving author became obligatory and this again resulted in an alteration in English law under the provisions of the Copyright Act, 1956. The Stockholm Convention contains an equivalent provision: Article 7 *bis*.

1116 **Protected works.** We now turn to consider what are the works which must be protected. Article 1 states that the countries to which the Convention applies are constituted into a Union for the protection of the rights of authors in their "literary and artistic works." Article 2 (1) then provides that the expression "literary and artistic works" shall include every production in the literary, scientific, and artistic domain, whatever may be the mode or form of its expression, such as books, pamphlets, and other writings; lectures, addresses, sermons and other works of the same nature; dramatic or dramatico-musical works, choreographic works and entertainments in dumb show, musical compositions with or without words; cinematographic works to which are assimilated works expressed by a process analogous to cinematography; works of drawing, painting, architecture, sculpture, engraving and lithography; photographic works to which are assimilated works expressed by a process analogous to photography; works of applied art, illustrations; maps, plans, sketches, and three-dimensional works relative to geography, topography, architecture or science. This definition presents something of a trap to the English lawyer accustomed to the general words "literary, dramatic, musical and artistic works" in the English Copyright Act who may therefore think that the words "literary and artistic works" appearing in the Convention do not include dramatic or musical works. Prior to the Revised Convention, there was no obligation to protect choreographic works or works of architecture, but, in countries where such works received protection, the other Union countries were entitled to the benefit of such protection. Photographic and cinematographic works were included in the definition of "literary and artistic works" for the first time by the Brussels Convention. Photographic works were previously protected under Article 3 which was not repeated in the Brussels Convention. Prior to the Brussels Convention cinematographic productions were protected under Article 14, but only as literary or artistic works if the author had given the work an original character; in the absence of such an original character they were protected as photographic works. This qualification on their protection was adopted in the Copyright Act, 1911, and the change brought about by the Brussels Convention has been followed in the Copyright Act, 1956, by the introduction of a special section dealing with the copyright in cinematograph films.[26] This definition has slight changes from that in the Brussels Convention, in particular the deletion of the words "the acting form of which is fixed in writing or otherwise" after

[26] Copyright Act, 1956, s. 13.

the reference to " entertainments in dumb show." This is because Article 2 (2) of Stockholm provides that it shall be a matter for legislation in the countries of the Union to prescribe that works in general, or any specified categories of works, shall not be protected unless they have been fixed in some material form.[27]

The Stockholm Convention expressly provides, however, that the protection of the Convention is not to apply to news of the day, nor to miscellaneous facts having the character of mere items of press information: Article 2 (8). Article 9 (3) of the Brussels Convention was slightly differently worded in that it provided that the protection of the Convention was not to apply to news of the day nor to miscellaneous information having the character of mere items of news. Thus, no copyright protection is afforded by the Convention to news or facts constituting press information. There are no equivalent provisions of English law, and material published in the press is equally protected as other literary material, subject only to the qualification that information is not protected as such by copyright law, but only the form in which the information is expressed.

1117 **Translations, adaptations and arrangements, collections, works of applied art.** Article 2 (3) of the Convention then goes on to provide that " Translations, adaptations, arrangements of music and other alterations of a literary or artistic work shall be protected as original works without prejudice to the copyright in the original work." The countries of the Union are therefore bound to make provision for the protection of the above-mentioned works and also for collections such as encyclopedias and anthologies: Article 2 (5). On the other hand, it is a matter for legislation in the countries of the Union to determine the protection to be granted to official texts of a legislative, administrative and legal nature, and to official translations of such texts: Article 2 (4).

The provisions of Article 2 as to adaptations must be read in conjunction with Article 12, which declares that authors of literary or artistic works are to enjoy the exclusive right of authorising adaptations, arrangements and other alterations of their works. It is a matter of domestic legislation as to how far works of applied art and industrial designs and models are protected, subject to Article 7 (4): Article 2 (7). Article 7 (4) [28] provides for a minimum term of protection of twenty-five years from the making of a work of applied art.

1118 **Speeches.** Lectures and speeches first received protection, as such, under the Rome Convention; previously, unless constituting

[27] See *ibid.* s. 48 (1), " dramatic work " and s. 49 (4).
[28] See § 1111, *supra.*

literary works, they would not have been within the provisions of the existing Conventions. As a consequence it is provided (Article 2 *bis*) that the domestic legislation of any country may limit protection in respect of political or legal speeches and may determine the conditions under which lectures and addresses delivered in public may be reproduced by the press, broadcast, communicated to the public by wire and made the subject of public communication as envisaged in Article 11 *bis* (1);[29] when such use is justified by the informatory purpose. Article 2 *bis* of the Brussels Convention was limited to reproduction by the press. On the other hand, such Article was not restricted to public lectures and addresses nor did it contain a reference to the use being justified by the informatory purpose.

1119 **Translation rights.** It will be noticed that translations are to be protected, and this, apparently, whether the same are authorised or not, subject to the rights of the author of the original work: Article 2 (3). Article 8 deals with the rights of the author of the original work, stipulating that " Authors of literary and artistic works protected by this Convention shall enjoy the exclusive right of making and of authorising the translation of their works throughout the term of protection of their rights in the original works."

The question of translations is of prime importance from the international point of view, for it is only by means of translations that an author of a literary or scientific work can practically make his work known in a country speaking another language than his own. Complete rights in respect of authorising translations were only gained for the first time under the Berlin Convention. The original Convention only gave the exclusive right of translation for a period of ten years from publication of the original work, and this only to authors who were subjects of a Union country. The additional Act of Paris gave to such authors the exclusive right of translation during the whole period of copyright in the original article, subject, however, to the condition that an authorised translation, in the language for which protection was claimed, should be published in a Union country within ten years from the first publication of the original work. Under the Berlin, Rome, Brussels and Stockholm Conventions authors—whether citizens of a Union country or not—who first published in a Union country enjoy the exclusive right of authorising a translation during the entire period of copyright in the original work, free from any such conditions as to publication of an authorised translation. Under the Stockholm Convention authors of a Union country would enjoy this right even if they had published in a non-Union country. However, a number of countries have declined to

[29] See § 1126, *post*.

adopt these provisions.[30] Citizens of non-Union countries, however, have no right to protection against translations of their unpublished works.

1120 **Reproduction rights.** Prior to Stockholm the Convention did not contain a provision expressly recognising a right of reproduction, notwithstanding that such a right was commonplace in the legislation of many countries of the Union. To correct this anomaly the Stockholm Convention now provides that authors of literary and artistic works protected by the Convention are to have the exclusive right of authorising the reproduction of these works in any manner or form: Article 9 (1). Further, that any sound or visual recording is to be considered as a reproduction for the purposes of the Convention: Article 9 (3). However, the Stockholm Convention goes on to provide that the countries of the Union may permit the reproduction of such works in special cases, provided that such reproduction does not conflict with a normal exploitation of the work and does not unreasonably prejudice the legitimate interests of the author.[31] Because of the introduction of Article 9 it has not been necessary to repeat Article 13 (1) of Brussels giving authors of musical works the right to authorise the recording of such works.

1121 **Exceptions. (a) Quotations.** The Stockholm Convention contains, in Articles 10 and 10 *bis*, provisions relating to exceptions from the rights granted by the Convention. Thus, Article 10 (1) provides that it is to be permissible to make quotations from published works, provided that their making is compatible with fair practice and their extent does not exceed that justified by the purpose, including quotations from newspaper articles and periodicals in the form of press summaries. This is wider than Article 10 (1) of the Brussels Convention, which was new and only permitted quotations from newspaper articles and periodicals, and " short " quotations at that. However, when a work is quoted, the source and name of the author, if given, must be mentioned: Article 10 (3).[32] Again, Article 10 (2), which revises Article 10 (2) of the Brussels Convention, provides that it is to be a matter for legislation in the countries of the Union and for special agreements existing or to be concluded between them, to permit the utilisation, to the extent justified by the purpose, of literary or artistic works by way of illustration in publications, broadcasts or sound or visual recordings for teaching, provided such utilisation is compatible with fair practice. Again this is subject to mention being made of the source and name of the author, if given: Article 10 (3).[33]

30 See *post*, § 1142.
31 See Copyright Act, 1956, ss. 6, 7, 8, 9, 40, 41 and 42.
32 See Copyright Act, 1956, s. 6.
33 See Copyright Act, 1956, ss. 6 (6) and 41.

1122 **(b) Reporting current events.** Article 10 *bis* (1) provides that it is to be a matter for the legislation in the countries of the Union to permit the reproduction by the press, the broadcasting or the communication to the public by wire of articles published in newspapers or periodicals on current economic, political or religious topics, and of broadcast works of the same character, in cases in which the reproduction, broadcasting or such communication thereof is not expressly reserved, providing the source is indicated. The legal consequences of a breach of this obligation is to be determined by the legislation of the country where protection is claimed. Article 9 (2) of the Brussels Convention contained a similar provision except that it was confined to reproduction by the press. Article 10 *bis* (2) provides further that it is also to be a matter for such legislation to determine the conditions under which, for the purpose of reporting current events by means of photography, cinematography, broadcasting or communication to the public by wire, literary or artistic works seen or heard in the course of the event may, to the extent justified by the informatory purpose, be reproduced and made available to the public. This provision is wider than Article 10 *bis* of the Brussels Convention, which was new and which it replaces, and, in particular, is no longer limited to " short extracts " from literary and artistic works. However, the use is limited to the extent justified by the informatory purpose and the works must have been seen or heard in the course of the event.[34]

1123 **(c) Compulsory licences to record.** Article 13 (1) of the Brussels Convention, which provided that the authors of musical works were to have the exclusive rights of recording such works and the public performance by means of mechanical instruments of the work thus recorded, is not repeated in the Stockholm Convention as the first right is now covered by Article 9 of the Stockholm Convention and the second right by Article 11 of the Stockholm Convention. However, the Stockholm Convention, like the Brussels Convention, contains provisions permitting the countries of the Union to impose reservations and conditions on the rights of authors of musical works to record their works, so as to permit compulsory licences to record such music: Art. 13 (1). However, such Article now makes clear that compulsory licences may also extend to words accompanying the music,[35] whereas, under Article 13 of the Brussels Convention, this was not clear. But such reservations and conditions are not to be prejudicial to the rights of the authors of the music and words to obtain equitable remuneration. The Copyright Act, 1911, gave the right to record on royalty terms in respect of any work which had

[34] See Copyright Act, 1956, s. 6 (3).
[35] See Copyright Act, 1956, s. 8 (5).

previously been recorded, and this right is repeated in the Copyright Act, 1956.[36]

1124 **Performing rights and recitation rights.** The performing rights of authors of dramatic, dramatico-musical and musical works are required to be protected by Article 11 of the Stockholm Convention. Under the original Convention these rights had to be specially reserved by notice on the title page, if the work was published, but the Berlin, Rome and Brussels Conventions provided that authors, to enjoy protection, should not be bound to forbid the public presentation or performance thereof. This provision has been deleted in the Stockholm Convention as being superfluous. The Stockholm Convention now makes clear that the public performance of a work by gramophone records is included so that that part of Article 13 (1) of the Brussels Convention relating thereto has not been repeated in the Stockholm Convention. Apart from public performance the Article also covers any communication to the public of the performance of such works. By the same Article, authors of dramatic or dramatico-musical works are required to be protected during the existence of their rights in the original works, against the unauthorised public performance or communication of translations of their works.

Rights relating to the recitation of literary works are given to the authors thereof by Article 11 *ter* of the Stockhom Convention which has expanded Article 11 *ter* of the Brussels Convention to equate recitation rights to performing rights under Article 11. Thus Article 11 *ter* covers the public recitation of literary works and also any communication to the public of the recitation of such works. Also by the same Article, authors of literary works are required to be protected during the existence of their rights in the original works against the unauthorised public recitation or communication of translations of their works.

1125 **Performing Right Tribunal.** In connection with Article 11 of the Brussels Convention the United Kingdom delegation at Brussels declared that they accepted the provisions of Article 11 on the understanding that H.M. Government remained free to enact such legislation as they might consider necessary, in the public interest, to prevent or deal with any abuse of the monopoly rights conferred upon owners of copyright by the law of the United Kingdom. It is in reliance upon this declaration that the Copyright Act, 1956, has introduced a Performing Right Tribunal with powers to modify and enforce licences granted by licensing bodies for the public performance of works controlled by such bodies.[37] This declaration

[36] s. 8.
[37] Copyright Act, 1956, ss. 23 to 30.

was not repeated at Stockholm but it was agreed that countries were free to enact measures to restrict public abuses of monopoly.

1126 **Broadcasting rights.** The Rome Convention first introduced provisions with regard to radio communication, but these were substantially amplified by the Brussels Convention and repeated in the Stockholm Convention. By Article 11 *bis* of the Stockholm Convention it is provided that authors of literary and artistic works are to have the exclusive right of authorising the communication of their works to the public by wireless, the communication of their works to the public by wire or by rebroadcasting of the broadcast of the work when the communication is made by an organisation other than the original one, and the communication of their works to the public by loudspeaker or other instrument transmitting the broadcast of the work. The conditions for the exercise of these rights is left to the legislation of individual countries, provided that such legislation does not affect the right of the author to obtain equitable remuneration.

The Convention, therefore, confers upon authors three distinct rights in respect of broadcast performances of their works: namely, first the right to restrict the original broadcast, secondly the right to restrict any diffusion of the broadcast by an independent receiving authority, and thirdly, the right to restrict the public performance of the broadcast at the receiving end. The first two rights are clearly conferred by the Copyright Act, 1956,[38] but, after considerable discussion during the passing of the Act, the right to restrict the operation of a diffusion service was considerably qualified by section 40 (3) of that Act.

1127 **Records of broadcasts.** It is further provided, by Article 11 *bis* (3), that a permission to broadcast is not to imply permission to record the broadcast, but there then follows a somewhat ambiguous paragraph as follows:

> " It shall, however, be a matter for legislation in the countries of the Union to determine the regulations for ephemeral recordings made by a broadcasting organisation by means of its own facilities and used for its own broadcasts. The preservation of these recordings in official archives may, on the ground of their exceptional documentary character, be authorised by such legislation."

Section 6 (7) of the Act of 1956 is designed to give effect to the provisions of the Article as to ephemeral recordings, but there is no provision for the preservation of recordings in official archives.

1128 **Cinematograph rights.** As has already been pointed out [39] cinematographic works are now treated as of the class of literary and

[38] ss. 2 (5) (*d*) and (*e*) and 3 (5) (*c*) and (*d*).

[39] *Ante*, § 1116.

artistic works receiving general protection under Article 2. But the rights of authors of literary or artistic works whose material may be included in a cinematograph film are dealt with in Article 14, and it is expressly stated by Article 14 *bis* (1), previously Article 14 (2) of the Brussels Convention that the protection of a cinematographic work as an original work is without prejudice to the rights of the author of the work adapted or reproduced. The author is required to be given the exclusive right of authorising, first the cinematographic adaptation and reproduction of his works, and the distribution of the works thus adapted or reproduced and, secondly, the right of public performance and communication to the public by wire of the works thus adapted or reproduced. The latter right is new in the Stockholm Convention. Article 14 further provides that the adaptation into any other artistic form of a cinematographic production derived from literary or artistic works is without prejudice to the authorisation of the author of the cinematographic production, to remain subject to the authorisation of the authors of the original works. Section 13 of the Act of 1956 provides that where the copyright of a cinematograph film has expired, a person who causes the film to be seen and heard in public does not thereby infringe any copyright subsisting in any literary, dramatic, musical or artistic work. Since the film copyright expires at the end of fifty years from publication, it may well do so before the expiration of copyright in the dramatic or musical work reproduced in the film and, therefore, it is difficult to see how this provision of the Act of 1956 accords with Article 14 of the Convention.

1129 **Sound tracks of films.** Article 14 (3) provides that the provisions of Article 13 (1) are not to apply and Article 13 (1) entitles member countries to impose reservations and conditions upon the right of authors of musical works and associated works to restrict the recording of their works. Article 14 (3), therefore, seems designed to prevent countries restricting in any manner the rights of authors of musical works to have these works included in the sound tracks of cinematograph films. While there was some doubt whether under section 19 (2) of the Copyright Act, 1911, the compulsory licence provisions thereby enacted could be utilised for the purpose of cinematograph films, it is clear that the similar provisions of section 8 of the Copyright Act, 1956, do not apply since they apply only where a manufacturer intends to sell a record by retail.

There does not seem anything in Article 14 (3) to deal with the reverse case, namely, the question whether a composer who authorised the recording of his music on the sound track of a film thereby threw open his work to the compulsory licence provisions for the making of gramophone records thereof. But the Act of 1956 appears to have made it clear that a licence to incorporate in a sound track does not have this effect, since the condition of the compulsory licence is that records have been previously made for the purposes of retail sale.[40]

1130 **Cinematograph films.** It has been mentioned above[41] that cinematographic works are included in the class of works protected under Article 2, and that Article 14 *bis* (1) provides that such protection is without prejudice to the copyright in any work adapted or reproduced. Article 14 *bis* (1) goes on to make clear what was previously understood to be the position, namely that the owner of the copyright in a cinematographic work is to have the same rights as the author of an original work, including the rights under Article 14.[42]

Article 14 *bis* (2) (*a*), which is new, leaves the question of ownership of the copyright in a cinematographic work to the legislation of the country where protection is claimed. However, the rest of Article 14 *bis* (2) and Article 14 *bis* (3), which also are new, contain provisions dealing with the rights of authors of contributions to a cinematographic work in countries where they are included among the owners of the copyright in such a work. Section 13 (4) and (10) of the Copyright Act, 1956, however, provides that the maker of a cinematograph film, that is the person by whom the arrangements necessary for the making of the film are undertaken, is the initial owner of the copyright in the film.

1131 **"Droit moral."** The Rome Convention, for the first time, introduced provisions intended to extend an author's rights beyond those generally comprehended in the term "copyright." These provisions comprehend what is known on the Continent as the author's "droit moral." These provisions were extended by the Brussels Convention, Article 6 *bis*, and provided first that, even after the assignment of his copyright, the author should have the right during his lifetime to claim authorship of the work, and to object to any "distortion, mutilation or other alteration thereof or any other action in relation to the said work which would be prejudicial to his honour or reputation." Secondly, it was provided that the rights granted to the author as aforesaid should, after his death, be maintained at least until the expiry of the copyright. The means of redress was left to the national law and this is repeated in the Stockholm Convention.

The Stockholm Convention, in Article 6 *bis*, whilst preserving the author's right to claim authorship of the work (the paternity right), has made slight changes in the wording of the right to object to mutilation (the integrity right) which now covers the right to object

[40] Copyright Act, 1956, s. 8 (1) (*a*).
[41] *Ante*, §§ 1116 and 1128.
[42] *Ante*, §§ 1128 and 1129.

to any "distortion, mutilation or other modification of, or other derogatory action in relation to, the said work, which would be prejudicial to his honour or reputation." A further amendment introduced by Article 6 *bis* of the Stockholm Convention is to make the grant of such rights compulsory at least until the expiration of the copyright, rather than during the author's lifetime and optional thereafter until the expiration of copyright as under Article 6 *bis* of the Brussels Convention.

1132 It will be observed, first, that both the Brussels Convention and the Stockholm Convention make the grant of such rights compulsory for the period prescribed and, secondly, that both Conventions require the rights to be safeguarded by the legislation of the country where protection is claimed. It would seem to follow from this that, not only are countries of the Union bound to grant such rights, but that they must be granted by statute law. So far as this country is concerned, the only statute law at all concerned with either of these rights is section 43 of the Copyright Act, 1956. But even this section, whilst going some way to grant an integrity right, only does so in respect of artistic works. Further, not only does such section not grant a paternity right to authors but, instead, makes it an offence to ascribe paternity to a non-author. Other than this, and actions for passing off, defamation and slander of goods, it would not seem that English law affords protection for the rights provided for in Article 6 *bis*.[43]

It would appear, therefore, that this country has not complied with the obligations of Article 6 *bis*, and it is interesting to note in this regard that the Report of the Copyright Committee, 1952, states that in the twenty years since the Rome Convention was accepted,

[43] See "'Droit moral.' Has it a place in English law?," *Nordiskt Immateriellt Rattsskydd*, Hafte 2, 1967, p. 194; and see *Millar* v. *Taylor* (1769) 4 Burr. 2303; *Doyle* v. *Wright* [1928–35] Macg.Cop.Cas. 243; *Gilbert* v. *The Star Newspaper Co., Ltd.* (1894) 11 T.L.R. 4; *Southey* v. *Sherwood* (1817) 2 Mer. 435; *Chaplin* v. *Leslie Frewin (Publishers), Ltd.* [1966] Ch. 71; *Harris and Co.* v. *Warren and Phillips* [1917–23] Macg.Cop.Cas. 44; *Coogan* v. *Odhams Press, Ltd.* [1928–35] Macg.Cop.Cas. 1; *Doan* v. *American Book Co.* [1901–04] Macg. Cop.Cas. 1; *Kipling* v. *Putnam's Sons* [1901–04] Macg.Cop.Cas. 37; *Byron (Lord)* v. *Johnston* (1816) 2 Mer. 29; *Ridge* v. *The English Illustrated Magazine, Ltd.* [1911–16] Macg.Cop.Cas. 91; *Tolnay* v. *Criterion Film Productions, Ltd.* [1936] 2 All E.R. 1625; *Johnstone* v. *Bernard Jones Publications, Ltd.* [1938] Ch. 599; *McQuire* v. *Western Morning News Co., Ltd.* [1903] 2 K.B. 100; *Crookes* v. *Petter* (1860) 6 Jur.(N.S.) 1131; *Booth* v. *Edward Lloyd, Ltd.* (1910) 26 T.L.R. 549; *Moseley* v. *Stanley Paul & Co.* [1917–23] Macg.Cop.Cas. 341; *Glyn* v. *Western Feature Film Co.* [1916] 1 Ch. 261; *Archbold* v. *Sweet* (1832) 1 Moo. & R. 162; *Cox* v. *Cox* (1853) 11 Hare 118; *Lee* v. *Gibbings* (1892) 67 L.T. 263; *Humphreys* v. *Thomson & Co., Ltd.* [1905–10] Macg.Cop.Cas. 148; *American Law Book Co.* v. *Chamberlayne* [1905–10] Macg.Cop.Cas. 246; *Springfield* v. *Thame* (1903) 89 L.T. 242; *Carlton Illustrators* v. *Coleman & Co., Ltd.* [1911] 1 K.B. 771; *Preston* v. *Raphael Tuck, etc., Ltd.* [1926] Ch. 667; *Westinghouse Brake, etc., Ltd.* v. *The Varsity Eliminator Co., Ltd.* (1935) 52 R.P.C. 295; *Joseph* v. *National Magazine Co., Ltd.* [1959] Ch. 14; *Frisby* v. *British Broadcasting Corporation* [1967] Ch. 932.

no other Union country had complained that this country had failed to discharge its obligations under Article 6 *bis*.[44] Whether this country will take steps to comply with its obligations in the future is a matter for conjecture, but it is to be noted that Article 36 of the Stockholm Convention, which is new, provides that it is understood that, at the time a country deposits its instrument of ratification or accession, it will be in a position, under its domestic law, to give effect to the provisions of the Convention. However, Article 6 *bis* (2) does provide that those countries whose legislation, at the moment of their ratification of or accession to the Stockholm Convention, does not provide for the protection after the death of the author of all the rights in Article 6 *bis* (1), may provide that some of these rights may, after his death, cease to be maintained.

1133 **" Droit de suite."** A further new right, which was introduced for the first time in the Brussels Convention, deals with what is known on the Continent as the " droit de suite." Article 14 *ter* of the Stockholm Convention, replacing Article 14 *bis* of the Brussels Convention, provides that the author or, after his death, the persons or institutions authorised by national legislation are, with respect to original works of art and original manuscripts to enjoy the inalienable right to an interest in any sale of the work subsequent to the first transfer thereof. This matter, however, is left to the legislation of individual members and cannot be claimed in any country introducing such legislation by an author belonging to a country which does not have such legislation. There appears to be no present intention to introduce such legislation into the United Kingdom.[45]

1134 **Procedure.** The remedy of a person whose work has been pirated is to be governed by the local law. Article 4 (2) of Brussels, now Article 5 (2) of Stockholm, provides that, " apart from the provisions of this Convention, the extent of protection, as well as the means of redress afforded to the author to protect his rights, shall be governed exclusively by the laws of the country where protection is claimed." [46] However, seizure of the pirated copies is a remedy which ought to be secured to authors by the legislation of every Union country, for Article 16 [47] provides as follows:

[44] *Cmd.* 8662, para. 220.

[45] See as to " droit de suite " in France and certain other countries, " The 'droit de suite' " by Robert Plaisant, *Copyright*, August 1969, No. 8, p. 157.

[46] An important and instructive case came before the Paris Court of Appeal which, affirming the decision of the Seine Civil Tribunal, held that the manager of the Paris branch and representative in Paris of an Argentine newspaper was liable in damages for putting on sale in France copies of the newspaper printed in Buenos Aires, and containing pirated portions of a novel written by a French author. This liability, the court stated, would exist " even if the legislation of the country of publication accorded no protection to copyright ": *Foley* v. *Cazaux, Le Droit d'Auteur* (1913), p. 100.

[47] See also Article 13 (3) as to seizure of recordings.

"(1) Infringing copies of a work shall be liable to seizure in any country of the Union where the work enjoys legal protection.

(2) The provisions of the preceding paragraph shall also apply to reproductions coming from a country where the work is not protected, or has ceased to be protected.

(3) The seizure shall take place in accordance with the legislation of each country."

Notwithstanding the provisions of the Convention, each Union country is to be at liberty "to permit, to control, or to prohibit, by legislation or regulation, the circulation, presentation, or exhibition of any work or production in regard to which the competent authority may find it necessary to exercise that right" (Article 17).

1135 **Presumptions.** Article 15 of the Stockholm Convention, as did Article 15 of the Brussels Convention, provides for certain presumptions.[48] Thus, Article 15 (1) provides that, in order that the author of a literary or artistic work protected by the Convention shall, in the absence of proof to the contrary, be regarded as such and consequently entitled to institute infringement proceedings in the countries of the Union, it is to be sufficient for his name to appear on the work in the usual manner.

Article 15 (1) is to be applicable even if the name is a pseudonym, where the pseudonym adopted by the author leaves no doubt as to his identity. Article 15 (3), however, provides that, in the case of anonymous and pseudonymous works, other than those referred to in Article 15 (1), the publisher whose name appears on the work, in the absence of proof to the contrary, is to be deemed to represent the author, and in that capacity he is to be entitled to protect and enforce the author's rights. These provisions are to cease to apply when the author reveals his identity and establishes his claim to authorship of the work.

Article 15 of the Stockholm Convention also contains certain new provisions. Thus, Article 15 (2) provides that the person or body corporate whose name appears on a cinematographic work "in the usual manner" shall, in the absence of proof to the contrary, be presumed to be the maker of such work. This provision will necessitate an amendment of section 20 of the Copyright Act, 1956.

Again, Article 15 (4) provides that, in the case of unpublished works where the identity of the author is unknown, but where there is every ground to presume that he is a national of a country of the Union, it is to be a matter for legislation in that country to designate the competent authority who shall represent the author and shall be entitled to protect and enforce his rights in the countries of the Union. Amendment of the Copyright Act, 1956, will be necessary to permit such authorities to bring proceedings in this country.

48 See Copyright Act, 1956, s. 20.

1136 **Retrospective effect.** An alteration was made as regards retrospective effect in the Berlin Convention and is repeated in the Rome, Brussels and Stockholm Conventions. Under the original Convention it was provided that its provisions should apply to all works which at the time of its coming into force had "not yet fallen into the public domain in their country of origin." The Berlin, Rome, Brussels and Stockholm Conventions (Article 18 (1)) only except works which have, at the moment of their coming into force, fallen into the public domain in their country of origin "through the expiry of the term of protection." Works, therefore, which have in the country of their origin lost their protection owing to failure to comply with formalities, such as registration and so forth, are intended to be protected under the Conventions, as also, apparently, are works which were previously entitled to no protection whatsoever, for instance (in some countries), works of architecture and photographs.[49] On the other hand, Article 18 (2) provides that if, through the expiry of the term of protection which was previously granted, a work has fallen into the public domain of the country where protection is claimed, that work is not to be protected anew. These provisions are to apply also in the case of new accessions to the Union, and to cases in which protection is extended by the application of Article 7 or by the abandonment of reservations: Article 18 (4).

Article 18 (3), however, provides that the application of the principle laid down in Article 18 (1) and (2) is to take effect subject to any provisions contained in special Conventions to that effect existing or to be concluded between countries of the Union, and that in the absence of such provisions, the respective countries are to determine, so far as they are respectively concerned, the conditions of application of such principle.

1137 **Convention not to limit wider protection.** Article 19 of the Stockholm Convention expressly states that the Convention is not to preclude authors from the benefit of any greater protection granted by the local law, and Article 20 preserves the right of member countries to make special agreements with other member countries giving greater protection to their respective nationals than is required under the Convention.

1138 **Administrative provisions and final clauses.** Articles 22 to 26 of the Stockholm Convention contain the administrative provisions and

[49] The Copyright Act, 1911, did not comply with the provisions as to retrospective effect and, in adhering to the Revised Convention, Great Britain made a reservation upon the point. This reservation was not maintained when Great Britain ratified the Rome Convention, presumably on the ground that it was not necessary to do so in view of the fact that the Convention did not make necessary any alteration of English law previously in force. The Act of 1956 appears, in substance, to comply with this Article.

Articles 27 to 38, the final clauses of the Convention, contain certain general provisions. Article 24 of the Stockholm Convention provides that the administrative tasks with respect to the Union are to be performed by the International Bureau, being the International Bureau of Intellectual Property referred to in the Convention establishing the World Intellectual Property Organisation [50]: Article 22 (2) (ii).

This latter Convention was framed at Stockholm in 1967 and was signed by this country on July 14, 1967. The objects of the Organisation established by such Convention are stated to be to promote the protection of intellectual property throughout the world through co-operation among States and, where appropriate, in collaboration with any other international organisation, and to ensure administrative co-operation among the various Unions, including the Berne Union: Article 3. Article 12 (1) of this Convention provides that the Organisation is to enjoy on the territory of each Member State, in conformity with the laws of that State, such legal capacity as may be necessary for the fulfilment of the Organisation's objectives and for the exercise of its functions. Accordingly this country has provided by statutory instrument,[51] which comes into operation on the date on which the Convention enters into force with respect to this country, that the Organisation is to have the legal capacities of a body corporate. The Convention was ratified by this country on February 26, 1969, and entered into force on April 26, 1970.

1139 **Protocol regarding developing countries.** As has been mentioned,[52] the Stockholm revision of the Berne Convention introduced the controversial Protocol Regarding Developing Countries which provides that any developing country which ratifies or accedes to the Convention may make reservations in respect of certain matters, which would have the effect of giving less protection in that country than is afforded in other countries of the Union. Because of this controversy, however, although Article 21 makes the Protocol an integral part of the Convention, this is subject to the provisions of Article 28 which enable any country ratifying or acceding to the Convention to declare that its ratification or accession is not to apply to the substantive provisions of the Convention and the Protocol.

1140 **Mode of operation of Protocol.** Article 1 of the Protocol provides that any country regarded as a developing country in conformity with the established practice of the General Assembly of the United Nations which ratifies or accedes to the Stockholm Convention, and

50 Cmnd. 4408, see text *post*, Appendix C, § 1826, and see *Copyright*, August 1967, No. 8, p. 154.

51 The World Intellectual Property Organisation (Immunities and Privileges) Order 1968 (S.I. 1968 No. 890).

52 § 1097, *ante*.

which, having regard to its economic situation and its social or cultural needs, does not consider itself immediately in a position to make provision for the protection of all the rights provided for by the Convention, may declare that it will, for a period of the first ten years during which it is a party thereto, avail itself of any or all of the stipulated reservations.

However, where a country no longer needs to maintain any or all of such reservations, it can withdraw such reservation or reservations: Article 2. On the other hand, any country which has made such reservations and which, at the end of the prescribed period of ten years, having regard to its economic situation and its social or cultural needs, still does not consider itself in a position to withdraw such reservations, may continue to maintain any or all of the reservations until it ratifies or accedes to the next revision of the Convention: Article 3. Further, Article 4 provides that, if a country ceases to be regarded as a developing country, it shall no longer have the right to maintain any of such reservations six years after the prescribed notification of such cessation.

1141 **Reservations. (a) Term.**[53] The first reservation enables a developing country to substitute for the term of fifty years in Article 7 (1), (2) and (3) a different term, provided it is not less than twenty-five years. Article 7 (1) prescribes the basic term of protection, Article 7 (2) the term for cinematographic works and Article 7 (3) the term for anonymous and pseudonymous works. Also to substitute for the term of twenty-five years in Article 7 (4) in respect of photographic works and works of applied art, a different term, provided it is not less than ten years.

1142 **(b) Translation rights.**[54] The second reservation permits the substitution for Article 8, which gives to authors the exclusive right to make and authorise the translation of their works during the term of protection of their rights in the original works, of provisions cutting down the author's translation rights in certain circumstances. Thus, the exclusive right of translation is to cease if the author has not availed himself of it, within ten years from the date of first publication of the original work, by publishing or causing to be published, in one of the countries of the Union, a translation in the language for which protection is to be claimed.

Further, in certain circumstances, compulsory licences to publish translations may be obtained. Thus, if after the expiration of three years from the date of first publication of the work, or of any longer period determined by national legislation of the developing country concerned, a translation of the work has not been published in that

[53] See § 1110 *et seq.*, *ante*.
[54] See § 1119, *ante*.

country into the national, or official, or regional language or languages of that country by or with the authority of the owner of the translation rights, any " national " of such country may obtain a non-exclusive licence of a limited kind from the " competent authority " to translate the work and publish the translation in any of such languages in which it has not been published. A licence may also be granted if all previous editions of a particular translation in that country are out of print. But such a licence is not to be granted when the author has withdrawn from circulation all copies of the work.

However, the " national " must either have requested and been denied permission to make and publish a translation, or been unable to find the owner of the translation rights and made applications for a licence to the persons prescribed by the Protocol. Further, the owner of the translation rights must be compensated for the prescribed period, the translation must be a correct translation and the original title and name of the author of the work must be printed on all copies of the published translation. Finally, the Protocol provides for termination of the licence if, during the term of ten years from the date of first publication, the author publishes or causes to be published a translation in the country where the licence has been granted.

143 **(c) Reproduction rights.**[55] The third reservation introduces compulsory licences in respect of reproduction rights by allowing the application of Article 9 (1), which gives authors the exclusive right of authorising the reproduction of their works in any manner or form, subject to certain compulsory licence provisions. These provisions are similar to those mentioned above in respect of translation rights, though such licences are limited to reproduction and publication of the work for educational or cultural purposes. Further, the licence will terminate if the author publishes or causes to be published his work in the country where the licence has been granted.

144 **(d) Broadcasting rights.**[56] The fourth reservation permits the substitution for Article 11 *bis* (1) and (2) of certain provisions which have the effect of cutting down an author's broadcasting rights. Thus, under the Protocol, authors are only to have the exclusive right of authorising the broadcasting of their works and the communication to the public of such broadcasts and then only if such communication is made for profit-making purposes.

145 **(e) General.** The fifth reservation is of a general nature and permits the restriction, exclusively for teaching, study and research

55 See § 1120, *ante*.
56 See § 1126, *ante*.

in all fields of education, of the protection of works, subject to the authors being compensated in conformity with standards of payment made to national authors.

1146 **Present members of the Copyright Union.**[57] At the moment of writing the following countries form the Copyright Union[58]: Argentina, Australia, Austria, Belgium, Brazil, Bulgaria, Cameroon, Canada, Ceylon, Chile, Congo (Brazzaville), Congo (Kinshasa), Cyprus, Czechoslovakia, the City of the Vatican, Dahomey, Denmark, Finland, France, including overseas departments and territories, Gabon, German Federal Republic (and Land Berlin), Great Britain, including her colonies and possessions, Greece, Hungary, Iceland, India, the Republic of Ireland, Israel, Italy, Ivory Coast, Japan, Lebanon, Liechtenstein, Luxembourg, Madagascar (Malagasy Republic), Mali, Malta, Mexico, Monaco, Morocco, Netherlands and her colonies, New Zealand, Niger, Norway, Pakistan, Philippines, Poland, Portugal and Portuguese overseas provinces, Rumania, Senegal, Spain, Sweden, Switzerland, Thailand, Tunisia, Turkey, Union of South Africa, Uruguay, Western Samoa and Yugoslavia.

1147 **Entry into force of Stockholm Convention.** Because of the controversy over the introduction into the Stockholm revision of the Berne Convention of the Protocol Regarding Developing Countries,[59] which is made an integral part of the Stockholm Convention (Article 21), such Convention permits any country of the Union ratifying or acceding to the Convention to declare that its ratification or accession is not to apply to the substantive provisions of the Convention (Articles 1 to 21) and the Protocol: Article 21 (1) (*b*) (i). Alternatively such a country may declare that its ratification or accession is not to apply to the administrative provisions of the Convention (Articles 22 to 26): Article 28 (1) (*b*) (ii). Ratification or accession in either way will carry with it the final clauses of the Stockholm Convention (Articles 27 to 38): Article 28 (3). There are, therefore, two distinct ways in which a country of the Union may become a party to the Stockholm Convention but, as a result, at the time of writing, none of the major developed countries has ratified or acceded to the substantive provisions of the Stockholm Convention. However, any country which has excluded one of the two groups of provisions may later extend the effect of its ratification or accession to that group: Article 28 (1) (*d*).

[57] Upper Volta has denounced the Berne Convention, revised at Brussels, with effect from September 20, 1970.

[58] Not all members of the Union have ratified the Brussels Convention, some remaining bound by provisions of earlier Conventions. As to the position of individual countries see *Copyright Laws and Treaties of the World*, prepared by UNESCO.

[59] See § 1097, *ante*.

148 **The substantive provisions and the Protocol.** Articles 1 to 21 and the Protocol come into force with respect to the first five countries which have ratified or acceded without declaring that their ratification or accession shall not apply to such Articles and Protocol, three months after the deposit of the fifth instrument of ratification or accession: Article 28 (2) (*a*).

149 **The Protocol.** However, the Protocol may be applied before the entry into force of the Stockholm Convention (Article 28 (2) (*d*)) and, therefore, Article 28 (2) (*a*) is made subject to the provisions of Article 5 of the Protocol. Article 5 provides that any country of the Union may declare, at any time before becoming bound by Articles 1 to 21 and the Protocol, either (a) in the case of a developing country, that it intends to apply the provisions of the Protocol to works whose country of origin is a country of the Union which admits the application of the reservations under the Protocol, or (b) that it admits the application of the provisions of the Protocol to works of which it is the country of origin by countries which, on becoming bound by Articles 1 to 21 and by the Protocol, or on making a declaration of application of the Protocol by virtue of the provision of (a), have made reservations permitted by the Protocol. If a country has already separately accepted the Protocol in accordance with Article 5 thereof, its declaration under Article 28 (1) (*b*) (i) may only relate to Articles 1 to 20: Article 28 (1) (*c*).

150 **The administrative provisions.** The administrative provisions of the Stockholm Convention, Articles 22 to 26, come into force with respect to the first seven countries which have ratified or acceded without declaring that their ratification or accession does not apply to such Articles, three months after the deposit of the seventh instrument of ratification or accession: Article 28 (2) (*b*).

151 **Relations between countries of the Union.** As a result of these complicated provisions for ratification or accession the position between individual countries of the Union will depend on how many countries ratify or accede, and to what their ratification or accession relates. There are also separate provisions dealing with accession by non-Union countries: Article 29. But, subject to any such ratifications or accessions, the position between countries of the Union remains the same as before the Stockholm revision. Thus Article 32 (1) of the Stockholm Convention provides that that Convention shall, as regards the relations between the countries of the Union "and to the extent that it applies," replace the Berne Convention and the subsequent revisions. However, such Article also provides that the previous Conventions shall continue to be applicable, in their entirety or to the extent that the Stockholm Convention does

not replace them by virtue of the earlier provisions of that Article, in relations with countries of the Union who do not ratify or accede to the Stockholm Convention.

1152 **Declarations and notifications.** The Stockholm Convention provides for various other declarations or notifications. For instance, Article 7 (7) provides that any country of the Union bound by the Rome Convention, which grants shorter terms of protection than those provided for in Article 7 of the Stockholm Convention, may maintain such terms when ratifying or acceding to the Stockholm Convention. Again, Article 33, which provides, in paragraph (1), for the settling of disputes about the interpretation or application of the Stockholm Convention, provides, in paragraph (2), that a country, when ratifying or acceding to the Stockholm Convention, may declare that it does not consider itself bound by paragraph (1). Further, Article 38 (2) provides that countries of the Union not bound by Articles 22 to 26 (the administrative provisions of the Stockholm Convention) may, until five years after the entry into force of the Convention establishing the World Intellectual Property Organisation [60] exercise, if they so desire, the rights provided under such Articles as if they were bound by such Articles, by giving written notification thereof as prescribed by Article 38 (2).

1153 **Present state of ratifications or accessions.** At the moment of writing, the only countries which have adhered to the substantive provisions of the Stockholm Convention and the Protocol are Germany (Democratic Republic), Pakistan, Rumania and Senegal. The substantive provisions are therefore not yet in force.

On the other hand, the administrative provisions of the Stockholm Convention are now in force, the following countries having adhered thereto: Canada, Denmark, Finland, Germany (Democratic Republic), Germany (Federal Republic), Ireland, Israel, Pakistan, Rumania, Senegal, Spain, Sweden, Switzerland and the United Kingdom.

The validity of the instrument of accession deposited by the German Democratic Republic is disputed. Rumania's ratification was accompanied by declarations under Articles 7 (7) and 33 (2). Pakistan and Senegal have made declarations under Article 5 (1) (*a*) of the Protocol. Bulgaria and Sweden have made declarations under Article 5 (1) (*b*) of the Protocol. Pakistan's accession was accompanied by a declaration that Pakistan availed itself of the reservations in Article 1 of the Protocol other than that in Article 1 (*a*). Finally, the following countries have availed themselves of the provisions of Article 38 (2): Belgium, Brazil, Bulgaria, Cameroon, Czechoslovakia,

[60] See § 1138, *ante*.

Dahomey, France, Gabon, Greece, Holy See, Hungary, Italy, Ivory Coast, Japan, Luxembourg, Malta, Morocco, Netherlands, Niger, Norway, Portugal, South Africa, Tunisia, Turkey and Yugoslavia.

3.—THE UNIVERSAL COPYRIGHT CONVENTION

1154 **Object of Convention.** Largely with the object of creating a bridge between the Berne Convention countries on the one hand and the Pan-American Convention countries on the other hand,[61] and particularly in the hope that the United States might be persuaded to enter into copyright relations with the Berne Union countries, a draft International Convention was prepared under the auspices of UNESCO, which resulted in the Universal Copyright Convention, signed at Geneva on September 6, 1952. As has been mentioned,[62] recommendations have been made for the holding of a revision Conference in mid-1971 for the purpose of revising this Convention in an attempt to resolve the unfortunate situation which has arisen over the Protocol regarding developing countries to the Stockholm revision of the Berne Convention.

1155 **Main provisions.** Basically, the effect of the Universal Copyright Convention [63] is that each contracting State undertakes to give to the unpublished works of the nationals of all other contracting States the same protection as it gives to the unpublished works of its own nationals, and further undertakes to give to the published works of nationals of the other contracting States wherever first published, and to published works of the nationals of any country if first published in one of the other contracting States, the same rights as it gives to works first published in its own territory. Furthermore, such published works, if first published outside the territory of the contracting State in question and not being the work of a national author, are to enjoy such protection without formality, such as registration or the deposit of copies, provided only that all copies published bear the symbol © accompanied by the name of the copyright proprietor and the year of first publication, placed in such manner and location as to give reasonable notice of claim of copyright.[64] The Convention is not to apply to works which at the effective date of the Convention in a contracting State where protection is claimed are permanently in the public domain in that State.

1156 **Term of copyright.** The Convention provides for a minimum term of protection, namely, the life of the author and twenty-five years

61 § 1160, *post*.
62 § 1099, *ante*.
63 See text, *post*, Appendix C, § 1730.
64 The positioning of such notice on various types of works is considered in the UNESCO Copyright Bulletin, 1957, Vol. X, No. 2 at p. 247.

after his death. It is, however, provided that any contracting State which, upon the effective date of the Convention in that State, does not compute the term of protection upon the basis of the life of the author, shall be entitled to compute the term of protection from the date of first publication of the work or from its registration prior to publication, provided that the term of protection is not to be less than twenty-five years from the date of first publication or registration. " Publication " is defined in the Convention as meaning the reproduction in tangible form and the general distribution to the public of copies of a work from which it can be read or otherwise visually perceived.

1157 **Minimum protection required.** As to the nature of the protection to be afforded, the Convention provides that each contracting State shall give adequate and effective protection to the rights of authors and copyright proprietors in literary, scientific and artistic works, including writings, music, dramatic and cinematographic works, and paintings, engravings and sculpture. It is further provided that copyright is to include the exclusive right to make, publish and authorise the making and publication of translations of works, but the contracting State may make provision for compulsory licences to translate if, after the expiration of a period of seven years from the date of first publication, a translation has not been published in the language of the contracting State.

1158 While promising protection on the general lines above indicated therefore, this Convention does not describe the details of protection which are to be afforded by the contracting States and substantially leaves the mode and extent of protection to the separate legislation of each State. It only extended further than the Berne Convention in requiring protection to be given to published works, not only if first published in a contracting State, but if first published anywhere, if the author is a national of a contracting State.[65] To meet this requirement of the Convention, and in order to enable the United Kingdom to ratify the Convention, the Copyright Act of 1956 has altered the law of the United Kingdom so as to protect the published works of nationals of contracting States although first published outside the United Kingdom and the Convention area.[66]

1159 **Countries which have ratified the Universal Copyright Convention.** The Universal Copyright Convention has been ratified by the following countries [67]: Andorra, Argentina, Australia, Austria, Belgium, Brazil, Cambodia, Canada, Chile, Costa Rica, Cuba, Czechoslovakia,

[65] But see now Article 3 (1) of the Stockholm Convention, § 1101, *ante*.
[66] Copyright Act, 1956, ss. 2 (2) and 3 (3).
[67] The effective date for Great Britain was September 27, 1957; for the effective dates for other countries see General Table of Laws, § 1271, *post*.

Denmark, Ecuador, Finland, France, German Federal Republic (and Land Berlin), Ghana, Great Britain, Greece, Guatemala, Haiti, Holy See, Hungary, Iceland, India, Irish Republic, Israel, Italy, Japan, Kenya, Laos, Lebanon, Liberia, Liechtenstein, Luxembourg, Malawi, Malta, Mauritius, Mexico, Monaco, Netherlands, New Zealand, Nicaragua, Nigeria, Norway, Pakistan, Panama, Paraguay, Peru, Philippines,[68] Portugal, Spain, Sweden, Switzerland, Tunisia, United States of America, Venezuela, Yugoslavia, Zambia.

4.—PAN-AMERICAN CONVENTIONS

1160 There are certain American Conventions—the Montevideo Convention and the various Pan-American Conventions, to none of which is Great Britain a party. The Montevideo Convention (January 11, 1889) adopts a wholly different principle to that of the Berne Convention, conferring upon an author belonging to one country of the Union in the other countries of the Union the rights which he enjoys in the country where he first publishes, not the rights which authors enjoy in the country where the infringement takes place, so that under this Convention the law of the country of origin follows the work into the other countries of the Union. It appears that the Montevideo Convention applies as between Argentina on the one hand and Austria, Belgium, France, German Federal Republic, Hungary, Italy and Spain on the other; between Bolivia on the one hand and Austria, German Federal Republic and Hungary on the other; and between Paraguay on the one hand and Austria, Belgium, France, German Federal Republic, Hungary, Italy and Spain on the other.

The Pan-American Conventions are those of Mexico City (1902), Rio de Janeiro (1906), Buenos Aires (1910) and Havana (1928).[69] The later of these Conventions are both modifications of the original Convention of 1902, and all adopt the Berne principle of according national protection to works published in any of the countries of the Union. But under the Convention of 1902, in order to obtain copyright in another country, it was an " indispensable " condition that the author or his representatives should address a petition to the official department of each government, claiming the recognition of the right. This was modified by the later Conventions, and, under the Convention of 1910, it simply provided that " the acknowledgment of a copyright obtained in one State, in conformity with its laws, shall produce its effects of conferring full right in all the other States without the necessity of complying with any other formality, provided

[68] The accession of the Philippines appears to have been withdrawn: the effective date for the Philippines was November 19, 1955.

[69] The full text of these Conventions will be found in " Copyright Laws and Treaties of the World," prepared by UNESCO, as will that of a Convention concluded between Hungary and Russia which came into force on January 1, 1968.

always there shall appear in the work a statement that indicates the reservation of the property right." The Convention of 1902 was ratified by Guatemala (1902), Salvador (1902), Costa Rica (1903), Honduras (1904), Nicaragua (1904), Dominica (1907), and the United States (1908). The Convention of 1906 was ratified by Guatemala (1909), Honduras (1908), Salvador (1910), Nicaragua (1909), Costa Rica (1908), Ecuador (1909), Chile (1910), Panama (1911) and Brazil (1911). The Convention of 1910 has been ratified by the United States, Dominica, Guatemala, Honduras, Panama, Nicaragua, Ecuador, Brazil, Costa Rica, Uruguay, Peru Paraguay, Haiti, Colombia, Argentina, Bolivia and Chile. The Convention of 1928 has been ratified by Costa Rica, Ecuador, Guatemala, Nicaragua and Panama. A further Pan-American Convention was concluded at Washington in 1946 under the terms of which rights of copyright set out in some detail are to be conferred as between the signatory countries without formality or restriction. This Convention has been ratified by Argentina, Bolivia, Brazil, Chile, Costa Rica, Cuba, Dominica, Ecuador, Guatemala, Haiti, Honduras, Mexico, Nicaragua and Paraguay.

[The next paragraph is 1161]

CHAPTER 25

PROTECTION OF WORKS OF FOREIGN ORIGIN

1.—GENERAL

1161 **Implementation of treaties and Conventions.** It is clear that the parties to treaties and Conventions can give effect to them, either by making the treaty, which they have ratified, part of the municipal law of the country, or by making separate legislation to carry its provisions into effect. This country, prior to the Act of 1911, had adopted the first alternative since, by Orders in Council made under the International Copyright Acts of 1844 and 1886, the original Berne Convention and the Act of Paris were given full effect in this country and were interpreted by the courts.[1] These Acts, however, were repealed by the Act of 1911 in the dominions to which the Act applied, and the scheme of the Act of 1911 was to give to British works rights as large as those required by the Convention and, by Orders in Council, to extend these rights to foreign works. The Brussels Convention is, therefore, not the subject of interpretation by the courts of this country, except in so far as reference is made in the Orders in Council to certain sections.[2]

1162 **Power to apply the Act of 1956 to other countries.** By section 32 of the Copyright Act, 1956, Her Majesty is authorised, by Order in Council, to make provision for applying any of the provisions of that Act, in the case of a country to which these provisions do not extend, so as to secure that those provisions:

(a) apply in relation to literary, dramatic, musical or artistic works, sound recordings, cinematograph films or editions first published in that country as they apply to such works first published in the United Kingdom;

(b) apply in relation to persons who, at a material time, are citizens or subjects of that country as they apply in relation to British subjects;

(c) apply in relation to persons who, at a material time, are domiciled or resident in that country as they apply in relation to persons domiciled or resident in the United Kingdom;

1 *e.g., in Hanfstaengl* v. *Empire Palace* [1894] 3 Ch. 109.

2 *Cf. Baron R. de Marienwert* v. *Adminstrator of Austrian Property* [1924] 2 Ch. 282; *The Cairnbahn* [1914] P. 25; *Walker* v. *Baird* [1892] A.C. 491; or in case of ambiguity see *Hogg* v. *Toye and Co., Ltd.* [1935] Ch. 497 at 520 and *Warwick Film Productions, Ltd.* v. *Eisinger* [1969] 1 Ch. 508 at 521; see also *Cheney* v. *Conn* [1968] 1 W.L.R. 242 and *Monte Ulia (Owners)* v. *Banco (Owners)* [1971] 2 W.L.R. 335.

(d) apply in relation to bodies incorporated under the laws of that country as they apply in relation to bodies incorporated under the laws of any part of the United Kingdom; and

(e) apply in relation to television broadcasts and sound broadcasts made from places in that country by one or more organisations constituted in or under the laws of that country as they apply in relation to television broadcasts and sound broadcasts made by the British Broadcasting Corporation or the Independent Television Authority.

Any such Order in Council may be made subject to exceptions and modifications, and may apply either generally or in relation to specified classes of works or classes of cases.

1163 **Countries to which the Act of 1956 may be applied.** The power to make such Orders is, however, limited, in that an Order is not to be made applying any of the provisions of the Act of 1956 in the case of a country, other than a country which is a party to a Convention relating to copyright to which the United Kingdom is also a party; "unless Her Majesty is satisfied that, in respect of the class of works or other subject matter to which those provisions relate, provision has been or will be made under the laws of that country whereby adequate protection will be given to owners of copyright under this Act." This limitation is in slightly different language from that contained in the similar provisions in section 29 of the Act of 1911, which stated that before making an order: "His Majesty shall be satisfied that that foreign country has made, or has undertaken to make, such provisions, if any, as it appears to His Majesty expedient to require for the protection of works entitled to copyright under this Act."

1164 **Self-governing dominions.** It is further to be observed that, whilst section 29 of the Act of 1911 enabled Orders in Council to be made in respect of works originating in "a foreign country," section 32 of the Act of 1956 applies to works originating in any country. This is because the Act of 1911 extended, or was capable of being extended, throughout the British Empire, including the self-governing dominions, whereas the Act of 1956 is only capable of being extended to the Isle of Man, the Channel Islands and any colony.[3] Consequently, protection to works originating in a self-governing dominion or member of the Commonwealth has to be provided by Order in Council in the same way as in the case of a foreign country.

1165 **Power to curtail protection.** The Copyright Act, 1956,[4] gives power to deprive citizens of countries, not giving adequate protection

[3] Copyright Act, 1956, s. 31.
[4] Copyright Act, 1956, s. 35.

to British works, of copyright under that Act. This power arises if the laws of a country fail to give adequate protection to British works, or to one or more classes of such works. A "British work," for this purpose, means a work of which the author, at the time when the work was made, was a qualified person.[5] Where the circumstances contemplated arise, an Order in Council may be made providing that copyright under the Act of 1956 shall not subsist in works, or classes of works, first published after a date specified in the Order, if at the time of their first publication the authors were citizens or subjects of the country designated by the Order, and not at that time persons domiciled or resident in the United Kingdom, or in another country to which the Act extends, or were bodies incorporated under the laws of the country designated by the Order. Such an Order may be made in respect of literary, dramatic, musical and artistic works, sound recordings and cinematograph films. The section only applies to published works because the unpublished works of foreign authors could, in any case, only obtain protection by an Order in Council under section 32 of the Act of 1956, and could be penalised merely by revoking or varying such an Order. What this section contemplates is the exclusion from copyright protection of works first published in the United Kingdom which would otherwise obtain automatic protection under the main provisions of the Act.

1166 **International organisations.** Section 33 of the Act of 1956[6] further makes provision for conferring copyright by Order in Council upon original literary, dramatic, musical or artistic works made by or under the direction or control of an international organisation, and whether or not such organisation has the legal capacity of a body corporate. The section also applies where such a work is first published by or under the direction or control of such an organisation.

1167 **Order in Council under Act of 1911.** A general Order in Council was made on June 24, 1912,[7] for the purpose of applying the Act of 1911, in accordance with section 29, to works originating in countries of the Copyright Union, and subsequent Orders were made, as necessity arose, by reason of countries joining the Union or altering their reservations to the Convention. By an Order in Council[8] dated March 16, 1933, all previous Orders were revoked, but without prejudice to existing rights, and the provisions of section 29 of the Act were applied to all countries of the Copyright Union. Under this Order, as under previous Orders, the term of protection was limited

[5] s. 35 (5).

[6] This does not apply to works made or published before the commencement of the Act (Sched. 7, para. 27). See § 1873, *post*.

[7] S.R. & O. 1912 No. 913.

[8] S.R. & O. 1933 No. 253; Copinger, *Copyright*, 8th ed., p. 459.

to that conferred by the law of the country of origin of the work, and limitations were imposed in respect of those countries which had made reservations to the Convention. In respect of existing works it was provided that rights extinguished by virtue of section 5 of the International Copyright Act, 1886, that is by virtue of non-publication in the English language within ten years, should not be revived by the Order, and that the copyright in musical works should include mechanical rights where no contrivances had been made or sold in His Majesty's dominions before the dates mentioned in the Schedule.

1168 **Preservation of Orders in Council made under the Act of 1911.** In order to prevent Orders in Council made under the Act of 1911 lapsing immediately upon the commencement of the Act of 1956 and its repeal of the Act of 1911, it was provided, in paragraph 40 of the Seventh Schedule of the Act of 1956, that such Orders, and all the provisions of the Act of 1911 required for the purposes of any proceedings arising out of the operation of such continuance, are to continue in force until the occurrence of whichever of the following events first occurs, that is to say:

(a) the revocation of the Order under the Act of 1911;
(b) the coming into operation of an Order under the Act of 1956 in the case of the foreign country in question; and
(c) the expiration of the period of two years from the repeal of the Act of 1911.

1169 **Orders in Council under the Act of 1956.** By an Order in Council made under section 32 of the Copyright Act, 1956, and coming into operation on September 27, 1957,[9] the Copyright Act, 1956, was applied to works originating in the countries specified in the First Schedule to that Order, being countries which had adhered to the Berne or Universal Copyright Conventions, in relation to all classes of works covered by that Act other than television broadcasts and sound broadcasts. This Order was amended by further Orders [10] coming into operation on various dates. Another Order made in 1964,[11] which came into operation on May 21, 1964, replaced these Orders and now deals with all classes of works, including sound and television broadcasts. Dealing first with works, other than broadcasts, the Copyright Act, 1956, is applied in relation to such works first published in such countries, and in relation to the citizens or subjects of such countries, and to persons domiciled or resident in such countries, and in relation to bodies incorporated under the laws of

[9] S.I. 1957 No. 1523. See *post*, Appendix D, § 1862. The date is the date at which the Universal Copyright Convention took effect so far as Great Britain is concerned, § 1159, note 67, *ante*.
[10] See § 1862, *post*.
[11] The Copyright (International Conventions) Order, 1964 (S.I. 1964 No. 690) now amended, *post*, Appendix D, § 1874.

such countries.[12] The general effect of the Order, therefore, is that all such works will be treated as if they had been first published in the United Kingdom, or had been made by British subjects. It will be recalled that, under sections 2 (2) and 3 (3) of the Copyright Act, 1956, a published work may enjoy copyright protection, not only by reason of the place of publication, but also because the author was a qualified person when the work was first published, and similar provision is made in regard to sound recordings and cinematograph films.[13] Consequently, under the Order, copyright may be enjoyed in the United Kingdom in respect of published works, not only because they have been first published in a country to which the Order applies, but also, if not so published, because the author or maker falls within the provisions of the Order.

1170 **Differences where work created after Order.** So far as concerns works first created after the commencement of the 1957 Order there are only two respects in which the copyright so created differs from that in a work of United Kingdom origin. The first concerns the term of such copyright and is general, and the second is of a limited character in respect of the copyright in sound recordings.

1171 **Term of copyright.** It was provided, in the 1957 Order, that the term of copyright in a work protected under the provisions of that Order was not to exceed that granted by the country of origin of the work without formality, other than that specified in the Universal Copyright Convention, to a British work of the same class. "British work" meant a work made by a British subject resident in the United Kingdom, or by a company incorporated under the laws of the United Kingdom, and which, if published, was first published in the United Kingdom.

However, this provision was cancelled by an Order [14] coming into operation on August 11, 1958, so that the normal term under the Act of 1956 now applies to all such works. But this amending Order was not to revive copyrights, so that it may still be necessary to consider the provisions of the original Order if, under such provisions, the term would have expired between September 27, 1957, and August 11, 1958. This will involve knowledge of the relevant foreign law, and of the meaning of "country of origin" in the Order.

1172 **Meaning of "country of origin."** Owing to the requirements of the various Conventions and the complications ensuing as a result of the simultaneous publication of works in a number of countries, the

[12] Certain countries adhered to Conventions subsequent to the 1957 Order and accordingly the 1964 Order applies to them as from later dates.

[13] Copyright Act, 1956, ss. 12 (1) and 13 (1).

[14] The Copyright (International Conventions) (Amendment) Order, 1958 (S.I. 1958 No. 1254).

expression "country of origin" receives a complicated definition in the 1957 Order which may be shortly summarised as follows:

In the case of a work which has been published in a country belonging to either of the Conventions it means, if first published in such a country and not simultaneously published elsewhere, that country.

In the case of simultaneous publication, which means, in the case of publications occurring before the commencement of that Order, publications within fourteen days of one another, and, in any other case, within a period of thirty days of one another, there are four classes of case. If a work is simultaneously published in a Berne country and a non-Berne country, the country of origin is the Berne country. If the work is simultaneously published in a Universal Copyright Convention country and a country which is not a member of either Convention, the country of origin is the Universal Copyright Convention country. If a work is simultaneously published in several Berne countries, the country of origin is the country giving the shortest term of protection. If a work is simultaneously published in a number of Universal Copyright Convention countries and not in a Berne country, the country of origin is the country giving the shortest term of protection.

In the case of a work which is unpublished or first published in a country which does not belong to either Convention, the country of origin is the country whose laws give the longest term of protection to such a work of the following, namely, the country of which the author was a subject or citizen, the country in which the author was domiciled, the country in which the author was resident or, where the author or maker was a body corporate, the country in which such body was incorporated.

1173 **Sound recordings.** The provision about sound recordings is that, in relation to any country other than Australia, Brazil, Canada, Ceylon, Cyprus, Czechoslovakia, Denmark, Ecuador, Federal Republic of Germany (and Land Berlin), India, Republic of Ireland, Israel, Italy, Mexico, New Zealand, Nigeria, Norway, Pakistan, Paraguay, Spain, Sweden, Switzerland and Western Samoa, the acts restricted by the copyright in a sound recording are not to include causing the record to be heard in public or broadcasting the recording.[15]

1174 **Existing works.** The provisions of the 1964 Order apply to works existing at the commencement of the 1957 Order, subject as aforesaid and to certain further qualifications.

In the first place, copyright will not subsist by virtue of the 1964 Order in any work by reason only of its publication before the

[15] Copyright (International Conventions) Order, 1964 (S.I. 1964 No. 690), Art. 3 and Sched. III, now amended, *post*, §§ 1875, 1880.

commencement of the 1957 Order in a country which is a party to the Universal Copyright Convention, but which is not a country of the Berne Copyright Union.[16] This, combined with the operation of paragraph 1 of the Seventh Schedule to the Act of 1956, Article 2 (1) of the 1964 Order [17] and paragraph 5 of the Fourth Schedule to the 1957 Order, will have the effect that works first published in a Universal Copyright Convention country, not being a Berne Convention country, before the commencement of the 1957 Order, will not enjoy United Kingdom copyright, notwithstanding that their authors may have been subjects of a country to which the 1957, now the 1964, Order applies, at the date of publication. There is an exception to this in the case of works first published in the United States during the periods of the two wars which already enjoy copyright in the United Kingdom by virtue of the Wartime Orders hereafter mentioned.[18] Such works will also enjoy the full term of United Kingdom copyright, notwithstanding the provisions about the term of copyright hereinbefore mentioned. There is also an exception in respect of Kenya, Malawi, Zambia, Ghana and Nigeria.[19] Although these countries are parties to the Universal Copyright Convention, but not to the Berne Copyright Union, their works enjoyed United Kingdom copyright as members of Her Majesty's Dominions prior to their independence.

1175 **Translations.** It is further provided by the 1964 Order,[20] that nothing in the Act of 1956, as applied by that Order, is to be construed as reviving any right to make, or restrain the making of, or any right in respect of, translations, if such right had ceased before the commencement of that Order. This refers, in particular, to certain provisions of the Order in Council (Copyright (Rome Convention) Order, 1933) made under the Act of 1911 restricting the translation rights in works originating in Greece, Estonia, Japan, Japanese Territories, Thailand and Yugoslavia because these countries also restricted translation rights.[20a]

1176 **1956 Act to apply as if references to commencement of Act were references to commencement of Order.** Again there is a general provision in the 1964 Order,[21] that, in the Seventh Schedule to the Act of 1956, references to the commencement of that Act, or to the repeal of any provision of the Copyright Act, 1911, are to be treated, in relation to any work in which copyright subsists by virtue of the 1964 Order, as references to the commencement of the 1957 Order.

16 *Ibid.* Art. 2 (2) and see Art. 2 (3) and Sched. 2.
17 And see *ibid.* Art. 2 (3) and Sched. 2.
18 *Ibid.* Art. 2 (4) (*b*), *post,* § 1184.
19 *Ibid.* Art. 2 (4) (*a*).
20 *Ibid.* Art. 6: see also Art. 1, proviso (v), Copyright (International Conventions) Order, 1957 (S.I. 1957 No. 1523).
20a Art. 2, proviso (ii) (*b*); see also proviso (vi).
21 Copyright (International Conventions) Order, 1964 (S.I. 1964 No. 690), Art. 2 (1), and see Art. 2 (3) and Sched. 2.

1177 **As to royalty terms for recorded music.** The 1957 Order contained provisions [21a] affecting the right to record music on royalty terms, which had the effect that, in the case of works published before certain dates set out in a Table to the Order, such works might be recorded on royalty terms, notwithstanding that they had not been previously recorded in the United Kingdom. Furthermore, in the case of such works which had been recorded and records sold in the United Kingdom before the relevant date, such works should be mechanically free. Where copyright was conferred by the Order for the first time on a musical work, then, for the purposes of the last-mentioned provision, the date of the Order was to be the relevant date. This provision is not repeated in the 1964 Order.

1178 **As to copyright in sound recordings.** There was also in the 1957 Order a provision [21a] about the copyright in sound recordings. This referred back, through paragraph 13 of the Seventh Schedule to the Copyright Act, 1956, to section 19 (8) of the Copyright Act, 1911, which gave copyright under the Act of 1911, in respect of existing sound recordings, provided that the making thereof would not have infringed copyright in some other sound recording if that Act had been in force at the time of the making thereof. This provision of the 1957 Order seemed intended to apply the dates mentioned in the Fourth Schedule thereto, or the date of the commencement of that Order, as the case might be, for the date of the commencement of the Act of 1911 in paragraph 13 of the Seventh Schedule to the Act of 1956. This provision also is not repeated in the 1964 Order.

1179 **Revocation of previous Orders.** The 1957 Order [22] revoked all the previous Orders in Council relating to works of foreign origin, but it was provided that where, by virtue of any of such Orders, copyright subsisted in a work immediately before the commencement of the 1957 Order and copyright did not subsist therein by the 1957 Order it should continue to subsist as if such Order had not been revoked. The effect of this provision was not altogether clear. The intention clearly was to keep alive copyright in works of foreign origin in which copyright subsisted at the commencement of the 1957 Order, but which would not acquire copyright under the Act of 1956 by virtue of the prior provisions of that Order. It seems that the only effect of this provision was to preserve the copyright in such works during the two years mentioned in paragraph 40 (2) (*c*) of the Seventh Schedule to the Copyright Act, 1956. It, also, is not repeated in the 1964 Order.

[21a] Copyright (International Conventions) Order, 1957 (S.I. 1957 No. 1523), Art. 1, proviso (iv) and Sched. 4.

[22] *Ibid.* Art. 3.

1180 **Broadcasts.** The 1964 Order provides [22a] that the provisions of section 14 of the Copyright Act, 1956, so far as they relate to sound broadcasts, are to apply in relation to sound broadcasts made from places in a number of named countries by any organisation constituted under the laws of such countries. It also provides [23] that the provisions of section 14, so far as they relate to television broadcasts, are to apply in relation to television broadcasts made from places in another series of countries by any organisation constituted under the laws of such countries.

1181 **Preservation of existing rights.** Finally both the 1957 and 1964 Orders contain general provisions preserving existing rights of persons who, before the commencement of each Order, have incurred expenditure or liability in connection with the reproduction or performance of any work.[24]

1182 **British colonies.** The position of the British colonies and dependencies with regard to countries belonging to the Copyright Union will be considered in the next chapter.

2.—UNITED STATES

1183 **Position under old law.** There was no treaty between Great Britain and the United States on the subject of copyright, and it was not until 1891, after the passage of the Act commonly called the "Chace Act," that British authors could obtain any effective protection for their works in that country. The Chace Act was repealed by the Copyright Act, 1909, under which British authors could obtain a certain measure of protection for their works, by virtue of a proclamation by the President of the United States to the effect that the British law grants to citizens of the United States the benefit of copyright on substantially the same basis as its own citizens.[25] American citizens were in fact able to obtain copyright in their works by first publishing them in England, or simultaneously [26] in England or a Convention country and America; and they could, no doubt, sue in England in respect of any publication in breach of trust or confidence.[27] Further, by an Order in Council dated February 3, 1915,[28] made under section 29 of the Act of 1911, the protection of that Act

22a Copyright (International Conventions) Order, 1964 (S.I. 1964 No. 690). Art 8 and Sched. V.

23 *Ibid.* Art. 9 and Sched. VI.

24 *Ibid.* Arts. 4 and 10 and Copyright (International Conventions) Order, 1957 (S.I. 1957 No. 1523), Art. 2.

25 See *post*, § 1252.

26 As to the meaning of this expression, see *ante*, § 76. The time for publication was extended during the war by an Order of February 9, 1920, § 1859, *post*.

27 *Ante*, § 88.

28 S.R. & O. 1915 No. 130. See Copinger, *Copyright*, 8th ed., p. 468.

was extended to works of classes (*b*) and (*c*) of that section. But works first published in America had no protection in this country.

1184 **Wartime legislation.** By an Order in Council dated February 9, 1920,[29] the Copyright Act, 1911, was applied to works, first published in the United States between August 1, 1914 and the termination of the war, which had not been republished in the British Empire (except the self-governing dominions) prior to February 2, 1920. It would appear that, if an authorised publication was made in the area in question after the fourteen days allowed by the Act of 1911, but before February 2, 1920, advantage could not be taken of this Order. By an Order in Council[30] dated August 6, 1942, as amended by an Order in Council[30] dated October 9, 1950, the Copyright Act, 1911, was applied to works first published in the United States between September 3, 1939, and December 29, 1950, which had not been published in the same area within fourteen days of the publication in the United States. In order to take advantage of this Order publication must have been made not later than December 28, 1950.[31] The 1942 Order came into operation on the date of its publication in the *London Gazette*.[32] While persons taking action before the commencement of the 1942 Order, on the assumption that no copyright existed, are given certain protection for accrued rights and interests, it remained obscure whether, if an authorised publication was in fact made, the owner thereof had a title by relation back.

1185 **Present position of United States works.** Copyright under the Copyright Act, 1956, is now conferred in respect of works of United States origin by reason of that country's adherence to the Universal Copyright Convention,[33] but the provisions of the Orders conferring this right are not retrospective in relation to published works except in so far as such works have already acquired copyright under these wartime Orders. Of course many existing works will obtain United Kingdom protection, under the Copyright Act, 1956, by having been simultaneously published in the United Kingdom or a Berne Convention country, without the necessity of reliance upon such Orders in Council.

3.—WORKS OF ENEMY ORIGIN

1186 **1914–1918 War legislation.** Prior to the commencement of the 1914-18 War, Germany, as a member of the Berne Convention,

[29] S.R. & O. 1920 No. 257, *post,* Appendix D, § 1859.
[30] S.R. & O. 1942 No. 1579; S.I. 1950 No. 1641, *post,* Appendix D, § 1861. The four Orders were repealed by the 1957 Order, but see *post,* § 1863.
[31] See *Plantation Wood (Lancing), Ltd.'s Applications for a Trade Mark* [1958] R.P.C. 400.
[32] March 10, 1944.
[33] See § 1169, *ante.*

and Austria-Hungary by a special copyright treaty,[34] had been given, by Orders in Council, rights in this country in respect of works published in those countries, or whose authors were subjects of or residents in those countries. Where works were made or published before the outbreak of the war, the copyright in this country, if the property of an enemy, became liable under the Trading with the Enemy Acts, 1914 to 1918, to be vested in the Public Trustee as the Custodian of Enemy Property.[35] With regard to works made or published in an enemy country after the outbreak of the war, it was doubted whether any copyright in this country was acquired, though the Orders in Council creating such copyright do not appear to have been revoked. To remove these doubts it was provided by the Trading with the Enemy (Copyright) Act, 1916,[36] that the copyright created by the aforesaid Orders in Council in enemy works should subsist and should be vested in the Custodian of Enemy Property. A large number of enemy copyrights were vested in the Custodian in the course of the war, and licences were granted in respect of the publication of such works in this country. The Treaties of Peace provided for the revesting of such copyrights, but subject to severe disabilities. The terms upon which the revesting took place are set out, as regards Germany and Austria, in an Order in Council of November 9, 1920,[37] made under the powers conferred by the Trading with the Enemy Act, 1914, and the Treaty of Peace Orders, 1919 and 1920, and, as regards Hungary, in an Order in similar terms dated August 16, 1921. These Orders reserved power to the Board of Trade to grant licences, but the provisions of these Orders were revoked in 1930,[38] so that, subject to any licences which may have been granted, it appears that the owner of the work is now again beneficially entitled to it. In order, however, to follow the title to such works, it may still be necessary to consider the effect of this legislation upon German, Austrian and Hungarian works made or published before the termination of the war, that is, in the case of Germany, before January 10, 1920,[39] in the case of Austria, July 16, 1920,[40] and in the case of Hungary, August 31, 1921,[41] since such works, if vested in the Custodian at any time, became revested, subject to the disabilities and restrictions created by the Peace Treaties and set out in the Orders in Council above referred to.

34 Since both Austria and Hungary are now members of the Berne Convention it has not been thought necessary to set out this treaty, or the Order in Council made in conformity with it, in the present edition. They will be found set out in full in the fifth edition of this work.

35 4 & 5 Geo. 5, c. 87, s. 4 (1); 8 & 9 Geo. 5, c. 31, s. 8.

36 6 & 7 Geo. 5, c. 32.

37 S.R. & O. 1920 (No. 2119).

38 Order in Council May 17, 1930 (S.R. & O. 1930 (No. 341)).

39 By Order in Council of February 9, 1920, made under the Termination of the Present War (Definition) Act, 1918 (8 & 9 Geo. 5, c. 59)

40 By Order in Council, July 22, 1920, made under that Act.

41 By Order in Council, August 10, 1921, made under that Act.

1187 **1939–1945 War legislation.** By section 5 of the Patents, Designs, Copyright and Trade Marks (Emergency) Act, 1939,[42] provision is made for the preservation of enemy copyrights and the continuing in force of Orders in Council made under the Copyright Act in relation to enemy countries. The result is that the war did not affect the creation or continuance of British copyrights in works originating in enemy countries. The 1939 Act [43] also continued in force licences granted by enemies to persons resident in the United Kingdom, subject to control. The 1939 Act [44] also gave power to the comptroller to grant licences in respect of enemy copyrights, and to vary existing licences.[45] In consequence of these provisions few copyrights were vested in the Custodian under the ordinary trading with the enemy legislation, matters being dealt with by leaving the copyrights vested in enemies and granting licences as required. Certain German copyrights may, however, be affected by virtue of the Enemy Property Act, 1953,[46] in consequence of the exercise by, or on behalf of, the Crown of the rights thereby conferred.

[The next paragraph is 1201]

[42] 2 & 3 Geo. 6, c. 107.
[43] s. 1.
[44] ss. 1 and 2.
[45] The nature and effect of these powers was discussed in *Novello & Co., Ltd.* v. *Eulenburg (E.), Ltd.* [1950] 1 All E.R. 44 and *Novello & Co., Ltd.* v. *Hinrichsen Edition, Ltd.* [1951] Ch. 595, 1026.
[46] 1 & 2 Eliz. 2, c. 57.

CHAPTER 26

PROTECTION OF WORKS ORIGINATING IN THE BRITISH COMMONWEALTH

1.—POSITION BEFORE THE ACT OF 1911

1201 **Colonial Conference, 1910.** In the year 1910, during the presence of representatives of the British colonies and dependencies in England, a conference of those representatives was held upon the subject-matter of copyright in the British dominions. Mr. Sydney Buxton, the then President of the Board of Trade, urged upon the representatives the extreme desirability of obtaining a uniform code of copyright laws which should apply throughout the King's dominions. At this conference certain resolutions were passed, generally recognising this desirability, but insisting, at the same time, that, at any rate, self-governing colonies ought not to be bound by any Imperial Copyright Act, or be made party to any convention or treaty entered into by the home government, without the assent of those colonies, and that all colonies ought to have the right to make local modifications in the law.[1] Accordingly, the Copyright Act, 1911, was extended in general terms throughout H.M. dominions, but the self-governing dominions were given rights to decide whether or not it should operate within their territories. In fact, as hereinafter appears, they all adopted the Act of 1911 and, in consequence, the Act of 1911 operated throughout the British Commonwealth. The Copyright Act, 1956, however, is framed so that it can only extend to the United Kingdom and Colonial and Protected territories. The Act of 1911 therefore will continue to operate in the self-governing dominions unless and until they pass new copyright legislation of their own and, unless they elect to do so in the same terms as the Act of 1956, the advantages of a uniform code throughout the British Commonwealth will be lost.[1a]

1202 **Law prior to Act of 1911.** Having regard to questions of title affecting older works, it is still necessary to understand the law as it existed prior to the Act of 1911. The Literary Copyright Act, 1842, expressly extended copyright to every part of the British dominions,[2] but none of the Acts relating to artistic or dramatic copyright contained any similar provision. The Fine Arts Copyright Act, 1862, did refer to the British dominions, giving copyright in all works made in the British dominions or elsewhere,[3] but it was held that there

[1] Report of Colonial Conference, 1910 (Cd. 5272).

[1a] See § 1221, *post.*

[2] s. 29.

[3] s. 1.

was nothing in that Act to extend the copyright throughout the British dominions, the provisions of sections 8 and 10 providing for the recovery of the penalties in England, Scotland and Ireland, and forbidding the importation into the United Kingdom of copies made in any part of the British dominions indicating a contrary intention.[4]

Whilst, therefore, a British author publishing a literary work in the United Kingdom obtained, under the Literary Copyright Act, 1842, an imperial copyright, extending throughout the British dominions, and was thus enabled to prevent piracies in any colony, a British artist, first publishing in the United Kingdom, obtained no imperial copyright, but, if he desired to prevent infringements in a colony, needed to acquire local copyright according to the laws of the particular colony.

1203 **Rights of colonial authors in United Kingdom.** Conversely, it was held that the Literary Copyright Act, 1842, did not confer copyright in the United Kingdom on works first published in the colonies.[5] This grievance was, however, removed by the International Copyright Act, 1886, which, by section 8, provided that the Copyright Acts should, subject to the provisions of the Act of 1886, apply to a literary or artistic work first produced in a *British possession* in like manner as they applied to a work first produced in the United Kingdom, provided (a) that the enactments respecting the registry of the copyright in such work should not apply if the law of such possession provided for the registration of such copyright; and (b) that where such work was a book, the delivery to any persons or body of persons of a copy of any such work should not be required. If, therefore, in the particular colony there was no provision for registration, then the registration needed to be effected in this country.

The result, therefore, was that any work produced in the colonies became entitled to the same copyright as it would have obtained if it had been first produced in the United Kingdom, but that although literary works published in the United Kingdom obtained copyright throughout the dominions, this was not the case with regard to artistic works.

1204 **Foreign reprints.** By section 17 of the Literary Copyright Act, 1842, all persons, other than the proprietor of the copyright or persons authorised by him, were forbidden to import into any part of the British dominions, for sale or hire, any printed book first composed or written or printed and published within the United Kingdom, wherein there should be copyright, and reprinted in any country or place out of the British dominions under penalty of £10, and

[4] *Graves (Henry) & Co., Ltd.* v. *Gorrie* [1903] A.C. 496.
[5] *Routledge* v. *Low* (1868) L.R. 3 H.L. 100.

double the value of the books.[6] Complaints arose, especially from Canada, with regard to this prohibition. It was contended that, in the sparsely populated colonies, where the circulating library system did not prevail, the price of English books was practically prohibitive, whilst English publishers feared to issue special cheap colonial editions, because they would not be able to prevent their re-importation into Great Britain. With a view to remedying these grievances, in 1847 there was passed an Act, commonly known as the Foreign Reprints Act,[7] enabling the Crown, by Order in Council, to suspend the prohibition against importation into the colonies of English copyright works, subject to their making suitable provisions for the protection of British authors. Under this Act numerous Orders in Council were issued by virtue of which cheap foreign reprints of copyright works were permitted to be imported into various colonies.

2.—UNDER THE ACT OF 1911

1205 **Provisions of the Copyright Act, 1911.** The provisions of the Copyright Act, 1911, relating to the British possessions were contained in sections 25 to 28. The countries subject to the Crown were divided into three classes: (a) dominions of the Crown, other than self-governing colonies; (b) self-governing colonies, meaning thereby the Dominion of Canada, the Commonwealth of Australia, the Dominion of New Zealand, the Union of South Africa, and Newfoundland [8]; and (c) protectorates and Cyprus.

1206 **Non-self-governing colonies and protectorates.** The provisions of the Act of 1911 relating to the colonies, other than the self-governing dominions, and to the protectorates and Cyprus, were comparatively simple. Section 25 (1) enacted that that Act, " except such of the provisions thereof as are expressly restricted to the United Kingdom,[9] shall extend throughout His Majesty's dominions," subject to a saving in respect of a self-governing dominion. Section 28 enabled His Majesty by Order in Council to extend the Act to any territories under his protection, and to Cyprus, " and, on the making of any such Order, this Act shall, subject to the provisions of the Order, have effect as if the territories to which it applies or Cyprus were part of His Majesty's dominions to which this Act extends." The legislature of any British possession to which the Act extended had, however, power to modify, or add to, any of the provisions of the Act in its application to the possession.[10]

6 And see the Customs Consolidation Act, 1876 (39 & 40 Vict. c. 36), ss. 151 and 152; and *Black* v. *Imperial Book Co., Ltd.* (1903) 5 Ontario L.R. 184; (1905) 21 T.L.R. 540.

7 Its official title is the Colonial Copyright Act, 1847.

8 Copyright Act, 1911, s. 35 (1).

9 *i.e.*, Copyright Act, 1911, ss. 11 and 12, relating to summary remedies.

10 Copyright Act, 1911, s. 27: and see *Rediffusion (Hong Kong), Ltd.* v. *Att.-Gen. of Hong Kong* [1970] A.C. 1136.

Thus, for the purposes of copyright, the colonies, other than the self-governing colonies, were treated as parts of the United Kingdom, and British copyright extended to all such colonies, and vice versa colonial copyright extended to the United Kingdom, except those modifications and additions to the British Act which the legislature of any colony should make, those only applying locally. Similarly, the following protectorates, to which by an Order in Council [11] dated June 24, 1912, the British Act was extended, were equally considered for copyright purposes to be part of the United Kingdom, namely, Cyprus, the Bechuanaland Protectorate, East Africa Protectorate, Gambia Protectorate, Gilbert and Ellice Islands Protectorate, Northern Nigeria Protectorate, Northern Territories of the Gold Coast, Nyasaland Protectorate, Northern Rhodesia, Southern Rhodesia, Sierra Leone Protectorate, Somaliland Protectorate, Southern Nigeria Protectorate, Solomon Islands Protectorate, Swaziland and Uganda Protectorate. Further, the British Act was extended to Palestine by an Order in Council of March 21, 1924, to Tanganyika by an Order in Council of April 16, 1924, to the Federated Malay States by Order in Council [12] of February 12, 1931, and to British Cameroons by Order in Council of March 16, 1933. Most of such colonies and protectorates passed local laws regarding the seizure by the customs of infringing copies and introducing penal provisions similar to those contained in section 11 of the Act of 1911, such laws being authorised by section 27 of that Act.

The Copyright Act, 1911, came into force in the above-mentioned possessions on July 1, 1912, except that it came into force in the Isle of Man on July 5, 1912, in India on October 30, 1912, in Papua on February 1, 1913, and in Jersey on March 8, 1913. The Act of 1911 came into force in the above-mentioned protectorates at the dates referred to in the respective Orders.

1207 **Self-governing dominions.** The self-governing dominions all became dominions to which the Act of 1911 extended.[13] Section 25 (1) of the Act of 1911 provided that that Act should not extend to the self-governing dominions unless declared by the legislature of any dominion so to apply, either without modifications, or with modifications relating exclusively to procedure and remedies, or necessary for its application to the dominion. Newfoundland adopted the Act of 1911 without modifications. The Commonwealth of Australia and the Union of South Africa made certain modifications.

Canada and New Zealand did not adopt this procedure, but passed independent Acts on similar lines to the Act of 1911. By section 25 (2) of the Act of 1911 is was provided that, if the Secretary of State

11 See § 1858, *post*.
12 See § 1860, *post*.
13 As regards the Republic of Ireland, see § 1209, *post*.

certified, by notice published in the *London Gazette*, that any self-governing dominion had passed legislation under which works, the authors whereof were, at the date of the making of the works, British subjects resident elsewhere than in the dominion or (not being British subjects) were resident in the parts of His Majesty's dominions to which that Act extended, enjoyed within the dominion rights substantially identical with those conferred by that Act, then, whilst such legislation continued in force, the dominion should, for the purposes of the rights conferred by that Act, be treated as if it were a dominion to which that Act extended.

1208 The Canadian Act of 1923 complied with the provisions of this section in its terms, and the New Zealand Act of 1913 also complied with them when coupled with an Order of the Executive Council made thereunder of March 27, 1914. The Secretary of State in fact certified, in respect of both dominions, under section 25 (2), in 1923 as to Canada and in 1914 as to New Zealand.[14]

1209 **The Republic of Ireland.** By an Order in Council dated October 27, 1930, made in pursuance of the Irish Free State (Consequential Provisions) Act, 1922,[15] the Irish Free State was deemed to be a self-governing dominion for the purposes of the Copyright Act, 1911, and, by a further Order in Council dated October 27, 1930, made in pursuance of section 26 (3) of the Copyright Act, 1911, the Act of 1911 was declared to apply to works first published in the Irish Free State and to works of which the authors were, at the time of making the work, resident in the Irish Free State, provided that there was to be no right to prevent the translation into English of literary or dramatic works in Irish if an authorised translation was not made within ten years from publication. This Order in Council was preserved by the provisions of paragraph 40 (4) of the Seventh Schedule to the Copyright Act, 1956, but was repealed by the Copyright (International Conventions) Order, 1957,[16] which applied the Copyright Act, 1956, to the Republic of Ireland as a Berne Convention country.

The Copyright Act, 1911, was repealed in the Irish Free State by an Irish Free State Act [17] passed in 1927 but, since this was thought to create doubts as to subsisting copyrights,[18] a further Act was passed in

14 See *Mansell* v. *Star Printing, etc., Ltd.* [1937] A.C. 872 and *Walt Disney Productions* v. *(H.) John Edwards Publishing Co. Pty., Ltd.* (1954) 71 W.N.(N.S.W.) 150.

15 13 Geo. 5, c. 2.

16 *Post*, Appendix D, § 1862: see now Copyright (International Conventions) Order, 1964, *post*, Appendix D, § 1874.

17 Industrial and Commercial Property (Protection) Act, 1927, No. 16 of 1927. See Appendix E of the 9th ed. of this work.

18 *Performing Right Society, Ltd.* v. *Bray U.D.C.* [1930] A.C. 377.

1929 [19] declaring that, so far as was necessary for the subsistence in the Irish Free State of copyrights, the Act of 1911 and every Order made thereunder should be deemed to continue to have full force and effect in the Irish Free State. A new Copyright Act was passed on April 8, 1963, to replace the existing law [20]; it has considerable resemblances to the United Kingdom Act of 1956.

1210 **Repeal by dominions of pre-1911 legislation.** It is to be noted that section 26 (1) of the Act of 1911 gave to the legislature of any self-governing dominion power to repeal any enactment relating to copyright including the Act of 1911. All the dominions repealed the legislation prior to the Act of 1911 which applied to them.

3.—UNDER THE ACT OF 1956

1211 **Repeal of Act of 1911 in the United Kingdom.** Paragraph 41 of the Seventh Schedule to the Copyright Act, 1956, provides that, in so far as the Act of 1911, or any Order in Council made thereunder, forms part of the law of any country other than the United Kingdom at a time after that Act has been wholly or partly repealed in the law of the United Kingdom, it shall, so long as it forms part of the law of that country, be construed and have effect as if that Act had not been so repealed.[21] The repeal of the Act of 1911 in the United Kingdom, therefore, did not affect its operation, either in colonial territory, or in the self-governing dominions.

1212 **Extension of the Act of 1956 to other countries.** Power is given, by section 31 of the Copyright Act, 1956, to extend that Act, and Orders in Council made under that Act, by Order in Council, to the Isle of Man, any of the Channel Islands, any colony,[22] any country outside H.M. dominions in which for the time being Her Majesty has jurisdiction, and any country consisting partly of one or more colonies and partly of one or more such countries as are last mentioned. Such Orders in Council may extend the Act of 1956 subject to exceptions and modifications. The Act of 1956, and Orders in Council thereunder, have been extended, by Orders in Council, to the Isle of Man as from May 31, 1959,[23] Sarawak as from January 1, 1960,[24] Gibraltar as from June 1, 1960,[25] Fiji as from February 1,

[19] Copyright (Preservation) Act, 1929, No. 25 of 1929. See Appendix E of the 9th ed. of this work.

[20] Copyright Act (No. 10 of 1963).

[21] See as to repeal of the Act of 1911 as part of the law of any country in the Commonwealth, the Copyright Act, 1956 (Transitional Extension) Order, 1959 (S.I. 1959 No. 103).

[22] See *Rediffusion (Hong Kong), Ltd.* v. *Att.-Gen. of Hong Kong* [1970] A.C. 1136.

[23] The Copyright (Isle of Man) Order, 1959 (S.I. 1959 No. 861) and the Copyright (Isle of Man) Order, 1970 (S.I. 1970 No. 1437).

[24] The Copyright (Sarawak) Order, 1959 (S.I. 1959 No. 2215).

[25] The Copyright (Gibraltar) Order, 1960 (S.I. 1960 No. 847).

1961,[26] Uganda as from January 1, 1962,[27] Zanzibar as from January 1, 1962,[28] Bermuda as from August 6, 1962,[29] North Borneo as from August 6, 1962,[30] the Bahamas as from October 11, 1962,[31] the Virgin Islands as from October 11, 1962,[32] the Falkland Islands as from June 10, 1963,[33] St. Helena and dependencies as from June 10, 1963,[34] Seychelles as from June 10, 1963,[35] Kenya as from July 4, 1963,[36] Mauritius as from May 21, 1964,[37] Montserrat as from November 5, 1965,[38] St. Lucia as from November 5, 1965,[39] Bechuanaland as from December 4, 1965,[40] Cayman Islands as from December 4, 1965,[41] Grenada as from January 1, 1966,[42] British Guiana as from February 5, 1966,[43] British Honduras as from June 16, 1966,[44] and Saint Vincent as from July 5, 1967.[45] Each Order contains exceptions and modifications which vary according to local circumstances.

1213 **Effect where the Act of 1956 is so extended.** To the extent that the Act of 1956 and Orders in Council thereunder have been so extended, common conditions for obtaining copyright protection exist throughout the area to which that Act and Orders in Council are so extended. Thus the definition of "qualified person," in section 1 (5) of the Act of 1956, includes, a person domiciled or resident in the United Kingdom or in another country to which any provision of that Act extends, and a body incorporated under the laws of any such country. Further, "first publication," in section 2 (2) of that Act, includes first publication in the United Kingdom or in another country to which the section extends. Similar provisions occur in sections 12 (2), 13 (2) and 15 (1) of the Act of 1956.

1214 **Power of such other countries to modify the Act of 1956.** While the legislature of any country to which any provisions of the Act

26 The Copyright (Fiji) Order, 1961 (S.I. 1961 No. 60).
27 The Copyright (Uganda) Order, 1961 (S.I. 1961 No. 2462); but see now Uganda Copyright Act, 1964.
28 The Copyright (Zanzibar) Order, 1961 (S.I. 1961 No. 2463), as amended by the Copyright (Zanzibar) (Amendment) Order, 1962 (S.I. 1962 No. 629).
29 The Copyright (Bermuda) Order, 1962 (S.I. 1962 No. 1642).
30 The Copyright (North Borneo) Order, 1962 (S.I. 1962 No. 1643).
31 The Copyright (Bahamas) Order, 1962 (S.I. 1962 No. 2184).
32 The Copyright (Virgin Islands) Order, 1962 (S.I. 1962 No. 2185).
33 The Copyright (Falkland Islands) Order, 1963 (S.I. 1963 No. 1037).
34 The Copyright (St. Helena) Order, 1963 (S.I. 1963 No. 1038).
35 The Copyright (Seychelles) Order, 1963 (S.I. 1963 No. 1039).
36 The Copyright (Kenya) Order, 1963 (S.I. 1963 No. 1147): but see now Kenya Copyright Act, 1966.
37 The Copyright (Mauritius) Order, 1964 (S.I. 1964 No. 689).
38 The Copyright (Montserrat) Order, 1965 (S.I. 1965 No. 1858).
39 The Copyright (St. Lucia) Order, 1965 (S.I. 1965 No. 1859).
40 The Copyright (Bechuanaland) Order, 1965 (S.I. 1965 No. 2009).
41 The Copyright (Cayman Islands) Order, 1965 (S.I. 1965 No. 2010).
42 The Copyright (Grenada) Order, 1965 (S.I. 1965 No. 2158).
43 The Copyright (British Guiana) Order, 1966 (S.I. 1966 No. 79).
44 The Copyright (British Honduras) Order, 1966 (S.I. 1966 No. 685).
45 The Copyright (Saint Vincent) Order, 1967 (S.I. 1967 No. 974).

of 1956 have been extended, as aforesaid, may modify or add to those provisions in their operation as part of the law of that country, no such modifications or additions, except in so far as they relate to procedure and remedies, are to be made so as to apply to any work or other subject-matter unless the qualification of authorship or publication arises with reference to that other country.[46] In fact numerous modifications of a minor character are embodied in the Orders in Council above referred to.

1215 **Proceedings in the U.K.** It is further provided[47] that, for the purposes of any proceedings under the Act of 1956 in the United Kingdom, where the proceedings relate to an act done in a country to which any provisions of that Act extend subject to exceptions, modifications or additions, the procedure and remedies are to be in accordance with that Act in its operation as part of the law of the United Kingdom; but, if the act does not constitute an infringement of copyright in its operation as part of the law of the country where the act was done, it is not to be treated as constituting an infringement of copyright under that Act in its operation as part of the law of the United Kingdom. Presumably the usual conditions will apply in respect of service out of the jurisdiction but, subject to this, it appears that a defendant may be sued in the United Kingdom in respect of an infringement in a colony, provided that the act of infringement would have been an infringement by the law of the colony if the proceedings had been brought there, but the procedure and remedies will be those of the United Kingdom.

1216 **Position as to colonial territories and self-governing dominions distinguished.** So far as the colonial territories are concerned when the necessary Orders in Council are made, the position will remain similar to that existing under the Act of 1911. But, so far as concerns the self-governing dominions, these are outside the operation of the Act of 1956, and works originating in their territory are only protected in the United Kingdom in the same manner as works originating in foreign countries are protected, that is to say, by Order in Council under section 32 of the Copyright Act, 1956, applying the provisions of the Act of 1956 to works originating in such countries.

1217 **Position in period before Orders in Council made.** To provide for the interim period after the commencement of the Act of 1956, and before Orders are made, extending or applying that Act to colonial and self-governing territories, provision is made in paragraph 39 of the Seventh Schedule to that Act. The effect of this paragraph

[46] Copyright Act, 1956, s. 31 (3): and see *Rediffusion (Hong Kong) Ltd.* v. *Att.-Gen. of Hong Kong* [1970] A.C. 1136.
[47] s. 31 (4).

appears to be that, until any such Order is made, the Act of 1956 is treated as extending to the territory in question whether it is a self-governing territory or not. The Copyright (International Conventions) Order, 1957, which came into operation on September 27, 1957,[48] applied the Act of 1956 in respect of works originating in the self-governing dominions and the same is now provided in the Copyright (International Conventions) Order, 1964.[49] Works originating in other Commonwealth territories remain protected by virtue of paragraph 39 until the making of Orders in Council extending the Act of 1956 thereto.

1218 **The Republic of Ireland.** As stated above,[50] the Republic of Ireland was treated as a self-governing dominion to which the Copyright Act of 1911 did not extend and copyright protection was afforded to works originating in that country by an Order in Council made under section 26 (3) of the Copyright Act, 1911. After the commencement of the Copyright Act, 1956, therefore, paragraph 40 (4) of the Seventh Schedule to that Act applies in relation to the Irish Republic, and it was accordingly treated as a foreign country in respect of which an Order in Council under section 29 of the Copyright Act, 1911, had been made. But the Republic of Ireland was one of the countries in respect of which protection was given by virtue of the Copyright (International Conventions) Order, 1957,[48] and now the Copyright (International Conventions) Order, 1964.[51] The Copyright Act, 1956, itself, in defining "qualified person," includes an individual who is a citizen of the Republic of Ireland, but not a body corporate incorporated under the laws of the Republic, and the Republic of Ireland is not a country to which that Act extends for the purpose of the provisions regarding first publication.

1219 **International arrangements with dominions.** With regard to any international arrangements which were made by the United Kingdom, it was provided that any Order in Council, made under section 29 of the Act of 1911 [52] was to apply to all His Majesty's dominions, except the self-governing dominions and any other possession specified in the Order.[53] Accordingly, the various Orders in Council which were made under that section [54] applied the Convention to all the dominions, colonies and possessions of the Crown, with the exception of the self-governing dominions, and also to Cyprus and the protectorates to which the Copyright Act was by Order in Council extended.[55] With regard to the self-governing dominions the Act of

48 *Post*, Appendix D, § 1862.
49 *Ante*, § 1169, and Appendix D, § 1874, *post*.
50 *Ante*, § 1209.
51 Appendix D, § 1874, *post*.
52 See, *ante*, § 1167.
53 Copyright Act, 1911, s. 30 (1) and (3).
54 See Appendix D, § 1858.
55 See § 1206, *ante*.

1911 authorised the Governor in Council of any such dominion to which that Act extended to make, as respects that dominion, the like Orders as the Crown in Council was, under sections 29 and 30 of that Act, authorised to make with regard to dominions other than self-governing dominions, and the provisions of those sections were, with the necessary modifications, to apply accordingly.[56] Orders in Council were, under this power, or a similar power in their own Acts, made by Australia, New Zealand, Newfoundland and the Union of South Africa, while the same effect was produced by the terms of the Canadian Act itself.

1220 As the Copyright Act, 1956, cannot be extended to the self-governing dominions, international protection therein depends upon the Copyright Act, 1911, and Orders in Council made thereunder so long as that Act is in force therein. If the self-governing dominions pass new Copyright Acts of their own, the nature of international protection therein will fall to be determined according to the provisions of those Acts.

1221 The following countries have now passed their own Copyright Acts, repealing the Copyright Act, 1911, or its equivalent: India in 1957, Ghana in 1961, Pakistan in 1962, New Zealand in 1962, Sierra Leone in 1965, Zambia in 1965, Malawi in 1965, South Africa in 1965, Tanzania in 1966, and Malta in 1967. Uganda and Kenya have passed their own Copyright Acts repealing the Copyright Act, 1956, in 1964 and 1966 respectively.[57] Malaysia has passed its own Copyright Act, repealing the Copyright Acts, 1911 and 1956, in 1969.[58]

[The next paragraph is 1230]

56 Copyright Act, 1911, s. 30 (2).
57 See § 1858, *post*.
58 See § 1860, *post*.

Part VI

COPYRIGHT LAWS OF COMMONWEALTH AND FOREIGN COUNTRIES

CHAPTER 27

COPYRIGHT LAW OF UNITED STATES OF AMERICA

1.—GENERAL

1230 In the United States, copyright in a published work depends entirely upon the legislation of Congress,[1] but unpublished works are protected by the common law, as in England prior to the Act of 1911. The Constitution of March 4, 1789, authorised Congress " to promote the progress of science and useful arts by securing for limited terms to authors and inventors the exclusive right to their respective writings and discoveries," and this provision is the source of the federal legislative power in matters of copyright. Several earlier laws were passed by Congress relating to copyright, but all these were repealed in 1870, and the entire law on the subject was embodied in an Act of 1873, which remained in force until 1909, with certain amendments made in the law, notably by the Act of 1891, commonly known as the Chace Act.

1231 **Copyright Act, 1909.** In the year 1909 was passed " an Act to amend and consolidate the Acts respecting copyright," which repealed all laws or parts of laws in conflict with its provisions.[2] This Act was amended in 1912, 1914 and 1919 and the copyright law of the United States was then codified in an Act of March 4, 1947,[3] which has been amended on a number of occasions and, as so amended, now governs the copyright law in the United States.

1232 **Subjects of copyright.** The subjects of copyright under the Act are: (a) books, (b) periodicals, (c) lectures, sermons and addresses, (d) dramatic and dramatico-musical compositions, (e) musical compositions, (f) maps, (g) works of art, (h) reproductions of works of art, (i) drawings or plastic works of a scientific or technical character, (j) photographs, (k) prints and pictorial illustrations, (l) motion-picture photo-plays, (m) motion pictures other than photo-plays.[4]

1233 **Industrial designs.** There has been considerable discussion of the qualification of ornamental designs for industrial articles to be registered. The leading case, *Mazer* v. *Stein*[5] decided that a

[1] See *Metro-Goldwyn-Mayer, etc., Corp.* v. *Bijou Theatre Co.* (1932) 50 F. (2d) 70.
[2] s. 63.
[3] Title 17, U.S. Code. Printed in Appendix E, *post.*
[4] s. 5.
[5] (1954) 347 U.S. 201.

statuette, which had been registered as a work of art, did not lose copyright protection by being used as a lamp base. Since this decision many works of art have been registered, notwithstanding that they have been embodied in articles of an industrial character. On the other hand objects of simple utility will not be so registered unless they can be justified as works of art.

1234 **Sound recordings.** It should be noted that gramophone records are not registrable for statutory protection. Therefore neither the copying of actual records, nor the performance in public of the music embodied therein, is an infringement of statutory copyright. Of course such acts may well infringe the statutory rights of the copyright owner of the music, but neither the gramophone manufacturers, nor the performing artistes have any remedy, though it is understood that in some states the copying of records may be regarded as a common law wrong.

1235 **Unpublished works.** Common law copyright is expressly preserved,[6] but statutory copyright may also be obtained in unpublished works, " of which copies are not reproduced for sale." [7]

1236 **Persons entitled to copyright.** The persons entitled by the Act to copyright protection for their works are the author or proprietor, or his executors, administrators or assigns.[8] But, except on the conditions discussed below, copyright is not extended to the work of an author or proprietor who is a citizen or subject of a foreign state or nation. Moreover, except as aforesaid, the text of any book in the English language has to be printed from type set up in the U.S.A. In case of a work produced " for hire," the employer is treated as the author.[9] And, in the case of a collective work,. the proprietor is entitled to copyright therein.[8]

1237 **Term of copyright.** The term of copyright in the United States is an original term of twenty-eight years from the date of first publication, with a right of renewal for a second period of twenty-eight years. In view of current proposals for a general extension of the renewal term, as part of an overall revision of Title 17, U.S. Code,[10] as an interim measure, an Act [11] was passed in 1962 extending until December 31, 1965, all renewal copyrights which would have expired between September 19, 1962, and December 31, 1965. As a result

[6] s. 2.
[7] s. 12.
[8] s. 9.
[9] s. 26.
[10] For a commentary on the progress of such revision see " Letter from the United States," *Copyright*, No. 10, October 1969, p. 185.
[11] P.L. 87–668.

of the delay in enacting the necessary legislation to achieve such revision, further extensions have been granted, the effect of which is to extend until December 31, 1971, all renewal copyrights which would have expired between September 19, 1962, and December 31, 1971.[11a]

This right of renewal belongs, in the case of a posthumous or a composite work, such as a periodical or encyclopedia, to the proprietor of the work, and, in other cases, to (a) the author, if still living; (b) the widow, widower, or children of the author, if the author is not living; (c) the author's executor, if such widow, widower, or children be not living; (d) if the author, widow, widower, and children are all dead, and the author left no will, his next-of-kin. Application for renewal must be made and registered within one year prior to the expiration of the first term.[12] But, in the case of works of United Kingdom authorship falling for renewal on or after September 3, 1939, the period was extended.[13] The assign of the author is not able to claim this renewal,[14] but can enforce against the author, though not against the representatives of a deceased author, an agreement to assign the renewed copyright. A number of United States decisions had decided that an assignment of copyright should not be construed as being intended to pass the renewal right unless such right was specifically mentioned, but it has been held that these decisions were inapplicable to an English contract, which must be construed in accordance with English rules of construction.[15]

1238 **Assignment of copyright.** Copyright is distinct from the property in the material object copyrighted, and, prima facie, a transfer of the material object does not transfer the copyright.[16] Copyright may be assigned by any instrument in writing signed by the proprietor of the copyright,[17] but, if executed in a foreign country, must be acknowledged by the assignor before a consular officer or secretary of legation of the United States authorised by law to administer oaths or perform notarial acts.[18] All assignments must be registered.[19] Non-registration is no defence to an action for infringement, but may render the transaction void against a purchaser for value without notice. It is the theory of United States transfer law that copyright is indivisible. Accordingly book rights cannot be transferred without serial rights, dramatic rights and motion-picture rights. The normal

11a By P.L. 89–142, P.L. 90–141, P.L. 90–416, P.L. 91–147 and P.L. 91–555; see Appendix E, §§ 1913, *post*.

12 s. 24.

13 See amending Act of 1941 and Presidential Proclamation of March 10, 1944. *Post*, Appendix E, § 1950.

14 *Fox Film Corp.* v. *Knowles* (1922) 261 U.S. 326.

15 *Campbell Connelly & Co., Ltd.* v. *Noble* [1963] 1 W.L.R. 252.

16 s. 27.

17 s. 28.

18 s. 29.

19 ss. 30 and 31.

practice, therefore, is to assign the whole copyright to the publisher, who will grant back to the author an exclusive licence in respect of the rights not intended to be transferred.

1239 **Publication.** The Act contains no precise definition of "publication," but, by section 26, "the date of publication" is, in the case of a work of which copies are reproduced for sale or distribution, to be "the earliest date when copies of the first authorised edition were placed on sale, sold, or publicly distributed by the proprietor of the copyright or under his authority." Publication, therefore, only takes place with the concurrence of the proprietor of the copyright, and it would seem that, for books at least, there must be an issue of copies. Representation on the stage of a play is not a publication of it, nor is the public performance of a musical composition publication. It is not very clear whether the public exhibition of a work of art is a publication—it would seem to depend upon the circumstances. In the case of *American Tobacco Co.* v. *Werckmeister*,[20] it was held that public exhibition, in a place where copying was forbidden, did not amount to publication, but the court added "we do not mean to say that the public exhibition of a painting or statue where all might see and freely copy it, might not amount to publication within the statute, regardless of the artist's purpose or notice of reservation of rights which he takes no measure to protect." It is thought that the issue of records of a musical work does not amount to publication of it. It results from the foregoing that many works may be publicly disseminated, by various forms of performance or exhibition, without losing perpetual protection at common law.

1240 **Copyright notice.** Copyright is obtained by publication "with the notice of copyright . . . affixed to each copy thereof published or offered for sale in the United States by authority of the copyright proprietor." [21] By section 19 it is provided that this copyright notice "shall consist either of the word 'Copyright' the abbreviation 'Copr.,' or the symbol ©, accompanied by the name of the copyright proprietor, and if the work be a printed literary, musical, or dramatic work, the notice shall include also the year in which the copyright was secured by publication." In the case of copies of works (f) to (k) mentioned in section 5,[22] the notice may consist of the letter C enclosed with a circle, thus ©, accompanied by the initials, monogram, mark, or symbol of the copyright proprietor, provided that on some accessible portion of such copies, or of the margin, back, permanent base, or pedestal, or of the substance on which such copies shall be

[20] (1907) 207 U.S. 284.

[21] s. 10. The notice may be omitted in the case of foreign made copies not offered for sale in the United States, though it has been suggested that the notice should appear on the work when first published, wherever such publication takes place.

[22] *Ante*, § 1232.

mounted, his name shall appear.[23] In the case of books or other printed publications, the notice must be upon the title page or the page immediately following; in the case of a periodical, either upon the title page or upon the first page of text of each separate number, or under the title heading; or, in the case of a musical work, either upon its title page or the first page of music; provided that one notice of copyright in each volume, or in each number of a newspaper or periodical published, is to be sufficient.[24]

1241 **Effect of omission of copyright notice.** Accidental omission of the copyright notice from some copies does not invalidate the copyright, but damages are not in that case recoverable against an innocent infringer, and an injunction may be refused, except on the terms of reimbursing the expenses of an innocent infringer.[25] On the other hand, no relief seems possible if the copyright notice is in the wrong place or a wrong form.[26]

1242 **Registration and deposit.** The next step is to register the copyright, which is effected by deposit at the Copyright Office of two complete copies of the best edition of the work,[27] with a proper application for registration and a money order for the amount of registration fee. A partnership may be registered.[28] The Act requires this deposit to be made "promptly," but this has to be read in conjunction with the next section which refers to the period of three months.[29] Such deposit is a sufficient publication to make the work subject to copyright within the Act, although not a publication within section 26.[30]

1243 **Failure to make deposit.** The effect of a failure to deposit the necessary copies and to register the copyright is not to invalidate the copyright in the first instance, but only to prevent any action for infringement being brought until such deposit and registration have been effected.[31] But notice may be given by the Registrar of Copyrights requiring the deposit to be made, and, upon failure to comply with this notice within three months—or six months in the case of a foreign country—the proprietor of the copyright will be liable to a fine, and the copyright will become void.[32]

[23] The old form of copyright notice will be sufficient in the case of works in which copyright subsisted on July 1, 1909: s. 19.
[24] s. 20.
[25] s. 21.
[26] *Freeman* v. *Trade Register* (1909) 173 Fed.Rep. 419; *Bowker on Copyright* (Amer.), p. 131. As to false copyright notices, see ss. 105 and 106.
[27] s. 13.
[28] *Campbell* v. *Wireback* (1920) 269 Fed.Rep. 372.
[29] *Freedman* v. *Milnag, etc., Corp.* (1937) 20 F.S. 802. As to foreign works, see *post*, § 1252 *et seq.*
[30] *Cardinal Film Corporation* v. *Beck* (1918) 248 Fed.Rep. 368.
[31] s. 13.
[32] s. 14.

1244 **Deposit in case of unpublished work.** In the case of unpublished works, statutory copyright may be obtained by deposit of one complete copy, in the case of a lecture, sermon, address, dramatic or musical work; a positive print, in the case of a photograph; a photographic reproduction, in the case of works of art, etc.[33] If, however, the work be afterwards published, deposit must be made in the ordinary way.[33]

1245 **The "manufacturing provisions."** In addition to the above formalities, printed "books," except the original text [34] of a book of foreign origin in a language other than English, must, except where the provisions of the Universal Copyright Convention apply, comply with the "manufacturing provisions" of the Act. That is to say, they must be "printed from type set within the limits of the United States, either by hand or by the aid of any kind of typesetting machine, or from plates made within the limits of the United States from type set therein, or, if the text be reproduced by lithographic process, or photo-engraving process, then by a process wholly performed within the limits of the United States, and the printing of the text and binding of the said book shall be performed within the limits of the United States." [35] These requirements also extend to the illustrations of the book, and to separate lithographs or photo engravings, except when, in either case, the subjects represented are located in a foreign country and illustrate a scientific work or reproduce a work of art.[35]

These provisions were even more stringent than those contained in the Act of 1891, inasmuch as they require that, not only shall the printing be done in the United States, but the type must be set and the binding done within the country. An affidavit to this effect must be made at the time of depositing the necessary copies,[36] and, apparently, failure to comply with the manufacturing provisions involves loss of the copyright.

1246 **Rights of owner of copyright.** The proprietor of the copyright has the exclusive right (a) to print, reprint, publish, copy, and vend the work; (b) to translate, dramatise, arrange, or adapt the work; (c) to deliver in public for profit a lecture, sermon, or address; (d) publicly to perform the work.[37]

1247 **Reproduction by records, etc.** Authors of works published after July 1, 1909, are also given the sole right to authorise the reproduction of their works by means of mechanical instruments,[38] but subject to

33 s. 12.
34 It is to be noted that the exemption only applies to the "original text." Apparently the French translation of a German book, for instance, must comply with the manufacturing provisions: Bowker, p. 155.
35 s. 16.
36 s. 17.
37 s. 1.
38 s. 1. As to foreign works, see *post*, § 1252.

the condition, as regards musical works, that once the owner of the copyright has permitted such reproduction, any other person may make similar use of the coprighted work upon payment of a fixed royalty of two cents on every record.[37] The records themselves are not entitled to copyright.

1248 **For profit.** There is, however, a distinction regarding the performing right, namely that, in the case of a musical work, performance is only an infringement if "for profit." This includes playing music at hotels and restaurants, but not charitable performances, even for raising funds. There is a special exemption for "jukeboxes," although clearly coin-operated record players are normally operated "for profit." [39]

1249 **Fair use.** The owner's rights have been limited in a series of judicial decisions on the principle of "fair use." Such exceptions fall under the headings of quotation for review or criticism, quotation for illustration in scientific works, parody, news summary, reproduction for study, reproduction for purposes of legal proceedings, fortuitous reproduction in newsreels.

1250 **Damages.** Section 101 of the Act is directed to damages. In view of the obvious difficulty, in copyright cases, of proving the actual damage suffered, a minimum penalty of $250 is provided, and it has been held that this may be recovered without legal proof of damage.[40]

1251 **Prohibition against importation.** The provisions of the Act as regards importation of copyright works are somewhat unusual, inasmuch as they expressly permit the importation of copyright books under certain circumstances. Section 107 provides, generally, against the importation of "piratical copies," and even of copies authorised to be imported by the owner of the copyright which have not been produced in accordance with the manufacturing provisions of the Act. But, except as regards piratical copies, the prohibition is not to apply to (a) works in raised characters for the use of the blind; (b) foreign-made periodicals containing authorised copyright matter; (c) authorised editions of works in foreign languages of which only an English translation has been copyrighted in the United States; (d) authorised copies published abroad when imported under special circumstances. These permit the importation of authorised copies for individual use and not for sale, provided not more than one copy be imported at one time; by or for the United States, or by or for certain educational authorities, including free libraries, not more than one copy at a time; or when parts of libraries or collections are

[39] s. 1 (*e*).
[40] *Hendricks Co. Inc.* v. *Thomas Pub. Co.* (1917) 242 Fed.Rep. 37.

purchased and imported *en bloc* for the use of such authorities as before mentioned, or form parts of personal baggage belonging to persons or families arriving from foreign countries, and are not intended for sale.

2.—WORKS OF FOREIGN ORIGIN

1252 **The Chace Act, 1891.** Until recent times, a foreign author or publisher had no rights as against an American publisher who reprinted or issued in America a work first published outside America. Common law protection for unpublished works has always been available to authors of any nationality. The first Copyright Act of 1790 was expressly applicable only to citizens of the United States or persons resident there, and this provision was maintained in all subsequent amendments of the law until the Chace Act of 1891. Under that Act, foreigners could obtain American copyright, provided they were citizens or subjects of a foreign state or nation which permitted to Americans " the benefit of copyright on substantially the same basis as its own citizens," or of a state or nation which is a " a party to an international agreement which provides for reciprocity in the granting of copyright by the term of which agreement the United States of America may, at its pleasure, become a party to such an agreement."

1253 **Present law.** Aliens who are domiciled in the United States may acquire statutory protection for their works in the same way as American citizens.[41] Secondly, by Presidential proclamation pursuant to section 9 (*b*) of the Act, the citizens or subjects of a number of foreign countries giving reciprocal protection to United States works may also acquire statutory protection for their works in the same way as American citizens. Thirdly and more recently, since the United States adhered to the Universal Copyright Convention, a more complex series of provisions apply.[42]

1254 **Gramophone records.** With regard to the exclusive right to make contrivances by which a work may be mechanically produced, it is provided [43] that, as regards musical works, this right shall not apply to " the works of a foreign author or composer unless the foreign state or nation of which such author or composer is a citizen or subject grants, either by treaty, convention, agreement, or law, to citizens of the United States similar rights."

1255 **Proclamations.** Presidential proclamations have been issued according the right to acquire general copyright in the United States

[41] s. 9 (*a*).
[42] *Post*, § 1262.
[43] s. 1.

to citizens of a number of countries including Great Britain and her possessions and colonies, including the self-governing dominions, and the following other countries—Argentina, Austria, Belgium, Brazil, Chile, Costa Rica, Cuba, Czechoslovakia, Denmark, Finland, France, Germany, Greece, Israel, Italy, Irish Republic, Luxembourg, Mexico, Monaco, The Netherlands and her possessions, Norway, Philippines, Poland, Portugal, Rumania, Spain, Sweden, Switzerland and Tunis. The right to obtain gramophone and similar rights is now accorded to the citizens of the same countries.

1256 **Special wartime provisions.** An amending Act of 1919 added a provision to section 9 to enable authors who, owing to war conditions, had been unable to register their copyright in the United States before first publication abroad, to obtain copyright by so doing within fifteen months of the declaration of peace, provided that it was proclaimed that they were nationals of a country which extended reciprocal rights to citizens of the United States. Proclamations were made that such rights had been extended to citizens of the United States by Great Britain (apart from the self-governing dominions), Denmark, Germany, Austria, Hungary, Italy and New Zealand. A further amendment to the said section was made by an Act of 1941 enabling a proclamation to be made extending, for the benefit of nationals of a country affording reciprocal rights, the time for performance of all formalities required by the law of the U.S.A. for such a period as the President should consider proper. A proclamation was issued in March, 1944,[44] giving the benefit of this amendment to residents in Great Britain and in a number of British possessions, and extending the time until further proclamation. In July 1967 a proclamation was made in favour of German citizens.

1257 **Formalities to be observed.** But, so far as concerns all the foregoing provisions, foreign authors were required to observe all the formalities to which United States authors were subject.

Foreign works had, therefore, to be registered at the Copyright Office in Washington, and every copy had to bear the necessary copyright notice.[45] There were, however, two modifications of the law in favour of foreigners, first, in respect of deposit of copies [46] and, second, as regards the manufacturing provisions.[47]

1258 **Deposit of one copy sufficient.** We have seen that the native author must deposit two complete copies of the best edition of his work. Section 12 of the Act of 1909 was amended in 1914, and section

44 *Post,* Appendix E, § 1950.
45 *Ante,* § 1240.
46 *Ante,* § 1242.
47 *Ante,* § 1245.

13 of the present Act now provides that, if the work is by an author who is a citizen or subject of a foreign state or nation, and has been published in a foreign country, only *one* complete copy of the best edition then published in such foreign country need be deposited.

1259 **Manufacturing provisions.** As has been pointed out, all books, except the original text of books of foreign origin written in a language *other than English*, are required to comply with the " manufacturing provisions " of the Act.[48] Thus, a book published by a British, or other foreign author, in the English language, must be printed from type set within the United States, and the printing and binding must also be performed within the limits of that country. This is a particularly onerous condition of copyright, and accounted for the fact that the great majority of English books were, prior to the alteration of the law produced by United States adherence to the Universal Copyright Convention, entirely unprotected in America.

1260 **Ad interim protection.** Section 22 of the Act, as amended in 1949,[49] afforded a substantial concession by enabling authors to obtain an *ad interim* protection for their works published abroad in the English language prior to the date of their publication in the United States. In order to obtain this *ad interim* protection, which is to have all the force and effect of copyright under the Act, deposit must be made at the Copyright Office, not later than six months after the publication of the work abroad, of a complete copy of the foreign edition,[50] with a request for the reservation of the copyright. The protection continues for five years after first publication abroad.[51] This provisional copyright becomes permanent when, within the period of provisional protection, an authorised edition of the book is published within the United States complying with the manufacturing provisions of the Act.[52] Thus, books in the English language can obtain *ad interim* protection for a period of five years from first publication abroad. Of course, if an American edition with notice of copyright can be published simultaneously with the English edition, there will be no necessity to apply for *ad interim* protection, and this is the course which is adopted by many of the larger publishing firms having offices in both countries.

1261 **Manufacturing provisions do not apply to artistic, dramatic, or musical works.** It must further be remembered that the manufactur-

[48] *Ante*, § 1245.
[49] The amendment altered the periods of deposit and protection from sixty days to six months and from four months to five years.
[50] It is not necessary that this copy should have the copyright notice required by s. 9 (Copyright Rules, r. 26).
[51] s. 22.
[52] s. 23.

ing provisions only apply to "books," and, moreover, to "the printed book or periodical specified in section 5, subsections (*a*) and (*b*)," [53] so that, not only are artistic works exempted from those provisions, but also dramatic and musical compositions, which are specified in subsections (*d*) and (*e*) of section 5, notwithstanding that such works have been printed in book form.[54] The proprietors of the copyright in such works can, therefore, obtain copyright for their foreign editions upon complying with the general formalities of the Act, without having them manufactured in the United States. First publication upon American soil is not expressly stated to be essential, provided the work has the requisite copyright notice and deposit of one copy with the requisite copyright notice has been made "promptly" at the Copyright Office in America.[55] But the doubt has been expressed whether a book, published in another country prior to publication in the United States, has not fallen into the public domain, and thus forfeited copyright protection in the United States.[56]

1262 **Universal Copyright Convention.** The position, however, of the protection afforded by the United States to works originating abroad was completely altered as a result of United States accession to the Universal Copyright Convention which was, in fact, ratified by the United States on September 16, 1955. This requires adherent countries to give protection without formality. Accordingly, by an amendment to section 9 of the Act, made by an amending Act of August 1954, a third case in which copyright under the Act may extend to the work of an author or proprietor, who is a citizen or subject of a foreign state or nation, was introduced. The amendment, subsection (*c*), provides that, when the Convention is in force between the United States and the foreign state or nation of which such author is a citizen or subject, or in which the work was first published, any work to which copyright is extended pursuant to this subsection is to be exempt from (1) the requirement that a foreign state or nation must grant to United States citizens mechanical reproduction rights similar to those specified therein; (2) the obligatory deposit requirements of the Act; (3) the manufacturing provisions; (4) the import prohibitions to the extent that they are related to the manufacturing provisions; and (5) the requirements of sections 19 and 20 of the Act relating to the copyright notice. Where this subsection applies, the only formality required, in order that a work may obtain copyright in the United States, is that "from the time of first publication all the copies of the work published with the authority of the author

53 *Ante,* § 1245.
54 *Ditson (O.) Co.* v. *Littleton* (1895) 67 Fed.Rep. 905; *Hervieu* v. *Ogilvie (J. S.) Pub. Co.* (1909) 169 Fed.Rep. 978.
55 *Ante,* § 1242.
56 Bowker, p. 127.

or other copyright proprietor shall bear the symbol © accompanied by the name of the copyright proprietor and the year of first publication placed in such manner and location as to give reasonable notice of claim of copyright." It would appear clear that this requirement involves the application of the symbol upon all copies wherever published. It is to be observed that the details of the notice required under the Act itself, in sections 19 and 20, are not made applicable to the notice under this section, though they may afford some indication of what is a " manner and location " such as to give reasonable notice of claim. It is to be observed that the notice has to appear upon all copies of the work published, which would seem to include the case of publication in a newspaper or periodical, and that the notice required is the name of the copyright proprietor, so that, if a contribution is published by licence, the notice with the name of the copyright owner must appear on the contribution as well as any notice attached to the periodical giving the owner of the general copyright in the periodical.

1263 **Effect on works having ad interim copyright.** It is further provided, by section 9, subsection (*c*) that, upon the coming into force of the Convention in a foreign state or nation, every book or periodical of a citizen or subject thereof, in which *ad interim* copyright was subsisting at the effective date of the said coming into force, is to have copyright for twenty-eight years from the date of first publication abroad without the necessity of complying with the further formalities specified in section 23 of the Act. This refers to the manufacturing provisions. Presumably, where this provision applies, the provisions of the Act itself about copyright notice, and not those of the amending subsection, are the relevant ones. As this provision is made with regard to works in existence at the date of the coming into force of the Convention, it would seem that the remaining provisions of the subsection are not intended to be restrospective, or to apply to works first published anywhere before the coming into force of the Convention, but this is a matter for decision by the United States courts.

1264 **Works to which new provisions not applicable.** It is further provided, by section 9, subsection (*c*), that the provisions of such subsection are not to extend to works of an author who is a citizen of, or domiciled in, the United States of America, regardless of place of first publication, or to works first published in the United States. This involves that works of non-American authors should not be first published in the United States, if Convention protection in the United States is desired.

1265 **When Convention came into force.** As provided by Article 9 (ix) of the Convention, the Convention came into force between the

United States and the United Kingdom, on September 27, 1957, that is three months after the United Kingdom deposited its instrument of ratification.

1266 **Treaties and Conventions.** America is not a party to the Berne Convention, but she is a party to the Pan-American Convention of 1902, including the modifications made to that Convention at Buenos Aires in 1910.[57] She also has special Copyright Treaties with China (1946), with Hungary (1912) and with Thailand (Siam) (1937).

1267 It would appear that enemy subjects did not lose their rights during the 1914–1918 war, though a law of October 6, 1917, imposed compulsory licences,[58] and it is apprehended that a similar situation arose in the 1939–1945 war.[59]

[The next paragraph is 1271]

57 *Ante*, § 1160.
58 See an article in the *Droit d'Auteur*, April 15, 1925.
59 See § 1256, *ante*, and *Copyright*, No. 10, October 1967, p. 249.

CHAPTER 28

COPYRIGHT LAWS OF COMMONWEALTH AND FOREIGN COUNTRIES

GENERAL TABLE OF LAWS [1]

	Country	Date of Principal Law	Period of Protection	Convention or other protection for United Kingdom works[2]	Effective date for UNESCO Convention
1271	Afghanistan	1950	20 years from registration	None—local registration	
	Albania	1947	Life of the author and limited rights thereafter	None	
	Andorra	None	Radio-Andorra regulated by private agreements	UNESCO	Sept. 16, 1955
	Argentina	1933	50 years from death of author	Brussels and UNESCO	Feb. 13, 1958
	Australia	1968	50 years from end of year in which author died. Photographs 50 years from end of year of publication	Brussels and UNESCO	May 1, 1969
	Austria	1936	50 years from death of author	Brussels and UNESCO	July 2, 1957
	Belgium	1886	50 years from death of author	Stockholm C, Brussels and UNESCO	Aug. 31, 1960
	Bolivia	1909	30 years from death of author	None—local registration and deposit	
	Brazil	1916	60 years from death of author	Stockholm C, Brussels and UNESCO	Jan. 13, 1960

[1] In many cases the principal law has been amended and in some cases the period of protection has been extended. This Table is intended as a general guide only and more detailed information can be obtained from *Copyright Laws and Treaties of the World*, published by UNESCO.

[2] For the purposes of this Table, countries which have ratified or acceded to the entire Stockholm revision of the Berne Convention, including the Protocol Regarding Developing Countries, are indicated thus "Stockholm A." Those countries which have declared that their ratification or accession does not apply to Articles 1 to 21 and such Protocol, are indicated thus "Stockholm B." Those countries which have given notification under Article 38 (2) are indicated thus "Stockholm C." Those countries which have made a declaration under Article 5 (1) (*a*) of such Protocol are indicated thus "Stockholm D." Those countries which have made a declaration under Article 5 (1) (*b*) of such Protocol are indicated thus "Stockholm E." See §§ 1152 and 1153, *ante*.

Country	Date of Principal Law	Period of Protection	Convention or other protection for United Kingdom works	Effective date for UNESCO Convention
Bulgaria	1951	The life of the author and limited rights thereafter	Stockholm C and E and Rome	
Cambodia	1934	Uncertain	UNESCO	Sept. 16, 1955
Cameroon	Uncertain	Uncertain	Stockholm C and Brussels	
Canada	1952	50 years from death of author	Stockholm B, Rome and UNESCO	Aug. 10, 1962
Ceylon	1911	50 years from death of author	Rome	
Chile	1925	50 years from death of author	Brussels and UNESCO	Sept. 16, 1955
China	1928	30 years from death of author	None—local registration	
Colombia	1946	80 years from death of author	Local registration apparently required	
Congo (Brazzaville)	1957	50 years from December 31 of the year of the author's death	Brussels	
Congo (Kinshasa)	Uncertain	Uncertain	Brussels	
Costa Rica	1896	50 years from death of author	UNESCO	Sept. 16, 1955
Cuba [3]	1879	80 years from death of author	UNESCO	June 18, 1957
Cyprus	1911	50 years from death of author	Rome	
Czechoslovakia	1965	50 years from December 31 of the year of the author's death	Stockholm C, Rome and UNESCO	Jan. 6, 1960
Dahomey	Uncertain	Uncertain	Stockholm C and Brussels	
Denmark	1961	50 years from death of author	Stockholm B, Brussels and UNESCO	Feb. 9, 1962
Dominican Republic	1947	30 years from death of author	None—local registration	
Ecuador	1957	50 years from death of author	UNESCO	June 5, 1957
El Salvador	1963	50 years from death of author	None	
Ethiopia	1960	The life of the author and limited rights thereafter	None	
Finland	1961	50 years from death of author	Stockholm B, Brussels and UNESCO	April 16, 1963

[3] The present position as to protection in Cuba is uncertain.

Country	Date of Principal Law	Period of Protection	Convention or other protection for United Kingdom works	Effective date for UNESCO Convention
France	1957	50 years from December 31 of the year of the author's death	Stockholm C, Brussels and UNESCO	Jan. 14, 1956
Gabon	Uncertain	Uncertain	Stockholm C and Brussels	
German Democratic Republic	1965	50 years from December 31 of year of author's death	None[4]	
German Federal Republic (and Land Berlin)	1965	70 years from death of author	Stockholm B, Brussels and UNESCO	Sept. 16, 1955
Ghana	1961	The end of the year in which the author dies or 25 years from end of year of publication whichever is later	UNESCO	Aug. 22, 1962
Greece	1920	50 years from December 31, of the year of the author's death	Stockholm C, Brussels and UNESCO	Aug. 24, 1963
Guatemala	1954	50 years from death of author	UNESCO	Oct. 28, 1964
Haiti	1968	Life of author and 25 years	UNESCO	Sept. 16, 1955
Holy See	1960	The end of the 50th calendar year from the death of the author	Stockholm C, Brussels and UNESCO	Oct. 5, 1955
Honduras	1919	10, 15 or 20 years from issue of patent according to importance of work	None—local registration as patents	
Hungary	1969	50 years from death of author	Stockholm C, Rome and UNESCO	Jan. 23, 1971
Iceland	1905	50 years from death of author	Rome and UNESCO	Dec. 18, 1956
India	1957	50 years from January 1, following death of author	Brussels and UNESCO	Jan. 21, 1958
Indonesia	1912	50 years from death of author	None	
Iran	1970	30 years from death of author	Uncertain	

[4] The present convention status of the German Democratic Republic is uncertain.

Country	Date of Principal Law	Period of Protection	Convention or other protection for United Kingdom works	Effective date for UNESCO Convention
Ireland, Republic of	1963	50 years from December 31 of year of the author's death	Stockholm B, Brussels and UNESCO	Jan. 20, 1959
Israel	1911	50 years from January 1, following the death of the author	Stockholm B, Brussels and UNESCO	Sept. 16, 1955
Italy	1941	The end of the 50th calendar year from the death of the author	Stockholm C, Brussels and UNESCO	Jan. 24, 1957
Ivory Coast	Uncertain	Uncertain	Stockholm C, and Brussels	
Japan	1970	50 years from beginning of year after author's death	Stockholm C, Rome and UNESCO	April 28, 1956
Jordan	1912	30 years from death of author	None	
Kenya	1966	25 years from end of year in which author dies	UNESCO	Sept. 7, 1966
Korea	1957	30 years from January 1, following death of author	None—local registration	
Laos	1957	50 years from December 31, of the year of the author's death	UNESCO	Sept. 16, 1955
Lebanon	1924	50 years from death of author	Rome and UNESCO	Oct. 17, 1959
Liberia	1911	25 years after death of author	UNESCO	July 27, 1956
Libya	1968	25 years from death of author or 50 years from first publication whichever is the longer	Protection under local law	
Liechtenstein	1928	50 years from death of author	Brussels and UNESCO	Jan. 22, 1959
Luxembourg	1898	50 years from death of author	Stockholm C, Brussels and UNESCO	Oct. 15, 1955
Madagascar (Malagasy Republic)	1957	50 years from December 31, of the year of the author's death	Brussels	

Country	Date of Principal Law	Period of Protection	Convention or other protection for United Kingdom works	Effective date for UNESCO Convention
Malawi	1965	25 years from death of author	UNESCO	Oct. 26, 1965
Malaysia	1969	25 years after end of year in which author dies	Protection under local law	
Mali	Uncertain	Uncertain	Brussels	
Malta	1967	25 years after end of year in which author dies	Stockholm C, Rome and UNESCO	Nov. 19, 1968
Mauritius	Uncertain	Uncertain	UNESCO	Mar. 12, 1968
Mexico	1963	30 years from death of author	Brussels and UNESCO	May 12, 1957
Monaco	1948	50 years from death of author	Brussels and UNESCO	Sept. 16, 1955
Morocco	1970	50 years from the end of the year in which author died	Stockholm C and Brussels	
Nepal	1966	50 years from death of author	None—local registration	
Netherlands	1912	50 years from death of author	Stockholm C, Rome and UNESCO	June 22, 1967
New Zealand	1962	50 years from the end of calendar year in which author died	Rome and UNESCO	Sept. 11, 1964
Nicaragua	1904	Life of the author with limited rights thereafter	UNESCO	Aug. 16, 1961
Niger	Uncertain	Uncertain	Stockholm C and Brussels	
Nigeria	1911	50 years from death of author	UNESCO	Feb. 14, 1962
Norway	1961	50 years from end of the year of death of author	Stockholm C, Brussels and UNESCO	Jan. 23, 1963
Pakistan	1962	50 years from January 1, following the death of the author	Stockholm A [5] and D, Rome and UNESCO	Sept. 16, 1955
Panama	1916	80 years from death of author	UNESCO	Oct. 17, 1962
Paraguay	1951	50 years from death of author	UNESCO	Mar. 11, 1962
Peru	1961	50 years from January 1, following the death of the author	UNESCO	Oct. 16, 1963

[5] Pakistan's accession was accompanied by a declaration in which Pakistan availed itself of the reservations provided in Art. 1 of the Protocol with the exception of that in para. (*a*) of that Article.

Country	Date of Principal Law	Period of Protection	Convention or other protection for United Kingdom works	Effective date for UNESCO Convention
Philippines	1924	30 years from registration and a further 30 years on renewal	Brussels and UNESCO	Nov. 19, 1955 [6]
Poland	1952	20 years from death of author	Rome	
Portugal	1966	50 years from death of author	Stockholm C, Brussels and UNESCO	Dec. 25, 1956
Rumania	1956	The life of the author and limited rights thereafter	Stockholm A [7] and Rome	
Senegal	Uncertain	Uncertain	Stockholm A and D and Brussels	
Sierra Leone	1965	50 years from the end of the calendar year in which the author died	Protection under local law	
South Africa	1965	50 years from the end of the calendar year in which the author died	Stockholm C and Brussels	
Spain	1879	80 years from death of author	Stockholm B, Brussels and UNESCO	Sept. 16, 1955
Sweden	1960	End of 50th year after year author died	Stockholm B and E, Brussels and UNESCO	July 1, 1961
Switzerland	1922	50 years from death of author	Stockholm B, Brussels and UNESCO	Mar. 30, 1956
Syria	1924	50 years from death of author	None—local deposit	
Tanzania	1966	25 years from death of author	Protection under local law	
Thailand	1931	30 years from death of author	Berlin	
Tunisia	1966	50 years from death of author	Stockholm C, Brussels and UNESCO	June 19, 1969
Turkey	1951	50 years from death of author	Stockholm C and Brussels	

6 The accession of the Philippines to the UNESCO Convention appears to have been withdrawn.

7 Rumania's ratification was accompanied by a declaration made in conformity with Art. 7 (7) and a declaration made in conformity with Art. 33 (2).

Country	Date of Principal Law	Period of Protection	Convention or other protection for United Kingdom works	Effective date for UNESCO Convention
Uganda	1964	50 years from end of year in which author dies	Protection under local law	
United Arab Republic	1954	50 years from death of author	None	
United States of America	1947	28 years from publication and a further 28 years on renewal [8]	UNESCO	Sept. 16, 1955
U.S.S.R. [9]	1964	15 years from January 1 of year of the death of author	None	
Upper Volta	Uncertain	Uncertain	None [10]	
Uruguay	1937	40 years from death of author	Brussels	
Venezuela	1962	50 years from January 1 of year after death of author	UNESCO	Sept. 30, 1966
Western Samoa [11]	1962	50 years from the end of calendar year in which author died	Rome	
Yugoslavia	1968	50 years from death of author	Stockholm C, Brussels and UNESCO	May 11, 1966
Zambia	1965	25 years from death of author	UNESCO	June 1, 1965

[The next paragraph is 1281]

[8] See § 1237, *ante*.

[9] A resolution of the Supreme Soviet on December 8, 1961, decided to approve new Bases of Legislation affecting copyright and to bring them into force on May 1, 1962. It also recommended the establishment of Procedure to bring into force these Bases in respect of the civil law of the U.S.S.R. and to bring the legislation of the U.S.S.R. into conformity with them. This appears to have been done: see " General Study: Copyright in the U.S.S.R." by R. Gorelik, UNESCO Copyright Bulletin, Vol. III, No. 4, 1969, p. 32. The 1964 law came into force on October 1, 1969.

[10] Upper Volta has denounced the Berne Convention, revised at Brussels, with effect from September 20, 1970.

[11] The position as to Samoa is uncertain. The New Zealand Copyright Act, 1913, repealed by the New Zealand Copyright Act, 1962, applied to Samoa by virtue of the Samoa Act, 1921.

Part VII

FORMS AND PRECEDENTS

FORMS

A.—General Descriptions.

(i) Of Rights.
(ii) Of Works.

B.—Licence Forms.

(i) Descriptions of Rights.
(ii) Term.
(iii) General.

C.—Forms for Publishing Agreements.

D.—Forms for Theatre and Film Agreements.

PRECEDENTS

1.—General.

(i) Assignment of Copyright (General Form).
(ii) Assignment of Copyright (Short Form).
(iii) Licence (General Form).
(iv) Licence (Short Form).
(v) Agreement for Sale.
(vi) Agreement for Sale where Assignments Postponed.
(vii) Assignment or Licence of Future Copyright.

2.—Publishing Agreements.

(i) Copyright Assigned for Single Payment.
(ii) Royalty Agreement.
(iii) Publishing on Commission Basis.
(iv) Profit-sharing Agreement.
(v) Agreement to Write and Assign Copyright in a Work.
(vi) Agreement with Respect to a New Edition.

3.—Theatre and Film Agreements.

(i) Licence for a Single Performance of a Play.
(ii) Agreement for a Single Run of a Play at a Theatre on Royalty Terms—Options.
(iii) Limited Copyright in a Play vested in Producer.
(iv) Licence to make a Film of a Novel.
(v) Agreement as to Film where Copyright in Novel and Play on which it is Based are vested in Different Persons.

FORMS

A.—General Descriptions

1281 (i) *Of Rights* [1]

ll rights e United dom

The copyright (which expression shall mean the exclusive right to do all acts which under the provisions of the Copyright Act, 1956, are restricted by the copyright in a [literary work *or as may be*]) in the United Kingdom [and in any other country to which the said Act extends], in [*insert description of work*].

ll rights parts of vorld

The copyright and all other rights of a like nature now conferred in respect of the work hereinafter mentioned by the law in force [in any part of the world] [*or* in the Republic of France] [*or* in the United States of America or any State thereof *or as may be*] in [*insert description of the work*].

forming

The sole right to perform [including] [*or* but not including] performances by means of sound broadcasting and television and by causing the work to be transmitted to subscribers to a diffusion service [2] [*insert description of the work*] in public [in any part of the world *or as may be*].

ight to and sh

The sole right to print and publish in any form and [in any language] [*or* in the English language only *or as may be*] in [any part of the world *or as may be*] the whole or any part of [*insert description of the work*].

ansla-

The sole right to translate into the [ ] language and to print and publish in [any part of the world *or as may be*] such translation of [*insert description of the work*].

amatisa-

The sole right [in any part of the world *or as may be*] to convert [*insert description of the work*] into a dramatic work and to print and publish [and to perform in public] such dramatic work.

[1] The Copyright Act, 1956, introduces certain novelties in language in its definitions, such as including the right to dramatise and the right to translate under the words "making any adaptation of the work" and including the making of records and cinematograph films under the words "reproducing the work." Since the Act extends only to the United Kingdom and Colonies, while copyright documents usually have a wider scope, it is preferable not to use such special definitions unless United Kingdom rights only are intended to be covered.

[2] For the purposes of the Copyright Act, 1956, these acts are not to constitute "performance" (s. 48 (5)), but in a contractual instrument it is thought "performance" might have a wider meaning. It will be safer either to include or exclude these acts expressly.

7. Film right — The sole right [in any part of the world *or as may be*] to reproduce [*insert description of the work*] in the form of cinematograph films [and to perform the said work in public by means of such films].

8. Gramophone records — The sole right [in any part of the world *or as may be*] to make records of [ ] by means of which [*insert description of the work*] may be automatically reproduced.

1282 (ii) *Of Works*

9. Any work — The [literary] [dramatic] [musical] *or* [artistic] work entitled [ ].

10. Work identified — A work [written] [composed] [prepared *or as may be*] by A.B. of [ ] a copy whereof has for the purpose of identification been signed by [ ] under date [ ] and deposited with [ ].

11. Parts of a collective work — The several parts of the work entitled [ ] of which A.B. of [ ] is the author.

12. Letterpress only — The letterpress but not the illustrations of the work entitled [ ].

13. New edition — All the new copyright material constituted by the alterations and additions made in the [ ] edition of [*insert description of work*] to the form, subject-matter, notes and indexes of the [ ] edition of the said work.

14. New arrangement — The new arrangement of the musical work entitled [ ] made by A.B. of [ ].

15. Film — The cinematograph film entitled [ ] and the dramatic action thereof.

16. Sound recordings — The sound recordings embodied in records made by A.B. Ltd. and numbered [ ] in their catalogue of the musical works entitled [ ].

17. Painting — A painting [entitled] [representing] [ ] and painted by A.B. of [ ].

18. Sculpture — A work of sculpture [entitled] [representing] [ ] and made by [ ].

19. Photograph — A photograph representing [ ] of which the original negative [was made by [ ]] [*or* is deposited with [ ]].

rchi- al plans — The plans for a building at [ ] a complete copy whereof has been signed by [ ].

uilding — The features of artistic character and design in a building at [ ].

horeo- ic work — A choreographic work produced by [ ] a copy of the notation identifying which [has been signed by] [*or* is annexed hereto].

B.—LICENCE FORMS

1283

(i) *Descriptions of Rights* [3]

eneral — The [sole and exclusive] right to [*insert any of the rights in Form A, Clauses* 3–8].

ook form — The [sole and exclusive] right to print and publish the work in book form in any part of the world in the [ ] language.

rial — The [sole and exclusive] right to print and publish the work in serial form in the [ ] newspaper.

Or

First British serial rights in the work entitled [ ], that is to say, the exclusive right to publish the work in a newspaper or magazine primarily published in Great Britain before publication thereof elsewhere or in any other form [provided always that this right shall lapse if not exercised prior to the of next].[4]

ny n — The [sole and exclusive right] to print and publish the work in the first and all subsequent editions [and reprints] of [ ].

ight to sis — The [sole and exclusive] right in any part of the world to make and publish and to authorise the making and publishing of a synopsis of not exceeding [ ] words in length of the said work or any parts or part thereof.

ight to h as a story — The [sole and exclusive] right in any part of the world to make and publish and to authorise the making and publishing of the said work in the form of a short story or serial story.

[3] Having regard to the difficulty of determining whether an assignment or a licence is intended, any grant of a licence should either be expressed to be " by way of licence only " or clause 29 should be used.

[4] This clause or very similar terms are frequently used in journalism but the exact customary meaning is not altogether certain. It is suggested that the clause should be used in full when practicable. The clause can be readily adapted for " first serial rights " " second British serial rights," etc.

7. Right to make records

The [sole and exclusive] right to make records whereby the said work may be automatically reproduced [but not] [*or* and] to perform the said work in public by means of such records.

8. Film right

The [sole and exclusive] right to reproduce the words and music of the said work in the form of cinematograph films [but not] [*or* and] to perform the same in public by means of such films or otherwise.

Or

The mechanical right in the said musical work, that is to say, the right to authorise the embodiment of the same in a record and the right to embody the same in the sound-track of a cinematograph film, provided that the same constitutes only background or incidental music in respect of such film.

9. Right to make film or record of musical work as part of film

The right to reproduce the said work as part of the film now in course of production and entitled [ ] but not otherwise [but not] [*or* and] to perform the said work in public [as part of such film].

10. Right to reproduce artistic work

The [sole and exclusive] right to make reproductions in any form of the said artistic work.

11. Limited right to reproduce photograph

The right to reproduce the said photograph once only [in the first edition only of] the said proposed book.

12. Right to reproduce drawing for purpose of named work

The right to reproduce the said drawing as often as may be required in the first and any subsequent edition of the work entitled [ ].

13. Importation

The right to import into and sell in [ ] [not exceeding] copies of the work.

14. Performance in public at a theatre

The [sole and exclusive] right to perform the said work in public at the [ ] Theatre.

15. Performance in public as a separate work

The [sole and exclusive] right to perform the said work in public as a separate work but not as part of any other work.

16. Performance in public as part of a work only

The [sole and exclusive] right to perform the said work in public as part of the work entitled [ ] but not separately.

erform- n with hed only

The [sole and exclusive] right to perform the said song in public with the music published therewith but not with any other music.

imited e as to form- rt of

The [sole and exclusive] right to perform in public the words and music of any songs forming part of the musical play entitled [ ] but so that not more than [ ] of such songs shall be performed in public at one time.

road- g

The [sole and exclusive] right to perform the said work in public by means of sound broadcasting [and television] [provided that this licence shall not be deemed to confer any right upon the licensee] [*or* and] to authorise any other person receiving such broadcast and television performances to perform the said work in public by re-broadcasting or otherwise.

ight to m s

The [sole and exclusive] right to perform in public records made by [ ] of the work entitled [ ] [but not] [*or* and] to perform the said work in public by means of such records [without the consent of the owner of the right to perform the said work in public].

ight to rise

And to authorise other persons [in the same area *or as may be*] to do any of the acts aforesaid.

1284 (ii) *Term*

ixed

For the period commencing on the of and terminating on the of

otice

Until the Licence shall be determined by notice or otherwise as hereinafter provided.

eek

For the week commencing on the of

erm of ght

During [the remainder of] the term of copyright subsisting in the said work.

o long nber of man- pt up

For so long as performances in public at least of the said work shall be given in pursuance of this Licence in a consecutive period of months [and the royalties herein prescribed are duly paid].

27. Terminable on bankruptcy, etc.

This Licence shall determine:

(a) on the death or bankruptcy of the Licensee.

(b) in the event of a resolution being passed or an order being made for the winding up of the Licensee.

(c) on the receipt by the Licensee of a notice in writing from the Grantor of his intention to determine this Licence.

28. Notice; formal clause

The Grantor may at any time after of by notice in writing to the Licensee determine the Licence hereby granted [as from a date not less than months after the date of such notice].

1285

(iii) *General*

29. No assignment implied

The grant to the Licensee herein contained shall be deemed to be by way of licence only and shall not confer upon the Licensee any right or interest in the copyright of the said work.

30. Personal to Licensee

The rights hereby granted shall be personal to the Licensee who shall not be entitled to authorise any other person to exercise the same.

31. Personal to Licensee and his servants

The rights hereby granted may be exercised by the Licensee or any persons in his employ but the Licensee shall not be entitled to authorise any other person to exercise the same.

32. Licence to persons authorised

The rights hereby granted shall be exercisable by the Licensee or by any person authorised by him.

33. Licence assignable or not

The Licensee shall [not] be entitled to assign the benefit of this Licence.

34. Agreement by Grantor to assign benefit to person acquiring business of Licensee

In the event of the business of the Licensee being transferred to another person firm or company then if such person firm or company shall offer to enter into an agreement with the Grantor on the same terms (as far as applicable) as those of this agreement the Grantor shall grant to such person firm or company the same licences and rights as are hereby granted to the Licensee.

35. Agreement by Grantor not to assign benefit

The Grantor shall not during the period of the Licence hereby granted make any assignment of any of the rights affected by the said Licence [without the previous consent in writing of the Licensee].

The Grantor shall at all times keep the Licensee indemnified against all claims demands actions or proceedings by any person made or brought against the Licensee in respect of any exercise by the Licensee during the said period of any of the rights comprised in the Licence hereby granted and against all damages costs and expenses paid or incurred by the Licensee [and from all loss or damage suffered by the Licensee] as a result of any such claim demand action or proceeding.

286

C.—FORMS FOR PUBLISHING AGREEMENTS

The Publisher shall print and publish the said work [*or* an edition of copies of the said work] at his sole risk and expense [on or before the of 19] [and shall use his best endeavours to sell the same] [provided that nothing herein contained shall preclude the Publisher from publishing or selling or being interested in the publication or sale of any other works dealing whether specifically or sectionally or generally with the subject-matter of the Author's said work and the Author shall not have any right of action against the Publisher in respect of the publication or sale of such other works by the Publisher or in respect of his interest in the publication or sale of such other works].

The Publisher shall have a full discretion as to the method of publication of the said work and as to the form size get-up and advertising thereof [and as to the price at which copies are to be sold].

The said work shall be printed in [*insert provisions as to size of page and of print, etc.*].

The Publisher shall print and publish an edition of copies of the said work in [*insert provisions as to size and type of printing of a luxury edition*] to be sold at a retail price of per copy and an edition of copies of the said work [*insert provisions as to ordinary edition*] to be sold at a retail price of per copy.

The Author shall correct and revise with due dispatch in the usual manner the proofs [of the said work] [*or* of the first and each subsequent edition of the said work] and will complete and see the same through the press.

Should the Author fail to deliver the complete manuscript of the said work by the Author shall pay to the Publisher a sum of £ per week until the complete manuscript is so delivered as and by way of liquidated damages for such non-delivery.

7. Cost of corrections charged to Author

If the cost of alterations and corrections in the proof sheets and revisions shall exceed an average cost of   per sheet of sixteen pages such excess shall be borne and paid by the Author or shall be deducted out of any sums payable to him hereunder.

8. Free copies

The Author shall be entitled to   copies of the said work free of charge.

9. Author to approve advertisements

No paper cover or advertisement shall be issued by the Publisher in respect of the said work unless the design and letterpress thereof shall have been first approved by the Author [provided that such approval shall not be unreasonably withheld].

10. Publisher to secure U.S.A. copyright

The Publisher shall use his best endeavours to secure copyright protection for the said work in the United States of America.

Or

The Publisher shall secure that all copies of the work shall bear the symbol © accompanied by the name of the copyright proprietor and the year of first publication placed in such manner and location as to give reasonable notice of claim to copyright.[5]

11. Retail price per copy

The said work shall be sold in the United Kingdom of Great Britain and Northern Ireland at the retail price of   per copy and in all other parts of the world at such price as the Publisher may from time to time in his discretion think proper.

12. Retail price per copy. Another form

The said work shall be sold—

(a) in Great Britain Northern Ireland and the Republic of Ireland at the retail price of   per copy.

(b) in the Dominion of Canada and the United States of America at the retail price of   per copy.

(c) in all other parts of the British Commonwealth at a retail price of   per copy.

(d) in other parts of the world at such a price as may from time to time be agreed between the Author and the Publisher.

13. Licence

The copyright in the said work shall remain vested in the Author but the Publisher shall have the sole and exclusive right for a period of   years from the date hereof to print and publish the said

[5] This is now essential to secure copyright without other formality in the U.S.A.

work [in book form] [in any part of the world] [*or* " in Great Britain and Northern Ireland " *or as may be, see Forms A* (*i*), *Clauses* 1 *and* 2] [*add, if desired,* " and to broadcast the said work in any part of the world." *If this addition is made, provision as to broadcasting royalties must be inserted*].

ump ay-

The Publisher shall pay to the Author on the day on which the said work is published the sum of £

ayment gle

The Publisher shall pay to the Author in respect of the said article on the day on which the said work shall be published a sum calculated at £ for every words of the said article.

oyalty d sum py, orm

The Publisher shall pay to the Author a royalty of for every copy of the said work sold by the Publisher [*or* of for each of the first copies of the said work sold by the Publisher and for every copy in excess of sold by the Publisher].

oyalty[6] centage ng short

The Publisher shall pay to the Author a royalty of per cent. of the retail price in respect of all copies of the said work sold by the Publisher.

oyalty g in nt

The Publisher shall pay to the Author a royalty of—

(a) per copy in respect of every copy of the said work sold by the Publisher in Great Britain and Northern Ireland and the Republic of Ireland.

(b) per copy in respect of every copy of the said work sold by the Publisher in Canada and the United States of America.

(c) per copy in respect of every copy of the said work sold by the Publisher in any other part of the British Commonwealth.

(d) per copy on the retail selling price at which copies are sold in respect of any copies of the said work sold in any other part of the world.

(e) per cent. of the net sum received by the Publisher in respect of copies or sheets sold by the Publisher outright for resale in

(f) per cent. of the net sum received by the Publisher in respect of any sub-licence granted by him for publication of the work in

[6] Special provision will be required in this and the following clauses where it is contemplated that there will be sales to Book Clubs on special terms. A special royalty or lump sum arrangement may be made for a cheap edition to be acquired by a Book Club.

19. Royalty increasing in proportion to number of copies sold

The Publisher shall pay to the Author a royalty of per cent. of the retail price of the first copies of the said work sold by the Publisher per cent. on the next copies of the said work sold by the Publisher and per cent. on all copies of the said work sold by the Publisher in excess of copies.

20. Royalty varying with retail selling price

The Publisher shall pay to the Author a royalty of per cent. of the retail price of all copies of the said work sold at per copy and of per cent. of the retail price of all copies of the said work sold at per copy.

Or

[*after a provision as to royalties on the original price of issue, add*] and if the said work shall be reissued at a retail price of [less than per copy] [*or* less than half the original retail price] a royalty of per copy.

21. No royalty on review copies

No royalties shall be payable in respect of any copies given away for review or other purposes [provided that not more than copies shall be given away without the previous consent of the Author].

22. Payment for serial rights, etc.

The Publisher shall pay to the Author royalties at the rates hereafter specified on all sums received by the Publisher in connection with the exercise of the respective rights set opposite thereto which the Publisher is accordingly hereby authorised and licensed by the Author to dispose of as the Publisher may think fit.

per cent.	First serial rights.
per cent.	Second serial rights.
per cent.	Translation rights.
per cent.	Broadcasting rights.
per cent.	Right to record on gramophone records or similar contrivances.
per cent.	Digest rights.
per cent.	Anthology rights.
per cent.	For the reproduction of extracts, quotations, single illustrations, or other artistic material.[7]

23. Royalties not dependent on payment to Publisher

Royalties shall be paid in respect of all copies sold by the Publisher whether the price thereof is received by the Publisher or not.

[7] This clause is intended to deal only with what in relation to a particular work may be regarded as minor rights. In the case of more important subsidiary rights clauses 37 or 38 below should be used.

yalties ent nent isher

Royalties shall only be paid in respect of sums actually received by the Publisher.

vance

The Publisher shall pay to the Author [on the signing hereof] [*or* on delivery of the manuscript] the sum of £ as advance and on account of royalties payable hereunder but no part thereof shall be returnable whether or not an equivalent amount of royalty is earned.

nual ts

Accounts shall be delivered by the Publisher to the Author annually on the of and the Publisher shall pay to the Author on or before the next succeeding of the amount shown due on such account.

riodi- ounts

Accounts in respect of the period ending [six] months after the date of publication of the work and in respect of every successive period of [six] months thereafter shall be delivered by the Publisher to the Author showing the amount due to the Author in accordance with the provisions hereof in respect of the period covered by each such account. The said accounts shall be delivered within [one] month after the termination of each such period and the Publisher shall within [three] months after the termination of each such period pay to the Author the amount due to him in respect of such period.

rticu- be d in ts

Every account shall show the number of copies of the said works sold by the Publisher during the period covered by such account and the price at which each such copy was sold and all other particulars necessary for the ascertainment of any sums to be paid to the Author under the provisions hereof.

thor spect

The Author shall have the right himself or by any accountant appointed by him from time to time on reasonable notice to the Publisher to inspect all books, vouchers and documents in the possession of the Publisher relating to the sale of copies of the said work [and relating to the expenses of production and publication of the said work].

ovi- r g for- ebit

In case the expenses of the Publisher in respect of any accounting period calculated as hereinbefore provided shall exceed the gross profits calculated as hereinbefore provided in respect of such period such excess shall be carried forward and added to the expenses of the Publisher in the next accounting period provided always that if there shall be such an excess [after all the copies hereby agreed to be published have been sold or disposed of] [*or* at the determination of this agreement] then such excess shall be borne [exclusively by the Publisher] [*or* by the Publisher and the Author in equal shares *or as may be*].

31. Power of Publisher to sell off copies

At the expiration of years from the date hereof [and at the expiration of years from the date of publication of any subsequent edition of the said work] the Publisher shall be at liberty to sell off at such price and in such manner as he may think desirable all copies [of the said work] [*or* respectively of the first and any such subsequent edition of the said work].

32. New edition

If at any time before the expiration of the said period of years the Publisher shall give notice in writing to the Author that he intends to print a new edition of the said work then provided that he shall actually publish such new edition within months after the date of such notice all the provisions hereof shall apply in respect of such new edition and the said sole and exclusive licence shall be extended for a further period of years from the date of such notice.

33. Termination for failure to publish

If the said work shall not be published before the of [*or* if any such new edition as aforesaid shall not be published within months after the date of such notice as aforesaid] then on the of [*or* at the expiration of the said period of months] this agreement and the sole and exclusive licence hereby granted shall determine.

34. Termination for breach or insolvency

If the Publisher shall [become bankrupt] [*or* be wound up otherwise than for the purposes of amalgamation or reconstruction] [or if the Publisher shall commit any breach of the provisions of this agreement and shall fail to remedy the same within of notice requiring him to do so] this agreement and the sole and exclusive licence hereby granted shall determine.

35. Publisher appointed sole agent to negotiate other rights

The Author appoints the Publisher to be his sole and exclusive agent for a period of years from the date hereof to negotiate for and in respect of the disposal by way of licence assignment or otherwise of all rights in the said work in all parts of the world (other than the rights therein hereby granted to the Publisher) on the terms that the Author shall pay to the Publisher a commission of per cent. on all sums received by the Author in respect of any assignment licence or other disposition of rights in the said work made during the said period.

ption
iire
r's
work

The Author shall submit to the Publisher for consideration [all works of fiction of over   words in length written by him during a period of   years from the date hereof] [*or* the next three works of fiction completed by him after the date hereof] and if the Publisher by notice in writing to the Author within   weeks of the submission thereof to the Publisher expresses a desire to acquire the same the Author shall grant in respect thereof to the Publisher the same rights as are hereby granted in respect of the said work upon the same terms as are herein contained [provided always that if the Publisher shall fail to acquire any work submitted to him as aforesaid the agreement contained in this clause shall thereafter cease to have effect].

ption to
e cer-
ghts
ap sum
nt

(i) The Publisher shall have the option to be exercised by notice in writing to be given to the Author within   months after the date of the publication of the said work to acquire on the terms hereinafter mentioned: (a) for the sum of £   the sole right to translate the said work into any foreign language and to print and publish any such translation in any part of the world; (b) for the sum of £   the sole right in any part of the world to convert the said work into one or more dramatic works and to print and publish and to perform in public either on the stage or by broadcasting (sound and television) such dramatic work or works; (c) for the sum of £   the sole right in any part of the world to make one or more cinematograph films reproducing the said work and to perform the said work in public by means of such films; (d) for the sum of £   the sole right to broadcast (by sound and television) the work or any part thereof; or any one or more of such sole rights.

(ii) If the Publisher shall duly give notice to the Author of his desire to acquire any of the said sole rights and shall pay to the Author within   months of the date of such notice the consideration to be paid in respect thereof the Author shall thereafter upon the request and at the expense of the Publisher do all such acts and execute all such documents as may be necessary to vest such sole rights in the Publisher for the whole of the term of copyright subsisting therein or such part thereof as is capable of assignment.

ption to
e rights
alty

(a) If the Publisher shall within   months after the date of publication of the said work by the Publisher give to the Author notice in writing of his intention to exercise any of the options hereby granted and pay to the Author the several sums hereafter mentioned in respect thereof then:—

(i) on payment of the sum of £   the Publisher shall during the period of   from the date hereof have the sole and exclusive right to print and publish or to authorise others to print and publish translations of the said work in any part of the world;

(ii) on payment of the sum of £ the Publisher shall during the period of from the date hereof have the sole and exclusive right to print and publish or to authorise others to print and publish the said work in serial form in any part of the world [8];

(iii) on payment of the sum of £ the Publisher shall during the period of from the date hereof have the sole and exclusive right in any part of the world to convert the said work into one or more dramatic works and to print and publish and to perform in public such dramatic work or works on the stage or by broadcasting (sound and television) and to authorise others to do any of the acts aforesaid;

(iv) on payment of the sum of £ the Publisher shall during the period of from the date hereof have the sole and exclusive right in any part of the world to make one or more cinematograph films reproducing the said work and to perform the said work in public by means of such film or films and to authorise others to do any of the acts aforesaid.

(b) The Publisher shall pay to the Author upon all sums received by the Publisher in respect of any exercise of any of the rights vested in the Publisher by virtue of any of the said options:—

(i) in the case of any exercise of the rights referred to in sub-clause (a) (i) a royalty of per cent.;

(ii) in the case of any exercise of the rights referred to in sub-clause (a) (ii) a royalty of per cent.;

(iii) in the case of any exercise of the rights referred to in sub-clause (a) (iii) a royalty of per cent.;

(iv) in the case of any exercise of the rights referred to in sub-clause (a) (iv) a royalty of per cent.

Provided always that the sum paid to the Author upon the taking up by the Publisher of any of the said options shall be deemed paid on account of any royalties payable in respect of that option but shall not be returnable in any event.

[8] Publication of the whole work as a supplement to a newspaper is not a proper exercise of serialisation rights: *Jonathan Cape, Ltd.* v. *Consolidated Press, Ltd.* [1954] 1 W.L.R. 1313. " Second serial rights " are now frequently granted usually for particular territories. This expression has not been interpreted by the courts but presumably means a licence to publish in serial form in the prescribed territory after a serialisation has already taken place therein. The grantor of such rights is well advised to stipulate that a first serialisation shall appear before some prescribed date, since otherwise " second serialisation rights " may prove of little value.

(c) The provisions herein contained as to accounts and payment of royalties hereunder shall apply to royalties payable under this clause.

(d) The rights hereby granted to the Publisher shall be deemed to be granted by way of licence only.

(e) The Author shall not make any assignment or grant any licence in respect of any of the rights mentioned in this clause until after the expiration of the said period of months from the date of publication of the said work or (in respect of any such rights as the Publisher may elect to acquire) until the determination of the period during which the licence hereby granted is to extend.

xtracts pying aries

The Publisher shall be entitled to grant licences for the publication of short extracts or quotations from the said work or for the copying of the said work by such libraries as are referred to in section 7 of the Copyright Act, 1956, and the Regulations made thereunder in any case in which copying without licence would be authorised by that section if the librarian did not know and could not by reasonable inquiry ascertain the name and address of the person entitled to authorise copying and shall in any such case pay to the Author per cent. of all sums received.

urther nce

(i) The Author shall at any time and from time to time hereafter at the request of the Publisher [*or* The Author hereby irrevocably appoints the Publisher his attorney in his name and on his behalf to] execute all such instruments, institute, be a party to or defend either alone or in concert with the Publisher all such proceedings and do all such acts or things as the Publisher may require for the purpose in any part of the world to which this agreement extends of establishing, protecting, enforcing or recovering damages or penalties in respect of any of the rights hereby conferred upon the Publisher provided that the Publisher shall pay and keep the Author indemnified against the whole [*or* part] of any cost or expenses paid or incurred by the Author in or as a result of his doing or being a party to any of the acts or proceedings aforesaid in pursuance of this clause [and provided further that the Author shall not be required to incur any cost or expense under this clause unless he shall be provided by the Publisher with a full and sufficient indemnity in respect of any such cost or expense].

(ii) All sums recovered by the Author in respect of any infringement of any of the rights comprised in this agreement [shall be paid to the Publisher] [*or* shall belong to the Author and the Publisher in equal shares] [*or* shall belong to the Publisher but shall be deemed proceeds of the said work upon which royalties are payable as herein provided].

41. Indemnity

The Author shall keep the Publisher indemnified against all actions proceedings claims or demands made against the Publisher by reason of anything contained in the said work constituting an infringement of copyright or being defamatory and against all costs damages or expenses in respect of any such action proceeding claim or demand.

42. Warranty

The author warrants that he is the owner of the copyright in the said work [and that copyright subsists therein] and that he has not made any assignment of or granted any licence in respect of any of the rights in the said work comprised in this agreement.

43. Fire risk

The Publisher shall be under no liability to the Author for any loss which the Author may suffer by reason of the loss or damage by fire of any copies of the said work while in the Publisher's possession or under his control and the Publisher shall not be required to repair or replace such copies but the Publisher will assist the Author at the Author's expense to insure and keep himself insured against the risk of such loss.

Or

The Publisher shall at its expense secure the insurance against loss or damage by fire of stocks of the said work while in the Publisher's possession or control and shall account to the Author for a sum equivalent to the Author's royalty out of moneys recovered from the insurer.

44. Definition of parties

In this agreement where the context admits the expression " the Author " shall include his personal representatives and the expression " the Publisher " shall include any person firm or company in whom the publishing business now carried on by the Publisher shall for the time being be vested.

1287 D.—Forms for Theatre and Film Agreements

1. Warranty

The Author warrants that he is the owner of the copyright in the said work and is entitled to grant the licence hereinafter contained and that no part thereof is defamatory of any person.

2. Author to complete work

The Author shall with all reasonable dispatch proceed to complete the said work to the satisfaction of the Producer with such alterations and additions as to the Producer may reasonably require.

3. Author to make alterations

The Author shall make all such alterations or additions to the said work as the Producer may reasonably from time to time require during the course of the proposed production of the said work.

thor to altera- for ses of

The Author shall use his best endeavours to supply to the Producer with all reasonable dispatch such alterations or additions to the text of the said work as the Producer shall reasonably require for the purpose of the production of the said film.

altera- ithout nt of or

No alteration of or addition to [the text] [*or* score] [*and/or* title] of the said work may be made without the previous consent of the Author [such consent not to be unreasonably withheld].

erty to

The Producer shall be at liberty in the exercise of the licence hereby granted without consulting the Author to make such alterations or interpolations in or variations of the [text] [*or* score] [*and/or* title] of the said work as he from time to time may think fit [and to use the said work in conjunction with the work of any other Author].

thor's to be tised

The Producer shall arrange for the Author's name to be shown on the said film and shall use his best endeavours to secure that the Author's name shall be referred to in all advertisements of the said film issued by him Provided Always that the Producer shall not be liable or responsible for any error or neglect in any of the above matters due to any act or default of any of his employees servants subcontractors associated companies or other persons and that he shall be at liberty to give credit for the production or authorship of the said film to any other person or persons as well as the Author.

y to be ced by d date

The Producer shall produce the said play at the Theatre on or before the of

y to be ced for d run

The Producer shall within of the date hereof produce the said play for a run in the evening bill at a first class West End theatre with a first class cast.

icence nined if ot ced

[If the said play is not produced before the] [*or* If in any consecutive period of months less than performances in public of the said play are given in pursuance of this Licence] this Licence shall determine.

gree- deter- le if ot pro- by d date

If production of the said film shall not be commenced by the of the Author may by notice in writing to the Producer determine this agreement and in this event the Producer shall be under no further liability to the Author but any sums already paid to the Author shall be retained by him [and the Producer shall reassign to the Author any rights assigned by him hereunder].

12. Cast to be approved by Author

The cast for the production of the said play shall be subject to the approval of the Author [such approval not to be unreasonably withheld].

13. Author to be present at rehearsals

The Author shall be entitled to be present at all rehearsals of the said work.

14. Royalty on Box Office receipts

The Producer shall pay to the Author a royalty of   per cent. on the gross Box Office receipts (less library commission) for all performances of the said work at the Theatre.

15. Royalty varying with receipts

The Producer shall pay to the Author in respect of every performance of the said work given in pursuance of this Licence:

(a) In the case of every performance at a theatre in the West End of London a royalty on the gross Box Office receipts (less library commission)

(1) of   per cent. of the first £   of such receipts received in each week or part of a week;

(2) of   per cent. of the next £   of such receipts received in each week or part of a week; and

(3) of   per cent. of any excess of such receipts over £   received in any week or part of a week.

(b) In the case of performance at any other theatre or place of entertainment   per cent. of the gross Box Office receipts (less library commission).

16. Royalty in respect of sub-licence

If the Producer shall grant a sub-licence for the performance of the said work in public in accordance with the provisions hereof he shall pay to the Author   per cent. of all sums received by him in respect of such sub-licence as and when he shall receive such sums.

17. General royalty on all performances

The Producer shall pay to the Author   per cent. of all moneys received by him in respect of any performance in public of any work which involves the exercise of any of his rights comprised in the licence hereby granted.

18. Payment for film rights by percentage of receipts

In consideration of the premises the Producer has paid to the Author on the signing hereof the sum of £   (the receipt whereof the Author hereby acknowledges) and shall pay to the Author   per cent. of all sums received by the Producer in respect of any sale letting for hire or other disposition of any film made in pursuance of this agreement or in case the Producer shall grant to some person the right to make any film in pursuance of this agreement per cent. of all sums received by the Producer as the consideration for such grant.

ayment m by ments

In consideration of the premises the Producer has paid to the Author on the signing hereof the sum of £ (the receipt whereof the Author hereby acknowledges) and shall pay to the Author [on delivery by him to the Producer of the completed manuscript of the said work] [*or* on the date when the Producer shall commence production of the said film or on the expiration of months from the date hereof (whichever shall first happen)] the further sum of £ [and on the date when the Producer shall complete production of the said film or on the expiration of months from the date hereof (whichever shall first happen) the further sum of £].

ayment count

The Producer shall pay to the Author forthwith the sum of £ The said sum shall be accepted by the Author on account of any royalties subsequently payable to him under the provisions of this Licence but the said sum shall not be repayable notwithstanding that the royalties hereunder do not amount to the said sum.

ccounts

The Producer shall render to the Author a quarterly account on the usual quarter days of all moneys received by him during the preceding period in respect of which royalties are payable to the Author hereunder and shall pay to the Author the amount due in accordance with the provisions hereof within days after such account shall be rendered. The first such account shall be rendered on the first usual quarter day after the said work shall have first been performed in public in pursuance of this Licence.

roducer n- d with ution en joint rs

The Producer shall not be concerned as to the distribution of the royalties payable hereunder between the Authors and all accounts shall be deemed to have been duly rendered and all sums payable hereunder shall be deemed to have been duly paid if the same shall be rendered or paid to either of the Authors or to the personal representatives of either of them.

o casting

The Producer shall not permit any performance of the said work to be the subject of a sound or television broadcast.

eturn of at end nce

Upon the determination of this agreement the Producer shall deliver to the Author all copies of the said play in the possession of the Producer [provided that the Author shall pay to the Producer for all copies thereof made by the Producer the sum of per copy] [*and/or* provided that any prompt copy of the said play containing stage directions or other matter inserted by the Producer or other persons in his employ may be retained by the Producer].

25. Option to acquire additional rights

(i) If the Producer shall within months after the first performance in public of the said work in pursuance of this agreement give to the Author notice in writing of his intention to exercise the option hereby granted and pay to the Author the sum of £ the Producer shall thereafter have the sole and exclusive right [*insert description and term of the right; see Forms B*].

(ii) The provisions as to royalties herein contained shall apply with regard to all performances of the said work given in exercise of the rights referred to in this sub-clause and the said sum of £ shall be accepted by the Author on account of such royalties but no part thereof shall be returnable to the Producer.

26. Option to acquire different rights on different terms

(a) If the Producer shall produce the said play in pursuance of this Licence on or before the of and shall within months after the date of commencement of such production before the termination of the run of the play hereby authorised give to the Author notice in writing of his intention to exercise any of the options hereby granted and pay the Author the several sums hereafter mentioned in respect thereof then:

(i) on payment of the sum of £ the Producer shall have the sole and exclusive right to perform or authorise the performance of the said work in public in the United Kingdom of Great Britain and Northern Ireland during the period [*insert period as in Forms B. (ii), Clause* 22 *or* 26];

(ii) on payment of the sum of £ the Producer shall have the sole and exclusive right to perform or authorise the performance of the said work in public in the United States of America during the period [*insert period as in Forms B. (ii), Clause* 22 *or* 26].

(iii) on payment of the sum of £ the Producer shall have the sole and exclusive right to make or authorise the making of cinematograph film or films reproducing the said work and to perform or authorise the performance of the said work in public by means of such films in any part of the world during the period [*insert period as in Forms B. (ii), Clause* 22 *or* 25].

(b) The producer shall pay to the Author

(i) a royalty calculated as hereinafter mentioned on the gross Box Office receipts [less library commission] in respect of any performance of the play given in exercise of any of the said options under managership of the Producer either alone or jointly with some other person that is to say [*insert details of royalties as in Forms D., Clause* 15] and

(ii) per cent of all sums received by the Producer in respect of any sub-licence or authority given by him in exercise of any of the said options.

(c) The provisions herein contained as to accounts and payment of royalties shall apply to all sums payable under this Clause.

(d) *and* (e) [*Forms C., Clause* 38 (*d*) *and* (*e*), *substituting* " Producer " *for* " Publisher."]

PRECEDENTS

1.—GENERAL

88–1409 (i) *Assignment of Copyright* (*General Form*) [9]

THIS ASSIGNMENT made the of 19 BETWEEN A.B. of of the one part and C.D. of of the other part

WITNESSETH that [in consideration of the sum of £ paid by the said C.D. to the said A.B. (the receipt whereof the said A.B. hereby acknowledges)] [*or* in pursuance of the agreement between them in this behalf and at the request of the said C.D. *or as the case may be*] the said A.B. as beneficial owner hereby assigns unto the said C.D. *ALL THAT* [*insert description of right and work using Forms A.* (*i*) *and* (*ii*)] for all the residue of the term of copyright therein and all renewals or extensions thereof.

AS WITNESS etc.

410 (ii) *Assignment of Copyright* (*Short Form*)

In consideration of the sum of £ (which I hereby acknowledge to have been received by me) I A.B. of hereby as beneficial owner assign to C.D. of [*insert description of rights and work using Forms A.* (*i*) *and* (*ii*)] *Signed*

411 (iii) *Licence* (*General Form*) [10]

AN AGREEMENT made the of 19 BETWEEN A.B. of (hereinafter called " the Grantor ") of the one part and

[9] See Copyright Act, 1956, s. 36. An assignment must be in writing, but need not be under seal. It must be stamped in the same way as an assignment of any other property.

[10] An " exclusive licence " is defined in the Copyright Act, 1956, s. 19 (9), as meaning a licence in writing signed by or on behalf of an owner or prospective owner of copyright authorising the licensee, to the exclusion of all other persons, including the grantor of the licence, to exercise a right. Such a licence confers on the licensee the right to sue an infringer: see § 382, *ante*.

C.D. of (hereinafter called "the Licensee" which expression shall include the person or persons for the time being entitled to the benefit of this Licence) of the other part.

WHEREBY it is agreed as follows:

1. The Licensee shall during the period (hereinafter called "the said period") commencing at the date hereof and terminating on the of or such earlier date as hereinafter provided have the sole and exclusive right [*insert description of rights and of work using Forms A.* (*i*) *and* (*ii*) *and B.* (*i*)].

2. [*Agreement to be by way of licence only. Forms B., Clause* 29.]

3. [*Grantor not to assign. Forms B., Clause* 35.]

4. [*If desired, provision that licence to be personal to licensee. Forms B., Clause* 30, 31 *or* 32. *Alternatively Forms B., Clause* 33.]

5. [*If desired, agreement with or power of attorney to licensee to enforce all remedies. Forms C., Clause* 40, *substituting* "Grantor" *and* "Licensee" *for* "Author" *and* "Publisher." *In sub-clause* (ii) *insert* "during the term of this licence" *after* "infringement" *and use the first alternative ending to sub-clause* (ii).]

6. [*Provision as to indemnity. Forms C., Clause* 41.]

7. [*Provision as to determination of licence. Forms B., Clause* 27 *or* 28.]

8. [*Provisions as to consideration. Forms C., Clause* 17, *or as may be required.*]

AS WITNESS etc.

1412 (iv) *Licence* (*Short Form*)

In consideration of the sum of £ now paid to me (the receipt whereof I hereby acknowledge) I hereby irrevocably authorise Messrs. A.B. & Co. to [*insert description of rights and of work using Forms A.* (*i*) *and* (*ii*) *and B.* (*i*)] during the period commencing on and terminating on [*or as in Forms B.* (ii)] and I undertake not to grant any similar licence [for the same area] during the same period.

Signed

1413 (v) *Agreement for Sale*

AN AGREEMENT made the of 19 BETWEEN A.B. of of the one part and C.D. of of the other part whereby the said A.B. agrees to sell and the said C.D. agrees to purchase for the sum of £ [*insert description of rights and of work using Forms A.* (*i*) *and* (*ii*) *and B.* (*i*) *as* "the sole right to print and publish in any form in the English language in any part of the world the literary work entitled "].

AS WITNESS etc.

1414 (vi) *Agreement for Sale of Copyright in a Work where Assignments to be Postponed*

AN AGREEMENT made the of 19 BETWEEN A.B. of (hereinafter called "the Vendor" which expression where the context admits shall include his personal representatives) of the one part and C.D. of (hereinafter called "the Purchaser" which expression where the context admits shall include the person or persons for the time being entitled by assignment devolution or otherwise to the benefit of this agreement) of the other part.

WHEREBY in consideration of the sum of £ paid by the Purchaser to the Vendor (the receipt whereof the Vendor hereby acknowledges) the Vendor agrees with the Purchaser

1. That the Vendor shall at any time and from time to time hereafter upon the request and at the expense of the Purchaser execute all such documents and do all such acts as the Purchaser may require in order to assign to and vest in the Purchaser [*insert rights and description of work, using Forms A.* (*i*) *and* (*ii*) *and B.* (*i*)].

2. [*Insert Forms C., Clause* 40, *substituting* "Vendor" *and* "Purchaser" *for* "Author" *and* "Publisher" *and* "hereby agreed to be sold to the Purchaser" *for* "hereby conferred upon the Publisher."]

AS WITNESS etc.

1415 (vii) *Assignment or Licence of Future Copyright* [11]

In consideration of A.B. grants to C.D. the sole and exclusive right [by way of exclusive licence and not of assignment] to [*insert rights to be granted using Forms A.* (*i*) *and B.* (*i*)] a literary work about to be written by the said A.B. to the intent that the said rights therein shall forthwith upon the completion of the work vest in the said C.D.

Signed [*by or on behalf of A.B.*]

2.—PUBLISHING AGREEMENTS

1416 (i) *Copyright Assigned for Single Payment*

THIS AGREEMENT is made the of 19 BETWEEN A.B. of (hereinafter called "the Author") of the one part and C.D. of (hereinafter called "the Publisher") of the other part.

WHEREAS the Author is the author of and the owner of the copyright in an unpublished work entitled (hereinafter called "the said work")

[11] By s. 37 of the Copyright Act, 1956, an agreement made in relation to any future copyright, and signed by or on behalf of the prospective owner of the copyright, whereby the prospective owner purports to assign, or to grant a licence, in respect of such future copyright, shall as in the section provided (see § 353, *ante*) cause the copyright, when it comes into existence, to vest in accordance with the agreement. It should be noted that an agreement in this form will not necessarily have the same effect outside the United Kingdom.

NOW IT IS AGREED as follows:

1. The Publisher shall print and publish the said work at his sole risk and expense on or before the of 19

2. If the Publisher shall duly publish the said work on or before the said of 19 and shall pay to the Author within one month after the date of publication the sum of £ the Author shall at the request of the Publisher assign to the Publisher the sole right to print and publish the said work in any form in [*insert description of area. See Forms A., Clauses* 1 *and* 2].

3. [*Author to revise proofs. Forms C., Clause* 5.]

4. [*Excess cost of revision to be borne by Author. Forms C., Clause* 7.]

5. [*Option to acquire further rights, if desired. Forms C., Clause* 37.]

6. [*Definition. Forms C., Clause* 44.]

AS WITNESS etc.

1417 (ii) *Royalty Agreement*

THIS AGREEMENT is made the of 19 BETWEEN [*Parties and Recital as in Precedent* (i)].

1. [*Publisher to Print. Forms C., Clause* 1.]

2. [*Provisions as to form of publication, if required. Forms C., Clause* 2 *or* 3.]

3. [*Provision requiring advertisements and get-up to be submitted to the Author, if required. Forms C., Clause* 9.]

4. [*Provision as to securing copyright in U.S.A. Forms C., Clause* 10.]

5. [*Provisions as to prices at which copies to be sold. Forms C., Clause* 11 *or* 12.]

6. [*Licence. Forms C., Clause* 13.]

7. [*Royalty provisions. Forms C., Clauses* 16, 17, 18, 19 *or* 20 *and* 25.]

8. [*No royalty on copies to be given away. Forms C., Clause* 21.]

9. [*Author to have certain copies free of charge. Forms C., Clause* 8.]

10. [*Provision as to whether royalties are to depend upon actual receipts by Publisher. Forms C., Clause* 23 *or* 24.]

11 *and* 12. [*Provisions as to accounts. Forms C., Clause* 26 *or Clauses* 27 *and* 28.]

13. [*Power to check accounts. Forms C., Clause* 29.]

14. [*Publisher's indemnity. Forms C., Clause* 41.]

15. [*Restriction on assignment by Author. Forms B., Clause* 35, *substituting* " Author " *and* " Publisher " *for* " Grantor " *and* " Licensee."]

16. [*Option to Publisher to print new edition, if required. Forms C., Clause* 32.]

17. [*Option to Publisher to acquire other rights in the work, if required. Forms C., Clause* 37 *or* 38.]

18. [*Option to Publisher to acquire other works of the Author. Forms C., Clause* 36.]

19. [*Publisher to be sole agent in respect of dealings with the work. Forms C., Clause* 35.]

20. [*Author to join in proceedings to protect copyright. Forms C., Clause* 40.]

21. [*Determination of agreement, if publication delayed. Forms C., Clauses* 33, 34.]

22. [*Power to sell off copies. Forms C., Clause* 31.]

23. [*Provision as to fire risk, if required. Forms C., Clause* 43.]

24. [*Definition of* " Author " *and* " Publisher " *as in Forms C., Clause* 44, *or define* " Author " *as including his personal representatives, and insert provisions for determination of licence on death or bankruptcy (or winding up if a company) of the Publisher. See Forms B., Clause* 27, *and Forms C., Clause* 34, *and insert Forms B., Clause* 34, *if desired, substituting* " Author " *and* " Publisher " *for* " Grantor " *and* " Licensee."]

AS WITNESS etc.

1418 (iii) *Publishing on a Commission Basis*

THIS AGREEMENT is made the of 19 BETWEEN [*Parties and Recital as in Precedent* (i)].

1. [*Publisher to publish by a certain date. Forms C., Clause* 1.]

2. [*Provisions as to form of publication. Forms C., Clause* 4.]

3. The Publisher shall spend a sum of not less than £ on advertising the said work [*or* The Publisher shall carry out at the expense of the Author such advertising in connection with the publication of the said work as the Author may from time to time direct].

4. [*Provisions as to price at which copies to be sold. Forms C., Clause* 11 *or Clause* 12.]

5. The Author shall pay to the Publisher immediately after the signing of this agreement the sum of £ which shall be accepted by the Publisher in full satisfaction of all expenses incurred by the Publisher in printing and publishing and advertising the said work [provided that *add Forms C., Clause* 6].

[*Alternative form for* 5.]

5. The Author shall pay to the Publisher per sheet of sixteen pages for the cost of printing and paper and per hundred copies for binding and shall pay to the Publisher the actual cost of advertising plus per cent. Such payments shall be made as and when the costs are incurred by the Publisher.

6. The Publisher shall be entitled to a commission of per cent. on all sums received by him in respect of sales of copies of the said work and subject thereto shall pay all sums received by him as aforesaid to the Author.

[*Alternative form replacing* 5 *and* 6; *renumber accordingly.*]

6. (i) The Publisher shall deduct and retain out of all sums received by him in respect of sales of copies of the said work

(a) a commission of per cent. on all such sums

(b) the expenses of the production publication and advertising of the said work

and shall pay the balance of all sums to the Author.

(ii) In ascertaining the expenses of production and publication [*continue as in Precedent* (iv), *Clause* 10, *omitting the words referring to* " period ".]

(iii) If at the expiration of years from the date of publication of the said work the sums received by the Publisher as aforesaid shall be less than the expenses of production publication and advertising the Author shall thereupon pay to the Publisher the sum necessary to make up the difference together with an amount equal to per cent. of all sums theretofore incurred by the Publisher in respect of sales of copies of the said work and the Publisher shall pay to the Author all sums subsequently received by the Publisher in respect of sales of copies of the said work less a commission of per cent. thereon.

7. [*Accounts. Forms C., Clause* 27.]

8. [*Particulars to be shown in accounts. Forms C., Clause* 28.]

9. [*Right to inspect books. Forms C., Clause* 29.]

10. [*Publisher's indemnity. Forms C., Clause* 41.]

11. [*Right to sell off copies at end of period. Forms C., Clause* 31.]

12. [*If desired, Publisher to be sole agent to deal with rights. Forms C., Clause* 35, *omitting words in brackets.*]

13. The Publisher shall upon the request and at the expense of the Author keep all copies of the said work in his possession insured against fire but shall not be personally liable for the loss or destruction of any of the said copies however caused [*or Forms C., Clause* 43].

14. [*Definition of* " Author " *and* " Publisher." *Forms C., Clause* 44.]

As Witness etc.

1419 (iv) *Profit Sharing Agreement*

This Agreement is made the of 19 Between [*Parties and Recital as in Precedent* (i)].

1. [*Publisher to print. Forms C., Clause* 1.]

2. [*Provision as to form of publication if required. Forms C., Clauses* 2, 3 *or* 4.]

3. [*Provision requiring advertisements and get-up to be submitted to the Author if required. Forms C., Clause* 9.]

4. [*Provision as to securing copyright in U.S.A. Forms C., Clause* 10.]

5. [*Provision as to price, if discretion to Publisher omitted from Clause* 2. *Forms C., Clause* 11 *or Clause* 12.]

6. [*Licence. Forms C., Clause* 13.]

7. The Author shall be entitled to parts of the net profits (as hereinafter calculated) of the publication of the said edition and the Publisher shall be entitled to the remaining parts thereof [*add Forms C., Clause* 7, *if required*].

8. The net profits of the publication of the work during any period shall be ascertained by deducting from the gross profits of the said work during such period the expenses of production and publication of the said work paid or incurred by the Publisher during such period.

9. In ascertaining the gross profits of the said work during any period

[the Publisher shall account for all sums actually received by him during the said period in respect of sales of copies of the said work]

[*or* the Publisher shall account for the price (being the wholesale bookseller's price less a commission of per cent.) of all copies of the said work sold during the said period whether actually paid for or not]

[*or* the Publisher shall account]

[(a) in respect of all copies of the said work sold by him to be retailed at the price of per copy at the retail price thereof less per cent.

(b) in respect of all copies of the said work sold by him to be retailed at a less price than per copy at the retail price less per cent., and

(c) in respect of all copies sold by him for retail outside the United Kingdom or as remainders and at a price not directly based upon the retail selling price at the actual price agreed to be paid to the Publisher]

[*or* for all copies of the said work sold by him during the said period whether actually paid for or not].

[provided always that the Publisher shall be entitled to a deduction of per cent. of the sums credited to such account in respect of any such period for bad debts].

10. In ascertaining the expenses of production and publication in respect of any period

[the Publisher shall be entitled to charge for all sums paid or expended by him during such period for or in respect of the printing publication sale and advertisment of the work]

[*or* the same shall be deemed to include the actual cost of printing paper binding illustrating and advertising the said work]

[*and/or* where the Publisher does any part of the work of printing a publication on his own premises the cost thereof shall be calculated at current firm and reasonable trade charges]

[*or* the Publisher shall not be entitled to make any charge in respect of his ordinary overhead or office expenses]

[*or* the Publisher shall be entitled to charge in respect of his ordinary overhead or office expenses per cent. of the gross profits of the said work during the said period].

11. [*Provisions as to delivery of accounts and payment. Forms C., Clause* 26 *or Clause* 27.]

12. [*Particulars to be included in accounts. Forms C., Clause* 28.]

13. [*Right to inspect. Forms C., Clause* 29.]

14. [*Provision for carrying forward debit balance. Forms C., Clause* 30.]

15. [*Author to revise proofs. Forms C., Clause* 5.]

16. [*Excess costs of revision to be borne by Author. Forms C., Clause* 7.]

17. [*Indemnity to Publisher. Forms C., Clause* 41.]

18. [*Restriction on assignment by Author. Forms B., Clause* 35, *substituting* " Author " *and* " Publisher " *for* " Grantor " *and* " Licensee."]

19. [*Option to Publisher to print new edition if required. Forms C., Clause* 32.]

20. [*Determination of agreement if publication delayed. Forms C., Clause* 33.]

21. [*Power to sell off copies. Forms C., Clause* 31.]

22. [*Fire Risk. Forms C., Clause* 43.]

23. [*Definition. Forms C., Clause* 44, *or define* " Author " *as including his personal representatives, and insert provisions for determination of licence on death or bankruptcy (or winding up if a company) of the Publisher. See Forms B., Clause* 28, *and insert Forms B., Clause* 34, *if desired, substituting* " Author " *and* " Publisher " *for* " Grantor " *and* " Licensee."]

As Witness etc.

1420 (v) *Agreement to Write and Assign Copyright in a Work*

An Agreement made the of 19 Between [*Parties as in Precedent* (i)].

Whereby it is Agreed as follows:

1. The Author in consideration of the agreements on the part of the Publisher hereinafter contained hereby agrees with the Publisher

(1) That he will write a work (hereinafter called " the said work ") to be entitled and to contain from to printed pages of size [*or* from to words *or as may*

be] and will supply the manuscript of the said work properly prepared for the Printer to the Publisher on or before the day of 19 and will thereafter correct the proof sheets supplied to him by the Publisher with all reasonable dispatch and will complete the work and see the same through the press.

(2) That the copyright in the said work shall vest in the Publisher on completion of the said work and the Author will execute such confirmatory assignments at the request and expense of the Publisher as the Publisher shall require in order to vest in the Publisher such copyright in all parts of the world.[12]

2. In consideration of the premises the Publisher agrees with the Author

(1) To print and publish the said work within months after the manuscript of the said work has been supplied as aforesaid and to bear all the charges of printing and publishing the same.

(2) To supply to the Author copies of the said work free of charge.

(3) To pay to the Author on the day upon which the said work is published the sum of £

[Provided Always that if the Author shall not supply to the Publisher the manuscript of the said work on or before the date aforesaid (time being of the essence of the contract) the Publisher may by notice in writing to the Author terminate this agreement forthwith but without prejudice to the rights of the Publisher in respect of any then antecedent breach by the Author of the provisions hereof.]

3. [*Publisher's indemnity. Forms C., Clause* 41.]

4. [*Definition of* " Author " *and* " Publisher." *Forms C., Clause* 44.]

AS WITNESS etc.

1421 (vi) *Agreement with respect to a New Edition*

AN AGREEMENT made the of 19 BETWEEN [*Parties as in Precedent* (i)].

WHEREBY IT IS AGREED as follows:

1. In consideration of the agreements on the part of the Publisher hereafter contained the Author agrees with the Publisher

(1) To prepare a new edition of the work known as (hereinafter called " the said work ") by making all such corrections deletions and additions as may be necessary or reasonable for the purpose of bringing the same up to date.

(2) To make all such alterations or additions to the index of the said work as may be necessary.

[12] See note 11, § 1415, *ante*.

(3) To provide sufficient new matter to replace matter deleted or as an addition to the said work so that the said new edition when completed shall contain between and pages (being pages of the same size and containing on the average the same amount of matter on each page as those of the current edition) of subject-matter and index.

(4) To supply to the Publisher properly prepared for the printer all alterations and additions to the subject-matter on or before the of 19 .

(5) To correct all proof sheets within a reasonable time after the same shall have been supplied to him and to supply the corrected index to the Publisher within a reasonable time after the whole signatures of the text shall be ready for him for that purpose.

(6) That the copyright in all parts of the world in all work done by the Author in connection with the said new edition shall vest in the Publisher on completion thereof and the Author will upon the request and at the expense of the Publisher assign and confirm to the Publisher all such copyright.

2. In consideration of the premises the Publisher agrees with the Author

(1) To afford the Author all reasonable facilities for enabling him to carry out the agreement on his part hereinbefore contained.

(2) To supply the Author free of charge with bound copies of the said new edition of the said work.

(3) If the Author shall duly carry out the agreements on his part hereinbefore contained to pay to the Author on publication of the said new edition of the said work or on the of 19 (whichever shall be the earlier date) the sum of £ [*add if desired proviso to Clause* 2 (3) *of Precedent* (v)].

3. [*Covenant of indemnity by Author, if required. Forms C., Clause* 41, *substituting* " in all work by him in connection with the said new edition " *for* " in the said work."]

As Witness etc.

1422 3.—Theatre and Film Agreements

(i) *Licence for a Single Performance of a Play*

In consideration of the sum of £ now paid by [*the Producer*] to [*the Author*] (the receipt whereof [*the Author*] hereby acknowledges) [*the Producer*] shall have the right to perform in public at the Theatre for the evening performance the play entitled provided that [*the Producer*] shall not permit the said performance to be broadcast by wireless.

Date *Signed by both parties.*

1423 (ii) *Agreement for Single Run of a Play at a Theatre on Royalty Terms—Options*

THIS AGREEMENT is made the of 19 BETWEEN A.B. of (hereinafter called " the Author ") of the one part and C.D. of (hereinafter called " the Producer ") of the other part.

WHEREAS the Author is the owner of the copyright in a work entitled (hereinafter called " the said work ")

NOW IT IS AGREED as follows:

1. The Producer shall have the right to produce the said work at the Theatre for a continuous run provided that the said work shall be first produced at the said Theatre on or before the of 19

2. [*Provisions as to alterations. Forms D., Clauses* 3, 5, *or* 6.]

3. [*Provision as to cast, if required. Forms D., Clause* 12.]

4. [*Author to be present at rehearsals. Forms D., Clause* 13.]

5. [*Royalty on box office receipts. Forms D., Clause* 14.]

6. [*Advance on account of royalties. Forms D., Clause* 20.]

7. [*Accounts and payment. Forms D., Clause* 21.]

8. [*Return of copies. Forms D., Clause* 24.]

9. [*Indemnity to Producer. Forms C., Clause* 41, *substituting* " Producer " for " Publisher."]

10. [*Option to acquire further rights. Forms D., Clause* 26.]

AS WITNESS etc.

1424 (iii) *Limited Copyright in a Play vested in the Producer*

THIS AGREEMENT is made the of 19 BETWEEN [*Parties as in Precedent* (ii)].

WHEREAS (1) The Author is the owner of the copyright in a work entitled (hereinafter called " the said work ").

(2) The Author has agreed to assign to the Producer the rights hereby assigned and to enter into the agreement hereinafter contained in consideration of the payment by the Producer of the sum of £

NOW THIS AGREEMENT WITNESSETH as follows:

1. In consideration of the payment to the Author by the Producer of the sum of £ (the receipt whereof is hereby acknowledged) the Author hereby as beneficial owner assigns to the Producer the right to perform the said work in public in Great Britain and Northern Ireland [*or as may be*] on the stage [but not by means of any mechanical or electrical contrivance or by sound or television broadcasting] for all the residue of the term of copyright subsisting therein or so much thereof as is capable by law of being assigned.

2. [*Author's warranty of title. Forms D., Clause* 1.]

3. [*Indemnity to Producer. Forms C., Clause* 41, *substituting* " Producer " for " Publisher."]

4. [*Option to acquire further rights. Adapt Forms C., Clause* 37, *inserting rights as desired, using Forms A.* (*i*) *or B.* (*i*).]

Or

[*Appointment of Producer as sole agent in respect of other rights in the work. Forms C., Clause* 35, *substituting* " Producer " *for* " Publisher " *and, if desired, limiting rights by substituting* " all rights for the performance of the said work in public by means of mechanical contrivances or otherwise " *in place of* " all rights in the said work."]

AS WITNESS etc.

1425 (iv) *Licence to make a Film of a Novel*

THIS AGREEMENT is made the of 19 BETWEEN [*Parties as in Precedent* (ii)].

WHEREAS

(1) The Author is the owner of the copyright in a work entitled (hereinafter called " the said work ").

(2) The Producer is desirous of making a [sound] [*or* silent] film (hereinafter called " the said film ") of the said work.

NOW IT IS AGREED as follows:

1. [*Author's warranty. Forms D., Clause* 1.]

2. The Author hereby grants to the Producer the rights following, that is to say:

(a) the sole and exclusive right to convert the said work into a dramatic work for the purpose only of making a [sound] [*or* silent] film of such dramatic work,

(b) the sole and exclusive right to reproduce the said work in a [sound] [*or* silent] film,

(c) the right to make copies of the said work or any part thereof for any purpose connected with the production of the said film,

(d) the sole and exclusive right to use the name of the said work as the name of the said film and for the purpose of advertising the said film,

(e) the sole and exclusive right to perform the said work in public by means of the said film.

(f) [*Right to publish synopsis, if required. Forms B., Clause* 5.]

(g) [*Right to publish work in short story or serial form, if required. Forms B., Clause* 6.]

3. The rights hereby granted shall extend to all parts of the world and shall continue for the full term of copyright in the said work but are limited to the production of the said film and do not extend to any other film.

4. [*Grants deemed to be by way of licence only. Forms B., Clause* 29, *substituting* "Producer" *for* "Licensee."]

5. The Producer shall be at liberty to assign the benefit of this agreement or of any of the rights hereby conferred.

6. The Author shall, if required by the Producer, co-operate in the production of the scenario for the said film but the Author shall not be entitled to insist upon co-operating in such production [*or insert Forms D., Clause* 4].

7. [*Producer to be at liberty to make alterations. Forms D., Clause* 6.]

8. [*Licence determined if production delayed. Forms D., Clause* 11.]

9. [*Provisions as to payment. Forms D., Clause* 18 *or Clause* 19.]

10. [*Provision for further assurance and recovery of claims. Forms C., Clause* 40, *substituting* "Producer" *for* "Publisher."]

11. [*Indemnity. Forms C., Clause* 41.]

12. [*Author's name to be advertised. Forms D., Clause* 7.]

AS WITNESS etc.

1426 (v) *Agreement as to Film where Copyright in Novel and Play on which it is Based are vested in Different Persons*

THIS AGREEMENT is made the of 19

BETWEEN A.B. of (hereinafter called "the Author") of the 1st part C.D. of (hereinafter called "the Playwright") of the 2nd part and E.F. of (hereinafter called "the Producer") of the 3rd part.

WHEREAS

(1) The Author is the owner of the copyright in a novel entitled (hereinafter called "the said work").

(2) The Playwright is the owner of the copyright in a play entitled (hereinafter called "the said play") which is a dramatisation of the said work made with the consent of the Author.

(3) The Producer is desirous of acquiring in respect of the said work and the said play the rights hereinafter mentioned in consideration of the several payments hereinafter described.

NOW THIS AGREEMENT WITNESSETH as follows:

1. The Author (so far as the rights hereby agreed to be assigned form part of the copyright in the said work) and the Playwright (so far as the rights hereby agreed to be assigned form part of the copyright in the said play) shall (subject as hereinafter provided) upon the request and at the expense of the Producer assign to the Producer:

(a) the sole right to reproduce the said work and the said play in the form of a cinematograph film,

(b) the sole right to perform the said work in public by means of such cinematograph film.

2. The said rights shall be assigned to the Producer for the whole term of copyright therein or so much thereof as is capable by law of being assigned and shall extend to all parts of the world.

3. (a) The Author (as to the said work) and the Playwright (as to the said play) hereby grant to the Producer:

(i) the sole right to make copies of the said work and of the said play or of any part or parts thereof respectively for any purpose connected with the production of any film produced in exercise of the rights hereinbefore agreed to be granted to the Producer:

(ii) the sole and exclusive right to use the name of the said work and of the said play as the name of or for the purpose of advertising any film produced in exercise of the rights hereinbefore agreed to be granted to the Producer.

(iii) [*Right to publish synopsis, if required. Forms B., Clause* 5.]

(iv) [*Right to publish work and/or play in short story or serial form, if required. Forms B., Clause* 6.]

(b) The rights granted in this clause shall be deemed to be by way of licence only, but shall extend to all parts of the world during [the whole term of copyright in the said work and the said play respectively] and the benefit thereof may be assigned by the Producer.

4. [*Provision as to Author's name. Forms D., Clause* 7, *adding* "and Playwright's" *where required.*]

5. The Producer having paid to the Author the sum of £ and to the Playwright the sum of £ on the signing hereof (the receipt of which respective sums of £ and £ the Author and the Playwright hereby respectively acknowledge) the Producer shall on the of or at the time when any of the rights hereby agreed to be assigned shall be first exercised (whichever shall be the earlier date) pay to the Author the further sum of £ and to the Playwright the further sum of £ and if the said sums shall not be paid on the date aforesaid either the Author or the Playwright shall be at liberty to terminate this agreement by notice in writing to the Producer. In the event of this agreement being so terminated the Producer shall cease to be entitled to any rights hereunder, but the sums already paid to the Author and the Playwright shall not be returnable.

6. Neither the Author nor the Playwright shall be required to make any assignment hereunder until all sums payable hereunder to them have been duly paid.

7. [*Provision for further assurance. Forms C., Clause* 40 *with necessary amendments of parties.*]

8. [*Indemnity to Producer. Forms C., Clause* 41 *with necessary amendments of parties.*]

AS WITNESS etc.

[The next paragraph is 1430]

Appendix A

UNITED KINGDOM STATUTES

PART I

Copyright Act, 1956

(4 & 5 Eliz. 2, c. 74)

ARRANGEMENT OF SECTIONS

PART I

COPYRIGHT IN ORIGINAL WORKS

An Act to make new provision in respect of copyright and related matters, in substitution for the provisions of the Copyright Act, 1911, and other enactments relating thereto; to amend the Registered Designs Act, 1949, with respect to designs related to artistic works in which copyright subsists, and to amend the Dramatic and Musical Performers' Protection Act, 1925; and for purposes connected with the matters aforesaid. [5th November, 1956]

PART I

COPYRIGHT IN ORIGINAL WORKS

1431 **Nature of copyright under this Act**

1.—(1) In this Act "copyright" in relation to a work (except where the context otherwise requires) means the exclusive right, by virtue and subject to the provisions of this Act, to do, and to authorise other persons to do, certain acts in relation to that work in the United Kingdom or in any other country to which the relevant provision of this Act extends.

The said acts, in relation to a work of any description, are those acts which, in the relevant provision of this Act, are designated as the acts restricted by the copyright in a work of that description.

(2) In accordance with the preceding subsection, but subject to the following provisions of this Act, the copyright in a work is infringed by any person who, not being the owner of the copyright, and without the licence of the owner thereof, does, or authorises another person to do, any of the said acts in relation to the work in the United Kingdom or in any other country to which the relevant provision of this Act extends.

(3) In the preceding subsections references to the relevant provision of this Act, in relation to a work of any description, are references to the provision of this Act whereby it is provided that (subject to compliance with the conditions specified therein) copyright shall subsist in works of that description.

(4) The preceding provisions of this section shall apply, in relation to any subject-matter (other than a work) of a description to which any provision of Part II of this Act relates, as they apply in relation to a work.

(5) For the purposes of any provision of this Act which specifies the conditions under which copyright may subsist in any description of work or other subject-matter, " qualified person "—

(*a*) in the case of an individual, means a person who is a British subject or British protected person or a citizen of the Republic of Ireland or (not being a British subject or British protected person or a citizen of the Republic of Ireland) is domiciled or resident in the United Kingdom or in another country to which that provision extends, and

(*b*) in the case of a body corporate, means a body incorporated under the laws of any part of the United Kingdom or of another country to which that provision extends.

In this subsection " British protected person " has the same meaning as in the British Nationality Act, 1948.

32 **Copyright in literary, dramatic and musical works**

2.—(1) Copyright shall subsist, subject to the provisions of this Act, in every original literary, dramatic or musical work which is unpublished, and of which the author was a qualified person at the time when the work was made, or, if the making of the work extended over a period, was a qualified person for a substantial part of that period.

(2) Where an original literary, dramatic or musical work has been published, then, subject to the provisions of this Act, copyright shall subsist in the work (or, if copyright in the work subsisted immediately before its first publication, shall continue to subsist) if, but only if,—

(*a*) the first publication of the work took place in the United Kingdom, or in another country to which this section extends, or

(*b*) the author of the work was a qualified person at the time when the work was first published, or

(*c*) the author had died before that time, but was a qualified person immediately before his death.

(3) Subject to the last preceding subsection, copyright subsisting in a work by virtue of this section shall continue to subsist until the end of the period of fifty years from the end of the calendar year in which the author died, and shall then expire:

Provided that if before the death of the author none of the following acts had been done, that is to say,—

(*a*) the publication of the work,

(*b*) the performance of the work in public,

(*c*) the offer for sale to the public of records of the work, and
(*d*) the broadcasting of the work,

the copyright shall continue to subsist until the end of the period of fifty years from the end of the calendar year which includes the earliest occasion on which one of those acts is done.

(4) In the last preceding subsection references to the doing of any act in relation to a work include references to the doing of that act in relation to an adaptation of the work.

(5) The acts restricted by the copyright in a literary, dramatic or musical work are—

(*a*) reproducing the work in any material form;
(*b*) publishing the work;
(*c*) performing the work in public;
(*d*) broadcasting the work;
(*e*) causing the work to be transmitted to subscribers to a diffusion service;
(*f*) making any adaptation of the work;
(*g*) doing, in relation to an adaptation of the work, any of the acts specified in relation to the work in paragraphs (*a*) to (*e*) of this subsection.

(6) In this Act " adaptation "—

(*a*) in relation to a literary or dramatic work, means any of the following, that is to say,—

(i) in the case of a non-dramatic work, a version of the work (whether in its original language or a different language) in which it is converted into a dramatic work;

(ii) in the case of a dramatic work, a version of the work (whether in its original language or a different language) in which it is converted into a non-dramatic work;

(iii) a translation of the work;

(iv) a version of the work in which the story or action is conveyed wholly or mainly by means of pictures in a form suitable for reproduction in a book, or in a newspaper, magazine or similar periodical; and

(*b*) in relation to a musical work, means an arrangement or transcription of the work,

1433 so however that the mention of any matter in this definition shall not affect the generality of paragraph (*a*) of the last preceding subsection.

Copyright in artistic works

3.—(1) In this Act " artistic work " means a work of any of the following descriptions, that is to say,—

(*a*) the following, irrespective of artistic quality, namely paintings, sculptures, drawings, engravings and photographs;
(*b*) works of architecture, being either buildings or models for buildings;
(*c*) works of artistic craftsmanship, not falling within either of the preceding paragraphs.

(2) Copyright shall subsist, subject to the provisions of this Act, in every original artistic work which is unpublished, and of which the author was a qualified person at the time when the work was made, or, if the making of the work extended over a period, was a qualified person for a substantial part of that period.

(3) Where an original artistic work has been published, then, subject to the provisions of this Act, copyright shall subsist in the work (or, if copyright in the work subsisted immediately before its first publication, shall continue to subsist) if, but only if,—

(*a*) the first publication of the work took place in the United Kingdom, or in another country to which this section extends, or

(*b*) the author of the work was a qualified person at the time when the work was first published, or

(*c*) the author had died before that time, but was a qualified person immediately before his death.

(4) Subject to the last preceding subsection, copyright subsisting in a work by virtue of this section shall continue to subsist until the end of the period of fifty years from the end of the calendar year in which the author died, and shall then expire:

Provided that—

(*a*) in the case of an engraving, if before the death of the author the engraving had not been published, the copyright shall continue to subsist until the end of the period of fifty years from the end of the calendar year in which it is first published;

(*b*) the copyright in a photograph shall continue to subsist until the end of the period of fifty years from the end of the calendar year in which the photograph is first published, and shall then expire.

(5) The acts restricted by the copyright in an artistic work are—

(*a*) reproducing the work in any material form;

(*b*) publishing the work;

(*c*) including the work in a television broadcast;

(*d*) causing a television programme which includes the work to be transmitted to subscribers to a diffusion service.

1434 **Ownership of copyright in literary, dramatic, musical and artistic works**

4.—(1) Subject to the provisions of this section, the author of a work shall be entitled to any copyright subsisting in the work by virtue of this Part of this Act.

(2) Where a literary, dramatic or artistic work is made by the author in the course of his employment by the proprietor of a newspaper, magazine or similar periodical under a contract of service or apprenticeship, and is so made for the purpose of publication in a newspaper, magazine or similar periodical, the said proprietor shall be entitled to the copyright in the work in so far as the copyright relates to publication of the work in any newspaper, magazine or similar periodical, or to reproduction of the work for the purpose of its being so published; but in all other respects the author shall be entitled to any copyright subsisting in the work by virtue of this Part of this Act.

(3) Subject to the last preceding subsection, where a person commissions the taking of a photograph, or the painting or drawing of a portrait, or the making of an engraving, and pays or agrees to pay for it in money or money's worth, and the work is made in pursuance of that commission, the person who so commissioned the work shall be entitled to any copyright subsisting therein by virtue of this Part of this Act.

(4) Where, in a case not falling within either of the two last preceding subsections, a work is made in the course of the author's employment by another person under a contract of service or apprenticeship, that other person shall be entitled to any copyright subsisting in the work by virtue of this Part of this Act.

(5) Each of the three last preceding subsections shall have effect subject, in any particular case, to any agreement excluding the operation thereof in that case.

(6) The preceding provisions of this section shall all have effect subject to the provisions of Part VI of this Act.

1435 **Infringements by importation, sale and other dealings**

5.—(1) Without prejudice to the general provisions of section one of this Act as to infringements of copyright, the provisions of this section shall have effect in relation to copyright subsisting by virtue of this Part of this Act.

(2) The copyright in a literary, dramatic, musical or artistic work is infringed by any person who, without the licence of the owner of the copyright, imports an article (otherwise than for his private and domestic use) into the United Kingdom, or into any other country to which this section extends, if to his knowledge the making of that article constituted an infringement of that copyright, or would have constituted such an infringement if the article had been made in the place into which it is so imported.

(3) The copyright in a literary, dramatic, musical or artistic work is infringed by any person who, in the United Kingdom, or in any other country to which this section extends, and without the licence of the owner of the copyright,—

(*a*) sells, lets for hire, or by way of trade offers or exposes for sale or hire any article, or

(*b*) by way of trade exhibits any article in public,

if to his knowledge the making of the article constituted an infringement of that copyright, or (in the case of an imported article) would have constituted an infringement of that copyright if the article had been made in the place into which it was imported.

(4) The last preceding subsection shall apply in relation to the distribution of any articles either—

(*a*) for purposes of trade, or

(*b*) for other purposes, but to such an extent as to affect prejudicially the owner of the copyright in question,

as it applies in relation to the sale of an article.

(5) The copyright in a literary, dramatic or musical work is also infringed by any person who permits a place of public entertainment to be used for a performance in public of the work, where the performance constitutes an infringement of the copyright in the work:

Provided that this subsection shall not apply in a case where the person permitting the place to be so used—

(*a*) was not aware, and had no reasonable grounds for suspecting, that the performance would be an infringement of the copyright, or

(*b*) gave the permission gratuitously, or for a consideration which was only nominal or (if more than nominal) did not exceed a reasonable estimate of the expenses to be incurred by him in consequence of the use of the place for the performance.

(6) In this section " place of public entertainment " includes any premises which are occupied mainly for other purposes, but are from time to time made available for hire to such persons as may desire to hire them for purposes of public entertainment.

1436 General exceptions from protection of literary, dramatic and musical works

6.—(1) No fair dealing with a literary, dramatic or musical work for purposes of research or private study shall constitute an infringement of the copyright in the work.

(2) No fair dealing with a literary, dramatic or musical work shall constitute an infringement of the copyright in the work if it is for purposes of criticism or review, whether of that work or of another work, and is accompanied by a sufficient acknowledgment.

(3) No fair dealing with a literary, dramatic or musical work shall constitute an infringement of the copyright in the work if it is for the purpose of reporting current events—

(*a*) in a newspaper, magazine or similar periodical, or

(*b*) by means of broadcasting, or in a cinematograph film,

and, in a case falling within paragraph (*a*) of this subsection, is accompanied by a sufficient acknowledgment.

(4) The copyright in a literary, dramatic or musical work is not infringed by reproducing it for the purposes of a judicial proceeding, or for the purposes of a report of a judicial proceeding.

(5) The reading or recitation in public by one person of any reasonable extract from a published literary or dramatic work, if accompanied by a sufficient acknowledgment, shall not constitute an infringement of the copyright in the work:

Provided that this subsection shall not apply to anything done for the purposes of broadcasting.

(6) The copyright in a published literary or dramatic work is not infringed by the inclusion of a short passage therefrom in a collection intended for the use of schools, if—

(*a*) the collection is described in its title, and in any advertisements thereof issued by or on behalf of the publisher, as being so intended, and

(*b*) the work in question was not published for the use of schools, and

(*c*) the collection consists mainly of material in which no copyright subsists, and

(*d*) the inclusion of the passage is accompanied by a sufficient acknowledgment:

Provided that this subsection shall not apply in relation to the copyright in a work if, in addition to the passage in question, two or more other excerpts from works by the author thereof (being works in which copyright subsists at the time when the collection is published) are contained in that collection, or are contained in that collection taken together with every similar collection (if any) published by the same publisher within the period of five years immediately preceding the publication of that collection.

(7) Where by virtue of an assignment or licence a person is authorised to broadcast a literary, dramatic or musical work from a place in the United Kingdom, or in another country to which section two of this Act extends, but (apart from this subsection) would not be entitled to make reproductions of it in the form of a record or of a cinematograph film, the copyright in the work is not infringed by his making such a reproduction of the work solely for the purpose of broadcasting the work:

Provided that this subsection shall not apply if—

(*a*) the reproduction is used for making any further reproduction therefrom, or for any other purpose except that of broadcasting in accordance with the assignment or licence, or (*b*) the reproduction is not destroyed before the end of the period of twenty-eight days beginning with the day on which it is first used for broadcasting the work in pursuance of the assignment or licence, or such extended period (if any) as may be agreed between the person who made the reproduction and the person who (in relation to the making of reproductions of the description in question) is the owner of the copyright.

(8) The preceding provisions of this section shall apply to the doing of any act in relation to an adaptation of a work as they apply in relation to the doing of that act in relation to the work itself.

(9) The provisions of this section shall apply where a work, or adaptation of a work, is caused to be transmitted to subscribers to a diffusion service as they apply where a work or adaptation is broadcast.

(10) In this Act " sufficient acknowledgment " means an acknowledgment identifying the work in question by its title or other description and, unless the work is anonymous or the author has previously agreed or required that no acknowledgment of his name should be made, also identifying the author.

1437 **Special exceptions as respects libraries and archives**

7.—(1) The copyright in an article contained in a periodical publication is not infringed by the making or supplying of a copy of the article, if the copy is made or supplied by or on behalf of the librarian of a library of a class prescribed by regulations made under this subsection by the Board of Trade, and the conditions prescribed by those regulations are complied with.

(2) In making any regulations for the purposes of the preceding subsection the Board of Trade shall make such provision as the Board may consider appropriate for securing—

(*a*) that the libraries to which the regulations apply are not established or conducted for profit;

(*b*) that the copies in question are supplied only to persons satisfying the librarian, or a person acting on his behalf, that they require them for purposes of research or private study and will not use them for any other purpose;

(*c*) that no person is furnished under the regulations with two or more copies of the same article;

(*d*) that no copy extends to more than one article contained in any one publication; and

(*e*) that persons to whom copies are supplied under the regulations are required to pay for them a sum not less than the cost (including a contribution to the general expenses of the library) attributable to their production,

and may impose such other requirements (if any) as may appear to the Board to be expedient.

(3) The copyright in a published literary, dramatic or musical work, other than an article contained in a periodical publication, is not infringed by the making or supplying of a copy of part of the work, if the copy is made or supplied by or on behalf of the librarian of a library of a class prescribed by regulations made under this subsection by the Board of Trade, and the conditions prescribed by those regulations are complied with:

Provided that this subsection shall not apply if, at the time when the copy is made, the librarian knows the name and address of a person entitled to authorise the making of the copy, or could by reasonable inquiry ascertain the name and address of such a person.

(4) The provisions of subsection (2) of this section shall apply for the purposes of the last preceding subsection:

Provided that paragraph (*d*) of the said subsection (2) shall not apply for those purposes, but any regulations made under the last preceding subsection shall include such provision as the Board of Trade may consider appropriate for securing that no copy to which the regulations apply extends to more than a reasonable proportion of the work in question.

(5) The copyright in a published literary, dramatic or musical work is not infringed by the making or supplying of a copy of the work, or of part of it, by or on behalf of the librarian of a library of a class prescribed by regulations made under this subsection by the Board of Trade, if—

(*a*) the copy is supplied to the librarian of any library of a class so prescribed;

(*b*) at the time when the copy is made, the librarian by or on whose behalf it is supplied does not know the name and address of any person entitled to authorise the making of the copy, and could not by reasonable inquiry ascertain the name and address of such a person; and

(*c*) any other conditions prescribed by the regulations are complied with:

Provided that the condition specified in paragraph (*b*) of this subsection shall not apply in the case of an article contained in a periodical publication.

(6) Where, at a time more than fifty years from the end of the calendar year in which the author of a literary, dramatic or musical work died, and more than one hundred years after the time, or the end of the period, at or during which the work was made,—

(*a*) copyright subsists in the work, but

(*b*) the work has not been published, and

(*c*) the manuscript or a copy of the work is kept in a library, museum or other institution where (subject to any provisions regulating the institution in question) it is open to public inspection,

the copyright in the work is not infringed by a person who reproduces the work for purposes of research or private study, or with a view to publication.

(7) Where a published literary, dramatic or musical work (in this subsection referred to as " the new work ") incorporates the whole or part of a work (in this subsection referred to as " the old work ") in the case of which the circumstances specified in the last preceding subsection existed immediately before the new work was published, and—

(*a*) before the new work was published, such notice of the intended publication as may be prescribed by regulations made under this subsection by the Board of Trade had been given, and

(*b*) immediately before the new work was published, the identity of the owner of the copyright in the old work was not known to the publisher of the new work,

then for the purposes of this Act—

(i) that publication of the new work, and

(ii) any subsequent publication of the new work, either in the same or in an altered form,

shall, in so far as it constitutes a publication of the old work, not be treated as an infringement of the copyright in the old work or as an unauthorised publication of the old work:

Provided that this subsection shall not apply to a subsequent publication incorporating a part of the old work which was not included in the new work as originally published, unless (apart from this subsection) the circumstances specified in the last preceding subsection, and in paragraphs (*a*) and (*b*) of this subsection, existed immediately before that subsequent publication.

(8) In so far as the publication of a work, or of part of a work, is, by virtue of the last preceding subsection, not to be treated as an infringement of the copyright in the work, a person who subsequently broadcasts the work, or that part thereof, as the case may be, or causes it to be transmitted to subscribers to a diffusion service, or performs it in public, or makes a record of it, does not thereby infringe the copyright in the work.

(9) In relation to an article or other work which is accompanied by one or more artistic works provided for explaining or illustrating it (in this subsection referred to as " illustrations "), the preceding provisions of this section shall apply as if—

(*a*) wherever they provide that the copyright in the article or work is not infringed, the reference to that copyright included a reference to any copyright in any of the illustrations;

(*b*) in subsections (1) and (2), references to a copy of the article included references to a copy of the article together with a copy of the illustrations or any of them;

(*c*) in subsections (3) to (5), references to a copy of the work included references to a copy of the work together with a copy of the illustrations or any of them, and references to a copy of part of the work included references to a copy of that part of the work together with a copy of any of the illustrations which were provided for explaining or illustrating that part; and

(*d*) in subsections (6) and (7), references to the doing of any act in relation to the work included references to the doing of that act in relation to the work together with any of the illustrations.

(10) In this section " article " includes an item of any description.

1438 **Special exception in respect of records of musical works**

8.—(1) The copyright in a musical work is not infringed by a person (in this section referred to as " the manufacturer ") who makes a record of the work or of an adaptation thereof in the United Kingdom, if—

(*a*) records of the work, or, as the case may be, of a similar adaptation of the work, have previously been made in, or imported into, the United Kingdom for the purposes of retail sale, and were so made or imported by, or with the licence of, the owner of the copyright in the work;

(*b*) before making the record, the manufacturer gave to the owner of the copyright the prescribed notice of his intention to make it;

(*c*) the manufacturer intends to sell the record by retail, or to supply it for the purpose of its being sold by retail by another person, or intends to use it for making other records which are to be so sold or supplied; and

(*d*) in the case of a record which is sold by retail, the manufacturer pays to the owner of the copyright, in the prescribed manner and at the prescribed time, a royalty of an amount ascertained in accordance with the following provisions of this section.

(2) Subject to the following provisions of this section, the royalty mentioned in paragraph (*d*) of the preceding subsection shall be of an amount equal to six and one-quarter per cent. of the ordinary retail selling price of the record, calculated in the prescribed manner:

Provided that, if the amount so calculated includes a fraction of a farthing, that fraction shall be reckoned as one farthing, and if, apart from this proviso, the amount of the royalty would be less than three-farthings, the amount thereof shall be three-farthings.

(3) If, at any time after the end of the period of one year beginning with the coming into operation of this section, it appears to the Board of Trade that the ordinary rate of royalty, or the minimum amount thereof, in accordance with the provisions of the last preceding subsection, or in accordance with those provisions as last varied by an order under this subsection, has ceased to be equitable, either generally or in relation to any class of records, the Board may hold a public inquiry in the prescribed manner; and if, in consequence of such an inquiry, the Board are satisfied of the need to do so, the Board may make an order prescribing such different rate or amount, either generally or in relation to any one or more classes of records, as the Board may consider just:

Provided that—

(*a*) no order shall be made under this subsection unless a draft of the order has been laid before Parliament and approved by a resolution of each House of Parliament; and

(*b*) where an order comprising a class of records (that is to say, either a general order or an order relating specifically to that class, or to that class together with one or more other classes of records) has been made under this subsection, no further order comprising that class of records shall be made thereunder less than five years after the date on which the previous order comprising that class (or, if more than one, the last previous order comprising that class) was made thereunder.

(4) In the case of a record which comprises (with or without other material, and either in their original form or in the form of adaptations) two or more musical works in which copyright subsists—

(*a*) the minimum royalty shall be three-farthings in respect of each of those works, or, if a higher or lower amount is prescribed by an order under the last preceding subsection as the minimum royalty, shall be that amount in respect of each of those works; and

(*b*) if the owners of the copyright in the works are different persons, the royalty shall be apportioned among them in such manner as they may agree or as, in default of agreement, may be determined by arbitration.

(5) Where a record comprises (with or without other material) a performance of a musical work, or of an adaptation of a musical work, in which words are sung, or are spoken incidentally to or in association with the music, and either no copyright subsists in that work or, if such copyright subsists, the conditions specified in subsection (1) of this section are fulfilled in relation to that copyright, then if—

(*a*) the words consist or form part of a literary or dramatic work in which copyright subsists, and

(*b*) such previous records as are referred to in paragraph (*a*) of subsection (1) of this section were made or imported by, or with the licence of, the owner of the copyright in that literary or dramatic work, and

(*c*) the conditions specified in paragraphs (*b*) and (*d*) of subsection (1) of this section are fulfilled in relation to the owner of that copyright,

the making of the record shall not constitute an infringement of the copyright in the literary or dramatic work:

Provided that this subsection shall not be construed as requiring more than one royalty to be paid in respect of a record; and if copyright subsists both in the musical work and in the literary or dramatic work, and their owners are different persons, the royalty shall be apportioned among them (or among them and any other person entitled to a share thereof in accordance with the last preceding subsection) as they may agree or as, in default of agreement, may be determined by arbitration.

(6) For the purposes of this section an adaptation of a work shall be taken to be similar to an adaptation thereof contained in previous records if the two adaptations do not substantially differ in their treatment of the work, either in respect of style or (apart from any difference in numbers) in respect of the performers required for performing them.

(7) Where, for the purposes of paragraph (*a*) of subsection (1) of this section, the manufacturer requires to know whether such previous records as are mentioned in that paragraph were made or imported as therein mentioned, the manufacturer may make the prescribed inquiries; and if the owner of the copyright fails to reply to those inquiries within the prescribed period, the previous records shall be taken to have been made or imported, as the case may be, with the licence of the owner of the copyright.

(8) The preceding provisions of this section shall apply in relation to records of part of a work or adaptation as they apply in relation to records of the whole of it:

Provided that subsection (1) of this section—

(*a*) shall not apply to a record of the whole of a work or adaptation unless the previous records referred to in paragraph (*a*) of that subsection were records of the whole of the work or of a similar adaptation, and

(*b*) shall not apply to a record of part of a work or adaptation unless those previous records were records of, or comprising, that part of the work or of a similar adaptation.

(9) In relation to musical works published before the first day of July, nineteen hundred and twelve, the preceding provisions of this section shall apply as if paragraph (*a*) of subsection (1), paragraph (*b*) of subsection (5), subsections (6) and (7), and the proviso to the last preceding subsection, were omitted:

Provided that this subsection shall not extend the operation of subsection (5) of this section to a record in respect of which the condition specified in paragraph (*b*) of that subsection is not fulfilled, unless the words comprised in the record (as well as the musical work) were published before the first day of July, nineteen hundred and twelve, and were so published as words to be sung to, or spoken incidentally to or in association with, the music.

(10) Nothing in this section shall be construed as authorising the importation of records which could not lawfully be imported apart from this section; and accordingly, for the purposes of any provision of this Act relating to imported articles, where the question arises whether the making of a record made outside the United Kingdom would have constituted an infringement of copyright if the record had been made in the United Kingdom, that question shall be determined as if subsection (1) of this section had not been enacted.

(11) In this section "prescribed" means prescribed by regulations made under this section by the Board of Trade; and any such regulations made for the purposes of paragraph (*d*) of subsection (1) of this section may provide that the taking of such steps as may be specified in the regulations (being such steps as the Board consider most convenient for ensuring the receipt of the royalties by the owner of the copyright) shall be treated as constituting payment of the royalties in accordance with that paragraph.

1439 General exceptions from protection of artistic works

9.—(1) No fair dealing with an artistic work for purposes of research or private study shall constitute an infringement of the copyright in the work.

(2) No fair dealing with an artistic work shall constitute an infringement of the copyright in the work if it is for purposes of criticism or review, whether of that work or of another work, and is accompanied by a sufficient acknowledgment.

(3) The copyright in a work to which this subsection applies which is permanently situated in a public place, or in premises open to the public, is not infringed by the making of a painting, drawing, engraving or photograph of the work, or the inclusion of the work in a cinematograph film or in a television broadcast.

This subsection applies to sculptures, and to such works of artistic craftsmanship as are mentioned in paragraph (*c*) of subsection (1) of section three of this Act.

(4) The copyright in a work of architecture is not infringed by the making of a painting, drawing, engraving or photograph of the work, or the inclusion of the work in a cinematograph film or in a television broadcast.

(5) Without prejudice to the two last preceding subsections, the copyright in an artistic work is not infringed by the inclusion of the work in a cinematograph film or in a television broadcast, if its inclusion therein is only by way of background or is otherwise only incidental to the principal matters represented in the film or broadcast.

(6) The copyright in an artistic work is not infringed by the publication of a painting, drawing, engraving, photograph or cinematograph film, if by virtue of any of the three last preceding subsections the making of that painting, drawing, engraving, photograph or film did not constitute an infringement of the copyright.

(7) The copyright in an artistic work is not infringed by reproducing it for the purposes of a judicial proceeding or for the purposes of a report of a judicial proceeding.

(8) The making of an object of any description which is in three dimensions shall not be taken to infringe the copyright in an artistic work in two dimensions, if the object would not appear, to persons who are not experts in relation to objects of that description, to be a reproduction of the artistic work.

(9) The copyright in an artistic work is not infringed by the making of a subsequent artistic work by the same author, notwithstanding that part of the earlier work—

(*a*) is reproduced in the subsequent work, and

(*b*) is so reproduced by the use of a mould, cast, sketch, plan, model or study made for the purposes of the earlier work,

if in making the subsequent work the author does not repeat or imitate the main design of the earlier work.

(10) Where copyright subsists in a building as a work of architecture, the copyright is not infringed by any reconstruction of that building; and where a building has been constructed in accordance with architectural drawings or plans in which copyright subsists, and has been so constructed by, or with the licence of, the owner of that copyright, any subsequent reconstruction of the building by reference to those drawings or plans shall not constitute an infringement of that copyright.

(11) The provisions of this section shall apply in relation to a television programme which is caused to be transmitted to subscribers to a diffusion service as they apply in relation to a television broadcast.

1440 Special exception in respect of industrial designs

10.—[(*1*) *Where copyright subsists in an artistic work, and a corresponding design is registered under the Registered Designs Act, 1949 (in this section referred to as " the Act of 1949 "), it shall not be an infringement of the copyright in the work—*

(a) *to do anything, during the subsistence of the copyright in the registered design under the Act of 1949, which is within the scope of the copyright in the design, or*

(b) *to do anything, after the copyright in the registered design has come to an end, which, if it had been done while the copyright in the design subsisted, would have been within the scope of that copyright as extended to all associated designs and articles:*

Provided that this subsection shall have effect subject to the provisions of the First Schedule to this Act in cases falling within that Schedule.

(2) *Where copyright subsists in an artistic work, and—*

(a) *a corresponding design is applied industrially by or with the licence of the owner of the copyright in the work, and*

(b) *articles to which the design has been so applied are sold, let for hire, or offered for sale or hire, and*

(c) *at the time when those articles are sold, let for hire, or offered for sale or hire, they are not articles in respect of which the design has been registered under the Act of 1949,*

the following provisions of this section shall apply.

(3) *Subject to the next following subsection,—*

(a) *during the relevant period of fifteen years, it shall not be an infringement of the copyright in the work to do anything which, at the time when it is done, would have been within the scope of the copyright in the design if the design had, immediately before that time, been registered in respect of all relevant articles; and*

(b) *after the end of the relevant period of fifteen years, it shall not be an infringement of the copyright in the work to do anything which, at the time when it is done, would, if the design had been registered immediately before that time, have been within the scope of the copyright in the design as extended to all associated designs and articles.*

In this subsection " the relevant period of fifteen years " means the period of fifteen years beginning with the date on which articles, such as are mentioned in paragraph (b) *of the last preceding subsection, were first sold, let for hire, or offered for sale or hire in the circumstances mentioned in paragraph* (c) *of that subsection; and " all relevant articles ", in relation to any time within that period, means all articles falling within the said paragraph* (b) *which had before that time been sold, let for hire, or offered for sale or hire in those circumstances.*]

[(2) Where copyright subsists in an artistic work, and—

(*a*) a corresponding design is applied industrially by or with the licence of the owner of the copyright in the work, and

(*b*) articles to which the design has been so applied are sold, let for hire, or offered for sale or hire whether in the United Kingdom or elsewhere, and

the following provisions of this section shall apply.

(3) Subject to the next following subsection, after the end of the relevant period of fifteen years it shall not be an infringement of the copyright in the work to do anything which at the time when it was done would, if a corresponding design had been registered under the Registered Designs Act 1949 (in this section referred to as " the Act of 1949 ") immediately before that time, have been within the scope of the copyright in the design as extended to all associated designs and articles.

In this subsection " the relevant period of fifteen years " means the period of fifteen years beginning with the date on which articles, such as are mentioned in paragraph (*b*) of the last preceding subsection, were first sold, let for hire or offered for sale or hire, whether in the United Kingdom or elsewhere.]

(4) For the purposes of subsections (2) and (3) of this section, no account shall be taken of any articles in respect of which, at the time when they were sold, let for hire, or offered for sale or hire, the design in question was excluded from registration under the Act of 1949 by rules made under subsection (4) of section one of that Act (which relates to the exclusion of designs for articles which are primarily literary or artistic in character); and for the purposes of any proceedings under this Act a design shall be conclusively presumed to have been so excluded if—

(*a*) before the commencement of those proceedings, an application for the registration of the design under the Act of 1949 in respect of those articles had been refused;

(*b*) the reason or one of the reasons stated for the refusal was that the design was excluded from such registration by rules made under the said subsection (4); and

(*c*) no appeal against that refusal had been allowed before the date of the commencement of the proceedings or was pending on that date.

(5) The power of the Board of Trade to make rules under section thirty-six of the Act of 1949 shall include power to make rules for the purposes of this section for determining the circumstances in which a design is to be taken to be applied industrially.

(6) In this section, references to the scope of the copyright in a registered design are references to the aggregate of the things, which, by

virtue of section seven of the Act of 1949, the registered proprietor of the design has the exclusive right to do, and references to the scope of the copyright in a registered design as extended to all associated designs and articles are references to the aggregate of the things which, by virtue of that section, the registered proprietor would have had the exclusive right to do if—

(*a*) when that design was registered, there had at the same time been registered every possible design consisting of that design with modifications or variations not sufficient to alter the character or substantially to affect the identity thereof, and the said proprietor had been registered as the proprietor of every such design, and

(*b*) the design in question, and every other design such as is mentioned in the preceding paragraph, had been registered in respect of all the articles to which it was capable of being applied.

(7) In this section " corresponding design ", in relation to an artistic work, means a design which, when applied to an article, results in a reproduction of that work.

AMENDMENT

This section and the First Schedule were amended by the Design Copyright Act, 1968 (1968 c. 68). The amendments consisted of deleting subs. (1), amending subs. (2) and substituting a new subs. (3). The original subss. (1), (2) and (3) are printed in italics. The word " and " at the end of subs. (2) (*b*) was not deleted by the 1968 Act.

1441 **Provisions as to anonymous and pseudonymous works, and works of joint authorship**

11.—(1) The preceding provisions of this Part of this Act shall have effect subject to the modifications specified in the Second Schedule to this Act in the case of works published anonymously or pseudonymously.

(2) The provisions of the Third Schedule to this Act shall have effect with respect to works of joint authorship.

(3) In this Act " work of joint authorship " means a work produced by the collaboration of two or more authors in which the contribution of each author is not separate from the contribution of the other author or authors.

PART II

COPYRIGHT IN SOUND RECORDINGS, CINEMATOGRAPH FILMS, BROADCASTS, ETC.

1442 **Copyright in sound recordings**

12.—(1) Copyright shall subsist, subject to the provisions of this Act, in every sound recording of which the maker was a qualified person at the time when the recording was made.

(2) Without prejudice to the preceding subsection, copyright shall subsist, subject to the provisions of this Act, in every sound recording which has been published, if the first publication of the recording took place in the United Kingdom or in another country to which this section extends.

(3) Copyright subsisting in a sound recording by virtue of this section shall continue to subsist until the end of the period of fifty years from the

end of the calendar year in which the recording is first published, and shall then expire.

(4) Subject to the provisions of this Act, the maker of a sound recording shall be entitled to any copyright subsisting in the recording by virtue of this section:

Provided that where a person commissions the making of a sound recording, and pays or agrees to pay for it in money or money's worth, and the recording is made in pursuance of that commission, that person, in the absence of any agreement to the contrary, shall, subject to the provisions of Part VI of this Act, be entitled to any copyright subsisting in the recording by virtue of this section.

(5) The acts restricted by the copyright in a sound recording are the following, whether a record embodying the recording is utilised directly or indirectly in doing them, that is to say,—

(*a*) making a record embodying the recording;
(*b*) causing the recording to be heard in public;
(*c*) broadcasting the recording.

(6) The copyright in a sound recording is not infringed by a person who does any of those acts in the United Kingdom in relation to a sound recording, or part of a sound recording, if—

(*a*) records embodying that recording, or that part of the recording, as the case may be, have previously been issued to the public in the United Kingdom, and

(*b*) at the time when those records were so issued, neither the records nor the containers in which they were so issued bore a label or other mark indicating the year in which the recording was first published:

Provided that this subsection shall not apply if it is shown that the records in question were not issued by or with the licence of the owner of the copyright, or that the owner of the copyright had taken all reasonable steps for securing that records embodying the recording or part thereof would not be issued to the public in the United Kingdom without such a label or mark either on the records themselves or on their containers.

(7) Where a sound recording is caused to be heard in public—

(*a*) at any premises where persons reside or sleep, as part of the amenities provided exclusively or mainly for residents or inmates therein, or

(*b*) as part of the activities of, or for the benefit of, a club, society or other organisation which is not established or conducted for profit and whose main objects are charitable or are otherwise concerned with the advancement of religion, education or social welfare,

the act of causing it to be so heard shall not constitute an infringement of the copyright in the recording:

Provided that this subsection shall not apply—

(i) in the case of such premises as are mentioned in paragraph (*a*) of this subsection, if a special charge is made for admission to the part of the premises where the recording is to be heard; or

(ii) in the case of such an organisation as is mentioned in paragraph (*b*) of this subsection, if a charge is made for admission to the place where the recording is to be heard, and any of the proceeds of the charge are applied otherwise than for the purposes of the organisation.

(8) For the purposes of this Act a sound recording shall be taken to be made at the time when the first record embodying the recording is produced, and the maker of a sound recording is the person who owns that record at the time when the recording is made.

(9) In this Act " sound recording " means the aggregate of the sounds embodied in, and capable of being reproduced by means of, a record of any description, other than a sound-track associated with a cinematograph film; and " publication ", in relation to a sound recording, means the issue to the public of records embodying the recording or any part thereof.

1443 **Copyright in cinematograph films**

13.—(1) Copyright shall subsist, subject to the provisions of this Act, in every cinematograph film of which the maker was a qualified person for the whole or a substantial part of the period during which the film was made.

(2) Without prejudice to the preceding subsection, copyright shall subsist, subject to the provisions of this Act, in every cinematograph film which has been published, if the first publication of the film took place in the United Kingdom or in another country to which this section extends.

(3) Copyright subsisting in a cinematograph film by virtue of this section—

(*a*) in the case of a film which is registrable under [Part II of the Films Act, 1960,] shall continue to subsist until the film is registered thereunder, and thereafter until the end of the period of fifty years from the end of the calendar year in which it is so registered;

(*b*) in the case of a film which is not so registrable, shall continue until the film is published, and thereafter until the end of the period of fifty years from the end of the calendar year which includes the date of its first publication, or, if copyright in the film subsists by virtue only of the last preceding subsection, shall continue as from the date of first publication until the end of the period of fifty years from the end of the calendar year which includes that date,

and then shall expire:

Provided that if the Parliament of Northern Ireland passes legislation for purposes similar to those of [Part II of the Films Act, 1960,] then, in the case of a cinematograph film which is registered under that legislation, at a time when it has not been registered under the said Part II, the copyright shall continue to subsist until the end of the period of fifty years from the end of the calendar year which includes the date on which the film is registered under that legislation, and shall then expire.

(4) Subject to the provisions of Part VI of this Act, the maker of a cinematograph film shall be entitled to any copyright subsisting in the film by virtue of this section.

(5) The acts restricted by the copyright in a cinematograph film are—

(*a*) making a copy of the film;

(*b*) causing the film, in so far as it consists of visual images, to be seen in public, or, in so far as it consists of sounds, to be heard in public;

(*c*) broadcasting the film;

(*d*) causing the film to be transmitted to subscribers to a diffusion service.

(6) The copyright in a cinematograph film is not infringed by making a copy of it for the purposes of a judicial proceeding, or by causing it to be seen or heard in public for the purposes of such a proceeding.

(7) Where by virtue of this section copyright has subsisted in a cinematograph film, a person who, after that copyright has expired, causes the film to be seen, or to be seen and heard, in public does not thereby infringe any copyright subsisting by virtue of Part I of this Act in any literary, dramatic, musical or artistic work.

(8) In the case of any such film as is mentioned in paragraph (*a*) of [subsection (1) of section 38 of the Films Act, 1960] (which relates to newsreels), the copyright in the film is not infringed by causing it to be seen or heard in public after the end of the period of fifty years from the end of the calendar year in which the principal events depicted in the film occurred.

(9) For the purposes of this Act a cinematograph film shall be taken to include the sounds embodied in any sound-track associated with the film, and references to a copy of a cinematograph film shall be construed accordingly:

Provided that where those sounds are also embodied in a record, other than such a sound-track or a record derived (directly or indirectly) from such a sound-track, the copyright in the film is not infringed by any use made of that record.

(10) In this Act—

"cinematograph film" means any sequence of visual images recorded on material of any description (whether translucent or not) so as to be capable, by the use of that material,—

(*a*) of being shown as a moving picture, or

(*b*) of being recorded on other material (whether translucent or not), by the use of which it can be so shown;

"the maker", in relation to a cinematograph film, means the person by whom the arrangements necessary for the making of the film are undertaken;

"publication", in relation to a cinematograph film, means the sale, letting on hire, or offer for sale or hire, of copies of the film to the public;

"copy", in relation to a cinematograph film, means any print, negative, tape or other article on which the film or part of it is recorded,

and references in this Act to a sound-track associated with a cinematograph film are references to any record of sounds which is incorporated in any print, negative, tape or other article on which the film or part of it, in so far as it consists of visual images, is recorded, or which is issued by the maker of the film for use in conjunction with such an article.

(11) References in this section to [Part II of the Films Act, 1960,] shall be construed as including references to any enactments for the time being in force amending or substituted for the provisions of the said [Part II and, in relation to any time before the commencement of that Act, as references to the enactments replaced by those provisions.]

AMENDMENT

The words in square brackets were substituted by the Films Act, 1960 (8 & 9 Eliz. 2, c. 57).

1444 **Copyright in television broadcasts and sound broadcasts**

14.—(1) Copyright shall subsist, subject to the provisions of this Act,—

(*a*) in every television broadcast made by the British Broadcasting Corporation (in this Act referred to as " the Corporation ") or by the Independent Television Authority (in this Act referred to as " the Authority ") from a place in the United Kingdom or in any other country to which this section extends, and

(*b*) in every sound broadcast made by the Corporation or the Authority from such a place.

(2) Subject to the provisions of this Act, the Corporation or the Authority, as the case may be, shall be entitled to any copyright subsisting in a television broadcast or sound broadcast made by them; and any such copyright shall continue to subsist until the end of the period of fifty years from the end of the calendar year in which the broadcast is made, and shall then expire.

(3) In so far as a television broadcast or sound broadcast is a repetition (whether the first or any subsequent repetition) of a television broadcast or sound broadcast previously made as mentioned in subsection (1) of this section (whether by the Corporation or by the Authority), and is made by broadcasting material recorded on film, records or otherwise,—

(*a*) copyright shall not subsist therein by virtue of this section if it is made after the end of the period of fifty years from the end of the calendar year in which the previous broadcast was made; and

(*b*) if it is made before the end of that period, any copyright subsisting therein by virtue of this section shall expire at the end of that period.

(4) The acts restricted by the copyright in a television broadcast or sound broadcast are—

(*a*) in the case of a television broadcast in so far as it consists of visual images, making, otherwise than for private purposes, a cinematograph film of it or a copy of such a film;

(*b*) in the case of a sound broadcast, or of a television broadcast in so far as it consists of sounds, making, otherwise than for private purposes, a sound recording of it or a record embodying such a recording;

(*c*) in the case of a television broadcast, causing it, in so far as it consists of visual images, to be seen in public, or, in so far as it consists of sounds, to be heard in public, if it is seen or heard by a paying audience;

(*d*) in the case either of a television broadcast or of a sound broadcast, re-broadcasting it.

(5) The restrictions imposed by virtue of the last preceding subsection in relation to a television broadcast or sound broadcast made by the Corporation or by the Authority shall apply whether the act in question is done by the reception of the broadcast or by making use of any record, print, negative, tape or other article on which the broadcast has been recorded.

(6) In relation to copyright in television broadcasts, in so far as they consist of visual images, the restrictions imposed by virtue of subsection (4) of this section shall apply to any sequence of images sufficient to be seen as a moving picture; and accordingly, for the purpose of establishing

an infringement of such copyright, it shall not be necessary to prove that the act in question extended to more than such a sequence of images.

(7) For the purposes of subsection (4) of this section a cinematograph film or a copy thereof, or a sound recording or a record embodying a recording, shall be taken to be made otherwise than for private purposes if it is made for the purposes of the doing by any person of any of the following acts, that is to say,—

(*a*) the sale or letting for hire of any copy of the film, or, as the case may be, of any record embodying the recording;
(*b*) broadcasting the film or recording;
(*c*) causing the film or recording to be seen or heard in public.

(8) For the purposes of paragraph (*c*) of subsection (4) of this section, a television broadcast shall be taken to be seen or heard by a paying audience if it is seen or heard by persons who either—

(*a*) have been admitted for payment to the place where the broadcast is to be seen or heard, or have been admitted for payment to a place of which that place forms part, or
(*b*) have been admitted to the place where the broadcast is to be seen or heard in circumstances where goods or services are supplied there at prices which exceed the prices usually charged at that place and are partly attributable to the facilities afforded for seeing or hearing the broadcast:

Provided that for the purposes of paragraph (*a*) of this subsection no account shall be taken—

(i) of persons admitted to the place in question as residents or inmates therein, or
(ii) of persons admitted to that place as members of a club or society, where the payment is only for membership of the club or society and the provision of facilities for seeing or hearing television broadcasts is only incidental to the main purposes of the club or society.

(9) The copyright in a television broadcast or sound broadcast is not infringed by anything done in relation to the broadcast for the purposes of a judicial proceeding.

(10) In this Act " television broadcast " means visual images broadcast by way of television, together with any sounds broadcast for reception along with those images, and " sound broadcast " means sounds broadcast otherwise than as part of a television broadcast; and for the purposes of this Act a television broadcast or sound broadcast shall be taken to be made by the body by whom, at the time when, and from the place from which, the visual images or sounds in question, or both, as the case may be, are broadcast.

1445 **Copyright in published editions of works**

15.—(1) Copyright shall subsist, subject to the provisions of this Act, in every published edition of any one or more literary, dramatic or musical works in the case of which either—

(*a*) the first publication of the edition took place in the United Kingdom, or in another country to which this section extends, or
(*b*) the publisher of the edition was a qualified person at the date of the first publication thereof:

Provided that this subsection does not apply to an edition which reproduces the typographical arrangement of a previous edition of the same work or works.

(2) Subject to the provisions of this Act, the publisher of an edition shall be entitled to any copyright subsisting in the edition by virtue of this section; and any such copyright shall continue to subsist until the end of the period of twenty-five years from the end of the calendar year in which the edition was first published, and shall then expire.

(3) The act restricted by the copyright subsisting by virtue of this section in a published edition is the making, by any photographic or similar process, of a reproduction of the typographical arrangement of the edition.

(4) The copyright under this section in a published edition is not infringed by the making by or on behalf of a librarian of a reproduction of the typographical arrangement of the edition, if he is the librarian of a library of a class prescribed by regulations made under this subsection by the Board of Trade, and the conditions prescribed by those regulations are complied with.

1446 **Supplementary provisions for purposes of Part II**

16.—(1) The provisions of this section shall have effect with respect to copyright subsisting by virtue of this Part of this Act in sound recordings, cinematograph films, television broadcasts and sound broadcasts, and in published editions of literary, dramatic and musical works; and in those provisions references to the relevant provision of this Part of this Act, in relation to copyright in a subject-matter of any of those descriptions, are references to the provision of this Part of this Act whereby it is provided that (subject to compliance with the conditions specified therein) copyright shall subsist in that description of subject-matter.

(2) Any copyright subsisting by virtue of this Part of this Act is infringed by any person who, without the licence of the owner of the copyright, imports an article (otherwise than for his private and domestic use) into the United Kingdom, or into any other country to which the relevant provision of this Part of this Act extends, if to his knowledge the making of that article constituted an infringement of that copyright, or would have constituted such an infringement if the article had been made in the place into which it is so imported.

(3) Any such copyright is also infringed by any person who, in the United Kingdom, or in any other country to which the relevant provision of this Part of this Act extends, and without the licence of the owner of the copyright,—

(*a*) sells, lets for hire, or by way of trade offers or exposes for sale or hire any article, or

(*b*) by way of trade exhibits any article in public,

if to his knowledge the making of the article constituted an infringement of that copyright, or (in the case of an imported article) would have constituted an infringement of that copyright if the article had been made in the place into which it was imported.

(4) The last preceding subsection shall apply in relation to the distribution of any articles either—

(*a*) for purposes of trade, or

(*b*) for other purposes, but to such an extent as to affect prejudicially the owner of the copyright in question,

as it applies in relation to the sale of an article.

(5) The three last preceding subsections shall have effect without prejudice to the general provisions of section one of this Act as to infringements of copyright.

(6) Where by virtue of this Part of this Act copyright subsists in a sound recording, cinematograph film, broadcast or other subject-matter, nothing in this Part of this Act shall be construed as affecting the operation of Part I of this Act in relation to any literary, dramatic, musical or artistic work from which that subject-matter is wholly or partly derived; and copyright subsisting by virtue of this Part of this Act shall be additional to, and independent of, any copyright subsisting by virtue of Part I of this Act:

Provided that this subsection shall have effect subject to the provisions of subsection (7) of section thirteen of this Act.

(7) The subsistence of copyright under any of the preceding sections of this Part of this Act shall not affect the operation of any other of those sections under which copyright can subsist.

PART III

REMEDIES FOR INFRINGEMENTS OF COPYRIGHT

1447 **Action by owner of copyright for infringement**

17.—(1) Subject to the provisions of this Act, infringements of copyright shall be actionable at the suit of the owner of the copyright; and in any action for such an infringement all such relief, by way of damages, injunction, accounts or otherwise, shall be available to the plaintiff as is available in any corresponding proceedings in respect of infringements of other proprietary rights.

(2) Where in an action for infringement of copyright it is proved or admitted—

(*a*) that an infringement was committed, but

(*b*) that at the time of the infringement the defendant was not aware, and had no reasonable grounds for suspecting, that copyright subsisted in the work or other subject-matter to which the action relates,

the plaintiff shall not be entitled under this section to any damages against the defendant in respect of the infringement, but shall be entitled to an account of profits in respect of the infringement whether any other relief is granted under this section or not.

(3) Where in an action under this section an infringement of copyright is proved or admitted, and the court, having regard (in addition to all other material considerations) to—

(*a*) the flagrancy of the infringement, and

(*b*) any benefit shown to have accrued to the defendant by reason of the infringement,

is satisfied that effective relief would not otherwise be available to the plaintiff, the court, in assessing damages for the infringement, shall have power to award such additional damages by virtue of this subsection as the court may consider appropriate in the circumstances.

(4) In an action for infringement of copyright in respect of the construction of a building, no injunction or other order shall be made—

(*a*) after the construction of the building has been begun, so as to prevent it from being completed, or

(*b*) so as to require the building, in so far as it has been constructed, to be demolished.

(5) In this Part of this Act " action " includes a counterclaim, and references to the plaintiff and to the defendant in an action shall be construed accordingly.

(6) In the application of this Part of this Act to Scotland, " injunction " means an interdict and " interlocutory injunction " means an interim interdict, " accounts " means count, reckoning and payment, " an account of profits " means an accounting and payment of profits, " plaintiff " means pursuer, " defendant " means defender and " costs " means expenses.

1448 **Rights of owner of copyright in respect of infringing copies, etc.**

18.—(1) Subject to the provisions of this Act, the owner of any copyright shall be entitled to all such rights and remedies, in respect of the conversion or detention by any person of any infringing copy, or of any plate used or intended to be used for making infringing copies, as he would be entitled to if he were the owner of every such copy or plate and had been the owner thereof since the time when it was made:

Provided that if, by virtue of subsection (2) of section three of the Limitation Act, 1939 (which relates to successive conversions or detentions), or of any corresponding provision which may be enacted by the Parliament of Northern Ireland, the title of the owner of the copyright to such a copy or plate would (if he had then been the owner of the copy or plate) have been extinguished at the end of the period mentioned in that subsection or corresponding provision, he shall not be entitled to any rights or remedies under this subsection in respect of anything done in relation to that copy or plate after the end of that period.

(2) A plaintiff shall not be entitled by virtue of this section to any damages or to any other pecuniary remedy (except costs) if it is proved or admitted that, at the time of the conversion or detention in question,—

(*a*) the defendant was not aware, and had no reasonable grounds for suspecting, that copyright subsisted in the work or other subject-matter to which the action relates, or

(*b*) where the articles converted or detained were infringing copies, the defendant believed, and had reasonable grounds for believing, that they were not infringing copies, or

(*c*) where the article converted or detained was a plate used or intended to be used for making any articles, the defendant believed, and had reasonable grounds for believing, that the articles so made or intended to be made were not, or (as the case may be) would not be, infringing copies.

(3) In this Part of this Act " infringing copy "—

(*a*) in relation to a literary, dramatic, musical or artistic work, or to such a published edition as is mentioned in section fifteen of this Act, means a reproduction otherwise than in the form of a cinematograph film,

(*b*) in relation to a sound recording, means a record embodying that recording,

(*c*) in relation to a cinematograph film, means a copy of the film, and (*d*) in relation to a television broadcast or a sound broadcast, means a copy of a cinematograph film of it or a record embodying a sound recording of it,

being (in any such case) an article the making of which constituted an infringement of the copyright in the work, edition, recording, film or broadcast, or, in the case of an imported article, would have constituted an infringement of that copyright if the article had been made in the place into which it was imported; and " plate " includes any stereotype, stone, block, mould, matrix, transfer, negative or other appliance.

(4) In the application of this section to Scotland, for any reference to the conversion or detention by any person of an infringing copy there shall be substituted a reference to an intromission by any person with an infringing copy, and for any reference to articles converted or detained there shall be substituted a reference to articles intromitted with.

1449 **Proceedings in case of copyright subject to exclusive licence**

19.—(1) The provisions of this section shall have effect as to proceedings in the case of any copyright in respect of which an exclusive licence has been granted and is in force at the time of the events to which the proceedings relate.

(2) Subject to the following provisions of this section—

(*a*) the exclusive licensee shall (except against the owner of the copyright) have the same rights of action, and be entitled to the same remedies, under section seventeen of this Act as if the licence had been an assignment, and those rights and remedies shall be concurrent with the rights and remedies of the owner of the copyright under that section;

(*b*) the exclusive licensee shall (except against the owner of the copyright) have the same rights of action, and be entitled to the same remedies, by virtue of the last preceding section as if the licence had been an assignment; and

(*c*) the owner of the copyright shall not have any rights of action, or be entitled to any remedies, by virtue of the last preceding section which he would not have had or been entitled to if the licence had been an assignment.

(3) Where an action is brought either by the owner of the copyright or by the exclusive licensee, and the action, in so far as it is brought under section seventeen of this Act, relates (wholly or partly) to an infringement in respect of which they have concurrent rights of action under that section, the owner or licensee, as the case may be, shall not be entitled, except with the leave of the court, to proceed with the action, in so far as it is brought under that section and relates to that infringement, unless the other party is either joined as a plaintiff in the action or added as a defendant:

Provided that this subsection shall not affect the granting of an interlocutory injunction on the application of either of them.

(4) In any action brought by the exclusive licensee by virtue of this section, any defence which would have been available to a defendant in the action, if this section had not been enacted and the action had been brought by the owner of the copyright, shall be available to that defendant as against the exclusive licensee.

(5) Where an action is brought in the circumstances mentioned in subsection (3) of this section, and the owner of the copyright and the exclusive

licensee are not both plaintiffs in the action, the court, in assessing damages in respect of any such infringement as is mentioned in that subsection,—

(*a*) if the plaintiff is the exclusive licensee, shall take into account any liabilities (in respect of royalties or otherwise) to which the licence is subject, and

(*b*) whether the plaintiff is the owner of the copyright or the exclusive licensee, shall take into account any pecuniary remedy already awarded to the other party under section seventeen of this Act in respect of that infringement, or, as the case may require, any right of action exercisable by the other party under that section in respect thereof.

(6) Where an action, in so far as it is brought under section seventeen of this Act, relates (wholly or partly) to an infringement in respect of which the owner of the copyright and the exclusive licensee have concurrent rights of action under that section, and in that action (whether they are both parties to it or not) an account of profits is directed to be taken in respect of that infringement, then, subject to any agreement of which the court is aware, whereby the application of those profits is determined as between the owner of the copyright and the exclusive licensee, the court shall apportion the profits between them as the court may consider just, and shall give such directions as the court may consider appropriate for giving effect to that apportionment.

(7) In an action brought either by the owner of the copyright or by the exclusive licensee,—

(*a*) no judgment or order for the payment of damages in respect of an infringement of copyright shall be given or made under section seventeen of this Act, if a final judgment or order has been given or made awarding an account of profits to the other party under that section in respect of the same infringement; and

(*b*) no judgment or order for an account of profits in respect of an infringement of copyright shall be given or made under that section, if a final judgment or order has been given or made awarding either damages or an account of profits to the other party under that section in respect of the same infringement.

(8) Where, in an action brought in the circumstances mentioned in subsection (3) of this section, whether by the owner of the copyright or by the exclusive licensee, the other party is not joined as a plaintiff (either at the commencement of the action or subsequently), but is added as a defendant, he shall not be liable for any costs in the action unless he enters an appearance and takes part in the proceedings.

(9) In this section " exclusive licence " means a licence in writing, signed by or on behalf of an owner or prospective owner of copyright, authorising the licensee, to the exclusion of all other persons, including the grantor of the licence, to exercise a right which by virtue of this Act would (apart from the licence) be exercisable exclusively by the owner of the copyright, and " exclusive licensee " shall be construed accordingly; " the other party ", in relation to the owner of the copyright, means the exclusive licensee, and, in relation to the exclusive licensee, means the owner of the copyright; and " if the licence had been an assignment " means if, instead of the licence, there had been granted (subject to terms and conditions corresponding as nearly as may be with those subject to

which the licence was granted) an assignment of the copyright in respect of its application to the doing, at the places and times authorised by the licence, of the acts so authorised.

1450 **Proof of facts in copyright actions**

20.—(1) In any action brought by virtue of this Part of this Act—

(*a*) copyright shall be presumed to subsist in the work or other subject-matter to which the action relates, if the defendant does not put in issue the question whether copyright subsists therein, and

(*b*) where the subsistence of the copyright is proved or admitted, or is presumed in pursuance of the preceding paragraph, the plaintiff shall be presumed to be the owner of the copyright, if he claims to be the owner of the copyright and the defendant does not put in issue the question of his ownership thereof.

(2) Subject to the preceding subsection, where, in the case of a literary, dramatic, musical or artistic work, a name purporting to be that of the author appeared on copies of the work as published, or, in the case of an artistic work, appeared on the work when it was made, the person whose name so appeared (if it was his true name or a name by which he was commonly known) shall, in any action brought by virtue of this Part of this Act, be presumed, unless the contrary is proved,—

(*a*) to be the author of the work, and

(*b*) to have made the work in circumstances not falling within subsection (2), subsection (3) or subsection (4) of section four of this Act.

(3) In the case of a work alleged to be a work of joint authorship, the last preceding subsection shall apply in relation to each person alleged to be one of the authors of the work, as if references in that subsection to the author were references to one of the authors.

(4) Where, in an action brought by virtue of this Part of this Act, with respect to a literary, dramatic, musical or artistic work, subsection (2) of this section does not apply, but it is established—

(*a*) that the work was first published in the United Kingdom, or in another country to which section two, or, as the case may be, section three, of this Act extends, and was so published within the period of fifty years ending with the beginning of the calendar year in which the action was brought, and

(*b*) that a name purporting to be that of the publisher appeared on copies of the work as first published,

then, unless the contrary is shown, copyright shall be presumed to subsist in the work and the person whose name so appeared shall be presumed to have been the owner of that copyright at the time of the publication.

For the purposes of this subsection a fact shall be taken to be established if it is proved or admitted, or if it is presumed in pursuance of the following provisions of this section.

(5) Where in an action brought by virtue of this Part of this Act with respect to a literary, dramatic, musical or artistic work it is proved or admitted that the author of the work is dead,—

(*a*) the work shall be presumed to be an original work unless the contrary is proved, and (*b*) if it is alleged by the plaintiff that a publication specified in the allegation was the first publication of the work, and that it took place in a country and on a date so specified, that publication shall be presumed, unless the contrary is proved, to have been the first publication of the work, and to have taken place in that country and on that date.

(6) Paragraphs (*a*) and (*b*) of the last preceding subsection shall apply where a work has been published, and—

(*a*) the publication was anonymous, or was under a name alleged by the plaintiff to have been a pseudonym, and

(*b*) it is not shown that the work has ever been published under the true name of the author, or under a name by which he was commonly known, or that it is possible for a person without previous knowledge of the facts to ascertain the identity of the author by reasonable inquiry,

as those paragraphs apply in a case where it is proved that the author is dead.

(7) In any action brought by virtue of this Part of this Act with respect to copyright in a sound recording, if records embodying that recording or part thereof have been issued to the public, and at the time when those records were so issued they bore a label or other mark comprising any one or more of the following statements, that is to say,—

(*a*) that a person named on the label or mark was the maker of the sound recording;

(*b*) that the recording was first published in a year specified on the label or mark;

(*c*) that the recording was first published in a country specified on the label or mark,

that label or mark shall be sufficient evidence of the facts so stated except in so far as the contrary is proved.

1451 **Penalties and summary proceedings in respect of dealings which infringe copyright**

21.—(1) Any person who, at a time when copyright subsists in a work,—

(*a*) makes for sale or hire, or

(*b*) sells or lets for hire, or by way of trade offers or exposes for sale or hire, or

(*c*) by way of trade exhibits in public, or

(*d*) imports into the United Kingdom, otherwise than for his private and domestic use,

any article which he knows to be an infringing copy of the work, shall be guilty of an offence under this subsection.

(2) Any person who, at a time when copyright subsists in a work, distributes, either—

(*a*) for purposes of trade, or

(*b*) for other purposes, but to such an extent as to affect prejudicially the owner of the copyright,

articles which he knows to be infringing copies of the work, shall be guilty of an offence under this subsection.

(3) Any person who, at a time when copyright subsists in a work, makes or has in his possession a plate, knowing that it is to be used for making infringing copies of the work, shall be guilty of an offence under this subsection.

(4) The preceding subsections shall apply in relation to copyright subsisting in any subject-matter by virtue of Part II of this Act, as they apply in relation to copyright subsisting by virtue of Part I of this Act.

(5) Any person who causes a literary, dramatic or musical work to be performed in public, knowing that copyright subsists in the work and that the performance constitutes an infringement of the copyright, shall be guilty of an offence under this subsection.

(6) The preceding provisions of this section apply only in respect of acts done in the United Kingdom.

(7) A person guilty of an offence under subsection (1) or subsection (2) of this section shall on summary conviction—

(*a*) if it is his first conviction of an offence under this section, be liable to a fine not exceeding forty shillings for each article to which the offence relates;

(*b*) in any other case, be liable to such a fine, or to imprisonment for a term not exceeding two months:

Provided that a fine imposed by virtue of this subsection shall not exceed fifty pounds in respect of articles comprised in the same transaction.

(8) A person guilty of an offence under subsection (3) or subsection (5) of this section shall on summary conviction—

(*a*) if it is his first conviction of an offence under this section, be liable to a fine not exceeding fifty pounds;

(*b*) in any other case, be liable to such a fine, or to imprisonment for a term not exceeding two months.

(9) The court before which a person is charged with an offence under this section may, whether he is convicted of the offence or not, order that any article in his possession which appears to the court to be an infringing copy, or to be a plate used or intended to be used for making infringing copies, shall be destroyed or delivered up to the owner of the copyright in question or otherwise dealt with as the court may think fit.

(10) An appeal shall lie to a court of quarter sessions from any order made under the last preceding subsection by a court of summary jurisdiction; and where such an order is made by the sheriff there shall be a like right of appeal against the order as if it were a conviction.

1452 Provision for restricting importation of printed copies

22.—(1) The owner of the copyright in any published literary, dramatic or musical work may give notice in writing to the Commissioners of Customs and Excise (in this section referred to as " the Commissioners ")—

(*a*) that he is the owner of the copyright in the work, and

(*b*) that he requests the Commissioners, during a period specified in the notice, to treat as prohibited goods copies of the work to which this section applies:

Provided that the period specified in a notice under this subsection shall not exceed five years and shall not extend beyond the end of the period for which the copyright is to subsist.

(2) This section applies, in the case of a work, to any printed copy made outside the United Kingdom which, if it had been made in the United Kingdom, would be an infringing copy of the work.

(3) Where a notice has been given under this section in respect of a work, and has not been withdrawn, the importation into the United Kingdom, at a time before the end of the period specified in the notice, of any copy of the work to which this section applies shall, subject to the following provisions of this section, be prohibited:

Provided that this subsection shall not apply to the importation of any article by a person for his private and domestic use.

(4) The Commissioners may make regulations prescribing the form in which notices are to be given under this section, and requiring a person giving such a notice, either at the time of giving the notice or at the time when the goods in question are imported, or at both those times, to furnish the Commissioners with such evidence, and to comply with such other conditions (if any), as may be specified in the regulations; and any such regulations may include such incidental and supplementary provisions as the Commissioners consider expedient for the purposes of this section.

(5) Without prejudice to the generality of the last preceding subsection, regulations made under that subsection may include provision for requiring a person who has given a notice under subsection (1) of this section, or a notice purporting to be a notice under that subsection,—

(*a*) to pay such fees in respect of the notice as may be prescribed by the regulations;

(*b*) to give to the Commissioners such security as may be so prescribed, in respect of any liability or expense which they may incur in consequence of the detention, at any time within the period specified in the notice, of any copy of the work to which the notice relates, or in consequence of anything done in relation to a copy so detained;

(*c*) whether any such security is given or not, to keep the Commissioners indemnified against any such liability or expense as is mentioned in the last preceding paragraph.

(6) For the purposes of section eleven of the Customs and Excise Act, 1952 (which relates to the disposal of duties), any fees paid in pursuance of regulations made under this section shall be treated as money collected on account of customs.

(7) Notwithstanding anything in the Customs and Excise Act, 1952, a person shall not be liable to any penalty under that Act (other than forfeiture of the goods) by reason that any goods are treated as prohibited goods by virtue of this section.

PART IV

PERFORMING RIGHT TRIBUNAL

1453 Establishment of tribunal

23.—(1) There shall be established a tribunal, to be called the Performing Right Tribunal (in this Act referred to as " the tribunal "), for the purpose of exercising the jurisdiction conferred by the provisions of this Part of this Act.

(2) The tribunal shall consist of a chairman appointed by the Lord Chancellor, who shall be a barrister, advocate or solicitor of not less than seven years' standing or a person who has held judicial office, and of not

less than two nor more than four other members appointed by the Board of Trade.

[(*3*) *A person shall be disqualified for being appointed, or being, a member of the tribunal so long as he is a member of the Commons House of Parliament, or of the Senate or House of Commons of Northern Ireland.*]

(4) The provisions of the Fourth Schedule to this Act shall have effect with respect to the tribunal.

(5) There shall be paid to the members of the tribunal such remuneration (whether by way of salaries or fees), and such allowances, as the Board of Trade, with the approval of the Treasury, may determine in the case of those members respectively.

(6) The Board of Trade may appoint such officers and servants of the tribunal as the Board, with the approval of the Treasury as to numbers and remuneration, may determine.

(7) The remuneration and allowances of members of the tribunal, the remuneration of any officers and servants appointed under the last preceding subsection, and such other expenses of the tribunal as the Board of Trade with the approval of the Treasury may determine, shall be paid out of moneys provided by Parliament.

AMENDMENT

Subsection (3) was repealed by the House of Commons Disqualification Act, 1957 (5 & 6 Eliz. 2, c. 20) which provides instead that a person is disqualified for membership of the House of Commons and the Senate and the House of Commons of Northern Ireland, who for the time being is a member of the Performing Right Tribunal.

1454 General provisions as to jurisdiction of tribunal

24.—(1) Subject to the provisions of this Part of this Act, the function of the tribunal shall be to determine disputes arising between licensing bodies and persons requiring licences, or organisations claiming to be representative of such persons, either—

(*a*) on the reference of a licence scheme to the tribunal, or

(*b*) on the application of a person requiring a licence either in accordance with a licence scheme or in a case not covered by a licence scheme.

(2) In this Part of this Act " licence " means a licence granted by or on behalf of the owner, or prospective owner, of the copyright in a literary, dramatic or musical work, or in a sound recording or a television broadcast, being—

(*a*) in the case of a literary, dramatic or musical work, a licence to perform in public, or to broadcast, the work or an adaptation thereof, or to cause the work or an adaptation thereof to be transmitted to subscribers to a diffusion service;

(*b*) in the case of a sound recording, a licence to cause it to be heard in public, or to broadcast it;

(*c*) in the case of a television broadcast, a licence to cause it, in so far as it consists of visual images, to be seen in public and, in so far as it consists of sounds, to be heard in public.

(3) In this Part of this Act " licensing body "—

(*a*) in relation to such licences as are mentioned in paragraph (*a*) of the last preceding subsection, means a society or other organisation which has as its main object, or one of its main objects, the negotiation or granting of such licences, either as owner or prospective owner of copyright or as agent for the owners or prospective owners thereof;

(*b*) in relation to such licences as are mentioned in paragraph (*b*) of the last preceding subsection, means any owner or prospective owner of copyright in sound recordings, or any person or body of persons acting as agent for any owners or prospective owners of copyright in sound recordings in relation to the negotiation or granting of such licences; and

(*c*) in relation to such licences as are mentioned in paragraph (*c*) of the last preceding subsection, means the Corporation or the Authority or any organisation appointed by them, or either of them, in accordance with the provisions of the Fifth Schedule to this Act:

Provided that paragraph (*a*) of this subsection shall not apply to an organisation by reason that its objects include the negotiation or granting of individual licences, each relating to a single work or the works of a single author, if they do not include the negotiation or granting of general licences, each extending to the works of several authors.

(4) In this Part of this Act " licence scheme ", in relation to licences of any description, means a scheme made by one or more licensing bodies, setting out the classes of cases in which they, or the persons on whose behalf they act, are willing to grant licences of that description, and the charges (if any), and terms and conditions, subject to which licences would be granted in those classes of cases; and in this subsection " scheme " includes anything in the nature of a scheme, whether described therein as a scheme or as a tariff or by any other name.

(5) References in this Part of this Act to terms and conditions are references to any terms and conditions other than those relating to the amount of a charge for a licence; and references to giving an opportunity to a person of presenting his case are references to giving him an opportunity, at his option, of submitting representations in writing, or of being heard, or of submitting representations in writing and being heard.

1455 **Reference of licence schemes to tribunal**

25.—(1) Where, at any time while a licence scheme is in operation, a dispute arises with respect to the scheme between the licensing body operating the scheme and—

(*a*) an organisation claiming to be representative of persons requiring licences in cases of a class to which the scheme applies, or

(*b*) any person claiming that he requires a licence in a case of a class to which the scheme applies,

the organisation or person in question may refer the scheme to the tribunal in so far as it relates to cases of that class.

(2) The parties to a reference under this section shall be—

(*a*) the organisation or person at whose instance the reference is made;

(*b*) the licensing body operating the scheme to which the reference relates; and

(*c*) such other organisations or persons (if any) as apply to the tribunal to be made parties to the reference and, in accordance with the next following subsection, are made parties thereto.

(3) Where an organisation (whether claiming to be representative of persons requiring licences or not) or a person (whether requiring a licence or not) applies to the tribunal to be made a party to a reference, and the tribunal is satisfied that the organisation or person has a substantial interest in the matter in dispute, the tribunal may, if it thinks fit, make that organisation or person a party to the reference.

(4) The tribunal shall not entertain a reference under this section by an organisation unless the tribunal is satisfied that the organisation is reasonably representative of the class of persons which it claims to represent.

(5) Subject to the last preceding subsection, the tribunal, on any reference under this section, shall consider the matter in dispute, and, after giving to the parties to the reference an opportunity of presenting their cases respectively, shall make such order, either confirming or varying the scheme, in so far as it relates to cases of the class to which the reference relates, as the tribunal may determine to be reasonable in the circumstances.

(6) An order of the tribunal under this section may, notwithstanding anything contained in the licence scheme to which it relates, be made so as to be in force either indefinitely or for such period as the tribunal may determine.

(7) Where a licence scheme has been referred to the tribunal under this section, then, notwithstanding anything contained in the scheme,—

(*a*) the scheme shall remain in operation until the tribunal has made an order in pursuance of the reference, and

(*b*) after such an order has been made, the scheme shall remain in operation, in so far as it relates to the class of cases in respect of which the order was made, so long as the order remains in force:

Provided that this subsection shall not apply in relation to a reference as respects any period after the reference has been withdrawn, or has been discharged by virtue of subsection (4) of this section.

1456 **Further reference of scheme to tribunal**

26.—(1) Where the tribunal has made an order under the last preceding section with respect to a licence scheme, then, subject to the next following subsection, at any time while the order remains in force,—

(*a*) the licensing body operating the scheme, or

(*b*) any organisation claiming to be representative of persons requiring licences in cases of the class to which the order applies, or

(*c*) any person claiming that he requires a licence in a case of that class,

may refer the scheme again to the tribunal in so far as it relates to cases of that class.

(2) A licence scheme shall not, except with the special leave of the tribunal, be referred again to the tribunal under the preceding subsection at a time earlier than—

(*a*) the end of the period of twelve months beginning with the date on which the order in question was made, in the case of an order made so as to be in force indefinitely or for a period exceeding fifteen months, or

(*b*) the beginning of the period of three months ending with the date of expiry of the order, in the case of an order made so as to be in force for fifteen months or less.

(3) The parties to a reference under this section shall be—

(*a*) the licensing body, organisation or person at whose instance the reference is made;

(*b*) the licensing body operating the scheme to which the reference relates, if the reference is not made at their instance; and

(*c*) such other organisations or persons (if any) as apply to the tribunal to be made parties to the reference and, in accordance with the provisions applicable in that behalf by virtue of subsection (5) of this section, are made parties thereto.

(4) Subject to the next following subsection, the tribunal, on any reference under this section, shall consider the matter in dispute, and, after giving to the parties to the reference an opportunity of presenting their cases respectively, shall make such order in relation to the scheme as previously confirmed or varied, in so far as it relates to cases of the class in question, either by way of confirming, varying or further varying the scheme, as the tribunal may determine to be reasonable in the circumstances.

(5) Subsections (3), (4), (6) and (7) of the last preceding section shall apply for the purposes of this section.

(6) The preceding provisions of this section shall have effect in relation to orders made under this section as they have effect in relation to orders made under the last preceding section.

(7) Nothing in this section shall be construed as preventing a licence scheme, in respect of which an order has been made under the last preceding section, from being again referred to the tribunal under that section, either—

(*a*) at any time, in so far as the scheme relates to cases of a class to which the order does not apply, or

(*b*) after the expiration of the order, in so far as the scheme relates to cases of the class to which the order applied while it was in force.

1457 **Applications to tribunal**

27.—(1) For the purposes of this Part of this Act a case shall be taken to be covered by a licence scheme if, in accordance with a licence scheme for the time being in operation, licences would be granted in cases of the class to which that case belongs:

Provided that where, in accordance with the provisions of a licence scheme,—

(*a*) the licences which would be so granted would be subject to terms and conditions whereby particular matters would be excepted from the licences, and

(*b*) the case in question relates to one or more matters falling within such an exception,

that case shall be taken not to be covered by the scheme.

(2) Any person who claims, in a case covered by a licence scheme, that the licensing body operating the scheme have refused or failed to grant him a licence in accordance with the provisions of the scheme, or to procure the grant to him of such a licence, may apply to the tribunal under this section.

(3) Any person who claims that he requires a licence in a case not covered by a licence scheme, and either—

(*a*) that a licensing body have refused or failed to grant the licence, or to procure the grant thereof, and that in the circumstances it is unreasonable that the licence should not be granted, or

(*b*) that any charges, terms or conditions subject to which a licensing body propose that the licence should be granted are unreasonable,

may apply to the tribunal under this section.

(4) Where an organisation (whether claiming to be representative of persons requiring licences or not) or a person (whether requiring a licence or not) applies to the tribunal to be made a party to an application under the preceding provisions of this section, and the tribunal is satisfied that the organisation or person has a substantial interest in the matter in dispute, the tribunal may, if it thinks fit, make that organisation or person a party to the application.

(5) On any application under subsection (2) or subsection (3) of this section the tribunal shall give to the applicant and to the licensing body in question and to every other party (if any) to the application an opportunity of presenting their cases respectively; and if the tribunal is satisfied that the claim of the applicant is well founded, the tribunal shall make an order declaring that, in respect of the matters specified in the order, the applicant is entitled to a licence on such terms and conditions, and subject to the payment of such charges (if any) as—

(*a*) in the case of an application under subsection (2) of this section, the tribunal may determine to be applicable in accordance with the licence scheme, or

(*b*) in the case of an application under subsection (3) of this section, the tribunal may determine to be reasonable in the circumstances.

(6) Any reference in this section to a failure to grant or procure the grant of a licence shall be construed as a reference to a failure to grant it, or to procure the grant thereof, within a reasonable time after being requested to do so

57a **[Applications for review by tribunal of orders**

27A.—(1) Where the tribunal has made an order under subsection (5) of the last preceding section, then subject to the next following subsection, at any time while the order remains in force,—

(*a*) the licensing body in question, or

(*b*) the original applicant

may apply to the tribunal to review its original order.

(2) An application shall not be made pursuant to subsection (1) of this section, except with the special leave of the tribunal, at a time earlier than—

(*a*) the end of a period of twelve months beginning with the date on which the original order was made, in the case of an order made so as to be in force indefinitely or for a period exceeding fifteen months, or

(*b*) the beginning of the period of three months ending with the date of expiry of the order in the case of an order made so as to be in force for fifteen months or less.

(3) The parties to an application under this section shall be—

(*a*) the parties to the original application proceedings; and

(*b*) any organisation or person who is made party thereto pursuant to subsection (5) of this section.

(4) The tribunal, on any application under this section, after giving all the parties an opportunity of presenting their cases shall make such order in relation to the application either by way of confirming or varying the order in question as—

(*a*) in the case of an order made pursuant to an application under subsection (2) of the last preceding section, the tribunal may determine to be applicable in accordance with the licence scheme, or

(*b*) in the case of an order made pursuant to an application under subsection (3) of the last preceding section, the tribunal may determine to be reasonable in the circumstances.

(5) Subsection (4) of section 27 (applications by organisations and persons to be made party to proceedings) shall apply in relation to proceedings under this section as it applies in relation to proceedings under that section.

(6) The preceding provisions of this section shall have effect in relation to orders made under this section as they have in relation to orders made under the last preceding section.]

AMENDMENT

This section was inserted by the Copyright (Amendment) Act, 1971 (c. 4).

1458 Exercise of jurisdiction of tribunal in relation to diffusion of foreign broadcasts

28.—(1) Where, on a reference to the tribunal under this Part of this Act relating to licences to cause works to be transmitted to subscribers to a diffusion service in the United Kingdom, the tribunal is satisfied—

(*a*) that the licences are required wholly or partly for the purpose of distributing programmes broadcast, from a place outside the United Kingdom, by an organisation other than the Corporation and the Authority, and

(*b*) that, under the arrangements in accordance with which the programmes are broadcast by that organisation, charges are payable by or on behalf of the organisation to another body, as being the body entitled under the relevant copyright law to authorise the broadcasting of those works from that place,

the tribunal shall, subject to the next following subsection, exercise its powers under this Part of this Act as the tribunal may consider appropriate for securing that the persons requiring the licences are exempted from the payment of any charges for them in so far as the licences are required for the purpose of distributing those programmes.

(2) If on such a reference as is mentioned in the last preceding subsection the tribunal is satisfied as to the matters mentioned in paragraphs (*a*) and (*b*) of that subsection, but it is shown to the satisfaction of the tribunal that the charges payable by or on behalf of the organisation, as mentioned in paragraph (*b*) of that subsection,—

(*a*) make no allowance for the fact that, in consequence of the broadcasting of the works in question by that organisation, the persons requiring the licences may be enabled to cause those works to be transmitted to subscribers to diffusion services in the United Kingdom, or (*b*) do not adequately reflect the extent to which it is likely that those persons will cause those works to be so transmitted in consequence of their being so broadcast,

the last preceding subsection shall not apply, but the tribunal shall exercise its powers under this Part of this Act so as to secure that the charges payable for the licences, in so far as the licences are required for the purpose mentioned in the last preceding subsection, are on a scale not exceeding that appearing to the tribunal to be requisite for making good the deficiency (as mentioned in paragraph (*a*) or paragraph (*b*) of this subsection, as the case may be) in the charges payable by or on behalf of the organisation broadcasting the works.

(3) The preceding provisions of this section shall have effect, with the necessary modifications, in relation to applications under this Part of this Act as they have effect in relation to references thereunder.

(4) In this section " the relevant copyright law ", in relation to works broadcast from a place outside the United Kingdom, means so much of the laws of the country in which that place is situated as confers rights similar to copyright under this Act or as otherwise relates to such rights; and any reference to works includes a reference to adaptations thereof.

1459 **Effect of orders of tribunal, and supplementary provisions relating thereto**

29.—(1) Where an order made on a reference under this Part of this Act with respect to a licence scheme is for the time being in force, any person who, in a case covered by the scheme as confirmed or varied by the order, does anything which—

(*a*) apart from this subsection would be an infringement of copyright, but

(*b*) would not be such an infringement if he were the holder of a licence granted in accordance with the scheme, as confirmed or varied by the order, in so far as the scheme relates to cases comprised in the order,

shall, if he has complied with the requirements specified in the next following subsection, be in the like position, in any proceedings for infringement of that copyright, as if he had at the material time been the holder of such a licence.

(2) The said requirements are—

(*a*) that, at all material times, the said person has complied with the terms and conditions which, in accordance with the licence scheme as confirmed or varied by the order, would be applicable to a licence covering the case in question, and

(*b*) if, in accordance with the scheme as so confirmed or varied, any charges are payable in respect of such a licence, that at the material time he had paid those charges to the licensing body operating the scheme, or, if at that time the amount payable could not be ascertained, he had given an undertaking to the licensing body to pay the charges when ascertained.

(3) Where the tribunal has made an order under section twenty-seven [or section twenty-seven A] of this Act declaring that a person is entitled to a licence in respect of any matters specified in the order, then if—

(*a*) that person has complied with the terms and conditions specified in the order, and (*b*) in a case where the order requires the payment of charges, he has paid those charges to the licensing body in accordance with the order, or, if the order so provides, has given to the licensing body an undertaking to pay the charges when ascertained,

he shall be in the like position, in any proceedings for infringement of copyright relating to any of those matters, as if he had at all material times been the holder of a licence granted by the owner of the copyright in question on the terms and conditions specified in the order.

(4) In the exercise of its jurisdiction in respect of licences relating to television broadcasts, the tribunal shall have regard (among other matters) to any conditions imposed by the promoters of any entertainment or other event which is to be comprised in the broadcasts; and, in particular, the tribunal shall not hold a refusal or failure to grant a licence to be unreasonable if it could not have been granted consistently with those conditions:

Provided that nothing in this subsection shall require the tribunal to have regard to any such conditions in so far as they purport to regulate the charges to be imposed in respect of the grant of licences, or in so far as they relate to payments to be made to the promoters of any event in consideration of the grant of facilities for broadcasting.

(5) Where, on a reference to the tribunal under this Part of this Act,—

(*a*) the reference relates to licences in respect of copyright in sound recordings or in television broadcasts, and

(*b*) the tribunal is satisfied that any of the licences in question are required for the purposes of organisations such as are mentioned in paragraph (*b*) of subsection (7) of section twelve of this Act,

the tribunal may, if it thinks fit, exercise its powers under this Part of this Act so as to reduce, in the case of those organisations, to such extent as the tribunal thinks fit, the charges which it determines generally to be reasonable in relation to cases of the class to which the reference relates, or, if it thinks fit, so as to exempt those organisations from the payment of any such charges.

(6) The last preceding subsection shall have effect, with the necessary modifications, in relation to applications under this Part of this Act as it has effect in relation to references thereunder.

(7) In relation to copyright in a literary, dramatic or musical work, any reference in this section to proceedings for infringement of copyright includes a reference to proceedings brought by virtue of subsection (5) of section twenty-one of this Act.

AMENDMENT

The words in square brackets in sub-s. (3) were inserted by the Copyright (Amendment) Act, 1971 (c. 4).

1460 **Reference of questions of law to the court**

30.—(1) Any question of law arising in the course of proceedings before the tribunal may, at the request of any party to the proceedings, be referred by the tribunal to the court for decision, whether before or after the tribunal has given its decision in the proceedings:

Provided that a question shall not be referred to the court by virtue of this subsection in pursuance of a request made after the date on which the tribunal gave its decision, unless the request is made before the end of such period as may be prescribed by rules made under the Fourth Schedule to this Act.

(2) If the tribunal, after giving its decision in any proceedings, refuses any such request to refer a question to the court, the party by whom the

request was made may, within such period as may be prescribed by rules of court, apply to the court for an order directing the tribunal to refer the question to the court.

(3) On any reference to the court under this section with respect to any proceedings before the tribunal, and on any application under the last preceding subsection with respect to any such proceedings, every party to the proceedings before the tribunal shall be entitled to appear and to be heard.

(4) Where, after the tribunal has given its decision in any proceedings, the tribunal refers to the court under this section a question of law which arose in the course of the proceedings, and the court decides that the question was erroneously determined by the tribunal,—

(*a*) the tribunal, if it considers it requisite to do so for the purpose of giving effect to the decision of the court, shall give to the parties to the proceedings a further opportunity of presenting their cases respectively;

(*b*) in any event, the tribunal shall reconsider the matter in dispute in conformity with the decision of the court;

(*c*) if on such reconsideration it appears to the tribunal to be appropriate to do so, the tribunal shall make such order revoking or modifying any order previously made by it in the proceedings, or, in the case of proceedings under section twenty-seven of this Act where the tribunal refused to make an order, shall make such order under that section, as on such reconsideration the tribunal determines to be appropriate.

(5) Any reference of a question by the tribunal to the court under this section shall be by way of stating a case for the opinion of the court; and the decision of the court on any such reference shall be final.

(6) In this section " the court "—

(*a*) in relation to any proceedings of the tribunal in England or Wales, or in Northern Ireland, means the High Court; and

(*b*) in relation to any proceedings of the tribunal in Scotland, means the Court of Session.

AMENDMENT

By virtue of s. 7 of and Sched. 1 to the Northern Ireland Act, 1962 (10 & 11 Eliz. 2, c. 30), s. 30 of the Copyright Act, 1956, in its application to proceedings in Northern Ireland, is to have effect with the omission, from subs. (2), of the words " within such period as may be prescribed by rules of court."

PART V

EXTENSION OR RESTRICTION OF OPERATION OF ACT

1461 **Extension of Act to Isle of Man, Channel Islands, colonies and dependencies**

31.—(1) Her Majesty may by Order in Council direct that any of the provisions of this Act specified in the Order (including any enactments for the time being in force amending or substituted for those provisions) shall extend, subject to such exceptions and modifications (if any) as may be specified in the Order, to—

(*a*) the Isle of Man;

(*b*) any of the Channel Islands;

(*c*) any colony;

(*d*) any country outside Her Majesty's dominions in which for the time being Her Majesty has jurisdiction;
(*e*) any country consisting partly of one or more colonies and partly of one or more such countries as are mentioned in the last preceding paragraph.

(2) The powers conferred by the preceding subsection shall be exercisable in relation to any Order in Council made under the following provisions of this Part of this Act, as those powers are exercisable by virtue of that subsection in relation to the provisions of this Act.

(3) The legislature of any country to which any provisions of this Act have been extended may modify or add to those provisions, in their operation as part of the law of that country, in such manner as that legislature may consider necessary to adapt the provisions to the circumstances of that country:

Provided that no such modifications or additions, except in so far as they relate to procedure and remedies, shall be made so as to apply to any work or other subject-matter in which copyright can subsist unless—

(*a*) in the case of a literary, dramatic, musical or artistic work, the author of the work, or, in the case of a sound recording or a cinematograph film, the maker of the recording or film, was domiciled or resident in that country at the time when, or during the period while, the work, recording or film was made, or
(*b*) in the case of a published edition of a literary, dramatic or musical work, the publisher of the edition was domiciled or resident in that country at the date of its first publication, or
(*c*) in the case of a literary, dramatic, musical or artistic work, or of a sound recording or a cinematograph film or a published edition, it was first published in that country, or
(*d*) in the case of a television broadcast or sound broadcast, it was made from a place in that country.

(4) For the purposes of any proceedings under this Act in the United Kingdom, where the proceedings relate to an act done in a country to which any provisions of this Act extend subject to exceptions, modifications or additions,—

(*a*) the procedure applicable to the proceedings, including the time within which they may be brought, and the remedies available therein, shall be in accordance with this Act in its operation as part of the law of the United Kingdom; but
(*b*) if the act in question does not constitute an infringement of copyright under this Act in its operation as part of the law of the country where the act was done, it shall (notwithstanding anything in this Act) be treated as not constituting an infringement of copyright under this Act in its operation as part of the law of the United Kingdom.

1462 Application of Act to countries to which it does not extend

32.—(1) Her Majesty may by Order in Council make provision for applying any of the provisions of this Act specified in the Order, in the case of a country to which those provisions do not extend, in any one or more of the following ways, that is to say, so as to secure that those provisions—

(*a*) apply in relation to literary, dramatic, musical or artistic works, sound recordings, cinematograph films or editions first published in that country as they apply in relation to literary, dramatic, musical or artistic works, sound recordings, cinematograph films or editions first published in the United Kingdom;

(*b*) apply in relation to persons who, at a material time, are citizens or subjects of that country as they apply in relation to persons who, at such a time, are British subjects;

(*c*) apply in relation to persons who, at a material time, are domiciled or resident in that country as they apply in relation to persons who, at such a time, are domiciled or resident in the United Kingdom;

(*d*) apply in relation to bodies incorporated under the laws of that country as they apply in relation to bodies incorporated under the laws of any part of the United Kingdom;

(*e*) apply in relation to television broadcasts and sound broadcasts made from places in that country, by one or more organisations constituted in, or under the laws of, that country, as they apply in relation to television broadcasts and sound broadcasts made from places in the United Kingdom by the Corporation or the Authority.

(2) An Order in Council under this section—

(*a*) may apply the provisions in question as mentioned in the preceding subsection, but subject to exceptions or modifications specified in the Order;

(*b*) may direct that the provisions in question shall so apply either generally or in relation to such classes of works, or other classes of cases, as may be specified in the Order.

(3) Her Majesty shall not make an Order in Council under this section applying any of the provisions of this Act in the case of a country, other than a country which is a party to a Convention relating to copyright to which the United Kingdom is also a party, unless Her Majesty is satisfied that, in respect of the class of works or other subject-matter to which those provisions relate, provision has been or will be made under the laws of that country whereby adequate protection will be given to owners of copyright under this Act.

463 **Provisions as to international organisations**

33.—(1) Where it appears to Her Majesty that one or more sovereign Powers, or the government or governments thereof, are members of an organisation, and that it is expedient that the provisions of this section should apply to that organisation, Her Majesty may by Order in Council declare that the organisation is one to which this section applies.

(2) Where an original literary, dramatic, musical or artistic work is made by or under the direction or control of an organisation to which this section applies in such circumstances that—

(*a*) copyright would not subsist in the work apart from this subsection, but

(*b*) if the author of the work had been a British subject at the time when it was made, copyright would have subsisted in the work immediately after it was made and would thereupon have vested in the organisation,

copyright shall subsist in the work as if the author had been a British subject when it was made, that copyright shall continue to subsist so long as the work remains unpublished, and the organisation shall, subject to the provisions of this Act, be entitled to that copyright.

(3) Where an original literary, dramatic, musical or artistic work is first published by or under the direction or control of an organisation to which this section applies, in such circumstances that, apart from this subsection, copyright does not subsist in the work immediately after the first publication thereof, and either—

(*a*) the work is so published in pursuance of an agreement with the author which does not reserve to the author the copyright (if any) in the work, or

(*b*) the work was made in such circumstances that, if it had been first published in the United Kingdom, the organisation would have been entitled to the copyright in the work,

copyright shall subsist in the work (or, if copyright in the work subsisted immediately before its first publication, shall continue to subsist) as if it had been first published in the United Kingdom, that copyright shall subsist until the end of the period of fifty years from the end of the calendar year in which the work was first published, and the organisation shall, subject to the provisions of Part VI of this Act, be entitled to that copyright.

(4) The provisions of Part I of this Act, with the exception of provisions thereof relating to the subsistence, duration or ownership of copyright, shall apply in relation to copyright subsisting by virtue of this section as they apply in relation to copyright subsisting by virtue of the said Part I.

(5) An organisation to which this section applies which otherwise has not, or at some material time otherwise had not, the legal capacities of a body corporate shall have, and shall be deemed at all material times to have had, the legal capacities of a body corporate for the purpose of holding, dealing with and enforcing copyright and in connection with all legal proceedings relating to copyright.

1464 **Extended application of provisions relating to broadcasts**

34. Her Majesty may by Order in Council provide that, subject to such exceptions and modifications (if any) as may be specified in the Order, such provisions of this Act relating to television broadcasts or to sound broadcasts as may be so specified shall apply in relation to the operation of wireless telegraphy apparatus by way of the emission (as opposed to reception) of electro-magnetic energy—

(*a*) by such persons or classes of persons, other than the Corporation and the Authority, as may be specified in the Order, and

(*b*) for such purposes (whether involving broadcasting or not) as may be so specified,

as they apply in relation to television broadcasts, or, as the case may be, to sound broadcasts, made by the Corporation and the Authority.

1465 **Denial of copyright to citizens of countries not giving adequate protection to British works**

35.—(1) If it appears to Her Majesty that the laws of a country fail to give adequate protection to British works to which this section applies, or fail to give such protection in the case of one or more classes of such works (whether the lack of protection relates to the nature of the work or the country of its author or both), Her Majesty may make an Order in Council designating that country and making such provision in relation thereto as is mentioned in the following provisions of this section.

(2) An Order in Council under this section shall provide that, either generally or in such classes of cases as are specified in the Order, copyright under this Act shall not subsist in works to which this section applies which were first published after a date specified in the Order, if at the time of their first publication the authors thereof were—

(*a*) citizens or subjects of the country designated by the Order, not being at that time persons domiciled or resident in the United Kingdom or in another country to which the relevant provision of this Act extends, or

(*b*) bodies incorporated under the laws of the country designated by the Order.

(3) In making an Order in Council under this section Her Majesty shall have regard to the nature and extent of the lack of protection for British works in consequence of which the Order is made.

(4) This section applies to the following works, that is to say, literary, dramatic, musical and artistic works, sound recordings and cinematograph films.

(5) In this section—

"British work" means a work of which the author, at the time when the work was made, was a qualified person for the purposes of the relevant provision of this Act;

"author", in relation to a sound recording or a cinematograph film, means the maker of the recording or film;

"the relevant provision of this Act", in relation to literary, dramatic and musical works means section two, in relation to artistic works means section three, in relation to sound recordings means section twelve, and in relation to cinematograph films means section thirteen, of this Act.

PART VI

MISCELLANEOUS AND SUPPLEMENTARY PROVISIONS

1466 **Assignments and licences in respect of copyright**

36.—(1) Subject to the provisions of this section, copyright shall be transmissible by assignment, by testamentary disposition, or by operation of law, as personal or moveable property.

(2) An assignment of copyright may be limited in any of the following ways, or in any combination of two or more of those ways, that is to say,—

(*a*) so as to apply to one or more, but not all, of the classes of acts which by virtue of this Act the owner of the copyright has the exclusive right to do (including any one or more classes of acts not separately designated in this Act as being restricted by the copyright, but falling within any of the classes of acts so designated);

(*b*) so as to apply to any one or more, but not all, of the countries in relation to which the owner of the copyright has by virtue of this Act that exclusive right;

(*c*) so as to apply to part, but not the whole, of the period for which the copyright is to subsist;

and references in this Act to a partial assignment are references to an assignment so limited.

(3) No assignment of copyright (whether total or partial) shall have effect unless it is in writing signed by or on behalf of the assignor.

(4) A licence granted in respect of any copyright by the person who, in relation to the matters to which the licence relates, is the owner of the copyright shall be binding upon every successor in title to his interest in the copyright, except a purchaser in good faith for valuable consideration and without notice (actual or constructive) of the licence or a person deriving title from such a purchaser; and references in this Act, in relation to any copyright, to the doing of anything with, or (as the case may be) without, the licence of the owner of the copyright shall be construed accordingly.

1467 **Prospective ownership of copyright**

37.—(1) Where by an agreement made in relation to any future copyright, and signed by or on behalf of the prospective owner of the copyright, the prospective owner purports to assign the future copyright (wholly or partially) to another person (in this subsection referred to as " the assignee "), then if, on the coming into existence of the copyright, the assignee or a person claiming under him would, apart from this subsection, be entitled as against all other persons to require the copyright to be vested in him (wholly or partially, as the case may be), the copyright shall, on its coming into existence, vest in the assignee or his successor in title accordingly by virtue of this subsection and without further assurance.

(2) Where, at the time when any copyright comes into existence, the person who, if he were then living, would be entitled to the copyright is dead, the copyright shall devolve as if it had subsisted immediately before his death and he had then been the owner of the copyright.

(3) Subsection (4) of the last preceding section shall apply in relation to a licence granted by a prospective owner of any copyright as it applies in relation to a licence granted by the owner of a subsisting copyright, as if any reference in that subsection to the owner's interest in the copyright included a reference to his prospective interest therein.

(4) The provisions of the Fifth Schedule to this Act shall have effect with respect to assignments and licences in respect of copyright (including future copyright) in television broadcasts.

(5) In this Act " future copyright " means copyright which will or may come into existence in respect of any future work or class of works or other subject-matter, or on the coming into operation of any provisions of this Act, or in any other future event, and " prospective owner " shall be construed accordingly and, in relation to any such copyright, includes a person prospectively entitled thereto by virtue of such an agreement as is mentioned in subsection (1) of this section.

1468 **Copyright to pass under will with unpublished work**

38. Where under a bequest (whether specific or general) a person is entitled, beneficially or otherwise, to the manuscript of a literary, dramatic or musical work, or to an artistic work, and the work was not published before the death of the testator, the bequest shall, unless a contrary intention is indicated in the testator's will or a codicil thereto, be construed as including the copyright in the work in so far as the testator was the owner of the copyright immediately before his death.

1469 Provisions as to Crown and Government departments

39.—(1) In the case of every original literary, dramatic, musical or artistic work made by or under the direction or control of Her Majesty or a Government department,—

(*a*) if apart from this section copyright would not subsist in the work, copyright shall subsist therein by virtue of this subsection, and

(*b*) in any case, Her Majesty shall, subject to the provisions of this Part of this Act, be entitled to the copyright in the work.

(2) Her Majesty shall, subject to the provisions of this Part of this Act, be entitled—

(*a*) to the copyright in every original literary, dramatic or musical work first published in the United Kingdom, or in another country to which section two of this Act extends, if first published by or under the direction or control of Her Majesty or a Government department;

(*b*) to the copyright in every original artistic work first published in the United Kingdom, or in another country to which section three of this Act extends, if first published by or under such direction or control.

(3) Copyright in a literary, dramatic or musical work, to which Her Majesty is entitled in accordance with either of the preceding subsections,—

(*a*) where the work is unpublished, shall continue to subsist so long as the work remains unpublished, and

(*b*) where the work is published, shall subsist (or, if copyright in the work subsisted immediately before its first publication, shall continue to subsist) until the end of the period of fifty years from the end of the calendar year in which the work was first published, and shall then expire.

(4) Copyright in an artistic work to which Her Majesty is entitled in accordance with the preceding provisions of this section shall continue to subsist until the end of the period of fifty years from the end of the calendar year in which the work was made, and shall then expire:

Provided that where the work in question is an engraving or a photograph, the copyright shall continue to subsist until the end of the period of fifty years from the end of the calendar year in which the engraving or photograph is first published.

(5) In the case of every sound recording or cinematograph film made by or under the direction or control of Her Majesty or a Government department,—

(*a*) if apart from this section copyright would not subsist in the recording or film, copyright shall subsist therein by virtue of this subsection, and

(*b*) in any case, Her Majesty shall, subject to the provisions of this Part of this Act, be entitled to the copyright in the recording or film, and it shall subsist for the same period as if it were copyright subsisting by virtue of, and owned in accordance with, section twelve or, as the case may be, section thirteen of this Act.

(6) The preceding provisions of this section shall have effect subject to any agreement made by or on behalf of Her Majesty or a Government department with the author of the work, or the maker of the sound

recording or cinematograph film, as the case may be, whereby it is agreed that the copyright in the work, recording or film shall vest in the author or maker, or in another person designated in the agreement in that behalf.

(7) In relation to copyright subsisting by virtue of this section—

(*a*) in the case of a literary, dramatic, musical or artistic work, the provisions of Part I of this Act, with the exception of provisions thereof relating to the subsistence, duration or ownership of copyright, and

(*b*) in the case of a sound recording or cinematograph film, the provisions of Part II of this Act, with the exception of provisions thereof relating to the subsistence or ownership of copyright,

shall apply as those provisions apply in relation to copyright subsisting by virtue of Part I or, as the case may be, Part II of this Act.

(8) For the avoidance of doubt, it is hereby declared that the provisions of section three of the Crown Proceedings Act, 1947 (which relates to infringements of industrial property by servants or agents of the Crown) apply to copyright under this Act.

(9) In this section "Government department" means any department of Her Majesty's Government in the United Kingdom or of the Government of Northern Ireland, or any department or agency of the Government of any other country to which this section extends.

1470 **Broadcasts of sound recordings and cinematograph films, and diffusion of broadcast programmes**

40.—(1) Where a sound broadcast or television broadcast is made by the Corporation or the Authority, and a person, by the reception of that broadcast, causes a sound recording to be heard in public, he does not thereby infringe the copyright (if any) in that recording under section twelve of this Act.

(2) Where a television broadcast or sound broadcast is made by the Corporation or the Authority, and the broadcast is an authorised broadcast, any person who, by the reception of the broadcast, causes a cinematograph film to be seen or heard in public shall be in the like position, in any proceedings for infringement of the copyright (if any) in the film under section thirteen of this Act, as if he had been the holder of a licence granted by the owner of that copyright to cause the film to be seen or heard in public by the reception of the broadcast.

(3) Where a television broadcast or sound broadcast is made by the Corporation or the Authority, and the broadcast is an authorised broadcast, any person who, by the reception of the broadcast, causes a programme to be transmitted to subscribers to a diffusion service, being a programme comprising a literary, dramatic or musical work, or an adaptation of such a work, or an artistic work, or a cinematograph film, shall be in the like position, in any proceedings for infringement of the copyright (if any) in the work or film, as if he had been the holder of a licence granted by the owner of that copyright to include the work, adaptation or film in any programme caused to be transmitted by him to subscribers to that service by the reception of the broadcast.

(4) If, in the circumstances mentioned in either of the two last preceding subsections, the person causing the cinematograph film to be seen or heard, or the programme to be transmitted, as the case may be, infringed the copyright in question, by reason that the broadcast was not an authorised broadcast,—

(*a*) no proceedings shall be brought against that person under this Act in respect of his infringement of that copyright, but

(*b*) it shall be taken into account in assessing damages in any proceedings against the Corporation or the Authority, as the case may be, in respect of that copyright, in so far as that copyright was infringed by them in making the broadcast.

(5) For the purposes of this section, a broadcast shall be taken, in relation to a work or cinematograph film, to be an authorised broadcast if, but only if, it is made by, or with the licence of, the owner of the copyright in the work or film.

1471 Use of copyright material for education

41.—(1) Where copyright subsists in a literary, dramatic, musical or artistic work, the copyright shall not be taken to be infringed by reason only that the work is reproduced, or an adaptation of the work is made or reproduced,—

(*a*) in the course of instruction, whether at a school or elsewhere, where the reproduction or adaptation is made by a teacher or pupil otherwise than by the use of a duplicating process, or

(*b*) as part of the questions to be answered in an examination, or in an answer to such a question.

(2) Nothing in the preceding subsection shall apply to the publication of a work or of an adaptation of a work; and, for the purposes of section five of this Act, the fact that to a person's knowledge the making of an article would have constituted an infringement of copyright but for the preceding subsection shall have the like effect as if, to his knowledge, the making of it had constituted such an infringement.

(3) For the avoidance of doubt it is hereby declared that, where a literary, dramatic or musical work—

(*a*) is performed in class, or otherwise in the presence of an audience, and

(*b*) is so performed in the course of the activities of a school, by a person who is a teacher in, or a pupil in attendance at, the school,

the performance shall not be taken for the purposes of this Act to be a performance in public if the audience is limited to persons who are teachers in, or pupils in attendance at, the school, or are otherwise directly connected with the activities of the school.

(4) For the purposes of the last preceding subsection a person shall not be taken to be directly connected with the activities of a school by reason only that he is a parent or guardian of a pupil in attendance at the school.

(5) The two last preceding subsections shall apply in relation to sound recordings, cinematograph films and television broadcasts as they apply in relation to literary, dramatic and musical works, as if any reference to performance were a reference to the act of causing the sounds or visual images in question to be heard or seen.

(6) Nothing in this section shall be construed—

(*a*) as extending the operation of any provision of this Act as to the acts restricted by copyright of any description, or

(*b*) as derogating from the operation of any exemption conferred by any provision of this Act other than this section.

(7) In this section " school "—

(*a*) in relation to England and Wales, has the same meaning as in the Education Act, 1944;

(*b*) in relation to Scotland, has the same meaning as in the Education (Scotland) Act, 1946, except that it includes an approved school within the meaning of the Children and Young Persons (Scotland) Act, 1937; and

(*c*) in relation to Northern Ireland, has the same meaning as in the Education Act (Northern Ireland), 1947;

and " duplicating process " means any process involving the use of an appliance for producing multiple copies.

1472 **Special provisions as to public records**

42.—(1) Where any work in which copyright subsists, or a reproduction of any such work, is comprised in—

(*a*) any records belonging to Her Majesty which are under the charge and superintendence of the Master of the Rolls by virtue of an Order in Council under section two of the Public Record Office Act, 1838, and are open to public inspection in accordance with rules made under that Act, or

(*b*) any public records to which the Public Records Act (Northern Ireland), 1923, applies, being records which are open to public inspection in accordance with rules made under that Act,

the copyright in the work is not infringed by the making, or the supplying to any person, of any reproduction of the work by or under the direction of any officer appointed under the said Act of 1838 or the said Act of 1923, as the case may be.

(2) In the preceding subsection " records "—

(*a*) in paragraph (*a*) of that subsection has the same meaning as in the Public Record Office Act, 1838;

(*b*) in paragraph (*b*) of that subsection has the same meaning as in the Public Records Act (Northern Ireland), 1923.

(3) Any reference in this section to the Public Records Act (Northern Ireland), 1923, shall be construed as including a reference to that Act as for the time being amended or re-enacted (with or without modifications) by any enactment of the Parliament of Northern Ireland.

AMENDMENT

The Public Record Office Act, 1838, was repealed by s. 13 of and Sched. 4 to the Public Records Act, 1958 (6 & 7 Eliz. 2, c. 51) and by virtue of s. 11 of and Sched. 3 to that Act, as respects any reproduction made after the commencement of that Act, the reference in s. 42 (1) (*a*) of the Copyright Act, 1956, to records of the description there mentioned is to be taken as a reference to public records which are open to public inspection in pursuance of the provisions of the 1958 Act.

1473 **False attribution of authorship**

43.—(1) The restrictions imposed by this section shall have effect in relation to literary, dramatic, musical or artistic works; and any reference in this section to a work shall be construed as a reference to such a work.

(2) A person (in this subsection referred to as " the offender ") contravenes those restrictions as respects another person if, without the licence

of that other person, he does any of the following acts in the United Kingdom, that is to say, he—

(*a*) inserts or affixes that other person's name in or on a work of which that person is not the author, or in or on a reproduction of such a work, in such a way as to imply that the other person is the author of the work, or

(*b*) publishes, or sells or lets for hire, or by way of trade offers or exposes for sale or hire, or by way of trade exhibits in public, a work in or on which the other person's name has been so inserted or affixed, if to the offender's knowledge that person is not the author of the work, or

(*c*) does any of the acts mentioned in the last preceding paragraph in relation to, or distributes, reproductions of a work, being reproductions in or on which the other person's name has been so inserted or affixed, if to the offender's knowledge that person is not the author of the work, or

(*d*) performs in public, or broadcasts, a work of which the other person is not the author, as being a work of which he is the author, if to the offender's knowledge that person is not the author of the work.

(3) The last preceding subsection shall apply where, contrary to the fact, a work is represented as being an adaptation of the work of another person as it applies where a work is so represented as being the work of another person.

(4) In the case of an artistic work which has been altered after the author parted with the possession of it, the said restrictions are contravened, in relation to the author, by a person who in the United Kingdom, without the licence of the author,—

(*a*) publishes, sells or lets for hire, or by way of trade offers or exposes for sale or hire the work as so altered, as being the unaltered work of the author, or

(*b*) publishes, sells or lets for hire, or by way of trade offers or exposes for sale or hire a reproduction of the work as so altered, as being a reproduction of the unaltered work of the author,

if to his knowledge it is not the unaltered work, or, as the case may be, a reproduction of the unaltered work, of the author.

(5) The three last preceding subsections shall apply with respect to anything done in relation to another person after that person's death, as if any reference to that person's licence were a reference to a licence given by him or by his personal representatives:

Provided that nothing in those subsections shall apply to anything done in relation to a person more than twenty years after that person's death.

(6) In the case of an artistic work in which copyright subsists, the said restrictions are also contravened, in relation to the author of the work, by a person who in the United Kingdom—

(*a*) publishes, or sells or lets for hire, or by way of trade offers or exposes for sale or hire, or by way of trade exhibits in public, a reproduction of the work, as being a reproduction made by the author of the work, or

(*b*) distributes reproductions of the work as being reproductions made by the author of the work,

if (in any such case) the reproduction or reproductions was or were to his knowledge not made by the author.

(7) The preceding provisions of this section shall apply (with the necessary modifications) with respect to acts done in relation to two or more persons in connection with the same work.

(8) The restrictions imposed by this section shall not be enforceable by any criminal proceedings; but any contravention of those restrictions, in relation to a person, shall be actionable at his suit, or, if he is dead, at the suit of his personal representatives, as a breach of statutory duty.

(9) Any damages recovered under this section by personal representatives, in respect of a contravention committed in relation to a person after his death, shall devolve as part of his estate, as if the right of action had subsisted and had been vested in him immediately before his death.

(10) Nothing in this section shall derogate from any right of action or other remedy (whether civil or criminal) in proceedings instituted otherwise than by virtue of this section:

Provided that this subsection shall not be construed as requiring any damages recovered by virtue of this section to be disregarded in assessing damages in any proceedings instituted otherwise than by virtue of this section and arising out of the same transaction.

(11) In this section " name " includes initials or a monogram.

1474 **Amendments of Registered Designs Act, 1949**

44.—(1) In section six of the Registered Designs Act, 1949, (under which the disclosure of a design in certain circumstances is not to be a reason for refusing registration), the following subsections shall be inserted after subsection (3):

" (4) Where copyright under the Copyright Act, 1956, subsists in an artistic work, and an application is made by, or with the consent of, the owner of that copyright for the registration of a corresponding design, that design shall not be treated for the purposes of this Act as being other than new or original by reason only of any use previously made of the artistic work, unless—

(*a*) the previous use consisted of or included the sale, letting for hire, or offer for sale or hire of articles to which the design in question (or a design differing from it only as mentioned in subsection (2) of section one of this Act) had been applied industrially, other than articles of a description specified in rules made under subsection (4) of section one of this Act, and

(*b*) that previous use was made by, or with the consent of, the owner of the copyright in the artistic work.

(5) Any rules made by virtue of subsection (5) of section ten of the Copyright Act, 1956 (which relates to rules for determining the circumstances in which a design is to be taken to be applied industrially) shall apply for the purposes of the last foregoing subsection."

(2) The following subsection shall be added at the end of section eight of the said Act of 1949 (which relates to the period of copyright in registered designs):

" (3) Where in the case of a registered design it is shown—

(*a*) that the design, at the time when it was registered, was a corresponding design in relation to an artistic work in which copyright subsisted under the Copyright Act, 1956;

(*b*) that, by reason of a previous use of that artistic work, the design would not have been registrable under this Act but for subsection (4) of section six of this Act; and (*c*) that the copyright in that work under the Copyright Act, 1956, expired before the date of expiry of the copyright in the design,

the copyright in the design shall, notwithstanding anything in this section, be deemed to have expired at the same time as the copyright in the artistic work, and shall not be renewable after that time."

(3) In section eleven of the said Act of 1949 (which relates to cancellation of the registration of designs), the following subsection shall be inserted after subsection (2):

" (2A) At any time after a design has been registered, any person interested may apply to the registrar for the cancellation of the registration of the design on the grounds—

(*a*) that the design, at the time when it was registered, was a corresponding design in relation to an artistic work in which copyright subsisted under the Copyright Act, 1956;

(*b*) that, by reason of a previous use of that artistic work, the design would not have been registrable under this Act but for subsection (4) of section six of this Act; and

(*c*) that the copyright in that work under the Copyright Act, 1956, has expired;

and the registrar may make such order on the application as he thinks fit."

(4) In subsection (3) of the said section eleven, for the words " the last foregoing subsection " there shall be substituted the words " either of the two last foregoing subsections."

(5) In subsection (1) of section forty-four of the said Act of 1949 (which relates to the interpretation of that Act)—

(*a*) after the definition of " article " there shall be inserted the words " ' artistic work ' has the same meaning as in the Copyright Act, 1956 "; and

(*b*) after the definition of " copyright " there shall be inserted the words " ' corresponding design ' has the same meaning as in section ten of the Copyright Act, 1956 ".

1475 Amendment of Dramatic and Musical Performers' Protection Act, 1925

[**45.** *In the Dramatic and Musical Performers' Protection Act, 1925,—*

(a) *after section one there shall be inserted the two sections set out in Part I of the Sixth Schedule to this Act; and*

(b) *after section three there shall be inserted the two sections set out in Part II of that Schedule;*

and the provisions of that Act specified in Part III of that Schedule shall have effect subject to the amendments set out in relation thereto in the second column of the said Part III (being minor amendments of that Act and amendments consequential upon the insertion therein of the sections referred to in paragraphs (a) *and* (b) *of this section).*]

AMENDMENT

This provision and the Sixth Schedule were repealed by the Dramatic and Musical Performers' Protection Act, 1958 (6 & 7 Eliz. 2, c. 44), which also repealed the Dramatic and Musical Performers' Protection Act, 1925 (15 & 16 Geo. 5, c. 46).

1476 **Savings**

46.—(1) Any rights conferred on universities and colleges by the Copyright Act, 1775, which continued to subsist in accordance with section thirty-three of the Copyright Act, 1911, notwithstanding the repeal of the said Act of 1775, shall continue to subsist in accordance with the said Act of 1775 notwithstanding any repeal effected by this Act:

Provided that no proceedings shall be brought under the Copyright Act, 1775, but the provisions of Part III of this Act shall apply for the enforcement of those rights as if they were copyright subsisting by virtue of this Act.

(2) Nothing in this Act shall affect any right or privilege of the Crown subsisting otherwise than by virtue of an enactment; and nothing in this Act shall affect any right or privilege of the Crown or of any other person under any enactment (including any enactment of the Parliament of Northern Ireland), except in so far as that enactment is expressly repealed, amended or modified by this Act.

(3) Nothing in this Act shall affect the right of the Crown or of any person deriving title from the Crown to sell, use or otherwise deal with articles forfeited under the laws relating to customs or excise, including any articles so forfeited by virtue of this Act or of any enactment repealed by this Act.

(4) Nothing in this Act shall affect the operation of any rule of equity relating to breaches of trust or confidence.

(5) Subject to the preceding provisions of this section, no copyright, or right in the nature of copyright, shall subsist otherwise than by virtue of this Act or of some other enactment in that behalf.

1477 **General provisions as to Orders in Council, regulations, rules and orders, and as to Board of Trade**

47.—(1) Any power to make regulations, rules or orders under this Act shall be exercisable by statutory instrument.

(2) Any statutory instrument containing—

(*a*) any Order in Council or regulations made under this Act, or

(*b*) any rules made by the Lord Chancellor under the Fourth Schedule to this Act,

shall be subject to annulment in pursuance of a resolution of either House of Parliament.

(3) Any Order in Council, or other order, made under any of the preceding provisions of this Act may be varied or revoked by a subsequent Order in Council or order made thereunder.

(4) Where a power to make regulations or rules is conferred by any provision of this Act, regulations or rules under that power may be made either as respects all, or as respects any one or more, of the matters to which the provision relates; and different provision may be made by any such regulations or rules as respects different classes of cases to which the regulations or rules apply.

[(5) *Anything required or authorised by or under this Act to be done by, to or before the Board of Trade may be done by, to or before the President of the Board of Trade, any Minister of State with duties concerning the affairs of the Board, any secretary, under-secretary or assistant secretary of the Board, or any person authorised in that behalf by the President.*]

(6) In this section " order " does not include an order of a court or of the tribunal.

AMENDMENT

Subs. (5) was repealed by s. 18 of and Sched. 4. to the Industrial Expansion Act, 1968, (1968, c. 32), s. 14 of which provides that anything authorised or required by or under that Act or any other enactments (including an enactment of the Parliament of Northern Ireland), whether passed before or after that Act, to be done by, to or before the Board of Trade may be done by, to or before the President of the Board or any person acting with his authority.

See as to concurrent exercise of functions by the Secretary of State, The Secretary of State for Trade and Industry Order, 1970 (1970 S.I. No. 1537).

1478 Interpretation

48.—(1) In this Act, except in so far as the context otherwise requires, the following expressions have the meanings hereby assigned to them respectively, that is to say:

" adaptation," in relation to a literary, dramatic or musical work, has the meaning assigned to it by section two of this Act;

" artistic work " has the meaning assigned to it by section three of this Act;

" assignment," in relation to Scotland, means an assignation;

" building " includes any structure;

" cinematograph film " has the meaning assigned to it by section thirteen of this Act;

" construction " includes erection, and references to reconstruction shall be construed accordingly;

" the Corporation " and " the Authority " have the meanings assigned to them by section fourteen of this Act;

" country " includes any territory;

" dramatic work " includes a choreographic work or entertainment in dumb show if reduced to writing in the form in which the work or entertainment is to be presented, but does not include a cinematograph film, as distinct from a scenario or script for a cinematograph film;

" drawing " includes any diagram, map, chart or plan;

" engraving " includes any etching, lithograph, woodcut, print or similar work, not being a photograph;

" future copyright " and " prospective owner " have the meanings assigned to them by section thirty-seven of this Act;

" judicial proceeding " means a proceeding before any court, tribunal or person having by law power to hear, receive and examine evidence on oath;

" literary work " includes any written table or compilation;

" manuscript," in relation to a work, means the original document embodying the work, whether written by hand or not;

" performance " includes delivery, in relation to lectures, addresses, speeches and sermons, and in general, subject to the provisions of subsection (5) of this section, includes any mode of visual or acoustic presentation, including any such presentation by the operation of wireless telegraphy apparatus, or by the exhibition of a cinematograph film, or by the use of a record, or by any other means, and references to performing a work or an adaptation of a work shall be construed accordingly;

"photograph" means any product of photography or of any process akin to photography, other than a part of a cinematograph film, and "author," in relation to a photograph, means the person who, at the time when the photograph is taken, is the owner of the material on which it is taken;

"qualified person" has the meaning assigned to it by section one of this Act;

"record" means any disc, tape, perforated roll or other device in which sounds are embodied so as to be capable (with or without the aid of some other instrument) of being automatically reproduced therefrom, and references to a record of a work or other subject-matter are references to a record (as herein defined) by means of which it can be performed;

"reproduction," in the case of a literary, dramatic or musical work, includes a reproduction in the form of a record or of a cinematograph film, and, in the case of an artistic work, includes a version produced by converting the work into a three-dimensional form, or, if it is in three dimensions, by converting it into a two-dimensional form, and references to reproducing a work shall be construed accordingly;

"sculpture" includes any cast or model made for purposes of sculpture;

"sound recording" has the meaning assigned to it by section twelve of this Act;

"sufficient acknowledgment" has the meaning assigned to it by section six of this Act;

"television broadcast" and "sound broadcast" have the meanings assigned to them by section fourteen of this Act;

"wireless telegraphy apparatus" has the same meaning as in the Wireless Telegraphy Act, 1949;

"work of joint authorship" has the meaning assigned to it by section eleven of this Act;

"writing" includes any form of notation, whether by hand or by printing, typewriting or any similar process.

(2) References in this Act to broadcasting are references to broadcasting by wireless telegraphy (within the meaning of the Wireless Telegraphy Act, 1949), whether by way of sound broadcasting or of television.

(3) References in this Act to the transmission of a work or other subject-matter to subscribers to a diffusion service are references to the transmission thereof in the course of a service of distributing broadcast programmes, or other programmes (whether provided by the person operating the service or other persons), over wires, or other paths provided by a material substance, to the premises of subscribers to the service; and for the purposes of this Act, where a work or other subject-matter is so transmitted,—

(*a*) the person operating the service (that is to say, the person who, in the agreements with subscribers to the service, undertakes to provide them with the service, whether he is the person who transmits the programmes or not) shall be taken to be the person causing the work or other subject-matter to be so transmitted, and (*b*) no person, other than the person operating the service, shall be taken to be causing it to be so transmitted, notwithstanding that he provides any facilities for the transmission of the programmes:

Provided that, for the purposes of this subsection, and of references to which this subsection applies, no account shall be taken of a service of distributing broadcast or other programmes, where the service is only incidental to a business of keeping or letting premises where persons reside or sleep, and is operated as part of the amenities provided exclusively or mainly for residents or inmates therein.

(4) References in this Act to the doing of any act by the reception of a television broadcast or sound broadcast made by the Corporation or the Authority are references to the doing of that act by means of receiving the broadcast either—

(*a*) from the transmission whereby the broadcast is made by the Corporation or the Authority, as the case may be, or

(*b*) from a transmission made by the Corporation or the Authority, as the case may be, otherwise than by way of broadcasting, but simultaneously with the transmission mentioned in the preceding paragraph,

whether (in either case) the reception of the broadcast is directly from the transmission in question or from a re-transmission thereof made by any person from any place, whether in the United Kingdom or elsewhere; and in this subsection " re-transmission " means any re-transmission, whether over paths provided by a material substance or not, including any re-transmission made by making use of any record, print, negative, tape or other article on which the broadcast in question has been recorded.

(5) For the purposes of this Act, broadcasting, or the causing of a work or other subject-matter to be transmitted to subscribers to a diffusion service, shall not be taken to constitute performance, or to constitute causing visual images or sounds to be seen or heard; and where visual images or sounds are displayed or emitted by any receiving apparatus, to which they are conveyed by the transmission of electromagnetic signals (whether over paths provided by a material substance or not),—

(*a*) the operation of any apparatus whereby the signals are transmitted, directly or indirectly, to the receiving apparatus shall not be taken to constitute performance or to constitute causing the visual images or sounds to be seen or heard; but

(*b*) in so far as the display or emission of the images or sounds constitutes a performance, or causes them to be seen or heard, the performance, or the causing of the images or sounds to be seen or heard, as the case may be, shall be taken to be effected by the operation of the receiving apparatus.

(6) Without prejudice to the last preceding subsection, where a work or an adaptation of a work is performed, or visual images or sounds are caused to be seen or heard, by the operation of any apparatus to which this subsection applies, being apparatus provided by or with the consent of the occupier of the premises where the apparatus is situated, the occupier of those premises shall, for the purposes of this Act, be taken to be the person giving the performance, or causing the images or sounds to be seen or heard, whether he is the person operating the apparatus or not.

This subsection applies to any such receiving apparatus as is mentioned in the last preceding subsection, and to any apparatus for reproducing sounds by the use of a record.

(7) Except in so far as the context otherwise requires, any reference in this Act to an enactment shall be construed as a reference to that enactment as amended or extended by or under any other enactment.

1479 **Supplementary provisions as to interpretation**

49.—(1) Except in so far as the context otherwise requires, any reference in this Act to the doing of an act in relation to a work or other subject-matter shall be taken to include a reference to the doing of that act in relation to a substantial part thereof, and any reference to a reproduction, adaptation or copy of a work, or a record embodying a sound recording, shall be taken to include a reference to a reproduction, adaptation or copy of a substantial part of the work, or a record embodying a substantial part of the sound recording, as the case may be:

Provided that, for the purposes of the following provisions of this Act, namely subsections (1) and (2) of section two, subsections (2) and (3) of section three, subsections (2) and (3) of section thirty-three, section thirty-eight, and subsections (2) to (4) of section thirty-nine, this subsection shall not affect the construction of any reference to the publication, or absence of publication, of a work.

(2) With regard to publication, the provisions of this subsection shall have effect for the purposes of this Act, that is to say,—

(*a*) the performance, or the issue of records, of a literary, dramatic or musical work, the exhibition of an artistic work, the construction of a work of architecture, and the issue of photographs or engravings of a work of architecture or of a sculpture, do not constitute publication of the work;

(*b*) except in so far as it may constitute an infringement of copyright, or a contravention of any restriction imposed by section forty-three of this Act, a publication which is merely colourable, and not intended to satisfy the reasonable requirements of the public, shall be disregarded;

(*c*) subject to the preceding paragraphs, a literary, dramatic or musical work, or an edition of such a work, or an artistic work, shall be taken to have been published if, but only if, reproductions of the work or edition have been issued to the public;

(*d*) a publication in the United Kingdom, or in any other country, shall not be treated as being other than the first publication by reason only of an earlier publication elsewhere, if the two publications took place within a period of not more than thirty days;

and in determining, for the purposes of paragraph (*c*) of this subsection, whether reproductions of a work or edition have been issued to the public, the preceding subsection shall not apply.

(3) In determining for the purposes of any provision of this Act—

(*a*) whether a work or other subject-matter has been published, or

(*b*) whether a publication of a work or other subject-matter was the first publication thereof, or

(*c*) whether a work or other subject-matter was published or otherwise dealt with in the lifetime of a person,

no account shall be taken of any unauthorised publication or of the doing of any other unauthorised act; and (subject to subsection (7) of section seven of this Act) a publication or other act shall for the purposes of this subsection be taken to have been unauthorised—

(i) if copyright subsisted in the work or other subject-matter and the act in question was done otherwise than by, or with the licence of, the owner of the copyright, or

(ii) if copyright did not subsist in the work or other subject-matter, and the act in question was done otherwise than by, or with the licence of, the author (or, in the case of a sound recording or a cinematograph film, or an edition of a literary, dramatic or musical work, the maker or publisher, as the case may be) or persons lawfully claiming under him:

Provided that nothing in this subsection shall affect any provisions of this Act as to the acts restricted by any copyright or as to acts constituting infringements of copyrights, or any provisions of section forty-three of this Act.

(4) References in this Act to the time at which, or the period during which, a literary, dramatic or musical work was made are references to the time or period at or during which it was first reduced to writing or some other material form.

(5) In the case of any copyright to which (whether in consequence of a partial assignment or otherwise) different persons are entitled in respect of the application of the copyright—

(*a*) to the doing of different acts or classes of acts, or

(*b*) to the doing of one or more acts or classes of acts in different countries or at different times,

the owner of the copyright, for any purpose of this Act, shall be taken to be the person who is entitled to the copyright in respect of its application to the doing of the particular act or class of acts, or, as the case may be, to the doing thereof in the particular country or at the particular time, which is relevant to the purpose in question; and, in relation to any future copyright to which different persons are prospectively entitled, references in this Act to the prospective owner of the copyright shall be construed accordingly.

(6) Without prejudice to the generality of the last preceding subsection, where under any provision of this Act a question arises whether an article of any description has been imported or sold, or otherwise dealt with, without the licence of the owner of any copyright, the owner of the copyright, for the purpose of determining that question, shall be taken to be the person entitled to the copyright in respect of its application to the making of articles of that description in the country into which the article was imported, or, as the case may be, in which it was sold or otherwise dealt with.

(7) Where the doing of anything is authorised by the grantee of a licence, or a person deriving title from the grantee, and it is within the terms (including any implied terms) of the licence for him to authorise it, it shall for the purposes of this Act be taken to be done with the licence of the grantor and of every other person (if any) upon whom the licence is binding.

(8) References in this Act to deriving title are references to deriving title either directly or indirectly.

(9) Where, in the case of copyright of any description,—

(*a*) provisions contained in this Act specify certain acts as being restricted by the copyright, or as constituting infringements thereof, and

(*b*) other provisions of this Act specify certain acts as not constituting infringements of the copyright,

the omission or exclusion of any matter from the latter provisions shall not be taken to extend the operation of the former provisions.

(10) Any reference in this Act to countries to which a provision of this Act extends includes a country to which that provision extends subject to exceptions, modifications or additions.

1480 **Transitional provisions, and repeals**

50.—(1) The transitional provisions contained in the Seventh Schedule to this Act shall have effect for the purposes of this Act; and the provisions of the Eighth Schedule to this Act shall have effect in accordance with those transitional provisions.

(2) Subject to the said transitional provisions, the enactments specified in the Ninth Schedule to this Act are hereby repealed to the extent specified in the third column of that Schedule.

1481 **Short title, commencement and extent**

51.—(1) This Act may be cited as the Copyright Act, 1956.

(2) This Act shall come into operation on such day as the Board of Trade may by order appoint; and different days may be appointed for the purposes of different provisions of this Act, and, for the purposes of any provision of this Act whereby enactments are repealed, different days may be appointed for the operation of the repeal in relation to different enactments, including different enactments contained in the same Act.

(3) It is hereby declared that this Act extends to Northern Ireland.

SCHEDULES

1482 **Section 10**

FIRST SCHEDULE

FALSE REGISTRATION OF INDUSTRIAL DESIGNS

1. The provisions of this Schedule shall have effect where—

(*a*) copyright subsists in an artistic work, and proceedings are brought under this Act relating to that work;

(*b*) a corresponding design has been registered under the Act of 1949, and the copyright in the design subsisting by virtue of that registration has not expired by effluxion of time before the commencement of those proceedings; and

(*c*) it is proved or admitted in the proceedings that the person registered as the proprietor of the design was not the proprietor thereof for the purposes of the Act of 1949, and was so registered without the knowledge of the owner of the copyright in the artistic work.

2. For the purposes of those proceedings (but subject to the next following paragraph) the registration shall be treated as never having been effected, and accordingly, in relation to that registration, [*subsection (1) of section ten of this Act shall not apply, and*] nothing in section seven of the Act of 1949 shall be construed as affording any defence in those proceedings.

3. Notwithstanding anything in the last preceding paragraph, if in the proceedings it is proved or admitted that any act to which the proceedings relate—

(*a*) was done in pursuance of an assignment or licence made or granted by the person registered as proprietor of the design, and

(*b*) was so done in good faith in reliance upon the registration, and without notice of any proceedings for the cancellation of the registration or for rectifying the entry in the register of designs relating thereto,

[*subsection (1) of section ten of this Act shall apply in relation to that act for the purposes of the first-mentioned proceedings*] [this shall be a good defence to such proceedings].

4. In this Schedule "the Act of 1949" means the Registered Designs Act, 1949, and "corresponding design" has the meaning assigned to it by subsection (7) of section ten of this Act.

AMENDMENT

Paras. 2 and 3 were amended by the Design Copyright Act, 1968 (1968, c. 68) by deleting the words in italics and by substituting new words at the end of para. 3 as shown in square brackets.

1483 **Section 11**

SECOND SCHEDULE

DURATION OF COPYRIGHT IN ANONYMOUS AND PSEUDONYMOUS WORKS

1. Where the first publication of a literary, dramatic, or musical work, or of an artistic work other than a photograph, is anonymous or pseudonymous, then subject to the following provisions of this Schedule—

(*a*) subsection (3) of section two of this Act, or, as the case may be, subsection (4) of section three of this Act, shall not apply, and

(*b*) any copyright subsisting in the work by virtue of either of those sections shall continue to subsist until the end of the period of fifty years from the end of the calendar year in which the work was first published, and shall then expire.

2. The preceding paragraph shall not apply in the case of a work if, at any time before the end of the period mentioned in that paragraph, it is possible for a person without previous knowledge of the facts to ascertain the identity of the author by reasonable inquiry.

3. For the purposes of this Act a publication of a work under two or more names shall not be taken to be pseudonymous unless all those names are pseudonyms.

1484 **Section 11**

THIRD SCHEDULE

WORKS OF JOINT AUTHORSHIP

1. In relation to a work of joint authorship, the references to the author in subsections (1) and (2) of section two of this Act, in subsections (2) and (3) of section three of this Act, and in paragraph 2 of the Second Schedule to this Act, shall be construed as references to any one or more of the authors.

2. In relation to a work of joint authorship, other than a work to which the next following paragraph applies, references to the author in subsection (3) of section two, in subsection (4) of section three, and in subsection (6) of section seven, of this Act, shall be construed as references to the author who died last.

3.—(1) This paragraph applies to any work of joint authorship which was first published under two or more names, of which one or more (but not all) were pseudonyms.

(2) This paragraph also applies to any work of joint authorship which was first published under two or more names all of which were pseudonyms, if, at

any time within the period of fifty years from the end of the calendar year in which the work was first published, it is possible for a person without previous knowledge of the facts to ascertain the identity of any one or more (but not all) of the authors by reasonable inquiry.

(3) In relation to a work to which this paragraph applies, references to the author in subsection (3) of section two of this Act, and in subsection (4) of section three of this Act, shall be construed as references to the author whose identity was disclosed, or, if the identity of two or more of the authors was disclosed, as references to that one of those authors who died last.

(4) For the purposes of this paragraph the identity of an author shall be taken to have been disclosed if either—

(*a*) in his case, the name under which the work was published was not a pseudonym, or

(*b*) it is possible to ascertain his identity as mentioned in subparagraph (2) of this paragraph.

4.—(1) In relation to a work of joint authorship of which one or more of the authors are persons to whom this paragraph applies, subsection (1) of section four of this Act shall have effect as if the author or authors, other than persons to whom this paragraph applies, had been the sole author, or (as the case may be) sole joint authors, of the work.

(2) This paragraph applies, in the case of a work, to any person such that, if he had been the sole author of the work, copyright would not have subsisted in the work by virtue of Part I of this Act.

5. In the proviso to subsection (6) of section six of this Act, the reference to other excerpts from works by the author of the passage in question—

(*a*) shall be taken to include a reference to excerpts from works by the author of that passage in collaboration with any other person, or

(*b*) if the passage in question is from a work of joint authorship, shall be taken to include a reference to excerpts from works by any one or more of the authors of that passage, or by any one or more of those authors in collaboration with any other person.

6. Subject to the preceding provisions of this Schedule, any reference in this Act to the author of a work shall (unless it is otherwise expressly provided) be construed, in relation to a work of joint authorship, as a reference to all the authors of the work.

1485 **Sections 23, 30, 47** FOURTH SCHEDULE

Provisions as to Performing Right Tribunal

1.—(1) Subject to the provisions of this paragraph, the members of the tribunal shall hold office for such period as may be determined at the time of their respective appointments; and a person who ceases to hold office as a member of the tribunal shall be eligible for re-appointment.

(2) Any member of the tribunal may at any time by notice in writing to the Board of Trade, or, in the case of the chairman of the tribunal, to the Lord Chancellor, resign his appointment.

(3) The Board of Trade, or, in the case of the chairman of the tribunal, the Lord Chancellor, may declare the office of any member of the tribunal vacant on the ground of his unfitness to continue in office or incapacity to perform the duties thereof.

2. If any member of the tribunal is, by reason of illness, absence or other reasonable cause, for the time being unable to perform the duties of his office, either generally or in relation to any particular proceedings, the Board of Trade, or, in the case of the chairman of the tribunal, the Lord Chancellor, may appoint some other duly qualified person to discharge the duties of that member for any period, not exceeding six months at one time, or, as the case

may be, in relation to those proceedings; and a person so appointed shall, during that period or in relation to those proceedings, have the same powers as the person in whose place he is appointed.

3. If at any time there are more than two members of the tribunal, in addition to the chairman, then, for the purposes of any proceedings, the tribunal may consist of the chairman together with any two or more of those members.

4. If the members of the tribunal dealing with any reference or application are unable to agree as to the order to be made by the tribunal, a decision shall be taken by the votes of the majority; and, in the event of an equality of votes, the chairman shall be entitled to a second or casting vote.

5. The tribunal may order that the costs or expenses of any proceedings before it incurred by any party shall be paid by any other party, and may tax or settle the amount of any costs or expenses to be paid under any such order or direct in what manner they are to be taxed.

6.—(1) The Lord Chancellor may make rules as to the procedure in connection with the making of references and applications to the tribunal, and for regulating proceedings before the tribunal and, subject to the approval of the Treasury, as to the fees chargeable in respect of those proceedings.

(2) Any such rules may apply in relation to the tribunal—

(*a*) as respects proceedings in England and Wales, any of the provisions of the Arbitration Act, 1950, and

(*b*) as respects proceedings in Northern Ireland, any of the provisions of the Arbitration Act (Northern Ireland), 1937.

(3) Any such rules may include provision—

(*a*) for prescribing the period within which, after the tribunal has given its decision in any proceedings, a request may be made to the tribunal to refer a question of law to the court;

(*b*) for requiring notice of any intended application to the court under subsection (2) of section thirty of this Act to be given to the tribunal and to the other parties to the proceedings, and for limiting the time within which any such notice is to be given;

(*c*) for suspending, or authorising or requiring the tribunal to suspend, the operation of orders of the tribunal, in cases where, after giving its decision, the tribunal refers a question of law to the court;

(*d*) for modifying, in relation to orders of the tribunal whose operation is suspended, the operation of any provisions of Part IV of this Act as to the effect of orders made thereunder;

(*e*) for the publication of notices, or the taking of any other steps, for securing that persons affected by the suspension of an order of the tribunal will be informed of its suspension;

(*f*) for regulating or prescribing any other matters incidental to or consequential upon any request, application, order or decision under section thirty of this Act.

(4) Provision shall be made by rules of court for limiting the time for instituting proceedings under subsection (2) of section thirty of this Act, and for authorising or requiring the court, where it makes an order directing the tribunal to refer a question of law to the court, to provide in the order for suspending the operation of any order made by the tribunal in the proceedings in which the question of law arose.

(5) In this paragraph "the court" has the same meaning as in section thirty of this Act.

7. As respects proceedings in Scotland, the tribunal shall have the like powers for securing the attendance of witnesses and the production of documents, and with regard to the examination of witnesses on oath, as if the tribunal were an arbiter under a submission.

8. Without prejudice to any method available by law for the proof of orders of the tribunal, a document purporting to be a copy of any such order, and to be certified by the chairman of the tribunal to be a true copy thereof, shall, in any legal proceedings, be sufficient evidence of the order unless the contrary is proved.

1486 **Sections 24, 37**

FIFTH SCHEDULE

APPOINTMENT OF TELEVISION COPYRIGHT ORGANISATIONS BY BRITISH BROADCASTING CORPORATION AND INDEPENDENT TELEVISION AUTHORITY

1. In this Schedule—

(*a*) references to a right to which this Schedule applies are references to the copyright (including any future copyright) in any television broadcast, in so far as the copyright relates, or when it comes into existence will relate, to the acts specified in paragraph (*c*) of subsection (4) of section fourteen of this Act;

(*b*) references to the purposes of this Schedule are references to the purposes of negotiating or granting licences in respect of rights to which this Schedule applies.

2. The Corporation and the Authority may jointly appoint an organisation for the purposes of this Schedule; and if they do so, no other organisation shall be appointed by them or either of them for those purposes until the appointment of that organisation has been duly terminated.

3. Subject to the last preceding paragraph, the Corporation or the Authority, or each of them, may appoint an organisation for the purposes of this Schedule; and if an organisation is so appointed by the Corporation or by the Authority, no other organisation shall be appointed for the purposes of this Schedule by the Corporation or the Authority, as the case may be, until the appointment of that organisation has been duly terminated.

4. A right to which this Schedule applies shall not be assignable by the Corporation or by the Authority except to an organisation duly appointed for the purposes of this Schedule; and where such a right has been assigned to such an organisation, it shall not be assignable by the organisation except to the Corporation or the Authority, as the case may be, or to another organisation subsequently appointed for the purposes of this Schedule.

5.—(1) Neither the Corporation nor the Authority shall authorise any organisation or person, other than any person in their employment under a contract of service, to negotiate or act for them with respect to the granting of licences in respect of rights to which this Schedule applies, except an organisation duly appointed for the purposes of this Schedule.

(2) An organisation appointed for the purposes of this Schedule shall not authorise any other organisation or person, other than any person in their employment under a contract of service, to negotiate or act for them, or for the Corporation or the Authority, with respect to the granting of licences in respect of rights to which this Schedule applies.

6. The appointment, or the termination of the appointment, of an organisation for the purposes of this Schedule shall not have effect unless, not less than fourteen days before the appointment or termination is to take effect, a notice is published in the London Gazette, the Edinburgh Gazette and the Belfast Gazette, specifying the name and address of the organisation, and the date on which the appointment or termination is to take effect, and stating whether the appointment, or termination of appointment, is made by the Corporation or the Authority or by both of them.

7. Where notice of the appointment of an organisation for the purposes of this Schedule has been given under the last preceding paragraph, the organisation shall be taken for the purposes of this Act to be authorised to act in accordance with the appointment until their appointment is duly terminated in pursuance of a notice published in accordance with that paragraph.

1487 **Section 45** [*SIXTH SCHEDULE*

Amendment of Dramatic and Musical Performers' Protection Act, 1925

Part I

New Sections 1a and 1b

Penalties for making, etc., cinematograph films without consent of performers

1A. *Subject to the provisions of this Act, if any person knowingly—*

(a) *makes a cinematograph film, directly or indirectly, from or by means of the performance of any dramatic or musical work without the consent in writing of the performers, or*

(b) *sells or lets for hire, or distributes for the purposes of trade, or by way of trade exposes or offers for sale or hire, a cinematograph film made in contravention of this Act, or*

(c) *uses for the purposes of exhibition to the public a cinematograph film made in contravention of this Act,*

he shall be guilty of an offence under this Act, and shall be liable on summary conviction to a fine not exceeding fifty pounds:

Provided that, where a person is charged with an offence under paragraph (a) *of this section, it shall be a defence to prove that the cinematograph film was made for his private and domestic use only.*

Penalties for broadcasting without consent of performers

1B. *Subject to the provisions of this Act, any person who, otherwise than by the use of a record or a cinematograph film, knowingly broadcasts a performance of any dramatic or musical work, or any part of such a performance, without the consent in writing of the performers shall be guilty of an offence under this Act, and shall be liable on summary conviction to a fine not exceeding fifty pounds.*

PART II

NEW SECTIONS 3A AND 3B

Special defences

1488 3A. *Notwithstanding anything in the preceding provisions of this Act, it shall be a defence to any proceedings under this Act to prove—*

(a) *that the record, cinematograph film or broadcast to which the proceedings relate was made only for the purpose of reporting current events, or*

(b) *that the inclusion of the performance in question in the record, cinematograph film or broadcast to which the proceedings relate was only by way of background or was otherwise only incidental to the principal matters comprised or represented in the record, film or broadcast.*

Consent on behalf of performers

3B. *Where in any proceedings under this Act it is proved—*

(a) *that the record, cinematograph film or broadcast to which the proceedings relate was made with the consent in writing of a person who, at the time of giving the consent, represented that he was authorised by the performers to give it on their behalf, and*

(b) *that the person making the record, film or broadcast had no reasonable grounds for believing that the person giving the consent was not so authorised,*

the provisions of this Act shall apply as if it had been proved that the performers had themselves consented in writing to the making of the record, film or broadcast.

PART III

MINOR AND CONSEQUENTIAL AMENDMENTS

1489 *Provision amended* — *Amendment*

Section one ... *At the beginning of the section there shall be inserted the words " Subject to the provisions of this Act"; and at the end of the section, for the words " not made for purposes of trade" there shall be substituted the words " made for his private and domestic use only."*

Section three ... *For the words " records or" there shall be substituted the words " records, cinematograph films."*

Section four ... *At the end of the definition of the expression " record" there shall be inserted the words " including the sound-track of a cinematograph film"; and at the end of the section there shall be inserted the following definitions:*

" The expression ' cinematograph film' means any print, negative, tape or other article on which a performance of a dramatic or musical work or part thereof is recorded for the purposes of visual reproduction, and any reference to the making of a cinematograph film is a reference to the carrying out of any process whereby such a performance or part thereof is so recorded;

The expression ' broadcast' means broadcast by wireless telegraphy (within the meaning of the Wireless Telegraphy Act, 1949), whether by way of sound broadcasting or of television."]

AMENDMENT

The provisions of this Schedule and section 45 were repealed by the Dramatic and Musical Performers' Protection Act, 1958 (6 & 7 Eliz. 2, c. 44), which also repealed the Dramatic and Musical Performers' Protection Act, 1925 (15 & 16 Geo. 5, c. 46).

1490 **Section 50**

SEVENTH SCHEDULE

TRANSITIONAL PROVISIONS

PART I

PROVISIONS RELATING TO PART I OF ACT

Conditions for subsistence of copyright

1. In the application of sections two and three to works first published before the commencement of those sections, subsection (2) of section two, and subsection (3) of section three, shall apply as if paragraphs (*b*) and (*c*) of those subsections were omitted.

Duration of copyright

2. In relation to any photograph taken before the commencement of section three, subsection (4) of that section shall not apply, but, subject to subsection (3) of that section, copyright subsisting in the photograph by virtue of that section shall continue to subsist until the end of the period of fifty years from the end of the calendar year in which the photograph was taken, and shall then expire.

Ownership of copyright

3.—(1) Subsections (2) to (4) of section four shall not apply—

(*a*) to any work made as mentioned in subsection (2) or subsection (4) of that section, if the work was so made before the commencement of that section, or (*b*) to any work made as mentioned in subsection (3) of that section, if the work was or is so made in pursuance of a contract made before the commencement of that section.

(2) In relation to any work to which the preceding sub-paragraph applies, subsection (1) of section four shall have effect subject to the proviso set out in paragraph 1 of the Eighth Schedule to this Act (being the proviso to subsection (1) of section five of the Act of 1911).

Infringements of copyright

1491 4. For the purposes of section five, the fact that, to a person's knowledge, the making of an article constituted an infringement of copyright under the Act of 1911, or would have constituted such an infringement if the article had been made in the place into which it is imported, shall have the like effect as if, to that person's knowledge, the making of the article had constituted an infringement of copyright under this Act.

5. Subsection (7) of section six does not apply to assignments made or licences granted before the commencement of that section.

6.—(1) References in section eight to records previously made by, or with the licence of, the owner of the copyright in a work include references to records previously made by, or with the consent of, the owner of the copyright in that work under the Act of 1911.

(2) The repeal by this Act of any provisions of section nineteen of the Act of 1911, or of the provisions of the Copyright Order Confirmation (Mechanical Instruments: Royalties) Act, 1928, shall not affect the operation of those provisions, or of any regulations or order made thereunder, in relation to a record made before the repeal.

7.—(1) In relation to a painting, drawing, engraving, photograph or cinematograph film made before the commencement of section nine, subsection (6) of that section shall apply if, by virtue of subsection (3) or subsection (4) of that section, the making of the painting, drawing, engraving, photograph or film would not have constituted an infringement of copyright under this Act if this Act had been in operation at the time when it was made.

(2) In subsection (10) of section nine, the reference to construction by, or with the licence of, the owner of the copyright in any architectural drawings or plans includes a reference to construction by, or with the licence of, the person who, at the time of the construction, was the owner of the copyright in the drawings or plans under the Act of 1911, or under any enactment repealed by that Act.

8.—(1) Section ten and the First Schedule to this Act do not apply to artistic works made before the commencement of that section.

(2) Copyright shall not subsist by virtue of this Act in any artistic work made before the commencement of section ten which, at the time when the work was made, constituted a design capable of registration under the Registered Designs Act, 1949, or under the enactments repealed by that Act, and was used, or intended to be used, as a model or pattern to be multiplied by any industrial process.

(3) The provisions set out in paragraph 2 of the Eighth Schedule to this Act (being the relevant provisions of the Copyright (Industrial Designs) Rules, 1949) shall apply for the purposes of the last preceding sub-paragraph.

9.—(1) Where, before the repeal by this Act of section three of the Act of 1911, a person has, in the case of a work, given the notice requisite under the proviso set out in paragraph 3 of the Eighth Schedule to this Act (being the proviso to the said section three), then, as respects reproductions by that person of that work after the repeal of that section by this Act, that proviso shall have effect as if it had been re-enacted in this Act as a proviso to subsection (2) of section one:

Provided that the said proviso shall so have effect subject to the provisions set out in paragraphs 4 and 5 of the Eighth Schedule to this Act (being so much of subsection (1) of sections sixteen and seventeen respectively of the Act of 1911 as is applicable to the said proviso), as if those provisions had also been re-enacted in this Act.

(2) For the purposes of the operation of the said proviso in accordance with the preceding sub-paragraph, any regulations made by the Board of Trade thereunder before the repeal of section three of the Act of 1911 shall have effect as if they had been made under this Act, and the power of the Board of Trade to make further regulations thereunder shall apply as if the proviso had been re-enacted as mentioned in the preceding sub-paragraph.

Works of joint authorship

1492 10.—(1) Notwithstanding anything in section eleven, or in the Third Schedule to this Act, copyright shall not subsist by virtue of Part I of this Act in any work of joint authorship first published before the commencement of section eleven, if the period of copyright had expired before the commencement of that section.

(2) In this paragraph " the period of copyright " means whichever is the longer of the following periods, that is to say,—

(*a*) the life of the author who died first and a term of fifty years after his death, and

(*b*) the life of the author who died last.

Part II

Provisions relating to Part II of Act

Sound recordings

1493 11. In the case of a sound recording made before the commencement of section twelve, subsection (3) of that section shall apply with the substitution, for the period mentioned in that subsection, of the period of fifty years from the end of the calendar year in which the recording was made.

12. Subsection (6) of section twelve shall not apply to a sound recording made before the commencement of that section.

13. Notwithstanding anything in section twelve, copyright shall not subsist by virtue of that section in a sound recording made before the first day of July, nineteen hundred and twelve, unless, immediately before the commencement of that section, a corresponding copyright subsisted, in relation to that recording, by virtue of subsection (8) of section nineteen of the Act of 1911 (which relates to records made before the commencement of that Act).

Cinematograph films

14. Section thirteen shall not apply to cinematograph films made before the commencement of that section.

15. Where a cinematograph film made before the commencement of section thirteen was an original dramatic work within the definition of " dramatic work " set out in paragraph 9 of the Eighth Schedule to this Act (being the definition thereof in the Act of 1911), the provisions of this Act, including the provisions of this Schedule other than this paragraph, shall have effect in relation to the film as if it had been an original dramatic work within the meaning of this Act; and the person who was the author of the work for the purposes of the Act of 1911 shall be taken to be the author thereof for the purposes of the said provisions as applied by this paragraph.

16. The provisions of this Act shall have effect in relation to photographs forming part of a cinematograph film made before the commencement of section thirteen as those provisions have effect in relation to photographs not forming part of a cinematograph film.

Television broadcasts and sound broadcasts

17 Copyright shall not subsist by virtue of section fourteen in any television broadcast or sound broadcast made before the commencement of that section.

18. For the purposes of subsection (3) of section fourteen, a previous television broadcast or sound broadcast shall be disregarded if it was made before the commencement of that section.

Supplementary

19. For the purposes of subsections (2) to (4) of section sixteen, the fact that, to a person's knowledge, the making of an article constituted an infringement of copyright under the Act of 1911, or would have constituted such an infringement if the article had been made in the place into which it is imported, shall have the like effect as if, to that person's knowledge, the making of the article had constituted an infringement of copyright under this Act.

PART III

PROVISIONS RELATING TO PART III OF ACT

1494 20. Nothing in section seventeen shall apply to any infringement of copyright under the Act of 1911, or shall affect any proceedings under that Act, whether begun before or after the commencement of that section.

21. Section eighteen shall not apply with respect to any article made, or, as the case may be, imported, before the commencement of that section; but, notwithstanding the repeal by this Act of section seven of the Act of 1911 (which contains provisions corresponding to subsection (1) of section eighteen), proceedings may (subject to the provisions of that Act) be brought or continued by virtue of the said section seven in respect of any article made or imported before the repeal, although the proceedings relate to the conversion or detention thereof after the repeal took effect.

22. Section nineteen shall not apply to any licence granted before the commencement of that section, and shall not affect any proceedings under the Act of 1911, whether begun before or after the commencement of that section.

23. For the purposes of section twenty-one the definition of " infringing copy " in section eighteen shall apply as if any reference to copyright in that definition included a reference to copyright under the Act of 1911.

24. Where before the commencement of section twenty-two a notice had been given in respect of a work under section fourteen of the Act of 1911 (which contains provisions corresponding to section twenty-two), and that notice had not been withdrawn and had not otherwise ceased to have effect before the commencement of section twenty-two, the notice shall have effect after the commencement of that section as if it had been duly given thereunder:

Provided that a notice shall not continue to have effect by virtue of this paragraph after the end of the period of six months beginning with the commencement of section twenty-two.

PART IV

PROVISIONS RELATING TO PART IV OF ACT

1495 25. The provisions of Part IV of this Act shall apply in relation to licence schemes made before the commencement of that Part as they apply in relation to licence schemes made thereafter, as if references in Part IV of this Act to copyright included references to copyright under the Act of 1911.

26. In section twenty-seven, references to a refusal or failure to grant or procure the grant of a licence, or to a proposal that a licence should be granted, do not include a refusal or failure which occurred, or a proposal made, before the commencement of that section.

PART V

PROVISIONS RELATING TO PART V OF ACT

1496 27. In section thirty-three, subsection (2) shall not apply to works made before the commencement of that section, and subsection (3) shall not apply to works first published before the commencement of that section.

PART VI

PROVISIONS RELATING TO PART VI OF ACT

Assignments, licences and bequests

1497 28.—(1) Where by virtue of any provision of this Act copyright subsists in a work, any document or event which—

(*a*) was made or occurred before the commencement of that provision, and

(*b*) had any operation affecting the title to copyright in the work under the Act of 1911, or would have had such an operation if the Act of 1911 had continued in force,

shall have the corresponding operation in relation to the copyright in the work under this Act:

Provided that, if the operation of any such document was or would have been limited to a period specified in the document, it shall not have any operation in relation to the copyright under this Act, except in so far as that period extends beyond the commencement of the provision of this Act by virtue of which copyright subsists in the work.

(2) For the purposes of the operation of a document in accordance with the preceding sub-paragraph,—

(*a*) expressions used in the document shall be construed in accordance with their effect immediately before the commencement of the provision in question, notwithstanding that a different meaning is assigned to them for the purposes of this Act; and

(*b*) subsection (1) of section thirty-seven shall not apply.

(3) Without prejudice to the generality of sub-paragraph (1) of this paragraph, the proviso set out in paragraph 6 of the Eighth Schedule to this Act (being the proviso to subsection (2) of section five of the Act of 1911) shall apply to assignments and licences having effect in relation to copyright under this Act in accordance with that sub-paragraph, as if that proviso had been re-enacted in this Act.

(4) In relation to copyright under this Act in a sound recording or in a cinematograph film, the preceding provisions of this paragraph shall apply subject to the following modifications, that is to say,—

(*a*) in the case of a sound recording, references to the copyright under the Act of 1911 shall be construed as references to the copyright under that Act in records embodying the recording, and

(*b*) in the case of a cinematograph film, references to the copyright under the Act of 1911 shall be construed as references to any copyright under that Act in the film (in so far as it constituted a dramatic work for the purposes of the Act of 1911) or in photographs forming part of the film.

(5) In this paragraph " operation affecting the title," in relation to copyright under the Act of 1911, means any operation affecting the ownership of that copyright, or creating, transferring or terminating an interest, right or licence in respect of that copyright.

29.—(1) Section thirty-eight shall not apply to a bequest contained in the will, or a codicil to the will, of a testator who died before the commencement of that section.

(2) In the case of an author who died before the commencement of section thirty-eight, the provisions set out in paragraph 7 of the Eighth Schedule to this Act (being subsection (2) of section seventeen of the Act of 1911) shall have effect as if it had been re-enacted in this Act.

Crown and Government departments

1498 30. Subsection (4) of section thirty-nine shall apply in relation to photographs taken before the commencement of that section as if the proviso to that subsection were omitted.

31.—(1) In the application of subsection (5) of section thirty-nine to a sound recording made before the commencement of that section, paragraph (*b*) of that subsection shall apply as if for the period mentioned in that paragraph there were substituted the period of fifty years from the end of the calendar year in which the recording was made.

(2) With respect to cinematograph films made before the commencement of section thirty-nine—

(*a*) subsection (5) of that section shall not apply, but

(*b*) in the case of a cinematograph film made as mentioned in that subsection, but before the commencement of section thirty-nine, if it was an original dramatic work as mentioned in paragraph 15 of this Schedule, the provisions of subsections (1) to (3) of section thirty-nine shall apply in accordance with that paragraph, and

(*c*) in relation to photographs forming part of such a cinematograph film the provisions of subsections (1), (2) and (4) of section thirty-nine (as modified by the last preceding paragraph) shall apply as they apply in relation to photographs not forming part of a cinematograph film.

False attribution of authorship

1499 32.—(1) Paragraphs (*b*) and (*c*) of subsection (2) of section forty-three shall apply to any such act as is therein mentioned, if done after the commencement of that section, notwithstanding that the name in question was inserted or affixed before the commencement of that section.

(2) Subject to the preceding sub-paragraph, no act done before the commencement of section forty-three shall be actionable by virtue of that section.

(3) In this paragraph " name " has the same meaning as in section forty-three.

Other provisions

1500 33.—(1) In the application of subsection (2) of section forty-nine to a publication effected before the commencement of that section, the reference in paragraph (*d*) to thirty days shall be treated as a reference to fourteen days.

(2) For the purposes of the application of subsection (3) of section forty-nine to an act done before the commencement of a provision of this Act to which that subsection applies, references to copyright include references to copyright under the Act of 1911, and, in relation to copyright under that Act, references to the licence of the owner are references to the consent or acquiescence of the owner.

Part VII

Works made before 1st July, 1912

1501 34.—(1) This part of this Schedule applies to works made before the first day of July, nineteen hundred and twelve.

(2) In this Part of this Schedule " right conferred by the Act of 1911," in relation to a work, means such a substituted right as, by virtue of section twenty-four of the Act of 1911, was conferred in place of a right subsisting immediately before the commencement of that Act.

35. Notwithstanding anything in Part I of this Schedule, neither subsection (1) or subsection (2) of section two, nor subsection (2) or subsection (3) of section three, shall apply to a work to which this Part of this Schedule applies, unless a right conferred by the Act of 1911 subsisted in the work immediately before the commencement of section two or section three, as the case may be.

36.—(1) Where, in the case of a dramatic or musical work to which this Part of this Schedule applies, the right conferred by the Act of 1911 did not include the sole right to perform the work in public, then, in so far as copyright subsists in the work by virtue of this Act, the acts restricted by the copyright shall be treated as not including those specified in sub-paragraph (3) of this paragraph.

(2) Where, in the case of a dramatic or musical work to which this Part of this Schedule applies, the right conferred by the Act of 1911 consisted only of the sole right to perform the work in public, then, in so far as copyright subsists in the work by virtue of this Act, the acts restricted by the copyright shall be treated as consisting only of those specified in sub-paragraph (3) of this paragraph.

(3) The said acts are—

(*a*) performing the work or an adaptation thereof in public;

(*b*) broadcasting the work or an adaptation thereof;

(*c*) causing the work or an adaptation thereof to be transmitted to subscribers to a diffusion service.

37. Where a work to which this Part of this Schedule applies consists of an essay, article or portion forming part of and first published in a review, magazine or other periodical or work of a like nature, and immediately before the commencement of section two a right of publishing the work in a separate form subsisted by virtue of the provision set out in paragraph 8 of the Eighth Schedule to this Act (being the note appended to the First Schedule to the Act of 1911), that provision shall have effect, in relation to that work, as if it had been re-enacted in this Act with the substitution, for the word " right " where it first occurs, of the word " copyright."

38.—(1) Without prejudice to the generality of sub-paragraph (1) of paragraph 28 of this Schedule, the provisions of this paragraph shall have effect where—

(*a*) the author of a work to which this Part of this Schedule applies had, before the commencement of the Act of 1911, made such an assignment or grant as is mentioned in paragraph (*a*) of the proviso to subsection (1) of section twenty-four of that Act (which relates to transactions whereby the author had assigned, or granted an interest in, the copyright or performing right in a work for the full term of that right under the law in force before the Act of 1911), and

(*b*) copyright subsists in the work by virtue of any provision of this Act.

(2) If, before the commencement of that provision of this Act, any event occurred, or notice was given, which in accordance with paragraph (*a*) of the said proviso had any operation affecting the ownership of the right conferred by the Act of 1911 in relation to the work, or creating, transferring or terminating an interest, right or licence in respect of that right, that event or notice shall have the corresponding operation in relation to the copyright in the work under this Act.

(3) Any right which, at a time after the commencement of that provision of this Act, would, by virtue of paragraph (*a*) of the said proviso, have been exercisable in relation to the work, or to the right conferred by the Act of 1911, if this Act had not been passed, shall be exercisable in relation to the work or to the copyright therein under this Act, as the case may be.

(4) If, in accordance with paragraph (*a*) of the said proviso, the right conferred by the Act of 1911 would have reverted to the author or his personal representatives on the date referred to in that paragraph, and the said date falls after the commencement of the provision of this Act whereby copyright subsists in the work, then on that date—

(*a*) the copyright in the work under this Act shall revert to the author or his personal representatives, as the case may be, and

(*b*) any interest of any other person in that copyright which subsists on that date by virtue of any document made before the commencement of the Act of 1911 shall thereupon determine.

PART VIII

GENERAL AND SUPPLEMENTARY PROVISIONS

1502 39.—(1) The provisions of this paragraph shall have effect for the construction of any reference in any provision of this Act—

(*a*) to countries to which that provision extends, or

(*b*) to qualified persons.

(2) Where, at any time after the commencement of any provisions of this Act, a provision which contains such a reference—

(*a*) has not yet been extended by virtue of section thirty-one to a country to which the Act of 1911 extended (or which, by virtue of that Act, was to be treated as a country to which it extended), and

(*b*) has not been applied in the case of that country by virtue of section thirty-two,

then, with respect to any time before the provision is so extended or applied, the reference shall be construed as if the provision did extend to that country.

(3) For the purpose of determining whether copyright subsists in any work or other subject-matter at a time when a provision containing such a reference has been extended to a country other than the United Kingdom, the reference shall be construed, in relation to past events, as if that provision had always been in operation and had always extended to that country.

(4) In relation to photographs taken before the commencement of section three, and to sound recordings made before the commencement of section twelve, the definition of "qualified person" in subsection (5) of section one shall apply as if, in paragraph (*b*) of that subsection, for the words "body incorporated under the laws of" there were substituted the words "body corporate which has established a place of business in".

40.—(1) The provisions of the two next following sub-paragraphs shall apply where—

(*a*) immediately before the date on which any provisions of the Act of 1911 (in this paragraph referred to as "the repealed provisions") are repealed in the law of the United Kingdom by this Act, the repealed provisions have effect as applied by an Order in Council made in respect of a foreign country under section twenty-nine of the Act of 1911; and

(*b*) no Order in Council under section thirty-two of this Act, applying any provisions of this Act in the case of that country, is made so as to come into force on or before that date.

(2) The repealed provisions, as applied by the Order in Council under section twenty-nine of the Act of 1911 (or by that Order as varied by any subsequent Order thereunder), shall continue to have effect, notwithstanding the repeal, until the occurrence of whichever of the following events first occurs, that is to say—

(*a*) the revocation of the Order in Council under section twenty-nine of the Act of 1911;

(*b*) the coming into operation of an Order in Council under section thirty-two of this Act applying any of the provisions of this Act in the case of the foreign country in question;

(*c*) the expiration of the period of two years beginning with the date mentioned in the preceding sub-paragraph.

(3) For the purposes of continuing, varying or terminating the operation of the repealed provisions in accordance with the last preceding sub-paragraph, and for the purposes of any proceedings arising out of the operation of those provisions in accordance with that sub-paragraph, all the provisions of the Act of 1911 (including the power to revoke or vary Orders in Council under section twenty-nine of that Act) shall be treated as continuing in force as if none of those provisions had been repealed by this Act.

(4) In relation to a country in respect of which an Order in Council has been made under subsection (3) of section twenty-six of the Act of 1911 (which relates to countries therein referred to as self-governing dominions to which that

Act does not extend), the preceding provisions of this paragraph shall apply as they apply in relation to a foreign country, with the substitution, for references to section twenty-nine of the Act of 1911, of references to the said subsection (3).

41. In so far as the Act of 1911 or any Order in Council made thereunder forms part of the law of any country other than the United Kingdom, at a time after that Act has been wholly or partly repealed in the law of the United Kingdom, it shall, so long as it forms part of the law of that country, be construed and have effect as if that Act had not been so repealed.

42. The mention of any particular matter in the preceding provisions of this Schedule with regard to the repeal of any of the provisions of the Act of 1911 shall not affect the general application to this Act of section thirty-eight of the Interpretation Act, 1889 (which relates to the effect of repeals), either in relation to the Act of 1911 or to any other enactment repealed by this Act.

43. For the purposes of the application, by virtue of any of the preceding paragraphs of this Schedule, of any of the provisions set out in the Eighth Schedule to this Act,—

(*a*) the expressions of which definitions are set out in paragraph 9 of that Schedule (being the definitions of those expressions in the Act of 1911) shall, notwithstanding anything in this Act, be construed in accordance with those definitions; and

(*b*) where, for those purposes, any of those provisions is to be treated as if re-enacted in this Act, it shall be treated as if it had been so re-enacted with the substitution, for the words " this Act ", wherever the reference is to the passing or the commencement of the Act of 1911, of the words " the Copyright Act, 1911 ".

1503 44. Without prejudice to the operation of any of the preceding provisions of this Schedule—

(*a*) any enactment or other document referring to an enactment repealed by this Act shall be construed as referring (or as including a reference) to the corresponding enactment of this Act;

(*b*) any enactment or other document referring to copyright, or to works in which copyright subsists, if apart from this Act it would be construed as referring to copyright under the Act of 1911, or to works in which copyright subsists under that Act, shall be construed as referring (or as including a reference) to copyright under this Act, or, as the case may be, to works or any other subject-matter in which copyright subsists under this Act;

(*c*) any reference in an enactment or other document to the grant of an interest in copyright by licence shall be construed, in relation to copyright under this Act, as a reference to the grant of a licence in respect of that copyright.

45.—(1) Except in so far as it is otherwise expressly provided in this Schedule, the provisions of this Act apply in relation to things existing at the commencement of those provisions as they apply in relation to things coming into existence thereafter.

(2) For the purposes of any reference in this Schedule to works, sound recordings or cinematograph films made before the commencement of a provision of this Act, a work, recording or film, the making of which extended over a period, shall not be taken to have been so made unless the making of it was completed before the commencement of that provision.

46.—(1) Any reference in this Schedule to a numbered section shall, unless the reference is to a section of a specified Act, be construed as a reference to the section bearing that number in this Act.

(2) Any reference in this Schedule to the commencement of a provision of this Act is a reference to the date on which that provision comes into operation as part of the law of the United Kingdom.

47.—(1) In this Schedule " photograph " has the meaning assigned to it in the definition set out in paragraph 9 of the Eighth Schedule to this Act, and not the meaning assigned to it by section forty-eight.

(2) In this Schedule " the Act of 1911 " means the Copyright Act, 1911.

1504 **Section 50**

EIGHTH SCHEDULE

PROVISIONS OF COPYRIGHT ACT, 1911, AND RULES, REFERRED TO IN SEVENTH SCHEDULE

1. *Proviso to s.* 5 (1) *of the Copyright Act,* 1911 (*referred to in paragraph* 3 *of Seventh Schedule*):

Provided that—

(*a*) where, in the case of an engraving, photograph, or portrait, the plate or other original was ordered by some other person and was made for valuable consideration in pursuance of that order, then, in the absence of any agreement to the contrary, the person by whom such plate or other original was ordered shall be the first owner of the copyright; and

(*b*) where the author was in the employment of some other person under a contract of service or apprenticeship and the work was made in the course of his employment by that person, the person by whom the author was employed shall, in the absence of any agreement to the contrary, be the first owner of the copyright, but where the work is an article or other contribution to a newspaper, magazine, or similar periodical, there shall, in the absence of any agreement to the contrary, be deemed to be reserved to the author a right to restrain the publication of the work, otherwise than as part of a newspaper, magazine, or similar periodical.

2. *Rule* 2 *of the Copyright* (*Industrial Designs*) *Rules,* 1949 (*referred to in paragraph* 8 *of Seventh Schedule*):

A design shall be deemed to be used as a model or pattern to be multiplied by any industrial process—

(*a*) when the design is reproduced or is intended to be reproduced on more than fifty single articles, unless all the articles in which the design is reproduced or is intended to be reproduced together form only a single set of articles as defined in subsection (1) of section 44 of the Registered Designs Act, 1949, or

(*b*) when the design is to be applied to—

(i) printed paper hangings,

(ii) carpets, floor cloths or oil cloths, manufactured or sold in lengths or pieces,

(iii) textile piece goods, or textile goods manufactured or sold in lengths or pieces, or

(iv) lace, not made by hand.

3. *Proviso to s.* 3 *of the Copyright Act,* 1911 (*referred to in paragraph* 9 *of Seventh Schedule*):

Provided that at any time after the expiration of twenty-five years, or in the case of a work in which copyright subsists at the passing of this Act thirty years, from the death of the author of a published work, copyright in the work shall not be deemed to be infringed by the reproduction of the work for sale if the person reproducing the work proves that he has given the prescribed notice in writing of his intention to reproduce the work; and that he has paid in the prescribed manner to, or for the benefit of, the owner of the coypright royalties in respect of all copies of the work sold by him calculated at the rate of ten per cent. on the price at which he publishes the work; and, for the purposes of this proviso, the Board of Trade may make regulations prescribing the mode in which notices are to be given, and the particulars to be given in such notices, and the mode, time, and frequency of the payment of royalties, including (if they think fit) regulations requiring payment in advance or otherwise securing the payment of royalties.

4. *S.* 16 (1) *of the Copyright Act,* 1911 (*referred to in paragraph* 9 *of Seventh Schedule*):

In the case of a work of joint authorship . . . references in this Act to the period after the expiration of any specified number of years from the death of the author shall be construed as references to the period after the expiration of the like number of years from the death of the author who dies first or after the death of the author who dies last, whichever period may be the shorter . . .

5. *S.* 17 (1) *of Copyright Act,* 1911 (*referred to in paragraph* 9 *of Seventh Schedule*):

In the case of a literary, dramatic or musical work, or an engraving, in which copyright subsists at the date of the death of the author or, in the case of a work of joint authorship, at or immediately before the date of the death of the author who dies last, but which has not been published, nor, in the case of a dramatic or musical work, been performed in public, nor, in the case of a lecture, been delivered in public, before that date,... the proviso to section three of this Act shall... apply as if the author had died at the date of such publication or performance or delivery in public as aforesaid.

1505 6. *Proviso to s.* 5 (2) *of the Copyright Act,* 1911 (*referred to in paragraph* 28 *of Seventh Schedule*):

Provided that, where the author of a work is the first owner of the copyright therein, no assignment of the copyright, and no grant of any interest therein, made by him (otherwise than by will) after the passing of this Act, shall be operative to vest in the assignee or grantee any rights with respect to the copyright in the work beyond the expiration of twenty-five years from the death of the author, and the reversionary interest in the copyright expectant on the termination of that period shall, on the death of the author, notwithstanding any agreement to the contrary, devolve on his legal personal representatives as part of his estate, and any agreement entered into by him as to the disposition of such reversionary interest shall be null and void, but nothing in this proviso shall be construed as applying to the assignment of the copyright in a collective work or a licence to publish a work or part of a work as part of a collective work.

7. *S.* 17 (2) *of the Copyright Act,* 1911 (*referred to in paragraph* 29 *of Seventh Schedule*):

The ownership of an author's manuscript after his death, where such ownership has been acquired under a testamentary disposition made by the author and the manuscript is of a work which has not been published nor performed in public nor delivered in public, shall be prima facie proof of the copyright being with the owner of the manuscript.

8. *Note to First Schedule to the Copyright Act,* 1911 (*referred to in paragraph* 37 *of Seventh Schedule*):

In the case of an essay, article, or portion forming part of and first published in a review, magazine, or other periodical or work of a like nature, the right shall be subject to any right of publishing the essay, article, or portion in a separate form to which the author is entitled at the commencement of this Act, or would, if this Act had not been passed, have become entitled under section eighteen of the Copyright Act, 1842.

9. *Definitions in s.* 35 (1) *of the Copyright Act,* 1911 (*referred to in paragraphs* 15, 43 *and* 47 *of Seventh Schedule*):

"literary work" includes maps, charts, plans, tables, and compilations;

"dramatic work" includes any piece for recitation, choreographic work or entertainment in dumb show the scenic arrangement or acting form of which is fixed in writing or otherwise, and any cinematograph production where the arrangement or acting form or the combination of incidents represented give the work an original character;

"performance" means any acoustic representation of a work and any visual representation of any dramatic action in a work, including such a representation made by means of any mechanical instrument;

"photograph" includes photo-lithograph and any work produced by any process analogous to photography;

"collective work" means—

(a) any encyclopaedia, dictionary, year book, or similar work;

(b) a newspaper, review, magazine, or similar periodical; and

(c) any work written in distinct parts by different authors, or in which works or parts of works of different authors are incorporated;

"delivery" in relation to a lecture, includes delivery by means of any mechanical instrument;

"lecture" includes address, speech and sermon.

Note—In this Schedule "this Act" means the Copyright Act, 1911.

1506 **Section 50** NINTH SCHEDULE

ENACTMENTS REPEALED

Session and Chapter	*Short Title*	*Extent of Repeal*
25 & 26 Vict. c. 68.	The Fine Arts Copyright Act, 1862.	The whole Act.
2 Edw. 7. c. 15.	The Musical (Summary Proceedings) Copyright Act, 1902.	The whole Act.
6 Edw. 7. c. 36.	The Musical Copyright Act, 1906.	The whole Act.
1 & 2 Geo. 5. c. 46.	The Copyright Act, 1911.	The whole Act, except sections fifteen, thirty-four and thirty-seven thereof.
18 & 19 Geo. 5. c. lii.	The Copyright Order Confirmation (Mechanical Instruments: Royalties) Act, 1928.	The whole Act.
11 & 12 Geo. 6. c. 7.	The Ceylon Independence Act, 1947.	Paragraph 10 of the Second Schedule.

Table of Statutes referred to in this Act

Short Title	*Session and Chapter*
Copyright Act, 1775	15 Geo. 3. c. 53.
Public Record Office Act, 1838	1 & 2 Vict. c. 94.
Interpretation Act, 1889	52 & 53 Vict. c. 63.
Copyright Act, 1911	1 & 2 Geo. 5. c. 46.
Dramatic and Musical Performers' Protection Act, 1925	15 & 16 Geo. 5. c. 46.
Children and Young Persons (Scotland) Act, 1937 ...	1 Edw. 8. & 1 Geo. 6. c. 37.
Cinematograph Films Act, 1938	1 & 2 Geo. 6. c. 17.
Limitation Act, 1939	2 & 3 Geo. 6. c. 21.
Education Act, 1944	7 & 8 Geo. 6. c. 31.
Education (Scotland) Act, 1946	9 & 10 Geo. 6. c. 72.
Crown Proceedings Act, 1947	10 & 11 Geo. 6. c. 44.
British Nationality Act, 1948	11 & 12 Geo. 6. c. 56.
Wireless Telegraphy Act, 1949	12, 13 & 14 Geo. 6. c. 54.
Registered Designs Act, 1949	12, 13 & 14 Geo. 6. c. 88.
Arbitration Act, 1950	14 Geo. 6. c. 27.
Customs and Excise Act, 1952	15 & 16 Geo. 6. & 1 Eliz. 2. c. 44.

PART II

Copyright Act, 1911 [1]

(1 & 2 Geo. 5, c. 46)

An Act to amend and consolidate the Law relating to Copyright.
[16th December, 1911.]

PART I.—IMPERIAL COPYRIGHT

Rights

1507 **Copyright**

1.—(1) Subject to the provisions of this Act, copyright shall subsist throughout the parts of His Majesty's dominions to which this Act extends for the term hereinafter mentioned in every original literary dramatic musical and artistic work, if—

(*a*) in the case of a published work, the work was first published within such parts of His Majesty's dominions as aforesaid; and

(*b*) in the case of an unpublished work, the author was at the date of the making of the work a British subject or resident within such parts of His Majesty's dominions as aforesaid;

but in no other works, except so far as the protection conferred by this Act is extended by Orders in Council thereunder relating to self-governing dominions to which this Act does not extend and to foreign countries.

(2) For the purposes of this Act, " copyright " means the sole right to produce or reproduce the work or any substantial part thereof in any material form whatsoever, to perform, or in the case of a lecture to deliver, the work or any substantial part thereof in public; if the work is unpublished, to publish the work or any substantial part thereof; and shall include the sole right,—

(*a*) to produce, reproduce, perform, or publish any translation of the work;

(*b*) in the case of a dramatic work, to convert it into a novel or other non-dramatic work;

(*c*) in the case of a novel or other non-dramatic work, or of an artistic work, to convert it into a dramatic work, by way of performance in public or otherwise;

(*d*) in the case of a literary, dramatic, or musical work, to make any record, perforated roll, cinematograph film, or other contrivance by means of which the work may be mechanically performed or delivered,

and to authorise any such acts as aforesaid.

(3) For the purposes of this Act, publication, in relation to any work, means the issue of copies of the work to the public, and does not include the performance in public of a dramatic or musical work, the delivery in public of a lecture, the exhibition in public of an artistic work, or the construction of an architectural work of art, but, for the purposes of

[1] This Act was repealed by the Copyright Act, 1956, *ante*, as from June 1, 1957 (S.I. 1957 No. 863 *post*, § 1610) with the exception of ss. 15, 34, 37.

Comparative Tables showing the correspondence of this Act to the Act of 1956, and of the Act of 1956 to this Act, are printed at §§ 1546 and 1547, *post*.

this provision, the issue of photographs and engravings of works of sculpture and architectural works of art shall not be deemed to be publication of such works.

1508 Infringement of copyright

2.—(1) Copyright in a work shall be deemed to be infringed by any person who, without the consent of the owner of the copyright, does anything the sole right to do which is by this Act conferred on the owner of the copyright: Provided that the following acts shall not constitute an infringement of copyright:

(i) Any fair dealing with any work for the purposes of private study, research, criticism, review, or newspaper summary:

(ii) Where the author of an artistic work is not the owner of the copyright therein, the use by the author of any mould, cast, sketch, plan, model, or study made by him for the purpose of the work, provided that he does not thereby repeat or imitate the main design of that work:

(iii) The making or publishing of paintings, drawings, engravings, or photographs of a work of sculpture or artistic craftsmanship, if permanently situate in a public place or building, or the making or publishing of paintings, drawings, engravings, or photographs (which are not in the nature of architectural drawings or plans) of any architectural work of art:

(iv) The publication in a collection, mainly composed of non-copyright matter, bona fide intended for the use of schools, and so described in the title and in any advertisements issued by the publisher, of short passages from published literary works not themselves published for the use of schools in which copyright subsists: provided that not more than two of such passages from works by the same author are published by the same publisher within five years, and that the source from which such passages are taken is acknowledged:

(v) The publication in a newspaper of a report of a lecture delivered in public, unless the report is prohibited by conspicuous written or printed notice affixed before and maintained during the lecture at or about the main entrance of the building in which the lecture is given, and, except whilst the building is being used for public worship, in a position near the lecturer; but nothing in this paragraph shall affect the provisions in paragraph (i) as to newspaper summaries:

(vi) The reading or recitation in public by one person of any reasonable extract from any published work.

(2) Copyright in a work shall also be deemed to be infringed by any person who—

(*a*) sells or lets for hire, or by way of trade exposes or offers for sale or hire; or

(*b*) distributes either for the purposes of trade or to such an extent as to affect prejudicially the owner of the copyright; or

(*c*) by way of trade exhibits in public; or

(*d*) imports for sale or hire into any part of His Majesty's dominions to which this Act extends,

any work which to his knowledge infringes copyright or would infringe copyright if it had been made within the part of His Majesty's dominions in or into which the sale or hiring, exposure, offering for sale or hire, distribution, exhibition, or importation took place.

(3) Copyright in a work shall also be deemed to be infringed by any person who for his private profit permits a theatre or other place of entertainment to be used for the performance in public of the work without the consent of the owner of the copyright, unless he was not aware, and had no reasonable ground for suspecting, that the performance would be an infringement of copyright.

1509 **Term of copyright**

3. The term for which copyright shall subsist shall, except as otherwise expressly provided by this Act, be the life of the author and a period of fifty years after his death:

Provided that at any time after the expiration of twenty-five years, or in the case of a work in which copyright subsists at the passing of this Act thirty years, from the death of the author of a published work, copyright in the work shall not be deemed to be infringed by the reproduction of the work for sale if the person reproducing the work proves that he has given the prescribed notice in writing of his intention to reproduce the work, and that he has paid in the prescribed manner to, or for the benefit of, the owner of the copyright royalties in respect of all copies of the work sold by him calculated at the rate of ten per cent. on the price at which he publishes the work; and, for the purposes of this proviso, the Board of Trade may make regulations prescribing the mode in which notices are to be given, and the particulars to be given in such notices, and the mode, time, and frequency of the payment of royalties, including (if they think fit) regulations requiring payment in advance or otherwise securing the payment of royalties.

1510 **Compulsory licences**

4. If at any time after the death of the author of a literary, dramatic, or musical work which has been published or performed in public a complaint is made to the Judicial Committee of the Privy Council that the owner of the copyright in the work has refused to republish or to allow the republication of the work or has refused to allow the performance in public of the work, and that by reason of such refusal the work is withheld from the public, the owner of the copyright may be ordered to grant a licence to reproduce the work or perform the work in public, as the case may be, on such terms and subject to such conditions as the Judicial Committee may think fit.

1511 **Ownership of copyright, etc.**

5.—(1) Subject to the provisions of this Act, the author of a work shall be the first owner of the copyright therein:

Provided that—

(*a*) where, in the case of an engraving, photograph, or portrait, the plate or other original was ordered by some other person and was made for valuable consideration in pursuance of that order, then, in the absence of any agreement to the contrary, the person by whom such plate or other original was ordered shall be the first owner of the copyright; and (*b*) where the author was in the employment of some other person under a contract of service or apprenticeship and the work was made in the course of his employment by that person, the person by whom the author was employed shall, in the absence of any agreement to the contrary, be the first owner of the copyright, but where the work is an article or other contribution to a newspaper, magazine, or similar periodical, there shall, in the absence of any agreement to the contrary, be deemed to be reserved to the author a right to restrain the publication of the work, otherwise than as part of a newspaper, magazine, or similar periodical.

(2) The owner of the copyright in any work may assign the right, either wholly or partially, and either generally or subject to limitations to the United Kingdom or any self-governing dominion or other part of His Majesty's dominions to which this Act extends, and either for the whole term of the copyright or for any part thereof, and may grant any interest in the right by licence, but no such assignment or grant shall be valid unless it is in writing signed by the owner of the right in respect of which the assignment or grant is made, or by his duly authorised agent:

Provided that, where the author of a work is the first owner of the copyright therein, no assignment of the copyright, and no grant of any interest therein, made by him (otherwise than by will) after the passing of this Act, shall be operative to vest in the assignee or grantee any rights with respect to the copyright in the work beyond the expiration of twenty-five years from the death of the author, and the reversionary interest in the copyright expectant on the termination of that period shall, on the death of the author, notwithstanding any agreement to the contrary, devolve on his legal personal representatives as part of his estate, and any agreement entered into by him as to the disposition of such reversionary interest shall be null and void, but nothing in this proviso shall be construed as applying to the assignment of the copyright in a collective work or a licence to publish a work or part of a work as part of a collective work.

(3) Where, under any partial assignment of copyright, the assignee becomes entitled to any right comprised in copyright, the assignee as respects the right so assigned, and the assignor as respects the rights not assigned, shall be treated for the purposes of this Act as the owner of the copyright, and the provisions of this Act shall have effect accordingly.

Civil Remedies

512 **Civil remedies for infringement of copyright**

6.—(1) Where copyright in any work has been infringed, the owner of the copyright shall, except as otherwise provided by this Act, be entitled to all such remedies by way of injunction or interdict, damages, accounts, and otherwise, as are or may be conferred by law for the infringement of a right.

(2) The costs of all parties in any proceedings in respect of the infringement of copyright shall be in the absolute discretion of the court.

(3) In any action for infringement of copyright in any work, the work shall be presumed to be a work in which copyright subsists and the plaintiff shall be presumed to be the owner of the copyright, unless the defendant puts in issue the existence of the copyright, or, as the

case may be, the title of the plaintiff, and where any such question is in issue, then—

(*a*) if a name purporting to be that of the author of the work is printed or otherwise indicated thereon in the usual manner, the person whose name is so printed or indicated shall, unless the contrary is proved, be presumed to be the author of the work;

(*b*) if no name is so printed or indicated, or if the name so printed or indicated is not the author's true name or the name by which he is commonly known, and a name purporting to be that of the publisher or proprietor of the work is printed or otherwise indicated thereon in the usual manner the person whose name is so printed or indicated shall, unless the contrary is proved, be presumed to be the owner of the copyright in the work for the purposes of proceedings in respect of the infringement of copyright therein.

1513 **Rights of owner against persons possessing or dealing with infringing copies, etc.**

7. All infringing copies of any work in which copyright subsists, or of any substantial part thereof, and all plates used or intended to be used for the production of such infringing copies, shall be deemed to be the property of the owner of the copyright, who accordingly may take proceedings for the recovery of the possession thereof or in respect of the conversion thereof.

1514 **Exemption of innocent infringer from liability to pay damages, etc.**

8. Where proceedings are taken in respect of the infringement of the copyright in any work and the defendant in his defence alleges that he was not aware of the existence of the copyright in the work, the plaintiff shall not be entitled to any remedy other than an injunction or interdict in respect of the infringement if the defendant proves that at the date of the infringement he was not aware and had no reasonable ground for suspecting that copyright subsisted in the work.

1515 **Restriction on remedies in the case of architecture**

9.—(1) Where the construction of a building or other structure which infringes or which, if completed, would infringe the copyright in some other work has been commenced, the owner of the copyright shall not be entitled to obtain an injunction or interdict to restrain the construction of such building or structure or to order its demolition.

(2) Such of the other provisions of this Act as provide that an infringing copy of a work shall be deemed to be the property of the owner of the copyright, or as impose summary penalties, shall not apply in any case to which this section applies.

1516 **Limitation of actions**

10. An action in respect of infringement of copyright shall not be commenced after the expiration of three years next after the infringement.

Summary Remedies

1517 **Penalties for dealing with infringing copies, etc.**

11.—(1) If any person knowingly—

(*a*) makes for sale or hire any infringing copy of a work in which copyright subsists; or (*b*) sells or lets for hire, or by way of trade exposes or offers for sale or hire any infringing copy of any such work; or

(*c*) distributes infringing copies of any such work either for the purposes of trade or to such an extent as to affect prejudicially the owner of the copyright; or

(*d*) by way of trade exhibits in public any infringing copy of any such work; or

(*e*) imports for sale or hire into the United Kingdom any infringing copy of any such work:

he shall be guilty of an offence under this Act and be liable on summary conviction to a fine not exceeding forty shillings for every copy dealt with in contravention of this section, but not exceeding fifty pounds in respect of the same transaction; or, in the case of a second or subsequent offence, either to such fine or to imprisonment with or without hard labour for a term not exceeding two months.

(2) If any person knowingly makes or has in his possession any plate for the purpose of making infringing copies of any work in which copyright subsists, or knowingly and for his private profit causes any such work to be performed in public without the consent of the owner of the copyright, he shall be guilty of an offence under this Act, and be liable on summary conviction to a fine not exceeding fifty pounds, or, in the case of a second or subsequent offence, either to such fine or to imprisonment with or without hard labour for a term not exceeding two months.

(3) The court before which any such proceedings are taken may, whether the alleged offender is convicted or not, order that all copies of the work or all plates in the possession of the alleged offender, which appear to it to be infringing copies or plates for the purpose of making infringing copies, be destroyed or delivered up to the owner of the copyright or otherwise dealt with as the court may think fit.

(4) Nothing in this section shall, as respects musical works, affect the provisions of the Musical (Summary Proceedings) Copyright Act, 1902, or the Musical Copyright Act, 1906.

518 Appeals to quarter sessions

12. Any person aggrieved by a summary conviction of an offence under the foregoing provisions of this Act may in England and Ireland appeal to a court of quarter sessions and in Scotland under and in terms of the Summary Jurisdiction (Scotland) Acts.

519 Extent of provisions as to summary remedies

13. The provisions of this Act with respect to summary remedies shall extend only to the United Kingdom.

Importation of Copies

520 Importation of copies

14.—(1) Copies made out of the United Kingdom of any work in which copyright subsists which if made in the United Kingdom would infringe copyright, and as to which the owner of the copyright gives notice in writing by himself or his agent to the Commissioners of Customs and Excise, that he is desirous that such copies should not be imported into the United Kingdom, shall not be so imported, and shall, subject to the provisions of this section, be deemed to be included in the table of prohibitions and restrictions contained in section forty-two of the Customs Consolidation Act, 1876, and that section shall apply accordingly.

(2) Before detaining any such copies or taking any further proceedings with a view to the forfeiture thereof under the law relating to the Customs, the Commissioners of Customs and Excise may require the regulations under this section, whether as to information, conditions, or other matters, to be complied with, and may satisfy themselves in accordance with those regulations that the copies are such as are prohibited by this section to be imported.

(3) The Commissioners of Customs and Excise may make regulations, either general or special, respecting the detention and forfeiture of copies the importation of which is prohibited by this section, and the conditions, if any, to be fulfilled before such detention and forfeiture, and may, by such regulations, determine the information, notices, and security to be given, and the evidence requisite for any of the purposes of this section, and the mode of verification of such evidence.

(4) The regulations may apply to copies of all works the importation of copies of which is prohibited by this section, or different regulations may be made respecting different classes of such works.

(5) The regulations may provide for the informant reimbursing the Commissioners of Customs and Excise all expenses and damages incurred in respect of any detention made on his information, and of any proceedings consequent on such detention; and may provide for notices under any enactment repealed by this Act being treated as notices given under this section.

(6) The foregoing provisions of this section shall have effect as if they were part of the Customs Consolidation Act, 1876: Provided that, notwithstanding anything in that Act, the Isle of Man shall not be treated as part of the United Kingdom for the purposes of this section.

(7) This section shall, with the necessary modifications, apply to the importation into a British possession to which this Act extends of copies of works made out of that possession.

AMENDMENT

In subsection (1) the words "and shall, subject to the provisions of this section" onwards were repealed by the Customs and Excise Act, 1952 (15 & 16 Geo. 6 and 1 Eliz. 2, c. 44), s. 320, Sched. 12, Part I.

Delivery of Books to Libraries

1521 **Delivery of copies to British Museum and other libraries**

15.—(1) The publisher of every book published in the United Kingdom shall, within one month after the publication, deliver, at his own expense, a copy of the book to the trustees of the British Museum, who shall give a written receipt for it.

(2) He shall also, if written demand is made before the expiration of twelve months after publication, deliver within one month after receipt of that written demand or, if the demand was made before publication, within one month after publication, to some depôt in London named in the demand a copy of the book for, or in accordance with the directions

of, the authority having the control of each of the following libraries, namely: the Bodleian Library, Oxford, the University Library, Cambridge, the [National Library of Scotland] and the Library of Trinity College, Dublin, and subject to the provisions of this section the National Library of Wales. In the case of an encyclopaedia, newspaper, review, magazine, or work published in a series of numbers or parts, the written demand may include all numbers or parts of the work which may be subsequently published.

(3) The copy delivered to the trustees of the British Museum shall be a copy of the whole book with all maps and illustrations belonging thereto, finished and coloured in the same manner as the best copies of the book are published, and shall be bound, sewed, or stitched together, and on the best paper on which the book is printed.

(4) The copy delivered for the other authorities mentioned in this section shall be on the paper on which the largest number of copies of the book is printed for sale, and shall be in the like condition as the books prepared for sale.

(5) The books of which copies are to be delivered to the National Library of Wales shall not include books of such classes as may be specified in regulations to be made by the Board of Trade.

(6) If a publisher fails to comply with this section, he shall be liable on summary conviction to a fine not exceeding five pounds and the value of the book, and the fine shall be paid to the trustees or authority to whom the book ought to have been delivered.

(7) For the purposes of this section, the expression " book " includes every part or division of a book, pamphlet, sheet of letterpress, sheet of music, map, plan, chart or table separately published, but shall not include any second or subsequent edition of a book unless such edition contains additions or alterations either in the letterpress or in the maps, prints, or other engravings belonging thereto.

OPERATION AND AMENDMENT

This section is not repealed by the Copyright Act, 1956.

A proviso added to subsection (1) by the Copyright (British Museum) Act, 1915 (5 & 6 Geo. 5, c. 38), was repealed by the British Museum Act, 1932 (22 & 23 Geo. 5, c. 34), s. 2 (2).

The National Library of Scotland was substituted in subsection (2) for the Library of the Faculty of Advocates at Edinburgh by the National Library of Scotland Act, 1925 (15 & 16 Geo. 5, c. 73), s. 5.

Special Provisions as to certain Works

1522 Works of joint authors

16.—(1) In the case of a work of joint authorship, copyright shall subsist during the life of the author who first dies and for a term of fifty years after his death, or during the life of the author who dies last, whichever period is the longer, and references in this Act to the period after the expiration of any specified number of years from the death of the author shall be construed as references to the period after the expiration of the like number of years from the death of the author who dies first or after the death of the author who dies last, whichever period may be the shorter, and in the provisions of this Act with respect to the grant of compulsory licences a reference to the date of the death of the author who dies last shall be substituted for the reference to the date of the death of the author.

(2) Where, in the case of a work of joint authorship, some one or more of the joint authors do not satisfy the conditions conferring copyright laid down by this Act, the work shall be treated for the purposes of this Act as if the other author or authors had been the sole author or authors thereof:

Provided that the term of the copyright shall be the same as it would have been if all the authors had satisfied such conditions as aforesaid.

(3) For the purposes of this Act, " a work of joint authorship " means a work produced by the collaboration of two or more authors in which the contribution of one author is not distinct from the contribution of the other author or authors.

(4) Where a married woman and her husband are joint authors of a work the interest of such married woman therein shall be her separate property.

AMENDMENT

In subs. (4) the word " separate " was repealed by the Law Reform (Married Women and Tortfeasors) Act, 1935 (25 & 26 Geo. 5, c. 30), s. 5, Sched. 2.

1523 **Posthumous works**

17.—(1) In the case of a literary dramatic or musical work, or an engraving, in which copyright subsists at the date of the death of the author or, in the case of a work of joint authorship, at or immediately before the date of the death of the author who dies last, but which has not been published, nor, in the case of a dramatic or musical work, been performed in public, nor, in the case of a lecture, been delivered in public, before that date, copyright shall subsist till publication, or performance or delivery in public, whichever may first happen, and for a term of fifty years thereafter, and the proviso to section three of this Act shall, in the case of such a work, apply as if the author had died at the date of such publication or performance or delivery in public as aforesaid.

(2) The ownership of an author's manuscript after his death, where such ownership has been acquired under a testamentary disposition made by the author and the manuscript is of a work which has not been published nor performed in public nor delivered in public, shall be prima facie proof of the copyright being with the owner of the manuscript.

1524 **Provisions as to Government publications**

18. Without prejudice to any rights or privileges of the Crown, where any work has, whether before or after the commencement of this Act, been prepared or published by or under the direction or control of His Majesty or any Government department, the copyright in the work shall, subject to any agreement with the author, belong to His Majesty, and in such case shall continue for a period of fifty years from the date of the first publication of the work.

1525 **Provisions as to mechanical instruments**

19.—(1) Copyright shall subsist in records, perforated rolls, and other contrivances by means of which sounds may be mechanically reproduced, in like manner as if such contrivances were musical works, but the term of copyright shall be fifty years from the making of the original plate from which the contrivance was directly or indirectly derived, and the person who was the owner of such original plate at the time when such plate was made shall be deemed to be the author of the work, and, where such owner is a body corporate, the body corporate shall be deemed for the purposes of this Act to reside within the parts of His Majesty's dominions to which this Act extends if it has established a place of business within such parts.

(2) It shall not be deemed to be an infringement of copyright in any musical work for any person to make within the parts of His Majesty's dominions to which this Act extends records, perforated rolls, or other contrivances by means of which the work may be mechanically performed, if such person proves—

(*a*) that such contrivances have previously been made by, or with the consent or acquiescence of, the owner of the copyright in the work; and

(*b*) that he has given the prescribed notice of his intention to make the contrivances, and has paid in the prescribed manner to, or for the benefit of, the owner of the copyright in the work royalties in respect of all such contrivances sold by him, calculated at the rate hereinafter mentioned:

Provided that—

(i) nothing in this provision shall authorise any alterations in, or omissions from, the work reproduced, unless contrivances reproducing the work subject to similar alterations and omissions have been previously made by, or with the consent or acquiescence of, the owner of the copyright, or unless such alterations or omissions are reasonably necessary for the adaptation of the work to the contrivances in question; and

(ii) for the purposes of this provision, a musical work shall be deemed to include any words so closely associated therewith as to form part of the same work, but shall not be deemed to include a contrivance by means of which sounds may be mechanically reproduced.

(3) The rate at which such royalties as aforesaid are to be calculated shall—

(*a*) in the case of contrivances sold within two years after the commencement of this Act by the person making the same, be two and one-half per cent.; and

(*b*) in the case of contrivances sold as aforesaid after the expiration of that period, five per cent.

on the ordinary retail selling price of the contrivance calculated in the prescribed manner, so however that the royalty payable in respect of a contrivance shall, in no case, be less than a halfpenny for each separate musical work in which copyright subsists reproduced thereon, and, where the royalty calculated as aforesaid includes a fraction of a farthing, such fraction shall be reckoned as a farthing:

Provided that, if, at any time after the expiration of seven years from the commencement of this Act, it appears to the Board of Trade that such rate as aforesaid is no longer equitable, the Board of Trade may, after holding a public inquiry, make an order either decreasing or increasing that rate to such extent as under the circumstances may seem just, but any order so made shall be provisional only and shall not have any effect unless and until confirmed by Parliament; but, where an order revising the rate has been so made and confirmed, no further revision shall be made before the expiration of fourteen years from the date of the last revision.

(4) If any such contrivance is made reproducing two or more different works in which copyright subsists and the owners of the copyright therein are different persons, the sums payable by way of royalties under this section shall be apportioned amongst the several owners of the copyright in such proportions as, failing agreement, may be determined by arbitration.

(5) When any such contrivances by means of which a musical work may be mechanically performed have been made, then, for the purposes of this section, the owner of the copyright in the work shall, in relation to any person who makes the prescribed inquiries, be deemed to have given his consent to the making of such contrivances if he fails to reply to such inquiries within the prescribed time.

(6) For the purposes of this section, the Board of Trade may make regulations prescribing anything which under this section is to be prescribed, and prescribing the mode in which notices are to be given and the particulars to be given in such notices, and the mode, time, and frequency of the payment of royalties, and any such regulations may, if the Board think fit, include regulations requiring payment in advance or otherwise securing the payment of royalties.

(7) In the case of musical works published before the commencement of this Act, the foregoing provisions shall have effect, subject to the following modifications and additions:

(*a*) The conditions as to the previous making by, or with the consent or acquiescence of, the owner of the copyright in the work, and the restrictions as to alterations in or omissions from the work, shall not apply:

(*b*) The rate of two and one-half per cent. shall be substituted for the rate of five per cent. as the rate at which royalties are to be calculated, but no royalties shall be payable in respect of contrivances sold before the first day of July, nineteen hundred and thirteen, if contrivances reproducing the same work had been lawfully made, or placed on sale, within the parts of His Majesty's dominions to which this Act extends before the first day of July, nineteen hundred and ten:

(*c*) Notwithstanding any assignment made before the passing of this Act of the copyright in a musical work, any rights conferred by this Act in respect of the making, or authorising the making, of contrivances by means of which the work may be mechanically performed shall belong to the author or his legal personal representatives and not to the assignee, and the royalties aforesaid shall be payable to, and for the benefit of, the author of the work or his legal personal representatives:

(*d*) The saving contained in this Act of the rights and interests arising from, or in connexion with, action taken before the commencement of this Act shall not be construed as authorising any person who has made contrivances by means of which the work may be mechanically performed to sell any such contrivances, whether made before or after the passing of this Act, except on the terms and subject to the conditions laid down in this section:

(*e*) Where the work is a work on which copyright is conferred by an Order in Council relating to a foreign country, the copyright so conferred shall not, except to such extent as may be provided by the Order, include any rights with respect to the making of records, perforated rolls, or other contrivances by means of which the work may be mechanically performed.

(8) Notwithstanding anything in this Act, where a record, perforated roll, or other contrivance by means of which sounds may be mechanically reproduced has been made before the commencement of this Act, copyright shall, as from the commencement of this Act, subsist therein in like manner and for the like term as if this Act had been in force at the date of the making of the original plate from which the contrivance was directly or indirectly derived:

Provided that—

(i) the person who, at the commencement of this Act, is the owner of such original plate shall be the first owner of such copyright; and

(ii) nothing in this provision shall be construed as conferring copyright in any such contrivance if the making thereof would have infringed copyright in some other such contrivance, if this provision had been in force at the time of the making of the first-mentioned contrivance.

1526 **Provision as to political speeches**

20. Notwithstanding anything in this Act, it shall not be an infringement of copyright in an address of a political nature delivered at a public meeting to publish a report thereof in a newspaper.

1527 **Provisions as to photographs**

21. The term for which copyright shall subsist in photographs shall be fifty years from the making of the original negative from which the photograph was directly or indirectly derived, and the person who was the owner of such negative at the time when such negative was made shall be deemed to be the author of the work, and, where such owner is a body corporate, the body corporate shall be deemed for the purposes of this Act to reside within the parts of His Majesty's dominions to which this Act extends if it has established a place of business within such parts.

1528 **Provisions as to designs registrable under 7 Edw. 7, c. 29**

22.—(1) This Act shall not apply to designs capable of being registered under the Patents and Designs Act, 1907, except designs which, though capable of being so registered, are not used or intended to be used as models or patterns to be multiplied by any industrial process.

(2) General rules under section eighty-six of the Patents and Designs Act, 1907, may be made for determining the conditions under which a design shall be deemed to be used for such purposes as aforesaid.

1529 **Works of foreign authors first published in parts of His Majesty's dominions to which Act extends**

23. If it appears to His Majesty that a foreign country does not give, or has not undertaken to give, adequate protection to the works of British authors, it shall be lawful for His Majesty by Order in Council to direct that such of the provisions of this Act as confer copyright on works first published within the parts of His Majesty's dominions to which this Act extends, shall not apply to works published after the date specified in the Order, the authors whereof are subjects or citizens of such foreign country, and are not resident in His Majesty's dominions, and thereupon those provisions shall not apply to such works.

1530 **Existing works**

24.—(1) Where any person is immediately before the commencement of this Act entitled to any such right in any work as is specified in the first column of the First Schedule to this Act, or to any interest in such a right, he shall, as from that date, be entitled to the substituted right set forth in the second column of that schedule, or to the same interest in such a substituted right, and to no other right or interest, and such substituted right shall subsist for the term for which it would have subsisted if this Act had been in force at the date when the work was made and the work had been one entitled to copyright thereunder:

Provided that—

(*a*) if the author of any work in which any such right as is specified in the first column of the First Schedule to this Act subsists at the commencement of this Act has, before that date, assigned the right or granted any interest therein for the whole term of the right, then at the date when, but for the passing of this Act, the right would have expired the substituted right conferred by this section shall, in the absence of express agreement, pass to the author of the work, and any interest therein created before the commencement of this Act and then subsisting shall determine; but the person who immediately before the date at which the right would so have expired was the owner of the right or interest shall be entitled at his option either—

(i) on giving such notice as hereinafter mentioned, to an assignment of the right or the grant of a similar interest therein for the remainder of the term of the right for such consideration as, failing agreement, may be determined by arbitration; or

(ii) without any such assignment or grant, to continue to reproduce or perform the work in like manner as theretofore subject to the payment, if demanded by the author within three years after the date at which the right would have so expired, of such royalties to the author as, failing agreement, may be determined by arbitration, or, where the work is incorporated in a collective work and the owner of the right or interest is the proprietor of that collective work, without any such payment;

The notice above referred to must be given not more than one year nor less than six months before the date at which the right would have so expired, and must be sent by registered post to the author, or, if he cannot with reasonable diligence be found, advertised in the *London Gazette* and in two London newspapers:

(*b*) where any person has, before the twenty-sixth day of July nineteen hundred and ten, taken any action whereby he has incurred any expenditure or liability in connexion with the reproduction or performance of any work in a manner which at the time was lawful, or for the purpose of or with a view to the reproduction or performance of a work at a time when such reproduction or performance would, but for the passing of this Act, have been lawful, nothing in this section shall diminish or prejudice any rights or interest arising from or in connexion with such action which are subsisting and valuable at the said date, unless the person who by virtue of this section becomes entitled to restrain such reproduction or performance agrees to pay such compensation as, failing agreement, may be determined by arbitration.

(2) For the purposes of this section, the expression " author " includes the legal personal representatives of a deceased author.

(3) Subject to the provisions of section nineteen subsections (7) and (8) and of section thirty-three of this Act, copyright shall not subsist in any work made before the commencement of this Act, otherwise than under, and in accordance with, the provisions of this section.

Application to British Possessions

1531 **Application of Act to British dominions**

25.—(1) This Act, except such of the provisions thereof as are expressly restricted to the United Kingdom, shall extend throughout His Majesty's dominions: Provided that it shall not extend to a self-governing dominion, unless declared by the Legislature of that dominion to be in force therein either without any modifications or additions, or with such modifications and additions relating exclusively to procedure and remedies, or necessary to adapt this Act to the circumstances of the dominion, as may be enacted by such Legislature.

(2) If the Secretary of State certifies by notice published in the *London Gazette* that any self-governing dominion has passed legislation under which works, the authors whereof were at the date of the making of the works British subjects resident elsewhere than in the dominion or (not being British subjects) were resident in the parts of His Majesty's dominions to which this Act extends, enjoy within the dominion rights substantially identical with those conferred by this Act, then, whilst such legislation continues in force, the dominion shall, for the purposes of the rights conferred by this Act, be treated as if it were a dominion to which this Act extends; and it shall be lawful for the Secretary of State to give such a certificate as aforesaid, notwithstanding that the remedies for enforcing the rights, or the restrictions on the importation of copies of works, manufactured in a foreign country, under the law of the dominion, differ from those under this Act.

1532 **Legislative powers of self-governing dominions**

26.—(1) The Legislature of any self-governing dominion may, at any time, repeal all or any of the enactments relating to copyright passed by Parliament (including this Act) so far as they are operative within that dominion: Provided that no such repeal shall prejudicially affect any legal rights existing at the time of the repeal, and that, on this Act or any part thereof being so repealed by the Legislature of a self-governing dominion, that dominion shall cease to be a dominion to which this Act extends.

(2) In any self-governing dominion to which this Act does not extend, the enactments repealed by this Act shall, so far as they are operative

in that dominion, continue in force until repealed by the Legislature of that dominion.

(3) Where His Majesty in Council is satisfied that the law of a self-governing dominion to which this Act does not extend provides adequate protection within the dominion for the works (whether published or unpublished) of authors who at the time of the making of the work were British subjects resident elsewhere than in that dominion, His Majesty in Council may, for the purpose of giving reciprocal protection, direct that this Act, except such parts (if any) thereof as may be specified in the Order, and subject to any conditions contained therein, shall, within the parts of His Majesty's dominions to which this Act extends, apply to works the authors whereof were, at the time of the making of the work, resident within the first-mentioned dominion, and to works first published in that dominion; but, save as provided by such an Order, works the authors whereof were resident in a dominion to which this Act does not extend shall not, whether they are British subjects or not, be entitled to any protection under this Act except such protection as is by this Act conferred on works first published within the parts of His Majesty's dominions to which this Act extends:

Provided that no such Order shall confer any rights within a self-governing dominion, but the Governor in Council of any self-governing dominion to which this Act extends, may, by Order, confer within that dominion the like rights as His Majesty in Council is, under the foregoing provisions of this subsection, authorised to confer within other parts of His Majesty's dominions.

For the purposes of this subsection, the expression "a dominion to which this Act extends" includes a dominion which is for the purposes of this Act to be treated as if it were a dominion to which this Act extends.

1533 **Power of Legislatures of British possessions to pass supplemental legislation**

27. The Legislature of any British possession to which this Act extends may modify or add to any of the provisions of this Act in its application to the possession, but, except so far as such modifications and additions relate to procedure and remedies, they shall apply only to works the authors whereof were, at the time of the making of the work, resident in the possession, and to works first published in the possession.

1534 **Application to protectorates**

28. His Majesty may, by Order in Council, extend this Act to any territories under his protection and to Cyprus, and, on the making of any such Order, this Act shall, subject to the provisions of the Order, have effect as if the territories to which it applies or Cyprus were part of His Majesty's dominions to which this Act extends.

Part II.—International Copyright

1535 **Power to extend Act to foreign works**

29.—(1) His Majesty may, by Order in Council, direct that this Act (except such parts, if any, thereof as may be specified in the Order) shall apply—

(*a*) to works first published in a foreign country to which the Order relates, in like manner as if they were first published within the parts of His Majesty's dominions to which this Act extends;

(*b*) to literary, dramatic, musical, and artistic works, or any class thereof, the authors whereof were at the time of the making of the work subjects or citizens of a foreign country to which the Order relates, in like manner as if the authors were British subjects;

(*c*) in respect of residence in a foreign country to which the Order relates, in like manner as if such residence were residence in the parts of His Majesty's dominions to which this Act extends;

and thereupon, subject to the provisions of this Part of this Act and of the Order, this Act shall apply accordingly:

Provided that—

(i) before making an Order in Council under this section in respect of any foreign country (other than a country with which His Majesty has entered into a convention relating to copyright), His Majesty shall be satisfied that that foreign country has made, or has undertaken to make, such provisions, if any, as it appears to His Majesty expedient to require for the protection of works entitled to copyright under the provisions of Part I of this Act;

(ii) the Order in Council may provide that the term of copyright within such parts of His Majesty's dominions as aforesaid shall not exceed that conferred by the law of the country to which the Order relates;

(iii) the provisions of this Act as to the delivery of copies of books shall not apply to works first published in such country, except so far as is provided by the Order;

(iv) the Order in Council may provide that the enjoyment of the rights conferred by this Act shall be subject to the accomplishment of such conditions and formalities (if any) as may be prescribed by the Order;

(v) in applying the provision of this Act as to ownership of copyright, the Order in Council may make such modifications as appear necessary having regard to the law of the foreign country;

(vi) in applying the provisions of this Act as to existing works, the Order in Council may make such modifications as appear necessary, and may provide that nothing in those provisions as so applied shall be construed as reviving any right of preventing the production or importation of any translation in any case where the right has ceased by virtue of section five of the International Copyright Act, 1886.

(2) An Order in Council under this section may extend to all the several countries named or described therein.

1536 **Application of Part II to British possessions**

30.—(1) An Order in Council under this Part of this Act shall apply to all His Majesty's dominions to which this Act extends except self-governing dominions and any other possession specified in the Order with respect to which it appears to His Majesty expedient that the Order should not apply.

(2) The Governor in Council of any self-governing dominion to which this Act extends may, as respects that dominion, make the like orders

as under this Part of this Act His Majesty in Council is authorised to make with respect to His Majesty's dominions other than self-governing dominions, and the provisions of this Part of this Act shall, with the necessary modifications, apply accordingly.

(3) Where it appears to His Majesty expedient to except from the provisions of any Order any part of his dominions not being a self-governing dominion, it shall be lawful for His Majesty by the same or any other Order in Council to declare that such Order and this Part of this Act shall not, and the same shall not, apply to such part, except so far as is necessary for preventing any prejudice to any rights acquired previously to the date of such Order.

PART III.—SUPPLEMENTAL PROVISIONS

1537 Abrogation of common law rights

31. No person shall be entitled to copyright or any similar right in any literary, dramatic, musical, or artistic work, whether published or unpublished, otherwise than under and in accordance with the provisions of this Act, or of any other statutory enactment for the time being in force, but nothing in this section shall be construed as abrogating any right or jurisdiction to restrain a breach of trust or confidence.

1538 Provisions as to Orders in Council

32.—(1) His Majesty in Council may make Orders for altering, revoking, or varying any Order in Council made under this Act, or under any enactments repealed by this Act, but any Order made under this section shall not affect prejudicially any rights or interests acquired or accrued at the date when the Order comes into operation, and shall provide for the protection of such rights and interests.

(2) Every Order in Council made under this Act shall be published in the *London Gazette* and shall be laid before both Houses of Parliament as soon as may be after it is made, and shall have effect as if enacted in this Act.

1539 Saving of university copyright

33. Nothing in this Act shall deprive any of the universities and colleges mentioned in the Copyright Act, 1775, of any copyright they already possess under that Act, but the remedies and penalties for infringement of any such copyright shall be under this Act and not under that Act.

1540 Saving of compensation to certain libraries

34. There shall continue to be charged on, and paid out of, the Consolidated Fund of the United Kingdom such annual compensation as was immediately before the commencement of this Act payable in pursuance of any Act as compensation to a library for the loss of the right to receive gratuitous copies of books:

Provided that this compensation shall not be paid to a library in any year, unless the Treasury are satisfied that the compensation for the previous year has been applied in the purchase of books for the use of and to be preserved in the library.

OPERATION

This section is not repealed by the Copyright Act, 1956.

1541 **Interpretation**

35.—(1) In this Act, unless the context otherwise requires,—

"Literary work" includes maps, charts, plans, tables, and compilations;

"Dramatic work" includes any piece for recitation, choreographic work or entertainment in dumb show, the scenic arrangement or acting form of which is fixed in writing or otherwise, and any cinematograph production where the arrangement or acting form or the combination of incidents represented give the work an original character;

"Artistic work" includes works of painting, drawing, sculpture and artistic craftsmanship, and architectural works of art and engravings and photographs;

"Work of sculpture" includes casts and models;

"Architectural work of art" means any building or structure having an artistic character or design, in respect of such character or design, or any model for such building or structure, provided that the protection afforded by this Act shall be confined to the artistic character and design, and shall not extend to processes or methods of construction;

"Engravings" include etchings, lithographs, wood-cuts, prints, and other similar works, not being photographs;

"Photograph" includes photo-lithograph and any work produced by any process analogous to photography;

"Cinematograph" includes any work produced by any process analogous to cinematography;

"Collective work" means—

(*a*) an encyclopaedia, dictionary, year book, or similar work;

(*b*) a newspaper, review, magazine, or similar periodical; and

(*c*) any work written in distinct parts by different authors, or in which works or parts of works of different authors are incorporated;

"Infringing," when applied to a copy of a work in which copyright subsists, means any copy, including any colourable imitation, made, or imported in contravention of the provisions of this Act;

"Performance" means any acoustic representation of a work and any visual representation of any dramatic action in a work, including such a representation made by means of any mechanical instrument;

"Delivery," in relation to a lecture, includes delivery by means of any mechanical instrument;

"Plate" includes any stereotype or other plate, stone, block, mould, matrix, transfer, or negative used or intended to be used for printing or reproducing copies of any work, and any matrix or other appliance by which records, perforated rolls or other contrivances for the acoustic representation of the work are or are intended to be made;

"Lecture" includes address, speech, and sermon;

"Self-governing dominion" means the Dominion of Canada, the Commonwealth of Australia, the Dominion of New Zealand, the Union of South Africa, and Newfoundland.

(2) For the purposes of this Act (other than those relating to infringements of copyright), a work shall not be deemed to be published or performed in public, and a lecture shall not be deemed to be delivered in public, if published, performed in public, or delivered in public, without the consent or acquiescence of the author, his executors administrators or assigns.

(3) For the purposes of this Act, a work shall be deemed to be first published within the parts of His Majesty's dominions to which this Act extends, notwithstanding that it has been published simultaneously in some other place, unless the publication in such parts of His Majesty's dominions as aforesaid is colourable only and is not intended to satisfy the reasonable requirements of the public, and a work shall be deemed to be published simultaneously in two places if the time between the publication in one such place and the publication in the other place does not exceed fourteen days, or such longer period as may, for the time being, be fixed by Order in Council.

(4) Where, in the case of an unpublished work, the making of a work has extended over a considerable period, the conditions of this Act conferring copyright shall be deemed to have been complied with, if the author was, during any substantial part of that period, a British subject or a resident within the parts of His Majesty's dominions to which this Act extends.

(5) For the purposes of the provisions of this Act as to residence, an author of a work shall be deemed to be a resident in the parts of His Majesty's dominions to which this Act extends if he is domiciled within any such part.

1542 **Repeal**

36. Subject to the provisions of this Act, the enactments mentioned in the Second Schedule to this Act are hereby repealed to the extent specified in the third column of that schedule:

Provided that this repeal shall not take effect in any part of His Majesty's dominions until this Act comes into operation in that part.

1543 **Short title and commencement**

37.—(1) This Act may be cited as the Copyright Act, 1911.

(2) This Act shall come into operation—

(*a*) in the United Kingdom, on the first day of July nineteen hundred and twelve or such earlier date as may be fixed by Order in Council;

(*b*) in a self-governing dominion to which this Act extends, at such date as may be fixed by the Legislature of that dominion;

(*c*) in the Channel Islands, at such date as may be fixed by the States of those islands respectively;

(*d*) in any other British possession to which this Act extends, on the proclamation thereof within the possession by the Governor.

OPERATION

This section is not repealed by the Copyright Act, 1956.

SCHEDULES

1544 **Section 24**

FIRST SCHEDULE

EXISTING RIGHTS

Existing Right	Substituted Right
(*a*) *In the case of Works other than Dramatic and Musical Works.*	
Copyright	Copyright as defined by this Act.*
(*b*) *In the case of Musical and Dramatic Works.*	
Both copyright and performing right	Copyright as defined by this Act.*
Copyright, but not performing right	Copyright as defined by this Act, except the sole right to perform the work or any substantial part thereof in public.
Performing right, but not copyright	The sole right to perform the work in public, but none of the other rights comprised in copyright as defined by this Act.

For the purposes of this Schedule the following expressions, where used in the first column thereof, have the following meanings:

"Copyright," in the case of a work which according to the law in force immediately before the commencement of this Act has not been published before that date and statutory copyright wherein depends on publication, includes the right at common law (if any) to restrain publication or other dealing with the work;

* In the case of an essay, article, or portion forming part of and first published in a review, magazine, or other periodical or work of a like nature, the right shall be subject to any right of publishing the essay, article, or portion in a separate form to which the author is entitled at the commencement of this Act, or would, if this Act had not been passed, have become entitled under section eighteen of the Copyright Act, 1842.

"Performing right," in the case of a work which has not been performed in public before the commencement of this Act, includes the right at common law (if any) to restrain the performance thereof in public.

1545 **Section 36** SECOND SCHEDULE

ENACTMENTS REPEALED

Session and Chapter	Short Title	Extent of Repeal
8 Geo. 2. c. 13	The Engraving Copyright Act, 1734.	The whole Act.
7 Geo. 3. c. 38	The Engraving Copyright Act, 1767.	The whole Act.
15 Geo. 3. c. 53	The Copyright Act, 1775.	The whole Act.
17 Geo. 3. c. 57	The Prints Copyright Act, 1777.	The whole Act.
54 Geo. 3. c. 56	The Sculpture Copyright Act, 1814.	The whole Act.
3 & 4 Will. 4. c. 15.	The Dramatic Copyright Act, 1833.	The whole Act.
5 & 6 Will. 4. c. 65.	The Lectures Copyright Act, 1835.	The whole Act.
6 & 7 Will. 4. c. 59.	The Prints and Engravings Copyright (Ireland) Act, 1836.	The whole Act.
6 & 7 Will. 4. c. 110.	The Copyright Act, 1836.	The whole Act.
5 & 6 Vict. c. 45.	The Copyright Act, 1842.	The whole Act.
7 & 8 Vict. c. 12.	The International Copyright Act, 1844.	The whole Act.
10 & 11 Vict. c. 95.	The Colonial Copyright Act, 1847.	The whole Act.
15 & 16 Vict. c. 12.	The International Copyright Act, 1852.	The whole Act.
25 & 26 Vict. c. 68.	The Fine Arts Copyright Act, 1862.	Sections one to six. In section eight the words "and pursuant to any Act for the protection of copyright engravings," and "and in any such Act as aforesaid." Sections nine to twelve.
38 & 39 Vict. c. 12.	The International Copyright Act, 1875.	The whole Act.
39 & 40 Vict. c. 36.	The Customs Consolidation Act, 1876.	Section forty-two, from "Books wherein" to "such copyright will expire." Sections forty-four, forty-five, and one hundred and fifty-two.
45 & 46 Vict. c. 40.	The Copyright (Musical Compositions) Act, 1882.	The whole Act.
49 & 50 Vict. c. 33.	The International Copyright Act, 1886.	The whole Act.
51 & 52 Vict. c. 17.	The Copyright (Musical Compositions) Act, 1888.	The whole Act.

Session and Chapter	Short Title	Extent of Repeal
52 & 53 Vict. c. 42.	The Revenue Act, 1889.	Section one, from " Books first published " to " as provided in that section."
6 Edw. 7. c. 36.	The Musical Copyright Act, 1906.	In section three the words " and which has been registered in accordance with the provisions of the Copyright Act, 1842, or of the International Copyright Act, 1844, which registration may be effected notwithstanding anything in the International Copyright Act, 1886."

46 COMPARATIVE TABLE—I

COPYRIGHT ACT, 1911
COMPARED WITH
COPYRIGHT ACT, 1956

1911	1956	1911	1956	1911	1956
s. 1 (1) (*a*)	ss. 2 (2), 3	s. 5 (1) (*b*)	s. 4 (2), (5)	s. 19 (6)	s. 8 (11)
	(3)	(2)	36 (1), (2),	(7)	(9)
(*b*)	1 (5), 2		(3)	(8)	omitted
	(1), 3 (2)	proviso	omitted	20	omitted
(2)	1 (1), 2	(3)	49 (5)	21	3 (4)
	(5), 3 (5)	6 (1)	17 (1)	22	ss. 10, 44
	46 (1),	(2)	omitted	23	s. 35
	48 (1),	(3)	20 (1)	24	omitted
	49 (1)	(*a*)	20 (2)	25	ss. 1 (1), 31
(*a*) (*b*) (*c*)	s. 2 (6)	(*b*)	20 (4)	26	omitted
(*d*)	ss. 2 (5), 3	7	18 (1)	27	s. 31 (3)
	(5), 48 (1)	8	ss. 17 (2), 18	28	(1)
(3)	s. 49 (2)		(2)	29	32
2 (1)	1 (2)	9 (1)	s. 17 (4)	30	omitted
(i)	6 (1), (2),	(2)	omitted	31	46 (4), (5)
	(3)	10	omitted	32	47
	9 (1), (2)	11	21	33	46 (1)
(ii)	9 (9)	12	21 (10)	34	not repealed
(iii)	9 (3),	13	21 (6)	35 (1)	ss. 3 (1), 13
	(4), (6)	14	22		(10)
(iv)	6 (6)	15	not repealed		18 (3), 48
(v) (vi)	omitted	16	11, Sch. 3		(1)
(2) (*a*)	5 (3)	(4)	16 (3)		s. 49 (2), (3)
(*b*)	(4)	17 (1)	ss. 2 (3), 3		
(*c*)	(3)		(4)	(2)	49 (3)
(*d*)	(2)	(2)	s. 38	(3)	(2)
(3)	(5)	18	39	(4)	(9)
3	ss. 2 (3), 3	19 (1)	12 (1)	(5)	1 (5) (*a*)
	(4)	(2)	8 (1), (5),		
proviso	omitted		(6), (8)	36	omitted
4	omitted	(3)	(2)	37	not repealed
5 (1)	s. 4 (1)	(3)	(3)	Sch. 1	omitted
(*a*)	(3), (5)	proviso		Sch. 2	omitted
		(4)	(4)		
		(5)	(7)		

1547

COMPARATIVE TABLE—II

Copyright Act, 1956

compared with

Copyright Act, 1911

1956	1911	1956	1911	1956	1911
s. 1 (1)	s. 1 (2)	s. 9 (1), (2)	s. 2 (1) (i)	s. 31 (2)	——
(2)	2 (1)	(3), (4)	(iii)	(3)	s. 27
(3), (4)	——	(5)	——	32	29
(5)	1 (1) (*b*)	(6)	2 (1) (iii)	ss. 33, 34	——
2 (1)	(*b*)	(7), (8)	——	s. 35	23
(2)	(*a*)	(9)	2 (1) (ii)	36	5 (2)
(3)	ss. 3, 17	(10), (11)	——	37	——
(4)	——	10	——	38	17 (2)
(5)	s. 1 (2)	11 (1)	——	39	18
(6)	(2)	(2), (3)	16	ss. 40–45	——
3 (1)	35 (1)	12	19 (1)	s. 46 (1)	33
(2)	1 (1) (*b*)	ss. 13–16	——	(2)	18
(3)	(*a*)	s. 17 (1)	6 (1)	(3)	——
(4)	ss. 3, 17, 21	(2)	(8)	(4), (5)	31
(5)	s. 1 (2)	(3)	——	47	32
4 (1)	5 (1)	(4)	9 (1)	48 (1)	35 (1)
(2)	(*b*)	18 (1)	7	(2)–(7)	——
(3)	(*a*)	(2) (*a*)	8	49 (1)	1 (2)
(4)	(*b*)	(*b*) (*c*)	——	(2)	ss. 1 (3), 35 (3)
(5)	5 (1)	(3)	35 (1)		
(6)	——	19	——	(3)	s. 35 (2)
5	2 (2), (3)	20 (1), (2)	6 (3)	(4)	(4)
6 (1), (2),		(3)	——	(5)	5 (3)
(3)	(1) (i)	(4)	6 (3)	(6)–(10)	——
(4)	——	(5), (6)	——	50	24
(5)	2 (1) (ii)	21	ss. 11, 12	51	——
(6)	(iv)	22	s. 14	Schs. 1, 2	——
(7)–(10)	——	ss. 23–30	——	Sch. 3	16
7	——	s. 31 (1)	28	Schs. 4–9	——
8	19 (2)–(7)				

Part III

Other United Kingdom Statutes

Interpretation Act, 1889

(52 & 53 Vict. c. 63)

1548 **Effect of repeal in future Acts**

38.—(1) Where this Act or any Act passed after the commencement of this Act repeals and re-enacts, with or without modification, any provisions of a former Act, references in any other Act to the provisions so repealed, shall, unless the contrary intention appears, be construed as references to the provisions so re-enacted.

(2) Where this Act or any Act passed after the commencement of this Act repeals any other enactment, then, unless the contrary intention appears, the repeal shall not—

(*a*) revive anything not in force or existing at the time at which the repeal takes effect; or

(*b*) affect the previous operation of any enactment so repealed or anything duly done or suffered under any enactment so repealed; or

(*c*) affect any right, privilege, obligation, or liability acquired, accrued, or incurred under any enactment so repealed; or

(*d*) affect any penalty, forfeiture, or punishment incurred in respect of any offence committed against any enactment so repealed; or

(*e*) affect any investigation, legal proceeding, or remedy in respect of any such right, privilege, obligation, liability, penalty, forfeiture, or punishment as aforesaid;

and any such investigation, legal proceeding, or remedy may be instituted, continued, or enforced, and any such penalty, forfeiture, or punishment may be imposed, as if the repealing Act had not been passed.

* * *

British Museum Act, 1932

(22 & 23 Geo. 5, c. 34)

An Act to enable the Trustees of the British Museum to except certain publications from the provisions of subsection (1) of section fifteen of the Copyright Act, 1911. [12th July, 1932.]

1549 **Power of Trustees to except certain publications from s. 15 (1) of 1 & 2 Geo. 5, c. 46**

1.—(1) Notwithstanding anything in subsection (1) of section fifteen of the Copyright Act, 1911, the publisher of any publication of a class to which this Act for the time being applies shall not be required to deliver a copy of the publication to the Trustees of the British Museum (hereafter in this Act referred to as " the Trustees ") unless a written demand for the delivery thereof is made by the Trustees; and the Trustees shall not be required to accept or give a receipt for a copy of any publication which is not required to be delivered to them.

(2) The Trustees may by regulations—

(*a*) apply this Act to publications of such classes as may be specified in the regulations, being publications of all or any of the descriptions set out in the Schedule to this Act;

(*b*) except any particular publication from any class of publication to which this Act is applied by the regulations, or to which this Act has been applied by previous regulations.

(3) All regulations made under this Act shall be laid before each House of Parliament as soon as may be after they are made, and if either House, within the next subsequent twenty-eight days on which that House has sat after the regulations are laid before it, resolves that the regulations be annulled, the regulations shall thenceforth be void, but without prejudice to anything previously done thereunder or to the making of any new regulations.

1550 **Short title and repeal**

2.—(1) This Act may be cited as the British Museum Act, 1932.

(2) The Copyright (British Museum) Act, 1915 (which empowers the Board of Trade on the application of the Trustees to except publications wholly or mainly in the nature of trade advertisements from the provisions of subsection (1) of section fifteen of the Copyright Act, 1911), is hereby repealed:

Provided that, notwithstanding the repeal of that Act, any regulations made thereunder shall continue in force and shall have effect as if they had been made by the Trustees under this Act and as if this Act were thereby applied to publications of the descriptions therein specified.

SCHEDULE

PUBLICATIONS TO WHICH ACT MAY BE APPLIED

Publications wholly or mainly in the nature of trade advertisements.

Registers of voters prepared under the Representation of the People Act, 1918, as amended by any subsequent enactment.

Specifications of inventions prepared for the purposes of the Patents and Designs Act, 1907, as amended by any subsequent enactment.

Publications wholly or mainly in the nature of time tables of passenger transport services, being publications prepared for local use.

Publications wholly or mainly in the nature of calendars.

Publications wholly or mainly in the nature of blank forms of accounts, or blank forms of receipts, or other blank forms of a similar character.

Wall sheets printed with alphabets, mottoes, religious texts or other matter for the purpose of elementary instruction.

*   *   *

Limitation Act, 1939

(2 & 3 Geo. 6, c. 21)

Actions of contract and tort and certain other actions.

1551 **Limitation of actions of contract and tort, and certain other actions**

2.—(1) The following actions shall not be brought after the expiration of six years from the date on which the cause of action accrued, that is to say:

(*a*) actions founded on simple contract or on tort;

*   *   *

(2) An action for an account shall not be brought in respect of any matter which arose more than six years before the commencement of the action.

*   *   *

(7) This section shall not apply to any claim for specific performance of a contract or for an injunction or for other equitable relief, except in so far as any provision thereof may be applied by the Court by analogy in like manner as the corresponding enactment repealed by this Act has heretofore been applied.

1552 **Limitation in case of successive conversions and extinction of title of owner of converted goods**

3.—(1) Where any cause of action in respect of the conversion or wrongful detention of a chattel has accrued to any person and, before he recovers possession of the chattel, a further conversion or wrongful detention takes place, no action shall be brought in respect of the further conversion or detention after the expiration of six years from the accrual of the cause of action in respect of the original conversion or detention.

(2) Where any such cause of action has accrued to any person and the period prescribed for bringing that action and for bringing any action in respect of such a further conversion or wrongful detention as aforesaid has expired and he has not during that period recovered possession of the chattel, the title of that person to the chattel shall be extinguished.

* * *

Wireless Telegraphy Act, 1949

(12, 13 and 14 Geo. 6, c. 54)

1553 **Interpretation**

19.—(1) In this Act, except where the context otherwise requires, the expression "wireless telegraphy" means the emitting or receiving, over paths which are not provided by any material substance constructed or arranged for that purpose, of electro-magnetic energy of a frequency not exceeding three million megacycles a second, being energy which either—

(*a*) serves for the conveying of messages, sound or visual images (whether the messages, sound or images are actually received by any person or not), or for the actuation or control of machinery or apparatus; or

(*b*) is used in connection with the determination of position, bearing or distance, or for the gaining of information as to the presence, absence, position or motion of any object or of any objects of any class,

and references to stations for wireless telegraphy and apparatus for wireless telegraphy or wireless telegraphy apparatus shall be construed as references to stations and apparatus for the emitting or receiving as aforesaid of such electro-magnetic energy as aforesaid:

Provided that where—

(i) a station or apparatus for wireless telegraphy cannot lawfully be used without a wireless telegraphy licence or could not lawfully be used without such a licence but for regulations under section one of this Act; and

(ii) any such electro-magnetic energy as aforesaid which is received by that station or apparatus serves for the conveying of messages, sound or visual images; and

(iii) any apparatus is electrically coupled with that station or apparatus for the purpose of enabling any person to receive any of the said messages, sound or visual images,

the apparatus so coupled shall itself be deemed for the purposes of this Act to be apparatus for wireless telegraphy.

(2) In this Act, the expression "station for wireless telegraphy" includes the wireless telegraphy apparatus of a ship or aircraft, and the expression "electric line" has the same meaning as in the Electric Lighting Act, 1882.

(3) Any reference in this Act to the emission of electro-magnetic energy, or to emission (as opposed to reception), shall be construed as including a reference to the deliberate reflection of electro-magnetic energy by means of any apparatus designed or specially adapted for that purpose, whether the reflection is continuous or intermittent.

* * *

(6) Any reference in this Act to the sending or the conveying of messages includes a reference to the making of any signal or the sending or conveying of any warning or information, and any reference to the reception of messages shall be construed accordingly.

* * *

Registered Designs Act, 1949 [3]

(12, 13 & 14 Geo. 6, c. 88)

Registrable designs and proceedings for registration

1554 **Designs registrable under Act**

1.—(1) Subject to the following provisions of this section, a design may, upon application made by the person claiming to be the proprietor, be registered under this Act in respect of any article or set of articles specified in the application.

(2) Subject to the provisions of this Act, a design shall not be registered thereunder unless it is new or original and in particular shall not be so registered in respect of any article if it is the same as a design which before the date of the application for registration has been registered or published in the United Kingdom in respect of the same or any other article or differs from such a design only in immaterial details or in features which are variants commonly used in the trade.

(3) In this Act the expression "design" means features of shape, configuration, pattern or ornament applied to an article by any industrial process or means, being features which in the finished article appeal to and are judged solely by the eye, but does not include a method or principle of construction or features of shape or configuration which are dictated solely by the function which the article to be made in that shape or configuration has to perform.

(4) Rules made by the Board of Trade under this Act may provide for excluding from registration thereunder designs for such articles, being articles which are primarily literary or artistic in character, as the Board think fit.

1555 **Proprietorship of designs**

2.—(1) Subject to the provisions of this section, the author of a design shall be treated for the purposes of this Act as the proprietor of the design:

[3] The sections of this Act, as amended by the Copyright Act, 1956, likely to be of particular interest to owners of artistic copyright are printed here.

Provided that where the design is executed by the author for another person for good consideration, that other person shall be treated for the purposes of this Act as the proprietor.

(2) Where a design, or the right to apply a design to any article, becomes vested, whether by assignment, transmission or operation of law, in any person other than the original proprietor, either alone or jointly with the original proprietor, that other person, or as the case may be the original proprietor and that other person, shall be treated for the purposes of this Act as the proprietor of the design or as the proprietor of the design in relation to that article.

1556 **Proceedings for registration**

3.—(1) An application for the registration of a design shall be made in the prescribed form and shall be filed at the Patent Office in the prescribed manner.

(2) For the purpose of deciding whether a design is new or original, the registrar may make such searches, if any, as he thinks fit.

(3) The registrar may refuse any application for the registration of a design or may register the design in pursuance of the application subject to such modifications, if any, as he thinks fit.

(4) An application which, owing to any default or neglect on the part of the applicant, has not been completed so as to enable registration to be effected within such time as may be prescribed shall be deemed to be abandoned.

(5) Except as otherwise expressly provided by this Act, a design when registered shall be registered as of the date on which the application for registration was made, or such other date (whether earlier or later than that date) as the registrar may in any particular case direct:

Provided that no proceedings shall be taken in respect of any infringement committed before the date on which the certificate of registration of the design under this Act is issued.

(6) An appeal shall lie from any decision of the registrar under subsection (3) of this section.

1557 **Registration of same design in respect of other articles, etc.**

4.—(1) Where the registered proprietor of a design registered in respect of any article makes an application—

(*a*) for registration in respect of one or more other articles, of the registered design, or

(*b*) for registration in respect of the same or one or more other articles, of a design consisting of the registered design with modifications or variations not sufficient to alter the character or substantially to affect the identity thereof,

the application shall not be refused and the registration made on that application shall not be invalidated by reason only of the previous registration or publication of the registered design:

Provided that the period of copyright in a design registered by virtue of this section shall not extend beyond the expiration of the original and any extended period of copyright in the original registered design.

(2) Where any person makes an application for the registration of a design in respect of any article and either—

(*a*) that design has been previously registered by another person in respect of some other article; or

(*b*) the design to which the application relates consists of a design previously registered by another person in respect of the same or some other article with modifications or variations not sufficient to alter the character or substantially to affect the identity thereof,

then, if at any time while the application is pending the applicant becomes the registered proprietor of the design previously registered, the foregoing provisions of this section shall apply as if at the time of making the application the applicant had been the registered proprietor of that design.

* * *

1558 **Provisions as to confidential disclosure, etc.**

6.—(1) An application for the registration of a design shall not be refused, and the registration of a design shall not be invalidated, by reason only of—

(*a*) the disclosure of the design by the proprietor to any other person in such circumstances as would make it contrary to good faith for that other person to use or publish the design;

(*b*) the disclosure of the design in breach of good faith by any person other than the proprietor of the design; or

(*c*) in the case of a new or original textile design intended for registration, the acceptance of a first and confidential order for goods bearing the design.

(2) An application for the registration of a design shall not be refused and the registration of a design shall not be invalidated by reason only—

(*a*) that a representation of the design, or any article to which the design has been applied, has been displayed, with the consent of the proprietor of the design, at an exhibition certified by the Board of Trade for the purposes of this subsection;

(*b*) that after any such display as aforesaid, and during the period of the exhibition, a representation of the design or any such article as aforesaid has been displayed by any person without the consent of the proprietor; or

(*c*) that a representation of the design has been published in consequence of any such display as is mentioned in paragraph (*a*) of this subsection,

if the application for registration of the design is made not later than six months after the opening of the exhibition.

(3) An application for the registration of a design shall not be refused, and the registration of a design shall not be invalidated, by reason only of the communication of the design by the proprietor thereof to a Government department or to any person authorised by a Government department to consider the merits of the design, or of anything done in consequence of such a communication.

[(4) Where copyright under the Copyright Act, 1956, subsists in an artistic work, and an application is made by, or with the consent of, the owner of that copyright for the registration of a corresponding design, that design shall not be treated for the purposes of this Act as being other than new or original by reason only of any use previously made of the artistic work, unless—

(*a*) the previous use consisted of or included the sale, letting for hire, or offer for sale or hire of articles to which the design in question (or a design differing from it only as mentioned in subsection (2) of section one of this Act) had been applied industrially, other than articles of a description specified in rules made under subsection (4) of section one of this Act, and

(*b*) that previous use was made by, or with the consent of, the owner of the copyright in the artistic work.

(5) Any rules made by virtue of subsection (5) of section ten of the Copyright Act, 1956 (which relates to rules for determining the circumstances in which a design is to be taken to be applied industrially) shall apply for the purposes of the last foregoing subsection.] [4]

Effect of registration, etc.

1559 **Right given by registration**

7.—(1) The registration of a design under this Act shall give to the registered proprietor the copyright in the registered design, that is to say, the exclusive right in the United Kingdom and the Isle of Man to make or import for sale or for use for the purposes of any trade or business, or to sell, hire or offer for sale or hire, any article in respect of which the design is registered, being an article to which the registered design or a design not substantially different from the registered design has been applied, and to make anything for enabling any such article to be made as aforesaid, whether in the United Kingdom or the Isle of Man or elsewhere.

(2) Subject to the provisions of this Act and of subsection (3) of section three of the Crown Proceedings Act, 1947, the registration of a design shall have the same effect against the Crown as it has against a subject.

1560 **Period of copyright**

8.—(1) Copyright in a registered design shall, subject to the provisions of this Act, subsist for a period of five years from the date of registration.

(2) The registrar shall extend the period of copyright for a second period of five years from the expiration of the original period and for a third period of five years from the expiration of the second period if an application for extension of the period of copyright for the second or third period is made in the prescribed form before the expiration of the original period or the second period, as the case may be, and if the prescribed fee is paid before the expiration of the relevant period or if such application is made and the said fee is paid within such further period (not exceeding six months) as may be specified in a request made to the registrar and accompanied by the prescribed additional fee.

[(3) Where in the case of a registered design it is shown—

(*a*) that the design, at the time when it was registered, was a corresponding design in relation to an artistic work in which copyright subsisted under the Copyright Act, 1956;

[4] Subsections (4) and (5) were added by the Copyright Act, 1956, s. 44 (1).

(*b*) that, by reason of a previous use of that artistic work, the design would not have been registrable under this Act but for subsection (4) of section six of this Act; and

(*c*) that the copyright in that work under the Copyright Act, 1956, expired before the date of expiry of the copyright in the design,

the copyright in the design shall, notwithstanding anything in this section, be deemed to have expired at the same time as the copyright in the artistic work, and shall not be renewable after that time.] [5]

1561 **Exemption of innocent infringer from liability for damages**

9.—(1) In proceedings for the infringement of copyright in a registered design damages shall not be awarded against a defendant who proves that at the date of the infringement he was not aware, and had no reasonable ground for supposing, that the design was registered; and a person shall not be deemed to have been aware or to have had reasonable grounds for supposing as aforesaid by reason only of the marking of an article with the word " registered " or any abbreviation thereof, or any word or words expressing or implying that the design applied to the article has been registered, unless the number of the design accompanied the word or words or the abbreviation in question.

(2) Nothing in this section shall affect the power of the court to grant an injunction in any proceedings for infringement of copyright in a registered design.

1562 **Compulsory licence in respect of registered design**

10.—(1) At any time after a design has been registered any person interested may apply to the registrar for the grant of a compulsory licence in respect of the design on the ground that the design is not applied in the United Kingdom by any industrial process or means to the article in respect of which it is registered to such an extent as is reasonable in the circumstances of the case; and the registrar may make such order on the application as he thinks fit.

(2) An order for the grant of a licence shall, without prejudice to any other method of enforcement, have effect as if it were a deed executed by the registered proprietor and all other necessary parties, granting a licence in accordance with the order.

(3) No order shall be made under this section which would be at variance with any treaty, convention, arrangement or engagement applying to the United Kingdom and any convention country.

(4) An appeal shall lie from any order of the registrar under this section.

1563 **Cancellation of registration**

11.—(1) The registrar may, upon a request made in the prescribed manner by the registered proprietor, cancel the registration of a design.

(2) At any time after a design has been registered any person interested may apply to the registrar for the cancellation of the registration of the design on the ground that the design was not, at the date of the registration thereof, new or original, or on any other ground on which the registrar could have refused to register the design; and the registrar may make such order on the application as he thinks fit.

[5] Subsection (2) is printed as amended by s. 1 of the Patents and Designs (Renewals, Extensions and Fees) Act, 1961 (9 and 10 Eliz. 2, c. 25). Subsection (3) was added by the Copyright Act, 1956, s. 44 (2).

[(2A) At any time after a design has been registered, any person interested may apply to the registrar for the cancellation of the registration of the design on the grounds—

(*a*) that the design, at the time when it was registered, was a corresponding design in relation to an artistic work in which copyright subsisted under the Copyright Act, 1956;

(*b*) that, by reason of a previous use of that artistic work, the design would not have been registrable under this Act but for subsection (4) of section six of this Act; and

(*c*) that the copyright in that work under the Copyright Act, 1956, has expired;

and the registrar may make such order on the application as he thinks fit.] [6]

(3) An appeal shall lie from any order of the registrar under [either of the two last foregoing subsections].

* * *

Register of designs, etc.

1564 **Register of designs**

17.—(1) There shall be kept at the Patent Office under the control of the registrar a register of designs, in which there shall be entered the names and addresses of proprietors of registered designs, notices of assignments and of transmissions of registered designs, and such other matters as may be prescribed or as the registrar may think fit.

(2) Subject to the provisions of this Act and to rules made by the Board of Trade thereunder, the register of designs shall, at all convenient times, be open to inspection by the public; and certified copies sealed with the seal of the Patent Office of any entry in the register shall be given to any person requiring them on payment of the prescribed fee.

(3) The register of designs shall be prima facie evidence of any matters required or authorised by this Act to be entered therein.

(4) No notice of any trust, whether expressed, implied or constructive, shall be entered in the register of designs, and the registrar shall not be affected by any such notice.

1565 **Certificate of registration**

18.—(1) The registrar shall grant a certificate of registration in the prescribed form to the registered proprietor of a design when the design is registered.

(2) The registrar may, in a case where he is satisfied that the certificate of registration has been lost or destroyed, or in any other case in which he thinks it expedient, furnish one or more copies of the certificate.

1566 **Registration of assignments, etc.**

19.—(1) Where any person becomes entitled by assignment, transmission or operation of law to a registered design or to a share in a registered design, or becomes entitled as mortgagee, licensee or otherwise to any other interest in a registered design, he shall apply to the registrar

[6] Subsection (2A) and the words in square brackets in subsection (3) were added by the Copyright Act, 1956, s. 44 (3) and (4).

in the prescribed manner for the registration of his title as proprietor or co-proprietor or, as the case may be, of notice of his interest, in the register of designs.

(2) Without prejudice to the provisions of the foregoing subsection, an application for the registration of the title of any person becoming entitled by assignment to a registered design or a share in a registered design, or becoming entitled by virtue of a mortgage, licence or other instrument to any other interest in a registered design, may be made in the prescribed manner by the assignor, mortgagor, licensor or other party to that instrument, as the case may be.

(3) Where application is made under this section for the registration of the title of any person, the registrar shall, upon proof of title to his satisfaction—

(*a*) where that person is entitled to a registered design or a share in a registered design, register him in the register of designs as proprietor or co-proprietor of the design, and enter in that register particulars of the instrument or event by which he derives title; or

(*b*) where that person is entitled to any other interest in the registered design, enter in that register notice of his interest, with particulars of the instrument (if any) creating it.

(4) Subject to any rights vested in any other person of which notice is entered in the register of designs, the person or persons registered as proprietor of a registered design shall have power to assign, grant licences under, or otherwise deal with the design, and to give effectual receipts for any consideration for any such assignment, licence or dealing:

Provided that any equities in respect of the design may be enforced in like manner as in respect of any other personal property.

(5) Except for the purposes of an application to rectify the register under the following provisions of this Act, a document in respect of which no entry has been made in the register of designs under subsection (3) of this section shall not be admitted in any court as evidence of the title of any person to a registered design or share of or interest in a registered design unless the court otherwise directs.

1567 **Rectification of register**

20.—(1) The court may, on the application of any person aggrieved, order the register of designs to be rectified by the making of any entry therein or the variation or deletion of any entry therein.

(2) In proceedings under this section the court may determine any question which it may be necessary or expedient to decide in connection with the rectification of the register.

(3) Notice of any application to the court under this section shall be given in the prescribed manner to the registrar, who shall be entitled to appear and be heard on the application, and shall appear if so directed by the court.

(4) Any order made by the court under this section shall direct that notice of the order shall be served on the registrar in the prescribed manner; and the registrar shall, on receipt of the notice, rectify the register accordingly.

1568 **Power to correct clerical errors**

21.—(1) The registrar may, in accordance with the provisions of this section, correct any error in an application for the registration or in the representation of a design, or any error in the register of designs.

(2) A correction may be made in pursuance of this section either upon a request in writing made by any person interested and accompanied by the prescribed fee, or without such a request.

(3) Where the registrar proposes to make any such correction as aforesaid otherwise than in pursuance of a request made under this section, he shall give notice of the proposal to the registered proprietor or the applicant for registration of the design, as the case may be, and to any other person who appears to him to be concerned, and shall give them an opportunity to be heard before making the correction.

1569 **Inspection of registered designs**

22.—(1) Subject to the following provisions of this section and to any rules made by the Board of Trade in pursuance of subsection (2) of section five of this Act, the representation or specimen of a design registered under this Act shall be open to inspection at the Patent Office on and after the day on which the certificate of registration is issued.

(2) In the case of a design registered in respect of an article of any class prescribed for the purposes of this subsection, no representation or specimen of the design filed in pursuance of the application shall, until the expiration of such period after the day on which the certificate of registration is issued as may be prescribed in relation to articles of that class, be open to inspection at the Patent Office except by the registered proprietor, a person authorised in writing by the registered proprietor, or a person authorised by the registrar or by the court:

Provided that where the registrar proposes to refuse an application for the registration of any other design on the ground that it is the same as the first-mentioned design or differs from that design only in immaterial details or in features which are variants commonly used in the trade, the applicant shall be entitled to inspect the representation or specimen of the first-mentioned design filed in pursuance of the application for registration of that design.

(3) In the case of a design registered in respect of an article of any class prescribed for the purposes of the last foregoing subsection, the representation or specimen of the design shall not, during the period prescribed as aforesaid, be inspected by any person by virtue of this section except in the presence of the registrar or of an officer acting under him; and except in the case of an inspection authorised by the proviso to that subsection, the person making the inspection shall not be entitled to take a copy of the representation or specimen of the design or any part thereof.

(4) Where an application for the registration of a design has been abandoned or refused, neither the application for registration nor any representation or specimen of the design filed in pursuance thereof shall at any time be open to inspection at the Patent Office or be published by the registrar.

1570 **Information as to existence of copyright**

23. On the request of any person furnishing such information as may enable the registrar to identify the design, and on payment of the prescribed fee the registrar shall inform him whether the design is registered, and if so, in respect of what articles, and whether any extension of the period of copyright has been granted and shall state the date of registration and the name and address of the registered proprietor.

1571 **Evidence of entries, documents, etc.**

24.—(1) A certificate purporting to be signed by the registrar and certifying that any entry which he is authorised by or under this Act to make has or has not been made, or that any other thing which he is so authorised to do has or has not been done shall be prima facie evidence of the matters so certified.

(2) A copy of any entry in the register of designs or of any representation, specimen or document kept in the Patent Office or an extract from the register or any such document, purporting to be certified by the registrar and to be sealed with the seal of the Patent Office, shall be admitted in evidence without further proof and without production of the original.

* * *

Legal proceedings and Appeals

1572 **Remedy for groundless threats of infringement proceedings**

26.—(1) Where any person (whether entitled to or interested in a registered design or an application for registration of a design or not) by circulars, advertisements or otherwise threatens any other person with proceedings for infringement of the copyright in a registered design, any person aggrieved thereby may bring an action against him for any such relief as is mentioned in the next following subsection.

(2) Unless in any action brought by virtue of this section the defendant proves that the acts in respect of which proceedings were threatened constitute or, if done, would constitute, an infringement of the copyright in a registered design the registration of which is not shown by the plaintiff to be invalid, the plaintiff shall be entitled to the following relief, that is to say:—

(*a*) a declaration to the effect that the threats are unjustifiable;
(*b*) an injunction against the continuance of the threats; and
(*c*) such damages, if any, as he has sustained thereby.

(3) For the avoidance of doubt it is hereby declared that a mere notification that a design is registered does not constitute a threat of proceedings within the meaning of this section.

* * *

Powers and Duties of Registrar

1573 **Exercise of discretionary powers of registrar**

29. Without prejudice to any provisions of this Act requiring the registrar to hear any party to proceedings thereunder, or to give to any such party an opportunity to be heard, the registrar shall give to any applicant for registration of a design an opportunity to be heard before exercising adversely to the applicant any discretion vested in the registrar by or under this Act.

1574 **Costs and security for costs**

30.—(1) The registrar may, in any proceedings before him under this Act, by order award to any party such costs as he may consider reasonable, and direct how and by what parties they are to be paid; and any such order may be made a rule of court.

(2) If any party by whom application is made to the registrar for the cancellation of the registration of a design or for the grant of a licence in respect of a registered design, or by whom notice of appeal is given from any decision of the registrar under this Act, neither resides nor carries on business in the United Kingdom or the Isle of Man, the registrar, or, in the case of appeal, the Appeal Tribunal, may require him to give security for the costs of the proceedings or appeal, and in default of such security being given may treat the application or appeal as abandoned.

1575 **Evidence before registrar**

31.—(1) Subject to rules made by the Board of Trade under this Act the evidence to be given in any proceedings before the registrar under this Act may be given by affidavit or statutory declaration; but the registrar may if he thinks fit in any particular case take oral evidence in lieu of or in addition to such evidence as aforesaid, and may allow any witness to be cross-examined on his affidavit or declaration.

(2) Subject to any such rules as aforesaid, the registrar shall in respect of the examination of witnesses on oath and the discovery and production of documents have all the powers of an official referee of the Supreme Court, and the rules applicable to the attendance of witnesses in proceedings before such a referee shall apply to the attendance of witnesses in proceedings before the registrar.

1576 **Power of registrar to refuse to deal with certain agents**

32.—(1) Rules made by the Board of Trade under this Act may authorise the registrar to refuse to recognise as agent in respect of any business under this Act—

(*a*) any individual whose name has been erased from, and not restored to, the register of patent agents kept in pursuance of rules made under the Patents Act, 1949;

(*b*) any individual who is for the time being suspended in accordance with those rules from acting as a patent agent;

(*c*) any person who has been convicted of an offence under section eighty-eight of the Patents Act, 1949;

(*d*) any person who is found by the Board of Trade (after being given an opportunity to be heard) to have been convicted of any offence or to have been guilty of any such misconduct as, in the case of an individual registered in the register of patent agents aforesaid, would render him liable to have his name erased therefrom;

(*e*) any person, not being registered as a patent agent, who in the opinion of the registrar is engaged wholly or mainly in acting as agent in applying for patents in the United Kingdom or elsewhere in the name or for the benefit of a person by whom he is employed;

(*f*) any company or firm, if any person whom the registrar could refuse to recognise as agent in respect of any business under this

Act is acting as a director or manager of the company or is a partner in the firm.

(2) The registrar shall refuse to recognise as agent in respect of any business under this Act any person who neither resides nor has a place of business in the United Kingdom or the Isle of Man.

* * *

Rules, etc.

1577 **General power of Board of Trade to make rules, etc.**

36.—(1) Subject to the provisions of this Act, the Board of Trade may make such rules as they think expedient for regulating the business of the Patent Office in relation to designs and for regulating all matters by this Act placed under the direction or control of the registrar or the Board, and in particular, but without prejudice to the generality of the foregoing provision—

(*a*) for prescribing the form of applications for registration of designs and of any representations or specimens of designs or other documents which may be filed at the Patent Office, and for requiring copies to be furnished of any such representations, specimens or documents;

(*b*) for regulating the procedure to be followed in connection with any application or request to the registrar or in connection with any proceeding before the registrar and for authorising the rectification of irregularities of procedure;

(*c*) for regulating the keeping of the register of designs;

(*d*) for authorising the publication and sale of copies of representations of designs and other documents in the Patent Office;

(*e*) for prescribing anything authorised or required by this Act to be prescribed by rules made by the Board.

(2) Rules made under this section may provide for the establishment of branch offices for designs and may authorise any document or thing required by or under this Act to be filed or done at the Patent Office to be filed or done at the branch office at Manchester or any other branch office established in pursuance of the rules.

1578 **Provisions as to rules and Orders**

37.—(1) Any rules made by the Board of Trade under this Act shall be advertised twice in the Journal.

(2) Any rules made by the Board of Trade in pursuance of section fifteen or section sixteen of this Act, and any order made, direction given, or other action taken under the rules by the registrar, may be made, given or taken so as to have effect as respects things done or omitted to be done on or after such date, whether before or after the coming into operation of the rules or of this Act, as may be specified in the rules.

(3) Any power to make rules conferred by this Act on the Board of Trade or on the Appeal Tribunal shall be exercisable by statutory instrument; and the Statutory Instruments Act, 1946, shall apply to a statutory instrument containing rules made by the Appeal Tribunal in like manner as if the rules had been made by a Minister of the Crown.

(4) Any statutory instrument containing rules made by the Board of Trade under this Act shall be subject to annulment in pursuance of a resolution of either House of Parliament.

(5) Any Order in Council made under this Act may be revoked or varied by a subsequent Order in Council.

* * *

1579 **Interpretation**

44.—(1) In this Act, except where the context otherwise requires, the following expressions have the meanings hereby respectively assigned by them, that is to say—

" Appeal Tribunal " means [the Appeal Tribunal constituted and acting in accordance with section 28 of this Act as amended by the Administration of Justice Act, 1969.] [7]

" article " means any article of manufacture and includes any part of an article if that part is made and sold separately;

[" artistic work " has the same meaning as in the Copyright Act, 1956;] [8]

" assignee " includes the personal representative of a deceased assignee, and references to the assignee of any person include references to the assignee of the personal representative or assignee of that person;

" copyright " has the meaning assigned to it by subsection (1) of section seven of this Act;

[" corresponding design " has the same meaning as in section ten of the Copyright Act, 1956;] [8]

" court " means the High Court;

" design " has the meaning assigned to it by subsection (3) of section one of this Act;

" Journal " means the journal published by the comptroller under the Patents Act, 1949;

" prescribed " means prescribed by rules made by the Board of Trade under this Act;

" proprietor " has the meaning assigned to it by section two of this Act;

" registered proprietor " means the person or persons for the time being entered in the register of designs as proprietor of the design;

" registrar " means the Comptroller-General of Patents Designs and Trade Marks;

" set of articles " means a number of articles of the same general character ordinarily on sale or intended to be used together, to each of which the same design, or the same design with modifications or variations not sufficient to alter the character or substantially to affect the identity thereof, is applied.

(2) Any reference in this Act to an article in respect of which a design is registered shall, in the case of a design registered in respect of a set of articles, be construed as a reference to any article of that set.

[7] The definition of " Appeal Tribunal " is printed as amended by the Administration of Justice Act, 1969 (1969, c. 58), s. 35 (1) and Sched. 1.

[8] The definitions of " artistic work " and " corresponding design " were added by the Copyright Act, 1956, s. 44 (5).

(3) Any question arising under this Act whether a number of articles constitute a set of articles shall be determined by the registrar; and notwithstanding anything in this Act any determination of the registrar under this subsection shall be final.

(4) For the purposes of subsection (1) of section fourteen and of section sixteen of this Act, the expression " personal representative ", in relation to a deceased person, includes the legal representative of the deceased appointed in any country outside the United Kingdom.

* * *

1580 **Dramatic and Musical Performers' Protection Act, 1958**

(6 & 7 Eliz. 2, c. 44)

An Act to consolidate the Dramatic and Musical Performers' Protection Act, 1925, and the provisions of the Copyright Act, 1956, amending it. [23rd July, 1958]

1581 **Penalization of making, etc., records without consent of performers**

1. Subject to the provisions of this Act, if a person knowingly—

(*a*) makes a record, directly or indirectly from or by means of the performance of a dramatic or musical work without the consent in writing of the performers, or

(*b*) sells or lets for hire, or distributes for the purposes of trade, or by way of trade exposes or offers for sale or hire, a record made in contravention of this Act, or

(*c*) uses for the purposes of a public performance a record so made,

he shall be guilty of an offence under this Act, and shall be liable, on summary conviction, to a fine not exceeding forty shillings for each record in respect of which an offence is proved, but not exceeding fifty pounds in respect of any one transaction:

Provided that, where a person is charged with an offence under paragraph (*a*) of this section, it shall be a defence to prove that the record was made for his private and domestic use only.

1582 **Penalization of making, etc., cinematograph films without consent of performers**

2. Subject to the provisions of this Act, if a person knowingly—

(*a*) makes a cinematograph film, directly or indirectly, from or by means of the performance of a dramatic or musical work without the consent in writing of the performers, or

(*b*) sells or lets for hire, or distributes for the purposes of trade, or by way of trade exposes or offers for sale or hire, a cinematograph film made in contravention of this Act, or

(*c*) uses for the purposes of exhibition to the public a cinematograph film so made;

he shall be guilty of an offence under this Act, and shall be liable, on summary conviction, to a fine not exceeding fifty pounds:

Provided that, where a person is charged with an offence under paragraph (*a*) of this section, it shall be a defence to prove that the cinematograph film was made for his private and domestic use only.

1583 **Penalization of broadcasting without consent of performers**

3. Subject to the provisions of this Act, a person who, otherwise than by the use of a record or cinematograph film, knowingly broadcasts a performance of a dramatic or musical work, or any part of such a performance, without the consent in writing of the performers, shall be guilty of an offence under this Act, and shall be liable, on summary conviction, to a fine not exceeding fifty pounds.

1584 **Penalization of making or having plates, etc., for making records in contravention of Act**

4. If a person makes, or has in his possession, a plate or similar contrivance for the purpose of making records in contravention of this Act, he shall be guilty of an offence under this Act, and shall be liable, on summary conviction, to a fine not exceeding fifty pounds for each plate or similar contrivance in respect of which an offence is proved.

1585 **Power of court to order destruction of records, etc., contravening Act**

5. The court before which any proceedings are taken under this Act may, on conviction of the offender, order that all records, cinematograph films, plates or similar contrivances in the possession of the offender which appear to the court to have been made in contravention of this Act, or to be adapted for the making of records in contravention of this Act, and in respect of which the offender has been convicted, be destroyed, or otherwise dealt with as the court may think fit.

1586 **Special defences**

6. Notwithstanding anything in the preceding provisions of this Act, it shall be a defence to any proceedings under this Act to prove—

(*a*) that the record, cinematograph film or broadcast to which the proceedings relate was made only for the purpose of reporting current events, or

(*b*) that the inclusion of the performance in question in the record, cinematograph film or broadcast to which the proceedings relate was only by way of background or was otherwise only incidental to the principal matters comprised or represented in the record, film or broadcast.

1587 **Consent on behalf of performers**

7. Where in any proceedings under this Act it is proved—

(*a*) that the record, cinematograph film or broadcast to which the proceedings relate was made with the consent in writing of a person who, at the time of giving the consent, represented that he was authorised by the performers to give it on their behalf, and

(*b*) that the person making the record, film or broadcast had no reasonable grounds for believing that the person giving the consent was not so authorised,

the provisions of this Act shall apply as if it had been proved that the performers had themselves consented in writing to the making of the record, film or broadcast.

1588 **Interpretation**

8.—(1) In this Act, unless the context otherwise requires, the following expressions have the meanings hereby respectively assigned to them, that is to say,—

"broadcast" means broadcast by wireless telegraphy (within the meaning of the Wireless Telegraphy Act, 1949), whether by way of sound broadcasting or of television;

"cinematograph film" means any print, negative, tape or other article on which a performance of a dramatic or musical work or part thereof is recorded for the purposes of visual reproduction;

"performance of a dramatic or musical work" includes any performance, mechanical or otherwise, of any such work, being a performance rendered or intended to be rendered audible by mechanical or electrical means;

"performers", in the case of a mechanical performance, means the persons whose performance is mechanically reproduced;

"record" means any record or similar contrivance for reproducing sound, including the sound-track of a cinematograph film.

(2) Any reference in this Act to the making of a cinematograph film is a reference to the carrying out of any process whereby a performance of a dramatic or musical work or part thereof is recorded for the purposes of visual reproduction.

1589 **Short title, extent, repeal and commencement**

9.—(1) This Act may be cited as the Dramatic and Musical Performers' Protection Act, 1958.

(2) It is hereby declared that this Act extends to Northern Ireland.

(3) The Dramatic and Musical Performers' Protection Act, 1925, and section forty-five of, and the Sixth Schedule to, the Copyright Act, 1956, are hereby repealed.

(4) This Act shall come into operation at the expiration of a period of one month beginning with the date of its passing.

* * *

1590 **Performers' Protection Act, 1963**

(c. 53)

An Act to amend the law relating to the protection of performers so as to enable effect to be given to a Convention entered into at Rome on 26th October 1961. [31st July 1963]

1591 **Performances to which principal Act [9] applies**

1.—(1) The principal Act shall have effect as if for references therein to the performance of a dramatic or musical work there were substituted references to the performance of any actors, singers, musicians, dancers or other persons who act, sing, deliver, declaim, play in or otherwise perform literary, dramatic, musical or artistic works, and the definition

[9] The Preamble to the 1963 Act defines the Dramatic and Musical Performers' Protection Act, 1958 (6 & 7 Eliz. 2, c. 44), for the purposes of the 1963 Act, as "the principal Act."

contained in section 8 (1) of that Act of the expression "performance of a dramatic or musical work" (by which that expression is made to include a performance rendered or intended to be rendered audible by mechanical or electrical means) shall be construed accordingly.

(2) For the avoidance of doubt it is hereby declared that the principal Act applies as respects anything done in relation to a performance notwithstanding that the performance took place out of the United Kingdom, but this shall not cause anything done out of the United Kingdom to be treated as an offence.

1592 **Sales, etc., of records made abroad**

2. For the purposes of paragraphs (*b*) and (*c*) of section 1 of the principal Act (by which sales of, and other dealings with, records made in contravention of the Act are rendered punishable), a record made in a country outside the United Kingdom directly or indirectly from or by means of a performance to which the principal Act applies shall, where the civil or criminal law of that country contains a provision for the protection of performers under which the consent of any person to the making of the record was required, be deemed to have been made in contravention of the principal Act if, whether knowingly or not, it was made without the consent so required and without the consent in writing of the performers.

1593 **Relaying of performances**

3.—(1) A person who, otherwise than by the use of a record or cinematograph film or the reception of a broadcast, knowingly causes a performance to which the principal Act applies, or any part of such a performance, to be transmitted without the consent in writing of the performers—

(*a*) to subscribers to a diffusion service; or
(*b*) over wires or other paths provided by a material substance so as to be seen or heard in public,

shall be guilty of an offence, and shall be liable, on summary conviction, to a fine not exceeding fifty pounds.

(2) Section 48 (3) of the Copyright Act, 1956 (which explains the meaning of references in that Act to the transmission of a work or other subject-matter to subscribers to a diffusion service) shall apply for the purposes of the preceding subsection as it applies for the purposes of that Act.

(3) Section 6 of the principal Act (which provides for special defences) shall have effect as if the preceding subsections were inserted immediately before that section, and that section and section 7 of the principal Act (which provides for the giving of consent on behalf of performers) shall have effect as if for the words "or broadcast" in each place where they occur there were substituted the words "broadcast or transmission".

1594 **Giving of consent without authority**

4.—(1) Where—

(*a*) a record, cinematograph film, broadcast or transmission is made with the consent in writing of a person who, at the time of giving the consent, represented that he was authorised by the performers to give it on their behalf when to his knowledge he was not so authorised, and (*b*) if proceedings were brought against the person to whom the consent was given, the consent would by virtue of section 7 of the principal Act afford a defence to those proceedings,

the person giving the consent shall be guilty of an offence, and shall be liable, on summary conviction, to a fine not exceeding fifty pounds.

(2) The said section 7 shall not apply to proceedings under this section.

1595 **Citation, construction, commencement and extent**

5.—(1) This Act may be cited as the Performers' Protection Act, 1963, and the principal Act and this Act may be cited together as the Performers' Protection Acts, 1958 and 1963.

(2) This Act shall be construed as one with the principal Act.

(3) This Act shall come into operation at the expiration of the period of one month beginning with the date of its passing, and shall apply only in relation to performances taking place after its commencement.

(4) It is hereby declared that this Act extends to Northern Ireland.

* * *

[The next paragraph is 1606]

Appendix B

UNITED KINGDOM ORDERS

1606 **British Museum (Delivery of Books) Regulation**

(S.R. & O. 1915 No. 773)

DATED AUGUST 9, 1915

The Board of Trade on the application of the Trustees of the British Museum, and by virtue of the powers given them by section 1 of the Copyright (British Museum) Act, 1915, hereby make the following Regulation, to come into operation as from the date hereof:

There shall be excepted from the provisions of section 15 (1) of the Copyright Act, 1911, whereby the publisher of any book published in the United Kingdom is required within one month after the publication to deliver, at his own expense, a copy of the book to the Trustees of the British Museum, the following publications, *viz.*:

Trade Advertisements,
Trade Cards,
Trade Catalogues,
Trade Circulars,
Trade Coupons,
Trade Designs,
Trade Forms,
Trade Labels,
Trade Leaflets,
Trade Plans,
Trade Posters,
Trade Price Lists,
Trade Prospectuses,
Trade Show Cards,
Trade Wrappers.

1607 **National Library of Wales (Delivery of Books) Regulations, 1924**

(S.R. & O. 1924 No. 400; as amended in square brackets in Regulation 2 by S.I. 1956 No. 1978 [1])

DATED APRIL 7, 1924

The Board of Trade in pursuance of section 15 (5) of the Copyright Act, 1911, hereby make the following regulations:

(1) These Regulations may be cited as the National Library of Wales (Delivery of Books) Regulations, 1924, and shall come into operation on the 1st day of May, 1924.

(2) The books, of which copies are to be delivered to the National Library of Wales in pursuance of section 15 of the Copyright Act, 1911, shall not include any book of the following classes, *viz.*:

Books (other than books written wholly or mainly in Welsh or any other Celtic language, or relating wholly or mainly to the antiquities, language, literature, philology, history, religion, arts, crafts, or industries of the Welsh or other Celtic peoples, or relating wholly or mainly to the natural history of Wales), of which:

(i) The number of copies in the published edition does not exceed 300; or, if the published edition has been imported from a foreign country does not exceed 100; or

(ii) The number of copies in the published edition does not exceed 400 and the published price of each volume exceeds [£10]; or

(iii) The number of copies in the published edition does not exceed 600 and the published price of each volume exceeds [£20].

[1] Which came into operation on December 31, 1956.

(3) For the purposes of these regulations the published edition of a book includes all copies of the same work published by the same publisher or his successor in business in a form substantially the same with respect to printing, illustrations and general condition.

The National Library of Wales (Delivery of Books) Regulations, 1912 [S.R. & O. 1912 No. 635], are hereby revoked.

1608 **British Museum (Publications Not Required) Regulation**

(S.R. & O. 1935 No. 278)

DATED OCTOBER 12, 1932

The Trustees of the British Museum, being empowered under the British Museum Act, 1932, by regulations to apply the said Act to publications of such classes as may be specified in such regulations being publications of the descriptions set out in the Schedule to the said Act and thereby to except certain publications from subsection (1) of section 15 of the Copyright Act, 1911, hereby make the following regulation within their said powers. The delivery by publishers of publications falling under the following categories is no longer required, unless a written demand for delivery of them or any of them is made by the Trustees:

Publications wholly or mainly in the nature of trade advertisements.

Registers of voters prepared under the Representation of the People Act, 1918, as amended by any subsequent enactment.

Specifications of inventions prepared for the purposes of the Patents and Designs Act, 1907, as amended by any subsequent enactment.

Publications wholly or mainly in the nature of time tables of passenger transport services, being publications prepared for local use.

Publications wholly or mainly in the nature of calendars.

Publications wholly or mainly in the nature of blank forms of accounts, or blank forms of receipts, or other blank forms of a similar character.

Wall sheets printed with alphabets, mottoes, religious texts or other matter for the purpose of elementary instruction.

1609 **Designs Rules, 1949**

(S.I. 1949 No. 2368)

Made - - - -	16*th December*, 1949
Laid before Parliament	22*nd December*, 1949
Coming into Operation	2*nd January*, 1950

By virtue of the provisions of the Registered Designs Act, 1949, the Board of Trade do hereby make the following Rules:

Short Title and Commencement

1. These Rules may be cited as the Designs Rules, 1949, and shall come into operation on the 2nd day of January, 1950.

Designs Excluded from Registration under Section 1 (4)

26. There shall be excluded from registration under the Act designs to be applied to any of the following articles, namely:

(1) works of sculpture other than casts or models used or intended to be used as models or patterns to be multiplied by any industrial process.

(2) wall plaques and medals.

(3) printed matter primarily of a literary or artistic character, including bookjackets, calendars, certificates, coupons, dressmaking patterns, greetings cards, leaflets, maps, plans, postcards, stamps, trade advertisements, trade forms, and cards, transfers, and the like.

1610 **Copyright Act, 1956 (Commencement) Order, 1957**

(S.I. 1957 No. 863)

Made - - - - 17*th May*, 1957

The Board of Trade in pursuance of the powers conferred upon them by section 51 (2) of the Copyright Act, 1956, hereby make the following order:

1. The Copyright Act, 1956, shall come into operation on the 1st day of June, 1957.

2. This Order may be cited as the Copyright Act, 1956 (Commencement) Order, 1957.

1611 **Copyright (Notice of Publication) Regulations, 1957**

(S.I. 1957 No. 865)

Made - - - -	17*th May*, 1957
Laid before Parliament	24*th May*, 1957
Coming into Operation	1*st June*, 1957

The Board of Trade in pursuance of the powers conferred upon them by subsection (7) of section 7 of the Copyright Act, 1956, hereby make the following Regulations:

1. Notice of an intended publication of a new work for the purposes of subsection (7) of section 7 of the Act shall be given by advertisement in a daily or Sunday newspaper with a national circulation in the United Kingdom.

2. Notice shall be given twice, on the first occasion to appear not less than three months, and on the second not less than two months, before the intended date of publication, with an interval of not less than one month between the two occasions.

3. Such notice shall be signed by or on behalf of the person giving it and shall include the following particulars:

(*a*) the name and address of the person intending to publish and a statement of his intention to publish;

(*b*) the title (if any) and a description of the old work and the date or estimated date of making;

(*c*) the name of the author of the old work, if known to the person intending to publish;

(*d*) the name and address of the library, museum or institution in which the manuscript or a copy of the old work is kept;

(*e*) the name of the person from whom the library, museum or institution in which the manuscript or a copy of the old work is kept acquired it or a statement that the person intending to publish has failed after reasonable inquiries to discover the name of that person;

(*f*) an invitation to any person claiming to be the owner of the copyright in the old work to give notice of his claim to the person intending to publish.

4. In these Regulations—
" the Act " means the Copyright Act, 1956, and
" old work " and " new work " have the meanings assigned to those expressions in subsection (7) of section 7 of the Act.

5. The Interpretation Act, 1889, shall apply to the interpretation of these Regulations as it applies to the interpretation of an Act of Parliament.

6. These Regulations may be cited as the Copyright (Notice of Publication) Regulations, 1957, and shall come into operation on the 1st day of June, 1957.

1612 **Copyright Royalty System (Records) Regulations, 1957**

(S.I. 1957 No. 866)

Made - - - -	*17th May,* 1957
Laid before Parliament	*24th May,* 1957
Coming into Operation	*1st June,* 1957

The Board of Trade in pursuance of the powers conferred upon them by subsections (1), (2), (7) and (11) of section 8 of the Copyright Act, 1956, hereby make the following Regulations:

Notice

1.—(1) The notice required by subsections (1) and (5) of section 8 of the Act shall contain the following particulars:

(*a*) the name and address of the person by whom the notice is given, hereinafter called " the manufacturer ";

(*b*) the name of the work to which the notice refers, hereinafter called " the work," a description sufficient to identify it and the name of the author or publisher;

(*c*) a statement that the manufacturer intends to make records of the work or an adaptation thereof and the address at which he intends to make such records;

(*d*) sufficient particulars to identify a record of the work or an adaptation thereof made in or imported into the United Kingdom in such circumstances that section 8 of the Act applies to the records which the manufacturer intends to make;

(*e*) the type or types of record on which it is intended to reproduce the work or adaptation, and an estimate of the number of records of each type initially intended to be sold or otherwise supplied for the purpose of retail sale;

(*f*) the ordinary retail selling price (as hereinafter defined) of the records, or, where it is intended to reproduce the work on more than one type of record, the ordinary retail selling price of each type of record, the manufacturer intends to make and the amount of the royalty payable on each record;

(*g*) the earliest date at which any of the records will be delivered to a purchaser or otherwise supplied as aforesaid;

(*h*) whether any other musical, literary or dramatic work is to be reproduced on the same record with the work and, in relation to any such other work, the particulars specified in sub-paragraph (*b*) of this paragraph.

(2) The notice shall, not less than fifteen days before any record on which the work is reproduced is delivered to a purchaser or otherwise supplied as aforesaid, be sent by registered post[2] or published by advertisement as follows:

(*a*) if the name and an address within the United Kingdom of the owner of the copyright, or his agent for the receipt of notice, are known or can by reasonable inquiry be ascertained, the notice shall be sent to such owner or agent at such address;

(*b*) if such name and address are not known and cannot by reasonable inquiry be ascertained, an advertisement shall be inserted in the *London Gazette* giving the particulars specified in paragraphs (*a*), (*b*), (*c*) and (*d*) of Regulation 1 and stating an address from which the particulars specified in paragraphs (*e*), (*f*), (*g*) and (*h*) may be obtained.

Payment of royalties

613 **2.**—(1) Royalties may be paid in such manner and at such times as are specified in any agreement which may be made between the manufacturer and the owner of the copyright.

(2) In the absence of any agreement to the contrary, the following provisions of this Regulation shall apply to the manner in and time at which royalties shall be paid and the steps to be taken to ensure the receipt of royalties by the owner of the copyright.

(3) (*a*) If within seven days of the date of the notice prescribed in Regulation 1 the owner of the copyright intimates to the manufacturer, by notice in writing sent by registered post,[2] some convenient place within the United Kingdom from which adhesive labels can be obtained, the manufacturer shall by notice in writing specify the number and denomination of the labels he requires and at the same time tender a sum equivalent to the amount of royalty represented by the labels required.

(*b*) If, within six days of receipt of the notice required by sub-paragraph (*a*) of this paragraph to be given by the manufacturer, the

[2] By the Copyright Royalty System (Records) (Amendment) Regulations, 1962 (S.I. 1962 No. 2076) which came into operation on September 26, 1962, any reference to registered post, in these Regulations is to be construed as including a reference to the recorded delivery service.

copyright owner supplies the labels required, the manufacturer shall not deliver to a purchaser or otherwise supply for the purpose of its being sold by retail any record made by him to which the notice prescribed in Regulation 1 refers unless there is attached thereto, or (if the type of record is such that it is not reasonably practicable to attach an adhesive label thereto) to the container in which it is intended to be delivered to a retail purchaser, a label supplied as aforesaid and representing the amount of the royalty payable in respect of that record.

(4) (*a*) If the owner of the copyright does not take the steps specified in sub-paragraphs (*a*) and (*b*) of paragraph (3) of this Regulation within the times therein respectively specified, the manufacturer may deliver to a purchaser or otherwise supply as aforesaid any record to which the notice specified in Regulation 1 hereof refers without complying with the requirements of paragraph (3) of this Regulation.

(*b*) The manufacturer shall keep an account of all records delivered by him to a purchaser or otherwise supplied as aforesaid in accordance with this paragraph and the amount of the royalties due to the owner of the copyright in respect thereof shall be transferred to a special account and held in trust for the owner of the copyright.

(5) If the manufacturer takes in relation to any records the steps specified in paragraph (3) or (4), as the case may be, of this Regulation, the taking of those steps shall be deemed to constitute the payment of royalties on those records in accordance with paragraph (*d*) of subsection (1) of section 8 of the Act.

(6) For the purposes of this Regulation " the date of the notice prescribed in Regulation 1 " means—

(i) in cases where the notice is required to be sent by registered post [2] the date when the notice would in ordinary course of post be delivered;

(ii) in cases where the notice is required to be advertised in the *London Gazette*, the date of such advertisement.

(7) The adhesive label supplied as aforesaid shall be an adhesive label, square in shape, the design to be entirely enclosed within a circle and the side of the label to be not greater than three-quarters of an inch in length. The label shall not contain the effigy of the Sovereign or any other person, nor any word, mark or design such as to suggest that the label is issued by or under the authority of the Government for the purpose of denoting any duty payable to the Government.

Ordinary retail selling price

1614 **3.** The ordinary retail selling price of any record shall be calculated at the marked or catalogued selling price of single records to the public, or if there is no such marked or catalogued selling price, at the highest price at which single records are ordinarily to be sold to the public, exclusive of purchase tax in either case.

Inquiries

1615 **4.**—(1) The inquiries referred to in subsection (7) of section 8 of the Act shall be directed to the owner of the copyright by name or (if his name is not known and cannot by reasonable inquiry be ascertained) in general terms as the owner of the copyright in the work in respect of which the inquiries are made and shall contain—

(*a*) a statement of the name of the musical, literary or dramatic work in respect of which the inquiries are made, a description sufficient to identify it and of the name of the author or publisher;

(*b*) a statement of the name and address of the person making the inquiries;

(*c*) an allegation that a record of the work or an adaptation thereof has previously been made in or imported into the United Kingdom for the purposes of retail sale, with the trade name (if known) and a description of such record sufficient to identify it;

(*d*) an inquiry whether the record so described was made in or imported into the United Kingdom for the purposes of retail sale by or with the licence of the owner of the copyright.

(2) The inquiries shall be sent by registered post [2] or published by advertisement as follows:

(*a*) if an address within the United Kingdom of the owner of the copyright or his agent is known or can by reasonable inquiry be ascertained, the inquiries shall be sent to such address;

(*b*) if such an address is not known and cannot by reasonable inquiry be ascertained, the inquiries shall be advertised in the *London Gazette*.

(3) The prescribed time for reply to such inquiries shall be:

(*a*) to an inquiry duly sent by registered post [2] seven days after the date when the inquiry would in ordinary course of post be delivered;

(*b*) to an inquiry duly advertised in the *London Gazette*, seven days after the date of such advertisement.

Interpretation

1616 **5.** In these Regulations " the Act " means the Copyright Act, 1956.

6. The Interpretation Act, 1889, shall apply to the interpretation of these Regulations as it applies to the interpretation of an Act of Parliament.

Citation and operation

7. These Regulations may be cited as the Copyright Royalty System (Records) Regulations, 1957, and shall come into operation on the 1st day of June, 1957.

1617 **Copyright (Industrial Designs) Rules, 1957**

(S.I. 1957 No. 867)

Made - - - -	17*th May*, 1957
Laid before Parliament	24*th May*, 1957
Coming into Operation	1*st June*, 1957

The Board of Trade, in pursuance of the powers conferred upon them by section 36 of the Registered Designs Act, 1949, and subsection (5) of section 10 of the Copyright Act, 1956, hereby make the following rules:

Industrial Application of Designs

1. A design shall be taken to be applied industrially for the purposes of section 10 of the Copyright Act, 1956, if it is applied—

(*a*) to more than fifty articles all of which do not together constitute a single set of articles as defined in subsection (1) of section 44 of the Registered Designs Act, 1949; or

(*b*) to goods manufactured in lengths or pieces, other than hand-made goods.

Interpretation

2.—(1) Reference in these rules to the application of a design to any articles or goods means the application of the design to those articles or goods by a process of printing or embossing or by any other process whatsoever, and shall be deemed to include a reference to the reproduction of the design on or in those articles or goods in the course of their production.

(2) The Interpretation Act, 1889, shall apply to the interpretation of these Rules as it applies to the interpretation of an Act of Parliament, and as if these Rules and the Rules hereby revoked were Acts of Parliament.

Revocation, Citation and Commencement

3.—(1) The Copyright (Industrial Designs) Rules, 1949,[3] are hereby revoked.

(2) These Rules may be cited as the Copyright (Industrial Designs) Rules, 1957, and shall come into operation on the 1st day of June, 1957.

1618 **Copyright (Libraries) Regulations, 1957**

(S.I. 1957 No. 868)

Made - - - -	17*th May*, 1957
Laid before Parliament	24*th May*, 1957
Coming into Operation	1*st June*, 1957

The Board of Trade in pursuance of the powers conferred upon them by subsections (1), (3) and (5) of section 7 and subsection (4) of section 15 of the Copyright Act, 1956, hereby make the following Regulations:

Prescribed Classes of Library

1619 **1.** Each of the classes of library specified in the First Schedule hereto shall be a class prescribed for the purposes of subsections (1) and (3) of section 7 of the Act:

Provided that this Regulation shall not apply to any library established or conducted for profit.

2.—(1) Each of the classes of library specified in the First or Second Schedule hereto shall be a class prescribed for the purposes of subsection (5) of section 7 of the Act and, for the purposes of paragraph (*a*) of that subsection (which relates to the librarian to whom a copy is supplied), any class of library so specified shall, where appropriate, be deemed to

[3] S.I. 1949 No. 2367.

include any library of a similar class situated outside the United Kingdom.

(2) This Regulation shall apply to any library of a class so specified, whether established or conducted for profit or not.

3. Each of the classes of library specified in the First or Second Schedule hereto shall be a class prescribed for the purposes of subsection (4) of section 15 of the Act.

Prescribed Conditions

1620 **4.** The following conditions shall be conditions prescribed for the purposes of subsections (1) and (3) of section 7 of the Act (which relate, respectively, to copies of articles in periodical publications and copies of parts of other works)—

(*a*) no copy of any work or any part of a work shall be made for or supplied to any person unless he has delivered to the librarian concerned, or to some person appointed by the librarian for that purpose, a declaration and undertaking in writing in relation to that work or part, substantially in accordance with the form set out in the Third Schedule hereto and signed in the manner therein indicated;

(*b*) for the purposes of subsection (1) (which relates to copies of articles in periodical publications) no copy extending to more than one article in any one publication shall be made;

(*c*) for the purposes of subsection (3) (which relates to copies of parts of other works) no copy extending to more than a reasonable proportion of a work shall be made;

(*d*) persons to whom copies are supplied shall be required to pay for such copies a sum not less than the cost (including a contribution to the general expenses of the library) attributable to their production.

1621 **5.** The following conditions shall be the conditions prescribed for the purposes of subsection (5) of section 7 of the Act (which relates to the making and supplying of copies of any works or parts of works to librarians)—

(*a*) no copy of a work or a part of a work shall be made for or supplied to the librarian of any library, if a copy of that work or that part has already been supplied to any person as a librarian of that library, unless the librarian by or on behalf of whom the copy is made is satisfied that the copy already supplied has been lost, destroyed or damaged;

(*b*) librarians to whom copies are supplied shall be required to pay for such copies a sum not less than the cost (including a contribution to the general expenses of the library) attributable to their production;

(*c*) no copy shall be supplied to the librarian of a library that is established or conducted for profit.

1622 **6.** Nothing in the preceding Regulations shall be taken to authorise the librarian of any library to make or supply a copy of any work or part of a work (other than an article in a periodical publication) for or to any other person (whether that person is the librarian of another library or not) if at the time when the copy is made the librarian knows the name and address of a person entitled to authorise the making of the copy or could by reasonable inquiry ascertain the name and address of such person.

1623 7.—(1) The provisions of paragraph (2) of this Regulation shall be the conditions prescribed for the purposes of subsection (4) of section 15 of the Act (which relates to reproductions of the typographical arrangements of published editions of works).

(2) A reproduction of the typographical arrangement of a published edition of a work or a part thereof may be made or supplied in pursuance of subsection (4) of section 15 only in the circumstances and upon the conditions in and upon which a copy of that work or part may, by virtue of the provisions of Part I of the Act, be made or supplied without infringing the copyright in that work under Part I:

Provided that for the purposes of subsection (4) of section 15 of the Act a reproduction of the typographical arrangement of a published edition of a work may be made without infringing the copyright in the published edition notwithstanding that the librarian by or on behalf of whom the reproduction is made knows, at the time it is made, the name and address of a person who is entitled to authorise the making of such a copy or such a reproduction or could by reasonable inquiry ascertain the name and address of such a person.

Interpretation

1624 **8.** In these Regulations "the Act" means the Copyright Act, 1956, and "work" means a published literary, dramatic or musical work.

9. The Interpretation Act, 1889, shall apply to the interpretation of these Regulations as it applies to the interpretation of an Act of Parliament.

Citation and Commencement

1625 **10.** These Regulations may be cited as the Copyright (Libraries) Regulations, 1957, and shall come into operation on the 1st day of June, 1957.

FIRST SCHEDULE

1626 I. Any library (including the British Museum) to which section 15 of the Copyright Act, 1911, applies.

II. Any library of a school (as defined by section 41 (7) of the Act), university, college of a university, university college, or (in relation to England, Wales and Northern Ireland) any library of an establishment for further education (within the meaning assigned to that expression by section 41 of the Education Act, 1944,[4] and by section 39 of the Education Act (Northern Ireland), 1947,[5] respectively) or (in relation to Scotland) any library of an educational establishment (within the meaning assigned to that expression by section 143 of the Education (Scotland) Act, 1946 [6]).

III. Any library administered by a Library Authority under the Public Libraries Acts 1892 to 1919,[7] or the Public Libraries (Scotland) Acts, 1887 to 1955,[8] or the Public Libraries Acts (Northern Ireland) 1855 to 1924.[9]

[4] 7 & 8 Geo. 6, c. 31.
[5] 10 & 11 Geo. 6, c. 3.
[6] 9 & 10 Geo. 6, c. 50.
[7] 55 & 56 Vict. c. 53; 56 & 57 Vict. c. 11; 1 Edw. 7, c. 19; 9 & 10 Geo. 5, c. 93.
[8] 50 & 51 Vict. c. 42; 57 & 58 Vict. c. 20; 62 & 63 Vict. c. 5; 10 & 11 Geo. 5, c. 45; 3 & 4 Eliz. 2, c. 27.
[9] 18 & 19 Vict. c. 40; 40 & 41 Vict. c. 15; 47 & 48 Vict. c. 39; 57 & 58 Vict. c. 38; 2 Edw. 7, c. 20; 14 & 15 Geo. 5, c. 10 (N.I.).

IV. Any Parliamentary library or library administered as part of a Government Department (including any Department of the Government of Northern Ireland).

V. Any library conducted for, or administered by any establishment or organisation conducted for, the purpose of facilitating or encouraging the study of all or any of the following: religion, philosophy, science (including any natural or social science), technology, medicine, history, literature, languages, education, bibliography, fine arts, music or law.

1627 SECOND SCHEDULE

Any library which makes works in its custody available to the public free of charge.

1628 THIRD SCHEDULE

FORM OF DECLARATION AND UNDERTAKING

To

The Librarian of

the Library

(Address)

1. I [ ] of [ ]

hereby request you to make and supply to me *[a copy of (*particulars of article*)] *[a copy of (*particulars of work of which a part is required to be supplied and particulars of that part*)], which I require for the purposes of research or private study.

2. I have not previously been supplied with a copy of *[the said article] *[the said part of the said work] by any librarian.

3. I undertake that if a copy is supplied to me in compliance with the request made above, I will not use it except for the purposes of research or private study.

Signature†.......................................

Date ....

* Delete whichever is inappropriate.

† This must be the personal signature of the person making the request. A stamped or typewritten signature, or the signature of an agent, is *NOT* sufficient.

1629 **Copyright (Customs) Regulations, 1957**

(S.I. 1957 No. 875)

Made - - - -	20*th May*, 1957
Laid before Parliament	27*th May*, 1957
Coming into Operation	1*st June*, 1957

The Commissioners of Customs and Excise in pursuance of the powers conferred on them by subsection (4) of section twenty-two of the Copyright Act, 1956, hereby make the following Regulations:

1. The notice required by subsection (1) of section twenty-two shall be in the form No. 1 or form No. 2 set out in the Schedule hereto. A separate notice on form No. 1 shall be given in respect of each work. A separate notice on form No. 2 shall be given in respect of each importation, whether of one or more works.

2. A fee of two pounds two shillings in respect of each notice shall be paid to the Commissioners at the time such notice is given.

3. The owner of the copyright in any published literary, dramatic or musical work for which a notice has been given shall notify the Commissioners in writing of any change in ownership or other change affecting the notice, within twenty-eight days of such change and further notice shall be given as the Commissioners may require. On a change of ownership of copyright, whether notified to the Commissioners or not, any notice already given shall be deemed to have been withdrawn as from the expiry of twenty-eight days from the change of ownership.

4. The owner of the copyright in any work, and any agent of his, who gives a notice shall either at the time of giving the notice or at the time when the work is imported, or at both such times, furnish to the Commissioners such evidence and information within such time and in such form as they may require, and shall produce within such time as they may specify such books or other documents as they may require. If such evidence and information is not furnished and if such books or other documents are not produced as required by the Commissioners, the notice shall be deemed to have been withdrawn as from such time as the Commissioners shall specify.

5. The owner of the copyright in any work, and any agent of his, who gives notice, shall give to the Commissioners security or further security, within such time and in such manner, whether by bond, deposit of a sum of money or otherwise, as the Commissioners may require, against all actions, proceedings, claims and demands whatsoever which may be taken or made against, or costs and expenses which may be incurred by, them in consequence of the detention of any copy to which the notice relates. Such security or further security shall be given at the time the notice is given or at such other time as the Commissioners may require. If such security or further security is not given within the time or in the manner required by the Commissioners, the notice shall be deemed to have been withdrawn as from the expiry of the time so required.

1630 6. In every case—

(*a*) in which the Commissioners have not required the security or further security referred to in Regulation 5 to be given, or
(*b*) in which the Commissioners have taken security and that security is insufficient, or
(*c*) in which the notice is deemed to have been withdrawn under Regulation 3, 4 or 5,

the owner of the copyright in any work, and any agent of his, who has given a notice shall jointly and severally keep the Commissioners indemnified against all actions, proceedings, claims and demands whatsoever which may be taken or made against them, and shall repay to the Commissioners all costs and expenses which may be incurred by them in consequence of the detention of, or anything done in relation to, any copy of a work to which the notice relates. Any such costs, expenses, damages or other sums may be recovered as a debt due to the Crown.

7. The Interpretation Act, 1889, shall apply for the interpretation of these Regulations as it applies for the interpretation of an Act of Parliament.

8. The Regulations dated the 19th June, 1912,* and the 13th March, 1923,† made by the Commissioners of Customs and Excise are hereby revoked.

9. These Regulations may be cited as the Copyright (Customs) Regulations, 1957, and shall come into operation on the 1st day of June, 1957.

* S.R. & O. 1912 No. 1714. † S.R. & O. 1923 No. 556.

THE SCHEDULE

FORM No. 1

1631 COPYRIGHT ACT, 1956

Notice relating to copyright in any published literary, dramatic or musical work

To the Commissioners of Customs and Excise.

I, ... of ....
hereby give you notice that copyright in the original work specified in the Schedule hereto now subsists under the Copyright Act, 1956, and that [10] ...... the owner of the copyright in the said work and that [11] .... request(s) that copies of the said work printed out of the United Kingdom shall be treated as prohibited goods, and shall not be imported into the United Kingdom for a period up to and including [12] ....

Dated this .... day of 19

Signature ....

[13] ....

SCHEDULE

Title of work ....
Description of work, if not a book ....
Full name of author or authors [14] ....
Whether author or authors alive. If not, date of death [15] ....
Country and date of first publication [16] ....
Status of author at date of first publication [17] ....

[10] If notice is given by the owner insert " I am," or if a company, the name of the company and the word " is "; if given by an agent insert name of owner and the word " is."

[11] " I," or " he "; or if a company the name of the company.

[12] The period shall not exceed five years and shall not extend beyond the period for which the copyright is to subsist.

[13] If an agent insert " Agent of owner," or if a company insert the name of the company and status in the company of the signatory.

[14] If the author is anonymous or pseudonymous, insert words to this effect and state for what period the copyright exists.

[15] Delete if author anonymous or pseudonymous.

[16] If copyright is claimed by virtue of section 2 (2) (*a*) of the Copyright Act, 1956, it is enough to state the country and date of first publication (see section 49 (2) (*d*) of the Act for the meaning of " first publication " for this purpose).

[17] If copyright is claimed by virtue of section 2 (2) (*b*) or 2 (2) (*c*) of the Copyright Act, 1956, state the grounds on which it is claimed that the author was a qualified person either (a) when the work was first published, or (b) if he died before the date of the first publication, immediately before he died. (" Qualified person " is defined in section 1 (5) of the Act.)

STATUTORY DECLARATION

I, ... of ....
do solemnly and sincerely declare that the contents of this notice are true, and I make this solemn declaration conscientiously believing the same to be true and by virtue of the provisions of the Statutory Declarations Act, 1835.

Declared by the above-named ....
at ....
this ....
day of ....19 ,
before me ....
A Commissioner for Oaths.

FORM No. 2

1632 COPYRIGHT ACT, 1956

Notice relating to a particular importation

To the Commissioners of Customs and Excise.

I, ... of ....
hereby give you notice that copyright in the original work(s) specified in the Schedule hereto now subsists under the Copyright Act, 1956, and that [18] ...... the owner(s) of the copyright in the said work(s), and that the under-mentioned copies of the said work(s) made out of the United Kingdom, that is to say
[19]
are about to be imported into the port/airport [20] of [21] ....
on or about the .... day of .... next in the [22]
.... from ....

And I request that the said copies be treated as prohibited goods and dealt with accordingly.

Dated this .... day of 19

Signature ....

[23] ....

SCHEDULE

Title of work(s) ....
Description of work(s), if not a book ....
Full name of author or authors [24] ....
Whether author or authors alive. If not, date of death [25] ....

[18] If notice is given by the owner insert " I am "; if given by a company insert name of the company and the word " is "; if given by an agent insert name of owner and the word " is."

[19] Describe the copies, number of packages, marks used, and any other particulars necessary for their identification.

[20] Delete that which is inapplicable.

[21] Insert name of port or airport.

[22] Insert name or indication of ship or aircraft.

[23] If an agent insert " Agent of Owner(s)." If a company insert the name of the company and status in the company of the signatory.

[24] If the author(s) is/are anonymous or pseudonymous, insert words to this effect and state for what period the copyright exists.

[25] Delete if author(s) anonymous or pseudonymous.

Country and date of first publication of work(s) [26] ....
....
Status of author or authors at date of first publication [27] ....

STATUTORY DECLARATION

I, ... of ....
do solemnly and sincerely declare that the contents of this notice are true, and I make this solemn declaration conscientiously believing the same to be true and by virtue of the provisions of the Statutory Declarations Act, 1835.

Declared by the above-named ....
at ....
this ....
day of ....19 ,
before me ....
A Commissioner for Oaths.

1633 **Performing Right Tribunal Rules, 1965**

(S.I. 1965 No. 1506 [28])

Made - - - -	*28th July* 1965
Laid before Parliament	*9th August* 1965
Coming into Operation	*1st September* 1965

I, Gerald, Baron Gardiner, Lord High Chancellor of Great Britain, in exercise of the powers conferred upon me by paragraph 6 of Schedule 4 to the Copyright Act 1956, and with the approval of the Treasury in regard to the fees prescribed by these rules in respect of proceedings before the Performing Right Tribunal, and after having consulted the Council on Tribunals in accordance with section 8 of the Tribunals and Inquiries Act 1958, do hereby make the following Rules:

Citation and commencement

1. These Rules may be cited as the Performing Right Tribunal Rules 1965, and shall come into operation on 1st September 1965.

Interpretation

1634 **2.**—(1) In these Rules, unless the context otherwise requires—

"the Act" means the Copyright Act 1956 [as amended] and a section referred to by number means the section so numbered in the Act;

"the Tribunal" means the Performing Right Tribunal;

"the Chairman" means the Chairman, or any person for the time being appointed to act as Chairman, of the Tribunal;

"costs", in relation to proceedings in Scotland, means "expenses";

[26] If copyright is claimed by virtue of section 2 (2) (*a*) of the Copyright Act, 1956, it is enough to state the country and date of first publication (see section 49 (2) (*d*) of the Act for the meaning of "first publication" for this purpose).

[27] If copyright is claimed by virtue of section 2 (2) (*b*) or 2 (2) (*c*) of the Copyright Act, 1956, state the grounds on which it is claimed that the author was a qualified person either (a) when the work was first published, or (b) if he died before the date of first publication, immediately before he died. ("Qualified person" is defined in section 1 (5) of the Act.)

[28] Which revoked and replaced the Performing Right Tribunal Rules, 1957 (S.I. 1957 No. 924), as amended by S.I. 1959 No. 1170 and S.I. 1960 No. 2428. The amendments shown in square brackets were made by S.I. 1971 No. 636.

"the office" and "the Secretary" mean respectively the office and the Secretary for the time being of the Tribunal;

"originator" means an organisation, licensing body or person who has referred a scheme to the Tribunal under section 25 (1) or 26 (1), or who has applied to the Tribunal under section 27 (2) or (3) [or section 27A (1) or (6)];

"intervener" means an organisation or person who has applied under section 25 (3), [26 (3), 27 (4) or 27A (5)] to be made a party to proceedings before the Tribunal;

"party" includes an intervener whose application is pending;

"credentials" means—

(*a*) the validity of an organisation's claim to be representative of a class of persons, or

(*b*) the possession by an intervener of a sufficient interest in the matter in dispute.

(2) A form referred to by number means the form so numbered in Schedule 1 to these Rules.

(3) The Interpretation Act 1889 shall apply to the interpretation of these Rules as it applies to the interpretation of an Act of Parliament.

Commencement of proceedings

1635 **3.**—(1) A licence scheme may be referred under section 25 or referred again under section 26, and an application for a declaration that the applicant is entitled to a licence may be made under section 27 [and an application for the review of an order may be made under section 27A], by serving on the Secretary a notice substantially in accordance with Form 1, [2, 3 or 3A], as the case may be.

(2) The originator shall, at the same time, serve on the Secretary a statement in writing setting out the case he intends to make together with a list of the documents relevant to the reference or application which are, or have been, in his possession.

(3) The Secretary shall, as soon as may be practicable, serve copies of the originator's notice, statement of case and list of documents—

(*a*) in the case of a reference under section 25 or an application under section 27, on the licensing body named in the notice, or

(*b*) in the case of a further reference under section 26, on every party [other than the originator] to the reference on which the Tribunal made the latest previous order with respect to the licence scheme.

[or

(*c*) in the case of an application under section 27A, on every party to the application other than the originator.]

Application for special leave under section 26 (2) [*or* 27A (2)]

1636 **4.**—(1) An application under section 26 (2) [or 27A (2)] for the special leave of the Tribunal may be made by serving on the Secretary a notice substantially in accordance with Form 4 [or 4A, as the case may be].

(2) The Secretary shall, as soon as may be practicable, serve copies of the notice on every party to the reference [or application, as the case may be, on which the Tribunal made the last relevant order.] and any such party may, within 14 days of the service upon him of such notice, make representations in writing to the Tribunal in connection with the application.

(3) The Tribunal, after considering any such representations and, if it thinks fit, after having given the applicant and any such party who has made such representations an opportunity of being heard, shall grant or dismiss the application as it may think just.

Advertisement of reference or application

1637 **5.**—(1) Except where the Chairman otherwise directs, the Secretary shall give notice by advertisement in such manner as the Chairman may think fit of every reference under section 25 or 26 and of every application under section 27 [or 27A].

(2) An advertisement under the last foregoing paragraph of this rule shall state—

(*a*) the names and addresses of the originator and (if it is not the originator) the licensing body and any organisation or person on whom copies of the notice of reference or application have been served;

(*b*) the nature of the reference or application;

(*c*) the time, not being less than 21 days from the latest publication of the advertisement, within which—

(i) an organisation or person may apply to the Tribunal to be made a party to the proceedings, and

(ii) an objection to the originator's credentials may be made in accordance with the next following rule.

Objection to originator's credentials

1638 **6.**—(1) In the case of a reference under section 25 or 26, a licensing body, or an organisation or person on whom notice of the reference has been served in accordance with rule 3, or an intervener, intending to object to the originator's credentials shall, within such time as may be specified for this purpose in the advertisement published under the last foregoing rule, serve on the Secretary a notice of objection substantially in accordance with Form 5.

(2) If notice of objection to the originator's credentials has been served on the Secretary in accordance with the last foregoing paragraph of this rule, or if the Tribunal intends to make such objection of its own motion, the Secretary shall, on the expiration of the time limited under rule 5 (2) (*c*), serve upon every party to the proceedings notice substantially in accordance with Form 6, and the proceedings shall (unless the Tribunal or the Chairman shall otherwise direct on the grounds that no reasonable cause of objection has been disclosed) be stayed from the date of such notice until further order.

(3) As soon as may be practicable after service of notice under the last foregoing paragraph of this rule, the Chairman shall give directions for the purpose of the consideration by the Tribunal of the objection. Such consideration shall, unless the Chairman otherwise directs, take place at an oral hearing before the Tribunal and the Tribunal shall give to the originator, any objector and any other party an opportunity of being heard or of making representations in writing.

(4) If, after considering the objection, the Tribunal is not satisfied of the originator's credentials, it shall direct that no further proceedings shall be taken by any party in connection with the reference, otherwise than in relation to any order for costs which the Tribunal may make under rule 24.

(5) If, after considering the objection, the Tribunal is satisfied of the originator's credentials, it shall direct that the reference shall proceed and the Tribunal or the Chairman may give such consequential directions as to the extension of the time limited for taking any step required or authorised under these Rules, or as to any further matter, as it or he may think fit.

(6) When the Tribunal has arrived at its decision on the objection, or where the objection has been withdrawn or is not proceeded with, the Secretary shall give notice substantially in accordance with Form 7 to every party to the proceedings.

(7) In computing the time limited by these Rules for the taking of any step in the proceedings, no account shall be taken, save in so far as the Tribunal or the Chairman may direct, of any period elapsing between the date of the notice served under paragraph (2) of this rule and the date from which the Tribunal directs, under paragraph (5) of this rule, that the reference shall proceed.

Applications to be made a party

1639 **7.**—(1) An application to the Tribunal by any organisation or person to be made a party to a reference under section 25 or 26, or to an application [under section 27 or 27A], may be made by serving on the Secretary notice of intervention substantially in accordance with Form 8.

(2) Notice under the last foregoing paragraph of this rule shall not be served after the expiration of the time limited under rule 5 (2) (*c*):

Provided that the Tribunal or the Chairman may give leave, subject to such conditions as it or he may think fit, to serve such notice notwithstanding the expiration of the time so limited.

(3) On being served with notice under paragraph (1) of this rule, the Secretary shall, as soon as may be practicable—

(*a*) serve copies of the notice on every other party to the proceedings, and

(*b*) serve on the intervener copies of—

(i) the originator's statement of case and list of documents, and

(ii) any other notice of intervention which has been served upon him.

Objections to intervener's credentials

1640 **8.**—(1) Any party intending to object to an intervener's credentials shall, within 14 days of being served with a copy of the notice of intervention under the last foregoing rule, serve on the Secretary a notice of objection substantially in accordance with Form 9.

(2) The Secretary shall, as soon as may be practicable, serve on every other party to the proceedings a copy of any notice of objection served on him under the last foregoing paragraph of this rule.

(3) If the Tribunal intends of its own motion to object to an intervener's credentials, the Secretary shall, on the expiration of the time limited under rule 5 (2) (*c*), serve on the intervener notice substantially in accordance with Form 10 and shall serve copies of such notice on every other party.

(4) Subject to any direction to the contrary that the Chairman may give under rule 12, an objection to an intervener's credentials shall not operate as a stay of the proceedings and shall be considered by the Tribunal at the same time as the reference or application in question.

[*Written answer*]

1641 **9.**—(1) A licensing body [or other party] on whom there has been served a copy of the originator's statement of case in accordance with rule 3 (3), shall, within 42 days of such service, serve on the Secretary a written answer to the originator's statement together with a list of the documents relevant to the reference or application which are, or have been, in its possession.

(2) The Secretary shall, as soon as may be practicable, serve copies of such answer and list of documents on every other party.

Interveners' cases

1642 **10.**—(1) Every intervener shall, within 21 days of the expiration of the time limited under rule 5 (2) (*c*), serve upon the Secretary a statement in writing setting out the case he intends to make together with a list of the documents relevant to the reference or application which are, or have been, in his possession.

(2) The Secretary shall, as soon as may be practicable, serve upon every other party copies of every intervener's statement of case and list of documents.

Amendment of statement of case and answer

1643 **11.**—(1) Subject to paragraph (3) of this rule, a party may at any time amend his statement of case or answer by serving on the Secretary the amended statement or answer.

(2) On being served with an amended statement of case or answer, the Secretary shall, as soon as may be practicable, serve copies thereof on every other party.

(3) No amended statement of case or answer shall, without the leave of the Tribunal or the Chairman, be served after such date as the Chairman may direct under rule 12.

Directions

1644 **12.**—(1) As soon as may be practicable after every party has delivered his statement of case or answer, or the time limited by these rules for doing so has expired, the Chairman shall appoint a date and place for the attendance of the parties for the purposes of his giving directions as to the further conduct of the proceedings.

(2) The Secretary shall give to every party not less than 14 days' notice of the date and place appointed under the last foregoing paragraph of this rule.

(3) On the appointment, the Chairman shall, after giving to every party attending the appointment an opportunity of being heard, and after considering any representations in writing made by any party, give such directions as he thinks fit with a view to the just, expeditious and economical disposal of the proceedings and, without prejudice to the generality of the foregoing, may give directions as to—

(i) the date and place of the oral hearing if one is desired by any party;

(ii) the procedure to be followed in regard to the submission and exchange of written arguments if no party requires an oral hearing;

(iii) the date after which no amended statement of case or answer may be delivered without leave;

(iv) the preparation and delivery by the originator of a schedule, to be agreed by all parties, setting out the issues to be determined by the Tribunal and the contentions of each party in relation thereto;

(v) the admission of any facts or documents;

(vi) the discovery and inspection of documents;

(vii) the giving of evidence on affidavit;

(viii) the consideration by the Tribunal of any objection made to an intervener's credentials.

(4) The Chairman may postpone, or adjourn to a later date to be appointed by him, the giving of any directions under this rule.

(5) At any time after directions nave been given under this rule, the Chairman may, whether or not any application in that behalf has been made under the next following rule, give such further directions as he may think fit.

(6) If any party fails to comply with any direction or order given or made under this or the next following rule, the Chairman may give such consequential directions as may be necessary and may order such party to pay any costs occasioned by his default.

Interlocutory applications

1645 **13.**—(1) Except where the Tribunal or the Chairman, whether generally or in any particular case, otherwise directs or these Rules otherwise provide, every interlocutory application shall be disposed of by the Chairman.

(2) The application shall be made by notice in writing to the Secretary and shall state the grounds upon which it is made.

(3) Unless the notice is accompanied by the written consent of all parties to the order or direction applied for, the Secretary shall serve copies of the application on every other party to the proceedings.

(4) Any party who objects to the application may, within 7 days after being served with a copy thereof, send written notice of objection to the Secretary and to the applicant and in that case, before disposing of the application, the Chairman shall consider any such objection and may, if he thinks fit, give all parties concerned an opportunity of being heard.

Consolidation of proceedings

1646 **14.** Where there is pending before the Tribunal more than one reference under section 25 or 26 relating to the same licence scheme, or more than one application under section 27 [or 27A] relating to the same licensing body, the Chairman may, if he thinks fit, either of his own motion or on an application made under the last foregoing rule, order that some or all of the references or applications, as the case may be, shall be considered together, and may give such consequential directions as may be necessary:

Provided that the Chairman shall not make an order under this rule of his own motion without giving all parties concerned a reasonable opportunity of objecting to the proposed order.

Procedure and evidence at hearing

1647 **15.**—(1) Every party to a reference or application which is considered at an oral hearing before the Tribunal shall be entitled to attend the hearing and to address the Tribunal and to call evidence.

(2) The hearing shall be in public.

(3) Evidence before the Tribunal shall be given orally or, if the parties so agree or the Tribunal or the Chairman so orders, by affidavit, but the Tribunal may at any stage of the proceedings require the personal attendance of any deponent for examination and cross-examination.

Representation and rights of audience

1648 **16.**—(1) Subject to paragraph (6) of this rule, a party to proceedings before the Tribunal may authorise some other person to act for him in the proceedings.

(2) The appointment of an agent under the last foregoing paragraph of this rule shall be made in writing and shall not be effective until written notice thereof shall have been given to the Secretary.

(3) Only one agent shall be appointed to act for a party at any one time.

(4) For the purpose of service on a party of any document, or of the taking of any step required or authorised by these Rules, an agent appointed by a party shall be deemed to continue to have authority to act for such party until the Secretary has received written notice of the termination of his appointment.

(5) On receiving notice of the appointment of an agent, or of the termination of such an appointment, the Secretary shall send a copy thereof to every other party.

(6) A party may be represented at any hearing, whether before the Tribunal or the Chairman, by counsel or solicitor, or by any other person allowed by the Tribunal or the Chairman to appear on his behalf, or may, save in the case of a corporation or unincorporated body, appear in person.

Withdrawal of reference or application

1649 **17.** The originator may withdraw a reference under section 25 or 26, or an application under section 27 [or 27A], at any time before it has been finally disposed of, by notice in writing served on the Secretary (who shall serve copies thereof on every other party to the proceedings), but such withdrawal shall be without prejudice to the Tribunal's power to make an order as to the payment of costs incurred up to the time of service of the notice:

Provided that, on the application of a licensing body named therein or of any other party, the Tribunal may proceed with the reference or application notwithstanding its purported withdrawal and may for this purpose substitute such party as originator and give such consequential directions as may be necessary.

Decision of the Tribunal

1650 **18.**—(1) The final decision of the Tribunal on a reference under section 25 or 26, or an application under section 27 [or 27A], shall be given in writing and shall include a statement of the Tribunal's reasons, and where on any such reference the Tribunal has varied the scheme there shall be annexed to the decision a copy of the scheme as so varied.

(2) Except where the operation of the order is suspended under rule 20, the Secretary shall send to every party to the proceedings a copy of the Tribunal's decision and shall cause a copy to be made available at the office for public inspection at such times as the Chairman may direct.

(3) The Chairman may in any case direct that short particulars of the decision shall be advertised in such manner as he may think fit.

Application for reference of question of law to the court

1651 **19.**—(1) A request to refer a question of law to the court under section 30 (1) shall (unless made at the hearing) be made by notice in writing to the Secretary and may be made at any time before or within 14 days after the Tribunal has given its decision in the proceedings in which the question arises.

(2) The Tribunal shall, as soon as may be practicable, consider any such request and shall notify its decision thereon to the party by whom the request was made.

Effect of references to the court

1652 **20.**—(1) Where the Tribunal refers a question of law to the court after giving its decision in any proceedings, it may, if it thinks fit, suspend the operation of any order made in the proceedings; and in that case the Secretary shall give notice of the suspension to all parties to the proceedings and, if particulars of the order have been advertised, shall cause notice of the suspension to be advertised in the same manner.

(2) Where a question of law has been referred to the court, the Tribunal shall not make any further order on the reference or application in connection with which the question arose until the court has given its decision thereon.

Effect of suspenson of order

1653 **21.** If the operation of any order is suspended by the Tribunal under the last foregoing rule or by the court, then, while the order remains suspended, section 29 (1) and (3) shall not have effect in relation to the order, but section 25 (7) (*b*) (and section 26 (5) to the extent that it applies section 25 (7) (*b*) for the purposes of section 26) shall continue to have effect as if the order had not been suspended.

Application of Arbitration Acts

1654 **22.** The provisions of sections 12, 14, 17 and 26 of the Arbitration Act 1950 [30] shall apply in the case of proceedings before the Tribunal in England and Wales, and the provisions of sections 13, 14, 16, 21 and 24 of, and paragraphs 4, 5 and 8 of Schedule 1 to, the Arbitration Act (Northern Ireland) 1937 [31] shall apply in the case of proceedings before the Tribunal in Northern Ireland, as those provisions respectively apply to an arbitration where no contrary intention is expressed in the arbitration agreement.

Enforcement of Tribunal's orders in Scotland

1655 **23.** Any decision of the Tribunal may be recorded in the Books of Council and Session for execution, and may be enforced accordingly.

Costs

1656 **24.** The costs of and incidental to any proceedings shall be in the discretion of the Tribunal, which may direct that any party against whom an order for costs is made shall pay to any other party a lump sum by way of costs, or such proportion of the costs as may be just and in the last-mentioned case the Tribunal may assess the sum to be paid or may direct that it be assessed by the Chairman, or taxed by a taxing officer of the Supreme Court or the Supreme Court of Northern Ireland, or by the Auditor of the Court of Session.

Fees

1657 **25.** The fees specified in Schedule 2 to these Rules shall be payable in respect of the matters therein mentioned.

Service of documents

1658 **26.**—(1) Any notice or other document required by these Rules to be served on or sent to any person may be sent to him by pre-paid post at

[30] 14 Geo. 6, c. 27.
[31] 1 Edw. 8 & 1 Geo. 6, c. 8 (N.I.).

his address for service, or, where no address for service has been given, at his registered office, principal place of business or last-known address, and every notice or other document required to be served on or sent to the Tribunal may be sent by pre-paid post to the Secretary at the office.

(2) Any notice or other document required to be served on a licensing body or organisation which is not a body corporate may be sent to the secretary, manager or other similar officer.

(3) The Tribunal or the Chairman may direct that service of any notice or other document be dispensed with or effected otherwise than in the manner provided by these rules.

(4) Service of any notice or document on a party's solicitor or agent shall be deemed to be service on such party, and service on a solicitor or agent acting for more than one party shall be deemed to be service on every party for whom such solicitor or agent acts.

Time

1659 **27.**—(1) The time for doing any act may (whether it has already expired or not) be extended—

(*a*) with the leave of the Tribunal or the Chairman, or

(*b*) by the consent in writing of all parties, except where the Tribunal or Chairman has fixed the time by order or (if the time is prescribed by these Rules) has directed that it may not be extended or further extended without leave:

Provided that the time limited under rule 19 (1) shall not be extended without leave.

(2) A party in whose favour time is extended by consent under the last foregoing paragraph of this rule shall, as soon as may be practicable after the necessary consents have been obtained, give the Secretary written notice thereof.

(3) Where the last day for the doing of any act falls on a day on which the office is closed and by reason thereof the act cannot be done on that day, it may be done on the next day on which the office is open.

Office hours

1660 **28.** The office shall be open at such times as the Chairman may direct.

Failure to comply with directions

1661 **29.** If any party fails to comply with any direction given, in accordance with these Rules, by the Tribunal or the Chairman, the Tribunal may, if it considers that the justice of the case so requires, direct that such party be debarred from taking any further part in the proceedings without leave of the Tribunal.

Power of Tribunal to regulate procedure

1662 **30.** Subject to the provisions of the Act and these Rules, the Tribunal shall have power to regulate its own procedure.

Transitional provisions and revocation of previous rules

1663 **31.**—(1) In relation to any proceedings which are pending when these Rules come into operation, the Tribunal or the Chairman may direct that they shall apply subject to such modifications as it or he may, in the circumstances, consider desirable.

(2) The Performing Right Tribunal Rules 1957,[32] the Performing Right Tribunal (Amendment) Rules 1959 [33] and the Performing Right Tribunal (Amendment) Rules 1960 [34] are hereby revoked, but without prejudice to anything done thereunder.

SCHEDULE 1

Rule 3 (1) FORM 1

COPYRIGHT ACT 1956
PERFORMING RIGHT TRIBUNAL

NOTICE OF REFERENCE UNDER SECTION 25

1664 To:—The Secretary
Performing Right Tribunal

1. TAKE NOTICE that [*name and address of organisation or person making the reference*] (hereinafter called "the originator") hereby refers to the Tribunal the licence scheme hereinafter described, operated by the [*name and address of licensing body*] (hereinafter called "the licensing body"), which is a licensing body for the purposes of the Copyright Act, 1956.

2. The scheme to which this notice relates (hereinafter referred to as "the scheme") is [*short description of scheme*].

3. The originator is
*[an organisation claiming to be representative of persons requiring licences in cases]
*[a person claiming that he requires a licence in a case] to which the scheme applies.

**4. The originator is an organisation representing [*here give particulars of the persons whom the originator claims to represent and the grounds on which it claims to represent them*].

5. There are delivered herewith:—
(*a*) a statement setting out the originator's case in support of this reference, and
(*b*) a list of the documents relevant to this reference which are, or have been, in the originator's possession.

6. All communications about this reference should be addressed to
*[the originator at the address shown above]
*[*name and address*—Solicitor(s)/Agent(s) for the originator].

Signed ....
Status of
signatory‡ ....
Date ....

* Delete whichever is inapplicable.
** Delete if inapplicable.
‡ Insert as appropriate:
"Originator"
"An officer of the originator"
"Solicitor(s) for the originator"
"Agent(s) for the originator"

[32] S.I. 1957 No. 924.
[33] S.I. 1959 No. 1170.
[34] S.I. 1960 No. 2428.

Rule 3 (1)

FORM 2

COPYRIGHT ACT 1956
PERFORMING RIGHT TRIBUNAL

NOTICE OF FURTHER REFERENCE UNDER SECTION 26

1665 To:—The Secretary
Performing Right Tribunal

1. TAKE NOTICE that [*name and address of licensing body, organisation or person making the further reference*] (hereinafter called "the originator") hereby refers to the Tribunal the licence scheme
*[confirmed]
*[varied]
by the Tribunal by an order dated [ ], and bearing the reference number [ ].

2. There are delivered herewith:—
(*a*) a statement setting out the originator's case in support of this reference, and
(*b*) a list of documents relevant to this reference which are, or have been, in the originator's possession.

3. All communications about this further reference should be addressed to
*[the originator at the address shown above]
*[*name and address*—Solicitor(s)/Agent(s) for the originator]

Signed ....
Status of
signatory‡ ....
Date ....

* Delete whichever is inapplicable.
‡ Insert as appropriate:
"Originator"
"An officer of the originator"
"Solicitor(s) for the originator"
"Agent(s) for the originator"

Rule 3 (1)

FORM 3

COPYRIGHT ACT 1956
PERFORMING RIGHT TRIBUNAL

NOTICE OF APPLICATION UNDER SECTION 27

1666 To:—The Secretary
Performing Right Tribunal

1. TAKE NOTICE that [*name and address of person making the application*] (hereinafter called "the originator") hereby applies to the Tribunal under section 27 *[(2)] *[(3)] of the Copyright Act 1956.

2. The originator requires a licence [*purpose for which licence is required*].

3. There are delivered herewith:—
(*a*) a statement setting out the originator's case in support of this application, and
(*b*) a list of documents relevant to this application which are, or have been, in the originator's possession.

4. All communications about this application should be addressed to
*[the originator at the address shown above]
*[*name and address*—Solicitor(s)/Agent(s) for the originator]

Signed ....
Status of
signatory‡ ....
Date ....

* Delete whichever is inapplicable.
‡ Insert as appropriate:
" Originator "
" An officer of the originator "
" Solicitor(s) for the originator "
" Agent(s) for the originator."

Rule 3 (1) FORM 3A

COPYRIGHT ACT 1956
PERFORMING RIGHT TRIBUNAL

NOTICE OF APPLICATION UNDER SECTION 27A

1666a To:—The Secretary
Performing Right Tribunal

1. TAKE NOTICE that [*name and address of person making the application*] (hereinafter called " the originator ") hereby applies to the Tribunal under section 27A *[(1)] *[(6)] of the Copyright Act 1956.

2. There are delivered herewith:—

(*a*) a statement setting out the originator's case in support of this application, and

(*b*) a list of documents relevant to this application which are, or have been, in the originator's possession.

3. All communications about this application should be addressed to
*[the originator at the address shown above]
*[*name and address*—Solicitor(s)/Agent(s) for the originator]

Signed ....
Status of
signatory‡ ....
Date ....

* Delete whichever is inapplicable.
‡ Insert as appropriate:
" Originator "
" An officer of the originator "
" Solicitor(s) for the originator "
" Agent(s) for the originator "

Rule 4 (1) FORM 4

COPYRIGHT ACT 1956
PERFORMING RIGHT TRIBUNAL

NOTICE OF APPLICATION FOR SPECIAL LEAVE
OF TRIBUNAL UNDER SECTION 26 (2)

1667 To:—The Secretary
Performing Right Tribunal

1. TAKE NOTICE that [*name and address of applicant*] (hereinafter called " the applicant ") hereby applies for the special leave of the Tribunal to refer again to the Tribunal the licence scheme

*[confirmed]
*[varied]
by the Tribunal by an order dated [ ], and bearing the reference number [ ].

2. The applicant is
*[the licensing body operating the scheme]
*[an organisation claiming to be representative of persons requiring licences in cases of the class to which the said order applies]
*[a person claiming that he requires a licence in a case of the class to which the said order applies].

3. [*Grounds on which the applicant desires to refer the scheme to the Tribunal before the time mentioned in Section* 26 (2)].

4. All communications about this application should be addressed to
*[the applicant at the address shown above]
*[*name and address*—Solicitor(s)/Agent(s) for the applicant]

Signed ....
Status of
signatory‡ ....
Date ....

* Delete whichever is inapplicable.
‡ Insert as appropriate:
" Applicant "
" An officer of the applicant "
" Solicitor(s) for the applicant "
" Agent(s) for the applicant."

Rule 4 (1) FORM 4A

COPYRIGHT ACT 1956
PERFORMING RIGHT TRIBUNAL

NOTICE OF APPLICATION FOR SPECIAL LEAVE OF TRIBUNAL UNDER SECTION 27A (2)

To:—The Secretary
Performing Right Tribunal

1. TAKE NOTICE that [*name and address of applicant*] (hereinafter called " the applicant ") hereby applies for the special leave of the Tribunal to make an application to it to review its order dated [ ], and bearing the reference number [ ].

2. The applicant is
*[the licensing body operating the scheme]
*[the applicant in the proceedings in which the said order was made].

3. [*Grounds on which the applicant desires to apply to the Tribunal before the time mentioned in Section* 27A (2)].

4. All communications about this application should be addressed to
*[the applicant at the address shown above]
*[*name and address*—Solicitor(s)/Agent(s) for the applicant]

Signed ....
Status of
signatory‡ ....
Date ....

*Delete whichever is inapplicable.
‡ Insert as appropriate:
" Applicant "
" An officer of the applicant "
" Solicitor(s) for the applicant "
" Agent(s) for the applicant."

Rule 6 (1) FORM 5

COPYRIGHT ACT 1956
PERFORMING RIGHT TRIBUNAL

PARTY'S NOTICE OF OBJECTION TO
ORIGINATOR'S CREDENTIALS

1668 To:—The Secretary
Performing Right Tribunal

1. TAKE NOTICE that, in connection with the proceedings instituted by notice of reference dated [ ] and given by
[*name of originator*],
[*name of party making the objection*], being
*[the licensing body named in the notice of reference]
*[*[a person] *[an organisation] on whom a copy of the notice of reference was served on [*date of service*] under rule 3 of the Performing Right Tribunal Rules]
*[an intervener in the proceedings by virtue of notice of intervention given on [*date of notice of intervention*]]
objects to the originator's credentials.

2. This objection is made on the grounds that [*grounds on which it is contended that the originator is not reasonably representative of the class of persons it claims to represent*].

Signed ....
Status of
signatory‡ ....
Date ....

* Delete whichever is inapplicable.
‡ Insert as appropriate:
" Objector "
" An officer of the objector "
" Solicitor(s) for the objector '
" Agent(s) for the objector."

Rule 6 (2) FORM 6

COPYRIGHT ACT 1956
PERFORMING RIGHT TRIBUNAL

TRIBUNAL'S NOTICE OF MAKING OF AN OBJECTION
TO ORIGINATOR'S CREDENTIALS

1669 To:— [*name of party*]

1. TAKE NOTICE that, in connection with the proceedings instituted by notice of reference dated [ ] and given by [*name of originator*], an objection has been made to the originator's credentials by
*[the Tribunal]
*[*name of objector*].

2. The objection is made on the grounds that [*grounds on which it is contended that the originator is not reasonably representative of the class of persons it claims to represent*].

3. The arrangements for the consideration of the objection by the Tribunal will be
*[notified to you as soon as may be practicable]
*[as follows].

4. As from the date of this notice—
   (i) the proceedings will be stayed, and
   (ii) time, as limited by the Performing Right Tribunal Rules for the taking of any step in the proceedings, will cease to run, until further notice.

Signed ....
Secretary to the Tribunal
Date ....

* Delete whichever is inapplicable.

Rule 6 (6) FORM 7

COPYRIGHT ACT 1956
PERFORMING RIGHT TRIBUNAL

NOTICE OF DISPOSAL OF OBJECTION TO ORIGINATOR'S CREDENTIALS

1670 To:— [*name of party*]

TAKE NOTICE that, in connection with the proceedings instituted by notice of reference dated [ ] and given by [*name of originator*], and with the objection to the originator's credentials, of which you were informed by notice dated [ ]:

*1. [*If the Tribunal has considered the objection and is satisfied of the originator's credentials*]
The Tribunal has considered the objection and is satisfied of the originator's credentials, and, accordingly as from [*date from which Tribunal directs that stay is to be lifted*]:—
   (i) the stay imposed on the proceedings on [*date of notice under rule* 6 (2)] will cease to operate, and
   (ii) time, as limited by the Performing Right Tribunal Rules for the taking of any step in the proceedings, will begin to run again.

*2. [*If the Tribunal has considered the objection and is not satisfied of the originator's credentials*]
The proceedings are determined as from the date of this notice, save for the purpose of any order the Tribunal may make as to costs.

*3. [*If the objection has been withdrawn or is not proceeded with*]
The objection *[has been withdrawn] *[is not being proceeded with], and, accordingly, as from [*date from which Tribunal directs that stay is to be lifted*]:—
   (i) the stay imposed on the proceedings on [*date of notice under rule* 6 (2)] will cease to operate, and
   (ii) time, as limited by the Performing Right Tribunal Rules for the taking of any step in the proceedings, will begin to run again.

*4. [*If the Tribunal gives any supplementary directions under rule* 6 (5)]
The Tribunal has given the following directions under rule 6 (5):—
[*directions given*]

Signed ....
Secretary to the Tribunal
Date ....

* Delete if inapplicable

Rule 7 (1) FORM 8

COPYRIGHT ACT 1956
PERFORMING RIGHT TRIBUNAL

NOTICE OF INTERVENTION

1671 To:—The Secretary
Performing Right Tribunal

1. TAKE NOTICE that [*name and address of intervener*] (hereinafter called " the intervener ") wishes to be made a party to the *[reference] *[application] advertised in [*name of newspaper or journal and date of issue*] under reference number [ ].

2. The intervener has a substantial interest in the matter in dispute for the following reasons [*give reasons*].

3. All communications about this intervention should be addressed to
*[the intervener at the address shown above]
*[*name and address*—Solicitor(s)/Agent(s) for the intervener]

Signed ....
Status of
signatory‡ ....
Date ....

* Delete whichever is inapplicable.
‡ Insert as appropriate:
" Intervener "
" An officer of the intervener "
" Solicitor(s) for the intervener "
" Agent(s) for the intervener."

Rule 8 (1) FORM 9

COPYRIGHT ACT 1956
PERFORMING RIGHT TRIBUNAL

PARTY'S NOTICE OF OBJECTION
TO INTERVENER'S CREDENTIALS

1672 To:—The Secretary
Performing Right Tribunal

1. TAKE NOTICE that, in connection with the proceedings instituted by notice of *[reference] *[application] dated [ ] and given by [*name of originator*], and with the notice of intervention in these proceedings given by [*name of intervener*] and dated [ ],
[*name of party making the objection*], being
*[the originator]
*[the licensing body named in the notice of *[reference] *[application]]
*[*[a person] *[an organisation] on whom a copy of the notice of reference has been served under rule 3 of the Performing Right Tribunal Rules]
*[an intervener in the proceedings by virtue of a notice of intervention dated],
objects to the intervener's credentials.

2. A copy of the notice of intervention was served on the objector on [*date*].

3. This objection is made on the grounds that [*grounds on which it is contended that the intervener has no substantial interest in the matter in dispute*].

Signed ....

Status of

signatory‡ ....

Date ....

* Delete whichever is inapplicable.

‡ Insert as appropriate:
" Objector "
" An officer of the objector "
" Solicitor(s) for the objector "
" Agent(s) for the objector."

Rule 8 (3) FORM 10

COPYRIGHT ACT 1956
PERFORMING RIGHT TRIBUNAL

TRIBUNAL'S NOTICE OF OBJECTION TO
INTERVENER'S CREDENTIALS

1673 To:— [*name of intervener*]

1. TAKE NOTICE that, in connection with the proceedings instituted by notice of *[reference] *[application] dated [ ] and given by [*name of originator*], and with your notice of intervention in those proceedings dated [ ], the Tribunal objects to your credentials.

2. This objection is made on the grounds that [*grounds on which it is contended that the intervener has no substantial interest in the matter in dispute*].

3. Unless the Chairman otherwise directs, the objection will be considered by the Tribunal at the same time as the *[reference] *[application].

Signed ....
Secretary to the Tribunal

Date ....

* Delete whichever is inapplicable.

SCHEDULE 2

1674 Rule 25 TABLE OF FEES

	£
1.—(1) On serving notice in Form 1, 2, 3 or 3A	6·00
(2) On serving notice in Form 4, 4A, 5, 8 or 9	2·00
(3) On every interlocutory application	1·00
(4) On a request for the reference of a question of law to the Court	2·00

2. The fees specified in the Table shall be paid to the Secretary at the time of service on him of the relevant notice:

Provided that, in the case of Fee No. (4), if the request is made otherwise than by notice in writing, the fee shall be paid to the Secretary on his demand.

3. If the proceedings are disposed of without a hearing, one half of Fee No. (1) shall be repaid to the originator.

Treasury Circular
Dated January 9, 1958, as amended [35]

1675 1. I am directed by the Lords Commissioners of Her Majesty's Treasury to refer to the Copyright Act, 1956, which came into effect on June 1, 1957, and which replaces the Copyright Act, 1911 (with the exception of certain provisions not directly relating to copyright). The new Act re-enacts in substance the provisions of the 1911 Act relating to Crown copyright and, in addition, contains certain new provisions relating to sound recordings and cinematograph films made by or under the direction or control of Her Majesty or of a Government Department. It also makes changes in the law relating to privately owned copyright. Section 39 of the Copyright Act, 1956, deals with Crown copyright and replaces section 18 of the Copyright Act, 1911.

2. The practice to be followed with regard to Crown copyright was defined, following the Copyright Act, 1911, in a Treasury Minute dated June 28, 1912. Although the Copyright Act, 1956, does not generally alter the position of Crown copyright, the increase in the volume and scope of official publications since 1912 and the development of new methods of reproduction make a restatement of policy on this subject desirable.

3. Crown copyright is vested by Royal letters patent in the Controller of Her Majesty's Stationery Office and permission to reproduce from official material, published or unpublished, may be given only by him, or by Departments to whom delegated authority to deal with particular classes of applications has been given. Authority to permit reproduction from official films and certain photographs has been delegated by the Controller to the Central Office of Information. All applications for permission to reproduce official material not covered by a specific delegated authority should be referred to the Controller, who will normally consult the Department of origin of the material before authorising its use.

4. For copyright purposes, Government publications may be divided into the following classes:

(1) Bills and Acts of Parliament, Statutory Rules and Orders and Statutory Instruments.
(2) Other Parliamentary papers, including Reports of Select Committees of both Houses and Papers laid before Parliament by Statute and by Command.
(3) The Official Report of the House of Lords and House of Commons Debates (Hansard).
(4) Non-Parliamentary publications, comprising all papers of Government Departments not contained in the first three classes.
(5) Charts and Ordnance Maps.

5. It is in the public interest that the information contained in publications falling in the first three classes should be diffused as widely as possible, and legal rights of the Crown in respect of copyright in them will not normally be enforced. But all Crown rights in respect of them are reserved, and will be asserted in cases considered by the Controller of Her Majesty's Stationery Office as exceptional—for example, in the case of reproduction of any part of any publication in these classes in undesirable contexts, or reproduction of the whole or a substantial part of any such publication, either as a separate document or as a major part of another work, in such a way as to result in a significant loss to public funds. Copies of Acts of Parliament, Statutory Rules and Orders and Statutory Instruments, other than those reproduced by or by the order of the Stationery Office, must not purport to be published by authority. Applicants desiring to make reproductions from the Official Report of Parliamentary Debates (Hansard) should be warned that any person or body publishing unofficial reports of proceedings in Parliament, even though they are verbatim reports of speeches as reported in the Official Report, may not enjoy, in proceedings for defamation, privilege as extensive as that enjoyed

[35] A new paragraph 5 was substituted by a Treasury Circular dated March 1, 1965.

by the Official Report. Reproductions from the Official Report in connection with advertising are not permitted.

6. The fourth class comprises a wide range of Government publications, including many which explain the operation of Acts of Parliament, or make available the results of research, and other activities of departments. It is desirable that this information should be widely known; but official publication is the usual channel for this purpose and, subject to the exercise of the discretions described in the next paragraph, My Lords see no reason why free reproduction should be allowed of this kind of material for commercial purposes. The exercise of Crown copyright is also necessary to protect official material from misuse by unfair or misleading selection, undignified associations, or undesirable use for advertising purposes. The rights of the Crown will therefore normally be enforced for publications in this class, which will bear an indication that Crown copyright is reserved. Acknowledgment of source and of the permission of the Controller of Her Majesty's Stationery Office should be required, and suitable fees imposed for reproduction. In assessing fees the Controller will give consideration to the value of the material to the applicant, and the extent to which private reproduction will affect the revenue from sales of the official publication, subject always to his discretion to waive or reduce fees in appropriate circumstances.

7. The Controller will waive or reduce fees in respect of applications for reproductions for professional, technical or scientific purposes where profit is not a primary purpose of reproduction, and consideration of reduction or remission of fees will also be given to reproductions in works of scholarship, in the journals of learned societies and similar non-profit-making bodies, for educational purposes and in other cases where the need for the fullest dissemination of official information is paramount and the commercial or other aspects are relatively unimportant.

8. The above considerations apply to the material in the fifth class. The routine administration of Crown copyright relating to charts and ordnance maps is subject in practice to appropriate arrangements for delegation between the Controller of Her Majesty's Stationery Office and the Admiralty and Ordnance Survey departments.

[The next paragraph is 1681]

Appendix C

COPYRIGHT CONVENTIONS AND AGREEMENTS

1681 STOCKHOLM COPYRIGHT CONVENTION, 1967 [1]

THE International Convention for the Protection of Literary and Artistic Works signed at Berne on 9th September, 1886, revised at Berlin in 1908, at Rome in 1928 and at Brussels in 1948 was further revised at a Conference which met in Stockholm on 11th June, 1967 and closed on the 14th July, 1967.

This document contains a comparison of the English texts of the Conventions as revised at Brussels and at Stockholm, with some explanatory notes.

Wherever possible corresponding provisions have been positioned side by side. Wording in the Brussels text which has been altered or omitted is printed in italics. New wording used in corresponding provisions in the Stockholm text and new provisions in that text are indicated by capital letters.

The Stockholm Conference was the first occasion on which the English text as well as the French was agreed by all participants. The fact that there are changes in the English from the translations previously published does not necessarily mean that the French (previously the only authentic text) has been changed.

[1] This comparative text is printed by kind permission of the Industrial Property and Copyright Department of the Department of Trade and Industry. For text of Stockholm Convention alone, see Cmnd. 4412. As to the position of the United Kingdom, see § 1098 *ante*. The following is a brief indication of the matters dealt with by the Convention.

Article 1	Constitution of Union
Article 2	Definitions of works
Article 2 (*bis*)	Speeches, etc.
Articles 3, 4, 5 and 6	What Authors the Convention protects
Article 6 (*bis*)	*Droit moral*
Articles 7 and 7 (*bis*)	Term of protection
Article 8	Translation rights
Article 9	Author's reproduction rights
Articles 10 and 10 (*bis*)	Quotation
Articles 11 and 11 (*ter*)	Performing rights
Article 11 (*bis*)	Broadcasting rights
Article 12	Radio-diffusion rights
Article 13	Compulsory licences
Article 14 and 14 (*bis*)	Cinematograph rights
Article 14 (*ter*)	*Droit de suite*
Article 15	Anonymous and pseudonymous works
Article 16	Seizure of infringing copies
Article 17	Governments' rights to control exhibitions, etc.
Article 18	Retrospective provisions
Article 19	Wider protection not prejudiced
Article 20	Special arrangements between governments
Article 21	Protocol regarding developing countries
Articles 22 and 23	Assembly
Article 24	International Bureau
Article 25	Finance
Articles 26 and 27	Revisions
Articles 28 and 29	Joining Union
Article 30	Reservations
Article 31	Territories
Articles 32 and 34	Previous Conventions
Article 33	Disputes
Article 35	Right to denounce
Article 36	Domestic law
Article 37	Text of Convention
Article 38	Transitional Provisions
Protocol Regarding	Developing Countries

Brussels

1682 ARTICLE 1

The countries to which this Convention applies constitute a Union for the protection of the rights of authors *over* their literary and artistic works.

Stockholm

ARTICLE 1

The countries to which this Convention applies constitute a Union for the protection of the rights of authors IN their literary and artistic works.

Note. This is a drafting change in the English text only.

Brussels

1683 ARTICLE 2

(1) The *term* "literary and artistic works" shall include every production in the literary, scientific and artistic domain, whatever may be the mode or form of its expression, such as books, pamphlets and other writings; lectures, addresses, sermons and other works of the same nature; dramatico-musical works; choreographic works and entertainments in dumb show, *the acting form of which is fixed in writing or otherwise*; musical compositions with or without words; cinematographic works *and works produced* by a process analogous to cinematography; works of drawing, painting, architecture, sculupture, engraving and lithography; photographic works *and works produced* by a process analogous to photography; works of applied art; illustrations, *geographical charts*, plans, sketches and *plastic* works relative to geography, topography, architecture or science.

(2) Translations, adaptations, arrangements of music and other alterations of a literary or artistic work shall be protected as original works without prejudice to the *rights of the author of* the original work. It shall, *however*, be a matter for legislation in the countries

Stockholm

ARTICLE 2

(1) The EXPRESSION "literary and artistic works" shall include every production in the literary, scientific and artistic domain, whatever may be the mode or form of its expression, such as books, pamphlets and other writings; lectures, addresses, sermons and other works of the same nature; dramatic or dramatico-musical works; choreographic works and entertainments in dumb show; musical compositions with or without words; cinematographic works TO WHICH ARE ASSIMILATED WORKS EXPRESSED by a process analogous to cinematography; works of drawing, painting, architecture, sculpture, engraving and lithography; photographic works to WHICH ARE ASSIMILATED WORKS EXPRESSED by a process analogous to photography; works of applied art; illustrations, MAPS, plans, sketches and THREE-DIMENSIONAL works relative to geography, topography, architecture or science.

(2) IT SHALL, HOWEVER, BE A MATTER FOR LEGISLATION IN THE COUNTRIES OF THE UNION TO PRESCRIBE THAT WORKS IN GENERAL OR ANY SPECIFIED CATEGORIES OF WORKS SHALL NOT BE PROTECTED UNLESS THEY HAVE BEEN FIXED IN SOME MATERIAL FORM.

(3) Translations, adaptations, arrangements of music and other alterations of a literary or artistic work shall be protected as original works without prejudice to the COPYRIGHT IN the original work.

Brussels

ART. 2—*cont.*

of the Union to determine the protection to be granted to *translations of official texts of a legislative, administrative and legal nature.*

(3) Collections of literary or artistic works such as encyclopaedias and anthologies which by reason of the selection and arrangement of their contents constitute intellectual creations shall be protected as such without prejudice to the *rights of the authors in respect of* each of the works forming part of such collections.

(4) The works mentioned in this Article shall enjoy protection in all countries of the Union. This protection shall operate for the benefit of the author and his *legal representatives and assignees.*

(5) It shall be a matter for legislation in the countries of the Union to determine the extent of the application of their laws to works of applied art and industrial designs and models, as well as the conditions under which such works, designs and models shall be protected. Works protected in the country of origin solely as designs and models shall be entitled in *other countries of the Union only to such protection as shall be accorded to designs and models in such countries.*

Stockholm

ART. 2—*cont.*

(4) It shall be a matter for legislation in the countries of the Union to determine the protection to be granted to OFFICIAL TEXTS OF A LEGISLATIVE, ADMINISTRATIVE AND LEGAL NATURE, AND TO OFFICIAL TRANSLATIONS OF SUCH TEXTS.

(5) Collections of literary or artistic works such as encyclopaedias and anthologies which, by reason of the selection and arrangement of their contents, constitute intellectual creations shall be protected as such, without prejudice to the COPYRIGHT IN each of the works forming part of such collections.

(6) The works mentioned in this Article shall enjoy protection in all countries of the Union. This protection shall operate for the benefit of the author and his SUCCESSORS IN TITLE.

(7) SUBJECT TO THE PROVISIONS OF ARTICLE 7 (4) OF THIS CONVENTION it shall be a matter for legislation in the countries of the Union to determine the extent of the application of their laws to works of applied art and industrial designs and models, as well as the conditions under which such works, designs and models shall be protected. Works protected in the country of origin solely as designs and models shall be entitled in ANOTHER COUNTRY OF THE UNION ONLY TO SUCH SPECIAL PROTECTION AS IS GRANTED IN THAT COUNTRY TO DESIGNS AND MODELS; HOWEVER, IF NO SUCH SPECIAL PROTECTION IS GRANTED IN THAT COUNTRY, SUCH WORKS SHALL BE PROTECTED AS ARTISTIC WORKS.

(8) The protection of this Convention shall not apply to news of the day nor to miscellaneous FACTS

Brussels

ART. 2—*cont.*

Stockholm

ART. 2—*cont.*

having the character of mere items of PRESS INFORMATION.

Note. Paragraph (2) of the revised text makes it clear that countries may demand, in all cases, that a work shall be " fixed " before protection is granted. This is of particular importance with regard to live television broadcasts which could be considered as " works expressed by a process analogous to cinematography." The United Kingdom protects live broadcasts under the European Agreement of 1960 and the Rome Convention of 1961, but not under the Berne Convention. By section 49 (4) of the Copyright Act, 1956, a work is " made " when it is " first reduced to writing or some other material form."

Paragraph (4) leaves countries free to refuse protection, not only to translations of certain official texts, but to the texts themselves.

Paragraph (7) now provides that countries which, unlike the United Kingdom, protect a work of applied art as an artistic work must give such a work at least 25 years' protection. If a work of applied art is protected in its country of origin solely as a design or model it can claim only such protection in other union countries. However, if the other union country has no special law for the protection of designs and models, it must give the protection obtained by the copyright law.

The new paragraph (8) has been transferred from Article 9 (3) of the Brussels text. The amendments made in the English text are a more accurate translation of the French.

Brussels

1684 ARTICLE 2 *bis*

(1) It shall be a matter for legislation in the countries of the Union to exclude wholly or in part from the protection *afforded* by the preceding Article political speeches and speeches delivered in the course of legal proceedings.

(2) It shall also be a matter for legislation in the countries of the Union to determine the conditions under which lectures, addresses, *sermons* and other works of the same nature may be reproduced by the press.

(3) *Nevertheless, the author alone* shall *have* the right of making a collection of his works mentioned in the *above* paragraphs.

Stockholm

ARTICLE 2 *bis*

(1) It shall be a matter for legislation in the countries of the Union to exclude, wholly or in part, from the protection PROVIDED by the preceding Article political speeches and speeches delivered in the course of legal proceedings.

(2) It shall also be a matter for legislation in the countries of the Union to determine the conditions under which lectures, addresses and other works of the same nature WHICH ARE DELIVERED IN PUBLIC may be reproduced by the press, BROADCAST, COMMUNICATED TO THE PUBLIC BY WIRE AND MADE THE SUBJECT OF PUBLIC COMMUNICATION AS ENVISAGED IN ARTICLE 11 BIS (1) OF THIS CONVENTION, WHEN SUCH USE IS JUSTIFIED BY THE INFORMATORY PURPOSE.

(3) Nevertheless, the author shall ENJOY the EXCLUSIVE right of making a collection of his works mentioned in the PRECEDING paragraphs.

Note. Paragraph (2) has been enlarged to put broadcasting and wire diffusion on the same footing as the press. At the same time its scope has been restricted to public lectures, etc., and to use for *public* information.

Brussels

1685 ARTICLE 3

Stockholm

ARTICLE 3

(1) THE PROTECTION OF THIS CONVENTION SHALL APPLY TO

(a) AUTHORS WHO ARE NATIONALS OF ONE OF THE COUNTRIES OF THE UNION, FOR THEIR WORKS, WHETHER PUBLISHED OR NOT:

(b) AUTHORS WHO ARE NOT NATIONALS OF ONE OF THE COUNTRIES OF THE UNION, FOR THEIR WORKS FIRST PUBLISHED IN ONE OF THOSE COUNTRIES, OR SIMULTANEOUSLY IN A COUNTRY OUTSIDE THE UNION AND IN A COUNTRY OF THE UNION.

(2) AUTHORS WHO ARE NOT NATIONALS OF ONE OF THE COUNTRIES OF THE UNION BUT WHO HAVE THEIR HABITUAL RESIDENCE IN ONE OF THEM SHALL, FOR THE PURPOSES OF THIS CONVENTION, BE ASSIMILATED TO NATIONALS OF THAT COUNTRY.

(3) THE EXPRESSION " PUBLISHED WORKS " MEANS WORKS PUBLISHED WITH THE CONSENT OF THEIR AUTHORS, WHATEVER MAY BE THE MEANS OF MANUFACTURE OF THE COPIES, PROVIDED THAT THE AVAILABILITY OF SUCH COPIES HAS BEEN SUCH AS TO SATISFY THE REASONABLE REQUIREMENTS OF THE PUBLIC, HAVING REGARD TO THE NATURE OF THE WORK. THE PERFORMANCE OF A DRAMATIC, DRAMATICO-MUSICAL, CINEMATOGRAPHIC OR MUSICAL WORK, THE PUBLIC RECITATION OF A LITERARY WORK, THE COMMUNICATION BY WIRE OR THE BROADCASTING OF LITERARY OR ARTISTIC WORKS, THE EXHIBITION OF A WORK OF ART AND THE CONSTRUCTION OF A WORK OF ARCHITECTURE SHALL NOT CONSTITUTE PUBLICATION.

(4) A WORK SHALL BE CONSIDERED AS HAVING BEEN PUBLISHED SIMULTANEOUSLY IN SEVERAL COUNTRIES IF IT HAD BEEN PUBLISHED IN TWO OR MORE COUNTRIES WITHIN THIRTY DAYS OF ITS FIRST PUBLICATION.

Brussels

1686 ARTICLE 4

(1) *Authors who are nationals of any of the countries of the Union shall enjoy in countries other than the country of origin of the work, for their works, whether unpublished or first published in a country of the Union, the rights which their respective laws do now or may hereafter grant to their nationals, as well as the rights specially granted by this present Convention.*

(2) *The enjoyment and the exercise of these rights shall not be subject to any formality; such enjoyment and such exercise shall be independent of the existence of protection in the country of origin of the work. Consequently, apart from the provisions of this Convention, the extent of protection, as well as the means of redress afforded to the author to protect his rights, shall be governed exclusively by the laws of the country where protection is claimed.*

(3) *The country of origin shall be considered to be, in the case of published works, the country of first publication, even in the case of works published simultaneously in several countries of the Union which grant the same term of protection; in the case of works published simultaneously in several countries of the Union which grant different terms of protection, the country of which the legislation grants the shortest term of protection. In the case of works published simultaneously in a country outside the Union and in a country of the Union, the latter country shall be considered exclusively as the country of origin. A work shall be considered as having been published simultaneously in several countries which has been published in two or more countries within thirty days of its first publication.*

Stockholm

ARTICLE 4

THE PROTECTION OF THIS CONVENTION SHALL APPLY, EVEN IF THE CONDITIONS OF ARTICLE 3 ARE NOT FULFILLED, TO

(a) AUTHORS OF CINEMATOGRAPHIC WORKS, THE MAKER OF WHICH HAS HIS HEADQUARTERS OR HABITUAL RESIDENCE IN ONE OF THE COUNTRIES OF THE UNION;

(b) AUTHORS OF WORKS OF ARCHITECTURE, ERECTED IN A COUNTRY OF THE UNION OR OF OTHER ARTISTIC WORKS INCORPORATED IN A BUILDING OR OTHER STRUCTURE LOCATED IN A COUNTRY OF THE UNION.

Brussels

ART. 4—*cont.*

(4) *For the purposes of Articles 4, 5 and 6, "published works" shall be understood to be works copies of which have been issued and made available in sufficient quantities to the public, whatever may be the means of manufacture of the copies. The presentation of a dramatic, dramatico-musical or cinematographic work, the performance of a musical work, the public recitation of a literary work, the transmission or the radio-diffusion of literary or artistic works, the exhibition of a work of art and the construction of a work of architecture shall not constitute publication.*

(5) *The country of origin shall be considered to be, in the case of unpublished works, the country to which the author belongs. However, in the case of works of architecture, or of graphic and plastic works forming part of a building, the country of the Union where these works have been built or incorporated in a building shall be considered as the country of origin.*

Stockholm

ART. 4—*cont.*

1687 ARTICLE 5 (Brussels)

Authors who are nationals of one of the countries of the Union, and who first publish their works in another country of the Union, shall have in the latter country the same rights as native authors.

ARTICLE 5 (Stockholm)

(1) AUTHORS SHALL ENJOY, IN RESPECT OF WORKS FOR WHICH THEY ARE PROTECTED UNDER THIS CONVENTION, IN COUNTRIES OF THE UNION OTHER THAN THE COUNTRY OF ORIGIN, THE RIGHTS WHICH THEIR RESPECTIVE LAWS DO NOW OR MAY HEREAFTER GRANT TO THEIR NATIONALS, AS WELL AS THE RIGHTS SPECIALLY GRANTED BY THIS CONVENTION.

(2) THE ENJOYMENT AND THE EXERCISE OF THESE RIGHTS SHALL NOT BE SUBJECT TO ANY FORMALITY; SUCH ENJOYMENT AND SUCH EXERCISE SHALL BE INDEPENDENT OF THE EXISTENCE OF PROTECTION IN THE COUNTRY OF ORIGIN OF THE

Brussels

ART. 5—*cont.*

Stockholm

ART. 5—*cont.*

WORK. CONSEQUENTLY, APART FROM THE PROVISIONS OF THIS CONVENTION, THE EXTENT OF PROTECTION, AS WELL AS THE MEANS OF REDRESS AFFORDED TO THE AUTHORS TO PROTECT HIS RIGHTS, SHALL BE GOVERNED EXCLUSIVELY BY THE LAWS OF THE COUNTRY WHERE PROTECTION IS CLAIMED.

(3) PROTECTION IN THE COUNTRY OF ORIGIN IS GOVERNED BY DOMESTIC LAW. HOWEVER, WHEN THE AUTHOR IS NOT A NATIONAL OF THE COUNTRY OF ORIGIN OF THE WORK FOR WHICH HE IS PROTECTED UNDER THIS CONVENTION, HE SHALL ENJOY IN THAT COUNTRY THE SAME RIGHTS AS NATIONAL AUTHORS.

(4) THE COUNTRY OF ORIGIN SHALL BE CONSIDERED TO BE

(a) IN THE CASE OF WORKS FIRST PUBLISHED IN A COUNTRY OF THE UNION, THAT COUNTRY; IN THE CASE OF WORKS PUBLISHED SIMULTANEOUSLY IN SEVERAL COUNTRIES OF THE UNION WHICH GRANT DIFFERENT TERMS OF PROTECTION, THE COUNTRY WHOSE LEGISLATION GRANTS THE SHORTEST TERM OF PROTECTION;

(b) IN THE CASE OF WORKS PUBLISHED SIMULTANEOUSLY IN A COUNTRY OUTSIDE THE UNION AND IN A COUNTRY OF THE UNION, THE LATTER COUNTRY;

(c) IN THE CASE OF UNPUBLISHED WORKS OR OF WORKS FIRST PUBLISHED IN A COUNTRY OUTSIDE THE UNION, WITHOUT SIMULTANEOUS PUBLICATION IN A COUNTRY OF THE UNION, THE COUNTRY OF THE UNION OF WHICH THE AUTHOR IS A NATIONAL, PROVIDED THAT:

(i) WHEN THESE ARE CINEMATOGRAPHIC WORKS THE MAKER OF WHICH HAS HIS HEADQUARTERS OR HIS HABITUAL RESIDENCE IN A COUNTRY OF THE UNION, THE COUNTRY OF ORIGIN SHALL BE THAT COUNTRY, AND

Brussels

ART. 5—*cont.*

Stockholm

ART. 5—*cont.*

(ii) WHEN THESE ARE WORKS OF ARCHITECTURE ERECTED IN A COUNTRY OF THE UNION OR OTHER ARTISTIC WORKS INCORPORATED IN A BUILDING OR OTHER STRUCTURE LOCATED IN A COUNTRY OF THE UNION, THE COUNTRY OF ORIGIN SHALL BE THAT COUNTRY.

Note. Articles 4, 5 and 6 (1) of the Brussels text have been re-drafted to some extent and re-arranged in a more logical order to form Articles 3, 4 and 5.

Article 3 defines the criteria for eligibility for protection. These have been broadened to provide that the work of a national of a Union country is protected even when first publication takes place in a non-Union country; and that a national of a non-Union country who is habitually resident in a Union country is to be treated as if he were a national of that country. The definition of " published works " in paragraph (3) (compare Article 4 (4) of the Brussels text) now has general application, but it has been limited to works published with the consent of the author and clarified to make it more appropriate to all kinds of works (*e.g.* films).

Article 4 provides additional eligibility criteria for authors of cinematograph works and works of architecture. These are new provisions and, as regards works of architecture, ratification of the revised Convention would involve a minor change in U.K. law.

Paragraph (1) of Article 5 defines the scope of the protection to be enjoyed by a work which is eligible for protection and makes no change. Paragraph (2) corresponds to Article 4 (2) of the Brussels text and now applies to nationals of Union and non-Union countries. Paragraph (3) combines Articles 5 and 6 (1) of the Brussels text with some minor changes. Paragraph (4) substantially reproduces the effect of Articles 4 (3) and 4 (5) of the Brussels text.

Brussels

1688 ARTICLE 6

(1) *Authors who are not nationals of one of the countries of the Union, and who first publish their works in one of those countries, shall enjoy in that country the same rights as native authors, and in the other countries of the Union the rights granted by this Conven tion.*

(2) *Nevertheless,* where any country outside the Union fails to protect in an adequate manner the works of authors who are nationals of one of the countries of the

Stockholm

ARTICLE 6

(1) Where any country outside the Union fails to protect in an adequate manner the works of authors who are nationals of one of the countries of the Union, the

Brussels

ART. 6—*cont.*

Union, the latter country may restrict the protection given to the works of authors who are, at the date of the first publication thereof, nationals of the other country and are not *effectively domiciled* in one of the countries of the Union. If the country of first publication avails itself of this right, the other countries of the Union shall not be required to grant to works thus subjected to special treatment a wider protection than that granted to them in the country of first publication.

(3) No restrictions introduced by virtue of the preceding paragraph shall affect the rights which an author may have acquired in respect of a work published in a country of the Union before such restrictions were put into force.

(4) The countries of the Union which restrict the grant of copyright in accordance with this Article shall give notice thereof to the *Government of the Swiss Confederation* by a written declaration specifying the countries in regard to which protection is restricted, and the restrictions to which rights of authors who are nationals of those countries are subjected. The *Government of the Swiss Confederation* shall immediately communicate this declaration to all the countries of the Union.

Stockholm

ART. 6—*cont.*

latter country may restrict the protection given to the work of authors who are, at the date of the first publication thereof, nationals of the other country and are not HABITUALLY RESIDENT in one of the countries of the Union. If the country of first publication avails itself of this right, the other countries of the union shall not be required to grant to works thus subjected to special treatment a wider protection than that granted to them in the country of first publication.

(2) No restrictions introduced by virtue of the preceding paragraph shall affect the rights which an author may have acquired in respect of a work published in a country of the Union before such restrictions were put into force.

(3) The countries of the Union which restrict the grant of copyright in accordance with this Article shall give notice thereof to the DIRECTOR GENERAL OF THE WORLD INTELLECTUAL PROPERTY ORGANIZATION (HEREINAFTER DESIGNATED AS THE "DIRECTOR GENERAL") by a written declaration specifying the countries in regard to which protection is restricted, and the restrictions to which rights of authors who are nationals of those countries are subjected. The DIRECTOR GENERAL shall immediately communicate this declaration to all the countries of the Union.

Note. This Article roproduces, with minor changes, paragraphs (2), (3) and (4) of Article 6 of the Brussels text.

The change in paragraph (3) is a result of the establishment, at the Stockholm Conference, of the World Intellectual Property Organisation.

Brussels

1689 ARTICLE 6 *bis*

(1) Independently of the author's *copyright*, and even after the transfer of the said *copyright*, the author shall have the right, *during*

Stockholm

ARTICLE 6 *bis*

(1) Independently of the author's ECONOMIC RIGHTS, and even after the transfer of the said RIGHTS, the author shall have the right to

Brussels

ART. 6 *bis—cont.*

his lifetime, to claim authorship of the work and to object to any distortion, mutilation or other *alteration thereof, or any other action* in relation to the said work which would be prejudicial to his honour or reputation.

(2) *In so far as the legislation of the countries of the Union permits, the rights granted to the author in accordance with the preceding paragraph shall, after his death, be maintained, at least until the expiry of the copyright*, and shall be exercisable by the persons or institutions authorised by the *said* legislation. *The determination of the conditions under which the rights mentioned in this paragraph shall be exercised shall be governed by the legislation of the countries of the Union.*

(3) The means of redress for safeguarding the rights granted by this Article shall be governed by the legislation of the country where protection is claimed.

Stockholm

ART. 6 *bis—cont.*

claim authorship of the work and to object to any distortion, mutilation or other MODIFICATION OF, OR OTHER DEROGATORY ACTION in relation to, the said work, which would be prejudicial to his honour or reputation.

(2) THE RIGHTS GRANTED TO THE AUTHOR IN ACCORDANCE WITH THE PRECEDING PARAGRAPH SHALL, AFTER HIS DEATH, BE MAINTAINED, AT LEAST UNTIL THE EXPIRY OF THE ECONOMIC RIGHTS, and shall be exercisable by the persons or institutions authorized by the legislation OF THE COUNTRY WHERE PROTECTION IS CLAIMED. HOWEVER, THOSE COUNTRIES WHOSE LEGISLATION AT THE MOMENT OF THEIR RATIFICATION OF OR ACCESSION TO THIS ACT, DOES NOT PROVIDE FOR THE PROTECTION AFTER THE DEATH OF THE AUTHOR OF ALL THE RIGHTS SET OUT IN THE PRECEDING PARAGRAPH, MAY PROVIDE THAT SOME OF THESE RIGHTS MAY, AFTER HIS DEATH, CEASE TO BE MAINTAINED.

(3) The means of redress for safeguarding the rights granted by this Article shall be governed by the legislation of the country where protection is claimed.

Note. This Article now provides that countries must protect the moral rights of an author during the full term of copyright instead of during the author's lifetime. However, countries whose laws do not, at the time of accession to the Stockholm Act, provide for protection after the author's death of all the moral rights specified in paragraph (1) shall be obliged only to protect some of them for the full period. This would involve some amendment of United Kingdom law (*e.g.* section 43 of the Copyright Act, 1956).

Brussels

1690 ARTICLE 7

(1) The term of protection granted by this Convention shall be the life of the author and fifty years after his death.

(2) *However, where one or more countries of the Union grant a*

Stockholm

ARTICLE 7

(1) The term of protection granted by this Convention shall be the life of the author and fifty years after his death.

Brussels

ART. 7—*cont.*

term of protection in excess of that provided by paragraph (1), *the term shall be governed by the law of the country where protection is claimed, but shall not exceed the term fixed in the country or origin of the work.*

(3) *In the case of cinematographic and photographic works, as well as works produced by a process analogous to cinematography or photography, and in the case of works of applied art, the term of protection shall be governed by the law of the country where protection is claimed, but shall not exceed the term fixed in the country of origin of the work.*

(4) In the case of anonymous and pseudonymous works the term of protection *shall be fixed at fifty years from the date of their publication.* However, when the pseudonym adopted by the author leaves no doubt as to his identity, the term of protection shall be that provided in paragraph (1). If the author of an anonymous or pseudonymous work discloses his identity during the above-mentioned period, the term of protection applicable shall be that provided in paragraph (1).

Stockholm

ART. 7—*cont.*

(2) HOWEVER, IN THE CASE OF CINEMATOGRAPHIC WORKS, THE COUNTRIES OF THE UNION MAY PROVIDE THAT THE TERM OF PROTECTION SHALL EXPIRE FIFTY YEARS AFTER THE WORK HAS BEEN MADE AVAILABLE TO THE PUBLIC WITH THE CONSENT OF THE AUTHOR, OR, FAILING SUCH AN EVENT WITHIN FIFTY YEARS FROM THE MAKING OF SUCH A WORK, FIFTY YEARS AFTER THE MAKING.

(3) In the case of anonymous or pseudonymous works, the term of protection GRANTED BY THIS CONVENTION SHALL EXPIRE FIFTY YEARS AFTER THE WORK HAS BEEN LAWFULLY MADE AVAILABLE TO THE PUBLIC. However, when the pseudonym adopted by the author leaves no doubt as to his identity, the term of protection shall be that provided in paragraph (1). If the author of an anonymous or pseudonymous work discloses his identity during the above-mentioned period, the term of protection applicable shall be that provided in paragraph (1). THE COUNTRIES OF THE UNION SHALL NOT BE REQUIRED TO PROTECT ANONYMOUS OR PSEUDONYMOUS WORKS IN RESPECT OF WHICH IT IS REASONABLE TO PRESUME THAT THEIR AUTHOR HAS BEEN DEAD FOR FIFTY YEARS.

(4) IT SHALL BE A MATTER FOR LEGISLATION IN THE COUNTRIES OF THE UNION TO DETERMINE THE TERM OF PROTECTION OF PHOTOGRAPHIC WORKS AND THAT OF WORKS OF APPLIED ART IN SO FAR AS THEY ARE PROTECTED AS ARTISTIC WORKS; HOWEVER, THIS TERM SHALL LAST AT LEAST UNTIL THE

Brussels

ART. 7—*cont.*

(5) *In the case of posthumous works which do not fall within the categories of works included in paragraphs* (3) *and* (4) *the term of the protection afforded to the heirs and the legal representatives and assignees of the author shall end at the expiry of fifty years after the death of the author.*

(6) The term of protection subsequent to the death of the author and the terms provided by paragraphs (3), (4) and (5) shall run from the date of *his* death *or of publication*, but such terms shall always be deemed to begin on the 1st January of the year following *the event which gives rise to them.*

Stockholm

ART. 7—*cont.*

END OF A PERIOD OF TWENTY-FIVE YEARS FROM THE MAKING OF SUCH A WORK.

(5) The term of protection subsequent to the death of the author and the terms provided by paragraphs (2), (3) and (4), shall run from the date of death OR OF THE EVENT REFERRED TO IN THOSE PARAGRAPHS, but such terms shall always be deemed to begin on the 1st January of the year following THE DEATH OR SUCH EVENT.

(6) THE COUNTRIES OF THE UNION MAY GRANT A TERM OF PROTECTION IN EXCESS OF THOSE PROVIDED BY THE PRECEDING PARAGRAPHS.

(7) THOSE COUNTRIES OF THE UNION BOUND BY THE ROME ACT OF THIS CONVENTION, WHICH GRANT, IN THEIR NATIONAL LEGISLATION IN FORCE AT THE TIME OF SIGNATURE OF THE PRESENT ACT, SHORTER TERMS OF PROTECTION THAN THOSE PROVIDED FOR IN THE PRECEDING PARAGRAPHS, SHALL HAVE THE RIGHT TO MAINTAIN SUCH TERMS WHEN RATIFYING OR ACCEDING TO THE PRESENT ACT.

(8) IN ANY CASE, THE TERM SHALL BE GOVERNED BY THE LEGISLATION OF THE COUNTRY WHERE PROTECTION IS CLAIMED; HOWEVER, UNLESS THE LEGISLATION OF THAT COUNTRY OTHERWISE PROVIDES, THE TERM SHALL NOT EXCEED THE TERM FIXED IN THE COUNTRY OF ORIGIN OF THE WORK.

Note. Article 7 of the Brussels text has been re-arranged and now some new provisions have been introduced. Minimum terms of protection have been laid down for cinematographic works, photographic works and works of applied art in so far as they are protected as artistic works. This would involve a minor change in the United Kingdom law as regards cinematographic works only under which the term of protection runs from registration rather than the first public showing.

An exception from the general rule prescribed by paragraph (1) is permitted for those countries which are at present bound by the Rome Act of the Convention.

	Brussels	*Stockholm*
1691	ARTICLE 7 *bis*	ARTICLE 7 *bis*
	In the case of a work of joint authorship the term of protection shall be calculated from the date of the death of the last surviving author.	THE PROVISIONS OF THE PRECEDING ARTICLE SHALL ALSO APPLY IN THE CASE OF A WORK OF JOINT AUTHORSHIP, PROVIDED THAT THE TERMS MEASURED FROM THE DEATH OF THE AUTHOR SHALL BE CALCULATED FROM THE DEATH OF THE LAST SURVIVING AUTHOR.
1692	ARTICLE 8	ARTICLE 8
	Authors of literary and artistic works protected by this Convention shall *have* the exclusive right of making and of authorising the translation of their works throughout the term of protection of their rights in the original works.	Authors of literary and artistic works protected by this Convention shall ENJOY the exclusive right of making and of authorising the translation of their works throughout the term of protection of their rights in the original works.
1693	ARTICLE 9	ARTICLE 9
	(1) *Serial novels, short stories and all other works, whether literary, scientific or artistic, whatever their purpose, and which are published in the newspapers or periodicals of one of the countries of the Union shall not be reproduced in the other countries without the consent of the authors.*	(1) AUTHORS OF LITERARY AND ARTISTIC WORKS PROTECTED BY THIS CONVENTION SHALL HAVE THE EXCLUSIVE RIGHT OF AUTHORIZING THE REPRODUCTION OF THESE WORKS, IN ANY MANNER OR FORM.
	(2) *Articles on current economic, political or religious topics may be reproduced by the press unless the reproduction thereof is expressly reserved; nevertheless, the source must always be clearly indicated. The legal consequence of the breach of this obligation shall be determined by the laws of the country where protection is claimed.*	(2) IT SHALL BE A MATTER FOR LEGISLATION IN THE COUNTRIES OF THE UNION TO PERMIT THE REPRODUCTION OF SUCH WORKS IN CERTAIN SPECIAL CASES, PROVIDED THAT SUCH REPRODUCTION DOES NOT CONFLICT WITH A NORMAL EXPLOITATION OF THE WORK AND DOES NOT UNREASONABLY PREJUDICE THE LEGITIMATE INTERESTS OF THE AUTHOR.

Brussels

ART. 9—*cont.*

(3) *The protection of this Convention shall not apply to news of the day nor to miscellaneous information having the character of mere items of news.*

Stockholm

ART. 9—*cont.*

(3) ANY SOUND OR VISUAL RECORDING SHALL BE CONSIDERED AS A REPRODUCTION FOR THE PURPOSES OF THIS CONVENTION.

Note. This Article, which is new, provides that authors shall have the exclusive right of authorising the reproduction of their works, including the making of sound or visual recordings. Paragraph (2) defines in general terms the exceptions to this right which countries may prescribe in their domestic laws. No change in United Kingdom law is involved.

Brussels

1694 ARTICLE 10

(1) *It shall be permissible in all the countries of the Union to make short quotations from newspaper articles and periodicals, as well as to include them in press summaries.*

(2) *The right to include excerpts from literary or artistic works in educational or scientific publications, or in chrestomathies, in so far as this inclusion is justified by its purpose, shall be a matter for legislation in the countries of the Union, and for special Arrangements existing or to be concluded between them.*

(3) *Quotations and excerpts shall be accompanied by an acknowledgment of the source and by the name of the author, if his name appears thereon.*

Stockholm

ARTICLE 10

(1) IT SHALL BE PERMISSIBLE TO MAKE QUOTATIONS FROM A WORK WHICH HAS ALREADY BEEN LAWFULLY MADE AVAILABLE TO THE PUBLIC, PROVIDED THAT THEIR MAKING IS COMPATIBLE WITH FAIR PRACTICE, AND THEIR EXTENT DOES NOT EXCEED THAT JUSTIFIED BY THE PURPOSE, INCLUDING QUOTATIONS FROM NEWSPAPER ARTICLES AND PERIODICALS IN THE FORM OF PRESS SUMMARIES.

(2) IT SHALL BE A MATTER FOR LEGISLATION IN THE COUNTRIES OF THE UNION, AND FOR SPECIAL AGREEMENTS EXISTING OR TO BE CONCLUDED BETWEEN THEM, TO PERMIT THE UTILIZATION, TO THE EXTENT JUSTIFIED BY THE PURPOSE, OF LITERARY OR ARTISTIC WORKS BY WAY OF ILLUSTRATION IN PUBLICATIONS, BROADCASTS OR SOUND OR VISUAL RECORDINGS FOR TEACHING, PROVIDED SUCH UTILIZATION IS COMPATIBLE WITH FAIR PRACTICE.

(3) WHERE USE IS MADE OF WORKS IN ACCORDANCE WITH THE PRECEDING PARAGRAPHS OF THIS ARTICLE, MENTION SHALL BE MADE OF THE SOURCE AND OF THE NAME OF THE AUTHOR, IF IT APPEARS THEREON.

Note. Paragraph (1) of the Brussels text has been widened in scope. The quotations may be made, not only from newspaper articles and periodicals, but from *any* work and, provided this making is compatible with fair practice and their extent does not exceed that justified by the purpose, they need not necessarily be " short."

Paragraph (2) of the Brussels text has been revised. The word "excerpts" in the English text was a mistranslation since the French word "emprints"—"borrowings"—includes the whole work. This provision, however, extends only for teaching purposes and the use must be by way of illustration and compatible with fair practice. Use is also allowed, not only in a publication, but also in a broadcast or recording.

Brussels

1695 ARTICLE 10 *bis*

It shall be a matter for legislation in countries of the Union to determine the conditions under which recording, reproduction, and public communication of short extracts from literary and artistic works may be made for the purpose of reporting current events by means of photography or cinematography or by radio-diffusion.

Stockholm

ARTICLE 10 *bis*

(1) IT SHALL BE A MATTER FOR LEGISLATION IN THE COUNTRIES OF THE UNION TO PERMIT THE REPRODUCTION BY THE PRESS, THE BROADCASTING OR THE COMMUNICATION TO THE PUBLIC BY WIRE, OF ARTICLES PUBLISHED IN NEWSPAPERS OR PERIODICALS ON CURRENT ECONOMIC, POLITICAL OR RELIGIOUS TOPICS, AND OF BROADCAST WORKS OF THE SAME CHARACTER, IN CASES IN WHICH THE REPRODUCTION, BROADCASTING OR SUCH COMMUNICATION THEREOF IS NOT EXPRESSLY RESERVED. NEVERTHELESS, THE SOURCE MUST ALWAYS BE CLEARLY INDICATED; THE LEGAL CONSEQUENCES OF A BREACH OF THIS OBLIGATION SHALL BE DETERMINED BY THE LEGISLATION OF THE COUNTRY WHERE PROTECTION IS CLAIMED.

(2) IT SHALL ALSO BE A MATTER FOR LEGISLATION IN THE COUNTRIES OF THE UNION TO DETERMINE THE CONDITIONS UNDER WHICH, FOR THE PURPOSE OF REPORTING CURRENT EVENTS BY MEANS OF PHOTOGRAPHY, CINEMATOGRAPHY, BROADCASTING OR COMMUNICATION TO THE PUBLIC BY WIRE, LITERARY OR ARTISTIC WORKS SEEN OR HEARD IN THE COURSE OF THE EVENT MAY, TO THE EXTENT JUSTIFIED BY THE INFORMATORY PURPOSE, BE REPRODUCED AND MADE AVAILABLE TO THE PUBLIC.

Note. Article 9 (2) of the Brussels text permitted the press to reproduce articles on current topics unless the author had expressly reserved his rights. This provision has now been transferred to paragraph (1) of Article 10 and extended to include broadcasting and wire-diffusion.

Paragraph (2) replaces Article 10 *bis* of the Brussels text. It is widened to cover also the use of works in the reporting of events by wire communication, and, although the user is not limited to "short extracts", the work used must be one seen or heard in the course of the event which is reported. The extent of the use must be no more than is justified by the informatory purpose.

Brussels

1696 ARTICLE 11

(1) The authors of dramatic, dramatico-musical or musical works shall enjoy the exclusive right of authorising: i. the *public presentation and* public performance of their works; ii. *the public distribution by any means* of the *presentation and* performance of their works. *The application of the provisions of Articles* 11 *bis and* 13 *is, however, reserved.*

(2) Authors of dramatic or dramatico-musical works, during the full term of their rights *over* the original works, shall enjoy the same rights with respect to translations thereof.

(3) *In order to enjoy the protection of this Article, authors shall not be bound, when publishing their works, to forbid the public presentation or performance thereof.*

Stockholm

ARTICLE 11

(1) Authors of dramatic, dramatico-musical and musical works shall enjoy the exclusive right of authorizing:

(i) the public performance of their works, INCLUDING SUCH PUBLIC PERFORMANCE BY ANY MEANS OR PROCESS;

(ii) ANY COMMUNICATION TO THE PUBLIC of the performance of their works.

(2) Authors of dramatic, or dramatico-musical works shall enjoy during the full term of their rights IN the original works, the same rights with respect to translation thereof.

Note. The changes in paragraphs (1) and (2) of the Brussels text are merely of a drafting nature. It has been made clear that performances by gramophone records are covered. The final sentence of paragraph (1) and paragraph (3) have been deleted as superfluous.

The United Kingdom declaration made at the Brussels Conference was not repeated. But see note on Article 17.

Brussels

1697 ARTICLE 11 *bis*

(1) Authors of literary and artistic works shall *have* the exclusive right of authorising: i. the *radio-diffusion* of their works or the communication thereof to the public by any other means of wireless diffusion of signs, sounds or images; ii. any communication to the public, *whether over wires or not*, of the *radio-diffusion* of the work, when this communication is made by a body other than the original one; iii. the *communication*

Stockholm

ARTICLE 11 *bis*

(1) Authors of literary and artistic works shall ENJOY the exclusive right of authorizing:

(i) the BROADCASTING of their works or the communication thereof to the public by any other means of wireless diffusion of signs, sounds or images;

(ii) any communication to the public BY WIRE OR BY REBROADCASTING of the BROADCAST of the work,

Brussels

ART. 11 *bis—cont.*

to the public by loudspeaker or any other *similar* instrument transmitting, by signs, sounds or images, the *radio-diffusion* of the work.

(2) It shall be a matter for legislation in the countries of the Union to determine the conditions under which the rights mentioned in the preceding paragraph may be exercised, but these conditions shall apply only in the countries where they have been prescribed. They shall not in any circumstances be prejudicial to the moral right of the author, nor to his right to obtain *just* remuneration which, in the absence of agreement, shall be fixed by competent authority.

(3) *Except where otherwise provided*, permission granted in accordance with paragraph (1) of this Article shall not imply permission to record the *radio-diffused* work by means of instruments recording sounds or images. It shall, however, be a matter for legislation in the countries of the Union to determine the regulations for ephemeral recordings made by a broadcasting body by means of its own facilities and used for its own *emissions*. The preservation of these recordings in official archives may, on the ground of their exceptional documentary character, be authorised by such legislation.

Stockholm

ART. 11 *bis—cont.*

when this communication is made by an organization other than the original one;

(iii) the PUBLIC COMMUNICATION by loudspeaker or any other ANALOGOUS instrument transmitting by signs, sounds or images, the BROADCAST of the work.

(2) It shall be a matter for legislation in the countries of the Union to determine the conditions under which the rights mentioned in the preceding paragraph may be exercised, but these conditions shall apply only in the countries where they have been prescribed. They shall not in any circumstances be prejudicial to the moral rights of the author, nor to his right to obtain EQUITABLE remuneration which, in the absence of agreement, shall be fixed by competent authority.

(3) IN THE ABSENCE OF ANY CONTRARY STIPULATION, permission granted in accordance with paragraph (1) of this Article shall not imply permission to record, by means of instruments recording sounds or images, the work BROADCAST. It shall, however, be a matter for legislation in the countries of the Union to determine the regulations for ephemeral recordings made by a broadcasting organisation by means of its own facilities and used for its own BROADCASTS. The preservation of these recordings in official archives may, on the ground of their exceptional documentary character, be authorised by such legislation.

Note. Only drafting changes in the English text have been made.

Brussels

1698 ARTICLE 11 *ter*

Authors of literary works shall enjoy the exclusive right of authorising the public recitation of their works.

Stockholm

ARTICLE 11 *ter*

(1) Authors of literary works shall enjoy the exclusive right of authorising:

(i) the public recitation of their

Brussels

ART. 11 *ter—cont.*

Stockholm

ART. 11 *ter—cont.*

works, INCLUDING SUCH PUBLIC RECITATION BY ANY MEANS OR PROCESS:

(ii) ANY COMMUNICATION TO THE PUBLIC OF THE RECITATION OF THEIR WORKS.

(2) AUTHORS OF LITERARY WORKS SHALL ENJOY, DURING THE FULL TERM OF THEIR RIGHTS IN THE ORIGINAL WORKS, THE SAME RIGHTS WITH RESPECT TO TRANSLATIONS THEREOF.

Note. Article 11 *ter* of the Brussels text has been re-drafted to bring the author's rights in respect of recitations into line with their performing right given by Article 11.

Brussels

1699 ARTICLE 12

Authors of literary, *scientific* or artistic works shall enjoy the exclusive right of authorising adaptations, arrangements and other alterations of their works.

Stockholm

ARTICLE 12

Authors of literary or artistic works shall enjoy the exclusive right of authorising adaptations, arrangements and other alterations of their works.

Brussels

1700 ARTICLE 13

(1) *Authors of musical works shall have the exclusive right of authorising: i. the recording of such works by instruments capable of reproducing them mechanically; ii. the public performance by means of such instruments of works thus recorded.*

(2) *Reservations and conditions relating to the application of the rights mentioned in the preceding paragraph may be determined by legislation in each country of the Union, in so far as it may be concerned*: but all such reservations and conditions shall apply only in the countries which have prescribed them and shall not, in any circumstances, be prejudicial to the author's right to obtain *just* remuneration which, in the absence of agreement, shall be fixed by competent authority.

Stockholm

ARTICLE 13

(1) EACH COUNTRY OF THE UNION MAY IMPOSE FOR ITSELF RESERVATIONS AND CONDITIONS ON THE EXCLUSIVE RIGHT GRANTED TO THE AUTHOR OF A MUSICAL WORK AND TO THE AUTHOR OF ANY WORDS, THE RECORDING OF WHICH TOGETHER WITH THE MUSICAL WORK HAS ALREADY BEEN AUTHORISED BY THE LATTER, TO AUTHORISE THE SOUND RECORDING OF THAT MUSICAL WORK, TOGETHER WITH SUCH WORDS, IF ANY: but all such reservations and conditions shall apply only in the countries which have imposed them and shall not, in any circumstances, be prejudicial to the rights of these authors to obtain EQUITABLE

Brussels

ART. 13—*cont.*

(3) *The provisions of paragraph (1) of this Article shall not be retroactive and consequently shall not be applicable in a country of the Union to works which, in that country, may have been lawfully adapted to mechanical instruments before the coming into force of the Convention signed at Berlin on the 13th November 1908, and, in the case of a country having acceded to the Convention since that date or acceding to it in the future, before the date of its accession.*

(4) Recordings made in accordance with paragraphs (*2*) *and* (*3*) of this Article and imported without permission from the parties concerned into a country where they are *not lawfully allowed* shall be liable to seizure.

Stockholm

ART. 13—*cont.*

remuneration which, in the absence of agreement, shall be fixed by competent authority.

(2) RECORDINGS OF MUSICAL WORKS MADE IN A COUNTRY OF THE UNION IN ACCORDANCE WITH ARTICLE 13 (3), OF THE CONVENTION SIGNED AT ROME ON JUNE 2, 1928, AND AT BRUSSELS ON JUNE 26, 1948, MAY BE REPRODUCED IN THAT COUNTRY WITHOUT THE PERMISSION OF THE AUTHOR OF THE MUSICAL WORK UNTIL A DATE TWO YEARS AFTER THAT COUNTRY BECOMES BOUND BY THIS ACT.

(3) Recordings made in accordance with paragraphs (1) and (2) of this Article and imported without permission from the parties concerned into a country where they are TREATED AS INFRINGING RECORDINGS shall be liable to seizure.

Note. Paragraph (1) of the Brussels text has been deleted as unnecessary. The right to authorise the making of records is now contained in Article 9 and the right of authorising public performance by records is absorbed in Article 11.

The new paragraph (1) replaces paragraph (2) of the Brussels text which has been amended to make clear that the compulsory licence may also extend to the words accompanying the music.

Paragraph (3) of the Brussels text contained transitional provisions whereby recordings of certain old works could continue to be made without the author's consent. The new paragraph (2) provides that these provisions shall cease to be effective in a country two years after it becomes bound by the Stockholm Act.

Brussels

1701 ARTICLE 14

(1) Authors of literary, *scientific* or artistic works shall have the exclusive rights of authorising: i. the cinematographic adaptation and reproduction of these works, and the distribution of the works thus adapted or reproduced: ii. the public *presentation and* performance of the works thus adapted or reproduced.

Stockholm

ARTICLE 14

(1) Authors of literary or artistic works shall have the exclusive right of authorising:

(i) the cinematographic adaptation and reproduction of these works, and the distribution of the works thus adapted or reproduced:

(ii) the public performance AND COMMUNICATION TO THE

Brussels

ART. 14—*cont.*

(2) Without prejudice to the rights of the author of the work adapted or reproduced, a cinematographic work shall be protected as an original work.

(3) The adaptation *under* any other artistic form of *cinematographic productions* derived from literary, scientific or artistic works shall, without prejudice to the authorisation of *their authors*, remain subject to the authorisation of the *author* of the original *work*.

(4) *Cinematographic adaptations of literary, scientific or artistic works shall not be subject to the reservations and conditions contained in Article* 13, *paragraph* (2).

(5) *The provisions of this Article shall apply to reproduction or production effected by any other process analogous to cinematography.*

Stockholm

ART. 14—*cont.*

PUBLIC BY WIRE of the works, thus adapted or reproduced.

(2) The adaptation INTO any other artistic form of a CINEMATOGRAPHIC PRODUCTION derived from literary or artistic works shall, without prejudice to the authorisation of THE AUTHOR OF THE CINEMATOGRAPHIC PRODUCTION remain subject to the authorisation of the AUTHORS of the original WORKS.

(3) THE PROVISIONS OF ARTICLE 13 (1), SHALL NOT APPLY.

Note. Paragraph (1) gives authors a new right of authorising the communication to the public by wire of works adapted and reproduced on films. The relaying by wire of a broadcast of a work incorporated in a film is covered by Article 11 *bis*. No change in United Kingdom law is involved.

Paragraph (2) of the Brussels text is now in new Article 14 *bis*.

Brussels

1702

Stockholm

ARTICLE 14 *bis*

(1) WITHOUT PREJUDICE TO THE COPYRIGHT IN ANY WORK WHICH MAY HAVE BEEN ADAPTED OR REPRODUCED, A CINEMATOGRAPHIC WORK SHALL BE PROTECTED AS AN ORIGINAL WORK. THE OWNER OF COPYRIGHT IN A CINEMATOGRAPHIC WORK SHALL ENJOY THE SAME RIGHTS AS THE AUTHOR OF AN ORIGINAL WORK, INCLUDING THE RIGHTS REFERRED TO IN THE PRECEDING ARTICLE.

(2) (a) OWNERSHIP OF COPYRIGHT IN A CINEMATOGRAPHIC WORK SHALL BE A MATTER FOR LEGISLATION IN

Brussels | *Stockholm*

ART. 14 *bis—cont.*

THE COUNTRY WHERE PROTECTION IS CLAIMED.

(b) HOWEVER, IN THE COUNTRIES OF THE UNION WHICH, BY LEGISLATION, INCLUDE AMONG THE OWNERS OF COPYRIGHT IN A CINEMATOGRAPHIC WORK AUTHORS WHO HAVE BROUGHT CONTRIBUTIONS TO THE MAKING OF THE WORK SUCH AUTHORS, IF THEY HAVE UNDERTAKEN TO BRING SUCH CONTRIBUTIONS, MAY NOT, IN THE ABSENCE OF ANY CONTRARY OR SPECIAL STIPULATION, OBJECT TO THE REPRODUCTION, DISTRIBUTION, PUBLIC PERFORMANCE, COMMUNICATION TO THE PUBLIC BY WIRE, BROADCASTING OR ANY OTHER COMMUNICATION TO THE PUBLIC OR TO THE SUBTITLING OR DUBBING OF TEXTS OF THE WORK.

(c) THE QUESTION WHETHER OR NOT THE FORM OF THE UNDERTAKING REFERRED TO ABOVE SHOULD, FOR THE APPLICATION OF THE PRECEDING SUBPARAGRAPH (b), BE IN A WRITTEN AGREEMENT OR A WRITTEN ACT OF THE SAME EFFECT, SHALL BE A MATTER FOR THE LEGISLATION OF THE COUNTRY WHERE THE MAKER OF THE CINEMATOGRAPHIC WORK HAS HIS HEADQUARTERS OR HABITUAL RESIDENCE. HOWEVER, IT SHALL BE A MATTER FOR THE LEGISLATION OF THE COUNTRY OF THE UNION WHERE PROTECTION IS CLAIMED TO PROVIDE THAT THE SAID UNDERTAKING SHALL BE IN A WRITTEN AGREEMENT OR A WRITTEN ACT OF THE SAME EFFECT. THE COUNTRIES WHOSE LEGISLATION SO PROVIDES SHALL NOTIFY THE DIRECTOR GENERAL BY MEANS OF A WRITTEN DECLARATION WHICH WILL BE IMMEDIATELY COMMUNICATED BY HIM TO ALL THE OTHER COUNTRIES OF THE UNION.

(d) BY "CONTRARY OR SPECIAL STIPULATION" IS MEANT ANY RESTRICTIVE CONDITION WHICH IS RELEVANT TO THE AFORESAID UNDERTAKING.

Brussels

Stockholm

ART. 14 *bis—cont.*

(3) UNLESS THE NATIONAL LEGISLATION PROVIDES TO THE CONTRARY, THE PROVISIONS OF PARAGRAPH 2 (b) ABOVE SHALL NOT BE APPLICABLE TO AUTHORS OF SCENARIOS, DIALOGUES AND MUSICAL WORKS CREATED FOR THE MAKING OF THE CINEMATOGRAPHIC WORK, NOR TO THE PRINCIPAL DIRECTOR THEREOF. HOWEVER, THOSE COUNTRIES OF THE UNION, WHOSE LEGISLATION DOES NOT CONTAIN RULES PROVIDING FOR THE APPLICATION OF THE SAID PARAGRAPH (2) (b) TO SUCH DIRECTOR, SHALL NOTIFY THE DIRECTOR GENERAL BY MEANS OF A WRITTEN DECLARATION WHICH WILL BE IMMEDIATELY COMMUNICATED BY HIM TO ALL THE OTHER COUNTRIES OF THE UNION.

Note. The first sentence of new paragraph (1) reproduces Article 14 (2) of the Brussels Act. The second sentence spells out what was implicit in the Brussels Act.

Paragraph (2) in a new provision: (a) leaves countries free to decide who shall own copyright in a film (*e.g.* the maker as in the United Kingdom or those who have contributed to the making of the film as in France), (b) provides that in countries which give copyright in a film to the contributors the latter may not, in the absence of a contrary agreement, object to the exploitation of the film.

Paragraph (3) provides that unless the national legislation of the country provides to the contrary, the presumption introduced by (b) shall not, however, apply to scenario and script writers, composers and film directors.

The changes will have the effect of bringing the continental systems of film copyright more into line with that obtaining in the United Kingdom.

Brussels

1703 ARTICLE 14 *bis*

(1) The author, or after his death the persons or institutions authorised by national legislation, shall, *in* respect *of* original works of art and original manuscripts of writers and composers, enjoy the inalienable right to an interest in any sale of the work subsequent to the first *disposal of the work* by the author.

Stockholm

ARTICLE 14 *ter*

(1) The author, or after his death the persons or institutions authorised by national legislation, shall, WITH respect TO original works of art and original manuscripts of writers and composers, enjoy the inalienable right to an interest in any sale of the work subsequent to the first TRANSFER by the author of the work.

Brussels

ART. 14 *bis—cont.*

(2) The protection provided by the preceding paragraph may be claimed in a country of the Union only if legislation in the country to which the author belongs so permits, and to the *degree* permitted by the country where this protection is claimed.

(3) The procedure for collection and the amounts shall be matters for determination by national legislation.

Stockholm

ART. 14 *ter—cont.*

(2) The protection provided by the preceding paragraph may be claimed in a country of the Union only if legislation in the country to which the author belongs so permits, and to the EXTENT permitted by the country where this protection is claimed.

(3) The procedure for collection and the amounts shall be matters for determination by national legislation.

Note. Apart from drafting changes, this Article corresponds to Article 14 *bis* of the Brussels text.

United Kingdom law does not provide for the right.

Brussels

1704 ARTICLE 15

(1) In order that the author of a literary or artistic work protected by this Convention shall, in the absence of proof to the contrary, be regarded as such, and consequently be entitled to institute infringement proceedings in countries of the Union, it shall be sufficient for his name to appear on the work in the usual manner. This paragraph shall be applicable even if this name is a pseudonym, where the pseudonym adopted by the author leaves no doubt as to his identity.

(2) In the case of anonymous and pseudonymous works, other than those referred to in the *preceding* paragraph, the publisher whose name appears on the work shall, in the absence of proof to the contrary, be *regarded as representing* the author, and in this capacity he shall be entitled to protect and enforce the author's rights. The provisions of this

Stockholm

ARTICLE 15

(1) In order that the author of a literary or artistic work protected by this Convention shall, in the absence of proof to the contrary, be regarded as such, and consequently be entitled to institute infringement proceedings in the countries of the Union, it shall be sufficient for his name to appear on the work in the usual manner. This paragraph shall be applicable even if this name is a pseudonym, where the pseudonym adopted by the author leaves no doubt as to his identity.

(2) THE PERSON OR BODY CORPORATE WHOSE NAME APPEARS ON A CINEMATOGRAPHIC WORK IN THE USUAL MANNER SHALL, IN THE ABSENCE OF PROOF TO THE CONTRARY, BE PRESUMED TO BE THE MAKER OF THE SAID WORK.

(3) In the case of anonymous and pseudonymous works, other than those referred to in paragraph (1) above, the publisher whose name appears on the work shall, in the absence of proof to the contrary, be DEEMED TO REPRESENT the author, and in this capacity he shall be entitled to protect and enforce the author's rights. The provisions of this paragraph shall cease to

Brussels

ART. 15—*cont.*

paragraph shall cease to apply if the author reveals his identity and establishes his claim to authorship of the work.

Stockholm

ART. 15—*cont.*

apply when the author reveals his identity and establishes his claim to authorship of the work.

(4) (a) IN THE CASE OF UNPUBLISHED WORKS WHERE THE IDENTITY OF THE AUTHOR IS UNKNOWN, BUT WHERE THERE IS EVERY GROUND TO PRESUME THAT HE IS A NATIONAL OF A COUNTRY OF THE UNION, IT SHALL BE A MATTER FOR LEGISLATION IN THAT COUNTRY TO DESIGNATE THE COMPETENT AUTHORITY WHO SHALL REPRESENT THE AUTHOR AND SHALL BE ENTITLED TO PROTECT AND ENFORCE HIS RIGHTS IN THE COUNTRIES OF THE UNION.

(b) COUNTRIES OF THE UNION WHICH MAKE SUCH DESIGNATION UNDER THE TERMS OF THIS PROVISION SHALL NOTIFY THE DIRECTOR GENERAL BY MEANS OF A WRITTEN DECLARATION GIVING FULL INFORMATION CONCERNING THE AUTHORITY THUS DESIGNATED. THE DIRECTOR GENERAL SHALL AT ONCE COMMUNICATE THIS DECLARATION TO ALL OTHER COUNTRIES OF THE UNION.

Note. Paragraph (2) is a new provision under which it is presumed that the person named on a film is the maker. This will involve minor amendment of United Kingdom law.

Paragraph (4) is also new. A country may designate a competent authority to represent the author and enforce his rights in other countries in cases where the work is unpublished and the identity of the author unknown but there is every reason to presume that he was a national of that country. This, too, will involve amendment of United Kingdom law to enable such an authority to bring action here.

Brussels

1705 ARTICLE 16

(1) *Works infringing copyright may be seized by the competent authorities of* any country of the Union where the *original* work enjoys legal protection.

(2) *In these countries the seizure* may also apply to reproductions imported from a country where the work is not protected.

Stockholm

ARTICLE 16

(1) INFRINGING COPIES OF A WORK SHALL BE LIABLE TO SEIZURE IN any country of the Union where the work enjoys legal protection.

(2) THE PROVISIONS OF THE PRECEDING PARAGRAPH SHALL also apply to reproductions coming from a country where the work is not protected, or has ceased to be protected.

Brussels

ART. 16—*cont.*

(3) The seizure shall take place in accordance with the legislation of each country.

Stockholm

ART. 16—*cont.*

(3) The seizure shall take place in accordance with the legislation of each country.

Note. Paragraph (1) of the Brussels Act has been re-drafted to reflect more clearly the principles behind the provision, namely that infringing copies are to be seized on the request of the author of the work infringed.

1706

Brussels

ARTICLE 17

The provisions of this Convention cannot in any way affect the right of the Government of each country of the Union to permit, to control, or to prohibit by legislation or regulation, the circulation, presentation, or exhibition of any work or production in regard to which the competent authority may find it necessary to exercise that right.

Stockholm

ARTICLE 17

The provisions of this Convention cannot in any way affect the right of the Government of each country of the Union to permit, to control, or to prohibit by legislation or regulation, the circulation, presentation, or exhibition of any work or production in regard to which the competent authority may find it necessary to exercise that right.

Note. This Article, which is unchanged, deals mainly with powers of censorship. It was agreed at Stockholm that questions of ordre public are always a matter for domestic legislation and that countries are free to enact measures to restrict possible abuses of monopoly.

1707

Brussels

ARTICLE 18

(1) This Convention shall apply to all works which at the moment of its coming into force have not yet fallen into the public domain in the country of origin through the expiry of the term of protection.

(2) If, however, through the expiry of the term of protection which was previously granted, a work has fallen into the public domain of the country where protection is claimed, that work shall not be protected anew.

(3) The application of this principle shall be *in accordance with the* provisions contained in special Conventions to that effect existing or to be concluded between countries of the Union. In the

Stockholm

ARTICLE 18

(1) This Convention shall apply to all works which, at the moment of its coming into force, have not yet fallen into the public domain in the country of origin through the expiry of the term of protection.

(2) If, however, through the expiry of the term of protection which was previously granted, a work has fallen into the public domain of the country where protection is claimed, that work shall not be protected anew.

(3) The application of this principle shall be SUBJECT TO ANY provisions contained in special conventions to that effect existing or to be concluded between countries of the Union. In the absence of

Brussels

ART. 18—*cont.*

absence of such provisions, the respective countries shall determine, each in so far as it is concerned, the *manner in which the said principle is to be applied.*

(4) The *above* provisions shall apply *equally* in the case of new accessions to the Union, and *in the event of protection being extended* by the application of Article 7 or by abandonment of reservations.

Stockholm

ART. 18—*cont.*

such provisions, the respective countries shall determine, each in so far as it is concerned, the CONDITIONS OF APPLICATION OF THIS PRINCIPLE.

(4) The PRECEDING provisions shall ALSO apply in the case of new accessions to the Union and TO CASES IN WHICH PROTECTION IS EXTENDED by the application of Article 7 or by the abandonment of reservations.

1708 ARTICLE 19

Brussels: The provisions of this Convention shall not preclude the making of a claim to the benefit of any *wider provisions* which may be *afforded* by legislation in a country of the Union.

Stockholm: ARTICLE 19

The provisions of this Convention shall not preclude the making of a claim to the benefit of any GREATER PROTECTION which may be GRANTED by legislation in a country of the Union.

1709 ARTICLE 20

Brussels: The Governments of the countries of the Union reserve *to themselves* the right to enter into special *Arrangements between each other*, in so far as such *Arrangements shall confer upon authors* more *extended* rights than those granted by the Convention, or *embody* other provisions not contrary to this Convention. The provisions of existing *Arrangements* which satisfy these conditions shall remain applicable.

Stockholm: ARTICLE 20

The Governments of the countries of the Union reserve the right to enter into special AGREEMENTS AMONG THEMSELVES in so far as such AGREEMENTS GRANT TO authors more EXTENSIVE rights than those granted by the Convention, or CONTAIN other provisions not contrary to this Convention. The provisions of existing AGREEMENTS which satisfy these conditions shall remain applicable.

1710 ARTICLE 21

(1) SPECIAL PROVISIONS REGARDING DEVELOPING COUNTRIES ARE INCLUDED IN A PROTOCOL ENTITLED "PROTOCOL REGARDING DEVELOPING COUNTRIES."

(2) SUBJECT TO THE PROVISIONS OF ARTICLE 28 (1) (b) (i) and (c), THE PROTOCOL REGARDING DEVELOPING COUNTRIES FORMS AN INTEGRAL PART OF THE PRESENT ACT.

Note. This is a new provision, the effect of which is that a country which ratifies or accedes to the Stockholm Act, without excluding the provisions of Articles 1 to 21 from the effect of its ratification or accession, becomes bound by the terms of the Protocol.

Brussels | *Stockholm*

1711

ARTICLE 22

(1) (a) THE UNION SHALL HAVE AN ASSEMBLY CONSISTING OF THOSE COUNTRIES OF THE UNION WHICH ARE BOUND BY ARTICLES 22 TO 26.

(b) THE GOVERNMENT OF EACH COUNTRY SHALL BE REPRESENTED BY ONE DELEGATE, WHO MAY BE ASSISTED BY ALTERNATE DELEGATES, ADVISORS, AND EXPERTS.

(c) THE EXPENSES OF EACH DELEGATION SHALL BE BORNE BY THE GOVERNMENT WHICH HAS APPOINTED IT.

(2) (a) THE ASSEMBLY SHALL:

(i) DEAL WITH ALL MATTERS CONCERNING THE MAINTENANCE AND DEVELOPMENT OF THE UNION AND THE IMPLEMENTATION OF THIS CONVENTION;

(ii) GIVE DIRECTIONS CONCERNING THE PREPARATION FOR CONFERENCES OF REVISION TO THE INTERNATIONAL BUREAU OF INTELLECTUAL PROPERTY (HEREINAFTER DESIGNATED AS " THE INTERNATIONAL BUREAU ") REFERRED TO IN THE CONVENTION ESTABLISHING THE WORLD INTELLECTUAL PROPERTY ORGANISATION (HEREINAFTER DESIGNATED AS " THE ORGANISATION "), DUE ACCOUNT BEING TAKEN OF ANY COMMENTS MADE BY THOSE COUNTRIES OF THE UNION WHICH ARE NOT BOUND BY ARTICLES 22 TO 26.

(iii) REVIEW AND APPROVE THE REPORTS AND ACTIVITIES OF THE DIRECTOR GENERAL OF THE ORGANIZATION CONCERNING THE UNION AND GIVE HIM ALL NECESSARY INSTRUCTIONS CONCERNING MATTERS WITHIN THE COMPETENCE OF THE UNION;

(iv) ELECT THE MEMBERS OF THE EXECUTIVE COMMITTEE OF THE ASSEMBLY;

Brussels	*Stockholm*
	ART. 22—*cont.*
	(v) REVIEW AND APPROVE THE REPORTS AND ACTIVITIES OF ITS EXECUTIVE COMMITTEE, AND GIVE INSTRUCTIONS TO SUCH COMMITTEE;
	(vi) DETERMINE THE PROGRAM AND ADOPT THE TRIENNIAL BUDGET OF THE UNION, AND APPROVE ITS FINAL ACCOUNTS;
	(vii) ADOPT THE FINANCIAL REGULATIONS OF THE UNION;
	(viii) ESTABLISH SUCH COMMITTEES OF EXPERTS AND WORKING GROUPS AS MAY BE NECESSARY FOR THE WORK OF THE UNION;
	(ix) DETERMINE WHICH COUNTRIES NOT MEMBERS OF THE UNION AND WHICH INTERGOVERNMENTAL AND INTERNATIONAL NON-GOVERNMENT ORGANISATIONS SHALL BE ADMITTED TO ITS MEETINGS AS OBSERVERS;
	(x) ADOPT AMENDMENTS TO ARTICLES 22 TO 26;
	(xi) TAKE ANY OTHER APPROPRIATE ACTION DESIGNED TO FURTHER THE OBJECTIVES OF THE UNION;
	(xii) EXERCISE SUCH OTHER FUNCTIONS AS ARE APPROPRIATE UNDER THIS CONVENTION;
	(xiii) SUBJECT TO ITS ACCEPTANCE, EXERCISE SUCH RIGHTS AS ARE GIVEN TO IT IN THE CONVENTION ESTABLISHING THE ORGANISATION.
	(b) WITH RESPECT TO MATTERS WHICH ARE OF INTEREST ALSO TO OTHER UNIONS ADMINISTERED BY THE ORGANISATION, THE ASSEMBLY SHALL MAKE ITS DECISIONS AFTER HAVING HEARD THE ADVICE OF THE CO-ORDINATION COMMITTEE OF THE ORGANISATION.
	(3) (a) EACH COUNTRY MEMBER OF THE ASSEMBLY SHALL HAVE ONE VOTE.

Brussels	*Stockholm*
	ART. 22—*cont.*

(b) ONE-HALF OF THE COUNTRIES MEMBERS OF THE ASSEMBLY SHALL CONSTITUTE A QUORUM.

(c) NOTWITHSTANDING THE PROVISIONS OF SUBPARAGRAPH (b), IF, IN ANY SESSION, THE NUMBER OF COUNTRIES REPRESENTED IS LESS THAN ONE-HALF BUT EQUAL TO OR MORE THAN ONE-THIRD OF THE COUNTRIES MEMBERS OF THE ASSEMBLY, THE ASSEMBLY MAY MAKE DECISIONS BUT, WITH THE EXCEPTION OF DECISIONS CONCERNING ITS OWN PROCEDURE, ALL SUCH DECISIONS SHALL TAKE EFFECT ONLY IF THE FOLLOWING CONDITIONS ARE FULFILLED. THE INTERNATIONAL BUREAU SHALL COMMUNICATE THE SAID DECISIONS TO THE COUNTRIES MEMBERS OF THE ASSEMBLY WHICH WERE NOT REPRESENTED AND SHALL INVITE THEM TO EXPRESS IN WRITING THEIR VOTE OR ABSTENTION WITHIN A PERIOD OF THREE MONTHS FROM THE DATE OF THE COMMUNICATION. IF, AT THE EXPIRATION OF THIS PERIOD, THE NUMBER OF COUNTRIES HAVING THUS EXPRESSED THEIR VOTE OR ABSTENTION ATTAINS THE NUMBER OF COUNTRIES WHICH WAS LACKING FOR ATTAINING THE QUORUM IN THE SESSION ITSELF, SUCH DECISIONS SHALL TAKE EFFECT PROVIDED THAT AT THE SAME TIME THE REQUIRED MAJORITY STILL OBTAINS.

(d) SUBJECT TO THE PROVISIONS OF ARTICLE 26 (2), THE DECISIONS OF THE ASSEMBLY SHALL REQUIRE TWO-THIRDS OF THE VOTES CAST.

(e) ABSTENTIONS SHALL NOT BE CONSIDERED AS VOTES.

(f) A DELEGATE MAY REPRESENT, AND VOTE IN THE NAME OF, ONE COUNTRY ONLY.

(g) COUNTRIES OF THE UNION NOT MEMBERS OF THE ASSEMBLY SHALL BE ADMITTED TO ITS MEETINGS AS OBSERVERS.

(4) (a) THE ASSEMBLY SHALL MEET ONCE IN EVERY THIRD CALENDAR

Brussels | *Stockholm*

ART. 22—*cont.*

YEAR IN ORDINARY SESSION UPON CONVOCATION BY THE DIRECTOR GENERAL AND, IN THE ABSENCE OF EXCEPTIONAL CIRCUMSTANCES, DURING THE SAME PERIOD AND AT THE SAME PLACE AS THE GENERAL ASSEMBLY OF THE ORGANISATION.

(b) THE ASSEMBLY SHALL MEET IN EXTRAORDINARY SESSION UPON CONVOCATION BY THE DIRECTOR GENERAL, AT THE REQUEST OF THE EXECUTIVE COMMITTEE OR AT THE REQUEST OF ONE-FOURTH OF THE COUNTRIES MEMBERS OF THE ASSEMBLY.

(5) THE ASSEMBLY SHALL ADOPT ITS OWN RULES OF PROCEDURE.

Note. This is a new provision. Its main effect is to shift responsibility for the Berne Union from the Swiss Government to the member States acting together in an Assembly. This will meet every three years to decide the programme and budget for the next three years and to take any other decision concerning matters within the competence of the Berne Union, except for revision of the substantive clauses of the Convention. The Assembly also has a voice in the affairs of the new organisation (the World Intellectual Property Organisation) *e.g.* the appointment of the Director General requires a majority vote in the Assembly of the Berne Union.

Brussels | *Stockholm*

1712 ARTICLE 23

(1) THE ASSEMBLY SHALL HAVE AN EXECUTIVE COMMITTEE.

(2) (a) THE EXECUTIVE COMMITTEE SHALL CONSIST OF COUNTRIES ELECTED BY THE ASSEMBLY FROM AMONG COUNTRIES MEMBERS OF THE ASSEMBLY. FURTHERMORE, THE COUNTRY ON WHOSE TERRITORY THE ORGANISATION HAS ITS HEADQUARTERS SHALL, SUBJECT TO THE PROVISIONS OF ARTICLE 25 (7) (b), HAVE AN EX OFFICIO SEAT ON THE COMMITTEE.

(b) THE GOVERNMENT OF EACH COUNTRY MEMBER OF THE EXECUTIVE COMMITTEE SHALL BE REPRESENTED BY ONE DELEGATE, WHO MAY BE ASSISTED BY ALTERNATE DELEGATES, ADVISORS, AND EXPERTS.

Brussels | *Stockholm*

ART. 23—*cont.*

(c) THE EXPENSES OF EACH DELEGATION SHALL BE BORNE BY THE GOVERNMENT WHICH HAS APPOINTED IT.

(3) THE NUMBER OF COUNTRIES MEMBERS OF THE EXECUTIVE COMMITTEE SHALL CORRESPOND TO ONE-FOURTH OF THE NUMBER OF COUNTRIES MEMBERS OF THE ASSEMBLY. IN ESTABLISHING THE NUMBER OF SEATS TO BE FILLED, REMAINDERS AFTER DIVISION BY FOUR SHALL BE DISREGARDED.

(4) IN ELECTING THE MEMBERS OF THE EXECUTIVE COMMITTEE, THE ASSEMBLY SHALL HAVE DUE REGARD TO AN EQUITABLE GEOGRAPHICAL DISTRIBUTION AND TO THE NEED FOR COUNTRIES PARTY TO THE SPECIAL AGREEMENTS WHICH MIGHT BE ESTABLISHED IN RELATION WITH THE UNION TO BE AMONG THE COUNTRIES CONSTITUTING THE EXECUTIVE COMMITTEE.

(5) (a) EACH MEMBER OF THE EXECUTIVE COMMITTEE SHALL SERVE FROM THE CLOSE OF THE SESSION OF THE ASSEMBLY WHICH ELECTED IT TO THE CLOSE OF THE NEXT ORDINARY SESSION OF THE ASSEMBLY.

(b) MEMBERS OF THE EXECUTIVE COMMITTEE MAY BE RE-ELECTED, BUT NOT MORE THAN TWO-THIRDS OF THEM.

(c) THE ASSEMBLY SHALL ESTABLISH THE DETAILS OF THE RULES GOVERNING THE ELECTION AND POSSIBLE RE-ELECTION OF THE MEMBERS OF THE EXECUTIVE COMMITTEE.

(6) (a) THE EXECUTIVE COMMITTEE SHALL:

(i) PREPARE THE DRAFT AGENDA OF THE ASSEMBLY;

(ii) SUBMIT PROPOSALS TO THE ASSEMBLY RESPECTING THE DRAFT PROGRAM AND TRIENNIAL BUDGET OF THE UNION, PREPARED BY THE DIRECTOR GENERAL;

Brussels

Stockholm

ART. 23—*cont.*

(iii) APPROVE, WITHIN THE LIMITS OF THE PROGRAM AND THE TRIENNIAL BUDGET, THE SPECIFIC YEARLY BUDGETS AND PROGRAMS PREPARED BY THE DIRECTOR GENERAL;

(iv) SUBMIT, WITH APPROPRIATE COMMENTS, TO THE ASSEMBLY THE PERIODICAL REPORTS OF THE DIRECTOR GENERAL AND THE YEARLY AUDIT REPORTS ON THE ACCOUNTS;

(v) IN ACCORDANCE WITH THE DECISIONS OF THE ASSEMBLY AND HAVING REGARD TO CIRCUMSTANCES ARISING BETWEEN TWO ORDINARY SESSIONS OF THE ASSEMBLY, TAKE ALL NECESSARY MEASURES TO ENSURE THE EXECUTION OF THE PROGRAM OF THE UNION BY THE DIRECTOR GENERAL;

(vi) PERFORM SUCH OTHER FUNCTIONS AS ARE ALLOCATED TO IT UNDER THIS CONVENTION.

(b) WITH RESPECT TO MATTERS WHICH ARE OF INTEREST ALSO TO OTHER UNIONS ADMINISTERED BY THE ORGANIZATION, THE EXECUTIVE COMMITTEE SHALL MAKE ITS DECISIONS AFTER HAVING HEARD THE ADVICE OF THE COORDINATION COMMITTEE OF THE ORGANIZATION.

(7) (a) THE EXECUTIVE COMMITTEE SHALL MEET ONCE A YEAR IN ORDINARY SESSION UPON CONVOCATION BY THE DIRECTOR GENERAL, PREFERABLY DURING THE SAME PERIOD AND AT THE SAME PLACE AS THE COORDINATION COMMITTEE OF THE ORGANIZATION.

(b) THE EXECUTIVE COMMITTEE SHALL MEET IN EXTRAORDINARY SESSION UPON CONVOCATION BY THE DIRECTOR GENERAL, EITHER ON HIS OWN INITIATIVE, OR AT THE REQUEST OF ITS CHAIRMAN OR ONE-FOURTH OF ITS MEMBERS.

(8) (a) EACH COUNTRY MEMBER OF THE EXECUTIVE COMMITTEE SHALL HAVE ONE VOTE.

Brussels | *Stockholm*

Stockholm

ART. 23—*cont.*

(b) ONE-HALF OF THE MEMBERS OF THE EXECUTIVE COMMITTEE SHALL CONSTITUTE A QUORUM.

(c) DECISIONS SHALL BE MADE BY A SIMPLE MAJORITY OF THE VOTES CAST.

(d) ABSTENTIONS SHALL NOT BE CONSIDERED AS VOTES.

(e) A DELEGATE MAY REPRESENT, AND VOTE IN THE NAME OF, ONE COUNTRY ONLY.

(9) COUNTRIES OF THE UNION NOT MEMBERS OF THE EXECUTIVE COMMITTEE SHALL BE ADMITTED TO ITS MEETINGS AS OBSERVERS.

(10) THE EXECUTIVE COMMITTEE SHALL ADOPT ITS OWN RULES OF PROCEDURE.

Note. This Article sets up an Executive Committee, the members of which are elected by the Assembly. This Committee is to meet annually mainly for the purpose of ensuring that the programme laid down by the Assembly is carried out within the budgetary limits. It will also play a significant part in the activities of the new Organisation.

The Executive Committee replaces the Permanent Committee of the Berne Union, which was established by resolution at the Brussels Conference, and has wider powers.

1713

Brussels

ARTICLE 21

(1) *The International Office established under the name of the "Office of the International Union for the Protection of Literary and Artistic Works" shall be maintained.*

(2) *That Office shall be placed under the high authority of the Government of the Swiss Con-*

Stockholm

ARTICLE 24

(1) (a) THE ADMINISTRATIVE TASKS WITH RESPECT TO THE UNION SHALL BE PERFORMED BY THE INTERNATIONAL BUREAU, WHICH IS A CONTINUATION OF THE BUREAU OF THE UNION UNITED WITH THE BUREAU OF THE UNION ESTABLISHED BY THE INTERNATIONAL CONVENTION FOR THE PROTECTION OF INDUSTRIAL PROPERTY.

(b) IN PARTICULAR, THE INTERNATIONAL BUREAU SHALL PROVIDE THE SECRETARIAT OF THE VARIOUS ORGANS OF THE UNION.

(c) THE DIRECTOR GENERAL OF THE ORGANIZATION SHALL BE THE CHIEF EXECUTIVE OF THE UNION AND SHALL REPRESENT THE UNION.

Brussels

ART. 21—*cont.*

federation, which shall regulate its Organization and supervise its working.

(3) *The Official language of the Office shall be the French language.*

ARTICLE 22

(1) *The International Office shall collect information of every kind relating to the protection of the rights of authors over their literary and artistic works. It shall coordinate and publish such information.*

It shall undertake the study of questions of general interest to the Union, and, by the aid of documents placed at its disposal by the different Administrations, it shall edit a periodical publication in the French language on questions which concern the purpose of the Union. The Governments of the countries of the Union reserve to themselves the power to authorise by agreement the publication by the Office of an edition in one or more other languages if, by experience, this should be shown to be necessary.

(2) *The International Office shall always place itself at the disposal of members of the Union in order to provide them with any special information which they may require relating to the protection of literary and artistic works.*

Stockholm

ART. 24—*cont.*

(2) THE INTERNATIONAL BUREAU SHALL ASSEMBLE AND PUBLISH INFORMATION CONCERNING THE PROTECTION OF COPYRIGHT. EACH COUNTRY OF THE UNION SHALL PROMPTLY COMMUNICATE TO THE INTERNATIONAL BUREAU ALL NEW LAWS AND OFFICIAL TEXTS CONCERNING THE PROTECTION OF COPYRIGHT.

(3) THE INTERNATIONAL BUREAU SHALL PUBLISH A MONTHLY PERIODICAL.

(4) THE INTERNATIONAL BUREAU SHALL, ON REQUEST, FURNISH INFORMATION TO ANY COUNTRY OF THE UNION ON MATTERS CONCERNING THE PROTECTION OF COPYRIGHT.

(5) THE INTERNATIONAL BUREAU SHALL CONDUCT STUDIES, AND SHALL PROVIDE SERVICES, DESIGNED TO FACILITATE THE PROTECTION OF COPYRIGHT.

(6) THE DIRECTOR GENERAL AND ANY STAFF MEMBER DESIGNATED BY HIM SHALL PARTICIPATE, WITHOUT THE RIGHT TO VOTE, IN ALL MEETINGS OF THE ASSEMBLY, THE EXECUTIVE COMMITTEE, AND ANY OTHER

Brussels

ART. 22—*cont.*

(3) *The Director of the International Office shall make an annual report on his administration, which shall be communicated to all the members of the Union.*

Stockholm

ART. 24—*cont.*

COMMITTEE OF EXPERTS OR WORKING GROUP. THE DIRECTOR GENERAL OR A STAFF MEMBER DESIGNATED BY HIM, SHALL BE EX OFFICIO SECRETARY OF THESE BODIES.

(7) (a) THE INTERNATIONAL BUREAU SHALL, IN ACCORDANCE WITH THE DIRECTIONS OF THE ASSEMBLY AND IN COOPERATION WITH THE EXECUTIVE COMMITTEE, MAKE THE PREPARATIONS FOR THE CONFERENCES OF REVISION OF THE PROVISIONS OF THE CONVENTION OTHER THAN ARTICLES 22 TO 26.

(b) THE INTERNATIONAL BUREAU MAY CONSULT WITH INTERGOVERNMENTAL AND INTERNATIONAL NON-GOVERNMENTAL ORGANIZATIONS CONCERNING PREPARATIONS FOR CONFERENCES OF REVISION.

(c) THE DIRECTOR GENERAL AND PERSONS DESIGNATED BY HIM SHALL TAKE PART, WITHOUT THE RIGHT TO VOTE, IN THE DISCUSSIONS AT THESE CONFERENCES.

(8) THE INTERNATIONAL BUREAU SHALL CARRY OUT ANY OTHER TASKS ASSIGNED TO IT.

Note. The existing Bureau of the Union (under the new title of the International Bureau) is to form one of the organs of the new World Intellectual Property Organisation and is to continue to act as the Secretariat of the Berne Union.

Brussels

1714 ARTICLE 23

(1) *The expenses of the Office of the International Union shall be shared by the countries of the Union. Until a fresh arrangement is made, they shall not exceed the amount of one hundred and twenty thousand gold francs a year. This amount may be increased, if necessary, by unanimous decision of the*

Stockholm

ARTICLE 25

(1) (a) THE UNION SHALL HAVE A BUDGET.

(b) THE BUDGET OF THE UNION SHALL INCLUDE THE INCOME AND EXPENSES PROPER TO THE UNION, ITS CONTRIBUTION TO THE BUDGET OF EXPENSES COMMON TO THE UNIONS, AND, WHERE APPLICABLE, THE SUM MADE AVAILABLE TO THE

Brussels

ART. 23—*cont.*

countries of the Union or of one of the Conferences provided for in Article 24.

(2) *The Share of the total expense to be paid by each country shall be determined by the division of the countries of the Union and those subsequently acceding to the Union into six classes, each of which shall contribute in the proportion of a certain number of units, viz.:*

1st Class	*25 units*
2nd „	*20 „*
3rd „	*15 „*
4th „	*10 „*
5th „	*5 „*
6th „	*3 „*

Stockholm

ART. 25—*cont.*

BUDGET OF THE CONFERENCE OF THE ORGANIZATION.

(c) EXPENSES NOT ATTRIBUTABLE EXCLUSIVELY TO THE UNION BUT ALSO TO ONE OR MORE OTHER UNIONS ADMINISTERED BY THE ORGANIZATION SHALL BE CONSIDERED AS EXPENSES COMMON TO THE UNIONS. THE SHARE OF THE UNION IN SUCH COMMON EXPENSES SHALL BE IN PROPORTION TO THE INTEREST THE UNION HAS IN THEM.

(2) THE BUDGET OF THE UNION SHALL BE ESTABLISHED WITH DUE REGARD TO THE REQUIREMENTS OF COORDINATION WITH THE BUDGETS OF THE OTHER UNIONS ADMINISTERED BY THE ORGANIZATION.

(3) THE BUDGET OF THE UNION SHALL BE FINANCED FROM THE FOLLOWING SOURCES:

(i) CONTRIBUTIONS OF THE COUNTRIES OF THE UNION;

(ii) FEES AND CHARGES DUE FOR SERVICES PERFORMED BY THE INTERNATIONAL BUREAU IN RELATION TO THE UNION;

(iii) SALE OF, OR ROYALTIES ON, THE PUBLICATIONS OF THE INTERNATIONAL BUREAU CONCERNING THE UNION;

(iv) GIFTS, BEQUESTS, AND SUBVENTIONS;

(v) RENTS, INTERESTS, AND OTHER MISCELLANEOUS INCOME.

(4) (a) FOR THE PURPOSE OF ESTABLISHING ITS CONTRIBUTION TOWARDS THE BUDGET, EACH COUNTRY OF THE UNION SHALL BELONG TO A CLASS, AND SHALL PAY ITS ANNUAL CONTRIBUTIONS ON THE BASIS OF A NUMBER OF UNITS FIXED AS FOLLOWS:

Class I	25
Class II	20
Class III	15
Class IV	10
Class V	5
Class VI	3
Class VII	1

Brussels

ART. 23—*cont.*

(3) *These coefficients shall be multiplied by the number of countries of each class, and the total product thus obtained will give the number of units by which the total expense is to be divided. The quotient will give the amount of the unit of expense.*

(4) *Each country shall declare, at the time of its accession, in which of the said classes it desires to be placed, but it may subsequently declare that it wishes to be placed in another class.*

Stockholm

ART. 25—*cont.*

(b) UNLESS IT HAS ALREADY DONE SO, EACH COUNTRY SHALL INDICATE, CONCURRENTLY WITH DEPOSITING ITS INSTRUMENT OF RATIFICATION OR ACCESSION, THE CLASS TO WHICH IT WISHES TO BELONG. ANY COUNTRY MAY CHANGE CLASS. IF IT CHOOSES A LOWER CLASS, THE COUNTRY MUST ANNOUNCE IT TO THE ASSEMBLY AT ONE OF ITS ORDINARY SESSIONS. ANY SUCH CHANGE SHALL TAKE EFFECT AT THE BEGINNING OF THE CALENDAR YEAR FOLLOWING THE SESSION.

(c) THE ANNUAL CONTRIBUTION OF EACH COUNTRY SHALL BE AN AMOUNT IN THE SAME PROPORTION TO THE TOTAL SUM TO BE CONTRIBUTED TO THE ANNUAL BUDGET OF THE UNION BY ALL COUNTRIES AS THE NUMBER OF ITS UNITS IS TO THE TOTAL OF THE UNITS OF ALL CONTRIBUTING COUNTRIES.

(d) CONTRIBUTIONS SHALL BECOME DUE ON THE FIRST OF JANUARY OF EACH YEAR.

(e) A COUNTRY WHICH IS IN ARREARS IN THE PAYMENT OF ITS CONTRIBUTIONS SHALL HAVE NO VOTE IN ANY OF THE ORGANS OF THE UNION OF WHICH IT IS A MEMBER IF THE AMOUNT OF ITS ARREARS EQUALS OR EXCEEDS THE AMOUNT OF THE CONTRIBUTIONS DUE FROM IT FOR THE PRECEDING TWO FULL YEARS. HOWEVER, ANY ORGAN OF THE UNION MAY ALLOW SUCH A COUNTRY TO CONTINUE TO EXERCISE ITS VOTE IN THAT ORGAN IF, AND AS LONG AS, IT IS SATISFIED THAT THE DELAY IN PAYMENT IS DUE TO EXCEPTIONAL AND UNAVOIDABLE CIRCUMSTANCES.

(f) IF THE BUDGET IS NOT ADOPTED BEFORE THE BEGINNING OF A NEW FINANCIAL PERIOD, IT SHALL BE AT THE SAME LEVEL AS THE BUDGET OF THE PREVIOUS YEAR, IN ACCORDANCE WITH THE FINANCIAL REGULATIONS.

Brussels

ART. 23—*cont.*

Stockholm

ART. 25—*cont.*

(5) THE AMOUNT OF THE FEES AND CHARGES DUE FOR SERVICES RENDERED BY THE INTERNATIONAL BUREAU IN RELATION TO THE UNION SHALL BE ESTABLISHED, AND SHALL BE REPORTED TO THE ASSEMBLY AND THE EXECUTIVE COMMITTEE, BY THE DIRECTOR GENERAL.

(6) (a) THE UNION SHALL HAVE A WORKING CAPITAL FUND WHICH SHALL BE CONSTITUTED BY A SINGLE PAYMENT MADE BY EACH COUNTRY OF THE UNION. IF THE FUND BECOMES INSUFFICIENT, AN INCREASE SHALL BE DECIDED BY THE ASSEMBLY.

(b) THE AMOUNT OF THE INITIAL PAYMENT OF EACH COUNTRY TO THE SAID FUND OR OF ITS PARTICIPATION IN THE INCREASE THEREOF SHALL BE A PROPORTION OF THE CONTRIBUTION OF THAT COUNTRY FOR THE YEAR IN WHICH THE FUND IS ESTABLISHED OR THE INCREASE DECIDED.

(c) THE PROPORTION AND THE TERMS OF PAYMENT SHALL BE FIXED BY THE ASSEMBLY ON THE PROPOSAL OF THE DIRECTOR GENERAL AND AFTER IT HAS HEARD THE ADVICE OF THE COORDINATION COMMITTEE OF THE ORGANIZATION.

(7) (a) IN THE HEADQUARTERS AGREEMENT CONCLUDED WITH THE COUNTRY ON THE TERRITORY OF WHICH THE ORGANIZATION HAS ITS HEADQUARTERS, IT SHALL BE PROVIDED THAT, WHENEVER THE WORKING CAPITAL FUND IS INSUFFICIENT, SUCH COUNTRY SHALL GRANT ADVANCES. THE AMOUNT OF THESE ADVANCES AND THE CONDITIONS ON WHICH THEY ARE GRANTED SHALL BE THE SUBJECT OF SEPARATE AGREEMENTS, IN EACH CASE, BETWEEN SUCH COUNTRY AND THE ORGANIZATION. AS LONG AS IT REMAINS UNDER THE OBLIGATION TO GRANT ADVANCES, SUCH COUNTRY SHALL HAVE AN EX OFFICIO SEAT ON THE EXECUTIVE COMMITTEE.

Brussels

ART. 23—*cont.*

(5) *The Swiss Administration shall prepare the budget of the office, supervise its expenditure, make the necessary advances, and draw up the annual account, which shall be communicated to all the other Administrations.*

Stockholm

ART. 25—*cont.*

(b) THE COUNTRY REFERRED TO IN SUBPARAGRAPH (a) AND THE ORGANIZATION SHALL EACH HAVE THE RIGHT TO DENOUNCE THE OBLIGATION TO GRANT ADVANCES, BY WRITTEN NOTIFICATION. DENUNCIATION SHALL TAKE EFFECT THREE YEARS AFTER THE END OF THE YEAR IN WHICH IT HAS BEEN NOTIFIED.

(8) THE AUDITING OF THE ACCOUNTS SHALL BE EFFECTED BY ONE OR MORE OF THE COUNTRIES OF THE UNION OR BY EXTERNAL AUDITORS, AS PROVIDED IN THE FINANCIAL REGULATIONS. THEY SHALL BE DESIGNATED, WITH THEIR AGREEMENT, BY THE ASSEMBLY.

Note. The financial arrangements of the Berne Union have been substantially changed. The permissible maximum expenditure, instead of being written into the Convention and so requiring unanimity to change it, is in future to be decided by the Assembly, which also takes over the responsibility of the Swiss Government specified in Article 23 (5) of the Brussels text. An additional Class for contribution purposes has been introduced and a working capital fund established.

Brussels

1715

Stockholm

ARTICLE 26

(1) PROPOSALS FOR THE AMENDMENTS OF ARTICLES 22, 23, 24, 25, AND THE PRESENT ARTICLE, MAY BE INITIATED BY ANY COUNTRY MEMBER OF THE ASSEMBLY, BY THE EXECUTIVE COMMITTEE, OR BY THE DIRECTOR GENERAL. SUCH PROPOSALS SHALL BE COMMUNICATED BY THE DIRECTOR GENERAL TO THE MEMBER COUNTRIES OF THE ASSEMBLY AT LEAST SIX MONTHS IN ADVANCE OF THEIR CONSIDERATION.

(2) AMENDMENTS TO THE ARTICLES REFERRED TO IN PARAGRAPH (1) SHALL BE ADOPTED BY THE ASSEMBLY. ADOPTION SHALL REQUIRE

Brussels

Stockholm

ART. 26—*cont.*

THREE-FOURTHS OF THE VOTES CAST, PROVIDED THAT ANY AMENDMENT OF ARTICLE 22, AND OF THE PRESENT PARAGRAPH, SHALL REQUIRE FOUR-FIFTHS OF THE VOTES CAST.

(3) ANY AMENDMENT TO THE ARTICLES REFERRED TO IN PARAGRAPH (1) SHALL ENTER INTO FORCE ONE MONTH AFTER WRITTEN NOTIFICATIONS OF ACCEPTANCE, EFFECTED IN ACCORDANCE WITH THEIR RESPECTIVE CONSTITUTIONAL PROCESSES, HAVE BEEN RECEIVED BY THE DIRECTOR GENERAL FROM THREE-FOURTHS OF THE COUNTRIES MEMBERS OF THE ASSEMBLY AT THE TIME IT ADOPTED THE AMENDMENT. ANY AMENDMENT TO THE SAID ARTICLES THUS ACCEPTED SHALL BIND ALL THE COUNTRIES WHICH ARE MEMBERS OF THE ASSEMBLY AT THE TIME THE AMENDMENT ENTERS INTO FORCE, OR WHICH BECOME MEMBERS THEREOF AT A SUBSEQUENT DATE, PROVIDED THAT ANY AMENDMENT INCREASING THE FINANCIAL OBLIGATIONS OF COUNTRIES OF THE UNION SHALL BIND ONLY THOSE COUNTRIES WHICH HAVE NOTIFIED THEIR ACCEPTANCE OF SUCH AMENDMENT.

1716 ARTICLE 24

(1) *This Convention may be submitted to revision for the purpose of introducing improvements intended to perfect the system of the Union.*

(2) *Questions of this kind, as well as those which in other respects concern the development of the Union, shall be considered in Conferences to be held successively in the countries of the Union by delegates of the said countries. The Administration of the country where a Conference is to meet shall, with the assistance of the International Office, prepare the programme of the Conference. The Director of the Office shall attend the sessions of the*

ARTICLE 27

(1) THIS CONVENTION SHALL BE SUBMITTED TO REVISION WITH A VIEW TO THE INTRODUCTION OF AMENDMENTS DESIGNED TO IMPROVE THE SYSTEM OF THE UNION.

(2) FOR THIS PURPOSE, CONFERENCES SHALL BE HELD SUCCESSIVELY IN ONE OF THE COUNTRIES OF THE UNION AMONG THE DELEGATES OF THE SAID COUNTRIES.

Brussels

ART. 24—*cont.*

Conferences, and may take part in the discussions, but without the right to vote.

(3) *No alteration in this Convention shall be binding on the Union except by the unanimous consent of the countries composing it.*

Stockholm

ART. 27—*cont.*

(3) SUBJECT TO THE PROVISIONS OF ARTICLE 26 WHICH APPLY TO THE AMENDMENT OF ARTICLES 22 TO 26, ANY REVISION OF THIS CONVENTION, INCLUDING THE PROTOCOL REGARDING DEVELOPING COUNTRIES, SHALL REQUIRE THE UNANIMITY OF THE VOTES CAST.

Note. A distinction has now been made between revision of the substantive clauses and amendment of the administrative clauses (*i.e.* Articles 22–26). Revision of the former is to continue to be a matter for Diplomatic Conferences and to require unanimity. In order that amendments dealing with administrative matters may be handled more easily and quickly, such amendments are to be decided by the Assembly.

Brussels

1717 ARTICLE 25

(1) *Countries outside the Union which make provision for the legal protection of the rights forming the object of this Convention may accede thereto upon request.*

(2) *Such accession shall be notified in writing to the Government of the Swiss Confederation, who shall communicate it to all the other countries of the Union.*

(3) *Such accession shall imply full acceptance of all the clauses and admission to all the advantages provided by this Convention, and shall take effect one month after the date of the notification made by the Government of the Swiss Confederation to the other countries of the Union, unless some later date has been indicated by the acceding country. It may, nevertheless, contain an indication that the acceding country wishes to substitute, provisionally at least, for Article* 8, *which relates to translations, the provisions of Article* 5 *of the Convention of* 1886 *revised at Paris in* 1896, *on*

Stockholm

ARTICLE 28

(1) (a) ANY COUNTRY OF THE UNION WHICH HAS SIGNED THIS ACT MAY RATIFY IT, AND, IF IT HAS NOT SIGNED IT, MAY ACCEDE TO IT. INSTRUMENTS OF RATIFICATION AND ACCESSION SHALL BE DEPOSITED WITH THE DIRECTOR GENERAL.

(b) ANY COUNTRY OF THE UNION MAY DECLARE IN ITS INSTRUMENT OF RATIFICATION OR ACCESSION THAT ITS RATIFICATION OR ACCESSION SHALL NOT APPLY:

(i) TO ARTICLES 1 TO 21 AND THE PROTOCOL REGARDING DEVELOPING COUNTRIES, OR

(ii) TO ARTICLES 22 TO 26.

(c) IF A COUNTRY OF THE UNION HAS ALREADY SEPARATELY ACCEPTED THE PROTOCOL REGARDING DEVELOPING COUNTRIES IN ACCORDANCE WITH ARTICLE 5 OF SUCH PROTOCOL, ITS DECLARATION UNDER ITEM (i) OF THE PRECEDING SUBPARAGRAPH MAY RELATE ONLY TO ARTICLES 1 TO 20.

(d) ANY COUNTRY OF THE UNION WHICH IN ACCORDANCE WITH SUBPARAGRAPHS (b) AND (c), HAS EXCLUDED FROM THE EFFECTS OF ITS RATIFICATION OR ACCESSION ONE OF

Brussels

ART. 25—*cont.*

the understanding that those provisions shall apply only to translations into the language or languages of that country.

Stockholm

ART. 28—*cont.*

THE TWO GROUPS OF PROVISIONS REFERRED TO IN THOSE SUBPARAGRAPHS MAY AT ANY LATER TIME DECLARE THAT IT EXTENDS THE EFFECTS OF ITS RATIFICATION OR ACCESSION TO THAT GROUP OF PROVISIONS. SUCH DECLARATION SHALL BE DEPOSITED WITH THE DIRECTOR GENERAL.

(2) (a) SUBJECT TO THE PROVISIONS OF ARTICLE 5 OF THE PROTOCOL REGARDING DEVELOPING COUNTRIES, ARTICLES 1 TO 21 AND THE SAID PROTOCOL SHALL ENTER INTO FORCE WITH RESPECT TO THE FIRST FIVE COUNTRIES OF THE UNION WHICH HAVE DEPOSITED INSTRUMENTS OF RATIFICATION OR ACCESSION WITHOUT MAKING THE DECLARATION PERMITTED BY PARAGRAPH (1) (b) (i), THREE MONTHS AFTER THE DEPOSIT OF THE FIFTH SUCH INSTRUMENT OF RATIFICATION OR ACCESSION.

(b) ARTICLES 22 TO 26 SHALL ENTER INTO FORCE, WITH RESPECT TO THE FIRST SEVEN COUNTRIES OF THE UNION WHICH HAVE DEPOSITED INSTRUMENTS OF RATIFICATION OR ACCESSION WITHOUT MAKING THE DECLARATION PERMITTED BY PARAGRAPH (1) (b) (ii), THREE MONTHS AFTER THE DEPOSIT OF THE SEVENTH SUCH INSTRUMENT OF RATIFICATION OR ACCESSION.

(c) SUBJECT TO THE INITIAL ENTRY INTO FORCE, PURSUANT TO THE PROVISIONS OF SUBPARAGRAPHS (a) AND (b), OF EACH OF THE TWO GROUPS OF PROVISIONS REFERRED TO IN PARAGRAPH (1) (b) (i) AND (ii), AND SUBJECT TO THE PROVISIONS OF PARAGRAPH (1) (b), ARTICLES 1 TO 26 AND THE PROTOCOL REGARDING DEVELOPING COUNTRIES SHALL, WITH RESPECT TO ANY COUNTRY OF THE UNION, OTHER THAN THOSE REFERRED TO IN SUBPARAGRAPHS (a) AND (b), WHICH DEPOSITS AN INSTRUMENT OF RATIFICATION OR ACCESSION OR ANY COUNTRY OF THE

Brussels

Art. 25—*cont.*

Stockholm

Art. 28—*cont.*

UNION WHICH DEPOSITS A DECLARATION PURSUANT TO PARAGRAPH (1) (d), ENTER INTO FORCE THREE MONTHS AFTER THE DATE OF NOTIFICATION BY THE DIRECTOR GENERAL OF SUCH DEPOSIT, UNLESS A SUBSEQUENT DATE HAS BEEN INDICATED IN THE INSTRUMENT OR DECLARATION DEPOSITED. IN THE LATTER CASE, THIS ACT SHALL ENTER INTO FORCE WITH RESPECT TO THAT COUNTRY ON THE DATE THUS INDICATED.

(d) THE PROTOCOL REGARDING DEVELOPING COUNTRIES MAY BE APPLIED, PURSUANT TO ARTICLE 5 THEREOF, PRIOR TO THE ENTRY INTO FORCE OF THIS ACT, FROM THE DATE OF ITS SIGNATURE.

(3) WITH RESPECT TO ANY COUNTRY OF THE UNION WHICH DEPOSITS AN INSTRUMENT OF RATIFICATION OR ACCESSION, ARTICLES 27 TO 38 SHALL ENTER INTO FORCE ON THE EARLIER OF THE DATES ON WHICH ANY OF THE GROUPS OF PROVISIONS REFERRED TO IN PARAGRAPH (1) (b) ENTERS INTO FORCE WITH RESPECT TO THAT COUNTRY PURSUANT TO PARAGRAPH (2) (a), (b) OR (c).

1718 Article 27

(1) *This Convention shall replace, in relations between the countries of the Union, the Convention of Berne of the 9th September 1886, and the subsequent revisions thereof. The Instruments previously in force shall continue to be applicable in relations with countries which do not ratify this Convention.*

(2) *The countries on whose behalf this Convention is signed may retain the benefit of the reservations which they have previously formulated, on condition that they make a declaration to that effect at the time of the deposit of their ratifications.*

Article 29

(1) ANY COUNTRY OUTSIDE THE UNION MAY ACCEDE TO THIS ACT AND THEREBY BECOME A MEMBER OF THE UNION. INSTRUMENTS OF ACCESSION SHALL BE DEPOSITED WITH THE DIRECTOR GENERAL.

(2) (a) WITH RESPECT TO ANY COUNTRY OUTSIDE THE UNION WHICH DEPOSITS ITS INSTRUMENT OF ACCESSION ONE MONTH OR MORE BEFORE THE DATE OF ENTRY INTO FORCE OF ANY PROVISIONS OF THE PRESENT ACT, THIS ACT SHALL ENTER INTO FORCE, UNLESS A SUBSEQUENT

Brussels

ART. 27—*cont.*

(3) *Countries which are at present members of the Union, but on whose behalf this Convention is not signed, may accede to it at any time, in the manner provided for in Article 25. In that event they shall enjoy the benefit of the provisions of the preceding paragraph.*

ARTICLE 28

(1) *This Convention shall be ratified, and the ratification deposited at Brussels, not later than the 1st July 1951. The ratifications, with the dates thereof and all declarations which may accompany them, shall be communicated by the Belgian Government to the Government of the Swiss Confederation, which shall notify the other countries of the Union thereof.*

(2) *This Convention shall come into force, between the countries which have ratified it, one month after the 1st July 1951. Nevertheless, if before that date it has been ratified by at least six countries of the Union, it shall come into force between those countries one month after the notification to them by the Government of the Swiss Confederation of the deposit of the sixth ratification and, in the case of countries which ratify thereafter, one month after the notification of each of such ratifications.*

(3) *Until the 1st July 1951, countries outside the Union may join it by acceding either to the Convention signed at Rome on the 2nd June 1928, or to this Convention. On or after the 1st July 1951, they may accede only to this Convention. The countries of the Union which shall not have ratified this Convention by the 1st July 1951, may accede thereto in accordance with the procedure provided by Article 25. In this event they shall be entitled to the benefit of the provisions of Article 27, paragraph (2).*

Stockholm

ART. 29—*cont.*

DATE HAS BEEN INDICATED IN THE INSTRUMENT OF ACCESSION, ON THE DATE UPON WHICH PROVISIONS FIRST ENTER INTO FORCE PURSUANT TO ARTICLE 28 (2) (a) OR (b); PROVIDED THAT:

(i) IF ARTICLES 1 TO 21 DO NOT ENTER INTO FORCE ON THAT DATE, SUCH COUNTRY SHALL, DURING THE INTERIM PERIOD BEFORE THE ENTRY INTO FORCE OF SUCH PROVISIONS, AND IN SUBSTITUTION THEREFOR, BE BOUND BY ARTICLES 1 TO 20 OF THE BRUSSELS ACT,

(ii) IF ARTICLES 22 TO 26 DO NOT ENTER INTO FORCE ON THAT DATE, SUCH COUNTRY SHALL, DURING THE INTERIM PERIOD BEFORE THE ENTRY INTO FORCE OF SUCH PROVISIONS, AND IN SUBSTITUTION THEREFOR, BE BOUND BY ARTICLES 21 TO 24 OF THE BRUSSELS ACT.

IF A COUNTRY INDICATES A SUBSEQUENT DATE IN ITS INSTRUMENT OF ACCESSION, THIS ACT SHALL ENTER INTO FORCE WITH RESPECT TO THAT COUNTRY ON THE DATE THUS INDICATED.

(b) WITH RESPECT TO ANY COUNTRY OUTSIDE THE UNION WHICH DEPOSITS ITS INSTRUMENT OF ACCESSION ON A DATE WHICH IS SUBSEQUENT TO, OR PRECEDES BY LESS THAN ONE MONTH, THE ENTRY INTO FORCE OF ONE GROUP OF PROVISIONS OF THE PRESENT ACT, THIS ACT SHALL, SUBJECT TO THE PROVISO OF SUBPARAGRAPH (a), ENTER INTO FORCE THREE MONTHS AFTER THE DATE ON WHICH ITS ACCESSION HAS BEEN NOTIFIED BY THE DIRECTOR GENERAL, UNLESS A SUBSEQUENT DATE HAS BEEN INDICATED IN THE INSTRUMENT OF ACCESSION. IN THE LATTER CASE, THIS ACT SHALL ENTER INTO FORCE WITH RESPECT TO THAT COUNTRY ON THE DATE THUS INDICATED.

Brussels

ART. 28—*cont.*

Stockholm

ART. 29—*cont.*

(3) WITH RESPECT TO ANY COUNTRY OUTSIDE THE UNION WHICH DEPOSITS ITS INSTRUMENT OF ACCESSION AFTER THE DATE OF ENTRY INTO FORCE OF THE PRESENT ACT IN ITS ENTIRETY, OR LESS THAN ONE MONTH BEFORE SUCH DATE, THIS ACT SHALL ENTER INTO FORCE THREE MONTHS AFTER THE DATE ON WHICH ITS ACCESSION HAS BEEN NOTIFIED BY THE DIRECTOR GENERAL, UNLESS A SUBSEQUENT DATE HAS BEEN INDICATED IN THE INSTRUMENT OF ACCESSION. IN THE LATTER CASE, THIS ACT SHALL ENTER INTO FORCE WITH RESPECT TO THAT COUNTRY ON THE DATE THUS INDICATED.

Note. Articles 28 and 29 of the Stockholm Act deal separately with countries of the Union and countries outside the Union. The former have the option of excluding from the effects of their ratification or accession either the substantive clauses or the administrative clauses (*i.e.* Articles 22–26). If they exclude the former they will not be bound by those clauses (in particular, the Protocol regarding developing countries). Failure to accept the administrative clauses by a country of the Union means that, after a transitional period, such country cannot take part in proceedings of the Assembly and cannot join the new World Intellectual Property Organisation. Countries outside the Union are not given any option.

Brussels

Stockholm

1719 ARTICLE 30

(1) SUBJECT TO THE POSSIBILITIES OF EXCEPTIONS PROVIDED FOR IN THE FOLLOWING PARAGRAPH, IN ARTICLES 28 (1) (b) AND 33 (2), AND THE PROTOCOL REGARDING DEVELOPING COUNTRIES, RATIFICATION OR ACCESSION SHALL AUTOMATICALLY ENTAIL ACCEPTANCE OF ALL THE CLAUSES AND ADMISSION TO ALL THE ADVANTAGES OF THIS ACT.

(2) (a) ANY COUNTRY OF THE UNION RATIFYING OR ACCEDING TO THIS ACT MAY RETAIN THE BENEFIT OF THE RESERVATIONS IT HAS PREVIOUSLY FORMULATED ON CONDITION THAT IT MAKES A DECLARATION TO THAT EFFECT AT THE TIME OF THE DEPOSIT OF ITS INSTRUMENT OF RATIFICATION OR ACCESSION.

Brussels

Stockholm

ART. 30—*cont.*

(b) ANY COUNTRY OUTSIDE THE UNION MAY, IN ACCEDING TO THIS ACT, DECLARE THAT IT INTENDS TO SUBSTITUTE, TEMPORARILY AT LEAST, FOR ARTICLE 8 CONCERNING THE RIGHT OF TRANSLATION, THE PROVISIONS OF ARTICLE 5 OF THE UNION CONVENTION OF 1886, AS REVISED IN PARIS IN 1896, ON THE CLEAR UNDERSTANDING THAT THE SAID PROVISIONS ARE APPLICABLE ONLY TO TRANSLATION INTO THE LANGUAGE OR LANGUAGES OF THE SAID COUNTRY. ANY COUNTRY OF THE UNION HAS THE RIGHT TO APPLY, IN RELATION TO THE RIGHT OF TRANSLATION OF WORKS WHOSE COUNTRY OF ORIGIN IS A COUNTRY AVAILING ITSELF OF SUCH A RESERVATION, A PROTECTION WHICH IS EQUIVALENT TO THE PROTECTION GRANTED BY THE LATTER COUNTRY.

(c) ANY COUNTRY MAY WITHDRAW SUCH RESERVATIONS AT ANY TIME BY NOTIFICATION ADDRESSED TO THE DIRECTOR GENERAL.

Note. Paragraph (1) of the new Article prescribes the general rule that no reservations are allowed, except those specified.

The two exceptions provided by paragraph (2) preserve the possibility of reservations given by Articles 27 (2) and 25 (3) of the Brussels Act. Both these reservations relate to translations.

Brussels

1720 ARTICLE 26

(1) *Any country of the Union may at any time in writing notify the Swiss Government that this Convention shall apply to its overseas territories, colonies, protectorates, territories under its trusteeship, or to any other territory for the international relations of which it is responsible, and the Convention shall thereupon apply to all the territories named in such notification, as from a date determined in accordance with Article 25, paragraph (3). In the absence of such notification, the Convention shall not apply to such territories.*

Stockholm

ARTICLE 31

(1) ANY COUNTRY MAY DECLARE IN ITS INSTRUMENT OF RATIFICATION OR ACCESSION, OR MAY INFORM THE DIRECTOR GENERAL BY WRITTEN NOTIFICATION ANY TIME THEREAFTER, THAT THIS CONVENTION SHALL BE APPLICABLE TO ALL OR PART OF THOSE TERRITORIES, DESIGNATED IN THE DECLARATION OR NOTIFICATION, FOR THE EXTERNAL RELATIONS OF WHICH IT IS RESPONSIBLE.

Brussels

ART. 26—*cont.*

(2) *Any country of the Union may at any time in writing notify the Government of the Swiss Confederation that this Convention shall cease to apply to all or any of the territories which have been made the subject of a notification under the preceding paragraph, and the Convention shall cease to apply in the territories named in such notification twelve months after its receipt by the Government of the Swiss Confederation.*

(3) *All notifications given to the Government of the Swiss Confederation in accordance with the provisions of paragraphs (1) and (2) of this Article shall be communicated by that Government to all the countries of the Union.*

Stockholm

ART. 31—*cont.*

(2) ANY COUNTRY WHICH HAS MADE SUCH A DECLARATION OR GIVEN SUCH A NOTIFICATION MAY, AT ANY TIME, NOTIFY THE DIRECTOR GENERAL THAT THIS CONVENTION SHALL CEASE TO BE APPLICABLE TO ALL OR PART OF SUCH TERRITORIES.

(3) (a) ANY DECLARATION MADE UNDER PARAGRAPH (1) SHALL TAKE EFFECT ON THE SAME DATE AS THE RATIFICATION OR ACCESSION IN WHICH IT WAS INCLUDED, AND ANY NOTIFICATION GIVEN UNDER SUCH PARAGRAPH SHALL TAKE EFFECT THREE MONTHS AFTER ITS NOTIFICATION BY THE DIRECTOR GENERAL.

(b) ANY NOTIFICATION GIVEN UNDER PARAGRAPH (2) SHALL TAKE EFFECT TWELVE MONTHS AFTER ITS RECEIPT BY THE DIRECTOR GENERAL.

Note. The changes made in Article 26 of the Brussels text bring the provision into conformity with modern territorial application clauses and provide that deposits shall be made with the Director General.

Brussels

Stockholm

1721 ARTICLE 32

(1) THE PRESENT ACT SHALL, AS REGARDS THE RELATIONS BETWEEN THE COUNTRIES OF THE UNION, AND TO THE EXTENT THAT IT APPLIES, REPLACE THE BERNE CONVENTION OF SEPTEMBER 9, 1886, AND THE SUBSEQUENT ACTS OF REVISION. THE ACTS PREVIOUSLY IN FORCE SHALL CONTINUE TO BE APPLICABLE, IN THEIR ENTIRETY OR TO THE EXTENT THAT THE PRESENT ACT DOES NOT REPLACE THEM BY VIRTUE OF

Brussels	*Stockholm*
	ART. 32—*cont.* THE PRECEDING SENTENCE, IN RELATIONS WITH COUNTRIES OF THE UNION WHICH DO NOT RATIFY OR ACCEDE TO THIS ACT.
	(2) COUNTRIES OUTSIDE THE UNION, WHICH BECOME PARTY TO THIS ACT, SHALL, SUBJECT TO THE PROVISIONS OF PARAGRAPH (3), APPLY IT WITH RESPECT TO ANY COUNTRY OF THE UNION NOT PARTY TO THIS ACT OR WHICH, ALTHOUGH PARTY TO THIS ACT, HAS MADE A DECLARATION PURSUANT TO ARTICLE 28 (1) (b) (i). SUCH COUNTRIES RECOGNIZE THAT THE SAID COUNTRY OF THE UNION, IN ITS RELATIONS WITH THEM: (i) MAY APPLY THE PROVISIONS OF THE MOST RECENT ACT TO WHICH IT IS PARTY, AND (ii) HAS THE RIGHT TO ADAPT THE PROTECTION TO THE LEVEL PROVIDED FOR BY THIS ACT.
	(3) ANY COUNTRY WHICH, IN RATIFYING OR ACCEDING TO THE PRESENT ACT, HAS MADE ANY OF OR ALL THE RESERVATIONS PERMITTED UNDER THE PROTOCOL REGARDING DEVELOPING COUNTRIES MAY APPLY THEM IN ITS RELATIONS WITH OTHER COUNTRIES OF THE UNION WHICH ARE NOT PARTY TO THIS ACT OR WHICH, ALTHOUGH PARTY TO THIS ACT, HAVE MADE A DECLARATION AS PERMITTED BY ARTICLE 28 (1) (b) (i), PROVIDED THAT THE LATTER COUNTRIES HAVE ACCEPTED THE APPLICATION OF THE SAID RESERVATIONS.

Note. Apart from a change of working necessitated by the option given to countries of the Union by Article 28 (1) (b), paragraph (1) corresponds exactly to Article 27 (1) of the Brussels text.

Paragraph (2) is new. It provides that a country which joins the Berne Union by acceding to the Stockholm Act shall, subject to paragraph (3), apply it in its relations with countries not party to that Act, while recognising that the latter countries may apply the most recent Act to which they are party and adapt the protection to the level of the Stockholm Act.

Paragraph (3) is also new and provides an exception to the general rules of paragraphs (1) and (2). Developing countries, whether they are old or new members of the Union, can only invoke the terms of the Protocol in respect of works the country of origin of which is a country not party to substantive changes in the Stockholm Act (*i.e.* Articles 1 to 21) if that country agrees.

Brussels

1722 ARTICLE 27 *bis*

A dispute between two or more countries of the Union concerning the interpretation or application of this Convention, not settled by negotiation shall be brought before the International Court of Justice for determination by it, unless the countries concerned agree on some other method of settlement. The country requesting that the dispute should be brought before the Court shall inform the International Office: the Office shall bring the matter to the attention of the other countries of the Union.

Stockholm

ARTICLE 33

(1) ANY DISPUTE BETWEEN TWO OR MORE COUNTRIES OF THE UNION CONCERNING THE INTERPRETATION OR APPLICATION OF THIS CONVENTION, NOT SETTLED BY NEGOTIATION, MAY, BY ANY ONE OF THE COUNTRIES CONCERNED, BE BROUGHT BEFORE THE INTERNATIONAL COURT OF JUSTICE BY APPLICATION IN CONFORMITY WITH THE STATUTE OF THE COURT, UNLESS THE COUNTRIES CONCERNED AGREE ON SOME OTHER METHOD OF SETTLEMENT. THE COUNTRY BRINGING THE DISPUTE BEFORE THE COURT SHALL INFORM THE INTERNATIONAL BUREAU; THE INTERNATIONAL BUREAU SHALL BRING THE MATTER TO THE ATTENTION OF THE OTHER COUNTRIES OF THE UNION.

(2) EACH COUNTRY MAY,. AT THE TIME IT SIGNS THIS ACT OR DEPOSITS ITS INSTRUMENT OF RATIFICATION OR ACCESSION, DECLARE THAT IT DOES NOT CONSIDER ITSELF BOUND BY THE PROVISIONS OF PARAGRAPH (1). WITH REGARD TO ANY DISPUTE BETWEEN SUCH COUNTRY AND ANY OTHER COUNTRY OF THE UNION, THE PROVISIONS OF PARAGRAPH (1) SHALL NOT APPLY.

(3) ANY COUNTRY HAVING MADE A DECLARATION IN ACCORDANCE WITH THE PROVISIONS OF PARAGRAPH (2) MAY, AT ANY TIME, WITHDRAW ITS DECLARATION BY NOTIFICATION ADDRESSED TO THE DIRECTOR GENERAL.

Note. Apart from drafting changes, Article 27 *bis* has been amended to allow countries to contract out of its provisions.

Brussels

1723

Stockholm

ARTICLE 34

AFTER THE ENTRY INTO FORCE OF THIS ACT IN ITS ENTIRETY, A COUNTRY MAY NOT ACCEDE TO EARLIER ACTS OF THIS CONVENTION.

Brussels

1724 Article 29

(1) *This Convention shall remain in force for an indefinite period. Nevertheless, each country of the Union shall be entitled to denounce it at any time, by means of a notification in writing addressed to the Government of the Swiss Confederation.*

(2) *This denunciation, which shall be communicated by the Government of the Swiss Confederation to all the other countries of the Union, shall take effect only in respect of the country making it, and twelve months after the receipt of the notification of denunciation addressed to the Government of the Swiss Confederation. The Convention shall remain in full force and effect for the other countries of the Union.*

(3) *The right of denunciation provided by this Article shall not be exercised by any country before the expiry of five years from the date of its ratification or accession.*

Stockholm

Article 35

(1) THIS CONVENTION SHALL REMAIN IN FORCE WITHOUT LIMITATION AS TO TIME.

(2) ANY COUNTRY MAY DENOUNCE THIS ACT BY NOTIFICATION ADDRESSED TO THE DIRECTOR GENERAL. SUCH DENUNCIATION SHALL CONSTITUTE ALSO DENUNCIATION OF ALL EARLIER ACTS AND SHALL AFFECT ONLY THE COUNTRY MAKING IT, THE CONVENTION REMAINING IN FULL FORCE AND EFFECT AS REGARDS THE OTHER COUNTRIES OF THE UNION.

(3) DENUNCIATION SHALL TAKE EFFECT ONE YEAR AFTER THE DAY ON WHICH THE DIRECTOR GENERAL HAS RECEIVED THE NOTIFICATION.

(4) THE RIGHT OF DENUNCIATION PROVIDED BY THIS ARTICLE SHALL NOT BE EXERCISED BY ANY COUNTRY BEFORE THE EXPIRATION OF FIVE YEARS FROM THE DATE UPON WHICH IT BECOMES A MEMBER OF THE UNION.

Note. Article 29 (3) of the Brussels text has been revised to limit the five-year rule to new members of the Union.

Brussels

1725

Stockholm

Article 36

(1) ANY COUNTRY PARTY TO THIS CONVENTION UNDERTAKES TO ADOPT, IN ACCORDANCE WITH ITS CONSTITUTION, THE MEASURES NECESSARY TO ENSURE THE APPLICATION OF THIS CONVENTION.

(2) IT IS UNDERSTOOD THAT, AT THE TIME A COUNTRY DEPOSITS ITS INSTRUMENT OF RATIFICATION OR ACCESSION, IT WILL BE IN A POSITION UNDER ITS DOMESTIC LAW TO GIVE EFFECT TO THE PROVISIONS OF THIS CONVENTION.

Note. This new provision makes explicit what was only implicit in the Brussels text.

Brussels

1726 ARTICLE 30

(1) *Countries which introduce into their legislation the term of protection of fifty years provided by Article 7, paragraph (1), of this Convention shall give notice thereof in writing to the Government of the Swiss Confederation, which shall immediately communicate it to all the other countries of the Union.*

(2) *The same procedure shall be followed in the case of countries abandoning the reservations made or maintained by them in accordance with Articles 25 and 27.*

Stockholm

Note. Article 30 has been cancelled. Its provisions are no longer needed.

Brussels

1727 ARTICLE 31

The Official Acts of the Conferences shall be established in French. An equivalent text shall be established in English. In case of dispute as to the interpretation of the Acts, the French text shall always prevail. Any country or group of countries of the Union shall be entitled to have established by the International Office an authoritative text of the said Acts in the language of its choice, and by arrangement with the Office. These texts shall be published in the Acts of the Conferences, annexed to the French and English texts.

Stockholm

ARTICLE 37

(1) (a) THIS ACT SHALL BE SIGNED IN A SINGLE COPY IN THE FRENCH AND ENGLISH LANGUAGES AND SHALL BE DEPOSITED WITH THE GOVERNMENT OF SWEDEN.

(b) OFFICIAL TEXTS SHALL BE ESTABLISHED BY THE DIRECTOR GENERAL AFTER CONSULTATION WITH THE INTERESTED GOVERNMENTS, IN THE GERMAN, ITALIAN, PORTUGUESE AND SPANISH LANGUAGES, AND SUCH OTHER LANGUAGES AS THE ASSEMBLY MAY DESIGNATE.

(c) IN CASE OF DIFFERENCES OF OPINION ON THE INTERPRETATION OF THE VARIOUS TEXTS, THE FRENCH TEXT SHALL PREVAIL.

(2) THIS ACT SHALL REMAIN OPEN FOR SIGNATURE AT STOCKHOLM UNTIL JANUARY 13, 1968.

(3) THE DIRECTOR GENERAL SHALL TRANSMIT TWO COPIES, CERTIFIED BY THE GOVERNMENT OF SWEDEN, OF THE SIGNED TEXT OF THIS ACT TO THE GOVERNMENTS OF ALL COUNTRIES OF THE UNION AND, ON REQUEST, TO THE GOVERNMENT OF ANY OTHER COUNTRY.

Brussels

ART. 31—*cont.*

Stockholm

ART. 37—*cont.*

(4) THE DIRECTOR GENERAL SHALL REGISTER THIS ACT WITH THE SECRETARIAT OF THE UNITED NATIONS.

(5) THE DIRECTOR GENERAL SHALL NOTIFY THE GOVERNMENTS OF ALL COUNTRIES OF THE UNION OF SIGNATURES, DEPOSITS OF INSTRUMENTS OR RATIFICATION OR ACCESSION AND ANY DECLARATIONS INCLUDED IN SUCH INSTRUMENTS OR MADE PURSUANT TO ARTICLE 28 (1) (d), ENTRY INTO FORCE OF ANY PROVISIONS OF THIS ACT, NOTIFICATIONS OF DENUNCIATION, AND NOTIFICATIONS PURSUANT TO ARTICLE 31.

1728 ARTICLE 38

(1) UNTIL THE FIRST DIRECTOR GENERAL ASSUMES OFFICE, REFERENCES IN THIS ACT TO THE INTERNATIONAL BUREAU OF THE ORGANISATION OR TO THE DIRECTOR GENERAL SHALL BE DEEMED TO BE REFERENCES TO THE BUREAU OF THE UNION OR ITS DIRECTOR, RESPECTIVELY.

(2) COUNTRIES OF THE UNION NOT BOUND BY ARTICLES 22 TO 26 MAY, UNTIL FIVE YEARS AFTER THE ENTRY INTO FORCE OF THE CONVENTION ESTABLISHING THE ORGANISATION, EXERCISE, IF THEY SO DESIRE, THE RIGHTS PROVIDED UNDER ARTICLES 22 TO 26 OF THIS ACT AS IF THEY WERE BOUND BY THOSE ARTICLES. ANY COUNTRY DESIRING TO EXERCISE SUCH RIGHTS SHALL GIVE WRITTEN NOTIFICATION TO THIS EFFECT TO THE DIRECTOR GENERAL: THIS NOTIFICATION SHALL BE EFFECTIVE ON THE DATE OF ITS RECEIPT. SUCH COUNTRIES SHALL BE DEEMED TO BE MEMBERS OF THE ASSEMBLY UNTIL THE EXPIRATION OF THE SAID PERIOD.

(3) AS LONG AS ALL THE COUNTRIES OF THE UNION HAVE NOT BECOME MEMBERS OF THE ORGANISATION, THE INTERNATIONAL BUREAU

Brussels | *Stockholm*

ART. 38—*cont.*

OF THE ORGANISATION SHALL ALSO FUNCTION AS THE BUREAU OF THE UNION, AND THE DIRECTOR GENERAL AS THE DIRECTOR OF THE SAID BUREAU.

(4) ONCE ALL THE COUNTRIES OF THE UNION HAVE BECOME MEMBERS OF THE ORGANISATION, THE RIGHTS, OBLIGATIONS, AND PROPERTY, OF THE BUREAU OF THE UNION SHALL DEVOLVE ON THE INTERNATIONAL BUREAU OF THE ORGANISATION.

Note. This new Article sets out the transitional provisions.

1729 PROTOCOL REGARDING DEVELOPING COUNTRIES

ARTICLE 1

ANY COUNTRY REGARDED AS A DEVELOPING COUNTRY IN CONFORMITY WITH THE ESTABLISHED PRACTICE OF THE GENERAL ASSEMBLY OF THE UNITED NATIONS WHICH RATIFIES OR ACCEDES TO THE ACT OF THIS CONVENTION OF WHICH THIS PROTOCOL FORMS AN INTEGRAL PART AND WHICH, HAVING REGARD TO ITS ECONOMIC SITUATION AND ITS SOCIAL OR CULTURAL NEEDS, DOES NOT CONSIDER ITSELF IMMEDIATELY IN A POSITION TO MAKE PROVISION FOR THE PROTECTION OF ALL THE RIGHTS AS PROVIDED IN THE ACT, MAY, BY A NOTIFICATION DEPOSITED WITH THE DIRECTOR GENERAL, AT THE TIME OF MAKING A RATIFICATION OR ACCESSION, WHICH INCLUDES ARTICLE 21 OF THE ACT, DECLARE THAT IT WILL, FOR A PERIOD OF THE FIRST TEN YEARS DURING WHICH IT IS A PARTY THERETO, AVAIL ITSELF OF ANY OR ALL OF THE FOLLOWING RESERVATIONS:

(a) SUBSTITUTE FOR THE TERM OF FIFTY YEARS REFERRED TO IN PARAGRAPHS (1), (2) AND (3) OF ARTICLE 7 OF THIS CONVENTION A DIFFERENT TERM, PROVIDED THAT IT SHALL NOT BE LESS THAN TWENTY-FIVE YEARS: AND SUBSTITUTE FOR THE TERM OF TWENTY-FIVE YEARS REFERRED TO IN PARAGRAPH (4) OF THE SAID ARTICLE A DIFFERENT TERM, PROVIDED THAT IT SHALL NOT BE LESS THAN TEN YEARS;

(b) SUBSTITUTE FOR ARTICLE 8 OF THIS CONVENTION THE FOLLOWING PROVISIONS:

(i) AUTHORS OF LITERARY AND ARTISTIC WORKS PROTECTED BY THIS CONVENTION SHALL ENJOY IN COUNTRIES OTHER THAN THE COUNTRY OF ORIGIN OF THEIR WORKS THE EXCLUSIVE RIGHT OF MAKING AND OF AUTHORISING THE TRANSLATION OF THEIR WORKS THROUGHOUT THE TERM OF PROTECTION OF THEIR RIGHTS IN THE ORIGINAL WORKS. NEVERTHELESS, THE EXCLUSIVE RIGHT OF TRANSLATION SHALL CEASE TO EXIST IF THE AUTHOR SHALL NOT HAVE AVAILED HIMSELF OF IT, DURING A TERM OF TEN YEARS FROM THE DATE OF THE FIRST PUBLICATION OF THE ORIGINAL WORK, BY PUBLISHING OR CAUSING TO BE PUBLISHED,

IN ONE OF THE COUNTRIES OF THE UNION, A TRANSLATION IN THE LANGUAGE FOR WHICH PROTECTION IS TO BE CLAIMED:

(ii) IF, AFTER THE EXPIRATION OF A PERIOD OF THREE YEARS FROM THE DATE OF THE FIRST PUBLICATION OF A LITERARY OR ARTISTIC WORK, OR OF ANY LONGER PERIOD DETERMINED BY NATIONAL LEGISLATION OF THE DEVELOPING COUNTRY CONCERNED, A TRANSLATION OF SUCH WORK HAS NOT BEEN PUBLISHED IN THAT COUNTRY INTO THE NATIONAL OR OFFICIAL OR REGIONAL LANGUAGE OR LANGUAGES OF THAT COUNTRY BY THE OWNER OF THE RIGHT OF TRANSLATION OR WITH HIS AUTHORISATION, ANY NATIONAL OF SUCH COUNTRY MAY OBTAIN A NON-EXCLUSIVE LICENCE FROM THE COMPETENT AUTHORITY TO TRANSLATE THE WORK AND PUBLISH THE WORK SO TRANSLATED IN ANY OF THE NATIONAL OR OFFICIAL OR REGIONAL LANGUAGES IN WHICH IT HAS NOT BEEN PUBLISHED: PROVIDED THAT SUCH NATIONAL, IN ACCORDANCE WITH THE PROCEDURE OF THE COUNTRY CONCERNED, ESTABLISHES EITHER THAT HE HAS REQUESTED, AND BEEN DENIED, AUTHORISATION BY THE PROPRIETOR OF THE RIGHT TO MAKE AND PUBLISH THE TRANSLATION, OR THAT, AFTER DUE DILIGENCE ON HIS PART, HE WAS UNABLE TO FIND THE OWNER OF THE RIGHT. A LICENCE MAY ALSO BE GRANTED ON THE SAME CONDITIONS IF ALL PREVIOUS EDITIONS OF A TRANSLATION IN SUCH LANGUAGE IN THAT COUNTRY ARE OUT OF PRINT;

(iii) IF THE OWNER OF THE RIGHT OF TRANSLATION CANNOT BE FOUND, THEN THE APPLICANT FOR A LICENCE SHALL SEND COPIES OF HIS APPLICATION TO THE PUBLISHER WHOSE NAME APPEARS ON THE WORK AND, IF THE NATIONALITY OF THE OWNER OF THE RIGHT OF TRANSLATION IS KNOWN, TO THE DIPLOMATIC OR CONSULAR REPRESENTATIVE OF THE COUNTRY OF WHICH SUCH OWNER IS A NATIONAL, OR TO THE ORGANISATION WHICH MAY HAVE BEEN DESIGNATED BY THE GOVERNMENT OF THAT COUNTRY. THE LICENCE SHALL NOT BE GRANTED BEFORE THE EXPIRATION OF A PERIOD OF TWO MONTHS FROM THE DATE OF THE DISPATCH OF THE COPIES OF THE APPLICATION;

(iv) DUE PROVISION SHALL BE MADE BY DOMESTIC LEGISLATION TO ASSURE TO THE OWNER OF THE RIGHT OF TRANSLATION A JUST COMPENSATION, TO ASSURE PAYMENT AND TRANSMITTAL OF SUCH COMPENSATION, SUBJECT TO NATIONAL CURRENCY REGULATIONS, AND TO ASSURE A CORRECT TRANSLATION OF THE WORK;

(v) THE ORIGINAL TITLE AND THE NAME OF THE AUTHOR OF THE WORK SHALL BE PRINTED ON ALL COPIES OF THE PUBLISHED TRANSLATION. THE LICENCE SHALL BE VALID ONLY FOR PUBLICATION OF THE TRANSLATION IN THE TERRITORY OF THE COUNTRY OF THE UNION WHERE IT HAS BEEN APPLIED FOR. COPIES SO PUBLISHED MAY BE IMPORTED AND SOLD IN ANOTHER COUNTRY OF THE UNION IF ONE OF THE NATIONAL OR OFFICIAL OR REGIONAL LANGUAGES OF SUCH OTHER COUNTRY IS THE SAME LANGUAGE AS THAT INTO WHICH THE WORK HAS BEEN SO TRANSLATED, AND IF THE DOMESTIC LAW IN SUCH OTHER COUNTRY MAKES PROVISION FOR SUCH LICENCES AND DOES NOT PROHIBIT SUCH IMPORTATION AND SALE. WHERE THE FOREGOING CONDITIONS DO NOT EXIST, THE IMPORTATION AND SALE OF SUCH COPIES IN A COUNTRY OF THE UNION SHALL BE GOVERNED BY ITS DOMESTIC LAW AND ITS AGREEMENTS. THE LICENCE SHALL NOT BE TRANSFERABLE BY THE LICENSEE;

(vi) THE LICENCE SHALL NOT BE GRANTED WHEN THE AUTHOR HAS WITHDRAWN FROM CIRCULATION ALL COPIES OF THE WORK;

(vii) SHOULD, HOWEVER, THE AUTHOR AVAIL HIMSELF OF THE RIGHT UNDER SUBPARAGRAPH (i) ABOVE DURING THE TERM OF TEN YEARS FROM THE DATE OF FIRST PUBLICATION, THE LICENCE SHALL TERMINATE FROM THE DATE ON WHICH THE AUTHOR PUBLISHES OR CAUSES TO BE PUBLISHED HIS TRANSLATION IN THE COUNTRY WHERE THE LICENCE HAS BEEN GRANTED, PROVIDED, HOWEVER, THAT ANY COPIES OF THE TRANSLATION ALREADY MADE BEFORE THE LICENCE IS TERMINATED MAY CONTINUE TO BE SOLD;

(viii) SHOULD, HOWEVER, THE AUTHOR NOT AVAIL HIMSELF OF THE RIGHT UNDER SUBPARAGRAPH (i) ABOVE DURING THE SAID TERM OF TEN YEARS, COMPENSATION UNDER THE NON-EXCLUSIVE LICENCE REFERRED TO ABOVE SHALL CEASE TO BE DUE FOR ANY USES MADE AFTER THE EXPIRY OF SUCH TERM;

(ix) SHOULD THE AUTHOR BE ENTITLED TO EXCLUSIVE TRANSLATION RIGHTS IN A COUNTRY BY HAVING PUBLISHED OR CAUSED TO BE PUBLISHED A TRANSLATION OF THE WORK IN THAT COUNTRY WITHIN TEN YEARS FROM THE DATE OF FIRST PUBLICATION, BUT SHOULD THEREAFTER DURING THE TERM OF THE AUTHOR'S COPYRIGHT IN THE WORK ALL EDITIONS OF THE AUTHORISED TRANSLATION IN THAT COUNTRY BE OUT OF PRINT, THEN A NON-EXCLUSIVE LICENCE TO TRANSLATE THE WORK MAY BE OBTAINED FROM THE COMPETENT AUTHORITY IN THE SAME MANNER AND SUBJECT TO THE SAME CONDITIONS AS ARE PROVIDED WITH RESPECT TO THE NON-EXCLUSIVE LICENCE REFERRED TO IN SUBPARAGRAPHS (ii) TO (vi) ABOVE, BUT SUBJECT TO THE PROVISIONS OF SUBPARAGRAPH (vii) ABOVE;

(c) APPLY THE PROVISIONS OF ARTICLE 9 (1) OF THIS CONVENTION SUBJECT TO THE FOLLOWING PROVISIONS:

(i) IF, AFTER THE EXPIRATION OF A PERIOD OF THREE YEARS FROM THE DATE OF THE FIRST PUBLICATION OF A LITERARY OR ARTISTIC WORK, OR OF ANY LONGER PERIOD DETERMINED BY NATIONAL LEGISLATION OF THE DEVELOPING COUNTRY CONCERNED, SUCH WORK HAS NOT BEEN PUBLISHED IN THAT COUNTRY IN THE ORIGINAL FORM IN WHICH IT WAS CREATED, BY THE OWNER OF THE RIGHT OF REPRODUCTION OR WITH HIS AUTHORISATION, ANY NATIONAL OF SUCH COUNTRY MAY OBTAIN A NON-EXCLUSIVE LICENCE FROM THE COMPETENT AUTHORITY TO REPRODUCE AND PUBLISH SUCH WORK FOR EDUCATIONAL OR CULTURAL PURPOSES; PROVIDED THAT SUCH NATIONAL, IN ACCORDANCE WITH THE PROCEDURE OF THE COUNTRY CONCERNED, ESTABLISHES EITHER THAT HE HAS REQUESTED, AND BEEN DENIED, AUTHORISATION BY THE PROPRIETOR OF THE RIGHT TO PRODUCE AND PUBLISH SUCH WORK FOR EDUCATIONAL OR CULTURAL PURPOSES, OR THAT, AFTER DUE DILIGENCE ON HIS PART, HE WAS UNABLE TO FIND THE OWNER OF THE RIGHT. A LICENCE MAY ALSO BE GRANTED ON THE SAME CONDITIONS IF ALL PREVIOUS EDITIONS OF SUCH WORK IN ITS SAID ORIGINAL FORM IN THAT COUNTRY ARE OUT OF PRINT;

(ii) IF THE OWNER OF THE RIGHT OF REPRODUCTION CANNOT BE FOUND, THEN THE APPLICANT FOR A LICENCE SHALL SEND COPIES OF HIS APPLICATION TO THE PUBLISHER WHOSE NAME APPEARS

ON THE WORK AND, IF THE NATIONALITY OF THE OWNER OF THE RIGHT OF REPRODUCTION IS KNOWN, TO THE DIPLOMATIC OR CONSULAR REPRESENTATIVE OF THE COUNTRY OF WHICH SUCH OWNER IS A NATIONAL, OR TO THE ORGANISATION WHICH MAY HAVE BEEN DESIGNATED BY THE GOVERNMENT OF THAT COUNTRY. THE LICENCE SHALL NOT BE GRANTED BEFORE THE EXPIRATION OF A PERIOD OF TWO MONTHS FROM THE DATE OF THE DISPATCH OF THE COPIES OF THE APPLICATION;

(iii) DUE PROVISION SHALL BE MADE BY DOMESTIC LEGISLATION TO ASSURE TO THE OWNER OF THE RIGHT OF REPRODUCTION A JUST COMPENSATION, TO ASSURE PAYMENT AND TRANSMITTAL OF SUCH COMPENSATION, SUBJECT TO NATIONAL CURRENCY REGULATIONS, AND TO ASSURE AN ACCURATE REPRODUCTION OF THE WORK;

(iv) THE ORIGINAL TITLE AND THE NAME OF THE AUTHOR OF THE WORK SHALL BE PRINTED ON ALL COPIES OF THE PUBLISHED REPRODUCTION. THE LICENCE SHALL BE VALID ONLY FOR PUBLICATION IN THE TERRITORY OF THE COUNTRY OF THE UNION WHERE IT HAS BEEN APPLIED FOR. COPIES SO PUBLISHED MAY BE IMPORTED AND SOLD IN ANOTHER COUNTRY OF THE UNION FOR EDUCATIONAL OR CULTURAL PURPOSES IF THE DOMESTIC LAW IN SUCH OTHER COUNTRY MAKES PROVISION FOR SUCH LICENCES AND DOES NOT PROHIBIT SUCH IMPORTATION AND SALE. WHERE THE FOREGOING CONDITIONS DO NOT EXIST, THE IMPORTATION AND SALE OF SUCH COPIES IN A COUNTRY OF THE UNION SHALL BE GOVERNED BY ITS DOMESTIC LAW AND ITS AGREEMENTS. THE LICENCE SHALL NOT BE TRANSFERABLE BY THE LICENSEE;

(v) THE LICENCE SHALL NOT BE GRANTED WHEN THE AUTHOR HAS WITHDRAWN FROM CIRCULATION ALL COPIES OF THE WORK;

(vi) SHOULD, HOWEVER, THE AUTHOR AVAIL HIMSELF OF THE RIGHT TO REPRODUCE THE WORK, THE LICENCE SHALL TERMINATE FROM THE DATE ON WHICH THE AUTHOR PUBLISHES OR CAUSES TO BE PUBLISHED HIS WORK IN ITS SAID ORIGINAL FORM IN THE COUNTRY WHERE THE LICENCE HAS BEEN GRANTED, PROVIDED, HOWEVER, THAT ANY COPIES OF THE WORK ALREADY MADE BEFORE THE LICENCE IS TERMINATED MAY CONTINUE TO BE SOLD;

(vii) SHOULD THE AUTHOR PUBLISH OR CAUSE HIS WORK TO BE PUBLISHED IN ITS SAID ORIGINAL FORM IN A COUNTRY, BUT SHOULD THEREAFTER DURING THE TERM OF THE AUTHOR'S COPYRIGHT IN THE WORK ALL AUTHORISED EDITIONS IN SUCH ORIGINAL FORM IN THAT COUNTRY BE OUT OF PRINT, THEN A NON-EXCLUSIVE LICENCE TO REPRODUCE AND PUBLISH THE WORK MAY BE OBTAINED FROM THE COMPETENT AUTHORITY IN THE SAME MANNER AND SUBJECT TO THE SAME CONDITIONS AS ARE PROVIDED WITH RESPECT TO THE NON-EXCLUSIVE LICENCE REFERRED TO IN SUBPARAGRAPH (i) TO (v) ABOVE, BUT SUBJECT TO THE PROVISIONS OF SUBPARAGRAPH (vi) ABOVE;

(d) SUBSTITUTE FOR PARAGRAPHS (1) AND (2) OF ARTICLE 11 *bis* OF THIS CONVENTION THE FOLLOWING PROVISIONS:

(i) AUTHORS OF LITERARY AND ARTISTIC WORKS SHALL ENJOY THE EXCLUSIVE RIGHT OF AUTHORISING THE BROADCASTING OF THEIR WORKS AND THE COMMUNICATION TO THE PUBLIC OF THE BROADCAST OF THE WORKS IF SUCH COMMUNICATION IS MADE FOR PROFIT-MAKING PURPOSES;

(ii) THE NATIONAL LEGISLATIONS OF THE COUNTRIES OF THE UNION MAY REGULATE THE CONDITIONS UNDER WHICH THE RIGHT MENTIONED IN THE PRECEDING SUBPARAGRAPH SHALL BE EXERCISED, BUT THE EFFECT OF THOSE CONDITIONS WILL BE STRICTLY LIMITED TO THE COUNTRIES WHICH HAVE PUT THEM IN FORCE. SUCH CONDITIONS SHALL NOT IN ANY CASE PREJUDICE THE MORAL RIGHTS OF THE AUTHOR, NOR THE RIGHT WHICH BELONGS TO THE AUTHOR TO OBTAIN AN EQUITABLE REMUNERATION WHICH SHALL BE FIXED, FAILING AGREEMENT, BY THE COMPETENT AUTHORITY;

(e) RESERVE THE RIGHT, EXCLUSIVELY FOR TEACHING, STUDY AND RESEARCH IN ALL FIELDS OF EDUCATION, TO RESTRICT THE PROTECTION OF LITERARY AND ARTISTIC WORKS, PROVIDED DUE PROVISION SHALL BE MADE BY DOMESTIC LEGISLATION TO ASSURE TO THE AUTHOR A COMPENSATION WHICH CONFORMS TO STANDARDS OF PAYMENT MADE TO NATIONAL AUTHORS; THE PAYMENT AND TRANSMITTAL OF SUCH COMPENSATION SHALL BE SUBJECT TO NATIONAL CURRENCY REGULATIONS. COPIES OF A WORK PUBLISHED PURSUANT TO RESERVATIONS UNDER THIS PARAGRAPH MAY BE IMPORTED AND SOLD IN ANOTHER COUNTRY OF THE UNION FOR PURPOSES AS AFORESAID IF THAT COUNTRY HAS INVOKED THE SAID RESERVATIONS AND DOES NOT PROHIBIT SUCH IMPORTATION AND SALE. WHERE THE FOREGOING CONDITIONS DO NOT EXIST, THE IMPORTATION AND SALE OF SUCH COPIES IN A COUNTRY OF THE UNION WHICH CANNOT TAKE ADVANTAGE OF THIS PROTOCOL ARE PROHIBITED IN THE ABSENCE OF AGREEMENT OF THE AUTHOR OR HIS SUCCESSOR IN TITLE.

Note. This Protocol was added to the Convention at the Stockholm Conference.

Paragraph (a) permits the normal copyright terms (see Article 7) to be reduced. Paragraph (d) deals with the broadcasting and the public communication of a broadcast of an author's works, the author retaining his exclusive right over the public communication of broadcasts (as distinct from the broadcasts themselves) only in those cases where the communication is for profit.

Paragraphs (b), (c) and (e) are concerned with compulsory licences to translate and publish.

Under paragraphs (b) and (c) just compensation is payable to the author under any licence granted and a licence cannot be granted unless the licensee has been unable to negotiate terms with the author. The author can restore his exclusive rights by publishing in the developing country (in the case of translations within 10 years of first publication), but a licence can again be obtained if the author's publication goes out of print. The translation made under a licence must be into the language of the developing country.

Reproduction under paragraph (c) is permissible for educational and cultural purposes.

Under paragraph (e) not only reproduction, but translation, performance and broadcasting of a work is possible in the more limited field of teaching, study and research and in this case the payment to the author must conform to national standards.

Importation and sale of works reproduced or translated under licence is generally prohibited, except for other developing countries which also invoke the Protocol.

ARTICLE 2

ANY COUNTRY WHICH NO LONGER NEEDS TO MAINTAIN ANY OR ALL THE RESERVATIONS MADE IN ACCORDANCE WITH ARTICLE 1 OF THIS PROTOCOL SHALL WITHDRAW SUCH RESERVATION OR RESERVATIONS BY NOTIFICATION DEPOSITED WITH THE DIRECTOR GENERAL.

ARTICLE 3

ANY COUNTRY WHICH HAS MADE RESERVATIONS IN ACCORDANCE WITH ARTICLE 1 OF THIS PROTOCOL, AND WHICH AT THE END OF THE PERIOD OF TEN YEARS PRESCRIBED THEREIN, HAVING REGARD TO ITS ECONOMIC SITUATION AND ITS SOCIAL OR CULTURAL NEEDS, STILL DOES NOT CONSIDER ITSELF IN A POSITION TO WITHDRAW THE RESERVATIONS UNDER THE SAID ARTICLE 1, MAY CONTINUE TO MAINTAIN ANY OR ALL THE RESERVATIONS UNTIL IT RATIFIES OR ACCEDES TO THE ACT ADOPTED BY THE NEXT REVISION CONFERENCE OF THIS CONVENTION.

ARTICLE 4

IF, IN CONFORMITY WITH THE ESTABLISHED PRACTICE OF THE GENERAL ASSEMBLY OF THE UNITED NATIONS, A COUNTRY SHOULD CEASE TO BE REGARDED AS A DEVELOPING COUNTRY, THE DIRECTOR GENERAL SHALL GIVE NOTIFICATION OF SUCH CESSATION TO THE COUNTRY CONCERNED AND TO ALL OF THE OTHER COUNTRIES OF THE UNION. AT THE EXPIRY OF A PERIOD OF SIX YEARS FROM THE DATE OF SUCH NOTIFICATION THE SAID COUNTRY SHALL NO LONGER HAVE THE RIGHT TO MAINTAIN ANY OF THE RESERVATIONS UNDER THIS PROTOCOL.

ARTICLE 5

(1) ANY COUNTRY OF THE UNION MAY DECLARE, AS FROM THE SIGNATURE OF THIS CONVENTION, AND AT ANY TIME BEFORE BECOMING BOUND BY ARTICLES 1 TO 21 OF THIS CONVENTION AND BY THIS PROTOCOL

(i) IN THE CASE OF A COUNTRY REFERRED TO IN ARTICLE 1 OF THIS PROTOCOL, THAT IT INTENDS TO APPLY THE PROVISIONS OF THIS PROTOCOL TO WORKS WHOSE COUNTRY OF ORIGIN IS A COUNTRY OF THE UNION WHICH ADMITS THE APPLICATION OF THE RESERVATIONS UNDER THE PROTOCOL, OR

(ii) THAT IT ADMITS THE APPLICATION OF THE PROVISIONS OF THE PROTOCOL TO WORKS OF WHICH IT IS THE COUNTRY OF ORIGIN BY COUNTRIES WHICH, ON BECOMING BOUND BY ARTICLES 1 TO 21 OF THIS CONVENTION, AND BY THIS PROTOCOL, OR ON MAKING A DECLARATION OF APPLICATION OF THIS PROTOCOL BY VIRTUE OF THE PROVISION OF SUBPARAGRAPH (i), HAVE MADE RESERVATIONS PERMITTED UNDER THIS PROTOCOL.

(2) THE DECLARATION SHALL BE MADE IN WRITING AND SHALL BE DEPOSITED WITH THE DIRECTOR GENERAL. THE DECLARATION SHALL BECOME EFFECTIVE FROM THE DATE IT IS DEPOSITED.

Note. Article 5 concerns the interim period between the date on which a country signs the Stockholm Act and the date on which it becomes bound by it.

In this period a developing country may apply the Protocol in respect of works originating in another country of the Berne Union only if that country agrees.

ARTICLE 6

ANY COUNTRY WHICH IS BOUND BY THE PROVISIONS OF THIS PROTOCOL AND WHICH HAS MADE A DECLARATION OR NOTIFICATION UNDER ARTICLE 31 (1) OF THIS CONVENTION IN RESPECT OF TERRITORIES WHICH, ON THE DATE OF THE SIGNATURE OF THIS CONVENTION, ARE NOT RESPONSIBLE FOR THEIR EXTERNAL RELATIONS, AND THE SITUATION OF WHICH CAN BE REGARDED AS ANALOGOUS TO THAT OF THE COUNTRIES REFERRED TO IN ARTICLE 1 OF THIS PROTOCOL, MAY NOTIFY THE DIRECTOR GENERAL THAT THE PROVISIONS OF THIS PROTOCOL SHALL APPLY TO ALL OR PART OF THOSE TERRITORIES AND MAY IN SUCH NOTIFICATION DECLARE THAT ANY SUCH TERRITORY WILL AVAIL ITSELF OF ANY OR ALL THE RESERVATIONS PERMITTED BY THIS PROTOCOL.

Note. This provides that a country which has accepted the obligations of the Stockholm Act may when joining one of its dependent territories declare that this territory, if it is developing, will avail itself of the Protocol.

1730 **Universal Copyright Convention** [2]

Geneva, September 6, 1952

The Contracting States,

Moved by the desire to assure in all countries copyright protection of literary, scientific and artistic works,

Convinced that a system of copyright protection appropriate to all nations of the world and expressed in a universal convention, additional to, and without impairing international systems already in force, will ensure respect for the rights of the individual and encourage the development of literature, the sciences and the arts,

Persuaded that such a universal copyright system will facilitate a wider dissemination of works of the human mind and increase international understanding,

Have agreed as follows:

ARTICLE I

1731 Each Contracting State undertakes to provide for the adequate and effective protection of the rights of authors and other copyright proprietors in literary, scientific and artistic works, including writings, musical, dramatic and cinematographic works, and paintings, engravings and sculpture.

ARTICLE II

1732 1. Published works of nationals of any Contracting State and works first published in that State shall enjoy in each other Contracting State the same protection as that other State accords to works of its nationals first published in its own territory.

2. Unpublished works of nationals of each Contracting State shall enjoy in each other Contracting State the same protection as that other State accords to unpublished works of its own nationals.

3. For the purpose of this Convention any Contracting State may, by domestic legislation, assimilate to its own nationals any person domiciled in that State.

[2] Cmd. 8912. The effective date for Great Britain was September 27, 1957.

ARTICLE III

1733 1. Any Contracting State which, under its domestic law, requires as a condition of copyright, compliance with formalities such as deposit, registration, notice, notarial certificates, payment of fees or manufacture or publication in that Contracting State, shall regard these requirements as satisfied with respect to all works protected in accordance with this Convention and first published outside its territory and the author of which is not one of its nationals, if from the time of the first publication all the copies of the work published with the authority of the author or other copyright proprietor bear the symbol © accompanied by the name of the copyright proprietor and the year of first publication placed in such manner and location as to give reasonable notice of claim of copyright.

2. The provisions of paragraph 1 of this Article shall not preclude any Contracting State from requiring formalities or other conditions for the acquisition and enjoyment of copyright in respect of works first published in its territory or works of its nationals wherever published.

3. The provisions of paragraph 1 of this Article shall not preclude any Contracting State from providing that a person seeking judicial relief must, in bringing the action, comply with procedural requirements, such as that the complainant must appear through domestic counsel or that the complainant must deposit with the court or an administrative office, or both, a copy of the work involved in the litigation; provided that failure to comply with such requirements shall not affect the validity of the copyright, nor shall any such requirement be imposed upon a national of another Contracting State if such requirement is not imposed on nationals of the State in which protection is claimed.

4. In each Contracting State there shall be legal means of protecting without formalities the unpublished works of nationals of other Contracting States.

5. If a Contracting State grants protection for more than one term of copyright and the first term is for a period longer than one of the minimum periods prescribed in Article IV, such State shall not be required to comply with the provisions of paragraph 1 of this Article III in respect of the second or any subsequent term of copyright.

ARTICLE IV

1734 1. The duration of protection of a work shall be governed, in accordance with the provisions of Article II and this Article, by the law of the Contracting State in which protection is claimed.

2. The term of protection for works protected under this Convention shall not be less than the life of the author and 25 years after his death.

However, any Contracting State which, on the effective date of this Convention in that State has limited this term for certain classes of works to a period computed from the first publication of the work, shall be entitled to maintain these exceptions and to extend them to other classes of works. For all these classes the term of protection shall not be less than twenty-five years from the date of first publication.

Any Contracting State which, upon the effective date of this Convention in that State, does not compute the term of protection upon the basis of the life of the author, shall be entitled to compute the term of protection from the date of the first publication of the work or from its registration prior to publication, as the case may be, provided the term of protection shall not be less than twenty-five years from the date of first publication or from its registration prior to publication, as the case may be.

If the legislation of a Contracting State grants two or more successive terms of protection, the duration of the first term shall not be less than one of the minimum periods specified above.

3. The provisions of paragraph 2 of this Article shall not apply to photographic works or to works of applied art; provided, however, that the term of protection in those Contracting States which protect photographic works, or works of applied art in so far as they are protected as artistic works, shall not be less than ten years for each of said classes of works.

4. No Contracting State shall be obliged to grant protection to a work for a period longer than that fixed for the class of works to which the work in question belongs, in the case of unpublished works by the law of the Contracting State of which the author is a national, and in the case of published works by the law of the Contracting State in which the work has been first published.

For the purposes of the application of the preceding provision, if the law of any Contracting State grants two or more successive terms of protection, the period of protection of that State shall be considered to be the aggregate of those terms. However, if a specified work is not protected by such State during the second or any subsequent term for any reason, the other Contracting State shall not be obliged to protect it during the second or any subsequent term.

5. For the purposes of the application of paragraph 4 of this Article, the work of a national of a Contracting State, first published in a non-Contracting State, shall be treated as though first published in the Contracting State of which the author is a national.

6. For the purposes of the application of paragraph 4 of this Article, in case of simultaneous publication in two or more Contracting States, the work shall be treated as though first published in the State which affords the shortest term; any work published in two or more Contracting States within thirty days of its first publication shall be considered as having been published simultaneously in said Contracting States.

Article V

1735 1. Copyright shall include the exclusive right of the author to make, publish, and authorise the making and publication of translations of works protected under this Convention.

2. However, any Contracting State may, by its domestic legislation, restrict the right of translation of writings, but only subject to the following provisions:

If, after the expiration of a period of seven years from the date of the first publication of a writing, a translation of such writing has not been published in the national language or languages, as the case may be, of the Contracting State, by the owner of the right of translation or with his authorisation, any national of such Contracting State may obtain a non-exclusive licence from the competent authority thereof to translate the work and publish the work so translated in any of the national languages in which it has not been published; provided that such national, in accordance with the procedure of the State concerned, establishes either that he has requested, and been denied, authorisation by the proprietor of the right to make and publish the translation, or that, after due diligence on his part, he was unable to find the owner of the right. A licence may also be granted on the same conditions if all previous editions of a translation in such language are out of print.

If the owner of the right of translation cannot be found, then the applicant for a licence shall send copies of his application to the publisher whose name appears on the work and, if the nationality of the owner of the right of translation is known, to the diplomatic or consular representative of the State of which such owner is a national, or to the organisation which may have been designated by the government of that State. The licence shall not be granted before the expiration of a period of two months from the date of the despatch of the copies of the application.

Due provision shall be made by domestic legislation to assure to the owner of the right of translation a compensation which is just and conforms to international standards to assure payment and transmittal of such compensation, and to assure a correct translation of the work.

The original title and the name of the author of the work shall be printed on all copies of the published translation. The licence shall be valid only for publication of the translation in the territory of the Contracting State where it has been applied for. Copies so published may be imported and sold in another Contracting State if one of the national languages of such other State is the same language as that into which the work has been so translated, and if the domestic law in such other State makes provision for such licences and does not prohibit such importation and sale. Where the foregoing conditions do not exist, the importation and sale of such copies in a Contracting State shall be governed by its domestic law and its agreements. The licence shall not be transferred by the licensee. The licence shall not be granted when the author has withdrawn from circulation all copies of the work.

Article VI

1736 "Publication," as used in this Convention, means the reproduction in tangible form and the general distribution to the public of copies of a work from which it can be read or otherwise visually perceived.

Article VII

1737 This Convention shall not apply to works or rights in works which, at the effective date of the Convention in a Contracting State where protection is claimed, are permanently in the public domain in the said Contracting State.

Article VIII

1738 1. This Convention, which shall bear the date of September 6, 1952, shall be deposited with the Director-General of the United Nations Educational, Scientific and Cultural Organisation and shall remain open for signature by all States for a period of 120 days after that date. It shall be subject to ratification or acceptance by the signatory States.

2. Any State which has not signed this Convention may accede thereto.

3. Ratification, acceptance or accession shall be effected by the deposit of an instrument to that effect with the Director-General of the United Nations Educational, Scientific and Cultural Organisation.

Article IX

1739 1. This Convention shall come into force three months after the deposit of twelve instruments of ratification, acceptance or accession, among which there shall be those of four States which are not members of the International Union for the Protection of Literary and Artistic Works.

2. Subsequently, this Convention shall come into force in respect of each State three months after that State has deposited its instrument of ratification, acceptance or accession.

Article X

1740 1. Each State party to this Convention undertakes to adopt, in accordance with its Constitution, such measures as are necessary to ensure the application of this Convention.

2. It is understood, however, that at the time an instrument of ratification, acceptance or accession is deposited on behalf of any State, such State must be in a position under its domestic law to give effect to the terms of this Convention.

Article XI

1741 1. An Intergovernmental Committee is hereby established with the following duties:

(*a*) to study the problems concerning the application and operation of this Convention;

(*b*) to make preparation for periodic revisions of this Convention;

(*c*) to study any other problems concerning the international protection of copyright, in co-operation with the various interested international organisations, such as the United Nations Educational, Scientific and Cultural Organisation, the International Union for the Protection of Literary and Artistic Works, and the Organisation of American States;

(*d*) to inform the Contracting States as to its activities.

2. The Committee shall consist of the representatives of twelve Contracting States to be selected with due consideration to fair geographical representation and in conformity with the Resolution relating to this article, annexed to this Convention.

The Director-General of the United Nations Educational, Scientific and Cultural Organisation, the Director of the Bureau of the International Union for the Protection of Literary and Artistic Works and the Secretary-General of the Organisation of American States, or their representatives, may attend meetings of the Committee in an advisory capacity.

Article XII

1742 The Intergovernmental Committee shall convene a conference for revision of this Convention whenever it deems necessary, or at the request of at least ten Contracting States, or of a majority of Contracting States if there are less than twenty Contracting States.

Article XIII

1743 Any Contracting State may, at the time of deposit of its instrument of ratification, acceptance or accession, or at any time thereafter, declare by notification addressed to the Director-General of the United Nations Educational, Scientific and Cultural Organisation that this Convention shall apply to all or any of the countries or territories for the international relations of which it is responsible and this Convention shall thereupon apply to the countries or territories named in such notification after the expiration of the term of three months provided for in Article IX. In the absence of such notification, this Convention shall not apply to any such country or territory.

Article XIV

1744 1. Any Contracting State may denounce this Convention in its own name or on behalf of all or any of the countries or territories as to which a notification has been given under Article XIII. The denunciation shall be made by notification addressed to the Director-General of the United Nations Educational, Scientific and Cultural Organisation.

2. Such denunciation shall operate only in respect of the State or of the country or territory on whose behalf it was made and shall not take effect until twelve months after the date of receipt of the notification.

Article XV

1745 A dispute between two or more Contracting States concerning the interpretation or application of this Convention, not settled by negotiation, shall unless the States concerned agree on some other method of settlement, be brought before the International Court of Justice for determination by it.

Article XVI

1746 1. This Convention shall be established in English, French and Spanish. The three texts shall be signed and shall be equally authoritative.

2. Official texts of this Convention shall be established in German, Italian and Portuguese.

Any Contracting State or group of Contracting States shall be entitled to have established by the Director-General of the United Nations Educational, Scientific and Cultural Organisation other texts in the language of its choice by arrangement with the Director-General.

All such texts shall be annexed to the signed texts of this Convention.

Article XVII

1747 1. This Convention shall not in any way affect the provisions of the Berne Convention for the Protection of Literary and Artistic Works or membership in the Union created by that Convention.

2. In application of the foregoing paragraph, a Declaration has been annexed to the present article. This Declaration is an integral part of this Convention for the States bound by the Berne Convention [3] on January 1, 1951, or which have or may become bound to it at a later date. The signature of this Convention by such States shall also constitute signature of the said Declaration, and ratification, acceptance or accession by such States shall include the Declaration as well as the Convention.

Article XVIII

1748 This Convention shall not abrogate multilateral or bilateral copyright conventions or arrangements that are or may be in effect exclusively between two or more American Republics. In the event of any difference either between the provisions of such existing conventions or arrangements and the provisions of this Convention, or between the provisions of this Convention and those of any new convention or arrangement which may be formulated between two or more American Republics after this Convention comes into force, the convention or arrangement most recently formulated shall prevail between the parties thereto. Rights in works acquired in any Contracting State under existing conventions or arrangements before the date this Convention comes into force in such State shall not be affected.

[3] " Switzerland No. 1 (1887)," C. 5167.

ARTICLE XIX

1749 This Convention shall not abrogate multilateral or bilateral conventions or arrangements in effect between two or more Contracting States. In the event of any difference between the provisions of such existing conventions or arrangements and the provisions of this Convention, the provisions of this Convention shall prevail. Rights in works acquired in any Contracting State under existing conventions or arrangements before the date on which this Convention comes into force in such State shall not be affected. Nothing in this article shall affect the provisions of Articles XVII and XVIII of this Convention.

ARTICLE XX

1750 Reservations to this Convention shall not be permitted.

ARTICLE XXI

1751 The Director-General of the United Nations Educational, Scientific and Cultural Organisation shall send duly certified copies of this Convention to the States interested, to the Swiss Federal Council and to the Secretary-General of the United Nations for registration by him.

He shall also inform all interested States of the ratifications, acceptances and accessions which have been deposited, the date on which this Convention comes into force, the notifications under Article XIII of this Convention, and denunciations under Article XIV.

APPENDIX DECLARATION

relating to Article XVII

1752 The States which are members of the International Union for the Protection of Literary and Artistic Works, and which are signatories to the Universal Copyright Convention,

Desiring to reinforce their mutual relations on the basis of the said Union and to avoid any conflict which might result from the co-existence of the Convention of Berne and the Universal Convention,

Have, by common agreement, accepted the terms of the following declaration:

(*a*) Works which, according to the Berne Convention, have as their country of origin a country which has withdrawn from the International Union created by the said Convention, after January 1, 1951, shall not be protected by the Universal Copyright Convention in the countries of the Berne Union;

(*b*) The Universal Copyright Convention shall not be applicable to the relationships among countries of the Berne Union in so far as it relates to the protection of works having as their country of origin, within the meaning of the Berne Convention, a country of the International Union created by the said Convention.

RESOLUTION CONCERNING ARTICLE XI

1753 The Intergovernmental Copyright Conference,

Having considered the problems relating to the Intergovernmental Committee provided for in Article XI of the Universal Copyright Convention,

resolves:

1. The first members of the Committee shall be representatives of the following twelve States, each of those States designating one representative and an alternate: Argentina, Brazil, France, Germany, India, Italy, Japan, Mexico, Spain, Switzerland, United Kingdom and United States of America.

2. The Committee shall be constituted as soon as the Convention comes into force in accordance with Article XI of this Convention.

3. The Committee shall elect its Chairman and one Vice-Chairman. It shall establish its rules of procedure having regard to the following principles:—

(*a*) the normal duration of the term of office of the representatives shall be six years; with one-third retiring every two years;

(*b*) before the expiration of the term of office of any members, the Committee shall decide which States shall cease to be represented on it and which States shall be called upon to designate representatives; the representatives of those States which have not ratified, accepted or acceded shall be the first to retire;

(*c*) the different parts of the world shall be fairly represented;

and expresses the wish
that the United Nations Educational, Scientific and Cultural Organisation provide its Secretariat.

In faith whereof the undersigned, having deposited their respective full powers, have signed this Convention.

* * *

1754 **Protocol 1 annexed to the Universal Copyright Convention concerning the application of that Convention to the works of Stateless Persons and Refugees**

The States parties hereto, being also parties to the Universal Copyright Convention (hereinafter referred to as the " Convention ") have accepted the following provisions:

1. Stateless persons and refugees who have their habitual residence in a State party to this Protocol shall, for the purposes of the Convention, be assimilated to the nationals of that State.

2.—(*a*) This Protocol shall be signed and shall be subject to ratification or acceptance, or may be acceded to, as if the provisions of Article VIII of the Convention applied hereto.

(*b*) This Protocol shall enter into force in respect of each State on the date of deposit of the instrument of ratification, acceptance or accession of the State concerned or on the date of entry into force of the Convention with respect to such State, whichever is the later.

In faith whereof the undersigned, being duly authorised thereto, have signed this Protocol.

Done at Geneva this sixth day of September, 1952, in the English, French and Spanish languages, the three texts being equally authoritative, in a single copy which shall be deposited with the Director-General of U.N.E.S.C.O. The Director-General shall send certified copies to the signatory states, to the Swiss Federal Council and to the Secretary-General of the United Nations for registration.

* * *

1755 **Protocol 2 annexed to the Universal Copyright Convention, concerning the application of that Convention to the works of certain International Organisations**

The State parties hereto, being also parties to the Universal Copyright Convention (hereinafter referred to as the " Convention "),

Have accepted the following provisions:

1.—(*a*) The protection provided for in Article II (1) of the Convention shall apply to works published for the first time by the United Nations, by the Specialised Agencies in relationship therewith, or by the Organisation of American States;

(*b*) Similarly, Article II (2) of the Convention shall apply to the said organisation or agencies.

2.—(*a*) This Protocol shall be signed and shall be subject to ratification or acceptance, or may be acceded to, as if the provisions of Article VIII of the Convention applied hereto.

(*b*) This Protocol shall enter into force for each State on the date of deposit of the instrument of ratification, acceptance or accession of the State concerned or on the date of entry into force of the Convention with respect to such State, whichever is the later.

In faith whereof the undersigned, being duly authorised thereto, have signed this Protocol.

Done at Geneva, this sixth day of September, 1952, in the English, French and Spanish languages, the three texts being equally authoritative, in a single copy which shall be deposited with the Director-General of U.N.E.S.C.O.

The Director-General shall send certified copies to the signatory States, to the Swiss Federal Council and to the Secretary-General of the United Nations for registration.

* * *

1756 **Protocol 3 annexed to the Universal Copyright Convention concerning the effective date of Instruments of Ratification or Acceptance of or Accession to that Convention**

States parties hereto,

Recognising that the application of the Universal Copyright Convention (hereinafter referred to as the " Convention ") to States participating in all the international copyright systems already in force will contribute greatly to the value of the Convention;

Have agreed as follows:

1. Any State party hereto may, on depositing its instrument of ratification or acceptance of or accession to the Convention, notify the Director-General of the United Nations Educational, Scientific and Cultural Organisation (hereinafter referred to as " Director-General ") that that instrument shall not take effect for the purposes of Article IX of the Convention until any other State named in such notification shall have deposited its instrument.

2. The notification referred to in paragraph 1 above shall accompany the instrument to which it relates.

3. The Director-General shall inform all States signatory or which have then acceded to the Convention of any notifications received in accordance with this Protocol.

4. This Protocol shall bear the same date and shall remain open for signature for the same period as the Convention.

5. It shall be subject to ratification or acceptance by the signatory States. Any State which has not signed this Protocol may accede thereto.

6.—(*a*) Ratification or acceptance or accession shall be effected by the deposit of an instrument to that effect with the Director-General.

(*b*) This Protocol shall enter into force on the date of deposit of not less than four instruments of ratification or acceptance or accession. The Director-General shall inform all interested States of this date. Instruments deposited after such date shall take effect on the date of their deposit.

In faith whereof the undersigned, being duly authorised thereto, have signed this Protocol.

Done at Geneva, the sixth day of September, 1952, in the English, French and the Spanish languages, the three texts being equally authoritative, in a single copy which shall be annexed to the original copy of the Convention. The Director-General shall send certified copies to the signatory States, to the Swiss Federal Council and to the Secretary-General of United Nations for registration.

* * *

1757

EUROPEAN AGREEMENT ON THE PROTECTION OF TELEVISION BROADCASTS [4]

Strasbourg, June 22, 1960

The Governments signatory hereto, being Members of the Council of Europe,

Considering that the object of the Council is to achieve a greater unity between its Members;

Considering that exchanges of television programmes between the countries of Europe are calculated to further the achievement of that object;

Considering that these exchanges are hampered by the fact that the majority of television organisations are at present powerless to restrain the re-broadcasting, fixation or public performance of their broadcasts, whereas the organisers of musical or dramatic performances or the like, and the promoters of sports meetings, make their consent to broadcasting to other countries conditional upon an undertaking that the relays will not be used for purposes other than private viewing;

Considering that the international protection of television broadcasts will in no way affect any rights of third parties in these broadcasts;

Considering that the problem is one of some urgency, in view of the installations and links now being brought into service throughout Europe, which are such as to make it easy from the technical point of view for European television organisations to exchange their programmes;

Considering that, pending the conclusion of a potentially universal Convention on " neighbouring rights " at present in contemplation, it is

[4] Cmnd. 1163. Ratified by the United Kingdom on March 9, 1961, and came into force on July 1, 1961.

fitting to conclude a regional Agreement restricted in scope to television broadcasts and of limited duration.

Have agreed as follows:

ARTICLE 1

1758 Broadcasting organisations constituted in the territory and under the laws of a Party to this Agreement or transmitting from such territory shall enjoy, in respect of all their television broadcasts:

1. in the territory of all Parties to this Agreement, the right to authorise or prohibit:
   (*a*) the re-broadcasting of such broadcasts;
   (*b*) the diffusion of such broadcasts to the public by wire;
   (*c*) the communication of such broadcasts to the public by means of any instrument for the transmission of signs, sounds or images;
   (*d*) any fixation of such broadcasts or still photographs thereof, and any reproduction of such a fixation; and
   (*e*) re-broadcasting, wire diffusion or public performance with the aid of the fixations or reproductions referred to in sub-paragraph (*d*) of this paragraph, except where the organisation in which the right vests has authorised the sale of the said fixations or reproductions to the public;

2. in the territory of any other Party to this Agreement, the same protection as that other Party may extend to organisations constituted in its territory and under its laws or transmitting from its territory, where such protection is greater than that provided for in paragraph 1 above.

ARTICLE 2

1759 1. Subject to paragraph 2 of Article 1, and Articles 13 and 14, the protection provided for in paragraph 1 of Article 1 shall continue until the end of the tenth calendar year following the year in which the first broadcast was made from the territory of a Party to this Agreement.

2. No Party to this Agreement shall be required, in pursuance of paragraph 2 of Article 1, to accord to the broadcasts of any broadcasting organisations constituted in the territory and under the laws of another Party to this Agreement or transmitting from the territory of another Party longer protection than that granted by the said other Party.

ARTICLE 3

1760 1. Parties to this Agreement, by making a declaration as provided in Article 10, and in respect of their own territory, may:

(*a*) withhold the protection provided for in sub-paragraph 1 (*b*) of Article 1;

(*b*) withhold the protection provided for in sub-paragraph 1 (*c*) of Article 1, where the communication is not to a paying audience within the meaning of their domestic law;

(*c*) withhold the protection provided for in sub-paragraph 1 (*d*) of Article 1, where the fixation or reproduction of the fixation is made for private use, or solely for educational purposes;

(*d*) withhold the protection provided for in sub-paragraphs 1 (*d*) and (*e*) of Article 1, in respect of still photographs or reproductions of such photographs;

(*e*) withhold the protection provided for in this Agreement from television broadcasts by broadcasting organisations constituted in their territory and under their laws or transmitting from such territory, where such broadcasts enjoy protection under their domestic law;

(*f*) restrict the operation of this Agreement to broadcasting organisations constituted in the territory and under the laws of a Party to this Agreement and also transmitting from the territory of such party.

2. It shall be open to the aforesaid Parties, in respect of their own territory, to provide exceptions to the protection of television broadcasts:

(*a*) for the purpose of reporting current events, in respect of the re-broadcasting, fixation or reproduction of the fixation, wire diffusion or public performance of short extracts from a broadcast which itself constitutes the whole or part of the event in question;

(*b*) in respect of the making of ephemeral fixations of television broadcasts by a broadcasting organisation by means of its own facilities and for its own broadcasts.

3. The aforesaid Parties may, in respect of their own territory, provide for a body with jurisdiction over cases where the right of communication to the public referred to in sub-paragraph 1 (*c*) of Article 1 has been unreasonably refused, or granted on unreasonable terms, by the broadcasting organisation in which the said right vests.

Article 4

1761 1. Fixations of a broadcast in which protection under this Agreement subsists, or still photographs thereof, as well as reproductions of such photographs, made in a territory to which this Agreement does not apply and imported into the territory of a Party to this Agreement where they would be unlawful without the consent of the broadcasting organisation in which the right vests, shall be liable to seizure in the latter territory.

2. The provisions of the last preceding paragraph shall apply to the importation into the territory of a Party to this Agreement of still photographs of a broadcast in which protection under this Agreement subsists and of reproductions of such photographs, where such photographs or reproductions are made in the territory of another Party to this Agreement by virtue of sub-paragraph 1 (*d*) of Article 3.

3. Seizure shall be effected in accordance with the domestic law of each Party to this Agreement.

4. No Party to this Agreement shall be required to provide protection in respect of still photographs, or the reproduction of such photographs, of broadcasts made by a broadcasting organisation constituted in the territory and under the laws of another Party to this Agreement or transmitting from such territory, if the said other Party has availed itself of the reservation provided for in sub-paragraph 1 (*d*) of Article 3.

ARTICLE 5

1762 The protection afforded by this Agreement shall apply both in relation to the visual element and in relation to the sound element of a television broadcast. It shall not affect the sound element when broadcast separately.

ARTICLE 6

1763 1. The protection provided for in Article 1 shall not affect any rights in respect of a television broadcast that may accrue to third parties, such as authors, performers, film makers, manufacturers of phonographic records or organisers of entertainments.

2. It shall likewise be without prejudice to any protection of television broadcasts that may be accorded apart from this Agreement.

ARTICLE 7

1764 1. This Agreement shall be open to signature by the Members of the Council of Europe, who may become Parties to it either by

(*a*) signature without reservation in respect of ratification; or

(*b*) signature with reservation in respect of ratification, followed by the deposit of an instrument of ratification.

2. Instruments of ratification shall be deposited with the Secretary-General of the Council of Europe.

ARTICLE 8

1765 1. This Agreement shall enter into force one month after the date on which three Members of the Council of Europe shall, in accordance with Article 7 thereof, have signed it without reservation in respect of ratification or shall have ratified it.

2. In the case of any Member of the Council of Europe who shall subsequently sign the Agreement without reservation in respect of ratification or who shall ratify it, the Agreement shall enter into force one month after the date of such signature or deposit of the instrument of ratification.

ARTICLE 9

1766 1. After this Agreement has come into force, any European Government which is not a Member of the Council of Europe or any non-European Government having political ties with a Member of the Council of Europe may accede to it, subject to the prior approval of the Committee of Ministers of the Council of Europe.

2. Such accession shall be effected by the deposit of an instrument of accession with the Secretary-General of the Council of Europe and shall take effect one month after the date of deposit.

ARTICLE 10

1767 Signature, ratification or accession shall imply full acceptance of all the provisions of this Agreement; provided always that any country may declare,[5] at the time of signature or of deposit of its instrument of

[5] The instrument of ratification deposited with the Secretary-General of the Council of Europe by the Permanent Representative of the United Kingdom contains the following reservations:

"(1) The Government of the United Kingdom of Great Britain and Northern Ireland withhold the protection provided for in sub-paragraph (b) of paragraph 1 of Article 1 of the said Agreement;

"(2) The Government of the United Kingdom of Great Britain and Northern ratification or accession, that it intends to avail itself of one or more of the options in paragraph 1 of Article 3 above.

ARTICLE 11

1768 The Secretary-General of the Council of Europe shall notify Members of the Council, the Governments of any countries which may have acceded to this Agreement and the Director of the Bureau of the International Union for the Protection of Literary and Artistic Works:

(*a*) of any signatures, together with any reservations as to ratification, of the deposit of instruments of ratification and of the date of entry into force of this Agreement;

(*b*) of the deposit of any instruments of accession in accordance with Article 9;

(*c*) of any declaration or notification received in accordance with Articles 12, 13 or 14;

(*d*) of any decision of the Committee of Ministers taken in pursuance of paragraph 2 of Article 12.

ARTICLE 12

1769 1. This Agreement shall apply to the metropolitan territories of the Parties.

2. Any Party may, at the time of signature, of the deposit of its instrument of ratification or accession, or at any later date, declare by notice addressed to the Secretary-General of the Council of Europe that this Agreement shall extend to any or all of the territories for whose international relations it is responsible.

3. Any Government which has made a declaration under paragraph 2 of this Article extending this Agreement to any territory for whose international relations it is responsible may denounce the Agreement separately in respect of that territory in accordance with Article 14 thereof.

ARTICLE 13

1770 1. This Agreement shall cease to be effective, except in regard to fixations already made, at such time as a Convention on " neighbouring rights ", including the protection of television broadcasts and open to European countries, amongst others, shall have entered into force for at least a majority of the Members of the Council of Europe that are themselves Parties to the Agreement.

2. The Committee of Ministers of the Council of Europe shall at the appropriate time declare that the conditions laid down in the preceding

Ireland withhold the protection provided for in sub-paragraph (c) of paragraph 1 of Article 1 of the said Agreement, where the communication is not to a paying audience within the meaning of the domestic law of the United Kingdom of Great Britain and Northern Ireland;

" (3) The Government of the United Kingdom of Great Britain and Northern Ireland withhold the protection provided for in sub-paragraph (d) of paragraph 1 of Article 1 of the said Agreement, where the fixation or reproduction of the fixation is made for private use or solely for educational purposes;

" (4) The Government of the United Kingdom of Great Britain and Northern Ireland withhold the protection provided for in sub-paragraphs (d) and (e) of paragraph 1 of Article 1 of the said Agreement, in respect of still photographs or reproductions of such photographs;

" (5) The Government of the United Kingdom of Great Britain and Northern Ireland restrict the operation of the said Agreement to broadcasting organisations constituted in the territory and under the laws of a Party to the said Agreement and also transmitting from the territory of such Party."

paragraph have been fulfilled, thereby entailing the termination of this Agreement.

ARTICLE 14

1771 Any Contracting Party may denounce this Agreement by giving one year's notice to that effect to the Secretary-General of the Council of Europe.

In witness whereof, the undersigned,[6] being duly authorised thereto, have signed this Agreement.

Done at Strasbourg, this 22nd day of June, 1960, in English and French, both texts being equally authoritative, in a single copy, which shall remain in the archives of the Council of Europe and of which the Secretary-General shall send certified copies to each of the signatory and acceding Governments and to the Director of the Bureau of the International Union for the Protection of Literary and Artistic Works.

* * *

1772 **PROTOCOL TO THE EUROPEAN AGREEMENT ON THE PROTECTION OF TELEVISION BROADCASTS**[7]

The member States of the Council of Europe, signatory hereto.

Considering the desirability of amending the European Agreement on the Protection of Television Broadcasts, signed at Strasbourg on 22nd June 1960,[8] hereinafter referred to as " the Agreement ";

Considering that the International Convention for the Protection of Performers, Producers of Phonograms and Broadcasting Organisations, signed in Rome on 26th October 1961, entered into force on 18th May 1964,[9]

Have agreed as follows:

ARTICLE 1

1773 1. Paragraph 1 of Article 2 of the Agreement shall be amended as follows:

> " Subject to paragraph 2 of Article 1, and Articles 13 and 14, the protection provided for in paragraph 1 of Article 1 shall last not less than a period of twenty years from the end of the year in which the broadcast took place."

2. Paragraph 2 of Article 2 of the Agreement shall be deleted.

ARTICLE 2

1774 1. Sub-paragraph 1 (*a*) of Article 3 of the Agreement shall be amended as follows:

> " (*a*) withhold the protection provided for in sub-paragraph 1 (*b*) of Article 1 as regards broadcasting organisations constituted in their territory or transmitting from such territory, and restrict the exercise of such protection, as regards broadcasts by broadcasting organisations constituted in the territory of another Party to this Agreement or transmitting from such territory, to a percentage of

6 At the time of signature by the United Kingdom, the following declaration was made:

" Her Majesty's Government understand the word ' signature ' in the first line of Article 10 to refer only to signature without reservation as to ratification."

7 Cmnd. 2744. Signed without reservation in respect of ratification by the United Kingdom on February 23, 1965, and entered into force on March 24, 1965.

8 § 1757, *ante*.

9 § 1791, *post*.

the transmissions by such organisations, which shall not be less than 50% of the average weekly duration of the broadcasts of each of these organisations."

2. Sub-paragraph 1 (*e*) of Article 3 of the Agreement shall be amended as follows:

"(*e*) without prejudice to sub-paragraph 1 (*a*) of this Article, withhold all protection provided for in this Agreement from television broadcasts by broadcasting organisations constituted in their territory and under their laws or transmitting from such territory, where such broadcasts enjoy protection under their domestic law."

3. Paragraph 3 of Article 3 of the Agreement shall be amended as follows:

"3. The aforesaid Parties may, in respect of their own territory, provide for a body with jurisdiction over cases where the right of diffusion to the public by wire referred to in sub-paragraph 1 (*b*) of Article 1, or the right of communication to the public referred to in sub-paragraph 1 (*c*) of Article 1, has been unreasonably refused or granted on unreasonable terms by the broadcasting organisation in which the said right vests."

4. Any State which in accordance with Article 10 of the Agreement has, before the entry into force of this Protocol, availed itself of the option in sub-paragraph 1 (*a*) of Article 3 of the Agreement may, notwithstanding anything in paragraph 1 of the present Article, maintain the application of such option.

Article 3

1775 Article 13 of the Agreement shall be deleted and replaced by the following:

"1. This Agreement shall remain in force indefinitely.

2. Nevertheless, as from 1st January 1975, no State may remain or become a Party to this Agreement unless it is also a Party to the International Convention for the Protection of Performers, Producers of Phonograms and Broadcasting Organisations signed in Rome on 26th October 1961."

Article 4

1776 1. The Governments signatory to the Agreement and the Governments having acceded thereto may become Parties to this Protocol by the procedure laid down in Article 7 or Article 9 of the Agreement, according to whether they are member States of the Council of Europe or not.

2. This Protocol shall enter into force one month after the date on which all the Parties to the Agreement have signed this Protocol without reservation in respect of ratification, or deposited their instrument of ratification or accession in accordance with the provisions of the preceding paragraph.

3. As from the date on which this Protocol enters into force, no State may become a Party to the Agreement without becoming also a Party to this Protocol.

Article 5

1777 The Secretary-General of the Council of Europe shall notify member States of the Council, other States Parties to the Agreement, and the

Director of the Bureau of the International Union for the Protection of Literary and Artistic Works of any signature of this Protocol, together with any reservations as to ratification, and of the deposit of any instrument of ratification of the Protocol or of accession to it, and of the date referred to in paragraph 2 of Article 4 of this Protocol.

In witness whereof the undersigned, being duly authorised thereto have signed this Protocol

Done at Strasbourg, this 22nd day of January 1965 in English and in French, both texts being equally authoritative, in a single copy which shall remain deposited in the archives of the Council of Europe. The Secretary-General of the Council of Europe shall transmit certified copies to each of the signatory and acceding states.

1778 EUROPEAN AGREEMENT CONCERNING PROGRAMME EXCHANGES BY MEANS OF TELEVISION FILMS [10]

Paris, December 15, 1958

The Governments signatory hereto, being Members of the Council of Europe.

Considering that the aim of the Council of Europe is to achieve a greater unity between its Members;

Considering that it is important in the interests of European cultural and economic unity that programmes may be exchanged by means of television films between the member countries of the Council of Europe as freely as possible;

Considering that national legislations allow different conclusions as regards the legal nature of television films and as regards the rights which they grant in respect of such films;

Considering that it is necessary to resolve the difficulties arising from this situation;

Having regard to Article 20 of the Berne Convention for the Protection of Literary and Artistic Works, by the terms of which the Governments of the countries of the Union reserve to themselves the right to enter into special arrangements which do not embody stipulations contrary to that Convention,

Have agreed as follows:

Article 1

1779 In the absence of any contrary or special stipulation within the meaning of Article 4 of the present Agreement, a broadcasting organisation under the jurisdiction of a country which is a Party to this Agreement has the right to authorise in the other countries which are Parties thereto the exploitation for television of television films of which it is the maker.

Article 2

1780 1. All visual or sound and visual recordings intended for television shall be deemed to be television films within the meaning of the present Agreement.

[10] Cmnd. 1509. Signed by the United Kingdom without reservation in respect of ratification on December 15, 1958, and entered into force on July 1, 1961.

2. A broadcasting organisation shall be deemed to be the maker if it has taken the initiative in, and responsibility for, the making of a television film.

Article 3

1781 1. If the television film has been made by a maker other than the one defined in Article 2, paragraph 2, the latter is entitled, in the absence of contrary or special stipulations within the meaning of Article 4, to transfer to a broadcasting organisation the right provided in Article 1.

2. The provision contained in the preceding paragraph applies only if the maker and the broadcasting organisation are under the jurisdiction of countries which are Parties to the present Agreement.

Article 4

1782 By " contrary or special stipulation " is meant any restrictive condition agreed between the maker and persons who contribute to the making of the television film.

Article 5

1783 This Agreement shall not affect the following rights, which shall be entirely reserved:

(*a*) any moral right recognised in relation to films;
(*b*) the copyright in literary, dramatic or artistic works from which the television film is derived;
(*c*) the copyright in a musical work, with or without words, accompanying a television film;
(*d*) the copyright in films other than television films;
(*e*) the copyright in the exploitation of television films otherwise than on television.

Article 6

1784 1. This Agreement shall be open to signature by the Members of the Council of Europe, who may accede to it either by:

(*a*) signature without reservation in respect of ratification; or
(*b*) signature with reservation in respect of ratification, followed by the deposit of an instrument of ratification.

2. Instruments of ratification shall be deposited with the Secretary-General of the Council of Europe.

Article 7

1785 1. This Agreement shall enter into force thirty days after the date on which three Members of the Council shall, in accordance with Article 6 thereof, have signed it without reservation in respect of ratification or shall have ratified it.

2. In the case of any Member of the Council who shall subsequently sign the Agreement without reservation in respect of ratification or who shall ratify it, the Agreement shall enter into force thirty days after the date of such signature or deposit of the instrument of ratification.

Article 8

1786 1. After this Agreement has come into force, any country which is not a Member of the Council of Europe may accede to it, subject to the prior approval of the Committee of Ministers of the Council of Europe.

2. Such accession shall be effected by the deposit of an instrument of accession with the Secretary-General of the Council of Europe, and shall take effect thirty days after the date of deposit.

ARTICLE 9

1787 Signature without reservation in respect of ratification, ratification or accession shall imply full acceptance of all the provisions of this Agreement.

ARTICLE 10

1788 The Secretary-General of the Council of Europe shall notify Members of the Council, the Governments of any countries which may have acceded to this Agreement and the Director of the Bureau of the International Union for the protection of literary and artistic works:

(*a*) of the date of entry into force of this Agreement and the names of any Members of the Council which have become Parties thereto;

(*b*) of the deposit of any instruments of accession in accordance with Article 8 of the present Agreement;

(*c*) of any declaration or notification received in accordance with Articles 11 and 12 thereof.

ARTICLE 11

1789 1. This Agreement shall apply to the metropolitan territories of the Contracting Parties.

2. Any Contracting Party may, at the time of signature, ratification or accession, or at any later date, declare by notice addressed to the Secretary-General of the Council of Europe that this Agreement shall apply to any territory or territories mentioned in the said declaration and for whose international relations it is responsible.

3. Any declaration made in accordance with the preceding paragraph may, in respect of any territory mentioned in such a declaration, be withdrawn under the conditions laid down in Article 12 of this Agreement.

ARTICLE 12

1790 1. This Agreement shall remain in force for an unlimited period.

2. Any Contracting Party may denounce this Agreement at one year's notice by notification to this effect to the Secretary-General of the Council of Europe.

In witness whereof, the undersigned, being duly authorised thereto, have signed this Agreement.

Done at Paris, this 15th day of December 1958, in English and French, both texts being equally authoritative, in a single copy, which shall remain in the archives of the Council of Europe and of which the Secretary-General shall send certified copies to each of the signatory and acceding Governments and to the Director of the International Bureau for the Protection of Literary and Artistic Works.

1791 **INTERNATIONAL CONVENTION FOR THE PROTECTION OF PERFORMERS, PRODUCERS OF PHONOGRAMS AND BROADCASTING ORGANISATIONS** [11]

Rome, October 26, 1961

The Contracting States, moved by the desire to protect the rights of performers, producers of phonograms, and broadcasting organisations,

Have agreed as follows:

ARTICLE 1

1792 Protection granted under this Convention shall leave intact and shall in no way affect the protection of copyright in literary and artistic works. Consequently, no provision of this Convention may be interpreted as prejudicing such protection.

ARTICLE 2

1793 1. For the purposes of this Convention, national treatment shall mean the treatment accorded by the domestic law of the Contracting State in which protection is claimed:

(*a*) to performers who are its nationals, as regards performances taking place, broadcast, or first fixed, on its territory;

(*b*) to producers of phonograms who are its nationals, as regards phonograms first fixed or first published on its territory;

(*c*) to broadcasting organisations which have their headquarters on its territory, as regards broadcasts transmitted from transmitters situated on its territory.

2. National treatment shall be subject to the protection specifically guaranteed, and the limitations specifically provided for, in this Convention.

ARTICLE 3

1794 For the purposes of this Convention:

(*a*) "Performers" means actors, singers, musicians, dancers, and other persons who act, sing, deliver, declaim, play in, or otherwise perform literary or artistic works;

(*b*) "Phonogram" means any exclusively aural fixation of sounds of a performance or of other sounds;

(*c*) "Producer of phonograms" means the person who, or the legal entity which, first fixes the sounds of a performance or other sounds;

(*d*) "Publication" means the offering of copies of a phonogram to the public in reasonable quantity;

(*e*) "Reproduction" means the making of a copy or copies of a fixation;

(*f*) "Broadcasting" means the transmission by wireless means for public reception of sounds or of images and sounds;

(*g*) "Rebroadcasting" means the simultaneous broadcasting by one broadcasting organisation of the broadcast of another broadcasting organisation.

[11] Cmnd. 2425. Ratified by the United Kingdom on October 30, 1963, and entered into force on May 18, 1964.

ARTICLE 4

1795 Each Contracting State shall grant national treatment to performers if any of the following conditions is met:

(*a*) the performance takes place in another Contracting State;
(*b*) the performance is incorporated in a phonogram which is protected under Article 5 of this Convention;
(*c*) the performance, not being fixed on a phonogram, is carried by a broadcast which is protected by Article 6 of this Convention.

ARTICLE 5

1796 1. Each Contracting State shall grant national treatment to producers of phonograms if any of the following conditions is met:

(*a*) the producer of the phonogram is a national of another Contracting State (criterion of nationality);
(*b*) the first fixation of the sound was made in another Contracting State (criterion of fixation);
(*c*) the phonogram was first published in another Contracting State (criterion of publication).

2. If a phonogram was first published in a non-contracting State but if it was also published, within thirty days of its first publication, in a Contracting State (simultaneous publication), it shall be considered as first published in the Contracting State.

3. By means of a notification deposited with the Secretary-General of the United Nations, any Contracting State may declare that it will not apply the criterion of publication or, alternatively, the criterion of fixation. Such notification may be deposited at the time of ratification, acceptance or accession, or at any time thereafter; in the last case, it shall become effective six months after it has been deposited.

ARTICLE 6

1797 1. Each Contracting State shall grant national treatment to broadcasting organisations if either of the following conditions is met:

(*a*) the headquarters of the broadcasting organisation is situated in another Contracting State;
(*b*) the broadcast was transmitted from a transmitter situated in another Contracting State.

2. By means of a notification deposited with the Secretary-General of the United Nations, any Contracting State may declare that it will protect broadcasts only if the headquarters of the broadcasting organisation is situated in another Contracting State and the broadcast was transmitted from a transmitter situated in the same Contracting State. Such notification may be deposited at the time of ratification, acceptance or accession, or at any time thereafter; in the last case, it shall become effective six months after it has been deposited.

ARTICLE 7

1798 1. The protection provided for performers by this Convention shall include the possibility of preventing:

(*a*) the broadcasting and the communication to the public, without their consent, of their performance, except where the performance used in the broadcasting or the public communication is itself already a broadcast performance or is made from a fixation;

(*b*) the fixation, without their consent, of their unfixed performance;

(*c*) the reproduction, without their consent, of a fixation of their performance:

(i) if the original fixation itself was made without their consent;

(ii) if the reproduction is made for purposes different from those for which the performers gave their consent;

(iii) if the original fixation was made in accordance with the provisions of Article 15, and the reproduction is made for purposes different from those referred to in those provisions.

2.—(1) If broadcasting was consented to by the performers, it shall be a matter for the domestic law of the Contracting State where protection is claimed to regulate the protection against rebroadcasting, fixation for broadcasting purposes, and the reproduction of such fixation for broadcasting purposes.

(2) The terms and conditions governing the use by broadcasting organisations of fixations made for broadcasting purposes shall be determined in accordance with the domestic law of the Contracting State where protection is claimed.

(3) However, the domestic law referred to in sub-paragraphs (1) and (2) of this paragraph shall not operate to deprive performers of the ability to control, by contract, their relations with broadcasting organisations.

Article 8

1799 Any Contracting State may, by its domestic laws and regulations, specify the manner in which performers will be represented in connexion with the exercise of their rights if several of them participate in the same performance.

Article 9

1800 Any Contracting State may, by its domestic laws and regulations, extend the protection provided for in this Convention to artistes who do not perform literary or artistic works.

Article 10

1801 Producers of phonograms shall enjoy the right to authorise or prohibit the direct or indirect reproduction of their phonograms.

Article 11

1802 If, as a condition of protecting the rights of producers of phonograms, or of performers, or both, in relation to phonograms, a Contracting State, under its domestic law, requires compliance with formalities, these shall be considered as fulfilled if all the copies in commerce of the published phonogram or their containers bear a notice consisting of the symbol ℗, accompanied by the year date of the first publication, placed in such a manner as to give reasonable notice of claim of protection; and if the copies or their containers do not identify the producer or the licensee of the producer (by carrying his name, trade mark or other appropriate designation), the notice shall also include the name of the owner of the rights of the producer; and, furthermore, if the copies or their containers do not identify the principal performers, the notice shall also include the name of the person who, in the country in which the fixation was effected, owns the rights of such performers.

Article 12

1803 If a phonogram published for commercial purposes, or a reproduction of such phonogram, is used directly for broadcasting or for any communication to the public, a single equitable remuneration shall be paid by the user to the performers, or to the producers of the phonograms, or to both. Domestic law may, in the absence of agreement between these parties, lay down the conditions as to the sharing of this remuneration.

Article 13

1804 Broadcasting organisations shall enjoy the right to authorise or prohibit:

(*a*) the rebroadcasting of their broadcasts;

(*b*) the fixation of their broadcasts;

(*c*) the reproduction:

(i) of fixations, made without their consent, of their broadcasts;

(ii) of fixations, made in accordance with the provisions of Article 15, of their broadcasts, if the reproduction is made for purposes different from those referred to in those provisions;

(*d*) the communication to the public of their television broadcasts if such communication is made in places accessible to the public against payment of an entrance fee; it shall be a matter for the domestic law of the State where protection of this right is claimed to determine the conditions under which it may be exercised.

Article 14

1805 The term of protection to be granted under this Convention shall last at least until the end of a period of twenty years computed from the end of the year in which:

(*a*) the fixation was made—for phonograms and for performances incorporated therein;

(*b*) the performance took place—for performances not incorporated in phonograms;

(*c*) the broadcast took place—for broadcasts.

Article 15

1806 1. Any Contracting State may, in its domestic laws and regulations, provide for exceptions to the protection guaranteed by this Convention as regards:

(*a*) private use;

(*b*) use of short excerpts in connexion with the reporting of current events;

(*c*) ephemeral fixation by a broadcasting organisation by means of its own facilities and for its own broadcasts;

(*d*) use solely for the purposes of teaching or scientific research.

2. Irrespective of paragraph 1 of this Article, any Contracting State may, in its domestic laws and regulations, provide for the same kinds of limitations with regard to the protection of performers, producers and phonograms and broadcasting organisations, as it provides for, in its domestic laws and regulations, in connexion with the protection of copyright in literary and artistic works. However, compulsory licences may be provided for only to the extent to which they are compatible with this Convention.

ARTICLE 16

1807 1. Any State, upon becoming party to this Convention, shall be bound by all the obligations and shall enjoy all the benefits thereof. However a State may at any time, in a notification deposited with the Secretary-General of the United Nations, declare that:

(*a*) as regards Article 12:

(i) it will not apply the provisions of that Article;

(ii) it will not apply the provisions of that Article in respect of certain uses;

(iii) as regards phonograms the producer of which is not a national of another Contracting State, it will not apply that Article;

(iv) as regards phonograms the producer of which is a national of another Contracting State, it will limit the protection provided for by that Article to the extent to which, and to the term for which, the latter State grants protection to phonograms first fixed by a national of the State making the declaration; however, the fact that the Contracting State of which the producer is a national does not grant the protection to the same beneficiary or beneficiaries as the State making the declaration shall not be considered as a difference in the extent of the protection;

(*b*) as regards Article 13, it will not apply item (*d*) of that Article; if a Contracting State makes such a declaration, the other Contracting States shall not be obliged to grant the right referred to in Article 13, item (*d*), to broadcasting organisations whose headquarters are in that State.

2. If the notification referred to in paragraph 1 of this Article is made after the date of the deposit of the instrument of ratification, acceptance or accession, the declaration will become effective six months after it has been deposited.

ARTICLE 17

1808 Any State which, on October 26, 1961, grants protection to producers of phonograms solely on the basis of the criterion of fixation may, by a notification deposited with the Secretary-General of the United Nations at the time of ratification, acceptance or accession, declare that it will apply, for the purposes of Article 5, the criterion of fixation alone and, for the purposes of paragraph 1 (*a*) (iii) and (iv) of Article 16, the criterion of fixation instead of the criterion of nationality.

ARTICLE 18

1809 Any State which has deposited a notification under paragraph 3 of Article 5, paragraph 2 of Article 6, paragraph 1 of Article 16 or Article 17, may, by a further notification deposited with the Secretary-General of the United Nations, reduce its scope or withdraw it.

ARTICLE 19

1810 Notwithstanding anything in this Convention, once a performer has consented to the incorporation of his performance in a visual or audio-visual fixation, Article 7 shall have no further application.

ARTICLE 20

1811 1. This Convention shall not prejudice rights acquired in any Contracting State before the date of coming into force of this Convention for that State.

2. No Contracting State shall be bound to apply the provisions of this Convention to performances or broadcasts which took place, or to phonograms which were fixed, before the date of coming into force of this Convention for that State.

ARTICLE 21

1812 The protection provided for in this Convention shall not prejudice any protection otherwise secured to performers, producers of phonograms and broadcasting organisations.

ARTICLE 22

1813 Contracting States reserve the right to enter into special agreements among themselves in so far as such agreements grant to performers, producers of phonograms or broadcasting organisations more extensive rights than those granted by this Convention or contain other provisions not contrary to this Convention.

ARTICLE 23

1814 This Convention shall be deposited with the Secretary-General of the United Nations. It shall be open until June 30, 1962 for signature by any State invited to the Diplomatic Conference on the International Protection of Performers, Producers of Phonograms and Broadcasting Organisations which is a party to the Universal Copyright Convention or a member of the International Union for the Protection of Literary and Artistic Works.

ARTICLE 24

1815 1. This Convention shall be subject to ratification or acceptance by the signatory States.

2. This Convention shall be open for accession by any State invited to the Conference referred to in Article 23, and by any State Member of the United Nations, provided that in either case such State is a party to the Universal Copyright Convention or a member of the International Union for the Protection of Literary and Artistic Works.

3. Ratification, acceptance or accession shall be effected by the deposit of an instrument to that effect with the Secretary-General of the United Nations.

Article 25

1816 1. This Convention shall come into force three months after the date of deposit of the sixth instrument of ratification, acceptance or accession.

2. Subsequently, this Convention shall come into force in respect of each State three months after the date of deposit of its instrument of ratification, acceptance or accession.

Article 26

1817 1. Each Contracting State undertakes to adopt, in accordance with its Constitution, the measures necessary to ensure the application of this Convention.

2. At the time of deposit of its instrument of ratification, acceptance or accession, each State must be in a position under its domestic law to give effect to the terms of this Convention.

Article 27

1818 1. Any State may, at the time of ratification, acceptance or accession, or at any time thereafter, declare by notification addressed to the Secretary-General of the United Nations that this Convention shall extend to all or any of the territories for whose international relations it is responsible, provided that the Universal Copyright Convention or the International Convention for the Protection of Literary and Artistic Works applies to the territory or territories concerned. This notification shall take effect three months after the date of its receipt.

2. The notifications referred to in paragraph 3 of Article 5, paragraph 2 of Article 6, paragraph 2 of Article 16 and Articles 17 and 18, may be extended to cover all or any of the territories referred to in paragraph 1 of this Article.

Article 28

1819 1. Any Contracting State may denounce this Convention, on its own behalf, or on behalf of all or any of the territories referred to in Article 27.

2. The denunciation shall be effected by a notification addressed to the Secretary-General of the United Nations and shall take effect twelve months after the date of receipt of the notification.

3. The right of denunciation shall not be exercised by a Contracting State before the expiry of a period of five years from the date on which the Convention came into force with respect to that State.

4. A Contracting State shall cease to be a party to this Convention from that time when it is neither a party to the Universal Copyright

Convention nor a member of the International Union for the Protection of Literary and Artistic Works.

5. This Convention shall cease to apply to any territory referred to in Article 27 from that time when neither the Universal Copyright Convention nor the International Convention for the Protection of Literary and Artistic Works applies to that territory.

Article 29

1820 1. After this Convention has been in force for five years, any Contracting State may, by notification addressed to the Secretary-General of the United Nations, request that a conference be convened for the purpose of revising the Convention. The Secretary-General shall notify all Contracting States of this request. If, within a period of six months following the date of notification by the Secretary-General of the United Nations, not less than one half of the Contracting States notify him of their concurrence with the request, the Secretary-General shall inform the Director-General of the International Labour Office, the Director-General of the United Nations Educational, Scientific and Cultural Organization and the Director of the Bureau of the International Union for the Protection of Literary and Artistic Works, who shall convene a revision conference in co-operation with the Intergovernmental Committee provided for in Article 32.

2. The adoption of any revision of this Convention shall require an affirmative vote by two-thirds of the States attending the revision conference, provided that this majority includes two-thirds of the States which, at the time of the revision conference, are parties to the Convention.

3. In the event of adoption of a Convention revising this Convention in whole or in part, and unless the revising Convention provides otherwise:

(*a*) this Convention shall cease to be open to ratification, acceptance or accession as from the date of entry into force of the revising Convention;

(*b*) this Convention shall remain in force as regards relations between or with Contracting States which have not become parties to the revising Convention.

Article 30

1821 Any dispute which may arise between two or more Contracting States concerning the interpretation or application of this Convention and which is not settled by negotiation shall, at the request of any one of the parties to the dispute, be referred to the International Court of Justice for decision, unless they agree to another mode of settlement.

Article 31

1822 Without prejudice to the provisions of paragraph 3 of Article 5, paragraph 2 of Article 6, paragraph 1 of Article 16 and Article 17, no reservation may be made to this Convention.

Article 32

1823 1. An Intergovernmental Committee is hereby established with the following duties:

(*a*) to study questions concerning the application and operation of this Convention; and
(*b*) to collect proposals and to prepare documentation for possible revision of this Convention.

2. The Committee shall consist of representatives of the Contracting States, chosen with due regard to equitable geographical distribution. The number of members shall be six if there are twelve Contracting States or less, nine if there are thirteen to eighteen Contracting States and twelve if there are more than eighteen Contracting States.

3. The Committee shall be constituted twelve months after the Convention comes into force by an election organised among the Contracting States, each of which shall have one vote, by the Director-General of the International Labour Office, the Director-General of the United Nations Educational, Scientific and Cultural Organization and the Director of the Bureau of the International Union for the Protection of Literary and Artistic Works, in accordance with rules previously approved by a majority of all Contracting States.

4. The Committee shall elect its Chairman and officers. It shall establish its own rules of procedure. These rules shall in particular provide for the future operation of the Committee and for a method of selecting its members for the future in such a way as to ensure rotation among the various Contracting States.

5. Officials of the International Labour Office, the United Nations Educational, Scientific and Cultural Organization and the Bureau of the International Union for the Protection of Literary and Artistic Works, designated by the Directors-General and the Director thereof, shall constitute the Secretariat of the Committee.

6. Meetings of the Committee, which shall be convened whenever a majority of its members deems it necessary, shall be held successively at the headquarters of the International Labour Office, the United Nations Educational, Scientific and Cultural Organization and the Bureau of the International Union for the Protection of Literary and Artistic Works.

7. Expenses of members of the Committee shall be borne by their respective Governments.

Article 33

1824 1. The present Convention is drawn up in English, French and Spanish, the three texts being equally authentic.

2. In addition, official texts of the present Convention shall be drawn up in German, Italian and Portuguese.

Article 34

1825 1. The Secretary-General of the United Nations shall notify the States invited to the Conference referred to in Article 23 and every State Member of the United Nations, as well as the Director-General of the International Labour Office, the Director-General of the United Nations Educational, Scientific and Cultural Organization and the Director of the Bureau of the International Union for the Protection of Literary and Artistic Works:

(*a*) of the deposit of each instrument of ratification, acceptance or accession;

(*b*) of the date of entry into force of the Convention;

(*c*) of all notifications, declarations [12] or communications provided for in this Convention;

(*d*) if any of the situations referred to in paragraphs 4 and 5 of Article 28 arise.

2. The Secretary-General of the United Nations shall also notify the Director-General of the International Labour Office, the Director-General of the United Nations Educational, Scientific and Cultural Organization and the Director of the Bureau of the International Union for the Protection of Literary and Artistic Works of the requests communicated to him in accordance with Article 29, as well as of any communication received from the Contracting States concerning the revision of the Convention.

IN FAITH WHEREOF, the undersigned, being duly authorised thereto, have signed this Convention.

DONE at Rome, this twenty-sixth day of October 1961, in a single copy in the English, French and Spanish languages. Certified true copies shall be delivered by the Secretary-General of the United Nations to all the States invited to the Conference referred to in Article 23 and to every State Member of the United Nations, as well as to the Director-General of the International Labour Office, the Director-General of the United Nations Educational, Scientific and Cultural Organization and the Director of the Bureau of the International Union for the Protection of Literary and Artistic Works.

[12] The United Kingdom ratification was accompanied by the following declaration:

(1) in respect of Article 5 (1) (*b*) and in accordance with Article 5 (3) of the Convention, the United Kingdom will not apply, in respect of phonograms, the criterion of fixation;

(2) in respect of Article 6 (1) and in accordance with Article 6 (2) of the Convention, the United Kingdom will protect broadcasts only if the headquarters of the broadcasting organisation is situated in another Contracting State and the broadcast was transmitted from a transmitter situated in the same Contracting State;

(3) in respect of Article 12 and in accordance with Article 16 (1) of the Convention,

(*a*) the United Kingdom will not apply the provisions of Article 12 in respect of the following uses:

(i) the causing of a phonogram to be heard in public at any premises where persons reside or sleep, as part of the amenities provided exclusively or mainly for residents or inmates therein except where a special charge is made for admission to the part of the premises where the phonogram is to be heard,

(ii) the causing of a phonogram to be heard in public as part of the activities of, or for the benefit of, a club, society or other organisation which is not established or conducted for profit and whose main objects are charitable or are otherwise concerned with the advancement of religion, education or social welfare, except where a charge is made for admission to the place where the phonogram is to be heard, and any of the proceeds of the charge are applied otherwise than for the purpose of the organisation;

(*b*) as regards phonograms the producer of which is not a national of another Contracting State or as regards phonograms the producer of which is a national of a Contracting State which has made a declaration under Article 16 (1) (*a*) (i) stating that it will not apply the provisions of Article 12, the United Kingdom will not grant the protection provided for by Article 12, unless, in either event, the phonogram has been first published in a Contracting State which has made no such declaration.

1826

CONVENTION ESTABLISHING THE WORLD INTELLECTUAL PROPERTY ORGANIZATION [13]

Stockholm, July 14, 1967 to January 13, 1968

THE CONTRACTING PARTIES,

Desiring to contribute to better understanding and co-operation among States for their mutual benefit on the basis of respect for their sovereignty and equality,

Desiring, in order to encourage creative activity, to promote the protection of intellectual property throughout the world,

Desiring to modernize and render more efficient the administration of the Unions established in the fields of the protection of industrial property and the protection of literary and artistic works, while fully respecting the independence of each of the Unions,

AGREE AS FOLLOWS:

ARTICLE 1

1827

Establishment of the Organization

The World Intellectual Property Organization is hereby established.

ARTICLE 2

1828

Definitions

For the purposes of this Convention:

(i) " Organization " shall mean the World Intellectual Property Organization (WIPO);

(ii) " International Bureau " shall mean the International Bureau of Intellectual Property;

(iii) " Paris Convention " shall mean the Convention for the Protection of Industrial Property signed on March 20, 1883, including any of its revisions;

(iv) " Berne Convention " shall mean the Convention for the Protection of Literary and Artistic Works signed on September 9, 1886, including any of its revisions;

(v) " Paris Union " shall mean the International Union established by the Paris Convention;

(vi) " Berne Union " shall mean the International Union established by the Berne Convention;

(vii) " Unions " shall mean the Paris Union, the Special Unions and Agreements established in relation with that Union, the Berne Union, and any other international agreement designed to promote the protection of intellectual property whose administration is assumed by the Organization according to Article 4 (iii);

(viii) " intellectual property " shall include the rights relating to:
- — literary, artistic and scientific works,
- — performances of performing artists, phonograms, and broadcasts,
- — inventions in all fields of human endeavour,
- — scientific discoveries,
- — industrial designs,

[13] Cmnd. 4408. Ratified by the United Kingdom on February 26, 1969, and entered into force on April 26, 1970.

— trademarks, service marks, and commercial names and designations,
— protection against unfair competition,

and all other rights resulting from intellectual activity in the industrial, scientific, literary or artistic fields.

ARTICLE 3

1829 **Objectives of the Organization**

The objectives of the Organization are:

(i) to promote the protection of intellectual property throughout the world through co-operation among States and, where appropriate, in collaboration with any other international organization,
(ii) to ensure administrative co-operation among the Unions.

ARTICLE 4

1830 **Functions**

In order to attain the objectives described in Article 3, the Organization, through its appropriate organs, and subject to the competence of each of the Unions:

(i) shall promote the development of measures designed to facilitate the efficient protection of intellectual property throughout the world and to harmonize national legislations in this field;
(ii) shall perform the administrative tasks of the Paris Union, the Special Unions established in relation with that Union, and the Berne Union;
(iii) may agree to assume, or participate in, the administration of any other international agreement designed to promote the protection of intellectual property;
(iv) shall encourage the conclusion of international agreements designed to promote the protection of intellectual property;
(v) shall offer its co-operation to States requesting legal-technical assistance in the field of intellectual property;
(vi) shall assemble and disseminate information concerning the protection of intellectual property, carry out and promote studies in this field, and publish the results of such studies;
(vii) shall maintain services facilitating the international protection of intellectual property and, where appropriate, provide for registration in this field and the publication of the data concerning the registrations;
(viii) shall take all other appropriate action.

ARTICLE 5

1831 **Membership**

(1) Membership in the Organization shall be open to any State which is a member of any of the Unions as defined in Article 2 (vii).

(2) Membership in the Organization shall be equally open to any State not a member of any of the Unions, provided that:

(i) it is a member of the United Nations, any of the Specialized Agencies brought into relationship with the United Nations, or the International Atomic Energy Agency, or is a party to the Statute of the International Court of Justice,[14] or

(ii) it is invited by the General Assembly to become a party to this Convention.

ARTICLE 6

1832 **General Assembly**

(1) (*a*) There shall be a General Assembly consisting of the States party to this Convention which are members of any of the Unions.

(*b*) The Government of each State shall be represented by one delegate, who may be assisted by alternate delegates, advisors, and experts.

(*c*) The expenses of each delegation shall be borne by the Government which has appointed it.

(2) The General Assembly shall:

(i) appoint the Director-General upon nomination by the Co-ordination Committee;

(ii) review and approve reports of the Director-General concerning the Organization and give him all necessary instructions;

(iii) review and approve the reports and activities of the Co-ordination Committee and give instructions to such Committee;

(iv) adopt the triennial budget of expenses common to the Unions;

(v) approve the measures proposed by the Director-General concerning the administration of the international agreements referred to in Article 4 (iii);

(vi) adopt the financial regulations of the Organization;

(vii) determine the working languages of the Secretariat, taking into consideration the practice of the United Nations;

(viii) invite States referred to under Article 5 (2) (ii) to become party to this Convention;

(ix) determine which States not Members of the Organization and which intergovernmental and international non-governmental organizations shall be admitted to its meetings as observers;

(x) exercise such other functions as are appropriate under this Convention.

(3) (*a*) Each State, whether member of one or more Unions, shall have one vote in the General Assembly.

(*b*) One-half of the States members of the General Assembly shall constitute a quorum.

(*c*) Notwithstanding the provisions of sub-paragraph (*b*), if, in any session, the number of States represented is less than one-half but equal to or more than one-third of the States members of the General Assembly, the General Assembly may make decisions but, with the exception of decisions concerning its own procedure, all such decisions shall take effect only if the following conditions are fulfilled. The International Bureau shall communicate the said decisions to the States members of the General Assembly which were not represented and shall invite them to express in writing their vote or abstention within a period of three months from the date of the communication. If, at the expiration of this period, the number of States having thus expressed their vote or abstention attains the number of States which was lacking for attaining the quorum in the session itself, such decisions shall take effect provided that at the same time the required majority still obtains.

14 "Treaty Series No. 67 (1946)," Cmd. 7015.

(*d*) Subject to the provisions of sub-paragraphs (*e*) and (*f*), the General Assembly shall make its decisions by a majority of two-thirds of the votes cast.

(*e*) The approval of measures concerning the administration of international agreements referred to in Article 4 (iii) shall require a majority of three-fourths of the votes cast.

(*f*) The approval of an agreement with the United Nations under Articles 57 and 63 of the Charter of the United Nations [15] shall require a majority of nine-tenths of the votes cast.

(*g*) For the appointment of the Director-General (paragraph (2) (i)), the approval of measures proposed by the Director-General concerning the administration of international agreements (paragraph (2) (v)), and the transfer of headquarters (Article 10), the required majority must be attained not only in the General Assembly but also in the Assembly of the Paris Union and the Assembly of the Berne Union.

(*h*) Abstentions shall not be considered as votes.

(*i*) A delegate may represent, and vote in the name of, one State only.

(4) (*a*) The General Assembly shall meet once in every third calendar year in ordinary session, upon convocation by the Director-General.

(*b*) The General Assembly shall meet in extraordinary session upon convocation by the Director-General either at the request of the Co-ordination Committee or at the request of one-fourth of the States members of the General Assembly.

(*c*) Meetings shall be held at the headquarters of the Organization.

(5) States party to this Convention which are not members of any of the Unions shall be admitted to the meetings of the General Assembly as observers.

(6) The General Assembly shall adopt its own rules of procedure.

Article 7

1833 **Conference**

(1) (*a*) There shall be a Conference consisting of the States party to this Convention whether or not they are members of any of the Unions.

(*b*) The Government of each State shall be represented by one delegate, who may be assisted by alternate delegates, advisors, and experts.

(*c*) The expenses of each delegation shall be borne by the Government which has appointed it.

(2) The Conference shall:

(i) discuss matters of general interest in the field of intellectual property and may adopt recommendations relating to such matters, having regard for the competence and autonomy of the Unions;

(ii) adopt the triennial budget of the Conference;

(iii) within the limits of the budget of the Conference, establish the triennial programme of legal-technical assistance;

(iv) adopt amendments to this Convention as provided in Article 17;

(v) determine which States not Members of the Organization and which intergovernmental and international non-governmental organizations shall be admitted to its meetings as observers;

(vi) exercise such other functions as are appropriate under this Convention.

[15] "Treaty Series No. 67 (1946)," Cmd. 7015.

(3) (*a*) Each Member State shall have one vote in the Conference.

(*b*) One-third of the Member States shall constitute a quorum.

(*c*) Subject to the provisions of Article 17, the Conference shall make its decisions by a majority of two-thirds of the votes cast.

(*d*) The amounts of the contributions of States party to this Convention not members of any of the Unions shall be fixed by a vote in which only the delegates of such States shall have the right to vote.

(*e*) Abstentions shall not be considered as votes.

(*f*) A delegate may represent, and vote in the name of, one State only.

(4) (*a*) The Conference shall meet in ordinary session, upon convocation by the Director-General, during the same period and at the same place as the General Assembly.

(*b*) The Conference shall meet in extraordinary session, upon convocation by the Director-General, at the request of the majority of the Member States.

(5) The Conference shall adopt its own rules of procedure.

ARTICLE 8

1834 **Co-ordination Committee**

(1) (*a*) There shall be a Co-ordination Committee consisting of the States party to this Convention which are members of the Executive Committee of the Paris Union, or the Executive Committee of the Berne Union, or both. However, if either of these Executive Committees is composed of more than one-fourth of the number of the countries members of the Assembly which elected it, then such Executive Committee shall designate from among its members the States which will be members of the Co-ordination Committee, in such a way that their number shall not exceed the one-fourth referred to above, it being understood that the country on the territory of which the Organization has its headquarters shall not be included in the computation of the said one-fourth.

(*b*) The Government of each State member of the Co-ordination Committee shall be represented by one delegate, who may be assisted by alternate delegates, advisors, and experts.

(*c*) Whenever the Co-ordination Committee considers either matters of direct interest to the programme or budget of the Conference and its agenda, or proposals for the amendment of this Convention which would affect the rights or obligations of States party to this Convention not members of any of the Unions, one-fourth of such States shall participate in the meetings of the Co-ordination Committee with the same rights as members of that Committee. The Conference shall, at each of its ordinary sessions, designate these States.

(*d*) The expenses of each delegation shall be borne by the Government which has appointed it.

(2) If the other Unions administered by the Organization wish to be represented as such in the Co-ordination Committee, their representatives must be appointed from among the States members of the Co-ordination Committee.

(3) The Co-ordination Committee shall:

(i) give advice to the organs of the Unions, the General Assembly, the Conference, and the Director-General, on all administrative, financial and other matters of common interest either to two or more of the Unions, or to one or more of the Unions and the

Organization, and in particular on the budget of expenses common to the Unions;

(ii) prepare the draft agenda of the General Assembly;

(iii) prepare the draft agenda and the draft programme and budget of the Conference;

(iv) on the basis of the triennial budget of expenses common to the Unions and the triennial budget of the Conference, as well as on the basis of the triennial programme of legal-technical assistance, establish the corresponding annual budgets and programmes;

(v) when the term of office of the Director-General is about to expire, or when there is a vacancy in the post of the Director-General, nominate a candidate for appointment to such position by the General Assembly; if the General Assembly does not appoint its nominee, the Co-ordination Committee shall nominate another condidate; this procedure shall be repeated until the latest nominee is appointed by the General Assembly;

(vi) if the post of the Director-General becomes vacant between two sessions of the General Assembly, appoint an Acting Director-General for the term preceding the assuming of office by the new Director-General;

(vii) perform such other functions as are allocated to it under this Convention.

(4) (*a*) The Co-ordination Committee shall meet once every year in ordinary session, upon convocation by the Director-General. It shall normally meet at the headquarters of the Organization.

(*b*) The Co-ordination Committee shall meet in extraordinary session, upon convocation by the Director-General, either on his own initiative, or at the request of its Chairman or one-fourth of its members.

(5) (*a*) Each State, whether a member of one or both of the Executive Committees referred to in paragraph (1) (*a*), shall have one vote in the Co-ordination Committee.

(*b*) One-half of the members of the Co-ordination Committee shall constitute a quorum.

(*c*) A delegate may represent, and vote in the name, of one State only.

(6) (*a*) The Co-ordination Committee shall express its opinions and make its decisions by a simple majority of the votes cast. Abstentions shall not be considered as votes.

(*b*) Even if a simple majority is obtained, any member of the Co-ordination Committee may, immediately after the vote, request that the votes be the subject of a special recount in the following manner: two separate lists shall be prepared, one containing the names of the States members of the Executive Committee of the Paris Union and the other the names of the States members of the Executive Committee of the Berne Union; the vote of each State shall be inscribed opposite its name in each list in which it appears. Should this special recount indicate that a simple majority has not been obtained in each of those lists, the proposal shall not be considered as carried.

(7) Any State Member of the Organization which is not a member of the Co-ordination Committee may be represented at the meetings of the Committee by observers having the right to take part in the debates but without the right to vote.

(8) The Co-ordination Committee shall establish its own rules of procedure.

ARTICLE 9

1835 **International Bureau**

(1) The International Bureau shall be the Secretariat of the Organization.

(2) The International Bureau shall be directed by the Director-General, assisted by two or more Deputy Directors-General.

(3) The Director-General shall be appointed for a fixed term, which shall be not less than six years. He shall be eligible for reappointment for fixed terms. The periods of the initial appointment and possible subsequent appointments, as well as all other conditions of the appointment, shall be fixed by the General Assembly.

(4) (*a*) The Director-General shall be the chief executive of the Organization.

(*b*) He shall represent the Organization.

(*c*) He shall report to, and conform to the instructions of, the General Assembly as to the internal and external affairs of the Organization.

(5) The Director-General shall prepare the draft programmes and budgets and periodical reports on activities. He shall transmit them to the Governments of the interested States and to the competent organs of the Unions and the Organization.

(6) The Director-General and any staff member designated by him shall participate, without the right to vote, in all meetings of the General Assembly, the Conference, the Co-ordination Committee, and any other committee or working group. The Director-General or a staff member designated by him shall be *ex officio* secretary of these bodies.

(7) The Director-General shall appoint the staff necessary for the efficient performance of the tasks of the International Bureau. He shall appoint the Deputy Directors-General after approval by the Co-ordination Committee. The conditions of employment shall be fixed by the staff regulations to be approved by the Co-ordination Committee on the proposal of the Director-General. The paramount consideration in the employment of the staff and in the determination of the conditions of service shall be the necessity of securing the highest standards of efficiency, competence, and integrity. Due regard shall be paid to the importance of recruiting the staff on as wide a geographical basis as possible.

(8) The nature of the responsibilities of the Director-General and of the staff shall be exclusively international. In the discharge of their duties they shall not seek or receive instructions from any Government or from any authority external to the Organization. They shall refrain from any action which might prejudice their position as international officials. Each Member State undertakes to respect the exclusively international character of the responsibilities of the Director-General and the staff, and not to seek to influence them in the discharge of their duties.

ARTICLE 10

1836 **Headquarters**

(1) The headquarters of the Organization shall be at Geneva.

(2) Its transfer may be decided as provided for in Article 6 (3) (*d*) and (*g*).

ARTICLE 11

1837 **Finances**

(1) The Organization shall have two separate budgets: the budget of expenses common to the Unions, and the budget of the Conference.

(2) (*a*) The budget of expenses common to the Unions shall include provision for expenses of interest to several Unions.

(*b*) This budget shall be financed from the following sources:

(i) contributions of the Unions, provided that the amount of the contribution of each Union shall be fixed by the Assembly of that Union, having regard to the interest the Union has in the common expenses;

(ii) charges due for services performed by the International Bureau not in direct relation with any of the Unions or not received for services rendered by the International Bureau in the field of legal-technical assistance;

(iii) sale of, or royalties on, the publications of the International Bureau not directly concerning any of the Unions;

(iv) gifts, bequests, and subventions, given to the Organization, except those referred to in paragraph (3) (*b*) (iv);

(v) rents, interests, and other miscellaneous income, of the Organization.

(3) (*a*) The budget of the Conference shall include provision for the expenses of holding sessions of the Conference and for the cost of the legal-technical assistance programme.

(*b*) This budget shall be financed from the following sources:

(i) contributions of States party to this Convention not members of any of the Unions;

(ii) any sums made available to this budget by the Unions, provided that the amount of the sum made available by each Union shall be fixed by the Assembly of that Union and that each Union shall be free to abstain from contributing to the said budget;

(iii) sums received for services rendered by the International Bureau in the field of legal-technical assistance;

(iv) gifts, bequests and subventions, given to the Organization for the purposes referred to in sub-paragraph (*a*).

(4) (*a*) For the purpose of establishing its contribution towards the budget of the Conference, each State party to this Convention not member of any of the Unions shall belong to a class, and shall pay its annual contributions on the basis of a number of units fixed as follows:

Class A	10
Class B	3
Class C	1

(*b*) Each such State shall, concurrently with taking action as provided in Article 14 (1), indicate the class to which it wishes to belong. Any such State may change class. If it chooses a lower class, the State must announce it to the Conference at one of its ordinary sessions. Any such change shall take effect at the beginning of the calendar year following the session.

(*c*) The annual contribution of each such State shall be an amount in the same proportion to the total sum to be contributed to the budget of the Conference by all such States as the number of its units is to the total of the units of all the said States.

(*d*) Contributions shall become due on the first of January of each year.

(*e*) If the budget is not adopted before the beginning of a new financial period, the budget shall be at the same level as the budget of the previous year, in accordance with the financial regulations.

(5) Any State party to this Convention not member of any of the Unions which is in arrears in the payment of its financial contributions under the present Article, and any State party to this Convention member of any of the Unions which is in arrears in the payment of its contributions to any of the Unions, shall have no vote in any of the bodies of the Organization of which it is a member, if the amount of its arrears equals or exceeds the amount of the contributions due from it for the preceding two full years. However, any of these bodies may allow such a State to continue to exercise its vote in that body if, and as long as, it is satisfied that the delay in payment arises from exceptional and unavoidable circumstances.

(6) The amount of the fees and charges due for services rendered by the International Bureau in the field of legal-technical assistance shall be established, and shall be reported to the Co-ordination Committee, by the Director-General.

(7) The Organization, with the approval of the Co-ordination Committee, may receive gifts, bequests, and subventions, directly from Governments, public or private institutions, associations or private persons.

(8) (*a*) The Organization shall have a working capital fund which shall be constituted by a single payment made by the Unions and by each State party to this Convention not member of any Union. If the fund becomes insufficient, it shall be increased.

(*b*) The amount of the single payment of each Union and its possible participation in any increase shall be decided by its Assembly.

(*c*) The amount of the single payment of each State party to this Convention not member of any Union and its part in any increase shall be a proportion of the contribution of that State for the year in which the fund is established or the increase decided. The proportion and the terms of payment shall be fixed by the Conference on the proposal of the Director-General and after it has heard the advice of the Co-ordination Committee.

(9) (*a*) In the headquarters agreement concluded with the State on the territory of which the Organization has its headquarters, it shall be provided that, whenever the working capital fund is insufficient, such State shall grant advances. The amount of these advances and the conditions on which they are granted shall be the subject of separate agreements, in each case, between such State and the Organization. As long as it remains under the obligation to grant advances, such State shall have an *ex officio* seat on the Co-ordination Committee.

(*b*) The State referred to in sub-paragraph (*a*) and the Organization shall each have the right to denounce the obligation to grant advances, by written notification. Denunciation shall take effect three years after the end of the year in which it has been notified.

(10) The auditing of the accounts shall be effected by one or more Member States, or by external auditors, as provided in the financial regulations. They shall be designated, with their agreement, by the General Assembly.

ARTICLE 12

1838 **Legal Capacity ; Privileges and Immunities**

(1) The Organization shall enjoy on the territory of each Member State, in conformity with the laws of that State, such legal capacity as may be necessary for the fulfilment of the Organization's objectives and for the exercise of its functions.

(2) The Organization shall conclude a headquarters agreement with the Swiss Confederation and with any other State in which the headquarters may subsequently be located.

(3) The Organization may conclude bilateral or multilateral agreements with the other Member States with a view to the enjoyment by the Organization, its officials, and representatives of all Member States, of such privileges and immunities as may be necessary for the fulfilment of its objectives and for the exercise of its functions.

(4) The Director-General may negotiate and, after approval by the Co-ordination Committee, shall conclude and sign on behalf of the Organization the agreements referred to in paragraphs (2) and (3).

ARTICLE 13

1839 **Relations with other Organizations**

(1) The Organization shall, where appropriate, establish working relations and co-operate with other intergovernmental organizations. Any general agreement to such effect entered into with such organizations shall be concluded by the Director-General after approval by the Co-ordination Committee.

(2) The Organization may, on matters within its competence, make suitable arrangements for consultation and co-operation with international non-governmental organizations and, with the consent of the Governments concerned, with national organizations, governmental or non-governmental. Such arrangements shall be made by the Director-General after approval by the Co-ordination Committee.

ARTICLE 14

1840 **Becoming Party to the Convention**

(1) States referred to in Article 5 may become party to this Convention and Member of the Organization by:

(i) signature without reservation as to ratification, or

(ii) signature subject to ratification followed by the deposit of an instrument of ratification, or

(iii) deposit of an instrument of accession.

(2) Notwithstanding any other provision of this Convention, a State party to the Paris Convention, the Berne Convention, or both Conventions, may become party to this Convention only if it concurrently ratifies or accedes to, or only after it has ratified or acceded to:

either the Stockholm Act of the Paris Convention in its entirety or with only the limitations set forth in Article 20 (1) (*b*) (i) thereof, or the Stockholm Act of the Berne Convention in its entirety or with only the limitation set forth in Article 28 (1) (*b*) (i) thereof.

(3) Instruments of ratification or accession shall be deposited with the Director-General.

ARTICLE 15

1841 **Entry into Force of the Convention**

(1) This Convention shall enter into force three months after ten States members of the Paris Union and seven States members of the Berne Union have taken action as provided in Article 14 (1), it being understood that, if a State is a member of both Unions, it will be counted in both groups. On that date, this Convention shall enter into force also in respect of States which, not being members of either of the two Unions, have taken action as provided in Article 14 (1) three months or more prior to that date.

(2) In respect to any other State, this Convention shall enter into force three months after the date on which such State takes action as provided in Article 14 (1).

ARTICLE 16

1842 **Reservations**

No reservations to this Convention are permitted.

ARTICLE 17

1843 **Amendments**

(1) Proposals for the amendment of this Convention may be initiated by any Member State, by the Co-ordination Committee, or by the Director-General. Such proposals shall be communicated by the Director-General to the Member States at least six months in advance of their consideration by the Conference.

(2) Amendments shall be adopted by the Conference. Whenever amendments would affect the rights and obligations of States party to this Convention not members of any of the Unions, such States shall also vote. On all other amendments proposed, only States party to this Convention members of any Union shall vote. Amendments shall be adopted by a simple majority of the votes cast, provided that the Conference shall vote only on such proposals for amendments as have previously been adopted by the Assembly of the Paris Union and the Assembly of the Berne Union according to the rules applicable in each of them regarding the adoption of amendments to the administrative provisions of their respective Conventions.

(3) Any amendment shall enter into force one month after written notifications of acceptance, effected in accordance with their respective constitutional processes, have been received by the Director-General from three-fourths of the States members of the Organization, entitled to vote on the proposal for amendment pursuant to paragraph (2), at the time the Conference adopted the amendment. Any amendments thus accepted shall bind all the States which are Members of the Organization at the time the amendment enters into force or which become Members at a subsequent date, provided that any amendment increasing the financial obligations of Member States shall bind only those States which have notified their acceptance of such amendment.

ARTICLE 18

1844 **Denunciation**

(1) Any Member State may denounce this Convention by notification addressed to the Director-General.

(2) Denunciation shall take effect six months after the day on which the Director-General has received the notification.

ARTICLE 19

1845 **Notifications**

The Director-General shall notify the Governments of all Member States of:

(i) the date of entry into force of the Convention,
(ii) signatures and deposits of instruments of ratification or accession,
(iii) acceptances of an amendment to this Convention, and the date upon which the amendment enters into force,
(iv) denunciations of this Convention.

ARTICLE 20

1846 **Final Provisions**

(1) (*a*) This Convention shall be signed in a single copy in English, French, Russian and Spanish, all texts being equally authentic, and shall be deposited with the Government of Sweden.

(*b*) This Convention shall remain open for signature at Stockholm until January 13, 1968.

(2) Official texts shall be established by the Director-General, after consultation with the interested Governments, in German, Italian and Portuguese, and such other languages as the Conference may designate.

(3) The Director-General shall transmit two duly certified copies of this Convention and of each amendment adopted by the Conference to the Governments of the States members of the Paris or Berne Unions, to the Government of any other State when it accedes to this Convention, and, on request, to the Government of any other State. The copies of the signed text of the Convention transmitted to the Governments shall be certified by the Government of Sweden.

(4) The Director-General shall register this Convention with the Secretariat of the United Nations.

ARTICLE 21

1847 **Transitional Provisions**

(1) Until the first Director-General assumes office, references in this Convention to the International Bureau or to the Director-General shall be deemed to be references to the United International Bureaux for the Protection of Industrial, Literary and Artistic Property (also called the United International Bureaux for the Protection of Intellectual Property (BIRPI)), or its Director, respectively.

(2) (*a*) States which are members of any of the Unions but which have not become party to this Convention may, for five years from the date of entry into force of this Convention, exercise, if they so desire, the same rights as if they had become party to this Convention. Any State desiring to exercise such rights shall give written notification to this effect to the Director-General; this notification shall be effective on the date of its receipt. Such States shall be deemed to be members of the General Assembly and the Conference until the expiration of the said period.

(*b*) Upon expiration of this five-year period, such States shall have no right to vote in the General Assembly, the Conference, and the Co-ordination Committee.

(*c*) Upon becoming party to this Convention, such States shall regain such right to vote.

(3) (*a*) As long as there are States members of the Paris or Berne Unions which have not become party to this Convention, the International Bureau and the Director-General shall also function as the United International Bureaux for the Protection of Industrial, Literary and Artistic Property, and its Director, respectively.

(*b*) The staff in the employment of the said Bureaux on the date of entry into force of this Convention shall, during the transitional period referred to in sub-paragraph (*a*), be considered as also employed by the International Bureau.

(4) (*a*) Once all the States members of the Paris Union have become Members of the Organization, the rights, obligations, and property, of the Bureau of that Union shall devolve on the International Bureau of the Organization.

(*b*) Once all the States members of the Berne Union have become Members of the Organization, the rights, obligations, and property, of the Bureau of that Union shall devolve on the International Bureau of the Organization.

[The next paragraph is 1858]

Appendix D

UNITED KINGDOM ORDERS IN COUNCIL

Orders in Council Applying or Extending the Provisions of the Copyright Acts, 1911 and 1956, to Works Originating Outside the United Kingdom

1858 **Order in Council dated June 24, 1912**

Extending the Copyright Act, 1911, to Certain British Protectorates [1]

(S.R. & O. 1912 No. 912)

At the Court at Buckingham Palace, the 24th day of June, 1912.

Present,

The King's Most Excellent Majesty

Lord President.	Sir Henry W. Primrose.
Earl Beauchamp.	Mr. C. F. G. Masterman.
Lord Richard Cavendish.	Sir David Brynmor Jones.
Viscount Allendale.	Sir James Henry Dalziel.
Lord Chamberlain.	Sir Albert Spicer, Bart.

Whereas it is, among other things, provided by the Copyright Act, 1911, that His Majesty may, by Order in Council, extend the said Act to any territories under His Protection and to Cyprus, and that on the making of any such Order the said Act shall, subject to the provisions of the Order, have effect as if the territories to which it applies or Cyprus were part of His Majesty's dominions to which the said Act extends:

Now, therefore, His Majesty, by and with the advice of His Privy Council, is pleased to order, and it is hereby ordered, as follows:

1. The Copyright Act, 1911, shall apply to Cyprus [2] and to the following territories under His Majesty's protection, namely, the Bechuanaland Protectorate,[3] East Africa Protectorate,[4] Gambia Protectorate,[5] Gilbert and Ellice Islands Protectorate, Northern Nigeria Protectorate,[6] Northern Territories of the Gold Coast,[7] Nyasaland Protectorate,[8]

1 Similar orders were made as to the Cameroons under British Mandate by an Order in Council dated March 16, 1933 (S.R. & O. 1933 No. 254), and as to Tanganyika by an Order in Council dated April 16, 1924 (S.R. & O. 1924 No. 521). See as to Tanganyika, Tanganyika Independence Act, 1961 (10 Eliz. 2, c. 1), Sched. II, paras. 13 and 14, Tanzania Act, 1969 (1969, c. 29) and § 1221, *ante*. See as to Jamaica, Jamaica Independence Act, 1962 (10 & 11 Eliz. 2, c. 40), Sched. II, para. 13, as to Trinidad and Tobago, Trinidad and Tobago Independence Act, 1962 (10 & 11 Eliz. 2, c. 54), Sched. II, para. 13, as to Malta, Malta Independence Act, 1964 (1964, c. 86), Sched. II, para. 13 and § 1221, *ante*, as to Basutoland, Lesotho Independence Act, 1966 (1966, c. 24), Sched., para. 9 and as to Barbados, Barbados Independence Act, 1966 (1966, c. 37), Sched. II, para. 12.

2 As to Cyprus, see Cyprus Act, 1960 (8 & 9 Eliz. 2, c. 52), Sched. II, para. 13.

3 As to Bechuanaland Protectorate, see Botswana Independence Act, 1966 (1966, c. 23).

4 Kenya. Repealed as to Kenya by an Order in Council dated June 26, 1963 (S.I. 1963 No. 1147). See Kenya Independence Act, 1963 (1963, c. 54); and see § 1221, *ante* and § 1875, *post*.

5 As to Gambia Protectorate, see Gambia Independence Act, 1964 (1964, c. 93), Sched. II, para. 12.

6 As to Nigeria, see Nigeria Independence Act, 1960 (8 & 9 Eliz. 2, c. 55), Sched. II, paras. 12 and 13, and § 1875, *post*.

7 As to the territories of the Gold Coast, see Ghana Independence Act, 1957 (5 & 6 Eliz. 2, c. 6), Sched. II, para. 12; and see § 1221, *ante* and § 1875, *post*.

8 As to Nyasaland Protectorate, see Malawi Independence Act, 1964 (1964, c. 46), Sched. II, para. 13 and see § 1221, *ante* and § 1875, *post*.

Northern Rhodesia,[9] Southern Rhodesia, Sierra Leone Protectorate,[10] Somaliland Protectorate, Southern Nigeria Protectorate,[6] Solomon Islands Protectorate, Swaziland,[11] Uganda Protectorate,[12] and Weihaiwei.[13]

2. In Article 12 of "The Somaliland Order in Council, 1899," [14] the word "Copyright" is hereby revoked and shall be deleted.

1859 **Order in Council dated February 9, 1920**

UNDER THE COPYRIGHT ACT, 1911 (1 & 2 GEO. 5, c. 46), FURTHER REGULATING COPYRIGHT RELATIONS WITH THE UNITED STATES OF AMERICA AS REGARDS WORKS FIRST PUBLISHED BETWEEN AUGUST 1, 1914, AND THE TERMINATION OF THE WAR [15]

(S.R. & O. 1920 No. 257)

At the Court at Buckingham Palace, the 9th day of February, 1920.

PRESENT,

The King's Most Excellent Majesty

Lord President.	Lord Colebrooke.
Earl Curzon of Kedleston.	Sir Frederick Ponsonby.

Whereas by reason of conditions arising out of the war difficulties have been experienced by citizens of the United States of America in complying with the requirements of the Copyright Act, 1911, as to first publication within the parts of His Majesty's dominions to which the Act extends of their works first published in the United States of America during the war:

And whereas His Majesty is advised that the Government of the United States of America has undertaken, upon issue of this Order, to extend the protection afforded by the United States Law of December 18, 1919, entitled "An Act to amend sections 8 and 21 of the Copyright Act, approved March 4, 1909," to British subjects:

And whereas by reason of the said undertaking of the Government of the United States of America His Majesty is satisfied that the said Government has made, or has undertaken to make, such provision as it is expedient to require for the protection of works first made or published between the 1st August, 1914, and the termination of the war in the parts of His Majesty's dominions to which this Order applies, and entitled to copyright under Part I of the Copyright Act, 1911:

And whereas by the Copyright Act, 1911, authority is conferred upon His Majesty to extend, by Order in Council, the protection of the said Act to certain classes of foreign works within any part of His

[9] As to Northern Rhodesia, see Zambia Independence Act, 1964 (1964, c. 65), Sched. I, para. 9 and see § 1221, *ante* and § 1875, *post*.

[10] As to Sierra Leone, see Sierra Leone Independence Act, 1961 (9 & 10 Eliz. 2, c. 16), Sched. III, para. 13 and 14 and § 1221, *ante*.

[11] As to Swaziland, see Swaziland Independence Act, 1968 (1968, c. 56), Sched., para. 9.

[12] Repealed as to Uganda by an Order in Council dated December 21, 1961 (S.I. 1961 No. 2462). See Uganda Independence Act, 1962 (10 & 11 Eliz. 2, c. 57) and § 1221, *ante*.

[13] Repealed as to Weihaiwei by Order in Council dated November 27, 1930 (S.R. & O. 1930 No. 1144).

[14] Revoked by S.R. & O. 1930 No. 222.

[15] Revoked by S.I. 1957 No. 1523, but see § 1185, *ante*.

Majesty's dominions, other than self-governing dominions, to which the said Act extends:

And whereas by reason of these premises it is desirable to provide protection within the said dominions for literary or artistic works first published in the United States of America between August 1, 1914, and the termination of the war which have failed to accomplish the formalities prescribed by the Copyright Act, 1911, by reason of conditions arising out of the war:

Now, therefore, His Majesty, by and with the advice of His Privy Council, and by virtue of the authority conferred upon him by the Copyright Act, 1911, is pleased to order, and it is hereby ordered, as follows:

1. The Copyright Act, 1911, shall, subject to the provisions of the said Act and of this Order, apply to works first published in the United States of America between the 1st August, 1914, and the termination of the war, which have not been republished prior to the commencement of this Order in the parts of His Majesty's dominions to which this Order applies, in like manner as if they had been first published within the parts of His Majesty's dominions to which the said Act extends:

Provided that the enjoyment by any work of the rights conferred by the Copyright Act, 1911, shall be conditional upon publication of the work in the dominion to which this Order relates not later than six months after the termination of the war, and shall commence from and after such publication, which shall not be colourable only, but shall be intended to satisfy the reasonable requirements of the public.

2. The provisions of section 15 of the Copyright Act, 1911, as to the delivery of books to libraries, shall apply to works to which this Order relates upon their publication in the United Kingdom.

3. In the case of musical works to which this Order relates and provided that no contrivances by means of which the work may be mechanically performed have before the commencement of this Order been lawfully made, or placed on sale, within the parts of His Majesty's dominions to which this Order applies, copyright in the work shall include all rights conferred by the said Act with respect to the making of records, perforated rolls and other contrivances by means of which the work may be mechanically performed.

4. This Order shall apply to all His Majesty's dominions, colonies and possessions with the exception of those hereinafter named, that is to say:

The Dominion of Canada;
The Commonwealth of Australia;
The Dominion of New Zealand;
The Union of South Africa;
Newfoundland.

5. Nothing in this Order shall be construed as depriving any work of any rights which have been lawfully acquired under the provisions of the Copyright Act, 1911, or any Order in Council thereunder.

6. This Order shall take effect as from the 2nd day of February, 1920, which day is in this Order referred to as the commencement of this Order.

And the Lords Commissioners of His Majesty's Treasury are to give the necessary orders accordingly.

1860 **Copyright (Federated Malay States) Order, 1931** [16]

(1931 No. 105)

At the Court at Buckingham Palace, the 12th day of February, 1931

PRESENT,

The King's Most Excellent Majesty

Earl of Desart.	Sir Dinshah Mulla.
Mr. Secretary Henderson.	Mr. Kennedy.
Sir Charles Trevelyan.	Mr. Morrison.

Whereas by the Copyright Act, 1911, authority is conferred upon His Majesty to extend by Order in Council the protection of the said Act to certain classes of foreign works within any part of His Majesty's dominions, other than self-governing dominions, to which the said Act extends:

And whereas His Majesty is satisfied that the Rulers of the Federated Malay States have made, or have undertaken to make, such provisions as it appears to His Majesty expedient to require for the protection of works entitled to copyright under the provisions of Part I of the said Act:

Now, therefore, His Majesty, by and with the advice of His Privy Council, and by virtue of the authority conferred upon Him by the Copyright Act, 1911, is pleased to order and it is hereby ordered as follows:

1. The Copyright Act, 1911, including the provisions as to existing works, shall subject to the provisions of the said Act and of this Order apply—

(*a*) to works first published in the Federated Malay States, in like manner as if they had been first published within parts of His Majesty's dominions to which the said Act extends;

(*b*) to literary, dramatic, musical and artistic works the authors whereof were at the time of the making of the work subjects of the Rulers of the Federated Malay States, in like manner as if the authors had been British subjects;

(*c*) in respect of residence in the Federated Malay States, in like manner as if such residence had been residence in the parts of His Majesty's dominions to which the said Act extends.

2. Where any musical work to which this Order applies has been published before the date of this Order but no contrivances by means of which the work may be mechanically performed have before the said date been lawfully made or placed on sale within the parts of His Majesty's dominions to which this Order applies, copyright in the work shall include all rights conferred by the said Act with respect to the making of records, perforated rolls and other contrivances by means of which the work may be mechanically performed.

3. In the application to works to which this Order applies of sections 1 (2) (*d*) and 19 of the Copyright Act, 1911, the date of this Order shall be substituted for the commencement of the Act and for the

[16] Extended to Southern Rhodesia by Order in Council dated April 9, 1932 (S.R. & O. 1932 No. 255). As to Malaya, see Federation of Malaya Independence Act, 1957 (5 & 6 Eliz. 2, c. 60), Sched. I, paras. 14, 15; as to the federation of North Borneo, Sarawak and Singapore with Malaya, see Malaysia Act, 1963 (c. 35), Sched. II, para. 1 (*a*); as to Singapore becoming an independent sovereign state separate from and independent of Malaysia, see Singapore Act, 1966 (1966, c. 29); and see § 1221, *ante*.

passing of the Act in section 19 (7) and 19 (8) wherever those expressions occur.

4. Where any person has, before the date of this Order, taken any action whereby he has incurred any expenditure or liability in connection with the reproduction or performance of any work in a manner which at the time was lawful, or for the purpose of or with a view to the reproduction or performance of a work at a time when such reproduction or performance would, but for the making of this Order, have been lawful, nothing in this Order shall diminish or prejudice any rights or interest arising from or in connection with such action which are subsisting and valuable at the said date unless the person who, by virtue of this Order, becomes entitled to restrain such reproduction or performance agrees to pay such compensation as failing agreement may be determined in accordance with the provisions of the Copyright Act, 1911.

5. This Order shall apply to all parts of His Majesty's dominions, including any territories under His Majesty's protection, to which the Copyright Act, 1911, extends, except to the self-governing dominions and to Southern Rhodesia.

6. This Order shall be construed as if it formed part of the Copyright Act, 1911.

7. This Order may be cited as the Copyright (Federated Malay States) Order, 1931.

1861 **Copyright (United States of America) Order, 1942**

(1942 No. 1579 as amended in square brackets by S.I. 1950 No. 1641) [17]
At the Court at Buckingham Palace, the 6th day of August, 1942.

PRESENT,

The King's Most Excellent Majesty

Lord President. Secretary Sir Archibald Sinclair.
Lord Macmillan. Mr. Williams.

Whereas by reason of conditions arising out of the war difficulties have been experienced by citizens of the United States of America in complying with the requirements of the Copyright Act, 1911, as to first publication within the parts of His Majesty's dominions to which the Act extends of their works first published in the United States of America during the war:

And whereas His Majesty is advised that the Government of the United States of America has undertaken to grant such extension of time as may be deemed appropriate for the fulfilment of the conditions and formalities prescribed by the laws of the United States with respect to the works of British subjects first produced or published outside the United States and subject to copyright or to renewal of copyright under the laws of the United States including works subject to ad interim copyright:

And whereas by reason of the said undertaking of the Government of the United States of America His Majesty is satisfied that the said Government has made, or has undertaken to make, such provision as it is expedient to require for the protection of works first made or published during the period commencing on the 3rd day of September, 1939, and ending one year after the termination of the present war within the parts of His Majesty's dominions to which this Order applies and entitled to copyright under Part I of the Copyright Act, 1911:

[17] Revoked by S.I. 1957 No. 1523, but see § 1185, *ante*.

And whereas by the Copyright Act, 1911, authority is conferred upon His Majesty to extend, by Order in Council, the protection of the said Act to certain classes of foreign works within any part of His Majesty's dominions, other than the self-governing dominions, to which the Act extends:

And whereas by reason of these premises it is desirable to provide protection within the parts of His Majesty's dominions to which this Order applies for literary or artistic works first published in the United States of America during the period commencing on the 3rd day of September, 1939, and ending one year after the termination of the present war which have failed to accomplish the formalities prescribed by the Copyright Act, 1911, by reason of conditions arising out of the war:

Now, therefore, His Majesty, by and with the advice of His Privy Council, and by virtue of the authority conferred upon Him by the Copyright Act, 1911, and of all other powers enabling Him in that behalf, is pleased to direct and doth hereby direct as follows:

1. The Copyright Act, 1911, shall, subject to the provisions of the said Act and of this Order, apply to works first published in the United States of America during the period commencing on the 3rd day of September, 1939 [and ending on the 29th day of December 1950], which have not been republished in the parts of His Majesty's dominions to which this Order applies within fourteen days of the publication in the United States of America, in like manner as if they had been first published within the parts of His Majesty's dominions to which the said Act extends:

Provided that the enjoyment by any such work of the rights conferred by the Copyright Act, 1911, shall be conditional upon publication of the work within the parts of His Majesty's dominions to which this Order relates [not later than the 28th day of December, 1950], and shall commence from and after such publication, which shall not be colourable only, but shall be intended to satisfy the reasonable requirements of the public.

2. The provisions of section 15 of the Copyright Act, 1911, as to the delivery of books to libraries, shall apply to works to which this Order relates upon their publication in the United Kingdom.

3. Nothing in this Order shall be construed as depriving any work of any rights which have been lawfully acquired under the provisions of the Copyright Act, 1911, or any Order in Council thereunder.

4. Where any person has, before the commencement of this Order, taken any action whereby he has incurred any expenditure or liability in connection with the reproduction or performance of any work which at the time was lawful, or for the purpose of or with a view to the reproduction or performance of a work at a time when such reproduction or performance would, but for the making of this Order, have been lawful, nothing in this Order shall diminish or prejudice any rights or interest arising from or in connection with such action which were subsisting and valuable at the said date, unless the person who by virtue of this Order becomes entitled to restrain such reproduction or performance agrees to pay such compensation as, failing agreement, may be determined by arbitration.

5. The Interpretation Act, 1889, shall apply to the interpretation of this Order as if it were an Act of Parliament.

6. This Order may be cited as the Copyright (United States of America) Order, 1942.

7. This Order shall come into operation on the date of its publication in the London Gazette, which day is in this Order referred to as the commencement of this Order. [The date of publication was March 10, 1944.]

1862 **Copyright (International Conventions) Order, 1957** [18]

(S.I. 1957 No. 1523)

Made - - - - *23rd August,* 1957
Laid before Parliament *29th August,* 1957
Coming into Operation *27th September,* 1957

At the Court at Balmoral, the 23rd day of August, 1957

PRESENT,

The Queen's Most Excellent Majesty in Council

Whereas it is provided by section 32 of the Copyright Act, 1956, that Her Majesty may by Order in Council apply any provisions of that Act in the case of any country to which those provisions do not extend:

And whereas it is further provided by the said section 32 that the power of applying any of those provisions shall not be exercised in the case of a country, other than a country which is a party to a Convention relating to copyright to which the United Kingdom is also a party, unless Her Majesty is satisfied that, in respect of the class of works or other subject-matter to which those provisions relate, provision has been or will be made under the laws of that country whereby adequate protection will be given to owners of copyright under that Act:

And whereas the countries mentioned in Part I of the First Schedule hereto are members of the Berne Copyright Union as parties to the Conventions relating to copyright therein respectively specified:

And whereas the countries mentioned in Part II of the said First Schedule are parties to a Convention relating to copyright concluded at Geneva on the sixth day of September, one thousand nine hundred and fifty-two (hereinafter referred to as "the Universal Copyright Convention"):

And whereas the United Kingdom is a party to each of the said Conventions except the Convention concluded at Brussels on the twenty-sixth day of June, one thousand nine hundred and forty-eight (hereinafter referred to as "the Brussels Convention"):

And whereas it is intended that the United Kingdom shall, as soon as may be, accede to the Brussels Convention:

And whereas all the countries which are parties to the Brussels Convention except Turkey are bound to the United Kingdom as parties either to the Rome Convention mentioned in the First Schedule hereto or to the Universal Copyright Convention:

And whereas Her Majesty is satisfied in the case of Turkey (which is a party to the Brussels Convention but not to any of the said Conventions to which the United Kingdom is at present a party) that, in respect of the class of works and other subject-matter to which the provisions applied by this Order relate, provision has been made under the laws of Turkey whereby adequate protection will be given to the

[18] This Order and its amending Orders were revoked by S.I. 1964 No. 690, *post,* § 1874; but see *ante,* § 1171.

owners of copyright under the Copyright Act, 1956, when the United Kingdom accedes to the Brussels Convention:

And whereas none of the provisions of the Copyright Act, 1956, extend to any of the countries mentioned in the First Schedule hereto:

And whereas, notwithstanding the repeal of the Copyright Act, 1911, its provisions continue by virtue of paragraph 40 of the Seventh Schedule to the Copyright Act, 1956, to have effect in respect of the countries to which those provisions have been applied by certain Orders in Council made under sections 26 and 29 of the said Copyright Act, 1911, which Orders in Council include those mentioned in the Fifth Schedule hereto:

And whereas by virtue of paragraph 40 of the said Seventh Schedule the power to revoke the said Orders in Council conferred by section 32 of the Copyright Act, 1911, is to be treated as continuing in force:

Now, therefore, Her Majesty, by and with the advice of Her Privy Council, and by virtue of the authority conferred upon Her by section 32 of the Copyright Act, 1956, and by section 32 of the Copyright Act, 1911, and of all other powers enabling Her in that behalf, is pleased to order, and it is hereby ordered, as follows:

1863 **1.** Subject to the following provisions of this Order, the provisions of the Copyright Act, 1956 (hereinafter referred to as the "Act"), specified in the Second Schedule hereto, being the provisions relating to literary, dramatic, musical and artistic works, sound recordings, cinematograph films and published editions of literary, dramatic or musical works, shall apply in the case of each of the countries mentioned in the First Schedule hereto as follows:

(*a*) in relation to literary, dramatic, musical or artistic works, sound recordings, cinematograph films or published editions first published in that country, as they apply in relation to such works, recordings, films or editions first published in the United Kingdom;

(*b*) in relation to persons who, at a material time (as hereinafter defined), are citizens or subjects of, or domiciled or resident in, that country, as they apply in relation to persons who, at such a time, are British subjects or domiciled or resident in the United Kingdom;

(*c*) in relation to bodies incorporated under the laws of that country, as they apply in relation to bodies incorporated under the laws of any part of the United Kingdom:

Provided that

(i) copyright shall not subsist by virtue of this Order in any work or other subject-matter by reason only of its publication before the commencement of this Order in a country which is a party to the Universal Copyright Convention but which is not a country of the Berne Copyright Union [19];

[(ii) *the term of copyright in a work or other subject-matter which enjoys protection in the nature of copyright in its country of origin shall not exceed the term of protection enjoyed in the country of origin without registration, deposit or the performance of any other formalities (or, if the laws of that country require the performance of any formalities as a condition of*

The Order in applying the provisions of the Act of 1956 in the case of Nigeria and Ghana is to have effect as if this paragraph of the proviso were omitted; see S.I. 1962 No. 1641.

protection, without compliance with any formalities other than those specified in paragraph 1 of Article III of the Universal Copyright Convention, which is set out in the Third Schedule hereto) in respect of a British work or subject-matter (as hereinafter defined) of the class in question [20];]

(iii) in the case of any country other than Australia, Canada, Ceylon,[21] Denmark, the Federal Republic of Germany, India, the Republic of Ireland,[22] Israel, Italy,[23] New Zealand, Nigeria,[24] Norway, Pakistan, South Africa, Spain and Switzerland, the acts restricted by the copyright in a sound recording conferred by section 12 of the Act as applied by this Order shall not include—

(*a*) causing the recording to be heard in public;
(*b*) broadcasting the recording;

(iv) in relation to any work or other subject-matter made before the commencement of this Order, the provisions of the Act shall apply subject to the modifications specified in the Fourth Schedule hereto;

(v) nothing in the provisions of the Act as applied by this Order shall be construed as reviving any right to make, or restrain the making of, or any right in respect of, translations, if such right has ceased before the commencement of this Order;

(vi) paragraph[*s*] (i) [*and* (*ii*) [25]] of this proviso shall not apply to any work or subject-matter first published in the United States of America, if, immediately before the commencement of this Order, copyright under the Copyright Act, 1911, subsisted in such work or subject-matter by virtue of either an Order in Council dated the 9th day of February, 1920, regulating copyright relations with the United States of America,[26] or the Copyright (United States of America) Order, 1942,[27] as amended.[28]

1864 **2.** Where any person has, before the commencement of this Order, taken any action whereby he has incurred any expenditure or liability in connection with the reproduction or performance of any work or other subject-matter in a manner which at the time was lawful, or for the purpose of or with a view to the reproduction or performance of a work at a time when such reproduction or performance would, but for the making of this Order,[29] have been lawful, nothing in this Order shall diminish or prejudice any rights or interest arising from, or in connection with, such action which are subsisting and valuable immediately before such commencement unless the person who, by virtue of this Order, becomes entitled to restrain such reproduction or performance agrees to pay such compensation as, failing agreement, may be determined by arbitration.

20 This paragraph of the proviso was deleted by S.I. 1958 No. 1254, which came into operation on August 11, 1958.
21 Inserted by S.I. 1961 No. 1496.
22 Inserted by S.I. 1958 No. 1254.
23 Inserted by S.I. 1958 No. 2184.
24 Inserted by S.I. 1962 No. 1641.
25 Deleted by S.I. 1958 No. 1254; see n. 20, *supra*.
26 S. R. & O. 1920 No. 257, *ante*, § 1859.
27 S.R. & O. 1942 No. 1579, *ante*, § 1861.
28 S.I. 1950 No. 1641, *ante*, § 1861.
29 See as to Argentina S.I. 1958 No. 135, Nicaragua S.I. 1961 No. 1496, Paraguay S.I. 1962 No. 397, Panama S.I. 1962 No. 2183 and Peru S.I. 1963 No. 1625.

1865 3. The Orders mentioned in the Fifth Schedule hereto are hereby revoked so far as they form part of the law of the United Kingdom:

Provided that where, by virtue of any of the aforesaid Orders, copyright subsisted in a work immediately before the commencement of this Order and copyright does not subsist therein by Article 1 of this Order, it shall continue to subsist therein as if such Order had not been revoked.

1866 4. In this Order

[(1) "*British work or subject-matter*" *means a work or other subject-matter which was made by a person who was at the material time a British subject resident in the United Kingdom or a company incorporated under the laws of any part of the United Kingdom, and which (if published) was first published in the United Kingdom* [30];]

(2) "country of origin" means—

(*a*) in the case of a published work or subject-matter, if the country of first publication is a country mentioned in the First Schedule hereto, that country;

(*b*) in the case of a work or subject-matter published simultaneously in a country of the Berne Copyright Union and a country which is not in the said Union, the former country;

(*c*) in the case of a work or subject-matter which is published simultaneously in a country which is a party to the Universal Copyright Convention and a country which is neither a country of the Berne Copyright Union nor a party to the Universal Copyright Convention, the former country;

(*d*) in the case of a work or subject-matter which is published simultaneously in several countries of the Berne Copyright Union, the country whose laws give the shortest term of protection in such a work or subject-matter;

(*e*) in the case of a work or subject-matter which is published simultaneously in several countries which are parties to the Universal Copyright Convention (and none of which are members of the Berne Copyright Union), the country whose laws give the shortest term of protection in such a work or subject-matter;

(*f*) in the case of a work or subject-matter which is unpublished, or which is first published only in a country other than a country mentioned in the First Schedule hereto, the country whose laws give the longest term of protection in such a work or subject-matter, being

(i) a country of which the author or maker thereof was a citizen or subject at a material time;

(ii) a country in which the author or maker thereof was domiciled at a material time;

(iii) a country in which the author or maker thereof was resident at a material time; or

(iv) a country under the laws of which the author or maker thereof, being a body corporate, was incorporated at a material time;

(3) "country of the Berne Copyright Union" means any country mentioned in Part I of the First Schedule hereto;

[30] This paragraph was deleted by S.I. 1958 No. 1254; see n. 20, *supra*.

(4) " material time " means—

(i) in relation to an unpublished work or subject-matter, the time at which such work or subject-matter was made or, if the making thereof extended over a period, a substantial part of that period;

(ii) in relation to a published work or subject-matter, the time of first publication;

(5) " party to the Universal Copyright Convention " means any country mentioned in Part II of the First Schedule hereto;

(6) " published simultaneously " means—

(i) in the case of publications occurring before the commencement of this Order, published within a period of fourteen days;

(ii) in any other case, published within a period of thirty days.

5. The Interpretation Act, 1889, shall apply to the interpretation of this Order as it applies to the interpretation of an Act of Parliament.

6. This Order may be cited as the Copyright (International Conventions) Order, 1957, and shall come into operation on the 27th day of September, 1957.[30a]

FIRST SCHEDULE

PART I

COUNTRIES OF THE BERNE COPYRIGHT UNION[31]

1867 *Under a Convention concluded at Berlin on the* 13*th November,* 1908 (" *the Berlin Convention* "), *replacing between the parties thereto a Convention concluded at Berne on the* 19*th September,* 1886 (" *the Berne Convention* "), *as amended by an Additional Act* (" *the Additional Act* ") *agreed to on the* 4*th May,* 1896—

South Africa (in respect of South-West Africa only)
Thailand

Under a Convention concluded at Rome on the 2*nd June* (" *the Rome Convention* "), *replacing between the parties thereto the Berne Convention and the Additional Act and subsequent revisions thereof*—

Australia (and Papua, New Guinea, Nauru and Norfolk Island)
Bulgaria
Canada
Ceylon[32]
Czechoslovakia
Finland
Federal Republic of Germany (and Land Berlin)
Hungary
Iceland
Japan
Lebanon
Netherlands (and Surinam, Netherlands Antilles and New Guinea)

30a See as to Argentina S.I. 1958 No. 135, Nicaragua S.I. 1961 No. 1496, Paraguay S.I. 1962 No. 397, Panama S.I. 1962 No. 2183 and Peru S.I. 1963 No. 1625.

31 Indonesia and Syria were deleted from Part I of Sched. I by S.I. 1960 No. 200 and S.I. 1962 No. 397.

32 Added by S.I 1960 No. 200 which came into operation on February 19, 1960.

New Zealand (and Western Samoa)
Norway
Pakistan
Poland
Roumania
Spain (in respect of its Colonies only)

Under a Convention concluded at Brussels on the 26th June, 1948 ("*the Brussels Convention*"), *replacing between the parties thereto the Berne Convention and the Additional Act and subsequent revisions thereof—*

Austria
Belgium (and Belgian Congo and Ruanda-Urundi)
Brazil
Congo (Brazzaville) [33]
Dahomey [34]
Denmark [35]
France (and French territories overseas)
Gabon [36]
Greece
India [37]
Israel
Italy
Ivory Coast [38]
Liechtenstein
Luxembourg
Mali [39]
Monaco
Morocco
Niger [40]
Philippines
Portugal (including Portuguese provinces overseas)
Republic of Ireland [41]
Senegal [42]
South Africa
Spain
Sweden [43]
Switzerland
Tunisia
Turkey
Vatican City
Yugoslavia

Part II

Parties to the Universal Copyright Convention

Andorra
Argentina [44]
Austria

[33] Added by S.I. 1962 No. 1641 which came into operation on August 22, 1962.
[34] Added by S.I. 1961 No. 1496 which came into operation on August 16, 1961.
[35] Transferred from "Berne" by S.I. 1962 No. 397 which came into operation on March 11, 1962.
[36] Added by S.I. 1962 No. 628 which came into operation on April 4, 1962.
[37] Transferred from "Berne" by S.I. 1958 No. 2184 which came into operation on January 1, 1959.
[38] Added by S.I. 1961 No. 2461 which came into operation on January 1, 1962.
[39] Added by S.I. 1962 No. 1641 which came into operation on August 22, 1962.
[40] Added by S.I. 1962 No. 2183 which came into operation on October 17, 1962.
[41] Transferred from "Berne" by S.I. 1960 No. 200 which came into operation on February 19, 1960.
[42] Added by S.I. 1962 No. 2183 which came into operation on October 17, 1962.
[43] Transferred from "Berne" by S.I. 1961 No. 1496 which came into operation on August 16, 1961.
[44] Added by S.I. 1958 No. 135 which came into operation on February 13, 1958.

Belgium (and Ruanda-Urundi) [45]
Brazil [46]
Cambodia
Canada [47]
Chile
Costa Rica
Cuba
Czechoslovakia [48]
Denmark [49]
Ecuador
France
Federal Republic of Germany (and Land Berlin)
Ghana [50]
Haiti
Iceland
India [51]
Ireland, Republic of [52]
Israel
Italy
Japan
Laos
Lebanon [53]
Liberia
Liechtenstein [54]
Luxembourg
Mexico
Monaco
Nicaragua [55]
Nigeria [56]
Pakistan
Panama [57]
Paraguay [58]
Peru [59]
Philippines
Portugal
Spain
Sweden [60]
Switzerland
United States of America (and Alaska, Guam, Hawaii, Panama Canal Zone, Puerto Rico and the Virgin Islands of the United States of America)
Vatican City

SECOND SCHEDULE

1868 The provisions of Parts I and II of the Act, except section 14, and all the other provisions of the Act relevant thereto.

45 Added by S.I. 1961 No. 1496 which came into operation on August 16, 1961.
46 Added by S.I. 1960 No. 200 which came into operation on February 19, 1960.
47 Added by S.I. 1962 No. 1641 which came into operation on August 22, 1962.
48 Added by S.I. 1960 No. 200 which came into operation on February 19, 1960.
49 Added by S.I. 1962 No. 397 which came into operation on March 11, 1962.
50 Added by S.I. 1962 No. 1641 which came into operation on August 22, 1962.
51 Added by S.I. 1958 No. 1254 which came into operation on August 11, 1958.
52 Added by S.I. 1958 No. 2184 which came into operation on January 1, 1959.
53 Added by S.I. 1960 No. 200 which came into operation on February 19, 1960.
54 Added by S.I. 1958 No. 2184 which came into operation on January 1, 1959.
55 Added by S.I. 1961 No. 1496 which came into operation on August 16, 1961.
56 Added by S.I. 1962 No. 1641 which came into operation on August 22, 1962.
57 Added by S.I. 1962 No. 2183 which came into operation on October 17, 1962.
58 Added by S.I. 1962 No. 397 which came into operation on March 11, 1962.
59 Added by S.I. 1963 No. 1625 which came into operation on October 16, 1963.
60 Added by S.I. 1961 No. 1496 which came into operation on August 16, 1961.

THIRD SCHEDULE

ARTICLE III (1) OF THE UNIVERSAL COPYRIGHT CONVENTION

1869 "1. Any Contracting State which, under its domestic law, requires as a condition of copyright, compliance with formalities such as deposit, registration, notice, notarial certificates, payment of fees or manufacture or publication in that Contracting State, shall regard these requirements as satisfied with respect to all works protected in accordance with this Convention and first published outside its territory and the author of which is not one of its nationals, if from the time of the first publication all the copies of the work published with the authority of the author or other copyright proprietor bear the symbol © accompanied by the name of the copyright proprietor and the year of first publication placed in such manner and location as to give reasonable notice of claim of copyright."

FOURTH SCHEDULE

1870 1. In the case of any work to which the provisions of the Copyright Act, 1911, applied immediately before the commencement of this Order, section 8 (9) of the Act shall have effect as if for the references therein to the first day of July, nineteen hundred and twelve, there were substituted references to the date specified in column 2 of the Table set out at the end of this Schedule in relation to the country of origin of that work (being the date on which section 1 (2) (*d*) of the Copyright Act, 1911, first applied in relation to that country), and, in the case of any other work, the said section 8 (9) shall have effect as if for the references to that date there were substituted references to the commencement of this Order.

2. Where any musical work in which, immediately before the commencement of this Order, copyright subsisted by virtue of any Order made under section 29 of the Copyright Act, 1911, was published before the date specified in column 2 of the aforementioned Table in relation to the country of origin of that work (being the date on which section 1 (2) (*d*) of that Act first applied in relation to that country) the acts restricted by the copyright in that work shall not include making, or authorising the making of, a sound recording thereof, if before that date any record of that work had been lawfully made or placed on sale within the United Kingdom.

3. Where any musical work in which copyright did not subsist as mentioned in the preceding paragraph has been published before the commencement of this Order, the preceding paragraph shall have effect as if for the reference to the date therein mentioned there were substituted a reference to the commencement of this Order.

4. In the case of the sound recording embodied in any record to which the provisions of the Copyright Act, 1911, applied immediately before the commencement of this Order, the provisions of paragraph 13 of the Seventh Schedule to the Act shall apply in relation to the copyright in that sound recording as if for the reference therein to the first day of July, nineteen hundred and twelve, there were substituted a reference to the date specified in column 2 of the aforementioned Table in relation to the country of origin of that work (being the date on which section 19 of the Copyright Act of 1911 first applied in relation to that country), and, in the case of any other sound recording, the said paragraph 13 shall have effect as if for the reference to that date there were substituted a reference to the commencement of this Order.

5. In relation to any work or other subject-matter in which copyright subsists by virtue of this Order, the relevant provisions of the Seventh Schedule to the Act shall have effect as if for the references, wherever they occur therein, to the commencement of the Act or of any provision of the Act or to the repeal of any provision of the Copyright Act, 1911, or of any other enactment there were substituted references to the commencement of this Order.

1871 TABLE

Country of Origin (Column 1)	Date of application of relevant provisions of Copyright Act, 1911 (Column 2)
Australia	1st July, 1912
Belgium	1st July, 1912
Canada	1st July, 1912
France	1st July, 1912
Federal Republic of Germany (and Land Berlin)	1st July, 1912
India	1st July, 1912
Republic of Ireland	1st July, 1912
Japan	1st July, 1912
Luxembourg	1st July, 1912
Monaco	1st July, 1912
New Zealand	1st July, 1912
Norway	1st July, 1912
Pakistan	1st July, 1912
Portugal	1st July, 1912
South Africa	1st July, 1912
Spain	1st July, 1912
Switzerland	1st July, 1912
Tunisia	1st July, 1912
Denmark	17th March, 1913
Netherlands	17th March, 1913
Indonesia	11th April, 1913
Netherlands New Guinea, Curaçao	11th April, 1913
Surinam	13th June, 1913
Italy	1st April, 1914
Morocco (former French Zone)	16th November, 1917
Sweden	1st January, 1920
Poland	26th April, 1920
Austria	21st December, 1920
Greece	21st December, 1920
Czechoslovakia	27th May, 1921
Bulgaria	6th February, 1922
Brazil	21st April, 1922
Hungary	21st April, 1922
Lebanon	9th October, 1924
Syria	9th October, 1924
Roumania	1st January, 1927
Finland	7th May, 1928
Portuguese Colonies	7th May, 1929
Spanish Colonies	7th May, 1929
French Colonies and Protectorates under the authority of the French Ministry of the Colonies	27th October, 1930
Yugoslavia	27th October, 1930
Liechtenstein	7th October, 1931
Thailand	7th October, 1931
Iceland	23rd June, 1948
Morocco (former Spanish Zone)	21st February, 1935
Vatican City	3rd October, 1935
Belgian Congo and Ruanda-Urundi	8th March, 1949
Israel	4th April, 1950

FIFTH SCHEDULE

1872 An Order in Council dated the 3rd February, 1915, regulating copyright relations with the United States of America.[61]

An Order in Council dated the 9th day of February, 1920, further regulating copyright relations with the United States of America.[62]

The Copyright (Irish Free State) Order, 1930.[63]

The Copyright (Rome Convention) Order, 1933.[64]

The Copyright (Rome Convention) (Morocco (Spanish Zone)) Order, 1935.[65]

The Copyright (Rome Convention) (Vatican City) Order, 1935.[66]

The Copyright (Rome Convention) (Latvia) Order, 1937.[67]

The Copyright (United States of America) Order, 1942.[68]

The Copyright (Rome Convention) (Iceland) Order, 1948.[69]

The Copyright (Rome Convention) (Belgian Congo and Ruanda Urundi) Order, 1949.[70]

The Copyright (Rome Convention) (Israel) Order, 1950.[71]

The Copyright (United States of America) Order, 1942 (Amendment) Order, 1950.[72]

1873 **Copyright (International Organisations) Order, 1957**

(S.I. 1957 No. 1524)

Made - - - -	*23rd August,* 1957
Laid before Parliament	*29th August,* 1957
Coming into Operation	*27th September,* 1957

At the Court at Balmoral, the 23rd day of August, 1957

Present,

The Queen's Most Excellent Majesty in Council

Whereas it is provided by section 33 of the Copyright Act, 1956, that where it appears to Her Majesty that one or more sovereign Powers, or the government or governments thereof, are members of an organisation, and that it is expedient that the provisions of that section should apply to that organisation, Her Majesty may by Order in Council declare that the organisation is one to which that section applies:

And whereas it appears to Her Majesty that it is expedient that the provisions of the said section (under which, in the circumstances therein prescribed, copyright is to subsist in any original literary, dramatic, musical or artistic work made or published by or under the direction or control of any organisation to which the said section applies) should apply to the organisations mentioned in the Schedule hereto, being organisations of which sovereign Powers or the governments thereof are members:

Now, therefore, Her Majesty, by and with the advice of Her Privy Council, and by virtue of the authority conferred upon Her by section 33

[61] S.R. & O. 1915 No. 130.
[62] S.R. & O. 1920 No. 257, *ante,* § 1859.
[63] S.R. & O. 1930 No. 899.
[64] S.R. & O. 1933 No. 253.
[65] S.R. & O. 1935 No. 155.
[66] S.R. & O. 1935 No. 999.
[67] S.R. & O. 1937 No. 97.
[68] S.R. & O. 1942 No. 1579, *ante,* § 1861.
[69] S.I. 1948 No. 1327.
[70] S.I. 1949 No. 354.
[71] S.I. 1950 No. 508.
[72] S.I. 1950 No. 1641, *ante,* § 1861.

of the Copyright Act, 1956, and of all other powers enabling Her in that behalf, is pleased to declare, and it is hereby declared, as follows:

1. Each of the organisations mentioned in the Schedule hereto is an organisation to which section 33 of the Copyright Act, 1956 applies.

2. This Order may be cited as the Copyright (International Organisations) Order, 1957, and shall come into operation on the 27th day of September, 1957.

SCHEDULE

United Nations Organisation.
Specialised Agencies of the United Nations Organisation.
Organisation of American States.
Council of Europe.
Organisation for European Economic Co-operation.
The Baghdad Pact Organisation.[73]
The Western European Union.[73]

1874 **Copyright (International Conventions) Order, 1964**

(S.I. 1964 No. 690)

Made - - - -	12*th* *May,* 1964
Laid before Parliament	20*th* *May,* 1964
Coming into Operation	21*st* *May,* 1964

At the Court at Buckingham Palace, the 12th day of May, 1964

Present,

The Queen's Most Excellent Majesty in Council

Her Majesty, by and with the advice of Her Privy Council, and by virtue of the authority conferred upon Her by sections 31, 32 and 47 of the Copyright Act, 1956 (hereinafter referred to as "the Act"), and of all other powers enabling Her in that behalf, is pleased to order, and it is hereby ordered as follows:

PART I

1875 *Protection in respect of literary, dramatic, musical and artistic works, sound recordings, cinematograph films and published editions*

1. Subject to the following provisions of this Order, the provisions of Parts I and II of the Act (except section 14) and all the other provisions of the Act relevant thereto, being the provisions relating to literary, dramatic, musical and artistic works, sound recordings, cinematograph films and published editions of literary, dramatic or musical works, shall apply in the case of each of the countries mentioned in Schedule 1 hereto as follows:

(*a*) in relation to literary, dramatic, musical or artistic works, sound recordings, cinematograph films or published editions first published in that country, as they apply in relation to such works, recordings, films or editions first published in the United Kingdom;

[73] Added by S.I. 1958 No. 1052 which came into operation on July 7, 1958.

(*b*) in relation to persons who, at a material time (as hereinafter defined), are citizens or subjects of, or domiciled or resident in, that country, as they apply in relation to persons who, at such a time, are British subjects or domiciled or resident in the United Kingdom;

(*c*) in relation to bodies incorporated under the laws of that country, as they apply in relation to bodies incorporated under the laws of any part of the United Kingdom.

2.—(1) Subject to the following provisions of this Article, the relevant provisions of Schedule 7 to the Act shall, in relation to any work or other subject-matter in which copyright subsists bv virtue of this Part of this Order, have effect as if for references, wherever they occur therein, to the commencement of the Act or of any provision of the Act or to the repeal of any provision of the Copyright Act, 1911, or of any other enactment there were substituted references to 27th September, 1957 (being the date on which the Copyright (International Conventions) Order, 1957 [74] (hereinafter referred to as " the 1957 Order "), came into operation).

(2) Subject to the following provisions of this Article, copyright shall not subsist by virtue of this Part of this Order in any work or other subject-matter by reason only of its publication before 27th September, 1957, in a country which is a party to the Universal Copyright Convention but which is not a country of the Berne Copyright Union.

(3) In the case of any country mentioned in column 1 of Schedule 2 to this Order paragraphs (1) and (2) of this Article shall have effect as if there were substituted for the references therein to 27th September, 1957, references to the date set out against the name of that country in column 2 of that Schedule (being the date on which the provisions of the Act were first applied in the case of that country).

(4) This Article shall not apply—

(*a*) in the case of Kenya,[75] Malawi,[76] Zambia,[77] Ghana or Nigeria; or

(*b*) to any work or subject-matter first published in the United States of America, if, immediately before 27th September, 1957, copyright under the Copyright Act, 1911, subsisted in such work or subject-matter by virtue of either an Order in Council dated 9th February, 1920, regulating copyright relations with the United States of America,[78] or the Copyright (United States of America) Order, 1942,[79] as amended.[80]

3. The acts restricted by section 12 of the Act as applied by this Part of this Order shall not include—

(*a*) causing the recording to be heard in public; or

(*b*) broadcasting the recording;

except in the case of the countries mentioned in Schedule 3 to this Order.

4. Where any person has, before the commencement of this Order, taken any action whereby he has incurred any expenditure or liability in connection with the reproduction or performance of any work or other subject-matter in a manner which at the time was lawful, or for the

[74] S.I. 1957 No. 1523, *ante*, § 1862.
[75] Added by S.I. 1966 No. 1185.
[76] Added by S.I. 1965 No. 1857.
[77] Added by S.I. 1965 No. 1303.
[78] S.R. & O. 1920 No. 257, *ante*, § 1859.
[79] S.R. & O. 1942 No. 1579, *ante*, § 1861.
[80] S.I. 1950 No. 1641, *ante*, § 1861.

purpose of or with a view to the reproduction or performance of a work at a time when such reproduction or performance would, but for the making of this Part of this Order, have been lawful, nothing in this Part of this Order shall diminish or prejudice any right or interest arising from, or in connection with such action which is subsisting and valuable immediately before the commencement of this Order unless the person who, by virtue of this Part of this Order, becomes entitled to restrain such reproduction or performance agrees to pay such compensation, as failing agreement, may be determined by arbitration.

5. In this Part of this Order—

(*a*) " country of the Berne Copyright Union " means any country mentioned in Part 1 of Schedule 1 to this Order;

(*b*) " material time " means—

(i) in relation to any unpublished work or subject-matter, the time at which such work or subject-matter was made or, if the making thereof extended over a period, a substantial part of that period;

(ii) in relation to a published work or subject-matter, the time of first publication;

(*c*) " party to the Universal Copyright Convention " means any country mentioned in Part 2 of Schedule 1 to this Order.

6. Nothing in the provisions of the Act as applied by this Part of this Order shall be construed as reviving any right to make, or restrain the making of, or any right in respect of, translations, if such right has ceased before the commencement of this Order.

7. This Part of this Order, and Part III, so far as relevant thereto, shall extend to the countries mentioned in column 1 of Part 1 of Schedule 4 to this Order subject to the modifications specified in Part 2 of that Schedule.

Part II

Protection in respect of broadcasts

1876 **8.** The provisions of section 14 of the Act, so far as they relate to sound broadcasts, and all the other provisions of the Act relevant thereto, other than section 40 (3), shall apply, in the case of each of the countries mentioned in column 1 of Schedule 5 to this Order, in relation to sound broadcasts made from places in those countries by an organisation constituted in, or under the laws of, the country in which the sound broadcast is made, as they apply in relation to broadcasts made from places in the United Kingdom by the British Broadcasting Corporation; so, however, that paragraphs 17 and 18 of Schedule 7 to the Act shall have effect as if for the references therein to the commencement of section 14 of the Act there were substituted references to the respective dates set out in column 2 of Schedule 5 to this Order (being the dates on which the provisions of section 14 of the Act so far as they relate to sound broadcasts were first applied in the case of those countries).

9. The provisions of section 14 of the Act, so far as they relate to television broadcasts, and all the other provisions of the Act relevant thereto, other than section 37 (4), section 40 (3) and Schedule 5, shall apply in the case of each of the countries mentioned in column 1 of Schedule 6 to this

Order, in relation to television broadcasts made from places in those countries by an organisation constituted in, or under the laws of, the country in which the television broadcast was made, as they apply in relation to television broadcasts made from places in the United Kingdom by the British Broadcasting Corporation or the Independent Television Authority; so, however, that—

(*a*) section 24 (3) (*c*) of the Act shall have effect as if for the reference to the Corporation or the Authority or any organisation appointed by them there were substituted a reference to any owner or prospective owner of coypright in television broadcasts; and

(*b*) paragraphs 17 and 18 of Schedule 7 to the Act shall have effect as if for the references therein to the commencement of section 14 of the Act there were substituted references to the respective dates set out in column 2 of Schedule 6 to this Order, (being the dates on which the provisions of section 14 of the Act so far as they relate to television broadcasts were first applied in the case of those countries).

PART III

Supplemental

1877 **10.**—(1) The Orders mentioned in Part 1 of Schedule 7 to this Order are hereby revoked insofar as they form part of the law of the United Kingdom or any country to which this Order extends; and accordingly the Orders mentioned in column 2 of Part 1 of Schedule 4 to this Order (being the Orders whereby the Act and the 1957 Order were extended to the countries to which this Order extends) shall have effect as though there were omitted therefrom the respective provisions mentioned in column 4 of that Part of that Schedule (being the provisions extending the 1957 Order and other Orders hereby revoked to those countries):

Provided that, notwithstanding the revocation of the 1957 Order, and without prejudice to the effect of section 38 of the Interpretation Act, 1889 (which relates to the effect of repeals), as applied by Article 11 of this Order, Article 2 of the 1957 Order shall continue to apply in any case in which it applied before the commencement of this Order as it applied by virtue of the 1957 Order or any of the other Orders hereby revoked.

(2) The Orders mentioned in Part 2 of Schedule 7 to this Order are hereby revoked in the law of the United Kingdom.

11. The Interpretation Act, 1889, shall apply to the interpretation of this Order as if this Order and the Orders hereby revoked were Acts of Parliament.

12. This Order may be cited as the Copyright (International Conventions) Order, 1964, and shall come into operation on 21st May, 1964.

W. G. Agnew.

SCHEDULE 1

PART 1

1878 COUNTRIES OF THE BERNE COPYRIGHT UNION

Argentina [81]
Australia (and Papua, New Guinea, Nauru and Norfolk Island)
Austria

[81] Added by S.I. 1967 No. 877 which came into operation on June 15, 1967.

Belgium
Brazil
Bulgaria
Cameroon [82]
Canada
Ceylon
Congo (Brazzaville)
Congo (Leopoldville)
Cyprus
Czechoslovakia
Dahomey
Denmark
Finland
France (and French territories overseas)
Gabon
Federal Republic of Germany (and Land Berlin)
Greece
Hungary
Iceland
India
Republic of Ireland
Israel
Italy
Ivory Coast
Japan
Lebanon
Liechtenstein
Luxembourg
Malagasy Republic [83]
Mali
Malta [84]
Mexico [85]
Monaco
Morocco
Netherlands (and Surinam and Netherlands Antilles)
New Zealand
Niger
Norway
Pakistan
Philippines
Poland
Portugal (including Portuguese provinces overseas)
Roumania
Senegal
South Africa (and South West Africa)
Spain (and its Colonies)
Sweden
Switzerland
Thailand
Tunisia
Turkey
Upper Volta
Uruguay [86]
Vatican City
Western Samoa
Yugoslavia

[82] Added by S.I. 1965 No. 1303 which came into operation on July 1, 1965.
[83] Added by S.I. 1966 No. 684 which came into operation on June 16, 1966.
[84] Added by S.I. 1968 No. 1858 which came into operation on November 29, 1968.
[85] Added by S.I. 1967 No. 877 which came into operation on June 15, 1967.
[86] Added by S.I. 1967 No. 1151 which came into operation on August 4, 1967.

PART 2

PARTIES TO THE UNIVERSAL COPYRIGHT CONVENTION

Andorra
Argentina
Australia [87]
Austria
Belgium
Brazil
Cambodia
Canada
Chile
Costa Rica
Cuba
Czechoslovakia
Denmark
Ecuador
Finland
France
Federal Republic of Germany (and Land Berlin)
Ghana
Greece
Guatemala [88]
Haiti
Iceland
India
Republic of Ireland
Israel
Italy
Japan
Kenya [89]
Laos
Lebanon
Liberia
Liechtenstein
Luxembourg
Malawi [90]
Malta [91]
Mexico
Monaco
Netherlands [91]
New Zealand [88]
Nicaragua
Nigeria
Norway
Pakistan
Panama
Paraguay
Peru
Philippines
Portugal
Spain
Sweden
Switzerland
Tunisia [92]

[87] Added by S.I. 1970 No. 290 which came into operation on March 4, 1970.
[88] Added by S.I. 1964 No. 1651, which came into operation on October 28, 1964.
[89] Added by S.I. 1966 No. 1185 which came into operation on September 27, 1966.
[90] Added by S.I. 1965 No. 1857 which came into operation on November 5, 1965.
[91] Added by S.I. 1968 No. 1858 which came into operation on November 29, 1968.
[92] Added by S.I. 1970 No. 290 which came into operation on March 4, 1970.

United States of America (and Guam, Panama Canal Zone, Puerto Rico and the Virgin Islands of the United States of America)
Vatican City
Venezuela [93]
Yugoslavia [94]
Zambia [95]

SCHEDULE 2

1879 DATES ON WHICH PROVISIONS OF THE ACT WERE FIRST APPLIED BY PREVIOUS ORDERS OTHER THAN THE 1957 ORDER TO COUNTRIES BEING PARTIES TO THE UNIVERSAL COPYRIGHT CONVENTION BUT NOT MEMBERS OF THE BERNE COPYRIGHT UNION.

Country	Date on which the Act was first applied
Argentina	13th February, 1958
Guatemala	28th October, 1964 [88]
Nicaragua	16th August, 1961
Paraguay	11th March, 1962
Panama	17th October, 1962
Peru	16th October, 1963
Venezuela	18th November, 1966 [93]

SCHEDULE 3 [96]

1880 COUNTRIES IN THE CASE OF WHICH COPYRIGHT IN SOUND RECORDINGS INCLUDES EXCLUSIVE RIGHT TO PERFORM IN PUBLIC AND TO BROADCAST

Australia
Brazil [97]
Canada
Ceylon
Cyprus
Czechoslovakia [98]
Denmark
Ecuador
Federal Republic of Germany (and Land Berlin)
India
Republic of Ireland
Italy
Israel
Mexico
New Zealand
Nigeria
Norway
Pakistan
Paraguay [99]
Spain
Sweden
Switzerland
Western Samoa

93 Added by S.I. 1966 No. 1409 which came into operation on November 18, 1966.
94 Added by S.I. 1966 No. 684 which came into operation on June 16, 1966.
95 Added by S.I. 1965 No. 1303 which came into operation on July 1, 1965.
96 Congo (Brazzaville) was deleted from this Schedule by S.I. 1964 No. 1651. South Africa was deleted from this Schedule by S.I. 1965 No. 2159.
97 Added by S.I. 1965 No. 1857 which came into operation on November 5, 1965.
98 Added by S.I. 1964 No. 1194, which came into operation on August 14, 1964.
99 Added by S.I. 1970 No. 290 which came into operation on March 4, 1970.

SCHEDULE 4

1881 COUNTRIES TO WHICH PART I OF THIS ORDER EXTENDS AND MODIFICATIONS THEREOF IN RELATION TO SUCH EXTENSION

PART 1

Column 1 Country	Column 2 Relevant Order	Column 3 Operative date of Relevant Order	Column 4 Provisions omitted from Relevant Order
Isle of Man ...	The Copyright (Isle of Man) Order, 1959 (S.I. 1959/861; 1959 I, p. 748).	31st May, 1959	Paragraph 1 of Schedule 2.
Gibraltar ...	The Copyright (Gibraltar) Order, 1960 (S.I. 1960/847; 1960 I, p. 767).	1st Oct., 1960	The reference to the Copyright (International Conventions) Order, 1957, in Article 2, and paragraph 1 of Schedule 2.
Fiji	The Copyright (Fiji) Order, 1961 (S.I. 1961/60; 1961 I, p. 116).	1st June, 1961	The references to the Copyright (International Conventions) Order, 1957, and the Copyright (International Conventions) (Argentina) Order, 1958, in Article 2, and paragraphs 2 and 3 of Schedule 2.
Bermuda ...	The Copyright (Bermuda) Order, 1962 (S.I. 1962/1642; 1962 II, p. 1909).	6th Dec., 1962	The references to the Copyright (International Conventions) Order, 1957, and the Copyright (International Conventions) (Argentina) Order, 1958, in Article 2, and paragraphs 2 and 3 of Schedule 2.
The Bahama Islands	The Copyright (Bahamas) Order, 1962 (S.I. 1962/2184; 1962 III, p. 2964).	11th Feb., 1963	The references to the Copyright (International Conventions) Order, 1957, and the Copyright (International Conventions) (Argentina) Order, 1958, in Article 2, and paragraphs 2 and 3 of Schedule 2.
The Virgin Islands	The Copyright (Virgin Islands) Order, 1962 (S.I. 1962/2185; 1962 III, p. 2969).	11th Feb., 1963	The references to the Copyright (International Conventions) Order, 1957, and the Copyright (International Conventions) (Argentina) Order, 1958, in Article 2, and paragraphs 2 and 3 of Schedule 2.

Column 1 Country	Column 2 Relevant Order	Column 3 Operative date of Relevant Order	Column 4 Provisions omitted from Relevant Order
The Falkland Islands and its Dependencies	The Copyright (Falkland Islands) Order, 1963 (S.I. 1963/1037; 1963 II, p. 1761).	10th Oct., 1963	The references to the Copyright (International Conventions) Order, 1957, and the Copyright (International Conventions) (Argentina) Order, 1958, in Article 2, and paragraphs 2 and 3 of Schedule 2.
St. Helena and its Dependencies	The Copyright (St. Helena) Order, 1963 (S.I. 1963/1038; 1963 II, p. 1767).	10th Oct., 1963	The references to the Copyright (International Conventions) Order, 1957, and the Copyright (International Conventions) (Argentina) Order, 1958, in Article 2, and paragraphs 2 and 3 of Schedule 2.
Seychelles ...	The Copyright (Seychelles) Order, 1963 (S.I. 1963/1039; 1963 II, p. 1772).	10th Oct., 1963	The references to the Copyright (International Conventions) Order, 1957, and the Copyright (International Conventions) (Argentina) Order, 1958, in Article 2, and paragraphs 2 and 3 of Schedule 2.
Mauritius ...	The Copyright (Mauritius) Order, 1964 (S.I. 1964/691).	21st Nov., 1964	

PART 2

1. In so far as Part I of this Order forms part of the law of any country by virtue of Article 7 of this Order, Article 1 of this Order shall have effect as if for references therein to " the United Kingdom " there were substituted references to that country.

2. In so far as Part I of this Order forms part of the law of any such country as aforesaid, Article 2 of this Order shall have effect subject to the following modifications—

(*a*) there shall be substituted for the references in paragraphs (1) and (2) to 27th September, 1957, references to the following date, that is to say—

(i) in relation to any country mentioned in Schedule 1 to this Order and not mentioned in column 1 of Schedule 2 to this Order, and also in relation to any country mentioned in column 1 of Schedule 2 where the date set out in column 2 of that Schedule against the name of that country is a date earlier than the operative date of the relevant Order, there shall be substituted the operative date of that Order (being the date on which the Act was first extended to that country);

(ii) in relation to any other country mentioned in column 1 of Schedule 2 to this Order, there shall be substituted the date set out in column 2 of that Schedule against the name of that country (being the date on which the provisions of the Act were first applied in the case of that country);

(*b*) paragraph (3) shall be omitted; and

(*c*) there shall be substituted for the reference in paragraph (4) to 27th September, 1957, a reference to the operative date of the relevant Order.

3. In paragraphs 1 and 2 of this Part of this Schedule the "relevant Order" and the "operative date" of that Order respectively mean, in relation to any country to which Part I of this Order extends, the Order and the date mentioned against the name of that country, in columns 2 and 3 of Part I of this Schedule.

SCHEDULE 5

1882 Countries whose Organisations are Protected in Relation to Sound Broadcasts

Country	Date
Brazil	5th November, 1965 [1]
Congo (Brazzaville)	21st May, 1964
Czechoslovakia	14th August, 1964 [2]
Denmark	1st July, 1965 [3]
Ecuador	21st May, 1964
Federal Republic of Germany (and Land Berlin)	18th November, 1966 [4]
Mexico	21st May, 1964
Niger	21st May, 1964
Paraguay	26th February, 1970 [5]
Sweden	21st May, 1964

SCHEDULE 6

1883 Countries whose Organisations are Protected in Relation to Television Broadcasts

Country	Date
Belgium	8th March, 1968 [6]
Brazil	5th November, 1965 [1]
Cyprus	5th May, 1970 [7]
Czechoslovakia	14th August, 1964 [2]
Federal Republic of Germany (and Land Berlin)	18th November, 1966 [4]
France	1st July, 1961
Sweden	1st July, 1961
Denmark	1st February, 1962
Congo (Brazzaville)	21st May, 1964
Ecuador	21st May, 1964
Mexico	21st May, 1964
Norway	10th August, 1968 [6]
Niger	21st May, 1964
Paraguay	26th February, 1970 [5]

[1] Added by S.I. 1965 No. 1857.
[2] Added by S.I. 1964 No. 1194.
[3] Added by S.I. 1965 No. 1303.
[4] Added by S.I. 1966 No. 1409.
[5] Added by S.I. 1970 No. 290.
[6] Added by S.I. 1968 No. 1858.
[7] Added by S.I. 1970 No. 637.

SCHEDULE 7

Part 1

1884 Orders Revoked in the Law of the United Kingdom and other Countries to which Part I of this Order Extends

Order	S.I. number and reference
The Copyright (International Conventions) Order, 1957.	S.I. 1957/1523 (1957 I, p. 474).
The Copyright (International Conventions) (Argentina) Order, 1958.	S.I. 1958/135 (1958 I, p. 361).
The Copyright (International Conventions) (Amendment) Order, 1958.	S.I. 1958/1254 (1958 I, p. 358).
The Copyright (International Conventions) (Amendment No. 2) Order, 1958.	S.I. 1958/2184 (1958 I, p. 360).
The Copyright (International Conventions) (Amendment) Order, 1960.	S.I. 1960/200 (1960 I, p. 772).
The Copyright (International Conventions) (Amendment) Order, 1961.	S.I. 1961/1496 (1961 II, p. 3040).
The Copyright (International Conventions) (Amendment No. 2) Order, 1961.	S.I. 1961/2461 (1961 III, p. 4507).
The Copyright (International Conventions) (Amendment) Order, 1962.	S.I. 1962/397 (1962 I, p. 348).
The Copyright (International Conventions) (Amendment No.2) Order, 1962.	S.I. 1962/628 (1962 I, p. 631).
The Copyright (International Conventions) (Amendment No.3) Order, 1962.	S.I. 1962/1641 (1962 II, p. 1907).
The Copyright (International Conventions) (Amendment No. 4) Order, 1962.	S.I. 1962/2183 (1962 III, p. 2962).
The Copyright (International Conventions) (Amendment) Order, 1963.	S.I. 1963/1625 (1963 III, p. 3018).

Part 2

Orders Revoked in the Law of the United Kingdom

Order	S.I. number and reference
The Copyright (Foreign Television Broadcasts) Order, 1961.	S.I. 1961/993 (1961 II, p. 1917).
The Copyright (Foreign Television Broadcasts) (Amendment) Order, 1962.	S.I. 1962/165 (1962 I, p. 166).

[The next paragraph is 1890]

Appendix E

UNITED STATES OF AMERICA CODE AND PROCLAMATION

United States Code. Title 17—Copyrights [1]

Chapter 1—Registration of Copyrights

Exclusive rights as to copyrighted works

1890 **1.** Any person entitled thereto, upon complying with the provisions of this title, shall have the exclusive right:

(*a*) To print, reprint, publish, copy, and vend the copyrighted work;

(*b*) To translate the copyrighted work into other languages or dialects, or make any other version thereof, if it be a literary work; to dramatize it if it be a nondramatic work; to convert it into a novel or other nondramatic work if it be a drama; to arrange or adapt it if it be a musical work; to complete, execute, and finish it if it be a model or design for a work of art;

(*c*) To deliver, authorise the delivery of, read, or present the copyrighted work in public for profit if it be a lecture, sermon, address or similar production, or other nondramatic literary work; to make or procure the making of any transcription or record thereof by or from which, in whole or in part, it may in any manner or by any method be exhibited, delivered, presented, produced, or reproduced; and to play or perform it in public for profit, and to exhibit, represent, produce, or reproduce it in any manner or by any method whatsoever. The damages for the infringement by broadcast of any work referred to in this subsection shall not exceed the sum of $100 where the infringing broadcaster shows that he was not aware that he was infringing and that such infringement could not have been reasonably foreseen;

(*d*) To perform or represent the copyrighted work publicly if it be a drama or, if it be a dramatic work and not reproduced in copies for sale, to vend any manuscript or any record whatsoever thereof; to make or to procure the making of any transcription or record thereof by or from which, in whole or in part, it may in any manner or by any method be exhibited, performed, represented, produced, or reproduced; and to exhibit, perform, represent, produce or reproduce it in any manner or by any method whatsoever; and

(*e*) To perform the copyrighted work publicly for profit if it be a musical composition; and for the purpose of public performance for profit, and for the purposes set forth in subsection (*a*) hereof, to make any arrangement or setting of it or of the melody of it in any system of notation or any form of record in which the thought of an author may be recorded and from which it may be read or reproduced: *Provided,* That the provisions of this title, so far as they secure copyright controlling the parts of instruments serving to reproduce mechanically the musical work, shall include only compositions published and copyrighted after July 1, 1909, and shall not include the works of a foreign author or composer unless the foreign state or nation of which such author or composer is a citizen or subject grants, either by treaty, convention, agreement,

[1] As amended to September 7, 1957. See, however, footnotes 2 and 3, *post,* §§ 1897 and 1913.

or law, to citizens of the United States similar rights. And as a condition of extending the copyright control to such mechanical reproductions, that whenever the owner of a musical copyright has used or permitted or knowingly acquiesced in the use of the copyrighted work upon the parts of instruments serving to reproduce mechanically the musical work, any other person may make similar use of the copyrighted work upon the payment to the copyright proprietor of a royalty of 2 cents on each such part manufactured, to be paid by the manufacturer thereof; and the copyright proprietor may require, and if so the manufacturer shall furnish, a report under oath on the 20th day of each month on the number of parts of instruments manufactured during the previous month serving to reproduce mechanically said musical work, and royalties shall be due on the parts manufactured during any month upon the 20th of the next succeeding month. The payment of the royalty provided for by this section shall free the articles or devices for which such royalty has been paid from further contribution to the copyright except in case of public performance for profit. It shall be the duty of the copyright owner, if he uses the musical composition himself for the manufacture of parts of instruments serving to reproduce mechanically the musical work, or licenses others to do so, to file notice thereof, accompanied by a recording fee, in the copyright office, and any failure to file such notice shall be a complete defense to any suit, action, or proceeding for any infringement of such copyright.

In case of failure of such manufacturer to pay to the copyright proprietor within thirty days after demand in writing the full sum of royalties due at said rate at the date of such demand, the court may award taxable costs to the plaintiff and a reasonable counsel fee, and the court may, in its discretion, enter judgment therein for any sum in addition over the amount found to be due as royalty in accordance with the terms of this title, not exceeding three times such amount.

The reproduction or rendition of a musical composition by or upon coin-operated machines shall not be deemed a public performance for profit unless a fee is charged for admission to the place where such reproduction or rendition occurs.

Rights of author or proprietor of unpublished work

1891 **2.** Nothing in this title shall be construed to annul or limit the right of the author or proprietor of an unpublished work, at common law or in equity, to prevent the copying, publication, or use of such unpublished work without his consent, and to obtain damages therefor.

Protection of component parts of work copyrighted; composite works or periodicals

1892 **3.** The copyright provided by this title shall protect all the copyrightable component parts of the work copyrighted, and all matter therein in which copyright is already subsisting, but without extending the duration or scope of such copyright. The copyright upon composite works or periodicals shall give to the proprietor thereof all the rights in respect thereto which he would have if each part were individually copyrighted under this title.

All writings of author included

1893 **4.** The works for which copyright may be secured under this title shall include all the writings of an author.

Classification of works for registration

1894 **5.** The application for registration shall specify to which of the following classes the work in which copyright is claimed belongs:

(*a*) Books, including composite and cyclopedic works, directories, gazetteers, and other compilations.
(*b*) Periodicals, including newspapers.
(*c*) Lectures, sermons, addresses (prepared for oral delivery).
(*d*) Dramatic or dramatico-musical compositions.
(*e*) Musical compositions.
(*f*) Maps.
(*g*) Works of art; models or designs for works of art.
(*h*) Reproductions of a work of art.
(*i*) Drawings or plastic works of a scientific or technical character.
(*j*) Photographs.
(*k*) Prints and pictorial illustrations including prints or labels used for articles of merchandise.
(*l*) Motion-picture photoplays.
(*m*) Motion pictures other than photoplays.

The above specifications shall not be held to limit the subject-matter of copyright as defined in section 4 of this title, nor shall any error in classification invalidate or impair the copyright protection secured under this title.

Registration of prints and labels

1895 **6.** Commencing July 1, 1940, the Register of Copyrights is charged with the registration of claims to copyright properly presented, in all prints and labels published in connection with the sale or advertisement of articles of merchandise, including all claims to copyright in prints and labels pending in the Patent Office and uncleared at the close of business June 30, 1940. There shall be paid for registering a claim of copyright in any such print or label not a trade-mark $6, which sum shall cover the expense of furnishing a certificate of such registration, under the seal of the Copyright Office, to the claimant of copyright.

Copyright on compilations of works in public domain or of copyrighted works; subsisting copyrights not affected

1896 **7.** Compilations or abridgments, adaptations, arrangements, dramatisations, translations, or other versions of works in the public domain or of copyrighted works when produced with the consent of the proprietor of the copyright in such works, or works republished with new matter, shall be regarded as new works subject to copyright under the provisions of this title; but the publication of any such new works shall not affect the force or validity of any subsisting copyright upon the matter employed or any part thereof, or be construed to imply an exclusive right to such use of the original works, or to secure or extend copyright in such original works.

Copyright not to subsist in works in public domain, or published prior to July 1, 1909, and not already copyrighted, or Government publications; publication by Government of copyrighted material

1897 **8.** No copyright shall subsist in the original text of any work which is in the public domain, or in any work which was published in this country or any foreign country prior to July 1, 1909, and has not been already copyrighted in the United States, or in any publication of the United States Government, or any reprint, in whole or in part, thereof, except that the Postmaster-General may secure copyright on behalf of the United States in the whole or any part of the publications authorized by section 2506 of title 39.[2]

The publication or republication by the Government, either separately or in a public document, of any material in which copyright is subsisting shall not be taken to cause any abridgment or annulment of the copyright or to authorize any use or appropriation of such copyright material without the consent of the copyright proprietor.

Authors or proprietors, entitled; aliens

1898 **9.** The author or proprietor of any work made the subject of copyright by this title, or his executors, administrators, or assigns, shall have copyright for such work under the conditions and for the terms specified in this title: *Provided, however,* That the copyright secured by this title shall extend to the work of an author or proprietor who is a citizen or subject of a foreign state or nation only under the conditions described in subsections (*a*), (*b*), or (*c*) below:

(*a*) When an alien author or proprietor shall be domiciled within the United States at the time of the first publication of his work; or

(*b*) When the foreign state or nation of which such author or proprietor is a citizen or subject grants, either by treaty, convention, agreement, or law, to citizens of the United States the benefit of copyright on substantially the same basis as to its own citizens, or copyright protection, substantially equal to the protection secured to such foreign author under this title or by treaty; or when such foreign state or nation is a party to an international agreement which provides for reciprocity in the granting of copyright, by the terms of which agreement the United States may, at its pleasure, become a party thereto.

The existence of the reciprocal conditions aforesaid shall be determined by the President of the United States, by proclamation made from time to time, as the purposes of this title may require: *Provided,* That whenever the President shall find that the authors, copyright owners, or proprietors of works first produced or published abroad and subject to copyright or to renewal of copyright under the laws of the United States, including works subject to ad interim copyright, are or may have been temporarily unable to comply with the conditions and formalities prescribed with respect to such works by the copyright laws of the United States, because of the disruption or suspension of facilities essential for such compliance, he may by proclamation grant such extension of time as

[2] This section is printed as amended by Public Law 87–646 dated September 7, 1962; the changes are in form but not in substance. See, as to standard reference data prepared or made available by the Secretary of Commerce, Public Law 90–396, dated July 11, 1968.

he may deem appropriate for the fulfilment of such conditions or formalities by authors, copyright owners, or proprietors who are citizens of the United States or who are nátionals of countries which accord substantially equal treatment in this respect to authors, copyright owners, or proprietors who are citizens of the United States: *Provided further*, That no liability shall attach under this title for lawful uses made or acts done prior to the effective date of such proclamation in connection with such works, or in respect to the continuance for one year subsequent to such date of any business undertaking or enterprise lawfully undertaken prior to such date involving expenditure or contractual obligation in connection with the exploitation, production, reproduction, circulation, or performance of any such work.

The President may at any time terminate any proclamation authorized herein or any part thereof or suspend or extend its operation for such period or periods of time as in his judgment the interests of the United States may require.

(*c*) When the Universal Copyright Convention, signed at Geneva on September 6, 1952, shall be in force between the United States of America and the foreign state or nation of which such author is a citizen or subject, or in which the work was first published. Any work to which copyright is extended pursuant to this subsection shall be exempt from the following provisions of this title: (1) The requirement in section 1 (*e*) that a foreign state or nation must grant to United States citizens mechanical reproduction rights similar to those specified therein; (2) the obligatory deposit requirements of the first sentence of section 13; (3) the provisions of sections 14, 16, 17, and 18; (4) the import prohibitions of section 107, to the extent that they are related to the manufacturing requirements of section 16; and (5) the requirements of sections 19 and 20: *Provided, however*, That such exemptions shall apply only if from the time of first publication all the copies of the work published with the authority of the author or other copyright proprietor shall bear the symbol © accompanied by the name of the copyright proprietor and the year of first publication placed in such manner and location as to give reasonable notice of claim of copyright.

Upon the coming into force of the Universal Copyright Convention in a foreign state or nation as hereinbefore provided, every book or periodical of a citizen or subject thereof in which ad interim copyright was subsisting on the effective date of said coming into force shall have copyright for twenty-eight years from the date of first publication abroad without the necessity of complying with the further formalities specified in section 23 of this title.

The provisions of this subsection shall not be extended to works of an author who is a citizen of, or domiciled in the United States of America regardless of place of first publication, or to works first published in the United States.

Publication of work with notice

1899 **10.** Any person entitled thereto by this title may secure copyright for his work by publication thereof with the notice of copyright required by this title; and such notice shall be affixed to each copy thereof published or offered for sale in the United States by authority of the copyright proprietor, except in the case of books seeking ad interim protection under section 22 of this title.

Registration of claim and issuance of certificate

1900 **11.** Such person may obtain registration of his claim to copyright by complying with the provisions of this title, including the deposit of copies, and upon such compliance the Register of Copyrights shall issue to him the certificates provided for in section 209 of this title.

Works not reproduced for sale

1901 **12.** Copyright may also be had of the works of an author, of which copies are not reproduced for sale, by the deposit, with claim of copyright, of one complete copy of such work if it be a lecture or similar production or a dramatic, musical, or dramatico-musical composition; of a title and description, with one print taken from each scene or act, if the work be a motion-picture photoplay; of a photographic print if the work be a photograph; of a title and description, with not less than two prints taken from different sections of a complete motion picture, if the work be a motion picture other than a photoplay; or of a photograph or other identifying reproduction thereof, if it be a work of art or a plastic work or drawing. But the privilege of registration of copyright secured hereunder shall not exempt the copyright proprietor from the deposit of copies, under sections 13 and 14 of this title, where the work is later reproduced in copies for sale.

Deposit of copies after publication; action or proceeding for infringement

1902 **13.** After copyright has been secured by publication of the work with the notice of copyright as provided in section 10 of this title, there shall be promptly deposited in the copyright office or in the mail addressed to the Register of Copyrights, Washington, District of Columbia, two complete copies of the best edition thereof then published, or if the work is by an author who is a citizen or subject of a foreign state or nation and has been published in a foreign country, one complete copy of the best edition then published in such foreign country, which copies or copy, if the work be a book or periodical, shall have been produced in accordance with the manufacturing provisions specified in section 16 of this title; or if such work be a contribution to a periodical, for which contribution special registration is requested, one copy of the issue or issues containing such contribution; or if the work belongs to a class specified in subsections (*g*), (*h*), (*i*) or (*k*) of section 5 of this title, and if the Register of Copyrights determines that it is impracticable to deposit copies because of their size, weight, fragility, or monetary value he may permit the deposit of photographs or other identifying reproductions in lieu of copies of the work as published under such rules and regulations as he may prescribe with the approval of the Librarian of Congress; or if the work is not reproduced in copies for sale there shall be deposited the copy, print, photograph or other identifying reproduction provided by section 12 of this title, such copies or copy, print, photograph, or other reproduction to be accompanied in each case by a claim of copyright. No action or proceeding shall be maintained for infringement of copyright in any work until the provisions of this title with respect to the deposit of copies and registration of such work shall have been complied with.

Same; failure to deposit; demand; penalty

1903 **14.** Should the copies called for by section 13 of this title not be promptly deposited as provided in this title, the Register of Copyrights may at any time after the publication of the work, upon actual notice, require the proprietor of the copyright to deposit them, and after the said demand shall have been made, in default of the deposit of copies of the work within three months from any part of the United States, except an outlying territorial possession of the United States, or within six months from any outlying territorial possession of the United States, or from any foreign country, the proprietor of the copyright shall be liable to a fine of $100 and to pay to the Library of Congress twice the amount of the retail price of the best edition of the work, and the copyright shall become void.

Same; postmaster's receipt; transmission by mail without cost

1904 **15.** The postmaster to whom are delivered the articles deposited as provided in sections 12 and 13 of this title shall, if requested, give a receipt therefor and shall mail them to their destination without cost to the copyright claimant.

Mechanical work to be done in United States

1905 **16.** Of the printed book or periodical specified in section 5, subsections (*a*) and (*b*), of this title, except the original text of a book or periodical of foreign origin in a language or languages other than English, the text of all copies accorded protection under this title, except as below provided, shall be printed from type set within the limits of the United States, either by hand or by the aid of any kind of typesetting machine, or from plates made within the limits of the United States from type set therein, or, if the text be produced by lithographic process, or photoengraving process, then by a process wholly performed within the limits of the United States, and the printing of the text and binding of the said book shall be performed within the limits of the United States; which requirements shall extend also to the illustrations within a book consisting of printed text and illustrations produced by lithographic process, or photoengraving process, and also to separate lithographs or photoengravings, except where in either case the subjects represented are located in a foreign country and illustrate a scientific work or reproduce a work of art: *Provided, however,* That said requirements shall not apply to works in raised characters for the use of the blind, or to books or periodicals of foreign origin in a language or languages other than English, or to works printed or produced in the United States by any other process than those above specified in this section, or to copies of books or periodicals, first published abroad in the English language, imported into the United States within five years after first publication in a foreign state or nation up to the number of fifteen hundred copies of each such book or periodical if said copies shall contain notice of copyright in accordance with sections 10, 19 and 20 of this title and if ad interim copyright in said work shall have been obtained pursuant to section 22 of this title prior to the importation into the United States of any copy except those permitted by the provisions of section 107 of this title: *Provided further,* That the provisions of this section shall not affect the right of importation under the provisions of section 107 of this title.

Affidavit to accompany copies

1906 **17.** In the case of the book the copies so deposited shall be accompanied by an affidavit under the official seal of any officer authorized to administer oaths within the United States, duly made by the person claiming copyright or by his duly authorized agent or representative residing in the United States, or by the printer who has printed the book, setting forth that the copies deposited have been printed from type set within the limits of the United States or from plates made within the limits of the United States from type set therein; or, if the text be produced by lithographic process, or photoengraving process, that such process was wholly performed within the limits of the United States and that the printing of the text and binding of the said book have also been performed within the limits of the United States. Such affidavit shall state also the place where and the establishment or establishments in which such type was set or plates were made or lithographic process, or photoengraving process or printing and binding were performed and the date of the completion of the printing of the book or the date of publication.

Making false affidavit

1907 **18.** Any person who, for the purpose of obtaining registration of a claim to copyright, shall knowingly make a false affidavit as to his having complied with the above conditions shall be deemed guilty of a misdemeanor, and upon conviction thereof shall be punished by a fine of not more than $1,000, and all of his rights and privileges under said copyright shall thereafter be forfeited.

Notice; form

1908 **19.** The notice of copyright required by section 10 of this title shall consist either of the word "Copyright," the abbreviation "Copr.," or the symbol ©, accompanied by the name of the copyright proprietor, and if the work be a printed literary, musical, or dramatic work, the notice shall include also the year in which the copyright was secured by publication. In the case, however, of copies of works specified in subsections (*f*) to (*k*), inclusive, of section 5 of this title, the notice may consist of the letter C enclosed within a circle, thus ©, accompanied by the initials, monogram, mark, or symbol of the copyright proprietor: *Provided*, That on some accessible portion of such copies or of the margin, back, permanent base, or pedestal, or of the substance on which such copies shall be mounted, his name shall appear. But in the case of works in which copyright was subsisting on July 1, 1909, the notice of copyright may be either in one of the forms prescribed herein or may consist of the following words: "Entered according to Act of Congress, in the year , by A. B., in the office of the Librarian of Congress, at Washington, D.C.," or, at his option, the word "Copyright," together with the year the copyright was entered and the name of the party by whom it was taken out; thus, "Copyright, 19—, by A. B."

Same; place of application of; one notice in each volume or number of newspaper or periodical

1909 **20.** The notice of copyright shall be applied, in the case of a book or other printed publication, upon its title page or the page immediately following, or if a periodical either upon the title page or upon the first page of text of each separate number or under the title heading, or if a musical work either upon its title page or the first page of music. One notice of copyright in each volume or in each number of a newspaper or periodical published shall suffice.

Same; effect of accidental omission from copy or copies

1910 **21.** Where the copyright proprietor has sought to comply with the provisions of this title with respect to notice, the omission by accident or mistake of the prescribed notice from a particular copy or copies shall not invalidate the copyright or prevent recovery for infringement against any person who, after actual notice of the copyright, begins an undertaking to infringe it, but shall prevent the recovery of damages against an innocent infringer who has been misled by the omission of the notice; and in a suit for infringement no permanent injunction shall be had unless the copyright proprietor shall reimburse to the innocent infringer his reasonable outlay innocently incurred if the court, in its discretion, shall so direct.

Ad interim protection of book or periodical published abroad

1911 **22.** In the case of a book or periodical first published abroad in the English language, the deposit in the Copyright Office, not later than six months after its publication abroad, of one complete copy of the foreign edition, with a request for the reservation of the copyright and a statement of the name and nationality of the author and of the copyright proprietor and of the date of publication of the said book or periodical, shall secure to the author or proprietor an ad interim copyright therein, which shall have all the force and effect given to copyright by this title, and shall endure until the expiration of five years after the date of first publication abroad.

Same; extension to full term

1912 **23.** Whenever within the period of such ad interim protection an authorized edition of such books or periodicals shall be published within the United States, in accordance with the manufacturing provisions specified in section 16 of this title, and whenever the provisions of this title as to deposit of copies, registration, filing of affidavits, and the printing of the copyright notice shall have been duly complied with, the copyright shall be extended to endure in such book or periodical for the term provided in this title.

Duration; renewal and extension [3]

1913 **24.** The copyright secured by this title shall endure for twenty-eight years from the date of first publication, whether the copyrighted work bears the author's true name or is published anonymously or under an

[3] By Public Law 87–668, dated September 19, 1962, all renewal copyrights that would have expired between that date and December 31, 1965, were extended until the latter date. Further extensions have been granted by Public Law 89–142, dated August 28, 1965, up to December 31, 1967, by Public Law 90–141, dated November 16, 1967, up to December 31, 1968, by Public Law 90–416, dated July 23, 1968, up to December 31, 1969, by Public Law 91–147, dated December 16, 1969, up to December 31, 1970 and by Public Law 91–555, dated December 17, 1970, up to December 31, 1971, the effect of which is to extend until December 31, 1971, all renewal copyrights which would have expired between September 19, 1962, and December 31, 1971. These extensions result from proposals for the general revision of the United States copyright law and the delay in enacting the necessary legislation, under which, in general, copyright in a work will subsist for the life of the author and 50 years after his death; see § 1237, *ante*.

assumed name: *Provided,* That in the case of any posthumous work or of any periodical, cyclopedic, or other composite work upon which the copyright was originally secured by the proprietor thereof, or of any work copyrighted by a corporate body (otherwise than as assignee or licensee of the individual author) or by an employer for whom such work is made for hire, the proprietor of such copyright shall be entitled to a renewal and extension of the copyright in such work for the further term of twenty-eight years when application for such renewal and extension shall have been made to the copyright office and duly registered therein within one year prior to the expiration of the original term of copyright: *And provided further,* That in the case of any other copyrighted work, including a contribution by an individual author to a periodical or to a cyclopedic or other composite work, the author of such work, if still living, or the widow, widower, or children of the author, if the author be not living, or if such author, widow, widower, or children, be not living, then the author's executors, or in the absence of a will, his next of kin shall be entitled to a renewal and extension of the copyright in such work for a further term of twenty-eight years when application for such renewal and extension shall have been made to the copyright office and duly registered therein within one year prior to the expiration of the original term of copyright: *And provided further,* That in default of the registration of such application for renewal and extension, the copyright in any work shall determine at the expiration of twenty-eight years from first publication.

Renewal of copyrights registered in Patent Office under repealed law

1914 **25.** Subsisting copyrights originally registered in the Patent Office prior to July 1, 1940, under section 3 of the Act of June 18, 1874, shall be subject to renewal in behalf of the proprietor upon application made to the Register of Copyrights within one year prior to the expiration of the original term of twenty-eight years.

Terms defined

1915 **26.** In the interpretation and construction of this title " the date of publication " shall in the case of a work of which copies are reproduced for sale or distribution be held to be the earliest date when copies of the first authorized edition were placed on sale, sold, or publicly distributed by the proprietor of the copyright or under his authority, and the word " author " shall include an employer in the case of works made for hire.

Copyright distinct from property in object copyrighted; effect of sale of object, and of assignment of copyright

1916 **27.** The copyright is distinct from the property in the material object copyrighted, and the sale or conveyance, by gift or otherwise, of the material object shall not of itself constitute a transfer of the copyright, nor shall the assignment of the copyright constitute a transfer of the title to the material object; but nothing in this title shall be deemed to forbid, prevent, or restrict the transfer of any copy of a copyrighted work the possession of which has been lawfully obtained.

Assignments and bequests

1917 **28.** Copyright secured under this title or previous copyright laws of the United States may be assigned, granted, or mortgaged by an instrument in writing signed by the proprietor of the copyright, or may be bequeathed by will.

Same; executed in foreign country; acknowledgment and certificate

1918 **29.** Every assignment of copyright executed in a foreign country shall be acknowledged by the assignor before a consular officer or secretary of legation of the United States authorized by law to administer oaths or perform notarial acts. The certificate of such acknowledgment under the hand and official seal of such consular officer or secretary of legation shall be prima facie evidence of the execution of the instrument.

Same; record

1919 **30.** Every assignment of copyright shall be recorded in the copyright office within three calendar months after its execution in the United States or within six calendar months after its execution without the limits of the United States, in default of which it shall be void as against any subsequent purchaser or mortgagee for a valuable consideration, without notice, whose assignment has been duly recorded.

Same; certificate of record

1920 **31.** The Register of Copyrights shall, upon payment of the prescribed fee, record such assignment, and shall return it to the sender with a certificate of record attached under seal of the copyright office, and upon the payment of the fee prescribed by this title he shall furnish to any person requesting the same a certified copy thereof under the said seal.

Same; use of name of assignee in notice

1921 **32.** When an assignment of the copyright in a specified book or other work has been recorded the assignee may substitute his name for that of the assignor in the statutory notice of copyright prescribed by this title.

Chapter 2—Infringement Proceedings

Infringement

1922 **101.** If any person shall infringe the copyright in any work protected under the copyright laws of the United States such person shall be liable:

(*a*) *Injunction.* To an injunction restraining such infringement;

(*b*) *Damages and profits; Amount; Other Remedies.* To pay to the copyright proprietor such damages as the copyright proprietor may have suffered due to the infringement, as well as all the profits which the infringer shall have made from such infringement, and in proving profits the plaintiff shall be required to prove sales only, and the defendant shall be required to prove every element of cost which he claims, or in lieu of actual damages and profits, such damages as to the court shall appear to be just, and in assessing such damages the court may, in its discretion, allow the amounts as hereinafter stated, but in case of a newspaper reproduction of a copyrighted photograph, such damages shall not exceed the sum of $200 nor be less than the sum of $50, and in the case of the infringement of an undramatized or nondramatic work by means of motion pictures, where the infringer shall show that he was not aware that he was infringing, and that such infringement could not have been reasonably foreseen, such damages shall not exceed the sum of $100; and in the case of an infringement of a copyrighted dramatic or dramatico-musical work by a maker of motion pictures and his agencies for distribution thereof to exhibitors, where such infringer shows that he was not aware that he was infringing a copyrighted work, and that such infringements could not reasonably have been foreseen, the entire sum of such damages recoverable by the copyright proprietor from such infringing maker and his agencies for the distribution to exhibitors of such infringing motion picture shall not exceed the sum of $5,000 nor be less than $250, and such damages shall in no other case exceed the sum of $5,000 nor be less than the sum of $250, and shall not be regarded as a penalty. But the foregoing exceptions shall not deprive the copyright proprietor of any other remedy given him under this law, nor shall the limitation as to the amount of recovery apply to infringements occurring after the actual notice to a defendant, either by service of process in a suit or other written notice served upon him.

First. In the case of a painting, statue, or sculpture, $10 for every infringing copy made or sold by or found in the possession of the infringer or his agents or employees;

Second. In the case of any work enumerated in section 5 of this title, except a painting, statue, or sculpture, $1 for every infringing copy made or sold by or found in the possession of the infringer or his agents or employees;

Third. In the case of a lecture, sermon, or address, $50 for every infringing delivery;

Fourth. In the case of a dramatic or dramatico-musical or a choral or orchestral composition, $100 for the first and $50 for every subsequent infringing performance; in the case of other musical compositions $10 for every infringing performance;

(*c*) *Impounding During Action.* To deliver up on oath, to be impounded during the pendency of the action, upon such terms and conditions as the court may prescribe, all articles alleged to infringe a copyright;

(*d*) *Destruction of Infringing Copies and Plates.* To deliver up on oath for destruction all the infringing copies or devices, as well as all plates, molds, matrices, or other means for making such infringing copies as the court may order;

(*e*) *Royalties for Use of Mechanical Reproduction of Musical Works.* Whenever the owner of a musical copyright has used or permitted the use of the copyrighted work upon the parts of musical instruments serving to reproduce mechanically the musical work, then in case of infringement of such copyright by the unauthorized manufacture, use, or sale of interchangeable parts, such as disks, rolls, bands, or cylinders for use in mechanical music-producing machines adapted to reproduce the copyrighted music, no criminal action shall be brought, but in a civil action an injunction may be granted upon such terms as the court may impose, and the plaintiff shall be entitled to recover in lieu of profits and damages a royalty as provided in section 1, subsection (*e*), of this title: *Provided also,* That whenever any person, in the absence of a license agreement, intends to use a copyrighted musical composition upon the parts of instruments serving to reproduce mechanically the musical work, relying upon the compulsory license provision of this title, he shall serve notice of such intention, by registered mail, upon the copyright proprietor at his last address disclosed by the records of the copyright office, sending to the copyright office a duplicate of such notice; and in case of his failure so to do the court may, in its discretion, in addition to sums hereinabove mentioned, award the complainant a further sum, not to exceed three times the amount provided by section 1, subsection (*e*), of this title, by way of damages, and not as a penalty, and also a temporary injunction until the full award is paid.

Willful infringement for profit

1923 **104.** Any person who willfully and for profit shall infringe any copyright secured by this title, or who shall knowingly and willfully aid or abet such infringement, shall be deemed guilty of a misdemeanor, and upon conviction thereof shall be punished by imprisonment for not exceeding one year or by a fine of not less than $100 nor more than $1,000, or both, in the discretion of the court: *Provided, however,* That nothing in this title shall be so construed as to prevent the performance of religious or secular works such as oratorios, cantatas, masses, or octavo choruses by public schools, church choirs, or vocal societies, rented, borrowed, or obtained from some public library, public school, church choir, school choir, or vocal society, provided the performance is given for charitable or educational purposes and not for profit.

Fraudulent notice of copyright, or removal or alteration of notice

1924 **105.** Any person who, with fraudulent intent, shall insert or impress any notice of copyright required by this title, or words of the same purport, in or upon any uncopyrighted article, or with fraudulent intent shall remove or alter the copyright notice upon any article duly copyrighted shall be guilty of a misdemeanor, punishable by a fine of not less than $100 and not more than $1,000. Any person who shall knowingly issue or sell any article bearing a notice of United States copyright which has not been copyrighted in this country, or who shall knowingly import any article bearing such notice or words of the same purport, which has not been copyrighted in this country, shall be liable to a fine of $100.

Importation of article bearing false notice or piratical copies of copyrighted work

1925 **106.** The importation into the United States of any article bearing a false notice of copyright when there is no existing copyright thereon in the United States, or of any piratical copies of any work copyrighted in the United States, is prohibited.

Importation, during existence of copyright, of piratical copies, or of copies not produced in accordance with section 16 of this title

1926 **107.** During the existence of the American copyright in any book the importation into the United States of any piratical copies thereof or of any copies thereof (although authorized by the author or proprietor) which have not been produced in accordance with the manufacturing provisions specified in section 16 of this title, or any plates of the same not made from type set within the limits of the United States, or any copies thereof produced by lithographic or photoengraving process not performed within the limits of the United States, in accordance with the provisions of section 16 of this title, is prohibited: *Provided, however,* That, except as regards piratical copies, such prohibition shall not apply:

(*a*) To works in raised characters for the use of the blind.

(*b*) To a foreign newspaper or magazine, although containing matter copyrighted in the United States printed or reprinted by authority of the copyright proprietor, unless such newspaper or magazine contains also copyright matter printed or reprinted without such authorization.

(*c*) To the authorized edition of a book in a foreign language or languages of which only a translation into English has been copyrighted in this country.

(*d*) To any book published abroad with the authorization of the author or copyright proprietor when imported under the circumstances stated in one of the four subdivisions following, that is to say:

First. When imported, not more than one copy at one time, for individual use and not for sale; but such privilege of importation shall not extend to a foreign reprint of a book by an American author copyrighted in the United States.

Second. When imported by the authority or for the use of the United States.

Third. When imported, for use and not for sale, not more than one copy of any such book in any one invoice, in good faith by or for any society or institution incorporated for educational, literary, philosophical, scientific, or religious purposes, or for the encouragement of the fine arts, or for any college, academy, school, or seminary of learning, or for any State, school, college, university, or free public library in the United States.

Fourth. When such books form parts of libraries or collections purchased en bloc for the use of societies, institutions, or libraries designated in the foregoing paragraph, or form parts of the libraries or personal baggage belonging to persons or families arriving from foreign countries and are not intended for sale: *Provided,* That copies imported as above may not lawfully be used in any way to violate the rights of the proprietor of the American copyright or annul or limit the copyright protection secured by this title, and such unlawful use shall be deemed an infringement of copyright.

Forfeiture and destruction of articles prohibited importation

1927 **108.** Any and all articles prohibited importation by this title which are brought into the United States from any foreign country (except in the mails) shall be seized and forfeited by like proceedings as those provided by law for the seizure and condemnation of property imported into the United States in violation of the customs revenue laws. Such articles when forfeited shall be destroyed in such manner as the Secretary of the Treasury or the court, as the case may be, shall direct: *Provided, however,* That all copies of authorized editions of copyright books imported in the mails or otherwise in violation of the provisions of this title may be exported and returned to the country of export whenever it is shown to the satisfaction of the Secretary of the Treasury, in a written application, that such importation does not involve willful negligence or fraud.

Importation of prohibited articles; regulations; proof of deposit of copies by complainants

1928 **109.** The Secretary of the Treasury and the Postmaster General are hereby empowered and required to make and enforce individually or jointly such rules and regulations as shall prevent the importation into the United States of articles prohibited importation by this title, and may require, as conditions precedent to exclusion of any work in which copyright is claimed, the copyright proprietor or any person claiming actual or potential injury by reason of actual or contemplated importations of copies of such work to file with the Post Office Department or the Treasury Department a certificate of the Register of Copyrights that the provisions of section 13 of this title have been fully complied with, and to give notice of such compliance to postmasters or to customs officers at the ports of entry in the United States in such form and accompanied by such exhibits as may be deemed necessary for the practical and efficient administration and enforcement of the provisions of sections 106 and 107 of this title.

Injunctions; service and enforcement

1929 **112.** Any court mentioned in section 1338 of Title 28 or judge thereof shall have power, upon complaint filed by any party aggrieved, to grant injunctions to prevent and restrain the violation of any right secured by this title, according to the course and principles of courts of equity, on such terms as said court or judge may deem reasonable. Any injunction that may be granted restraining and enjoining the doing of anything forbidden by this title may be served on the parties against whom such injunction may be granted anywhere in the United States, and shall be operative throughout the United States and be enforceable by proceedings in contempt or otherwise by any other court or judge possessing jurisdiction of the defendants.

Transmission of certified copies of papers for enforcement of injunction by other court

1930 **113.** The clerk of the court, or judge granting the injunction, shall, when required so to do by the court hearing the application to enforce said injunction, transmit without delay to said court a certified copy of all the papers in said cause that are on file in his office.

Review of orders, judgments, or decrees

1931 **114.** The orders, judgments, or decrees of any court mentioned in section 1338 of Title 28 arising under the copyright laws of the United States may be reviewed on appeal in the manner and to the extent now provided by law for the review of cases determined in said courts, respectively.

Limitations

1932 **115.** (*a*) Criminal Proceedings.—No criminal proceedings shall be maintained under the provisions of this title unless the same is commenced within three years after the cause of action arose.

(*b*) Civil Actions.—No civil action shall be maintained under the provisions of this title unless the same is commenced within three years after the claim accrued.

Costs; attorney's fees

1933 **116.** In all actions, suits, or proceedings under this title, except when brought by or against the United States or any officer thereof, full costs shall be allowed, and the court may award to the prevailing party a reasonable attorney's fee as part of the costs.

Chapter 3—Copyright Office

Copyright office; preservation of records

1934 **201.** All records and other things relating to copyrights required by law to be preserved shall be kept and preserved in the copyright office, Library of Congress, District of Columbia, and shall be under the control of the register of copyrights, who shall, under the direction and supervision of the Librarian of Congress, perform all the duties relating to the registration of copyrights.

Register, Assistant Register, and subordinates

1935 **202.** There shall be appointed by the Librarian of Congress a Register of Copyrights, and one Assistant Register of Copyrights, who shall have authority during the absence of the Register of Copyrights to attach the copyright office seal to all papers issued from the said office and to sign such certificates and other papers as may be necessary. There shall also be appointed by the Librarian such subordinate assistants to the register as may from time to time be authorized by law.

Same; deposit of moneys received; reports

1936 **203.** The Register of Copyrights shall make daily deposits in some bank in the District of Columbia, designated for this purpose by the Secretary of the Treasury as a national depository, of all moneys received to be applied as copyright fees, and shall make weekly deposits with the Secretary of the Treasury, in such manner as the latter shall direct, of all copyright fees actually applied under the provisions of this title, and annual deposits of sums received which it has not been possible to apply as copyright fees or to return to the remitters, and shall also make monthly reports to the Secretary of the Treasury and to the Librarian of Congress of the applied copyright fees for each calendar month, together with a statement of all remittances received, trust funds on hand, moneys refunded, and unapplied balances.

Same; bond

1937 **204.** The Register of Copyrights shall give bond to the United States in the sum of $20,000, in form to be approved by the General Counsel for the Department of the Treasury and with sureties satisfactory to the Secretary of the Treasury, for the faithful discharge of his duties.

Same; annual report

1938 **205.** The Register of Copyrights shall make an annual report to the Librarian of Congress, to be printed in the annual report on the Library of Congress, of all copyright business for the previous fiscal year, including the number and kind of works which have been deposited in the copyright office during the fiscal year, under the provisions of this title.

Seal of copyright office

1939 **206.** The seal used in the copyright office on July 1, 1909, shall be the seal of the copyright office, and by it all papers issued from the copyright office requiring authentication shall be authenticated.

Rules for registration of claims

1940 **207.** Subject to the approval of the Librarian of Congress, the Register of Copyrights shall be authorized to make rules and regulations for the registration of claims to copyright as provided by this title.

Record books in copyright office

1941 **208.** The Register of Copyrights shall provide and keep such record books in the copyright office as are required to carry out the provisions of this title, and whenever deposit has been made in the copyright office of a copy of any work under the provisions of this title he shall make entry thereof.

Certificate of registration; effect as evidence; receipt for copies deposited

1942 **209.** In the case of each entry the person recorded as the claimant of the copyright shall be entitled to a certificate of registration under seal of the copyright office, to contain the name and address of said claimant, the name of the country of which the author of the work is a citizen or subject, and when an alien author domiciled in the United States at the time of said registration, then a statement of that fact, including his place of domicile, the name of the author (when the records of the copyright office shall show the same), the title of the work which is registered for which copyright is claimed, the date of the deposit of the copies of such work, the date of publication if the work has been reproduced in copies for sale, or publicly distributed, and such marks as to class designation and entry number as shall fully identify the entry. In the case of a book, the certificate shall also state the receipt of the affidavit, as provided by section 17 of this title, and the date of the completion of the printing, or the date of the publication of the book, as stated in the said affidavit. The Register of Copyrights shall prepare a printed form for the said certificate, to be filled out in each case as above provided for in the case of all registrations made after July 1, 1909, and in the case of all previous registrations so far as the copyright office record books shall show such facts, which certificate, sealed with the seal of the copyright office, shall, upon payment of the prescribed fee, be given to any person making application for the same. Said certificate shall be admitted in any court as prima facie evidence of the facts stated therein. In addition to such certificate the Register of Copyrights shall furnish, upon request, without additional fee, a receipt for the copies of the work deposited to complete the registration.

Catalog of copyright entries; effect as evidence

1943 **210.** The Register of Copyrights shall fully index all copyright registrations and assignments and shall print at periodic intervals a catalog of the titles of articles deposited and registered for copyright, together with suitable indexes, and at stated intervals shall print complete and indexed catalog for each class of copyright entries, and may thereupon, if expedient, destroy the original manuscript catalog cards containing the titles included in such printed volumes and representing the entries made during such intervals. The current catalog of copyright entries and the index volumes herein provided for shall be admitted in any court as prima facie evidence of the facts stated therein as regards any copyright registration.

Same; distribution and sale; disposal of proceeds

1944 **211.** The said printed current catalogs as they are issued shall be promptly distributed by the Superintendent of Documents to the collectors of customs of the United States and to the postmasters of all exchange offices of receipt of foreign mails, in accordance with revised list of such collectors of customs and postmasters prepared by the Secretary of the Treasury and the Postmaster General, and they shall also be furnished in whole or in part to all parties desiring them at a price to be determined by the Register of Copyrights for each part of the catalog not exceeding $25 for the complete yearly catalog of copyright entries. The consolidated catalogs and indexes shall also be supplied to all persons ordering them at such prices as may be fixed by the Register of Copyrights, and all subscriptions for the catalogs shall be received by the Superintendent of Documents, who shall forward the said publications; and the moneys thus received shall be paid into the Treasury of the United States and accounted for under such laws and Treasury regulations as shall be in force at the time.

Records and works deposited in copyright office open to public inspection; taking copies of entries

1945 **212.** The record books of the copyright office, together with the indexes to such record books, and all works deposited and retained in the copyright office, shall be open to public inspection; and copies may be taken of the copyright entries actually made in such record books, subject to such safeguards and regulations as shall be prescribed by the Register of Copyrights and approved by the Librarian of Congress.

Disposition of articles deposited in office

1946 **213.** Of the articles deposited in the copyright office under the provisions of the copyright laws of the United States, the Librarian of Congress shall determine what books and other articles shall be transferred to the permanent collections of the Library of Congress, including the law library, and what other books or articles shall be placed in the reserve collections of the Library of Congress for sale or exchange, or be transferred to other governmental libraries in the District of Columbia for use therein.

Destruction of articles deposited in office remaining undisposed of; removal of by author or proprietor; manuscripts of unpublished works

1947 **214.** Of any articles undisposed of as above provided, together with all titles and correspondence relating thereto, the Librarian of Congress and the Register of Copyrights jointly shall, at suitable intervals, determine what of these received during any period of years it is desirable or useful to preserve in the permanent files of the copyright office, and, after due notice as hereinafter provided, may within their discretion cause the remaining articles and other things to be destroyed: *Provided*, That there shall be printed in the Catalog of Copyright Entries from February to November, inclusive, a statement of the years of receipt of such articles and a notice to permit any author, copyright proprietor, or other lawful claimant to claim and remove before the expiration of the month of December of that year anything found which relates to any of his productions deposited or registered for copyright within the period of years stated, not reserved or disposed of as provided for in this title. No manuscript of an unpublished work shall be destroyed during its term of copyright without specific notice to the copyright proprietor of record, permitting him to claim and remove it.

Fees

1948 **215.** The Register of Copyrights shall receive, and the persons to whom the services designated are rendered shall pay, the following fees:

For the registration of a claim to copyright in any work, except a print or label used for articles of merchandise, $4; for the registration of a claim to copyright in a print or label used for articles of merchandise, $6; which fees shall include a certificate of registration under seal for each work registered: *Provided*, That only one registration fee shall be required in the case of several volumes of the same book published and deposited at the same time: *And provided further*, That with respect to works of foreign origin, in lieu of payment of the copyright fee of $4 together with one copy of the work and application, the foreign author or proprietor may at any time within six months from the date of first publication abroad deposit in the Copyright Office an application for registration and two copies of the work which shall be accompanied by a catalog card in form and content satisfactory to the Register of Copyrights.

For recording the renewal of copyright and issuance of certificate therefor, $2.

For every additional certificate of registration, $1.

For certifying a copy of an application for registration of copyright, and for all other certifications, $2.

For recording every assignment, agreement, power of attorney, or other paper not exceeding six pages, $3; for each additional page or less, 50 cents; for each title over one in the paper recorded, 50 cents additional.

For recording a notice of use, $2, for each notice of not more than five titles; and 50 cents for each additional title.

For any requested search of Copyright Office records, or works deposited, or services rendered in connection therewith, $3 for each hour of time consumed.

When the day for taking action falls on Saturday, Sunday, or a holiday

1949 **216.** When the last day for making any deposit or application, or for paying any fee, or for delivering any other material to the Copyright Office falls on Saturday, Sunday, or a holiday within the District of Columbia, such action may be taken on the next succeeding business day.

Proclamation dated March 10, 1944

1950 Extending period for renewing copyright and renewal of copyright, where formalities interrupted by war conditions.

A Proclamation

Whereas by the act of Congress approved 25th September, 1941, c. 421, 55 Stat. 732, the President is authorised, on the conditions prescribed in that Act, to grant an extension of time for the fulfilment of the conditions and formalities prescribed by the copyright laws of the United States of America with respect to works first produced or published outside the United States of America and subject to copyright or to renewal of copyright under the laws of the United States of America, including works subject to *ad interim* copyright, by nationals of countries which accord substantially equal treatment to citizens of the United States of America; and

Whereas His Britannic Majesty has issued an Order in Council, effective from this day, by the terms of which treatment substantially equal to that authorised by the aforesaid Act of 25th September, 1941, is accorded, within the British dominions, colonies, protectorates and mandated territories to which that Order applies, to literary and artistic works first produced or published in the United States of America; and

Whereas the aforesaid Order in Council applies to the United Kingdom of Great Britain and Northern Ireland, British India, British Burma, Southern Rhodesia, Aden Colony, Bahamas, Barbados, Basutoland, Bechuanaland Protectorate, Bermuda, British Guiana, British Honduras, British Solomon Islands Protectorate, Ceylon, Cyprus, Falkland Islands and Dependencies, Fiji, Gambia (Colony and Protectorate), Gibraltar, Gilbert and Ellice Islands Colony, Gold Coast ((a) Colony, (b) Ashanti, (c) Northern Territories), Hong Kong, Jamaica (including Turks and Caicos Islands and the Cayman Islands), Kenya (Colony and Protectorate), Leeward Islands (Antigua, Montserrat, St. Christopher and Nevis, Virgin Islands), Malta, Mauritius, Nigeria ((a) Colony, (b) Protectorate), Northern Rhodesia, Nyasaland Protectorate, Palestine (excluding Transjordan), St. Helena and Ascension, Seychelles, Sierra Leone (Colony and Protectorate), Somaliland Protectorate, Straits Settlements, Swaziland, Transjordan, Trinidad and Tobago, Uganda Protectorate and Windward Islands (Dominica, St. Vincent, Grenada, St. Lucia); and

Whereas the aforesaid Order in Council is annexed to and is part of an agreement embodied in notes exchanged this day between the Government of the United States of America and the Government of the United Kingdom of Great Britain and Northern Ireland; and

Whereas by virtue of a proclamation by the President of the United States of America, dated 9th April, 1910 (36 Stat. 2685), subjects of Great Britain and her possessions are, and since 1st July, 1909, have been, entitled to the benefits of the act of Congress approved 4th March, 1909, 35 Stat. 1075, relating to copyright, other than the benefits of section 1 (*e*) of that act; and

Whereas by virtue of a proclamation by the President of the United States of America dated 1st January, 1915 (38 Stat. 2044), the subjects of Great Britain and the British dominions, colonies and possessions, with the exception of Canada, Australia, New Zealand, South Africa and Newfoundland, are, and since 1st January, 1915, have been, entitled to all the benefits of section 1 (*e*) of the aforesaid act of 4th March, 1909; and

Whereas by virtue of a proclamation by the President of the United States of America dated 29th September, 1933 (48 Stat. 1713), citizens of Palestine (excluding Transjordan) are, and since 1st October, 1933, have been, entitled to all the benefits of the aforesaid act of 4th March, 1909:

Now, therefore, I, Franklin D. Roosevelt, President of the United States of America, under and by virtue of the authority vested in me by the aforesaid act of 25th September, 1941, do declare and proclaim:

That with respect to (1) works subject to copyright under the laws of the United States of America, including works eligible to *ad interim* copyright, which were first produced or published outside of the United States of America on or after 3rd September, 1939, by British nationals of the United Kingdom of Great Britain and Northern Ireland and of the British territories to which the aforesaid Order in Council applies, or by citizens of Palestine (excluding Transjordan); and (2) works of the same authors or copyright proprietors which were entitled to renewal of copyright under the laws of the United States of America on or after 3rd September, 1939, there existed and continues to exist such disruption or suspension of facilities essential to compliance with the conditions and formalities prescribed with respect to such works by the copyright laws of the United States of America as to bring such works within the terms of the aforesaid act of 25th September, 1941; and that accordingly the time within which compliance with such conditions and formalities may take place is hereby extended with respect to such works until the day on which the President of the United States of America shall, in accordance with that act, terminate or suspend the present declaration and proclamation.

It shall be understood that the term of copyright in any case is not and cannot be altered or affected by this proclamation, and that, as provided by the aforesaid act of 25th September, 1941, no liability shall attach under the Copyright Act for lawful uses made or acts done prior to the effective date of this proclamation in connexion with the above-described works, or in respect to the continuance for one year subsequent to such date of any business undertaking or enterprise lawfully undertaken prior to such date involving expenditure or contractual obligation in connexion with the exploitation, production, reproduction, circulation, or performance of any such work.

In witness whereof, I have hereunto set my hand and caused the seal of the United States of America to be affixed.

Done at the City of Washington this tenth day of March in the year of our Lord one thousand nine hundred forty-four, and of the Independence of the United States of America the one hundred and sixty-eighth.

FRANKLIN D. ROOSEVELT.

INDEX

[All references are to paragraph numbers.]

Index